The Concise
Encyclopedia of American Antiques

The Concise Encyclopedia of American Antiques

EDITED BY HELEN COMSTOCK

HAWTHORN BOOKS, Inc.
Publishers
New York

First Edition, October, 1965
Second Printing, January, 1966

THE CONTENTS

CONTENTS

Painting in the Nineteenth Century

Romantic realism: the early portrait tradition and the Hudson River School – the tonalists – genre – still-life – late portrait and figure painters – fantasy and mysticism – visual realism

By JOHN I. H. BAUR

Curator, Whitney Museum of American Art

Folk Painting

Definition of folk art – portraits – landscapes – genre not prevalent – historical subjects – wall decoration – sources of design – theorem painting – mourning pictures – glass painting

By NINA FLETCHER LITTLE

Author of *American Decorative Wall Painting*; also, *The Abby Aldrich Rockefeller Folk Art Collection*

Miniature Painting

First half of the eighteenth century – development under Copley, the Peales and others after 1750 – foreign influences – best period represented by Malbone and Fraser – later work in Philadelphia, New York, Boston and Baltimore

By JOSEPHINE L. ALLEN

Former associate curator, Metropolitan Museum of Art

Engravings

Eighteenth-century town views and historical subjects – portraits – aquatints – wood engravings

By ELIZABETH E. ROTH

First assistant, prints division, New York Public Library

FOREWORD

WHETHER the interest in American antiques had its origin at the time of the Philadelphia Centennial in 1876 or whether it was a manifestation of that same reappraisal of the past evident in England and France in the late-nineteenth century, which seems more likely, collections began to be formed shortly before 1900. The names of Eugene Bolles, Jacob Paxon Temple, Dwight Blaney and Richard A. Canfield are recalled among the early collectors, but it was not until the time of Francis P.Garvan, Louis Guerineau Myers, Mrs J.Insley Blair, Mrs Harry Horton Benkard and others who were assembling great collections in the 1920s that antiques began to receive general understanding and appreciation.

Books began to appear early in the century. Lockwood published his *Colonial Furniture* in 1903. The writings of Frances Clary Morse, Alice Morse Earl, Esther Singleton and Edwin Atlee Barber were pioneer works which today's collectors can read with profit. More specialised publications followed. In furniture there were books by Nutting (1926); Lyon (1924); Kettell (1929); Hornor (1935) and Miller (1937). Silver was introduced by the catalogue of the historic exhibition in Boston in 1906, followed by studies by Bigelow in 1917 and Miss Avery in 1930. Pewter was first covered in definitive form by Kerfoot in 1924; glass by Mrs Knittle in 1927; and textiles by Miss Morris in 1931. There have been important additions to the literature of all these fields, but not enough of them, and not enough revisions of early works to keep pace with discoveries. It is true that a number of monographs have appeared, among which books on silversmiths lead, while glass has had recent and excellent presentation by the McKearins, and pewter a monumental study by Dr. Laughlin. But it is often surprising and disappointing to new students and collectors to find how inadequate is the number of recent books on fundamental subjects. It is continually necessary to refer to periodicals, particularly the magazine *Antiques,* to *Old-Time New England* and the bulletins of museums, all of which present new material, while the broad survey of the field is difficult to find in many instances, particularly in regard to furniture, ceramics, silver and textiles. To answer the need for a new, comprehensive work on antiques the *Concise Encyclopedia of American Antiques* has been prepared. Its authors are members of the staffs of museums, libraries and historical societies, or authors of books in their particular fields. In general plan and format the *Encyclopedia* is related to the *Concise Encyclopedia of Antiques* of which four volumes have been published by Hawthorn Books, Inc. (1955, 1956, 1957, 1959). These four earlier volumes contain articles on American furniture, silver, glass and prints, but none of this material is reprinted in the present work.

It has not been possible to hold to the same period in regard to all subjects. The question of 'how old is an antique' can probably never be satisfactorily answered. Some of the objects discussed are of the mid- or late-nineteenth century, a few, such as mechanical toys and dime novels, are of the twentieth. However, it is well to remember

21

that the requirement, 'before 1830,' is a sound one, since that date, which coincides with the beginning of the machine age, saw the decline of the individual craftsman working in a tradition handed down from master to apprentice. Many of the contributors have felt obliged to carry their subjects to mid-century, as in regard to clocks; or the 1876 Philadelphia Centennial (printed textiles) ; or even the end of the century (painting, Victorian furniture, art glass) .

The completion of this *Encyclopedia* would not have been possible without the cooperation of members of the staff of *Antiques,* who have not only contributed some of the articles but have been continuously helpful. I wish especially to thank Alice Winchester, editor of *Antiques,* for allowing me to draw liberally on the magazine's invaluable file of photographs.

HELEN COMSTOCK
American Editor: *The Connoisseur*

FURNITURE 1640–1840

By MARVIN D. SCHWARTZ

FROM the beginning of colonization in America there was some conflict of interest between the settlers and the nations that nurtured the new colonies. Although colonization was undertaken by the mother countries for the dual purpose of acquiring raw materials and a market for manufactures, it was impractical for the settlers to depend entirely upon the homeland for manufactured goods. There were craftsmen available to produce some of what was required, so that in spite of prohibitions by the governing companies and nations, pewter, silver and furniture were made locally before the end of the seventeenth century.

Seventeenth century: one of the remarkable features of American furniture from the very beginning is its distinctiveness from the provincial styles of the British Isles. It has qualities that place it apart because of its consistent simplicity. The first style to be encountered is a late version of the Tudor style, which was current in the English provinces all through the seventeenth century. It is a style in which there are few furniture forms. Chests for storage and cupboards for display and storage were the only large case pieces. Several kinds of decoration are found on American chests of the seventeenth century. One is an arcade carved in the panels across the front of the chest with foliate pattern on the arches and the columns (Plates 1A, 2A). Another kind of decoration consists of the application of strips of molding which divide the panels across the front of the chest into patterns such as a modified cross or a hexagon. Turned wooden spindles and bosses are often applied between the panels. A number of related pieces have been traced to the Ipswich, Massachusetts, area, where the joiner, Thomas Dennis, made furniture in the

seventeenth century. A variation of the type has been associated with Connecticut; in these the applied decoration is combined with flat carving in a floral pattern interpreted as a sunflower surrounded by tulips. This has been called the Hartford or Sunflower chest (Plate 2C). In rare instances, seventeenth-century chests have been found with the floral decoration painted on (Plate 5A). One variation of the form has drawers added below the usual chest which adds height to the piece.

Small boxes for the storage of books and for the storage of toilet articles are also known. The box for books, more popularly known as the Bible box (Plate 4B), usually has a slanting lid which may have been used to hold books while they were being read, or as a surface for writing.

The same decoration is encountered on the small forms as on the larger ones. The seventeenth-century cupboard was used for storage and display. Two important variations exist, the court (Plate 3A) and the press cupboard (Plate 1A), which vary in the degree they provide for each of the two functions. The court cupboard was designed mainly for showing off objects. It consists of three shelves with a recessed cabinet between the middle and upper shelf. There are shallow drawers making a skirt below each shelf. The cabinet frequently has canted sides to increase the display area. The decoration on this form is elaborate. The shelves are supported by heavy baluster-like columns decorated with turned rings or carving. The flat areas are decorated either by the application of turned spindles and bosses or carving. The turnings are generally painted black to simulate ebony. Motifs in carving are floral or foliate. The black turnings on the rich dark brown stain of the oak were made even richer by the addition of brightly colored carpets and cushions which are mentioned in seventeenth-century inventories as being on such pieces.

The chair was not as common in middle-class homes of the seventeenth century as it became later. The inventories of Plymouth, Massachusetts, between 1633 and 1654, and those of Boston for relatively the same period, reveal that most homes had only a few chairs. The chair had special significance and was reserved for the master of the household or an important guest. Others sat on chests, benches or small joint stools. These stools (Plate 3C) had wooden seats, rectangular in shape, on turned legs joined by low stretchers.

Several varieties of seventeenth-century American chairs are known: the wainscot; the chair of turned posts and spindles; or slats; and the so-called Cromwellian or Farthingale chair. The wainscot chair (Plate 1C) has a back and seat of solid panels, with curving arms on turned supports and turned legs joined by straight stretchers. The back is decorated with flat incised carving in foliate, floral or geometric patterns. Occasionally a curving crest tops the back. This chair, which had been fashionable in the sixteenth century Elizabethan court, actually was one variation of a type that existed at least as early as the fourteenth century, but by the seventeenth century was found only in the provinces. Its heaviness makes it impressive, and the characteristic decoration reflects the Renaissance taste, which affected English culture rather late.

Chairs of turned posts and spindles or slats fall into three categories: the Carver, the Brewster and the slat-back. The Carver and Brewster both use spindles. Each is named for a founding father of Massachusetts because of a resemblance to chairs these men owned (now in the Pilgrim Society in Plymouth). The Carver (Plate 1B) is an armchair with a single tier of spindles making up the back. The turned decoration on the spindles and posts is simple. The seat is of rush. The Brewster (Plate 2B) is basically the same type of chair; the back has two tiers of small spindles across it, however, and under the arms and between the seat and the stretchers there are also rows of spindles. The origin of this type is

unclear. There are thirteenth-century Scandinavian examples related vaguely, and in the sixteenth century in England a three-legged version is encountered. The chair brought to the New World which became the President's Chair at Harvard is an example of this later group.

The table varied greatly in size and type. The trestle table might have a top as large as eight feet in length resting loosely on two or more trestles joined by a brace. Another type of rectangular table has four turned legs joined by low stretchers (Plate 4A). The skirt below the top often has a drawer. These vary in length, and the tops are square or oblong. Occasionally the skirt is molded. The gateleg table is a type that generally dates quite late in the period (Plate 5C). It is a narrow table with large drop leaves which are supported on a leg and stretchers that swing out. The top is round, oval, square or oblong when opened. Still another type is the chair table. Similar in construction to the wainscot chair, its back was made so that it could be pivoted down and rested on the arms of the chair to serve as a table top.

The furniture of the seventeenth century in America was made predominantly of oak, although pine and other soft woods were used where there was no great threat of heavy wear. Construction was simple and heavy; the mortise and tenon was used to join sides of large pieces of furniture as well as drawers, a continuation of a technique that goes back to medieval times. Painting and staining furniture in black, blue, red and green to emphasize flat carving or to bring out moldings on chests is common in this early furniture. This also is a technique that dates back to medieval times; however, the motifs and the decoration in this furniture are classical in source.

William and Mary style: toward the end of the seventeenth century a change of style can be discerned in American furniture. This was a late manifestation of tendencies occurring all through the century in England and the rest of Europe. These changes were in part the result of the economic development in Europe, which made it possible for the middle and upper classes to seek new and greater luxuries. One factor was the expansion of trade, with each nation reaching out for new markets, which resulted in a growing trade with the Far East and the importation of all kinds of exotic merchandise.

In America the style named for William and Mary lasted from 1690 to 1725. It combines elements of the English William and Mary style with tendencies that began earlier in the century in England.

The style very clearly reflects the taste for the luxurious and relates to the baroque; as in the baroque, classical motifs are interpreted with inventiveness which is most obvious in the designs of the legs as scrolls, spirals and columns. Another facet of the new taste is an interest in attractive surfaces. Walnut, with its fine grains, replaced oak as the predominant wood, and other woods were also chosen for the pattern of the grain. To obtain the best patterns, veneers were employed. Beautiful effects were achieved by cutting sections of the tree near the root into thin strips, for application as veneer. The burl of the walnut was favored for veneering case pieces. Inlaid strips of contrasting wood were used as borders, and occasionally larger designs were inlaid.

Oriental lacquered furniture inspired imitations in Europe, England and America. Since true lacquering is long and laborious, some of the processes were greatly simplified. In 1688 an English publication, *Treatise of Japanning and Varnishing*, by John Stalker and George Parker, was published with instructions on how to imitate lacquer work with Western varnishes. These were probably followed almost as avidly in America as in England. The results vary from close copies of the Oriental design to some fairly different designs. Japanners advertised in Boston in the early eighteenth century. Surviving examples of their work are rare, and the best are of the Queen Anne period, such as the highboy illustrated (Plate 8A).

One of the most important changes that came with the new style was the introduction of greater variety in furniture form. New forms for special purposes, such as the desk and the dressing table, were developed. In the seventeenth-century American home the simple box-like chest served as storage for everything, but toward the end of the century the chest of drawers evolved, finally raised on a stand or frame (Plate 7C). The earliest examples occurred before the transition to William and Mary, and there are examples in oak with panelled decoration, but the form is more typical of the later style.

Another variation is the chest of drawers on tall legs, correctly called the high chest, but popularly named the highboy during the nineteenth century. The high chest lends itself more readily to elegant design. In some William and Mary examples (Plate 6A) the chest has four legs across the front and two in the back. The legs are elaborately shaped and are joined just above the foot by a curving stretcher that goes around the piece. The upper part is rectangular with a flat top; occasionally a bolection molding is used at the top, as in the example illustrated, to conceal a narrow secret drawer that was probably designed for papers.

The low chest was made at table height and seems to have been devised to serve as a dressing table. On tall legs, like the high chest, it has one or two tiers of small drawers. In later periods, more often than in the William and Mary period, it was made to match the high chest. The mixing table is very similar in form. More often it has four legs, joined by crossed stretchers, than six, and to replace the center front legs there are turned ornaments attached to the skirt. Rare examples have tops of imported slate framed in marquetry (Plate 6B).

The desk evolves as a large form in this period by the addition to a chest of drawers of an upper section enclosed by a slant-top which contains pigeon holes, small drawers and a writing area. Occasionally a cupboard is added above for book storage. This has been called a scrutoire or escritoire; it is known as a bureau in England, or bureau-cabinet; the modern term is secretary. In another type of desk the slant-top enclosure is used on a frame of turned legs joined by stretchers, the desk-on-frame.

In the category of tables, gateleg tables (Plate 5C) seem to have been the most popular type in the period. They appear in a great variety of sizes, so that they evidently served many different purposes.

Chair design was affected quite radically by the change of style. The wainscot chair all but disappeared, Carvers and Brewsters became rare, and the slat-back was retired to the country. Taller, thinner proportions were characteristic of the new style in chairs (Plate 7B). There are relatively more side chairs than in the earlier period. Frequently a material from the Orient, cane, was used to make the seat and the back (Plate 7A). Most of the American examples are simplified versions of a type that was introduced in England after being popular in Portugal and the Netherlands. The typical American example has an elaborately carved cresting-rail, turned stiles and front legs carved in scroll or vase shapes.

The wing chair (Plate 5B), with back and arms completely upholstered, and a flanking, curving 'wing' coming out from the back over the arms, was introduced in this period as a bedroom chair.

The William and Mary style marked the beginning of variety in furniture form in America. It possessed a new lightness and elaborate decoration, such as fine carving and the application of rich veneers and inlays, being the American version of the baroque.

Queen Anne style: the Queen Anne style was at its height from 1725 to 1750 but persisted longer in rural areas. It combines influences from the style of the reign of Queen Anne, 1702–14, with later influences from the period of the early Georgian rulers. Naming the style in America after Queen Anne is unfortunate, because her reign was short and its style was not significant. The American counterpart marks the beginning of an eighteenth-century style that lasted until the Revolution. It developed at a time when the larger towns in the American colonies were becoming more prosperous and taste more sophisticated. Importation of expensive textiles, porcelains and other objects became increasingly important and the demand for more skilled work by local craftsmen was augmented. The furniture of the larger American towns reflected this greater sophistication in the technical improvement shown by cabinet-

makers. Fine details in construction, and finesse in carving became more evident than in earlier work.

A comparison of the Queen Anne style with contemporary movements in the arts reveals at once that it includes elements of the rococo. There is restraint and balance in line and ornament typical of the style which, however, is more classical than truly rococo. American Queen Anne furniture is characterized by a lightness in line and delicate symmetrical ornamentation. The favored wood was walnut, but mahogany, imported from the West Indies, was used to some degree. Veneers and inlay became less fashionable than fine solid wood with carved decoration. In the important centers, where walnut and mahogany were used, furniture occasionally continued to be japanned in imitation of Oriental lacquer (Plate 8A). Curves take a particularly prominent place in the shapes encountered during the Queen Anne period. The cabriole leg, a simple curving support inspired by the design of an animal leg, which had occurred on rare occasions in the William and Mary style, became quite important. There were few new furniture forms in the Queen Anne period, and most of those introduced in the previous period were employed.

The high chest underwent certain changes in the transition to the Queen Anne style. The top is less frequently flat than pedimented with a broken arch flanked by finials on either side (Plate 9B). Often the center drawers at the top and the bottom have shell decoration and occasionally pilasters flank either side of the upper section. The cabriole legs on which it stands terminate in a variety of ways: a simple round pad; a curving three-section design called the trifid (Plates 9A, 9C), or a pointed type called the slipper foot (Plate 10B), shown here with a carved tongue. Very rarely the Spanish foot (see Glossary), a variation of the scroll foot, is used with the cabriole leg. On the more elaborate pieces, the knees of the cabriole legs are decorated with shells (Plate 9C), or, in what appear to be late examples, the acanthus leaf. The typical examples of the period have a skirt that is scalloped, although frequently there are vestigial remains of the two center legs of the

William and Mary period in the form of drops attached to the skirt. Matching low chests were more common in this period. Apparently the chest of drawers became a little less popular.

There was a great increase in the variety of tables. Tables for tea and for china, of small dimensions and with fine detail, occur in a variety of shapes. The simplest type is rectangular (Plate 8c) with a top surrounded by an enclosing molding that makes it seem like a tray (the tray-top, or dished top). The corners of such tables are apt to be curved and the legs are sometimes decorated with a shell on the knee. On rare occasions the top is of marble rather than wood. For serving tea, a round table which could have its top tilted up to save space when it was not in use, was also introduced in the Queen Anne period. The top rests on a turned baluster terminating in a tripod of cabriole legs. A smaller version was used as a candlestand.

The gaming, or card table, is another small table that was developed in this period. This table has a folding top whose two hinged halves rest in layers when not being used. One or two legs swing out as supports when the table is opened for games. Occasionally there is a fifth leg or both rear legs can be extended. When the top is opened, a surface covered with baize or felt, with oval depressions for counters and a wooden area at each corner for a candlestick is exposed.

Although there is evidence to show that dining rooms were not common in the American Queen Anne period, a few special forms relating to dining developed. A table that would appear to have been a serving table appears. It is rectangular, or roughly so, with the back unfinished and the front usually curving. The tops are marble and there is a plain, thick skirt in several of the examples known. The most frequent top of dining tables is the kind with drop leaves supported by swinging cabriole legs. The tops are rectangular, oval or round.

The chair is a form that clearly reflects style, because it can be changed easily. The Queen Anne chair is light and graceful and made up of a series of curves (Plates 8B, 10B). It is quite different from the stiff, but elegant, William and Mary type. The back of a Queen Anne chair consists of a curving top rail, which in the center provides space for a shell. This rail is joined to stiles that often curve also, and from the center of the toprail to the seat there is a solid splat shaped like a vase or violin. The seat is horseshoe-shaped (also called compass seat), and the front legs are cabriole. The rear legs are generally plain and round, the stump-leg. In some examples stretchers brace the legs. The curving lines are emphasized by the curving of the individual wooden members. The back is often shaped to accommodate the human form.

Sofas or settees of this period have straight upholstered backs, which are sometimes plain across the top (Plate 10C) and sometimes scalloped (Plate 11A). Occasionally a settee is made up of two or three chair backs joined together.

Regional differences in American furniture become more apparent in the Queen Anne period than they had been earlier. These are summarized at the conclusion of the sections on the Chippendale and classical styles.

The curve is the most important element of Queen Anne furniture design, with simplicity and restraint significant characteristics. The forms are relatively the same as in the William and Mary style, but there is greater variety in size and greater lightness in line. Veneers became less important than fine solid woods. Walnut, a local wood that is hard and handsome, was gradually replaced by imported mahogany. The Queen Anne style is a restrained version of the rococo.

Chippendale style: the American Chippendale style, in many ways a continuation of the Queen Anne, may be dated from 1750 to 1780, the period in which the colonies came of age, culturally as well as politically. Thriving American towns kept as much in fashion as any in provincial England by following the latest trends in London. In spite of this similarity, it is interesting to see that the style of colonial America is as different from that of the provinces of the mother country in furniture as in the different accents of speech, which were also recognizable by that time.

The style is named after the English cabinetmaker, Thomas Chippendale, who published a volume of furniture designs in 1754. This book, *The Gentlemen and Cabinetmaker's Director*, published in three editions and translated into several languages, was known all over Europe and in some of the European colonies. The designs epitomized the rococo in England, when this style was at its height, with admittedly French inspiration. On the title page the reader is advised that the designs are in the Gothic, Chinese and Modern (meaning French) taste. Each of the tastes is basically French, the differences are in motif rather than spirit or source.

The American Chippendale style is more conservative than its name implies. Besides Chippendale's designs, earlier English styles serve as a source of inspiration, so that while it brings the incipient rococo tendencies of Queen Anne into a more prominent position, it is more restrained than English Chippendale. In general, the furniture forms of American Chippendale are likely to be somewhat more elaborately decorated continuations of Queen Anne forms rather than innovations.

Forms that started in the William and Mary period changed in design in the Queen Anne, and really only became more ornamented in American Chippendale furniture. The simple shell and the plain architectural detail with limited carving so popular in the Queen Anne period were replaced by more complicated foliate patterns on pieces that are relatively alike in line and function.

The curving cabriole leg continued to be common, but rather than terminating in such a simple form as the pad foot, the claw and ball, which had been introduced late on American Queen Anne furniture, became the usual solution. This type of foot was too old-fashioned in England to appear in the *Director*, where cabriole legs generally terminate in the scroll foot which appears in America only on rare occasions. Still another type of foot, and one that is more elaborate than the claw and ball, but less rococo than the scroll, the hairy paw, appears once in the *Director* and on some very fine American furniture (Plate 14B). It had been used in English furniture earlier.

One type of leg introduced for tables and chairs in the main is straight and in the Chinese taste. This is sometimes called the Marlborough leg, a term of uncertain origin, but known to have been in use in the eighteenth century. The leg is sometimes plain, sometimes fluted or molded, and occasionally cut-out frets are applied (Plate 15B).

The high chest is handled with relative conservatism. Not mentioned in the *Director*, it is a form that had grown unpopular in England. In America it found particular favor in Philadelphia. The form was a continuation of an earlier tradition, repeating the same general characteristics. In a few of the more outstanding examples, however, the decoration is in the latest fashion (Plate 14A). Strips of asymmetrical foliate patterns are applied across the skirt and in the area just below the broken arch pediment. Asymmetrically carved shells are on the top and bottom center drawers. Finials in the shape of flaming urns, a classical motif, flank the pediment, with the center finial a rococo scroll device called a cabochon. The knees of the cabriole legs are carved in an acanthus leaf pattern.

In England the high chest had been replaced by the chest-on-chest, and by a chest combined with an upper section that is a cupboard. These were introduced in the American colonies shortly after they were known in England. They were used everywhere, but some of the outstanding examples were made in New England, New York and Charleston, South Carolina (Plate 12A). Several Connecticut examples show simple ornamentation and are quite plain. In New York there are a few examples of the second type, sometimes called a linen press. These have features typical of the area, such as a fret frieze applied just under the cornice.

The chest of drawers, important in the William and Mary period, was almost forgotten in the Queen Anne period, but it was revived in Chippendale furniture. Some chests were straight fronted with chamfered front corners, or with engaged quarter columns at the front corners. These usually rested on claw and ball feet. This is a design followed in New York. More often, in keeping with the tendency toward greater elabora-

(A) Press cupboard of oak, pine and maple; New England, 1660–80. *Metropolitan Museum of Art, New York.*

(B) Armchair with Carver type back and rush seat; New York, late seventeenth century. *Metropolitan Museum of Art, New York.*

(C) Wainscot chair, oak; *c.* 1650. *Brooklyn Museum.*

A

B

C

PLATE I

(A) Carved oak chest of Thomas Dennis type; Ipswich, Massachusetts, 1660–80. *Israel Sack.*

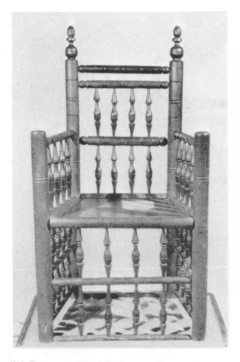

(B) Brewster-type chair, actually belonged to Governor William Bradford, d. 1657. *Pilgrim Hall, Plymouth, Massachusetts.*

(C) The 'Hartford', 'Connecticut' or 'Sunflower' chest; late seventeenth century. *Ex-coll. of Luke Vincent Lockwood, courtesy Parke-Bernet Galleries.*

PLATE 2

(A) Court cupboard of oak, pine and maple; Massachusetts, about 1675. *Metropolitan Museum of Art, New York.*

(B) Hadley chest marked IP for Joanna Porter (1687–1714) who married John Marsh, representative to the General Court in 1704. (Luther, *The Hadley Chest*, No. 65.) *C. Sanford Bull collection, Yale University Art Gallery.*

(C) Joint stool, maple; Ipswich, Massachusetts. 1660–80. *Israel Sack.*

A

B

C

PLATE 3

(A) Oak table; Plymouth, Massachusetts, *c.* 1650. (B) Bible box, painted green. *Brooklyn Museum.*
Greenwood collection, Smithsonian Institution.

(C) Hooded pine panel-back settle, seventeenth century. *Israel Sack.*

PLATE 4

(A) Painted chest, oak, pine and maple; graining on body, with panels, red, black and white; Massachusetts, *c.* 1700. *Brooklyn Museum.*

(B) Wing chair with rudimentary Spanish foot; *c.* 1700. *Blair collection, Metropolitan Museum of Art, New York.*

(C) Walnut double gateleg table; New England, 1690–1725. *Metropolitan Museum of Art, New York.*

PLATE 5

(B) Mixing table, slate and marquetry top, burl veneer and herringbone cross-banding; New England, 1690–1710.   *Coll. of C. K. Davis.*

(A) William and Mary high chest; burl maple; bolection molding; has drawer; 1700–25.   *Henry Ford Museum, Dearborn, Michigan.*

PLATE 6

(B) Leather upholstered side chair of maple and oak; Massachusetts, 1685–1700. *Metropolitan Museum of Art, New York.*

(A) William and Mary caned maple side chair; *c.* 1700. *Metropolitan Museum of Art, New York.*

(C) William and Mary high chest on rope-twist turned legs; late seventeenth century. *Metropolitan Museum of Art, New York.*

PLATE 7

(A) Japanned Queen Anne highboy, maple and white pine; Boston, c. 1735. *Metropolitan Museum of Art, New York.*

(B) Queen Anne walnut side chair; Rhode Island, c. 1740. *Israel Sack.*

(C) Tea table, dished top with incurved corners; New England, Queen Anne period, 1725–50. Downs's *American Furniture, No. 365. Henry Francis du Pont Winterthur Museum, Winterthur, Delaware.*

PLATE 8

(A) Philadelphia Queen Anne walnut side chair; 1725–50. *Antiques*, xlix, 49.

(B) Cherry bonnet top high chest; Rhode Island, *c.* 1745. *Ginsburg and Levy.*

(C) Walnut dressing table or lowboy; probably Maryland, 1745–60. Downs's *American Furniture, No. 324, Winterthur Museum.*

PLATE 9

(A) New England Queen Anne wing chair, 1725–50. *Blair collection; Metropolitan Museum.*

(B) Philadelphia Queen Anne walnut armchair; *c.* 1730–50. *Ex-Haskell collection; courtesy Parke-Bernet.*

(C) Queen Anne walnut leather-covered sofa, arrow-shape stretchers, carved web feet and scrolled knee blocks; Philadelphia 1740–50. Downs's *American Furniture*, No. 269, *Winterthur Museum.*

PLATE 10

(A) Chippendale upholstered settee of mahogany and maple; Massachusetts, *c.* 1765–75. *Metropolitan Museum of Art, New York.*

(B) New York mahogany oval drop-leaf dining table; *c.* 1770. *Metropolitan Museum of Art, New York.*

(C) Philadelphia mahogany pier or side table with top of black and white marble; carved fret on rounded frieze; *c.* 1760–75. *Metropolitan Museum of Art, New York.*

PLATE II

(B) Tripod tea table with piecrust edge and birdcage attachment; Philadelphia, 1765–80. *Karolik collection; Museum of Fine Arts, Boston.*

(A) Blockfront mahogany chest-on-chest, Townsend-Goddard, cabinetmakers; Newport, 1765–70. Downs's *American Furniture, No. 183, Winterthur Museum.*

(C) Tea table made by John Goddard, Newport, 1763, for Jabez Bowen. Downs's *American Furniture, No. 373, Winterthur Museum.*

PLATE 12

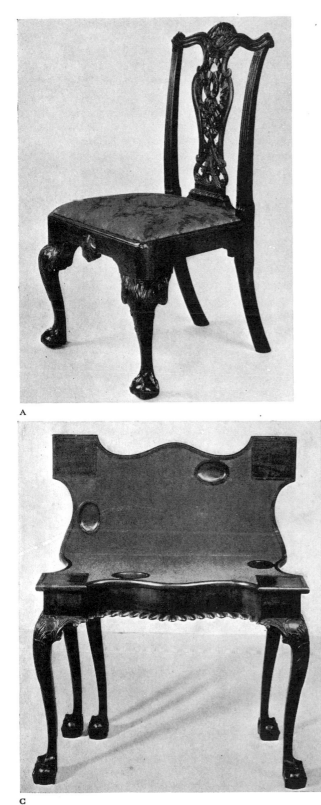

A

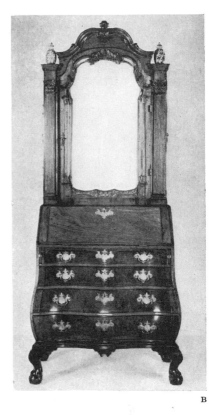

B

(A) Philadelphia mahogany ribbon-back side chair; design of back from Chippendale's *Director, c.* 1760. *Brooklyn Museum.*

(B) Massachusetts desk and bookcase in rococo style; with bombé base; possibly by John Cogswell, Boston, *c.* 1765–80. Downs's *American Furniture, No. 227, Winterthur Museum.*

(C) New York gaming table, serpentine form, with gadrooning on skirt; *c.* 1760–80. *Ex-Norvin Green collection; courtesy of Parke-Bernet.*

C

PLATE 13

A

B

C

(A) Philadelphia high chest; the Van Pelt high-boy, formerly in the Reif-snyder collection; *c.* 1765–80. Downs's *American Furniture*, No. *195*, Winter-thur Museum.

(B) One of the six so-called 'sample chairs' of Benjamin Randolph; design of back from Chip-pendale's *Director*, Plate IX, 1762 ed. Downs's *American Furniture*, No. *137*, Winterthur Museum.

(C) Philadelphia dressing table or lowboy with fine rococo ornament; made for the Gratz family, 1769; companion to the high chest also at Winterthur. Downs's *American Furniture*, No. *333*,Winterthur Museum.

PLATE 14

(A) Connecticut blockfront cherry desk signed by Benjamin Burnham of Norwich; dated 1769. *Metropolitan Museum of Art, New York.*

(B) Chippendale armchair with Marlborough leg; Boston, 1765–70. *Metropolitan Museum of Art, New York.*

(C) Charleston chest-on-chest with fret on frieze; of type attributed to Thomas Elfe, *c.* 1775. *Heyward-Washington House, Charleston Museum.*

A

B

C

PLATE 15

(A) Baltimore inlaid sideboard showing use of contrasting woods emphasizing ovals; panels with mitred corners; *c.* 1800. *Ginsburg and Levy.*

(B) New York Hepplewhite side chair with drapery and feather carved in splat; 1790–1800. *Karolik collection, Museum of Fine Arts, Boston.*

(C) New England Hepplewhite mahogany and satinwood bowfront chest of drawers on French bracket foot; 1790. *Coll. of Mrs Francis P. Garvan.*

PLATE 16

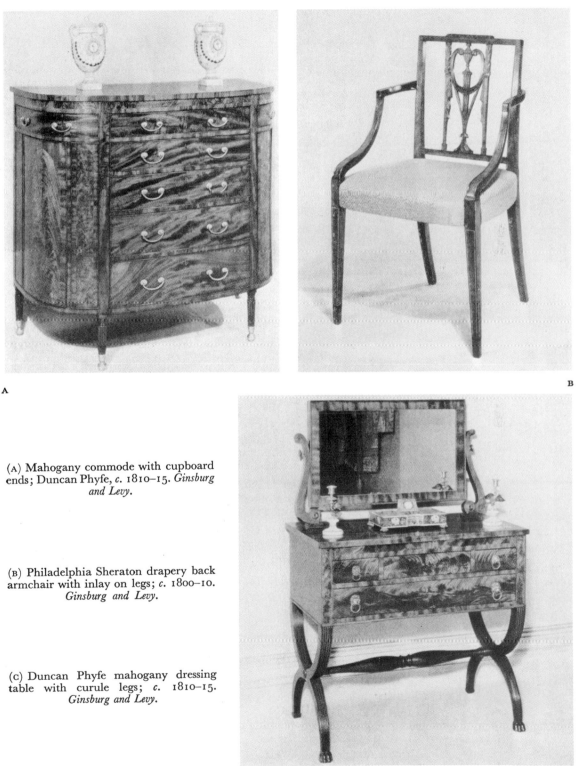

A

B

(A) Mahogany commode with cupboard ends; Duncan Phyfe, c. 1810–15. *Ginsburg and Levy*.

(B) Philadelphia Sheraton drapery back armchair with inlay on legs; c. 1800–10. *Ginsburg and Levy*.

(C) Duncan Phyfe mahogany dressing table with curule legs; c. 1810–15. *Ginsburg and Levy*.

C

PLATE 17

(A) New England Sheraton tambour secretary; attributed to John Seymour, Boston, *c.* 1810. *Ginsburg and Levy.*

(B) Martha Washington armchair, mahogany, *c.* 1790–1800. *Metropolitan Museum of Art, New York.*

(C) New York sewing table, mahogany and birdseye maple; *c.* 1815. *Coll. of Mrs Giles Whiting.*

(D) Mahogany sewing table, Salem, 1800–10. *Ginsburg and Levy.*

PLATE 18

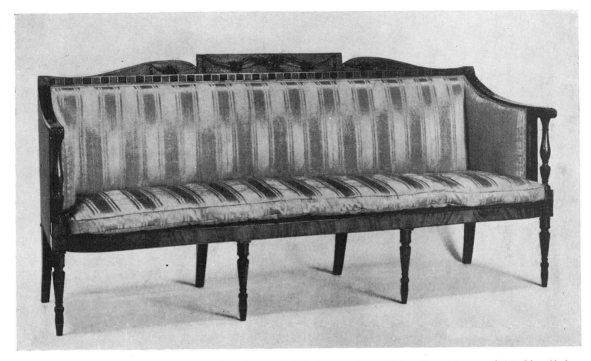

(A) Salem sofa with carving attributed to Samuel McIntire; *c.* 1800. *Metropolitan Museum of Art, New York.*

(B) Baltimore Hepplewhite inlaid mahogany card table; 1790–1800. *Karolik collection, Museum of Fine Arts, Boston.*

(C) Duncan Phyfe medallion back side chair; reeded stiles are one with the seat rail; *c.* 1800–10. *Ginsburg and Levy.*

PLATE 19

A

B

C

(A) Salem desk and bookcase with ivory finials and knobs; white and gold glass panels in bookcase section; c. 1800–10. *Ginsburg and Levy.*

(B) Mahogany armchair; attributed to Henry Connelly, Philadelphia, c. 1800. *Ginsburg and Levy.*

(C) Inlaid Pembroke with reeded legs; attributed to Duncan Phyfe, New York, 1790. *Ginsburg and Levy.*

PLATE 20

Victorian parlor from the Milligan house, Saratoga, New York; mid-nineteenth century. *Brooklyn Museum.*

PLATE 21

(A) Rosewood side chair; neo-gothic back designed by A.J.Davis, *c.* 1830. *Museum of The City of New York.*

(B) Carved walnut side chair inlaid with crotch walnut; by Thomas Brooks, Brooklyn, *c.* 1856–76. *Brooklyn Museum.*

(C) Rosewood table with marble top, inside frame inscription *J. H. Belter and Co. Antiques,* September 1848. *Photograph, courtesy of Metropolitan Museum of Art.*

PLATE 22

(A) Dresser by John Belter, New York; *c.* 1850.
Brooklyn Museum.

(B) Bed by John Belter, New York, showing laminated construction; *c.* 1850. *Brooklyn Museum.*

PLATE 23

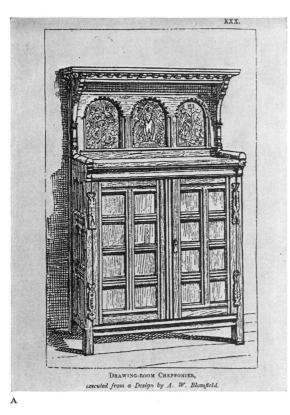

DRAWING-ROOM CHEFFONIER,
executed from a Design by A. W. Blomfield.

A

(A) Design for 'drawing-room cheffonier'; from East-lake's *Hints on Household Taste*, first American Edition, Boston, 1872.

(B) (C) Cast-iron garden furniture, James and Kirkland, New York, *c.* 1850. (Plate marked Janes, Beebe and Co., 356, Broadway, New York) *New York Public Library.*

No. 144.

B

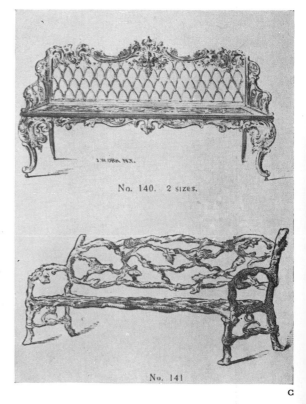

No. 140. 2 sizes.

No. 141

C

PLATE 24

(A) Three of the six basic Windsor types: low back; comb-back; fan-back. From *The American Windsor* by J. Stogdell Stokes, *Antiques*, April 1926.

(B) Hoop-back; New England armchair; loop-back. From *The American Windsor*, J. Stogdell Stokes, *Antiques*, April 1926.

PLATE 25

A

(A) New England writing arm Windsor showing old green paint; 1790–1800. *Shelburne Museum, Shelburne, Vermont.*

(B) A fine example of Philadelphia comb-back. *Coll. of C.K.Davis.*

(C) New York; *c.* 1797; label of John Dewitt; original leather seat. *Joe Kindig, Jr., and Son.*

B

C

PLATE 26

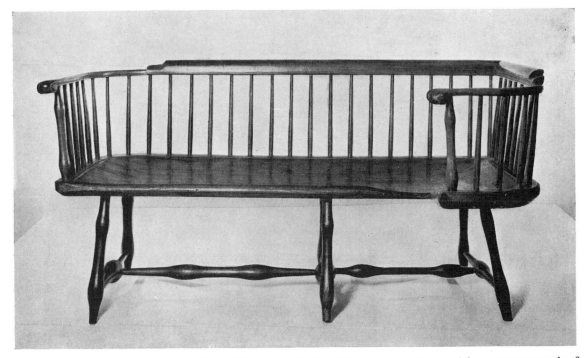

(A) Connecticut low-back settee with knuckle arm; refashioned from a seven-foot straight settee as a result of a fire. *Davenport collection, Williams College, Williamstown, Massachusetts.*

(B) New England writing arm Windsor with bamboo turning; c. 1770. *Davenport collection, Williams College, Williamstown, Massachusetts.*

PLATE 27

(A) New England armchair with braced, one-piece back and arms; fine knuckle ends; *c.* 1760. *Davenport collection, Williams College, Williamstown, Massachusetts.*

(B) Triple-back armchair with comb; arms have three-finger ends. *Davenport collection, Williams College, Williamstown, Massachusetts.*

(C) New England braced fan-back side chair; *c.* 1770. *Davenport collection, Williams College, Williamstown, Massachusetts.*

(D) Comb-back armchair with double curbed arm; New England, *c.* 1760. *Davenport collection, Williams College, Williamstown, Massachusetts.*

PLATE 28

Unpainted pine cupboard; late-eighteenth or early-nineteenth century. *All illustrations are from Old Sturbridge Village, Sturbridge, Massachusetts.*

PLATE 29

(A) Sunflower chest, taking its name from the rayed, aster-like flower in the carved oak center panel; vicinity of Hartford, seventeenth century.

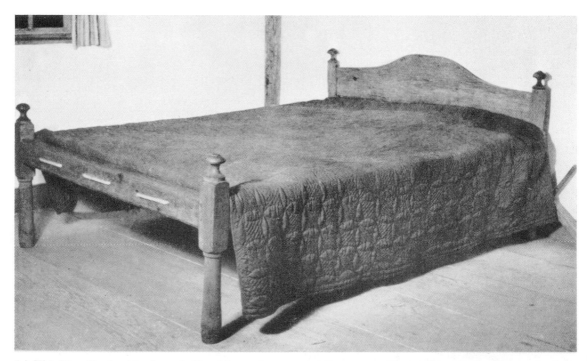

(B) This New England bed, probably eighteenth century, reflects an earlier tradition in the choice of oak for the posts and rails; headboards were usually pine.

PLATE 30

(A) Slat back chair; three, four and five slats, turned members and finials, rush or splint seats, arms and rockers gave variety to a basic form.

(B) Country Chippendale chair of curly maple. Often made in sets; local cabinetmakers made numerous interpretations for almost a century.

(C) Painted pine settle, narrowed to a single seat; settles were made for two centuries.

PLATE 31

(B) The hutch table with storage space in the seat was made in the seventeenth, eighteenth and nineteenth centuries; this one is pine, painted red; mid-eighteenth century.

(A) Tavern table, maple with marbleized top; pine bottle chest has grooved and painted decoration; the pipe box is decorated in green and gray.

PLATE 32

tion in decoration, the fronts of these chests were curved. The curve varied between ox-bow and serpentine. Occasionally the corners were chamfered. Each variation was popular for a time, and the shapes varied from region to region. In Massachusetts the curving front is occasionally accompanied by sides that swell toward the bottom in a kettle or bombé shape, seen in the desk section of the exceptionally graceful desk-bookcase at Winterthur (Plate 13B). This form was occasionally found in Connecticut. A variation of the curving front is the blockfront in which flattened curves in three vertical sections are either applied or cut from solid wood. In some outstanding examples made in Newport (Plate 12A) and Connecticut, these sections are topped by shells that are finely carved.

The desk remained a form that is a variation of the chest of drawers (Plate 15A). Its development is the same with similar enrichment of detail. The form with the bookcase added (Plate 13B) is better known as a Chippendale piece than earlier. Details of dentil molding on the doors of the bookcase, mirrored doors, fluted chamfered corners, architectural elements such as pilasters with richly carved Corinthian capitals are among the many devices used for enrichment.

Although little new development is seen in the forms of tables, there is greater variety in size and decoration in the Chippendale style. Oval, round or rectangular drop-leaf tables with cabriole legs continued in use as dining tables with subtle changes (Plate 11B). Acanthus leaf carving on the knees and claw and ball foot terminals were favored over the ordinarily plain legs of Queen Anne examples.

China or tea tables, rectangular in shape, seem to have been made in greater numbers. Again, it is the character of the decoration that changes. Carved ornament becomes more ostentatious, with elaborate acanthus leaf decoration on the legs and the skirt. The shape of the top is more often curved as a further concession to the new taste (Plate 12C). The tilt-top baluster base table, which serves as a candlestand when very small and a tea table when larger, was introduced as a form in which the baluster was plain, but Chippendale

examples have elaborately carved balusters and legs, and in some cases the top is scalloped and fitted with a molding around the edge. The scalloped top inspired the name 'pie-crust' for these elaborate tables (Plate 12B). A feature making the top turn is the 'bird-cage', a cube of approximately six inches, with solid top and bottom and sides consisting of small baluster or columnar pegs. The base fits into the 'cage' and the table top rests on it, connected by a hinge so that it can be tilted. The 'cage' can be turned on the base. The baluster on a tripod is also used as the base for fire-screens. The baluster is tall and thin and often elaborately carved. The screen is ordinarily needlework.

Another type of small table, the card or gaming table (Plate 13C), also becomes more elaborate in carved decoration without any significant changes in form. The serpentine front becomes more popular since it is so suitable to a form with carving. The outstanding new form is the Pembroke table, a rectangular breakfast table with short drop leaves. The name is not used in the *Director*, but it is found on bills of the time. Usually the legs of these tables are in the 'Chinese taste' and reinforced by crossed stretchers.

A larger form devised for use in serving a meal is the side table, the predecessor of the sideboard. The Chippendale examples often have marble tops (Plate 11C). There again, the form is one known in Queen Anne examples but now decorated with more elaborate carving. Occasionally the cabriole leg is replaced by the Marlborough.

Chairs changed radically in line, although the proportions remained virtually the same. The back is much more intricate, the curving top rail turns up at the ends in a 'cupid's bow' shape, and the center back support, the splat, is cut out and carved in a pattern often borrowed from the *Director* (Plates 13A, 14B). The rails and stiles frequently are carved in foliate patterns. This is all in contrast to the rich but simply curving Queen Anne back with its solid splat. The seat, which had been curved in a horseshoe shape, becomes straight sided. Besides the usual cabriole leg, the straight leg is also employed as a support (Plate 15B).

In the choice of designs for the back, there is a variety of pattern which often can be traced back to inspiration from one of the 'tastes' suggested by Chippendale. The use of a Gothic arcade, however, can not readily be distinguished from a Chinese or French pattern in all cases because of the liberties taken with the various motives. The objective was whimsical design rather than archeological precision. There were other designers besides Chippendale who provided designs in a very closely related spirit. Although entire books of designs might not be available, groups of engraved designs were. Another source was the actual furniture, which was at times imported. The advertisements are confusing on this score, because the allusions to importations tend to give us an exaggerated idea of their importance.

The curving lines of the rococo are aptly used in the backs of upholstered pieces. Sofas and settees have curving frames which were covered by rich imported fabrics (Plate 11A). In rare pieces a part of the upper frame is exposed and carved as in English examples of late rococo design.

Regional characteristics summarized: the differences in taste that developed in the various American colonies as an attribute of location are very complex. By the Queen Anne period they could be distinguished, and in Chippendale furniture the characteristics are perhaps even more apparent. In Massachusetts one finds very thin cabriole legs with the knees coming to a point in the center (Plate 11A). The skirts of tables and chairs of such pieces are narrow and there is a general tightness of line. The claw and ball foot, characteristic of the area, has claws that are turned back so that they appear to be grasping the ball tightly (Plate 11A). The ball is high in an almost oval shape. Almost completely contradictory is another trend in which elaborate carving and shapes are important. The bombé (Plate 13B), the serpentine and other types of shaped fronts are employed. In some cases finely carved details are added to make the form even more elaborate. The work of a Boston cabinetmaker, John Cogswell, is outstanding in its rich detail, while just across the river in Charlestown, Benjamin Frothingham produced furniture in which elegance is achieved through delicacy and simplicity.

Newport was the center of a very special style in this period. As a rich port town and already a summer resort, it had many wealthy residents, and its cabinetmakers were able to produce some masterpieces of technique and fine design. Since designs are quite conservative, hardly any truly rococo details are used. The finest and most typical work is in the blockfront pieces where shells are used to top the section of blocking (Plate 12A). These shells are superbly carved with great restraint. A group of tables made in Newport has carving on the cabriole legs in a design that combines leaf and shell in a simple intaglio pattern (Plate 12C). A concession to the rococo is seen in some tables where the Marlborough leg is used with rich classical detail in the form of fluting and reeding rather than Chinese ornament.

Another sign of the virtuosity of the Newport craftsmen is the way claw and ball feet are carved. The claws on the finest Newport examples are joined to the ball at the nails of the claw, with the rest of the claw raised above the ball so that light is seen between the ball and claw (Plate 12C). This is a minor but significant detail.

Newport and Boston influence can be seen along with New York and Philadelphia influence in Connecticut furniture. Connecticut developed a particular style in which various influences remained easily recognizable.

New York made heaviness a virtue in design. Rich New York carving always lacked delicacy, but rarely finesse. The skirts of New York tables and chests often have a molding of gadrooning (Plate 13C) and carving on the knees is cut deep, with an area of cross hatching frequently in a triangular shape at the center of the top of the knee. New York case pieces tend to be straight across the front with corners chamfered and fluted. The double chest often has a frieze of fretwork applied below the cornice. As in the Queen Anne period, New York chairs retain a closeness to English furniture in details such as the footed rear leg. The claw and ball typical of New York (Plate 13C) has the three front claws quite straight, with the two on the side appearing perpendicular to the center claw. The rear claw is often a continuation of the rear of the cabriole leg without any break or turn of line to distinguish the foot from the leg.

Philadelphia was the largest city in America for decades before the Revolution, and the center of fine craftsmanship. Philadelphia furniture tends to be elaborately carved and generally ornate. There is a squatness in proportion that emphasizes the richness of the ornament (Plate 14C). Forms, such as the high chest, may be conservative, but frequently the ornament is in the latest fashion and directly from an engraving (Plate 14A). The most elaborately carved and wonderfully shaped American chairs are of Philadelphia workmanship, and are closely related to the most ornate English examples (Plate 13A). The claw and ball foot in Philadelphia is squat and proportionately smaller than that of other centers.

One center of fashion south of Philadelphia was Charleston, where furniture was made in high style and fairly close to English design. Significantly, the high chest, out of fashion in London, was a form not used for Chippendale furniture in Charleston but the chest-on-chest was favored (Plate 15C). Ornamentation is used freely, with fretwork added to many plain surfaces.

In short, each of the centers of fashion in the American colonies developed a particular way of interpreting style. Within bounds of variety there are factors of similarity. No matter how ornate American furniture is, there remains an element of clear line. The American Chippendale style is a conservative, almost classical, version of the English rococo, with enough consistency and quality to be accepted as an integral style rather than as a provincial echo.

Classical style: about 1780 the classical style was introduced in America as a reaction to the rococo. This style is sometimes named for two English cabinetmakers who published books of furniture design, George Hepplewhite and Thomas Sheraton. Although neither of these men was responsible for original ideas, both provided neo-classical designs which America followed. The notion that American furniture can be separated into a Sheraton and a Hepplewhite style, however, presupposes basic differences which do not exist between the two.

The interest which began in the fifteenth century received in the classical art of Rome new vigor in the eighteenth. In 1738 excavations began near Rome at Herculaneum, and a decade later work on the most romantic of sites, Pompeii, was begun and continues to this day. This interest in the antique was reflected in the architectural design of Robert Adam, who introduced the new style in England shortly before 1760. Adam's innovation was in going to the antique for sources, whereas earlier eighteenth-century attempts at employing the classical usually sought inspiration from Renaissance and baroque models.

Besides designing houses, Adam frequently undertook furnishing their interiors. For this he commissioned important cabinetmakers to execute his furniture designs. Thomas Chippendale executed some of Adam's furniture at the time his *Director* was in vogue. Adam attempted to establish a vocabulary of design dominated by simplicity and straight lines. He used oval, round and straight motives in clear linear patterns that were entirely unlike the complicated floral, shell and foliate designs of the rococo.

Adam's new style was very quickly taken up by other architects. It was more than something personal, rather an expression of the mood of the era. The reaction to rococo exuberance is to be found elsewhere in Europe at the same time. In France the same kind of reaction occurred so that the style of Louis XVI in many ways is a parallel expression.

The books of furniture designs in the style came later. In 1788 two books of designs were published. One was by Thomas Shearer, who contributed illustrations for *The Cabinet-Maker's London Book of Prices*. The other, *The Cabinet-Maker and Upholsterer's Guide*, was by George Hepplewhite and was published by his widow, Alice. Hepplewhite's book was a really comprehensive view of the style. It included 300 items for the use of cabinet-makers. None of the designs was original, rather they were practical modifications of the more elaborate designs by Adam. Even the shield-back chair was not really his invention.

Three years later Thomas Sheraton began the publication of *The Cabinet-Maker's and Upholsterer's Drawing Book*. Both Sheraton and Hepplewhite were adaptors of the Adam style in which neo-classical ornament was applied to variations of furniture form that normally evolved from what went before. The ornament was antique but the basic lines of the furniture were not. Early in the nineteenth century a more faithfully classical style developed with the design of furniture based at least in part on ancient furniture forms, a contrast to earlier efforts. A design book influential in the spread of this second phase of the classical style was *Household Furniture and Decoration* by Thomas Hope, published in 1807. Hope was a scholar and architect, a friend of the French architect Percier, whose influence was important in the formation of the Directoire style in France. Hope owned a large collection of antiquities and had studied in Greece and Egypt. He attempted to recreate ancient forms. For chairs, couches and a few other types he was on safe ground, but more frequently adaptation was required to make the style fit forms that had not existed in ancient times. The year after Hope's work appeared, a less scholarly and more practical work was published by a cabinetmaker and upholsterer, George Smith. It was entitled *A Collection of Designs for Household Furniture and Interior Decoration*, and contained furniture in the Greek, Egyptian and Roman styles. This more archeologically correct style continued in fashion until Victorian times. Smith published a volume of designs in the same classical spirit in 1826 in which he offered designs to replace those that had become obsolete in his 1808 book. The new work combined Greek and Gothic in heavy forms. In the earlier part of the period the designs of Sheraton and Hepplewhite were important, and in the later Hope and Smith were influential. The presence of French craftsmen who worked in America after the Revolution was another factor.

The classical style brought about many changes in design and form. It is basically a style in which delicacy is important. Straight line and uncomplicated curves are the basis of design. The straight leg, tapering to a narrow foot, either round or rectangular in cross-section, is the most common. Veneer and inlay, which were not used in the Chippendale period, regained a place of importance. The most popular classical motives are: the patera, husk, generally called bellflower, and eagle in inlay; the thunderbolt, sheaf of wheat, drapery, baskets of fruit and vines in carving. Besides mahogany, lighter colored woods such as satinwood were used in contrasting veneers.

Changes in furniture forms include the replacement of the high chest and low chest by chests of drawers and wardrobe-like presses. The dining room, as a separate room, became more common and furniture specifically for it was developed. The sideboard (Plate 16A), the most notable example, is a form invented by Robert Adam and developed by Thomas Shearer. American cabinetmakers commonly borrowed from designs of Sheraton or Hepplewhite. Many smaller forms were employed in this period, either as variations or as innovations. The sewing table, or lady's work table, is an example of such innovation (Plate 18c).

The chest of drawers, a form revived in the Chippendale period, became more common after 1780, with very few changes to transform it into an expression of the new style. Both Hepplewhite and Sheraton suggested a number of designs. A popular simple design offered in the Hepplewhite *Guide* and again in the Sheraton *Drawing Book* with only minor variations was a curving swell or bow-front chest supported on French bracket feet, a kind of curving high bracket foot (Plate 16c). The front and sides are generally veneered in contrasting light and dark woods. Occasionally there is an inlaid design on the front in an oval either on the skirt or across a drawer, and a border.

A design specifically attributed to Thomas Sheraton is the chest on round legs which extend through the entire piece as columns projecting at the corners as on the sewing table

(Plate 18D). These columns are reeded or have turned decoration.

The dressing table, with fewer tiers of drawers than the chest, and a mirror attached above, is a form introduced in the classical period. It is a transformation of the low chest. In some examples it is closely related to the Sheraton chests, but its lines vary. The form continues through the entire period and in some late examples one finds the curule leg, an ancient Roman type where two legs on each side roughly form an X (Plate 17C).

The slant-top desk popular in the Chippendale period and earlier continued to be common in the classical style. Hepplewhite suggested the rather moderate changes to the slant-top which American cabinetmakers followed. The surface is veneered with decoration inlaid on occasion instead of being solid wood with carved decoration. The claw and ball or bracket feet are replaced by the curving high French bracket feet, which make the lines lighter and more graceful. There are more complicated variations introduced. The folding lid of the slant-top was replaced by a rolling cylinder top made of a solid piece or of a tambour consisting of strips of wood on canvas. The new top is often found as a development of the desk-on-frame, supported on tall legs rather than being combined with the chest of drawers.

A new type of desk has a tambour enclosing the pigeon holes and small drawers. In this case the strips are vertical and are moved horizontally in two sections from the center (Plate 18A). The writing area is made by opening a hinged lid that rests flat before the tambour.

Each type of desk is occasionally topped by a bookcase with glass doors (Plate 20A), and in a wider variation the sideboard and secretary are combined.

The bookcase as a separate piece of furniture is extremely rare before 1780. Afterwards it is less rare, but not common. Usually it consists of a glass enclosed upper section and a lower part with wooden doors.

In the category of tables there is great variety of form. Small types for various uses were introduced. The dining table underwent several changes. In the early nineteenth century the dining room became a more common phenomenon and tables seating large groups were developed. An extension table was worked out which could be dismantled into several smaller tables. Shapes vary and the legs are round or square in cross-section. Inlay decoration was used on the legs of some of the finer examples. Late examples occasionally have a series of balusters on curving legs to support the top. Often balusters have heavy carving.

The sofa table was made for a position near the sofa and is described in Sheraton's *Cabinet Dictionary* as a 'sofa writing table'. It is long and narrow with short drop leaves at either end. The table usually has legs at either end joined by simple stretchers. The position back of a sofa is a modern arrangement.

The Pembroke table was known first in the Chippendale period, and the classical version has the expected modifications in design (Plate 20C). A larger variation, with the four legs replaced by a central baluster, or its equivalent, is called a library table. It seems to have been used in the middle of a room.

Tables designed to be used against a wall, side tables, were designed relatively high. A few examples of earlier styles are known, but in the classical period they seem to have been more numerous. These only occasionally have marble tops, and they may very well have been more than serving tables in a dining room. Some probably were used in halls and parlors.

The wardrobe is a form that was known in America from the seventeenth century, but it was fairly uncommon among English colonists, who favored chests of drawers of various kinds. During the classical period, marked by the disappearance of the chest, there was an increase in the popularity of the wardrobe. There are several types, some including a lower section of drawers.

Chair design changed in line and decoration during the transition from Chippendale to the classical. Although there was little change in proportion, the new vocabulary of motives suggests greater lightness. There is some variety among the early examples, with the shield back (Plate 16B), the oval back and a rectangular back (Plate 17B) competing. American cabinetmakers theoretically followed Hepplewhite when they used the shield or oval back and Sheraton for the rectangular form. The differences from the designs in the book and the fact that both designers used these shapes make it difficult to trace the specific source of inspiration. The early classical style chairs generally have straight, tapering legs and frequently the seat is curved. One aspect of American conservatism in design is manifested in the fact that there are chairs in which the back is a compromise between the shield shape and the Chippendale 'cupid's bow'. There the top rail is curved almost like a shield and the side stiles are straight.

In both the conservative and more stylish examples there is either a center splat decorated in a classical motif or a series of columns curving in toward the bottom. Popular motifs for decoration of the splat are the urn, and feathers. The second type, with columns, is sometimes called a baluster back. Inlay is used less frequently than carved decoration on American chairs, with small garlands of flowers on the tapering legs and intricate festoons surrounding the urns or feathers.

On the rectangular or square back the same motifs are used. Generally columns flank a center splat, or an arcade goes all the way across. Urns and feathers are equally popular. The straight round leg with reeding and a straight seat are used. Carving, or carving combined with inlay, is usual.

A different approach to the use of antique sources is seen in chair design after 1800, when the general design was based on actual classical chairs. The back has a solid, thick curving top rail with thin stiles that are often of one piece with the seat rail and the splat is generally horizontal when used (Plate 19C). Occasionally a lyre, harp or simple X-shape serves as a back support.

The seats of these pieces are often curved and cane was revived as a substitute for upholstery on side chairs. These designs began as suggestions of Sheraton, but after 1807 the more accurate interpretations of classical chairs by Hope gradually came to the fore.

Sofa designs are lighter and simpler in the classical style. The camel back of Chippendale is replaced by a straight lined back or one with a simpler curve. In a number of designs wooden arm supports were used projecting from the upholstered portion (Plate 19A). Legs were in the usual classical shapes. In later examples a curving leg, called the saber leg, is frequently used. This is simple in 1810 and is reeded, but by 1830 the curve became an elaborately carved lion's paw or cornucopia. The line is virtually the same, although much heavier.

The day-bed was revived in the classical period, a favorite variation being the 'Récamier', named for the famous subject of David's portrait, who is portrayed on a similar French example. Another name was 'Grecian sofa'. This has a curving back and extended seat with a long arm rest on one side.

Regional traits in the classic period: after the Revolution the newly established states continued to vary their interpretations of furniture styles. The same dependence on English inspiration held, but a French influence was discernible after 1800. In some centers independence brought with it a closer relationship to English furniture, possibly because of the renewed migration.

Salem took over Boston's position of preeminence as a center of fine craftsmanship in Massachusetts during the Revolution. Afterwards its cabinetmakers provided furniture not only for the region but for export. Carving on Salem furniture is an important feature. Elaborately carved motifs such as a basket of fruit, the cornucopia, garlands of fruit or grapes are found with punch-marked backgrounds. The finest of this carving was executed by Samuel McIntire (Plate 19A) for the various cabinetmakers.

Boston, although less active after the Revolution, remained the scene of fine craftsmanship. The work of John Seymour is outstanding. His labeled tambour secretaries are among the finest examples of American furniture. The tambour is made of thin strips of wood with a delicate garland inlay. Inlays of ivory are used around the keyholes. The pilaster, the herringbone and the lunette inlays seen on his work may have been used by other Boston craftsmen also, so attribution on stylistic grounds is difficult. The bellflower inlay of three petals which Seymour used is easily confused with the bellflower of Baltimore, another very sophisticated center.

Rhode Island, which had been most important before the Revolution, was less influential after it. Fine cabinetmaking continued to be important, and in the work of such men as Holmes Weaver we find really elaborate inlays handled with great skill.

In New York the early classical style had the local characteristic of simplicity and strength. Most famous is the later cabinetmaker, Duncan Phyfe, who worked in New York from 1795 until his retirement in 1847. His early work often follows Sheraton's suggestions (Plates 17A, 20C). His characteristic chair has a thick top rail and stiles joined in one piece with the seat rail (Plate 19C). The carving on the top rail was executed in a few specific motifs. The thunderbolt, the sheaf of wheat and a festoon of drapery make up almost the whole repertoire. The lyre and the harp are motifs used as splats and as a substitute for a baluster on tables with a center support.

New York was a city in which French influence was strong. After the Revolutions in France and the French West Indies there was an influx of French immigrants. They were probably responsible for the abnormally strong French influence there. Charles Honoré Lannuier, an émigré who worked in New York, produced certain pieces of furniture with a strong French quality, in others repeating Sheraton designs.

Philadelphia elegance was manifested in works of four cabinetmakers, Daniel Trotter, Ephraim Haines, Joseph Barry and Henry Connelly (Plate 20B). Haines and Connelly worked in a style that suggested their use of Sheraton designs. Reeded legs with delicately carved Corinthian capitals and round spade feet are often encountered. The work of Barry reflects Sheraton influence also. On his label are designs borrowed from the *Drawing Book*, but his work reflects later influences as well. Philadelphia was not as significant in classical furniture design as it had been earlier.

Baltimore came into its own during the Revolution and afterwards as a quickly growing, prosperous community and was a center of fine cabinetmaking. Baltimore's elegance is at times confusingly close to English style but goes to extremes, as in the use of painted glass panels, and gilt decoration on light wood inlays, which is typical of the exuberance of 'nouveau riche' ornament in any period. The small desks with elaborate ornamentation that follow Sheraton's suggestions are more elaborate than any other American classical example. Inlay on panels showing contrasting woods is typical (Plates 16A, 19B).

The classical style in America had its primary influences from England and secondary ones from France. It reflected various phases of the neo-classical revival. Early neo-classical influence was restricted to ornament, later it spread to the choice of furniture forms. In the last years there was a change in proportions, although the same basic forms and motifs continued to be used. The last phase, which is heavy, is the most difficult to understand, since it is very easily thought of as the result of a decline in taste, but it must be seen in its own context as a counterpart of the architecture of the Greek Revival.

GLOSSARY

Acanthus: the leaf used in classical and Renaissance architectural design, particularly on Corinthian capitals. Adapted later as a motif in furniture design. Most important in Chippendale furniture as decorative motif on the knees of cabriole legs.

FIG. 1. Acanthus

Apple: a hard wood of a rich pink-brown color used especially for turnings in American furniture but also occasionally for case pieces.

Apron: the horizontal member below the seat rail of a chair or the underframing of a case piece. Ornamental in function, it is frequently scalloped or carved.

Ash: a cream-colored hard wood with oak-like graining. Used for upholstry frames because it is tough and elastic; used also in Windsor chairs. As a secondary wood, ash was favored in Newport case pieces.

Bail: a curving pull, often of brass, hanging from metal bolts and backed by a metal plate. Used for drawers from about 1700 on in America.

Ball foot: a round turned foot most popular in the William and Mary period.

Banister-back chair: tall side or arm chair with turned members. The back is made up of split balusters. A simplified William and Mary style chair popular in rural areas all through the eighteenth century.

Baroque: the major style of seventeenth-century Europe, characterized by sweeping curves, resplendent ornament and the inventive use of classical motifs. Reflected in the American William and Mary style.

Beech: a smooth, close-grained wood of light color less frequently used in America than England. Found in the underframes of New York Chippendale pieces and occasionally in New England Chippendale as well as early turned pieces.

Bellflower: a classical style motif; flower bud of three or five narrow pointed petals; carved or inlaid; the English husk motif.

Bell seat: a curving seat shaped a little like a bell, also called compass seat. Used especially in Philadelphia Queen Anne chairs.

Bible box: a rectangular box usually with a slant-top. Used to hold a Bible, books or writing materials. It was placed on a chest or table. A seventeenth-century form often made of oak and carved.

Bilbao (Bilboa): a wall mirror of colored marbles in the classical style; supposedly imported from the Spanish sea-port, Bilbao.

Bilsted: word used in colonial New York for sweet-gum wood.

Birch: hard, close-grained wood. Stained to substitute for mahogany in country furniture. Resembles satinwood in certain cuts. The American variety, *betual lenta*, was exported to England in second half of the eighteenth century.

Bird's-eye: a marking encountered on sugar maple. It consists of small spots reminiscent of birds' eyes.

Blister: a marking found in various woods such as maple, mahogany and pine.

Blockfront: a treatment of the front of a case piece favored in Newport, Rhode Island, in the Chippendale period and used elsewhere in New England; rarely in New York and Virginia. The front is made of thick boards cut so that in the center a section recedes in a flattened curve and on either side a section swells out in a flattened curve. The Newport examples and those by cabinet-makers under Newport influence generally have carved shells topping the receding and convex sections; known at the time as 'swell'd front'.

Boat bed: an Empire style bed shaped like a gondola; a variant of the sleigh bed.

Bonnet top: a type of broken arch pediment topping tall case furniture in which the entire top is covered. There are two varieties. In one the bonnet is solid wood behind the pediment, and in the other the pediment is repeated in the back with side covers joining the two pediments.

Bookcase: in America the bookcase appears first as the upper part of the secretary, and not until after 1780 does it occur as a separate form. Earliest records show cupboards and chests used to store books. In England the form existed by the middle of the seventeenth century.

Boston rocker: a rocking chair in the category of fancy painted chair, related to the Hitchcock type and developed from the Windsor. The back is made of turned spindles topped by a broad curving rail. Examples date from the 1820s, but from the 1840s the rockers were mass-produced.

Bow-front: a curving front used on case pieces in New England during the Chippendale period.

Bracket foot: a foot supporting a case piece and attached directly to the underframing. It consists of two pieces of wood, joined at the corner. The open side is generally cut out in a simple pattern. The corner end is sometimes straight, at other times curved in an ogee pattern.

Breakfast table: a small table with hinged side leaves that can be used by one or two people. After the Chippendale period the name Pembroke is often applied to the type.

Brewster chair: a seventeenth-century type of armchair of turned spindles and posts with rush seat (Plate 2B). The back has two tiers of spindles. There is a tier under the arms and one under the seat. The chair is usually of ash or maple. Named after William Brewster, elder of Plymouth Plantation, whose chair is preserved at Pilgrim Hall, Plymouth, Massachusetts. Similar to the Carver chair.

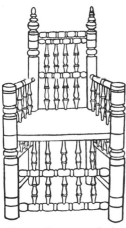

FIG. 2. Brewster chair

Bull's eye: a popular term for the small round mirror with convex or concave glass and an ornate gilt frame. The type was fashionable 1800–20, and often of English or French manufacture. An alternate meaning is the reference to clear glass with a large center drop or gather employed as window glass and in cabinets.

Bureau: in America, a chest of drawers, although in England the word means desk (the original French meaning).

Bureau table: a dressing table with drawers on short legs and a knee-hole recess.

Burl: a tree knot or protruding growth which can be sliced to reveal beautiful graining. Employed as a veneer; particularly popular in American William and Mary veneered pieces. Walnut and maple burls were used most frequently.

Butterfly table: a William and Mary style drop-leaf table with solid swinging supports shaped a little like butterfly wings. The supports are pivoted on the stretchers joining the

FIG. 3. Butterfly table

legs. Assumption that the type is of American origin is probably incorrect.

Cabriole leg: the curving tall furniture leg used in American Queen Anne and Chippendale furniture, and almost universally used in the eighteenth century. The adjective is from the French noun which is a dancing term meaning a goat leap, and is used in the idiom *faire le cabriole* to refer to the agility and grace of a person. The leg is inspired by an animal form, unlike the earlier scroll and turned shapes and is terminated in the claw and ball foot, the hairy paw or the scroll in the Chippendale period and earlier the claw and ball, the pad, trifid or slipper foot.

FIG. 4. Cabriole leg

Camel back: a popular term for the curving upholstered back of a chair or sofa; typical of the Chippendale style but used occasionally later.

Cane chair: a chair with a seat of tightly woven canes or rattans used in America first in about 1690, in William and Mary tall backed chairs (Plate 7A). The type occasionally occurred in Queen Anne but was revived in the classical style. Duncan Phyfe used it.

Caning was introduced from the Orient through the Netherlands.

Canted: sloping, at an angle.

Cartouche: a rococo decoration based on the scroll; encountered in America mainly on  Philadelphia Chippendale where it is used as center finial or in the center design for the skirts of case pieces. 'Philadelphia Peanut' is the popular term sometimes applied to it.

FIG. 5. Cartouche

Carver chair: a seventeenth-century type of armchair of turned posts and spindles with a rush seat (Plate 1B). The back has three spindles; the stretchers are plain. It is a simpler variant of the type which includes the Brewster chair. It is named for the first governor of Plymouth Plantation, John Carver, because his chair, preserved in Pilgrim Hall, Plymouth, Massachusetts, is of this type.

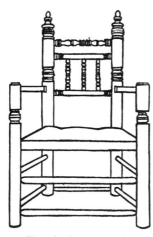

FIG. 6. Carver chair

Cedar: an evergreen related to the pine; its wood was used for drawers, linings and generally as a secondary wood. White cedar used in Philadelpia for drawer bottoms, red cedar found in New England furniture often, and occasionally the primary as well as secondary wood.

Cherry: a hard, close-grained wood used as a primary wood in New York and Con-necticut and less often in Pennsylvania, Virginia and Kentucky.

Chest of drawers: the chest of drawers developed as a refinement of the simple box-like chest in the late seventeenth century. It was generally table-high on short legs with four or five drawers. It was not common in the Queen Anne period but was revived, especially in New England, during the Chippendale period. Serpentine, oxbow and block-front shapes are found on New England Chippendale chests.

China cabinet: a form that did not become important in America until after 1800. Glass enclosed, it is generally the upper part of a chest of drawers or a cabinet enclosed by doors.

Classical style: basically any humanistic style emphasizing ancient Greek ideals, and in the arts a style inspired by Greek and Roman art and architecture. In American furniture the style reflected the innovations of Robert Adam, the English architect who was inspired by ancient Roman design. The design books of Hepplewhite and Sheraton helped communicate the style to America, where it has been called after them by dividing the style into two tendencies, the Hepplewhite and Sheraton. This is a difficult distinction to make.

Claw and ball foot: in American furniture a common termination for the cabriole leg in the Chippendale period; less frequently encountered in the earlier Queen Anne style. It is a bird's claw holding a ball flattened on the bottom. Originally Oriental, it was probably first introduced into Europe in the Lowlands. Popular on American furniture from about 1740 to 1780.

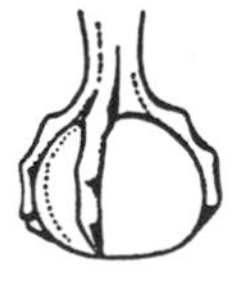

FIG. 7. Claw and ball foot

Concertina action: a device on card and gaming tables for extending the frame to support the table top when it is opened. The back half of the frame is made up of two hinged sections that fold in to reduce the frame size when the top is closed.

Connecticut chest: a seventeenth-century type of oak chest with one or two drawers below the chest area. The front of the chest is divided into panels carved in a flat floral pattern with an aster-like or sunflower device. The drawers and stiles are decorated with applied bosses and spindles painted black. Also called 'sunflower' chest; or Hartford chest (Plate 2c).

Corner chair: an armchair that could be placed in a corner. The arrangement of the legs is unusual, with one at each side, the third in the center of the back and the fourth in the center of the front. The chair back is generally only as high as the arm rest. The shape of the seat varies from a segment of a circle to an almost rectangular shape. The type was made in America through most of the eighteenth century. The seat is usually a good height for desk use.

Corner cupboard: a cupboard fitting into a corner, generally a movable piece. The front is sometimes curved. The cupboard is divided into an upper and lower section, the upper for display and the lower part for storage. The upper section often has glass doors and shelves; made between 1725 and 1820 in a variety of styles.

Couch: a seventeenth- and eighteenth-century term for daybed; not used as synonym for sofa or settee until recent times.

Court cupboard: among the earliest American forms, it was made for display and a minimum of storage (Plate 3A). Based on the English form introduced first in the sixteenth century, it is a rectangular piece, generally of oak, consisting of three shelves with a recessed enclosed cabinet, sometimes with splayed sides on the middle shelf. Decorated with applied turned spindles, bosses and elements suggesting architecture. The columns supporting the shelves are heavy turned baluster forms. The press cupboard is a variant with the lower area enclosed (Plate 1A). Both forms went out of fashion in the William and Mary period.

Courting mirror: a popular term applied to a group of crudely made glasses that have been found around Salem and other sea-port towns. Generally the looking glass is framed by strips of painted glass crossetted at the corners with a center crest on top. The strips are enclosed by metal moldings. Popularly supposed to be of Chinese make, but origin unknown; dating from the early nineteenth century.

Cromwellian chair: a seventeenth-century type of small side chair with the seat and a strip across the back upholstered, often in leather. Legs, stretchers and the exposed parts of the stiles are turned. American examples are rare, English and Continental examples more common. The name probably comes from the fact that the chair was mistakenly thought to have been introduced during the Puritan Revolution.

Cross stretchers: stretchers crossing diagonally to form an 'X'. Most often the stretchers are curved (Plate 6B). Used particularly in William and Mary furniture and in later classical pieces.

Cupid's bow: a term used to describe the typical top rail of a Chippendale chair back which curves up at the ends and dips slightly in the center.

Cypress: a light smooth close-grained wood that grows in the south. Used for drawer linings as well as entire pieces by southern cabinetmakers.

Day-bed: a chair with the seat extended for reclining. Introduced in the William and Mary period. The back can often be lowered. Popular in America until about 1750 and then revived after 1800 in a modified classical version.

Desk box: a rectangular box with sloping lid for the storage of books and writing materials; more popularly known as a Bible box (Plate 4B).

Document drawer: a thin narrow drawer in a desk for important papers.

Dowry chest (or Dower chest): is one made to store the trousseau of a prospective bride. Outstanding among American examples are the Hadley chest (Plate 3B), the Connecticut chest (Plate 2C) and the painted Pennsylvania-German chest.

Drake foot: *see* Duck foot.

Dresser: a wide cupboard with open shelves above for display, and an enclosed cabinet below.

Drop or Teardrop handle: a small curved cast brass drawer-pull in fashion between 1690 and 1720. It is attached to a brass plate often with scallop-shaped edge and etched in a foliate design. Also called pear-drop because of the shape.

Drop-leaf: a table with hinged leaves that can be raised to enlarge it. Supports for the leaves are either legs or other supports swung into position. In the category of drop-leaf table fit butterfly, corner, gateleg and Pembroke tables.

Drum table: a circular top table on a tripod base with a deep skirt that may contain drawers. The type exists only in the classical style and American examples appear late.

Duck foot: a foot used in the Queen Anne period as a terminal for cabriole legs with markings suggesting three toes. Favored in Pennsylvania. Also called the trifid, drake and web foot.

Dumb waiter: extremely rare in American furniture, the form is mentioned in England about 1750, although it does not appear in Chippendale's *Director*. Generally a tripod table with three tiers of turning shelves. Suggested by Sheraton in his *Cabinet Dictionary* (1803).

Eagle, American: included in the Great Seal of the United States adopted in 1782. A motif popular in furniture decoration after that. The eagle was a Roman symbol revived in the eighteenth century and common also in European ornament.

Ebonize: to stain wood to look like ebony. This was often done in the seventeenth century for the applied ornaments on oak furniture. Also used in William and Mary period when contrasting colors were sought in wood.

Fancy chair: a classical style painted chair popular between 1790 and 1850. Decoration is often stencilled. The designs are not standard and many different patterns were followed. Some versions have cane seats.

Federal style: the style of the early Republic dating from *c.* 1785 to 1830 and including influences from Robert Adam and other exponents of the classical style.

Flag seat: a seat of woven rush-like material.

Flame finial: used on American Queen Anne and Chippendale furniture, it is an urn with straight or spiral carving to represent flames issuing from it (Plate 9B).

Flemish scroll: a curving double scroll used on William and Mary style legs; also on the wide stretcher connecting the front legs.

Fluting: narrow vertical groovings used in classical architecture on columns and pilasters. In furniture fluting is employed where pilasters or columns are suggested and on straight legs. It is of particular importance in the classical style but is encountered in earlier work as well. The use of fluting combined with reeding is seen on Newport tables and chairs in the Chippendale style.

Fig. 8. Fluting

Four poster: a bed with four posts to support a canopy or tester.

Gadrooning: a carved ornamental edging of a repeated pattern which, on Chippendale furniture, is often no more than curving, alternating convex and concave sections. Particularly popular in New York and Philadelphia in the Chippendale period.

Gateleg: a form of drop-leaf table with swinging supports that are legs joined to the main frame of the table by upper and lower stretchers which make a gate. Used in the late seventeenth and early eighteenth centuries.

Gothic: a twelfth- to fifteenth-century style revived superficially in the eighteenth century. Chippendale offered designs in the 'Gothick Taste', occasionally followed by

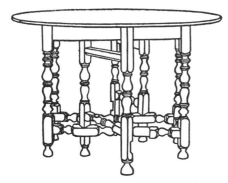

FIG. 9. Gateleg table

American craftsmen. These consisted of arcades of pointed arches and quatrefoils on chair backs. In the classical period there are also occasional designs employing Gothic motifs.

Hadley chest: a chest with one or two drawers and decoration consisting of overall floral carving in a simplified, almost abstract pattern (Plate 3B). These chests were painted originally. Identification of the original owners of some suggests that they served as dower chests in the area around Hadley, Massachusetts.

Handkerchief table: a single-leaf table with leaf and top triangular in shape. Closed, the table fits in a corner, opened it is a small square.

Hickory: a North American tree of the walnut family, hard, strong and heavy. The wood bends well and was used often for Windsor chair spindles.

Highboy: a modern term for the high or tall chest of drawers (Plates 6A, 8A, 9B). The earliest American examples occur about 1700 and the form disappears after the Revolution. The high chest is built in two parts, a lower commode or chest on tall legs on which the larger drawer section is mounted. The Queen Anne and Chippendale examples are generally topped by broken arch pediments with finials at either side and in the center. Architectural motifs such as pilasters and engaged columns are often used as decorative motifs on the main part.

Hitchcock chair: a type of fancy chair mass-produced by Lambert Hitchcock between 1820 and 1850 in Hitchcockville, Connecticut. The chair has an oval turned 'pillow-back' top rail, spindles to form the back, a shaped solid seat and turned legs. It is often painted black or green with gold stenciled decoration. The name is often applied loosely to any similar fancy chair.

Holly: a fine-grained white wood with small flecks used for inlay; stains easily.

Inlay: a technique of placing designs of contrasting colored wood or other materials in the solid wood surface of a piece of furniture. Introduced in America at the end of the seventeenth century and used through the Queen Anne period. Generally forgotten in the Chippendale period and revived in the classical style, when it became quite elaborate.

Japanning: European and American version of Oriental lacquering often substituting paint for the layers of varnish on lacquered wares. Raised *Chinoiserie* in plaster is generally the added decoration. The technique became popular in England late in the seventeenth century; a book of instructions, *Treatise of Japanning and Varnishing*, by Stalker and Parker, was published in 1688 in London. In America the technique was practised before 1715 and continued to be used throughout the century.

Kas: the Dutch word, *Kast*, for wardrobe incorrectly spelled. Used to refer to the wardrobes made by Dutch settlers. They are generally large, with wide moldings, heavy cornice and on ball feet. Their style is of the seventeenth century but they were made for a great part of the eighteenth.

Knotty pine: a low-grade pine used originally only for objects to be painted, now fashionable to use with the knots showing.

Labeled furniture: furniture bearing the paper label of a cabinetmaker which serves as a signature. Labels were applied in obscure places and often have been preserved.

Lacquer: a process of applying successive layers of varnish to wood. Developed in the

Orient in ancient times and introduced to the West in the seventeenth century.

Ladder back: a chair back with the vertical center splat replaced by a series of horizontal bars cut in curving lines. Usually this type of chair has straight legs. It originated in the Chippendale period, but persisted until the end of the eighteenth century.

Lowboy: a modern name applied to the dressing table mounted on tall legs. Often made to match the high chest or highboy. Contemporary names include dressing table, chamber table, low chest of drawers. It is a form introduced in the William and Mary period which persisted through the Chippendale period.

Lyre: a motif used as a splat in chair backs; also as the pedestal support of a table in the classical period. Duncan Phyfe particularly favored it.

Mahogany: a dense, dark heavy wood which in the eighteenth century was known in two varieties, the Spanish and the Honduras. The Spanish from Cuba, San Domingo and Puerto Rico was darker and harder than the variety from Honduras. Mahogany was an imported wood that became important in America close to 1750.

Maple: any one of the trees or shrubs of the genus *Acer*, growing in the northern temperate zone from Canada to North Carolina. Sugar or rock maple, the hard variety, has grains in the bird's-eye and blister patterns. Silver or white maple and the red or swamp maple are both softer and occasionally have curly grains as well as the tiger stripe. Maple has always been popular with American cabinetmakers. In the Pilgrim style, it was used for the turned additions to oak furniture. Later it played an important role both as a primary and secondary wood.

Marlborough leg: the straight leg introduced as in the 'Chinese Taste' by Thomas Chippendale. Decoration generally consists of cutting the surface with a molding plane. Occasionally strips of carved border or frets in a Chinese pattern are added.

Mortise and tenon: for joining two pieces of wood. The mortise is a cavity, usually rectangular; the tenon, an end shaped to fill the cavity exactly; characteristic of Philadelphia chairs, where seat rail joins the stiles.

FIG. 10. Mortise and tenon

Oak: a hard wood with coarse grain used as a primary wood in seventeenth-century furniture and as a secondary wood later. Its hardness made it difficult to carve but quite durable.

Oxbow front: curving front for case pieces in a reverse serpentine curve reminiscent of an oxbow. Used particularly in New England in the Chippendale period.

Pedestal table: a table on a round center support.

Pembroke table: a small table with short drop leaves supported on swinging wooden brackets. The term Pembroke is used in England first in the 1760s. Although Chippendale lists tables of this description as 'breakfast tables' in the *Director*, he used the term on bills. Sheraton said this type of table was named after the lady who first ordered it. It was particularly popular in the classical period and both Hepplewhite and Sheraton suggested designs for it.

Pennsylvania Dutch: the name applied to German settlers in Pennsylvania. Their furniture has many distinctive qualities since it assimilates English and German peasant styles. Their cabinetmakers worked in soft woods which they painted and often decorated with floral patterns and other motifs from the vocabulary of peasant design.

Pie-crust table: a round tilt-top tea table on a tripod base. The top has a scalloped edge finished with a carved molding which is suggestive of the notched rim of a pie crust; tables in the Chippendale style have pedestals elaborately carved. The tripod consists of three cabriole legs terminating generally in claw and ball feet (Plate 12B).

Pier table: a table designed to stand against the pier, the part of the wall between the windows. In America the term is used loosely to refer to a table designed for use against a wall, a side table.

Pilgrim furniture: term used to describe American seventeenth-century furniture.

Pine: a soft wood growing all over North America in twenty-eight variations of the species. Pine is easy to work but hard to preserve. It has been popular for painted furniture and as a secondary wood.

Poplar: *see* Tulip wood.

Press cupboard: a variation of the court cupboard (*q.v.*) with the lower section enclosed either by doors or drawers (Plate IA). A seventeenth-century form generally made of oak.

Puritan: a term applied to simpler seventeenth-century furniture.

Rail: the horizontal piece in framing or paneling. In a chair back, the top member supported on the stiles.

Reeding: narrow vertical convex moldings encountered in classical architecture as filler for fluting; used in classical style furniture on round legs and bed posts.

Fig. 11. Reeding

Rising sun: fan-shaped ornament which is a simplified version of the shell ornament used particularly on New England case pieces. The pattern is thought to resemble the sun's rays.

Rocking chair: a simple chair mounted on curving strips of wood. The origin is disputed as is the date when it came into use. A favorite unfounded story attributes its invention to Benjamin Franklin.

Rococo: the ornate whimsical eighteenth-century extension of the baroque style begun by the French. The American version only barely suggests the exuberance of the Continental rococo style. Ornament rococo in spirit is used on American Chippendale furniture, particularly in Philadelphia, but the lines of the furniture are more conservative.

Rosette: a round ornament in a floral design.

Roundabout: synonym for corner chair.

Rush seat: from a plant common in most northern countries; rushes were woven into seats for chairs in the seventeenth century in American country furniture. This continued into the nineteenth century.

Saber leg: a term used to describe a sharply curving leg in the classical style which has also been called scroll-shaped and even likened to the shape of a cornucopia. It is generally reeded. This leg is found on small sofas attributed to Duncan Phyfe.

Saddle seat: a seat shaped to fit the human form like a saddle. Used especially in Windsors, but occasionally encountered in elegant furniture.

Salem rocker: a painted rocker related to fancy chairs with a lower back than the Boston rocker.

Salem secretary: a classical style secretary with china cabinet as the upper part. There is generally a double-doored center part with a drawer that pulls out to serve as desk and flanking single-door sections.

Salem snowflake: a six pointed punched decoration resembling a star or a snowflake found as a background in the carved areas of Salem furniture.

Sample chairs: a group of six chairs thought to have been made by Benjamin Randolph, a Philadelphia cabinetmaker, as samples of his skill. The group of chairs (one wing and five side chairs) is in the most elegant Philadelphia Chippendale style.

Sawbuck table: a table with X-shaped legs used in rural areas.

Scroll top: a curved broken-arch pediment used on case pieces. Also called gooseneck, swan-neck, etc.

Scrutoire, escritoire: late seventeenth-century and eighteenth-century term for an enclosed desk, from the French. Also used for desk and bookcase (the English call it bureau).

Secretary: modern term for enclosed writing desk with a cabinet section above that can be used for the storage of books or china.

Settee: a seat with back and arms, a small sofa, for two or more people. The back may be upholstered or made up of several chair backs.

Settle: a bench with arms and a high back; the seat is often the lid of a chest. An early

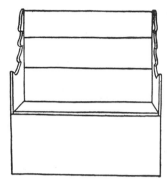

FIG. 12. Settle

form that was used through the eighteenth century in rural areas.

Sewing table: a small table with drawers (Plate 18c) and, frequently, a cloth bag to hold what is being sewn; introduced after 1780.

Shaker furniture: furniture produced in the factories of the Shaker communities which flourished in the middle of the nineteenth century. This furniture was simple, well constructed and extremely functional. The style was *retardataire*, using elements from earlier country furniture. It was among the first mass-produced furniture in which good construction was important. (*See* article on 'The Craftmanship of the American Shakers' by Edward Deming Andrews, p. 66.)

Shearer, George: English furniture designer, contemporary of Hepplewhite and Sheraton, whose work first appeared in the 1788 *Cabinet-Maker's London Book of Prices*. The sideboard, as usually made in the classical style, appeared first in his book of designs.

Sideboard: a dining-room piece for storage and serving; it is a wide chest of drawers usually including cupboard space below the drawers. The form was introduced in the classical period. Robert Adam, the

architect, designed its prototype combining knife boxes on pedestals with cabinet areas and sideboard tables. The table had been used earlier in sophisticated homes. The combination piece was further developed by George Shearer (*see above*) and was included in the design books of both Sheraton and Hepplewhite.

Slant-top desk: a desk on a chest of drawers or frame which has a writing area enclosed by a hinged lid that slopes at a 45-degree angle. Probably originally used closed with the sloping angle for writing. Early examples have the hinges at the upper end.

Slat back: a seventeenth-century style chair made of turned posts connected by horizontal slats across the back. Persisted in rural areas to the twentieth century.

Sleigh bed: a nineteenth-century bed in late classical style with high front and back, generally terminating in scroll-shaped rails that make it look a little like a sleigh.

FIG. 13. Slat back chair

Sofa table: a narrow table meant to be used near a sofa, in front or at sides. Introduced about 1800 and popular with Duncan Phyfe. Often there are small leaves at either end and drawers across the front.

Spanish foot: a scroll form with curving vertical ribs, most often the terminal for a turned leg. Used in the William and Mary and Queen Anne periods. As a terminal for the cabriole leg it is rare but occurs on a group of New Jersey pieces.

FIG. 14. Spanish foot

Spinning wheel: a machine for making yarn or thread, employing foot or hand power. As a piece for the home, it generally was made of turned parts. Used through the nineteenth century in rural areas.

Splint seat: a seat made of oak or hickory strips interlaced. Used in country furniture through the eighteenth century.

Spool: a turning in the shape of a row of spools which was employed for long, thin members such as legs. Introduced after 1820 and continued through the Victorian period in rural work.

Star: an ornamental motif used after the Revolution. It is encountered as brass inlay on late classical furniture under French influence.

Stile: an upright piece in framing or paneling. In a chair back, the vertical members on which the top rail rests.

Stump leg: a simple, thick rear leg curved at the corners; used on Queen Anne and Chippendale chairs, especially in Philadelphia.

FIG. 15.
Stump leg

Sunburst: a decorative carved motif which in American furniture is a half-circle with fluting or reeding in a fan pattern. Really derived from the rocaille or shell motif of the more elaborate rococo style.

Sunflower: carved ornamental floral motif popular on Connecticut chests.

Tavern table: a small rectangular table with one or two drawers in a single tier, and turned legs braced by turned stretchers. William and Mary characteristics persist through the eighteenth century on this form which was common in taverns.

Teardrop: *see* Drop handle.

Tulip wood: a soft light wood used as a secondary wood and in painted furniture; also called tulip poplar.

Turtle back: a plain curved ornamental boss used in the seventeenth century.

Veneering: a technique which involves gluing thin slices of wood on to a wooden carcase. The thin slices are cut to bring out a fine graining or figure. The technique was introduced in America in the William and Mary period and all but disappeared in the

Chippendale period. It was revived in the classical period.

Walnut: finely figured hard wood good for carving, veneering and turning. Black walnut was used particularly in the William and Mary and Queen Anne periods for elegant furniture, and replaced by mahogany when importations increased. It retained popularity in Pennsylvania and the south. White walnut, known better as butternut, grows between New England and Maryland. It is open-grained and light brown, and used mainly in country furniture.

Martha Washington chair: an upholstered-back armchair in the classical style with tapering straight legs (Plate 18B). The back is usually high and curved on top. The term was in use in the eighteenth century. Joseph Short of Newburyport advertised that he made Martha Washington chairs.

Martha Washington mirror: a Georgian-style looking glass with scroll top and bird finial combining wood color and gilt ornament, so-called because Mrs Washington is said to have owned one; also called 'Constitution' mirror, a term of unknown origin which is used without justification.

Martha Washington sewing table: an oval work table fitted with drawers in the center and compartments for cloth on either side; in the classical style. The connection with Martha Washington is remote.

Water leaf: a carved ornamental motif of narrow leaf with regular horizontal undulations divided by stem going down the center (Plate 18c). Used in classical style and favored by Duncan Phyfe as a leg decoration. In many ways it is the classical style counterpart of the acanthus leaf of the Chippendale period.

Web-foot: *see* Duck foot.

Wheat ears: or sheaf of wheat; a carved ornamental motif employed in the classical style. Both Samuel McIntire and Duncan Phyfe used it.

Wing chair: an upholstered chair with high back, stuffed arms and wing-shaped protectors at head level protruding from the back over the arms (Plate 10A). The chair was known in England during the seventeenth century and was probably introduced in America before 1725.

Winthrop desk: a Chippendale slant-top desk mistakenly named for one of the seventeenth-century governors of Massachusetts.

Work table: *see* Sewing table.

CABINETMAKERS

Affleck, Thomas: arrived from London in Philadelphia 1763, died 1795; most famous for his elaborate Chippendale pieces.

Allen, Josiah: worked in Charleston and appears in the *Directory* between 1809 and 1813.

Allison, Michael: worked in New York between about 1800 and 1810 in a style that has been occasionally confused with Duncan Phyfe's.

Appleton, Nathaniel: early nineteenth-century Salem cabinetmaker working in the classical style.

Ash, Gilbert: born 1717, died 1785; New York chair and cabinetmaker of importance. Evidently he studied in Philadelphia, because his chairs are constructed like Philadelphia examples. Several labeled and one signed piece make his work distinguishable.

Ash, Thomas: died 1815; New York chairmaker, son of Gilbert. Succeeded by son, Thomas. (New York City Directory, 1815.)

Axson, William, Jr.: worked in Charleston between about 1763 and his death in 1800. He did interior woodwork as well as furniture.

Backman, John: Lancaster County, Pennsylvania, cabinetmaker, leading member of a family of furniture makers; best-known work in the Chippendale style executed in the last quarter of the eighteenth century.

Badlam, Stephen: born 1751, died 1815. Worked in classical style. His name is stamped on several fine chairs. His masterpiece is the chest-on-chest made for Elias Hasket Derby of Salem, 1791.

Barry, Joseph B.: cabinetmaker in Philadelphia who worked in an elaborate style. His label of *c.* 1810 illustrates a group of Thomas Sheraton designs of 1793.

Belter, John: active 1844 to 1863. New York cabinetmaker of German birth. Famous for heavily carved Louis XV style Victorian furniture. He invented a technique of bending wood, lamination.

Beman, Reuben, Jr.: active 1785 to 1800. Worked in Kent, Connecticut in a *retardataire* Chippendale style.

Burling, Thomas: active before 1774 to 1801; worked in New York in a style more often derived from Chippendale than classical.

Burnham, Benjamin: Connecticut cabinetmaker active around 1769; his block-front desk in American Wing, Metropolitan Museum, has an inscription.

Calder, Alexander: cabinetmaker from Scotland active between 1796 and 1807 in Charleston, S.C.

Chapin, Aaron: worked in East Windsor and Hartford, Connecticut in the 1780s. A cousin of Eliphalet Chapin.

Chapin, Eliphalet: born 1741, died after 1807; born in East Windsor, Connecticut; worked for a time in Philadelphia before returning to Connecticut. Made fine case pieces in a modification of Philadelphia style.

Cheney, Silas E.: active in Litchfield, Connecticut, after the Revolution. Several sideboards are attributed to him.

Cogswell, John: active from 1769 to 1782 in Boston where his most important work is in bombé-shaped case pieces with rich carving.

Connelly, Henry: made fine classical style furniture in Philadelphia between 1800 and 1810. Worked with Ephraim Haines. A turned section with acanthus carving above reeded leg is characteristic.

Courtenay, Hercules: active around 1762; he advertised as a carver and gilder from London, and worked for Philadelphia cabinetmakers including Benjamin Randolph.

Dennis, Thomas: seventeenth-century Ipswich joiner to whom the key pieces of early New England furniture are attributed.

Disbrowe, Nicholas: born in England around 1612, the son of a joiner. Was in Hartford before 1639. Perhaps 'Hartford' and 'Sunflower' chests were developed by his apprentices and followers.

Dunlap, Samuel, II: the best-known member of a family of New Hampshire joiners who did paneling and furniture. His distinctive style included an interlaced cornice design and shells carved deeply. Most of his furniture is in maple.

Egerton, Matthew: Brunswick, New Jersey cabinetmaker probably active in both Chippendale and classical styles.

Elfe, Thomas: Charleston, South Carolina cabinetmaker active between 1747 and 1776. Many elaborately carved case pieces are attributed to him through references to Charleston families in his account books.

Elliott, John: Philadelphia cabinetmaker known particularly for looking glasses. He was active from about 1756 until his death in 1791, when his business was carried on by his son.

Folwell, John: Philadelphia cabinetmaker most famous for making the case for the orrery by David Rittenhouse. Folwell solicited subscriptions for an American counterpart of Chippendale's *Director*, to be called *The Gentlemen and Cabinet-maker's Assistant*, which was never published.

Frothingham· Benjamin: Charlestown, Massachusetts cabinetmaker working from about 1756 to 1809. He was a Revolutionary major and a friend of George Washington. He is known best for Chippendale furniture of restrained design and used blockfront and serpentine fronts for chests and desks.

Gaines, John: a cabinetmaker born in Ipswich, Massachusetts, 1704, who worked in Portsmouth, New Hampshire, between about 1724 and 1743. Known for chairs that combine William and Mary straight back with a Queen Anne violin-shaped splat.

Gillingham, James: Philadelphia cabinetmaker in the Chippendale style responsible for work of fine quality.

Goddard, John: 1723–85; son-in-law of Job Townsend of Newport, Rhode Island, and active as a cabinetmaker from the 1740s on. Three pieces contain original inscriptions stating that he made them. Other members of the family include Thomas Goddard, 1765–1858, and Stephen, 1764–1804, sons of John, who carried on their father's business, and Townsend Goddard, 1750–90, their older brother.

Gostelowe, Jonathan: *c.* 1744–95; Philadelphia cabinetmaker who produced elaborate Chippendale furniture. A labeled piece is in the Philadelphia Museum.

Haines, Ephraim: worked with Henry Connelly in production of superior classical style furniture in Philadelphia.

Hains, Adam: born 1768, active until at least 1815; this Philadelphia cabinetmaker worked in the Chippendale style after the Revolution.

Hosmer, Joseph: Concord, Massachusetts cabinetmaker, active around the time of the Revolution. He worked in a provincial style. His activity in the Revolution included leading an attack on the Concord bridge as a captain of the Minute Men at the outbreak of hostilities.

Lannuier, Charles Honoré: New York cabinetmaker who emigrated from France. He was active at the beginning of the nineteenth century in a style close to the French.

Lawton, Robert, Jr.: active in Newport in the 1790s. Several labeled examples of his work are known.

Lehman, Benjamin: a Philadelphia carpenter most famous for the compilation of a price list for cabinetwork, 1786, the manuscript for which, in the Pennsylvania Historical Society, gives an indication of the types and styles available at the time.

Lemon, William: Salem cabinetmaker flourishing around 1796.

McIntire, Samuel: 1757–1811; a carver active after the Revolution until 1811; his work on Salem furniture as well as in architecture is quite important. He supplied Salem cabinetmakers with carved details; basket of fruit, cornucopia and grape patterns are most characteristic.

Mills & Deming: classical style cabinetmakers in New York around 1790.

Phyfe, Duncan: 1768–1854; New York's most famous cabinetmaker; worked from the late 1780s to 1846 in successive versions of the classical style.

Pimm, John: Boston cabinetmaker working around 1740. He is known from an inscribed high chest with lacquer and gilt decoration in the Winterthur Museum.

Prince, Samuel: New York cabinetmaker who worked in the Chippendale style.

Randolph, Benjamin: Philadelphia cabinetmaker active from 1762 to around 1792, working in the Chippendale style. A group of 'sample' chairs with the most elaborate carving known on American furniture is attributed to him.

Sanderson, Elijah: active from 1771 to 1825 in Salem, Massachusetts. His furniture was exported to the south. He worked with his brother, Jacob; the two employed McIntire as a carver for their finest work.

Sass, Jacob: active in Charleston from 1774 to about 1828. A desk and bookcase exist with the ink inscription: *Made by Jacob Sass, October 1794.*

Savery, William: a Philadelphia cabinetmaker active from the 1740s to his death in 1787. Both simple and elaborate furniture have turned up with his label.

Seymour, John: a Boston cabinetmaker who worked in the classical style. Tambour doors, elaborate inlays, a liberal use of satinwood and an odd locking device are characteristics that make his furniture outstanding.

Shaw, John: Annapolis cabinetmaker advertising between 1773 and 1794, but living until after 1828. Several labeled pieces of his work are known.

Short, Joseph: Newburyport, Massachusetts cabinetmaker active from 1771 through 1819. He produced Chippendale and classical style furniture.

Skillin, John and Simeon: listed as carvers in the Boston Directory, 1798; shipcarvers; worked also for Elias Hasket Derby; were responsible for pediment figures on Badlam's chest-on-chest in the Garvan collection.

Stitcher & Clemmens: appear in the Baltimore City Directory in 1804. A labeled secretary is known.

Toppan, Abner: 1764–1836; Newbury, Massachusetts cabinetmaker who worked first in a belated Chippendale style, and then in the classical style.

Townsend: a family of cabinetmakers active in Newport, Rhode Island for about a century from before 1750 to the middle of the nineteenth. Most famous for elaborate shell decoration on blockfront pieces.

Townsend, Edmund: 1736–1811; son of Job Townsend, working in the family style. A kneehole bureau with his label shows him to be equal to the best of the family.

Townsend, Job: 1699–1765; earliest of the Newport, Rhode Island family of cabinetmakers; worked for important families of Newport and Providence.

Townsend, Stephen: active in Charleston, South Carolina between 1763 and after 1768. A partner of William Axson, Jr., for several years.

Trotter, Daniel: Philadelphia cabinetmaker in the Chippendale and classical styles; known for ladder-back chairs.

Tufft, Thomas: Philadelphia cabinetmaker active during the Chippendale period.

Walker, Robert: active around 1799 to 1833 and the only Charleston craftsman whose labeled pieces survive. Two are known, one of which is at the Charleston Museum.

Wayne, Jacob: Philadelphia cabinet-maker active after 1785; worked in the Chippendale style first, then in the classical.

Weaver, Holmes: 1769–1848; Newport, Rhode Island cabinetmaker in the classical style. He used elaborate inlays in a continuation of the Newport tradition of fine craftsmanship.

Willet, Marinus: 1740–1830; worked as a cabinetmaker in New York and distinguished himself as a colonel in the Revolution; advertised as a cabinetmaker in 1773 and 1774.

BOOKS FOR FURTHER READING

Burton, E. Milby: *Charleston Furniture, 1700–1825,* Charleston, S.C. (1956).

Downs, Joseph: *American Furniture, Queen Anne and Chippendale Periods,* New York (1952).

Horner, W.M., Jr.: *Blue Book of Philadelphia Furniture,* Philadelphia (1935).

Kettell, Russell H.: *Pine Furniture of Early New England,* Garden City (1929, re-issued 1952).

Lockwood, Luke Vincent: *Colonial Furniture in America,* third edition 1926, reissued New York (1951), 2 vols.

McClelland, Nancy: *Duncan Phyfe and the English Regency,* New York (1939).

Miller, E. G.: *American Antique Furniture,* Baltimore (1937), 2 vols. (re-issued 1948).

Nutting, Wallace: *Furniture Treasury,* vols. 1 and 2, Cambridge (1928); vol. 3, Framingham (1933); vols. 1 and 2 re-issued 1954 as one volume.

Southern Furniture, catalogue of the loan exhibition at Richmond, Va., 1952, *Antiques,* Jan., 1952.

Handbook of the American Wing, Metropolitan Museum of Art, New York (2nd ed. 1942). Revised edition in preparation.

Concise Encyclopedia of Antiques, vol. 1, pages 50–74. Hawthorn Books, New York, 1955.

Second Treasury of Early American Homes, Richard Pratt. Hawthorn Books, New York, 1954.

The illustrations on Plates 8, 9, 10, 12, 13, 14 from Joseph Down's *American Furniture, Queen Anne and Chippendale Periods,* Macmillan, 1952, are used by permission of The Macmillan Company, New York.

VICTORIAN FURNITURE

By MARVIN D. SCHWARTZ

THE American Victorian style, in existence from 1840 until about 1910, displays strong English influence, as the name implies. Designs and design books were simultaneously published in London and New York. Basically the Victorian is an eclectic style. Many different sources were used for inspiration with innovations introduced in construction and proportion. Most of the misunderstanding of this style comes from the fact that its originality is not accepted as anything more than lack of ability at imitating. Actually, the Victorian designers tried to remain close to their models but also wanted to create practical furniture and they changed the scale and some of the details to suit the rooms for which the furniture was intended.

The style has been referred to by Carol Meeks as one of 'Picturesque Eclecticism'. The emphasis is on visual elements. Covering and screening new types of construction with traditional motifs is general.

New designs were always based on previous periods. At times the sources were close at hand in the various eighteenth-century styles, but occasionally the more exotic and distant models such as Jacobean and Near Eastern were employed.

Very important to the development of furniture production was the partial industrialization that became typical of the craft in the United States. The large workshop, with the bare beginnings of mass-production and specialization, gradually became common in the centers where furniture was made. This was responsible, in part, for some of the changes in what might be considered traditional forms.

By 1840 many manufacturers in American cities were known to employ from forty to one hundred men, most of whom were unskilled workers. Furniture designs were created by the shop owner and a minimal number of skilled men were required to follow the designs. The larger shops produced inexpensive furniture that could be shipped easily. John of Cincinnati supplied many small Mississippi river towns with stylish furniture. The furniture of Hennesy of Boston was available in many smaller towns along the seacoast.

We can get some idea of the Victorian conception of styles from the writings of the American architect, A. J. Downing. In *Cottage Residences*, published in New York in 1842, he implies the use of more than one furniture style when he says, 'A person of correct architectural taste will ... confer on each apartment by expression of purpose, a kind of individuality. Thus in a complete cottage-villa, the hall will be grave and simple in character, a few plain seats its principal furniture; the library sober and dignified ...; the drawing room lively or brilliant, adorned with pictures. ...'

He continues in the same vein in another book, *The Architecture of Country Houses*, one edition of which was published in 1861 (others earlier): 'Furniture in *correct taste* is characterized by its being designed in accordance with certain recognized styles and intended to accord with apartments in the same style.' Downing goes on to describe the various styles and he includes Grecian (or French), Gothic, Elizabethan, Romanesque, and a version of the Renaissance style. Each has its place. The idea of using the different styles was criticized later by Charles Eastlake, an English architect who was influential in America. In 1872 he said, 'In the early part of the present century a fashionable conceit prevailed of fitting up separate apartments in large mansions each after a style of its own. Thus we had Gothic halls, Elizabethan chambers, Louis-Quatorze drawing rooms, etc. ...'

These various styles of the Victorian period were used at about the same time, but fashion determined when they were replaced and none lasted throughout the period.

The earliest significant style was a continuation of American Empire. This furniture was heavy in proportion and differed from the earlier models only in a few details. The wavy molding was a border introduced late; medallions and other small details of applied carving in leaf or floral motifs reduced the simplicity and classicism characteristic of earlier furniture. In the Victorian versions, drawers rarely have borders of molding but rather are flush with the front surface. Marble tops for small tables and bedroom chests are common. Bracket feet are a frequent support for heavy case pieces. On tall legs turning as well as heavy carving was employed. Popular as finer woods were mahogany, black walnut and rosewood. Simpler, less expensive pieces were made of maple, butternut or other hard woods which often are stained quite dark in red or brown. Veneers in prominent grains were used on case pieces as well as on the skirts of sofas and chairs.

In general there were few new forms developed. Among the new were such peculiarities as the Lazy Susan and the ottoman; however, the wardrobe and the bookcase, which were known only infrequently before, were better known in the Victorian period.

With the factory replacing the craftsman's workshop, techniques requiring less skill developed. Machine sawing and planing were used with hand-fitting and finishing. The lines were planned by someone higher in rank than the man who operated the saw or did the finishing. The larger scale operations made competition a more important factor than ever before with price more important than workmanship.

A Baltimore cabinetmaker, John Hall, published a book of furniture designs in 1840. One of the objectives of his book he describes by saying, 'Throughout the whole of the designs in this work, particular attention has been bestowed in an economical arrangement to save labor, which being an important point,

is presumed will render the collection exceedingly useful to the cabinetmaker.' The designs are Grecian, he says in his commentary and '... the style of the United States is blended with European taste ...'. This is the style that A. J. Downing refers to as Greek, modern and French and 'the furniture most generally used in private houses'. Contemporary cartoons and illustrations confirm his remark by usually including this kind of furniture. A popular woman's magazine of the time, Godey's *Lady's Book*, consistently presented suggestions for furniture in the style from the late 'forties to the 'sixties which was called 'cottage furniture'.

The Gothic style in Victorian furniture has two aspects. As a variation of the classical, it involves only the use of the pointed arch (Plate 22A) and related motifs in what is basically the classical style. As a more ambitious innovation, it involves the use of Gothic ornament in a more serious attempt to create a special style. The first approach was used by Chippendale, who included Gothic motifs in his rococo suggestions. Later, Sheraton included Gothic arcades in suggestions of designs, primarily neo-classical. This continued in early Victorian furniture in the Greek style. The other aspect was connected with the Gothic revival in architecture which, although begun in the eighteenth century, had an important effect on home building after 1830. Suitable to houses in the Gothic style was furniture repeating the motifs. Large bookcases, which seem almost like architectural elements, and hall chairs, high-backed side chairs carved elaborately, are often the most spectacular examples of the style.

Some of the finest examples were designed by architects for use in their buildings. Occasionally spiral turned columns, seventeenth century in inspiration, are combined with elements of earlier inspiration. The characteristic feature of the style is the pointed arch of simple or complicated form used with incised or pierced spandrels and bold raised moldings. The Gothic style is one favored for hall decoration and used less frequently in the parlor. Sets of bedroom furniture in the style are known. Tables are extremely rare in this style.

When referring to furniture of various kinds Downing says in *The Architecture of Country Houses*, 'There is, at the present moment, almost a mania in the cities for expensive French furniture and decorations. The style of royal palaces abroad is imitated in town houses of fifty foot front....' This style was often called Louis XIV, although it is a combination of various French styles from Louis XIV to Louis XVI (Plates 22B, C).

Revival of rococo style had started in France as a reaction to its classicism which was dominant shortly before the Revolution. With the Restoration came a desire for the good old days and a style related to them. Napoleon's Romanism was as distasteful as his political upsets. From France the revival spread to the rest of the Continent, England and the United States. In the Victorian home, where each room varied in style to suit its proper mood, the French style was most popular in the parlor, although bedroom furniture in the style is known.

The American Victorian pieces were smaller in proportion than the eighteenth-century models. The curving lines of the back stiles are often exaggerated so that the back is balloon-shaped. Cabriole legs are restrained in their curve. Console tables with marble tops come in scallop shapes. Curving fronts are typical for case pieces. Carving in rose, grape or leaf motifs with elaborate details in high relief is seen on chairs and sofas. On other forms this carving is flatter. Elaborate carving was frequently used on cabriole legs.

The curve becomes all important as a contrast to the straightness of the classical. Small boudoir pieces were made in this style as well as whole matching parlor sets which include a sofa or love seat, gentleman's armchair, lady's chair, four side chairs, an ottoman and center table (Plate 21). In a drawing room set there are additional pieces such as an extra sofa, more side chairs and possibly a matching *étagère*. There seem to be no dining-room pieces in this style. Introduced in America about 1840, it was important until some time in the 1870s. One of the most important cabinetmakers working in this manner was John Belter of New York (Plates

23A, B). Born in Germany, he opened a shop in the city of New York in 1844 and continued in business until his death in 1863. Belter's work was a distinctive variation of the Louis XV style. He invented a laminating process for curving wood that he used in making the sides of case pieces and chair and sofa backs. He destroyed the means of doing this laminating shortly before his death, so that it was never used later. Solid curving pieces are characteristic of Belter's shop, as is elaborate carving in high relief and balloon-shaped chair backs. Belter's parlor sets are best known, but he also made bedroom furniture.

The Louis XVI style was more specifically popular after 1865 when there was some reaction to the exuberance of the rococo revival evident in the Louis XV-inspired examples. The straight line and the fine detail are distinctly opposed to the heavier curving style.

Other revivals of interest occur in the early period, but to no great extent. Downing's suggestions include pieces in what he refers to as the Flemish style, but actually of William and Mary origin.

After 1870 there were several other adaptations of eighteenth-century models. The Adam and Sheraton styles served as inspiration for dining-room and parlor pieces done with greater faithfulness to the model and less of a re-interpretation for modern requirements.

The Renaissance style was introduced at the Crystal Palace exhibitions of 1851 (London) and 1853 (New York). It is a style heavy in proportion and generally straight in line. Decoration is elaborate and frequently inspired by architectural rather than furniture design. The pediment is used to top many of the forms, from chairs to large case pieces. Bold moldings, raised cartouches, raised and shaped panels, incised linear decoration and applied carving in garlands and medallions are all characteristic. Occasionally animal heads and sporting trophies appear on dining-room pieces. The style was used primarily for bedroom, library and dining-room pieces, but there are examples of parlor furniture also. This style continued to be important until about 1880.

Factory production inspired spool-turned

furniture, a particular type easy to produce for the lower-priced furniture market. In the main, designs were simple and the sizes were right for easy handling in lower middle class interiors. This furniture was decorated by turning on a lathe the legs, arms and supports and obtaining identical units repeated in any of a variety of motifs that include the bobbin, knob, button, sausage and vase and ring. The lines are generally rectangular and simple. This furniture did not include every form, but rather emphasized beds and tables.

The first seeds of modernism can be traced from the reactions against bad craftsmanship in the Victorian period. As a period of mass-production and keen competition, the Victorian period saw the development of truly bad design as well as some very good design that has been misunderstood. By attempting to make things cheaply without simplifying the design and method of production, some makers produced surprisingly unsuccessful results.

One of the first important reactions was the book, *Hints on Household Taste*, which had an American edition in 1872. The author was the English architect, Charles Lock Eastlake, who decried bad craftsmanship and the shams it involved. He sought to inspire simple honest work in solid woods. He disliked shoddy veneer and overly elaborate work. His argument was: 'I recommend the re-adoption of no specific type of ancient furniture which is unsuited, whether in detail or general design, to the habits of modern life. It is the spirit and principles of early manufacture which I desire to see revived and not the absolute forms in which they found embodiment.'

Eastlake proposed that craftsmen follow appropriate models that would not be difficult to execute. He disliked the overly ambitious attempts of the 'fifties in which the rococo was used to excess. The resultant style was simple and rectangular (Plate 24A). Most of what he suggested was to be executed in oak, a durable but inexpensive wood. Carving could be simple and turnings were to play an important role. This style was gradually more and more important on the American scene. Related suggestions follow in ensuing decades

and the oak furniture of the turn of the century by Gustav Stickley is probably basically of the same inspiration.

Attempts to find new and more appropriate sources of design resulted in furniture of exotic inspiration such as that of the so-called Turkish style, seen in overstuffed pieces for parlor use.

The Victorian period is marked by variety of inspiration, stimulated by the use of different styles to suggest different moods. In the first half of the period the changes from the original to the Victorian interpretation were probably greater. After 1880 there was a more faithful adherence to the lines of the models, although the results always differed from the originals. About the same time attempts to make furniture only vaguely connected with earlier styles were evident, and there was also a search for new sources of inspiration.

In the Victorian age mass-production was a key factor in the development of the kind of competition which made bad craftsmanship profitable. This resulted from cutting costs without considering the need for simplification in design. The contrast between good and bad craftsmanship was probably greater after the beginning of factory production.

CAST IRON FURNITURE

The manufacture of cast iron furniture in the United States began in the 1840s and continued until the first decade of the twentieth century. The manufacturers were firms making grille work, architectural ornaments and building fronts. Both indoor and outdoor furniture was produced, although, with few exceptions, the indoor furniture was popular for a much shorter time than the outdoor furniture. Cast-iron furniture for interiors was introduced in the 1850s, a little later than the garden furniture. It was designed as an imitation of wooden furniture in the various Victorian styles and was painted to simulate wood. The exceptions to this characterization were the beds and hatracks in which imaginative forms were developed. These two forms continued to be popular after cast-iron furniture for interiors had become unfashionable.

Garden furniture of cast iron was used for a longer period and the designs became standardized. The dominant influence was the romantic garden which had come into fashion at the end of the eighteenth century. It was created to appear wild, as if man had not had a hand in it. The furniture was designed to have a rustic look, to appear to be made of unhewn logs, or boughs of trees, vines or flowers (Plates 24B, C). The various patterns used seem to have been followed by many manufacturers. The same designs appear in early and late examples. The earliest catalogue known to contain an illustration of cast-iron garden furniture appeared in the 1840s in Philadelphia, but almost every American city of any size produced it some time during the nineteenth century. Often the mold contained the name of the manufacturer, and the piece can be dated by consulting city directories.

BOOKS FOR FURTHER READING

DREPPERD, CARL: *Handbook of Antique Chairs*, Garden City (1948).

LICHTEN, FRANCES: *Decorative Art of Victoria's Era*, New York (1950).

ORMSBEE, THOMAS H.: *Field Guide to American Victorian Furniture*, Boston (1952).

PRATT, RICHARD: *Second Treasury of Early American Homes*, Hawthorn Books, New York, 1954.

Concise Encyclopedia of Antiques, Vol. III, pages 17–29. Hawthorn Books, New York, 1957.

WINDSOR CHAIRS

By MARVIN D. SCHWARTZ

THE Windsor chair was introduced into the American colonies about 1725. The form originated in England and was particularly popular in Berkshire, where the town of Windsor is an important trading center. The chair developed from seventeenth-century country chairs and is unlike any Continental European chair. The American version, although obviously dependent on the English, developed individual characteristics.

The Windsor chair has a back of spindles, a solid wooden seat and turned splayed legs set right through the seat. There is a great deal of variety in the form of the back, the shape of the seat and the shape of the legs so that it is possible to name six categories of variation. These chairs originally were painted and generally they are made of several kinds of wood. The heavy plank seat is made of pine, the spindles are often hickory, with ash, white oak and maple used occasionally. Many colors are mentioned, but a dark green seems to have been favored. Indian red appears frequently, sometimes yellow and black, and white rarely (in spite of Wallace Nutting's abhorrence of white as a Windsor color).

Windsors are simple chairs that were primarily for garden and porch use, but they were reasonably priced and probably were used indoors by some. The variety and the place of use is suggested in an advertisement that Andrew Gauteir placed in the New York *Gazette or Weekly Post-boy*, April 18, 1765, which includes this statement: 'A large and neat assortment of Windsor chairs made in the best and neatest manner and well painted. Viz. Highback'd, low back'd and Sackback'd Chairs and Settees, or double seated, fit for Piazza or Gardens. ...'

The six categories (Plates 25A, B) that are generally distinguished today do not retain the names Gauteir used. They are:

1. *Low-back:* a chair with short spindles topped by a semi-circular rail that serves as top rail and arms (*a*).

2. *Comb-back:* the same as the low-back with a center addition of spindles on the rail topped by a curving thin cupid's-bow shaped rail (*b*).

3. *Fan-back:* a relatively high-backed chair with the top rail cupid's-bow shaped and spindles going from the seat to the top rail. It is most often a side chair and is closely related to the comb-back (*c*).

4. *Hoop-back (or bow-backed):* a low-backed chair with a curving addition topping the center portion (*d*).

5. *New England armchair:* another version of the hoop-back. In this chair the hoop includes the arms so that one continuous binding encloses all the spindles of the chair back (*e*).

6. *Loop-back:* a variation of the hoop-back with spindles going from seat to top rail. It is the counterpart of the fan-back and bears the same relation to the hoop-back as the fan-back bears to the comb-back. Most often this is a side chair (*f*).

These are not all the variations possible. Comb pieces are added to the curving loop-backs on occasion (Plate 28B), and at times there are other variations in shape such as the braced-back (Plate 28c).

One important type is the *writing arm Windsor* (Plates 26A, 27B) in which one arm has a curving shelf added as a small writing area. Often a drawer was included under it and also under the seat. Thomas Jefferson developed one variation of this type in which the seat revolves.

The technique of making the Windsor chair explains its sturdiness. The chairs were made with green wood that shrank later, making joints firmer and tighter than any obtained when seasoned wood is used. Woods were chosen for their ability to withstand wear, and, since the piece was to be painted, the differences would not show. Pine and whitewood were used for seats because they were soft and, therefore, easily modeled. Frequently the seat is saddle-shaped.

Legs are turned in a variety of designs and for turning maple, birch, ash and chestnut are good woods. Although some chairs have all lathed parts of the same wood, there are also examples in which different woods are employed for the upper parts. Ash, white oak and hickory do not tend to fracture when steamed and bent so that spindles and hoops frequently were made of one of these woods. Wedges and small wooden pins found in Windsors were made of seasoned wood. In any case, the Windsor was constructed as a chair that could withstand hard wear.

In Colonial America, Philadelphia was apparently the first place where Windsors were made, and it was a popular place for their manufacture. In New York Thomas Ash, advertising in 1775 as a Windsor chairmaker complained, 'As several hundred pounds have been sent out of this province for this article, he hopes the public will encourage the business. ...' The money probably went to Philadelphia, because the year before the New York *Gazette and Weekly Mercury* carried the announcement that 'John Kelso Windsor Chair-maker from Philadelphia ... Makes and sells all kinds of Windsor Chairs ... and as he served a regular apprenticeship in Philadelphia he is persuaded he can supply those who may be kind enough to favour him with their custom with as well-finished, strong, and neat work as ever appeared in this city. ...'

Five of the six types of chairs were made in Philadelphia and the fifth on the list, the New England armchair, is thought to have had its origin in the latter locality (Plate 28D). The Windsor chair developed in the various colonies with distinguishing characteristics that can be separated into two general types, the Philadelphia and the New England. The geographical differences are logical with one exception, New York chairmakers followed Philadelphia before the Revolution and New England later (Plate 26C).

Characteristic of the Philadelphia examples are legs in a blunt-arrow design (Plate 26B). This leg starts with a ball foot, then there is a narrow ring and bun division, a straight cylindrical section follows, and after another narrowing an almost vase-shaped section makes up the rest of the leg. The New England leg has no foot; generally the lower part is cone-shaped, and after a narrow division a vase-shaped section follows (Plate 28A). The Rhode Island and Connecticut chairs have greater differentiation between the parts. The Connecticut leg is heavier and the curve is simpler (Plate 27A). The Rhode Island leg has a curve in the lower part of the cone-shaped section and a more exaggerated curve in the vase. Philadelphia stretchers have large balls in the center, occasionally flanked by ring turnings. In New England the center of the stretchers bulge but not to a ball shape.

The seats of Philadelphia chairs are usually straight across the front and cut out in a deep saddle shape. In New England chair seats are more often curved across the front and relatively shallow. They are oval-shaped rather than U-shaped. In the spindles the Philadelphians employed tapering shapes which New Englanders most often ignored in favor of a spindle with bulbous enlargements about one-third of the way up from the seat.

Legs and spindles were turned in bamboo shapes on some examples as early as the late-eighteenth century (Plate 27B), but this style developed popularity in the nineteenth century. One unusual type of Windsor, the rod-back, has rail and stiles of the back, legs and stretchers in the same bamboo turned pattern. In some examples the top rail is wide and in a shape inspired by Sheraton, with a raised rectangular area in the center.

Windsor chairs also appear extended, as settees (Plate 27A) and 'double seats', a term that probably referred to what today is called a love seat. The same turned construction sometimes was used to make simple small tables.

From the advertisements of the eighteenth century, it becomes evident that Windsors were often made in the large coastal towns and exported. There were, however, some made in rural areas for local use.

The American Windsor was used in many different homes, from those of the simple farmer to those of country gentlemen such as George Washington. The back porch of Mount Vernon had a group of Windsors; and chairs for some bedrooms ordered in 1757 were very likely of the same type. As well as in homes, the chair was used in public buildings. In Philadelphia, the members of the Continental Congress sat on Windsors. The American type differs from the English version in being simpler. The English had more variety and allowed passing fads to influence the form. In English examples a center splat reflecting the Georgian style is frequently used. Cabriole legs are sometimes substituted for the turned legs. The American seat is most frequently made of pine and is thicker than the English seat. Because it might easily be split, the holes for the legs are placed closer to the center and the legs are splayed more than the English examples.

The American Windsor is a strong chair, of simple construction, that served many uses. It was important in the American colonies possibly as early as 1725, although most known examples should be dated from the late-eighteenth century to about the middle of the nineteenth. It is interesting to note, on the subject of dating, that the English author, F. Gordon Roe, finds American dates early in comparison to English dates.

BOOKS FOR FURTHER READING

DREPPERD, CARL: *Handbook of Antique Chairs*, Garden City, New York (1948).

KINDIG III, JOE: 'Upholstered Windsors', in *Antiques*, July, 1952.

NUTTING, WALLACE.: *American Windsors*, Framingham and Boston (1917).

PRATT, RICHARD: *Second Treasury of Early American Homes*, Hawthorn Books, New York, 1954.

STOKES, J.STOGDELL: 'The American Windsor', in *Antiques*, April, 1926.

WESTON, KARL E.: 'Windsor Chairs at Williams College', in *Antiques*, November, 1944.

All illustrations from photographs lent by *Antiques* Magazine.

COUNTRY FURNITURE IN NEW ENGLAND

By FRANK O. SPINNEY

THE term *country furniture* derives from the observation that there developed in rural New England in the seventeenth, eighteenth and early-nineteenth centuries a kind of furniture different enough in character and spirit from sophisticated urban styles to be classed as a type in itself.

Such a development was, of course, not unique to New England nor to this period. In many places and in many times there has developed a country, even a 'folk' style of furniture. In like manner there have frequently coexisted twin streams of popular and classical music, academic and non-academic art, and formal and cottage architecture.

The characteristics of New England's country furniture tell the story of a simple, self-sufficient life, with its conservatism, thriftiness, individualism, isolation, and dependence on local resources of materials and skills.

To understand the development of New England country furniture as a distinct style, it may be helpful to recall the pattern of that region's growth from its earliest settlements to the time in the nineteenth century when craftsmen were superseded by machines and factory-made furniture replaced the product of local artisans.

During the first uncertain years of colonization, life in the newly established settlements was rugged indeed. Theirs was truly a pioneering venture. With their backs to the sea, new arrivals faced an unexplored wild territory, a virtually unrelieved expanse of dense primeval forest out of which they were literally to hew their livelihoods, their homes and much of their furnishings. Clearing fields,

lumbering and building was heavy work. Settlements were planted and succeeded only because this work was performed. The homes of the men and women who did it were furnished with the barest necessities and sometimes not even those. Simple benches, a table, perhaps a chest brought with them on the voyage from England, a bed or a pallet thrown on the floor were about all the average household possessed. Some few pieces were brought by those able to afford it, but the ordinary settler had only what the housewright, the joiner or his own practical skill could make. From those first decades we have few physical survivals either of architecture or furnishings. Pieces of furniture that have come down to our day are usually the more elaborate and important ones, press and court cupboards, the Carver, Brewster and wainscot chairs, carved chests and an occasional table. All these are essentially country furniture, provincial versions of provincial pieces in the homeland. While most of the more elaborate New England pieces followed so closely their English prototypes that frequently their attribution hinges on the matter of the wood out of which they were made, there are certain ones, in which New Englanders take great pride, that have a definite stamp of local individuality. The Sunflower (Plate 30A) and Hadley Chests made along the Connecticut River, the Ipswich pieces of Thomas Dennis, and a few others are examples of New England's first native-born country furniture.

In the eighteenth century population grew rapidly. From a total of between 75,000 and 100,000 inhabitants in 1700, a doubling every two or three decades took place for nearly a hundred years. On the eve of the

Revolution, New England held close to three-quarters of a million people. The first Federal census in 1790 showed more than a million residents.

This growth of population, partly normal increase and partly immigration, meant a tremendous development of the interior parts of the region. Most of the increase went inland to set up homes in newly-granted towns back from the coast, in western Connecticut, central and western Massachusetts, Vermont and New Hampshire. The lure was land, virtually free acreage to those whose capital might be small but whose muscles and determination were large. It was this promise of land ownership that filled many ships from England and made New England a region where eight out of every ten persons were farmers.

The furniture needs of this growing population were nowhere near fully supplied by importations from England and elsewhere. In fact, purchases abroad declined not only relatively in respect to the growing number of people, but absolutely in terms of the amount of furniture brought in. Moreover, most imported furniture was undoubtedly of the more elegant type destined for the homes of wealthy city merchants and traders whose economic position and cultural ties enabled them to keep up with the latest English fashions. Even the importations were insufficient for these latter. Thus there arose in urban centers such as Boston, Salem, Providence, Newport and perhaps a dozen smaller places, groups of craftsmen who strove to meet the demand for silver, pewter, clocks, fabrics, art and furniture by the well-to-do and cultivated whose tastes were sophisticated and whose pocketbooks could afford the best. From these city craft shops came the Townsends, the Goddards, the Frothinghams, the Seymours, and others who created the masterpieces of New England cabinetwork.

It is easy to forget that even by 1810 there were only three cities in southern New England with over 10,000 population. These three with eleven smaller centers between 5,000 and 10,000 accounted for less than 15 percent of the total. In Maine, New Hampshire and Vermont, the proportion of rural population was even greater. Thus throughout the region close to 90 percent were farm and village people spread out in almost 600 small communities. In these areas, too, flourished craftsmen. Along with land, equally inviting to the newly-arrived immigrant or resident of the older coastal settlements, was the opportunity to ply a trade, housebuilding, blacksmithing, milling, tanning, potting and furniture-making to supply the needs of this vast and growing group.

The New England farmer was not a commercial farmer. With so small a part of the population living in the tiny urban areas, there was no real market for his products. Thus he raised his crops not to sell but for his own use. Small surpluses were traded for necessities he could not produce – spices, tea, coffee, powder and shot, iron, sugar, rum – and for the services of his neighbor craftsmen who accepted lumber, wool, tallow, beef and work for the product of their special skills. This money-poor, self-sufficient economy of the New England farmer is reflected in his simple farmhouse architecture, the interior decoration of his house and his furniture.

In such a milieu, isolated from the urban centers with their ties abroad, it is not strange that there developed a style of furniture that had a flavor of its own, reminiscent of but more vital than a mere country-cousin version of 'big city' fashions. It was created by artisans who shared and understood their customers' need for utility and economy, who were, with their neighbors, conservative and slow to take up new ideas, and who were dependent on local resources.

The men who made the tables, chairs, chests, stands, beds and coffins for their local customers were often only part-time craftsmen. In common with rural ministers, lawyers, doctors and other professional or craft workers, the cabinetmakers were frequently farmers who employed their special skill to supplement their return from the land. Their account books show them devoting perhaps a tenth or a quarter of their time to their trade. Pieces were produced on order, not for stock. They were jacks-of-all-trades in the field of woodwork, hewing out the frame of a house, constructing a workbench, making a window sash, turning a dish on a lathe, framing a picture or map, as well as constructing grain chests, dough troughs, candlestands, kitchen tables, desks, beds, bureaus, cupboards, settles, chairs and clock cases.

The materials used in their work were usually local in source. Often the pine, maple, birch, cherry and other woods were supplied by the customer from his own timber lot. Payment for the craftsman's work was frequently in the form of well-seasoned planks. To a certain degree the woods used varied somewhat from section to section (Plate 30B). Abundance or lack were factors as well as a local predilection. Thus what the Massachusetts cabinetmaker made in maple, the southern Maine or eastern New Hampshire craftsman often fabricated in birch. Poplar is a hallmark of a type of southern Connecticut piece. Cherry was the rural mahogany for many workers, while apple and pear wood were occasionally used. Unusual and unpredictable in source and supply was curly maple (Plate 31B). It was considered especially desirable and reserved for larger, more impressive pieces. Pine was the most common wood (Plate 29). It was used not only for concealed structural parts but for entire pieces. Oak, chestnut, walnut and other indigenous trees supplied materials on occasion.

The tools and techniques of the rural cabinetmaker were similar to those of his urban contemporaries. Perhaps the country worker had a smaller assortment of molding planes. Working alone, he may have had to use a pole or treadle lathe since he rarely had apprentices to turn the great wheel found in larger establishments. His techniques were the same, although perhaps he was not quite so careful when fitting a dovetail or cutting a tenon.

Workmanship was not usually of the highest quality. Experience, training and the intense continuous discipline of a large city shop where one's work was carefully scrutinized by the master-owner were not always a part of the rural craftsman's background. Today's eyes should not mistakenly glorify what is actually inability, carelessness or ignorance. Allowing for all of this, however, it

is remarkable how consistently good was most of the work produced.

The cost of this kind of work to the purchaser was modest. In searching the ledgers and account books of the obscure rural cabinetmaker, one senses that he commonly took his labor into account at approximately the same daily rate prevailing for general work in the locality. To this basic cost was added the value of materials. Bookkeeping practices of the day did not expose the profit involved, if any. Possibly the net result was more in the direction of full employment. One doubts that country furniture makers accumulated substantial estates.

The finishes applied to country furniture were varied, ranging from varnish and shellac surfacing to oil and wax, or commonly to no finish at all, leaving the piece to the customer's taste and energy. Paint was used widely (Plate 32B), strong earth colors, red, yellow, brown, put on sometimes almost as a stain and then again in a heavy coat whose vehicle, tradition and early recipes assert, was skimmed milk which hardened in casein fashion into a nearly impenetrable plating. In addition to solid blacks, greens, blues and grays, multicolored decorations were popular at times. Astonishing abstract designs, simulated graining and marbleizing, and decorative freehand or stenciled patterns were common paint finishes in the later periods (Plate 32A). Whether this can be properly considered as part of the furniture itself or not, it contributed to the distinctive character of much country furniture.

While the style of country furniture followed changes that occurred in fashionable circles, often there was a time lag due to isolation, conservatism and the feeling that a form that had proved its usefulness was still useful even though fashion had decreed otherwise. Thus the familiar hearthside settle (Plate 31C), popular in England in the seventeenth century, was made in New England in the 1820s long after it had become obsolete elsewhere. The country version of the Chippendale style (Plate 31B) was a rural favorite for decades after urban tastes had passed on to newer delights. To try to date tables and chairs of this type is hazardous, for

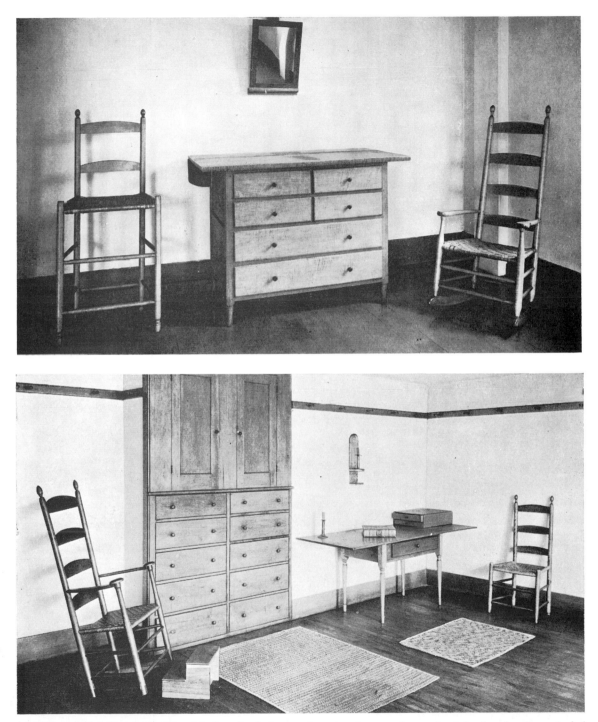

(A) Watervliet tailoress counter with drop leaf; drawer fronts and top curly maple stained red; pine paneled sides darker red; curly maple in mirror, also in posts and 'ladle' arms of rocking chair; high-seated chair for shop or counter use.

(B) Built-in drawers and cupboards in a room in the South family dwelling, New Lebanon; brethren's chair with foot-stool; on the table is a two-drawer lap or table desk.

PLATE 33

Simplicity of Shaker craftsmanship is seen in this 'round' stand from the Second family, New Lebanon, and matched side chairs from Enfield. Both are tilting chairs with finials identifying their origin. The stand is cherry, the hanging cupboard pine.

PLATE 34

Armed rocking chairs with mushroom arms and cushion rails for eldresses at Hancock; for comfort a shag mat hung from top rail. Tape seats were woven in various color patterns. Cherry and maple table has typical turnings, braces and long drawer.

PLATE 35

(A) New Lebanon trestle table 20 ft. long; four-board pine top 34 ins. wide; birch trestles; *c.* 1810.

(B) Sabbathday Lake sewing table has cutting board in drawer to be used also for writing. New Lebanon 'Shaker red' stand; swivel sewing stools.

PLATE 36

(A) Pepperrell family looking glass; *c.* 1700. *Henry Francis du-Pont Winterthur Museum.*

(B) New York looking glass; 1725–35. *Winterthur Museum.*

(C) Bleeker family looking glass; *c.* 1730–40. *Winterthur Museum.*

PLATE 37

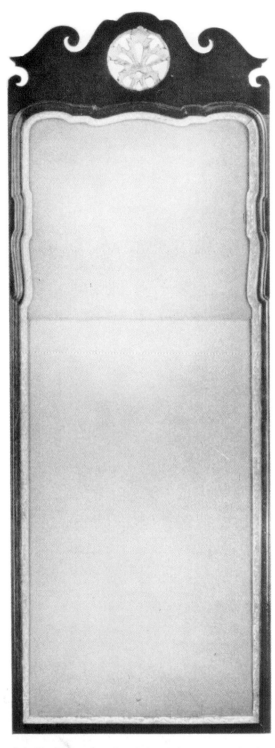

(A) Looking glass by John Elliott; *c.* 1762–67.
Winterthur Museum.

(B) Looking glass by William Wilmerding; 1794
Ginsburg and Levy.

(C) William Wilmerding label-detail. *John S.
Walton.*

PLATE 38

(A) Cadwalader family looking glass; *c.* 1768-76
Winterthur Museum.

(B) Dressing glass by Jonathan Gostelowe; 1789.
Mabel Brady Garvan collection, Yale University Art Gallery.
Photograph, courtesy of The Philadelphia Museum of Art.

PLATE 39

A

B

C

(A) Dressing glass probably carved by Samuel McIntire; *c.* 1800. *Museum of Fine Arts, Boston.*

(B) Derby family looking glass. *Mabel Brady Garvan collection, Yale University Art Gallery.*

(C) Classical looking glass; *c.* 1800. *Winterthur Museum.*

(D) Looking glass by Peter Grinnell & Son; *c.* 1800. *Israel Sack.*

D

PLATE 40

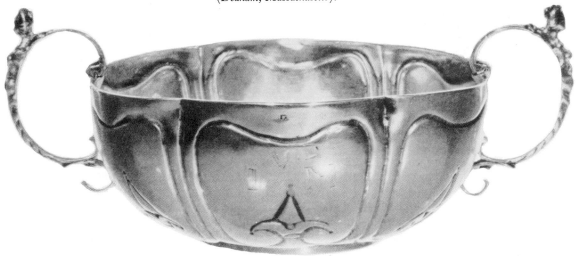

(A) Caudle cup by John Hull (1624–83) and Robert Sanderson (1608–93), Boston, in partnership *c.* 1650–80. Engraved date 1720 shows it to have been originally a domestic piece. Ht. 3$\frac{3}{16}$ ins. *The Dedham Churches (Dedham, Massachusetts).*

(B) Bowl by Jesse Kip (1660–1722), New York. Floral design on bottom more elaborate than ornament of the panels. Traditionally a racing trophy of 1699; initials of Jacob and Maria Van Dorn. D. 6 ins. *Henry Ford Museum, Dearborn, Michigan.*

PLATE 41

Tankard by Peter Van Dyck (1684–1750/1). 'Corkscrew' thumbpiece, cherub's mask and base molding with stamped ornament characteristic of New York. Ht. 7⅝ ins. *Henry Ford Museum, Dearborn, Michigan.*

PLATE 42

(A) Tankard by Nicholas Roosevelt (1715–69). New York tankards retained flat covers. Ht. 7¼ ins. *Coll. of Guy Warren Walker, Jr.*

(B) Tankard by Benjamin Hiller (born 1687/8), Boston. The slightly higher cover indicates eighteenth century. Ht. 6¹³⁄₁₆ ins. *Museum of Fine Arts, Boston.*

(C) Tankard by Jeremiah Dummer (1645–1718), Boston. Thumbpiece, low cover and handle tip characteristic of early New England. Ht. 6⅝ ins. *Henry Ford Museum, Dearborn, Michigan.*

(D) Tankard by Joseph Lownes (c. 1754–1820), Philadelphia. A gift from *The underwriters of London to Capt. John Cassin, c.* 1790. Ht. 7¾ ins. *Henry Ford Museum, Dearborn, Michigan.*

PLATE 43

Tankard by Benjamin Burt (1729–1805), Boston. Midband and domed cover appeared *c.* 1720 on New England tankards. Given to Timothy Hilliard, Harvard College tutor, 1769. Ht. 9 ins. *Henry Ford Museum, Dearborn, Michigan.*

PLATE 44

(A) Three casters (a pair and one other) by John Coney (1656–1722), Boston;
late mark. Ht. (pair) 5 ins. *Museum of Fine Arts, Boston.*

(B) Saucepan by Myer Myers (1723–95), New York, D. bowl 4 ins. *Coll. of Mr and
Mrs Mark Bortman.*

PLATE 45

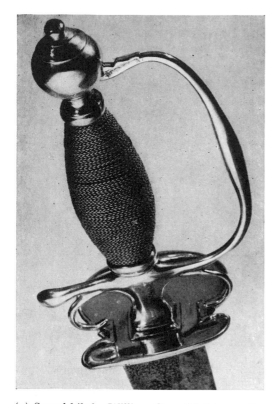

(A) Sword hilt by William Cowell (1682–1736), or his son (1713–61); Boston. L. 6 ins. *Henry Ford Museum, Dearborn, Michigan.*

(B) Mug by Jacob Gerritse Lansing (1681–1767), Albany. *DF* over *IN* for Jesse and Neeltje de Forest, married 1718. Ht. 4⅛ ins. *Henry Ford Museum, Dearborn, Michigan.*

(C) Chafing dish by Joseph Kneeland (1698–1740), Boston. Probably originally equipped with a wooden handle in a silver socket attached to a scroll support. Ht. 3⅜ ins. *Coll. of Mr and Mrs Mark Bortman.*

PLATE 46

(A) Salver by John Coburn (1725–1803) Boston. Form introduced after 1725; engraving suggests the 1760s. W. 5¾ ins. *Museum of Fine Arts, Boston.*

(B) Porringer by Thomas Savage (1664–1749), Boston, *c.* 1690; initials added mid-eighteenth century. D. (bowl) 3⅞ ins. *Privately owned.*

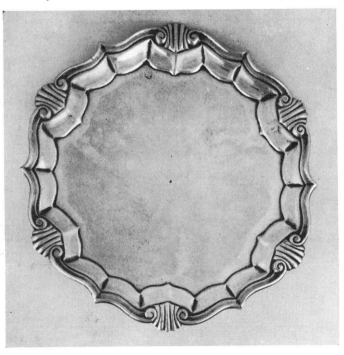

(c) Salver with shell border by Samuel Edwards (1705–62), Boston. Diam. 6¹³⁄₁₆ ins. *Privately owned.*

PLATE 47

(A) Salver by Ephraim Brasher (1744–1810), New York; three notched pad feet, gadrooned rim. Diam. 11$\frac{11}{16}$ ins. *Coll. of Guy Warren Walker, Jr.*

(B) Creampot by Daniel Parker (1726–85), Boston. Unusual masks on feet; Ht. 4 ins. *Museum of Fine Arts, Boston.*

(C) Teapot by Jacob Hurd (1703–58), Boston. Engraved with Sturgis arms. Ht. 5 ins. *Museum of Fine Arts, Boston.*

PLATE 48

they were made practically unaltered for the greater part of a century.

While the elements of each style change are recognizable in country furniture, there is often as well an overlapping of fashions in a single piece. Whether this was due to the hazily understood design, the experimentation of the maker, or the iron whim of a customer, it sometimes produced the appealing friendly quality that a mongrel dog possesses and a highly-bred canine may lack.

Starting with a current style, well defined and highly developed in fashionable circles by talented master-craftsmen, the country furniture equivalent, worked out, modified, simplified or added to, became in the shop of the rural cabinetmaker a new thing with its own individual qualities and its own charac-ter, reflecting the period and place of its creators and users. Retrieved now from the past, it tells a story of rural New England.

BOOKS FOR
FURTHER READING

BRIDENBAUGH, CARL: *The Colonial Craftsman*, New York and London (1950).

CORNELIUS, CHARLES O.: *Early American Furniture*, New York (1926).

KETTELL, RUSSELL HAWES: *The Pine Furniture of Early New England*, New York (1929).

PRATT, RICHARD: *Second Treasury of Early American Homes*, Hawthorn Books, New York (1954).

SPINNEY, FRANK O.: 'Country Furniture', *Antiques*, August, 1953.

Concise Encyclopedia of Antiques, Vol. 1, pp. 50–74, Hawthorn Books (1955).

THE CRAFTSMANSHIP OF THE AMERICAN SHAKERS

By EDWARD DEMING ANDREWS

The 'world's people' could adapt forms; the Shakers could create them. More than one generation would pass in America before this conception of logic with beauty would come into its own.

OLIVER W. LARKIN, *Art and Life in America*

For the sheer beauty of the direct solution, elemental but not primitive, there is little in America to surpass their designs.

JOSEPH ARONSON, *Book of Furniture and Decoration*

SHAKER furniture is religion in wood. It was made by craftsmen working in the spirit and holding the beliefs of a communitarian sect which had separated from the 'world' to seek a more spiritual way of life. The Shakers were separatists in a fundamental sense: dissenters from Anglicanism, Puritanism, even Quakerism – a people who, in their attempt to restore the primitive Christian church, repudiated private property, marriage, the bearing of arms, all worldliness. Joining in protest against what they considered the evils of the time, they affirmed new socio-religious principles, to ensure the development of which they established, in the late-eighteenth and early-nineteenth centuries, a system of semi-monastic communities largely insulated from the world around them.[1] It is within this framework, that of a separatist religious order, that its craftsmanship, as a distinctive American art form, must be considered.

Current in the Society was the saying that 'every force evolves a form'. What then, we must ask, *were* the forces that conditioned workmanship, that imbued the furniture and architecture of the Believers with a recognizable character? The answer can best be given in terms of five Shaker principles, closely interrelated to be sure, but each having a special bearing as a direct or indirect cause: the doctrines, namely, of order and use; separation from the world; separation of the sexes; community of goods, or 'united inheritance'; and perfectionism, or purity of life.

The earliest evidence of a standard of workmanship is found in the *Way Marks* of Joseph Meacham (1742–1796), the organizer of the Shaker Church and Ann Lee's successor as its head. In this guide to conduct and organization (*c.* 1790) 'Father' Joseph ruled that 'all things must be made ... according to their order and use', and that 'all work done, or things made in the church, ought to be faithfully and well done, but plain and without superfluity – neither too high nor too low'. In separating from a world of evil and disorder, in elevating themselves above the 'carnal' plane of existence, Meacham and other leaders considered the mission of 'Believers' to be the application, in social practice, of the Christian virtues of justice, peace and brotherhood. Organization was essential to the realization of such an ideal. 'Order,' the Shakers were constantly enjoined, 'is Heaven's first law.' And by order they meant not only the careful planning of the social, economic and religious structure, but the use of human and material resources for given ends. Order involved co-operative effort and specific responsibilities on the part of each member. It was equated, in the Shaker mind, with neatness and cleanliness, with Mother Ann's saying that 'there is no dirt in Heaven'. It meant, specifically, that labor, including the work of builders, joiners and other 'mechanics', should be directed to foreseen uses, should serve, as perfectly as possible, its appointed purposes. Meacham's injunction was an early statement of what today we call functionalism. In practice it meant that the use to which a building, or a piece of furniture, or a tool was to be put, predetermined its design. As a guiding precept, it had far-reaching implications.

The doctrine of 'united inheritance', or 'joint interest', has relevance here, for labor was consecrated to communal – and millennial-uses. The craftsman worked not to please his own fancy or the passing tastes of the world, but for the good of his brothers and sisters, the whole society, an order he believed would last a thousand years. Consecration of talent and possessions, 'the right use of property', was one of the seven moral principles of the church:[2] 'the true followers of Christ [an official statement reads] are one with him, as he is one with the Father. This oneness includes all they possess; for he who has devoted himself to Christ, soul, body and spirit, can by no means withhold his property.'[3] Since property, therefore, was a trust, not a personal possession – 'the earth is the Lord's and the fullness thereof' – it was the duty, the privilege indeed, of all Believers to be faithful stewards of their heritage, accountable to God for the improvement of their time and talents in this life. Laboring in such a spirit, the craftsman employed his skill, like a medieval artisan, to glorify a church eternal. The product, in turn, was part of the United Inheritance, to be held in perpetuity and used with scrupulous care.

Its communal function influenced craftsmanship in other ways. Meeting-houses, dwellings, barns, shops and furniture were designed for the convenience of societies divided into family groups of thirty to a hundred members. Such an organization necessitated commodious buildings, shops adapted to diverse occupational needs and furniture suited to group use – long trestle-tables and benches, built-in drawers, large cupboard-chests and tailoring counters, multiple-use kitchen and office furniture, spacious rooms. Group requirements, however, did not exclude the need for smaller, or specialized, cabinet work. Chairs were designed with given individuals in mind; small stands adapted to specific uses were consigned to the sewing and 'retiring' rooms; clocks promoted punctuality, and looking glasses neatness of person; desks of various types were needed by the family deacons and deaconesses, the eldership and the ministry. Joinery of all kinds was furnished on call from, and on specifications by, those entrusted with the 'temporal care'.

As a result, Shaker furniture presents a diversity of forms, within a general uniformity of style, which gives it lasting interest. Every piece has an unmistakable Shaker look, yet an individuality of its own. One explanation of the seeming paradox lies in the fact that the United Society was a decentralized organization, with each of its eighteen branches, and each family unit within the colony, semi-independent in its economy. At the outset the central order, or church family, at New Lebanon set up certain patterns and standards, in industry and the crafts, which other families in other societies were encouraged to follow. But in practice this did not result in outright copying or duplication. The distance separating communities was one factor making for differentiation. Another was the diversity in skills, methods and training of those 'mechanics' who, as converts, happened to be drawn into one community rather than another. There are peculiarities in Maine Shaker furniture, for instance – the turnings of table legs and chair finials, the high, narrow cupboards, etc. – which distinguish it from that of other New England colonies. One can recognize, by their finial turnings, the chairs made in Hancock from those, say, in New Lebanon, Enfield, New Hampshire or the Ohio communes. The size of a family, its financial status, the part played by furniture-making in its economy, all affected the crafts. Families bought from and sold to one another, and even engaged in friendly competition, a practice militating against standardization.

The multiplicity of patterns in Shaker craftsmanship derives from another source: the concept of 'use' mentioned above. If there was to be continual 'increase' in the gospel, individual as well as group potential must be utilized, with a concern, therefore, for the well-being of members as persons. This recognition of the worth of the individual is not unrelated to our central theme of craftsmanship. Take chairs, for instance. Chairs made for the 'world', an early industry dating back to the 1790s, eventually conformed to standardized designs. But the chairs intended for domestic use often have marked individuality. Armed rocking-chairs were made for the comfort of the aged and infirm, in sizes adapted to given users. Chairs for invalids had special characteristics. Children's chairs, weaving and tailoring chairs, footstools, settees for visitors to the novitiate order, etc., bear the stamp of particular intent. It was not unusual, also, for a craftsman, with the approval of the family 'Lead', to make a special piece, as a token of esteem or affection for some beloved brother or sister, elder or eldress. In the domestic economy of the sect, a sister was often assigned to look after the temporal needs of a given brother – his room, his clothes – in appreciation for which service some article of manufacture might be fashioned, as a symbol of gospel love, for the sister's comfort and convenience. A certain type of round-topped candle-stand, designed especially for the ministry, was called a 'ministry stand'. A color applied to the cots used by the 'Lead' was known as 'ministry green'. A sister or brother might take a fancy to a particular piece of furniture, which the family eldress or elder would thereupon consign to his, or her, use. Visiting the rooms of a unitary household, one is aware, by their appointments, that though, in theory, 'there was little importance in the individual', in practice the human personality was not lost.

Still another factor affecting both architecture and furniture design was the dual nature of their organization. The Shakers believed in a dual Deity – a Father-Mother God, Power and Holy Mother Wisdom – and a dual messiahship, Christ and Mother Ann. They believed in separation of the sexes, but also in their equality, with elders and eldresses, deacons and deaconesses, brethren and sisters sharing both privileges and obligations. Men and women lived together, but in opposite parts of the dwelling; they worshipped together, in song and dance, but in patterns which kept them apart; they worked for a common end, but in separate shops. The boys and girls received into the society under indenture agreements with their parents or guardians, lived with their caretakers in the Children's Order. The presiding ministry, two elders and two eldresses, engaged in manual labor with the rest, but in their own 'ministry's shop', a building adjacent to the meeting-house in which they had their private quarters. Churches, therefore, were built with at least three doors – one each for the brethren, sisters and ministry – and sometimes, as at New Lebanon, with two others for the males and females who often attended public meetings from the 'world'. Dwellings had separate doorways, stairs, halls and retiring rooms. Furniture, too, was differentiated on the basis of sex. Tables, chairs, desks, etc., consigned to the sisterhood were of lower height, and sometimes of more delicate construction, than those designed for the brethren.

Meacham's principle of 'plainness' derived from the Shaker belief that man could be purified, by degrees, from all his imperfections. The great imperfection was selfishness, the ego – 'Great I'. Man could rise above self, above his 'carnal' nature, only by devoting himself whole-heartedly, and with all his strength, to the love of God. Humility, honesty, innocence, charity, simplicity – these were the marks of the regenerate spirit. And of these 'foundations of the New Jerusalem' none had greater meaning, in the Shaker mind, than simplicity, a concept which Seth Wells, the author of *The Millennial Church*, defines in these words, that 'its thoughts, words and works are plain and simple. ... It is without ostentation, parade or any vain show, and naturally leads to plainness in all things.'[4] In the field of craftsmanship, which deliberately abjured the superfluous and useless, the concept had direct application. Carvings, inlays, veneers, moldings, excess turnings and surface 'embellishment' added nothing, the Shakers held, to the usefulness, the comfort, the 'goodness' of a piece of furniture or a building. Why obscure the beauty of the natural grain of woods with varnish? Why complicate the gentle curve with unnecessary turning, the broad plane with distracting ornament? That was what 'Father' Joseph meant by 'too high'. On the other hand, materials should be of 'substantial' quality and put to 'truly virtuous' use. According to the Gospel Orders, there was 'no room for half-way work, either in things inward or outward'. That was the inference of 'too low'. There is nothing somber, stilted or stereotyped about Shaker furniture. It has a harmony of proportion and refinement of line which give it a quiet, unassuming dignity. In perfect keeping with its setting, it makes a chaste contribution to the atmosphere of sanctity pervading the rooms of every Shaker dwelling.

Though the Believers were indeed seeking perfection, in works as in conduct, they did not contemplate a state in which there could be 'no increase for the better'. As in their covenants and relations with the world, their psalmody and mode of worship, their dress, their language and deportment, their theories regarding health and education – so in their architecture, industry and craftsmanship, they were constantly striving for 'improvement'. As regards their 'manner of building', a New Lebanon Shaker historian, citing the early handicaps of poverty and inexperience, explains that at first they had to build 'for the present, on a small scale, and in a cheap style ... with a rough way of building foundations ... little hall room ... crowded and steep stairs ... no jets to the eaves or ends of the roof,' etc. Therefore the structures were 'very inferior, and poorly adapted to the purpose for which they were needed'. He then records, by five-year intervals, the manifold advances: the door-caps or hoods, the recesses to the outside doors, the provisions for ventilation and sanitation, the tin roofs, the stone paths, the marble gate-posts and horse-blocks, the

cisterns and aqueducts, the chimney caps, the improvements in tools (buzz-saws and planing, mortising and boring machines, etc.) and the shops, sheds, barns and mills constructed for the 'convenience' of various trades.

In their industrial practices, likewise, the Shakers were alert to the more useful method, the tool better adapted to its purpose, the mechanism which would save time and labor – ready, if necessary, to adopt worldly inventions, but always ingenious in their own right, as proved by the many inventions or improvements credited to the order. A partial list would include the metal pen, the common clothespin, cut nails, the one-horse wagon, the flat broom (and machinery for turning broom handles and sizing broom-corn brush), a loom for weaving palm-leaf for bonnets, a silk-reeling machine, a revolving oven, a pea-sheller, a butter-worker and 'self-acting' cheese-press, a machine for twisting whip handles, an improved washing-machine and mangle, a turbine water-wheel and a screw propeller, the original 'Babbitt metal', the circular saw, threshing and fertilizing machines, a side-hill plow, an improved corn-drying kiln, machinery for planing and matching boards, a device for making basket splints, a sash balance, a chimney-cap and 'stoves of the Shaker improvement'. They were pioneers in the medicinal herb industry, constantly experimenting with processes to ensure the highest quality of product. They were probably the first people in America to distribute garden seeds in small packages, priced at three cents each and appropriately labeled or printed. Seldom did they patent any invention, believing that patent money savored of monopoly.

The instinct – if such it may be called – for experimentation, for finding a better, the more logical solution, is also exemplified by many functional details of construction: by the lappers or 'fingers' of oval boxes, for instance, which gave them strength and held the form; by the ball-and-socket device at the base of the rear posts of side-chairs, enabling the sitter to rock or tilt without wearing the carpet; by the large wooden casters applied to bed-posts so the cots could be rolled forward and back without effort; and by the clever contrivances for locking drawers, raising window-shades, and raising or lowering desks to a desired height. The arrangement of drawers and cupboards, in moveable pieces of furniture, to utilize fully a given space; the application of drop leaves to tables, counters and walls; the practice of building drawers and cupboards into the walls, and lining the walls with peg-boards – all testify to a love of economy and order.[5]

To introduce our theme we have quoted from two commentators, both of whom, in their evaluations, use the word 'beauty'. In the Shaker vocabulary, however, the term had minor importance. 'The divine man has no right to waste money upon what you would call beauty, in his house or his daily life, while there are people living in misery.' Such was the stand of Elder Frederick Evans, one of the chief spokesmen of the sect. The society was concerned, as we have noted, chiefly with order, use, the avoidance of super-fluities – a subject to which its Millennial Laws devote an entire section. From the first the emphasis was on neatness, good economy and industry. To labor was to pray. 'Put your hands to work,' Mother Ann had taught, 'and your hearts to God.' Even at a later period in their history, as the Shakers attempted to explain their philosophy, they talked in terms of the early values:

'Order is the creation of beauty.'

'Love of beauty has a wider field of action in association with Moral Force.'

'All beauty that has not a foundation in use soon grows distasteful, and needs continual replacement with something new.'

'That which has in itself the highest use possesses the greatest beauty.'

Yet one cannot say that the Believers neglected, or consciously repudiated, the beautiful. Evidence to the contrary is abundant: in their 'gift' for song and the painstaking calligraphy of their hymnals; in the soft reds, yellows and greens applied to furniture; in the yellow-greens of floors, and the warm browns or blue-greens of peg-racks, doors and window-frames; in their colored silk kerchiefs, and the natural dyes used in rugs and clothing; in their exquisite poplar

basketry; in their finely wrought ironware; in their neat fences, paths and 'smooth-shaven greens'; and most conspicuously, in the inspirational designs accompanying the 'era of manifestations', beginning in 1837, when they drew or painted their trees of life and other 'emblems of the heavenly sphere'.

It is a matter of definition. Visitors were always impressed by the *neatness* of the Shaker villages. Harriet Martineau commented on the 'frame dwellings ... finished with the last degree of nicety, even to the springs of the windows and the hinges of the doors'. John Finch testified that 'the neatness, cleanliness and order which you everywhere observe in their persons and their premises, and the cheerfulness and contented looks of the people afford the reflective mind continual pleasure'. For another English traveler, Hepworth Dixon, 'no Dutch town [had] a neater aspect ... the paint is all fresh; the planks are all bright; the windows are all clean. A white sheen is on everything, a happy quiet reigns around'. It was the opinion of Robert Wickliffe, a prominent American lawyer, that 'in architecture and neatness they are exceeded by no people upon the earth'. To these persons, order was indeed 'the creation of beauty'.

Whatever the medium – the village unit, the individual structure, the furnishings of the buildings, even to the slightest accessory – Shaker workmanship achieved the status of an art, art in the sense employed by Emerson as 'the spirit's voluntary use and combination of things to serve its end'. When the sage of Concord wrote, in another connection, that 'in the construction of any fabric or organism, any real increase of fitness to its end, is an increase in beauty'; or when Walt Whitman, in the preface to *Leaves of Grass*, asserted that whatever 'distorts honest shapes ... is a nuisance' – they were expressing Shaker doctrine. Long before the American sculptor, Horatio Greenough, was proclaiming that 'beauty is the promise of function', that embellishment is 'false beauty', and that when the essential is found the product is complete, his principles had been exemplified in Shaker practice. In England, Ruskin, Morris and Charles Eastlake, had they known, would surely have found, in the craftsmanship of these overseas communities, an application of their ideals.

In one of his *Kindergarten Chats*, Louis H. Sullivan, the American architect, observed that 'Behind every form we see there is a vital something or other which we do not see yet which makes itself visible to us in that very form'. In the case of Shaker craftsmanship that 'something' was the spirit of a people laboring to create a heaven on earth – a people with an end to serve.

(Edward Deming Andrews and his wife, Faith Andrews, have given to Yale University (1956) their Shaker collection in order to ensure not only its preservation but its maximal educational use. Assembled over a period of thirty years, the collection represents the finest in the craftsmanship and arts of an indigenous religious order. A comprehensive library of books, pamphlets, manuscripts, etc., and a selection of artifacts illustrative of the industrial pursuits of the United Society, contribute to its unique historical value. – EDITOR).

[1] The movement had its origin in Manchester, England. In 1758 its founder, Ann Lee, a youthful worker in the textile mills of the manor, had joined a Quaker society which had come under the influence of the French Prophets, and which, in turn, was to accept 'Mother' Ann's revelations regarding celibacy, the millennium and Christ's Second Appearing. Persecuted for their 'heretical' beliefs and such practices as dancing as a mode of worship, eight of these 'Shaking Quakers', led by the prophetess, emigrated to America in 1774. Ann died ten years later, but not before the struggling movement had been revitalized by the fires of revivalism in various parts of New York and New England. The first colony was founded at Niskeyuna, or Watervliet, near Albany, in 1780. The first community to be fully organized was at New Lebanon, New York, in 1788. Eventually eighteen societies, divided into some fifty-eight 'family' units, were established: at New Lebanon, Watervliet and Groveland in New York; Hancock, Tyringham, Shirley and Harvard, in Massachusetts; Enfield, Connecticut; Alfred and Sabbathday Lake, in Maine; Enfield and Canterbury, in New Hampshire; Union Village, Watervliet, Whitewater and North Union in Ohio; and Pleasant Hill and South Union in Kentucky. A few other societies existed for short periods. The movement reached its zenith about the time of the Civil War

when membership totalled about six thousand. Today only three colonies survive, at Hancock, Canterbury and Sabbathday Lake, with less than fifty members.

[2] The other principles were duty to God, duty to man, separation from the world, practical peace, simplicity of language and a virgin life.

[3] *Summary View of the Millennial Church*, Albany, 1823, p. 269.

[4] *Summary View, op. cit., p.* 249.

[5] A pine wash-stand recently added to the author's collection provides an apt illustration of Shaker functionalism. Parallel to one of the front legs is an inner post to which is attached, about two-thirds of the way down, a wooden plate – the post swivelling to allow the plate or disc to be swung freely forward. The plate was used to hold a slop pail, into which water from the wash basin could be emptied without the hazard of reaching underneath the top of the stand. A logical solution to a problem, entailing, to be sure, extra thought, extra effort – but that was the Shaker way.

BOOKS FOR FURTHER READING

ANDREWS, EDWARD DEMING, and ANDREWS, FAITH: *Shaker Furniture. The Craftsmanship of an American Communal Sect*, Yale University Press, New Haven, Connecticut (1937). (Reprinted by Dover Publications, Inc., New York, 1950.)

ANDREWS, EDWARD DEMING: 'Designed for Use: The Nature of Function in Shaker Craftsmanship', in *New York History*, July, 1950, Vol. XXXI, No. 3, Cooperstown, New York.

ANDREWS, EDWARD DEMING: 'Shaker Furniture', in *Interior Design*, May, 1954, Vol. 25, No. 5, New York.

ANDREWS, EDWARD DEMING, and ANDREWS, FAITH: 'Notes on Shaker Furniture', in *The Antiques Book* (ed. Alice Winchester), New York (1950). (A condensation of articles in the August, 1928, and April, 1929, issues of *Antiques*.)

ANDREWS, EDWARD DEMING: *The People Called Shakers: A Search for the Perfect Society*, Oxford University Press, New York (1953).

ANDREWS, EDWARD DEMING: 'The Communal Architecture of the Shakers', in *Magazine of Art*, No. 12, December, 1937, Vol. XXX, Washington, D.C. (1937).

ANDREWS, EDWARD DEMING: *The Community Industries of the Shakers*, Handbook No. 15, New York State Museum, Albany, New York (1932).

McCAUSLAND, ELIZABETH: 'The Shaker Legacy', in *The Magazine of Art*, December, 1944, Vol. XXXVII, Washington, D.C.

'Shaker Furniture in a Little Red Farmhouse', in *Living with Antiques* (ed. Alice Winchester), New York (1941).

All the illustrations to this article, Plates 33–6, are from photographs by William F. Winter, from *Shaker Furniture; The Craftsmanship of an American Communal Sect*, by Edward Deming and Faith Andrews, Yale University Press, New Haven, Connecticut, 1937.

LOOKING GLASSES USED
IN AMERICA

By MARTHA GANDY FALES

The early records: instructing farmers about to settle in frontier areas of the United States in 1789, Benjamin Rush pointed out, 'There are several expensive parts of household furniture that he should leave behind him for which he will have no use in the woods, such as a large looking glass. ...' This advice suggests the reason for the paucity of information about looking glasses in America in the early-seventeenth century. That they were in use by 1644 is substantiated, however, by the inventory of the estate of Joanna Cummings, of Salem, Massachusetts, which lists a looking glass valued at three shillings.

A study of the published probate records of Essex County, Massachusetts, discloses that between 1644 and 1681 at least ninety-four looking glasses were owned in that area. Before 1665 these glasses were usually valued between two and three shillings, with a few notable exceptions such as 'one faire gret looking glass, 6s.' owned by Thomas Trusler, in 1654 and 'a gilt looking glasse, 6s. 8d.' owned by the Reverend Nathaniel Rogers, of Ipswich, in 1655. After 1655 the glasses were more frequently valued up to seven to ten shillings.

These records reveal that usually the glasses were placed in the hall or the parlor, the main gathering room in the early homes. Less frequently, they were used in the chamber or bedroom. One of the earliest records of one person's owning more than one looking glass occurs in 1661 in the estate of Robert Gray, of Salem: 'In the parlor ... one large lookinge glass ... In the litle Chamber ... a lookinge glass and 3 pictures.'

By the eighteenth century their usage be-

came less limited, and the following advertisement appeared in *The Boston News-Letter* of April 25/May 2, 1715: 'Looking-Glasses of all sorts, Glass Sconces, Cabbinetts, Writing Desks, Bookcases with Desks, old Glasses new Silvered, and all sorts of Japan-work, Done and sold by William Randle at the Sign of the Cabinnett, a Looking-Glass Shop in Queen-Street ...'

A manuscript book containing inventories taken in New York City between 1742 and 1768 (Downs Manuscript Library, Winterthur Museum) indicates that out of twenty-one colonists of varied circumstances, nineteen possessed at least one looking glass. Notable among these are the three owned by Joseph Leddell, pewterer, in 1754: one listed simply as a looking glass, one 'with black frame', and one 'with japanned frame'. William Wright, chandler, possessed one old looking glass and a 'Small looking glass and sconces, old', in 1757. Rice Williams in 1758 had one small looking glass and a chimney glass.

At this time chimney glasses, or looking glasses placed above the fireplace on the chimney breast, were frequently found in American houses. A graphic account in the *Pennsylvania Gazette* of March 17, 1763, tells of a fire which broke out in the house of Captain Hampton in Elizabeth, New Jersey. 'The fire began in the mantle-tree, occasioned by a new fashioned fire place', and 'would have all consumed in a few minutes, had not Mr Hampton and his wife been alarmed by the fall of a large looking-glass, in the common parlor'. An early chimney glass probably made in New York about 1720–30 is in the Winterthur Museum. This glass is almost five feet across and only sixteen inches high. At each end the black walnut is cut in scrolled ears which hold brass candle arms.

Another type of looking glass was the pier glass, intended for use on the wall between two windows. 'All sorts of peer glasses' were advertised as early as 1732 in the *South Carolina Gazette*.

Benjamin Franklin's inventory taken in 1790 reveals a variety of looking glasses. In one chamber there was a dressing glass valued at £2 and in Mr Franklin's chamber, a pier glass worth £2 and a looking glass. There were a glass in the parlor, two looking glasses valued at £12 in the dining room, and one in the Blue Room. This indicates the wider use and the variety of looking glasses in America by the end of the eighteenth century.

That these were no longer simply utilitarian objects but also an important part of the decorative scheme is indicated by Abigail Adams's letter to her sister on June 9, 1790, in which she asks that her large looking glass be sent from her house in Braintree to Richmond Hill. 'This House,' she explains, 'is much better calculated for the Glasses, having all the Rooms Eleven foot high.' A similar reference is found in the diary of the Reverend William Bentley, of Salem, Massachusetts, in October 1801, when he speaks of a Mr West's house: 'The Mirrors were large and gave full view of every one who passed, and were intended for the house in town but were exchanged as those for this Seat were too large'. This is the earliest known use of the term *mirror* in American writings, *looking glass* being the proper term prior to that time.

Sheraton, in his *Cabinet Dictionary* published in London in 1803, defines the word *mirror* as an article of furniture, specifically as 'the circular convex glass in a gilt frame,' which was introduced at the turn of the century. Presumably it is this type of glass which was listed in the inventory of John C. Vanden Heuvel, of New York City, 1826 (Downs Manuscript Library, Winterthur Museum). In the drawing room were two mirrors worth $15 each, listed separately from a looking glass valued at $18 in the same room. The inventory of Gerard Beekman, also of New

York City, in 1833 still separated these items as they appeared in the back chamber; that is, '1 Looking Glass – $20', '2 mirrors – $10'. Certainly it was the convex mirror which Sheraton characterized as 'collecting the reflected rays into a point' that Phillip Hone spoke of in his diary on January 23, 1834, and which allowed him to make a play on words in describing the house of Mr *Ray* of New York as having 'splendid mirrors which reflect and multiply all the *rays*, great and small'.

By 1840 mirrors and looking glasses had become commonplace items in American homes. Two paintings by Henry Sargent, done in the early nineteenth century, provide one of the first visual records of the use of looking glasses in American interiors (Museum of Fine Arts, Boston). *The Tea Party* shows the use of horizontal, rectangular glasses above the fireplace in each of two parlors and a vertical, rectangular pier glass between the two windows of one parlor. *The Dinner Party* shows a similar, though simpler, pier glass between the windows in the dining room.

Imported looking glasses: many of the looking glasses used in early America were imported from abroad. In his articles on the 'English Export Trade in Furniture to Colonial America' in *Antiques* (June, October, 1935), R.W.Symonds reprints the statistics of the approximate number of English-made looking glasses exported to New England, New York, Pennsylvania, Virginia, Maryland and Carolina. The earliest record is for 1697, when 334 looking glasses were shipped to America. From that time until 1747, the last date cited, the number exported fluctuated sharply, ranging from a low of 6 in 1698 to a high of 1,112 looking glasses in 1723. Many English looking glasses made their way to America as presentation pieces. A notable example, now at the Winterthur Museum, made of fir wood with elaborate gesso and gilt decoration, was presented to Colonel Peter Schuyler, of Albany, at the time of his visit to London with the five Indian chiefs in 1709.

The goldsmith Francis Richardson sold many English looking glasses at his shop in

Philadelphia. In 1719 when he made a trip to London, he recorded in his account book (Downs Manuscript Library, Winterthur Museum) the purchase of two boxes of looking glasses: 'Bought of Joseph Tantom 20 Looking Glasses and 2 small Blanketts amounting 8 hund boards 4 Round with a Case ... 15/9/4.' Under his notes of people to see in London, Richardson also listed 'Cristepher Siphtha [sic] a Looking Glass maker at the Sign Looking Glass in Aldermondary'. Both these London furniture makers are listed by Sir Ambrose Heal: Christopher Sibthorpe, cabinetmaker, in Aldermanbury; and Joseph Tantum, cabinetmaker, in Gravel Lane, Houndsditch.

An indication of the variety of the glasses imported is seen in the advertisement of John Elliott in the *Pennsylvania Gazette* on October 20, 1768: 'A very large, neat and genteel assortment of looking-glasses, consisting of common sconces and piers, plain and with gilding, pediment sconces and piers, japanned sconces, gilt and white carved ditto, chimney glasses, dressing ditto, with drawers, swinging ditto, hanging ditto, with and without heads, shaving and pocket ditto, coach and chariot ditto, ditto for book case doors, &c ...'

Although, in this case, Elliott's glasses were imported from London, after the War of Independence looking glasses came from other sources. J.Billard, of Philadelphia, advertised in 1784 as 'just received from France, an Assortment of Looking Glasses in gilt mahogany and walnut frames', and De Blok and De Vos, of Baltimore, advertised in 1792 'an elegant assortment of Looking Glasses' from Hamburg. A type of glass in a frame veneered with pink marble has become known as a *Bilbao* mirror since it has been suggested that this type was brought back from trade with that Spanish city. Many of these glasses have been found in New England seaport towns such as Salem, Massachusetts, which had established trading connections with Bilbao early in the eighteenth century. However, Italian and Danish origins have also been ascribed to this type of looking glass.

Even in the early nineteenth century many

of the gilt *convex* mirrors surmounted with eagles were imported from England as well as France. Milbert in his early-nineteenth century *Itinéraire* points out that, while looking glasses, mirrors, and girandoles were made in America in large quantities, the most beautiful of those used here came from France and also from England.

American-made looking glasses: how early looking glasses were made in America is uncertain. From the beginning, plate glass had to be brought from the old country. William Wood in his *Nevv Englands Prospect* in 1634 suggested to future colonists, 'Glasse ought not to be forgotten of any that desire to benefit themselves, or the Country: if it be well leaded, and carefully pack't up, I know no commodity better for portage or sayle ...' Certainly from an early date there was some reframing of old glasses. This practice of utilizing the glass in a new-fashioned looking glass continued well after the Revolutionary War as indicated by the advertisements of Samuel Kneeland, one of which appeared in the Hartford, Connecticut, *American Mercury* on November 12, 1787, 'N.B. Old Looking Glasses repaired, fram'd and gilt in the neatest manner, so as to look equal to new ones.'

Styles and types: the earliest looking glasses probably were framed in simple cove-molded rectangular frames made of oak and pine, perhaps painted or, toward the end of the seventeenth century, veneered with walnut. In the last quarter of the seventeenth century a crest was added at the top, in a separate piece which is often missing today. Because the crest was cut from a thin piece of wood, it frequently warped and curved backward in spite of braces put on the back to correct this tendency. Often the crest was pierced in an elaborate pattern similar to the carved cresting rails on William and Mary chairs. The looking glass illustrated (Plate 37A) is one of the earliest surviving examples made in this country. The frame is made of white pine, native to New England, and is painted to give a tortoiseshell appearance.

This looking glass belonged originally to the Pepperell family of Kittery, Maine.

Another variety of looking glass with a crested design was that called today a *courting mirror*. These glasses were set in wide molded frames with stepped crests. Set in between the moldings were pieces of simply painted glass decorated with bright-colored leaves and flowers. Many of these glasses, though their origins are uncertain, are found today in New England along with the wooden cases in which they were carried.

In the early-eighteenth century the molding of the frame around the glass became more elaborate (Plate 37C), being rounded at the upper corners. By 1720 this molding had changed from the cove molding to a channeled molding. The most popular type of cresting on looking glasses of the first half of the eighteenth century was a solid, scrolled cresting. At this time a scrolled skirt was often added at the base of the looking glass as well. Often the beveled glass was set into the frame in two pieces since many of these glasses were as much as five feet high, and glass was precious, especially in large sheets. Because the upper section could not easily be used to reflect a particular image, the glass in that area was sometimes engraved with a floral pattern or a heraldic device. This was particularly true of glasses made between 1725 and 1750.

Toward the middle of the eighteenth century, japanning became a favorite method of decorating looking-glass frames. Such works as John Stalker's *Treatise of Japanning and Varnishing*, published in 1688 in Oxford, gave instructions for the imitation of Oriental lacquer work. The largest known American example with japanned decoration (Plate 37C) was probably made in New York between 1729 and 1740 and was owned by Jon Johannes Bleeker. Made of soft pine, it is decorated on a black ground with raised Oriental and European designs in gilt. It was in New York at this time, too, that Gerardus Duyckinck advertised in the *Weekly Journal* in 1736, 'Looking-glasses new Silvered and the Frames plaine, japand or Flowered ... made and sold, all manner of painting done.'

A simpler version (Plate 37B), originally used on the Luyster farm in Middletown, New York, and made between 1725 and 1735, has exotic gilt decoration on a cerulean-blue ground. Many glasses were made of walnut in these same designs and were not painted. One of the most popular designs of all, this style continued to be made throughout the eighteenth century and well into the nineteenth century. Such looking glasses can be dated only by their diminished crests, the use of later classical motifs, or the type of molding surrounding the glass itself.

By the middle decades of the eighteenth century, the molding of looking-glass frames became further elaborated by having an inner border which was carved and gilded. Especially in Philadelphia and also elsewhere, the cresting of these glasses was often decorated in the center with a gilded shell, at first a solid, symmetrical shell which, with the advent of the rococo taste, became pierced and asymmetrical. By this time mahogany was the favored primary wood. A fine example of this particular type of glass (Plate 38A) was made between 1762 and 1767 and labeled by JOHN ELLIOTT, SR, of Philadelphia. This same John Elliott with Isaac Gray owned the Philadelphia Glass Works about 1773–77, a natural association for a cabinetmaker who made numerous looking glasses. The first label Elliott used, while at his shop on Chestnut Street from 1756 to 1761, was printed in English and German. From 1762 to 1767 he was working on Walnut Street at the Sign of the Bell and Looking Glass, where he advertised in 1763 that he also 'quicksilvers and frames old glasses, and supplies people with new glasses to their own frames; and will undertake to cure any English looking glass that shows the face either too long or too broad or any other way distorted'.

The glass was indeed the valuable part of the object, and Edward Weyman announced in the *South Carolina Gazette* on March 24, 1759, that 'Prices are regulated according to the size' of the glass. In 1795 Wells and Morris, of Philadelphia, had 'Looking-Glass Plates, 10 by 17, 12 by 18, 13 by 20, 13 by 22, 14 by 24, for sale ...'.

Concurrently popular in the mid-eighteenth century was the *architectural* type of looking glass (Plate 38B) surmounted by a broken-arch pediment and a phoenix or eagle finial. This type of frame usually had pendent swags of leaves and flowers on each side, and often had the architectural outlines emphasized by gilt and carved egg-and-dart or leaf moldings. Bearing a close relationship to the architectural patterns of British designers like James Gibbs or Abraham Swan, these frames were quite suitable for filling wall panels similarly derived from the designs of these men. Crosseted corners in the upper section of the frame, more elaborate scrolling below the base of the glass, and rosettes with streamers in the volutes of the pediment are features which enhanced these designs.

Generally the glass in the architectural examples was in one section, as is the case in the one illustrated (Plate 38B). This looking glass is documented by a bill of sale dated 'New York, Augst. 25th 1794 Mr Jacob Everson Bo^{t}. of William Wilmerding 1 Looking Glass – £8 – .' The beaded oval decoration and delicate gilt branches in the pediment verify the date of 1794, although the rest of the frame reflects a style at its height in the third quarter of the century. WILLIAM WILMERDING advertised in New York City between 1789 and 1794. After 1798 he was listed in New York directories as a merchant. Wilmerding's label (Plate 38C), which appears on a looking glass owned by John S. Walton, New York, is most interesting as it shows a portable dressing box, a cheval glass with a pedimented crest, a dressing stand with an oval-shaped glass, a looking glass with a widely pitched pediment and eagle finial, and a looking glass surmounted by an urn filled with ears of wheat, a new style introduced in the last decade of the eighteenth century.

As the rococo taste became firmly established, frames became more elaborately scalloped, gilt ornament increased, the inner moldings became undulating and even pierced with rocaille details. Cartouches as well as gadrooned vases filled with three-dimensional flowers and occasionally *papier-mâché* figures filled the pediment.

One of the most beautiful examples of looking glasses in the rococo taste (Plate 39A) is the lightly carved white-and-gold frame which belonged to the Cadwalader family in Philadelphia. The delicate C-scrolls, fanciful columns, and pendent leaves and flowers are the very essence of the rococo style. A strikingly similar glass, undoubtedly from the same hand, was made for Richard Edwards, proprietor of the Taunton Furnace in Burlington County, New Jersey, by JOHN ELLIOTT, of Philadelphia, and bears the label which he used between 1768 and 1776. A third frame of this type is in the Metropolitan Museum of Art and is distinguished by having glass behind the open areas between the inner molding and the outer scrolls.

A contemporary of Elliott, JAMES REYNOLDS, advertised in Philadelphia 'carved and white, carved and gold, carved mahogany pier, sconce, pediment, mock pediment, ornamented, or raffle frames, box, swinging, or dressing glasses ...'. Thomas Jefferson in 1792 recorded in his account book that he 'gave James Reynolds ord[er]. on bank of U.S. for [$]141.33 in full for looking glasses', and again in 1793 he paid him $99.53 for framing looking glasses.

Shortly after the War of Independence the new classical style began to penetrate looking-glass designs. One of the earliest intrusions of this new taste was in the oval-shaped glass set into the older-style frame. A happy combination showing this transition is the dressing stand (Plate 39B) made by JONATHAN GOSTELOWE, a Philadelphia cabinetmaker noted for his serpentine chest of drawers. This *dressing glass* along with a chest of drawers was made in 1789 for Gostelowe's bride, Elizabeth H. Towers.

Federal period: with a similar oval-shaped glass, but showing the subsequent assimilation of the classical style, is the dressing glass (Plate 40A), the carving of which is attributed to SAMUEL MCINTIRE, of Salem, Massachusetts, about 1800. Delicate string inlay, veneers of flame wood, carved laurel swags, beading and cornucopias all betray the Federal period of design.

Another inlaid dressing glass, with French feet, was labeled by STEPHEN BADLAM, JR.

(1751–1815), a cabinet and looking-glass maker in Dorchester, Massachusetts. Probably these dressing glasses in the new style were similar to those advertised in 1784 by Willing, Morris and Swanwick as having been stolen from their Philadelphia counting house, 'Two oval Swinging Glasses with Mahogany frames and black and white string edges – one marked on the back 52s, 6, the other 35s.'

In the early-nineteenth century these dressing glasses followed furniture styles in the use of plain dark mahogany surfaces. Often they were supported on brass ball feet. At the same time the chest of drawers with an attached looking glass supported by a large scrolled frame became a more common furniture form, especially in the Boston and Salem area. This general type of furniture had been made in New York City during the Chippendale period in the form of a chest of drawers, the top drawer of which contained a collapsible looking glass and many compartments for organizing the accoutrements of dressing.

Looking glasses, now frequently made in pairs, similarly took up the new decoration, so that the frames for glasses made between 1790 and 1810 frequently were oval (Plate 40C), surmounted by fragile classical urns, banded with beading or flat water leaves carved around the base. From these urns sprang wired and gilded gesso ornaments of ears of wheat, rosettes, thin classical scrolls, laurel swags and acanthus leaves. At the base of the oval frames were more leaves, a patera and often the favored feather motif of the Prince of Wales. Usually the innermost molding immediately surrounding the glass was an edge of beading.

This type of frame was readily developed into the more heavily ornamented frame of the early-nineteenth century (Plate 40B). One example made for Elias Hasket Derby, of Salem, Massachusetts, has a naturalistic, carved eagle above the three-feathers motif, coarsely carved leaves, and entwined dolphins at the base. The molding immediately around the glass is reeded with a twisted-rope design in the center instead of beading. This is an enormous glass, slightly over six feet high,

which Abigail Adams undoubtedly would have preferred to see in a room where the walls were at least eleven feet high. Another large, oval-shaped glass, now in the Museum of Fine Arts, Boston, and owned originally by Elizabeth Derby, is attributed to JOHN DOGGETT, a well-known picture-frame and looking-glass maker in Roxbury, Massachusetts, whose trade label is itself inscribed within a frame which is surmounted by an eagle on three feathers and which has entwined dolphins at the base.

The final development in this type of looking glass was effected when the glass became round and convex, in the style of the French mirrors to which Sheraton referred in his *Dictionary*. Having large eagles at the top, which could be associated with the Great Seal of the United States, and outlined by heavy ball carving, an exaggeration of the classical beaded molding, these mirrors are often mistakenly cherished above others as American made, although they were largely imported from England and France during this Greek Revival period. When candle arms are added they are popularly called *girandoles*, a somewhat loose application of a term belonging to lighting devices.

At the same time, the architectural type of frame continued in the classical period with a flat cornice, gradually replacing the earlier broken-arch pediment. The term *tabernacle* has sometimes been applied to the flat cornice type. Classical columns flanked the glass, and the upper section was usually filled with painting. Detail on these frames became less refined after 1810, beading being replaced by heavy ball ornament, twisted-rope moldings, and surfaces left smooth and undecorated. A chaste example of an architectural-type looking glass made in 1810 (Plate 40D) is particularly interesting in that not only does it bear the label of PETER GRINNELL & SON, of Providence, Rhode Island, but also its painted glass or *églomisé* panel at the top is signed by the painter, 'B. CREHORE, Aug. 27, 1810'. The painted wall-of-Troy border around the rustic scene gives ample evidence that this frame belongs to the period of the Greek Revival.

An alternative method of decorating the

upper section of these frames was to substitute gilded plaster decoration for the *églomisé* panel. A labeled example of this sort made by John Doggett is in the Metropolitan Museum of Art, and has the figure of *Fame* above a floral festoon upheld by two trophies of the Prince of Wales feathers and a bowknot. John McElwee advertised in the *Pennsylvania Packet* on May 7, 1800, that he had 'Also for sale on a liberal credit, a quantity of Composition Ornaments, and Moulds of every pattern necessary for the Looking Glass business'.

During this final period in the first half of the nineteenth century, there were many well-known names among looking-glass makers. BARNARD CERMENATI worked at No. 10 State Street in Boston and Newburyport, Massachusetts, and in Portsmouth, New Hampshire. STILLMAN LATHROP, when he moved to Boston in 1806, continued his old business in Salem through an agent, George Dean. WAYNE & BIDDLE succeeded JAMES STOKES in Philadelphia and produced many architectural glasses with landscapes and seascapes in the *églomisé* panels. In New York, the DEL VECCHIOS – CHARLES, JOSEPH and JOHN – produced looking glasses during the first decades of the nineteenth century.

From obscure beginnings and a trade largely concerned with importing looking glasses and the repairing of old glasses, the seller of looking glasses became, by the nineteenth century, a distinguished, specialized artisan.

GLOSSARY

Bilbao mirror: name given to type of looking glass in frames veneered with sheets of pink marble imported from Europe to America at the end of the eighteenth century and in the early nineteenth century.

Chimney glass: looking glass designed to fit the chimney breast above the fireplace in a room.

Constitution mirror: rectangular looking glass in an architectural frame with a broken arch pediment and shaped apron; reason for the use of this term not known.

Courting mirror: looking glass of unknown origin, held in molded, step-crested frames set with panels of glass painted with multi-colored leaves and flowers, usually accompanied by crude wooden boxes in which they were carried.

Dressing glass: looking glass suspended between two upright members affixed to a box containing drawers and supported by brackets or knobs for feet.

Girandole: technically, candle supports, though this term is now used with reference to the type of convex, circular mirror surmounted by an eagle, with or without candle branches.

Mirror: generally any reflective, impervious surface, but specifically a circular, convex glass in a gilt frame.

Tabernacle mirror: generally applied to the Sheraton mirror with flat cornice under which is a row of gilt balls above a scene painted on glass; columns at sides.

BOOKS FOR FURTHER READING

DOWNS, JOSEPH: *American Furniture*. New York (1952).
MILLER, ERIC G., JR.: *American Antique Furniture*. Vol. II, Baltimore (1937).
NUTTING, WALLACE: *Furniture Treasury*, Vol. II (Framingham, Massachusetts).
Antiques Magazine: 1922 to date; see index.
Concise Encyclopedia of Antiques, Vol. III, pp. 159–164, Hawthorn Books, New York (1957).

All photographs from the Winterthur Museum are by Gilbert Ask.

SILVER 1640–1820

By KATHRYN C. BUHLER

THE art of the silversmith (or goldsmith, as the craftsmen called themselves) flourished early in colonial America, with a skill and sophistication not found in the other crafts. The styles were basically English, as the earliest goldsmith whose work has come down to us was, like many subsequent ones, trained in London. Robert Sanderson emigrated after a nine years' apprenticeship to arrive in Massachusetts in 1638. Richard Storer had served only five years in a London goldsmith's shop before he came to Boston in 1635, yet he was able to instruct his young half-brother, John Hull, in 'the trade of a goldsmith', until he 'through God's help obtained that ability in it, as I was able to get my living by it'. Storer's work, and that of John Mansfield, the first trained goldsmith in New England, are unknown today. Hull was one of the most active early Boston citizens, and upon being appointed mintmaster recorded again in his diary that the Court permitted him to take his friend, Robert Sanderson, to be his partner. Most of the silver fashioned by these men bears the mark of each partner, and most of it survives from having been given to churches (Plate 41A). Marks were not a requisite on plate fashioned in the colonies, and wrought plate was a commodity as valuable as its weight in coin, and more useful. Hence, a good proportion of the silver owned by the first churches had served a period of domestic use; and the tankard, caudle cup, beaker and standing cup are ecclesiastic as well as secular forms. Porringers are unknown today in church services; it is probable that this shallow bowl with a flat, pierced, horizontal handle was always a domestic piece (Plate 47B). Inventories disclose that it was always a popular one, whereas the seemingly equally domestic dram cup lost favor in the early-eighteenth century.

Spoons, too, a household's first possession in the precious metal, followed English styles; although those with *slipped in the stalk* or *puritan* handles are rare today, suggesting re-fashioning into the ensuing forms. Another seventeenth-century Boston worker in precious metal, William Rouse, has left a few pieces in distinctly English style; yet the journal of Jasper Danckaerts, visiting in Boston, reveals that he was 'Willem Ros, from Wesel. He had married an Englishwoman and carried on his business here. ... We were better off at his house, for although his wife was an Englishwoman, she was quite a good housekeeper.'

The first native craftsman was Jeremiah Dummer, born of English parents in 1645 and recorded as his apprentice in Hull's diary of 1659. Indentures for apprentices followed those of England, and in Boston the legally required term was seven years. Dummer's contract called for eight years. His work, too, was largely in English styles (Plate 43C); exceptions are his seventeenth-century columnar candlesticks like earlier French ones copied in England, and his punch bowl of 1692 which is Portuguese in derivation. He is credited with having introduced cut-card work and gadrooning into colonial silver-smithing. Some of

FIG. 1. Candlestick; John Coney

his contemporaries, documented apprentices of Hull as were the Samuels, Paddy and Clark, have left no known work; Timothy Dwight, similarly trained, is known by only two pieces yet each of a skill to make the scarcity of his work the more surprising. John Coney, whose work (Plate 45A) survives in greater quantity and variety than any of the others, reasonably seems to have learned his craft from the same source. His earliest sugar boxes are in rich Charles II style, as are his cherub-laden

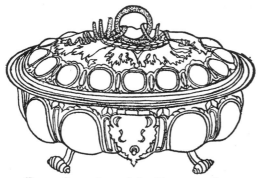

FIG. 2. Sugar box; John Coney, c. 1690

caudle cups or punch bowls, yet the majority of his pieces are simple.

Sanderson had three sons whom he trained, yet only one is known by his work today. Hull's sons all died in infancy; his daughter Hannah, however, married Samuel Sewall, who has

FIG. 3. Dish; John Coney

been called the colonial Samuel Pepys; his diary records activities of 'Cousin Dummer', 'Mr Coney', 'Tim' and their successors. Thomas Savage, whose small porringer's

handle (Plate 47B) is very much like the simple early ones by Dummer, was by witness

FIG. 4. Flagon; early-eighteenth century

of Sewall's diary the master of Samuel Haugh.

Dummer's generation saw the beginning of the craft in New York which, although

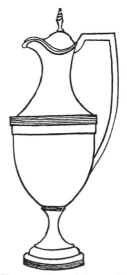

FIG. 5 Flagon; late-eighteenth century

then under English rule, still held to Dutch traditions. The very names of the earliest craftsmen, Van der Burgh, Onckelbag, Kip and Kierstede proclaim their origin. Cornelis van der Burgh was the first native New York goldsmith, and one who worked entirely in the seventeenth century, for he died in 1699.

FIG. 6. Inkstand ; John Coney, *c.* 1710

His best-known beaker – the basically Dutch form which had, however, been incorporated into English plate in Jacobean days – was engraved with illustrations by Adriaen van

der Venne from a Dutch book of poems; his broad two-handled paneled bowl shows the form most characteristic of New York plate. A simpler one, yet characteristically New York by its six embossed panels and similar caryatid handles, was made by Jesse Kip (Plate 41B) who is thought to have taught the craft to Cornelius Kierstede.

FIG. 7. Beaker ; *c.* van der Burgh

The Huguenot, Bartholomew Le-Roux, who is known to have been working in New York in 1689, wrought similar handles for his generous 'brandy bowl' now owned by Yale University but left the sides similarly unadorned save for the grooves to indicate panels. LeRoux trained his own sons, John and Charles and the Dutch-named Peter Van Dyck, who, in the manner of apprentices, married his master's daughter. Onckelbag and Kierstede in New York's first generation vie for the richest productions, although

Jacobus van der Spiegel's tankard at Yale University has no rival in its intricacy of engraving. Tankards were fashioned with great skill by all the Dutch New Yorkers although the form was not one found in their homeland. To the English vessel, elaboration of handle and base molding, and frequently of the cover too, gave a distinctly local style well exemplified in the one by Peter Van Dyck (Plate 42).

When, in the last years of the seventeenth century, the craft developed in Pennsylvania, the first tankards had simplified New York base moldings, although porringer handles were derived from New England styles. New York porringers almost always show a regional character; the first handles had intricate cuttings that left no room for the owners' initials proudly proclaimed on others, and in the eighteenth-century cuttings were starkly simple in a handle of distinct solidity. New York spoons, too, had been different in their first styles of cast shaped handles with hoof or caryatid terminal, whereas Philadelphia's earliest are the trifid-ends of which the greatest surviving number in the colonies are from New England.

Rhode Island, at the turn of the eighteenth century, was training goldsmiths, probably in Boston. Samuel Vernon, the first from that colony whose work has survived, occasionally employed the meander wire and stamped base molding of New York derivation. Connecticut became the home of Boston-trained John Potwine and the New Yorker, Cornelius Kierstede, who was without doubt that colony's unsurpassed craftsman. In the south, although English goldsmiths apparently seeking metal had arrived in Virginia earlier even than in New England, no goldsmiths are known to have plied their craft until the eighteenth century. In Virginia, which still preferred to order its fine plate in London, small wares and repairs continued to be the goldsmith's chief role until Revolutionary days. Cesar Ghiselin, who was Philadelphia's first goldsmith, moved to Annapolis to become Maryland's first – as Johannis Nys, in Philadelphia in the late 1690s, went on to start the craft in Delaware. In South Carolina, the Legares from New England and Stoutenburghs from New York started a craft of which little now remains.

Meantime, in the city of Boston, John Coney had taken a Huguenot lad to be his apprentice. Apollos Rivoire anglicized his name and as Paul Revere became famous through his son and namesake. Coney had had no sons to carry on; but John Burt, believed to have been his apprentice, had three sons to continue the proud craft, one of whom for the most part, less ambitious pieces were fashioned. Early in the eighteenth century, Salem, Newburyport and other towns supported goldsmiths, but important works seem to have been largely restricted to the main centers of the craft.

John Edwards was the scion of a three-generation craft tradition; his sons, Thomas and Samuel (Plate 47c), were almost exact contemporaries of Jacob Hurd. The last, by

FIG. 8. Cup; Jacob Hurd, c. 1740–1750

worked throughout the second half of the century. Although there were numerous goldsmiths in Boston at that period, the patriot Revere and Benjamin Burt (Plate 44) seem to have shared the earlier importance of John Coney and Jacob Hurd (Plate 48c). Edward Winslow had been an apprentice of Jeremiah Dummer, as had, undoubtedly, John Noyes and, probably, John Edwards. No parallel is found for Winslow's four sugar boxes, all dated in the early 1700s. Dummer, Winslow and Edwards, in partnership with Allen, fashioned the three surviving standing salts of colonial make. A third maker of sugar boxes in the early 1700s is thought to have been Daniel Greenough of New Hampshire where, the quality and variety of his work and importance of his clients, seems to have taken Coney's place in Boston for approximately a quarter of a century. His sons, Nathaniel and Benjamin Hurd, and his apprentice, Daniel Henchman (Plate 50A), all worked in the third quarter of the century and left an occasional rococo piece, though New England obviously still preferred simple lines and fine proportions. Jacob Hurd was commissioned by the maritime court to make its admiralty oar; the Court of Vice-Admiralty in New York ordered one from Charles LeRoux. The latter fashioned a gold box for Andrew Hamilton, an official presentation piece now owned by the Historical Society of Pennsylvania. An earlier gold gift had been made in 1693 by Cornelis van der Burgh for Governor Fletcher, but it is known only by documentation.

In Albany the Ten Eyck family (Plate 46B), of goldsmiths was flourishing; the early Koenraet had sent his son Jacob to be an apprentice of Charles LeRoux. A generation earlier Kiliaen Van Rensselaer, apprenticed to Jeremiah Dummer in Boston, had found living in that staid town to be rather simple. Kiliaen's work is unknown, but Koenraet and his sons, Jacob and Barent Ten Eyck, have left examples of their fine workmanship. Barent fashioned for Daniel Cruyn in 1755 a gorget engraved with the British Royal arms, also engraven on the Admiralty Oars. Throughout the eighteenth century, and in all colonial centers, British designs set the styles for colonial craftsmen. Samuel Sympson's *Book of Cyphers*, published in London in 1736, is known to have been used in New York and Rhode Island. John Singleton Copley painted Nathaniel Hurd with the 1724 edition of Guillim's *Display of Heraldry* at his elbow, and many craftsmen followed the heraldic designs in this oft-published work.

There are more portraits of silversmiths than of other craftsmen. Copley painted Revere in his shirt-sleeves, though at a highly polished work-bench, with a pear-form teapot in his capable hand; and depicted Rufus Greene, an apprentice of William Cowell who, in turn, had learned his craft with Dummer. Nathaniel Hurd sat for his miniature portrait on copper to Copley, and to an unidentified limner in watercolor on ivory. William Gilbert of New York sat to James Sharples, as did Joseph Anthony of Philadelphia to Gilbert Stuart; but none of these portraits proclaim the sitter's profession as Copley twice had done.

The shift to English styles in New York was undoubtedly broader in scope than the influence of such London-trained craftsmen in that town as Simeon Soumain (Plate 49C) and Daniel Christian Fueter, two well-known names in its goldsmithing annals. The latter advertised employing a chaser from Geneva, yet the average goldsmith was still carrying on his trade in all its branches.

Many were also spreading into other fields which were then, but not now, allied to it. Dentistry was an achievement of several goldsmiths, best known among them, no doubt, the patriot Revere. Nathaniel Hurd had turned to engraving so that, at his early demise in 1777, it was as an 'ingenious engraver' that he was extolled. Revere's engravings were sometimes executed carefully, but the best known of his were political cartoons, carelessly and hastily executed. He gave up his craft entirely for the five years of the Revolution, but resumed to work in the newest English fashion (Plate 51C) practised also by Benjamin Burt, both of whom continued into the early years of the 1800s. Revere printed continental currency; Ephraim Brasher (Plate 48A) of New York minted the famous and now very rare Brasher doubloon. Like the earliest mint in Massachusetts, it was not entirely legal, but extremely convenient. (See 'Coins and Medals', by Sydney P. Noe, Vol. II.) Myer Myers of New York (Plate 45B), whose work also spanned the rococo through classic styles, showed usually a preference for simplicity.

His dish ring is unique in known American silver, and his cake basket made for the same patrons, Samuel and Susanna Cornell, has come to public attention since the publication of Mrs Rosenbaum's recent book on Myers.

Philadelphia had three families of three-generation craftsmen who almost spanned the eighteenth century. Philip Syng, Jr, fashioned the standish (Fig. 15) used at the signing of the Declaration of Independence; his father and son, both of the same name, owe their present-day reputation to him. Francis Richardson had a namesake and a Joseph (Plates 49A, B) among his sons. The latter – who imported much English plate

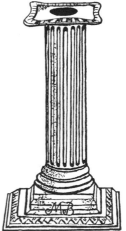

FIG. 9. Candlestick; J. and N. Richardson

and worked in richest styles – had sons Joseph (Plate 52A) and Nathaniel as successors. Peter, David and his son and grandson John were capable craftsmen but probably owe their reputation today to their family adherence to the craft rather than to their individual practise of it. Richard Humphreys was selected by the Continental Congress to fashion its rich presentation urn to Charles Thomson, Secretary of the Congress, and by George Washington to make camp cups.

The silversmithing family of Faris in Annapolis was founded by William who has been characterized as 'the most picturesque figure among eighteenth-century Maryland silversmiths'. His accomplishments included clock and watch making, portrait painting, and work as a cabinetmaker, dentist, innkeeper and tulip grower. He has left the only known manuscript book of silver designs in the colonies, and had three sons whom he trained in silversmithing.

Unique in America was Baltimore's endeavor in the early 1800s to establish a guild-system similar to that so long in existence in England and on the Continent. For a brief time, starting in 1814, silver made in Baltimore was marked at a hall and identified by a date letter; this compulsory marking was abolished in 1830. By coincidence, perhaps, this is the period when American silver was becoming, through the taste of the time and introduction of machinery, a commodity of far less appeal than that of the previous two centuries.

GLOSSARY

Annealing: the reheating of silver to keep it malleable while it is being worked. 'Nealing tongs' appear in goldsmiths' inventories.

Asparagus tongs: in the inventory of John Hancock in 1794, otherwise unknown in American silver.

Assay: in silver, the test made to prove that the metal was of required quality.

Bason: the usual spelling in the seventeenth and eighteenth centuries for the large vessel known in English plate as a 'rosewater dish'. The known American survivors are those given to churches to serve as baptismal basins; others in almost the form of the domestic ones were made for immediate church use. Most have a rather broad rim around a deep depression, usually domed in the center.

Bead: 'a globular ornament peculiar to Saxon architecture, carved in the mouldings' is the definition in the *Gentleman's Magazine* (LXXVII, 1802), and an applicable description to the ornament in silver from the last quarter of the eighteenth century. Earlier, in effect a graduated, beading appeared as handle ornament, known today as 'beaded rat-tail'.

Beaker: derived doubtless from earlier horn vessels, the cylindrical form sometimes with flaring rim of the seventeenth century developed to an inverted bell on a molded

FIG. 10. Beaker by Jacob Hurd, 1740   FIG. 11. Beaker by Benjamin Burt, 1798

foot in the early eighteenth. Late in the century small beakers with almost straight sides again became popular, with or without a molding at the base (Plate 52B). The same forms were used in America for domestic and ecclesiastical use.

Beer bowles and **beer cupps:** encountered in inventories but not distinctly recognizable today.

Bezel: the added inside rim to make a cover fit more firmly.

Biggin: recorded in the *Gentleman's Magazine* of 1803, 'Mr Biggin some years ago invented a new sort of coffee pot which has been ever since extensively sold under the name of coffee biggins.' None is known of American make at that period, but the principle is that of the drip pot.

Bottle tickets: small plaques, plain or ornamented, engraved or cut with the name of a beverage, with a chain to be hung on the neck of a decanter.

Bowl: an unknown item is the 'silver Bowl with two wooden handles' in an inventory of 1728; 'a wrought bowl which will hold five pints, with handles' is mentioned in 1758. *Slop bowls* and *slop basins* appear in inventories early in the eighteenth century but are identifiable chiefly in the second half.

Box: in New England *sugar box* was the name by which large caskets known in England as *sweetmeat boxes* were called. Early New York inventories mention *spice boxes*, none so far identified. *Tobacco* and *snuff boxes* were popular, as were very small *patch boxes* for a lady's beauty spots.

Bread baskets: the opulent form, usually of pierced work and on feet, although an example by Myer Myers is on a baseband,

FIG. 12. Bread basket; D. C. Fueter

with bail handle; today called a cake basket, as in the will of Dorothy Quincy Hancock Scott (1830): 'My large silver cake basket requesting her to have it used at the weddings ... as it has been heretofore.'

Bright-cut: a form of sharp cut decoration popular in the late eighteenth century.

Buckles: for knees, shoes, girdles and stocks were recorded in great quantity in gold, silver, paste, etc., but comparatively few have survived and even fewer with maker's marks.

Burnishing: *see* Planishing.

Butter tester: a device found in silver from the mid-eighteenth century akin in shape to a modern *apple corer*, and sometimes thus called erroneously.

Candlesticks: only two American silver pairs are so far known from the seventeenth century, both of wrought silver and based on English styles. John Coney's inventory in 1722 included 'candlestick moulds' and two types of his cast candlesticks, a third wrought one, are known. Silver candlesticks, however, were rare in the colonies judging from inventories and survivors.

Canes: unidentified today; inventories from 1697 refer to 'silver-headed canes'; in 1719 the Boston goldsmith, Samuel Haugh, had 'a silver ferril upon an Agget Canes head', and Revere's day-book in 1786 mentions a gold cane head.

Canister: usually considered a receptacle for tea; Edward Franklin's inventory of 1725 listed 'a Canister Boat for spoons', a form unknown today.

Cann: usually applied to the curve-sided small open drinking vessel with a single handle introduced in the second decade of the eighteenth century. Yet Lt.-Gov. William Stoughton of Boston mentioned in his will (probated in 1701) 'my little Silver drinking Cann'. *Pint* and *quart canns* were specified, singly and in pairs, sometimes the latter qualified by 'wine quart'.

Cast: pieces cast are those formed in a mold; candlesticks were sometimes cast, or the handle ornament of a tankard. Handles in caryatid form are cast, sometimes the foot of a cup or beaker was cast.

FIG. 13. Caster

Caster: vessel with pierced cover, the earliest cylindrical ones changing to vase form (Plate 45A). Frequently in sets of three and specified then as for sugar, pepper and mustard, one large and one small with piercings, and a mate to the latter with its holes only simulated.

Caudle: *see* Cups.

Chafing dish: a pierced receptacle on wooden feet and held by a horizontal wooden handle, in which coals could be placed for heating (Plate 46c). Many Boston examples are known in pairs; a New York inventory of 1700 mentioned 'a babye's chafingdish' which suggests a single one. The 'Iron chaffendishes' of Elizur Holyoke's inventory in 1711 suggest a more practical but less luxurious piece. Although the surviving examples are largely from the first half of the eighteenth century, Paul Revere made one in 1762. In 1779 'Two very elegant Table Chafing Dishes of the newest fashion, the only ones of the kind that have ever been imported into this place', advertised by Richard Humphreys (Philadelphia), suggest *dish crosses* with lamps.

Chalice: a communion cup usually with paten cover, given to the established churches in the new country. *See also* Communion cup.

Chasing: a form of decoration produced by chisels and hammers in distinction to the cutting away of an engraving tool; a raised ornament also termed embossing.

Chocolate cup: Boston's famed Peter Faneuil left '6 Lignum Vitae chocolate cups lin'd with Silver' in 1743, but they are unknown today.

Chocolate pot: although in Boston as early as 1670 a 'House for Coffee and Chucka-letto' was permitted, pots for these popular beverages are not known until the 1700s. In 1701 John Coney fashioned a chocolate pot for Sarah Tailer in gallipot form; his ensuing one was like a tall curved coffee pot, but the removable finial to provide a hole in the cover for a stirring rod continued to differentiate the two vessels.

Clasps: for books, pocketbooks and cloaks were shaped plaques on which, to judge by the few remaining ones, a goldsmith could show his imagination and skill in engraving. Clasps for necklaces and bracelets were usually oblong or elliptical and engraved. These are sometimes called lockets.

Coaster: a modern name for the *bottle stands*, fashioned in the late-eighteenth century, wherein decanters might be placed on the table to *coast* from one guest to another.

Cobbet pot: in Boston in 1667 John Wilson left 'one chased cobbet pott & Cover'. of silver but unknown shape and size. The *Oxford Dictionary on Historic Principles* lists *Cobbit* as an obsolete form of *Cobbard*, or *fire irons* – obviously not applicable to this puzzle.

Coffee pot: unknown in American silver of the seventeenth century, the first (Plate 49c) are cylindrical, and some have spout at right angles to handle, which, like those on tea and chocolate pots, was of wood. Curved bodies apparently preceded the pear-form (Plates 50A, B), but that both were made at the same time is evidenced in advertisements of 'double and single belly'd coffee pots ...'.

Creampot: the earliest colonial example known was made by John Edwards, with a small triangular spout and a molded foot. Shortly a similar pear-form body with an elongated lip (Plate 48B) was given three scroll feet, and in the last decade of the eighteenth century the single foot was resumed, but higher and frequently on a plinth (Plate 51c). *Cream ewers* and *cream urns* were descriptive of these; *cream cows* were advertised as imported in the 1770s, *cream cups* and *cream jugs* appear in the records of that decade also. *Cream pitchers* are mentioned in the 1790s, as were *cream pails* and *cream buckets*; the latter in Revere's ledger had a ladle.

Cruet stand: occasionally made in the colonies (one example has survived) and frequently imported from London. A frame to hold oil and vinegar cruets, usually with three casters too.

Cups: various forms and sizes appear; Lt.-Gov. Stoughton's gift to Harvard College was designated both as a *bowl* and a *grace-cup*; a seemingly similar one in Isaac Addington's will of 1713, 'my large Silver Cup with two handles & Cover' is known to have been in the gourd form of a caudle cup. Mary

Lumsden in 1688 left a 'two-ear'd silver cup', in the next decade Ruth Carter had a 'two-eared cup with feet'.

Caudle cups: popular in New England until the 1720s were gourd-shaped with two handles (Plate 41A), occasionally covered; two of New York make have recently come to public attention with the caryatid handles of early fashion.

Church cup: a designation in bequests for standing cups and beakers diverted from domestic to ecclesiastic use.

Communion cup: any cup used in the communion service.

Cordial cups: weighing about thirty ounces, with or without covers, are in early New York inventories but unidentified.

Dram cup: a small two-handled shallow bowl, similar to a *wine taster*, seldom made after the second decade of the eighteenth century.

Spout cup: used for feeding infants and invalids, generally superseded in the mid-eighteenth century by the papboat, al-

FIG. 14. Spout cup

though later examples are known. A narrow spout, with a tiny aperture in the body at its juncture, is placed at right angles to the handle, usually single, although a two-handled spout cup was made by Jeremiah Dummer.

Wine cup: mentioned in seventeenth-century inventories but whether of standing or tumbler form is unknown.

Cut card: sheet silver cut in shapes applied for strength or decoration, as at the base of a finial, joining of a handle, or surbase of a cup.

Cypher: *see* Engraving.

Dish: Revere made '4 silver dishes' in 1796 for presentation to the First Church in Boston in the form of the six given in 1764 by Thomas Hancock to the Brattle Street Church. These in turn are similar to the wholly domestic ones of Winslow's and Coney's make, which have been erroneously called 'alms dishes'. The Royal gifts to established churches included a 'receiver' in plate form. 'Issue plates' and 'trencher plates' of silver were recorded in private possession in the 1690s.

Dish ring: only one in spool form is known of colonial make, by Myer Myers of New York, yet in the 1660s 'wicker rings to sett Dishes on' were recorded in Boston, and in 1754 a *pewter ring stand* was advertised in New York.

Dish stand: importation of 'ex-s with slides and lamps for dish stands' and 'table crosses' with and without lamps were advertised in the second half of the eighteenth century, and a few, also known as dish crosses, with local maker's marks are known.

Drawing benches and wires: used in forming applied moldings and strap handles.

Emboss: ornament hammered from within in relief.

Engrave: ornament in which lines are cut in the silver. Initials were engraved as an aid in identification, or in a decorative cypher or monogram. Sometimes initials were enclosed in cartouches similar to those used to frame coats of arms. Guillim's *Display of Heraldry* in its 1724 edition is shown in Nathaniel Hurd's portrait by John Singleton Copley, and doubtless the volume, as were others of lettering, was used by many colonial gold-smiths. Sympson's *Book of Cyphers* wherein initials were intertwined and reversed is also known to have been used in the colonies.

Epergne: advertised in Boston in 1757 'A neat polish'd Epergne, with gadrooned and pierced Bason Saucers, and 4 saucers and 4

Nozzels and Pans wt. 191 oz. 13 dwt.' An extravagant piece of plate, the name derived from the French *épargne*; no American-made example known from early times.

Feathered: spoons 'feathered on the edge' in the second half of the eighteenth century had a narrow chased edge reminiscent of gadrooning.

Finial: on covers the more readily to lift them, in forms varying from simple turnings to acorns, pineapples and twisted 'flames'.

Fish slice: sometimes *fish trowel*, a flat shaped server, pierced and engraved, on a wooden handle; today more apt to be called a *pie knife*.

Flagon: a deep covered vessel with one handle used in silver in the colonies seemingly exclusively in churches. Introduced through royal gifts to Episcopal churches, it became popular in non-conformist churches as well. In the nineteenth century urn-shaped vessels with spouts were called flagons.

Fork: only rarely made of silver in the colonies. John Oxenbridge of Boston in 1675 had 'a fork spoon' presumably the sucket fork of which but few examples remain, with a small spoon bowl and two-tined fork at either end of a long shaft. Even in 1774, John Singleton Copley noted in a letter from Marseilles 'The forks are all silver ...' as if it were unusual in his experience.

Freedom box: usually in *tobacco box* size, but engraved with the arms of the city conferring its 'freedom' on a worthy citizen.

Gadroon: given in 1611 as 'from Goderon, a fashion of embossement used by Goldsmiths, etc. and tearmed knurling', is a design of reeds and flutes usually slightly spiraled; on the edge of a piece it gives the effect of rope-molding.

Geometric: porringer handles so designated have pierced design in angular forms.

Goblets: those pieces so recorded can be identified today as standing cups, *i.e.* bowls on tall stems.

Grater: a small pocket case with a rasped inner surface to grate nutmegs, freqeuntly in heart, acorn or urn form.

Graver: or **burin,** a tool for engraving.

Hammers: Coney's inventory in 1722 contained '112 Hammers for Raising, Pibling, Swolling, Hollowing, Creasing, Planishing &c.' as well as several 'Two-hand hammers' to give an idea of the painstaking care in hand-wrought silver.

Inkstands: *inckhorns* of silver are recorded in Boston in the 1670s, in 1696 'a silver ink box' was listed. Lt.-Gov. Stoughton in 1701 left a 'silver standish' and Mary

FIG. 15. Inkstand; Philip Syng, Jr.

Saltonstall in 1728 'an Ink Case' among her plate. Governor Belcher's triangular standish by John Coney (now in the Metropolitan Museum of Art, Fig. 6) and Philip Syng's used at the signing of the Declaration of Independence (Independence Hall, Philadelphia) are the best known today.

Instruments for surgery: made by silversmiths for the wealthy practitioners who could afford this most hygienic material. 'Rasors and Scissors tipt with silver' in the seventeenth century; *spatulas* and *probes*, the former perhaps another name for *tongue depressors*, were common in the eighteenth century toward the end of which *speaking trumpets* were made which survive. *Spectacle frames* were made in gold and silver.

Jewelry: was the province of the gold or silversmith, and a great variety unknown today is recorded in colonial courts. In 1693 James Lloyd's inventory listed '1 Hair Lockett set with Gold', almost a century earlier than surviving examples. Beads, bracelets, buttons for shirts and cuffs, necklaces and rings are the most frequently mentioned.

Keyhole: the name given today to the eighteenth-century porringer handle which continues to be made.

Ladle: a serving utensil usually on a long handle. In 1691 a 'basting ladle' was recorded; in the period 1761–97 Revere listed ladles for cream, soup, tureen, punch, mustard, and even one 'pepper ladle'.

Larding pin: a pointed instrument, angular in section, seemingly dating from the late-eighteenth century.

Limmel: the early form of *lemail*, or scrapings or filings of metal.

Marks: not required in the colonies, yet usually used by goldsmiths. The early ones followed the style of contemporary English makers' marks. Presumably because there was no central hall to record one's initials, when craftsmen were more numerous, early in the eighteenth century, it became the custom to use the surname. Silver marked WEBB was advertised at a time to indicate the use of his name by Edward Webb who died in 1718, yet Coney, living four years longer, is known only by initialed marks – one of which shows a coney as a rebus on his name under his crowned initials. John Burt (1692/3–1745) and Jacob Hurd (1702/3–58) each used his full name in two lines, as one of several marks.

Milk potts of silver seem to have been the same as creampots.

Monteith: a basin with a scalloped rim to cool glasses. John Coney made two in the early-eighteenth century. Daniel Henchman fashioned one in 1771 for the president of Dartmouth College (and his successors in that office), and Mrs Hannah Rowe of Boston left in 1805 'A large silver Bowl with a rim that takes off'.

Muffineer: a later name for casters.

Mug: a straight-sided single-handled open drinking vessel, frequently strengthened with a mid-band of applied molding (Plate 46B).

Mustard pot: with a spoon was recorded in the seventeenth century, but the form is unknown until Peter Van Dyck's ovate footed one in the Garvan Collection at Yale University.

Panakin: apparently the word now reduced to *pipkin*. A small saucepan with a wooden handle held in a horizontal socket.

Papboat: a child's feeding device, perhaps also used for invalids, a small shallow bowl with a long lip.

Paten: a small ecclesiastical footed dish.

Pepper box: a small cylindrical or octagonal piece with a pierced cover and single handle. More survive from the early than the late-eighteenth century.

Pibling: an obsolete form of *pebbling*. Coney's inventory included hammers for pibling, undoubtedly to produce the matted surface found on some of his early work.

Pitchers: early in the nineteenth century Paul Revere adapted in silver the Liverpool pottery pitchers favored by sea-captains;

FIG. 16. Pitcher; Paul Revere, *c.* 1800

copied copiously today for water pitchers, and in small sizes for cream, one can only speculate on their original use. Revere left three sizes of them in his own inventory, to judge by the listing; and large ones survive from his household.

Planishing: Bailey's *Dictionary* of 1728: 'to make plain as Silversmiths and Pewterers do'. Planishing hammers in goldsmiths' inventories were those with which the careful finishing to conceal hammer marks was effected.

Plate: generic term for silver. *See also* Dish.

Porringer: in the colonies, a shallow bowl with a horizontal pierced handle (Plate 47B). Earliest ones have straight sides curving to a flat bottom; very soon the sides were curved and had everted rims, the bottoms slightly domed at the center. New York porringers had elaborate handles or very simple ones; Philadelphia porringer handles usually followed New England styles. In the eighteenth century so-called 'keyhole' handles superseded the earlier forms. Porringers were made in child's size, pint and other sizes, and in pairs.

Prick work: a delicate and short-lived style of ornament to delineate owners' initials and the decorative device sometimes surrounding them.

FIG. 17. Punch bowl; C. Kierstede

FIG. 18. Punch bowl; Wm. Holmes, 1763

Punch bowls: open or covered bowls, the early ones with two handles. In New York a paneled bowl, usually with embossed flowers therein, was doubtless for punch or brandy

(Plate 41B); in Boston Dummer made one in Portuguese style with a lobed rim. Henry Flynt's inventoried 'Punch Bole & Cover' seems to have been his two-handled or grace-cup. The very large caudle cups by Coney with embossed flowers and cherubs may well have been punch bowls. Punch ladles and punch strainers were accompaniments, the latter a shallow pierced bowl with two long horizontal handles, usually of rectangular wire.

Purchase: *see* Thumbpiece.

Raising: the formation of a hollow piece beginning with a flat circle of silver, hammered in concentric circles over a succession of anvils, or stakes, and with frequent annealings, until even such a piece as a flagon was fashioned without a seam.

Rapiers: with silver-hilts were popular for dress occasions in the colonies; many show little variety whether made by early or late men of New England (Plate 46A) or New York.

Rings: to commemorate special occasions, and particularly as funeral mementoes, were a common task of the goldsmith.

Salts: the earliest salt recorded in the colonies: 'a very faire salt with 3 full knops on the top of it' was made in London and bequeathed to Harvard College in 1644. In the next decade Rebecca Bacon of Salem, Massachusetts, had '1 silver duble salt', in 1697 Ruth Carter of Boston had '1 high salt'. Three standing salts of New England craftsmanship, *c.*

FIG. 19. Salt

1700, are known; from early New York possession Dutch standing salts survive. Trencher salts and footed ones of the eighteenth century followed English styles.

Salver: Timothy Dwight (1654–91/2) left a large broad-rimmed salver on a trumpet-shaped foot; William Cowell (1682–1736) made one of similar size with a narrow molding on its flat circular dish. Smaller ones resembling church patens were made in pairs and in considerable quantity for domestic use through the first quarter of the eighteenth century. In the third decade square dishes on four short feet (Plate 47A), and also circular ones on three, superseded the single foot, but though the form of the piece was changed the name apparently was not.

Sauceboat: butter boat was another name; early in the eighteenth century an elliptical bowl had a handle at each side and a spout at each end and was on a splayed footband. Later a single lip on the end opposite a high handle balanced a body on three feet. Still later the single footband returned in higher form, to be optional.

Saucepan: in New York Gerrit Onckelbag used a long hollow silver handle on the globular body of one for which Jesse Kip made a very practical cover. One with wooden handle was made by Myers (Plate 45B). John Concy's saucepan, for his sister-in-law's family, the Dummers, has a turned wooden handle in a silver socket with cut-card on the capacious body rimmed with molding. Later saucepans were cylindrical with flaring lips and molded baseband. *See* Panakin.

Save-alls: are recorded with snuffers and extinguishers suggesting use with lighting equipment; Revere recorded in 1797 two with a total weight of 1 oz. 16 dwt., so it is not surprising that none are known to have survived.

Sconces: with silver candle brackets are rare. Two pairs of the latter by Knight Leverett (1703–53) and Jacob Hurd (1702/3 –58) in The Henry Francis du Pont Winterthur Museum are the only colonial ones now known.

Server: probably another name for salver.

Sewing equipment: thimbles, scissors, bands on pin balls, hooks, needle cases, bodkins, in gold and silver are known by record more than by surviving specimens.

Skewer: a long flat blade with a slight grip at one end tapers to a point; occasionally made by American silversmiths.

Skillet: Henry Flynt owned a silver 'camp skillet wt. 22 oz.' at his death in 1760, but no example is recognized.

Snuff boxes: all of silver or gold, or silver combined with other materials: steel, tortoiseshell, agate and the like, appear throughout colonial days and the eighteenth century.

Snuffer: a scissors-like device for trimming wick is not common in silver though a few survive.

Snuffer-stands: were usually horizontal rectangular trays on feet; an exception is the handsome upright one, with a box-like device for the now missing snuffer, by Cornelius Kierstede (1675–1757) of New York, in the Metropolitan Museum of Art.

Spectacle frames and cases: appear in inventories in the seventeenth and throughout the eighteenth century.

Spoon: except for a brief period in New York when cast spoon handles were patterned on Dutch styles, colonial spoons – beginning with the slip-end – follow the forms found in England. Early in the nineteenth century a 'coffin-end' spoon had a brief popularity. Sheaves of wheat or a basket of flowers were stamped on thin 'fiddle-tip' spoons in the 1820s. *Large spoons, porringer spoons* and *teaspoons* were the differentiations in the early days; in the mid-eighteenth century the word *tablespoon* appears, and presently *dessert spoons* were in the intermediate size of the earlier porringer spoon.

Stake: 'a small anvil us'd by smiths' is Bailey's definition of 1728.

Sterling: the quality of ·925 pure silver in an alloy usually with copper of ·075 base metal.

Strainer: *see* Punch. An egg strainer is in an inventory of 1728; tea strainers were mentioned in the 1750s. Strainer spoons with pointed handles or handles in the current spoon form are known; the former are sometimes (but apparently not contemporarily) called mote spoons.

Sugar box: *see* Box. In the furnishings of Mrs José Glover, attested by her servants in 1641, was 'a great silver trunke with 4 knop to stand on the table and with sugar'. *Sugar baskets, chests, dishes, fluted sugar vase* and *sugar urns* appear in the latter half of the eighteenth century.

Swage: a form into which silver might be stamped as the '2 Tests with plaine and flower'd Spoon Swages' of Edward Webb's inventory in 1718.

Sword: *see* Rapier.

Tankard: 'a drinking pot with hinged cover' according to Bailey's *Dictionary* of 1728 (Plates 42, 43, 44). Earliest known is the one by Robert Sanderson (1608–93) made for Isaac and Mary Vergoose, *c.* 1670, with only a very slight step on its flat lid which is engraved in floral design. A hollow scroll handle has a shield tip and a hole for the escape of air in soldering it to the body; the theory that it was a whistle is a pleasant myth. In New York tankards received elaborately stamped baseband ornament, and more elaborate handles than were customary in New England. Philadelphia tankards in the mid-eighteenth century were large and sometimes curved, a style not eagerly adopted in the other colonies. Midbands and finials on the covers were popular in New England in the eighteenth century; early in the nineteenth century spouts were added to many examples to convert them from drinking to pouring vessels in the first temperance movement. Thumb-pieces and handle tips gave scope to the goldsmiths' ingenuity. Sizes of tankards ranged from approximately a pint to over two quarts.

Tazza: a modern misnomer for salvers or wine bowls.

Teapot: small, almost globular ones with straight spouts and ornamented basebands and low domed covers survive from seventeenth-century New York. In Massachusetts,

Lt.-Gov. Stoughton's will in 1701 mentioned 'my silver teapot' but none is known today from Boston until John Coney's, with Mascarene arms. This has the high domed cover and curved spout of the early-eighteenth century. Shortly after a globular form (Plate 48c), with a flat cover and on a slightly splayed molded foot, was preferred until the mid-century. At the same time one usually finds in New York a pear-form, frequently with a median molding, on a straight or splayed molded footband, its high domed cover rimmed with molding. In both centers the inverted pear-shape, which is best known in Copley's portrait of Paul Revere, with a flat or slightly domed cover flush with the shoulder, preceded the change to cylindrical, or drum-form (Plate 51A) – short-lived in favor of flat-bottomed elliptical ones. For the last, stands were fashioned on four short feet to save polished table tops from heat. In the nineteenth century, urn-shaped pots on plinths (Plate 51B), and these sometimes on ball feet, were popular and more capacious.

Tea kettles: are very rare in colonial examples, but in general were enlargements of the current teapot form.

Teasts: Coney's inventory in 1722 had 'spoon teasts'; *see also* Swage.

Tea urns or coffee urns: appear in classic form, and seemingly are differentiated in name only by a patron's preference.

Thumbpiece: the projecting part above the hinge of a covered vessel whereby the cover might easily be opened with the thumb. On tankards these showed greater variety than on flagons; on a few early chocolate pots a vestigial thumbpiece is found. Corkscrew, cusped, dolphin and mask, scrolled, and open thumbpieces denote periods and places.

Tobacco: in silver in 1678, Thomas Thacher had a tobacco box and tobacco tongs. Coney's inventory included a 'Tobacco box anvil'; in 1725 there was lost in Boston 'a double Tobacco Stopper, tipt with silver in a crooked piece of wood'. In 1704 'a guinea deer's foot tipt with gold' was probably a tobacco stopper; *smoking tongs* were in the plate of David Mason in 1725. Silver pipes are recorded and survive in small numbers.

Toothpicks and **toothpick cases:** of silver and gold are not known to have survived although mentioned in the seventeenth and eighteenth centuries.

Touchstone: a piece of polished 'stone' on which a piece of silver of known quality could be rubbed to compare its mark with that of a piece being assayed.

Tumblers: presumably are the rounded based cups familiar in various sizes.

Tureen ladles: appear in Revere's ledgers, but silver tureens of colonial make are rare if existent. A few from the Federal period follow classic forms. John Singleton Copley wrote from Paris of 'Soupp ... in Silver Turenes' in 1774, which probably would not have been noteworthy had he known them at home.

Waiter: this term appears in the latter half of the eighteenth century in the colonies; one from 1797 identified in Revere's ledgers has bail handles at the ends of an oblong foot-less server.

Water pots: seemingly appear first in an advertisement in Philadelphia in 1782 as 'milk pots, water ditto ...' but the beverage was not catered for by colonial goldsmiths.

Whistles: with corals and bells for children are depicted in gold and silver in portraits and survive of eighteenth-century craftsmanship from the three centers: Boston, New York and Philadelphia.

Wine bowls, wine cups and **wine tumblers:** are recorded in American silver annals of colonial time, but not identified in form.

Wine labels: bottle tickets, but restricted to lighter beverages.

BOOKS FOR FURTHER READING

AVERY, C. LOUISE: *Early American Silver*, New York (1930).

BIGELOW, FRANCIS HILL: *Historic Silver of the Colonies and its Makers*, New York (1917, re-issued 1941).

BUHLER, KATHRYN C.: *American Silver*, New York (1950).

CLARKE, H.F.: *John Hull*, Portland, Me. (1940).

CLARKE, H.F.: *John Coney*, Cambridge, Mass. (1932).

ENSKO, STEPHEN G.C.: *American Silversmiths and their Marks III*, New York (1948).

FRENCH, HOLLIS: *Jacob Hurd and His Sons*, Cambridge, Mass. (1939).

PHILLIPS, JOHN MARSHALL: *American Silver*, New York (1949).

PLEASANTS AND SILL: *Maryland Silversmiths*, Baltimore (1930).

PRATT, RICHARD: *Second Treasury of Early American Homes*, Hawthorn Books, New York (1954).

ROSENBAUM, JEANETTE W.: *Myer Myers*, Philadelphia (1954).

Concise Encyclopedia of Antiques, Vol. II, pp. 149–161 Hawthorn Books, New York (1956).

PEWTER

By ERIC DE JONGE

DURING the Bronze Age, some four thousand years ago, man learned to fashion objects of pewter. When some experimenter added tin to the crucible containing molten copper, he created bronze, after thousands of years still one of mankind's most valuable alloys. When another early metallurgist reversed the process by adding copper to tin, he produced an almost equally important alloy, pewter.

The basic formula changed little through the ages. Additions of lead, antimony, or bismuth were made in varying proportions for economical reasons or better workability. Although it is repeatedly said that the sheen of highly burnished pewter is due to an addition of silver, this assertion may be relegated to the realm of fairy-tales. Whatever traces of silver are found in ancient pewter were due to impurities in the ore that could not be eliminated in the refinery.

Compared with the centuries-old history of pewter in all parts of the world, the history of pewter in America is a rather short one of only about two hundred years. Its history, however, as gathered from records, inventories, newspapers, and other printed or written sources in America, England and other European countries, encompasses so much American national and local history that its study is a fascinating one and the collecting of it not infrequently an all-consuming occupation.

The beginning in America: the record of Richard Graves who opened a pewterer's shop in Salem, Massachusetts, in 1635, is the earliest reference to a pewterer in the American colonies. Lacking at this time any other reference, this may be considered the beginning of pewter-making in America.

Fewer than ten pewterers plied their trade in the colonies before 1700 so far as is known today. This does not seem to have been a very auspicious beginning for a craft that was practised in almost every country of the world at that time, supplying mankind with utensils for households, taverns, churches, and ceremonies. For many years no tangible evidence of the handiwork of the early colonial pewterers was found. Excavations at Jamestown, Virginia, eventually brought forth the remnants of a pewter spoon that not only bore a name in its maker's touch, but, by an unbelievable stroke of luck, the locality where he worked. The pewterer, Joseph Copeland, worked during the years 1675–91 in Chuckatuck as well as in Jamestown, both in Virginia. This artifact (now in the museum at Jamestown) is still the only definitely ascertainable pewter specimen of seventeenth-century America. A few other pewter objects of the same period still lack a definite American attribution. The first definitely attributable pieces may be assigned to about 1725.

The seventeenth century was the great age of pewter in Europe. Better mining methods, faster transportation, the existence of more and better design books, and many other factors contributed to the increase in pewter-making. With currently lower prices, pewter-ware gradually supplanted treen and pottery household utensils used even in the homes of the more affluent. It was used extensively for ceremonies and in taverns; even the poorer classes could afford a few pewter spoons and plates.

The average colonist owned only the most necessary pewterware. Being well aware of the vast, unsettled territory which was open to him, he brought only the things which could be carried easily, chiefly clothing and some tools. In addition, he brought those utensils which he could not fashion himself, or could not readily acquire in a sparsely settled country, such as eating and drinking utensils. Instead of the breakable crockery, the hardier pewter, in the shapes of plates, bowls, beakers, spoons, was selected.

It could not have taken overly long before many of the plates and bowls were battered, or, being left too close to the open hearth, damaged beyond restoration by their owners. There being scarcely a more fragile utensil than a pewter spoon, time and usage took a tremendous toll. Some spoon molds must have been among the possessions of the colonists, to be lent on occasions to neighbors. Other bronze molds for recasting plates and bowls, or making hollowware, were far too valuable to be used occasionally by one who knew only the rudiments of the craft. The need for trained pewterers became apparent the more pewter utensils suffered by careless handling. Shipping, being infrequent and uncertain, could not be depended upon for quick replacements from England. Before long English pewterers became aware of the opportunities to themselves which the colonies offered, ownership of land and house and the free exercise of their craft. When the first pewterers arrived, it is a fair assumption that they did not have a great variety of molds; they brought along the simplest and most necessary.

American characteristics develop: free from any restrictive supervision, they could ingeniously use their few molds for any purpose to which they could be adapted. With the molds they had, they fashioned pewter objects for which their English or Continental contemporaries would have required still others. Since they could not compete with the multitude of forms and the variations of styles imported from England, the colonial pewterers concentrated on a few forms. Against the many different rim types of the English plates and the still more numerous rim types of other European countries, they offered only two types, the earlier smooth rim plate (Plate 60A) and the later single reed plate.

Another compelling reason for the limitation of forms and production was the fact that the colonies, in spite of great natural resources, were entirely lacking in the most important item of the pewterer's trade, tin ore. Like most other countries the colonies were dependent upon the supply from Cornwall, where the inexhaustible tin mines brought affluence to their owners and revenue to the mother country. The American colonies became a rich source of other raw materials for the English landholder and merchant, who in turn supplied the needs of a rapidly increasing population with great quantities of finished products. The importation of finished pewterware into America was astounding. According to Ledlie Laughlin's *Pewter in America*, it exceeded by far the combined importations of furniture, silver and tinware during the period 1720–67.

Under pressure exerted by the highly organized English pewterers' guilds, and in anticipation of additional revenue, the English authorities soon imposed an *ad valorem* custom duty of 5 percent upon imported raw tin bars, leaving the finished pewterware duty free. The disadvantages of this arbitrary rule were impossible to overcome.

While the cost of labor in the colonies was lower than in England, the additional duty on the raw material prevented colonial pewter from competing extensively with the duty free English product. The American craftsmen were forced largely to rework and recast the old pewter that was taken in in trade or brought to them by merchants who dealt in new pewter. The battered bowl, the broken spoon, unlike the fragments of broken crockery, represented definite value. They were not discarded, but saved for the day when the owner was able to go to a pewterer or merchant and pay only for the difference of weight between the discards and the new utensil, and for labor.

In the reworking of old pewter the pewterer proved himself to be very often an able craftsman. His wares were generally of good quality, and while the quality or workmanship does not compare in general with the product of English or Continental pewterers, many American specimens disclose excellent workmanship and the capabilities and ingenuity of their makers.

The larger towns being centers of trade, the majority of pewterers gravitated toward them, while rural areas depended upon an occasional pewterer working there for a limited time, and on the hawkers and peddlers who in later years were able to supply the needs for pewterware from the larger towns. With incomes curtailed by the restrictions, most pewterers were compelled to apply their skill to other trades as well. Only a few were able to devote their entire time to their craft and still fewer were comparatively well to do. To many, pewtering became a sideline while they worked as farmers, husbandmen, braziers, plumbers, tavernkeepers, merchants and in other trades. This they could do only in the colonies, as they would not have been permitted to work in other occupations under the stringent guild rules of other countries.

One of the many regulations that grew out of a set of rules for regulating the pewterer's craft in fourteenth-century London was the imposition of standards of quality, buying and selling, working conditions and, reaching deeply into man's inner sanctum, even dictating the behavior at home. At an even earlier date other European countries had issued similar regulations.

The enforcement of these standards was generally left to the officers of the pewterers' guilds who could punish the violator with fines, confiscation of his merchandise, and even expulsion from the craft. Agreements with other trade guilds forbade work in other crafts. These rules governed and influenced the life and work of every pewterer, and the effect of these ancient restrictions may have been one of the reasons the colonial pewterer continued to follow the old craft rules, even though free from supervision. Only in a few instances does there seem to have been official inspection.

The American pewterer was independent. He could work as he pleased; there were no dictates as to form or design, nor any objections to the number of apprentices or journeymen he engaged. If his pewter were of inferior quality, or his workmanship poor, only his customers could object. In spite of, or perhaps because of this freedom from supervision and restrictions, the American pewterer generally lived up to the best traditions of the craft. He did not need to be afraid to mark his products with his touch, and when we find American pewter unmarked, but definitely identifiable as American, it compares favorably in quality and workmanship with similar European pieces. It may be stated at this point that there is no truth in the belief that unmarked pewter can always be classified as American. If this were the case, the production of our colonial pewterers would have been so large that their need to work at other trades would have been unnecessary. Also, it could only have been produced by many more workers than are recorded, and had there in fact been so many active, there would be in existence much more information about the trade than has been preserved. Another factor against such an interpretation is the great range of forms and styles while American work was subject to a process of anglicization in every part of the colonies.

European influences: the early impact of English-trained pewterers and the monopoly of English-made pewterware were largely responsible for the adoption of English styles and forms, modified by the limitations in molds and material. These limitations were frequently responsible for the clean and unpretentious lines of American pewter which the collector today appreciates. So dominant was English influence that American pewterers who trained in other European countries gradually submitted to it. The pewter of the transitional period, in which the Continental and English characteristics were united, is of great interest to the student and collector.

There are evidences in a pewterer's technique which indicate his probable origin, lacking other biographical data. If no other information had been found, the hammermarks on Simon Edgell's pewter would point him out as an English-trained 'hammerman'. The practice of strengthening pewter by light hammerblows, producing the innumerable small indentations which give light to the surface with brilliant effect, had reached such heights in England that hammer-

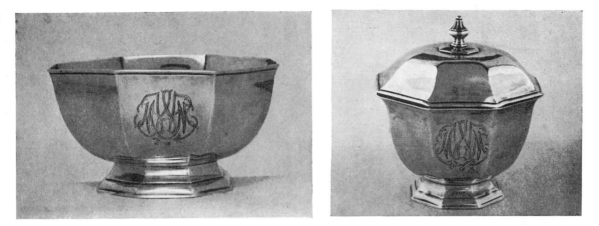

(A) and (B) Octagonal waste bowl and sugar bowl by Joseph Richardson (1711–84), Philadelphia. Cypher of Margaret Wistar. W. (waste bowl) 5¾ ins. Ht. (sugar bowl) 4¾ ins. *Coll. of Mrs Charles H. Taylor.*

(c) Coffee-pot and sugar bowl by Simeon Soumain (*c.* 1685–*c.* 1750), New York. Straight sides indicate first half of the century; rare to have accompanying sugar bowl. Ht. (pot) 10⅜ ins. *Museum of Fine Arts, Boston.*

PLATE 49

(A) Coffee-pot by Daniel Henchman (1730–75), Boston. Ht. 10⅞ ins. *Coll. of Philip H. Hammerslough.*

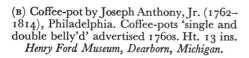

(B) Coffee-pot by Joseph Anthony, Jr. (1762–1814), Philadelphia. Coffee-pots 'single and double belly'd' advertised 1760s. Ht. 13 ins. *Henry Ford Museum, Dearborn, Michigan.*

PLATE 50

(A) Teapot by Joseph Anthony, Jr. (1762–1814), Philadelphia. Ht. 5$\frac{5}{16}$ ins. *Henry Ford Museum, Dearborn, Michigan.*

(B) Teapot by Robert and William Wilson, Philadelphia. Seems to antedate partnership in 1825. Ht. 12$\frac{1}{2}$ ins. *Museum of Fine Arts, Boston.*

(C) Creampot by Paul Revere (1735–1818), Boston. *c.* 1790–5. Ht. 7$\frac{1}{2}$ ins. *Coll. of Mr and Mrs Mark Bortman.*

PLATE 51

(A) Waste Bowl by Joseph Richardson, Jr. (1752–1831), Philadelphia. Ht. 5 ins. *Museum of Fine Arts, Boston.*

(B) Pair of Beakers by Alexander Gordon, known to have been working in New York in 1795 and, judging by these, at least a decade later. Ht. 4⅛ ins. *Coll. of Philip H. Hammerslough.*

PLATE 52

Pewter flagon by Henry Will, New York and Albany, 1761–93. Ht. 11½ ins. *Mabel Brady Garvan collection, Yale University Art Gallery.*

PLATE 53

(A) T.D. & S. Boardman flagon, New York, 1810–50; flagon by Johann Christopher Heyne, Lancaster, 1754–80; flagon by Samuel Danforth, Hartford, 1795–1816. *Brooklyn Museum.*

(B) Tankards: (*left*) attributed to Joseph Leddell or Joseph, Jr, New York, 1711–53 and 1740–54. Ht. 5½ ins.; (*center*) attributed to Francis Bassett II, New York, 1749-1800, Ht. 6 ins.; (*right*) Simon Edgell, Philadelphia, 1713–42, Ht. 5¾ ins. *Antiques, April 1941; from Coll. of Edward E. Minor.*

(C) Pair of chalices, (*left*) Peter Young, New York, Albany, 1772–83, paten by Joseph Danforth, Middletown, 1780–8; (*right*) pair of chalices by Timothy Brigden, Albany, 1816–19. *Brooklyn Museum.*

PLATE 54

(A) Beakers: (*left*) marked B.B.; (*center*) T.Boardman & Co., New York, 1822–4; (*right*) John Will, New York, 1752–66. *Brooklyn Museum.*

(B) Mugs: (*left*) Jacob Whitmore, Middletown, 1758–90; (*center*) William Will, Philadelphia, 1764–98; (*right*) Robert Palethorpe, Philadelphia, 1817–22. *Brooklyn Museum.*

(C) New England quart mugs: (*left to right*) Nathaniel Austin, Charlestown, 1763–1800; Gershom Jones, Providence, 1774–1809; David Melville, Newport, 1755–93; 'Semper Eadem' (IS: John Skinner, 1760–90), Boston; Benjamin Day, Newport, 1706–57. Shown in the *Loan Exhibition of American Pewter, 1939, Metropolitan Museum of Art.*

PLATE 55

(A) Porringers: (*front row, left*) John A. Brunstrom, Philadelphia, 1783–93; (*right*) Thomas Melville, Newport, 1793–6; (*center*) Richard Lee, New England, 1770–1823; (*top row, left*) unidentified; (*right*) T.D.Boardman, New York, 1805–50. *Brooklyn Museum.*

(B) Porringer, (*left*) William Billings, Providence, 1791–1806; (*center*) lidless tankard, Benjamin Day, Newport, 1706–57; porringer, (*right*) Samuel Hamlin, Hartford and Providence, 1767–1801. *Brooklyn Museum.*

(C) Pewter teapot by William Kirby, New York, 1760–93. *Metropolitan Museum of Art.*

PLATE 56

(A) Teapots: (*upper row, left*) Boardman & Co., New York, 1825–7; (*right*) octagonal teapot, Roswell Gleason, Dorchester, 1822–71; (*lower row, left*) Boardman & Hart, New York, 1805–50; (*right*) Taunton Britannia Mfg. Co., Taunton, 1830–5. *Twentieth Century Club Exhibition, Boston. Antiques, April, 1925.*

(B) Teapot by William Will, Philadelphia, 1764–98. *Metropolitan Museum of Art.*

PLATE 57

Coffee urn of unusual form by Roswell Gleason, Dorchester, 1822–71. *Brooklyn Museum.*

PLATE 58

(A) (*Top*) deep dish by Thomas Danforth III, Stepney, 1777–1818; (*below, left to right*) plate by Thomas Badger, Boston, 1737–1815; pitcher by Boardman & Hart, New York, 1827–31; porringer by Samuel Hamlin, Hartford and Providence, 1767–1801. *Old Sturbridge Village, Sturbridge, Massachusetts.*

(B) Pitcher by Parks Boyd, Philadelphia, 1795–1819. *Brooklyn Museum.*

PLATE 59

(A) Smooth rim plate by John Skinner, Boston, 1760–90. *Author's collection.*

(B) Covered pitcher by Daniel Curtis, Albany, 1822–40. *Mary Brady Garvan collection, Yale University Art Gallery.*

(C) Candlesticks: (*center*) pair by Taunton Britannia Mfg. Co, Taunton, 1830–5; (*left and right*) by Henry Hopper, New York, 1842–7; (*front*) by Morey & Smith, Boston, 1852–5. *Brooklyn Museum.*

PLATE 60

(A) A fine and unusually small early American weathervane, showing some old repair work; 9 by 11 ins.

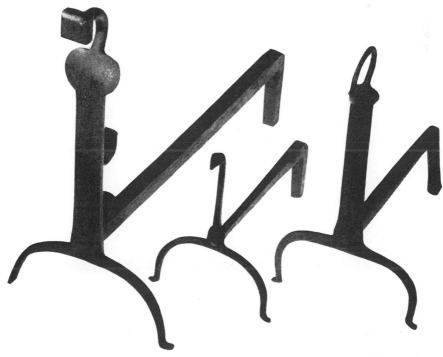

(B) Three graceful andirons. Note the attachments on one for holding a spit.
All illustrations by courtesy of The Henry Ford Museum, Dearborn, Michigan.

PLATE 61

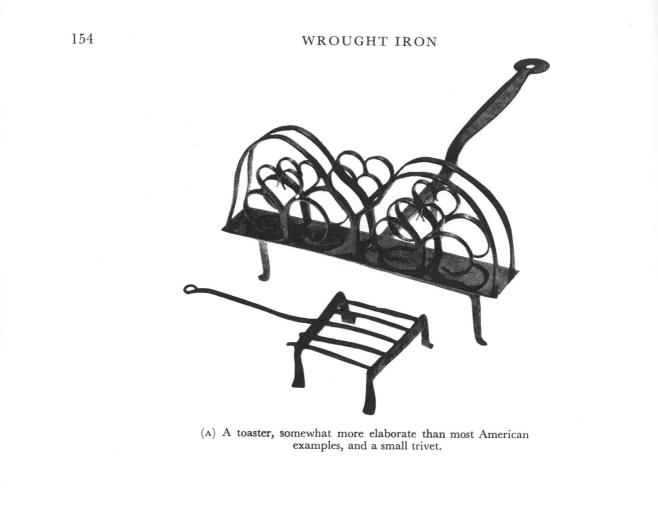

(A) A **toaster**, somewhat more elaborate than most American examples, and a small trivet.

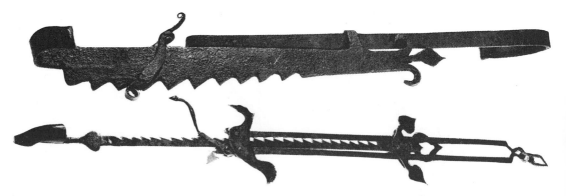

(B) Two different applications of the trammel. The heavier one is for suspending a pot from a fireplace crane and is from Fredericksburg, Virginia. The lighter one, probably from Pennsylvania, is a candle holder and is intended to be hung from the ceiling.

PLATE 62

(A) A decorative side hinge, probably of Pennsylvania-German origin.   (B) A simple Suffolk latch.

PLATE 63

(A) A Suffolk latch from Connecticut, the cusps of which are shaped in a variation of the pine tree pattern.

(B) Two early-nineteenth-century Norfolk latches. Although this type of latch was used in the eighteenth century it was less common then than the Suffolk type.

(c) A Suffolk latch from Pennsylvania; the cusps combine the heart and tulip motifs.

PLATE 64

men were considered the aristocracy of the craft. In other countries hammering did not achieve the importance it was accorded in England. Examples of American work by pewterers not trained in England show us, by comparison, the proficiency of the English in this art. The all over hammered plates and dishes of Edgell, the hammered tankard by Benjamin Day of Newport, are outstanding examples of the tradition. Also excellent, if to a slightly less degree, are the hammered booges on the flatware of the Bassetts, Wills, Danforths, and others, representations of excellent craftsmanship which they in turn taught their apprentices. The art of the hammerman dwindled in the Federal period, so it would seem this time-consuming art was sacrified to speedier production.

Habits and customs of ethnic groups persisted for a long time. Craftsmen were drawn together by these bonds, by the common tie of escape from economic and political oppression, and, last but not the least, by a common language. While the New England and southern colonies were settled predominantly by the English, other colonies attracted settlers from Central Europe. In continuing their Old World customs these groups influenced later generations. Central European trained pewterers were able to furnish their compatriots in the new country with pewterware that perhaps was not identical to, but approximated, familiar forms and designs. The accustomed forms prevailed until about the beginning of the nineteenth century. The steady anglicization of the population, the ascendancy of English pewter, and finally the gradual decline of pewtermaking extinguished the last traces of Continental influences on American pewter.

Nevertheless, the influence of the past was long discernible. The Dutch settlers of New Netherland retained the ingrained habits and customs of their original homeland. Traces of this are found for many generations in the working methods and ideas of New York artisans. There is no doubt that their homes, taverns and meeting-places were filled with the furnishings of Holland. Pewter, so frequently seen in Dutch paintings of the seventeenth century, had an important role in the domestic interior. No documentary proof of any pewterer having worked in New Netherland has survived. Yet pewterware must have been as much in evidence in New Amsterdam as in Holland. Being as vulnerable in one place as another, it must have required the ministrations of a skilled pewterer for repairs. The evidence of Dutch influence as to style prevailed long after New Amsterdam became New York. The roundness of the bowls of spoons, the sturdiness of hollowware and solidity of workmanship in general were not greatly changed by English influence.

Fusion of styles: Thomas Paschall, an English-trained pewterer, opened his shop in Philadelphia in 1682; he was followed by other, also English-trained, pewterers; amongst them was the excellent hammerman, Simon Edgell. Their pewter, in the English manner, suited well the demands of their fellow citizens, most of them of English origin. With the increasing arrival of Continental immigrants a change of taste took place. While the English type of pewter probably never wanted for buyers, Continental immigrants were able to supply their customers with pewterware adhering to other European forms. This resulted in the creation of so many varieties of shapes, designs and special features that the study of Pennsylvania pewter is often bewildering. There is the highly desirable English style of Cornelius Bradford and Simon Edgell (Plate 54B); the transitional features of the pewter of Andrew Brunstrom and Parks Boyd (Plate 59B); the astonishing versatility of Heyne, showing German-Swedish influences (Plate 54A); the highly individual work of William Will (Plate 57B); not to forget the mysterious maker whose pieces are marked *Love*.

Types: the American pewterer offered a wide range of styles in the different vessels and utensils demanded of him, although he could not match European pewter in variety. The colonial pewterer probably never cast any handles for brooms or feather dusters, as in eighteenth-century Europe, but they answered everyday demands and did exceedingly well in executing occasional orders for special purposes. The pewterer catering to the city trade was able to change styles more readily than his rural contemporary who very often did his pewtering in his spare time and had to supply the more conservative demands of his rural clientele. As far as the colonial pewterer was concerned, the rococo period never existed. Accepted established forms of the early-eighteenth century persisted, often long after they went out of fashion in other countries.

The popularity of the porringer (Plate 56B), a small, multi-purpose vessel that apparently made its way from New York to all parts of colonial America, increased steadily and endured far into the nineteenth century, after it had ceased to be a favorite in England and Continental Europe. Whatever ambition to decorate the American pewterer had was apparently lavished on the execution of the

Fig. 1. Porringer handles

porringer handle. With the shape of the body remaining fairly constant, the handle was fashioned in two distinct types, the pierced or open work, and the solid or tab handle. The former was derived from English prototypes; the latter bore definite Continental characteristics. In the ornamental features of the handles great variety of treatment was exhibited, limited only by the great expense of new molds. The English-type porringer naturally found ready acceptance in English areas, while the tab-handled porringer appealed to the many groups originating in

Central Europe. Generally a pewterer made porringers according to the preferences of his customers, one exception being the pewterers of Rhode Island, who, probably because of additional trade outlets, cast both types. Another exception was Thomas Danforth III of Connecticut, who, understandably, gave up his English-type porringer for the tab-handled upon setting up shop in Philadelphia.

The touch: the English or Continental pewterer was free to choose his own design for his trademark or touch. He followed certain patterns, dependent upon the style of the period, on national preferences, and on ordinances issued by governing authorities. Frequently his touch had to contain the numerals of the year in which he was admitted to mastership, or a design denoting the quality of his pewter. The American pewterer was not bound by these rules. While it was important to advertise his work, he was not compelled to strike his touch nor any quality mark, although the legend *London* was frequently struck to show that his pewter compared with the best of England's products or to let the unwary buyer accept the native pewterware as English made. Outside of the American colonies only a master pewterer was permitted a registered touch, a precious possession that he would include in the necessities which he brought to the colonies. Once in a land where no questions of his status were asked and where no proofs of official qualifications were demanded, he could use his touch or change it as he saw fit. The use of a touch was equally free to anyone else turning to pewtering. There is every indication that many a journeyman pewterer set himself up in business and marked his products as if he had qualified before his peers. Many of them became outstanding makers of American pewter.

In the choice of their touches the pewterers evidently followed the traditional patterns of their native countries. We find that the pre-Revolutionary touches closely resemble English and Continental devices, such as the rose and crown (Fig. 2); the lamb and dove motif; the golden fleece. There are lions in circles and ovals, in or out of columns (Fig. 3);

shields, urns, hallmarks, plain initials (Fig. 4) and many other symbols. John Will's angel touch, signifying first-quality pewter, was

FIG. 2.   FIG. 3.

Pre-Revolutionary touches

FIG. 4.

apparently identical to his touch as a master pewterer of his native Germany, except that now his die was American-made, since his German touch must have shown his given name *Johannes* instead of the anglicized *John*. After the Revolution the designs of the American touches lost their interesting individuality. Apparently, it was found patriotic as well as opportune to employ a device emphasizing the newly won freedom. The eagle of the Great Seal of the United States became a popular motif (Figs. 5 & 6). Dies changed upon the admission of a new state, the

FIG. 5.   FIG. 6.

Post-Revolutionary touches

number of stars or dots in the frame surrounding the eagle signifying that another

state had ratified the Constitution. This aids in the dating of pewter except where the stars form a continuous circle surrounding the eagle, as they were then meant for decoration only.

Not long after the turn of the nineteenth century another drastic change in the type of touch took place. The symbolic and heraldic motifs were completely cast aside to be replaced by the simple initials or name of the pewterer, at times surrounded by circular or

FIG. 7.

Nineteenth-century touches   FIG. 8.

rectangular frames (Figs. 7 & 8). The age of mass production had arrived, permitting no frills.

Britannia period: a steady increase in the amount of ceramics, glass and tinware, produced at reasonable prices in great quantities, had begun for a long time to affect pewterers everywhere. To meet this competition, pewterers intensified their search for methods to increase their output at competitive prices. Early in the eighteenth century English pewterers developed a pewter composition of tin, antimony and copper that proved to be exceptionally durable and workable; it was generally advertised as 'hard metal'. Further experiments created an alloy that could be cast and rolled into thin sheets without cracking. When it was subsequently discovered that this metal could be cold formed over wooden molds on a spinning lathe, costly bronze molds and expensive hand-finishing were eliminated, and semi-skilled laborers could be employed for the simple operations of mass fabrication. When in 1825 Hiram Yale of Wallingford, Connecticut, engaged English workmen to come to America, the spinning method succeeded here also. For a while the new process stemmed the decline in the sale of pewterware, or Britannia, as it was now called. But a new era had arrived, a time when almost every designer and artisan aspired to devise new and exaggerated forms and decorative features. Neither pewter nor the new 'hard metal' could be successfully adapted to these shapes, and for the present-day collector pewter made after 1850 is not of interest.

GLOSSARY

Alloy: a composition of two or more metals intimately mixed by fusion.

FIG. 9. Beaker

Antimony: a metallic element used for hardening of alloys.

Beaker: a form of drinking vessel, generally flaring slightly to the top and having no handle (Plate 55A).

Bismuth: a metal added to harden pewter. Also called tinglass.

Booge: the curved part of a plate, etc., that forms the connection between the rim and the bottom.

Britannia metal: a trade name given to a tin-antimony-copper alloy, lending itself to mass production by spinning. Although the name was used before 1800 it rightfully should be named 'hard metal' until August 10, 1842, when the English patent No. 9441 was granted to Richard Ford Sturges for the name and composition of 'Britannia Metal' (Plate 60c).

Dish: term used for plates upward of twelve inches.

Finial: the decorative and functional termination of covers of flagons, teapots, etc.

Flagon: a large vessel for dispensing liquids, with handle and cover, with or without spout (Fig. 10 and Plates 53, 54A).

Flatware: general term for plates, platters, dishes, etc.

Hallmarks: a series of designs struck by punches into metal indicating its maker, quality, date, origin, etc. Used by pewterers in imitation of silversmiths' marks.

Hammer marks: the indentations of a pewterer's hammer. Hammering was done to give the pewter greater density and as a means of strengthening the product.

FIG. 10. Flagon

Hollowware: a general term for vessels designed to hold liquids.

FIG. 11. Mug

Measure: a vessel of standard liquid capacity.

Mug: a handled drinking vessel without cover (Plate 55B).

Pear shape: a term used in identifying a curved or pyriform shape in hollowware (Plate 56c).

FIG. 12. Pear shape

Pewter: an alloy, chiefly of tin, with varying proportions of copper, lead, antimony or bismuth.

Plates: dishes ranging from six to twelve inches (Plate 59A).

Porringer: a small, handled bowl or basin used for liquid or semi-liquid food, ranging in size from two and a half to six inches (Plate 56A).

Porringer handles: one or more flat handles horizontally attached to a porringer, of often highly ornamented design (Fig. 1).

Punch: a die for striking the maker's touch or other identification or decorative marks into metal.

Rattail: the tapering extension of a spoon handle unto the underside of the bowl.

Single reed: a single molding around the edge of a plate rim as compared to multi-reeded rims, where two or more moldings form the edge (Plate 59A).

Smooth rim: a flat, unadorned plate rim, where the reinforcing molding appears on the underside of the rim (Plate 60A).

Spinning: a process by which a thin metal sheet is pressed against a wooden core in a spinning lathe to be forced into shape.

FIG. 13. Tankard

Tankard: a drinking vessel with handle and cover (Plate 54B).

Touch: the mark struck by a pewterer on his products

Tulip shape: a term used in identifying a bulbous shape in hollowware with not such a pronounced curve as pear shape (Fig. 14 and Plate 55B).

Wriggle-work: rare on American pewter. A decorative motif on pewter

FIG. 14.
Tulip-shaped tankard

incised by a rocking (wriggling) motion of a gouge along an outlined pattern.

GLOSSARY OF PEWTERERS
(Condensed)

Austin, Nathaniel: Charlestown, 1763–1800 (Plate 55C).

Austin, Richard: Boston, 1792–1817.

Badger, Thomas: Boston, 1737–1815 (Plate 59A).

Barnes, Blakslee: Philadelphia, 1812–17.

Bassett I, Francis: New York, 1715–40.

Bassett II, Francis: New York, 1749–1800 (Plates 54B).

Bassett, Frederick: New York, 1761–1800.

Bassett, John: New York, 1720–61.

Belcher, Joseph, and **Joseph, Jr:** Newport and New London, 1769–84.

Billings, William: Providence, 1791–1806 (Plate 56B).

Boardman, Luther: South Reading, 1836–42.

Boardman, Thomas Danforth and partners worked under many names in Hartford. Some of their pewter was marked N.-York, where they maintained a sales office, 1805–50 (Plates 54A, 55A, 56A, 57A).

Boyd, Parks: Philadelphia, 1795–1819 (Plate 59B).

Bradford, Cornelius: New York and Philadelphia, 1752–85.

Bradford, William, Jr: New York, 1719–85.

Brigden, Timothy: Albany, 1816–19 (Plate 54C).

Brunstrom, John Andrew: Philadelphia, 1783–93 (Plate 56A).

Calder, William: Providence, 1817–56.

Curtiss, Daniel: Albany, 1822–40 (Plate 60B).

Danforth I, Thomas: Taunton, 1727–33. First of the many Danforths who worked chiefly in Connecticut until the middle of the nineteenth century.

Day, Benjamin: Newport, 1706–57 (Plates 55C, 56B).

Derby, Thomas S.: Middletown, 1812–52.

Dunham, Rufus: Westbrook and Portland, 1837–82.

Edgell, Simon: Philadelphia, 1713–42 (Plate 54B).

Eggleston, Jacob: Middletown and Fayetteville, 1795–1807.

Ellsworth, William J.: New York, 1767–98.

Flagg & Homan: Cincinnati, 1842–54.

Gleason, Roswell: Dorchester, 1822–71 (Plates 57A, 58).

Green, Samuel: Boston, 1794–1818.

Griswold, Ashbil: Meriden, 1802–42.

Hamlin, Samuel: Hartford and Providence, 1767–1801 (Plates 56B, 59A).

Hamlin, Samuel E., Jr: Providence, 1801–56.

Harbeson, Benjamin and Joseph: Philadelphia and Lancaster, 1765–1800.

Heyne, Johann Christopher: Lancaster, 1754–80 (Plate 54A).

Hopper, Henry: New York, 1842–7 (Plate 60B)

Johnson, Jehiel: Middletown and Fayetteville, 1815–25.

Jones, Gershom: Providence, 1774–1809 (Plate 55C).

Kilbourn, Samuel: Baltimore, 1814–39.

Kirby, William: New York, 1760–93 (Plate 56C).

Leddell, Joseph and Joseph, Jr: New York, 1711–54 (Plate 54B).

Lee, Richard, and Richard, Jr: various places in New England, 1770–1823 (Plate 56A).

Leonard, Reed and Barton: Taunton, 1835–40.

Lightner, George: Baltimore, 1806–15.

'Love': Philadelphia, 1750–18??.

Melville, David: Newport, 1755–93 (Plate 55C).

Melville, Samuel and Thomas: Newport, 1793–1800.

Melville, Thomas: Newport, 1793–6 (Plate 56A).

Palethorp, John H.: Philadelphia, 1820–40.

Palethorp, Robert, Jr: Philadelphia, 1817–22 (Plate 55B).

Pierce, Samuel: Greenfield, 1792–1830.

Porter, Allen: Westbrook, 1830–40.

Porter, Freeman: Westbrook, 1835–60.

Putnam, James H.: Malden, 1830–5.

Richardson, George, Sr: Boston, 1818–28.

Sellew & Co.: Cincinnati, 1830–60.

'Semper Eadem': Boston, after 1750 (Plate 55C).

Skinner, John: Boston, 1760–90 (Plate 60A).

Smith, Eben: Beverly, 1813–56.

Southmayd, Ebenezer: Middletown and Castleton, 1790–1830.

Stafford, Spencer: Albany, 1794–1830.

Taunton Britannia Mfg. Co.: Taunton, 1830–5 (Plates 57A, 60C).

Trask, Israel: Beverly, 1807–56.

Trask, Oliver: Beverly, 1825–30.

Treadway, Amos: Middletown, 1760–90.

Weekes, James: New York and Poughkeepsie, 1820–35.

Whitlock, John H.: Troy, 1836–44.

Whitmore, Jacob: Middletown, 1758–90 (Plate 55B).

Will, Henry: New York, 1761–93 (Plate 53).

Will, John: New York, 1752–66 (Plate 55A).

Will, William: Philadelphia, 1764–98 (Plates 55B, 57B).

Yale, Hiram: Wallingford, 1822–35.

Yale, William, Jr, and Samuel: Meriden, 1813–20.

Young, Peter: New York and Albany, 1772–82 (Plate 54C).

BOOKS FOR FURTHER READING

COTTERELL, H.H.: *National Types of Old Pewter* (1925).
COTTERELL, H.H.: *Pewter Down the Ages* (1932).
COTTERELL, H.H.: *Old Pewter, its Makers and Marks* (1929).
KERFOOT, J.B.: *American Pewter* (1924).
LAUGHLIN, LEDLIE I.: *Pewter in America* (1940).
Antiques magazine, 1922 to date.
Bulletins of the Pewter Collectors' Club of America, 1934 to date.
Concise Encyclopedia of Antiques, Vol. I, pp. 142–7, Hawthorn Books, New York (1955).

WROUGHT IRON

By M. W. THOMAS, Jr

THE fabrication of American wrought iron can be said to have begun in 1607 when James Read, a blacksmith, went ashore at Jamestown, Virginia, with the first group of English settlers. Read's first American pieces were probably tools, since Captain John Smith reported a few months after the landing that the colonists had brought iron with them which 'we made into little chissels'. But these first American pieces, as with all wrought iron for years to come, must have been American in name only, for certainly the early smiths who emigrated to the colonies in Virginia and New England must have continued to fashion objects in exactly the same manner as they had learned in their native England. Indeed, among the artifacts recently excavated at Jamestown are thousands of wrought-iron objects and, as yet, no one has been able to tell which of these were made in the new country, and which were imported from home by the colonists.

In spite of the industriousness of the numerous colonial blacksmiths the supply of home-made wrought-iron hardware was never able to keep up with the demand, and hardware was one of the major exports of England to the colonies up until the Revolution and beyond. In fact, the mother country consistently discouraged home industry in the colonies in order to maintain a market for her own manufacturers. Early craftsmen were not noted for their literary ability and, in consequence, so little of the work of seventeenth-century American smiths is known that it is not possible to separate their products from English imports except in very rare instances. Thus, when the English background and training of many American smiths is considered together with the extensive importation of English wrought pieces, it is not surprising that an American style of work cannot be discerned with any degree of clarity until about the beginning of the eighteenth century. Add the fact that wrought iron is seldom dated and almost never signed and it becomes apparent that the would-be collector of early American hardware is faced with a considerable problem in authentication at the very outset. Yet, in spite of these difficulties, there is a great deal of wrought iron which shows characteristics which have come to be regarded as typically American. The question of the actual country of origin of these pieces still remains, and can probably never be settled in a wholly satisfactory manner, but we can say, with considerable confidence, that iron exhibiting certain characteristics is of a known type that was produced by American smiths. These characteristics are simplicity, lack of ostentatious ornamentation and an appearance of utility. The whorls, scrolls and other purely decorative effects so often found on ironwork of the old world are conspicuous by their absence on most American pieces. Even the objects made by the Pennsylvania-German smiths, probably the most intricate American ironwork, show a certain restraint that marks them as being of the new world. Nowhere is this tendency toward simplicity better exemplified than at Williamsburg, Virginia, the pre-Revolutionary capital of Britain's wealthiest and most aristocratic colony. Extensive archeological work in that town has brought to light thousands of pieces of wrought iron of all classifications in use during the eighteenth century. These artifacts are, almost without exception, simple, straightforward, and utilitarian in their design, be they carpenters' tools, door hinges, or carriage parts. The most sophisticated articles in the whole of the enormous collection are a few pairs of shutter hinges

163

from the 'Palace' of the Royal Governors. These have been decorated very modestly by a suggestion of foliation on the ends. The remainder of the iron house-hardware of that very imposing building is quite plain and hardly to be distinguished from the hardware used on the houses of some of the humbler residents of the town.

It is hard to explain this characteristic simplicity of American wrought iron. It has been suggested that over-elaboration was distasteful to the residents of a country where the frontier was at the doorstep; that the colonial spirit rebelled at anything that smacked of ostentation. The high price of the blacksmith's labor has been cited by others as a deterrent to ornamentation, and still others have suggested that the limited resources and skill of individual smiths may account for the plain appearance of most colonial ironwork. None of these suggestions, whether they be regarded singly or together, offer a really acceptable reason for the differences between English and American iron. The collector can only note that the differences exist and make use of them as an aid in identification.

The foregoing is not meant to imply that American iron is without esthetic appeal. Quite the reverse is true. The well-designed hinges (Plates 63A, 66), latches (Plates 63B, 64) and shutter fasteners (Plate 65B), used on early American houses supplement the architecture beautifully. A Connecticut door latch (Plate 64A) which has had its cusps shaped into the outline of a pine tree by a few cuts with a file and cold chisel exhibits a charm of its own, as does a Pennsylvania latch (Plate 64C) bearing the simple outline of a heart or tulip. Even the perfectly plain H and HL hinges of Virginia express the dignity and durability of the houses to which they are attached.

Though the colonist ofttimes complained about the high cost of ironwork, this complaint was caused by the high cost of blacksmith's labor rather than by a scarcity of material. All of the iron used in the first few years of the struggling new colonies in Virginia and Massachusetts had to be imported from the mother country but the early settlers were quick to set about finding a means of supply-

ing themselves. Recent archeological work has indicated that small test furnaces were built at Jamestown in the early years of that settlement and it is known that a full-fledged ironworks was being constructed at Falling Creek, Virginia, in 1621. This enterprise was, unfortunately, wiped out during the Indian massacre of 1622. This setback delayed iron production in Virginia for many years, but early in the eighteenth century furnaces were again in operation and by 1750 Virginia was exporting iron bars in considerable quantities to England, in addition to supplying her own smiths. In the North the industry was successfully established in the seventeenth century. A furnace was built in 1685 at Saugus Center, Massachusetts, and was successfully operated for many years. This smelter has recently been reconstructed by the American Iron and Steel Institute and is a fascinating reminder of early industry. By 1750 New England furnaces, as well as those of Pennsylvania and Virginia, were exporting great quantities of iron bars which were sometimes made into finished articles in England and shipped back to the country of origin for sale.

Practically all American hand-forged iron was made in the material known as wrought iron until about the middle of the nineteenth century when various grades of mild steel began to be widely used for blacksmith work. These mild steels, particularly the variety known as hot rolled, are generally used today by the few remaining blacksmiths for their everyday work and, on occasion, reproductions of antique pieces. The use of this material ofttimes furnishes the collector with a clue as to the age of a piece of ironwork, particularly if it is rusty. A typical object made of wrought iron rusts to a 'grainy' appearance with the grain generally running in the direction in which the piece was formed or 'drawn' by the smith. Mild steel rusts to an evenly pitted, 'orange peel' surface with no indication of grain. The collector should apply this test with caution, however, since it is not infallible. Some genuine old iron exhibits the surface appearance of steel and some genuine wrought iron is still available from Sweden and is being worked today. It should be noted that a limited amount of fine steel was available to the colonists and was used primarily in tools and weapons, and that cast iron has existed since the first furnace was built but that both of these topics are beyond the scope of this discussion.

Some of the finest American wrought iron is combined with, or embellished by, other materials such as wood, copper and brass. Candle-stands frequently have brass finials and drip pans, and lamps (Plate 68B) of various types ofttimes are equipped with brass or copper reservoirs. Fireplace implements, too, are commonly decorated with brass finials which add greatly to their appeal. Among the articles esteemed by many collectors are the countless variety of kitchen ladles, skimmers, spoons and forks which combine iron, brass or copper in their make up. Some of these pieces even have the contrasting metal cleverly inlaid in their handles and it is among this group of highly personalized utensils that the signed and dated piece is most often found.

The would-be collector of American wrought iron should acquaint himself with the various types of material which are likely to be encountered and which are worthy of acquiring. It is ofttimes found that a single category offers sufficient variety and interest to occupy the antiquarian for a lifetime and some fine collections have been assembled in this manner. Others have collected in a wholesale manner and, although expensive, this has resulted in several major museum displays. Still others have known deep satisfaction in collecting pieces of all categories to fit their private homes, disposing of individual pieces as better ones were found. Whatever method is adopted it will be found that iron can be grouped in the following general classifications:

Tools and implements: this category includes the tools of artisans and farmers as well as some of the implements of the soldier, except swords and firearms, which are too specialized to be considered here. Many tools are made of a combination of wood, wrought iron and steel so that the tool collector often confines himself to this one group of objects and is not thought of as a collector of wrought iron (Plate 67A).

Fireplace and kitchen equipment: this is probably the second largest and most diverse type of American iron. It includes such things as andirons (Plate 61B), trivets and toasters (Plate 62A), spits, hooks, pokers and trammels (Plate 62B), etc. A great deal of individuality is displayed by pieces of this type since they were often made to order to fit a given fireplace or cooking necessity. It should be noted that most iron pieces which were signed or dated will be found in this group.

Builders' hardware: hinges (Plates 63A, 66), hasps, shutter fasteners (Plate 65B), foot scrapers (Plate 65A) and the like constitute this group and it is here that regional characteristics most often come to light, partly because of the fact that many of these pieces are still attached to the houses for which they were made and peculiarities of different parts of the country can be noted by the astute collector. Nails, too, were an important product of the early smith and they offer an interesting small study by themselves.

Cabinet hardware: this group consists mostly of hinges and catches from chests, boxes and furniture. Though a small group, it often includes some exquisitely fashioned articles.

Locks and latches: these could be considered as a part of the foregoing categories but their great abundance and varying degrees of complexity make them worthy of a grouping of their own (Plates 63B, 64A, B, C). Most latches and latch-locks are wrought iron and many were custom-made for a particular door or cabinet; however, some of the more complicated locks combine brass, steel and other metals in their construction and exhibit many characteristics of factory production, thus, in a strict sense, eliminating themselves from inclusion in a wrought-iron collection.

Vehicular hardware: structural and decorative parts of coaches, carriages and wagons (Plate 67B) are included in this group to which little attention has been paid as yet. An exception to this statement might be made in the case of tool boxes from Conestoga wagons which have been avidly sought for and which are often fitted with ironwork of unusual decorative interest.

Ornamental iron: fences, gates, railings, weathervanes (Plate 61A) and similar pieces are included here. As might be expected, this group of rather expensive, custom-made objects often exhibits the ultimate in the iron-worker's skill. There are few collectors who specialize in these things, largely because of the difficulties in housing and displaying such bulky objects as well as the fact that they are usually an integral part of the structure for which they were designed and are not apt to be available unless a house is demolished. It should be noted that many of the beautiful iron railings and grill works in Charleston and New Orleans are not wrought pieces. They are cast and, as such, are examples of the founders' art rather than that of the black-smith.

Lighting devices: many types of lighting devices were made, wholly or in part, of wrought iron. These range from simple grease lamps (Plate 68B) to more elegant candle-stands and even, on occasion, to brackets or stands for gas and kerosene lights. Collections of wrought-iron lighting devices are not generally made as such, however, but are most often included with more comprehensive collections dealing with lighting.

For the student of American wrought iron there are many excellent museum collections on display. All of the larger 'outdoor' museums such as the ones at Shelburne, Vermont; Old Deerfield, Massachusetts; Old Sturbridge, Massachusetts; Williamsburg, Virginia and Greenfield Village at Dearborn, Michigan, have major collections of iron of all types. The period rooms in the larger art museums and most historic house museums as well as local historical societies have a certain amount of blacksmith work represented in their displays. At the Museum of the Bucks County Historical Society at Doylestown, Pennsylvania, and at Landis Valley, near Lancaster, Pennsylvania, there are truly enormous collections of wrought iron of all types. Further west, there is an extensive collection of implements in the Museum of the Ohio Historical Society at Columbus, Ohio, and a very large and comprehensive collection of wrought iron in the Henry Ford Museum at Dearborn, Michigan.

GLOSSARY

Andirons: implements for supporting logs in the fireplace. Commonly made of wrought iron, though there are many early examples in cast iron, brass and other materials. Andirons usually show some decorative features such as carefully formed finials, shanks and feet. Many are equipped with devices for holding a spit (Plate 61B) and occasionally a pair is found with cresset tops for holding a cup or mug to be warmed by the fire.

Betty lamp: a simple grease lamp, usually made of wrought iron, and consisting of a shallow cup with a vertical handle and an indentation in which a wick was placed. Those made of two cups, one below the other, are generally called Phoebe lamps.

Butterfly hinge: (Plate 66). *See* Dovetail hinge.

Cast iron: a form of iron containing a relatively high percentage of carbon (approximately 4 percent) and characterized by hardness and brittleness. Cast iron cannot be worked in a forge but is shaped by being poured into molds while in a molten state.

Cat: a form of trivet consisting of an iron ball with six equally spaced rods extending from it. No matter how it is placed in the fireplace three legs will support the device while the other three will support a cooking utensil.

Cob iron: a term somewhat loosely used as a synonym for andirons. Apparently its early meaning was an andiron equipped with a device for supporting a turnspit.

Cock's-head hinge: a form of H-hinge in which each termination is formed into the silhouette of a cock's head (Fig. 1).

Crab: a trivet (Plate 62A).

FIG. I.
Cock's-head hinge

Crane: an iron bracket affixed on two swivels inside a fireplace in such manner as to be capable of being swung in and out of the fireplace. Used to support cook pots.

Cresset: generally an iron basket affixed to a rod and designed to hold wood or other fuel for lighting purposes.

Cross garnet hinge: a type of strap hinge (Plate 66), one leaf of which is a horizontal strap and the other a vertical strap; when in position like a letter T lying on its side.

Dovetail hinge: a butterfly hinge, the leaves of which resemble two dovetails joined at the narrow part (Plate 66).

Escutcheon-lift latch: a trick latch resembling the common Norfolk type which is operated by lifting a sliding escutcheon plate rather than the more usual system of pressing a thumb plate.

FIG. 2.
Escutcheon-lift latch

Firedog: andiron, especially one of the lower and simpler sort.

Grisset: an elongated, cup-like, iron basin, generally with a handle, for holding grease so that rushes can be drawn through it to prepare rushlights. These devices are fairly rare, since rushlighting was not a usual system in early America.

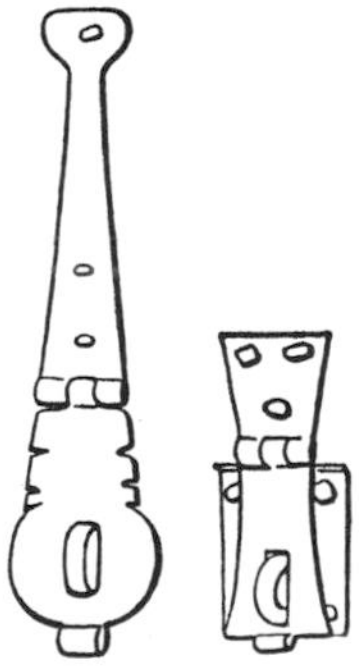

FIG. 3A and B.
Hasp

Hasp: a hinged strap generally used with a pin or lock to secure a door or chest.

H-hinge: a common type of early hinge the leaves of which are formed of vertical straps and affixed to each other by short horizontal straps in the center so as to resemble the letter H (Plate 66). HL hinges have an extra horizontal strap extending from one extremity of the H.

Knocker latch: a combination door knocker and latch. Turning the knocker opened the latch.

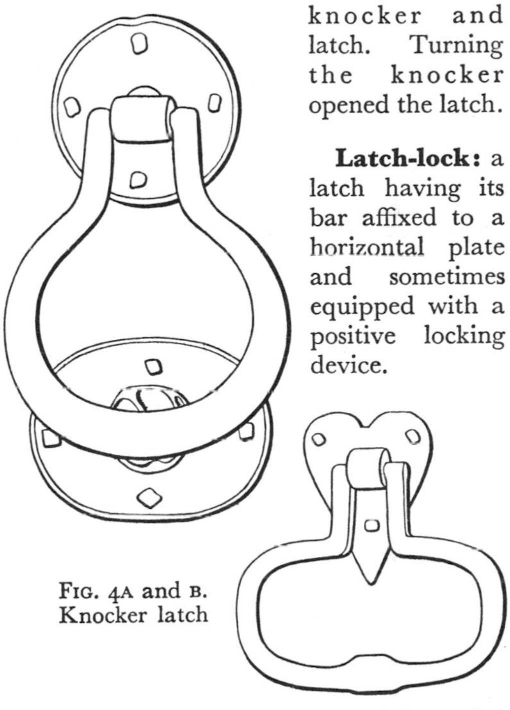

Latch-lock: a latch having its bar affixed to a horizontal plate and sometimes equipped with a positive locking device.

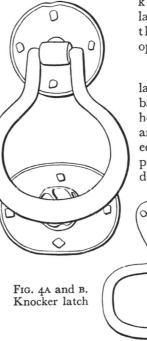

FIG. 4A and B.
Knocker latch

Norfolk latch: a type consisting of a handle affixed to a large, one-piece escutcheon plate (Plate 64B).

Pintle: a pivot pin for a hinge.

Pothook: an iron hook used to support a pot from a crane or trammel.

Rattail hinge: a type usually found on cupboards in which there is a downward extension, serving as a brace, of the pintle. This extension is curved and terminated with a decorative device.

Side hinge: a hinge consisting of only one leaf, usually placed in a vertical position, acting on a pintle (Plate 63A).

Skewer: small iron pin for holding meat on a spit.

Spider: a three-legged skillet, or sometimes a long-handled skillet.

Spit: an iron rod for holding meat before the fire for roasting. Also called turnspit.

Steel: a complicated alloy of iron and small amounts of other elements with a carbon content between that of wrought iron and cast iron. Its carbon content is sometimes

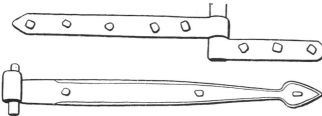

FIG. 5A and B. Strap hinge

used as a rough indication of its hardness, a high carbon steel (over 1 percent) being very hard and brittle while a low carbon, or mild, steel is less hard and more ductile. Steel can be worked at the forge while hot and can be hardened, or tempered, by quenching in water or oil. Steel was scarce and expensive in early America so its use was usually confined to cutting tools. Some early tools, such as axes, have wrought-iron bodies with steel cutting edges forge-welded into them.

Strap hinge: a simple hinge consisting of two horizontally placed iron straps.

Suffolk latch: a type consisting of a handle terminating in large decorative cusps but lacking an escutcheon plate (Plates 63B, 64C).

Trammel: an adjustable device (Plate 62B) for hanging a pot from a crane or the lug pole of a fireplace. Many lighting devices are also equipped with a trammel so that they may be raised or lowered.

Trivet: generally a three-legged stand for supporting cooking utensils in a fireplace but sometimes meaning any flat stand to hold a dish or other object (Plate 62A).

Wrought iron: literally iron which has been worked or formed by a blacksmith. The term has also come to mean a type of iron which contains practically no carbon but a considerable amount of slag which often gives it a grainy appearance. Wrought iron is readily worked and welded in the forge and is characterized by great toughness and ductility. Wrought iron cannot be hardened by heating and sudden cooling as steel can be, consequently it is unsuitable for the cutting edges of tools.

BOOKS FOR FURTHER READING

BRIDENBAUGH, CARL: *The Colonial Craftsman*, New York University Press, New York (1950).

DREPPERD, CARL W.: *Pioneer America – Its First Three Centuries*, Doubleday, Garden City, New York (1949).

GEERLINGS, GERALD K.: *Wrought Iron in Architecture*, Charles Scribner's Sons, New York (1929).

LINDSAY, J. SEYMOUR: *Iron and Brass Implements of the English and American Home*, The Medici Society, Boston (n.d.).

SONN, ALBERT H.: *Early American Wrought Iron*, Charles Scribner's Sons, New York (1928).

WALLACE, PHILIP B.: *Colonial Ironwork in Old Philadelphia*, Architectural Book Publishing Co., Inc., New York (1930).

The Chronicle, Published quarterly by The Early American Industries Association.

TIN, COPPER AND BRASS

By HENRY J. KAUFFMAN

THE **metals:** a study of American tin, copper and brass should be prefaced with some information about the physical qualities of these metals, for knowledge of their properties will assist the reader in understanding why different metals were selected for different objects. Although all of the metals are good conductors of heat, and all of them were consequently used to manufacture cooking utensils, nevertheless, for certain reasons, one was sometimes preferred to another. Because tin was cheap, it was used to make inexpensive 'pieced ware' like coffee pots; the malleability of copper rendered it suitable for making hand-hammered tea kettles; and brass, the only metal of the three that can be cast satisfactorily, was used for such objects as cast jelly kettles. Each metal has unique qualities. Tin is silvery-white, malleable and easily fused, and closely resembles pewter, for pewter is 80 to 90 percent tin. Tin was used in ancient times, but the production of tin-plate had to be deferred until a way to produce a thin sheet of iron was invented.

In the seventeenth century a small ingot of iron was hammered into a sheet by a man called a 'beater', but in the eighteenth century a machine was invented that rolled thin, uniform sheets. These sheets were cleaned and dipped into a vat of molten tin, so that a thin coating of tin rust-proofed the iron. This procedure produced a sheet that had the qualities of iron and some of the qualities of tin. Like iron, it was strong and rigid, and yet could be bent into many useful shapes. Like tin it was rust-proof, white and easily joined with solder. This useful and inexpensive medium was very popular with colonial craftsmen and was equally useful when the machine took over the production of stamped tin-ware.

Known to be one of the first metals used by man, copper was widely used in both Europe and America in the seventeenth, eighteenth and nineteenth centuries. Its principal assets are its resistance to rust, efficient conduction of heat, excellent malleability, and attractive red-orange color. It was particularly well adapted to making such articles as warming-pan and saucepans, where all of its qualities could be used to the satisfaction of the craftsman and his customer. The major objection to using copper for the making of cooking utensils was the disagreeable taste (perhaps poisonous effect) which foods acquired from it. Because of this reason the inside of copper culinary vessels was covered with a thin coating of tin (Plate 70B). The tinning was preceded by a thorough scraping and cleaning, then sal-ammoniac was applied to prevent oxidation during the application of the tin. When the tin coating was worn away in spots the entire vessel had to be retinned.

An alloy is a metal compounded of two or more metals to secure properties which one alone cannot provide. Such an alloy is brass, made of copper and zinc, the most frequent ratio being two parts of copper to one part of zinc. In early times brass was made by combining granules of copper with calcined calamine (impure zinc) in a crucible. The zinc, reduced to a metallic state by intense heat, combined with the copper and formed a lump in the bottom of the crucible. Several of these lumps were combined into a small ingot and sold to the craftsman or merchant. In 1781 James Emerson patented the process of directly fusing copper with zinc to make brass. The two-to-one ratio produces bright gold-colored metal that is soft to the hammer but hardens quickly and must be frequently annealed or softened. It also produces (with some small changes in its contents) a metal which is free-flowing when molten and can be cast in thin sections, required in the making of furniture brasses, or intricate shapes like candlesticks. Brass is one of the most valuable alloys known to man and has a number of desirable qualities. It is harder than copper; it is ductile and malleable; it takes a high polish; it is easily joined; and it does not disintegrate rapidly when exposed to the atmosphere. These qualities made it an attractive metal to the colonial artisans, who used it extensively for objects of utility and beauty.

The craftsmen: evidence of overlapping on the trades of the different metal workers can be found in the newspaper advertisement of E. Brotherton of Lancaster, Pennsylvania, obviously a manufacturer of objects made of sheet-tin, copper and brass:

'*E. Brotherton, Coppersmith, Brazier, and Tinplate Worker, Lately from England, Begs leave to inform the public ...*'

Probably the most obscure craftsman involved in this study is the brass-founder, described as follows in Hazen's *Panorama of Professions and Trades* (Philadelphia 1837):

'The appellation of founder is given to the superintendent of a blast furnace, and likewise to those persons who make castings, either of iron, or any other metal. In every case the term is qualified by a word prefixed, indicating the metal in which he operates, or the kind of castings which he may make: as brass-founder, iron-founder, or bell-founder. But whatsoever may be the material in which he operates, or the kind of castings he may produce, his work is performed on the same general principles.'

Besides a melting furnace, the brass-founder had to have a large supply of dampened sand and a pattern of the object which he planned to reproduce. Sand was rammed around the pattern in a box called a flask which could be opened for the removal of the pattern without disturbing the sand. After several flasks were prepared the molten metal was dipped from a crucible or a furnace and poured into the cavity in the sand. The casting of heavy objects like bells and cannons was done below ground level so that the molten metal could run directly from the furnace into the mould. Many objects were cast in bronze in essentially the same manner.

Perhaps the most specialized skill connected with the brass industry was metal spinning. In 1851 H.W.Haydn invented the process of spinning brass kettles and most of the spun ones were made in Connecticut during the last half of the nineteenth century. The procedure is to rotate a disc of brass on a lathe between a previously formed die on the headstock and a rotating device on the tailstock. A tool is pressed against the rotating disc until the disc conforms to the shape of the die. A large number of concentric circles is the usual evidence that an object has been spun.

Plain tinware: decorated and plain tinware were the two types made by American craftsmen. That a larger portion of the decorated has survived may be due to the fact that the paint gave added protection, and being largely ornamental, it was less used and better cared for. (For an account of the latter see *Japanned Tin-plate* by Shirley Spaulding DeVoe, Vol. I.)

The question as to what forms of plain tinware were made is answered by early newspaper advertisements and business catalogues. Though it might seem that such advertising would cater chiefly to city trade, this is not the case, for most of the advertisements mention that country merchants could be supplied on short notice and on good terms for cash. An interesting listing is that of Thomas Passmore who had a wholesale and retail tin manufactory at Seventh and Market Streets, Philadelphia. His advertisement appearing in the *Federal Gazette* on November 30, 1793, lists seventy-six specific items which he manufactured and concludes by saying that there were other items too numerous to mention. The unique aspect of his advertisement is that he arranged the items alphabetically and had at least one item for each letter except N, Q, R, X, Y and Z:

Ale tasters	Cheese trays
Argyles for gravy	Cream skimmers
Boxes for writing	Cheese toasters
Bathing machines	Cheese ovens
Bread baskets	Coffee biggins
Cranes	Coffee pots

Chocolate pots
Cyllenders
Candle boxes
Candle safes
Candle molds
Candle sticks
Canisters
Covers for plates
Cake pans and hoops
Dust pans
Dripping pans
Dressing boxes
Egg slicers
Extinguishers
Flour boxes
Fish kettles
Funnels
Fenders
Garden engines
Gingerbread cutters
Graters
Hash dishes
Hearing trumpets
Ice cream pots
Jacks
Jugs and tumblers
Kettles
Knife trays
Lanthorns
Lamps of all kinds
Moulds for blo-
    monges

Milk strainers
Money boxes
Meat skreens
Milk pails
Milk saucepans
Ovens
Oil pumps
Oil kettles
Pots and measures
Plate warmers
Punch strainers
Powder canisters
Pepper boxes
Pudding pots
Patty pans
Saucepans
Speaking trumpets
Sugar boxes
Snuff boxes
Suet strainers
Slicers
Scollops
Salvatonies
Steam kettles
Soup ladles
Stills
Staves suitable for
    ladies
Tureens
Tinder boxes
Ventilators
Water pots

These objects were usually round, square or rectangular in form, with wire inserted in the edges to make them strong and rigid. There were large articles like tin ovens and bathing machines, and small objects like nursing bottles (Plate 70A) and funnels. It is important to remember that in the early period large objects were often made of several pieces of tin-plate, for pieces of sufficient size were not easily obtainable. Unless an early piece was unusually well cared for, it should show some sign of disintegration such as rust. Distortion and poor soldering, however, are not necessarily evidences of great age.

Because tin-plate was a cheap and flexible medium there was rapid change of style, and the variety of shapes and joints indicates that the craftsmen were quick to grasp new ideas. Early pieces do not have factory-made spouts and handles like those of the 1850s and 1860s. Because he produced a custom-made object involving machine-made parts, the tinsmith stayed in business a long time. Many tin

shops were still operating at the beginning of the twentieth century, and even today a few can be found in rural areas.

It is obvious that a great many of the objects made of tin-plate were used in the home, more specifically in the kitchen. One of the most interesting accessories was the tin oven or roaster (Plate 69A) which stood before the fireplace with a large roast mounted on a spit. This was a long horizontal bar extending through each end, with some facility for manual or mechanical operation. The semi-circular form of the oven saved much heat lost by the earlier spit which did not have such a sheet-metal reflector. There were also small baking devices, using the same principle of reflected heat, to bake birds and small game.

The making of candles was an important project for the pioneer family, and candle-molds made of tin-plate facilitated the operation. That they must have been very widely used is attested by the fact that there were few attics on the eastern seaboard which could not boast of a few even in the late nineteenth century. Passmore made them in the eighteenth century, and the tin merchants, Hall & Carpenter of Philadelphia, sold machinery to make them as late as 1886. They were made in a variety of heights and unit combinations from two to fifty, units of two, four, six, eight and twelve being the most common. Of interest is it that tin candle-molds are very scarce in England; one antique dealer with a very large shop said that in his entire career he had only three.

The candle box (Plate 69C) was also made of tin-plate and hung by the fireplace to provide a small supply of candles within easy reach. The boxes were twelve to fourteen inches long and usually about four inches in diameter; though a few have punched designs in stars and other motifs, the functional use of wire and beading is all that decorates some of them.

Some of the early tinsmiths made ginger-bread cutters, and it seems safe to conclude that many of the Pennsylvania craftsmen were engaged in the production of the famous Dutch cooky cutter. To the indigenous designs of birds, tulips, hearts, etc., were added eagles, log cabins, Uncle Sams and Indians. The influence of Pennsylvania-German fractur can be seen in some of them, while others resemble the carved cake boards which were very popular in northern Europe. The popularity of the cooky cutter continued late in the nineteenth century, for the Hall & Carpenter catalogue carried them in their wholesale stock in 1886. At this late date the animal shapes retained the primitive feeling of the earlier designs, but the geometric patterns are uninteresting.

Museums like Old Sturbridge Village, Sturbridge, Massachusetts, and the Landis Valley Museum near Lancaster, Pennsylvania, have displays of tinware used on the farms and in small villages during the nineteenth century. They usually include objects such as colanders, measures, funnels, berry and meat presses, dippers, egg beaters, egg boilers, spice boxes, cheese molds, stencils, portable pumps, milk strainers, milk buckets, coffee pots, tea-kettles, wash basins, lamp fillers, milk buckets and an endless variety of lamps, lanterns and other lighting devices. Regarded by many people today as a metal of little value, tin-plate was a commodity precious to our ancestors.

Sheet-brass and copper: the survival of many objects made of sheet-brass and copper can be attributed to a number of reasons. The inherent quality and beauty of the metals influenced craftsmen to use them for the making of objects of importance. These items served a long time; they were well cared for, and did not disintegrate rapidly when they were discarded for a later and more fashionable object. This statement does not imply that fine and long-lasting objects were not made of tin-plate, but generally speaking the malleability, the color and the permanence of sheet-brass and copper gave them a favored position over tin. Silver was the only superior metal available to make comparable objects.

Perhaps no other object combines function and beauty so well as the warming pan of copper or brass. To function properly it had to be flat, so that it could be pushed rapidly between the sheets to take the chill from a cold bed. A flat surface provided space for the engraver to display his skill in decorative motifs on the lid, using designs of flowers, fowl or geometric patterns. The flat form of the warming pan was also well suited to standing or hanging on a wall where its decorative qualities were obvious. The handles of the eighteenth century examples were made of wood while earlier European types had gracefully forged handles of iron with loops on the ends for hanging. Though American craftsmen advertised them, the only maker whose products have been identified is Charles Hunneman, a Boston coppersmith. A few pans have appeared with initials I W and L C, but these makers have not been identified.

The copper weathervane of early date, of great interest to collectors, combines functionalism and good design (Plate 71A). This is an object in which the malleability and permanence of copper are important. After years of exposure the copper turns a fine verdigris-green. The earliest vanes were made of two convex pieces of copper, soldered together at the edges, forming a figure in low relief. The early ones, like Shem Drowne's *Indian*, belonging to the Massachusetts Historical Society, were probably knocked out with a mallet on a plank or a piece of lead. In the middle of the nineteenth century, however, such vanes were made by shaping a piece of sheet-copper in a mold of cast-iron, the mold having been cast from a pattern of wood which had been carved in full detail. The later vanes were in higher relief and more detailed than the earlier type. A variety of forms were produced, such as cocks, horses, ships, fish, grasshoppers and horse-drawn sulkies.

The copper tea-kettle deserves some consideration, for despite a long European tradition in the making of utensils, the coppersmiths of Pennsylvania and New York produced a flaring goose-neck type with a swinging handle that is peculiar to the area (Plate 71B). Many of them can be identified because the makers stamped them with an intaglio stamp. A few added the name of the city where they worked, and William Heiss, a Philadelphia coppersmith, included his street address.

Another significant item produced in quantity was the liquor still, for which there was a brisk demand throughout the grain-growing areas of Pennsylvania. It was easier and more lucrative to carry liquor to the Philadelphia market than cumbersome bags of grain. If the farmers were too poor to own a still for their individual use, a number pooled their resources and bought one for a community. Most of the stills show evidence of fine workmanship in the riveting and planished surfaces.

The pot, pan and kettle group are difficult to identify as American products because few of them are marked, and American styles closely resemble European styles. Known to exist is a saucepan that bears the name of William Bailey of York, Pennsylvania. Illustrated is one that was made by Crabb and Minshall (Plate 70c), the latter an independent maker in Baltimore before or after his association with Crabb. Many large apple-butter kettles were made in Lancaster, Pennsylvania, and distributed throughout America by a national chain store.

The most common article made of sheet brass was undoubtedly the spun brass kettle from Connecticut. After the first one was spun in 1851, kettles were produced in large quantities and sold by peddlers on the eastern seaboard. Other objects besides kettles were spun, for in the collection of Old Sturbridge Village at Sturbridge, Massachusetts, can be found a basin that has the typical concentric circles, and on the bottom the stamp usually found on spun kettles. A hammered brass kettle illustrated (Plate 72B) bears the name of William Heyser, a coppersmith from Chambersburg, Pennsylvania. There are many dish-based brass candlesticks, commonly called chambersticks, but few if any of them can be documented as American. Most of the bases are round, a few are elliptical, and a large number have rectangular bases.

Of sheet-brass and copper were made many other objects such as braziers, coal-hods (Plate 73A), oil-lamp fillers, measures (Plate 72A), funnels, fish kettles, chocolate pots, frying pans, housepouting, butter churns, footwarmers and many specialized objects for the hatting and dying trades. There were ob-jects for marine use, and a number of copper dry measures were used by official sealers of weights and measures.

Cast brass: it is doubtful if any product of the American craftsman is more difficult to identify as to origin than the object of cast brass. Despite the fact that many skilled men were engaged in the craft, the names of only a few are known, and extremely few of their products can be identified, an obscurity difficult to understand, yet existing.

Early costumes and newspaper advertisements indicate that brass buttons (Plate 74B) and buckles were in wide use in the eighteenth century. The following advertisement appeared in the *Pennsylvania Packet* in 1789:

'Wanted, a man who is capable of Moulding and casting large and small work, Particularly Buckles and Buttons, and that understands the management of Air and Blast furnaces. Also a man who has been bred to and Capable of working at the button trade in all its branches. ... To men, if found capable, large and extraordinary Wages will be given by Clarke & Co. No 1 Carters Alley, Philadelphia.'

Caspar Wistar (who came to Philadelphia in 1717) was one of the first craftsmen known to have engaged in the business of brass casting, and his product seems to have been confined to buttons. In the Lancaster County Court House a number of real estate transactions are recorded in which he is called the 'Brass button maker of Philadelphia'. His name is also associated with the glass industry. His son, Richard, continued the manufacture of brass buttons, and one of his newspaper advertisements concludes by saying:

'He likewise carries on the trade of making brass buttons, where merchants, shop-keepers, and others, can be supplied as usual.'

Most plentiful among objects of cast brass, and almost impossible to identify as to origin, are furniture mounts (Plate 76). The many English trade catalogues indicate a brisk exporting business, but there is proof that these pieces were made in America also. In 1795 Bolton & Grew of Boston advertised *Cabinet Brass Foundry Goods* and enumerated articles such as pulls, hinges, pendants, etc.

A number of signed drawer handles have been found, but the makers have not been identified as American or foreign.

The absence of a rough, cast texture on the back of furniture brasses indicates a stamped reproduction rather than an old casting.

Early cast brass and irons of American manufacture are quite rare, but in recent years a number of these have been found bearing names of American craftsmen. And-irons of iron, from which the name obviously originates, were enhanced by adding a finial and plate of brass as interiors of houses became richer. Into this category fall the attractive knife-blade andirons with penny feet and brass urn finials (Plate 75A). Some of this style have been found with the initials I C stamped on the brass plate at the bottom of the shaft, but the maker's name is not known. Late in the eighteenth century andirons of cast brass were popular and are appropriately used in a Georgian setting with Chippendale furniture. These have tall intricately patterned columns terminating in a variety of finials such as the urn, ball, steeple, lemon, and double-lemon pattern. They have a modified cabriole leg with a simple ball, snake or ball-and-claw foot. The most extravagant style had a twisted baluster and diamond-and-flame finial; a pair signed by Paul Revere is now in the Metropolitan Museum, New York (Plate 75B).

For use with late eighteenth- and early nineteenth-century furniture there are andirons with classic details. These have a long brass column mounted on a square base with an urn finial. The cabriole leg and ball feet are continued from the earlier style. A later pattern has a heavy brass turned column mounted on delicate legs and feet. Other firetools, principally shovels and tongs, had brass finials which matched the designs of the andiron finials. A few of these were marked by their makers, who have not, however, been established as American craftsmen.

Another important product of the brass-founder was the brass door-knocker. Popular in the eighteenth century was the modified S-type, while the urn and eagle patterns were popular in the early nineteenth century. Newspaper advertisements indicate they were made in America, but a signed one has not appeared.

A number of brass-founders made mathematical or surveying instruments, lancets, and the famous clockmaking Chandlees of Nottingham, Maryland, made a sundial that is signed. A few cast brass (or bronze) skillets are known to have been made in America; the Gay & Hunneman example illustrated (Plate 73C) is in the collection of Old Sturbridge Village. The absence in England of the common brass mold for making pewter spoons may indicate that they were essentially an American product, and the same may be said about the bronze molds used for making plates and hollow-ware. The origin of the many cast kettles remains a mystery, as does that of button and bullet molds, and a number of molds whose origin and function is only a matter of speculation.

Objects of cast brass can be easily reproduced, and it is difficult for a novice to tell the old from the new. The absence of makers' marks and of other identifying evidence, such as patina on pewter, forces the buyer to depend chiefly on the integrity of the dealer.

BOOKS FOR
FURTHER READING

BRAZIER, ESTHER: *Early American Decoration*, Pond-Ekberg Co. (1947).

FULLER, JOHN: *The Art of Coppersmithing*, David Williams Co., New York (1911).

HAMILTON, HENRY: *The English Brass and Copper Industries to 1800*, Longmans, Green & Co., London (1926).

KAUFFMAN, HENRY J.: *Early American Copper, Tin and Brass*, Medill McBride Co., New York (1950).

SMITH, R. GOODWIN: *English Domestic Metalwork*, F. Lewis Limited (1937).

JAPANNED TIN-PLATE

By SHIRLEY SPAULDING DeVOE

THERE were several tin centers in New England by the end of the eighteenth century, and they depended on England for their supply of tin-plate. It was exported to Boston in neat boxes containing sheets which measured 10 × 14 inches. From Boston it was carried by horse or oxen to the various tin shops. The Revolution halted the supply, but at the close of hostilities imports were again available.

The tin shops at first had no machinery. The utensils were made by hammering the metal over a hardwood mold with mallets. They were polished with wood ashes to brighten the plain tin. The shiny new pans and pails appealed to the housewife because they were light in weight. Iron was heavy and hard to clean and brass was expensive.

The size of the tin sheets naturally limited the size of the articles. The cutter had to measure accordingly and use the scrap for pepper and pill boxes or other small items. The octagonal or 'coffin' trays seem to have been the only trays made as long as sheet tin remained small. They were made in three sizes; half sheet, one sheet and two sheets. The latter was made with a center seam which was a clever way of producing a larger tray. The narrow gallery was a continuation of the floor of the tray and turned up five-eighths to one inch. Other articles were sugar boxes and sugar bowls, trinket and deed boxes, cylindrical and oval tea-caddies, bread trays, pap warmers, tea and coffee pots, the popular American apple dish, knitting-needle cases, banks and miniature domestic utensils for toys and many other objects.

Japanning was introduced into America about the end of the eighteenth century, which furthered the development of the industry. The articles were coated with asphaltum varnish, heat dried, then decorated. After reaching a peak in popularity about 1850, production waned and japanners wishing to remain in the craft turned to decorating sewing machines, carpet sweepers, typewriters and other household items.

The tin centers employed peddlers who at first traveled on foot, then on horseback. Baskets for holding the tin were fastened to the saddle. When the turnpikes opened after 1791, and more distance could be covered, wagons were used. Commonly painted red, they were especially designed to 'carry the most wares in the least space and were a maze of secret compartments, drawers and hooks'.

Goods were carried to the south, midwest and Canada. Cash was scarce so the barter and trade system was used. The Yankee peddler was a colorful character about whose shrewdness and adventurous ways much has been written. Many tinsmiths became prosperous through the clever bartering of their peddlers.

Of the many tin establishments, the best known are those of the Pattisons, Stevens, Filleys and Butlers.

The Pattisons are said to have started the American industry in 1740. They came from Ireland and settled in the Connecticut River Valley in what is now the town of Berlin. Edward and his brother William were English-trained tinsmiths who, when their business prospered, trained local men in the craft. In time these men established their own shops, some in other communities, and Connecticut became the largest producer of tinware in America.

The Berlin pieces (1825–50) most easily recognized are stenciled (Plate 77A). A privately owned collection of stencils has established the identity of apple dishes, coffin trays, large and small flat-top boxes and banks. Backgrounds for such items were often transparent red, blue, green and asphaltum. The bright tin under the transparent varnish made a rich translucent background. Opaque brown, yellow, green, white and red were used as well. Berlin workers liked a vermilion stripe as a change from the commonplace yellow.

Not as easily recognized are the Berlin painted designs with the exception of those attributed to Oliver Buckley. He is identified by the use of a central round spot of color, usually chrome orange, with smaller satellite spots encircling the center one. Brush strokes are superimposed on each spot, with heart-shaped leaves and beautiful brush strokes growing out of the center; they fill and soften the area between spots. The complete design retains an over-all circular pattern. Also attributed to Connecticut are running borders in red, green and black on bands of white (Plate 77B).

Zachariah Stevens abandoned the paternal blacksmith craft and became a tinsmith. His shop was in Stevens Plains, near Portland, Maine (Plates 79B, 80B). 'The industry grew by leaps and bounds until in the year 1832 there were eleven tin shops manufacturing 27,000 dollars' worth of tin annually.' Fire destroyed the shop in 1842.

Thomas Briscoe was one of the earliest tinners and peddlers who worked at Stevens Plains. Other remembered names are Walter Goodrich, Elisha and Elija North and the formerly mentioned Oliver Buckley. All four moved to Stevens Plains from Berlin. While the Connecticut influence can be seen in some Maine work, the Stevens designs were more realistic in form and softer in color, the result of adding white to the colors and more top detail on the flowers. Two overlapping large vermilion cherries were a specialty of Stevens Plains. The borders were original and full where space permitted, otherwise rick-rack and cable borders were used. Many of the finer articles had yellow and cream white backgrounds.

Zachariah's great-great-granddaughter, Esther Stevens Brazer, 1898–1945, successfully revived the old methods of japanning and decorating. By her teaching, research and collections of patterns and tinware, others are now able to continue further research and to perpetuate the craft.

Oliver Filley had been a peddler when he started what was to be an extensive business (Plate 79A). In 1800 he began the manufacture and sale of tinware, selling mostly in Vermont until 1809. Subsequently he had a branch in Philadelphia and one in Lansingburgh, New York. It was a family affair with a brother in the former and a cousin in the latter. Workers and painters were exchanged between the three shops as the need arose.

The Butler family settled in East Greenville, New York, after moving from Connecticut (Plates 78A, B). A son, Aaron, was sent back to Berlin to learn the tin trade. Upon finishing his apprenticeship, he returned to Greenville and opened a shop. His oldest daughter, Ann, learned to paint tin, using a rather individual style and signature. Ann taught her two younger sisters Minerva and Marilla. Ann's work is tight, crowded and covers most of the surface area. She liked dots as fillers and to sign her work with her name or initials, framed by heart-shaped borders.

A later factory was that of the American Tea Tray Works, 1860, at Albany, New York. Their products were Windsor oval trays in several sizes and were of imported sheet metal.

Another firm was the Litchfield Manufacturing Company, 1850–4, makers of *papier-mâché* (Plate 80A). Japanners were brought from Wolverhampton and Oxfordshire to ornament daguerreotype cases, boxes and furniture. Clock cases became their chief product. All were decorated with paint, pearlshell and metal-leaf in the English style of the mid-Victorian period. Trays were not produced.

Hull & Stafford of Clinton, Connecticut, 1850–70, were producing japanned toys, and no doubt other firms are still to be discovered by research.

From about 1820 English-trained stencilers were putting the finest decoration by that method on pianos and Empire furniture. As stenciling became more popular the fashion spread to the tin industry.

The American tin painters developed a forthright style that required little time for execution. It is marked by facile brush strokes and primary colors of pigment and varnish. Quick, shaded effects were cleverly done on fruits, flowers and leaves by applying light strokes on one half and dark on the other half of a motif. The base-motif was often a round, oval or scalloped form put on with vermilion or yellow. They left to the English-trained japanner the use of gold-leaf and work demanding high technical skill.

American japanned ware was almost entirely painted by girls. Some were daughters or relatives of the tinsmith or japanner. The designs in all the communities were similar in their unsophisticated quality. The color was fresh, bright and lasting, as has been proven by time. The homespun look of the articles and their use in rural areas has caused them to be called 'country tin'.

England supplied the world with tin; by 1800 twenty-five hundred tons were produced, and by 1860 a record of ten thousand tons was established. Not only tin-plate, but manufactured articles, plain and japanned, were exported to America. From the eighteenth century to the mid-nineteenth century, newspaper advertisements offered japanned trays, single and in sets, cash boxes and kitchen utensils for the American market.

Rectangular, oval, large octagonal and Chippendale trays elaborately painted or stenciled were as familiar in American homes as Staffordshire pottery. They are often mistaken for American but like the Staffordshire are English products. Jennens & Bettridge opened an office in New York at 218 Pearl Street, 1851-2. All American japanned tin was made of English sheet metal and in all probability blank trays were received in this country.

Because England controlled the market in tin-plate and flooded America with decorated tin the American industry was limited. Nevertheless, it grew out of this popular English industry and craft, and because of this relationship, and because there has been little in print until the recent publication of W.D. John's *Pontypool and Usk*, an account of the English japanned ware, which was such a familiar object in American homes, is given here.

ENGLISH JAPANNED WARE

When the English trading center of Bantam, Java, 1597, was supplying England with pepper, the East Indiamen brought home 'India skreens' as well as other lacquered pieces. Oriental objects continued to arrive from the Indies, China and Japan until, in the late-seventeenth century, England was flooded with Oriental goods. Furniture and cabinets made from screens were so popular that imitating lacquer became a craft. Sedan chairs, coaches and furniture which were made of wood were decorated by English artisans using their own methods and mediums. This new craft was called 'japan' work, as Japan then signified the Orient.

Pontypool in Monmouthshire was the first important center where japanning on metal was done. This came about through a sequence of inventions and improved methods over a period of thirty-five years. Because the English imported tin-plate from Saxony, Andrew Yarranton went there in 1665-7 to learn the foreign methods. On his return he presumably introduced the plating of iron with tin at Pontypool. In 1697 Major Hanbury invented the rolling mill for producing thin, smooth sheet iron which when tin-plated proved superior to the German plate. Finally, the Allgoods's invention of a permanent varnish which could be dried to a hard finish by controlled temperatures completed the fundamental steps. They established an industry that through fat and lean years continued until 1822, and exists to the present day in the Midlands.

The Pontypool works started producing commercially about 1720. Small objects were made, such as candlesticks, waiters, tobacco and snuff boxes, chestnut urns, teapots and caddies.

The use of the pierced edge and painted tortoiseshell ground was characteristic of Pontypool. Fine metal-leaf brush stroke borders and *chinoiseries* in low relief, called India work, as well as painted fruits and flowers, were typical.

In 1761 a family quarrel divided the business. Edward and Thomas Allgood moved to the neighboring town of Usk and established Allgood & Company. After 1822 it went out of the family, changed hands twice and closed in 1860.

Usk pieces show geometrical borders of fine gold lines, 'Stormont work' (serpentine lines which wander willy-nilly), stars of four lines crossing each other and dainty flower sprays in metal leaf.

While the Pontypool works were slowly getting started, production of tin-plate was moved to the Midland towns of Bilston and Wolverhampton. There the manufacture of japanned tin-plate and later *papier-mâché* grew to large proportions. The products were still called Pontypool. The name became a generic term and so it was used for many years. In 1834 four of the fourteen factories still described their work as Pontypool.

While Bilston is mentioned as the first Midland center, records are vague about the beginning. The 1818 registry lists fifteen japanners as well as workers in the kindred trades, which indicates a well established business. Bilston's principal products were blank trays, waiters, bread baskets, coal-vases and trays of the cheaper types which were exported to Russia, Norway, South America and the Spanish possessions. At one time Bilston alone exported fifty thousand trays a week to foreign markets.

The nearby town of Wolverhampton soon exceeded Bilston in its output. The center of the industry was an old Elizabethan mansion which in 1750 was converted into a factory known as the Old Hall Works. It housed several companies starting with Taylor & Jones who were succeeded by Ryton & Walton after 1810. Their descendants remained in possession until 1847, when the Old Hall went into bankruptcy. A twenty-one day auction disposed of the stock by the wagonload to buyers from London and other large towns.

Other firms as well as Old Hall made and decorated items for the ever increasing market, *i.e.* hand screens, inkstands, trays of all kinds, tea-caddies, coal-vases and a variety of *papier-mâché* furniture. In addition to the standard rectangular and oval gallery trays, new shapes and designs were constantly introduced with an eye to the export trade. Mechanical short-cuts were invented to speed up production, but handwork prevailed throughout. Henry Loveridge & Company, who produced in large quantity from 1840 to 1918, were the winners of the highest award at the London Exhibition of 1851.

The work spread to Birmingham where, in the 1730s, John Taylor, maker of snuff boxes, was the first successful japanner. His rival, John Baskerville, was making coach panels in 1741. Later, Henry Clay, who had been apprenticed to Baskerville, became very successful by his invention of paper ware. Clay needed coach panels lighter than iron and warp-proof as wood was not, to withstand stoving. He devised a way of compressing sheets of soft paper into a board. The material was dried over an iron core (mold) smoothed and japanned. Straight-edged trays or tea-boards were the next step. They were made over a mold similar in shape to a baking pan. At a much later date paper mills made and supplied japanners with mill board which eliminated the tedious handmade process.

In 1803 Clay moved his Birmingham business to King Street, London, where it remained until 1862. He was japanner to King George III and the Prince of Wales.

From 1818 to 1864 Jennens & Bettridge were Birmingham's foremost producers of japan ware. Most of their products were of paper in Clay's process which after 1830 they called *papier-mâché* for commercial reasons.

The japanned articles of the Midlands are too numerous to list. Along with the elaborate and decorative items were such utilitarian pieces as cash and pencil boxes, coal-hods and a variety of tin tubs. Most of the ordinary pieces were covered with black japan having fine and wide stripes as the sole ornament.

To the present day the manufacture of japanned metal is carried on in the Midlands. At least one company is at the same address as in 1888. Four, in and around Wolverhampton, were listed in the 1953 telephone directory.

In the early days business suffered for lack of transportation, especially where there were no waterways. Not as fortunate as Pontypool and Usk, the Midlands had no waterways and depended on pack horses and slow lumbering wagons. The japan master journeyed once a year to sell his products. He packed saddle bags with samples and patterns, the latter being flat, tin cut-outs or replicas of snuffer trays and tea caddies decorated exactly like the finished article. They were packed in space-saving flat cases of japanned tin. When the Worcestershire and Staffordshire canals were opened in 1769, the situation was greatly relieved and the products were sold to merchants in London and other important cities.

Many experienced workers were those who had been furniture and coach painters. Others were the best flower and arabesque painters lured from the Staffordshire potteries.

Finished apprentices became valuable and well known artisans in the craft. Most of them were very young boys who served for seven or more years with little thought given to health or education. Boys with ability were put with painters, others worked with girls and women at polishing surfaces, varnishing, stoving or the filing and grinding of pearl shell. The latter occupation was the cause of many early deaths from silicosis.

In the kindred trades were the makers of varnish, blank trays and bronze powders. Also tin workers, gold beaters and pearl shell workers. The Bilston registry for 1827 lists one 'stenseller', one caddy locksmith and one maker of candlestick springs.

A japanner coated the surfaces of the article with black asphaltum varnish. Later the word japanner also indicated one who produced as well as decorated. An artist painted centers, ordinary workmen did borders, and a filleter framed the article with stripes or lines.

All the workers moved from one town or company to another carrying designs with them. There were no copyrights, and anyone could imitate another's patterns.

A japanner could not work without varnish. Black varnish was customarily used for backgrounds (asphaltum and japan were practically synonymous) while clear varnish could be used with added red or yellow for size on which to lay metal leaf; or mixed with oil paints for painting, and left clear for a finish coat. Crystallized tin was coated with a clear yellow varnish.

Silver leaf (usually an alloy as silver tarnished under varnish) or aluminum after 1830, was washed with a yellow varnish to imitate gold-leaf. This was a common economy. Dutch metal, an alloy of copper and zinc, was another substitute for gold-leaf. Gold paint was never used.

Bronze powders in several shades were available after 1812. They were applied with swabs or 'bobs' made of chamois leather. The swabs varied in size. Larger ones were balls of cotton wrapped in chamois and fastened to a stick. The smallest were bits of chamois drawn through a quill. This free hand bronze method was worked on a nearly dry varnished surface. After 1820 bronze powders were applied through stencils on a similar surface. Often all the methods were combined in one decoration.

At the start of the eighteenth century pearl shell (abalone and great pearl oyster) was being viewed with interest by the japanners. Shell had been used as a decoration and ornament in the Orient for centuries. At the height of its popularity it was sold in London by the ton, the price depending on the quality.

When the workers had ground the shell to very thin pieces it was cut into motifs by several means : hydrochloric acid, knife or press tool. The cut motifs were placed on japan, and the surface of the shell was painted with transparent and opaque paint, and incorporated into the rest of the painted design.

Many short cuts for decorating were used. Cut cork was used in a process similar to linoleum block printing. Offset printing, which was devised for printing on tin-plate, was widely used in the late-nineteenth century. The design was transferred to a resilient blanket and applied to the flat tin surface. The tin was then pressed into the required shape. Many later trays had borders printed in gold which looked deceptively like handwork. The illusion was completed by the addition of handpainted centers.

The origin of French *tôle peinte* (painted sheet iron) is the same as that of the English japan work. The Oriental influence was strongly felt. There is a similarity to the English work in the shape and designs of some pieces thought to be French. This leads to the belief that plain and decorated English products were exported to France. It is known that japanners and painters traveled between the two countries, which confirms the belief and adds to the difficulty of identifying the work. Old French *tôle peinte* has been brought to America comparatively recently and seems not to have been in general use here in the period when the New England and New York tinsmiths were producing their wares. The terms *tôle*, or toleware, have come into rather general use, however, for all wares of this class regardless of place of production. Japanned tin-plate, or japanned tinware can be used more appropriately.

GLOSSARY

Asphaltum varnish: a bituminous product with other ingredients.

Berlin, Connecticut: largest tinware center in America, founded *c.* 1740 by the Pattisons and continued into nineteenth century.

Bilston: English industrial city in the Midlands, about two and a half miles from Wolverhampton. Next to Pontypool the earliest center.

Briscoe, Thomas: tinner and peddler of Stevens Plains, Maine; originally from Berlin, Connecticut.

Buckley, Oliver: tinsmith of Berlin, Connecticut. Born about 1781; went to Stevens Plains *c.* 1804; died 1872.

Butler: family of tinsmiths from Connecticut who established the business in East Greenville, New York. Aaron Butler was born about 1799 and died 1860. Associated with him were his daughters Ann, Minerva and Marilla (Plates 78A, B).

Coal vase: upright rectangular container for coal. Iron footed, with a slanting lid, it was painted on the lid and front.

Dutch metal: alloy of copper and zinc used in place of gold-leaf in decoration.

Filley, Oliver: manufacturer of tinware in Vermont, Philadelphia and Lansingburgh, New York (Plate 79A).

Goodrich, Walter: born 1802 and apprenticed at Berlin, Connecticut, at sixteen; went to Stevens Plains, Maine, where he worked for Oliver Buckley, 1824–7; in partnership as Goodrich & Thompson, 1830.

Hall & Stafford: made japanned toys 1850–70 at Clinton, Connecticut.

Japan: black asphaltum varnish for coating metal in imitation of lacquer.

Japanner: one who coats the surface with asphaltum varnish. Later it was used in a broader sense in regard to both decoration and manufacture.

Japanning: imitating effect of Oriental lacquered ware with varnish and oil paint.

Litchfield Manufacturing Company: 1850–4, Litchfield, Connecticut. Brought japanners from England; specialized in clock cases.

Nacre: mother-of-pearl.

North, Elisha and Elijah: learned trade in Connecticut and then worked at Stevens Plains, Maine.

Pattison, Edward and William: English trained tinsmiths who founded the industry in Connecticut *c.* 1740.

Pontypool: a city in Monmouthshire where japanning on sheet metal originated; a generic term for japanned articles.

Sheet tin or tin-plate: thinly rolled iron coated with tin.

Stevens, Zachariah: born 1778, died 1856; tinsmith of Stevens Plains, near Portland, Maine (Plate 79B).

Tôle: French for sheet iron, now in common use for any painted tinware, although *tôle peinte* is the complete form.

BOOKS FOR FURTHER READING

DICKINSON, GEORGE: *English Papier-Mâché*, London (1925).

JOHN, W.D.: *Pontypool and Usk*, Newport, Mon., England (1953).

JONES, W.H.: *Story of Japan and Tin-plating*, London (1900).

LAWLEY, GEORGE T.: *History of Bilston* (1893).

MANDER, GERALD: *Japanned Work in Wolverhampton* (1925).

PERIOD STOVES

By JOSEPHINE H. PEIRCE

In very early days a heated room was called a stove, although the room was not employed for living purposes. Later, an enclosed fireplace used for cooking or heating was known as a stove.

An early-nineteenth-century definition called it 'a contrivance or apparatus in which fires are made, with the view of conveying heat through a house, church or other building'.

Through the ages there has been an intimate connection of fire with the cultural growth of humanity, and the primitive need for fire has not been outgrown by the human race. Inventive genius was responsible for adjusting stoves to changing environment and the art of designers followed closely the forms and motifs used in architecture and furnishings, adapting them to stove materials.

Stoves have been made of logs (daubed inside and out with clay), cast iron, wrought iron, sheet iron, brick (sometimes with porcelain or tile exteriors), bronze, soapstone and steel.

Fuels utilized include wood, charcoal, peat, dung, coal, hay and straw, 'coal oil' or kerosene, and gas. Each fuel required special systems to use it to the best advantage.

For many years stoves were forgotten, considered old-fashioned and outdated. Recently many beautiful examples have come to light and an amazing number of people have become interested in them for their decorative value, as well as adjuncts to central heating.

Historians, novelists and other writers for many years have given people the idea that all early heating in North America came from huge and smoky fireplaces, and later from pot-bellied stoves. Nothing could be further from the truth.

GLOSSARY

Air-tight stoves: usually oval in shape and made of Russia sheet iron. They had a door at one end with a draft and a large opening with a hinged cover in the top through which large chunks of wood could easily be slipped. At times the lower area was lined with a heavier piece of the sheet iron. The first legs were made of half-round strips of iron which came with the bundles of sheet iron. Later models had cast iron bases into which cast legs were fitted. Urns or vases were often placed on top to be filled with water, or with perfumes or aromatic spices to offset the stuffiness and disagreeable smell of hot iron. The stoves were invented in 1836 by Isaac Orr of Washington, D.C. After 1842 self-regulating drafts were included.

Base-burning stoves: the first experiments with anthracite coal for fuel, soon after 1820, resulted in a new type of stove. Dr Eliphalet Nott called his a Saracenic Grate. It was an illuminated magazine stove consisting of an ash pit, a grate and a rectangular fire box lined with fire brick, with an opening through the rear of the brick lining for the escape of the products of combustion into a rectangular exit flue which was carried up nearly to the ceiling.

At the same time Jordan L. Mott in New York City was experimenting with a self-feeding magazine like a hopper with an inclined bottom which could only be used for nut coal. Many improvements were made in the grate and the method of feeding coal into the magazine, until in the 1850s the stoves attained consumer popularity. From then until the early-twentieth century, with improvements from time to time, base-burners (Plate 84D) became the standard of efficient heating, and were made by many manufacturers.

Bog-iron: bog-iron deposits were found in many parts of Massachusetts, along the borders of ponds which were spring fed, and blast furnaces were erected in several places to make use of the ore. While small utensils like pots, mortars and skillets were the usual items, records show that stoves were also cast in Saugus, Massachusetts, as early as 1647.

Box stoves: are just what the name implies – heating apparatus in the form of a box (Plates 83C, D). They were made in two ways: (1) separate plates (Plates 89A,B,C,D,) (*see* Five-plate, Six-plate (Plates 83B, C, D) and Ten-plate (Plate 83A); (2) cast in two sections: the base and hearth being one piece; the box another, with a hole for a funnel on top, and an opening at the front for a door.

Cannon stoves: the earliest cylinder stoves were made in Germany and Holland in the fifteenth century when plates of sheet iron were riveted together. In 1752 'Baron' Stiegel was casting cannon stoves in Pennsylvania. They were in three sections, the lowest containing a grate and draft door, and came in several sizes, suitable for churches, courtrooms, legislative halls and ships' cabins.

Cast iron stoves: the earliest cast iron stove extant was made in China in the later Han dynasty (A.D. 25–200). In Europe the first cast iron stoves were recorded in Alsace in 1475. Chinese stoves were cast in one piece and set on four cast legs. In Europe they were made of rectangular plates fastened together with gutter-shaped rims and short bolts. In later models the rim was cast in one piece with the plate; the weight of the top plate held the stove together. Both methods were used in Pennsylvania. (*See also* Five-plate stoves.)

Before the nineteenth century, plates were cast in the open sand. The iron, either melted directly from the ore or remelted from ingots (pig iron), was poured into the open unroofed cavity formed by pressing the face of a wooden pattern into a bed of dampened caster's sand so as to leave the upper surface of the impression exposed to the air.

Commemorative stoves: flasks and bottles to commemorate historic events were rather commonly made, but stoves with such designs are not as common. However, they can be found. Ten-plate stoves in Pennsylvania were made to commemorate two battles: the Bombardment of Fort McHenry, September 1, 1814; and the Battle of New Orleans, January 1, 1815. A six-plate box stove was made in 1848 for General Zachary Taylor, then a popular hero running for president. The Mexican battles he fought and won are listed on a banner encircling his likeness on each side of the stove.

Dumb stoves: also called radiator stoves and heating drums. The upper part exposes a large radiating surface, consisting of one, two or three chambers which are connected with pipes or columns, while the lower chamber has an opening in the lower plate which admits a pipe for heated air from a stove below (in the same room or a lower story). First patented *c.* 1838.

Another type patented in 1841 consists of a hollow statue set on a pedestal, which is the stove. The statue is a likeness of George Washington in a toga.

Fire frames: having the appearance and advantage of a fireplace, fire frames (Plate 82A) appeared early in the nineteenth century. They were made with three castings, forming a frame to be placed against the chimney, or a bricked-up fireplace. An opening was made in the chimney at the upper part of the frame to let the smoke pass into the chimney flue. The fire was made on a brick hearth, raised on andirons. Many times these frames were cast from the same patterns used for Franklin stoves but they were less expensive, easier to instal and had one great advantage – they did not smoke.

Five-plate stoves: also known as jamb stoves. They were cast iron boxes with five sides and an open end which fitted into an opening in the wall. The opening was at the rear or side of a fireplace in an adjoining room, usually the kitchen. The box protruded into the room it was to heat and the front end rested on legs or a platform.

Fuel, in the form of hot embers, was shoveled into the box from the fireplace and thus did double duty for cooking and heating.

Jamb stoves were common in Germany, and many sets of plates were brought to Pennsylvania, where they were used for patterns and installed as well. Decorations were, for the most part, illustrations of Biblical subjects with titles in the German language. They were manufactured in Pennsylvania from 1741 to 1768.

Four-o'clock stoves: term given to very small box stoves placed in bedrooms, where the fire was lighted at four o'clock to take the chill off the room before retiring.

Franklin stoves: cast iron fireplaces where the fire burns on an iron hearth (Plate 82c). Originally intended to be partially set inside a fireplace already built in order to save fuel and radiate more heat into the room. This was Benjamin Franklin's contribution to heating in 1742 but he soon found the stoves were more efficient outside the fireplace, or wherever they could be connected with a chimney.

The sides of some models are straight, others have a flare which helps radiate the heat. A sun-face with sixteen rays was the original decoration but it was changed many times. About 1770 classic ornament was used for decoration, following the architectural trend. After the Revolution, small profiles of Washington and Franklin replaced conventional rosettes. In all periods the decoration followed the prevailing styles.

The name 'Franklin' had great appeal, although no stoves were patented under that name until 1816, when James Wilson of Poughkeepsie was granted one. After that, patents were granted for Franklin Fireplace Stoves, Pipe Franklin Stoves, Open Fireplace Stoves with Andirons, Closed Franklin Stoves with Doors, Fold-door Franklin Stoves, Slide-door Franklin Stoves and Ben Franklin Stoves, all good sellers. Many can be found today.

Franklin-type stoves: stoves which can be opened in front to show the fire, but without the features of a real Franklin stove. Many of these have draft doors and ash pits below the grate.

Gallery stoves: very attractive galleries of pierced design in brass or iron were often placed on top of square or oval sheet-iron stoves, *c.* 1850.

Globe stove: a stove representing a mounted globe. It had a grate which could be raised or lowered in the pedestal. Patented February 8, 1834. (*See* Vase Stoves.)

The term 'Globe' was also used for a large size heater which warmed railroad depots, factories, stores and other public rooms.

Hay-burners: stoves of iron or brick especially made for burning hay in the prairie lands. Wood was unavailable, coal too expensive, and the fuel at hand was hay, cornstalks or sunflowers. The first patent is dated January 18, 1877, but they were used earlier.

Heat Radiator: a contrivance of sheet iron which had moveable dampers or heat-radiating tubes. It was inserted in a stovepipe in order to utilize more of the heat.

Holland stoves: known variously as draft-stoves, wind-stoves, ventilating-stoves and six-plate stoves. They were cast iron boxes connected with the chimney by a flue proceeding from the top. They also had a door opening into the room, in which was a draft hole of some sort. They stood away from the wall, and some had a hearth extension.

Illuminated stoves: had openings in the castings backed by sheets of mica, which allowed the flames to show through, giving a cheerful glow.

Jamb stoves: *See* Five-plate stoves.

Parlor cook stoves (Plate 81): in 1845 improvements were added to box stoves in the way of boiling holes to do cooking for a small family. Ovens were next included and decorations were designed to camouflage the utilitarian purpose. The boiling units were hidden by a hinged cover, topped with an ornamental urn or vase to hold perfume or spice to dispel the cooking odors. Oven doors were so liberally ornamented they hardly showed.

Base-burners, too, had models with built-in ovens and a boiling hole or two.

Smoke-consuming stoves: the principle was that of a reversed siphon, so smoke would descend through burning coals which then kindled it to flame, giving more heat. (*See* Vase stoves.)

Soapstone stoves: slabs of soapstone held together with an iron frame were made as early as 1797, from quarries in New Hampshire, Vermont and Massachusetts. When once heated through, the stone would hold the heat for many hours. Most were for burning wood, but a base-burning type was made in the 1860s for coal.

Stove room: term used for the room next to the kitchen, which in early days was the only room with a stove.

Ten-plate stoves (Plate 83A): were adapted from the six-plate stoves to allow the insertion of a small oven for baking. Four more plates were needed; top and bottom plates for the oven, and two doors, one on each side.

Two- and four-column stoves: box stoves with two (Plate 84A), and later four (Plate 84B), columns with a horizontal member, which had an opening for the stove pipe. At first the funnels were of plain stove pipe; later they were cast and handsomely decorated. Very often they were named and advertised by the design. For example, there were lyre stoves, jews'-harp stoves and dolphin (Plate 84A,B) stoves with variations. Two-column stoves were first made *c.* 1842.

Vase stoves: a vase-shaped iron vessel, which held the fuel, set upon a box which contained the grate. Benjamin Franklin made one in 1771 and called it a vase-machine. He used it in London for three winters. For it he adapted the smoke-consuming ideas first recorded by Louis Savot, who died in 1640. Patents have been granted ever since, for the principle is of great interest to present-day inventors.

BOOKS FOR
FURTHER READING

EDWARDS, FREDERICK, JR: *Our Domestic Fireplaces*, New Edition, London (1876).

ENCYCLOPEDIA AMERICANA, "Stoves," Vol. 25, 1955 edition, pp. 702–5b.

FRANKLIN, BENJAMIN: *An Account of the Newly Invented Pennsylvania Fireplace*, etc., Phila. (1744).

GAUGER, NICHOLAS: *La Méchanique de Feu*, translated by Dr Desaugliers, London (1716).

HOUGH, WALTER: *Fire as an Agent in Human Culture*, U.S. National Museum Bulletin, No. 139. Washington, D.C. (1925).

KNIGHT, EDWARD H.: *American Mechanical Dictionary* (1876), 3 Vols.

MERCER, DR HENRY CHAPMAN: *The Bible in Iron*, Revised edition edited by Horace M. Mann, Bucks County Historical Society, Pa. (1941).

PEIRCE, JOSEPHINE H.: *Fire on the Hearth*, Springfield, Mass. (1951).

PUTNAM, J. PICKERING: *The Open Fireplace in All Ages*, Boston (1881).

SHUFFREY, L.A.: *The English Fireplace*, B.T. Batsford, London and New York (1912).

SMITHSONIAN INSTITUTION, U.S. National Museum Bulletin, No. 141, *Heating and Lighting Devices*.

CHINA-TRADE PORCELAIN FOR THE AMERICAN MARKET

By ALICE WINCHESTER

CHINA-TRADE porcelain is the ceramic ware made and decorated in China for export to the Occident from the early-sixteenth century to the mid-nineteenth. Though it can be defined as simply as that, it is much misunderstood, for the facts about its identity and history have been badly confused with legend and false tradition, and it has been known by various conflicting names.

In the eighteenth century this same ware was called East India Company china, or East India china, or, simply, china, which indicated its origin. To the French it was, and still is, *porcelaine de la Compagnie des Indes*. In the nineteenth century it came to be called Lowestoft, or Oriental Lowestoft, and in the twentieth the designation Chinese export porcelain was added.

Much of the confusion that surrounds China-Trade porcelain can be laid at the door of William Chaffers, an able English scholar of the past century to whom we are indebted for much valuable information but who on this subject went astray. In his book *Marks and Monograms on Pottery and Porcelain*, first published in 1870 and still, in revised editions, a standard reference, Chaffers ascribed certain pieces of China-Trade porcelain to the small English factory at Lowestoft. While the Lowestoft product, which was limited in quantity, was a soft-paste porcelain and the plentiful Chinese ware was hard-paste, they had a superficial resemblance and apparently Chaffers was misled by local traditions. At any rate, he started a hare

which it has taken nearly a century to run to earth.

Though Chaffers's ascriptions were not, even at first, universally accepted, the name Lowestoft was soon widely adopted as a generic term for the export ware. Even when it came to be understood that the porcelain was actually Chinese, the misnomer still stuck.

Some years ago the name Chinese export porcelain was put forward in a serious effort to displace 'Lowestoft', and it is now frequently used. It is accurate, but nevertheless cumbersome, and is now giving way to the term which, though only recently proposed by John Goldsmith Phillips of the Metropolitan Museum of Art, had its origins in the eighteenth century when commerce with the East was known in America as the China Trade. The name China-Trade porcelain is not only simple and explicit but also evocative of the days when sailing ships beat their hazardous way around the Cape of Good Hope to bring the wonders of Cathay to the Western world.

The East India Companies: the China Trade had gone on for centuries before Americans were able to participate in it directly. In the early 1600s the Portuguese first established European trade relations with the East. They were followed by the Spanish, Dutch, Swedes, English and others who set up their East India Companies and sent their ships to India, China and the Eastern islands. Canton was the only Chinese port open to trade, and there by the late 1700s thirteen different nations were operating places of business, known as factories or *hongs*. The porcelain made 400 miles inland at the great ceramic center of Ch'ing-tê Chên played, to be sure, only a part in this profitable commerce, which was primarily concerned with tea and raw silk, but it was a useful part. Porcelain was highly prized in Europe, and it served as ballast in the ships, so that tea services, dinner services and ornamental pieces made to please Western taste were exported from China in constantly increasing quantities. Some reached the colonists in America, by way of England as the British trade laws required, but the story of China-Trade porcelain for the American market does not begin until after the Revolution.

The American China trade: once the United States had won independence and was free to trade directly with other countries than England, Americans lost no time in entering the China Trade. They did not found an East India Company: individual merchants sent out their own ships and each was a separate venture. The first to sail to the East was the *Empress of China*, a former privateer, which left New York for Canton on February 22, 1784, and arrived during the summer. Major Samuel Shaw, former aide-de-camp to General Knox, was supercargo on this voyage – an extremely important post, for on the supercargo depended not only financial success of the venture but also diplomatic relations with the Chinese. Shaw acquitted himself well, laying the groundwork for future trade between his country and China, and bringing home a cargo that inspired many American merchants to join in the hazardous but lucrative China Trade.

Ships set sail to the Orient from New York, Philadelphia, Boston, Norfolk, Charleston and other ports. By 1790 twenty-eight American ships had made the voyage. Before 1800 one merchant trader alone, Elias Hasket Derby of Salem, had sent out forty-five ventures. The China Trade became the most profitable branch of American shipping, and presently threatened the monopoly of Britain's powerful East India Company. It reached its peak with the development of the clipper ship in the 1840s, and by the time steam replaced sail its great colorful days were over. But long before then literally tons of Chinese porcelain, along with tea and spices, silks and cottons, lacquer and other exotic luxuries, had been brought into ports up and down the Eastern seaboard. Some survives still in the families for whom it was made.

Chinese porcelain for the American market: in general American-market porcelain from China is less elaborate and less varied than what was made for Europe. This is partly because it covers a shorter period, partly because the taste of this period was for the neo-classic, more restrained than the rococo of the preceding era. Moreover, by the time Yankees were trading to the East, the production of export porcelain had become a highly developed commercial operation and a large proportion of the ware was turned out in stock patterns of simple design instead of being specially made and decorated to individual order.

Forms: the forms were chiefly adapted from European models in ceramics or silver. Most commonly found are pieces from dinner services and tea services, punch bowls, mugs and barrel-shape flagons or pitchers. Among ornamental items, which are rarer, are pairs of covered urns and five-piece garnitures composed of tall beakers and covered vases. A single table service often had as many as 350 pieces, including dozens of plates in several sizes, platters, covered dishes, tureens. Teapots are most often cylindrical in this period, coffee pots tall and tapering, creamers of pear or helmet shape. Tea cups usually follow the low flaring shape of the Chinese tea bowl, without handles and with deep saucers; coffee and chocolate cups are deeper and straighter-sided, sometimes cylindrical, with handles.

Decoration: of greatest interest to collectors is the decoration that was applied to this Chinese porcelain. In fact, it is the decoration that determines whether a piece was made for the American or one of the European markets, since the ware itself is virtually all the same – smooth and white with a slightly grayish tinge. Differences in quality of ware are relatively minor; for example, some has a rather pebbly surface known as orange-peel glaze (Plate 92c).

Like the forms, the decorations were copied from Occidental models, and are of two main types: stock patterns and special-order designs. Most of the stock patterns were equally suitable, perhaps with minor variations, to both Europeans and Americans. They could be ordered from samples; a sample plate in the Victoria and Albert Museum shows four different types of border and two styles of monogram. For special-order pieces the design was sent out usually in the form of an engraving or drawing. With their well-known gift for copying, the Chinese enamelers reproduced these Western models with extraordinary accuracy, though there are amusing instances of misinterpretation, like the set said to be inscribed, *This is the middle.*

In American China-Trade porcelain, special-order pieces with decorations of unmistakable national or personal significance are far rarer than examples of stock patterns, and few of the stock patterns are exclusively American.

The principal stock patterns may be classified as: monogram, floral, ship, armorial and emblematic, and underglaze designs. Often two of these are combined, especially floral and monogram. Most of the special-order pieces also fall in one or more of these categories, but they have individual features that set them apart in the group of historical rarities.

Monogram designs: while Europeans had much Chinese porcelain lavishly decorated with their coats of arms, most Americans, not being armigerous, contented themselves with ware marked with their initials in a decorative monogram or cipher (Plates 86A, 89C). These initials were of course applied to suit the individual, but the shield or frame in which they were placed was usually a stock pattern. A favorite device

was a mantled shield, suggesting a coat of arms; this type is called pseudo-armorial (Plate 86c). Monograms were used in combination with all sorts of other designs, but they were also used with no other decoration than a simple border.

Up to the early 1800s borders were usually narrow lines of tiny floral or stylized motifs. The great favorite from about 1785 to about 1810 was a dark blue band sown with gold stars. Then a broader border came into fashion, sometimes dark blue with stars and floral reserves, sometimes a band of color overpainted with gilt.

Floral designs: by the time of the American trade with China, the eighteenth-century *famille rose* style of painted decoration had lost its earlier richness. Floral motifs were likely to be confined to scattered sprigs or sprays, and wreath or garland borders (Plate 86B). Often these were painted in charming natural colors, but sometimes only in blue, sepia, or black, perhaps with gilding. In contrast with this restrained treatment which kept most of the surface white is the Fitzhugh pattern, a floral design discussed in Underglaze Designs.

Ship designs: since it was the sailing ships that brought Americans this exotic china, it is not surprising that a very popular type of decoration was ship designs, also classified as *marine* or *nautical* (Plates 85, 89A, B).

Many of these were stock patterns, bought by English and other traders as well as Americans and adjusted to the individual case by addition of the appropriate flag and perhaps a name, initials, or motto. They are believed to have been copied from the small engravings of ships that ornamented bills of lading. There are, however, examples where the ship painting is obviously a portrait of a real ship, copied by the Chinese artist either from an engraving supplied by the purchaser or actually from one of the ships riding at anchor in the harbor of Canton.

Perhaps the most famous American ship item is a punch bowl on which appear, outside and in, pictures of a vessel under full sail, flying the Stars and Stripes, and inscribed

(A) A foot scraper of a common pattern.

(B) Three styles of typical American shutter fasteners.

PLATE 65

A cross-garnet hinge, a butterfly hinge and two H hinges with foliated ends.

PLATE 66

(A) A hewing axe on which a forge weld between a steel blade and a wrought-iron eye can be clearly seen.

(B) An unusual twisted iron singletree from a light cart or sleigh.

PLATE 67

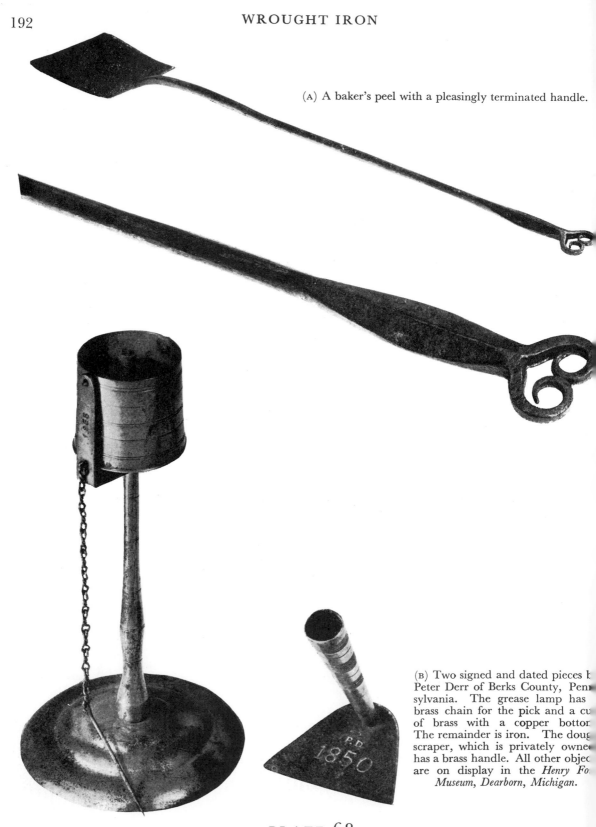

(A) A baker's peel with a pleasingly terminated handle.

(B) Two signed and dated pieces by Peter Derr of Berks County, Pennsylvania. The grease lamp has a brass chain for the pick and a cup of brass with a copper bottom. The remainder is iron. The dough scraper, which is privately owned, has a brass handle. All other objects are on display in the *Henry Ford Museum, Dearborn, Michigan.*

PLATE 68

(A) Tin oven; the handle at right was for rotating roast. Late-eighteenth or early-nineteenth century. *Metropolitan Museum of Art.*

(B) Tin weathervane in the form of a rooster, nineteenth century. *New York State Historical Association, Cooperstown, New York.*

(C) Tin candle box with hangers reinforced with wire. *Essex Institute, Salem.*

PLATE 69

(A) Tin nursing bottle; has tube inside which reaches to the bottom. *Author's collection.*

(B) Fish kettle, copper lined with tin. The ears for holding iron handle are of sheet copper riveted to body. *Old Sturbridge Village, Sturbridge, Massachusetts.*

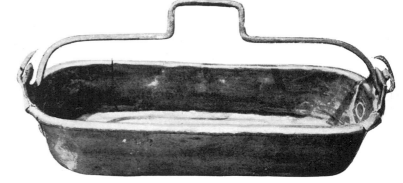

(C) Copper saucepan, stamped 'Crabb & Minshall'. One of the most attractive forms in sheet copper. *Dauphin County (Pennsylvania) Historical Society.*

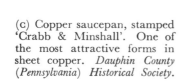

PLATE 70

(A) Copper weathervane, well executed; nineteenth century. *Florene Maine, Ridgefield, Connecticut.*

(B) Rare signed and dated copper tea kettle by William Heyser, Chambersburg, Pennsylvania, 1825. Knob is replacement. *Heyser collection.*

PLATE 71

(A) Copper and brass dry measure engraved 'Half bushel, W O Hickok. Harrisburg, Pa.' Numerals 47 in star between 'PA' and '1816'. *Author's collection*.

(B) Hammered brass kettles are scarce; this is stamped 'Heyser Chambersburg'; ears are of iron; handle probably replacement. *Coll. of Enos Horst*.

PLATE 72

(A) Brass coal hod of fine workmanship, American, *c.* 1800. *Metropolitan Museum of Art.*

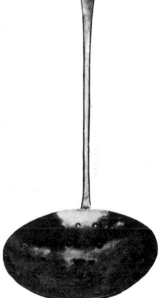

(B) New England brass skimmer stamped on back of handle 'Richard Lee', a rare maker whose work is highly prized. *Coll. of John J. Evans, Jr.*

(c) Cast brass skillet by Gay & Hunneman, Boston. *Old Sturbridge Village, Sturbridge, Massachusetts.*

PLATE 73

(A) *Martyr's Mirror*, published Ephrata, Pennsylvania, 1748; with brass corners and finely engraved clasps. This is one of the most important books published in America in the first half of the eighteenth century. *Author's collection.*

(B) Brass button with initials of George Washington, surrounded by those of the thirteen states, made probably in 1789 to commemorate his inaugural. *Metropolitan Museum of Art.*

PLATE 74

(A) Unusual brass andirons with iron rods extending through the brass balusters and riveted to top; seventeenth century. *Coll. of Joe Kindig, Jr.*

(B) Brass andirons with the mark of Paul Revere, Boston silversmith. In his later life he also worked in brass and copper. *Metropolitan Museum of Art.*

PLATE 75

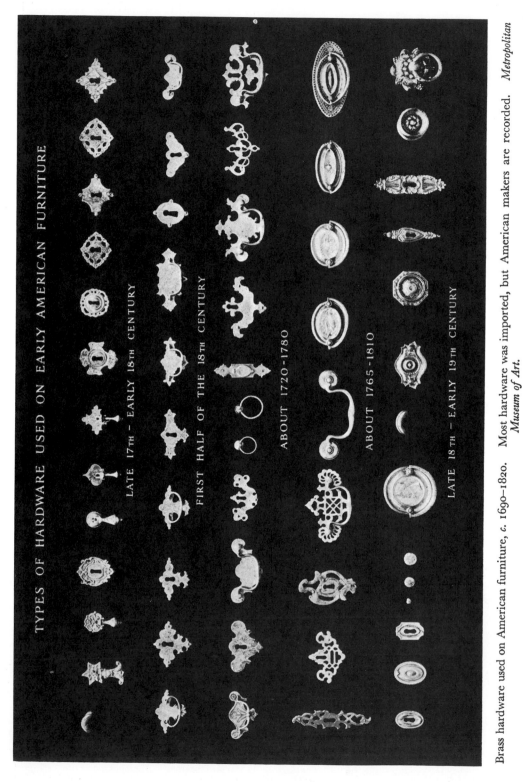

TYPES OF HARDWARE USED ON EARLY AMERICAN FURNITURE

LATE 17TH – EARLY 18TH CENTURY

FIRST HALF OF THE 18TH CENTURY

ABOUT 1720–1780

ABOUT 1765–1810

LATE 18TH – EARLY 19TH CENTURY

Brass hardware used on American furniture, c. 1690–1820.   Most hardware was imported, but American makers are recorded.   *Metropolitan Museum of Art.*

PLATE 76

(A) Stenciled examples from Berlin, Connecticut; the bank, blue on white; molasses pitcher, green on black; cuspidor, white smoked ground with blue border under stencil, red stripes. *Author's collection.*

(B) New England pieces decorated in bright green, red, yellow on the usual black. The white band as a background is thought to be a Connecticut characteristic. *Old Sturbridge Village, Sturbridge, Massachusetts.*

PLATE 77

(A) 'Coffin' tray, attributed to Butler shop, East Greenville, New York. *Coll. of Mrs Palmer, East Greenville; courtesy of Historical Society of Early American Decoration.*

(B) Deed box, attributed to Butler shop. *Courtesy of Historical Society of Early American Decoration.*

PLATE 78

(A) Deed box, attributed to New York State. *Coll. of A.P.Robertson; courtesy of Margaret M. Coffin.*

(B) Deed box, decorated probably by Zachariah Stevens of Stevens Plains, Maine. *Coll. of the late Esther Stevens Brazer; courtesy of the magazine Antiques.*

PLATE 79

(A) Papier-mâché table from the Litchfield Manufacturing Co., 1850–4.
Litchfield Historical Society.

(B) Teapot, Stevens Plains, Maine. *Coll. of Mrs S.V.Van Riper;*
courtesy of Historical Society of Early American Decoration.

PLATE 80

Ship Grand Turk At Canton 1786 (Plates 89A, B). Owned by Elias Hasket Derby of Salem, the *Grand Turk* was the second American ship to enter the China Trade and made in all forty-five prosperous voyages. This punch bowl, now in the Peabody Museum, Salem, Massachusetts, was a gift from a Chinese merchant to the captain on her first voyage. The ship picture, though more elaborate than many, is probably not a true portrait but a stock design adapted to the purpose.

Armorial and emblematic designs: one of the most popular motifs in decoration of every sort in the early days of the American Republic was the eagle, and on China-Trade porcelain it appears so often and in so many guises as to make up almost a separate category (Plates 87A, B, C, D, E, F). It may be classified as an armorial design, however, since it derives originally from the Great Seal of the United States, adopted in 1782. An exact copy of the official form is rare on porcelain. More often the national bird looks like a rather scrawny sparrow grasping arrows in one claw and laurel in the other, and bearing a shield on its breast – striped, monogrammed or flowered. Some eagles have been called the pigeon type; some are framed in a medallion or oval; a few unusually well-painted ones are shown with flags and emblems of war. Most of these eagle designs have narrow, simple borders. While the majority appear to have been stock patterns designed for the American market, the American eagles should not be confused with those of other breeds which are often seen on China-Trade porcelain, especially in the crest of an armorial design made for a European.

The arms of certain states also served as porcelain decoration. Most often found are the arms of New York which occur in several versions (Plate 88B). Those of Pennsylvania (Plate 86D) and New Jersey are the only others definitely known to have been used, and examples are much rarer.

A certain amount of porcelain was decorated with the insignia of the Society of the Cincinnati, that select group founded in 1783 by officers of the Continental Army, and while some examples were special-order pieces,

there were sets made in what might be called stock designs and advertised for sale in the American market. The most famous of these is one brought home by Captain Shaw on the first voyage of the *Empress of China* and acquired by George Washington (Plate 88A). It has the blue Fitzhugh border, and in the center a winged figure of Fame bearing the Cincinnati eagle badge. Many pieces from this set are now in the Winterthur Museum; examples are also at Mount Vernon and in the Metropolitan Museum of Art. The Cincinnati emblem was used on other sets, with a narrower, overglaze border, usually minus the figure of Fame, and plus a monogram.

The all-seeing eye, square and compass, and other emblems of the Masonic order appear on China-Trade porcelain in a variety of forms and combinations (Plate 88C). Masonic designs were popular in this country, but unless the occult symbols are accompanied by an American eagle or identifiable monogram there is no way to be certain that a given piece came originally to the American market rather than to Europe.

Underglaze designs: collectors of China-Trade porcelain today are most interested in pieces with painted, or enameled, decoration, but underglaze decoration, usually blue in the old Chinese tradition, was used on vast quantities of the ware imported over a long period. The three main types are called Nanking, Canton and Fitzhugh (the last said to be a Yankee version of Foochow). Actually these types were made, like other China-Trade porcelain, at Ch'ing-tê Chên, and their underglaze decoration was applied there, whereas the overglaze painting or enameling of most other types was done at Canton.

A pattern very popular in America was the profuse floral arrangement known as *Fitzhugh* (Plate 91A). The wide, distinctive border is composed of pomegranates, butterflies and latticework, and the center is filled with four large medallions of flowers and emblems. The border alone sometimes frames enameled motifs, as on George Washington's Cincinnati service. Enameled decoration is also combined with the complete design, usually in the form of a monogram, occasionally of an eagle, placed in the center. Though most often in underglaze blue, Fitzhugh occurs also with overglaze color—green, brown or orange.

Nanking and *Canton* are types closely similar to one another, whose all-over decoration in underglaze blue is a landscape or island scene, within a wide latticework border. The commonest scene on Canton (Plate 91B) was the inspiration of the familiar willow ware made in England – though believed to have been itself inspired by an English chinoiserie design. Nanking ware is of rather finer quality and often gilded.

Special-order pieces: the most highly prized examples of China-Trade porcelain for the American market are the unique items or sets painted to special order, often for presentation, of which a few may be mentioned here. Others are recorded elsewhere, especially in J.A.Lloyd Hyde's indispensable book on this ware, and in *Antiques* Magazine.

Several pieces of Cincinnati china belong in this category. The most impressive is a punch bowl made about 1786 for Colonel Richard Varick and now owned by the Washington Association of New Jersey, in Morristown (Plate 90A). The decoration, which circles the bowl, reproduces in minute detail the symbolic scenes and figures and complete inscription which appear on the engraved certificate of membership in the Society of the Cincinnati. Obviously Varick's own parchment must have been sent out as a model to the Chinese copyists.

Another impressive and historically important punch bowl is an eight-gallon one now in the Metropolitan Museum, which was, according to an inscription around the rim, *Presented by General Jacob Morton, to the Corporation of the City of New York July 4th 1812* (Plates 90B, C). On its sides are painted the arms of the city and of the nation, with scenes of ships and shores. Covering the inside is a finely painted view of New York from Brooklyn, copied from an engraving of 1802 by Samuel Seymour after William Birch. Another inscription around the base makes this as fully documented a piece of China-Trade porcelain as exists: *This Bowl was made by*

Syngchong in Canton Fungmanhe Pinxt. China-Trade porcelain was never marked, and this is the only known example whose maker and decorator are identified.

Martha Washington had her own set of porcelain, brought as a gift in 1796 by Andreas Everardus van Braam Houckgeest, a naturalized American and representative of the Dutch East India Company. The set, also known as the 'States china', has a border of links inscribed with the names of the fifteen states that existed at the time, and in a gold sunburst in the center the monogram MW (Plate 92A). Examples are at Mount Vernon and in the Metropolitan Museum.

Other pieces of China-Trade porcelain notable for their quality and their historic significance include such items as the punch bowl picturing the Pennsylvania Hospital in Philadelphia; and the one made for Captain Stephen Decatur with his portrait admirably copied from a St Mémin engraving, and an equally fine view of a naval engagement; flagons or toddy jugs bearing a portrait of George Washington copied from an engraving after a Gilbert Stuart portrait; and monogrammed pieces brought on the *Grand Turk's* first voyage which are decorated with mythological figures, a rare treatment in American-market ware.

European-market types collected in America: several types of China-Trade porcelain made originally for European markets are now eagerly sought in the American collectors' market. They include varied armorial designs; floral designs in the *famille rose* style (Plate 92C); sporting subjects; religious subjects; some mythological designs, such as *The Judgment of Paris*; genre scenes, of which *The Cherry Pickers* is a favorite; and an occasional patriotic item like the *Wilkes & Liberty* bowl which, though made for the English market, is equally appreciated here.

Late pieces and reproductions: while the great era of the China Trade closed soon after the mid-1800s, China went on making porcelain and American-market pieces were produced later. Certain patriotic designs related to the Revolution which may be found today seem to have been made about the time of the Centennial Exposition of 1876; for example, a scene of the Signing of the Declaration of Independence. These are inferior both in potting and painting to the earlier pieces but they may easily cause confusion.

Skilful reproductions of the Chinese porcelain have been made by two French manufacturers, Samson and Vivinis. Well-known instances are two separate copies by Samson of the Martha Washington 'States china', one put out in 1876 for the Centennial Exposition (Plate 92B), the other in 1893 for the Chicago World's Fair; and a Vivinis copy of the commemorative 'Washington urn' design originally produced soon after Washington's death in 1799. These simulate the Chinese ware surprisingly well but can be recognized, especially when compared with the originals.

A more dangerous pitfall for the unwary lies in items that have been tampered with, for it must be said that pieces of genuine old porcelain with false decoration are known. Significant motifs, such as the arms of New York, have been added to pieces originally quite plain to enhance their appeal. Such forgeries are, happily, not common.

BOOKS FOR FURTHER READING

No books are devoted exclusively to the China-Trade porcelain made for the American market but the reader will find helpful information on China-Trade ware in general in many standard works on ceramics, in exhibition catalogues, in numerous articles in *Antiques* Magazine (1922 on). He is also referred especially to
HYDE, J. A. LLOYD: *Oriental Lowestoft (Chinese Export Porcelain, Porcelaine de la Cie des Indes)*, 2nd ed., Newport, Monmouthshire, England (1954).
PHILLIPS, JOHN GOLDSMITH: *China-Trade Porcelain*, Harvard University Press, Cambridge (1956).
KEYES, HOMER EATON: *The Cincinnati and their Porcelain, Antiques*, Feb. 1930; *American Eagle Lowestoft, Antiques*, June 1930; *American Ship Lowestoft, Antiques*, June 1931; *Lowestoft: Exclusively American Antiques*, April 1932.
Concise Encyclopedia of Antiques, Vol. II, pp. 96-101, Hawthorn Books, New York (1956).

POTTERY
AND PORCELAIN

Part I. The wares made in America

By GREGOR NORMAN-WILCOX

'*I Like fine things, Even when They are not mine, And cannot become mine; I still enjoy them.*' This, translated from Pennsylvania dialect, appears on a *sgraffito* plate signed by Johannes Leman, made before 1830 at the Friedrich Hildebrand pottery near Tyler's Port, Montgomery County, Pennsylvania.

Everything needed for the production of pottery was present in America – everything but the most important, enough encouragement. Potter's clays were abundant. The common red-burning clays (for bricks, rooftiles, coarse redware) occurred in shales at or near the ground's surface, and their use since earliest days had called for only the simplest kilns and equipment. Buff-burning clays of finer texture were employed since the seventeenth century for experimental wares of every grade, and in the 1800s provided a range of factory-made wares from Bennington to Baltimore, and westward along the Ohio River.

White-burning pipe clay had been used by the aborigines. In a court trial of 1685 at Burlington, N.J., the potter, 'Wm. Winn Attested sayth that hee can finde noe Clay in the Countrey that will make white wear', but white tobacco pipes were made as early as 1690 in Philadelphia, where in 1720 they were advertised by Richard Warder 'Tobacco Pipe Maker living under the same Roof with Phillip Syng Gold Smith'. And by 1738 'an earth' (the true kaolin, white china-clay) was found by Andrew Duché 'on the back of Virginia', a vein of unaker running through the Carolinas into Georgia, exposed on riverbanks or along old stream beds.

Stoneware clays were absent in New England, but supplies were fetched by boat from northern New Jersey and Staten Island. At the Corselius (afterwards Crolius) pottery on Potbaker's Hill, 'the first stoneware kiln or furnace was built in this year 1730' on lower Manhattan Island. In January of that year in Philadelphia, Anthony Duché and his sons had petitioned the Assembly for support in 'the Art of making Stone-ware', to which they had been applying themselves 'for severall Years past'.

If the wanted clays were not near at hand, coastwise vessels and riverboats brought them. Materials for glaze or decoration were of simple and available sorts. Fuel for the potter's kiln was everywhere in this forested land.

Men with technical knowledge were here among the first. Brickmaking was reported by 1612 in Virginia, 1629 and 1635 in Salem and Boston. Rooftiles or 'tile Earth for House covering' appeared in Massachusetts court orders of 1646, and 'tylemakers' prospered in Virginia by 1649. The potter Philip Drinker arrived 1635 in Charlestown, and that same year at nearby Salem the 'potbakers' William Vinson (Vincent) and John Pride were recorded. One 'extraordinary potter' came in 1653 to Rensselaerwyk (Albany) on the ship *Graef*, and a Dirck Claesen 'Pottmaker' was established by 1657 at Potbaker's Corner, in New Amsterdam.

The thumping of the potter's wheel was soon heard in every colonial town of consequence, and for New England alone (says Lura W. Watkins) two hundred and fifty potters were recorded by 1800, twice that number by 1850. How many more were never mentioned at all?

Place-names like Potter's Creek, Clay City or Pottertown give a clue to the spread of activity – four states had a Jugtown, seven more a Kaolin.

All that was lacking was a proper market. In numbers the colonists were so few, a total of 200,000 by 1690 and the five leading towns accounting for only 18,600. The population nearly doubled every twenty years, so that by 1776 its total reached 2,500,000 (about equally divided between the five Southern and eight Northern provinces) and Philadelphia, with 40,000 souls, was the second city in the British dominions. Ninety percent of the population was on the land, and for the most part comprised a sort of village society. The complaint was everywhere the same as in Virginia, that 'for want of Towns, Markets, and Money, there is but little Encouragement for tradesmen and Artificers'. It was all very well for a Boston official to say (1718) that 'Every one Incourages the Growth and Manufactures of this Country and not one person but discourages the Trade from home, and says 'tis pitty any goods should be brought from England', but fashion preferred what was imported, and the colonial potter found little demand except for useful wares.

In the South (where tobacco was the cornerstone of the finances of Chesapeake society until 1750, followed by wheat and corn; where rice was the staple in Carolina from 1700, indigo from about 1745) the English character of plantation life was strongly marked. The local commodities were exchanged for English luxuries, and except for rude plantation crafts, nothing much was to be expected here. Andrew Duché and the mysterious Samuel Bowen, two early Savannah potters, were marvels who appeared far ahead of their time.

England's suppression of all colonial manufactures was a sternly established policy. General Thomas Gage expressed the official attitude when writing to Lord Barrington in 1772 that it would be 'for our interest to Keep the Settlers within reach of the Sea-Coast as long as we can; and to cramp their Trade as far as can be done prudentially'. But he was unaware to what an extent people had already moved inland, away from the agents who supplied English goods; nor had he perceived the rapid advance made in our own manufactures since the French and Indian Wars of 1754–63.

Yet potmakers lagged in this general improvement. Through the colonial years and far beyond, coarse red-clay pottery – jugs and jars, plates and bowls, mugs and milk-pans – formed the principal output of small potteries everywhere. New England's glacial clays made excellent redware (Plate 93C) which was partly supplemented by gray stoneware from the time of the Revolution, or more extensively after 1800 (Plate 96). Always popular, ordinary redware survived the competition offered by cheap and serviceable factory-made wares from the 1830s, and in country districts lasted through the nineteenth century, lingering within present memory.

REDWARE

In kitchen and dairy, or for table use alongside pewter and common woodenware or 'treen', the simple forms of this sturdy folk pottery were washed or splashed with pleasant color – glazed with browns and yellows, rich orange to salmon pink, copper-greens, a brownish black made from manganese. For this the least equipment was needed: a horse-powered mill for grinding and mixing clay, a self-built potter's wheel, a few wooden tools and perhaps some molds (Plate 94A). The maker might be no more than a seasonal or 'blue-bird' potter who worked when his other affairs permitted, and carried his output by wagon through the near vicinity; or the larger and fulltime potshops might employ untrained lads (William Scofield of Honeybrook got 'one skilled potter from every 16 apprentice boys') or migrant journeyman potters of uncertain grades.

There were no secrets in this simple manufacture. Since 1625–50, at the Jamestown colony, potters everywhere had made useful everyday ware of much the same sorts, in its own time used up, smashed up, never regarded as worth preserving.

Of this class, an early and curious milkpan pictured here for the first time (Plate 93A) is credited to Andrew Duché, who advertised (April 1735, the *South Carolina Gazette*) to supply 'Butter pots, milk-pans, and all other sorts of Earthenware of this country make'. The story of its discovery a decade ago was told by Ruth Monroe Gilmer in *Apollo* for May 1947.

Andrew Duché (1710–78), a Huguenot from Philadelphia, who worked 1731–5 'on the Bay' at Charleston, South Carolina, and at New Windsor, South Carolina, from 1735–7, finally enjoyed a short but important career 1738–43 at Savannah, Ga. (*see* Porcelain p. 139).

Found at Guyton (in the Salzburger area forty-five miles inland from Savannah) this heavy, thick and flatfooted pan was apparently made from riverbank clays, quoting its owner: 'the body densely textured and mottled reddish brown, as if made from shale and ball clay ... the glaze a clear strawcolored lead used all over ... the glazed bottom flat, without rim or ridge of any kind.'

Not long after Duché's time, another Southern pottery was established by a colony of Moravians who in 1753 moved from Bethlehem, Pennsylvania, to the wilderness region of Wachovia, North Carolina. Here the United Brethren founded a communal society served by Brother Gottfried Aust as potter. He fired his first kiln at the village of Bethabara in 1756, making redware, clay pipes, stove-tiles, and from 1761 conducted public sales which attracted buyers from a surprising distance (Rice, *Shenandoah Pottery*, pp. 271–7). The enterprise was transferred in 1768 to Salem, N.C., where by 1774 far superior wares were achieved, and production lasted to around 1830.

Still another venture in this region was the so-called Jugtown Pottery, in a settlement peopled *c.* 1740–50 at Steeds, North Carolina, by a group of colonists from Staffordshire. Apparently the plainest of 'dirt dishes' were made here (1750?) by Peter Craven, first of

his family, and latterly the place became known as Jugtown, for the common vessels it supplied to Southern distilleries. Languished and long forgotten, the pottery was revived in 1917 at a hamlet amusingly named Why Not?

Far north, New England must have been brimming with small but able potters. In 1775 (says John Ramsay in *American Potters and Pottery*) the two Essex County, Massachusetts, towns of Danvers and Peabody had seventy-five potters, and there were twenty-two Peabody potters at the Battle of Lexington.

Early New England potters and their wares were given ample and excellent record in Mrs Watkins's fairly recent book, in which the illustrations show what Puritan austerity characterized the general output. Simple and appropriate forms were enough, with richly colored glazes to satisfy the eye and only with occasional attempts at further decoration. Pictured here (Plate 93c) is a basin with trailed lines of yellow slip; a cooky jar girdled with an incised rigaree; and herb-pot with *Edward Towle* (its owner?) scratched on the cover.

Pennsylvania-German: for the Pennsylvania-'Dutch' (that is, *deutsch* or German) Frances Lichten has provided a full report in her *Folk Art of Rural Pennsylvania*. In the 'Dutch counties' settled in the eighteenth century by Swiss Mennonites, and by Germans from the Palatinate, pottery was made which was in wide contrast to New England work, marked by a love of color, a play of ideas, an engaging humor.

The flat Pennsylvania fruit pie dish or *poi-schissel* was a distinctive article; or the pots for applebutter called *epfel buther haffa;* the saucered flowerpots or *bluma haffa*. Fluted turk's-head cakemolds (Plate 94A) came in all sorts and sizes, and there were standing pottery grease-lamps not seen in New England, quaint banks and bird-whistles, double-walled tobacco jars displaying skilful pierced work. (See *Pennsylvania-German Folk Art* by Frances Lichten, p. 401).

Shenandoah Valley: just south of Pennsylvania, a numerous and flourishing group of potters worked throughout the nineteenth century in a hundred-mile stretch of the Shenandoah Valley. Foremost were the Bell family (Plate 95B) founded by Peter Bell who from 1800–45 produced 'erthingwear' at Hagerstown, Maryland, and Winchester, Virginia. His oldest son, John Bell (1800–80), worked 1833–80 at Waynesboro, Pennsylvania, and was followed by five sons who continued the business until 1899. John's brothers, Samuel and Solomon, were in partnership from 1833 at Strasburg, Virginia, where the factory continued until 1908.

Midwest: fairly typical of what was made through Ohio and Indiana, where a variety of pottery and stoneware clays were abundant, the washbowl and jug (Plate 94C) is stamped on one handle *Zoar*, on the other 1840. The Society of Separatists (called Zoarites) were one of many religious sects gathered in communal settlements that flowered and died in the nineteenth century, themselves coming in 1817 from Württemberg and prospering 1819–98 at Zoar, in Tuscarawas County, Ohio. In a long list of trades and crafts practised here, we find weavers and carpenters, a printshop and bindery, a fine blacksmith shop and of course a pottery. Red rooftiles (one is dated 1824) are still seen on a few houses, and in 1834 the Society was selling 'porringers' to farm folk in the vicinity. The services of an outsider were engaged, Solomon Purdy, a potter recorded 1820 at Putnam; 1840 at Atwater. Until 1852/3 the Zoar associates still produced common brownware, and black- or buff-glazed redware.

Decoration: last of the everyday wares, and different from the others, a buff pottery painted (sometimes stenciled) with manganese brown belonged to New Geneva, Pennsylvania. So wholly unlike the dutch-country pottery seen farther east, this sober stuff (Plate 95A) with hard, unglazed tan body was made 1860–90 by James Hamilton of New Geneva, in the southwestern corner of Pennsylvania, and very likely (see *Antiquarian* for September 1931) also across the river at the A. & W. Boughner pottery in Greensboro.

Long employed by redware potters everywhere, a simple and most effective method of decoration was by the use of diluted clay or 'slip', which from a cup fitted with one or several quills (Plate 94A) was trailed on the surface of a piece in flourishes or perhaps words like *Lemon Pie*, names like *Louisa* (Plate 94B). Made by George Wolfkiel at Hackensack, New Jersey, during the panic of 1837, were slipware platters woefully inscribed *Hard Times in Jersey*.

For such, a slab of clay was flattened with the wooden beater (one in Plate 94A shows a beautifully worn and polished thumbprint) and smoothed like piecrust with a wooden rolling pin. When half-dried, the raised lines of slip would be pressed into the soft or 'green' surface of the unfired dish, its edge would be trimmed and then notched with a wooden coggle-wheel.

Far more ambitious was *sgraffito* (scratched) ornament, for which redware was thinly coated with cream-color slip and this cut through to expose the darker body. Plates often showed a border inscription written with a sharp tool, and parts of the design might be enhanced with added colors (Plate 93B). Widely known in European peasant pottery, this technique was a favorite of the Pennsylvania-Germans from perhaps 1733 (a shaving basin, p. 197 in Barber's *Tulip Ware*) and furnishes surely the most decorative examples in American redware.

STONEWARE

The family of stonewares, a varied company, was made of finer and denser clays and fired in a kiln much hotter than for earthenware (above 2,000° F.), resulting in a hard body for which 'no other glazing need be used than what is produced by a little common salt strewed over the ware' (1785). The salt vapor supplied a roughish, glassy coating that was colorless. According to the clays used and the temperature of the kiln, wares ranged from the familiar gray body to buff or cream, even a dark brown.

Fine grades of stoneware approached the quality of porcelain, such as the 'white stone Tea-cups and sawcers' (thin-bodied white Staffordshire, later with scratch-blue decoration) sold 1724 in Boston, or the 'Basket-work't plates' (of saltglaze with embossed and pierced lattice borders) which arrived from England in 1758 and 1764. Next century a middle grade of 'figured stone pitchers' and Toby jugs of 'superior stone' in buff and brown earned praise and awards in 1829–30 for David Henderson of Jersey City.

The popular class of stonewares considered here were chiefly utility articles: common crocks, jugs or churns along with other things made for amusement, like whistles and money-banks, bird or animal figures. Most of it was gray ware, and after about 1800 the vessels were usually coated inside with brown Albany slip.

The favorite decoration was freehand painting in cobalt blue, or rarely brown. Initials and dates, birds or flowers and scrolls, might be emphasized with scratched lines or die-stamped flowerets (Plate 96A), though after about 1850 stenciled designs were widely used (Plate 96D).

Many redware potters made stoneware also, and from c. 1800 often marked their work with a die-stamped name and perhaps the place. But later than 1850 and especially in the midwest, crocks might show the name not of their maker but of some wholesaler to whom they were supplied.

Stoneware was developed because of fear of poison from lead-glazed wares. 'Preceding the glorious Revolution', said a long notice in the *Pennsylvania Mercury* on February 4, 1785, 'here and there, were a few scattered Potteries of Earthen-Ware, infamously bad and unwholesome, from their being partially glazed with a thin, cheap washing of Lead.' This lead glaze, attacked by acid foods, 'becomes a slow but sure poison, chiefly affecting the Nerves, that enfeebles the constitution, and produce paleness, tremors, gripes, palsies, &c.'. It was hinted that the Legislature should enact 'discountenancing the use of Lead in glazing Earthen-ware', and further that 'a small bounty, or exemption' might encourage stoneware potters.

Whatever justice there was in this alarm, it had long been discussed among potters. The apocryphal date 1722 appears on a large open-mouthed stoneware jar (Robert J. Sim, *Some Vanishing Phases of Rural Life in New Jersey*, p. 43). At least we have seen 'the first stoneware kiln or furnace' erected 1730 near the Collect Pond in New York, by William Crolyas (Crolius). And we have heard Anthony Duché that same year claiming to have made stoneware 'for severall Years past' in Philadelphia. Others soon sought to learn the mystery.

Isaac Parker of Charlestown (Boston) was one of these, a redware maker who eagerly sent for a man 'trained in the stoneware potter's art'. What arrived in Boston on July 14, 1742, aboard the brigantine *Mary* (Watkins, *Early New England Potters*, pp. 35–8) was James, son of Anthony Duché and brother of Andrew the porcelain maker. Two months later, Parker could report to the General Court that he had 'now' learned the secret of stoneware making. Parker died forthwith; but by December 1742 his widow Grace with James Duché as co-partner was granted a fifteen-year monopoly, and in April 1745 their firm (called Thomas Symmes & Co.) advertised 'blue and white stone ware of forty different kinds'. Duché disappeared next year, probably returned to Philadelphia, and death in 1754 released Mrs Parker from a failing enterprise.

Nor was the failure surprising, since New England afforded no stoneware clay and was put to the expense of getting it from New York. Indeed, the major source of supply for all American stoneware was for many years the rich deposit of fine blue-clay centered at South Amboy, New Jersey, and extending to Staten Island and Long Island.

From this bed Adam Staats, a potter of Horse Neck (Greenwich), Connecticut, dug clay in 1751, on a five year lease between 'the Said adam States' and the town trustees of Huntington, Long Island. He knew its qualities, having worked at Cheesequake or 'Chesquick' Creek (South Amboy) before appearing in 1743 in New York.

With seemingly one exception, other early stoneware makers, if not in the locality, were at least within easy range of the New Jersey blue-clay beds. This exception occurred far south, where the Moravians at Salem, North

Carolina, burnt their first kiln of stoneware (according to Brother Aust's diary) in May 1774, instructed by an English journeyman potter William Ellis, who came the year before from Pine Tree 'where he had been working'. At this inaccessibly inland town, local clays must have answered.

Naturally, these opening years of the Revolution saw vigorous increase in stoneware potting. First by a boycott to express political discontent, and then by war itself, the domestic market was largely cut off from its accustomed foreign sources of supply, the Thames-side potteries at Fulham and Lambeth, and the furnaces of the Rhine Valley.

Blue-painted gray stoneware shards carrying the dates 1775 and 1776 (*Antiques*, March 1944, pp. 122–5) have been found along Cheesequake Creek, presumably from a pottery operated by General James Morgan, who in 1779 filed a claim for '1 kiln of Stoneware not burnt' that British soldiers had destroyed. Also dated 1775, *July* 18/*JC* is a stoneware jug (Metropolitan Museum) from the New York factory of William Crolius II. By 1778 a certain Bernard Hamlen advertised for return of a horse strayed from his 'Stoneware Potting Manufactory at Trenton' (Clement, *Our Pioneer Potters*, p. 20).

By a potter who sometimes stamped his ware *C.Crolius Manhattan-Wells* and was working by 1794 (Plate 96A) is a brownish stoneware batter jug with die-stamped blue flowerets and leaves, scratched: *New York, Feb^v 17th 1798/Flowered by Clarkson Crolius/ Blue*. The New-York Historical Society, its owner, also possesses the maker's actual stamp and other tools. This was Clarkson, Sr (1773–1843), a grandson of William 'Crolyas', the stoneware potter of 1730. Clement, *Our Pioneer Potters*, reviews (pp. 21–5) the complicated record of the Crolius dynasty (fifteen potters in all) who worked in New York until *c.* 1870 when Clarkson, Jr, retired.

The first Crolius and one 'Johannes Remmi' or de Remy (John Remmey I) married the Cornelius sisters, Veronica and Anna. But a supposed business partnership of Remmey & Crolius in 1742–4 finds no supporting records. The Remmeys followed their separate way from 1735 until today. When the New York factory failed in 1819/20 one great-grandson continued at South Amboy until 1833; another had gone to Philadelphia about 1810, where (with a side venture at Baltimore from 1818–*c.*1835) the firm is still established.

A reason is easily seen for the flurry of new stoneware factories that appeared around 1805. From 1804–12 the seizure and impressment of ten thousand American seamen into the British Navy led to a series of Congressional Acts (1806–9) that prohibited trade with England. With the Embargo Act of 1807 (one of the causes of the War of 1812) imports dropped to one-third, and American potters had to supply a domestic market cut off from foreign sources.

Xerxes Price who stamped his jars *XP* was working at Sayreville (South Amboy) as early as 1802 and until 1830. Peter Cross whose mark was *P.Cross/Hartford* appeared 1805–*c.* 1818 in Connecticut. Samuel Wetmore in 1805 began the enterprise at Huntington, Long Island, that later would become Brown Brothers (Plate 96D). And from an unidentified maker (Watkins, *New England Potters*, p. 83) came sober brown-stained jars with '*BOSTON*.1804.' impressed (Plate 96B).

In Albany, the able Paul Cushman from 1809–32 made both redware and stoneware, on the hill 'a half mile west of Albany Gaol'. Not far east was Bennington, Vermont, where Captain John Norton in 1793 had started a potworks continued by the family for a century, until 1894. By tradition, stoneware was made here in 1800; in 1810 wagons were fetching clay across the hills from Troy, and in January 1815 the diary of Hiram Harwood says the Nortons 'were making ware of both kinds, stone and clay' (Spargo, *Potters of Bennington*, pp. 9, 11–13). But the flourishing period was from 1828–32 when the proprietors had begun to use clays from South Amboy and Long Island.

In the Ohio country, the earliest recorded stoneware potter was Joseph Rosier, working by 1814 near Zanesville; but by 1840 (says John Ramsay) there were more than fifty such potters through the area. Excellent clays were here in plenty, and potters of all sorts were attracted to the midwest. East Liverpool with its fine Ohio River clays was to overtake northern New Jersey, which itself has been called 'the Staffordshire of America'.

By this time stonewares were a factory-made product that devoted less attention to form, more to decoration. Typical are a 4-gallon crock made 1850–68 by Edmands & Co. (Plate 96c *left*) and the gray churn made 1850–70 in the State of New York (Plate 96c *right*), a freely drawn, blue-painted deer on one, a whimsical bird on the other. Still later the decorations might be stenciled, to save labor, as in the case of the eagle of Plate 96D in which is also seen the cylindrical shape much used for crocks after the mid-nineteenth century.

Government reports for 1900 showed an American output of stonewares valued at $1,800,000, but of redwares only $400,000 (Ramsay, p. 18), and the latter mostly from Ohio and Pennsylvania. The old order of work was indeed disappearing.

SOME BETTER WARES

In between the common grades of work on one hand, and porcelains on the other, American potters made constant boast of producing wares 'allowed by the nicest Judges to exceed any imported from England'. These were always 'on the very lowest Terms' – terms that were often based not on cash but barter, and perhaps 'the potter will take in Pay, pork, tar, wheat, corn or tobacco' (Maryland, 1756). Though claiming so much, theirs were mostly small and experimental ventures, poorly financed and showing a high mortality rate. Edward Rumney in July 1746 bravely undertook 'to sett up a Pottery' at Annapolis, having 'furnished himself with Persons exceedingly well skilled (in the making of) all sorts of Potts, Pans, Juggs, muggs &c.' Within four months his business was already offered at public vendue, even 'two Potters and several Horses'. A more ambitious project was that Factory in New-Boston, which advertised in October 1769 'for Apprentices to learn the Art of making Tortois-shell, Cream and Green-colour Plates' (or Queensware and so-called

green-edge Leeds). After this solitary notice, only silence. From the dismal number of such failures, Lord Sheffield's *Observations on the Commerce of the United States* (1791) seems not too prejudiced in saying: 'Manufactures of glass, of earthenware, and of stone mixed with clay, are all in an infant state.' Yet across this fairly cheerless scene moved many potters of sound experience. Who were these lost men? Some are known only from one passing mention in early records, or for a solitary example of ware 'said to be' by John Doe, a potter. Unlike the silversmiths, who were often men of public consequence, potters enjoyed relatively slight notice.

And where are their products, of which enormous amounts once existed? How to account for the total disappearance of examples from our first whiteware furnace (1688–92 at Burlington, New Jersey) where Dr Daniel Coxe said his agents made 'a great quantity of White and Chiney ware'? What has become of all the 'Pennsylvania *pencil'd* bowls and sugar dishes' praised for their 'beauty of colours and elegance of figures', the work of Alexander Bartram who 'has got a Pot-house' in Philadelphia and advertised 1767–73? Where is one specimen of 'General Washington's bust, ditto in Medallions, several images part of them not finished', which in 1784 were offered at the sale of Jeremiah Warder's kilns in the North Liberties (Philadelphia)?

An answer might be that because our work of the better grades must compete with the imported, it attempted close imitation, and nowadays the American ware (so seldom marked, until after 1800) languishes unrecognized, mistaken for English. Thomas Baker who advertised 1756 in St Mary's County, Maryland, was only one who made 'ware of the same kind as imported from Liverpool, or made in Philadelphia'.

In their day the 'compleat Setts of Blue-china, Enamuel'd ditto' shown in the Boston import lists of 1737 probably had no equal here. But the 'new fashion'd Turtle-shell Tereens' of Whieldon's ware (1754) were soon copied by colonial potters. The same were described as 'Tortorise-ware' in Boston and New York lists of 1771, along with other

Whieldon-Wedgwood types such as 'Colly flower, Mellon, Pine-apple, Aggitt'. Also in 1771 came 'Queen's Ware' to Boston, the 'Plain Cream-colour' to New York.

Creamware: nothing approached the popularity of creamware, or lasted longer. Its inventor Josiah Wedgwood called this (1767) 'the Cream color, alias Queensware, alias Ivory'.

John Bartlem or Bartlam ('one of our insolvent master potters', complained Wedgwood in 1765, who was hiring hands to go to his 'new Pottworks in South Carolina') was producing creamware by 1771 at Charleston. Messrs Bartlam & Co. in October 1770 had opened a manufactory on Meeting-street, 'the proper Hands &c. for carrying it on having lately arrived here from England'. Three months later it 'already makes what is called Queen's Ware, equal to any imported'. But a grant of £500 from the Assembly did not save it from disastrous labor troubles.

William Ellis, one of the Bartlam workmen, appeared December 1773 at Salem, North Carolina, where Brother Aust's diary said 'he understands how to glaze and burn Queens Ware'. The Moravians built a suitable kiln, and the following May 'Ellis made a burning of Queensware'. He departed the same year, and in 1783 Wedgwood referred to this Ellis as now 'of Hanley' (Staffordshire), calling him the sole survivor of Bartlam's enterprise.

Philadelphia became the center of creamware manufacture. Here in 1792 the Pennsylvania Society for Encouragement of Manufactures and the Useful Arts offered a $50 prize for specimens 'approaching nearest to queen's-ware'. John Curtis, having dissolved the partnership of Curtis & Roat in July 1790, continued with 'the cream-color'd' from 1791–1811 at his Pottery-Ware Manufactory in Front Street, Southwark. Three others soon appeared: Alexander Trotter (who in 1809 had 'lately established a Queens-ware pottery on an extensive scale'); the Columbian Pottery); Daniel Freytag (maker in 1810/11 of a 'fine earthenware, the paste resembling queen's-ware'); and David G.

Seixas (producing from 1816 a cream-color 'similar to the Liverpool').

In New York 'a new Cream Ware Manufactory' was established 1798 at Red Hook Landing, where J.Mouchet made Tivoli Ware 'with colored edges'. Nor had Alexander Trotter retired in 1812/13 (Spargo, p. 180), but reappeared 1815 in Pittsburgh, with Trotter & Co. advertising 'Queensware similar to the Philadelphia'.

The undiminishing popularity of this ware is reflected (*American Collector*, June 1940, p. 11) by one item in a ship's list of 1827: '532 doz. ordinary quality dinner plates, cream colored or blue and green edges', in a shipment of mixed pottery from Liverpool to Portsmouth, New Hampshire.

Another decade later, the Staffordshire potter James Clews arrived 1836 at Louisville, Kentucky, where creamware had been made since 1830 by the Lewis Pottery Co. With the backing of Vodrey & Lewis, Clews built a large factory downriver at Troy, Indiana, and the first kiln of the new Indiana Pottery Co. was fired in June 1837. A blue-printed snuff jar seen here (Plate 103A) with the mark *Clews's Manufacturer's* is a good sample of the ware made here only in 1837–8, Clews then returning to England because the local clays proved disappointing.

After that time, fine creamware was scarcely heard of, though poor and coarser wares of cream or ivory color were widely made, e.g. the 'attempts at cream colored' reported 1850–1900 at the Shaker colony in Amana, Iowa. The Bennett Pottery might be listed 1847 in the Pittsburgh directory as 'makers of domestic Queensware', but through the Ohio country this name was understood to mean a cream-bodied earthenware with rich brown glaze.

PORCELAIN

Allowance must always be made for the extravagant claims constantly offered by struggling potters who nervously looked for support. Small enterprises might make the loudest noise, asserting that they operated a China Manufactory and calling their ware porcelain, though they did not possess the requisite materials. Even if they did, it was one thing to know how, but another to produce a successful china.

The early 'pottery att Burlington for white and chiney ware' (1688–92) surely achieved no more than white tin-glazed delftware. Indeed, England herself had done no better at that time. Half a century must pass before porcelains of even an experimental grade were actually made here.

The ideal, of course, was true hard-paste porcelain like the Chinese, with which all potters had long been well familiar. This was the ware always preferred by fashionable and wealthy persons, who bought so much of it that by 1754 the General Court of Massachusetts passed an Act placing special excise on 'East-India Ware, called China-ware'.

It should be noted that in August 1738 samples of this Chinese ware were sent by the Earl of Egmont (most active of the Trustees of the colony of Georgia) to a certain master potter in Savannah. These samples were to serve as models for one Andrew Duché, already mentioned, first of the three pre-Revolutionary porcelain makers.

Duché (sometimes Duchee, Deshee, Deusha) was third son of the stoneware potter Antoine (Anthony) Duché. Born in 1710 in Philadelphia, he married twice in 1731, worked first at Charleston (1731–5) and then at New Windsor (1735–7) across the river from Augusta, finally at Savannah (1738–43) where he had been assured that 'all reasonable encouragement' would be given him by General James Oglethorpe, founder (1733) of the colony of Georgia. Indeed, he received a grant of £230 and built a pottery, where (say local records of 1743) he 'found out the secret to make as good porcelain as is made in China'.

Of his output, the 'one or two specimens in the United States' mentioned by George Savage (*18th-Century English Porcelains*, p. 149) are pictured here (Plates 93A, 97). The late Mr Hommel and Mrs Gilmer (*see* Books for Further Reading) have published extensive notes on Duché, the subject of happy excitement in research circles; and a further hoard of unpublished facts, graciously made available by Mrs Gilmer, might have assisted persons skeptical of Duché's true achievements.

As for his porcelains, Oglethorpe in 1738 already reported to the Trustees that Duché had found 'an earth' (kaolin, china-clay) and baked it into china. By February in the next year he had discovered 'a whole mountain of stone' (petuntze?) in the Salzburger area, near Ebenezer; and in 1740 Duché found 'a quarry of Ironstone' on the five acre lot of William Gough. For while conducting his experiments to perfect porcelain, Duché supplied the vicinity with useful articles of common earthenware or Ironstone, and stove-tiles for the settlement forty miles inland.

On March 17, 1738, he had requested of the Trustees 'two ingenious pot painters', and special supplies including 'a Tun weight of Pig lead, 200 wt of blew smalt such as potters use, 300 wt of block Tin, and an Iron Mortar & pestle'. The wanted materials (though skimped in their amounts) were sent him in August, and the 'two servants' came in July 1739 on the ship *Two Brothers*. Duché here had all the requirements for blue-decorated porcelain, and skilled helpers to finish it.

Found in 1946 at Charleston, his unique bowl (Plate 97) is heavy for its size, slightly translucent but not resonant. Thanks to the Earl of Egmont's samples, its blue decoration resembles Chinese work but employs a local vernacular, with a band border of white oak leaves, a calyx of slim fern fronds below. If it bears no mark, Mrs Gilmer rightly asserts it is 'marked' all over. This bowl of experimental grade is just such as Duché would produce from the materials he had and working under the particular conditions.

The story of his after years belongs not here so much as in English accounts of porcelain making. Drawn into political squabbles, Duché came into disagreement with Colonel William Stephens who was secretary to the Trustees; ostensibly to plead the cause of the dissatisfied settlers, he left Savannah in March 1743 and appeared in London by May the next year.

Our concern with him centers on his contact with the proprietors of the Bow factory, Edward Heylin and Thomas Frye, who obtained the following December a patent for 'invention of manufacturing a certain material, whereby a Ware may be made of the same material as China'. Their secret (apparently communicated by Duché) was 'an earth, the produce of the Chirokee nation in America, called by the natives *unaker*'.

This same year, Duché waited upon William Cookworthy, who in a letter of May 1745 discusses 'the person who has discovered the china earth, calling it *kaulin* and saying that the finder is going for a Cargo of it'. Cookworthy has seen 'several samples of the china-ware of their making', and understands that the requisite earth is to be found 'on the back of Virginia'.

What profitable arrangements were made by Duché? We hear no more of him as a potter. From 1750–69 he is a 'merchant' and prosperous landowner in Norfolk, Virginia. In 1769 he returned to Philadelphia, and here (described as a 'gentleman') he died in 1778.

Much briefer is the account of a second porcelain maker, the elusive Samuel Bowen. In 1745 one Henry Gossman, aged eighteen, and 'son of a very poor helpless widow of Purisburg, South Carolina' (a Swiss Huguenot settlement on the river above Savannah), was apprenticed or 'bound to a potter'. This would appear to be Samuel Bowen, now occupying the potworks vacated by Duché two years before.

Not until November 1764 did an English newspaper (the *Bristol Journal*) report that 'This week, some pieces of porcelain manufactured in Georgia was imported', but added that 'the workmanship is far from being admired'. Two years later (says Alice Morse Earle) Samuel Bowen was awarded a gold medal from the English Society for the Encouragement of Arts, Manufactures and Commerce 'for his useful observations in china and industrious *application of them* in Georgia' (italics ours). Two years later, in March 1768, he was thanking the Georgia Commons 'for the Benefits he had received by their Recommendation of him'. Nothing further is known of Bowen.

Bonnin & Morris: recovering quickly from the French and Indian Wars (the American phase of the Seven Years War,

1756–63), the colonies had enjoyed since mid-century a rising prosperity, an established society and a higher standard of living. Philadelphia in 1770 was a rich and fashionable center, likely to support a porcelain factory. 'The China-Works now erecting in Southwark' (January 1, 1770) was 'compleated, and in motion' the following July, and for just short of two years gave continual report in newspaper advertisements (Prime, *Arts & Crafts*, pp. 114–24).

The China Proprietors were Gouse Bonnin (from Antigua) and a Philadelphia Quaker named George Anthony Morris. The latter retired April/May 1771 and removed to North Carolina where he died two years later, while Bonnin in November 1772 was sulkily 'embarking for England without the least prospect of ever returning to this continent'.

They were financed by a £500 advance from the father of Dr James Mease (Barber, pp. 98–100), who got nothing in return but a blue-painted dinner service, from which one broken basket in the Worcester manner is all that survives (Philadelphia Museum). This piece and four others, all with a factory-mark *P* in blue, were the 'known' output of Bonnin & Morris as fully reported in *Antiques* for Jan. 1944, pp. 14–16, Sept. 1946, p. 166, Sept. 1950, p. 199 and Feb. 1951, p. 139. The teapot here (Plate 89A, B) is a later discovery.

From the evidence, their ware seems to have been a fine grade of white earthenware, though their 'first Emission of Porcelain' was announced in January 1771, and that same month in an appeal to the Assembly they described the 'Manufacture of Porcelain or China Earthen Ware ... a sample of it we respectfully submit'. Indeed, they achieved a translucent porcelain (the example in *Antiques*, Feb. 1951).

Their clay came from White-Clay Creek, near Wilmington (Barber, p. 99) and they advertised in July 1770 for 'any quantity of horses or beeves shank bones', implying the attempt to make bone-china. But in August 1772 Bonnin had 'lately made experiments with some clay presented by a Gentleman of Charles Town, South-Carolina'. Could this have been John Bartlam? Although a few years earlier, Richard Champion of Bristol had received (1765) a 'box of porcelain-earth' from his brother-in-law Caleb Lloyd of Charleston. The firm's first notice (January 1770) had referred to 'the famous factory in Bow, near London', as if this were their ideal.

In October 1770 'nine master workmen' arrived in Captain Osborne's ship. Three months later 'a quantity of Zaffer or zaffera' was wanted, and by July the factory could supply 'any Quantity of Blue and White Ware'. As their agent, Archibald M'Elroy in Second-Street was exposing a 'General Assortment of AMERICAN CHINA' in January 1771 and next September 'both useful and ornamental Enamelled China'. The factory in January 1772 needed 'Painters, either in blue or enamel'.

Only their blue-printed wares are recognized today, such as a finely modeled sweet-meat dish (Plate 98c) found in New Jersey, or a teapot (Plate 98A, B) with charming *chinoiserie* and large initials *WP*. This latter came from a Philadelphia Quaker family in which it had always been known as 'the William Penn teapot', unaccountably, since the Proprietor was in his grave by 1718.

To the next name in American porcelains it is a leap of forty years. Mentioned in 1810 as 'of New Haven', a certain 'Henry Mead, physician' appeared in the New York directory for 1816–17. This was the alleged maker of a solitary all-white vase (Plate 19, Clement's *Our Pioneer Potters*) on the evidence of a paper label: *Finished in New York* 1816. A little late then, 'In 1819 the manufacture of Porcelain ... was commenced in New York by Dr H.Mead' (J.Leander Bishop, *History of American Manufactures*). No less confusing, the doctor's obituary notice (1843) said that 'he commenced at Jersey City'.

Records are far more satisfactory for the Jersey Porcelain & Earthenware Company, established December 1825 in Jersey City and sold in September 1828 to David Henderson. In 1826 this firm won a silver medal at the Franklin Institute, for the 'best china from American materials', though what competition might they have had? Fragments of hard-paste porcelain have been

unearthed on the factory site, and praise of a visitor to the factory in 1826 (Clement, p. 68) was for articles 'either of white biscuit, or of white and gold in the French style'. Dr Barber in 1902 described one gold-banded white bowl 'made in 1826', then in the Trumbull-Prime collection at Princeton but now lost.

Tucker porcelain: coming now to the first really successful chinaworks we need little more than to correct and abbreviate the oft-told accounts of that well documented Philadelphia enterprise of 1826–38, Tucker porcelains. More than half a century ago, Dr

FIG. 1. Tucker porcelain

Barber devoted a chapter (pp. 126–53) to these well appreciated wares, *Antiques*, June 1928, pp. 480–4, adding further reports.

Born of a prosperous Quaker family, William Ellis Tucker (1800–32) began in 1826 his earnest experiments in porcelain making, at the Old Water-Works building in Philadelphia. That year he bought (in brief partnership with one John Bird) a property near Wilmington, Delaware, that yielded feldspar, and another at 'Mutton Hollow in the state of New Jersey' that provided kaolin or blue-clay. In 1827 his porcelains won a silver medal at the 4th Franklin Institute exhibition, and in 1828 another, for ware comparing with 'the best specimens of French China'.

Examples of his earlier work are three pieces c. 1827 (Plate 99A) with painted scenes not in the familiar sepia, but darker brown. A cup showing the *Dam and Waterworks at*

Fairmount is apparently after the Thomas Birch drawing published 1824 (the same used on blue-printed Staffordshire pottery of 1825–30, Nos. 249–50 and 535–6 in Mrs Larsen's book). Seen here on a plate and cup, the *Old Schuylkill Bridge* occurs also on a cordate scent bottle owned by a Tucker descendant (*Antiques*, Oct. 1936, p. 167). Again the subject (Plate 110B) is used on blue Staffordshire and in very rich taste was employed on a Hemphill jug of about 1835 (*Antiques*, June 1928, p. 481).

In 1828 a younger brother, Thomas Tucker (born 1812), became an apprentice, and William himself formed a partnership (1828–9) with John Hulme, as Tucker & Hulme. From this time came a large tea service factory-marked and dated 1828 (*Antiques*, Oct. 1933, p. 134) with typical 'spider' border in gold, wrongly said to enjoy 'the distinction of being the first *complete sett* of china manufactured in this country'.

In 1831 Tucker established still another partnership Tucker & Hemphill (with Alexander Hemphill) and that year his porcelains won a silver medal at the American Institute, New York. William Tucker died in 1832, and from 1833–6 the factory was continued by Alexander's father, Judge Joseph Hemphill, with Thomas Tucker as manager. The Hemphill period displayed rich taste, with enamel painting in Sèvres style and a lavish use of gold. Its masterpiece was a large vase (Plate 100A) made 1835 by Thomas Tucker, the gilt-bronze handles designed by Friedrich Sachse and cast by C.Cornelius & Sons of Philadelphia.

The first quality of work about 1835 is seen (Plate 99B, c) in a mug with gold scrollwork and colored scene entitled *Baltimore* in black script underfoot. Five cups from a set of *Presidents* (Plate 100B) must be dated toward the factory's close, since Jackson's portrait is from the *National Portrait Gallery of Distinguished Americans*, published 1834–6. Judge Hemphill retired in 1837 and Thomas Tucker rented the factory a year, closing it in 1838.

After a curious lapse of a decade, when porcelains were wholly neglected, five factories deserve notice as producers of such ware on a commercial scale.

Bennington: in 1843 Julius Norton, a Vermont potter, brought from England one John Harrison, a modeler at the Copeland works, where the year before a waxy white porcelain called Parian or Statuary Ware had been perfected (*see* Glossary). Harrison's experiments from October 1843 to mid-1845 were interrupted by a disastrous fire, and he returned to Stoke. During 1845–7 the firm of Norton & Fenton set this work aside; but from 1847–50 the reorganized Lyman & Fenton was producing successful white wares, including Parian. An example is the Daisy jug (Plate 101B) in white porcelain, showing the Fenton's Works mark of 1847–8, though variants of this design continued for some years.

With new financing and expansion in 1851–2, Christopher Webber Fenton developed blue-and-white porcelains (Plate 101C) or rarely tan, still rarer the green-and-white. Much work was unsigned, but the familiar *U.S.P.* ribbon-mark of the United States Pottery Co. (1853–8) is found 'principally upon porcelain pitchers and vases, both the white and blue-and-white, and upon some Parian pieces' (Spargo, *The A.B.C.*, p. 19).

From the latter years of the factory, which closed in 1858, came whole dinner or tea services of heavy gold-banded porcelain (Spargo, *Potters of Bennington*, Plate XXVII). Kaolin had been obtained from Monkton, Vermont. Pitchers displayed at the Crystal Palace exhibition in New York (1853–4) were 'made of the flint from Vermont and Massachusetts, the feldspar from New Hampshire, and the china clays from Vermont and South Carolina.'

Greenpoint: first of two factories at Greenpoint (now Brooklyn), was Charles Cartlidge & Co., operating 1848–56. The proprietor was a Staffordshire (Burslem) man, who at once brought over his brother-in-law Josiah Jones to model 'biscuit busts of celebrated Americans'. A 9-inch likeness of General Zachary Taylor in 1848 (Barber, pp. 446–7) was followed by Daniel Webster, John Marshall and others, in what the firm always described as bisque porcelain. From buttons and cameos the firm's output ranged to inkstands and chessmen, cane heads and endless other novelties, which at the Crystal Palace in 1853 won a silver medal 'for the excellence of the porcelain body and the gilding'.

Second of the Greenpoint enterprises was that of William Boch & Brother, founded 1850, which exhibited at the Crystal Palace as makers of door hardware and bone-china table goods. Thomas Carl Smith who became manager in 1857, acquired the shaky business in 1861, reopened it as the Union Porcelain Works in 1862 and by 1864/5 had changed over to hard-paste porcelain.

Karl Müller came to the factory in 1874 as chief designer and modeler, creating many once famous subjects eyed nowadays with disfavor, and others of quality and virtue; among the latter was a bisque porcelain pitcher *The Poets* (Plate 101A) which in 1876 was a presentation piece to E. J. Brockett. Finely molded heads of *Milton, Ossian, Shakspeare* (*sic*), *Dante, Homer* and *Virgil* are seen with trophies and allegorical figures above and below. To the red-painted factory mark is added an impressed (later, printed) bird's head, the symbol adopted in 1876.

Other porcelain: of minor importance is the Southern Porcelain Manufacturing Co., established 1856 at Kaolin, South Carolina, by William H. Farrar who had been a Bennington stockholder. Numerous potters followed him here, the modeler Josiah Jones as manager in 1857, when the Cartlidge factory closed, and next year (when Bennington also failed) Fenton was there briefly on his way to Peoria, Illinois, where he built an unsuccessful works. Until fire destroyed the factory in 1863/4 only 'a fair porcelain' was produced at Kaolin, such as the coarsely designed *Corn* pitchers of 1859–61 (Barber, pp. 188–9). But to this site six miles from Augusta, potters were still attracted as they had been in Duché's time more than a century before.

From an inconspicuous beginning in Trenton, New Jersey, in 1863 there grew two years later the firm of Ott & Brewer, whose workshop, called the 'Etruria Pottery', proved the training ground for several potters of stature. For his own part, John Hart

Brewer produced in 1875–6 a series of fine Parian portrait busts of Washington, Franklin and U.S. Grant, modeled by Isaac Broome (Newark Museum, Clement's *Pottery and Porcelain of New Jersey*, Nos. 217–19 and Plate 44). The firm, dissolved in 1893, is especially remembered as a maker of American Belleek in the 1880s.

One of the Ott & Brewer apprentices was Walter Scott Lenox, later their decoration manager, who in 1889 formed the Ceramic Art Company, and in 1896 established the distinguished firm of Lenox, Inc. – since 1918 known as the makers of White House state services, and porcelains for the American embassies.

MOLDED WARES

The later porcelains (Plate 101) and the wares that follow (Plates 102, 103, 104) were of a new order. The factory period had arrived about 1830, product of an industrial revolution that showed a parallel in mechanization of the glass industry, as freeblown glass gave way to pressed. In the ceramics field, new types of pottery were no longer thrown on the potter's wheel but shaped in molds. Forms were now created by designers and mass-produced by professional workmen; the simple potshop was transformed into a factory, where output was large and the price small.

Parian: being made from liquid clay, Parian ware had to be poured into molds. Bennington had been first to introduce 'this exquisite material, the happy substitute for marble in statuettes' – indeed, in 1852 had advertised it by the latter name, as 'Figures in Parian Marble'. The snowy ware was everywhere a favorite after the 1850s, made from Vermont to the Carolinas, or in Ohio by William Bloor of East Liverpool in 1860. And so much was its formula varied, one often doubts whether to call an example Parian or bisque porcelain.

But fear and outrage had swept the workers, at seeing 'the old usages of the trade broken up' (Wedgwood and Ormsbee, p. 95). Labor strikes in 1834–43 were followed by a panic of Staffordshire workmen in 1845–6, when they thought their livelihood threatened by the invention of pot-making machines.

The nonpareil of all molded work was a ten-foot monument made 1851–2 at Bennington and displayed 1853 at the Crystal Palace (Barber, Fig. 74). In three tiers of marbled or 'scroddled' ware, of the color-flecked Fenton's Enamel, and of brown-streaked Rockingham, it was topped with the Parian figure of a 'woman in the act of presenting the Bible to an infant'. Just below, a portrait bust also in Parian represented Mr Fenton himself, peeking through a classic colonnade.

In America, David Henderson of Jersey City, who has been called 'the Wedgwood of America', was pioneer in the manufacture of molded wares. His fine buff stoneware jug marked *Uncle Toby*/1829 was advertised as *Toby Philipot* (sic) in 1830. A very similar but larger one (Plate 102B) was made 1838–45 at the Salamander Works (1825–96) in Woodbridge, New Jersey. This is a jug of rich chestnut-brown color with yellow-glazed interior. Pictured alongside it is the Daniel Greatbach model with grapevine handle, made at Bennington, with normal Rockingham glaze but mis-marked *Fenton's Enamel*/*Patented* 1849.

Rockingham: this was the common utility ware made by everyone from the 1840s to 1900, a yellowware dappled or streaked with lustrous manganese brown glaze. Its quality ranged from coarse splattered yellow to a rich brown tortoise shell, and this ware was used for every sort of article, doorknobs or pudding pans, hound-handled jugs or lamp bases, cuspidors or picture frames.

Little was marked, and 'Bennington' as a generic name is wrongly applied to wares the bulk of which were made elsewhere, principally at East Liverpool and down the Ohio River, or by the Bennetts of Pittsburgh and Baltimore, by a hundred factories large and small. At Bennington, Julius Norton first made Rockingham or 'flint' glaze (as it was generally called) in 1841. Henderson had produced it in 1829: 'Flint Ware both embossed and plain', in what the New York

Commercial Advertiser called 'elegant pitchers ... in a new style [which] if not too cheap will be accounted handsome'.

As an improvement on quiet brown Rockingham, a brilliant glaze flecked and streaked with colors was patented by Lyman, Fenton & Co. in November 1849 and examples carried a special *Fenton's Enamel* mark (Spargo, *The A.B.C.*, p. 21, mark D). Oddly, this *1849* mark is found also on common Rockingham, or even on white Parian, and continued in use all through the U.S. Pottery Co. period (1853–8).

This color-flecked glaze was not new; Fenton's patent only referred to a way of producing it with powdered colors. If an urn (Plate 102A) and the famous lion (Plate 102C) are examples of the best Bennington work, Fenton's enamel was widely pirated, being produced at East Liverpool as early as 1852 (Ramsay, p. 76). Pairs of Bennington lions in plain Rockingham or *1849* enamel, made with or without the platform and showing either a curly or the sanded 'cole-slaw' mane, appeared 1851–2 and are attributed to Daniel Greatbach, though he did not arrive at Bennington until December 1851 or January 1852, remaining as chief modeler until the factory closed (Spargo, *Bennington Potters*, pp. 227–8).

PRINTED WARES

Doubtless because the Staffordshire and Liverpool makers supplied such a torrent of cheap and attractive printed pottery, in an endless range of patterns and colors, the development of printed wares made scarcely a beginning here. True, a 'rolling press, for copper-plate printing; and other articles *made use of* in the China Factory' were advertised August 1774 when the Bonnin & Morris properties were offered. Apparently it was their intention to produce Worcester-type porcelains with printed blue decoration, but no examples are known today, if indeed they were made at all.

Not until 1839–43 are American-made subjects encountered (Clement, *Our Pioneer Potters*, Plates 10–13; the same as Nos. 128–32 in Newark Museum catalogue *Pottery and*

Porcelain of New Jersey), all four from the Henderson works, which since 1833 had been called the American Pottery Manufacturing Co.

In 1839 the pattern *Canova* was printed in light blue, cribbed from a design by John Ridgway of Hanley. The United States eagle and shield occurs on 6½-inch jugs also in light blue. In transfer print with added colors, the *Landing of Gen-Lafayette/at Castle Garden, New-York/16th August 1824* is seen on a larger jug and footed punchbowl at the New-York Historical Society, the same jug with a 15½-inch oval cistern appearing No. 243 in the Van Sweringen sale of 1938 at Parke-Bernet Galleries. In *Antiques*, May 1931, p. 361, this view is assigned to 1843, when historic Castle Garden (formerly Fort Clinton) was leased to Christopher Heiser.

Pictured here (Plate 103B) is a black-printed W.H.HARRISON memorial jug made in 1841, when the ninth president died after one month in the White House. Below the repeated portraits of Harrison (from the J.R. Lambdin portrait, engraved by R.W.Dodson and published 1836) is shown the American eagle; above is the 'log cabin' symbol of the Harrison-Tyler presidential campaign, with *The Ohio Farmer*. When the same subject was issued a year before, during that campaign against the New York aristocrat Martin Van Buren, the log cabin was lettered *To Let in 1841*.

The cabin so lettered, and the portrait entitled *Harrison & Reform*, occur on Staffordshire tea ware or copper-lustred mugs, the former marked *Manufactured/for Rob[t] H. Miller/ALEXANDRIA. D.C.*, an importer who advertised October 30, 1840, that he was expecting 'supplies of ware with Harrison and Log Cabin engravings, from designs sent out to the Potteries by himself' (*Antiques*, June 1944, p. 295, and Feb. 1945, p. 120).

The Henderson jug carries a black-printed mark AM. POTTERY/MANUF[G] C[O]/JERSEY CITY, and for it (says Lura W.Watkins) 'printing plates were executed by Thomas Pollock, an American engraver'.

Slightly earlier (1837-8) is a blue-printed creamware jar for snuff (Plate 103A) made to order of Hezekiah Starr, a tobacconist at No. 27 Calvert Street, Baltimore. Its mark *Clews's Manufacturer's* is also pictured.

James Clews the English potter had a factory at Cobridge (Burslem) which 'was noted for its cream-colored ware' in the 1820s, but to American collectors is chiefly known as a source of transfer-printed pottery showing American-historical views. When the J. & R. Clews factory closed in 1836, James (*c*. 1786-1856) came to this country and at Louisville, Kentucky, found the firm Vodrey & Lewis, makers of creamware since 1829.

Clews, being 'a man of fine presence and a fluent talker', persuaded Jacob Lewis and others to back him; the Louisville factory was closed, and a new Indiana Pottery Company established January 1837 across the river at Troy, Indiana. Neither the workmen nor the Ohio River Valley clays suited him, and after disappointing efforts to make creamware in 1837-8 he returned to England. The factory under various proprietors made yellow and Rockingham wares until finally demolished in 1875.

Our pot for *Macacbau, Scotch & Rappee SNUFF* (Plate 103A) is probably not unlike those creamware 'pickle, pomatum & druggist pots' made 1798 by J.Mouchet in New York. Another nearer its own time and area is the 10-inch brown-glazed jar, also found in Indiana, made for the tobacconist H. Thayer and carrying the mark of a Cincinnati maker *Franklin Factory/1834/S.Quigley* (*Antiques*, Aug. 1928, p. 162).

Only one more example of American printed ware deserves mention, a late blue platter, *Pickett's Charge, Gettysburg* (Ramsay, Fig. 86), with oakleaf border picturing four generals who served that day in July 1863. Its blue eagle mark is for Edwin Bennett of Baltimore, who worked 1841 at East Liverpool with his brother James (he was formerly with Clews at Troy) and from 1846 operated his own factory in Baltimore. His *Pickett's Charge* appeared in 1870 and was re-issued 1901.

LATE WARES

It might be felt that Rogers Groups (Plate 104A) have no place here, being not of fired clay but plaster casts taken from clay models. But in their day these enormously popular figure groups were fondly accepted as ceramic sculpture, an 'Art' expression that filled bare space in the Victorian parlor. And indeed they exerted a large influence upon potters who then produced Parian or other figure work.

John Rogers (1829–1904) created his patented story-telling groups in New York, from 1859–93. Cast in reddish plaster and painted a sad putty color, these low-priced groups were issued in vast editions, in 1886 *The Elder's Daughter* (Plate 104A) 'weight 100 lbs packed, price $12'. If sentimental, obvious and sometimes silly, the subjects were well modeled; and their themes were from the Civil War, from domestic life of the time, or popular legends. Collections may now be studied at the New-York Historical Society and at the Essex Institute, Salem.

Majolica: during this same period, a new pottery called Majolica won wide favor; a coarse earthen body with colored lead glazes, it appeared in useful wares, leaf-shaped dishes, and ornamental work of every description. In 1851 Minton had exhibited Majolica at the Crystal Palace, and Wedgwood was producing it by 1860. Meanwhile, American potters adopted it; Edwin Bennett by 1853 at Baltimore, and Carr & Morrison of New York in 1853–5. In the 1880s it was a staple of potters everywhere, from the Hampshire Pottery (James Taft's) at Keene, New Hampshire, to the Bennett and Morley firms in East Liverpool. Best known is *Etruscan Majolica*, made 1879–90 by Griffen, Smith & Hill at Phoenixville, Chester County, Pennsylvania.

An excellent example of Etruscan Majolica (Plate 104D) shows surprising likeness to the 'Colly flower tea potts' imported a century earlier (Boston, 1771). Developed 1754–9 by Wedgwood when a junior partner to Whieldon, cauliflower ware had a vogue 1760–80. The match for our later teapot is seen in the Burnap Collection (No. 320, catalogue, 1953, the Nelson-Atkins Gallery of Art, Kansas City, Mo.). According to John Ramsay 'the first cauliflower teapot' was made by James Carr in New York, Dr Barber adding that Carr

& Morrison (1853–88) only made Majolica 'for a period of about two years', 1853–5.

American Belleek: belonging with the porcelains, last of the late wares is American Belleek, a thin, highly translucent, feldspathic body which is cousin to Parian, finished with a pale pearly glaze. Irish Belleek (*see* Glossary) was seen at the Centennial Exhibition in 1876, and excited the admiration of American potters.

Some time between 1880 and 1882 the Trenton firm of Ott & Brewer brought over the potter William Bromley, who had developed Irish Belleek, and by 1882 produced 'the first piece of belleek porcelain made in America' (a square tray, No. 223 in Newark Museum, *Pottery and Porcelain of New Jersey*). A fancy shell-shaped pitcher (*ibid.*, No. 233) marked *W.S.L./1887* was produced at their works by Walter Lenox, who later brought two Belleek workmen to his own Ceramic Art Co. (1889–96) and further developed the ware at Lenox, Inc., from 1896. Edwin Bennett had achieved the production of Belleek by 1886 at Baltimore, and the Columbian Art Pottery (established 1893) made it by 1895 at Trenton.

Perhaps best of the American Belleek was 'Lotus Ware' (Plate 104B, C), a product of Knowles, Taylor & Knowles at East Liverpool, 1891–8. In 1887 Isaac W. Knowles had brought over Joshua Poole, manager of the Irish factory, and before 1889 made a finely molded and fragile ware that in the 1890s earned much favor.

Belleek and Majolica, or the Art tiles and 'studio wares' that flourished alongside Rookwood from the 1880s, cannot yet be classed as antiques. Yet with Tiffany glass and other late work of quality, they have gained wide acceptance among collectors. In 1879 the 3rd edition of W. C. Prime's *Pottery and Porcelain of All Times and Nations* (which devoted a total of six pages to 'Pottery and Porcelain in the United States') began with these words: 'Ten years ago there were probably not ten collectors of pottery and porcelain in the United States. Today there are perhaps ten thousand. ...' What would he think of the range and vigor of collecting today?

Part II. Anglo-American Pottery

EXCEPT for common wares produced here by countless small and mostly forgotten potbakers, the varied wants of the American colonists had been supplied almost wholly by British potters. Meissen or so-called Dresden figurines were known in the luxury trade, or even more those charming China-Trade porcelains nowadays called by the misnomer Chinese 'Lowestoft'. Rhenish stonewares had long answered a need for certain kitchen and dairy or tavern vessels. But until the time of the Revolution, English makers suffered little competition.

Danger signs appeared in the decade before 1775. Wedgwood's excellent creamware was very soon imitated by American potters; stoneware of a good grade was produced along Cheesequake Creek in northern New Jersey. At the Philadelphia chinaworks of Bonnin & Morris a brief but most noteworthy attempt at making 'porcelains' marked the years 1770–2. With what success we do not now know, potters from Boston to Salem, North Carolina, were claiming to supply Whieldon-type wares with the mottled tortoise shell glaze, or Leeds-type pottery with colored 'shell edge'. Seeing their own sales diminish, the English potters had reason to worry about a political unrest expressed in non-importation resolutions and a mounting boycott.

True, the American manufactures made small headway. Most persons fixedly believed in the superiority of any imported wares; the market for American output was a reluctant one. From the number of china menders' advertisements noted at this time, it is obvious that people clung to their outworn articles in a time of scarcity. Moreover, when war broke in 1775 the potters here had enormous difficulties; money and materials were wanting, the British occupations and naval blockade were a frustration, and younger workmen had gone into military service or those of royalist disposition were 'in exile' in Canada or the West Indies. No really vigorous and lasting growth in American manufactures would occur until those again unsettled years that preceded the War of 1812.

Farsighted and aggressive English potters, even during Revolutionary wartime, were ready with the first of those many wares now called Anglo-American Pottery; merchandise not only suiting the taste of the American market, but particularly addressed to it. Rebel muskets were still smoking when Wedgwood (who openly expressed sympathy with the colonists' cause) in 1779/80 produced basalt portrait medallions of Washington and Franklin, and in 1782 his sharpest competitor Henry Neale of Hanley offered likenesses even better. The Staffordshire men saw no objection to providing subjects that proclaimed the ideals of Liberty and Independence, or to picturing a frigate saucily labeled *The Trueblooded Yankee* (*reverse* of Plate 105D).

And just at this time things had been made far easier. New roads were built across Staffordshire in the 1760s, and from 1765–76 (largely by Wedgwood's energetic efforts) the cutting of canals to connect with the ports of Liverpool and Bristol reduced freight rates to one-seventh the previous cost. A flood of attractive wares that greatly appealed to American pride could now readily reach this eager market.

Liverpool: first of the Anglo-American wares were black-printed creamware jugs, plates and bowls showing portraits of our heroes and statesmen, maps of the colonies, naval scenes even of *America triumphing over Britain*. Allegorical figures of Freedom standing knee-deep in military devices (*An Emblem of America*) displayed verses addressed to Wisdom, Justice and Independence. The eagle adopted as our national emblem in 1782 (Plate 105D) appeared promptly and often, with flags and other patriotic motifs or framed with a chain carrying the names of the rebel colonies. Such jugs as one saluting *The Crooked But interesting Town of BOSTON* (Plate 105C) catered to regional pride.

McCauley's *Liverpool Transfer Designs* (see Books for Further Reading) records about three hundred of these subjects. Altogether they are known as Liverpool ware, and indeed this class of black-printed pottery (called 'the jet enamell'd') derived from the printed tiles made by Sadler & Green at Liverpool since the 1750s. When in 1756 these gentlemen applied for a patent, they had done such printing 'for upwards of seven years'.

Wedgwood and others for a while sent their fragile pottery the fifty perilous miles to Liverpool, for printing and return; but in 1763, Wedgwood 'bought the right to do his own printing' (Graham and Wedgwood, *Wedgwood: A Living Tradition*, p. 95) and the trade gradually became centered in Staffordshire. Indistinguishable unless marked, which is very seldom, Liverpool-type examples are sometimes impressed HERCULANEUM (for the Herculaneum Works at Liverpool itself, 1794–1841) or carry the signature of Staffordshire engravers, *F.Morris/Shelton* on jugs dated 1804, or jugs until the 1820s marked *Bentley, Wear & Bourne, Engravers and Printers, Shelton, Staffordshire* (Plate 106A).

The typical Liverpool jug from *c.* 1780 well into the nineteenth century was of gently curving barrel shape (Plates 105C, D) which about 1800 was used for *Peace, Plenty & Independence* designs, or for *Free Trade & Sailors' Rights*, that hinted the oncoming War of 1812. A nation in mourning for Washington's death (1799) could not buy enough *Apotheosis* designs, or memorial subjects inscribed: *Washington in Glory, America in Tears*.

Staffordshire: from about 1800 to 1825 a second generation of rather different jugs and plates appeared, made now in Staffordshire and of lower globular shape with a collar (Plate 106C). Wedgwood had introduced this shape as early as 1770, but it now became the standard one for a new set of heroes and victories furnished by the War of 1812. The subjects were mostly printed in black, sometimes in sepia or carmine, and often showed added decoration in pink or lilac lustre (Plates 105A, B, 106A, C).

For these and other printed subjects hereinafter discussed, much of our information is taken by permission from Mrs Larsen's unapproached *American Historical Views on Staffordshire China*, edition 1950 (*see* Books for Further Reading) and the Larsen checklist numbers given here.

In greater part, the War of 1812 subjects were drawn from *The Naval Monument*, published 1816. But the black-printed Clews plate with General Pike's portrait (Plate 106B) is after a Thomas Gimbrede engraving of 1814, the likeness also printed in blue or with a berry-pattern relief border, and found as well on yellow-bodied or Sunderland lustred jugs (Larsen Nos. 628, 782).

Naval engagements of 1812 and 1813 are pictured by Bentley, Wear & Bourne on a jug (Plate 106A) with pale green ground, its collar in marbled purple lustre. Here the victories of the brig *Enterprise* off the coast of Maine, and Stephen Decatur's frigate *United States* near Madeira (Larsen Nos. 739, 788), are recorded by the Staffordshire potter with seemingly no embarrassment. The same with a Bainbridge-Brown portrait jug (Plate 106C, Larsen Nos. 725, 727) representing American naval heroes who could not have been British favorites.

Against this avalanche of subjects so timely and enticing, it was with small result that our newspapers carried constant appeals to buy American-made goods. Advertisers cried in vain the 'Original American Manufacture' of their pottery, praising its quality and cheapness, nor was much benefit secured to them from the import tariffs of 1816, 1818 and 1824, or the so-called Tariff of Abominations in 1828. More English wares were imported monthly in 1825 than yearly in the 1790s.

If things were not bad enough already, in 1824 the aged Marquis de Lafayette returned for a triumphal tour of America, re-visiting the scenes of the Revolution, kneeling at the shrines now erected to his departed friend Washington. He was idolized and fêted everywhere, and any mementoes of Lafayette became a rage. And again showing excellent foresight, English potters almost beat him to these shores with an assortment of dishware dedicated to his fame.

Encircling a likeness of this popular idol, the words *Welcome Lafayette, the Nation's Guest/and Our Country's Glory* are seen on a small blue-printed plate with frilled or shell edge (Plate 107D). Born in 1757 and now approaching his seventieth year, Lafayette is pictured here by Clews (Larsen No. 619, from the 'Yorktown Portrait' by Geille) as a young man in Washington's time.

On a copper-lustred jug with pail-shaped body (Plate 107B) the Marquis appears again, wearing the Continental uniform and crowned with laurel by the figures of *Victory* and *Fame*, and indeed he was so crowned, at a ceremony marking his 1824 visit to Yorktown. This subject paired with the *Surrender of Cornwallis* (Plate 107A) was many times repeated on 4- to 9-inch jugs of two shapes and on 7- to 10-inch vases, Larsen Nos. 736, 765.

Once more, Lafayette is seen in distinguished company on a pair of mottled pink-lustre bowls (Plates 105A, B) by a controversial 'Ric^d. Hall & Son', Larsen No. 742 and comments pp. 254-5. Franklin is pictured from the Cochin 'fur cap' portrait of 1777, Washington from Stuart's 'Athenaeum' portrait, and Lafayette after Ary Scheffer. Inside is a handsome *Shipwrights' Arms* and on one side the eagle of the Great Seal of the United States, lettered *Republicans [Republics] are not always ungrateful* (quoting an Act of Congress that conferred benefits upon Lafayette).

Nor are these bowls to be confused with a group of London-made fakes very closely similar, made about fifty years ago. Coarser in quality and often with exaggerated black-stained crackle, the spurious pieces (bowls, cups and saucers, jugs, small portrait plaques) are sufficiently noticed (pp. 136-8 in Mc-Cauley) and appear as Nos. 155-62 and 187-9 in the Pennsylvania Museum catalogue to their 1916 *Exhibition of Fakes and Reproductions*. Examples were also pictured (ex-collection Lanier Washington, 1922) as Nos. 19-21 in the catalogue to the Hayes-MacDonald-Whitwell sale, October 30, 1930, in New York.

But the printed wares were only one department of Staffordshire manufactures. Probably the earliest Anglo-American item was made by Wedgwood & Bentley in 1777, the black basalt *Rattlesnake Seal* with motto *Don't Tread on Me*, taken from the first American Revolutionary flag of a year before (a daring talisman, not offered for sale but given to sympathizers, Wedgwood saying: 'I think it will be best to keep unchristian articles for Private Trade'). Later in the century, Prattware jugs showed the portraits of several American notables in colored relief; modelers from Ralph and Aaron Wood until Victorian days were making statuettes of Franklin and Washington, sometimes with their names exchanged; every imaginable subject that might appeal to American pride and patriotism was offered.

From this endless list, one example will suffice here, a blue-and-white pottery jug (in cheap imitation of Wedgwood's jasper ware) that is found in many variations. Its subjects are on one side the American eagle (Plate 107C) and on the *reverse* a Liberty head framed in laurel branches, an arc of stars above. The pattern had been found in tea wares of about 1800 (e.g. two sugarbowls with uncolored reliefs, *Antiques*, Oct. 1933, pp. 123-4, and Nov. 1937, p. 228) made in David Dunderdale's factory at Castleford, near Leeds. In these the eagle and Liberty head face now left, now right, with the eagle taken 'from the $10 gold-piece of 1798' or again as found 'on U.S. gold coins in 1795-1806'.

Jugs with the vineleaf collar may show light or dark blue grounds, or even copper lustre (one mistakenly described as blue, *Antiques*, Mar. 1939, p. 117). Their eagles may be splendid birds crowned properly with stars and cloud puffs, or starveling sparrowlike fowl, such as the one illustrated. In all the varied lot, it appears useless to attempt any dating from resemblance to a certain coin, from the number of stars used above Liberty's head, or by the shifting of arrows from the eagle's dexter to sinister claw (a change enacted 1805 by the Congress). These slight alterations did not concern the Staffordshire potter, who innocently copied whatever model came to hand. In fact, that the jug illustrated dates rather later is shown by a large feature below its spout, paired cornucopias, clasped hands, the caduceus (as a symbol of Commerce) and motto *Peace & Plenty*, altogether indicating the treaty of Ghent (1814) which ended the War of 1812.

See also section on 'Historical Ware', p. 151.

Gaudy Dutch: all the wares so far mentioned were to suit literal-minded persons who wanted a picture, a symbol, a phrase. But there were others who looked for something prettier. Such was the well named 'Gaudy Dutch', sure to have an enormous success from about 1810–30.

Gaudy Dutch pottery (Plate 108A, B, C, D) made no narrow appeal to pride or victory, but was addressed to the spritely taste of a particular folk, the color-loving Pennsylvania-Germans of southeastern Pennsylvania. Here was a fat, smiling farmland that provided bountiful and famous tables; the German folk lived well. And who could imagine golden *Pannhas* (scrapple) on a plain plate, or *Lattwoerick* (applebutter) in anything but a flowered bowl?

Gaudy Dutch was painted in underglaze blue and with many-colored overglaze enamels, using a bright yellow enamel in lieu of gold, in simple fashion, imitating the effect of Imari-patterned porcelains made 1780–1820 at Derby and Worcester. In its day practically unknown outside the Dutch-country, this was a ware exactly suiting prosperous and substantial folk who could pay for something nice (it was twice-fired and hand painted) but would regard a use of porcelains as pretentious.

Sixteen patterns plus many variants are listed, pp. 67–74, in Laidacker, Part I (*see* Books for Further Reading), of which nine are pictured here. *Butterfly*, *Urn* and *War Bonnet* are the patterns most wanted, in that order; commonest designs are *Grape*, *Oyster* and *Single Rose*. But common doesn't mean cheap; so great a leap in favor has Gaudy Dutch taken in recent years, single examples may fetch as much as a set of porcelain.

Found in plates and tea ware, Gaudy Dutch with its frantic mixtures of orange and pink, blue and bright yellow, green and red, was quite apparently a product of numerous workshops, the standard patterns occurring with little variations according to the maker. Very rarely are there any marks at all; Laidacker reports only the marks of two Burslem potters, RILEY (for John & Richard Riley, working 1802–27) and WOOD (Enoch Wood & Sons, working from 1819). The mark Riley is found on *Primrose*, *Zinnia*, *Single Rose* and *Strawflower* examples, and a Wood mark is recorded for the patterns *Grape* and *Single Rose*.

Sometimes classed with the Gaudy Dutch wares is a family of three members all called *Strawberry*, all three popular, but (unlike Gaudy Dutch itself) not primarily made for this market. Translucent bone-china tea-sets with delicate painting of strawberry vines, sometimes also with pink-lustre added, had been seen since the early 1800s. Toward 1820 appeared another sort, now of thin pottery with molded relief of bright strawberries and leaves, the teapots with gadroon edges and of that boxy, saddled form so familiar in plain silver- or copper-lustred wares. Finally, a third type of *Strawberry* was made about 1820–35, enamel-painted with strawberries and large leaves (as in Gaudy Dutch, a thick enamel that flakes off easily) and any background space filled with hairlike tendrils. This last was obviously from the same shops that produced the 'dutch' types, and indeed on the shoulder of a jug or teapot (Laidacker, p. 75) one finds the rose-meander border that belongs to *King's Rose* (Plate 108C).

Gaudy Welsh and Gaudy Ironstone: not at all related to Gaudy Dutch except in name, two later British-made cottage wares have enjoyed fast-growing appreciation in recent years. Both occur in a varied range of flowered patterns, usually with added detail in copper-lustre or gilding. The so-called Gaudy Welsh was a translucent tea ware, made about 1830–45 in the Swansea area. The other was a dense and heavy whiteware now called Gaudy Ironstone, appearing 1850–65 in tea and dinner wares, showing perhaps the marks of the Staffordshire potters Thos. Walker or E. Walley (of Cobridge) and often the impressed words PEARL WHITE or IRONSTONE. Laidacker (Part I, pp. 83–5) tells something of these two pleasant types, which have received little other mention.

Spatterware: another large family of painted wares now enjoying high popularity is Spatter (Plate 109). Made 1820–50 for the

American trade, it was not, like Gaudy Dutch, intended to please a regional taste but found wide sale among simple folk from Maine to Pennsylvania or into the midwest. The body was a common soft pottery, or later a 'pearl ware' and still later a heavy ironstone, and its delightful range of patterns (nearly forty) will be seen in plates and tea or dinner ware, water jugs and platters, toilet sets of matching washbowl and jug. Great collections have been formed by Mrs J.Watson Webb at Shelburne, Vermont, and by Henry Francis du Pont at Winterthur, Delaware. Notice that the Frank Forrestall Adams collection was all found in Maine (*Antiquarian*, Oct. 1930) while the A.C. Williams collection (*Antiques*, April 1930) was assembled through the Ohio and Pennsylvania area.

Sponged or 'spattered' work was nothing new, but often seen in English delft chargers of the seventeenth century and first half of the eighteenth, with perhaps the painted figures of an Adam and Eve standing in shrubbery of sponged green color. The same effective work reappeared about 1800, in Leeds and Staffordshire pottery (Plate 109A, which shows a W E D G W O O D mark). From such pieces soon came the assortment of cottage wares known as Spatter, quaint in design, lively and sometimes garish in color.

Again in Laidacker (Part I, pp. 77–80) will be found a general discussion of Spatter, a checklist of patterns and the names of many makers who produced such work. Most popular patterns are the red *Schoolhouse* (Plate 109D) which also occurs in blue or green, the *Peafowl* (Plate 109C) in its numerous variants, and the familiar *Tulip* (Plate 109D). Typical of late but no less attractive designs is a set of plates with *Bird on a Fence* (Plate 109B).

Staffordshire Pots and Potters (G.W. and F.A. Rhead, 1906) illustrates (p. 240) a group of *Peafowl* Spatter pieces, calling them 'sponged' ware, and takes pains to identify four trouble-making potters all named William Adams. Three cousins and the son of one, constantly confused, they worked at Tunstall, Burslem, Cobridge and Stoke. It was the last, William Adams (1798–1865) 'of Greenfield', whose mark A D A M S is frequently found on Spatter

made *c.* 1825–40 at the Stoke and Tunstall works.

Historical ware: but more than for any others, the first and faithful love of collectors has been for *Old Blue*, or *Historical Blue*. This was a cheap, transfer-printed picture pottery made through the 1820s, in medium to richly dark cobalt blue; if the ware itself was poor and blemished, any defects would be well covered. From 1830 well into the next decade came a further flood of subjects now in light colors, the popular 'pink Staffordshire' (carmine) or a light blue, sepia, black or green, even in two colors, one for the pattern and another for its border. Altogether there were about eight hundred subjects, which have enjoyed the unflagging attention of collectors for eighty years.

The literature of American-historical printed Staffordshire is extensive, from *The China Hunter's Club* in 1878 to the Earle, Barber and luxurious Halsey books at the end of the century, with reprints of several books to satisfy a new generation of collectors in the 1920s. The great omni-gatherum of all this mixed and scattered information did not appear until 1950, when a second edition of the superb *American Historical Views on Staffordshire China* was completed by Mrs Larsen.

This pottery printed in monochrome was of course more profitable than Gaudy Dutch or other handpainted wares, nor was its want of colors much noticed. The subjects were themselves interesting, and the rich blue looked so fine with pewter, or the pink and green with lacy pressed glassware of their own time. Enormous quantities were produced, certain subjects only occurring on jugs or sets of plates, others in tea services, two or three in complete dinner services (e.g. the Clews *Landing of Lafayette* or Rogers *Boston State House*).

A long list of Staffordshire makers are easily recognized from the distinctive borders they used (only seldom were these pirated, or the designs sold) and the same men issued countless English or Continental views, though for these the demand is now far less.

Attempting to describe the range of

American-historical subjects, one wonders what was forgotten. Everything is here, from handsome armorial designs (Plate 111A) to the picture of a toylike coal train (Plate 110B). If surely few American villagers of the 1820s had ever heard of the famed mansion *Harewood House* (Plate 110A) they could buy instead a view of the *Saw-Mill at Center Harbor, New Hampshire*. Indeed, it was remarkable what people wanted, perhaps a pictorial record of calamities, like *The Great Fire of the City of New York* (1835). Such titles as the Clews *Insane Asylum, New York*, or a Ridgway *Deaf & Dumb Asylum, Hartford*, which (oddly) was from the series called *Beauties of America*, represented an interest in the new architectural styles.

Views of towns and cities might be handsome, as Andrew Stevenson's platter, *New York* (Plate 111B, Larsen No. 97) from the W.G.Wall painting published 1823, or showed remote villages like *Vevay* in Indiana, or the hamlet *Riceborough, Georgia*. J. & R. Clews about 1830 pictured the hustling midwest town of *Pittsburgh* (Larsen Nos. 159–60) and this view on a platter was split to provide two plates, the left half with steamboat *Pennsylvania* (Plate 111C).

Historic events ran a gamut from *Landing of Columbus* (in a series of fifteen scenes made 1830 by Wm. Adams, apparently first of the light-color subjects, Larsen Nos. 345–59) to a *Landing of the Fathers at Plymouth* (Plate 110B) or in 1824 the *Landing of Gen. La Fayette at Castle Garden, New York* (Larsen No. 125).

Heroes and celebrities if not individually represented had one more chance of being seen, in the Medallion Series, prepared 1825 by Ralph Stevenson and his younger brother Andrew, to celebrate the opening of the Erie Canal. This was a large assortment of American views with a few English ones thrown in (Larsen Nos. 540–605) which on plates and platters now displayed a sort of special *collage*, with extra pictures inserted. The unique oakleaf-bordered platter *Harewood House* (Plate 110A, Larsen No. 549), carries an inserted *Entrance of the Erie Canal into the Hudson at Albany*, or sometimes the views at Little Falls or Rochester were used. Here in the border above are portrait medallions of

Jefferson, Washington, Lafayette and Governor Clinton. Small plates showed these personages separately; larger ones used all four, or paired them variously.

Needless to say, patriotic emblems had wide and lasting popularity. The eagle of the United States Seal appeared constantly, either in its proper armorial state or volant; examples of the latter are seen in Plate 112C, or in the so-called *Boston Harbor* (Larsen No. 360), where an eagle spreads his protecting wings above a harbor scene. The Clews *States* series of a dozen views in dark blue (Larsen Nos. 109–20) shows allegorical figures of *America* and *Independence* with a portrait medallion of Washington, all within a ribbon meander carrying the names of fifteen (sometimes eighteen) states. Perhaps handsomest of any printed Staffordshire subjects, a rare series, *Arms of the States*, was issued in 1829 by Thomas Mayer of Stoke, from designs drawn by Thomas Sully. Shown here is *Pennsylvania* (Plate 111A, Larsen No. 264), which is largest of all platters in this series. Oddly, only twelve States' Arms are known, no examples of the thirteenth (New Hampshire) having come to light.

Later, but of great interest, two *States* series (Larsen Nos. 460–71 and 472–84; also Laidacker, Part I, pp. 24–6) were produced by Mellor, Venables & Company, who worked at Burslem from 1843 or earlier. Mr Laidacker acquired in 1956 a forty-piece plain white tea service with IRONSTONE and *Royal Patent* marks, carrying small detached medallions of states' arms in hand-colored black transfer. Seven states were represented, a number increased to twenty in the second series, showing a dozen light-color American views taken from engravings after W.H. Bartlett, published 1837–9. These designs were in a border with small vignettes of states' arms. British Registry Office marks on this second series (Laidacker, p. 24) give the maker as *Mellor, Venables & Co.* in 1847, *J.Venables & Co.* in January 1852 and *Venables & Baines* a month later.

The very mixed list of other American subjects covered everything; ports and forts, banks and bourses, churches and college buildings, Washington's *Mount Vernon* and the *President's House* (Plate 111C). The expanding world of trade and travel provided its trains and river packets, its steamships from Fulton's *Clermont* to the *Boston Mails* series (Larsen Nos. 453–7) which in 1841 pictured the Cunard Line ships linking Liverpool with Boston.

Many of the subjects mentioned were issued in series, each group with its border of distinctive design. Ridgway offered twenty-two titles in the *Beauties of America*, Clews about twenty-five in the *Picturesque Views on the Hudson River*, Jackson a list of thirty-four subjects in light colors, or Wood nearly forty views in rich blue with the shell-border. Familiar scenery in the Catskills or along the Hudson was rivalled by 'new' places in the Midwest, from the falls of Niagara to the burbling *Headwaters of the Juniata, U.S.* (Plate 111C). If most were copied from paintings or from portfolios of prints, all were equally strange to the Staffordshire potter, who must therefore be forgiven if sometimes he mixed the titles printed on his views.

Appearing somewhat past their time, a few lingering subjects must be added to the list of American-historical titles, which normally ended with the 1840s. So popular had these pictures been, Staffordshire potters could not bear to discontinue them altogether.

Catering to the wild excitement of Gold Rush days, a catch-penny pattern called *California* (discussed p. 200 in Larsen) referred *to* this promised land, though indeed not giving an actual picture *of* it. A minor gold rush had followed the first discovery of this metal in March, 1842, on a remote *rancho* northwest of Los Angeles. Six years later, the great stampede of goldseekers ensued from James Marshall's goldstrike of January, 1848, at Sutter's Mill, near San Francisco. Before the end of 1848 people were hastily *en route* for California from all over the world.

Ironstone: entitled *California*, with *Pearl Stone Ware*, in a garter and carrying the British Registry codemark for April 2, 1849, ironstone dinner services printed in a dull slate-blue were made 1849–52. The maker's mark WEDGWOOD was doubtless used with intent

to mislead, the true maker of this highly popular pattern being John Wedg Wood of the Woodland Pottery, Tunstall. So much to the contrary of the raw and brawling life to be found there, his *California* depicted a dreamy land of classic temples and marble balustrades, with fantastic goldminers lazily drifting in gondolas upon tree-shaded lagoons.

If poor in quality, at least more truthful was a rare little set of black-printed Gold Rush cup plates (Plate 112B) with embossed rosette border. The first showed a three-masted ship with pennants flying, *Away to California*. In a companion view, *California Diggings*, the ship is at anchor, its jubilant passengers already at work with pick and shovel in the pure gold soil. There is a third plate called *Indian Chiefs*, showing two redmen and a shield of arms, their companion the California bear and at their feet a cornucopia spewing golden coins. The maker's mark is an impressed JT, possibly for John Tams (whose pottery at Longton was the Crown Works) or perhaps for John Twigg, who operated the Newhill Pottery from 1822–66 and had produced about 1845 a blue-printed *Mormon Temple at Nauvoo, Illinois*.

That enduring favorite, the eagle, seen in many adaptations from the United States Seal, is encountered in several late versions. Ironstone tea and dinner services of the pattern-name *Gem* (Plate 112C, Larsen No. 658) were black-printed and with a blurred or 'flow' blue border, made at Burslem by R. Hammersley. They show the Registry Office mark for April 23, 1868. A subject fairly similar but with broad flower-panel border was marked *Excelsior*, but is also known as *America* (Larsen No. 499), printed in medium blue by Thomas Ford & Company of Hanley and carrying a Registry-mark for November 21, 1846.

Strange and needless mystery attaches to another subject called *Alabama* (Larsen No. 649). In 1950 Mrs Larsen found 'no china available for analysis', but four years later, an ironstone basin and jug in this design were pictured in *Antiques*, July 1954, p. 66, as 'the first examples of this ware to come to our attention'. Actually these were long ago recorded, mentioned 1878 in *The China*

Hunter's Club and again in 1893 by Dr Barber (pp. 190–1, *Pottery and Porcelain of the United States*). Annie Trumbull Slosson in 1878 told of three sets, printed in gray, blue-gray and green. These originated in the Civil War period, and their maker was E.F.Bodley & Company of Burslem. *Alabama* refers to the Confederate warship of that name, aboard which a gray service was used at the officers' table (examples are at the University of the South, at Sewanee, Tennessee). The design is a medallion with crossed cannon and *C.S.N.* (Confederate States Navy) framed with sprays of the tobacco and cotton plants, and the motto below: *Aide-toi et Dieu t'Aidera* ('The Lord helps those who help themselves').

Latest of the Anglo-American wares was one not primarily our own, but occurring as the sub-group to an extensive range of titles long popular in the English market. The Fenton firm of Felix & Richard Pratt had patented in 1847 a process of color-printing on pottery and semi-porcelain using oil colors, a type of decoration first cousin to the colored George Baxter prints. Jesse Austin as their head engraver from 1847 to 1879 produced with his helpers nearly five hundred titles, chiefly employed in the printing of picture potlids—views of royal castles or such great English houses as Haddon Hall, copies after Landseer and other Royal Academy painters, scenes from literature or the Scriptures. Besides these picture potlids, the Pratts exhibited at the Crystal Palace in 1851 many other articles 'printed in a peculiar style' – vases and pitchers, plates and plaques, whole tea and dessert sets, which found their principal market in the United States. In this output the makers did not forget to include a dozen American titles. Earliest was the *Exhibition Buildings, New York*, 1853 (New York's Crystal Palace), with four more subjects produced for the Centennial Exhibition (Philadelphia, 1876) and one even for the Columbian Exposition (Chicago, 1893). Of a series of plates with wide borders variously colored 'Sèvres blue' or cyclamen pink, grass green or violet magenta, the *Philadelphia Exhibition*, 1876, is pictured here (Plate 112A). This was the great Art Building, and in it was displayed, said the *Tribune*, 'a rich exhibition

of international mediocrity'. Later it became the old Pennsylvania Museum known as Memorial Hall.

With this Centennial plate appeared also a view of the *Philadelphia Public Buildings*, 1876 (the city hall), one of Independence Hall entitled *The State House in Philadelphia*, 1776, and another view, *Interior of Independence Hall, Philadelphia*. Late these might be, but to all collectors of Anglo-American wares they are in a sense birthdate tokens. For the interest in antiques had its beginning at the Centennial Exhibition, where people in numbers became aware of our historical heritage. From talk of division, engendered in the previous decade by a War between the States, people now spoke instead of national unity, of patriotic pride. Mementoes of colonial and Revolutionary days or of our early republic were now 'discovered' as if seen for the first time.

A still later class of blue-printed wares (Plate 112C) was made around 1900 by the descendants of those potters who, in the 1820s, produced Old Blue; these so-called Commemoratives were not re-issues of old subjects, but new ones, offered to meet a large demand (after the Columbian Exposition of 1893) for sets of blue 'historical' plates to hang upon the wall or to stand on the plate-rails then in fashion. Their borders were new, except where, perhaps, Minton borrowed a Ridgway flower design of the 1830s, or Wedgwood framed a *Williams College* in the Large Scroll border used for a Riley series of the 1820s. The rich fruit-and-flower border seen in *Washington's Prayer at Valley Forge*, 1777 (Plate 112C), was taken from Hall's design employed about 1830 for the *Oriental Scenery* series.

No one might mistake these Commemoratives for earlier work – their glaze is glassier, the blue usually harsher. And almost always they were quite truthfully marked, with the names of maker and importer, sometimes with serial and copyright numbers and the telltale word ENGLAND which after 1891 was required by the McKinley Tariff Act.

In 1901 Minton made a series of about twenty views for a Philadelphia importer; Wedgwood a set of seventeen Albany views; and a *Pilgrims* series is mentioned among others in Laidacker, Part I, pp. 63–5. Sixty-two views were catalogued in the fine Wedgwood series that included *Carpenters' Hall, Philadelphia* and *Mount Vernon* (Plate 112C), these marked 'Copyright 1899' and codemarked 1902.

The rich-blue series including *Washington's Prayer* was made 1898–1910 at Stoke by S.Hancock & Sons, for the New York importers Rowland & Marcellus (not made by the latter, as said in Laidacker), comprising a list of about forty titles given in *Antiques* (Sept. 1942, pp. 155–6, and Nov. 1942, pp. 267–8). Altogether, the broad range of titles by various makers runs into uncounted hundreds, offering quite the same interest as Old Blue, in a now extended roll of town views, Revolutionary battle scenes, college buildings and capitols, churches and historic houses, historical portraits from William Penn to midnight-riding Paul Revere, or events from *De Soto Discovering the Mississippi* to a furious *Battle of Lake Erie*.

Though produced in enormous issues, the Commemoratives are already hard to find, and fetch sometimes surprising prices. Although not as yet antiques, cabinets of Old Blue have included them for the past fifty or sixty years, and it seems likely that future collectors will take an interest in them.

GLOSSARY

Albany slip: the diluted, creamy state of a fine clay found on the Hudson riverbank near Albany, New York. Of rich dark-brown color, sometimes used as a glaze, or after *c.* 1800 for coating the interior of salt-glazed stoneware vessels. In 1843 the New York Geological Survey said it was 'known and shipped all over the country'.

Art pottery: also called Studio Ware. Much ornamental work in what Dr Barber (writing in 1893) considered 'elegant decorative forms' appeared after the Centennial, 1876. Rookwood Faience (q.v.) was especially admired, also the wares of Chelsea Keramic Art Works (1872–89 at Chelsea, Massachusetts) developed by Hugh C.Robertson from 1891 as the Chelsea Pottery, from 1895 as

Dedham Pottery. Art Tiles (*see* Barber, pp. 343–84) flourished in the 1880s, notably John G.Low's from 1879 at Chelsea, Massachusetts.

Belleek: a light, fragile feldspathic porcelain cast in molds, with lustrous pearly glaze. Invented *c.* 1860 by William Goss of Stoke, improved by William Bromley at the Irish factory of David McBirney & Co. (founded 1857 at Belleek, Co. Fermanagh) which by 1865 won a medal at the Dublin Exhibition. Produced at many American factories 1882–1900 and called *Lotus Ware* by Knowles of East Liverpool (Plates 104B, C).

Bennington: a name widely, and wrongly, applied to brown Rockingham wares in general. The Vermont town had two establishments, a lesser stoneware works of the Norton family (1793–1894) and the enterprising factory of Christopher W. Fenton, 1845–58 (called the U.S. Pottery Co., from 1853). Fenton produced a diversity of wares, from common yellow and Flint Enamel (*q.v.*) to porcelains and Parian (Plates 101B, C and 102A, B, C).

FIG. 2
Bennington

Bisque: unglazed or 'biscuit' porcelain (Plate 101A).

Body: the composite materials of which potter's clay is made – the ware itself, usually pottery or stoneware; for porcelains the word *paste* is preferred (as hard-paste, soft-paste).

Bone china: an artifical porcelain utilizing white bone-ash as an ingredient. Known from 1748 (Thomas Frye's second patent at the Bow factory) and since about 1800 the standard English body. The best grades are hard, translucent, and a close approach to 'true' porcelain.

China-clay: a white-burning natural clay (kaolin) used with china-stone (petuntze, *q.v.*) to produce true porcelain. It was the *unaker* of the Cherokees, found 'on the back of Virginia' and through the Carolinas, into

Georgia. Wedgwood imported 'the Cherokee earth', and in 1777 wrote his partner that 'it is really used in all the Jaspers'.

China-stone: feldspar, decomposed gran¯ite (petuntze). Fuses at great heat, combining with china-clay to produce porcelain.

Chinese 'Lowestoft': a misnomer for China-Trade porcelains, the East India Company china, often decorated to special order with coats-of-arms, monograms, etc. In 1754 the Massachusetts General Court placed an excise on this popular 'East-India ware, called China-ware'. From 1785 to 1830 much was fetched on American vessels, appropriately painted with eagles and ships, Masonic symbols, States' arms and the like.

See preceding article 'China-Trade Porcelain' by Alice Winchester.

Clay: special plastic earths of varying grades and colors, from coarse red-burning clay fit for bricks or tile-making to the blue-clays required for stoneware, the fine white kaolin used for porcelains.

Cream-colored: (in the trade called C.C.) and Creamware. A lead-glazed earthenware, perfected by Wedgwood who first called it Queensware; much also made at Liverpool and Leeds. Of nice quality and smooth ivory surface, it displaced delft by 1780 and enjoyed a world market far into the nineteenth century. Was the most mentioned of American imports, our own potters constantly claiming to equal the English (Plate 103A).

Flint enamel: *Fenton's Enamel*, an improvement on the brown Rockingham glaze, patented 1849 by Lyman, Fenton & Co. of Bennington, Vermont, but soon copied by East Liverpool and other factories. Metallic powders dusted on the glaze produced streaks and flecks of color (Plates 102A, C). *See* Rockingham.

Gaudy Dutch: the popular name for a gaily decorated Staffordshire pottery produced *c.* 1810–30 for the American trade (Plate 108). *See* Anglo-American Pottery.

Gaudy Welsh: also Gaudy Ironstone. Later wares (*c.* 1830–45 and 1850–65) made in England for the American trade. *See* Anglo-American Pottery.

Glaze: a glassy surface coating of many types. Liquid lead glazes were most used, Ramsay giving a typical formula as 114 parts red lead, 39 parts silica sand, 10 parts white clay. Salt glaze (q.v.) characterized most stonewares. To what extent unknown, white 'chiney wear' glazed or coated with opaque tin-enamel (i.e. delft) was apparently produced 1688–92 at Burlington, New Jersey, and also by New York potbakers of that time.

Historical Blue: also 'Old Blue'. Staffordshire pottery transfer-printed with scenes of actual places, notable persons, historic events. These deep-blue prints of the 1820s were followed by light colors about 1830 and into the 1840s (Plates 107D, 110 and 111A, B). *See* Anglo-American Pottery.

Ironstone: dense and opaque white wares, produced experimentally 1740–3 by Andrew Duché at Savannah, Georgia, and as the well known 'Stone China' (from 1805) of Josiah Spode II. *Mason's Ironstone* was patented 1813 by C.J.Mason of Lane Delph, was highly successful and much copied by others. Similar wares of heavy grade were a staple of American makers from 1860 to 1900 under such names as White Granite, Opaque Porcelain, Flint China, with so-called Hotel China and Semi-Porcelain appearing about 1885.

Kaolin: china-clay, 'a natural compound which contains alumina, silica and water' (A.L.Hetherington).

Lead: was employed for lead-glazing either as a dry powder (galena, native lead sulphide) or a liquid (litharge, lead oxide). 'Baron' Stiegel the glassmaker was buying 'Litterage' for lead-glass in 1772. In scarce times, one Ohio potter obtained lead by collecting and burning the lead-foil with which Chinese tea was packaged.

Liverpool: a generic name given to creamware made 1780–1825 by Liverpool but also certain Staffordshire potters, especially in jugs black transfer-printed with

American-historical subjects (Plate 105). *See* Anglo-American Pottery.

Lotus Ware: (Plates 104B, C). *See* Belleek.

Lustre: a surface film of metal on pottery; platinum produced 'silver' lustre; gold produced pink and lilac if used on a light body, copper lustre if on a dark body. First use in American manufacture was by Abraham Miller, the enterprising Philadelphia potter who exhibited 1824 at the Franklin Institute 'platinated or lustre pitchers, the first made in the U.S.'.

Majolica: an earthenware with colored lead glazes, popular from the 1850s. Enormous quantities were distributed as premiums in the 1880s made by Bennett of Baltimore (for the Price Baking Powder Co.) and by Griffen, Smith & Hill of Phoenixville, Pennsylvania (for the Atlantic & Pacific Tea Co.) (Plate 104D).

Mocha Ware: or Banded Creamware. Lathe-turned work occurring *c.* 1790–1840 mostly in mugs and jugs, with bands of colored decoration in combed or fernlike designs. Much was imported, and the same called Moco Ware (with bands of rudely spattered slip) was made after 1850 by Edwin Bennett of Baltimore.

Parian: or Statuary Ware. Fine-grained, waxy feldspathic porcelain resembling white Parian marble, developed in the 1840s by

FIG. 3. Parian

Copeland and Minton; much admired at the Crystal Palace exhibitions in London and

New York (1851 and 1853). Soon a favorite of American makers, chiefly for portrait busts and parlor ornaments.

Petuntze: *see* China-stone.

Porcelain: translucent, vitrified ware made of china-clay and china-stone fused at great heat – the 'true' or hard-paste porcelain. Soft-paste and 'artificial' porcelains are of white clay with glassy frit, sometimes soap-rock (steatite, soapstone) or later bone-ash. From continual experiments, the formulas varied endlessly, and many marginal 'porcelains' are accepted if they show translucence.

Pottery: in the broadest sense is 'any receptacle or vessel made of clay' by the potter. But the name is saved for earthenwares fired at low temperature (600° C. or more) as distinguished from stoneware or porcelain, fired at much greater heat.

Queensware: *see* Cream-colored.

Redware: or Red-Clay Pottery. Simple lead-glazed wares of soft, porous body ranging

FIG. 4. Redware

in color from pinkish buff to reds and brown. *See also* Slipware, Sgraffito.

Registry Mark: appearing on English wares in two cycles, 1842–67 and 1868–83. A lozenge with code-letters and numerals assigned by the 'Registration of Designs' Office (*see Antiques*, March 1931, pp. 204–6).

Rockingham: a common yellow ware with lustrous brown manganese glaze, mottled or streaked. The popular misnomer is 'Bennington ware', but it was made at countless American factories from the 1840s

FIG. 5. Rockingham

onward. East Liverpool produced 'probably fifty percent of the total' (*see Antiques*, Jan. 1946, pp. 42–4) (Plate 102B).

Rookwood Faience: *see* Art Pottery. The Rookwood Pottery at Cincinnati, Ohio, was founded 1880 by Mrs Maria L. Nichols (later Mrs Bellamy Storer), first making table wares, but by 1889 receiving a gold medal at the Paris Exposition for its now widely recognized Art Wares.

Salt glaze: hard, transparent and faintly roughish glaze found on most stonewares, a glassy film formed by the settling of vapor produced when common rock salt is introduced to the kiln at the height of firing (Plate 96).

Sgraffito: incised or 'scratched' decora-

FIG. 6. Sgraffito

tion on redware, especially the Pennsylvania-German show plates; traditional in European peasant pottery and transplanted to the 'Dutch country', where it flourished from the mid-eighteenth far into the nineteenth century (Plate 93B).

Slipware: redware with decoration of flourishes, names etc., drawn in lines of

FIG. 7. Slipware

colored 'slip' (diluted clay) (Plates 93C and 94A, B).

Spatter: a cheerful range of wares with sponged color and painted designs, made *c.* 1820–50 in Staffordshire for the American market (Plate 109). *See* Anglo-American Pottery.

Stoneware: a variable family of hard, high-fired wares mostly salt-glazed, from the

FIG. 8. Stoneware

thin white Staffordshire stonewares of 1720–50 to heavy crocks and jugs of blue-painted gray stoneware so common in the nineteenth century (Plate 96).

Toby: the familiar figure-jug of Toby Philpot the toper, or other popular and amusing characters, favorites in English pottery since the 1740s. *Uncle Toby/ 1829* made by Henderson of Jersey City; produced at various American factories, including 'a whole series of Toby mugs and bottles' modelled 1852–8 by Greatbach at Bennington, Vermont (Plate 102B).

Transfer-printing: the process of decorating pottery from paper impressions taken off inked copperplate engravings, an English invention dating from the Battersea enamelworks (1753–6). Very limited application in this country, mentioned in records of the Bonnin & Morris factory (Philadelphia, 1771–2) and a few subjects produced around 1840 by Henderson of Jersey City (Plates 103, 105, 106, 107, 110, 111, 112). *See* Historical Blue; Liverpool.

Unaker: *see* China-clay; Kaolin.

Yellow Ware: utility ware (molds, baking dishes, etc.) of cream or buff clays with transparent glaze ranging from pale straw color to deep yellow; it became Rockingham (*q.v.*) when given a mottled brown manganese coloring. Widely made *c.* 1830–1900.

Zaffer: cobalt oxide in powder form, from which was made *smalt* (a powdered blue glass) the blue coloring used by potters. Bonnin & Morris in Jan. 1771 wanted 'a quantity of Zaffre' for their blue-painted porcelains. The potter John Bell wrote to his brother Samuel in 1848 that 'graffree is calcined cobalt or fly stone which is the same thing', warning him that this 'coulering matter is rank poison'.

BOOKS FOR FURTHER READING

Part I. The wares made in America

BARBER, EDWIN ATLEE: *The Pottery and Porcelain of the United States*, G.P.Putnam, New York (1893, 1902, 1909).

BARBER, EDWIN ATLEE: *Tulip Ware of the Pennsylvania-German Potters*, Pennsylvania Museum, Philadelphia (1903, 1926).

BRIDENBAUGH, CARL: *The Colonial Craftsman*, New York University Press, New York (1950).

CLEMENT, ARTHUR W.: *Our Pioneer Potters*, The Author, New York (1947).

JAMES, ARTHUR E.: *The Potters and Potteries of Chester County, Pennsylvania*, Chester County Historical Society, West Chester, Pa. (1945).

LICHTEN, FRANCES: *Folk Art of Rural Pennsylvania* (Chapter 'From the Earth Itself – Clay'), Scribner's, New York (1946).

PRIME, ALFRED COXE: *The Arts and Crafts in Philadelphia, Maryland and South Carolina, 1721–1785* (Chapter 'Pottery and Porcelain'), The Walpole Society (1929); also *Series Two, 1786–1800* (1932).

RAMSAY, JOHN: *American Potters and Pottery*, Hale, Cushman & Flint, Boston (1939).

RICE, A.H., AND STOUDT, JOHN B.: *The Shenandoah Pottery*, Shenandoah Publishing House, Strasburg, Pa. (1929).

SPARGO, JOHN: *The A.B.C. of Bennington Pottery Wares*, Bennington Historical Museum, Bennington, Vt. (1948).

SPARGO, JOHN: *Early American Pottery and China*, Century, New York (1926).

SPARGO, JOHN: *The Potters and Potteries of Bennington*, Houghton Mifflin and Antiques, Inc., Boston (1926).

WATKINS, LURA WOODSIDE: *Early New England Potters and Their Wares*, Harvard University Press, Cambridge (1950).

Catalogues, Bulletins, Magazines:

CLEMENT, ARTHUR W.: *Notes on American Ceramics, 1607–1943*, Handbook to the Museum Collections, Brooklyn Museum, Brooklyn (1944).

CLEMENT, ARTHUR W. AND BISHOP, EDITH: *The Pottery and Porcelain of New Jersey, 1688–1900*, Exhibition catalogue, Newark Museum, Newark, N.J. (1947).

GILMER, RUTH MONROE: 'Andrew Duché and His China, 1738–1743' (article pp. 128–30 in *Apollo* for May 1947).

GILMER, RUTH MONROE: 'Andrew Duché – America's First China Maker' (article pp. 63–5 in *Apollo* for September 1948).

HOMMEL, RUDOLPH P. ('G.A.R.Goyle'): 'First Porcelain Making in America' (four articles on Andrew Duché, in the *Chronicle* of the Early American Industries Association, Vol. I, Nos. 8–11, Nov. 1934 – May 1935).

McKEARIN, GEORGE S.: *Loan Exhibition of Early American Pottery and Early American Glass* from the Collection of George S. McKearin, held 1931 at the Grand Central Palace, New York, The Author, Hoosic Falls (1931).

McKEARIN, HELEN: *Early American Pottery and Porcelain*, Foreword to sales-catalogue of the Alfred B. Maclay Collection, Parke-Bernet Galleries, New York (1939).

The Magazine *Antiques*. Boston 1922–9 and New York 1929 to date, fully indexed.

Part II. Anglo-American pottery

CAMEHL, ADA WALKER: *The Blue-China Book*, Dutton, New York (1916); Tudor Publishing Co., New York (1946).

EARLE, ALICE MORSE: *China Collecting in America*, Scribner's, New York (1892); Empire State Book Co., New York (1924).

Parlor cook stove made by Augustus Quackenboss, Albany, *c.* 1850. Very fine casting. Top is hinged, and urn is made to hold perfume. *Stoves are privately owned, except as noted.*

PLATE 81

(A) Fire frame, early-nineteenth century.

(B) Yacht stove. Brass frame with blue and white tile, made by Murdock Parlor Grate Co., Boston, *c.* 1876. Smallest size 27 ins. high. *Henry Ford Museum, Dearborn, Michigan.*

(C) Franklin stove with flared sides, made by C. Newcomb & Co., Worcester, *c.* 1830.

PLATE 82

(B) Six-plate stove with three legs.   Fine casting, *c.* 1840.   *Newport, Rhode Island, Historical Society.*

(A) Ten-plate stove with baking oven, made at the Hereford Furnace, Bucks County, Pennsylvania, *c.* 1767.   *Henry Ford Museum, Dearborn, Michigan.*

(C) Six-plate box stove with four legs, *c.* 1845.

(D) Six-plate box stove made by Newcomb & Bowen, Worcester, Massachusetts, *c.* 1839.

PLATE 83

(A) Two-column box stove with dolphin columns, mounted with an eagle. Made by Leake & Low, Albany, 1844. *Henry Ford Museum, Dearborn, Michigan.*

(B) Four-column dolphin stove, No. 3 size. Made by Johnson, Geer & Cox, Troy, *c.* 1845. *Henry Ford Museum, Dearborn, Michigan.*

(C) Floral parlor stove, No. 2, made by Fuller, Warren & Morrison, Troy, *c.* 1853. *Henry Ford Museum, Dearborn, Michigan.*

(D) 'Art Laurel' base-burning stove with elaborate nickel trim. Illuminated model, made by the Art Stove Company, Detroit, Michigan, *c.* 1880. Ht. 67½ ins. *Henry Ford Museum, Dearborn, Michigan.*

PLATE 84

Flagon with ship decoration; reverse shows the ship in fair weather, flying American flag. *New-York Historical Society.*

PLATE 85

(A) Monogram and mythological; brought on the 'Grand Turk', 1786, for Deborah Fairfax Anderson. *Essex Institute.*

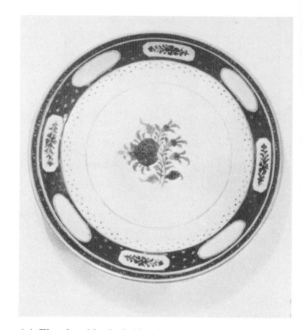

(B) Floral: wide dark blue border with floral reserves and gilt stars; early 1800s. *Mottahedeh; Antiques,* xxviii, 121.

(C) Pseudo-armorial; monogram in mantled shield; ship with American flag. Privately owned; *Antiques*, xix, 442.

(D) Armorial: arms of Pennsylvania. *New-York Historical Society.*

PLATE 86

(A) Armorial: eagle from the Great Seal of the United States. *Antiques*, xvii, 530.

(B) 'Pigeon' type eagle on a tea-pot. *Essex Institute.*

(C, D, E, F) Four variants of the American eagle on China-Trade porcelain; above, *Museum of Fine Arts, Boston*, and *Rhode Island School of Design*. Below, *J.A.Lloyd Hyde* and *Museum of Fine Arts, Boston.*

PLATE 87

(A) Emblematic: George Washington's Cincinnati porcelain, with underglaze Fitzhugh border. *Metropolitan Museum of Art.*

(B) Armorial: variant of arms of State of New York. *Antiques*, xv, 42.

(C) Emblematic: Masonic designs, with eagle, indicating this was made for the American market. *Antiques*, xxi, 173.

PLATE 88

(A and B) Ship decoration: the Grand Turk punch bowl, with view of interior inscribed 'Ship Grand Turk At Canton 1786'. *Peabody Museum, Salem, Massachusetts.*

(C) Emblematic: insignia of the Society of the Cincinnati, with monogram of original owner, Dr David Townsend of Boston, and floral motifs; 1790. *Henry N. Flynt.*

PLATE 89

(A) Richard Varick punch bowl; motifs and inscription from Varick's certificate of membership in the Society of the Cincinnati. *Washington Association of New Jersey, Morristown.*

(B and C) Punch bowl presented to the Corporation of the City of New York by General Jacob Morton, 1812. Interior shows view of city after engraving by Samuel Seymour. *Metropolitan Museum of Art.*

PLATE 90

(A) Underglaze decoration: Fitzhugh pattern in green with enameled American eagle. *Metropolitan Museum of Art.*

(B) Underglaze decoration: Canton type with scene in blue. *New-York Historical Society.*

PLATE 91

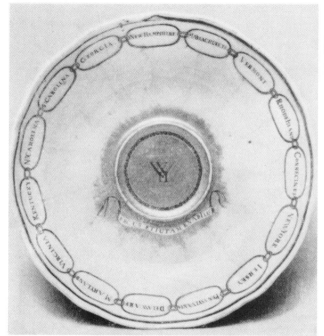

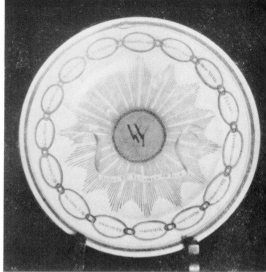

(B) French reproduction of 'States', probably 18
Antiques, xxi, 172.

(A) 'States' pattern, presented to Martha Washington, 1786.
Metropolitan Museum of Art.

(C) Tureen; orange-peel texture. This, with famille rose decoration, is one of the
European market types sought by American collectors today. *McCann collection,
Metropolitan Museum.*

PLATE 92

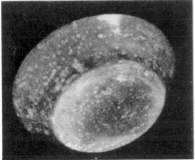

(A) Brown pottery milk-pan; straw-colored lead glaze. Detail of flat bottom. Credited to Andrew Duché, *c.* 1735–40. New Windsor, South Carolina, or Savannah, Georgia. D. 12½ ins. *Ruth Monroe Gilmer.*

(B) Pennsylvania Redware puzzle-jug; sgraffito decoration, inscribed 'SW 1775' and 'this and the / gever is thine / for ever.' Ht. about 8 ins. *Ex-coll. of Alfred B. Maclay, Parke-Bernet Galleries.*

(A) Detail.

(C) New England Redware: (*Left*) Pan with brown-splashed light brown interior, lines of yellow slip; (*Center*) Black-glazed cup; (*Center*) Cooky jar with bright brown glaze, girdle of incised rigaree; (*Right*) Herb pot splashed yellow, brown and orange; (*Right*) Herb pot with salmon glaze, cover scratched 'EDWARD TOWLE'. Cooky jar, Ht. 8 ins. *Author's collection.*

PLATE 93

(A) Tools of the Redware Potter: (*Left*) Wooden beater and coggle wheel; (*Left*) Plate showing use of trailed green slip; (*Center*) Orange-glazed 4-in. slip cup for three quills, scratched 'H. Scofield / Honeybrook', Pennsylvania 1888–1927; (*Right*) Turk's head cake mold, and plaster core for shaping a 7-in. mold. Beater L.11½ ins. *W. Dan Quattlebaum and Author's collection.*

(B) Three Redware dishes with inscriptions in trailed yellow slip. *Old Sturbridge Village, Sturbridge, Massachusetts.*

(C) Ohio washbowl and jug with buff-glazed interior, handles stamped 'ZOAR' and '1840'. Bowl D. 17 ins.; jug Ht. 11¾ ins. *Ex-coll. of Rhea Mansfield Knittle, Henry Ford Museum, Dearborn.*

PLATE 94

(A) (*Left*) Pennsylvania Redware churn with brown and olive glaze, and wooden dasher; (*Right*) brown-painted crock of unglazed tan pottery, made 1860–90 by James Hamilton at New Geneva, Pennsylvania. *Ex-coll. of Alfred B. Maclay, Parke-Bernet Galleries.*

(B) Bell Pottery, Shenandoah Valley: (*Left*) Celadon-glazed jelly mold stamped 'JOHN BELL', made for his sister at Winchester, Virginia, *c.* 1825; (*Left center*) Frog glazed brown and green; (*Center*) Orange-glazed plate stamped 'JOHN BELL / WAYNESBORO'; (*Right*) Cup and saucer, *c.* 1860, and brightly splashed jug, both by Samuel and Solomon Bell of Strasburg, Virginia. Plate D. 9 ins. *Author's collection.*

PLATE 95

(A) Blue-painted brown stoneware batter jug, 'New York Feby 17th 1798 / Flowered by Clarkson Crolius / Blue.' Ht. 11⅜ ins. *The New-York Historical Society.*

(B) Brown-stained stoneware 3-gallon jar stamped 'BOSTON. 1804'. *Old Sturbridge Village, Sturbridge, Massachusetts.*

(C) Blue-painted gray stoneware crock and churn, Edmands & Co. (working 1850–68 at Charlestown, Massachusetts) and Madison Woodruff (working 1849–c. 1870 at Cortland, New York). Ht. 13 and 19¼ ins. *Henry Ford Museum, Dearborn.*

(D) Crock with blue-stenciled eagle, 'Brown Brothers / Huntington, L.I.' (working 1863–1904). Ht. 9 ins. *Samuel E. Kamens.*

PLATE 96

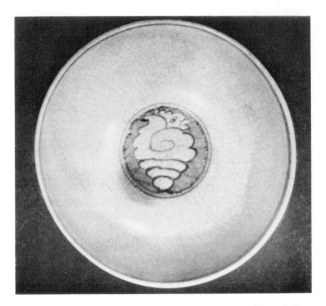

(A) Detail of the Duché bowl, interior with shell medallion perhaps from the Earl of Egmont's 'sample' Chinese porcelains, sent in 1738.

(B) Blue-painted bowl of experimental porcelain, made 1738–43 by Andrew Duché at Savannah, Georgia. D. 5¾ ins. Ht. 3 ins. *Ruth Monroe Gilmer.*

PLATE 97

(A) Fine earthenware or 'porcelain' teapot with blue painting, made 1771–2 in Philadelphia by Bonnin and Morris. Ht. 7 in. L. 9 ins.

(B) Reverse with initials 'WP' said to be for William Penn. *Mr and Mrs Arthur J. Sussel.*

(c) Blue-painted sweetmeat dish in style of Bow or Plymouth. Mark: 'P' in blue. Bonnin and Morris of Philadelphia, 1771–2. Ht. 5¼ ins. W. 7¼ ins. *Brooklyn Museum.*

PLATE 98

(A) Dam and Waterworks at Fairmount, and Old Schuylkill Bridge, brown-painted *c.* 1827 by William Ellis Tucker, Philadelphia. Plate Diam. 6¼ ins. *Mr and Mrs Arthur J. Sussel.*

(B, C) Tucker mug of the Hemphill period, about 1835, richly colored view titled *Baltimore* and gold scroll-work. Ht. 3⅝ ins. *Mr and Mrs Murray Braunfeld.*

PLATE 99

(A) 'The Tucker Masterpiece', porcelain vase in salmon and gold with colors, gilt-bronze handles. Made 1835 by Thomas Tucker. Ht. 21 ins. *Philadelphia Museum of Art.*

(B) John Quincy Adams, Andrew Jackson, James Monroe, John Adams, James Madison, portraits on violet-gray ground with wreath-molded foot. Tucker porcelain, 1835–8. *Ex-coll. of C. W. Lyon; photo, courtesy of Antiques.*

PLATE 100

(A) Bisque porcelain pitcher 'The Poets', glazed interior with leafage in gold and red; modelled in 1876 by Karl Müller, marks of 'Union Porcelain Works / Greenpoint, N.Y.' Ht. 7¾ ins. *Verna Ruth Quattlebaum.*

(B) Daisy and Tulip jug, raised mark 'Fenton's Works / Bennington, Vermont,' made 1847-8. Ht. 8 ins. *Ex-coll. of Alfred B. Maclay, Parke-Bernet Galleries.*

(C) 'Charter Oak' jug, white porcelain with blue pitted ground, 'U.S.P.' ribbon-mark, made *c.* 1853 at Bennington by the United States Pottery Co. *Ex-coll. of Alfred B. Maclay, Parke-Bernet Galleries.*

PLATE 101

(B) Toby jugs: the smaller one made 1852–8 at Bennington, Vermont, and the larger one 1838–45 at the Salamander Works at Woodbridge, New Jersey. Ht. 6½ and 12¾ ins. *Los Angeles County Museum.*

(A) Hot-water urn with pewter spigot, brown glaze flecked with green and blue, orange and yellow. Mark: 'Fenton's Enamel / Patented 1849 / Bennington Vᵗ.' Ht. 20¼ ins. *The Bennington Museum.*

(C) The Bennington Lion, brilliant flint enamel and sanded or 'Cole-slaw' mane, made 1851–2 and showing 1849 mark. Base 6 × 11 ins. Ht. 7¼ ins. *The Bennington Museum.*

PLATE 102

(A) Blue-printed creamware jar for snuff, and its mark: 'Clews's Manufacturer's'. Made 1837–8 by the Indiana Pottery Co. (James Clews) at Troy, Indiana. *George William Bierce.*

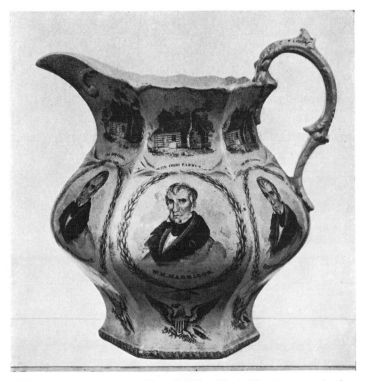

(B) Black-printed memorial jug, William Henry Harrison; made 1841 at Jersey City by the American Pottery Manufacturing Co. Ht. 10½ ins. *Ex-coll. of Alfred B. Maclay, Parke-Bernet Galleries.*

PLATE 103

(A) Parlor group 'The Elder's Daughter', issued October 1886 in New York by John Rogers; one of the popular Rogers Groups made 1859–93. Ht. 21 ins. *Los Angeles County Museum.*

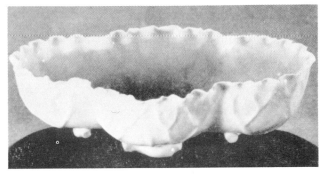

(B) American Belleek made 1891–8 at East Liverpool, Ohio, by Knowles, Taylor and Knowles. Mark in green: 'K.T.K. Co. LOTUS WARE.' L. 7½ ins. *Henry Ford Museum, Dearborn.*

(C) Belleek or 'Lotus Ware' shell, same makers and mark as (B). L. 4¾ ins. *Clement collection, Brooklyn Museum.*

(D) Cauliflower teapot, 'Etruscan Majolica', made 1879–90 at Phoenixville, Pennsylvania, by Griffen, Smith & Hill. Ht. 5¼ ins. *Clement collection, Brooklyn Museum.*

PLATE 104

(A) & (B) Pair of bowls, mottled pink lustre with black-printed medallions of Franklin, Washington, Lafayette. U.S. Arms and 'Republicans (Republics) are not always ungrateful'. D. 8 ins. *Ex-coll. Lorimer, Parke-Bernet Galleries.*

(C) Liverpool jug, black-printed *c.* 1790 'Success to the Crooked But interesting Town of Boston!'. Ht. 7¾ ins. *Ex-coll. Lorimer, Parke-Bernet Galleries.*

(D) Liverpool jug with U.S. Arms, reverse a frigate 'The Trueblooded Yankee'; rim and a large anchor below the spout in copper lustre. Ht. 8¼ ins. *Ex-coll. Lorimer, Parke-Bernet Galleries.*

PLATE 105

(A) 'The Enterprize and Boxer' and reverse 'The United States and Macedonian', c. 1818–20. Pale green with lustre collar, black-printed from engravings by Bentley, Wear & Bourne of Shelton. Ht. 5¾ ins. *Ex-coll. W.R.Hearst, Parke-Bernet Galleries.*

(B) Black-printed Staffordshire plate with blue frilled edge, marked 'CLEWS'. Gen. Zebulon M. Pike (1779–1813), the soldier and explorer for whom Pike's Peak was named. Diam. 10 ins. *Ex-colls. Hudnut and Hearst, Parke-Bernet Galleries.*

(C) Commodore William Bainbridge and reverse Ma... Gen. Jacob Brown, canary yellow jug with blac... printed portraits and lustre trim, c. 1815. Ht. 5¼ i... *Ex-coll. Lorimer, Parke-Bernet Galleries.*

PLATE 106

(B) The Lafayette/Cornwallis subjects of (A) used on a smaller copper-lustred jug. Ht. 6¼ ins. *Ex-coll. Lorimer, Parke-Bernet Galleries.*

(A) 'Cornwallis resigning his sword at Yorktown, October 19, 1781', and reverse 'Lafayette'. Copper-lustred vase, black transfer on canary yellow band, *c.* 1825. Ht. 7 ins. *Ex-coll. Hearst, Parke-Bernet Galleries.*

(C) Pottery jug with American patriotic symbols, cheap imitation of Wedgwood's blue jasper, made to celebrate the Treaty of Ghent (1814). Ht. 4½ ins. *Parke-Bernet Galleries.*

(D) Blue-printed plate, Lafayette, shell edge, impressed mark 'CLEWS' (Cobridge, *c.* 1825). Diam. 5½ ins. *Ex-colls. Nolen and Hearst, Parke-Bernet Galleries.*

PLATE 107

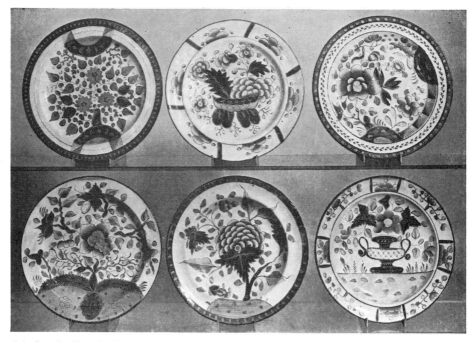

(A) Gaudy Dutch plates made *c.* 1820 for the Pennsylvania-German market, in order Strawflower, War Bonnet, Single Rose, Dove, Grape, Urn. Diam. 10 ins. *Ex-coll. Yeager, Parke-Bernet Galleries.*

(B) Coffee-pot in Butterfly, most-sought-for of Gaudy Dutch patterns. Ht. 9½ ins. *Parke-Bernet Galleries.*

(C) Coffee-pot in King's Ro pattern. Ht. 10½ ins. *Park Bernet Galleries.*

(D) Gaudy Dutch plates in Oyster pattern, showing usual painted border and blue transfer-printed border. Diams. 7½ and 8¼ ins. *Ex-coll. Yeager, Parke-Bernet Galleries.*

PLATE 108

SPATTER

(A) The parent of Spatter wares, a painted Peafowl plate with blue frill edge, green sponged foliage. Impressed WEDGWOOD mark, *c.* 1800–20. Diam. 8 ins. *Ex-coll. Lorimer, Parke-Bernet Galleries.*

(B) Ironstone plate of the 1840s, blue spatter and colors, 'Bird on a Fence'. Diam. 8½ ins. *Parke-Bernet Galleries.*

(C) Cup and saucer in Peafowl pattern, carmine spatter. *Parke-Bernet Galleries.*

(D) Spatter in typical patterns of 1820–40: The Star, Tulip and Red Schoolhouse. Plates Diam. 8 ins. *Parke-Bernet Galleries.*

PLATE 109

(A) Blue platter Harewood House, Yorkshire, with Erie Canal view at Albany, portrait medallions of Jefferson, Washington, Lafayette, Clinton; 1825; by Ralph Stevenson & (Aldborough Lloyd) Williams at Cobridge. L. 14¼ ins. *Ex-colls. Hudnut and Hearst, Parke-Bernet Galleries.*

(B) Blue plates 'Baltimore & Ohio Railroad' (*c.* 1828 by Enoch Wood & Sons); 'Upper Ferry Bridge over the River Schuylkill' (before 1829 by Joseph Stubbs). Diams. 10 and 8¾ ins. *Parke-Bernet Galleries.* Blue plate 'Landing of the Fathers at Plymouth' (2nd issue in 1821, Enoch Wood & Sons). Diam. 8¾ ins. *Los Angeles County Museum.*

PLATE 110

(A) Pennsylvania State Arms, from series in dark blue printed 1829 by Thomas Mayer. L. 20¾ ins. *Ex-colls. Kellogg and Hearst, Parke-Bernet Galleries.*

(B) Medium blue 'New York from Heights near Brooklyn', made 1823–9 in two variants by Andrew Stevenson, and a plate the same by Clews. L. 16½ ins. *Ex-coll. Haskell, Parke-Bernet Galleries.*

(C) Two carmine plates 'Headwaters of the Juniata, U.S.' (from series by William Adams & Sons) and 'The President's House, Washington' (from series by J. & J. Jackson). Purple plate with half-subject 'Pittsburgh' (from series 'Picturesque Views' by J. &. R. Clews). All, Diam. 10½ ins. *Parke-Bernet Galleries.*

PLATE III

(A) Color-printed plate 'Philadelphia Exhibition, 1876' (the Art Building) by Felix & Richard Pratt of Fenton. Diam. 7¼ ins. *Los Angeles County Museum.*

(B) Gold Rush cup plates 'Away to California' and 'California Diggings', *c.* 1850 by JT (Joseph Twigg?). Diam. 2¾ ins. *Author's collection.*

(C) Two blue-printed plates, 'Carpenters' Hall, Philadelphia,' and 'Mount Vernon' made 1902 by Wedgwood. Ironstone plate Gem pattern, codemarked 1868, by R. Hammersley of Burslem. Blue plate 'Washington's Prayer at Valley Forge, 1777', from series *c.* 1900 by S. Hancock & Sons of Stoke. Diam. of the last, 10 ins.; others 9 ins. *Los Angeles County Museum.*

PLATE 112

HALSEY, R.T.HAINES: *Pictures of Early New York on Dark Blue Staffordshire Pottery*, Dodd, Mead, New York (1899).

LAIDACKER, SAM: *Anglo-Anerican China, Part I* (American-historical views, Gaudy Dutch, Spatter, etc.) The Author, Bristol, Pa. (1938: revised 2nd ed. 1954). *Part II* ('Other than American Views'), The Author, Bristol, Pa. (1951).

LARSEN, ELLOUISE BAKER: *American Historical Views on Staffordshire China*, Doubleday, New York (1939; revised 2nd ed., 1950).

MANKOWITZ, WOLF, and HAGGAR, REGINALD: *Concise Encyclopedia of English Pottery and Porcelain*, Hawthorn Books, New York (1957).

McCAULEY, ROBERT H.: *Liverpool Transfer Designs on Anglo-American Pottery*, Southworth-Anthoensen, Portland, Me. (1942).

PRATT, RICHARD: *Second Treasury of Early American Homes*, Hawthorn Books, New York (1954).

WEDGWOOD, JOSIAH, AND ORMSBEE, THOMAS H.: *Staffordshire Pottery* (Part II, pp. 105–14 and 153–62), McBride, New York (1947).

GLASS

By CAROLYN SCOON

Early blown glass: in any discussion of American glass, it should first be noted that glassmaking in America had its roots in Europe and before that in the Mediterranean world thousands of years before Christ. The history of glassmaking goes back to the Egyptian period; ancient Alexandria, Tyre and Sidon were centers of the art. It then spread throughout the Roman Empire, survived the Dark Ages, kept alive in small isolated glasshouses, and was reborn again in Venice. From Venice, on the tide of the Renaissance, it was carried to France and the Low Countries, later into England, while a different tradition was preserved in the small forest glasshouses scattered throughout Germany. The two very different traditions of Germany and Britain were the main sources influencing American glass, which retained some of the characteristics of each while incorporating others. This, briefly summarized, is the background of American glass. It was an immigrant to America, as were the craftsmen who brought it here.

There were several attempts to establish glasshouses in the colonies in the seventeenth century but, due to the rigors of life in the wilderness where the supplying of bare necessities presented almost insurmountable difficulties to the settlers, they were failures, and little is known about them except what can be gleaned from documentary evidence. The first of these was at Jamestown, Virginia, in 1608, where a furnace was built just a little more than a year after the founding of the settlement, with the avowed intention of making glass for export. A second attempt at Jamestown in 1621 ended disastrously, due to disease, dissension and the hostility of the Indians. The site of these glasshouses has been excavated, and a recon-struction of a seventeenth-century establishment was opened in the spring of 1957 to mark the 350th anniversary of the first permanent settlement in the New World. Archeological exploration shows the outlines of furnaces and melting pots and a cullet pile which produced many fragments of glass of the type used in starting a new batch. Unfortunately, these fragments were not large enough to show what the original objects had been. No glass beads were found although documentary sources state that beads were to be made for trade with the Indians. Probably little if any glass was actually blown at Jamestown although some experimental batches must have been produced.

Only six glasshouses are recorded as in operation in America in the seventeenth century: the two at Jamestown; one in Salem, Massachusetts, 1641, which is supposed to have operated intermittently for as long as twenty years; two in New Amsterdam with which the names of Johannes Smedes and Evert Duyckinck are connected; and one is supposed to have operated in what became Philadelphia. None of these were successful and no examples of their wares have actually been authenticated. If any glass was actually blown at any of these places, it is logical to suppose that the products were window glass and bottles, blown from the ordinary light and dark green bottle glass.

Window glass and bottles were made in the ten or eleven eighteenth-century glasshouses established before the Revolutionary War, such as the two works of the Glass House Company of New York, one of which was in the city of New York, the other at New Windsor, Ulster County, New York, which operated from about 1752 to 1767.

South Jersey type: the most successful glass manufactory of the eighteenth century was established in 1739 by Caspar Wistar on the banks of Alloway's Creek in southern New Jersey. Wistar was a German who came to Philadelphia in 1717 and made a success of manufacturing brass buttons. He sent back to his native land for four expert glass-blowers, who taught the art of glassmaking to Wistar and his son, Richard, in return for a share of the profits. Richard took over both the glassworks and the button manufactory on the death of his father in 1752, and continued to operate the former profitably until the Revolutionary War brought on a business depression which resulted in his financial failure in 1780.

Although bottles and window glass were the commercial products of the works at Wistarburg, the glass sought by collectors and called 'early American' consists of the so-called 'off-hand' pieces made by the blowers for their families and friends. According to glasshouse tradition, a small corner pot was always set up for the personal use of the blowers. The aquamarine and pale green pieces were made from the metal used to make window glass; the darker-colored objects were made from bottle glass. Artificial colors, such as blue, were occasionally used, but deep reds or wines and opaque white were probably not used until the nineteenth century. A great variety of these off-hand pieces were made, including bowls and sugar bowls, pitchers, vases, candlesticks and many other items (Plates 113, 114, 115). Some were intended for table use; some were merely decorative examples of the ingenuity of the individual blower.

The decorative techniques found in the off-hand blown glass grew out of the process of free blowing and hand manipulation, following the centuries-old traditions of glass blowing still in use wherever fine hand-blown glass is made. The present day Steuben glass of the Corning Glass Works is an example. The decorative devices on the early glass include such applied decoration as prunts (Plate 114B), threading around the neck (Plate 114A), crimping of feet and handles (Plate 114C), and the so-called 'lily pad'

(Plates 113, 114A, C). Three varieties of lily-pad decoration have been listed, none of which have so far been found in European glass. In the first and earliest type, usually found on eighteenth- and early-nineteenth century pieces, slender vertical stems terminate in a bead. The second type, found in pieces dating from about 1830, from upper New York State factories, has a broader stem and circular or oval pad. Type three has a long, wave-like stem ending in a rather flat ovoid pad which actually looks like the lily pad for which it was named. This type seems to have been used on pieces made about the middle of the nineteenth century in New Hampshire, New York and occasionally in New Jersey. In later pieces, these motifs were used in combination with each other as well as singly. A swirled or looped design in two or more colors was also used.

These decorative devices were used at the second Jersey glasshouse. It was established by the Stanger brothers, who were former Wistar employees. This factory was started c. 1781 at what is now Glassboro, a center of glassmaking even in the twentieth century. Few pieces can be attributed with certainty either to Wistarburg or to the Stangers, but the training of apprentices in these and other houses in the area, and the subsequent migration of workers to newly established factories in New York, New England and to some extent in Ohio, accounts for the spread of the South Jersey tradition. Pieces embodying these techniques are called 'South Jersey type' even though made in different sections of the country and at a later date.

Stiegel-type glass: in 1750 Henry William Stiegel (1729–85) came from Germany to Lancaster County, Pennsylvania, and there established an iron foundry. This prospered and in 1763 he turned to glassmaking. By 1765, he had three glasshouses, two of them at Manheim, a town he founded. Over-expansion was the cause of his downfall and he went from wealth and distinction, when he lived in the lavish style which earned him the complimentary title of 'Baron', to imprisonment for debt. In 1774 his glassworks, together with the Kensington works, the first to try to make fine tableware in America, was closed.

Stiegel imported Venetian, German and English glassblowers, thus bringing together very different traditions of glassmaking. The Continental style of engraving on clear glass (Plate 116), and enameled decoration (Plate 117C), are so similar to the so-called 'peasant glass' made in Europe that no expert would care to make an attribution on style alone. Unfortunately, the same is true of the English-type glass produced at Manheim. These pieces, mostly tableware, were made of richly-colored metal; shades of purple or amethyst, blues and, more rarely, emerald-green, were the colors used. They were blown in plain or pattern molds, were then expanded by blowing to the desired size and were finally shaped by manipulation and tools. The principal pattern-molded designs attributed to Stiegel are the ribbed, fluted and the various diamond designs. The diamond-daisy design of the amethyst perfume or scent bottle (Plate 117D) and the daisy-in-hexagon design (Plate 118A) are believed to have originated at Manheim, since as yet no foreign counterparts are known. The paneled vases (Plate 118B) believed for so long to have been made at the Stiegel works, are now attributed to nineteenth-century New England factories – Boston, Cambridge and especially to the Sandwich works.

After Stiegel's collapse his workmen moved to other centers of glassmaking in Pennsylvania, Maryland, and later into Ohio, carrying with them the Stiegel tradition in the same manner as the South Jersey style traveled. The pieces made in this style, even those made in the early nineteenth century (Plate 118C), are called 'Stiegel type'.

Other eighteenth-century glasshouses: the Philadelphia Glass Works at Kensington, c. 1772–7, and the New Bremen Glass Manufactory of John Frederick Amelung, 1785–95, near Frederick, Maryland, were the only other glasshouses making fine tableware. While no examples from Kensington have been identified, a number of fine pieces from New Bremen are known (Plate 119). This was a presentation piece, made as a gift for August Koenig, a well-to-do merchant living in Baltimore about 1796. It shows the high degree of excellence attained by Amelung both in the quality of the metal – a light smokiness in color is characteristic – and in the decoration. Since Amelung came from Bremen, Germany, and most of his workmen were from the same region, his glass naturally follows the Continental style, both in form and in the use of copper-wheel engraved decoration. That he also made colored ware similar to Stiegel's has been proved by excavations on the site of the glasshouse. The salt illustrated (Plate 118D) is thought to be an example of this type of ware. The history of Amelung's venture is similar to that of Stiegel; he overestimated his market in relation to his production costs, and ended in debt and failure.

Nineteenth-century glassmaking: although the history of glassmaking in the United States is filled with stories of failure, it is also a history of continued struggle and final emergence into an established industry. At the beginning of the nineteenth century, about twelve glasshouses were in operation. By 1820 the number had increased to forty, and in 1830 approximately ninety had been started.

The geographical distribution followed the communication lines of emigration westward, mainly the Hudson River-Erie Canal route in New York and, in Pennsylvania, the Allegheny and Monongahela Rivers which meet at Pittsburgh to form the Ohio. A number of small factories, started in New England and northern New York, were near to the source of raw materials, wood for the furnaces and sand for glassmaking, but were too far from easy means of transportation for marketing their products to prosper. Roads were so poor as to make transportation by this means not only slow but costly. It is no wonder that Pittsburgh, situated so conveniently at the head of a great waterway system, became a great center of glassmaking. The discovery of coal in the region was another factor in its favor and helped to spell the doom of many of the eastern wood-burning furnaces.

Bakewell's glass works: the most famous of the glasshouses of the Pittsburgh area was Bakewell's. It was established in 1808 by Benjamin Bakewell and was formally called The Pittsburgh Flint Glass Works but is usually known simply as 'Bakewell's'. This firm was the first, as far as is known, to make cut glass on a commercially successful basis. However, English and Irish cut glass gave the new factory very stiff competition and they were forced to add window glass, bottles and probably molded tableware in both clear and colored glass to the list of products. In 1817 Bakewell made a set of decanters, tumblers and wine glasses for President Monroe. They continued the tradition of being glassmakers to the White House by providing a complete table service for Andrew Jackson while he was President. They also produced some commemorative ware of distinction, such as the tumbler with a portrait bust of DeWitt Clinton embedded in the base (Plate 120A). This tumbler is supposed to be part of a set which was presented to Clinton when he was Governor of New York and was presumably made in recognition of his efforts in the planning and completion of the Erie Canal in 1825. It is decorated with a band of plain panels alternating with panels of fine cut diamonds above a band of 'splits'.

Cut and engraved glass: it is possible that cut glass was made in the eighteenth century. Amelung advertised in 1791 that 'glass may be had, cut with letters, cyphers, crests, flowers, or devices agreeable to the fancy of the purchasers ...' although this is more likely to mean the shallow cutting known as engraving (Plate 116). However, there were cutting shops in all the large cities which depended on other factories for their blanks (*see* Glossary). About 1820 most works making fine glassware were also operating their own glass-cutting departments. At the same time, huge quantities of this ware were imported from abroad, contributing to the difficulty of attribution to specific factories and indeed even to specific countries. The New England Glass Company started in 1818 with twenty-four glass-cutting mills operated by steam and with expert cutters brought over from Ireland. Quite naturally, the pieces produced are hard to distinguish from glass made in such Irish factories as Waterford.

Cut glass reached the peak of its popularity after the Centennial Exhibition in Philadelphia in 1876. The Boston & Sandwich Glass Company, the New England, Mount Washington, Dorflinger's and Hobbs, Brockunier, all had handsome displays at the Fair, and Gillinder & Son of Philadelphia set up a complete glassworks, including a cutting shop, and gave away and sold thousands of Centennial souvenirs.

Cut glass had always been a symbol of wealth and elegance and out of the reach of most people. However, with the arrival of prosperity in the 1880s, almost every family was able to afford a few pieces of cut glass tableware and it was the most popular wedding present for many years. It was made in standard table settings consisting of all kinds of drinking vessels, ice cream dishes, plates of all kinds, finger bowls, pickle and relish dishes, etc., all made in many different patterns. As is often the case, popularity was the cause of the downfall of cut glass.

The designs and motifs cut into glass have remained more or less the same through the years because they are determined and limited by the process. Patterns may be made up of different combinations of motifs but they contain the same flutes, deep miter cuts called 'splits', panels and diamonds of all types, combined with circles, ovals or arcs, because these are the only ones which can be made on the cutter's lathe. The blanks on which the patterns are cut must be heavy and the metal must be of high quality, clear and brilliant. In the late nineteenth century, due to advances in manufacturing techniques, American cut glass was the equal of any in the world. Some examples of cut glass attributed to American factories are shown (Plates 120B, 121A).

Blown three mold glass: in the early nineteenth century fine Irish and English and indeed American cut glass was too expensive and in too short supply for any but the wealthy. However there was a growing market for glass tableware and, to meet this demand, an imitation of cut glass called 'blown three mold' was developed, probably in the United States, about 1812. Between 1820 and 1830 it was produced on a scale approaching mass production, but was itself superseded by the invention of mechanical pressing about 1825.

Blown three mold glass was blown in full-sized hinged metal molds with the pattern cut intaglio on the inner surface of the mold. Since it was *blown* into the mold, the pattern on the side away from the mold follows in reverse that on the mold side. This fact, together with the presence of fine mold marks and the softness and roundness of the edges of the pattern, are the distinguishing characteristics of this ware.

Since blown three mold glass was developed in imitation of cut glass, it is natural to find many patterns similar, and in some cases identical, to cut glass. This is most noticeable in the *Geometric* group, one of the more than one hundred and fifty patterns classified and recorded by Helen McKearin. The patterns of this group are composed mainly of ribbings and diamond-diapering in blocks and bands in different geometric combinations. The other two patterns, the *Arch* and the *Baroque*, are American originals with no known foreign counterparts. The small *Arch* group (about eight recorded patterns) have either a Roman or a Gothic arch as the most conspicuous motif (Plate 121B). The approximately twenty-five *baroque* patterns have simple arabesques and such motifs in bold relief as hearts, palmettes and shells (Plate 122A). The articles made in these two patterns seem to be limited to decanters and pitchers, with a few cruet bottles and tumblers. Those made in the *geometric* pattern (Plate 122B) were more varied and included many types of drinking vessels, dishes of different sizes, bowls, celery glasses and most types of tableware. Besides these, such items as inkwells, hats and lamp fonts were also produced. Most of these articles were of clear or colored flint (lead) glass, blue the most favored color, with amethyst and emerald-green used sparingly. However, some pieces were also made of bottle glass; olive-amber and olive-green decanters, bottles and inkwells were made from this type of glass (Plate 122C).

Blown three mold glass seems to have been made principally in eastern glasshouses, although Kent and Mantua, Ohio, are two Midwestern houses known to have produced this ware. The Boston and Sandwich Glass Company at Sandwich, Massachusetts, famous for pressed glass, was one of the largest producers of blown three mold; fragments of all three patterns have been found in excavations on the site of this glasshouse. The Marlboro Street Factory at Keene, New Hampshire; the works in Coventry, Connecticut, and the Mount Vernon Glass Company, Vernon, New York, are the only other factories to which patterns can definitely be attributed, although it seems probable that still other factories operating during this period, including those in the Pittsburgh district, must have joined in the competition for this market.

Early pressed glass: in 1825 John Palmer Bakewell, one of the sons of the founder of the Pittsburgh Flint Glass Works, took out a patent for the mechanical pressing of door and furniture knobs. Other factories had also been experimenting with different types of pressing apparatus and within a year more patents were granted for improvements in manufacturing. The process was soon extended to other items, effecting the final mechanization of the industry. It not only increased production but also reduced costs to such an extent that glass tableware was brought within reach of a great buying public.

Lacy glass: like blown three mold, pressed glass was an imitation of cut glass and the earliest patterns were derived from this source. However, a typically American type of pressed glass, called 'lacy glass', was developed about 1828, having characteristics obtainable only through this mechanical process. The intricacy and delicacy of the stippled background of tiny relief dots, derived from the diamond cut glass patterns, could not have been achieved in cut glass. Since the pressing process was new, and operators had not had time to learn how to overcome some of the mechanical difficulties, stippling and allover patterns also served the very practical purpose of making any imperfections less noticeable.

Briefly summarized, the process of pressing is as follows: molten metal is dropped into a patterned mold, a plunger is then forced into the mold pressing the glass into all parts and impressing the pattern on it. Since the plunger, or core, is smooth, the corresponding surface of the article is also smooth. The pattern side has a rather dull appearance but, seen through the smooth surface, it is full of sparkle and brilliance.

Cup-plates are among the most fascinating examples of lacy glass, not only because of their large number – nearly a thousand major designs and variants can be found – but also because of the historical significance of many of the patterns. These small plates (from about 2⅝ to 4⅝ inches in diameter) supported the tea cup while the beverage cooled in the porcelain saucer. They were one of the first articles to be pressed in quantity and their popularity seems to have continued well into the 1840s. The historical significance of the cup-plate patterns can only be matched by those of bottles and flasks, which are discussed in the following section by Helen McKearin. Subjects on cup-plates include portraits of George Washington, William Henry Harrison and the emblems of the 1840 presidential campaign; Henry Clay, a popular but unsuccessful presidential candidate; Major Samuel Ringgold, a Mexican War hero; and the Swedish singer, Jenny Lind, who was brought to America in 1850 by P.T.Barnum. Even the coronation of Queen Victoria and her marriage to Prince Albert were portrayed. So also were such events as the saving of the frigate *Constitution* (Plate 123A), and the completion of the Bunker Hill Monument in 1841. Another favorite design was the American eagle, made by a number of factories with plain or patterned borders (Plate 122D).

Cup-plates were also made in a variety of conventional patterns, denoted by the most conspicuous motif, such as *heart; rose; sunburst; thistle; shell* and the so-called *hairpin,*

as well as a number of purely geometric patterns. Among the last are the most beautiful examples of lacy glass because the intricate design and stippled background give the maximum sparkle and brilliance (Plate 123B).

Forms in pressed glass: one of the most familiar forms in pressed glass is the salt. The earliest were simple rectangles with feet at the corners and a single motif, such as a rose or basket of flowers on the sides and ends (Plate 124A). Lacy patterns include designs using scrolls, rosettes, shells and leaves. Salts did not lend themselves to historical subjects and only a few, illustrated by the Lafayette item made by the Boston & Sandwich Company, have been recorded (Plate 124B).

Lamps, candlesticks and vases were also made during the early pressed glass period, from the late 1820s through the 1850s. Earlier, a few of these were hand-blown or blown-molded (Plates 115, 117B) but, judging by their scarcity, their number was small. However, a much larger number of lamps and candlesticks exist with pressed bases but with hand-blown oil fonts and shafts. Those with stepped bases are usually hollow on the inside (Plate 124D). When a lacy base was used, the design is almost always on the under or inner side of the base. This type constitutes a transition from the entirely handmade article to the completely mechanical, but they were still expensive due to the handwork involved. Vases do not seem to have been made with either stepped or lacy bases but after about 1835, when these three items were made entirely by the pressing process, they became an important part of production. Pressed glass made up to about 1860 is rather heavy, with simple, effective designs, often based on the classical. This was also the period of the popular dolphin motif (Plate 124C) used for the standards of candlesticks, lamps and compotes. The greatest innovation was in the use of color and combinations of colors; many shades of blue, green, the popular vaseline and canary, amethyst, and translucent and opaque white. Only a few different molds were necessary which greatly reduced the cost of production; but the combinations were numerous and the use of different colors gave a feeling of even greater variety.

Makers of pressed glass: while the name Sandwich for the Boston & Sandwich Glass Company of Sandwich, Massachusetts, has become almost synonymous with pressed glass (Plate 125B), this type of glass was produced in increasing quantities by many other factories. Actually between 1829 and 1850, at least eight factories in New England, New York and Pennsylvania, and another eight of the Midwestern factories of the Ohio and West Virginia area were pressing glass on a commercial scale.

It is impossible to describe in detail here the activities of even some of the larger and more important glasshouses of the first half of the nineteenth century. The following list, which is arranged geographically and with emphasis on those houses to which examples can be attributed, will give some idea of the names and locations of the most noteworthy manufactories of the period.

Connecticut

COVENTRY GLASS WORKS, 1813–c. 1848; bottles, flasks, blown three mold.
PITKIN GLASS WORKS, Manchester, 1783–c. 1830; the earliest factory in the state; bottles and flasks.
WILLINGTON GLASS WORKS, West Willington, 1814–72; bottles, flasks, off-hand blown glass.

Massachusetts

BOSTON & SANDWICH GLASS WORKS, Sandwich, 1825–88; established by Deming Jarves, formerly of the New England Glass Company, excelled in a variety of ware; plain, cut, engraved and blown three mold tableware, pressed and lacy glass.
MOUNT WASHINGTON GLASS COMPANY, South Boston, 1837–94 (moved to New Bedford in 1869); blown, cut and pressed glass.
NEW ENGLAND GLASS COMPANY, Cambridge, 1818–80; established by Deming Jarves and associates; one of the foremost producers of all types of fine glassware, including cut, engraved, blown three mold, pressed glass, paperweights and Art glass.

New Hampshire

MARLBORO STREET FACTORY, Keene, 1815–50; the first flint glass factory in New England outside of the Boston area; bottles, flasks, blown three mold.
NEW HAMPSHIRE GLASS FACTORY, Keene, the 'North Works' on Washington Street, 1814–55; window glass.
STODDARD. There were four factories here at different times between 1842 and 1873, making bottles and flasks.

New Jersey

JERSEY GLASS COMPANY, Jersey City, 1824–c. 1862; cut, engraved and pressed glass.
STANGER BROTHERS, Millville; established 1781, carried over into the nineteenth century. By 1820, there were about eleven glasshouses in operation in this area making window glass and bottles, as well as individual off-hand blown ware; by 1836 the number had increased to forty.

New York

BROOKLYN FLINT GLASS WORKS, 1823–68 (moved to Corning); established by John L. Gilliland; fine cut glass and other types.
CLEVELAND GLASS WORKS, Oswego County, 1840–89; window glass, off-hand pieces.
ELLENVILLE GLASS COMPANY, Ulster County, 1836–late nineteenth century; bottles, demijohns, individual off-hand pieces.
LANCASTER GLASS WORKS, Erie County, 1849–late nineteenth century; flasks, individual off-hand pieces.
LOCKPORT GLASS WORKS, Niagara County, 1840–late nineteenth century; bottles, flasks, individual off-hand pieces.
NEW YORK (CITY), BLOOMINGDALE FLINT GLASS WORKS, 1820–40; established by Richard and John Fisher; fine cut glass.
REDFORD CROWN GLASS WORKS, Clinton County, 1831–51; window glass, off-hand pieces.
REDWOOD GLASS WORKS, Jefferson County, 1833–late nineteenth century; window glass, individual off-hand pieces.

SARATOGA, CONGRESSVILLE GLASS WORKS, 1865–c. 1890; spring water bottles.
SARATOGA (MOUNTAIN) GLASS WORKS, 1844–65; spring water bottles, flasks, blown three mold, individual off-hand pieces, formerly at Vernon.
VERNON, ONEIDA COUNTY, MOUNT VERNON GLASS WORKS, 1810–c. 1844 (moved to Saratoga); bottles, blown three mold, individual off-hand pieces.

Ohio

KENT, 1823–c. 1834; MANTUA, 1821–9; ZANESVILLE, 1815–c. 1845; factories in these three places made Stiegel-type colored flint glass, bottles and blown three mold ware.

Pennsylvania

NEW GENEVA GLASS WORKS, 1797–1847; established by Albert Gallatin and others, bottles, window glass and clear glass similar to that made by Amelung.
PITTSBURGH, BAKEWELL & COMPANY (PITTSBURGH FLINT GLASS COMPANY), 1809–80; fine cut and engraved tableware, bottles, pressed glass.
R.B.CURLING & SONS (FORT PITT GLASS WORKS), 1826–c. 1900; cut glass and pressed glass.
O'HARA & CRAIG (PITTSBURGH GLASS WORKS), 1797–c. 1886; window glass, bottles.
STOURBRIDGE FLINT GLASS WORKS, 1823–45; cut, engraved and pressed glass.

West Virginia

WHEELING: there were a number of factories established in this area including, RITCHIE & WHEAT, 1829–c. 1850, cut and pressed glass; M. & R.H.SWEENEY & COMPANY, 1831–67, cut and engraved glass.

Pressed tableware: lacy designs were expensive to produce because the intricacy of the stippled backgrounds meant higher costs in mold making. To overcome this difficulty, another type of pressed glass was developed about 1837. Again following cut glass patterns, this type used simple geometric motifs which could be adapted to all types of tableware. At first only the more necessary articles of tableware were made, but as the demand grew, complete table sets in many patterns and many colors were produced, including, besides the usual types of drinking glasses, egg cups, butter dishes, celery vases, compotes, lamps, candlesticks and vases. The earlier patterns, called the colonial group, were made from a heavy, brilliant metal in simple, effective designs like the *Ashburton*, *Argus*, *Excelsior*, *Diamond-Thumbprint* and *Waffle and Thumbprint*. These were produced in the late 1830s and early 1840s. This type of pattern was soon followed by designs somewhat more complicated in detail but still retaining the characteristics of cut glass, such as *Bull's Eye* and *Fleur-de-Lis* (Plate 128D), *Horn of Plenty*, *Comet* and *Sandwich Star*. One of the most popular groups of patterns of the 1850s was the *ribbed*, characterized by fine vertical ribbing and comprising such patterns as the *Ribbed Bellflower*, *Ivy* (Plate 128C), *Grape* and *Acorn*. The *Ribbed Bellflower* seems to have been one of the earliest patterns to have been made in complete sets. It is listed in a catalogue of the McKee Brothers of Pittsburgh, in 1868, and was probably made even earlier than this. In the 1860s such patterns as *Cable*, *Lincoln Drape*, *Frosted Roman Key*, and a number of *Grape* patterns were in vogue. While many of these patterns continued in style well into the 1860s and 1870s, the trend was away from simplicity toward elaboration. By 1870 the Victorian preference for naturalistic motifs was evident and designs were over-ornamented and often in high relief. Patterns of this period include the popular *Westward-Ho*, having an Indian finial on the cover and a log cabin on the body; *Lion* with a lion finial, and *Three Faces*, with three classical heads used as finials and as decoration on the stems of glasses and compotes. A group of patterns with conventional motifs was produced in the 1880s, including the *Daisy and Button* and several varieties of *Hobnail*. From 1870 on, these patterns were made in complete sets in colors as well as in clear glass.

Much of this later ware was lime glass, a metal much cheaper to produce but having almost as much brilliance as fine lead or flint glass. Lime glass was introduced by Hobbs, Brockunier & Company, Wheeling, West Virginia, in 1864, and other factories were soon forced into using it in order to meet the competition.

Books by Ruth Webb Lee, listed in Books for Further Reading, cover the subject of pressed, or pattern glass in thorough fashion, listing over three hundred patterns of pressed tableware.

Marble glass: the quest for the unusual led to the production of opaque glass like Marble or Purple Slag (Plate 128B) developed by Challinor, Taylor & Company, Tarentum, Pennsylvania, and made by them in great quantities in the 1870s and 1880s. The original name for this type in the catalogues of this firm was 'Mosaic Glass', showing that it was conceived as an imitation of mosaic pottery and was not produced by accident from the left-overs in the melting pot, as is popularly believed. It is very attractive in simple patterned pieces where the blending of the purple and white in a marbleized design shows to best advantage. This ware was made in sets in a fluted pattern and also in the flower and panel design (Plate 128B). The open-edged plates are especially attractive examples of this type. Pieces showing brown and white mixture, called *caramel* or *custard glass*, were also produced in the late nineteenth and early twentieth centuries.

Milk glass, or Milk-White Glass, was originally called 'Opaque White', 'Opaque', 'Opalescent' and 'Alabaster'. It was developed in imitation of porcelain. There are a few pieces of hand-blown opaque white glass from the early part of the nineteenth century, and more having opalescent tints from the early pressed glass period. But the Milk Glass which is collected today was first made on a large commercial scale in the 1870s and 1880s. There are some pieces with 1870 and 1872 patent dates but its greatest popularity came in the last two decades of the century and, in fact, reproductions of the most popular designs are still being turned out.

As usual, the earliest patterns are the best artistically. The *Saw Tooth, Sheaf of Wheat,*

and the *Berry* patterns are the same as the clear glass of the same names. The open-edge and lattice-edge plates and bowls are also very attractive examples of this ware. However, the most popular articles in milk glass are the covered animal dishes. These include hens (Plate 126A), roosters, ducks, swans, rabbits, dogs, cats and in fact a complete 'Barnyard Assortment' as listed in the catalogue. The majority of these dishes are all white but some are combined with blue with naturalistic touches, such as red combs on the roosters and glass eyes. The hen and rooster dishes were made by the Westmoreland Glass Company, Grapeville, Pennsylvania, and were sold filled with mustard. A number of animal dishes are marked 'McKee', a Pittsburgh factory. The Atterbury Company, also of Pittsburgh, patented a well-designed duck dish in 1887. The late Victorian taste for the sentimental was pleased by plates with kittens, puppies, owls and bunnies, which are realistically conceived and not particularly good in design.

Whimseys, miniatures and Victorian novelties: the term whimsey is used for odd or unusual pieces created by individual workmen to show their skill and inventiveness. It also applies to articles which differ from the standard or commercial types, such as hats, toys, canes, rolling-pins and button-hooks. These articles may be free blown, blown molded or blown three mold and might have originated in any window or bottle glass factories of the early nineteenth century.

The later pressed glass novelties were commercial products, used as premiums or as containers for mustard and other prepared products. Many of these novelties originated after the Centennial Exhibition in Philadelphia in 1876. There were match and toothpick holders in the form of boots, slippers, shoes, shoes on roller skates, coal scuttles and all kinds of animal dishes. Pin trays, ash trays, card trays and pickle dishes were made in the shape of fans, hands, boats and fish, all kinds of animals and other shapes in questionable taste. All were made in a variety of colors and patterns (Plate 127). *Daisy and Button* was one of the commonest patterns.

Paperweights: the art of making glass paperweights goes back to the techniques employed by Venetian workmen in making *latticinio* and striped glass in the famous Murano glasshouses of the Renaissance. However, the earliest signed and dated paperweights are those made in St Louis, France, in the 1840s. Other fine weights were made at Baccarat, and at Clichy near Paris and in the English factories.

Paperweights were produced in large numbers in several American glasshouses, but in most cases do not equal in quality and technical excellence the finest of those made in the European factories. Some of the best American weights were created by Nicholas Lutz, who came from the St Louis works to Sandwich. Many of his weights contain tiny colored fruits, apples, pears or cherries, with green leaves on a *latticinio* (lace-like) background. Sandwich weights of the 'candy' and *millefiori* type were made in considerable quantity as were flower designs such as the well-known *poinsettia*, the *dahlia*, *pansy* and *fuchsia* (Plate 126B).

The New England Glass Company made weights of similar design and excellence, such as the blown-glass apple and pear weights by François Pierre, a former workman at Baccarat. John L. Gilliland made beautiful paperweights at his Brooklyn factory. At the Millville, New Jersey, works of Whitall, Tatum & Company, quantities of weights were made from 1863 until 1912. One of the best known was the *Millville rose* made between 1905 and 1912. The *lily* was also a popular Millville design, the best examples dating from the 1870s. The Mount Washington Glass Works in South Boston, which moved to New Bedford in 1868 and became part of the Pairpont Company, produced some fine examples, as did the Dorflinger factory in White Mills, Pennsylvania, the Ravenna Glass Works of Ravenna, Ohio, and other midwestern houses.

The manufacture of these fascinating and beautiful examples of the glass-blower's art is too complicated to discuss here, but authoritative references are listed in Books for Further Reading.

Following the trend of the times, the art of paperweight-making declined in both workmanship and design. Many later weights contained such inscriptions as *Home Sweet Home*, *Remember Me*, and *From a Friend*, inscribed in milk-white on either clear or colored backgrounds. The form was finally taken over as an advertising medium with flat, rectangular weights which have printed reproductions of factories or products pasted on the under side.

Art glass: not all late nineteenth-century ware was of the pressed variety. The so-called 'Art or Fancy glass' was free blown or blown in a mold. However, its interest lies mainly in the high degree of technical excellence which was achieved and in the invention of new types of glass. The emphasis was on naturalistic designs and new forms in keeping with the tastes of the Victorian period. The search for new materials brought forth some interesting results, especially in the use of color.

Foremost among the new types was Peachblow. This ware was made in imitation of Chinese porcelain, and its production followed the sensational sale of Mrs Mary J. Morgan's collection of Chinese and Japanese porcelains in New York in 1886. At this sale an eight-inch vase brought a record $18,000, and the glass manufacturers were quick to capitalize on the resulting publicity. Hobbs, Brockunier & Company of Wheeling, copied it (Plate 125A) and soon other companies were making similar ware. The Wheeling product was a cased or plated glass with the outside color shading from a deep red to a yellowish tint and with a milk-white lining. Vase and bowl forms follow Oriental shapes but new types like salts, peppers, jugs, cruets and gas lamp shades were also made. The Wheeling Peachblow was usually made with a *matte* finish produced by an acid bath but it was also made with the natural glossy finish.

The New England and Mount Washington factories also made a ware called Peachblow but it was a homogeneous glass of the same composition throughout. The New England Company's Peachblow shades from creamy white and ivory to deep rose, while the Mount

Washington ware show light pastel shades of pale blue and rose-pink. The former company also made a variation of Peachblow, called Agata (*see* Glossary), in which the surface was treated to produce a mottled effect. It was always made with the glossy finish and shades from white to rose.

Another similar ware called Burmese glass, shading from rose-pink to yellow, was patented by the Mount Washington Glass Company in 1885. It was made in both decorative shapes and in a great variety of tableware. Amberina was a shaded glass but was translucent, while Peachblow and Burmese were opaque. Amberina was an amber glass containing the metal gold and shading from yellow-amber to dark red (Plate 129A). Other novelty glass of the last two decades of the nineteenth century were Aurene, Mother-of-Pearl or Satin, Pomona (Plate 128A), and Spangled glass. These types are described more fully in the glossary.

Imitations of ancient glass were the Vasa Murrhina (*see* Glossary) and the glass made by Louis C. Tiffany, son of the New York jeweller. At his Corona, Long Island works, Tiffany was finally able to produce a metal having the iridescence of long-buried glass. Tiffany believed that glassmaking was an art and that glass should be made by hand instead of by mechanical means, so he chose *Favrile*, meaning handwrought, for his trademark. Some fanciful and imaginative shapes were produced as well as a number of unusual colors such as bluish-green and gold and many shades of red. By combining different colors in the body of the object, and then twisting and spinning it while it was being blown, lines and patterns were produced suggestive of leaves, waves and peacock feathers (Plates 129B, 130). Besides vases of various shapes, he made goblets and wineglasses, bonbon dishes and many other decorative pieces.

A great deal of the Art glass was poorly designed according to present taste but it was an attempt to create beauty, and was not merely a mechanical product. It has a place in the history of American glass as the forerunner of the fine free-blown crystal being made today.

GLOSSARY

Agata: mottled finish used chiefly on Amberina glass, in which the article is coated with a metallic stain or mineral color, then spattered with a quickly evaporating liquid such as alcohol. Made by New England Glass Co., 1886.

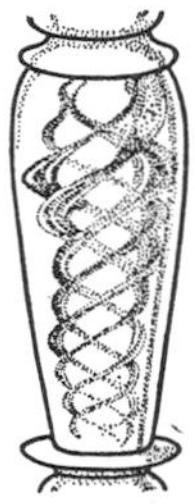

Air twist: spiral veins of air formed by extension of air bubbles, usually in stems of drinking vessels and shafts of candlesticks.

FIG. 1.
Air twist

Amberina: made from a gold-ruby compound, an amber glass mixture containing the metal gold; colors shade from yellow-amber to dark red. New England Glass Co., 1883.

Annealing: process of cooling glass slowly in an annealing oven.

Applied decoration: ornaments formed from a separate gather of metal and tooled into form.

Arch patterns: blown three mold patterns having a Gothic or Roman arch as the conspicuous motif (Plate 121B); pressed glass patterns also.

Art glass: late-nineteenth-century glass showing use of new materials and techniques; includes Peachblow, Burmese, Satin, Tiffany, etc.

Aurene: gold-ruby glass heated to different degrees resulting in iridescent shades of yellow, violet and pink. Steuben Glass Works.

Baluster: *see* Stems.

Baroque patterns: blown three mold patterns composed of bold motifs in relief; used instead of 'rococo' to distinguish typical American designs from French (Plate 122A).

Batch: mixture of raw materials ready for melting.

Blank: uncut vessel before it is decorated.

Blown molded: a gather of metal blown in a mold, either a dip mold or a part-size piece mold, to impress a design before an object is shaped. *See* Molded glass.

Blown three mold: collector's name for a category of inexpensive blown molded ware, made from about 1815 to 1835; blown in full-size piece molds with design cut on inside of mold; three categories of patterns: *geometric, arch* and *baroque*; distinguished from cut and pressed glass in that inner surfaces follow pattern of outer surfaces; developed in an effort to produce less expensive tableware than the fashionable Irish and English cut glass; was itself outmoded by pressed glass.

Blowpipe: long, hollow, iron tube used to hold a gather of molten glass.

Bottles: with window glass, the commercial product of glasshouses of eighteenth and early nineteenth centuries; of dark olive-green or olive-amber metal, blown in full-size two-piece molds;
1. *calabash:* ovoid body tapering into cylindrical neck with collared lip.
2. *case:* any bottle designed for use in a case or box, blown to size to fit a compartment as in a traveling case.
3. *carboy:* large demijohn; usually set in wooden tub; used mainly for corrosive liquids.
4. *chestnut:* free-blown bottles with long neck and fat chestnut-shaped body, ranging in size from a few ounces to a gallon or more; also called *Ludlow* because of a tradition of having been made in a Ludlow, Massachusetts, glasshouse; eighteenth and early nineteenth centuries.
5. *demijohn:* mainly a storage and shipping bottle, often with wicker jacket; free-blown or molded for symmetrical, globular form, with long neck and lip usually collared; quart to twenty-gallon sizes.
6. *nursing:* flattened ovoid flask rounded at the end, short neck with sheared lip; plain and pattern-molded; eighteenth and early nineteenth centuries.
7. *Stiegel-type pocket or perfume:* chunky bulbous form, slightly flattened wide sides; pattern-molded designs (Plate 117).

Bottle glass: *see* Green glass.

Burmese glass: said to contain the element uranium; shading from rose-pink to pale yellow; dull or glossy finish. Mount Washington Glass Co., New Bedford, Massachusetts; from 1885.

Camphor glass: white, cloudy appearance; known in blown-mold and pressed glass.

Case bottles: *see* Bottles.

Cased glass: two or more layers of glass differing in color; called overlay when design is cut through to body color; popular Bohemian glass technique.

Castor bottles: bottles to set in a castor or cruet frame for condiments; perforated metal tops.

Chain: applied, tooled, link-like decoration laid on around the body of a partially-formed object; also called *Guilloche*.

Checkered diamond: decorative motif of large diamond enclosing four small ones; possibly used by Stiegel at Manheim, Pennsylvania; at New Bremen in Maryland and in one or more early-nineteenth-century midwestern bottle houses, used principally for flasks and salts (Plate 118D).

Chestnut bottle: *see* Bottles.

Collars: heavy applied thread or ribbon laid on around lips of bottles and flasks, necks of decanters; also used to denote part of stem or shaft.

Compote: bowl on standard (stem and foot); also on domed or pedestal foot.

Crimping: dents or flutes impressed by a tool, usually diagonal, used on the foot or tip of handle (Plates 114A, C, 117A).

Crown glass: early form of window glass; commercial product with bottles of early glasshouses.

Cruet: lipped bottle with or without handles; *see* Castor bottles.

FIG. 2. Crimping

Crystal: refers to finest colorless or clear flint glass.

Cullet: cleaned, broken glass used in all new mixtures to promote fusion and improve quality of the metal.

Cup-plate: small plate, about $2\frac{5}{8}$ to $4\frac{5}{8}$ inches in diameter; used as saucer for cup while tea was cooling in pottery or porcelain saucer; made mainly in inexpensive wares such as pressed glass in second quarter of the nineteenth century (Plate 122D).

Cut glass: glass decorated by grinding designs and motifs with abrasives and polishing wheels; an old form of decoration brought to the United States from England and Ireland in late eighteenth century; patterns mainly geometric; simple in early nineteenth century, becoming over-complicated in late nineteenth century (Plates 120A, B, 121A).

Daisy-in-hexagon: decorative motif of daisy-like flower in a hexagon, believed to have been originated by Stiegel; found mainly on pocket or perfume bottles (Plate 118A).

Diamond-daisy: decorative motif of daisy-like flower within square diamond; also believed to be a Stiegel original (Plate 117D).

Dip mold: one-piece open-top fluted or ribbed mold, of varying sizes and depths.

Double-ogee bowl: shape of bowl displaying a double ogival curve, or distorted S-shape; found in Stiegel type salts.

Eagle, American: motif derived from the United States Seal or coins; commonly found in lacy glass (Plate 122D) and historical flasks.

End-of-day glass: misnomer for marble glass.

Engraved glass: decoration achieved by means of copper wheels of various sizes (Plates 116, 120A).

Etched glass: decoration achieved by means of corrosive acid applied to unprotected surfaces.

Favrile glass: name meaning 'hand-wrought' used for Art glass made by Louis Comfort Tiffany (1848–1933). *See* Tiffany glass.

Finial: knob or ornament on covers, either drawn or applied, usually with short stem; forms such as ball, ball and button, mushroom, spire, hen or swan-like bird.

Fire polishing: reheating of finished objects to obtain a smooth surface.

Flashed glass: thin coating of colored glass over layer of clear glass; a ruby stain in imitation of Bohemian glass, the most popular.

Flasks: bottle-shaped containers to hold liquids, perfume or liquor: varying in size from a few ounces to over a quart in capacity.
1. *Chestnut:* free-blown and pattern-molded, resembling a chestnut in shape; ranging in size from a few ounces to over a quart; mainly late eighteenth – early nineteenth centuries.
2. *Historical:* designs using historical figures or events. (*See* following article by Helen McKearin.)
3. *Pitkin:* generic term for pocket bottles or flasks, blown by German half-post method and pattern-molded in such ribbed designs as vertical, swirled and broken swirl; eighteenth century and early nineteenth century; identified by tradition with the Pitkin Glassworks, East Hartford, Connecticut, *c.* 1790–1830.

Flint glass: literally, glass made with silica of calcined flints; as far as is now known, not made in the United States but used as a trade-name for fine glassware. *See also* Lead glass.

Flip or **Flip glass:** collector's term for tumblers, usually of pint or more capacity; something of a misnomer, as probably rarely used to serve the beverage called flip (Plate 117C).

Fluting: term used when wider unit of a ridged design is concave: fan-fluting a blown three mold motif of short tapering flutes or panels.

Folded rims: *see* Rims.

Foot: base of vessel, usually circular, sometimes square; may be applied or drawn from the vessel's body and fashioned by tooling; may be flat, sloping, petaled or domed.

Free blown: glass formed by blowing and manipulation with hand tools, without the aid of molds; also called hand blown and off-hand blown.

Frit: partially fused ingredients, heated in furnace and kept on hand for melting.

Full-size mold: mold composed of two or more hinged pieces and the approximate size of the article which would receive no further expansion by blowing.

Gadroon or **Gadrooning:** method of decorating a foot or the base of a bowl in which a second gather of glass is pulled up over the original and tooled or molded to form a ribbed or swirled band (Plate 115).

Gather: blob of molten metal on end of blowpipe ready for blowing.

Geometric patterns: blown three mold patterns composed of such motifs as ribs, flutes, diamond, sunbursts, circles and ovals (Plate 122B, C); also pressed and cut glass patterns.

Green glass: glass in its natural color, neither rendered colorless nor artificially colored; generally made from coarser and less pure materials than those used for fine wares; soda, potash or lime the principal alkaline base; many bottles and window glass made from this glass.

Guilloche: *see* Chain.

Half-post: method of giving added strength by re-dipping the post (first gather) in pot of metal; case bottles and Pitkin flasks made by this method.

Hand blown: *see* Free blown.

Handles: applied after object is formed; may be solid or hollow, round or flat; with turned back or curled tip or crimped end; sometimes decorated by medial rib or different types of ribbing.

Historical glass: glass bearing decoration illustrating national or local events; portraits of heroes; emblems of agriculture; trade; transportation; chiefly flasks and pressed glass, such as cup plates.

Kewblas: colored glass over milk glass with coat of clear on top. Union Glass Works, Somerville, Massachusetts, 1890s.

Knop: solid or hollow knob in stem or shaft of a vessel.

Lacy glass: type of pressed glass made c. 1820–40; intricate relief designs on finely stippled, lace-like background; characteristically brilliant and sparkling; mainly cup plates and salts with some dishes and plates, and more rarely, bases of lamps and candlesticks (Plates 122D, 123B).

Lava glass: type of glass made in imitation of mosaic lava-ware pottery. Mount Washington Glass Works, South Boston, Massachusetts, 1878.

Lead glass: glass containing lead as a flux; called 'flint glass'.

Lily pad: applied decoration formed from a superimposed layer of glass attached to bottom of parison, pulled up and tooled into a pad-like form which gives rise to the name; used on South Jersey type glass (Plates 113, 114A, C).

Lime glass: glass containing lime; first produced in 1864; the metal is as clear as lead glass and cheaper but not so resonant or heavy.

Loopings or Draggings: decorative device achieved by applying threads of contrasting colors to body or parison, which are then dragged upward by a tool and rolled on marver to embed in body; used since ancient times; used in American glass on pieces of South Jersey type.

FIG. 3. Looping

Marble glass: also called 'Purple Slag' and, wrongly, 'End-of-Day Glass' because it was supposed to have been made from left-overs in furnace at end of day's work; pressed glass in variegated tints of purple and milk-white glass giving a marbleized effect. Challinor, Taylor & Co., Tarentum, Pennsylvania, 1870s and 1880s (Plate 128B).

Marver: polished metal slab supported by frame on which gather of metal is rolled.

Merese: glass wafer or button joining bowl and stem of a vessel or connecting parts of stem or shaft.

Metal: term for glass either in the molten or hard state.

Midwestern: collector's term for glass made in glasshouses of the midwest, principally in the Pittsburgh area, and in Ohio and West Virginia.

Milk glass or **Milk-white glass:** opaque white glass made in imitation of Chinese porcelain, produced by mixing oxide of tin with clear; free blown or, in late nineteenth century, pressed in a variety of objects (Plate 126A).

Molded glass: glass blown in a mold for pattern and given partial or final body shape by the mold; generally called blown molded.

Mother-of-pearl or **Satin glass:** core of opaque white glass blown in a pattern mold, given a coating of transparent glass and treated with acid to achieve satin finish. Phoenix Glass Company, Pittsburgh, Pennsylvania, 1885.

Neck rings: *see* Collars.

Nursing bottles: *see* Bottles.

Off-hand blown: *see* Free blown.

Ogival: expanded diamond in pattern-molded design; usually loosely formed diamonds above flutes.

Opalescent dewdrop (later called Hobnail): pressed in full-size molds; tips of nodules made of opalescent glass; made in various colors. Hobbs, Brockunier & Company, Wheeling, West Virginia, 1886.

Overlay: *see* Cased glass.

Paneling: molded contiguous round or oval-topped arches (Plate 118B).

Parison: inflated, unformed gather of metal.

Part-size mold: small two-piece hinged mold used to impress the design on the gather.

Pattern-molded: term used to designate glass molded for decorative pattern or design only in dip or part-size molds which is then expanded; used to differentiate glass so patterned from that blown in full-size molds.

Peach glass or **Peachblow:** peach-like tints shading from cream to rose, red to yellow, or blue to pink, made in imitation of a Chinese porcelain. Made by the New England Glass Company in 1885 but became very popular when Hobbs, Brockunier & Company of Wheeling brought out a copy of the Mary J. Morgan collection Chinese porcelain vase which brought $18,000 at auction in 1886. Their product was a cased glass with milk-white lining, whereas the Peachblow made by the New England Glass Company and by the Mount Washington Glass Works was the same composition throughout.

Pedestal foot: *see* Foot.

Piece mold: mold composed of two or more pieces; may be either part-size or full-size.

Pillar molded: ornamentation of pattern-molded ribs, either vertical or swirled.

Pinched trailing: *see* Quilling.

Pitkin flask: *see* Flasks.

Pocket bottle: *see* Bottles.

Pomona glass: stippled body achieved with acid combined with unstippled portion stained a straw color; frequently decorated with an applied garland of flowers; New England Glass Company, 1884 (Plate 128A).

Pontil or **Punty rod:** long solid iron rod, occasionally hollow, used to hold vessel while still hot during the finishing process.

Pontil mark: scar left on a completed vessel where it was snapped off the pontil or punty rod; sometimes polished off, so its presence or absence is not positive proof of age.

Pressed glass: glass pressed manually or mechanically in molds; molten glass is dropped into a patterned mold, a plunger is rammed into the mold, forcing glass into all parts of the mold and impressing the pattern on it; plunger or core has a smooth surface so that inside of piece being pressed is smooth in contrast to blown molded or blown three mold glass. Method said to have originated in United States. It is wrongly called 'Sandwich Glass' from the famous factory at Sandwich, Massachusetts, where it was first produced on a large commercial scale. By 1829, at least six eastern and four midwestern glasshouses were producing pressed glass.

Pressed pattern ware: pressed glass tableware made in complete table settings in many patterns. *See* Books for Further Reading for titles which give complete catalogue of patterns.

Prunts: applied blobs of glass tooled or molded into various forms (Plate 114B).

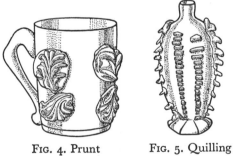

FIG. 4. Prunt   FIG. 5. Quilling

Purple slag: *see* Marble glass.

Quilling: ribbon of glass applied and pinched into pleats; also called 'pinched trailing'.

Ribbing: term used when the convex ribs in a design are wider than the interstices between them.

Rigaree: narrow applied ribbons of glass tooled in parallel lines.

Rims: edge finish of foot or bowl tops; may be *sheared* or *plain*, in which case the excess

glass is cut away evenly and the edge is smoothed by reheating; *folded*, in which the sheared edge is folded back; *gauffered* – a flaring, wide-scallop edge used on vases; *galleried* – treatment of nineteenth-century bowls in which the rim is drawn up to form a support for a set-in cover.

Rummer: drinking vessel with a globular bowl, short stem and plain foot; in effect, a short-stemmed goblet.

South Jersey type: term for off-hand pieces fashioned by free blowing and manipulation from bottle and window glass for the families and friends of the blowers; not

FIG. 6. Threading

made commercially; this type seems to have been blown not only in New Jersey but in most eastern bottle and window glasshouses until the complete mechanization of the industry in the 1870s; types of decoration included the lily pad, prunts, threading around necks of vessels, crimping of feet and handles and quilling (Plates 113, 114, 115).

Spangled glass: molten glass rolled over flakes of mica or metal particles which fused when heated. Made by Hobbs, Brockunier & Company, Wheeling, West Virginia, 1883; called 'Vasa Murrhina'; blue flecked with silver and gold and other combinations are known.

Stiegel type: term for type of glass first made at the Glasshouse of Henry William Stiegel, Manheim, Pennsylvania, *c.* 1765–74; three types known: *engraved* as in Plate 116; *enameled*, similar to the Continental type, Plate 117C; and *colored pattern ware* which follows the English tradition. These techniques or methods were used at other glasshouses established in the late eighteenth and early nineteenth centuries in New England, Ohio and Pennsylvania; this type of glass is called

'Stiegel type' whether made at Manheim or elsewhere in the United States (Plate 118c).

Stippling: minute raised dots forming the background in lacy glass which produced the glitter and sparkle characteristic of this type of glass.

Swagging: superimposed layer of glass tooled into wave-like forms.

Tiffany glass: a type of Art glass; made by Louis Comfort Tiffany (1848–1933) in New York in the late 1890s; many pieces marked *Favrile*. Process fused various colors by heat, then exposed the piece to fumes of vaporized metals; pieces were hand blown in fanciful forms; spinning and twisting during blowing process produced wavy lines suggestive of leaves, waves or peacock feathers; bluish-green and gold, light mother-of-pearl, red and other more unusual colors; is characteristically iridescent with a satiny finish, in imitation of ancient glass (Plates 129B, 130).

Tortoise shell: pale brownish-amber glass with darker splotches; another glass made in imitation of other ware which was popular in the late nineteenth century; attributed to the Sandwich Glass Company.

Whimsey: term used for odd or unusual pieces, such as hats, slippers, buttonhooks, made by individual workmen for themselves or their families; or the adaptation of a conventional form to some odd or unusual shape or use (Plate 127).

BOOKS FOR FURTHER READING

BELKNAP, E. McCAMLY: *Milk Glass*, New York (1949).

BERGSTROM, EVANGELINE H.: *Old Glass Paperweights*, New York (1948).

DANIEL, DOROTHY: *Cut and Engraved Glass 1771–1905*, New York (1950).

KNITTLE, RHEA M.: *Early American Glass*, New York (1927).

LEE, RUTH WEBB: *Sandwich Glass*, Pittsburg, Penn. (1931).

LEE, RUTH WEBB: *Early American Pressed Glass*, Northboro, Mass. (Enlarged and revised 1946).

LEE, RUTH WEBB: *Victorian Glass*, Northboro, Mass. (1944).

McKEARIN, GEORGE S. and HELEN: *American Glass*, New York (1941).

McKEARIN, HELEN and GEORGE S.: *Two Hundred Years of American Blown Glass*, New York (1950).

PRATT, RICHARD: *Second Treasury of Early American Homes*, Hawthorn Books, New York (1954).

WATKINS, LURA WOODSIDE: *American Glass and Glass Making*, New York (1950).

Concise Encyclopedia of Antiques, Vol. III, 73–89, Hawthorn Books, New York (1957).

The author wishes to make acknowledgment to Helen McKearin, not only for dependence on her books listed here, but for personal suggestions and guidance.

FIGURED BOTTLES
AND FLASKS

By HELEN McKEARIN

IT has not been established just when United States bottles and flasks were first blown and decorated in full-size piece molds, that is, metal molds of two or more pieces (leaves) hinged together, the inner surface of which bore an intaglio pattern and/or lettering and was the size and shape of the article for which it was made. However, regardless of other factors, early-nineteenth-century economics would have determined the supremacy of the full-size mold over the old free-blown techniques: apart from ensuring uniformity of shape, size and liquid capacity, as free-blowing did not, it was a labor-saving and time-saving device well on the road to mass-production.

While eighteenth-century advertisements sometimes seem to hint that bottles for nostrums may have been blown in lettered molds, the earliest recorded proof of their American use is an advertisement of May 17, 1809, in the *Federal Gazette and Baltimore Daily Advertiser* stating '... Dr Robertson's Family Medicines are put up in square flint glass bottles American Manufactured, with these words impressed on the glass – Dr Robertson's Family Medicines, prepared only by T.W. Dyott.' It may be that such bottles were used by Thomas W. Dyott from the beginning of his career in the field of medicine, 1807. If inscribed bottles were used by him they surely were by some of his many competitors.

From bottles with inscriptions it was a short step to bottles with decoration, one certainly taken during or immediately following the War of 1812. But, so far as we now know, the earliest reference which, presumably, designated flasks with relief decoration is an 1817 advertisement in the Hartford, Connecticut, *Times* of 'figured

Pocket Bottles, suitable for the southern market' made at John Mather's East Hartford glassworks. Mather, who started his works in 1805, undoubtedly was producing figured bottles before 1817 as, it is generally believed, was the Flint Glass Factory on Marlboro Street, Keene, New Hampshire. Whatever the date of the first appearance of these bottles the fact that infinite possibilities of design were assured by the now indispensable full-size mold must have been quickly recognized by bottlemakers and users. There can be no doubt that, as the general fashion of relief decoration settled into a style, flasks and bottles so ornamented soon became the typical American container for many liquids. In fact, it may be said that from about 1810 or 1815 through the 1860s at least, decorative, pictorial and historical bottles and flasks were a national style of packaging some hard and some less ardent liquors. It is believed at present that some of the Masonic and decorative flasks (such as Plates 131A, 132A) preceded the historical.

Although the number originated by United States moldmakers, glassmen and liquor dealers has not been ascertained, about five hundred bottles and flasks falling in one or another of the three main categories were listed in *Early American Bottles and Flasks*, 1926. Of the three hundred and ninety-eight from individual molds which were charted in *American Glass*,[1] 1941, some were unknown in 1926 and all but a few antedated 1850. Today variants of charted and listed flasks and bottles, as well as newly discovered designs and sizes within established design groups, have swelled the ranks. Moreover, although innumerable aquamarines, ambers, olive-ambers, and olive-greens – colors natural to glass – predominate, within many groups the limits of collectibility are stretched by artificial colors, primary and in many nuances of tone, tint and hue.

By far the majority of the known examples are *flasks*, as the term is used in the United States, a bottle type having flat or convex sides rising to a shoulder or tapering into a short neck and being elliptical or ovate in cross-section. Other shapes are classified as *bottles*. The most common among them is the so-called calabash like the *Louis Kossuth, McK. GI-112* (Plate 132B *centre*). It should be noted also that in the late eighteenth and early nineteenth centuries, for pint and half-pint sizes, the term *flask* seems to have been used interchangeably with *pocket bottle*. Moreover, these were the usual sizes until the 1840s. At least, none of the recorded full-size-molded quart flasks have as yet been unquestionably identified with the earlier period.

Decorative flasks: foremost among the charted decorative flasks are sunbursts, cornucopia and urn of produce or fruit, a few intricate geometric designs, and the scroll flasks. The last appeared later and form a group in which variations, often slight, indicate a large number of individual molds. Occasionally a purely decorative design was used to adorn the side opposite one of historical import. A definite factory attribution can be given to few; for example, only five of the thirty charted sunburst flasks. Types of sunburst, cornucopia and urn are shown (Plate 131A). The sunburst at left center, *McK.GVIII-15,* illustrates a variety of an early type, blown usually from lead glass, mainly at Keene between 1815 and 1820, that at the left, *McK.GVIII-25,* another and later type, probably of the 1820s–30s, represents one blown from bottle glass in an unidentified glassworks. On fifteen of eighteen charted flasks in the cornucopia group that motif graces one side and its natural companion, the urn of produce, the other. An interesting midwestern half-pint variety has an upside-down cornucopia spilling its plenty, and a geometric design, on the reverse. One of two flasks having the symbol of plenty on

each side is illustrated by the half-pint *McK.GIII-2,* at right center. It is attributed to Dyott's Kensington Glass Works, a proven source of the motif's use since Dyott advertised 'cornucopia flasks' in 1824. The flask at the right, produced at the Lancaster (New York) Glass Works established 1849, shows a mid-century urn, one rather linear in rendering as compared with the earlier more fully realized motif. The cornucopia on its reverse is likewise thinly drawn.

Pictorial flasks: as yet, this group is comparatively small, but its numbers are multiplying as the survey of flasks from 1850 into the 1870s progresses. Glasshouses and cabins, flora, fauna and even subjects showing man in some of his antics and sports provide most designs. Among them are hunters, fishermen, mounted and racing horsemen, hounds, banjo players, dancers and trees with and without foliage, as on the pint flask, *McK. GX-17* (Plate 131B *left*). None of those which have been charted seem to be earlier than the 1830s and many of those listed fall in the third quarter of the century.

Masonic emblems: of course, many of the motifs found on decorative and pictorial flasks are 'as old as the hills' and are not in any way essentially American, though possibly their presence on such containers may be. Perhaps the same may be said of the emblems of Freemasonry. However, excepting a New York City merchant's advertisement (1825) of Bristol (England) green glass Masonic pocket bottles, we have no evidence at present of Masonic flasks which might presumably be similar to those produced in the United States. Here, obviously, no line was drawn between a personal pocket bottle of fine flint (lead) glass engraved with Masonic emblems and those with blown-molded emblems, made for packaging as well as for 'toting' and sold over the counter; for the latter were produced in quantity mainly, as would be expected, since Masonry, while socially important and, until the 1830s, politically powerful everywhere in the United States, had an especial stronghold in New York and New England. Pint and half-pint flasks have been identified by archeological evidence with glassworks operating by 1810, 1813, 1814 and 1815 in these two areas. It is almost axiomatic that other contemporary works made similar flasks.

If the conjectured causes of the abrupt drop in production of Masonic flasks in the early 1830s be true ones then there can be no doubt that the creators of bottle and flask designs were sensitive to current social and political events. In this case production is believed to have fallen partly because of the scandal following the alleged kidnapping and murder by indignant and fearful Brothers of a Freemason who threatened to reveal – to publish – his order's secrets. Shortly afterward the furore enabled the latent anti-Masonic political parties to raise a voice which clearly was heard and heeded by many. In addition there was the spreading and daily more militant Temperance Movement which may have aroused the feeling among many Masons that the appearance of their emblems on common whisky bottles was not respectable.

During the period of their popularity at least forty-six varieties of Masonic flasks were produced. Only three have emblems on each side and they are extremely rare today. Five have the Pavement and Arch enclosing Farmers' Arms. One, probably the Kensington Agricultural and Masonic pocket bottle advertised by Dyott in 1822, had on the reverse the frigate *Franklin* and inscription FREE TRADE AND SAILORS RIGHTS. (The *Franklin* was at that time strategically stationed off the coast of South America 'looking after the interests of American merchants in Chile and Peru'. Another, *McK. GIV-32*, similar in form to the Kensington flask but first made about 1832, is illustrated here (Plate 132A *left*). On the reverse is the American eagle and inscription identifying its provenance and maker, ZANESVILLE/OHIO/J.SHEPARD & CO. Among the earliest were those produced at the Flint Glass Factory, Keene, of which *McK. GIV-2* (Plate 132A *center*) is one. On the reverse is an American eagle below a pennant inscribed E PLURIBUS UNUM and above a beaded oval frame with HS, presumably the initials of Henry Schoolcraft, a founder of the works and member of the firm

operating from December 1815 to February 1817.

Because Masonry was so closely tied to politics and also because, with only three exceptions, the flasks have designs of historical import on the other side, the Masonic flasks always have been included in the historical category, which is the largest. Its designs are essentially American. Besides the Masonics, those charted fall roughly into three principal groups: 1. emblems and designs related to our local and national civic and economic life; 2. portraits of heroes and designs associated with them or their deeds; 3. portraits of presidential candidates, emblems and slogans of political campaigns.

Historical: the date on which the first of these flasks appeared and the name of its originator may never be established. However, as in the case of labeled patent-medicine bottles, an advertisement from Thomas W. Dyott is as yet the first in which historical flasks can be identified. In 1812 scarcity of imported medicine bottles led Dyott to acquire an interest in the Olive Glass Works, New Jersey. He soon became sole agent for the Gloucester and Kensington factories as well, and in March 1822 secured sole or controlling interest in the latter. In that month he advertised 'American eagle, ship Franklin, Agricultural and Masonic Pocket Bottles'. That the mention of these bottles was casual, the tag end of innumerable unnotable wares (that is, unnotable to today's collectors) leads one to hope that Dr Dyott had been producing such flasks earlier. If Dyott had, probably others had done so too. For a little over a decade, until his bankruptcy in 1837, he contributed well designed historical and decorative flasks. His ambitious creation, the 'model community' of Dyottville, with its five glassworks was a potent factor in his downfall.

Presidential campaigns: eventually, under other ownerships, flasks and bottles once more were produced at Dyottville. However, the half-pints, pints and quarts identified today with Dyottville are of the 1840–50 period, associated mainly with General Zachary Taylor, Mexican War hero and presidential candidate in 1848. The pint flask, *McK. GI-38* (Plate 132B *right*), showing a classical bust of George Washington and inscription THE FATHER OF HIS COUNTRY, has on the reverse a profile bust of Taylor in uniform and the inscriptions DYOTT-VILLE GLASS WORKS PHILAD⁺ and GEN. TAYLOR NEVER SURRENDERS, one of the several Taylorisms much quoted during the campaign. Supposedly it was his blunt reply to the invitation of the Mexican General Santa Anna to capitulate. Twenty of the flasks depicting Taylor emanated from Dyott-ville and in a fascinating range of colors, natural and artificial. Of the remaining seven, five are attributed to the Baltimore Glass Works. Two have the portrait of Major Samuel Ringgold on the reverse, a Baltimorian, Mexican War hero and the first United States officer to die of wounds received in battle on foreign soil. The flask apparently was nationally, as well as locally, popular: it is common today except in a few colors such as cornflower-blue, amethyst and jade green.

Hard liquor was not new as a vote persuader in elections but its container was, and as such was popular long before the 1848 campaign. Four candidates were so presented before Zachary Taylor. Possibly in 1824, certainly in 1828, the likeness of John Quincy Adams appeared on a midwestern flask. Only about five survivors are known today and probably few were made, since John Q. Adams had little appeal for John Q. Public. But his chief opponent Andrew Jackson, best known as 'Old Hickory' and considered the people's advocate, was an appealing subject for flasks. Two of the eleven charted varieties were from eastern houses, the others from the midwest. Henry Clay, the perennial presidential candidate and father of the 'American System' (high tariffs to protect infant industry and national support of internal improvements), appeared on an 1824 pint flask advertised by a midwestern glassworks but, to this day, never identified. However, Clay is believed to have been portrayed in classical bust on three quart-size flasks produced in the early 1840s. Lastly there was General William Henry Harrison, 'Old

Tippecanoe'. The 1840 'Hard Cider and Log Cabin' campaign which put him in the White House, and after his sudden death in 1841, lodged his running mate, John Tyler, there, was perhaps the most turbulently exciting in our entire national lifetime. Emblems and symbols of the candidates were embodied in many fabrics. In glass, strangely enough, there were only two bottles, both in the form of little log cabins, and only two, possibly three, flasks, all of pint size. While campaign emblems and symbols appear on the flasks, Harrison's likeness is on only one.

Portraits: Taylor, Jackson and Harrison were Generals, heroes of wars, as well as successful presidential candidates. George Washington was certainly both but his political career antedated historical flasks, probably by more than a quarter century. However, for Taylor and Jackson and Henry Clay, Washington's portrait on the other side of the flask was doubtless intended to imply favorable comparison. Be that as it may, Washington is believed to be the American hero whose likeness was chosen first to decorate a flask, possibly by the irrepressibly imaginative Dr Dyott. Washington's portrait adorned at least sixty flasks, forty of which appeared before 1840 and depicted him in uniform as General Washington, military hero, 'Columbia's Matchless Son' rather than 'The Father of his Country'. The statesman-like classical bust was first used in the 1840s and occurs, usually with Taylor, on the many Dyottville half-pint, pint and quart flasks and quart flasks from the Lockport (New York), the Baltimore (Maryland) and the Bridgeton (New Jersey) Glass Works.

In addition to the preceding and a few unidentified portraits, the whisky-flask Hall of Fame contains those of six other men and one woman. That of Benjamin Franklin appears on five. One has the inscription ERIPUT COELO FULMEN, SCEPTRUMQUE TYRANNIS (He snatched the lightning from the heavens and the sceptre from tyrants); another, WHERE LIBERTY DWELLS THERE IS MY COUNTRY, a sentiment undoubtedly held but not yet proven to have been expressed by Franklin. On the reverse of all but one is the name and bust of T.W.Dyott, M.D. – he so honored himself. While not qualifying as a statesman, diplomat or military hero, his name doubtless was a household word in the cities and towns of the many states where his patent medicines were taken.

Among living notables commemorated on liquor flasks was General Lafayette in 1824–5, during his last visit to the country which had made him an honorary citizen in return for his role in making her a sovereign country. Another was De Witt Clinton, so much in the limelight at the same time, because his 'ditch', the Erie Canal, had proved practical. Lastly, there were two foreigners, one who took the country by storm and one who caused a storm in the country in 1850–2. They were – Jenny Lind, 'The Swedish Nightingale', and Louis Kossuth, the Hungarian patriot who found the country in general sympathetic, but unprepared to assist in repelling Russian aggression. On the reverse of the Kossuth bottle, *McK. GI-112* (Plate 132B *center*), is depicted the frigate *Mississippi* on which he embarked for the United States.

Local subjects: also in the historical category are a few flasks with more local than national significance. Among them are those depicting Baltimore's two tall monuments. The Battle Monument, commemorating the city's defenders against the British in the War of 1812, was placed on the reverse of two Washington flasks, one with the Taylorism A LITTLE MORE GRAPE CAPTAIN BRAGG, and one with Daniel Webster's slogan LIBERTY AND UNION. The Washington Monument, the first erected to George Washington, appears on nine. Its cornerstone was laid in 1815, but the figure of Washington did not crown it until 1829. Therefore it may be that the four flasks which show the monument without the statue of Washington were produced before 1829, namely one with General Taylor, two with Washington and one with a small shallop. With the statue, the Monument flasks (Plate 131B *right center*) have an ear of corn and slogan CORN FOR THE WORLD.

Agriculture and transportation: many motifs pertaining to the interwoven threads of the country's local and national economy were devised besides the ear of corn – *Farmers' Arms* as on *McK. GIV-32* (Plate 132A *left*), sheaves of grain, bunches of grapes, corn and stalk. The corn motifs were favored by the Baltimore Glass Works, as they and the slogan were appropriate for the city from which great quantities of corn and corn-meal were shipped to foreign markets. The ships which carried national produce on river, lake and ocean and protected our trade, as did the frigate *Franklin*, were logical subjects also and are found on a few flasks. Even the sloop or shallop, as on *McK. GX-8* (Plate 131B *left center*), represents a type of vessel used for eastern coastal and river traffic and by oystermen. On the reverse of this example is an eight-pointed ornament with tiny trefoil between points.

That exciting advance in transportation, the railroad, inspired at least thirteen individual molds for flasks. Three, assigned to the 1850s, have a crudely drawn steam locomotive on each side. Seven, of which some appeared about 1828 and were still popular in the 1860s, have a horse-drawn cart on rails on each side and the inscription SUCCESS TO THE RAILROAD. That, *McK. GV-5* (Plate 131B *right*), was blown in a mold which Harry Hall White's excavations on the factory sites proved was used at the Mt Vernon Glass Works, Vernon, New York, 1810-44, and then at Mt Pleasant, Saratoga, New York, 1844–c. 1865, to which site the Vernon factory was moved. Three railroad flasks have an American eagle on the reverse.

National emblems: the American eagle, the American star and the American flag were all vibrantly thrilling in the days when these flasks were popular, not viewed with the often unstirred complacency of today. The flag as well as the star appeared on only a few flasks. One is the furled flag with inscription FOR OUR COUNTRY on *McK. GII-53* (Plate 132A *right*), charted in the eagle group because on the other side is an American eagle, exceedingly alert and perched on a shield with an olive branch at left and palm at right of shield. The American eagle, one of the national symbols most overworked in the interests of trade and patriotism, appears on well over a hundred and fifty flasks and bottles, from the earliest datable – that is, the Keene Masonics like *McK. GIV-2* (Plate 132A *center*) – through the *Pike's Peaks* into the 1870s. On six, *Columbia,* the personification of the United States in the form of a Grecian lady wearing a Phrygian Liberty cap, graces the other side. Some renderings follow the United States Coat-of-Arms, some depict a stolid settled bird, others a vigorous, even belligerent, one. The version appearing each side of the pink flask *McK. GII-24* (Plate 132B *left*) was a popular midwestern type in the mid-century.

Throughout the entire period of the decorative, pictorial and historical flasks there was as great a variety in quality of design, fineness of rendering and detail as in the major designs themselves. However, from the point

of view of most collectors and students, a moldmaker's or a designer's lack of skill usually is more than compensated by the interest of a genre product of its times. ART of glass they are not, but they do represent a popular art in American glass.

[1] McK. numbers appearing in connection with flasks are from the charts in *American Glass.*

BOOKS FOR FURTHER READING

McKearin, George S. and Helen: *American Glass,* New York (1941).

McKearin, Helen and George S.: *Two Hundred Years of American Blown Glass,* New York (1950).

McKearin, Helen: *American Historical Flasks,* Corning (1953).

Rensselaer, Stephen Van: *Early American Bottles and Flasks* (1926).

White, Harry Hall: Articles in the Magazine *Antiques,* see Index of *Antiques.*

All examples illustrated are from the McKearin Collection.

NEEDLEWORK

By RUTH BRADBURY DAVIDSON

IN America the professional embroiderer has always been the exception. The great bulk of the needlework for which an American origin can be claimed was produced by amateurs – women who employed this age-old craft to beautify their homes and clothing or, in a later period, young ladies demonstrating the genteel accomplishments acquired at school. This accounts for the difficulty of giving exact dates to many of the oldest and most interesting examples that have survived. Embroidresses in remote parts of the country probably continued, as they do today, to work in styles long since abandoned elsewhere, whether for lack of newer models or simply because they liked the old ways best; they evidently copied nature as well as the transmitted pattern and drew on imagination as needleworkers have always done.

Names and dates in the embroidery are not always a certain means of identification. Leaving aside the possibility that such 'signatures' and dates may have been added recently, we can easily imagine how an especially ambitious project, begun by one worker, could have been carried on by her daughters, or even her granddaughters, who would work into it the name of their ancestress and some significant date of her life as a sort of domestic memorial. Not only is it impossible to trace the makers of many 'signed' pieces, but the towns, buildings and human figures depicted in needlework are only rarely to be identified with real places or people. And, it need hardly be pointed out, family histories not bolstered by other evidence are as unreliable here as in the case of other types of antiques.

It is difficult even to say when the story of American needlework properly begins. An early regulation in the Massachusetts Bay Colony forbade the wearing of 'cuttworke, embroidered or needle worke capps, bands, & rayles', indicating that at least some of the community were exposed to this temptation, but the objectionable finery may have been obtained from abroad. Inventories of the late 1600s, which indicate a rising standard of comfort, frequently list 'wrought', 'needle-worked' or 'Turkey' chairs, cushions, carpets, cupboard cloths, and hangings. Though many of these embroideries, like other furnishings of the colonists' homes, undoubtedly came from the mother country, there is just as much reason to think that some were made in America.

The *Turkey work* chairs, cushions and carpets mentioned in early wills and inventories represent a type of needlework that had come into fashion in England in the late sixteenth century. Simulating the colorful rugs imported from the Near East for the homes of wealthy Europeans, Turkey work was made by pulling heavy wool through canvas or coarse linen, knotting it, and cutting the ends to form a pile. Turkey work carpets were used for table covers, just as Oriental rugs were at this time. In an inventory of 1676, twelve Turkey work chairs are valued at 960 pounds of tobacco, twice the amount estimated for the same number of leather-covered chairs. Among the very few pieces of American furniture that have survived with their original Turkey work upholstery are two chairs, now in the Metropolitan Museum of Art, that date from about this time.

A set of embroidered bed hangings, also in the Metropolitan Museum, is probably typical of many that added warmth and cheerful color to the American homes of the late seventeenth century (Plate 134A). According to tradition, these hangings were made by the three successive wives of Dr

Gilson Clapp, an Englishman who came to this country about 1666 and settled near Westchester, New York. The story, like others that have come down the years with cherished pieces of embroidery, cannot be corroborated, but the work itself represents a type that came into style in England in the late 1500s and remained popular for nearly a century with women of the middle class provincial society from which most of the American colonists came. Embroidered with red wool in outline, blanket, and seed stitches, the panels have narrow scalloped borders enclosing a ground on which dogs, birds, squirrels, and stags pierced with arrows alternate with floral sprays in a close, all-over pattern. Motifs of this sort were originally copied from manuscripts and early printed books on natural history, herbals, and, in the case of the deer pierced with an arrow, books of emblems and devices; they were later redrawn for the use of embroiderers and published in such works as Shorleyker's *Schole House for the Needle* (1624) and the engravings of Peter Stent and John Overton, among others.

The painted and resist-dyed Indian chintzes imported into Europe from 1630 on opened up a rich source of design to the needle-worker. Before the middle of the century, small repeating patterns like that on the Metropolitan Museum hangings had been superseded by typical motifs from the chintzes – the great flowering tree that rises out of a low mound or hillock, with all sorts of exotic birds and butterflies in its scrolling branches and human figures standing on the schematized earth at its base, and the detached, naturalistic flower sprays scattered irregularly over the ground. Embroideries in this style are probably what most people think of first as *crewelwork* (Plate 134B), though the name is just as properly applied to those described above.

The word crewel actually designates the loosely-twisted, worsted yarns with which the design was worked. Early newspaper advertisements of crewels, 'cruells', etc., indicate that imported yarns were available in the major cities, but evidently much of the early needlework produced here was worked with materials spun, woven, and dyed at home. Crewels were supplied commercially in several grades, from coarse to fine; home-made yarns were bound to vary widely in weight and texture. The ground is usually linen or twilled cotton; homespun linen is most common in American examples. One invariable characteristic of crewelwork is that the ground material is never entirely obscured by the embroidery, though this may cover more or less of the space. It is generally held that in American work the motifs are smaller and sparser, more of the ground is left showing, and the whole effect is more 'open' than in English crewelwork. The patterns inspired by the Indian chintzes demanded a more naturalistic treatment than those in the preceding style, and were accordingly worked in yarns of various rather than a single hue. An exceptional example in shades of blue is illustrated (Plate 134C). At first rather somber, with many dark blues and greens relieved only by dull tan or mustard yellow, the color schemes lightened in the course of the following century. Early crewelwork was carried out in a variety of stitches, outline or stem stitch (often spoken of as crewel stitch), Oriental, and long and short stitch being the most usual. Chain stitch gained favor in the 1700s.

Besides bed hangings, coverlets, and curtains, cushions, chair covers, and many smaller objects were decorated with crewelwork. A notice in the *Boston Gazette* of 1749 calls attention to the loss by theft of a 'Woman's Fustian Petticoat, with a large work'd Embroidered Border, being Deer, Sheep, Houses, Forrest, &c.' Several petticoat bands preserved in museums today have patterns that might be described in the same words (Plate 134D).

Before the 1700s were well advanced, life in most parts of the American colonies had become relatively safe and easy. In the large cities, accumulating wealth brought leisure and the desire for agreeable surroundings in its train. Houses were built and furnished with primary consideration for the comfort and esthetic enjoyment of their occupants. Among the new forms that served this requirement, easy chairs, sofas, card tables, and firescreens in particular were well designed for the display of fine needlework, and the lady of the house, free of the heavier duties of earlier homemakers and able to call on the professional services of a tailor or mantua maker for the family's clothing, willingly took up the task of embellishing them. Contemporary newspaper advertisements offering instruction in various kinds of embroidery among other handicrafts speak for the popularity of this occupation. As early as 1719, an insertion in the *Boston News-Letter* announced that at the house of Mr George Brownell young gentlewomen and children would be taught 'all sorts of fine Work ... embroidery in a new way, Turkey work for Handkerchiefs two ways, fine new Fashion Purses, flourishing and plain work ... Brocaded work for Handkerchiefs and Short aprons upon Muslin', as well as dancing. Among the 'Curious works' taught in New York in 1731 by Martha Gazley, 'late of Great Britain', were 'Nun's-Work', and 'Philligree and Pencil Work upon Muslin', all probably types of embroidery, though this teacher also offered artificial fruit and flower making, wax work, and 'Raising of Paste'. 'Flowering', 'flourishing', 'Dresden flowering on catgut (canvas)', and 'shading with silk or worsted, on Cambrick, lawn, or Holland' may take in all the colorful floral embroidery found on women's gowns, petticoats, aprons, pockets, and other accessories of the period, as well as the fine work in silk on satin and velvet 'wedding' waistcoats for men.

Tent stitch and *cross stitch* are frequently mentioned. The first, known today as petit point, is worked on a firm but not too closely woven ground material in rows of short, slanting stitches, each stitch crossing diagonally an intersection of the threads of the ground (Plate 136A). Imitating the effect of woven tapestry and offering comparable strength and durability, this kind of work was much appreciated in the eighteenth century, as it is today, for the coverings of chairs and sofas, and it lent itself well to all-over patterns of small, naturalistic flowers and leaves that suited the light, graceful forms of Queen Anne and Chippendale furniture. *Cross stitch* scarcely requires description; worked in

woolen yarns, it was an alternative to tent stitch for upholstery in the 1700s.

A third type of needlework that was frequently used for upholstery and other purposes in this period was called *flame stitch* or *Hungarian stitch*. Its rainbow-like effects were created by making horizontal bands of short, parallel stitches from one side of the work to the other. All the stitches in one row are the same length, but the rows themselves may rise and fall in zigzag patterns of great complexity. Wool or silk yarns were used for flame stitch, depending on the purpose of the work.

Most of the newspaper advertisers who offered instruction in needlework also had materials and patterns to sell. A notice inserted in the *Boston News-Letter* in 1738 by a Mrs Condy reads significantly, 'All sorts of beautiful Figures on Canvas, for Tent Stick [*sic*]; the Patterns from London, but drawn by her much cheaper than English drawing.' David Mason, 'Japanner', was also ready to provide 'Coats of Arms, Drawings on Sattin or Canvis for Embroidering'. Mrs Condy supplied 'Silk Shades, Slacks, Floss, Cruells of all Sorts, the best White Chapple Needles, and everything for all Sorts of Work'. 'Shaded crewells' and 'worsted Slacks in Shades' were also advertised.

Outside the cities and in the more modest urban homes, women continued to decorate their curtains, chair covers, bed furniture and clothing with colorful crewels up to the end of the century and even later. Among fashionable city folk, however, this useful work had gone out of style. For one thing, the new Hepplewhite and Sheraton furniture that came in during the last quarter of the 1700s required more delicate coverings. Pattern-woven silks and satins were used on chairs and sofas in preference to needlework, and the needlewoman, relieved of this last duty, turned to decoration pure and simple, spending her new leisure on *needlework pictures* and similar 'fancy work'.

Pictorial subjects had, of course, been a frequent choice for furniture covers, fire screens and other objects worked with woolen yarns in tent stitch and cross stitch earlier in the century. A group of thirty-six embroidered panels from New England, presumably the work of young ladies at a Boston finishing school in the mid-1700s, is widely known as the *Fishing Lady* series (Plate 135A) from the name given to the central figure in the pastoral scene depicted. Considerable research has been devoted to tracing the source of this design, evidently one or more English prints.

The embroidered pictures of the late 1700s and early 1800s, however, differ from these last examples in their general spirit and intention as well as by the materials and techniques employed (Plates 135B, 136C). The designs, including landscapes, pastoral scenes, views of architecture and ships, maps, portraits, biblical and mythological subjects, memorials, flower pieces, and allegorical compositions, were worked mainly in floss or twisted silk in a variety of stitches. Large areas like sky or background, as well as faces and other details, were often painted in. The ground material might be fine linen, canvas, silk or satin. Such pictures were customarily framed like paintings, with a broad margin of black glass setting off the rather delicate colors of the embroidery. Perhaps the most typical of this group are the 'mourning pictures', depicting an urn or monument, often inscribed with a name or epitaph, a willow, symbol of sorrow, and one or more figures that may be meant to represent survivors of the deceased. Numbers of these are dedicated to the memory of George Washington. That the drawing of the figures is ordinarily competent points to the use of prepared designs, kept in stock by the vendors of other materials for needlework and traced or 'pounced' (by rubbing colored powder through a pricked paper pattern) on the ground material desired. Many of the most elaborate embroidered pictures are the work of school girls, and testify to the young needlewomen's completion of a course of formal instruction. The school conducted by the Sisters of Bethlehem, a Moravian religious order, in Pennsylvania was famous for the fine needlework developed and taught there in the eighteenth century.

In America as elsewhere, girls and young women had long made *samplers* to demonstrate their mastery of useful and decorative stitches and to record motifs and patterns for future use. Very few American samplers survive from the seventeenth century; the oldest, preserved in Pilgrim Hall in Plymouth, Massachusetts, was worked by Lora Standish, daughter of Captain Myles Standish, 1653. These early samplers, truly exemplars or patterns, as the name indicates, are long, narrow linen panels, on which the needlework is disposed in horizontal bands. Borders and small separate designs in various stitches, cut work (*reticello*), drawn thread work, and needle lace (*punto in aria*) are found on them. An alphabet or inscription or both is usual, and the maker's name and the date of the completion of the work were almost invariably added. In the course of the 1770s, the inscription, which might be a motto, a verse or verses from scripture, or a selection from some such volume as Isaac Watts's *Divine Songs for Children*, occupied an increasingly prominent place, until the sampler became virtually a vehicle for the lettering and numbers. By this time, the shape had changed as well, tending to be square or oblong with the length little greater than the width. A border, which might be either a slender, running vine or a wide band of flowers, framed the embroidered text, and any remaining space was filled in with such motifs as flowers, fruits and leaves, birds, animals, and human figures, all more or less crudely drawn and worked most often in cross stitch or tent stitch. Bright, gay colors were the rule. After the 1830s, both design and workmanship deteriorated. The wide availability of patterns and materials for the popular Berlin wool work of the mid-nineteenth century seems to have put an end to all more individual expressions in embroidery.

An effort has been made in this account to introduce the chief varieties of American needlework in some historical sequence, but it should not be forgotten that their periods of popularity overlapped and coincided with those of other techniques. Concurrently with the vogue for embroidered silk pictures there was a great fashion for *tambour* work, so-called from the shape of the two hoops between which the foundation material was stretched while being embroidered. A tambour needle, with a hooked end, was used, and the thread was drawn up through the material to form a chain stitch on the right side. Sheer muslin and crape were worked in tambour for ladies' caps. The same method, used on machine-made cotton or silk net, produced a lace-like effect that was much appreciated for wedding veils, shawls, fichus, and edgings (tambour lace). 'Darned net', embroidered with a needle of the usual sort, was used for the same purposes. Satin stitch was worked in white thread, most often silk or linen, on the gossamer white linen, cotton, and silk dress materials of the 1830s. Large handkerchiefs of the finest white linen were embellished with drawn thread work and incredibly fine satin stitch embroidery in white. Mull, a cobwebby silk muslin brought from India, was embroidered in silk with motifs copied from Indian shawls or chintzes.

The fashion for white on white extended to needlework in coarser materials that gave a very different effect. Heavy white cotton bedcovers were embroidered with long strands of *candlewicking*, the typical design of a basket of flowers or a patriotic motif framed by a flowering vine being worked in small running stitches that stand out on the surface of the material and are sometimes looped and cut to make protruding tufts.

Among other types of American needlework that interest collectors are the *towel covers* made by Pennsylvania-German housewives in the late eighteenth and early nineteenth centuries to hang over and conceal the common towel on its rack in the kitchen. These are long strips of linen, often made up of two or more small towels sewn together, decorated with simple cross stitch motifs representing birds, hearts, flowers, and human figures. Many are finished off with bands of lace or knotted fringe.

The rare *wool-on-wool* coverlets, of which a notable example is illustrated from Old Deerfield Village (136B), apparently represent another regional specialty. Practically all of the small group so far recorded are thought to come from the Connecticut River Valley. Their bold, all-over designs, carried out in woolen yarns on a ground of heavy woolen fabric, seem to acknowledge the same exotic source as the crewel embroideries on linen. Most of the known examples are dated, the earliest 1748, the latest 1826.

An interesting survival of European customs may be seen in the early embroidered *hatchments* preserved in some museums today (Plate 133). A hatchment was a coat of arms on a lozenge, meant to be carried in the funeral and displayed on the outside of the house of a person who had recently died. It consisted ordinarily of a diamond-shape wooden panel (or canvas stretched on a wooden frame of the same shape), painted black with the arms of the deceased on a shield in color. In New England, at least, hatchments were copied in embroidery as memorials; the designs were carried out in colored silks and gold and silver threads, which were couched or worked in long and short stitch and sometimes covered the entire surface of the panel.

BOOKS FOR FURTHER READING

The literature of American needlework is meager. Only two books can be cited:
BOLTON, ETHEL STANWOOD and COE, EVA JOHNSTON: *American Samplers*, Massachusetts Society of the Colonial Dames of America (1921).
HARBESON, GEORGIANA BROWN: *American Needlework*, Coward-McCann, New York (1938).

Numerous articles in *Antiques* discuss the various types of needlework mentioned here, particularly:
BOWEN, HELEN: "The Fishing Lady and Boston Common" (August 1923).
CABOT, NANCY GRAVES: "The Fishing Lady and Boston Common" (July 1941). "Engravings and Embroideries; The Sources of some Designs in the Fishing Lady Series" (December 1941).
PETO, FLORENCE: "Some Early American Crewelwork" (May 1951).
Concise Encyclopedia of Antiques, Vol. I, pp. 210–221, Hawthorn Books, New York (1955).

COTTON PRINTING

By D. GRAEME KEITH

THERE is much documentary evidence in wills and inventories, as early as the middle of the seventeenth century, which attests the use of printed calicoes and chintzes in the American colonies. While these generally were itemized as furnishing fabrics such as bedhangings, curtains and seat covers, printed fabrics were also used for apparel, particularly after the middle of the eighteenth century, reflecting the corresponding fashion for chintzes in Europe.

There can be little doubt that the English, following their mercantile policy, dominated the colonial market for printed fabrics and did all in their power to prevent their being manufactured in the colonies. Dry goods were an important part of the cargoes of most ships from England, and the rapidity with which such merchandise was commonly sold indicates the great demand which existed. Many a colonial visitor to England purchased, before returning home, English prints to furnish a room or to dress his lady. One of the early references to copperplate prints is to be found in a letter Benjamin Franklin wrote to his wife from London in 1758:

'There are also fifty-six yards of cotton, printed curiously from copper plates, a new invention, to make bed and window curtains; and seven yards of chair bottoms, printed in the same way, very neat. This was my fancy, but Mrs Stevenson tells me I did wrong not to buy both of the same color.'

After the Revolution and well into the nineteenth century, English and French printworks printed many fabrics whose designs were made especially for the American market. These employed emblems of the new republic, American historical subjects and occasionally views. They were chiefly furnishing fabrics and historical kerchiefs printed at this time to support the great demand for American subjects. Most of them correspond roughly in date to the blue transfer-printed Staffordshire china manufactured for the American market.

Despite the English ban on colonial manufactures, cottons and linens were printed on a small scale in the American colonies during the eighteenth century. The evidence for this is almost entirely of a documentary nature, chiefly advertisements. One of the earliest of these, appearing in 1712 in the *Boston Newsletter*, tells us that GEORGE LEASON and THOMAS WEBBER had opened a 'Callendar Mill and Dye House in Cambridge Street, Boston, near the Bowling-Green: Where all Gentlemen Merchants and others may have all sorts of Linnens, Callicoes, Stuffs or Silks Callendar'd; Prints all sorts of Linnens' (April 21, 1712). In 1720 JAMES FRANKLIN, printer and elder brother of Benjamin Franklin, advertised in the *Boston Gazette* that he also printed fabrics:

'Linnens, Calicoes, Silks, etc. printed in good figures, very lively, and durable colours, and without the offensive smell which commonly attends the linens printed here.'

That competition was keen and not always above reproach is indicated by another advertisement inserted a few weeks later in the same newspaper, apparently by James Franklin:

'The Printer hereof having dispers'd advertisements of his Printing Callicoes, etc. a certain Person in Charlestown, to rob him of the benefit of said advertisements and impose upon strangers, calls himself by the name of Franklin, having agreed with one in Queen Street, Boston, to take his work. These are to desire him to be satisfyed with his proper Name, or he will be proceeded against according to Law.'   (May 2, 1720)

In 1735, also in the *Boston Gazette*, appeared the advertisement of FRANCIS GRAY, 'Calicoe Printer from Holland; Prints all sorts of

Callicoes of several colors to hold washing, at his house in Roxbury near the Meeting-House' (June 16, 1735).

Many such notices appear in newspapers in New England and the middle colonies but it has been almost impossible, with the exception of the Philadelphia calico printer, JOHN HEWSON, to attribute surviving fabrics to any particular printer or even identify them surely as being printed in the colonies.

Textile printing tools are also occasionally the subject of advertisements, further confirming the fact that printing was carried on here in the eighteenth century. In 1713, the Boston engraver, FRANCIS DEWING, advertised that he: 'Engraveth and Printeth Copper Plates – likewise Cuts neatly and printeth Callicoes.' In a *Boston Newsletter* of 1773, an anonymous printer advertised:

'To be sold, very cheap for cash, by the person who prints dark callicoes, an excellent set of prints for the same. The person who has them to dispose of, would Instruct the Purchaser in the use of them if required ...'

Here one finds the use of the word 'prints' in its eighteenth century meaning to describe the blocks or copper plates used to print fabrics. The word is used in the same sense in a contemporary description of John Hewson's designer, Mr Lang 'designing and cutting prints for shawls'.

An early description of eighteenth-century calico printing, which well illustrates the primitive technique and the marginal nature of the operations of many of the early printers, appears in a manuscript written by Anthony Arnold about 1830, describing a short-lived calico printing enterprise in Rhode Island. The account refers to three woodblocks (Plate 138A, B), in the Rhode Island Historical Society, thought to have been cut by a German calico printer named HERMAN VANDAUSEN of East Greenwich, Rhode Island, but more probably cut by JEREMIAH EDDY:

'*Some Account of the First Beginning of the Calico Printing in Providence.*

In the year 1780 Alverson a painter & Jeremiah Eddy agreed to go into the Printing of cloth with oil colors, Jeremiah Eddy cut the tipes on the end of small pieces of hard wood and put on the paint on the tipes with a brush, stamping the cloth by hand in small flowers to please the eye, and the work was done in a shop belonging to Charles Lei, near Stone Pond. The health of Alverson becoming poor in the fall he gave up the business and Col. Benjamin Hopper took his place as a partner. They carried on the business until the Spring of 1781. They then dissolved the Partnership and about that time there came a German into Providence from the british servis who had worked in the printing business and he gave the said Eddy knowledge of Printing with water colors, he then cut larger tipes in blocks and pieces of boards of hard wood and printed running vines and large flowers and he printed hundreds of various figures, the women brought in their sheets made of Tow and lining taken from their beads, and had them printed and made into gounds, and in the fall of 1781 or the spring of 1782 the rumor of Peace, and the arrival of calicoes through various channells reduced the price so much that he gave up the business. Herewith is presented some of the Tipes that was used in 1780.

Anthony Arnold.'

Another brief Rhode Island calico printing enterprise was that established in 1794 by MESSRS SCHAUB, DUBOSQUE & TISSOT who block printed calico cloth imported from India. Not succeeding in this business, Peter Schaub associated himself with others in the manufacture of paper hangings in 1800.

New York newspapers yield comparatively meager evidence that textile printing was carried on in that state during the eighteenth century. One of the few names we meet with is that of MRS JOHN HAUGAN who advertised in 1761 that she 'stamped linen China blue or deep blue, or any other color that Gentlemen or Ladies fancies'. One would like to think that this reference to china blue had some connection with the perplexing problem of the so-called 'blue-resist' textiles, long thought to be of New York origin. These handsome furnishing fabrics with large patterns in one or more shades of blue enriched with designs of small white dots constitute a distinct class in themselves (Plate 137). This group, many of which are highly sophisticated in design, is generally dated in the first half of the eighteenth century because of the almost baroque sweep of many of the patterns. They are usually called American and are often attributed to New York State as so many of them have been found there. Others believe that they were imported from Europe or the Orient and indeed many of the designs show a strong Oriental influence. However, these fabrics seem to be unknown in England and Holland, both countries deeply involved in the eastern trade. They are equally perplexing on a technical level. Were they directly printed with blue or were the white areas covered with a resist, presumably applied with wood blocks, and the fabric then dyed? The great difficulty at that time of direct printing with indigo seems to make that possibility unlikely, while the fact that the pattern is on a white ground naturally suggests a block print. On the other hand, fabrics decorated by the resist process usually have designs in white on a colored ground. As the answers to these historical and technical questions remain so highly speculative, one can, for the present, only tentatively accept the fact of their apparently being known only in the American colonies as evidence pointing to an American origin for this important group of textiles.

Philadelphia was perhaps the most important center of calico printing in the colonies, although as far as we know, the craft did not establish itself there until nearly the end of the colonial period. A good deal is known about its first practitioner, one JOHN HEWSON (1744–1821), a London calico printer, 'master in several large manufactories for linen, cotton and calico printing, like wise cutting and stamping of copper plates for the same', who had been encouraged by Benjamin Franklin to establish a calico printing business in Philadelphia. He was among the first to have circumvented successfully the English prohibition on the export of machinery to the colonies. An advertisement in the *Pennsylvania Gazette*, cited by Gillingham, indicates that his print works and bleachery were fully established by July 1774:

'A CALICOE PRINTING MANUFACTORY, AND BLEACH YARD, is just opened, near the Glass-House, at the upper end of Kensington, about one mile from the city of Philadelphia:

JOHN HEWSON

The Proprietor thereof, begs to inform the public, that he has, at considerable expense, imported prints from London, and compleated works sufficient for carrying on the above business to perfection; should the public encourage him in his present undertaking, he hopes to merit their favour, as well in the execution as price, being brought up regularly to the business, at Bromley-Hill, near London one of the most considerable Manufactories and Bleachyards in England. He engages his work shall be equal in colour, and will stand washing, as well as any imported from London or elsewhere, otherwise, will require no pay ... his present sett of prints consists of patterns for printed calicoes and linens for gowns, &c, coverlids, handkerchiefs, nankeens, janes, and velverets, for waistcoats and breeches, &c. Orders from town or country are taken at the Manufactory, or by the following gentlemen, in Philadelphia, who have been pleased to encourage the work,-Mr Jonathan Zane, Mr Sharp Delany, Dr William Drewet Smith, in Second-Street; Joel Zane, between Race and Vine-Streets; Jonathan Zane, jun. in Vine-Street, between Third- and Fourth-streets, and at New-Ferry. Patterns of the different prints may be seen at the Manufactory, or on notice he will do himself the pleasure to wait on any person with them.'   (July 20, 1774)

Hewson identified himself with the cause of the colonists, and, during the Revolution was captured by the English who, of course, destroyed his manufactory. He escaped captivity and, after the English evacuated the city, returned to re-establish his business under the name of Hewson and Lang as announced in the *Pennsylvania Packet* of November 9, 1779:

'LINEN PRINTING

The subscribers beg leave to inform the public, that they have removed to Kensington, on purpose to carry on the business at the original factory ... the savage foe of Britain have made such destruction of their works and materials, that renders them unable to carry on the business in all its branches. The branch ... they mean to carry on, is the printing of blue handkerchiefs, with deep blue grounds and white spots; also very neat gown-patterns of the same colour ... Little need be said as to the abilities of the subscribers, as there are numbers of yards now in wear, done by them, equal to any done by the bostful Britons. The Works will be ready this week, and work received at the factory, by
HEWSON AND LANG.'

WILLIAM LANG was an English designer and engraver who had joined Hewson about that time. In 1789 the General Assembly of Pennsylvania granted him a seven-year loan of two hundred pounds with-

Bluish-aquamarine sugar bowl, Redford or Redwood Glass Works, *c.* 1835–50; lily pad decoration, hollow knop stem with coins dated 1829 and 1835 in hollow ball of cover, with chicken finial. Ht. 11 ins. *The Corning Museum of Glass.*

PLATE 113

(A) Pitcher; deep emerald-green; New York State, *c.* 1830–70; lily pad decoration, threaded neck, applied handle with crimped end, circular foot. Ht. 7½ ins. *The New-York Historical Society.*

(B) Aquamarine mug, South Jersey, *c.* 1835–60. Six applied leaf prunts, solid semi-ear-shaped handle with crimped end. Ht. 4⅜ ins. *The Corning Museum of Glass.*

(C) Aquamarine vase, South Jersey type, early-nineteenth century; lily pad decoration, solid applied handles with crimped ends, crimped circular foot. Ht. 7 ins. *The New-York Historical Society.*

PLATE 114

Pair of light-green glass candlesticks, South Jersey type, early-nineteenth century; gather of glass at base of socket tooled into gadrooning. Ht. 9⅛ ins. *The Metropolitan Museum of Art.*

PLATE 115

Stiegel type glass and cover; clear; late-eighteenth century; engraved tulip in pot on front, flower on back, flanged cover with ball finial. Ht. 12¾ ins. *The New-York Historical Society.*

PLATE 116

(A) Salt; dark olive-amber; Connecticut, early-nine-teenth century; bowl has flaring rim, cylindrical stem, crimped foot. Ht. 3⅛ ins. *The New-York Historical Society.*

(B) Dark amber candlestick; Coventry, Connecticut, 1838–48; spool baluster shaft, sloping foot. Ht. 6 ins. *The New-York Historical Society.*

(C) Stiegel type glass with enameled decoration in color; late-eighteenth century. *The Metropolitan Museum of Art.*

(D) Light amethyst perfume bottle, thought to have been made at Stiegel's Manheim Glass Works *c.* 1763–74; pattern-molded and expanded in a dia-mond daisy design. Ht. 5½ ins. *The New-York Historical Society.*

PLATE 117

(A) Perfume bottle attributed to Stiegel's Manheim glasshouse; the daisy-in-hexagon design has so far not been found in pieces of foreign origin. *The Henry Francis du Pont Winterthur Museum.*

(B) Amethyst vase, for many years called Stiegel but probably Boston & Sandwich Glass Company; nineteenth century. Twelve sunken panels around base. Ht. 8¾ ins. *The New-York Historical Society.*

(C) Amethyst salt; Stiegel-Midwestern type, early-nineteenth century; pattern-molded and expanded in diamond design, petaled foot. Ht. 3 ins. *The New-York Historical Society.*

(D) Sapphire-blue salt, possibly Amelung; late-eighteenth century; pattern-molded and expanded in checkered-diamond design. Knop-like stem, circular foot. Ht. 3 ins. *The New-York Historical Society.*

PLATE 118

Clear glass goblet, engraved; slight smoky tint, John Frederick Amelung's New Bremen Glass Manufactory. Presented to August Koenig, Baltimore merchant, from whose great-great-granddaughter it was acquired. Ht. 7¾ ins. *The Maryland Historical Society*.

PLATE 119

(A) Cut glass tumbler, Bakewell's Pittsburgh Flint Glass Works, *c.* 1825; band of plain panels alternating with panels of fine cut diamonds above a band of splits. Engraved DWC and white cameo bust of DeWitt Clinton encrusted in the base. One of a set presented to Clinton. Ht. 3⅜ ins. *The New-York Historical Society.*

(B) Clear cut glass butter dish, attributed to Brooklyn Flint Glass Works; early-nineteenth century; fan-cut edges. Ht. 4⅞ ins. *The New-York Historical Society.*

PLATE 120

(A) Cut glass decanter attributed to Dummer's Jersey City Works or Gilliland's Brooklyn Flint Glass Works *c.* 1845. Ht. 10¼ ins. *The New-York Historical Society.*

(B) **Clear glass** decanter, possibly New England Glass Co., *c.* 1815–30; blown three mold in arch pattern. *The New-York Historical Society.*

PLATE 121

(A) Light purple creamer, Boston and Sandwich Glass Company, 1825–35; blown three mold baroque pattern called horizontal palm leaf. Ht. 4½ ins. *The New-York Historical Society.*

(B) Sapphire-blue creamer, *c.* 1825–35; blown three mold geometric pattern in sunburst design. Ht. 4⅛ ins. *The New-York Historical Society.*

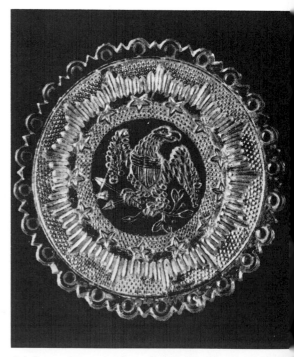

(C) Olive-amber inkwell, Marlboro Street Factory, Keene, New Hampshire, *c.* 1825–35; blown three mold geometric pattern. Ht. 1½ ins. *The New-York Historical Society.*

(D) Lacy glass cup-plate, Bakewell's Pittsburgh Flint Glass Works, *c.* 1825–40; eagle with blaze border. D. 3½ ins. *The New-York Historical Society.*

PLATE 122

(A) Dish with pressed design of the frigate *Constitution*, probably made *c.* 1840, Boston & Sandwich Glass Company. $7\frac{1}{8} \times 4\frac{1}{2}$ ins. *The New-York Historical Society.*

(B) Clear pressed glass tray, Boston & Sandwich Glass Company, *c.* 1830–40; lacy pattern of scrolled leaf and fleur-de-lis. $4\frac{7}{8} \times 6\frac{5}{8}$ ins. *The New-York Historical Society.*

PLATE 123

(A) Light green pressed glass salt, Jersey Glass Company, *c.* 1827–40; basket of flowers on sides, rose on ends, marked on bottom 'Jersey / Glass / Co. Nʳ.N. York'. Ht. 2 ins. *The New-York Historical Society.*

(B) Clear pressed glass salt, Boston & Sandwich Glass Company, *c.* 1827; boat-shaped; paddle wheels inscribed 'Lafayet', stern marked 'Sandwich / B&S Glass Co.' Ht. 1⅝ ins. *The New-York Historical Society.*

(C) Pressed glass candlestick, Boston & Sandwich Glass Company, *c.* 1840–50; opaque blue petal socket, opaque white dolphin shaft and square stepped base. Ht. 10 ins. *The New-York Historical Society.*

(D) Clear glass lamp, *c.* 1827; free blown oil font attached by a ring to square stepped pressed base. Ht. 8½ ins. *The New-York Historical Society.*

PLATE 124

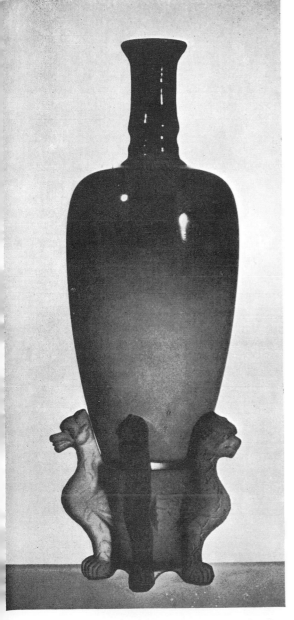

(A) Peach blow vase; Hobbs, Bruckunier & Co., Wheeling, West Virginia; *c.* 1886; copied from the Mary J. Morgan Chinese porcelain vase; white lining with casing of yellow shading to deep red; outside coating of clear glass; on pressed glass holder. Ht. 7⅞ ins. *The Corning Museum of Glass*.

(B) Light amethyst pressed glass vase, Boston & Sandwich Glass Company, *c.* 1835–60; circle and ellipse pattern, scalloped rim, hexagonal base. Ht. 7½ ins. *The New-York Historical Society*.

PLATE 125

(A) Milk glass covered dish, The Atterbury Company, Pittsburgh, Pennsylvania, 1880s; chicken with eggs design, open edge. Ht. 7 ins. *The New-York Historical Society.*

(B) Paper weight, Boston & Sandwich Glass Company, mid-nineteenth century; fuchsia red with blue, green and yellow stem on *latticinio* background. D. 2$\frac{7}{8}$ ins. *The New-York Historical Society.*

PLATE 126

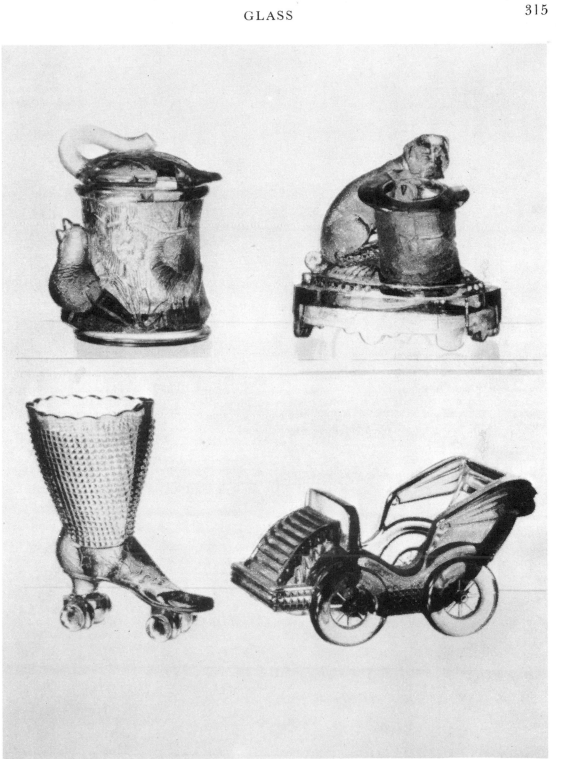

Light-blue glass novelties, late-nineteenth and early-twentieth centuries.   *The New-York Historical Society.*

PLATE 127

(A) Pomona vase; New England Glass Co., late-nineteenth century; pale amber with frosted surface; band of pale blue flowers and pale amber leaves; deeply scalloped rim and applied petaled foot. Ht. 6¼ ins. *The Corning Museum of Glass.*

(B) Marble glass or purple slag water pitcher, Challinor, Taylor & Company, 1870–90; pressed in flower and panel pattern. Ht. 8⅞ ins. *The New-York Historical Society.*

(C) Clear pressed glass goblet, c. 1850; ribbed ivy pattern. Ht. 6 ins. *The New-York Historical Society.*

(D) Clear pressed glass sugar bowl and cover, mid-nineteenth century; bull's-eye and fleur-de-lis pattern. Ht. 8⅝ ins. *The New-York Historical Society.*

PLATE 128

(A) Amberina decanter; New England Glass Co., late-nineteenth century; pale amber shading to deep red; pattern-molded and expanded in ribbing swirled to right. Ht. 10⅞ ins.. *The Corning Museum of Glass*.

(B) Free blown iridescent glass vase, late-nineteenth century; marked on base *L.C. Tiffany*. Ht. 18½ ins. *The New-York Historical Society*.

PLATE 129

Vase, Louis C. Tiffany *favrile* glass, 1875–96; peacock feather design. *The Metropolitan Museum of Art.*

PLATE 130

References are to McKearin's "American Glass"

(A) Half-pint flasks: (*Left*) Sunburst, light olive-amber, recorded also in olive-green and pale green; *c.* 1820–30 (McK. GVIII—25). (*Left center*) Flint Glass Works, Keene, New Hampshire; Sunburst, light sapphire, recorded also in pale, deep and peacock green (McK. GVIII–15). (*Right center*) Kensington Glass Works, Philadelpia; Cornucopia, clear rich green, recorded also in aquamarine, amber and bluish green (McK. GIII–2). (*Right*) Lancaster Glass Works, Lancaster, New York; Urn of Produce, emerald green; mid-nineteenth century (McK. GIII–14).

(B) (*Left*) Deep blue, recorded also in deep amber, olive-yellow and aquamarine; tree and foliage each side; 1830s and 1840s (McK. GX—17). (*Left center*) Possibly Bridgetown Glass Works, New Jersey; grey-blue, recorded also in aquamarine and deep green; *c.* 1830–40 (McK. GX–8). (*Right center*) Baltimore Glass Works, showing Washington Monument, Baltimore; olive-green, also recorded in aquamarine, clear green, olive-amber and olive-yellow; mid-nineteenth century (McK. GVI–7). (*Right*) From mold used at Mount Vernon Glass Works, Vernon, and Mount Pleasant, Saratoga, New York; inscribed SUCCESS TO THE RAILROAD; olive-amber, recorded also in olive-green and amber; *c.* 1828–65 (McK. GV–5).

PLATE 131

References are to McKearin's "American Glass"

(A) (*Left*) Zanesville, Ohio, J. Shepard & Co., Masonic Arch and Pavement, enclosing Farmer's Arms; red-amber, recorded also in golden amber, aquamarine, 'black' (dense amber), olive-yellow and golden-yellow; *c.* 1832 (McK. GIV–32). (*Center*) Flint Glass Works, Keene, New Hampshire; *c.* 1815–17 (McK. GIV–2). (*Right*) Coffin & Hay, Hammonton, New Jersey, flag and inscription FOR OUR COUNTRY; olive-green, recorded also in aquamarine, *c.* 1836 (McK. GII53).

(B) (*Left*) Possibly Louisville Glass Works, Louisville, Kentucky; amber, recorded also in aquamarine, 'black' (dense amber), blue, clear green, yellow-green, moonstone and olive-yellow; mid-nineteenth century (McK. GII–24). (*Center*) Made for S.S.Huffsey in mold by Doflein, Philadelphia; LOUIS KOSSUTH; deep green, recorded also in aquamarine, 'black' (dense olive-green), emerald and yellow-green; *c.* 1851 (McK. GI–112). (*Right*) Dyottville; Washington and inscription THE FATHER OF HIS COUNTRY; 'black' (dense wine), recorded also in dense amber, olive-green, olive-yellow; *c.* 1847–8 (McK. GI–38).

PLATE 132

Hatchment with the Grant arms embroidered in tan, red, green and blue silk and gold and silver threads; eighteenth century. *Ashley House, Old Deerfield, Massachusetts.*

PLATE 133

(A) Detail from late-seventeenth-century bed hangings embroidered in red wool. *Metropolitan Museum of Art.*

(B) Crewel-embroidered linen bedcover, probably mid-eighteenth century. *Old Deerfield.*

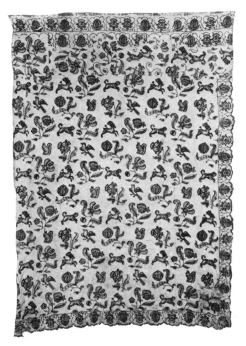

(c) Crewel in shades of blue; CER 1749 PTB worked in lower edge; by Catherine, wife of Peter Ten Broeck. *Ginsburg and Levy.*

(D) Detail, crewel embroidered petticoat band. *Museum of Fine Arts, Boston.*

PLATE 134

(A) The 'Fishing Lady' design in tent stitch on panel of a firescreen; mid-eighteenth century. *Mr and Mrs Henry N. Flynt.*

(B) Montpelier, the home of James Madison; worked in split stitch in silk with painted sky. *Ginsburg and Levy.*

PLATE 135

(A) Tent stitch; 'Mary Upelbe 1767' worked on lower edge; from Newburyport, Massachusetts. *Mr and Mrs Henry N. Flynt.*

(B) Wool on wool coverlet from the Connecticut River Valley; tan, blue and green on an embroidered dark brown ground. *Ashley House, Old Deerfield, Massachusetts.*

(C) Embroidered picture worked by Evelina Hull, Charlestown, Massachusetts, *c.* 1812. Silk thread on satin ground; painted detail. *Metropolitan Museum of Art.*

PLATE 136

Eighteenth-century resist printed cotton in two shades of indigo blue; a type used in colonial America; origin of 'blue-resist' unknown. *Rhode Island School of Design.*

PLATE 137

(A) Woodblocks for textile printing, cut probably by Jeremiah Eddy, *c.* 1780. (B) Modern rubbings taken by Mrs Robert M. Pettit. *Rhode Island Historical Society.*

(C) Cotton printed at LaGrange, Philadelphia Co., Pennsylvania, *c.* 1832; from Vol. 2 of Dunster's dye receipt books. *Rhode Island Historical Society.*

PLATE 138

otton bedspread printed by John Hewson (1744–1821). Philadelphia, late-eighteenth century. *Philadelphia Museum of Art.*

PLATE 139

Stenciled bolster cover made by Polly Parker Hardy; probably Massachusetts, *c.* 1840. *Cooper Union Museum.*

PLATE 140

(A) Edmund Barnes' dye receipt book, dated Dover, 1829; apparently kept when working for Cocheco. *Cooper Union Museum.*

(C) Probably Andrew Robeson or the American Print Works, Fall River, 1825–35. *Fall River Historical Society.*

(B) From book of swatches, probably Crocker, Richmond & Otis, Taunton, 1823–33. *Old Colony Historical Society, Taunton, Massachusetts.*

PLATE 141

(A) Merrimack Manufacturing Company, Lowell, Massachusetts; mid-nineteenth century. *Metropolitan Museum of Art.*

(B) Furniture chintz; Marqueston & Company Haverstraw, New York, 1850. *Metropolitan Museum of Art.*

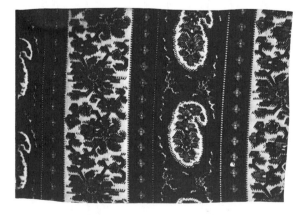

(c) 'Cashmere' print from Dunster's dye receipt books (No. 11); Cocheco; 1858. *Rhode Island Historical Society.*

(D) Centennial print; American Printing Company Fall River, 1876. *Elinor Merrell, New York.*

PLATE 142

Chintz appliqué counterpane. Motifs from chintz and printed cottons with embroidered details, dated 1782.
Henry Francis du Pont Winterthur Museum, Winterthur, Delaware.

PLATE 143

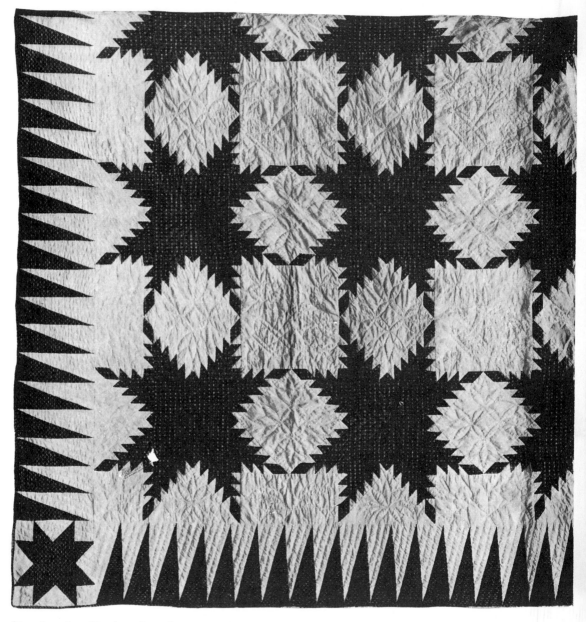

Pieced quilt. 'Feathered star' pattern. Red and white cotton, *c.* 1840. *Wadsworth Atheneum, Hartford, Connecticut.*

PLATE 144

out interest. He acknowledged this assistance in an advertisement under the name of JOHN HEWSON & COMPANY in the *Pennsylvania Journal* of April 15, 1789, wherein he also advertised that 'the Board of Managers of the Manufacturing Society of the City of Philadelphia adjudged to John Hewson the Plate of Gold proposed as a premium for the best specimen of Calico Printing done within the state'.

There exist a number of contemporary references to Hewson which reveal the esteem in which he was held. He played a prominent role in the Grand Federal Procession celebrated in Philadelphia on July 4, 1788. On the Manufacturing Society's float 'was fixed the apparatus of Mr Hewson printing muslins of an elegant chintz pattern, and Mr Lang designing and cutting prints for shawls; on the right was seated Mrs Hewson and her 4 daughters, pencilling a piece of neat sprigged chintz of Mr Hewson's printing, all dressed in cotton of their own manufacture ...'. He is said to have printed, at Mrs Washington's request, a handkerchief with General Washington on horseback as the central motif. No examples of this kerchief have been identified.

John Hewson died on October 14, 1821, leaving 'My printers utensils at the Printing Manufactory' and 'my gold medal' to his son John Hewson, Jr, who had managed the print works since 1810 when his father had retired. To his daughters he left several 'India chintz bedquilts' and 'one full chintz bedspread of my own printing' which are now in the Philadelphia Museum (Plate 139).

Other calico printers were active in Philadelphia during the last quarter of the eighteenth century. JOHN WALTERS & THOMAS BEDWELL advertised in 1775 that they conducted 'Linen Printing in all its branches ... at the Manufactory near the Three-Mile Stone, on Germantown Road', a business which apparently lasted but two years, for in 1777 Walters announced that he had given up the 'linen stamping business'. Other advertisements reveal that NATHANIEL NORGROVE (1777), HENRY ROYL & COMPANY (1784), OAKFORD & LA COLLAY (1797), and DAVY, ROBERTS & COMPANY were also engaged in the textile printing business. ROBERT TAYLOR advertised in 1786 that he 'intends carrying on the bleaching and printing business on the same principles they are conducted in Britain' ... adding that 'Pattern books will be lodged in different places for the convenience of the public'.

The nineteenth century: during the nineteenth century textile printing in the United States was greatly expanded and, by the third decade of the century, was practised on a truly industrial scale. This growth, encouraged by a protective tariff, was nurtured by the availability of cheap cotton and an abundance of water power, the introduction of machinery, and the productive and mechanical genius of the people of a young nation with an ever-expanding market for American manufactures. In 1789 SAMUEL SLATER had introduced mechanical spinning at Pawtucket, Rhode Island, by successfully transplanting to America Arkwright's complex spinning frame. Zachariah Allen, writing in 1835, described the difficulties of getting this yarn woven into cloth:

'In that comparatively thinly populated country, the difficulty of finding weavers became so extreme, as nearly to put a stop to the extension of cotton manufacture, the webs having been in some instances scattered over a whole region of country, frequently at a distance of 200 miles from the manufacturers; and nearly a year elapsed before some of them were returned.'

In 1814, at Waltham, this bottleneck was broken by the introduction of the power loom by FRANCIS CABOT LOWELL, who, after an extended visit to Lancashire (1810–13) had successfully reconstructed the power loom in America. Nathan Appleton, in his recollections of these early years of industrial expansion and invention, described their spellbound satisfaction as they watched the perfected loom in action:

'I recollect the state of admiration and satisfaction with which we sat by the hour watching the beautiful movement of this new and wonderful machine, destined as it evidently was, to change the character of all textile industries.'

The proprietors of the Waltham Company, which made sheetings soon expanded their interests to the manufacturing and printing of calicoes. Toward this end, the MERRI-MACK MANUFACTURING COMPANY was established at Lowell in 1822. By all previous American standards, this was indeed a gigantic enterprise. Where nothing but a few farm houses had stood before, there rose within a few years a sizeable, well laid out town which housed mills and print works which, by 1839, could manufacture more than a million yards of print cloth a year and would soon greatly increase this figure. The directors of the Merrimack Company turned to England to find a superintendent for their print works and induced J OHN D. PRINCE to come from Manchester as, in the following years, did many others, including designers, engravers, block and machine printers, color mixers and chemists. When Kirk Boot succeeded in finding Mr Prince, he asked him what salary he would expect. He replied, 'Five thousand dollars per year.' 'Why, that is more than we pay the Governor of Massachusetts,' protested Mr Boot. 'Can the Governor of Massachusetts print?' Mr Prince asked. He was hired on his own terms.

While many Merrimack prints doubtless survive (Plate 142A), few of these can be identified today. They frequently received awards at the annual exhibitions of American manufactures held at Boston, New York and Philadelphia. In 1839, at Boston, the committee for the 2nd Annual Exhibition of the Massachusetts Charitable Mechanic Association reported the Merrimack prints 'a gorgeous product. The width, durability and beauty of texture, the rich original designs, the superior execution and the brilliancy of coloring are beyond any work of the kind that has before been brought to the notice of the committee.'

Family letters and a swatch book of Merrimack prints in the possession of Mrs Nina Fletcher Little give us the name of her great-grandfather WILLIAM JARVIE (1807–84), a Scottish designer, who came to this country from Manchester, c. 1856, and had joined the staff of the Merrimack Company as 'a designer for their prints'. A letter of 1871, addressed to Jarvie by the treasurer of the company, gives evidence of a significant change in the designing set-up of the textile

industry, indicating that the selling agents in New York were taking over from the manufacturers the responsibility of designing the textiles they sold. Jarvie was therefore told in this letter that: 'Messrs Wheelwright, Anderson & Company have been appointed to sell our prints after January 1, 1872. You will therefore turn yourself, bag and baggage over to them and whatever there is in your department belonging to us.' This evolution later resulted in the emergence of the independent textile converter who today buys the cloth, provides the designs, chooses the printer and sells the finished goods.

Fall River, Massachusetts, also became an important textile manufacturing and printing center. ANDREW ROBESON (Plate 141C) began printing calicoes in the mid-1820s and soon established an enviable reputation for the excellence of his prints. In 1832 the judges for the Franklin Institute Exhibition reported that 'the premium went to Andrew Robeson for their printed cottons – for their fineness, coloring and elegance of execution'. In 1831 the AMERICAN PRINT WORKS was established, which after the mid-century became one of the largest print works in the world (Plate 142D). In the exhibition of 1840 at Philadelphia, the judges gave them the highest award: 'Printed cottons from the American Print Works, Fall River ... are noted for their beauty of designs, rich and agreeable effect in combination, delicacy and exactness in the execution that lead this season – the first premium.' The nearby GLOBE PRINT WORKS and BAY STATE PRINT WORKS, at Tiverton, also became large producers of printed fabrics. Another early print works was the firm of CROCKER, RICHMOND & OTIS at Taunton (Plate 141B). *Niles Weekly Register* informs us in 1825 that they printed '150 pieces of fine calicoes per day and 1,000 persons are employed in the establishment'. Their prints received a silver medal at the 1827 Franklin Institute Exhibition: 'but the Taunton goods were deemed the best in considering the colors, fabric and printing.' The Taunton prints received awards at nearly every Franklin Institute annual. In 1833, ten years after their establishment, the firm was sold to interests in

Bristol, Rhode Island, and was thereafter known as the BRISTOL PRINT WORKS. The Cooper Union has forty-eight dyers' receipt books containing many hundreds of swatches from the large print works connected with the PACIFIC MILLS at Lawrence, established in 1853. Another late manufacturer was HARVEY ARNOLD & COMPANY, established at North Adams in 1862, and known after 1876 as the ARNOLD PRINT WORKS, many of whose prints are in the collection of the Rhode Island School of Design.

The two chief textile printing companies in New Hampshire, located at Dover and Manchester, wove as well as printed cloth, as did the companies at Lowell and Fall River. The DOVER MANUFACTURING COMPANY, after 1827 known as the COCHECO MANU-FACTURING COMPANY, began printing calicoes in 1824 (Plates 141A, 142C). They received a silver medal at the Boston exhibition of 1839: 'In appearance their prints are strikingly like English work ... they are skillfully and delicately executed.' Two of a set of nine color receipt books kept by S. DUNSTER (Plates 138C, 142C), now in the Rhode Island Historical Society, contain many Cocheco prints of the periods 1830–2 and 1855–7. Prints from the MANCHESTER MILLS, renamed MANCHESTER PRINT WORKS in 1848, are to be found in pattern books in the Metropolitan Museum of New York and the Manchester Historical Society. They were among the first to manufacture and print delaines in this country (1846). Payroll accounts for the years 1848–51 tell us that JOSEPH BATES and JOHN GOODIER were employed by them as print designers.

Rhode Island, considered the cradle of the American textile industry, played a prominent role in textile printing. The first considerable print works there was that established by WILLIAM SPRAGUE in 1824 at Cranston, later known as A. & W. SPRAGUE and today as the CRANSTON PRINT WORKS. They began printing in 1824 with a two-color printing machine, adding other colors with wood blocks. JOHN DAY supplied the early patterns. In 1850, they were awarded a gold medal by the American Institute of the City of New York Exhibition 'for the best Madder print'. PHILLIP ALLEN & SONS at their works on Thurber's Lane, Providence, began printing in 1830. Twelve dyers' receipt books in the Rhode Island Historical Society, kept by DANIEL O. MCCARTHY, contain swatches of Allen prints for the period 1845–58, and the Providence Directory for 1847–8 list EDWARD BARLOW and THOMAS FOSTER as designers at Allen's print works and Joseph Bates as a 'designer to calico printers'. PHILLIP ALLEN also apparently had an interest in the WOONSOCKET COMPANY, many of whose prints of the 1850s and 1860s are to be found in two of the company's pattern books now in the Rhode Island School of Design. Another large Rhode Island printer, whose beginnings go back to about 1825, is the APPONAUG PRINT WORKS at Apponaug, but examples of their early prints have not been identified. A printer, who perhaps received the most awards at the Philadelphia and Boston exhibitions, was JACOB DUNNELL & COMPANY, established at Pawtucket in 1836, and later known as the DUNNELL MANUFAC-TURING COMPANY. One of those rare descriptions of early American Manufacturers appeared in the December, 1849, issue of the English *Journal of Design and Manufactures* concerning the Dunnell prints:

'MOUSSELINES DE LAINE, MUSLINS AND CALI-COES PRINTED BY JACOB DUNNELL & CO., PROVIDENCE, RHODE ISLAND, UNITED STATES OF AMERICA
We have received about 30 specimens of printing from the above house, and with them a gratifying letter, which conveys some valuable information as to the present condition of calicoe-printing in America. Notwithstanding the modest estimate of their own productions by Messrs Dunnell & Co., we must declare that they have agreeably surprised us by their general excellence, for, with the exception of the two specimens of chintz, which certainly are very puzzling, the workmanship of the whole is excellent. The *Mousselines de laine*, the material for which is imported by the house, are certainly first rate. The design of one is well drawn and the rose ... treated in an artistic and effective manner. Some of the muslins, too, are equally excellent – the material being manufactured in Portsmouth, New Hampshire ... The 'madders' are chiefly brown and grey ... Three or four of them are equal to anything we have seen of the same class during the current season, and there are one or two of which we should have inserted

specimens if it had been possible ... We should state that the cloth on which the madders are printed is manufactured in the immediate neighbourhood of Providence, and is of good average quality ... This firm rarely uses French designs, as they are generally unsuitable to the American market; they have several designers in their employ, and make the whole of their own designs, for their inducement to copy our designs is very slight. Before they could get their goods into the market, the English original would be selling at their doors.'

One of the early-nineteenth-century print works in Pennsylvania was MESSRS THORP, SIDALL & COMPANY near Germantown, who in 1809 introduced printing from engraved copper rollers imported from England. By 1822 engraved copper rollers were being made in Philadelphia by MASON & BALDWIN, manufacturers of bookbinders' tools. In 1826, they received honorable mention at the Franklin Institute exhibition for 'an engraved copper cylinder for calico printing'. S. Dunster's receipt book in the Rhode Island Historical Society includes a volume of prints of the 1830s printed at LA GRANGE in Philadelphia county. This may be the PERKINS & WENDELL which so often received premiums, particularly at the Philadelphia exhibitions (Plate 138c). The Franklin Institute and other exhibition judges frequently awarded premiums to print works in various states, whose prints prior to 1876 are not yet identified. Among these were the WARREN COMPANY near Baltimore (1827); EAGLE PRINT WORKS at Bellview, New Jersey (1829); JOSEPH RIPKA, Manayunk, Pennsylvania (1844); HUDSON CALICO PRINTING WORKS (J. & B. Marshall) Stockport, New York (1829); BRIGGS & COMPANY, Frankfort (1847); BENJAMIN COZZENS, Providence (1843); LODI PRINT WORKS (Robert Rennie), Lodi, New Jersey (1849); HAMILTON MANUFACTURING COMPANY, Lowell (1844) and GARNER & COMPANY (Plate 142B), Haverstraw, New York (1850).

GLOSSARY

Block printing: the application of color by means of wood with the design cut in relief. A 'coppered' block is one in which the design is outlined with brass or copper strips driven edgewise into the block, the areas intended to print solid color being filled with felt.

Calico (callicoe, calicoe, calicut): before the nineteenth century, a staple white or dyed cotton cloth imported via Calcutta. Later a similar fabric manufactured in Europe or America. Today, a cotton cloth printed with a small figure.

Chintz (chint, chits, chinse): a painted or printed calico from India. Today, a cotton printed in large designs in several colors, often glazed.

Copper plate printing: the application of color to cloth by means of an engraved flat copper plate the full width of the fabric. Used in England c. 1760; introduced a monochrome, pictorial style of printing.

Discharge printing: a 'dyed' style, first used c. 1806, in which the fabric is first dyed a solid color and then the design is printed as a chemical which bleaches out or discharges the color, producing a white design on a dyed ground.

Piece: a unit length of cloth about thirty yards long.

Resist printing: an ancient 'dyed' style in which the fabric is printed in the desired design with a substance which protects those areas of the cloth from the action of the dye. The patterns are usually white on a dyed ground, often indigo blue (Plate 137).

Roller or Machine printing: a revolutionary development in textile printing invented c. 1783, by David Bell but not generally used until shortly after 1800. Printing is done from an engraved copper surface in the form of a cylinder about 4 inches in diameter. This made possible a process of continuous printing and the use of several rollers in a single printing machine, each applying successively a different color or pattern to the cloth. Rollers were engraved by hand or impressed with 'mills' – cylinders of hardened steel with the design to be engraved raised in relief on their surface. Jacob Perkins, an American bank note engraver, is credited with the invention of this important engraving technique *c.* 1808. Pantograph engraving is an etching technique introduced in 1834. Roller printing was first introduced in this country at Philadelphia, *c.* 1809, and engraved rollers first manufactured in the same city by Mason & Baldwin.

Stenciling: a technique of applying color with a brush through openings cut in heavy waterproof paper, used in the decoration of furniture, tole and textiles. Most surviving examples date from the first half of the nineteenth century (Plate 140).

BOOKS FOR
FURTHER READING

BAGNALL, WILLIAM R.: *The Textile Industries of the United States* (1893).

CLARK, V.S.: *History of Manufactures in the United States* (1929).

CLOUZOT, H., and MORRIS, FRANCIS: *Painted and Printed Fabrics* (1927).

COOPER, T.: *A Practical Treatise on Dyeing and Callicoe Printing*, Philadelphia (1815).

LITTLE, FRANCES: *Early American Textiles* (1931).

WHITE, GEORGE S.: *Memoir of Samuel Slater* (1836).

QUILTS AND COVERLETS

By VIRGINIA D. PARSLOW

QUILTS and coverlets are primarily bed coverings created for warmth; while counterpanes and bedspreads are decorative covers for the bed produced with no thought of contributing to the comfort of the user. The quilts and coverlets of the nineteenth century, which were primarily utilitarian in their purpose, are the kinds most available to the collector today. They were produced in great quantity and a remarkable number have survived in good condition. Many of them are very attractive in color and pattern. The discriminating collector can make good use of them in the decoration of the home. Some knowledge, however, is desirable as to their period if they are to be fitted into their most appropriate setting. An understanding of the techniques involved in their production will make them more interesting and appreciated.

Most eighteenth-century quilts and counterpanes are very large, often nine to twelve feet square, as they were used on the high beds of the period and often covered the stacked featherbeds and pillows which were placed on the main bed during the day to be spread on floor and settle for sleeping at night. These early covers were usually made of simple homespun or of imported English, French or India printed or painted cottons and were often not quilted at all but used only as counterpanes.

As a rule the design of the textile will give a clue as to its approximate age. During the seventeenth and eighteenth centuries the designs of bed-covers tend to develop from a base and to flow outward and upward as in the typical Tree-of-Life design. They may be symmetrical horizontally but not vertically, and there are rarely borders. In the nineteenth century this gradually gave way to more formalized patterns. At first the central design remained free and was surrounded by symmetrical borders; but later, that too disappeared and the whole design became balanced. After 1825 the designs tend to become geometrical in repeating units. Naturally there was a great carry-over of these designs and much copying of older pieces so that a typical eighteenth-century design may well appear as late as 1860. In this case the materials used may date the piece. Fortunately many women were very proud of their work and both signed and dated their more elaborate productions.

Crewel embroidered bedspreads, or counterpanes, were produced in the eighteenth century. Often a complete set of bed furniture was embroidered, including canopy or tester, curtains and sometimes a skirt. The design was produced in the traditional English way with colored wools worked in various stitches on a homespun linen ground. The well-known Tree-of-Life design was most popular but often scattered motifs are found. These usually have the same Eastern feeling although the subject-matter may be the original idea of the maker.

Among the most interesting of the bed-covers, although rare, are the *wool-on-wool* covers or bedrugs (Plate 146c) which have large scrolling or Tree-of-Life motifs worked in woolen yarn on a background of natural colored woolen blanketing. While the technique is often mistaken for hooking, it is usually a product of the needle. Several strands of single-ply woolen yarn were stitched through the ground in a running stitch taking short stitches through the fabric and leaving loops of yarn on the surface. The entire surface is usually covered with a deep pile which is uncut. These textiles often resemble in appearance the woven pile bedrugs of Scandinavia which are called *Rya*.

Some have pile in various shades of blue with natural colored woolen; while others combine these with shades of yellow, brown and green. The designs appear to stem directly from the early crewel work. Sometimes the woolen sheeting or blanket used for the background is pieced together from fabric in several different weaves, suggesting that it may have been a secondary use of partly worn material. These bedrugs are usually seven or eight feet square. Most of them are round in the New England area, particularly in the Connecticut River Valley from Vermont, Massachusetts and Connecticut. Many are dated, the earliest 1724 and latest in the early nineteenth century. (*See also* 'Needlework', Vol. I, Plate 136B.)

When cotton cloth became available from the factory soon after 1815 it was used for counterpanes, just as had the earlier chintz, but it needed to be decorated by hand. It was sometimes printed at home by means of carved wooden blocks or stencils. These blockprinted or *stenciled counterpanes* were occasionally made into quilts and it is in this condition that they are most often found today. The designs are simple and resemble to great degree the appliquéd quilts of the period. The colors usually used were red, green and yellow. (*See* 'Cotton Printing in America', Vol. I, Plate 140.)

After 1800 many bedspreads were made of cotton cloth, the earliest hand-woven, embroidered in various stitches with cotton roving or *candlewicking*. These are all-white counterpanes, with sometimes simple, sometimes elaborate, designs and are often signed and dated. There is usually fringe applied to three sides. The designs become geometric after 1825 and there is often tufting combined with the embroidery stitches.

Closely resembling these embroidered spreads are the all-white *woven counterpanes*, made on the loom (Plate 147). A cotton roving was raised in loops over a wire to form the pattern on a background of plain cotton. Some of these were produced at home and some by professional weavers. The home-woven ones are usually seamed, while the others were woven full width and often numbered and dated. These woven tufted spreads can be distinguished from the embroidered variety by the heavy roving which is continuous across the width, forming a heavy rib where it is not looped on the surface for the design. Stars often form a part of the design with swag borders. These were made from about 1800 to 1820.

QUILTS

There were at this period also *all-white quilts* made to serve as counterpanes. The interlining of cotton wadding is very thin and the quilting stitches very fine. The pattern may be very elaborate and often extra padding was introduced from the back after the quilting was completed, in order to accent certain parts of the design. This usually consists of a large central medallion, urn, cornucopia or basket of fruit or flowers with a series of surrounding borders. Companion pieces, such as bureau covers, were often made as well as separate pieces to cover the pillows. These white quilts usually may be assigned to the first quarter of the nineteenth century.

The technique of quilting developed because three layers of cloth are warmer than one, and has been employed for centuries. Clothing has been made for both warmth and protection as in the quilted cotton garments of China and the quilted padding worn under medieval armor. Counterpanes have probably been quilted in every century from the fourteenth to the twentieth. In the seventeenth and eighteenth centuries bedhangings and tablecovers were also among the household articles quilted. Clothing also came in for its share of this technique and articles included petticoats or underskirts, waistcoats, slippers, jackets and dresses. Petticoats are the most usual surviving articles in this group and their patterns are inclined to follow rather closely the bedcoverings of the period.

In American bed quilts this technique of quilting is often combined with designs, pieced or patched (appliquéd), of colored fabrics in order to furnish a colorful, as well as warm, article of bed clothing. The important era of American quilt-making extended from about 1750 to 1860. Quite naturally, many more examples have survived from the nineteenth than from the eighteenth century.

The quilted woolen bedcovers, which are often called *Linsey-woolseys*, are not often made of that staple household fabric. Rather, they are composed of a top layer of woolen or glazed worsted fabric dyed dark blue, green or brown with a bottom layer of a coarser woolen material, either natural or a shade of yellow or buff. The filling is a soft layer of carded wool and the three layers are held together with quilting done with homespun linen thread. While some of these may date from the eighteenth century many were made during the first half of the nineteenth. The design of the quilting is often a simple one composed of interlocking circles or crossed diagonal lines giving a diamond pattern. The earlier woolen quilts are thinner and the designs tend to be finer and more elaborate. The size of these quilts may also be a clue to their age, as in the nineteenth century they tend to be blanket size, while in the eighteenth they are likely to be large bedcovers, occasionally with cutout corners for the bedposts.

While the eighteenth-century cotton counterpanes were made of whole cloth, usually imported, and therefore confined to the households of the well-to-do, the ordinary housewife soon came to realize that the expensive patterned chintzes would go much farther if they were first cut up into design units and applied to a linen or cotton ground (Plate 143). The central part of the design of the *chintz appliqué counterpane* was often the Tree, cut from the chintz generally in one piece and applied to the plain fabric ground with the birds and insects found in these designs applied separately. Borders were then cut from smaller figured chintz and sewn on all four, or sometimes only three, sides. There were often two or three of these bands, of varying patterns and colors, separated by bands of plain fabric. At a later period a back was added and a thin layer of carded cotton or wool placed between to be stitched in place by the finest of hand sewing. This was almost always a simple running stitch in

America; while in England and on the Continent a back-stitch was more generally used. The quilting often followed the outlines of the appliqué in the central design which set it off in a raised manner. The plain ground was often simply quilted in closely spaced diagonal rows.

In the later part of the eighteenth century came the first of the *pieced quilts*. The central design was often a large Rising Sun motif or Star of Bethlehem covering almost the entire bed with the familiar chintz floral patterns cut out and appliquéd to the square and triangular blocks of plain white fabric which filled in the star corners. A chintz border was usually added to complete the quilt top. This star pattern, which continued to be popular for a century or more, was composed of diamond-shaped pieces of small-patterned chintz and calico which were carefully arranged so that the colors radiated from the center to the points. After 1800 the appliqué filling the corners gave way to pieced blocks in a smaller star pattern (Plate 144). The sewing of these pieced patterns had to be most carefully done, as the seams had to be perfectly regular if the finished design was to lie flat and even.

The earliest colored quilts made of remnant patches must have been just that, with the odd-shaped pieces sewn down to a fabric backing; but by 1800 women began to use the more convenient method of making the quilt top in units of blocks and setting these together, either in parallel rows or diagonally, with strips of lattice-work or with alternate white blocks. These smaller units could be pieced or appliquéd very conveniently and then assembled and quilted in simple or elaborate designs. If plain white blocks were used in setting the pattern blocks together, these were often quilted elaborately; while the quilting in the pieced or appliquéd blocks followed rather closely the construction lines of the block.

The patterns for quilting were often marked on the fabric by snapping a chalk line for the diagonal lines or chalking around a cardboard pattern for the more elaborate designs. Household objects such as cups, saucers and plates were often used as patterns for simple quilting. Pencil, chalk, charcoal and soap were used for the marking. Background designs included: the Horizontal, the Cross Bar, Diagonal, Diamond and Double and Triple Cross-Bars and Diamonds. Running designs for borders and lattice strips included: Running Vine, Princess Feather, Rope, Ocean Wave and Serpentine. Designs for the plain blocks were: Feather Wreath, Clam Shell, Wheel of Fortune, Spider Web, Pineapple, Bouquet, Weeping Willow, Star Crescent, Heart, American Eagle, Fan, Star and Crown, Oak Leaf, Bellflower, Acanthus, Swirl and Dove of Peace. Many designs were based on the always adaptable feather motif.

Pieced quilts are generally geometric in design, as it is much easier to seam two small pieces of fabric together if the seams are straight and not curved. There are thousands of designs for these quilts and many have fanciful names. The same pattern was known by different names in various sections of the country and often the same name would be used for several totally unrelated patterns. There are Star patterns named for every state in the Union. A few of the more interesting names are:

Cross and Crown	Puss-in-the-Corner
Goose Tracks	Bourgoyne Surrounded
Hen and Chickens	Pine Tree
Bear's Track	Flying Dutchman
Peony	Feather Star (Plate 144)
Flying Geese	Drunkard's Path
Lincoln's Platform	Robbing Peter to Pay Paul
Stepping Stones	Dutchman's Puzzle
Morning Star	Wheel of Fortune
King David's Crown	Cats and Mice
Joseph's Coat	Hearts and Gizzards
Jacob's Ladder	Grandmother's Fan
Sunflower	Dresden Plate
Delectable Mountains	Winding Warp
Log Cabin	Turkey Tracks
Rose of Sharon	Irish Chain

These pieced or appliquéd quilts of the nineteenth century were usually made of plain colored or printed cotton fabrics combined with white. Many were made of random bits of carefully hoarded fabric and in this case some of the fabrics may be much earlier than the actual date of the making of the quilt. Often the quilt which is best preserved, because carefully kept for use on special occasions, is the one made of two or three colors of fabric which were especially purchased for its construction. Many quilts of this type were made during the 1830s and 1840s of turkey red and green cottons appliquéd on white grounds. It is probable that many of them were brides' quilts as, even though the customary dozen quilts were made of scraps, it would have been that final masterpiece for which new materials would most likely have been purchased. These quilts were often made of identical blocks in a basket or flower design and set together with white blocks on which were lavished the most elaborate quilting. Often each block is quilted in a different design.

The technique of making the quilt top in separate blocks led to a special type of quilt during the 1840s and 1850s. This was known variously as a *Signature, Autograph, Friendship, Bride, Presentation* or *Album* quilt (Plate 145). These quilts were made for a special person. Friends or well-wishers each supplied a pieced or appliquéd block of her own chosen pattern which she usually signed in India ink. These friends gathered for an afternoon and assembled and quilted the quilt which was then presented to the honored guest. They were often made for a favorite minister or a minister's wife. These are among the most interesting of the nineteenth-century quilts and, if the colors are compatible and the various blocks well chosen and arranged, they may be very lovely as well.

During the late Victorian era the patched covers of the seventeenth and eighteenth century were revived but in a more elaborate form. These were the *Crazy Quilts* made of scraps of silk, satin and velvet. Like their earlier counterparts they were made of small irregular shaped pieces appliquéd to a base fabric but now the seams were often covered with embroidery stitches and sometimes the patch itself had a design painted or embroidered upon it. These were often most unattractive in color and design but occasionally a good example is found. They were impractical as bedcoverings, due to the material from which they were made, so they were made up into smaller sizes for use as couch throws, piano covers and other parlour ornamentation of the period.

COVERLETS

Unlike quilts, which were made of already woven fabric, coverlets are woven into patterns on the loom. They may be either the product of the housewife and her family or of the professional weaver. During the early years of the settlement of this country not much patterned weaving could have been done. It was all the housewife could do to supply her large family with the everyday clothing and household fabrics which were necessary. The materials for their manufacture were scarce. Sheep were not raised in great numbers and flax was a time-consuming crop. Cotton was obtainable only in limited quantities and at a high price. The housewife spun the flax which she had raised into linen yarn and wove materials for sheets and shirts, underclothing and toweling. The refuse tow from its processing she converted into sacking and coarse tow cloth. She spun the wool from her sheep into yarn and wove it into heavy material for the clothing of the men and boys and outer garments for the whole family, as well as blankets for the bed. Only when the hardships of the first years had decreased and more time and material were available could she turn her hand to producing the patterned textiles which would adorn her home as well as keep her family warm and protected.

The patterns of these fabrics were not invented by her but were based on a long-continuing tradition. Perhaps she had brought with her some family textiles or perhaps only the written formula for their weaving. These weaving drafts were freely interchanged and traveled through all the colonies. It is likely that the first really intricately patterned fabrics were produced by professional weavers who emigrated to America from the various countries of Europe bringing with them the old patterns of their homeland. It is certain that the early-eighteenth-century pattern books printed in Germany were brought to this country and used. The weavers of England and Scotland who came were well trained if they had successfully completed their apprenticeship. They certainly brought with them the patterns which they had been taught to weave. This was true of all the migrant weavers, for German, French, Dutch, Scandinavian, Scottish and English all contributed their traditional textile designs and techniques to America.

In the category of woven coverlets must be included those woolen blankets also produced on the loom but decorated with embroidery so that they fufilled both the purpose of warmth and decoration. *Rose Blankets* are among these. They were woven of soft white wool in the simplest weave of the home loom. It is probable that the ones with a raised nap were woven at a slightly later date than the others either at home or in a factory. After weaving and finishing they were decorated with embroidery in colored woolen yarns. The pattern used was a stylized wheel design of loose stitches. This decoration was often in two corners and sometimes in all four. The colors used were those readily dyed at home with the natural dyestuffs generally available. Rose, green, yellow, tan, brown, black and sometimes blue are found. Rose blankets were being produced in the period from 1810 to 1840 in both New York and Pennsylvania and probably throughout New England. They were among the items of domestic manufacture which were being encouraged by the prizes awarded by agricultural societies of this period.

Material was also woven especially for making embroidered bedspreads. These often resemble plaid blankets in design. White or natural colored cotton was used with blue woolen yarn and woven in a twill weave. Then, after the strips were assembled, a design was embroidered in colored woolen yarns in the spaces of the plaid. A fringe was often added to finish the edge.

The coverlets produced in their entirety on the loom include several types and techniques. In the order of their complexity, they are: *overshot* (Plate 146A) also known as *float* weave; *summer-and-winter* weave; *block* or *double-weave geometric* (Plate 146B); and the two types of *flowered* coverlets (Plate 148) which are in the so-called *Jacquard* weave.

Due to the width of the home loom, coverlets were woven in two or more strips, each $2\frac{1}{2}$ to 3 yards long and seamed together when finished. They were usually about 84 inches wide if in two strips. Sometimes a separate woven fringe was sewn on the sides while the ends of the warp threads formed the fringe at the bottom.

Coverlets are found in shades of blue, blue and red, brown, brown and tan, black, madder rose or rust, yellow, green with rose or yellow, and more rarely in scarlet. The dyes used in producing these colors were the ones most readily available and the ones considered to be most permanent. The most satisfactory dyestuff available was indigo. This had to be purchased from a shop or from the peddler in the country but it was widely available from the earliest days. Much was grown in the south during the later half of the eighteenth century but a large amount was always imported. Indigo produces a fast blue color on all fibers and this may be varied considerably in shade. It was also used to produce shades of green by dyeing with it either before or after a yellow dye was applied. The process of dyeing with indigo was an unpleasant one because of the odor of the fermenting indigo vat, which demanded particular care as the vat had to be maintained at a constant warm heat to keep the fermentation from stopping. Other dyes were easier to apply. The brilliant scarlet was obtained from cochineal, an insect raised under cultivation in Mexico, by boiling the dried and powdered insects with a solution of tin dissolved in acid. As this dyestuff was probably the most expensive of all, it was not often used for home-woven coverlets. The common shades of red were obtained from madder root which could be purchased as a ground powder or could be raised in the garden. Dyeing with this material followed a standard procedure used for many natural dyestuffs. First the woolen yarn was boiled in a solution of alum or of alum and cream of tartar, and then in a bath with the madder root. Shades from rose to deep lacquer red and rust were obtained. This was the second most popular dye for coverlets as it was almost as fast to light and washing as indigo blue.

Yellow was obtained from goldenrod and sumac, tan from alder bark and butternut hulls and roots, dark brown from hickory or black walnut hulls and roots, and black by dyeing first with walnut and then with indigo. Other herbs, barks, roots and berries were used with the alum process for dyeing various shades. Most of these were rather dull in tone due to the natural impurities in the dyestuffs and most of them faded to some degree in time. Imported dyewoods from South and Central America generally available during the eighteenth and nineteenth centuries included logwood, Brazilwood and fustic, but the domestic weaver was inclined to trust to the familiar dyestuffs.

The simplest type of coverlet to produce was in the *overshot* weave (Plate 146A) which could be woven on the limited four-harness loom to be found in almost every home. It was made of linen warp and woolen weft in the eighteenth century and of cotton warp and woolen weft in the nineteenth. These coverlets are confined, by the limitations of the loom used, to simple geometric patterns, but there are literally thousands of patterns as the combinations of four blocks in different order and proportions are infinite. Like the names of quilt patterns, the names of coverlet patterns were often very fanciful, reflected the historical events of their day, or were based on the resemblance, either real or fancied, to some familiar object. The fact that these names show late American historical connections does not mean that they were created at that time. The same old pattern with its origin in Europe was renamed by the weaver to modernize it. Geographic and historical names include:

England Beauty	Downfall of Paris
Monmouth	London Beauty
Governor's Garden	King's Flower
Southern Beauty	Queen's Delight
Tennessee Flower	Western Beauty
Indian Trouble	Jackson's Purchase
Federal Knot	Federal City
Indian Wars	Whig Rose

Those bearing resemblance to familiar objects or merely fanciful include:

Double Bow Knot	Snail Trail and Cat
Church Windows	Tracks
Rose in the Bush	True Love's Vine
Snowball	Irish Chain
Blooming Leaf	Wheel of Fortune

Ladies' Delight	Snow Drop
Ladies' Fancy	Bachelor's Button
Free Mason and	Fox Trail
Felicity	Young Man's Delight
Cards and Wheels	Bachelor Among the
Nine Snowballs	Girls
Chariot Wheel	Forsaken Lover
Blazing Star	Gentleman's Fancy
Pine Bloom	

The overshot weave is a three-thread construction. There is one warp, usually a two-ply linen or cotton; a binder weft, usually the same material as the warp but often a single ply and slightly smaller in grist; and the pattern weft which is a colored woolen yarn. This may be either single or two-ply and is always larger than either the warp or the binder weft. The pattern of the overshot is three-tone; dark, light and half-tone. The dark spots or blocks which form the real design are composed of several pattern wefts where they overlie the basic cotton or linen ground. These are called 'floats', 'skips' or 'overshots'. The light spots are the basic ground fabric where the pattern threads lie below it and the half-tones are formed between the dark and light spots where the pattern weft is bound closely into the ground. Most frequently this type of coverlet is in a four-block pattern. The rectangular blocks may vary in size and proportion, but all the blocks in a horizontal row are the same height and all the blocks in a vertical row are the same width in any single piece of weaving. This weave was used in all of the Colonies and traveled westward with the settlers into the new states. Many of these coverlets are still in existence but most of those surviving were woven in the first half of the nineteenth century.

Coverlets were sometimes woven in the *summer-and-winter* weave, but this weave did not have as wide a distribution geographically as the overshot weave. These are found most often in New York and Pennsylvania. The opinion of many is that this weave was either brought to America by German immigrants of the early-eighteenth century or was developed by them after arrival. A weave closely resembling it and in identical patterns was common in the Schleswig-Holstein area in the seventeenth and eighteenth centuries, where it was used for bed curtains.

Summer-and-winter weave produces a fabric which is two-toned and reversible. On the side where the colored woolen pattern weft predominates it is dark and on the reverse side where the light warp and binder weft predominate it is light. From this it receives its name. It is in fact a small overshot weave in blocks which may be of any size and proportion and may overlap or combine. The pattern is still geometric but it may be more intricate than the overshot. The fabric is extremely flexible and the threads being so intimately bound together, it is structurally more sound and wears better than the overshot weave.

The same colors are found in this weave as in the others since they were the ones commonly available. Indigo blue is the most common, followed by madder rust and rose. More than one color of pattern weft is never used in summer-and-winter weave. This weave requires a loom slightly more elaborate than the overshot weave and therefore was used only by the more experienced home weaver. It is doubtful that it was often the product of the professional. These coverlets were probably produced during the first twenty-five or thirty years of the nineteenth century.

Another weave sometimes encountered in Pennsylvania resembles summer-and-winter and can be woven with the same patterns. The blocks, however, show a pattern of bird's-eye weave. It is probable that this technique is an interpretation of the linen patterns found in the German weaving books.

Block or *double woven geometric* coverlets are among the most beautiful preserved today (Plate 146B). These were undoubtedly most often the work of the professional craftsman as few homes would have contained the elaborate loom required for their manufacture. According to the account books of these professionals, they were producing block coverlets during the period from 1820 to 1840. At this same period the same men were weaving the even more elaborate flowered coverlets (Plate 148). These professional weavers were most often Scotsmen who imigrated to this country after having already learned their trade. It is reasonable to assume that such weaves were in use in Scotland but the patterns are identical with the ones used by the Germans for summer-and-winter weave and are to be found in the German weaving books of the eighteenth century as well as the Scottish weaving books of the early nineteenth century. In both of these published sources they seem to have been intended as patterns for linens.

In color they follow the style of the day, most often in deep indigo blue woolen yarn which was usually supplied by the housewife, combined with a natural colored cotton yarn which was factory spun and supplied by the weaver. Sometimes red and blue were used in the same coverlet, giving a red, white and blue coloring.

This technique produces a fabric which is really a combination of two fabrics in one. One is a plain-woven colored woolen while the other is a plain-woven natural colored cotton. Rarely is the second of linen. Two warps are required on the loom and these are woven together in such a way that the design is produced by the interchanging of the two basic fabrics. It is completely reversible, a block on the one side of colored woolen fabric being backed on the reverse by a block in natural cotton. Like the summer-and-winter weave, these blocks may overlap and combine but the pattern is always geometric. Block coverlets like summer-and-winter and overshot were woven on the narrow loom; so that two strips were always necessary to produce a full width coverlet.

The fancy *flowered* coverlets, now usually called *Jacquard* coverlets, were always the work of the professional weaver who often referred to them as *carpet coverlets*. Many of these were woven by Scottish weavers who were already weavers of carpets in the same double-weave and with similar patterns. The German weavers of Pennsylvania also produced many of them. They were being woven as early as 1818 in New York State but the earliest dated one to come to light so far is marked *1821*. They were probably first woven in New York and Pennsylvania and later in Kentucky, Ohio, Indiana and Illinois. In the opinion of some students the coverlets woven during the most active period, the 1830s and 1840s, were woven on the draw-loom; while later ones were woven on hand-operated looms with the help of the Jacquard attachment. It was not too difficult to install the Jacquard attachment on the old draw-loom but there was a patent carpet loom used in Scotland which was earlier than the Jacquard and might very well have been in use in this country in the 1830s. Many of these flowered coverlets were certainly woven by power in full width on looms with Jacquard attachments in the 1860s and 1870s. These later coverlets have one-piece patterns, usually with a large central medallion surrounded with elaborate borders. The designs are finer and less clear cut than the earlier coverlets. In this late period appear the scarlet-red coverlets which are suitable for rooms decorated in the Victorian manner.

The earliest of these flowered coverlets are always in the double-weave, but instead of being confined to geometric patterns, the weaver could use naturalistic designs. While many weavers used the same repeating medallion designs for the central portion of the coverlet, making one wonder if there were not a published pattern book now unknown, the borders were often most individual in treatment. These might contain designs of eagles, scrolls, festoons, flowers, birds, trees, buildings, portraits or mottoes and the weaver could include the name of the person for whom the coverlet was woven, the date, the place and his own signature. The earliest ones are likely to be more restrained in design and more pleasing to the eye.

Many of these coverlets produced in Pennsylvania and westward in Kentucky, Ohio and Indiana during the 1830s and 1840s are not in double-weave but in a single or damask weave. These are often in two or more colors of woolen yarn. Damask table linens in cotton and linen and cotton and wool were produced by some New York weavers in the identical designs of their double-woven coverlets.

BOOKS FOR FURTHER READING

ATWATER, MARY MEIGS: *The Shuttle-craft Book of American Hand-weaving*, New York (1928, 1946).

COLONIAL COVERLET GUILD: *Heirlooms from Old Looms*, Chicago (1940).

DUNTON, JR, M.D., WILLIAM RUSH: *Old Quilts*, Cantonville, Maryland (1946).

FINLEY, RUTH E.: *Old Patchwork Quilts and the Women Who Made Them*, Philadelphia (1929).

HALL, CARRIE, and KRETSINGER, ROSE G.: *The Romance of the Patchwork Quilt in America*, Idaho (1935).

HALL, ELIZA CALVERT, *A Book of Handwoven Coverlets*, Boston (1912).

ICKIS, MARGUERITE: *The Standard Book of Quilt Making and Collecting*, New York (1949).

LITTLE, FRANCES: *Early American Textiles*, New York (1931).

PETO, FLORENCE: *Historic Quilts*, New York (1939).

PETO, FLORENCE: *American Quilts and Coverlets*, New York (1949).

RABB, KATE MILAN: *Indiana Coverlets and Coverlet Weavers*, Indianapolis (1928).

REINERT, GUY F.: *Coverlets of the Pennsylvania Germans*, Allentown, Pa. (1949).

REINERT. GUY F.: *Yearbook of the Pennsylvania-German Folklore Society* (1948).

ROBERTSON, ELIZABETH WELLS: *American Quilts*, New York (1948).

WEBSTER, MARIE D.: *Quilts – Their Story and How to Make Them*, Garden City, New York (1915).

THE ORIENTAL 'CARPITT' IN COLONIAL AMERICA

By JOSEPH V. McMULLAN

Rugs from the Orient have enjoyed distinction in the West from earliest times. Rome, Byzantium, Venice, France and Flanders have in turn exerted extraordinary efforts to secure them. They came rather late to England, less than a century before the colonists brought with them to the new land an appreciation of the Oriental rug as an object of luxury.

Knowledge of the appearance of the early examples to reach Europe is gained from paintings. Italian frescoes of the fourteenth century depict almost exclusively simple repeat panels containing either stylized birds or animals. As the fifteenth century progressed animal styles continued, frequently more complex in execution and with such motifs as the dragon and phoenix, an early design migrant from China. At the same time, highly developed abstractions appeared in large numbers, based primarily on tree, shrub and flower motifs in which geometric drawing becomes evident. This second type soon became predominant.

Strong evidence of rug importations into western Europe is furnished by Van Eyck and Memling, whose paintings show rugs which parallel those depicted by such fifteenth-century Italian masters as Ghirlandajo.

Tudor England: the insular position of England and her distance from sources of supply delayed introduction of these rugs to any extent until the sixteenth century. It was time for a distinguished collector to appear and he was at hand – Henry VIII. His new palace of Hampton Court was not a fortress but matched in luxury the Fontainebleau of Francis I. Henry VIII had almost certainly seen a sufficient number of rugs on the Continent to excite his interest. He sought the proper connections and found that Cardinal Wolsey, through Rome and particularly through Venetian traders, could supply the needs of Hampton Court for the prized Oriental weavings.

From Holbein, court painter to the king, much can be learned regarding the color, design and scale of the rugs obtained. One of his portraits shows the king in characteristic stance on a Turkish rug with indented repeat medallions of a type now known as a 'Star' Ushakh, in a style which persisted into the eighteenth century. In Hans Eworth's portrayal of the royal family the floor is covered with another of Cardinal Wolsey's carpets, a well-known type with a central medallion on a rich red ground. This too is a Turkish rug from the vicinity of Ushakh, a type which has continued in more or less degenerate form almost to our own day (Plate 149).

In Holbein's *Ambassadors* at the National Gallery, London, two envoys stand one on either side of a table covered with a small rug differing in design from the rugs in the royal collection and almost entirely geometric in character. It probably came from an outlying village, not from one of the great weaving centers (Plate 153A).

The English nobility were quick to follow the royal example. The Montague family have at least two rugs of the 'Star' Ushakh type, one of which has embroidered in the end selvage the date *1580*. These two rugs are in the collection of the present Duke of Buccleuch and have been published many times.

In America: there are no seventeenth-century portraits of colonial owners of Oriental rugs, and not until the following century do these appear. It is therefore necessary to look elsewhere for some indication of their arrival in the colonies. For the time being, inventories provide us with the only information available, and as they are mentioned in inventory after inventory it is apparent that the colonists must have valued the Oriental as much as their contemporaries in England.

Contrary to general opinion, a number of colonists were men of some property on arrival, or soon created it through superior enterprise in their new environment. This was particularly true in New England where ships were built almost at once and ocean trade with the West Indies and Europe began to flourish. Successful merchants managed to acquire the means to supply themselves with 'Turkey carpitts' in comparatively short time. Such a one was William Clarke of Salem, the inventory of whose estate, taken after his death in 1647, just twenty-seven years after the landing of the Pilgrims at Plymouth, included the following: '1 Turkey carpitt' valued at £1, and '1 old Turkey carpitt' valued at 8 shillings. These are in contrast to entries of '1 Red Rugg, 1 Greene Rugg', etc., in the same inventory. This early example is the forerunner of many as the century advanced.

It is generally stated that carpets were used as a covering for tables and not on the floor, and it is undoubtedly true that many were so used. However, it seems wrong to argue that they were never used on the floor in the light of the following announcement from the *Boston Gazette*, March 26, 1754:

'To be sold at public vendu at the dwelling house of the late Ebenezer Holmes in King Street, Boston ... a large Turkey carpet measuring eleven and a half by eighteen and a half feet. ...'

This could obviously have been used only on the floor and in a room of considerable size.

The acquisition of Oriental carpets could be made at that time, legally, only through England, or beyond the legal pale through smuggling. A successful raid on a Dutch or Spanish merchantman might also have yielded such a prize.

An indication of the esteem in which the Turkey carpet was held is seen in an advertisement in the *Boston News-Letter* February 20, 1755:

'Stolen out of a house in Boston a Turkey carpet of various colors, about a yard and a half in length, and a yard in width fringed at each end. Three dollars reward.'

In pre-Revolutionary America the dollars were the Spanish milled dollars which were important in the financial dealings of the day and their value was considerable, so that the reward was actually a high one.

Colonies such as Pennsylvania and Virginia had many families of wealth and culture, but as these colonies had no such stringent laws regarding the inventories of the deceased as existed in New England more is to be learned from New England, particularly Massachusetts, in this respect.

Up to the present time, no American family has been able to offer one shred of evidence of an existing Oriental carpet which has come down to them from their seventeenth- or eighteenth-century ancestors.

Portraits showing Oriental rugs: the only visual evidence of the types of Oriental rugs known in early America is found in portraits, particularly in four that are very well known. These are:

1. John Smibert's *Portrait of Bishop Berkeley and his Entourage*, done in 1729, during Berkeley's two-year sojourn in America spent chiefly in Newport, Rhode Island. This, which is now in the Yale University Art Gallery, New Haven, Connecticut, shows the group seated at a table covered with an Oriental carpet (illustrated Vol. II, Plate 202A). This type is seen in Plate 150.

2. Robert Feke's *Portrait of Isaac Royall and his Family*, painted in 1741 (Plate 151A) is now owned by the Law School of Harvard University, Cambridge, Massachusetts. Isaac Royall's fine house at Medford is one of the historic New England houses open to the public. A copy of Feke's picture hangs over the mantel where the original once hung. Feke was familiar with Smibert's picture as he has copied the arrangement, and shows the carpet in a similar way on the table, but the carpet itself is entirely different, which argues for the actuality of the original in Royall's possession. Although of the same type it is of

later date than the rug in the Berkeley portrait.

3. John Singleton Copley's *Portrait of Colonel Jeremiah Lee*, 1768, shows the wealthy Marblehead merchant standing on a carpet of the type illustrated in Plate 152. This portrait is now in the Wadsworth Atheneum, Hartford, Connecticut. The Lee Mansion in Marblehead, one of the finest examples of Georgian domestic architecture in New England, is also open to the public.

4. Gilbert Stuart's 'Lansdowne' *Washington*, 1796, is not properly of the colonial period. It shows Washington standing on an eighteenth-century medallion 'Ushakh', definitely of a late eighteenth-century origin and lacking much of the refinement of the mid-eighteenth-century type (Plate 154B).

Terminology: it has become the custom to use the word *rug* for what our ancestors in England and America called the 'Turkey carpitt', and the word *carpet* is generally reserved today for the machine-made product, acquired in strips and used to cover an entire room. The carpets of the eighteenth century, and earlier, were more frequently used on the table, but as trade made them more common they were used on the floor. The advertisement of 1754 makes it clear that Boston had homes where Oriental rugs were used on the floor in mid-century. After the Revolution, when trade directly with the East and Near East was undertaken, Oriental rugs must have become still more familiar.

While carpets took their place on the floor, the 'rugg' remained what it had been, a cover for a bed. What is called today a coverlet was often recorded as a 'bed rug'. The steamer rug represents a survival of the old use of the term.

Collections: recognition of the importance of the Oriental rug in colonial and post-colonial decoration has advanced rapidly in recent years. Henry F. du Pont, in furnishing the matchless series of American rooms at the Winterthur Museum, Winterthur, Delaware, was a pioneer. The buildings of the restored colonial capital of Williamsburg, Virginia, show an admirable selection of authentic types in the Governor's Palace, the Wythe house, Brush-Everard house and elsewhere. The American Wing of the Metropolitan Museum in New York will soon have rugs especially chosen to agree with the period of each room. The houses in Fairmount Park, Philadelphia, under the care of the Philadelphia Museum of Art, the houses at Old Deerfield, Massachusetts, and at the Shelburne Museum, Shelburne, Vermont, as well as interiors in the museums in most of our large cities show the use of such rugs as were known in early America.

The illustrations: the subjects chosen for illustration on the following plates represent types related to those in the four portraits mentioned, or are of such frequent recurrence that their importation into America seems to have been inescapable. Important among them are the 'Ushakh' with medallion center, made from the seventeenth century through the eighteenth and into the nineteenth; the 'Transylvania' rugs with broad borders containing a cartouche pattern, the centers frequently with floral sprays and leafy spandrels; the 'Smyrna' rugs with overall palmette; and geometric designs from the Caucasus. From these examples it may be seen what types may suitably be used today in interiors with American furniture of the seventeenth and eighteenth centuries.

The author is indebted to Charles F. Montgomery, director of the Winterthur Museum, for the reference to the William Clarke inventory of 1647, and to Mrs Joseph Grover of Gloucester, Massachusetts, for the information contained in the *Boston News-Letter* of 1755, and the Ebenezer Holmes auction of 1754.

BOOKS FOR
FURTHER READING

BODE, WILHELM VON, and KUHNEL, ERNST: *Antique Rugs from the Near East*, 3rd revised edition, New York (1922).

DILLEY, ARTHUR URBANE: *Oriental Rugs and Carpets*, New York (1931).

DIMAND, MAURICE S.: *A Handbook of Muhammadan Art*, New York (1944).

GROTE-HASENBALG, WERNER: *Masterpieces of Oriental Rugs*, translated from the German, New York (1922).

McMULLAN, JOSEPH V.: 'The Turkey Carpet in Early America' in *Antiques*, March 1954.

POPE, ARTHUR UPHAM: Catalogue of a Loan Exhibition of Early Oriental Carpets, Chicago (1926).

PRATT, RICHARD: *Second Treasury of Early American Homes*, Hawthorn Books, New York (1954).

Concise Encyclopedia of Antiques, Vol. I, pp. 222-227, Hawthorn Books, New York (1955).

HOOKED RUGS

By VIRGINIA D. PARSLOW

ALL of the decorative floor rugs, exclusive of Oriental rugs, which have an appearance of a pile surface have been classified as hooked rugs. According to general acceptance, these may be dated as follows: antique, 1775–1825; early, 1825–75; late, 1875–1900. It is possible that a classification by technique would help to date some examples and would assist in placing them in their proper period settings. There are three main types of technique: sewn with yarn through the background; patches or shirred strips sewn on to the background; and strips of fabric or yarn hooked through the background.

Early settlers in America probably had no rugs on their floors with the exception of the skins of wild animals. The first European rugs with pile surfaces had been made centuries before in imitation of furs but were used on beds and not on floors. Since there was little time or material available for making even the necessary textiles, it must have been some time before rugs were made for the floors. This may well not have been before 1750 in the common household. Most of the hooked rugs still in existence seem to have come from Canada and New England, which would lead one to believe that the art first developed there. The earliest floor rugs seem to be the ones worked in the same manner as the bedrugs of the Connecticut River Valley which are dated from 1724 to 1800. This technique could well be the basis for all the rugs now known as hooked rugs.

Embroidered rugs were produced from 1800 to 1835 and were often of carpet size and worked in tent or cross-stitch with homespun wools. Since these had to be made of new materials, like the sewn rugs, they were never as numerous as the scrap rugs. Rugs, braided or woven on the loom, from rags were also used but their exact period remains unknown.

Carpets were homewoven about 1820 from multi-colored woolen yarns and were probably in use until about 1850. Double-woven carpets were being produced by the professional coverlet weavers in the 1820s and 1830s, but all large-sized floor coverings were very expensive and the average housewife produced smaller rugs from scrap material. It is probable that at first these were scraps of cloth sewn to a fabric base and later were strips hooked through the base.

Yarn sewn rugs are those in the bedrug technique which are sometimes described as *embroidered, needle-tufted* or *reed-stitched*. In this technique a homespun linen or tow ground fabric was used and the pile surface was formed of several strands of two-ply yarn. The yarn was sewn through the ground taking a short stitch and leaving a loop on the surface. Another stitch was taken close to the first and in a line following the curves of the design. Sometimes the pile is very long and sometimes exceedingly short. Rugs with short loops made of fine yarns may have been intended as table rugs (Plate 155A). This technique produces a very soft flexible rug.

It is easier to tell if a rug is sewn or hooked if it is unlined. A sewn rug gives the appearance of a line of short dashes from the back. The pile yarn comes through a space or hole in the ground material, runs along a short distance on the back and returns to the face through another space. It returns to the back a short distance from the point it last returned to the surface. In a hooked rug the pile yarn or rag goes to the surface and returns to the back through the same space, leaving a continuous line on the back with no open spaces between stitches.

The colors usually found in yarn sewn rugs are the ones made from natural dyestuffs. They are the same shades as are found in

350

woven blankets and coverlets. These are: madder reds, yellows, indigo blues, greens, tans and browns and brownish or bluish black. These are soft muted colors. Often there is evidence that the rug had a dark colored woolen fringe sewn to the edges. Rugs in this technique were probably first made some time in the middle of the eighteenth century and continued until about 1830. An occasional late one made after 1850 would include material dyed with cochineal in shades of pink to scarlet. These colors are rarely found in the earlier rugs.

The designs of these yarn rugs are occasionally geometrical but more often they bear close resemblance to the designs of eighteenth-century crewel work. There are often loose flowers in sprays or in jars or vases which fill most of the space (Plate 155B). There is little emphasis on the border which may be missing altogether.

Patched rugs may be constructed in two general ways. The basic fabric may be new or used homespun linen, tow or woolen cloth, or it may be cotton sacking. The scraps of woolen cloth may be sewn to the surface of this ground material in two ways. In the first technique, which has been called *button* or *patchwork*, the pile cloth was cut into small square or circular patches from one-half to one inch across. These were folded in fourths and sewn down at the folded point to the ground. When sewn close together the effect is the same as the hooked rugs which have been sheared.

The second way, sometimes called *Chenille* or *caterpillar* (Plate 156A), was to cut strips from one-quarter to one and a half inches wide which were shirred and sewn to the ground. Sometimes the wider strips, cut on the bias, were folded through the center and shirred before being sewn on, and sometimes the strips were shirred through the center and sewn on with the two edges standing straight up. They were also constructed by cutting the strips very narrow, on the straight of the goods, and sewing them on flat so that they form small cartridge-pleats and look very much like an unclipped hooked rug.

All rugs of this patched or shirred type seem to be made of about the same materials.

They are always woolen fabrics of either homespun and woven material or of the material available at the time as finished goods. The colors are likely to be much the same as the natural dyed yarns as so much home-produced fabric was used. Often in this type of rug there is found the scarlet cloth such as was used for capes and uniforms. This is a stiff napped material resembling felt which was dyed with the expensive and hard-to-procure cochineal. These patched rugs also show the remnants of the woolen fringe which was originally sewn around them. Most of the specimens seem to have originated between 1840 and 1860.

Their designs are mostly floral but with fairly wide borders containing scrolling leaf and simple flower forms. The rectangular center may contain designs of flowers in baskets; flower sprays of stylized forms worked in spirals of shirred strips; houses with trees; designs from Oriental rugs and in one specimen examined the geometric pattern was one of interlocking circles apparently formed by use of a saucer for a pattern.

Hooked rugs form the third group in regard to technique. The background material for these rugs was homespun linen, factory woven cotton or burlap. The cloth scraps were cut in strips and a hook was used to draw these up in loops from the back of the ground fabric. Sometimes the loops were cut when made, sometimes not, and in some rugs the loops were varied in length to give a raised or sculptured effect to parts of the design.

The best material for the pile was woolen rags and the more cotton fabric that is found in a rug the later in period it may generally be presumed to be. The ones hooked through a linen foundation are usually earlier than the ones with burlap. Burlap was probably not used to any extent before 1850. Almost any color may be found in a hooked rug. Usually they show the brighter hues of the mid- and late-nineteenth century and rarely is one found which has only the earlier natural dyes. Hooked rugs in general probably date from 1840 to 1900. They come not only from New England but from Pennsylvania and other states where the hooking is likely to be coarser and much cotton fabric included.

The designs used for hooked rugs encompass almost everything known to tradition. Among the simplest patterns, which were ideal for using up the accumulation of vari-colored scraps unsuitable for a formal design, are: *block* and *basketweave* which consist of squares or other geometrical forms, filled with stripes running at right angles to the stripes in adjacent forms; *wave* or *zigzag* where one color follows another in undulating rows looking like mosaic work; *inch square* with multi-colored squares resembling a simple quilt design from which it may well have come; *log cabin* which is definitely like the quilt pattern of the same name and shows the same variations of shading; *shell* or *fish scale* design which is a very old pattern of overlapping arcs. There are also repeating geometrical forms such as circles, squares, diamonds and medallions which are often filled with stylized flowers.

In the floral designs, the flowers in vase or jar or loose sprays or bands of flowers may occupy almost the entire rug area or may be confined to a central medallion with a scrolled border surrounding it (Plate 156B). The flowers became less stylized and more realistic as the Victorian era advanced.

Animal forms in hooked rugs may be early but are more common in the Victorian period. They include dogs, stags, parrots, lions, swans, cats with kittens and various unnamable species. Landscape designs are also found and these may include buildings or animals. Nautical designs are more common near the seacoast where some of them were probably made by sailors.

Patriotic, fraternal and symbolic designs are not so common and are, with the exception of the popular eagle of the 1820s, usually of rather late vintage. A common patriotic design celebrated the centennial of the Declaration of Independence in 1876. Along with these Victorian patterns go the rugs with mottoes, such as *God Bless Our Home*, *Good Luck*, etc. Many of the Victorian designs seem to be derived from the designs for Berlin work which were published in *Godey's Lady's Book* and *Peterson's Magazine*.

Commercial designs were certainly available by 1870 when one Edward Sands Frost, a tin peddler from Biddeford, Maine, was already selling his designs. These he printed in colors on burlap by means of metal stencils.

Hooked rugs are found in all shapes and sizes. There are half-round threshold or 'Welcome' mats and round, oval, square and rectangular rugs of all sizes from one and one-half feet square to large carpets and hall and stair runners.

BOOKS FOR FURTHER READING

KENT, WILLIAM WINTHROP: *Rare Hooked Rugs*, Springfield, Massachusetts (1941).

KENT, WILLIAM WINTHROP: *The Hooked Rug*, New York (1930).

RIES, ESTELLE H.: *American Rugs*, Cleveland, Ohio (1950).

WALKER, LYDIA LeBARON: *Homecraft Rugs*, New York (1929).

WAUGH, ELIZABETH and FOLEY, EDITH: *Collecting Hooked Rugs*, New York (1927).

EIGHTEENTH-CENTURY FLOORCLOTHS

By HELEN COMSTOCK

(Reprinted by permission from *Antiques*, January 1955)

IN Purdie and Dixon's *Virginia Gazette* for December 28, 1769, Joseph Kidd, 'Upholsterer, in Williamsburg', advertises that he 'hangs rooms with paper or damask, stuffs sophas, couches, and chairs, in the ueatest manner, makes all sorts of bed furniture, window curtains, and matrasses, and fits carpets to any room with the greatest exactness ... and paints floor cloths ... according to directions.'

From other advertisements of the period and from inventories we know that the floorcloths Mr Kidd painted – they were also called oilcloths – were fairly common in the eighteenth century. We know also that they were made of canvas or linen heavily coated with paint. In the first half of the eighteenth century they were decorated with a design in imitation of marble tiled floors, but later designs kept pace with the times. There is a reference to 'Wilton or Marble Cloths' in an advertisement of a variety of carpeting in the *Boston Gazette* for January 26, 1761; and as late as January 1, 1828, 'a large and elegant assortment of Painted floor Cloths, without seams, some in imitation of Brussels Carpeting' was offered in the *Boston Daily Advertiser*.

These floor coverings were so perishable that almost none have survived. There is one in the Pine Kitchen at Winterthur, but it is probably unique among museum collections. To know what sort of 'directions' Mr Kidd followed, then, we must rely on contemporary accounts. The eighteenth-century English encyclopedias consulted do not mention floorcloth, and Diderot, who has supplied so many records of early manufacturers, does

not help, since oilcloth (*toile cirée*) was not used on the floor in France. H.Havard says in his *Dictionnaire de l'ameublement* ... that the history of oilcloth is very ancient in France, going back to the fourteenth century, and in the eighteenth it was used for table covers and hangings. He does not mention its use on floors.

Wills and other records of the period have been somewhat more helpful. In the long and highly interesting inventory of the estate of Governor William Burnet of New York and Massachusetts, who died in 1728, there is mention not only of 'two old chequered canvas's to lay under a table' but of a 'large painted Canvas Square as the Room'. The latter was valued at eight pounds, a large sum for the period.

Many references to floorcloth in the records of York County, Virginia, have been discovered by the research division of Colonial Williamsburg. The earliest is in the inventory of the estate of Robert Davidson, recorded in 1739; '1 floor Cloth 15/'. A 'red painted floor cloth' is mentioned in 1769 in the estate of William Waters. Peyton Randolph's estate (1776) contained '1 floor cloth 20/, 1 passage do (ditto) 8/ ...' indicating their use in halls.

Floorcloths were not always painted to order. They were also imported ready-made, as indicated by the records of the Tucker family. An invoice for 'a painted floor cloth shipp'd by Donald & Burton for Edmund Logwood & sold by James Brown To the Hon[ble] St. George Tucker' describes the cloth as 19 feet, 6 inches by 15 feet, 9 inches; it may have covered the floor from wall to wall. With charges for packing, transportation, insurance, exchange, commissions and duty, this cost the owner over nineteen pounds.

George Washington's purchase of floorcloth is recorded in a list of household expenditures in New York and Philadelphia, written in his own hand, which is in the New York State Library: '1796, January 11, Roberts & Company, floorcloth $14.82.' *The Washington Family* by Edward Savage in the National Gallery shows a floor with black and white squares which have been said to represent a floorcloth, but it must be remembered that the setting is the conventional one of an eighteenth-century portrait painter, with classic column and drapery, rather than an actual interior. The tiled design for a floor was a European painter's convention which persisted from the seventeenth century and does not indicate the actual use of either tiles or floorcloth in colonial homes.

Paintings of the period, then, are not of much use in helping us to visualize these popular floor coverings. However, there is in the library at Williamsburg a book of engravings by John Carwitham of London, dated 1739, which shows us exactly how many

of them must have looked. The engravings show designs which could be used either for pavements of marble or for painted floorcloths.

The plates also offer many interesting views of interior and exterior architecture of the time. The name of the engraver, John Carwitham, will interest the print collector because of the 'Carwitham views' of New York, Boston and Philadelphia, which are among the most important of American historical prints. Carwitham never saw the cities in question, but, since the artist is unknown, his name, as engraver, has become attached to them.

BOOKS FOR FURTHER READING

(As little has been written of this subject, source material is to be found only in old inventories, newspapers and documents.)

Dow, G.F.: *The Arts and Crafts in New England, 1704–1775* (Compendium of Newspaper Advertisements), Topsfield, Mass. (1927).

PRIME, A.C., *The Arts and Crafts in Philadelphia, Maryland and South Carolina*, Series I and II (Newspaper advertisements), Topsfield, Mass. (1929–33).

LIGHTING DEVICES

By C. MALCOLM WATKINS

Devices for burning wood: in a new country, covered with inexhaustible timber, wood was an obvious light source. The burning log of the open fireplace, which shed far more light than a lamp or candle, was for long a basic illuminant, remaining so until modern times in the log cabins of the Appalachian highlanders[1] and in the slave and tenant houses of southern Negroes.[2]

Supplementing fireplace light, the early colonists used pine splints, following the custom of northern European peoples. Francis Higginson in 1630[3] wrote that 'our pine trees, that are the most plentiful of all wood, doth allow us plenty of candles, which are very useful in a house, and they are nothing else but the wood of the pine tree cloven into little slices something thin, which are as full of the moisture of turpentine and pitch that they burn clear as a torch'. Governor Winthrop of the Massachusetts Bay Colony said[4] that 'candlewood' splints were much used in New England, Virginia, and by the Dutch, and that they were burned on a flat stone or iron in 'the [chimney] corner', except when carried by hand about the house. 'Lightwood', as it was called in Virginia, was similarly burned in a pan stuck into the side of the fireplace.[5] 'Fire pans' are listed in Massachusetts inventories in the seventeenth century.[6] By the latter part of the eighteenth century, splints were confined to backcountry areas. In 1789 the Reverend Nathan Perkins of Hartford, lodging overnight in remote Jericho, Vermont, complained in his diary,[7] 'no candles pine splinters used in lieu of them ... bed poor and full of flees'.

Cressets, or fire baskets, were used out of doors for burning pine knots or, on whaling ships, pieces of blubber. Their use was widespread and of long duration. They are mentioned in seventeenth-century inventories[6]

and there are many persons alive today who have used cressets on the bows of row-boats for night fishing.

There is no evidence that metal holders or clamps especially designed to hold pine splints were employed in America, as they were in Europe. They are not mentioned in published inventories and no documented specimen is recorded.

Fatted rushes and rushlights: English, Scottish and Irish cottagers for centuries used prepared rushes for ordinary illumination. The classic account of how the *juncus effusus* was processed into a light source was given by Gilbert White in the *Natural History of Selborne* in 1789[8]. These fat-soaked rushes were burned in simple iron clip-like affairs, mounted on wooden blocks or on tripod bases, called rushlights. There is scant evidence that rushlights were used in America to any extent. Early inventories do not mention them, nor is there literary reference either to rushlights or rushes. However, the *juncus effusus* grows along the New England coast and a bundle of peeled rushes was discovered in a colonial Massachusetts house.[9] In the Charles L. Woodside collection there is an iron rushlight of typical English design which was found in the chimney of the late seventeenth-century Hazen garrison house in Haverhill, Massachusetts. There are also instances of the preparation of rushes in Ohio in the nineteenth century for lighting purposes.[10] Although undoubtedly the English colonists brought their familiar rushlights with them, the ease of obtaining candlewood, a sufficient substitute, probably discouraged their use.

Candles: candles were the superior and favored light source from the time of the first settlement to the end of the eighteenth century, remaining popular, in spite of later innovations, until their general displacement by kerosene lamps after the Civil War. At the beginning of settlement imported candles were available in the Massachusetts Bay Colony's supply store, and this was probably the case in other new colonies. By the time domestic animals were on hand to supply tallow, in addition to native bears and deer, candle-dipping and molding became a regular part of the colonial housewife's duties. In the coastal colonies the bayberry bush (*myrica cerifera*) produced a wax-yielding berry much favored for candles because of its hardness, sweetness and steady light-giving qualities. The tedious labor involved in picking the berries restricted their use, however. Beeswax was only rarely used for domestic candles, but for altar lights it was employed according to ancient custom and prescription. Molded ceremonial candles of beeswax have been made and used by the Moravians in Bethlehem, Pennsylvania, since 1756.[11]

The best candles were made of *spermaceti*, the crystalline wax found in the heads of sperm whales. They were expensive and beyond the means of the average householder, although they were favored for drawing-rooms by the well-to-do. Because of involved processing, they were made commercially, rather than at home. The first successful manufactory was established in Quincy, Massachusetts, in 1752. This became a unit in the United Company of Spermaceti Candlers, a monopoly which controlled production from Boston to Philadelphia until 1772.[12] After urban populations had grown in the eighteenth century, tallow candles were also made commercially by dipping racks of wicks from the ends of revolving spokes. Candle dipping at home was similar in principle, but there the wicks were suspended from long rods or 'broaches'.[13] Candle molds were convenient for small-scale domestic manufacture, occurring in a variety of shapes and arrangements and ranging in size from single tubes to multiple clusters. Although usually of tin, they were also made of pewter and pottery.

Candle wicks were usually of cotton yarn, varying in diameter inversely with the efficiency of the fuel, so that tallow candles had heavy wicks and spermaceti candles light ones. Rushes were also used for candle wicks, having been considered superior to cotton, since they were self-consuming. A bill from Joseph Loring and Sons of Boston, dated 1787, itemizes 'Rush candles at 11*d*.', and 'Candles at 9*d*.'. Rush candles, it should be understood, were not merely fat-soaked rushes as used in rushlights, but full-fledged candles.

Candleholders: candlesticks and associated forms are treated in the following section, where design is discussed by Ralph E. Carpenter. Here they are considered briefly in terms of function and technique and historical context.

Candle-holding devices are referred to more frequently than other lighting utensils in early inventories. Many well-equipped seventeenth-century households were without candleholders, and it may be supposed that candles were held in the hand in moving about the house and secured in a bit of soft tallow whenever stationary. As late as 1856 Frederick Law Olmsted, visiting the south, recorded several instances of candles being used sparingly and without candlesticks, of which the following is one:

'Mr Newman asked if I wanted a candle to undress by, I said yes, if he pleased, and waited for him to set it down. As he did not do so I walked towards him, lifting my hand to take it. 'No – I'll hold it,' said he, and then I perceived that he had no candle-stick, but held the little dip in his hand. I remembered also that no candle had been brought into the 'sitting-room', and that while we were at supper only one candle had stood upon the table, which had been immediately extinguished when we rose, the room being lighted from the fire.'[14]

Candlesticks were subject only to a minimum number of improvements, the ejector, or device to raise the candle to a desired level, having been the most exploited. 'Wire candlesticks' are mentioned in seventeenth-century inventories, and these were presumably of a type illustrated in contemporary Dutch paintings and found in collections today. They feature vertical wires mounted in iron supports, with an iron candle socket which can be raised or lowered on the wires.

Later eighteenth-century inventions included knob-lifted sockets which slid in vertical channels on the sides of metal candlesticks, and socket raisers which fitted in notches at the desired heights. Some were equipped with plungers operated from the bottom. An iron type which was popular from the late-eighteenth century until the beginning of the present one in rural areas was the 'hogscraper'. This had a slide-type ejector and a sharp-edged base which farmers found convenient for scraping bristles from hogs after slaughtering.

There were many types of candleholders and candlesticks for special uses. Weavers used iron candleholders which were S-shaped and hung from loom frames. Shoemakers employed wooden hanging L-shaped candleholders or, sometimes, home-made toggle-arm devices. Iron candle sockets with two spikes, one vertical and one horizontal, have been used until recently in the holds of Gloucester fishing boats.

Chandeliers were introduced in the seventeenth century, three 'hanging candlesticks' having been recorded in the Essex County Probate Records.[6] There are many eighteenth-century examples. Most of the rooms at Tuckahoe, the Virginia home of the Randolphs, are said to have been hung with chandeliers in 1779.[15] When Lord Howe was fêted in Philadelphia in 1776, twelve lustres with twenty spermaceti candles each hung in one of the rooms.[15] In 1748 Isaac Royall gave the town of Boston what was variously described as a 'branch of candlesticks', and 'branched candlestick'. It hung from the ceiling over the clerk's table in the Representatives' Chamber of the Town House.[16]

Churches were the principal repositories of chandeliers. St Michael's Church in Marblehead, Massachusetts, still displays the brass chandelier given it in 1732. The First Baptist Meeting House of Providence, Rhode Island, still possesses its twenty-four-candle Bristol glass chandelier, given it by Nicholas Brown II in 1795.[17] Country churches displayed less exotic chandeliers, made by local craftsmen, but often distinguished in design. The collections at Old Sturbridge Village include two wooden chandeliers with applied carved acanthus leaves and wire branches tipped with wooden sockets, originally used in a Buzzards Bay, Massachusetts, church. A more primitive example in the same collections hung in the Bunganuck Baptist Meeting House in Brunswick, Maine, in 1830. This consists of a turned wooden shaft, painted yellow and green, supporting angular arms which terminate in flat tin candleholders steadied by leaf-shaped supports.

Tin chandeliers were made in the late-eighteenth and early nineteenth centuries for tavern ballrooms (Plate 158D), as well as for churches. Products of country tinsmiths, these are usually characterized by central shafts formed of cone-shaped sections joined together, with radiating branches of tin arms terminating in sockets with saucer rims. The Smithsonian Institution has a set of three such chandeliers used in a Keene, New Hampshire, tavern.

Adjustable candlestands occur in seemingly limitless variety. Handsome iron stands were made in the late-eighteenth century, ornamented with brass knops and candle sockets. Some have double branches which move on vertical shafts, held in the desired position by ornamental tension springs. Others have single branches, while most have graceful three- or four-footed bases. They were made in American cities as well as in England.

Wooden adjustable stands vary from the unpractised handiwork of rural whittlers to the elegancies of skilled cabinetmakers. Some are crudely fitted with cross arms secured by wedges, others have ratchet devices, while a third category is fitted with threaded wooden uprights upon which candle arms can be elevated to the desired heights (Plate 158A). Although dating such devices is difficult and dependent usually on hints of formal style occurring in the work, most appear to have been made in the late-eighteenth or early-nineteenth centuries. There are virtually no written references to these contraptions, but the relatively large number of survivals suggests that they were once fairly common. Cruder specimens were presumably designed for workshops, rather than homes.

Save-alls constitute a special class of candleholder. These are designed to fit into the sockets of candlesticks and have prongs or wires on which candle stubs can be mounted so as to use up an entire candle. There are frequent early allusions to these devices.

Simple lamps: lamps are lighting devices which are designed to contain a liquid or liquefiable fuel and a wick or wicks for burning it. It is the most evolved type of light source, even in its primitive

FIG. 1. Simple lamp

forms. However, it remained primitive until the end of the eighteenth century, when radical improvements took place.

At the time of colonial settlement lamps were common on the Continent. In the Alpine regions of Europe iron lamps consisting of flat shallow pans were used for burning tallow or lard, the wicks having been laid on the bottoms of the pans, burning back into the fuel supply and melting the solid fat as they did so. Simple examples of this type hung from hooks, while elaborate ones with round, square, oval or foliated pans incorporated highly ornamental wrought-iron stands (Plate 157A).

In central and northern Europe, in Italy, and in parts of France, hanging lamps for burning oil were widely used. These were usually ovate or pear-shaped in outline, with flat bottoms and flaring or curving sides. Near the nose, or narrow end, each had an up-turned metal rest for the wick, representing a technical innovation which allowed excess oil to run back into the fuel supply. Some wick-support lamps, as these are classified by present-day collectors, were fitted with hinged or pivoted covers. The open, coverless type is found more commonly in southern Europe. Nearly all were designed to be hung and had a curved strap or bar of iron extending up and over the lamp proper. This was attached to a hook for hanging. Variants in the wick-support lamp are found in examples mounted on stands so as to be adjustable

Another class of lamp, having the same type of suspension as the hanging wick-

support lamp, occurred along the coastal regions of Europe from Spain to Iceland. This also had a pear-shaped reservoir as a rule, but differed in having a long beak-like trough without an internal wick support. The functional part of the lamp thus differed little from near eastern and north African wick-channel lamps in which the wicks lay in the narrow troughs. However, in the class under discussion an identical receptacle was secured directly under the reservoir to receive the dripping excess. Most often the drip pan was attached to the curving hanger bar on which there was a notched hook to hold the reservoir and allow it to be tipped as the oil supply diminished. They usually burned fish oil and are most commonly found in Spain, Cornwall and Scotland. In Cornwall they are called *chills* and in Scotland *crusies*. Although the pear shape occurs most commonly among those surviving, multi-wick lamps of the class, square or pentagonal in shape, are also found. A French variant is made of brass and has a birdcage-like superstructure and a vestigial drip pan below.

Tin and brass spout lamps, depicted by seventeenth-century Dutch genre painters, particularly Gerard Dou, were used in the Low Countries. These were cylindrical with a straight or tapering spout to hold the wick. A drip channel below the spout led into a receptacle below the reservoir.

Presumably, all these European types of lamps were brought to America during the early days of settlement, although there is little to tell us in documentary or archeological sources what precisely the earliest lamps were. There are occasional early references to lamps, such as Edward Winslow's advice to new colonists, written in 1621, to bring 'cotton yarn for your lamps'[18] or Higginson's comment that 'by the abundance of fish thereof [New England] can afford oil for lamps'.[3] Since the English were never such enthusiastic users of lamps as their Continental contemporaries, it is probable that splints and candles were preferred among them in the colonies. The Probate Records of Essex County[6] list occasional lamps in wills and inventories, but these are notable for their infrequent occurrences. It is significant that among the thousands of iron artifacts excavated from the site of Jamestown, Virginia, first permanent English settlement in America, not a single lamp has been found.

Crude 'grease' lamps, for use around the oven and the workshop, were evidently employed in the early colonies, as later under frontier conditions. These were called 'sluts', or 'slut lamps' (Plate 157B). A Salem, Massachusetts, shopkeeper left a 'slutt' among his effects in 1660[19] and the term still has meaning among those who have lived in the Appalachians or in the more recently settled areas of the west. In form they may be degenerate crusies, designed in the usual manner to be hung, but having no drip pan, wick support, or more than a vestigial wick trough. A New Hampshire specimen in the Woodside Collection is mounted on a vertical standard so that it can be rotated, or lifted an inch or so (Plate 157B right). The reservoir is a round bowl with a wick trough and pivoted cover. The Smithsonian has a skillet-like specimen welded to a fork-shaped stand, and many other wrought-iron types occur in endless variety. A cast-iron type, with a small but deep bowl-shaped reservoir mounted on a vertical post with saucer base and handle connecting bowl with base was made in early-nineteenth-century Ohio (Plate 157B left). Very often the 'slut' was merely a twisted rag placed at the edge of a saucer full of kitchen fat. A variant of the slut lamp, made in the past century, is the cast-iron baker's-lamp, consisting of a deep reservoir with hinged lid and heavy round, or boat-shaped, base. Some examples bear the names of iron foundries.

It remained for the Germans and Swiss to introduce on a large scale the Continental type of wick-support lamp, described above. They not only imported them, but made them here in quantity. The conservative Pennsylvania-German farmer liked his traditional iron lamp and continued to use it, often until the beginning of the present century. Most Pennsylvania examples collected today are nineteenth-century in origin, sometimes bearing the names of their manufacturers, such as Peter Derr, J.Eby, Hurxthal & Company, and others from the vicinity of Lancaster. They were called 'betty' lamps (Plate 157C), although they were also known as 'judies', 'kays', or 'frog lamps'.[20] The etymology of the word 'betty' has been the subject of much speculation, but without satisfactory solution.[21] Pennsylvania and Ohio tinsmiths also made betty lamps and adjustable stand lamps. In Pennsylvania the iron betty lamp was sometimes supported on a wooden stand, either crudely whittled at home or turned on a lathe and painted. Tin betty lamps sometimes had neatly fitting tin stands, such combinations having been designated 'Ipswich betty lamps' by some early writers on lighting devices because of a supposed association with the Massachusetts town of Ipswich. They are a Pennsylvania-German type, however, mostly of the nineteenth century. Potters, as well as metalsmiths, turned their attention to lamps, and many examples from Pennsylvania, Ohio and the Moravian settlements of North Carolina have survived.

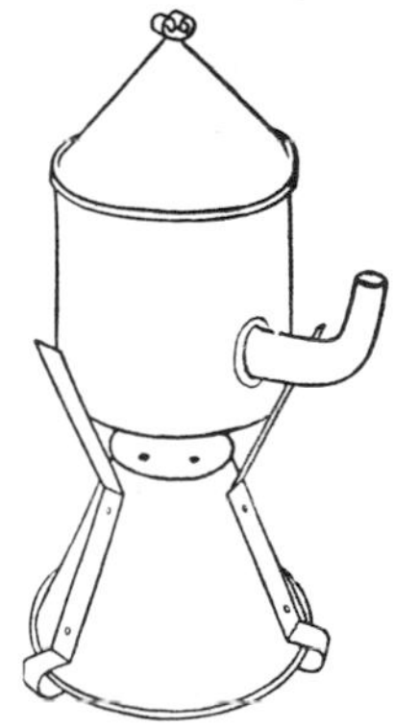

FIG. 2. Cape Cod spout lamp

Descendants of the Flemish spout lamp were used in the coastal communities of New England in the form of the *kyal*,[22] sometimes called 'Cape Cod spout lamp'. This was of tin and apparently was intended for shop or marine use. The Smithsonian collections have such lamps from New London, Connecticut, and New Bedford, Massachusetts, both whaling ports, and one from Marblehead, Massachusetts, the last having been used by a weaver, probably incidentally to its intended purpose.

Argand lamps: the most revolutionary innovation in artificial lighting prior to the electric light was the invention by the Swiss chemist Ami Argand of a controlled air-draft lamp in 1783. This was characterized by a vertical tubular burner with cylindrical wick, open at both ends. The heat of the circular flame created an internal draft which increased combustion and therefore the amount of light. Further efficiency was gained by adding a glass chimney. Franklin, Jefferson and Washington were among the first American purchasers of Argand lamps. Several handsome Sheffield specimens may still be seen at Mount Vernon and in the Smithsonian Institution's *Washingtoniana* collection (Plate 159A).

The Argand lamp, capable of burning sperm oil and other viscous fuels, was several times brighter than a candle. Count Rumford, writing in 1811,[23] commented, 'no decayed beauty ought ever to expose her face to the direct rays of an Argand lamp'. There were many modifications and improvements to the Argand lamp, embodying the basic principles of the burner, most of which found their way to America. One was the Carcel, or 'mechanical', lamp, a French invention of 1800 in which a clock-work pump kept the Argand burner flooded with oil. This most efficient, but expensive, lamp was still being advertised in 1845.[24] Another variant was the astral lamp, featuring a ring-shaped reservoir to minimize shadow (Plate 160A). This was most popular in the 1830s and 1840s as a reading lamp and was used in combination with etched-glass shades, sometimes ornamented with cut designs. The 'sinumbra' lamp was an

FIG. 3. A solar lamp

astral lamp whose reservoir had a wedge-shaped cross-section to reduce further the amount of shadow. Another, for parlor use, was the solar lamp, designed to burn lard oil. This was characterized by boring an inverted-saucer-shaped plate with a hole in the center, placing it over the Argand burner, creating a brilliant white column of flame. It was most favored in the 1840s and 1850s. Benjamin Thompson, the Massachusetts-born Count Rumford of the Holy Roman Empire, invented several lamps based on Argand's. His 'portable illuminator', a table lamp with flat wick surrounded by an air tube, designed with economy in view, seems to have been the only one of these introduced into America.

The whale-oil, or 'common', lamp: in 1787 John Miles of Birmingham patented his 'agitable' lamp.[25] Simple and seemingly obvious in design, it was nevertheless an innovation in its day. It consisted of a reservoir with a tightly-fitting burner, having one or more tubes for solid wicks. Because it could be made without difficulty of tin, brass (Plate 157D), pewter or glass, and because it was cheap and capable of burning abundant whale oil, it was immediately adopted in America. The 'patent' or 'agitable' or just 'common' lamp, as it was variously known, had the advantages of economy, cleanliness and symmetry. It has several forms, among them the following: peg lamps, which could be placed in candle sockets, thus making the new lamp adaptable to candlesticks and chandeliers; petticoat lamps of tin and sometimes brass, which were peg lamps with flaring 'petticoats' to enable them to stand independently or in candle sockets; saucer-base chamber lamps; standing lamps which combined the esthetic virtues of candlesticks with the utility of the new device. Before 1820 the glass manufacturers had adopted the 'agitable' lamp and made it an important part of their output. Blown-glass types ranged from tiny chamber lamps to splendid standing specimens with bell-shaped bases and knopped stems. After the introduction of mechanical pressing in 1827, glass whale oil lamps with pressed bases became common, remaining so until after the Civil War (Plate 159B). The pressed designs followed the evolution of glass-pressing techniques, beginning with simple bases pressed in cup-plate molds, going on to the 'lacy' style in combination with blown reservoirs, and continuing with the heavy patterns of the mid-century, which were produced almost entirely by mechanical techniques. The earliest glass lamps were fitted with stopper-type burners of tin and cork, often stamped 'patent'. These were made obsolete in a short time by pewter collars which were attached to the lamps by plaster of paris. These permitted use of the standard interchangeable screw-type burners found on metal lamps.

Fluid lamps: the rising cost of whale oil, particularly the superior-burning sperm oil, in the early-nineteenth century led to the invention of the first chemical 'burning fluid' by Isaiah Jennings in 1830. This consisted of alcohol and turpentine in the proportion of eight to one. There were several variants on Jennings's fluid in the next few years. In 1839 Augustus V.X. Webb of New York introduced distilled turpentine, without a diluting agent, designating it 'camphine'. Later, this name, often spelled camphene, was popularly, though inaccurately, applied to all the burning fluids.

Jennings designed and patented a modified Argand lamp for his 'burning fluid'. However, the fluids seem to have been burned indiscriminately at first in all sorts of lamps, including the common whale-oil lamp. As a result, there were terrible explosions, fires and deaths from burning. A new type of burner was introduced which was interchangeable with the standard whale-oil burner in common lamps. In these the wick tubes lead up from the lamp, instead of down into the reservoir, and are splayed so as to burn separately. Extinguisher caps are attached, so as to obviate blowing out the flame with the attendant danger of back-firing into the fuel supply (Plate 159B center).

The new burners abated but did not erase the dangers of explosion. In the 1840s and 1850s there were numerous patents on 'safety' lamps, among them John Newell's, which provided for a cylinder of fine wire-gauze screen to surround the wick inside the reservoir and for small perforations in the burner cap to allow gases to escape. These precautions were intended to 'prevent the passage of flame on the principle of Sir Humphry Davy's discovery relative to the passage of flame through perforated metal[26]. Horsford and Nichols, and others, employed modifications of this device.

There were several designs for burners which would vaporize the fluids and burn them as a gas. The Smithsonian collections include a three-branched chandelier of this type (Plate 160C), as well as a student's lamp. Some vapor burners had small pilot wicks beside them in order to preheat and volatilize the fluid. At the opposite extreme from vapor lamps were those for burning rosin. They were usually equipped with heaters to melt the rosin.

Lard and lard-oil lamps: as the population moved west into the interior there was increasing need for improved lard-burning lamps, since fish and chemical fuels were not readily available. This resulted in a spate of queer contraptions the purpose of which was always to keep a steady supply of lard in contact with the wick. These were often the products of country tinkers who seldom relied on scientific principle. They fall into three categories: those which are supposed to conduct heat into the fuel supply in order to keep it fluid; those which rely on gravity as well as heat conduction; those which depend upon mechanical pressure.

Lamps in the first category sometimes had simple burners with long copper wick tubes extending down into the fuel supply. Others, like that patented by Delamar Kinnear in 1850, embodied a pilot light from which a copper wire led into the lard. Inadequacies of the conduction system are revealed in the directions which came with Samuel Davis' lamp in 1854: 'If the lamp be cold, and there be no warm lard to start it, hold the lamp upside down, and with a match let it burn until the burner gets hot, then set the lamp down and put a little cold lard in the lid around the wick.' Zuriel Swope's patent provided for a daffodil-like funnel-and-tube arrangement which was supposed to pick up heat from the flame and convey it to the fuel supply.

Among the several lamps depending upon gravity as well as heat conduction was Dexter S. Chamberlain's lamp of 1854, whose reservoir tilted automatically to provide a constant fuel level. Typical of those employing mechanical pressure were Smith & Stonesifer's, Grannis's and Maltby & Neal's patents, which specified different kinds of pistons for forcing the lard to the wicks.

Kerosene lamps: in 1854 Abraham Gesner of Williamsburg, New York, patented his 'new liquid hydrocarbon, which I denominate "kerosene".' This refined petroleum virtually made obsolete everything in lighting that had preceded it, except gas. The full effect of this was not felt until after the discovery of the Pennsylvania oil fields in 1859,which yielded a plentiful supply of raw material, and the design of a kerosene burner patented about the same time by Michael Dietz.[23] So successful was the Dietz burner, depending, like Argand's, upon an air draft, that it still remains in use with little fundamental change. In the decade following the Civil War there were scores of patents for kerosene burners.

Kerosene lamps were larger than their predecessors and were the object of the labored artistry of Victorian designers in glass and metal. Towards the end of the century elaborate colored and painted glass kerosene lamps with cast brass-plated trim were distributed as soap premiums. They are collected today as 'gone-with-the-wind' lamps. Kerosene lamps of tin and pressed glass are still sold, but they hold little interest for the collector. There are also special developments, such as the Rochester burner, which finds use in summer cottages and out-of-the-way places beyond the reach of electricity.

Gas light: gas lighting, adopted for street lamps in Baltimore in 1817, and soon after in other large cities, was not widely introduced for domestic use until after the Civil War, and then, of course, only in urban areas. Gas chandeliers were being made by Cornelius in Philadelphia and others in the mid-century in elaborate Gothic-Revival forms. Towards the end of the century wall brackets were often fitted with well-made glass shades, some etched or engraved or cut, some of ruby and shaded 'amberina' glass. The fixtures themselves are seldom of interest except to the historian of technology.

Lanterns: lanterns are at least as old in form as the candles they sheltered. At the time of early settlement, and throughout the succeeding two centuries, the ordinary lantern was made of tinned sheet metal with panes of translucent horn – hence the early spelling *lant horn* (Plate 158B). In the Plymouth colony, three 'lant-horns' were listed among twenty-one estate inventories between 1633 and 1640.[27] Essex County inventories[6] show 'lanthorns' in about the same proportions.

More elegant forms of lanterns appeared in the eighteenth century, especially square and polygonal tin lanterns with glass panes. The famous lanterns used to signal Paul Revere from the belfry of the Old North Church in Boston were such, square in shape and embellished with stepped turrets and ornamental trim. They were not, as popular belief would have it, the cylindrical lanterns of pierced tin used around nineteenth-century farms and often mistakenly called 'Paul Revere lanterns'. Primitive home-made wooden lanterns (Plate 158C), were found everywhere, particularly in Pennsylvania.

FIG. 4. Miscalled Paul Revere lantern

John Miles's patent for agitable lamps extended also to lanterns, particularly of the pocket variety, having small rectangular reservoirs and whale-oil burners (Plate 160B). 'Miles' pocket Lanthornes' were advertised in the *Boston Gazette* on May 14, 1804. Somewhat later the glass industry devised lanterns with tin bases and tops connected by blown-glass sections which were either globose or slightly curved-out in profile. This type was adopted by the railroads, which often applied their names in engraved letters on the glass. After the mid-nineteenth century wire guards were added for protection.

There were many nineteenth-century innovations in lanterns, such as Miner's patent pocket lantern of 1865, but the principal improvement was the Dietz tubular lantern which brought a continuous blast of fresh air to the kerosene burner. This may be considered the last important development, for the Dietz tubular lantern remains the standard device of its kind today.

The best sources for further reading are all mentioned in the References.

REFERENCES

1. EATON, ALLEN H.: *Handicrafts of the Southern Highlands*, New York (1937).
2. OLMSTED, FREDERICK LAW: *A Journey in the Seaboard Slave States*, New York (1856).

3. HIGGINSON, FRANCIS: *New England's Plantation*, London (1630).

4. WINTHROP, JOHN: *Journal, History of New England, 1630–1649*, New York (1908).

5. HOUGH, WALTER: *Collection of Heating and Lighting Utensils in the United States National Museum*, p. 5. U.S.N.M. Bulletin 141, Washington (1928).

6. *The Probate Records of Essex County*, Massachusetts, Salem (1916).

7. PERKINS, REV. NATHAN: *A Narrative of a Tour through the State of Vermont from April 27 to June 12, 1789*. Woodstock, Vermont (1930).

8. WHITE, GILBERT: *The Natural History of Selborne*, London (1789; has been frequently reprinted since 1906).

9. *The Rushlight*, Vol. II, No. 3, p. 3.

10. 'More about Rushlights' (The editor's attic). *Antiques*, Vol. XLVI, No. 1, p. 284.

11. CUMMINGS, JOHN: 'Candles and their Place in History'. *The Rushlight*, Vol. XX, No. 3, pp. 558–61.

12. DOW, GEORGE FRANCIS: *Whale Ships and Whaling*, pp. 35–6. Salem (1925).

13. EARLE, ALICE MORSE: *Home Life in Colonial Days*, pp. 35–6, New York (1898).

14. OLMSTED (1856), pp. 85–8, *op. cit.*

15. LITTLE, NINA FLETCHER: 'References to Lighting in Colonial Records'. *The Rushlight*, Vol. VIII, No. 1 (n.p.).

16. *The Rushlight*, Vol. VI, No. 3 (n.p.).

17. 'Lighting of Old Churches'. *The Rushlight*, Vol. XIII, No. 1, p. 156.

18. WINSLOW, EDWARD: *Good News from New England*, London (1624).

19. WATKINS, C.MALCOLM: 'The Lamps of Colonial America', *Antiques*, Vol. XXXII, No. 4, pp. 187–91.

20. WATKINS, C.MALCOLM: *Artificial Lighting in America, 1830–1860*. Smithsonian *Report* for 1951, pp. 385–407. Washington, pp. 389–90.

21. WOODSIDE, CHARLES L.: 'Early American lamps', *Antiques*, Vol. XII, pp. 497–9. 'Further light on the Betty Lamp', *Antiques*, Vol. XV, No. 4, pp. 290–1.
GOYLE, G.A.R.: 'New Light on the Betty Lamp', *Antiques*, Vol. XIV, p. 219.

22. HOUGH (1928), p. 62, *op. cit.*

23. WATKINS (1951), p. 395, *op. cit.*

24. The Carcel lamp. Advertisement quoted from the *Boston Transcript*, November 17, 1845. *The Rushlight*, Vol. III, No. 4 (n.p.).

25. WATKINS, C.MALCOLM: 'The Whale-Oil Burner: its Invention and Development'. *Antiques*, Vol. XXVII, No. 4, pp. 148–9.

26. U.S. Patent No. 10,099, specifications for. Washington (1853).

27. BRIGGS, ROSE: 'Pilgrim Lighting from Old Colony Inventories', *The Rushlight*, Vol. XII, No. 3, pp. 2–17.

CANDLESTICKS, SCONCES, CHANDELIERS

By RALPH E. CARPENTER, Jr

Candles: candles and oil lamps were the two sources of light in seventeenth- and eighteenth-century America. Candles were preferred, because of convenience and better light, and were used by those who could afford them and by the poorer class when the material to make them was readily available.

The devices which held them were made of many materials – glass, silver, wood, pewter, tin, brass, iron and china. The design changed in unison with that of furniture and architecture. Candles were used in lanterns, lamps, candlesticks, chandeliers and sconces. These fixtures either rested on tables or hung from ceiling or walls.

Candlesticks: the most widely used of all devices were the iron and brass candlesticks, some domestic and some imported. In the homes of the wealthy were found silver, glass and china sticks, imported, except for an occasional pair of silver ones made by such silversmiths as Jeremiah Dummer (Plate 161B) and Jacob Hurd, both of Boston, and George Ridout of New York. Robberies of the period, reported in the newspapers, invariably identify silver candlesticks as English or French. Isaac Seixas, in 1754, in New York, was robbed of 'two French silver candlesticks'. In 1757, Jacob Franks lost by theft 'two pair of Silver Candlesticks, weight of each about twenty ounces'. 'All are Sterling Plate, having a Lion Stampt on the Bottom.' Silver candlesticks of American origin were extremely rare. From the advertisements, we know that brass and iron candlesticks were made in considerable quantities. We also find advertised 'Glass Candlesticks' (1762); 'complete sets of best China Candlesticks'

(1762); 'a beautiful variety of printed and gilt and plain cream-coloured candlesticks' (1772); 'very neat cut-glass candlesticks' (1772).

Chandeliers, sconces and girandoles: were often used in America, but they must have been imported because we do not find them recorded in the long lists prepared for advertisements by brass and other metal workers. The inventory of Jonathan Nichols, taken in 1754 in Newport, R.I., lists 'two brass sconces 60/-; two glass candlesticks £2-; nine candlesticks £11-; two pairs of snuffers'. In Boston, in 1758, John Welch, who was going back to England, sold his household furniture, including 'Large and Small Sconces and two dozen of Candle Moulds some large and ribbed'. In New York, on April 16, 1740, a list of household furnishings to be sold at auction included 'a pair of large Gilt fram'd Sconces'.

An inventory of a theatre in Federal Street, Boston, in 1793 includes chandeliers and elaborately designed free-standing girondoles ordered from England by Bulfinch, of which his agent was exceedingly proud. They were the work of Robert Cribb, Carver and Gilder, No. 288, Holborn, near Great Turnstile, and cost in London £37 16s. 10d. Josiah Taylor describes them in his letter to Charles Bulfinch, dated August 31, 1793. Some idea of the extent to which this type of fixture was used can be gained from a description of the Assembly Room of the theatre which included '3 glass chandalears, 4 large Johndoles with 4 arms each, 10 single Johndoles, 20 tin hanging candlesticks. In one night, lighting for the entire theatre required 23 lbs. of spermaceti candles – $12.50, 33 lbs. tallow

Friendship or album quilt. Pieced and appliquéd; Yonkers, dated 1847. *The New-York Historical Society, New York.*

PLATE 145

(A) Overshot coverlet. Wool and cotton, applied fringe at sides. *Vining collection, National Society Daughters of the American Revolution, Washington, D.C.*

(B) Block coverlet. Double-weave geometric, wool and cotton. *New York State Historical Association, Cooperstown, New York.*

(c) Bed rug. 'Tree-of-life' design, wool on wool; *c.* 1775. *National Society Daughters of the American Revolution, Washington, D.C.*

PLATE 146

Woven counterpane. Loop weave, all white cotton, probably by professional weaver; *c.* 1820. *Smithsonian Institution, Washington, D.C.*

PLATE 147

Flowered coverlet. Double-weave, wool and cotton. Woven by James Alexander, Orange County, New York. Dated 1822. *Old Museum Village of Smith's Clove, Monroe, New York.*

PLATE 148

Turkish, early-seventeenth century, 'Ushakh' showing medallion with arabesque spandrels; stylized cloud border; the ancestral type of rug in paintings by Smibert, 1729, and Feke, 1741.
Photo Metropolitan Museum.

All subjects illustrated are from the author's collection of more than two hundred rugs which have been presented to the Metropolitan Museum of Art, New York; Fogg Museum, Cambridge; Art Institute of Chicago; Museum of Fine Arts, Boston.

PLATE 149

Turkish 'Transylvania', late seventeenth century; similar to, but earlier than the rug in Smibert's portrait of the Berkeley family at Yale; has center design of angular floral sprays and leafy spandrels; the eight-pointed star in border disappears from later examples. *Photo Metropolitan Museum.*

PLATE 150

(A) At the Fogg Museum exhibition, The Turks in History, 1954; the author stands at a table covered with a 'Transylvania' of somewhat earlier date than the rug in Feke's portrait of the Royall family hanging above, in which the drawing of the border cartouche is not so fine. *Photo Fogg Museum.*

(B) 'Transylvania', eighteenth century; close to the Royall example; shows a simplification of the more elaborate seventeenth- and early-eighteenth-century renderings. *Photo Fogg Museum.*

PLATE 151

'Smyrna' rug, so-called from the city prominent in the trade; palmette design similar to a rug
which belonged to Jeremiah Lee of Marblehead and shown in Copley's portrait of him, 1768, now
in the Wadsworth Atheneum. *Photo Metropolitan Museum.*

PLATE 152

(B) Dated 1797; from the Caucasus; design probably based on a formal garden, also appears on Turkish rugs; blue ground with details red and blue on white. *Photo Fogg Museum.*

(A) 'Holbein variant', as named by Bode; this little rug, about 4 by 5 feet, represents village weaving with individual treatment of ancient motifs; rugs of this type were made over a long period and are wonderfully vigorous in design and color. *Photo Fogg Museum.*

PLATE 153

(A) Leafy palmette; known in west from the fifteenth to eighteenth century. *Photo Metropolitan Museum.*

(B) 'Ushakh'; design persistent from Holbein to Stuart. *Photo Metropolitan Museum.*

(C) Dated 1768; related to Plate 151 A and B, but more degenerate in design. *Photo Fogg Museum.*

(D) Long called Turkish, but from the Caucasus; design elements are Persian. *Photo Metropolitan Museum.*

PLATE 154

(A) Yarn sewn rug. Geometric design in blue, rust, yellow and green. May have been used as a table carpet.
Nina Fletcher Little, Brookline, Massachusetts.

(B) Yarn sewn rug. Floral design—natural colours.
New York State Historical Association, Cooperstown, New York.

PLATE 155

(A) Shirred strip rug. 'Caterpillar' technique. *New York State Historical Association, Cooperstown, New York.*

(B) Hooked rug. Floral design with leafy scroll border. Maine, mid-nineteenth century. *The Henry Francis du Pont Winterthur Museum, Winterthur, Delaware.*

PLATE 156

(A) Iron lamps, German and Swiss types, used in Pennsylvania. (*Left*) saucer type with swinging reservoir, possibly made in Pennsylvania. (*Center*) pan lamp, probably Alpine origin. (*Right*) polished steel; swinging reservoir; slanting wick support; for lard or kitchen fat; used until mid-nineteenth century and later. *Skinner Museum, South Hadley, Massachusetts.*

(B) Iron grease or slut lamps. (*Left*) cast iron; Adams County, Ohio, early-nineteenth century. (*Center*) baker's lamp, used to light ovens; hinged cover missing. After 1850. *Science Museum, Boston.* (*Right*) forged iron; sliding, spring-tension device probably salvaged from adjustable candle stand; found, southern New Hampshire. *Charles L. Woodside collection.*

(C) Nineteenth-century iron betty lamps. (*Left*) stamped 'E. Brown', dated 1835, used in Washington D.C. (*Center*) typical Pennsylvania, carried to western frontier and used in Newkirk, Oklahoma. (*Right*) found in stock of old Philadelphia hardware store, 1898. *Smithsonian Institution.*

(D) The 'agitable' or 'common' whale-oil lamp. Based on John Miles' patent of 1787, these brass versions are typical American products 1800–30. *Smithsonian Institution.*

PLATE 157

(A) Wooden can-
dle stand. Double
candle arm ad-
justed by turning
on threaded shaft.
*Old Sturbridge
Village.*

(B) Tin 'lanthorn'; panes of
translucent horn, a type used
during two centuries; found
among old ship's stores, Alexandria, Virginia. Early-nineteenth century. *Smithsonian
Institution.*

(C) Home-made wooden lantern
with glass panes; conical tin top
probably salvaged from pierced
tin lantern. New England, early-
nineteenth century. *Old Sturbridge Village.*

(D) Tin chandelier, origin unknown. *Old Sturbridge Village.*

PLATE 158

(A) George Washington's argand lamp from Mount Vernon; Sheffield plate, glass base, chimneys of blue glass. The two tubular burners were fed by a central oil supply in the urn-shaped reservoir. *Smithsonian Institution.*

(B) Blown glass lamps with pressed bases; cut and engraved decoration; 1815–30. (*Left*) stopper-type whale-oil burner of tin and cork. (*Center*) fluid burner with splayed wick-tubes leading up from reservoir and equipped with extinguisher caps; probably took the place of original whale-oil burner. (*Right*) has pewter burner which screws into a pewter collar fixed to the lamp. *Smithsonian Institution.*

PLATE 159

(B) Tin and glass lanterns.   (*Left*) kerosene, *c.* 1870.
(*Right*) whale-oil, *c.* 1840–50.   *Smithsonian Institution.*

(A) Astral lamp, a modified argand with ring-shaped or
'annular' reservoir; diminished shadow; *c.* 1830–40.
Smithsonian Institution.

(C) Chandelier for camphine or burning fluid. Glass shades missing. Used Lynchburg, Virginia, *c.* 1840. *Smithsonian Institution.*

PLATE 160

candles – $8.75, 6 gals. oil – $7.50 and 15 lbs. Hoggs lard $2.25 – a total of $31.00.' At the same time, in Philadelphia, the new theater was lighted by 'small 4 branched chandeliers placed on every second box' and 'supported by gilded iron S's'.

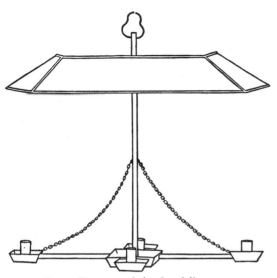

FIG. 1. Four-armed tin chandelier, 1793

Several American churches still retain the chandeliers installed when they were completed. The brass chandeliers of Trinity Church, Newport, Rhode Island, bear the inscription, *James Drew Exon 1728*. Whether he was the maker or the donor is not known. The First Baptist Church in Providence has the glass chandeliers imported from England about 1770 and St Paul's in New York still has those mentioned by Moreau de Saint Méry, who, in 1793, went to 'prayer meeting at 7:30 which was followed by organ music and singing with 162 lighted candles placed in chandeliers or in brackets'.

Glass chandeliers were also used in homes, such as the handsome English example of the period 1770–80 which was hung in the Miles Brewton House, Charleston, South Carolina at the time the house was built in the 1770s and is still in place. An example similar in style was acquired for the interior of the Tradd Street House, Charleston, now installed in the Minneapolis Institute of Fine Arts (Plate 162).

PRINCIPAL PERIODS IN STYLING AND USE

The principal periods in styling and use of the candlestick, sconce and chandelier may be summarized as follows:

1620–1700: brass, iron and pewter candlesticks in the turned Jacobean style were in general use. Wooden candlestands with ratchets were used on the floor. Much crude ironwork was available to hold candles.

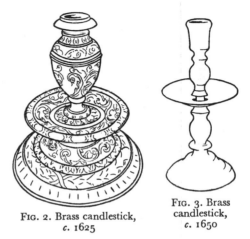

FIG. 2. Brass candlestick, c. 1625

FIG. 3. Brass candlestick, c. 1650

1700–30: the candlesticks of the eighteenth century assumed the type of turning in keeping with the William and Mary style. Iron tripods with brass bobèches and finials and trim were introduced and used throughout the eighteenth century. Imported brass chandeliers were used in public buildings and in the better homes. Brass sconces with arms, similar to the arms of the brass chandeliers, were used. Tin sconces and chandeliers appeared (Fig. 1).

1730–50: brass candlesticks in the Queen Anne style, both imported and domestic, were used in increasing numbers. Silver sticks in similar

FIG. 4. Candlestick, c. 1675

style were imported with a limited number of china ones. Glass ones of the early type were used in limited amounts. Chandeliers with turned wooden columns and iron wire arms and bobèches were made locally in considerable quantities. Brass chandeliers

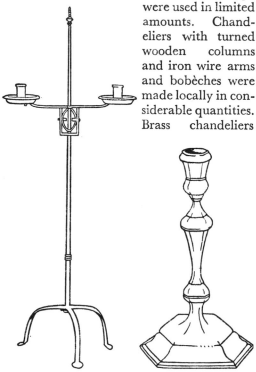

FIG. 5. Iron and brass candle-stand, early-eighteenth century

FIG. 6. Queen Anne brass candlestick, 1730-50

and sconces became increasingly popular. Also carved and gilt sconces and mirror sconces in the Queen Anne style began to adorn the better homes. In the poorer homes, crude home-made imitations of all these forms were employed.

1750–80: during this period, all of the forms of the preceding period continued in use, but with a transition in style from the baroque to the rococo of the Chippendale era. Glass and china candlesticks were imported in larger quantities. Glass chandeliers of the so-called Waterford type (Plate 162) were introduced in larger numbers as time went on. Brass chandeliers came from both England and Holland. Brass and iron candlesticks continued to be the most numerous of all devices.

1780–1800: first the classical designs of Adam, and then those of Hepplewhite and Sheraton, found favor with those who made chandeliers, sconces and candlesticks. The urn replaced the ball in the center column of the chandeliers; sconces became classical in appearance with eagles, columns and sheafs of wheat as motifs. Candlesticks acquired round or oval bases with tapered columns. The gadrooning of the previous period was replaced by beading, and architectural columns with the features of the three orders – Doric, Ionic and Corinthian – were incorporated in the designs. So-called bull's-eye mirrors with candle arms became popular (Plate 164A).

GLOSSARY

Chandelier: defined in Samuel Johnson's Dictionary (1755) 'a branch for candles'. An earlier definition (1736 – *Oxford Universal Dictionary*) defines it as 'an orna-

FIG. 7. George III brass candlestick, c. 1760

FIG. 8. Carved and gilded wall-sconce, c. 1800

mental branched support to hold a number of candles, usually hung from the ceiling' (Plate 162), indicating that chandeliers were not always hung. The term 'branch' was extensively used in the eighteenth century to describe arms to hold candles whether in a chandelier, sconce or girandole.

Extinguisher: a cone-shaped device with a handle used to put out lighted candles by excluding air.

Girandole: in 1769, this term meant 'a branched support for candles'. The difference between a sconce and a girandole is not clear, and in many instances the object was the same – only the name was different. In the nineteenth century, the term 'girandole' was popularly applied to the candelabrum hung with long prisms and also to the round (bull's-eye) mirrors with candle arms attached to the carved and gilt frame (Plate 164A).

Hurricane shade: cylindrical glass shade, open at both ends, for placing over a candlestick to protect from draft; used chiefly in the south, the West Indies and in India, where some of them have been found; apparently made in England for export, starting in the second half of the eighteenth century. The earliest are clear and undecorated; star cutting appears on eighteenth-century examples, followed by wheel engraved designs; ornamentation more elaborate in Victorian period. Also called wind glasses; the name *hurricane shade*, said to be of New England origin, is later.

FIG. 9. Hurricane shade

Sconce: a bracket-candlestick (Plate 164c) to fasten against the wall is a common definition, but a better indication of the particular meaning of the name 'sconce' in the eighteenth century is given by the definition in Johnson's *Dictionary* 'a pensile candlestick, generally with a looking-glass to reflect the light'.

(Note: Pensile – hanging in the air or in space.)

FIG. 10. Metal sconce, *c.* 1750

Snuffers: a pair of scissors to which a box is attached, used to receive the unburned portion of the wick (Plate 163A).

BOOKS FOR FURTHER READING

Dow, George Francis: *The Arts and Crafts in New England 1704-1775*, The Wayside Press (1927).

Hayward, Arthur H.: *Colonial Lighting*, Boston (1927).

Hedges, James B.: *The Browns of Providence Plantations*, Harvard University Press.

Proceedings of American Antiquarian Society, Vol. 65, Part I.

The Arts and Crafts in New York 1726-1776, The New-York Historical Society.

ANTIQUE BUTTONS

By LILLIAN SMITH ALBERT and JANE FORD ADAMS

Buttons worn by American colonists before 1750, not to mention any made here that early, are largely a matter of record only. Today's collector finds hardly any earlier than the Revolutionary War period.

From the beginning comparatively few buttons had marked regional characteristics. On the whole, buttons worn in Boston have been like those worn in London and as soon as factories became established in America, the products of Waterbury, Connecticut, duplicated those of Birmingham, England.

An American button is sometimes known for what it is only because it has been handed down as a family heirloom, or preserved on a manufacturer's sample board, or documented by museum records. George Washington's beautiful pink conch shell buttons at Mount Vernon illustrate the point (Plate 165K).

Interesting as such buttons always are and informative as they may occasionally be, they answer but few of the collector's questions. He needs to know what points to look for when examining buttons that have no credentials.

The three chief points are: design subject-matter which is uniquely American; American makers' marks; characteristics of material, construction and ornamentation which say to the knowing observer 'that's American'.

Emphasis here is on the distinguishing features of selected important types to 1876.

SEVENTEENTH CENTURY

Seventeenth-century references to buttons for Americans are more tantalizing than self-explanatory. John Eliot, it is recorded, ordered three gross of pewter buttons from England in 1651 for trade with the Indians; nothing more is known about them. Inventories often say only 'black' or 'coloured', leaving us to surmise that either needle-wrought or cloth-covered buttons are meant. Silver and gold 'pairs' can be identified as two buttons linked together to make a sleeve-band fastening.

EIGHTEENTH CENTURY

Sleeve buttons (Plate 165A): with the turn of the century names of goldsmiths and silversmiths, famous and obscure, emerge as makers of sleeve buttons. Examples by Jacob Hurd (Boston, 1702–58); James Boyer (Boston, 1723–41); Daniel Van Voorhis (Philadelphia, 1751–1824); Paul Revere, Sr. (who learned under John Coney and set up for himself in 1730); and John Burt (Boston, 1692–1745) are now in museum collections.

Sleeve buttons exhibiting other kinds of jeweler's work, as advertised by their makers, include enamel, plaited hair, mother-of-pearl, tortoise shell and the frequently offered pairs set with stones and crystal. The inventory of John Burt's estate, 1746, lists a 'parcel of christalls for buttons' valued at the considerable sum of thirty-two pounds.

John Fitch, steamboat inventor, made both silver and brass sleeve buttons. When a young man he paid his way on several trips with buttons made out of an old brass kettle. Later, while a captive of the British, he managed to obtain enough brass to make no less than three hundred pairs.

Philadelphia buttons: Caspar Wistar, best remembered now for his glass, was known everywhere during his lifetime for the kind of buttons he made. Beginning about 1720, he advertised 'Philadelphia Buttons' throughout the colonies. A son continued the successful business after Caspar's death in 1752.

Though descriptions must take the place of authenticated examples, we know they were solid brass of excellent finish, stoutly shanked and of great durability, like the finest English importations. 'Philadelphia' became the trade synonym for 'best' used by merchants and appropriated by competitors.

Assorted types: coat buttons covered with mohair were being made in Boston by 1740. Fifty years later a Connecticut firm experimented with button covers made of home-grown silk.

In mid-century at least one American made buttons in the accepted French way, by placing a thin silver cap over a horn mold.

Benjamin Randolph, celebrated Philadelphia cabinetmaker, advertised wooden buttons as his patriotic contribution to the buyer's strike on British goods in 1769.

Connecticut pewterers, including the Yales and the Danforths, itemized button sales in their order books. Martin Bull used 'hardened tin' for several thousand, 'very serviceable and of good appearance', about 1790.

Hand-operated molds (Plate 165B, C, D): Pewter, being a common household metal and one easily worked, lent itself to small-scale button production in the home. Hand-operated molds (constructed like contemporary bullet molds) performed the task of turning worn-out dishes into buttons quickly and easily.

Ordinarily the working parts of a mold were of brass, and the handles wood. A few have survived that have wooden working parts, brass being employed only for removable pattern forms that fit into the wooden chambers.

Molds producing up to a full dozen buttons at one pouring are known. Four-button models are most common. Usually two or more different sizes, shapes or patterns come from the same mold. Sizes run from under one-half inch to over one inch; shapes go from flat discs to highly rounded caps. All buttons are solid and heavily shanked. Plain fronts predominate, though patterns are not uncommon.

The number of imperfect button slugs unearthed at old camp sites prove that the Continental soldier outfitted himself at least partly with buttons of his own making. A mold carrying the device of the First Connecticut Regiment is preserved. It is a pocket-size tool and makes only one button at a time.

The fact that molds antedate the Revolution is shown by a handsome example of Pennsylvania-German provenance engraved *1755*. Their long continued use is attested by another dated *1816*.

Molds are as serviceable today as ever. Their collector-owners make and exchange unbroken castings – a connecting bar with buttons pendent.

Inaugural buttons, 'GW's' (Plate 165E, F, lower G): George Washington's inauguration in 1789 was the first historic occasion marked by American commemorative buttons, a type well established abroad at that time. His monogram, placed upon many, has given all Washington inaugural buttons the abbreviated name '*GW's*'.

In his book *Washington Historical Buttons* Alphaeus H. Albert illustrates and describes twenty-four authenticated patterns. Six other buttons honoring George Washington during his lifetime and many of later date are also included (Plate 165G upper). The motto LONG LIVE THE PRESIDENT adorns many. Two are dated *March fourth 1789*, the day set for the ceremony. One has *30 April 1789*, the actual date of the postponed event.

GW's hold first place in Americana for the collector of buttons. No pattern is plentiful; part are known by one example only. Unfortunately a word of warning is necessary. It is easy to be deceived by certain questionable claimants and by a near-replica sold for the centennial in 1889. Mr Albert's book gives full details.

A description of the buttons that the President himself wore on his inauguration suit comes to us in correspondence of the time. They were large gilt buttons with the Great Seal of the United States engraved upon them by William Rollinson of New York City. In Washington's own words they 'really do credit to the manufactures of this Country'.

Colonial-type (Plate 165H): *GW's* belong to a large and widely collected class now known as 'Colonials', an allusion to period, not geography. Colonials are hand wrought from hard malleable metals such as brass, copper and bronze; loop shanks are brazed on (not soldered); decoration is engraved, die-struck, stamped or engine turned. Size range 1–1½ ins.

Luxury buttons à la Versailles: buttons of extravagant cast were fashionable in Europe as the century progressed. French courtiers bankrupted themselves buying quantities of expensive buttons. The colonists may have done the same thing but, if so, where are the records or the buttons to indicate it?

Inventories and correspondence speak repeatedly of silver buttons, often of gold ones. But of intricate pieces of art and craftsmanship there is no mention. When it comes to actual buttons, only one small set can be pointed out to illustrate an American taste for elegance. This is a set of six, each with the enameled portrait of a military hero. Benedict Arnold, designated colonel (Plate 165I), dates their drawing as 1775–6. They can scarcely have been worn after his disgrace in 1780. Paul Jones (Plate 165J), Israel Putnam, Charles Lee, Robert Rogers and David Wooster are the other subjects. Such a set could have been made only for an American customer.

NINETEENTH CENTURY

Hard white buttons (Plate 165L): early in the nineteenth century small shops powered by water wheels sprang up along the Connecticut streams, particularly around Waterbury. One product, a durable pewter alloy which the button-makers called 'hard white', gained an acceptance that lasted thirty years or more.

Hard whites differed from the older pewters in construction as well as metal. The designs were struck and the shanks were wire loops embedded in a hump of pewter. They are of quite uniform appearance, the regular size was about one inch and the usual pattern (if any) was some elaboration of the star motif. Backmarks were characteristic, though sometimes omitted.

A partial list of names that serve to date and identify hard white buttons includes: A. Matthews; G.Smith; Laurence Merriman; Asbel Griswold; A.Goodyear; Judd & Woster; Grilley; Hotchkiss & Terrel; M. Fowler.

Contemporary buttons of identical pattern but made of steel seem to have been more highly regarded. At least the backmark *Imitation Steel* on hard whites suggests as much. Whether the steel examples were made here or abroad remains to be traced. Since, however, there are records of steel button manufacture in this country, they may prove to be as native as the pewters.

Lafayette presentation buttons: in 1824 Lafayette returned to the United States for a year's visit as guest of the nation. Lavish celebrations and showers of gifts marked the gala tour. A gift set of fourteen buttons made from a single nugget of virgin gold was created for him. The style was determined by current fashion, for it was intended that Lafayette should wear the buttons. He did, indeed, find them appropriate for a hand-woven blue woolen suit also presented to him.

They resembled fine coins, about quarter-eagle size, die struck obverse and reverse. On the front was the profile of his good friend George Washington. The backmark read *Presented to General Lafayette by L.H. & Scovill, Button Manufacturers, Waterbury, Con.*

Not a single gold button was sold, the only three extras being kept by the partners Leavenworth, Hayden and Scovill. The company did sell other buttons to commemorate the visit, however. Made of brass and highly gilded, they pictured the French hero himself. First advertised in 1824, they remained in demand for several years. Three sizes (none over an inch) were uniformly backmarked *L.H. & Scovill/Extra Rich*. About 1827 similar buttons picturing Washington proved popular. They were backmarked *L.H. & S./Extra* (Plate 165M).

In 1876 the Scovill firm introduced replicas of the presentation buttons, struck in brass from new dies. Mounted on an explanatory card and packaged two dozen to a box, many gross were sold (Plate 165N).

Subsequently repeated restrikes were made. The uninformed, coming upon these late buttons, may mistake them for rare historic relics. Note that brass buttons with the presentation backmark cannot be earlier than 1876. Since 1946 the date year has been impressed at the shank. Lafayette and Washington gilts of 1824–34 have the simpler marks given above. These are scarce but not rare.

Golden Age buttons (Plate 165 O, P): highly gilt buttons made for some thirty years (until they declined in fashion during the 1840s are described as 'Golden Age'. The name is appropriate not only because it fits the buttons. It also signifies the period during which American manufacturers, after much hard learning, were at last able to produce a gilt button competitive with the best offered by English master craftsmen.

Plain polished fronts, engraved, die-struck and hand-chased patterns were popular in turn. Conventional designs always predominated, flowers next, then fruits.

Golden Age buttons might be solid or shell construction, but they were always completely gilded, front, back and shank. Quality marks (*Rich Orange*, *Extra Gilt*, *Superfine*, etc.) and makers' names characterize their backs. A few major producers were: Scovill & Company; Benedict & Burnham; R. & W. Robinson; Wadham, Coe & Company; Ives, Scott & Company; W. H. Jones & Company.

'Jacksonians', of the period of Jackson's presidency, approximately, are a widely collected variety. Unlike other Golden Age types, pictorial subject-matter abounds here. Small size (seldom over a half-inch) is another peculiarity. Their one unique feature is a narrow metal band fitted tightly around the rim (Plate 165Q).

Most Golden Age names can be found on fine sporting, livery and uniform buttons as well as on costume buttons (Plate 165R, S). Frequent company reorganizations and new partnerships are reflected in backmarks. For accurate dating one must consult detailed lists as published in the *National Button Bulletin* and elsewhere.

Political buttons: a button presumably of English origin is the earliest reported with American political implications. It has the legend *William Pitt/No Stamp Act 1766* encircling a profile of the minister (Plate 166A).

John Clark of Boston was marking his buttons *Union and Liberty for all America* almost as early. About 1780 an American-made button was stamped *Unity Prosperity Independence* (Plate 165T).

Party buttons became a firmly established type in 1834 when the Whigs, under Henry Clay, adopted the Liberty Cap as their emblem. The solid metal buttons then worn could be stamped with political messages on both front and back. For example, a small gilt button has a Liberty Cap on Pike with *E pluribus unum* above, and *34* beneath; on the back *True Whigs of 76 & 34* (Plate 166B).

Clay seems to have been the first candidate to have his picture on buttons frankly designed for political propaganda (1832). During his long career as a presidential aspirant, different Clay buttons came and went (Plate 166C).

The 'Log Cabin and Hard Cider' campaign of 1840 produced buttons in unequaled supply. Dozens of patterns are recorded. The cabin (complete with cider barrel and American flag), the candidate himself, and the battle cry *Tippecanoe and Tyler Too* all appeared (Plate 166D, E lower).

In 1848 the rugged features of Zachary Taylor were accompanied by such slogans as *Rough and Ready*, *Hero of Buena Vista*, and *Never Surrender* (Plate 166E upper).

Other candidates who made some use of campaign buttons included Jackson (1828), Van Buren (1836), Pierce (1852) and, in 1868, both Grant and Seymour (Plate 166F, G, H).

A comic anti-Van Buren button with the slogan *You Can't Come It, Matty*, and two buttons ridiculing the Whigs are lamentably scarce.

Thomas Jefferson's likeness was struck on a Sheffield plate button bearing the backmark of Robert Martin. Sinec Martin's years as a Philadelphia button-maker were 1799–1808, this must be a commemorative piece produced during Jefferson's administration. It is notable for its beauty and historic interest, outstanding for its early mark, and excessively rare (Plate 166 I, lower).

Lincoln designs were less popular than one might expect. Fewer than ten button portraits of him are known and none are recognized as campaign items (Plate 166 I upper).

Sandwich glass buttons: this name so loosely applied to other glass articles has been misapplied to certain foreign-made glass buttons of 'lacy' design. Sandwich records show no button production but countless tiny discs ($\frac{3}{8}$–$\frac{1}{2}$ in.) identical with the molded glass centers in small 'jewel' buttons made elsewhere have been excavated on the site of the old works.

Norwalk pottery: distinctive pottery buttons were manufactured in Connecticut, notably at Norwalk and Prospect, during the second quarter of the century. Sometimes mistakenly called 'Bennington' from the similarity of the glazes, their correct name is 'Norwalk'.

Brick-red, sand-colored or white clay was molded into patternless round or oval shapes. The hard, bright glaze was mottled in browns (commonest), greens, blues or mixtures. Styles include sew-throughs, center-hole pin shanks, embedded metal shanks and discs mounted in metal – in that order of increasing supply.

Goodyear buttons (Plate 166H, J, K): on May 6, 1851, Nelson Goodyear obtained a United States patent for 'hard and inflexible rubber' specified as suitable for button-making. Hard rubber buttons soon proved highly acceptable on the American market and highly unacceptable abroad.

Over five hundred different patterns with the backmarks of the Novelty Rubber Company or the India Rubber Comb Company (only licensees) are catalogued. Plain and textile patterns in black are very plentiful. Reds, grays and natural tans (not to be con-

fused with deteriorated black) are unusual. Backmarks having *1849* are desirable. Good subjects include heads, birds, flowers, insects and dancing frogs.

These are highly rated: United States Army and Navy; campaign buttons of 1868; Gail Borden Milk Company (with name and emblem) doubly desirable as an early example of a company button regardless of material (Plate 166K lower, 1$\frac{3}{8}$ ins.)

Jenny Lind (Plate 166L lower): the singer's American tour, 1850–2, is commemorated by buttons of current fashion, small glass cameos mounted in simple metal frames. Her head, turned in various poses, is most easily recognized by the coiffure. Though conclusive proof is lacking, every indication of American manufacture exists.

Louis Kossuth (Plate 166L upper): the Hungarian patriot in exile enjoyed great acclaim during his American speaking tour of 1851–2. Two gilt buttons commemorate the visit. Both show Kossuth's handsome face set off by his striking beaver hat with plume. The larger button (25mm) identifies him by his erstwhile title 'Governor of Hungary' as well as by name. The smaller one (13mm) has the name only. Their respective backmarks are *O.W.Minard/H.W.Hayden's/Patent/1851/ Waterbury* and *H.W.H./Patent 1851*.

Tintype buttons (Plate 166M): tintype pictures, printed in sheets and cut apart for mounting in novelty jewelry, were ideal for fancy waistcoat buttons. The favorite subjects were pretty girls and celebrated heroes, particularly Civil War generals.

Early tintypes are smaller than a dime, the tiny portrait being enclosed in a narrow metal rim. Large, showy examples are of later (perhaps present-day) construction.

Coin buttons (Plate 166N): following the Dutch custom, early settlers attached button shanks to large silver coins. At a later period coins inspired button designs. During the 1820s and 1830s the eagle device (silver coin reverse) was widely copied with varying amounts of simplification for both uniform and costume buttons. These were solid, coin-like pieces, albeit gilt might belie the source and true size be disregarded. From the 1850s through the 1870s the current gold coins were drawn upon for some fifteen or twenty designs. These have shell construction, thin brass fronts turned over tin backs.

Philadelphia Centennial (Plate 166 o, P): no other public event in America has produced as many beautiful souvenir buttons as did the Philadelphia Centennial of 1876. Large sizes with stud fastenings predominate. Particularly fine ones picture the Exhibition buildings inlaid in pearl or silver on tortoise shell. The American eagle, Liberty Bell, Independence Hall and dates 1776–1876 abound on metal buttons.

Uniform buttons: by a coincidence of history, American soldiers began using military buttons at the very time such buttons came into being. Regulation buttons had been non-existent until 1762 when the French government introduced insignia designs, an idea quickly copied by England and her colonies. A selected list of the most important American military uniform buttons follows:

Continental Army (Plate 165C, D): pewter buttons bearing the monogram *USA* in different styles have been unearthed at every Revolutionary camp site explored. Contemporary pewter buttons have been identified as belonging to militia companies from New York, New Jersey, Massachusetts, Connecticut, Rhode Island and Maryland. Poor condition does not greatly depreciate these key pieces.

War of 1812 (Plate 166Q): pewter declined in favor as improvements in home manufacture of brass developed. Backmarks gained general adoption, providing for the first time a permanent record of origin. The pioneer Scovill Company filled repeated government orders for such half-forgotten branches of the Army as Light Artillery, Heavy Artillery, Riflemen and Dragoons.

Republic of Texas (Plate 166R lower): the Scovill firm made nine designs (apparently all that were authorized) for the short-lived Republic of Texas. Six were for the army, three for the navy. All bore the

Texas star. Part had the identifying legend *Republic of Texas*. The originals are rare and highly desirable. Late replicas can be recognized for what they are by the presence of *Mfg.* in the Scovill backmark.

Mid-century: saw the final stage of a change in uniform button construction that had been going on since the 1830s. One-piece – i.e. solid metal – had given place to two-piece – i.e. hollow 'shell' bodies. In general, this difference provides a crude guide for recognizing post-1830 examples.

State militia and National Guard buttons, some bearing state seals, were current. Army officers wore corps buttons for riflemen, artillery, dragoons, engineers, ordnance, infantry and voltigeurs. This last-named, little-remembered minor branch of the Army provides the one genuine rarity in the group (Plate 166R upper).

Civil War: Union buttons from the war years are indistinguishable from those worn earlier or later and hence have only sentimental importance. Confederate buttons, on the other hand, have intrinsic value. The Confederate field soldier, officers of each corps, the navy and a number of state militia units were outfitted (at least on paper) with authorized buttons. The design most frequently encountered is the monogram *CSA* in letters azure-lined. Very many of these buttons post-date the war by decades. The illustration is of an early example (Plate 166s).

Names of Southern outfitters found on some button backs include: Halfman & Taylor, Montgomery; Courtney & Tennent, Charleston, South Carolina; E.M. Lewis & Company, Richmond, Virginia; Hyde & Goodrich, New Orleans.

A few Confederate buttons are of crude local manufacture. Many came from northern factories. Some of the finest are of English make.

Civilian uniform: fire and police departments, railroad and steamship companies, clubs, schools and other groups began wearing distinctive uniform buttons before the middle of the century. Their acceptance was so slow, however, that as a field civilian uniform buttons offer little until late in the nineteenth century.

Aboriginal buttons: buttons were unknown to the Indians of the eastern seaboard when the white explorers came. The dispute as to whether or not certain inland tribes may have worn buttons in prehistoric times does not concern collectors. Navaho silver buttons (esteemed as they are today) are neither indigenous nor early. The development of Navaho silversmithing came almost entirely after 1876.

Buttons carved from walrus ivory by the Alaskan Eskimos are generally considered to be the only kind original to the North American continent. Archeologists recognize examples predating the first contact of the white man with the Arctic region.

Originally worn as an ornament of native dress, they are still made for that purpose and for export. High polish and machine finish make much of the late work easily recognizable. Many fine pieces can be dated only by an expert, if at all (Plate 166T).

BOOKS FOR FURTHER READING

ALBERT, ALPHAEUS H.: *Washington Historical Buttons* (1949).

ALBERT, ALPHAEUS H.: *Record of American Uniform and Historical Buttons* (In preparation).

ALBERT, LILLIAN SMITH: *A Button Collector's Journal* and *A Button Collector's Second Journal* (1941).

ALBERT, LILLIAN SMITH and ADAMS, JANE FORD: *The Button Sampler* (1951).

ALBERT, LILLIAN SMITH and KENT, KATHRYN: *The Complete Button Book* (1949).

CALVER, WILLIAM L. and BOLTON, REGINALD P.: *History Written With Pick and Shovel* (1950).

DAVIS, EDWARD H.: *The Lafayette Presentation Button, 1824* (1951).

EMILIO, LUIS FENOLLOSA: *The Emilio Collection of Military Buttons* (1911).

Bi-monthly magazine of the National Button Society, *The National Button Bulletin*.

EARLY TRADECARDS

By BELLA C. LANDAUER

TRADECARDS, originally intended to indicate on a small cardboard no more than a man's name, business and address, form an interesting record of a significant part of our European cultural inheritance. Artists and engravers elaborated these seemingly trifling items, and in England, France and Italy they sometimes transformed them into artistic and pictorially interesting compositions.

Two of the earliest American tradecard designers and engravers were PETER RUSHTON MAVERICK (1755–1811), and the English-born JAMES SMITHER (ac. 1768–c. 1800). The latter executed the well-known Francis Hopkinson tradecard (Plate 167A) advertising a *Large and Curious assortment of Superfine, Second and Coarse clothes, with all suitable trimmings*. It depicts sheep contentedly resting under a tree, and the lettering is adorned with a flow of scrolls. Smither and Maverick could scarcely have foreseen the powerful influence their capabilities would exert. Peter Rushton Maverick, his sons and his half brother, Samuel, contributed greatly to the development of engraving in America. PETER MAVERICK, who died in 1831, designed many tradecards, one of the most elaborate representing the West Point Foundry and Boring Mill. The factory dominates the scene, with cannon in the foreground, the entire composition framed by oak sprays bearing conspicuous acorns. Samuel Maverick's billhead of 1818 announces that 'all orders will be thankfully received and executed with neatness and dispatch', modestly refraining from mentioning good taste. Samuel's personal tradecard shows him turning the wheel while printing copper plates. The United States, virile country that it was, quickly responded by giving further opportunities to such artistic endeavors. There are many early examples of engraved tradecards.

ALEXANDER LAWSON, c. 1798, engraved a copper plate for a merchant's counting house tradecard. PAUL REVERE, the silversmith, was responsible for two tradecards, which were more utilitarian than ornamental. We find some even earlier cards which, though interesting, lack identification as to their artists. Some of these of unknown origin advertise the establishments of Richard Worley (1730–60); Samuel Taylor, a Philadelphia bookbinder (1767); Ebenezer Larkin's book and stationery store, Boston (June 1789); Jehosepht (*sic*) Polk (1795) saddler, also of Philadelphia.

JOHN SCOLES (ac. 1793–c. 1844) designed an attractive scene for William Bull, a saddler (Plate 168A). The well-known engravers CORNELIUS TIEBOUT (ac. 1789 c. 1830) and WILLIAM ROLLINSON (1762–1842) also contributed to the development of American tradecard design. An elaborate sporting scene was engraved by J.M.TAYLOR for A.Heaton, gun-maker (Plate 167C).

Plates of identified engravers during the nineteenth century include ELKANAH TISDALE's card for Peter Burtsell (1803); JOSEPH CALLENDER's advertising French, English and India goods for Willard Peele in Salem, Massachusetts; and J.YEAGER's attractive tradecards of Ann P. Shallus' circulating library in Philadelphia, 1817, engraved by FRANCIS SHALLUS. J.Greenwood, surgeon dentist, commissioned ROY of Paris in 1806 to design and engrave his professional card. Ten years later J. & J. HARPER engraved a 'Patent Comb' for Robert Gedney.

J.J.BARRALET, arriving in the United States in 1795, executed an ornate copper plate for the Dove Paper Company, which may have served either as a tradecard or as a decorative heading for ream paper. Another plate of equally uncertain character but vast charm was produced by the New York lithographer N.CURRIER for Plattner & Smith. Other specimens include a tradecard produced in 1839 by DOOLITTLE & MUNSON, drawn by C.FOSTER, executed for Thomas Emery of Cincinnati, Ohio; and J.NEALE's street scene for a New York apothecary (Plate 167B). In 1849 J.W.ORR engraved a card showing Rathbun's Hotel on Broadway, New York. WILLIAM HAMLIN of Rhode Island engraved (1850) a card notifying the public that he *Repairs and Rectifies Compasses, Quadrants, Sextants and Nautical, Optical and Mathematical Instruments. Also Engraving and Copperplate Printing.* Later, in the 1860s, there is a colored lithograph devoted to the Industrial Straw Works of White Bro. & Co., in Pennsylvania designed by J.MAGEE. John Slocum of Rhode Island had a copperplate engraving to advertise *Cordials, Warranted pure.* A very popular artist, GEORGE CRUIKSHANK, designed and etched (1871–3) a business announcement for J.W.Bouton, bookseller and importer of New York, and also one for Samuel P. Avery's Fine Art Room. The HATCH LITHOGRAPH COMPANY of New York and Boston furnished a plate for Walter A. Woods' Mowing and Reaping Machine Co. of Hoosick Falls, New York, c. 1875. There is an interesting card of 1877 for the New York Hygienic Hotel and Turkish Bath Establishment.

The reader should also note these names of artists and engravers which are apt to appear on early tradecards; J.M.ELFORD, DEL.; CHARLES CUSHING WRIGHT, ENG.; R. TILLER, JR, ENG.; A.J.DAVIS, DEL.; RAWDON WRIGHT & CO., ENG.; R.M.GAW, ENG.; T.MOORE, LITH.; GEO.W.TEUBNER, ENG.

Prior to the Civil War, a new medium was introduced in the making of tradecards, the art of embossing or *gaufrage* (Plate 168D). Strictly speaking, the term is applied only to raised impressions produced by means of engraved dies or plates brought forcibly to bear on the material to be embossed. This was done by various means, according to the nature of the substance acted on. *Gaufrage*, both blind and colored, was used for trade-

cards. *Some Embossed American Trade Cards* gives quite a formidable list of such specimens. The best-known artists in this special field were: HOWELL EVANS, Philadelphia Printer, 1843–52; ANDREW SCOTT, Philadelphia Printer, 1852; THE WERNER PRINTING COMPANY, Akron, Ohio, c. 1890; SAMUEL N.DICKINSON & COMPANY, Boston, 1841. However, E.KETTERLINUS of Philadelphia was by far the most prolific artist in this line of ornamentation. Modern embossing is apt to be limited to the blind variety, but the really fine examples abound in all the hues of the rainbow, and are further abundantly enriched with different metals. Perforated designs also greatly enhance the general effect. One of the personal show-cards of Ketterlinus (1855) reads thus: 'We invite the attention of Dealers and others to our splendid stock of embossed Show cards, Perfumery, Fabric, Wine and Liquor Labels, the largest and most varied assortment in the United States. Jar and Drawer labels printed in Gold Leaf and Bronze. Lettering navy, gold, bronze, green; framed in grey, red, gold; ornate design.'

A smaller group of cards called *Metamorphoses* also were derived from a European type. In the eighteenth century this peculiar mode originated; paper strips were cut and folded in booklet form, thereby producing various pictures. Each time the flaps turned, the scene varied, and as most metamorphoses were folded three times twelve changes of pictures were produced. This process was used for games, pamphlets and children's books. As early as 1814 we find SAMUEL WOOD in New York, publishing metamorphoses, and in 1839, T.H.CARTER of Boston issued a *Metamorphoscope.* Somewhat later advertisers adopted this method, but the results were oftentimes more grotesque than artistic. Still these examples are collectors' items.

After American humor and ingenuity began to assert themselves on the tradecard, classification becomes far more complicated. There are myriads of headings and the list seems endless. Another classification is the patriotic card, with a subdivision, *Washingtoniana*, which in itself supplies ample material for an entire book (Plate 167D). Then there is a large group of literary cards including innumerable Shakespeare items. Others are inspired by *Alice in Wonderland, Uncle Tom's Cabin, Don Quixote,* and the works of Oscar Wilde, O.Henry, Longfellow and Mark Twain. This list is far from complete.

There are so many Gilbert and Sullivan tradecards (*see* Plate 168B for *H.M.S. Pinafore*) that they have formed the nucleus for two collections, one at the Pierpont Morgan Library in New York and another at The New-York Historical Society. *The Mikado,* for example, was adopted by two soap companies, Satin Gloss and Lautz. Others who used *The Mikado* were two spool cotton firms, Clark and J. & P. Coats; also Rice's Flower Seeds; Straiton & Storms' cigars; Fox & Kelly's Dry Goods. Adams & Westlake announced a 'Mikado Stove'. Three corset houses drew on the same favorite for their inspiration, and although *Yum-Yum* and her two boon companions never wore such garments, they are pictured on the advertising cards of Madam Strange Comfort Corset, Tricora Corset and Thompson's Patent Glove Fitting Corset. Substituting watches for the fans on the Tricora corset card, the 'Three Little Maids from School' publicized the Waterbury watch. This firm not only used the pictures but also appropriated all the original verses and altered them to serve their purpose.

Other groups of tradecard motifs are devoted to the elephant, *Jumbo; Punch and Judy;* the *Statue of Liberty;* the *Obelisk,* or *Cleopatra's Needle* (Plate 168C), Indian scenes; philatelic reproductions; military events; the theater and ballet; aeronautical subjects; sports; transportation, and so on *ad infinitum.* These lists may appear dull but are essential to grasping the development of tradecards, a mighty form of modern advertising providing a history of industries, of commerce, of mechanical progress, changes in taste and style of living. Through them we are assisted in reconstructing much of the social development of the past.

BOOKS FOR FURTHER READING

LANDAUER, BELLA C.: *Gilbert and Sullivan Influence on American Tradecards,* pamphlet (1936).

LANDAUER, BELLA C.: *Some Terpsichorean Tradecards,* pamphlet (1940).

Early American Tradecards from the Collection of Bella C. Landauer, with critical notes by Adele Jenny (New York, 1927).

Tradecards from the Aeronautical Collection of Bella C. Landauer, pamphlet (1940).

Philatelic Advertising, pamphlet.

Soda Water in the 19th Century, pamphlet.

Some Alcoholic Americana, pamphlet (1932).

When Advertisers Discovered Shakespeare (1937).

The Indian Does Not Vanish in American Advertising (1940).

Trivial Washingtoniana (1941).

Embossing (1941).

Pre-frigidaire Ice Ephemera, pamphlet (1943).

LANDAUER, BELLA C.: "Jumbo's Influence on Advertising," in *The New York Historical Society Quarterly,* October 1934, pp. 43–52.

TRADE CATALOGUES

By LAWRENCE B. ROMAINE

O_F the hundreds of specialized fields of American collecting, both private and institutional, none offers greater opportunity for historic research and proper preservation than the trade catalogue. This one facet of industrial Americana is in its infancy, and has only received general recognition within the past twenty-five years. Fortunately a few farsighted historical research workers *did* recognize the value of the trade catalogues before the destructive paper drives of recent years. But for their imagination and common sense, we would today have no records whatever of hundreds of American inventions and manufactures long since lost to posterity in our fast and furious development.

Before the Revolution there were very few, if any, trade catalogues issued. Craftsmen and artisans advertised their wares in the newspapers, or issued lists, broadsides and circulars. Possibly Benjamin Franklin's *Poor Richard's Almanack* might be considered a catalogue or house organ for his print-works, but this requires a considerable stretch of the imagination. It is fairly safe to state that there were no trade catalogues as we know them offered prior to about 1760.

From 1800 until 1831, when Jocelyn, Darling & Co. of New York published *The American Advertising Directory, for Manufacturers and Dealers in American Goods*, the practise of sending out catalogues grew slowly. Manufactories were growing up all over the country and mass production suddenly appeared on the American horizon. Quite naturally the New England Yankee sought the markets of Ohio and the newly opened west, and soon found that illustrated lists of goods paid well as a supplement to the peddler. From 1830 to 1850, as type foundries produced better cuts, presses improved and the cost of paper decreased, manufacturers and merchants published larger and more complete catalogues. After 1850, with the new steam rotary presses and the tremendous expansion of industry, the post office found a new and growing source of revenue. About the time of the Philadelphia Centennial in 1876, the mail order business really went into high gear and has been gathering speed ever since.

From 1700 to 1800 there were but twenty-five different crafts and trades advertised in the New York City newspapers. For the same period, there were about seventy advertised in all New England newspapers. By 1831 the *American Advertising Directory* found four hundred and fifty odd trades and products. A recent compilation published in Washington lists just short of two thousand different American occupations. Each new invention has created specialists. The number of trade catalogues necessary to keep pace with our present luxurious way of life has of course increased a thousandfold. Our ancestors have thrown away old catalogues by the hundred, and we must dispose of billions. Our libraries and museums are faced with the battle of the bulk, for only the best examples in each line can possibly be saved for future research.

There is scarcely a chapter on any subject in this encyclopedia that can be thoroughly written without the aid of American trade catalogues, either directly or indirectly. Most of the reference volumes that stand on the shelves of our libraries are indebted to them for names, dates and illustrations. Future works of reference must also depend on this source of information for facts about many little-known craftsmen and manufacturers not as yet 'discovered'. Many authorities depend entirely on manuscript accounts, letters and records, but these do not supply the illustrations of plans and designs to be found in the old trade catalogues.

Value is a difficult word to define. Most people value what they have to pay for and tend to belittle what is given them. American trade catalogues have been, are, and I hope always will be, distributed free. The reason that the following short lists* of important titles are priceless is, I feel sure, because they were given away originally: Isaiah Thomas's catalogues of books, c. 1790; William Prince's catalogue of seeds, 1771; Thomas Moore's *Newly Invented Machine called the Refrigerator;* Baltimore 1803; lists of prices offered by various groups of carpenters, dyers, tin-plate workers and other craftsmen stipulating costs for such items as architraves, blow-horns, butter-kettles, beer measures, furniture, calicoes, glassware, and even watering pots, c. 1800–30; Michael Floy's catalogue of seeds, New York, 1823; Wheaton & Hickox, *Housekeeper's Own Book*, Worcester, Massachusetts, c. 1840. Of mid-century date and later are catalogues of W.M.Shute's Hat, Cap and Fur Store, Boston, c. 1850; Livingston, Copeland & Co. Novelty Works, Pitts-

FIG. 1. Hogg and Patterson *Opal Goods*, 1880

burgh, 1855; Harris's catalogue of copper weather-vanes for 1860; Curtis & Mitchell's type specimens, 1860; New Haven Clock Co.'s catalogue, 1860; Reading Hardware Works price list, 1866; A.Montgomery Ward's *Grangers Supplied* ... 1874; Chas. Palm & Co.,

* Recently reported:—Nat. Library of Medicine. J. Tweedy: *A Catalogue of Druggs*, Newport (1760).
   Massachusetts Horticultural Library. George Spriggs: *A Catalogue of Seeds*, Boston (1770).

1877 Sample Book of Ornaments for Buggy, Carriage and Sleigh; Hogg & Patterson's *Plain and Decorated Opal Goods*, 1880; Knickerbocker Ice Co. catalogue of wagons, with color plates, Philadelphia, 1884; The Rambler Automobile-Model C., 1902; Wm.F.Hasse's *Music Boxes*, 1894–5; Alpha Aero & Marine Engines, 1907 – and, bringing this list up to date, *All the King's Horses and All the King's Men*, offered by R.R.Donnelley & Sons of Chicago, just a very few years ago.

The library today that boasts such a chronologically complete pictorial catalogue record as the above is fortunate. If the collector and librarian of today thoroughly appreciate the fact that today's news is tomorrow's history, and select with discretion and taste the best examples of this atomic age, the next generation will have saved what the past has lost. Through the years our historical societies, libraries and museums have been able to save relatively few of these illustrated records of American ingenuity. There has always been a lag in appreciation. Even today there are institutions and private collectors completely ignoring this field after a set date of about 1870; only a few years ago this date was 1830 or 1840.

In 1947 the Grolier Society of New York published *One Hundred Influential American Books printed before 1900*, and in so doing brought to the attention of collectors, curators, dealers, directors and librarians the importance of the American catalogue. The outstanding example noted is the first mail order broadside list issued by Montgomery Ward & Co. in 1874. The compiler writes:

'No idea ever mushroomed so far from so small a beginning, or had so profound an influence on the economics of a continent, as the concept, original to America, of directly selling by mail, for cash. Aaron Montgomery Ward conceived the idea in 1869, was wiped out in the Chicago fire, but started Montgomery Ward & Co. with George S. Drake and R.C.Caulfield in August, 1872, on a capital of less than $5,000. 'In December Messrs Drake and Caulfield became alarmed, thinking they would lose their money, and wished to withdraw, and Mr Ward purchased their interest.' (Ward *MS.*) By 1878 total annual sales were $308,000; in 1944 total net sales were $621,000,000. We do not know how many copies were issued of the bijou 1874 pamphlet exhibited; the 1945 catalogues, if stacked on top of each other, would make a column 256 miles high.'

'The mail order catalogue has been perhaps the greatest single influence in increasing the standard of American middle-class living. It brought the benefit of the wholesale prices to city and hamlet, to the cross-roads and prairie; it inculcated cash payments as against crippling credit; it urged millions of housewives to bring into their homes and place upon their backs and, in their shelves and on their floors creature comforts which otherwise they could never have hoped for; and, above all, it substituted sound quality for shoddy. As a final bow, the mail order catalogue was, in too many homes, the only illustrated book.'

After emphasizing the importance and value of these catalogues as history, the next consideration is the answer to the perennial question – 'which catalogues are valuable?':

1. All *first* catalogues. In this group I would include all lists of merchandise offering newly created or invented fields of manufacture, such as the first refrigerator or ice box, 1803, the first mouse trap, the first washing machine or first automobile.

2. All catalogues offering new designs, models, devices and processes; hence a new model refrigerator, mouse trap, washing machine, automobile, carriage, locomotive, bridge, stove, printing press, toy or weathervane.

3. All those representing the country's expansion and development, such as the first Philadelphia fire engine, the first Cincinnati carriage works, the first St Louis drug house, or the first San Francisco milling machines.

4. All color-illustrated catalogues, especially before 1860, but up to 1900 on the basis of careful selection.

5. Many of the general jobbers' catalogues that were too often the 'only illustrated book'. A complete list of these would be far too long, but a selected few may be helpful: *Baltimore Bargain House, Busiest House in America;* Butler Brothers' *Our Drummer;* catalogues of R.H. Macy & Co.; Marshall, Field & Co.; Montgomery Ward & Co.; Sears' Roebuck & Co.; White, Van Glahn & Co. *Oldest in America – Since 1816,* New York, 1907; Charles Williams; and John Wanamaker.

Many of them offer a pictorial panorama of the buying fads and fancies of the nation from the Civil War through World War I.

No rules are perfect and all must be applied with common sense. I do not suggest that even the Library of Congress should try to preserve them all. One good example every decade under the last group would form a good reference library to the student and scholar for research. Nor do I suggest that a Texas library collect *Philadelphia fire engines.* A complete accumulation under any one heading would be practically impossible. However, a combination of subject and local interest should clarify plans for both institution and private collector. The old law of supply and demand will always control prices and values. There is no practical method of appraising the standards of future collecting.

It would be impossible to cover the entire alphabetical field from *apple pairers* to *whaling irons* in less than ten volumes. It would have been impossible even in 1831 to condense this subject to one small chapter and still illustrate the manufacturers' creations adequately. These notes are based on material known to exist in present collections, but new fields of interest will be indicated.

Catalogues should be divided into two major groups: those issued by the manufacturer, including the house organs; and those issued by the jobber and merchant. Chronologically, the manufacturers' lists and brochures were the first to appear. As the country expanded and markets developed, merchants adopted the general catalogue, and included between two large covers everything they could handle and sell from *axe* to *wig.* Collectors are often puzzled to find that catalogues of knife rests, foot scrapers, insulators, mouse traps, molders' tools or perhaps some special glassware are so rare. In most cases the answer is multiple manufacture, in others, pure economics. One small craftsman turning out mouse traps at the rate of half a dozen a day could not afford to print a catalogue. His small output was sold to a jobber or merchant who listed the traps in his general catalogue. Sometimes, in this way, the name of an individual inventor was never recorded at all.

(A) Iron lamp similar to the French bouillote lamp but of American origin; has long history of ownership in Rhode Island; shade of painted tin; candle box; mid-eighteenth century. The iron candlestick could be hung on the back of a chair; first half of eighteenth century. *Author's collection; photo Costain.*

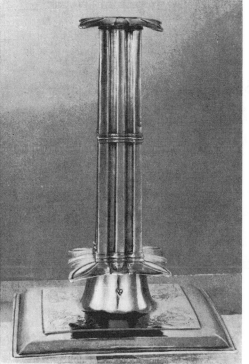

(B) Silver candlestick, one of a pair by Jeremiah Dummer, Boston, made to commemorate a marriage of the year 1686. *Garvan collection, Yale University Art Gallery.*

PLATE 161

English glass chandelier, *c.* 1770–80, similar in type to the chandelier which has been in the Miles Brewton house, Charleston, since its building, *c.* 1770. *Minneapolis Institute of Arts.*

PLATE 162

(A) Rare silver snuffer stand by Cornelius Kierstede, 1675–1757, of New York and New Haven. Ht overall 12 ins. *Metropolitan Museum of Art, New York.*

(B) American blown glass candlestick, olive green; Gallatin-Kramer New Geneva Glass Works, New Geneva, Pennsylvania; *c.* 1812. *Smithsonian Institution.*

(C) Pair of wooden candlesticks with shades; English, *c.* 1800; has come down in the Amory family of Boston. *Karolik collection, Museum of Fine Arts, Boston.*

PLATE 163

(A) Girandole or convex mirror with gilt frame and candlearms; probably English; has been owned by a New York family since about 1820; shown in the Greek Revival Exhibition, 1943. *Metropolitan Museum of Art, New York*

(B) English cut glass candlestick, 1800–20; Amory family, Boston. *Karolik collection, Museum of Fine Arts, Boston.*

(C) China-trade porcelain sconce in form of a hand, with brass candle socket; floral decoration in iron red and rose; c. 1780. *Old Deerfield, Massachusetts.*

PLATE 164

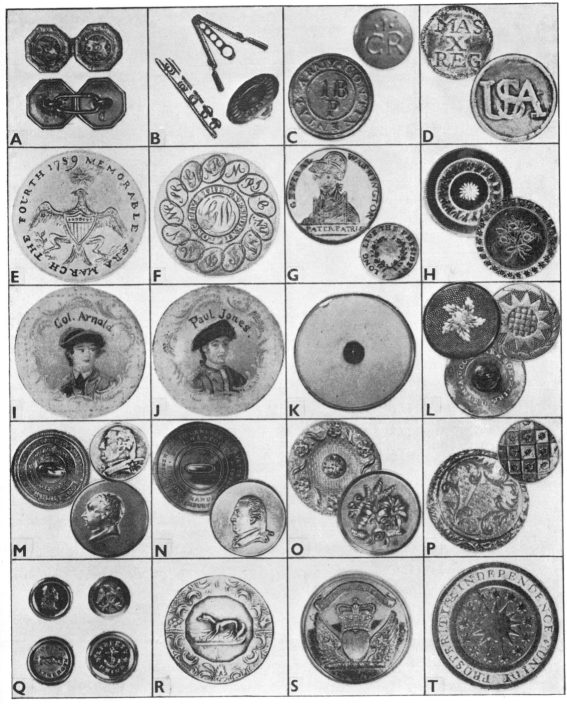

(A) Gold sleeve links. Jacob Hurd. *Courtesy: Wadsworth Atheneum.* (B) Hand-operated mold, actual length 7¼ ins. Full casting 3½ ins. Detached button ¾ in. (C and D) Pewter military buttons from hand-operated molds. (E) Washington Inaugural, dated eagle pattern. (F) G.W., linked-states border. (G) (*Upper*) Pater Patriæ; (*Lower*) small G.W. (H) Colonials. (I and J) De luxe enamels, *c.* 1775. (K) Conch shell disc with silver pinshank, 1¼ ins. (L) Pewter, stamped 'Hard White'. (M) Gilts. (*Upper right*) Washington, *c.* 1827; (*Upper left and lower right*) Lafayette, *c.* 1824. (N) Replica of Lafayette presentation button. Back enlarged. (O, P) Golden Age types. (P) (*Lower*) called 'Hunting-case watch gilt'. (Q) Jacksonians. (R) Sporting. (S) Livery. (T) Patriotic, *c.* 1780. Colonial type.

(*Actual size except where noted.*)   *National Button Society.*

PLATE 165

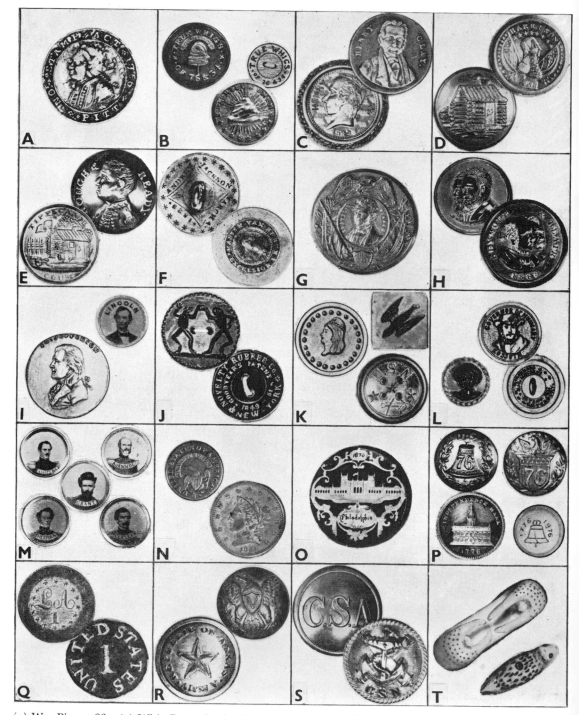

(A) Wm Pitt, 1766.   (B) Whig Party, back of lower reduced.   (C) Henry Clay.   (D and E) (Lower) 1840 campaign; (Upper) Zachary Taylor.   (F) Plain-front gilts with political back marks.   (Upper) Jackson; (Lower) Van Buren.   (G) Franklin Pierce.   (H) 1868 campaign.   (I) (Upper) Lincoln, tintype; (Lower) Jefferson, Sheffield plate.   (J and K) Goodyear rubber.   (L) (Upper) Kossuth; (Lower) Jenny Lind.   (M) Tintypes.   (N) Coin patterns. (O) Centennial stud, silver inlaid in tortoiseshell.   (P) Centennial motifs.   (Q) War of 1812.   (R) (Upper) Voltigeur; (Lower) Republic of Texas.   (S) Confederate—Army, Navy.   (T) Walrus ivory, Alaskan Eskimo.

(Actual size except where noted above, and T, lower example reduced by half.)   National Button Society.

PLATE 166

(A) Trade card of Francis Hopkinson, by Smither.

(B) Neely's Apothecary, Greenwich Lane, New York, engraved by J.Neale.

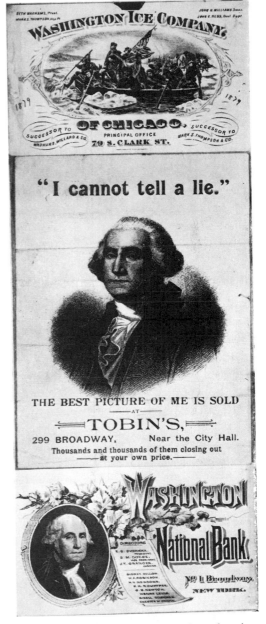

(D) Three 'Washington' engraved cards, nineteenth century.

(c) A.Heaton, Gun Maker, New York, engraved by Taylor.

All cards from Bella C. Landauer collection, The New-York Historical Society.

PLATE 167

(A) William Bull, Sadler, New York;
engraved by Scoles.

"What, never? No, never!
What, never? Hardly ever!"
Without Higgins' German Laundry Soap!

(B) Subjects from *H.M.S. Pinafore* and *The Mikado* were popular.

(C) One of the many cards showing
the obelisk, or Cleopatra's Needle,
soon after it was erected in Central
Park, New York.

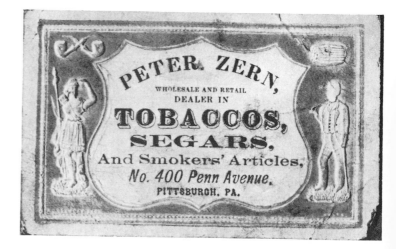

(D) Embossed card of Peter Zern, Tobacco Dealer.

All cards from Bella C. Landauer collection, The New-York Historical Society.

PLATE 168

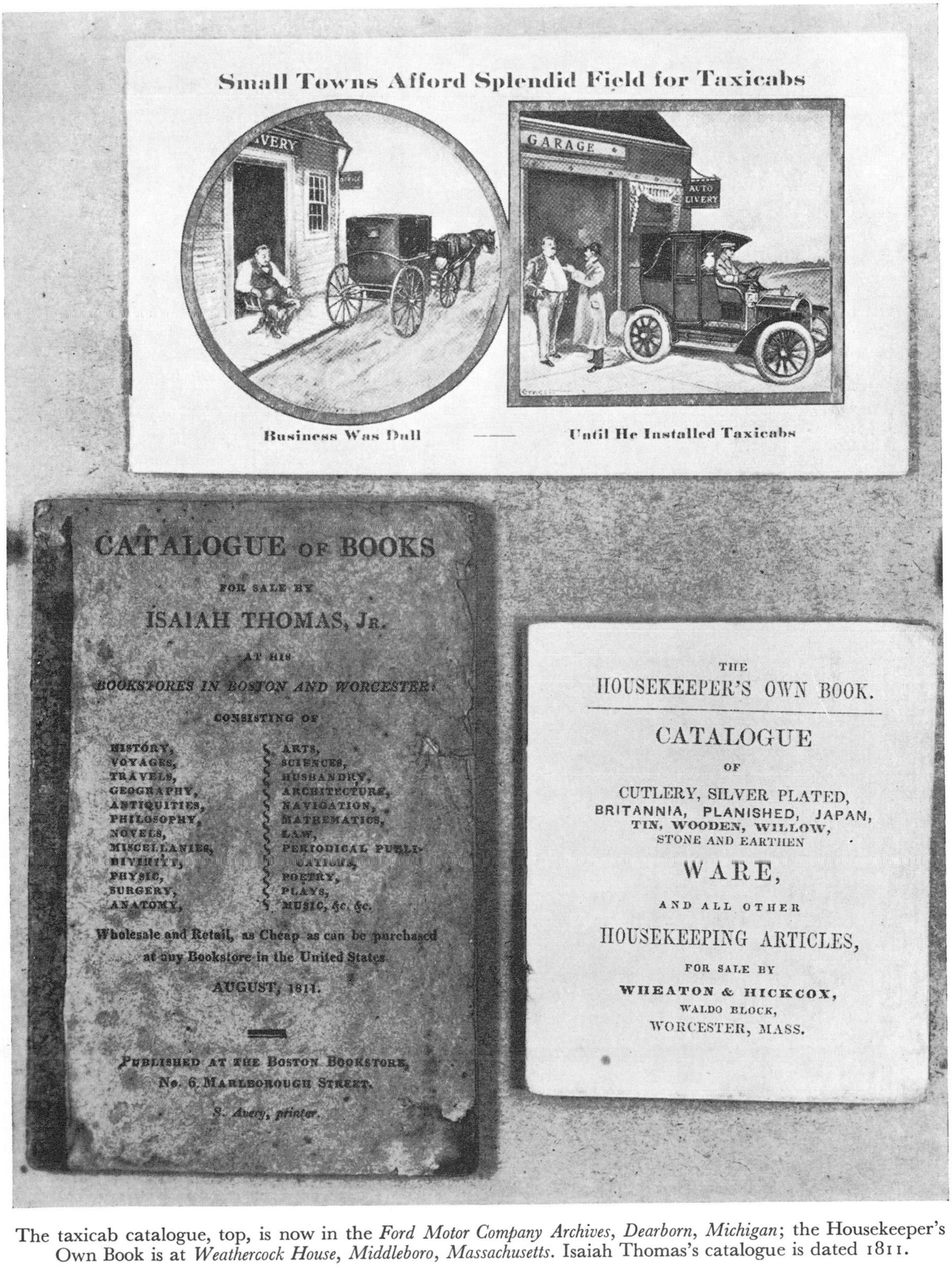

The taxicab catalogue, top, is now in the *Ford Motor Company Archives, Dearborn, Michigan*; the Housekeeper's Own Book is at *Weathercock House, Middleboro, Massachusetts*. Isaiah Thomas's catalogue is dated 1811.

PLATE 169

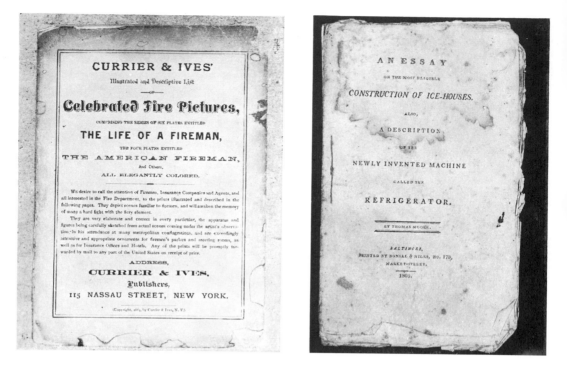

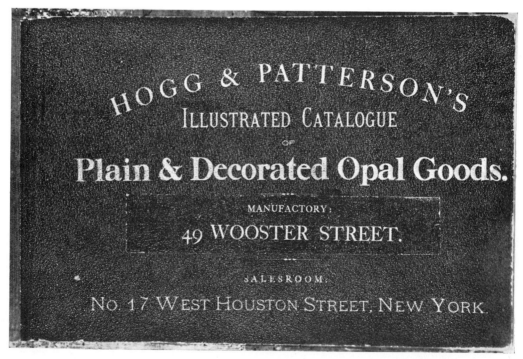

Currier & Ives catalogue at *Weathercock House;* Refrigerator essay, *Thomas W. Streeter collection, Morristown, New Jersey;* copies of Hogg & Patterson catalogue at the *Metropolitan Museum, Chicago Historical Society, Corning Museum of Glass,* and *Weathercock House.*

PLATE 170

(*Top left*) Ace of Spades, deck published by Thomas Crehore, Massachusetts, 1816. (*Top right*) Tripoli deck of Jazaniah Ford, Massachusetts, 1811. (*Lower left*) Jack of Spades, ivory finish, L.I.Cohen, New York, 1832. (*Lower right*) German style, A.Wiehl, New York, 1850. *All illustrations from the Author's collection.*

PLATE 171

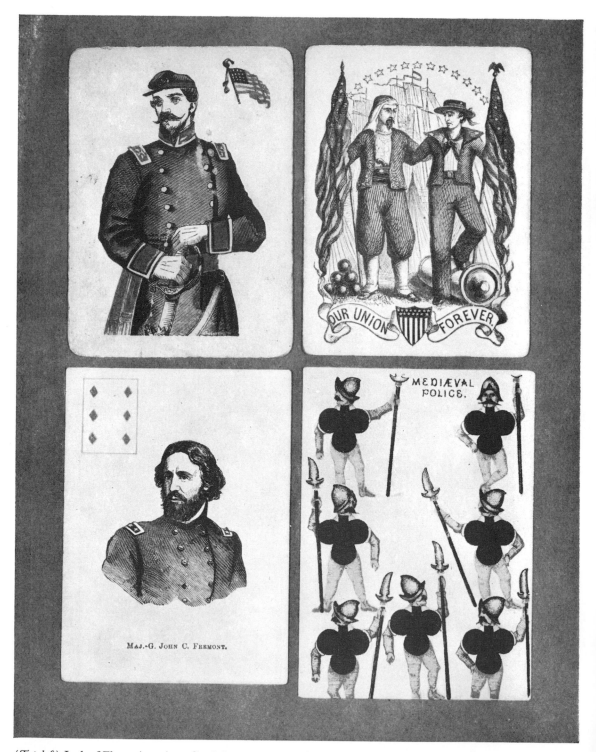

(*Top left*) Jack of Flags, American Card Company, New York, 1863. (*Top right*) Civil War deck, Samuel Hart, New York, 1864. (*Lower left*) Fremont on Civil War card, M. Nelson, New York, 1863. (*Lower right*) 'Transformation' deck, Tiffany, New York, 1876.

PLATE 172

(B) One of a pair of exceptionally large and elaborate sconces in gilded frames, Ht. 30 ins., w. 14 ins., made by Eunice Deering of Kittery, Maine, *c.* 1730; brass candleholder. The wax sheep are an unusual feature. *Metropolitan Museum of Art, New York.*

(A) One of a pair of quillwork sconces described in Frances Clary Morse's *Furniture of the Olden Time* and in the Anderson Galleries' catalogue of the Francis Hill Bigelow sale in 1924. The original candle arms by Knight Leverett were described by Mr Bigelow in his *Historic Silver of the Colonies,* but at the time of the sale they were no longer attached to the sconces; the present candle arms are of brass. Ht. 28½ ins., w. 11 ins. *Metropolitan Museum of Art, New York.*

PLATE 173

(A) One of a pair of quillwork sconces made by Ruth Read of Boston, *c.* 1720. Original candle arms; black-painted frame. Ht. 23½ ins. *Ex-coll. of George Reed, Francis Hill Bigelow, Natalie K. Blair. Cooper Union Museum.*

(B) Single quillwork sconce, small (17⅞ × 8⅝ ins.) and without candle arm, though one was evidently originally attached to the under side of the frame; black-painted frame. Probably made in Maine. *Metropolitan Museum of Art, New York.*

PLATE 174

(A) Maple burl scoop with bowl and handle in one piece, hardwood piggin with pine bottom, and pine soap dish. *Old Sturbridge Village.*

(B) Large covered bowl of maple burl, D. 14 ins. *Old Sturbridge Village.*

(C) Ash spoon, L. 12 ins. carved by Thomas Waldron Sumner of Brookline; inscribed 'TWS/-1791'. *Los Angeles County Museum.*

PLATE 175

(A) One of a pair of chalkware oranges in a spray of leaves; light green, yellow, red and black. Ht. 10 ins.; mid-nineteenth century. *The New-York Historical Society.*

(B) Chalkware goat, creamy yellow ground with black markings, red ears, mouth and nostrils. *Henry Ford Museum.*

(C) Chalkware lovebirds from a mold similar to that shown on the right; colors, dark green, yellow and red. *The New-York Historical Society.*

(D) Plaster-of-Paris mold for chalkware figure: pair of lovebirds, beak to beak. *Henry Ford Museum.*

PLATE 176

Collections: when Drepperd published his *Primer of American Antiques* in 1944, but three institutions had recognized the tremendous value of the American trade

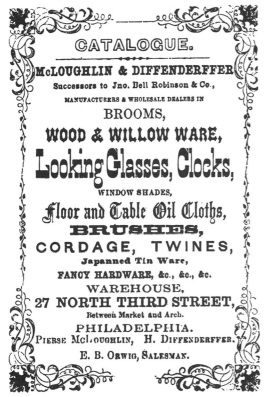

FIG. 2. Early Manufacturer's Catalogue

catalogue. Today this has changed and it has become very difficult to make a complete list of our historical societies, libraries and museums whose vast collections should be known both to the neophyte and seasoned collector. Each of our forty-eight state libraries and historical societies has its own collection of local manufacturers' catalogues. Some have set dates as noted before, but most of them have tried faithfully to fill in the neglected gaps from their beginnings to the present. Our museums throughout the country have also tried to preserve both the specific and general catalogues that best authenticate their exhibits of American crafts, trades and industries in the periods they cover. Our municipal and private libraries and museums have developed fine collections. In spite of

these combined efforts, however, we have expanded so fast that it will surely take all of our librarians and historians, as well as thousands of new collectors, to piece together what has been produced in the last fifty years.

A more specific guide to the location of present collections will be helpful. For the very earliest catalogues issued, from about 1790 to 1820, regardless of local interest or importance, the following should be consulted: American Antiquarian Society, Worcester, Massachusetts; The Metropolitan Museum of Art, New York; The New-York Historical Society Library; The Historical Societies of Pennsylvania and Philadelphia; Smithsonian Institution and the Library of Congress, Washington, D.C.

For outstanding collections from about 1820 to the present, general and specialized, in all their varying hues and sizes, local and national, private and institutional, from A to Z, consult: Baker Library at Harvard University, Cambridge; Brooklyn Museum; Chicago Historical Society; Cooper Union, New York; Old Sturbridge Village, Sturbridge, Massachusetts; Longwood Library, Kennett Square, Pennsylvania; New York University's Commerce Library, Washington Square, New York; the Library of Congress, Washington. These will cover the subject in general but there are many special fields. For American carriages, consult Margaret V. Wall at the Suffolk Museum in Stony Brook, Long Island, or the Shelburne Museum in Shelburne, Vermont. Data on a special glass house will very likely be found at the Corning Museum of Glass, Corning, New York. Information on a Model X Stanley Steamer may be in the Ford Motor Company archives, the Detroit Public Library, the Flint, Michigan Public Library or in Henry Austin Clark's vast collection at the Long Island Automobile Museum in Southampton, Long Island. Catalogues relating to the mills and millers of the last hundred and fifty years are at Eleutherian Mills, Wilmington, Delaware. For material on the so-called heavy industries, from mine to forge to steel, consult the library at the Bethlehem Steel Corporation, Bethlehem, Pennsylvania. The best files on horticultural and gardening catalogues may be found at the Queens Borough Public Library, Long Island, and at the Bailey Hortorium, Cornell University, Utica, New York.

Buttons: although there were few catalogues of buttons offered directly by the manufacturer, many of the general offerings contain fine plates and pertinent information: Butler Brothers; Sears Roebuck; Montgomery, Ward; White, Van Glahn; Charles Williams; 'A.B.C.' of Chicago; Baltimore Bargain House; Marshall Field; Butterick; R.H.Macy; John Wanamaker.

Cards: catalogues of tradecards and playing cards were issued by many printers and lithographers after 1840. Currier & Ives of New York had single page lists and others had folding panoramas of colored samples, these being of later date. Other sources of information for tradecards are the many type-specimen circulars, folders and catalogues in which business cards, comic and serious, were offered with examples of designs.

Ceramics: American and Anglo-American pottery has been thoroughly studied by many scholars. It is safe to say that they have been very conscious of the value of trade catalogues in this field. Catalogues are rare before about 1850, though later examples from merchants turn up fairly often.

Clocks and watches: American clocks and watches have been catalogued well and thoroughly by both the manufacturer and the jobber. The earliest examples appeared about 1850. Those issued by the manufacturers are rare, and even the general catalogues with everything included from bobèches to wedding rings are becoming scarce. In March 1885 the E.N.Welch Manufacturing Co. of Forestville, Connecticut, offered *Superior American Clocks*. The wise collector will keep one eye open for such as this, but will always train the other on the larger, general catalogues of the Baltimore Bargain House; Norris, Alister & Co. of Chicago; J.H.Purdy & Co. of Chicago; and jewelry catalogues from S.F.Myers Co.

Firearms: American firearms apparently entered the mail order catalogue field about

mid-nineteenth century. Ray Riling's monumental work, *The Powder Flask Book* (New Hope, Pennsylvania) shows the value of the trade catalogue in compiling a work of reference. He has made effective use of catalogues offered between 1850 and 1880 by the American Cap and Flask Co., Great Western Gun Works (1869–72), Waterbury Brass Co., James Bown & Sons and Edward K. Tryon.

Furniture: catalogues with lists or illustrations of furniture before 1800 are practically non-existent. There were a few guides and manuals but they were mostly English. From about 1830 there were a few pseudo-catalogues printed, but after about 1850 the furniture manufacturers went into the mail order business. A few examples:

Kehr, Kellner & Co. of New York. *Designs of Writing Desks, Tables, Secretaries manufactured at the American Desk Co.* (1873).
Harwood Mfg. Co., Boston. *Illustrated catalogue of Assembly Chairs, Settees, etc.* Boston (1883).
Morton D. Banks, Baltimore (1878). *Chamber, Parlour & Dining Room.*

The Metropolitan Museum has examples of earlier catalogues in this field.

Glass: American glass, an extensive field, has been well covered by Helen and George McKearin, Rhea Mansfield Knittle and Ruth Webb Lee. Their use of American glass manufacturers' catalogues is familiar to most collectors. That trade catalogues have been invaluable in compiling their works is obvious. There are however catalogues and firms that have not as yet been studied, a profitable field for future work. Representative are:

Baltimore Glass Works, Baker Bros. & Co., established 1790. *Bottles, Sundries, Glass Practice Balls*, Baltimore (1880).
Hogg & Patterson, *Opal Goods* (1880).
Maple City Glass Co., Honesdale, Pennsylvania, *Glass Tableware. No. 10. A galaxy of patterns in clear glass* (c. 1900).

Lighting Devices: the manufacturers of lighting devices followed the trend toward catalogues after 1850. Some of them, though of no practical use to the student of colonial lighting (see Arthur Hayward's *Colonial*

Lighting), are among the best ever offered, and those with colored lithographs very scarce. From the last days of the whale-oil lamp to the comforts of electricity, these catalogues are of great value. A few good examples are:

Celebrated No. Tubular Lanterns, n.p. (1860).
Bradley & Hubbard Mfg. Co., West Meriden, Connecticut (1877). *Kerosene Fixtures, Lamps, etc.* fine illustrations.
Wheeler Reflector Co., Boston & Chicago, *Chandeliers* (1885).

Lithographers: American lithographers have not been too prolific in turning out catalogues of their works, but there are a few. Harry T. Peters in *America on Stone*, made good use of the N.Currier, and Currier & Ives broadsheets, circular lists and catalogues. Although their workmanship helped to create most of the best catalogues in every field from the middle of the nineteenth century, their own specimen books are scarce. An occasional descriptive catalogue turns up and is a highly prized item. E.B. & E.C.Kellogg of Hartford, Connecticut, is represented by *Specimen Book of Fruits, Flowers & Ornamental Trees* (*c.* 1850). Few of this type have been saved.

Metalwork: just how carly American silversmiths and pewterers offered catalogues is not certain, but there are excellent examples after about 1840:

L.Boardman & Sons Works, East Haddam, Connecticut, for tableware (1870).
Simpson, Hall, Miller & Co., Wallingford, Connecticut, electro-plates, silverware, tea sets, paper weights, etc. (1878).
Meriden Britannia Co., Meriden, Connecticut, *Price List – Wine Stands, Candlesticks, Lamps,* etc., West Meriden (1867).
Gorham Mfg. Co., New York, Silversmiths' patterns, *Versailles, St Cloud, Cluny, Old Masters,* etc. (1889).
Reed & Barton, Artistic Workers in Silver & Gold, folio catalogue with color plates, designs; Taunton and New York (1884).

Ironwork, with the metal crafts in brass, copper and tin, is rich in catalogue material. The first ironwork hardware catalogues before 1800 were English, and there were very few illustrated in America before about the middle of the nineteenth century. A complete collection of the Birmingham, England, hardware catalogues may be seen at the Essex Institute in Salem, Massachusetts, and at Colonial Williamsburg, Williamsburg, Virginia. So many of the best illustrated catalogues cover several fields that many of the following should be considered as references to many early American industries, especially craftsmen's tools.

South Boston Iron Co. *List of Patterns corrected to Nov. 1, 1846*, Boston (1846).
Phoenix Iron Foundry, Eddy's Point, Providence, Rhode Island, *Pattern Book for 1839.*
J.W.Fiske, New York, *Artistic Wrought Iron Brass & Bronze.* 189 fine plates of designs, etc. New York (1891).
Hart, Bliven & Mead Mfg. Co. New York. *Foot Scrapers, Fancy Designs in Sad Iron Stands, Hardware,* etc., New York (1878).
Russell & Erwin Mfg. Co., New Britain, Connecticut, catalogue of designs & gadgets for barn, church & kitchen, bells to revolvers (1882). (This firm was one of the last to make old surface door locks with maple and oak cases.)
Reading Hardware Co., Reading, Pennsylvania, catalogue (1866).

Illustrations of japanned tin, or toleware appear in many catalogues, decorated with free hand and stenciled designs on everything from a trinket box to a toilet set, by both the tinsmith and the general merchant:

Smith, Burns & Co., *New York, Stamped, galvanised & Japanned Tinware. Medallion and Scenic Toilet Sets,* etc., New York (1872).
Bridge & Remington, *American Fancy Goods,* New York (1854).
F.A.Walker & Co. Boston, *Useful & Ornamental Goods* (1871).

Stoves: catalogues of stoves and heating devices including the kitchen range, which both heated and cooked in many a Yankee farmhouse (and still does), comprise a fertile field for references. The reader is referred to *Fire on the Hearth; the Evolution and Romance of the Heating-Stove* by Josephine H. Peirce, who has made a thorough search of the catalogues of all periods; her selection of illustrations from them provides a complete account.

Textiles: embroidery catalogues, with every possible pattern and design, have flooded the mails since approximately 1860. A few representative firms to keep in mind are Barbour Brothers, New York; Belding Brothers, New York to San Francisco;

Bentley Bros., New York; Mrs T.G. Farnham, New York; M.M. Fletcher Co., Chicago; Nonotuck Silk Co., Florence, Massachusetts; Frederick Herrschner, Chicago; J.F. Ingalls, Lynn, Massachusetts; S.W. Tilton Co., Boston. It is probable that the Slater Mill and its contemporaries did not issue catalogues of printed cottons and other cloth. The first apparently were offered after 1860.

Quilts, coverlets and hooked rugs were home industries, although the machine age produced a few manufactories that made poor imitations. There are a few catalogues of rug patterns, c. 1880–1900, and even more of the machines.

Tools: the subject of early American industries is a very extensive field, and the catalogues illustrating its many facets are legion. The earliest catalogues with illustrations of American tools are, strangely enough, those issued by the early seedsmen such as George C. Barrett of Boston in 1835; Michael Floy of New York, 1823; Hovey & Co., Boston, c. 1840; Rapalje & Briggs, Rochester, New York, 1850; William Prince & Son of Long Island; and Joseph Breck & Sons, Boston. Beginning about 1850, hardware catalogues illustrated almost every American tool and hand-machine. Catalogues by the manufacturer are scarce, but some turn up now and then, such as *Catalogue of Bench Planes and Moulding Tools* issued by the Arrowmammet Works of Middletown, Connecticut, in 1858. Charles Harrison's *Catalogue of Plumbers' Tools*, New York, 1879; and D.A. Newton & Co.'s *Hardware Specialties*, in which appear such curious inventions as the *American Meat and Vegitable Chopper*. Just when *early* American industries began, and how far the collector wants to carry his studies is up to the individual. The trade catalogues start about 1820 and end with the current automobile show. The source material for research in this field can never eliminate the circular, broadside, list and catalogue of both manufacturer and jobber.

Toys: mechanical toys have been advertised in catalogues which have been drawn on for illustrations in many recent works. *Cavalcade of Toys* by Ruth and Larry Freeman (Century House, 1942) offers an excellent example of using American trade catalogues for research. Many of the best inventions and creations in this field may be found in catalogues issued by Stirn & Lyon of New York; Selchow & Righter; Columbia Grey Iron Co.; Schoenut's Marvelous Toys; Unexcelled Fireworks Co.; and the Consolidated Fireworks Co. of America.

Others: stamp catalogues, which have been issued from 1850, are rather scarce. It would seem that the American circus has always advertised: the brochures describing acrobats and freaks are surely not mail order or trade catalogues, and yet their purpose is similar; they sold tickets instead of acrobats. Other fields are: music boxes; talking machines; wind mills; harvesting machinery; architectural accessories; hotel management; fashions; automobiles; carriages; and even trolley cars. There are American trade catalogues for them all, waiting to be collected and preserved by the institution and the private collector.

BOOKS FOR FURTHER READING

Dow, George Francis: *The Arts and Crafts in New England 1704–1775* (1927).
Drepperd, Carl W.: *The Primer of American Antiques*, New York (1944).
Gottesman, Mrs Rita Susswein: *The Arts and Crafts in New York 1726–1799*, 2 vols., The New-York Historical Society (1938 & 1954).
Larson, Henrietta M.: *Guide to Business History*, Harvard University Press (1950).
Peirce, Josephine H.: *Fire on the Hearth*, Springfield, Massachusetts.
Ramsey, Robert E.: *Effective House Organs*, Appleton, New York (1920).
The Colonial Scene, 1602–1800, Introduction by Edmund S. Morgan. Compiled by Lawrence C. Wroth and Clarence S. Brigham from the collections of the American Antiquarian Society and the John Carter Brown Library (1950).

PLAYING CARDS

By DR LAWRENCE KURZROK

AMERICAN playing cards, naturally enough, originally were imported from abroad, mainly from England, Spain and France. Spanish cards were the earliest, if we do not include the bone gambling devices of the Indians. However, because of the closer ties to England, English cards had a more lasting effect and the early playing card makers followed the English type. Court cards still resemble those of pre-Revolutionary War days.

It is extremely probable that James Franklin, older brother of Benjamin, printed playing cards about 1720. Benjamin himself cut discs from playing cards for his experiments with electricity. Amos Whitney manufactured playing cards in 1799, and Joseph Ford, nephew of Jazaniah Ford, card maker of Milton, operated the factory after 1832. The Whitney ace of spades was particularly interesting, showing in a medallion the early official eagle of Paul Revere and Samuel Hill. Across the top was the New England saying 'Use but Don't Abuse Me'. Other typical spade aces included an eagle hovering over a ribbon of stars. Among other early playing card makers or manufacturers were Jazaniah Ford of Milton, Massachusetts, and Thomas Crehore (Plate 171 top left) of Dorchester, Massachusetts. They made cards from about the end of the eighteenth century to 1832. Among the best-known cards by Ford were two commemorative decks, one in honor of Decatur (Plate 171 top right) and his victory at Tripoli, the other honoring the visit of Lafayette to America in 1824. In New York early designers and makers of playing cards were Dr Alexander Anderson, John Casenave and David Felt, a stationer. In 1832 L.I. Cohen (Plate 171 lower left) began to make playing cards, and in 1833 invented a machine for printing four colors in one impression; the process was kept secret for twelve years, and it revolutionized the manufacture of cards. Cohen made some very fine pasteboards, particularly in ivory finish, and these cards sold for as much as fifty cents or more a pack (Plate 171 lower left). He retired in 1854, leaving the business to his son and his nephew, under the firm name of Lawrence & Cohen. This company issued double-faced cards, which were a novelty in the United States. A little later, they produced a deck of cards with an index in each corner of the card, called 'squeezers'. Previously no identifications appeared on American cards. In 1871 Lawrence & Cohen united with Samuel Hart and Isaac Levy to form a corporation called the New York Consolidated Card Company. Hart (Plate 172 top right) had offices in Philadelphia as early as 1849 and made cards, some of which were very attractive, especially the ace of spades showing George and Martha Washington. He originated the round corner deck in America, a form which soon found favor. Also issued by him was a joker, which has been adopted almost universally. In 1848, Andrew Dougherty started as a card manufacturer in New York. The early issues were poor compared with Hart & Levy's, but soon there were marked improvements and Dougherty cards became popular. In 1875 Dougherty issued indexed cards under the name of *Triplicate*, with a special ace of spades. Cards for Mexican export, with the typical Spanish suits, were produced in 1849. About 1880 the New York Consolidated Card Company began to make cards with some interesting backs, showing portraits of Mary Anderson, the actress, and President Garfield. They also made a very fine and unusual deck at the time of the Paris Exhibition in 1900, showing sovereigns of Europe on the court cards.

In 1881 Russell, Morgan & Company was organized. The name of the company was changed to United States Printing Company and, in 1894, to United States Playing Card Company. This became the largest maker of playing cards in the world.

For several centuries playing card makers have tried to find a magic formula to sell their products. Unusual novelty cards made their appearance in historic (Plates 172 top left, top right, lower left), political, educational and so-called 'transformation' decks (Plate 172 lower right). Subjects were drawn from military or naval actions, as in the War with Tripoli (1811); portraits of Civil War generals and admirals (1865); portraits of famous authors (1870); characters from Dickens (1870); baseball (1870–88 and later); musical composers (1880); Goethe (1870); *Uncle Tom's Cabin* (1860); *Dr Busby and Yankee Trader* (1850); warships (1899); animals (1890); Tarot (1920); and a host of others.

The playing card manufacturers have capitalized on the popularity of figures in the limelight by issuing decks of cards showing actors and actresses. Some of these are very attractive, colored with gilt and illustrated with portraits of De Wolf Hopper, Julia Marlowe, Wilton Lackaye (1895), Charlie Chaplin and William S. Hart (1920). When Jim Jeffries was heavyweight boxing champion of the world, the story has it that he had a deck of cards made up for him showing scenes of his fights, also other fighters on the front of the cards and his picture on the back. These decks were reportedly given to his friends as souvenirs.

An attempt to change public taste came with the round card, especially the round deck by the Globe Playing Card Company in 1874. Round cards had been made as early as 1850 but despite efforts to popularize them they were not successful. As stated earlier, American court cards have followed the English style. There have been numerous attempts to change this and to introduce more modern faces and types. These efforts have consistently failed, though the cards produced thereby are attractive collector's items, such as the Fan-C-Pak in pastel colors; modernistic court cards; concave cards (about 1930);

New Era (1906); *Circus* (1905). The Wiehl deck (1850), a beautiful deck with German-type court cards, was probably for use in Pennsylvania and the German section of New York (Plate 171 lower right). An unusual deck appearing about 1920 shows court cards resembling those of Iceland, while on the back is a black cat. Using different colors for the four suits has also been tried, but did not become popular.

One of the most unusual types is the 'transformation'. This incorporates the pips or markings into a pictorial design on the face of each card. Lowerre in 1876, Hart in 1850, Tiffany in 1876 (Plate 172 lower right), all made interesting transformation decks with humorous figures or caricatures. The United States Playing Card Company issued the *Vanity Fair* and *Hustling Joe* decks. The tobacco companies took advantage of playing cards as an advertising medium and put out three packs of transformation cards, two in miniature size and one in the regular size. One was placed in each container of cigarettes by the Kinney Tobacco Company, while the larger cards were given as a premium. In addition, this company issued a miniature deck of transparent cards – when the cards were held up to the light, a picture appeared. A manufacturer of transparent cards was the Transparent Playing Card Company (1860). These cards come in the usual size, but the ace of spades, the joker and the court cards are not transparent. The tobacco industry issued some of the most sought-after cards. The Duke Company had a miniature deck with double lions on the back, which is sought by collectors. Lorillard put playing cards into packs of snuff and 5c *Ante* tobacco. Other companies such as Moore and Calvi, Maclin-Zimmer and Cullingworth produced almost a dozen decks of playing cards portraying the buxom beauties of the Mauve Decade. Snipe and Kid Cut Plug tobacco also were responsible for an interesting deck of beauties. Caffee in 1888 sold a presidential deck of cards, picturing the candidates in that year's national election.

Especially interesting are the war decks. The Decatur-Tripoli War deck shows Algerian costumes (Plate 171 top right). During the

Civil War no fewer than six different decks were brought out, with the court cards showing military figures. Anheuser-Busch Brewing Company issued a fine deck with its advertisement on the back, a picture of the brewery on the front of the ordinary cards, and national heroes of the Spanish-American War on the court cards. The 27th Division of the United States Army produced an odd pack during World War I, with the courts bearing caricatures of army officers.

Two groups of playing cards are collected avidly. These commemorate the international expositions or are views of scenery. At each exposition packs were sold illustrating the buildings and special exhibits. These include the Columbian (1893); Louisiana Purchase (1904); Pan-American (1901); Century of Progress Exposition at Chicago (1934); and the New York World's Fair (1939). Among the scenic packs are the railroad company issues showing scenes along their right of way. There are views of many states and cities all over America on special decks advertising particular areas.

Collections of card backs numbering well over 25,000 are not uncommon and have many interesting facets. Values of playing cards of all types depend primarily on the age and completeness of the pack. Strangely enough they do not command high prices and seldom bring more than a dollar or two. While unusual decks may sell for as much as twenty-five dollars, they seldom bring more than this sum. Their endless variety seems unlimited, even to the inveterate collector.

BOOKS FOR
FURTHER READING

Taylor, Rev. Ed. S.: *The History of Playing Cards*, John Camden Hotten, London (1865).

Van Rensslaer, Mrs John King: *A History of Playing Cards*, Dodd, Mead & Company, New York (1890).

Concise Encyclopedia of Antiques, Vol, III, pp. 201-204, Hawthorn Books, New York (1957).

MINOR ARTS: QUILLWORK, TREEN, CHALKWARE

By EDITH GAINES

Quillwork or paper filigree: this is made of paper strips about an eighth of an inch wide, fluted, twisted, or rolled into tight little scrolls which are then arranged in designs closely resembling mosaic work. Colored paper is used, or white may be painted or gilded at the edge; when gilding is used the effect is that of gold filigree; sometimes motifs are outlined in silver wire, and the work resembles silver filigree. The flutes and scrolls are pasted by one edge to a background of paper, silk or wood, and are combined with other substances to form elaborate designs.

According to Webster, the noun 'quillwork' is properly applied only to the 'ornamentation of skins, bark or fabrics, by overlaying with porcupine quills ... a highly developed art among some tribes of North American Indians'. The term is used to describe this type of paper work only in America; in England the same decorative device is known as paper filigree or rolled paper work. The American 'quillwork' may have been derived from another form of the word: quilling, says Webster, is 'a strip of lace, ribbon, or the like, fluted or folded, so as to somewhat resemble a row of quills; also, one of the folds or flutings so made'. Such flutings are found in American rolled paper work, and the name may have been applied to them rather than to the cone-shape spirals that also form part of these designs. It does seem to have been applied to this type of work fairly early; Benjamin Burt (Boston, 1729–1805) left to his niece 'a sconce of quill work wrought by her aunt'. 'Filigree' has

also been used in America to describe it, however. On the back of one of a pair of quillwork sconces offered at the Bigelow sale in 1924 was written 'Mr George Curwen has a similar specimen of filigree work made by Sarah Pickman, born in Salem December 1st, 1718, married George Curwen November 18, 1738, died June 2nd, 1810'. Dow (*The Arts & Crafts in New England, 1704–1775*, pp. 288–9) quotes an advertisement in the Boston *Evening Post* for February 15, 1748, which was repeated with minor variations until May 26, 1755: 'This may inform Young Gentlewomen ... that ... Mrs Hiller designs to open a Boarding-School ... where they may be taught wax work, Transparent and Filligree, Painting upon Glass, Japanning, Quill-Work, Feather-Work and Embroidering with Gold and Silver ...' If what Mrs Hiller taught was rolled paper work it is still not clear whether she called it 'Quill-Work' or 'Filligree'.

Paper filigree was used to decorate religious figures in England in the fifteenth and sixteenth centuries; its use was discontinued during the Reformation, and revived in the second half of the seventeenth century. It became popular as a pastime for ladies during the eighteenth century, and most specimens found today date from that period. Mrs Delany (Mary Granville) mentions 'paper mosaic' in many of her letters, and some authorities have assumed that she was referring to rolled paper work; however, a careful reading of contemporary descriptions of her work makes it clear that her paper mosaics were actually quite different from paper filigree. 'In the progress of her work, she pulls the [real] flower in pieces, examines anatomically the structure of its leaves, stems and buds; and having cut her papers to the shape of the several parts, she puts them together, giving them a richness and consistence, by laying one piece over another, and often a transparent piece over part of a shade, which softens it.' (*Observations relating to Picturesque Beauty in the Highlands of Scotland*, Vol. II, p. 190, quoted in *Mrs Delany's Letters*, 3rd ed., London, 1821.)

In Europe, paper filigree was used to decorate a wide variety of objects – picture and mirror frames, panels for pole screens, tea caddies, boxes and even an entire cabinet. Portraits, coats-of-arms and other pictures were created from the cleverly manipulated bits of paper. It was used in conjunction with metal threads and beads, shells, seeds, needlework, waxwork, printed or painted medallions and paintings on fabric. In America some of these were also used, but almost the only form of rolled paper work that has survived is the sconce. A coat-of-arms in the Metropolitan Museum of Art resembles European work in that it is formed of rolls of paper solidly grouped ('honeycombed', as it was described by Joseph Downs in the Museum's *Bulletin* for December 1938) to form the major part of the design, but the sconces are more loosely assembled. Known examples are so closely similar in design as to suggest at least a common model. They include waxwork, silver and copper wire, shells, beads, silk thread, feathers and a heavy sprinkling of mica to make the whole sparkle when the candles were lighted. The sconces are all glazed, and have frames of the types made for mirrors, some quite simple and others with a crudely cut cresting. Some have sockets at the base for S-shape candle arms. Winterthur Museum has a pair with the original silver candle branches by Jacob Hurd (Boston, 1702–58), and a pair in the Cooper Union Museum still have original candle branches. All seem to have been made in New England in the period between 1720 and 1740, a date supported by the style of the frames and candle branches as well as by such scanty documentation as exists.

Treen: small objects of wood once in common domestic or farm use, American treen is more elementary in design and execution than its European counterpart, which is often elaborately decorated and may even be mounted in metal. In this country molds and wall boxes were carved in ornamental designs, but among tablewares even such slight embellishment as that on the Sumner spoon (Plate 175c) is rare. For its appeal old American woodenware must rely on beauty of shape or material, or perhaps even more on its significance as a survival from the daily lives of past generations.

Treen (the word means 'made of tree') is almost impossible to date. At the time of its most widespread use its manufacture was a home affair, almost none of it carries identifying marks, and except for the lightness and smoothness which come with age and wear, there is no sure way to distinguish between a wooden utensil made by hand late in the nineteenth century and one that has survived since the eighteenth. The earliest forms were also the simplest, and the shapes of wooden utensils whittled, turned or gouged in the late nineteenth century in remote country regions or in the west are much the same as those in use two centuries earlier.

It is also difficult in many instances to identify aged woods. Vessels which have been used for storing or serving oils, fruits, milk or milk products, spices and syrups over any length of time will be discolored by these substances; and while such stains may help in determining the use to which a particular utensil has been put, they add to the difficulty of identifying the wood. The only sure method is microscopic examination.

Maple was the wood most frequently used, though treen made of pine, birch, ash, oak, beech, hickory, black walnut, cedar, poplar and basswood is also found. One wood that can always be identified is *lignum vitae*, a West Indian species producing particularly handsome pieces because of the contrast in color between its sapwood, which is light, and its dark heartwood. Even when an object is made entirely of the light sapwood it is impossible to mistake *lignum vitae* for anything else because of its weight: it is so heavy that it sinks in water. This density also adds to its desirability as a material for wooden wares, since it will not split (it is used today for ships' pulleys, mallets and other wooden objects that must withstand severe strains).

Another material valued for both beauty and resistance to splitting is the burl. A burl (or 'burr') is a sort of wart or growth on some trees, in which the grain, instead of running straight up and down, is twisted and turned in such a way as to strengthen the wood greatly. This eccentricity of the grain also makes burl wood highly ornamental. The beautiful Scottish mazers (ceremonial drinking vessels) are made of it. In America it was used mostly for bowls and mortars.

Farm, dairy and kitchen equipment such as the pieces shown in Plate 175A is much collected in America, but the most popular as well as the most attractive form of treen is table ware. For many years after the settlement of the colonies wood was the usual material for such utensils; it was everywhere available, easy to shape into the desired form, and simple to replace when it wore out.

Trenchers (wooden plates or platters) were used from the earliest days until (in backward areas and on the frontier) fairly late in the last century. The name apparently derives from a meaning, now obsolete, of the verb to trench: to carve or cut up. Trenchers made in America were usually either round or oval; square ones were used in England until the sixteenth century, when the round shape was introduced. Myles Standish left twelve trenchers among his household gear when he died, reflecting what was for his day a lavish way of life; one trencher for every two persons was considered adequate. A Connecticut deacon who owned a turning mill was accused of vanity because he provided each of his children with a separate trencher. Husbands and wives or two children commonly shared one, and a couple might announce a betrothal by eating from the same trencher.

Bowls – made of burl (Plate 175B) whenever possible – are often quite handsome pieces; some have covers with ornamental finials. They are round or oval, and sizes vary a good deal, from large ones intended for serving to small individual eating dishes.

Tankards are usually simple affairs constructed of hooped staves with a cover; sometimes there is a hole in the cover through which a heated toddy stick could be thrust. Another type of drinking vessel, the noggin, was carved all in one piece – body, spout and handle. Noggins look very much like pitchers, and were probably used as such in the larger sizes. The piggin (Plate 175A), a sort of bucket with one stave left long and sometimes slightly shaped for a handle, was also used as a drinking vessel in the smaller sizes.

Wooden salt bowls were very commonly used, and standing salts made for the more prosperous households are sometimes quite elaborate. Another form of treen to which a good deal of skill was devoted is the pounce box (pounce, a contraction of 'pumice', was the name given to a fine black sand sprinkled on wet ink to dry it); these are rare and highly desirable collectibles.

Mortars, like bowls, vary greatly in size and beauty. Crudely made examples up to three feet in height were used for pounding grain; eight or nine inches is the usual height for those designed for ordinary household use; and mortars for herbs and drugs may be no more than three inches high. *Lignum vitae* was a popular wood for the better specimens, and some very handsome ones survive. Matching pestles were sometimes made, but these were easily lost and few can be found today.

Wooden boxes served many purposes. These exist in many sizes and are round or oval in shape, painted or unpainted. Perhaps the most sought after are the nests of boxes (of maple with pine tops and bottoms) made by the Shakers, like all their products fine in design and meticulously made. Copper nails were used in all their boxes, and the method of lapping and joining the staves is particularly skilful.

Wall boxes for spoons, candles, spices, salt, pipes, knife cleaning and other uses are frequently found in attractive forms. Most American examples are quite simple and appeal by their graceful outlines, though the type of geometric carving called Frisian is known to exist on native specimens. More elaborate carving usually indicates a Euro-pean origin. Some Pennsylvania-German boxes have the bird, flower and animal motifs of that region painted on, cut out or inlaid.

Other examples of Pennsylvania-German decoration are found among the molds for butter, cheese, cake or cookies. These molds and examples from New England and else-where are the most purely decorative items in treenware to be found today. The earliest butter molds are crudely carved discs without handles, with designs similar to those found on Pennsylvania and Connecticut chests. During the first quarter of the nineteenth century hand-cut handles were added, and by mid-century these were turned on lathes. Later molds were completely factory-made.

Cake molds were often brought to America by families coming from Germany or Switzer-land. Purely American in origin, however, are such topical molds as the one celebrating Andrew Jackson's victory over the English at New Orleans in 1815; and there can be little doubt about the mahogany mold found in New York State with an Indian chief carved on one side and a papoose on the other.

Treenware should be kept clean, waxed, at a cool temperature and free from wood-worms. Light surface dirt can be removed with any good cleaning wax polish; water and a mild soap are safe if no animal glue has been used for repairs.

Chalkware: this name is commonly given in America to mantel ornaments made of plaster of Paris in imitation of the more expensive pottery and porcelain figures so popular in the eighteenth and nineteenth centuries. Questions have been raised as to the origin of this term for plaster images, but the simplest explanation is probably the true one: they look like chalk. In *The Adventures of Huckleberry Finn*, Mark Twain has Huck say, describing Colonel Grangerford's parlor, 'Well, there was a big outlandish parrot on each side of the clock, made out of something like chalk, and painted up gaudy', and any-one who has seen a chalkware parrot will agree that the description is apt. The gilding and coloring – mostly strong primary colors,

black, and brown – on surviving pieces has faded a good deal, but it must have been gaudy indeed when they were new.

For many years it was believed that these ornaments were made by the Pennsylvania Germans, partly because they were found in greatest quantity in that area and partly because of their naïveté and gay coloring. However, research indicates that they were first imported from Europe and then made throughout this country. Apparently Henry Christian Geyer of Boston was the first to advertise plaster figures made here, though earlier mention can be found of imported ones. Geyer advertised in the *Boston News-Letter* in 1768, and again in 1770, that 'be-sides carrying on the Stone Cutting Business as usual, he carries on the Art and Manu-factory of a fuser Simolacrorum, or the making of all sorts of images, viz. ... Kings & Queens. ... Likewise a Number of Busts, among which are, Mathew Prior, Homer, Milton, &c. – also a number of Animals, such as Parrots, Cats, Dogs, Lions, Sheep, with a number of others, too many to enumerate. ... All the above-mentioned Images, Animals, &c. are made of Plaister of Paris of this Country Produce. ... N.B. All Merchants, Masters of Vessels, Country Traders, Shop-keepers, &c. may be supplied with what Quantity of Figures they may have occasion for by giving timely Notice to said Geyer.' (Dow, *Arts & Crafts in New England, 1704–1775*, 1927, pp. 284–5.)

Collectors of chalkware will note many familiar items in Geyer's listing. Molds were made from existing figures, so the continuity of models is not surprising. Practically all extant chalkware is believed to date from the period from 1850 to 1890, but sketches of a plaster parrot and cat in William Hone's *Every-Day Book* (vol. II, pp. 310–15), publish-ed in London in 1829 and illustrating plaster figures sold in Hone's youth, might have been drawn from models to be found in any collection today. He does not show a picture of the familiar single orange with leaves (Plate 176A), but his description of it is clear: '... an "image" of a "fine bowpot", consisting of half a dozen green shapes like halbert tops for "make believe" leaves, spreading like a half opened fan, from a knot ... delicately concealed by a tawny coloured ball called an orange, which pretended to rest on a clumsy clump of yellowed plaster as on the mouth of a jar. ...'

Early in the nineteenth century peddlers were selling the plaster busts and figures on the streets of London and New York. *Cries of New York* (1812) describes the 'image vendor' thus: 'This man ... strives to please, by presenting a variety of images, or representations of animals, which he carries around to sell. ... They are made of plaster of Paris, which is a kind of stone that abounds at Nova Scotia.' (Nova Scotia is an important source of gypsum, the raw material of plaster of Paris.) And William Hone, in the work cited above, says that 'Buy my images!' or 'Pye m'imaitches!' was a familiar cry in the London of his youth as well as of the time (1827) when he was writing, 'by Italian lads carrying boards on their heads'.

It seems clear that most of the trade in chalkware was handled by Italians, here as well as abroad. *City Cries, or a Peep at Scenes in Town* (anonymous, Philadelphia, 1851) tells us: 'The itinerant seller of plaster casts is a regular street figure in all our great cities. By means of a few worn-out molds which he has brought from Italy, the poor man makes a stock of casts, and mounting them on a board, cries them about the streets. ... When he has followed this street traffic for a few years, he has amassed money enough to begin business on a larger scale; and accordingly he hires a shop, and commences the making and selling of all sorts of plaster casts. ... Instead of carrying a small shop on his head through the streets, he now sends forth a little army of his compatriots, poor expatriated Romans or Tuscans, regretting the glorious skies of Italy, while they are selling busts of the glorious heroes of America.' Nineteenth-century literature also gives us a glimpse of a member of the 'little army', operating in the territory where so many pieces of chalkware have been found: 'In the dusk of evening a loud rapping was heard at the front door ... the lady of the house on opening it nearly swooned away in terror on beholding before her ... a giant form nine feet

high. Her shrieks brought out her husband, who, on a closer examination, found it to be an Italian image seller with his wares on his head looking for a night's lodging' (William J. Buck, *Local Sketches & Legends of Bucks and Montgomery Counties, Pa.*, 1887).

The making of plaster images has been described as a folk art, but as the anonymous Philadelphia observer and even Geyer's advertisement make clear, it was mainly a commercial operation. Edwin T. Freedley (*Philadelphia & Its Manufactures*, 1858) also reports: 'Of Calcined Plaster (Plaster of Paris, we call it today) about 16,000 barrels are made yearly and consumed principally in Stucco work, architectural decorations, and in the manufacture of figurines, in which a large business is done by Italians.'

The process of manufacture was a fairly simple one. The molds were also made of plaster of Paris, which is sometimes called 'potter's stone' because it was, and is, used in much the same way in the manufacture of pottery and porcelain pieces. It was also used for making molds for wax images. One of the earliest 'how to' books, *Art Recreations* (E. J. Tilton & Company, Boston, 1860), gives minute instructions for making plaster of Paris molds to be used for plaster of Paris figures or wax ornaments. Since the method of making the mold was the same for both these substances, there may be some question as to the use for which surviving molds were intended, except in instances where the object is known to have been produced in only one.

Molds (Plate 176D) were made in two or more parts (depending on the intricacy of the model) from existing images or from real pieces of fruit, nuts and so on. When the mold was completed the parts were securely fastened together and plaster of 'the consistency of batter for cakes' was introduced and swirled rapidly around until it had hardened in a thin layer on the oiled inner surfaces of the mold. This is why most old chalkware pieces are so surprisingly light for their size. Some were filled with a cheaper type of plaster after being finished, to give them weight.

Chalkware was never glazed. The earliest pieces were sized and colored with oil paints; later, water colors were used. The coloring was always done by hand, so that there are variations even in two images forming a pair. (Almost everything came in pairs, with animals, birds, or people facing in opposite directions.) Coloring was sometimes done on only one side.

Much of the appeal of chalkware lies in its variety. Most familiar are the animals and birds – cats, dogs, roosters, sheep, goats (Plate 176B), single birds and pairs joined at the beak (Plate 176c), rabbits, deer reminiscent of Bennington as well as of saltglaze and later English models. There are squirrels with nuts, and cats with mice. Fruit occurs in single pieces, in groups, and arranged in pyramids atop large urns, sometimes with space for a watch in the center. Watch holders were made in many other forms as well, including that of rectangular mantel clocks. There are busts of popular heroes, and portraits complete with plaster frames tinted to look like walnut. Cottages and churches may have candle-holders inside and glass windows for the light to shine through.

Sources of the chalkware designs were many. The most obvious are the Staffordshire mantel ornaments from which many were copied and which probably provided molds for some. At least one model, the Bloomer girl, has been traced to a Currier & Ives print. There are a good number of religious subjects: ornaments in the form of niches survive, in some instances in the original design, and in others secularized by the substitution of a child, a bird or an animal in the space intended for a religious figure: Some of the larger groups – the urns with fruit, for example – may have been made for altar decorations; and, whatever use they may have been intended for, it is possible to assemble charming crèche groups of angels, lambs and babies in cradles.

BOOKS FOR FURTHER READING

Quillwork:

EDWARDS, RALPH: 'Filigree Paper Decoration', *Dictionary of English Furniture*, Vol. II (1954).

MORSE, FRANCES CLARY: *Furniture of the Olden Time* (1917).

NUTTING, WALLACE: *Furniture of the Pilgrim Century* (1924).

ROTHERY, GUY CADOGAN: 'Rolled Paper Work', *Antiques*, July 1929.

Treen:

BOICOURT, JANE: 'American Woodenware', *Antiques*, December 1951.

EARLE, ALICE MORSE: *Home Life in Colonial Days* (1922).

GOULD, MARY EARLE: *Early American Wooden Ware* (1942).

HYNSON, GARRET and NASH, SUSAN HIGGINSON: 'Design in Yankee Butter Molds', *Antiques*, February 1942.

MINER, EDITH: 'When Treen Ware Was "The" Ware', *Antiques*, December 1930.

PINTO, E. H.: *Treen or Small Woodware* (1949).

Chalkware:

ALLIS, MARY: 'The Last of the American Folk Arts', *American Collector*, January 1941.

HOMMEL, RUDOLF: 'Chalk Figures', *Hobbies*, November 1949.

McCLINTON, KATHARINE MORRISON: *Antique Collecting for Everyone* (1951).

SWORDS

By HAROLD L. PETERSON

Sword collecting has only recently become a popular hobby in America. Twenty-five years ago there were fewer than twenty serious students and collectors, and very little was known about the swords made or used in this country. The intervening years, however, have seen this situation change radically as increased knowledge has led to a wider appreciation and understanding of the sword as a weapon, a work of art, or an historical relic.

THE COLONIAL PERIOD AND THE REVOLUTION

Little is known about the early manufacture of swords in America. They may have been made or at least assembled here by 1650, but there are no surviving specimens of that age and no documentary proof that such was the case. The earliest American-made swords and documents relating to sword manufacture in this country date from the beginning of the eighteenth century. At that time almost all blades seem to have been imported, with only the hilts and scabbards being made here. During the Revolution blades of necessity were made in America, but even then a large portion of them were imported, principally from the Solingen area of Germany and from France.

Except for the silversmiths who also made sword hilts, only a few of America's eighteenth-century sword makers are known by name. Of these the most important were James Potter and John Bailey (Plate 179C) of New York City, Lewis Prahl of Philadelphia, and James Hunter who operated the Rappahannock Forge in Virginia. All of these men ex-cept Bailey made complete swords in quantity both for the Continental Army and for private individuals. Potter's and Prahl's swords are well known, but interestingly enough none of Hunter's has yet been identified. Bailey was a cutler and silversmith who specialized in hunting swords of quality. George Washington wore one of Bailey's swords through most of the Revolution.

The principal types of swords manufactured in America during the eighteenth century were the heavy saber, the cutlass, the hunting sword and the small sword. All were based on British patterns. Among these the sabers afford the greatest variety. Mounted in either brass or iron, some had the simplest of stirrup hilts with only a flat cap pommel, while others had more elaborate guards fashioned with additional bars or cut from a sheet of metal and pierced for decorative effects. There was also a variety of pommels: spheres, mushrooms, cones, ovoids, and the sculptured heads of birds, lions and dogs. These bird and animal heads offer most interesting examples of 'primitive' art, both in the modeling and in the engraving of the subjects. Interestingly, the head of the British lion was the most popular of these pommels, and it was made and used right through the Revolution and until the opening years of the nineteenth century. American hunting swords also frequently made use of these sculptured pommels. Almost all hunting swords and small swords hilted in America, however, were mounted in silver, and the workmanship on them is usually much more refined though the sculpture itself is still apt to be 'primitive' (Plate 179A, B, C, D).

SWORDS OF THE UNITED STATES

For students and collectors of swords made after the Revolution the situation is strikingly different from the earlier period. During the colonial period many civilians had worn swords but, except for diplomats, that practice had ceased, and the collector is forced to concentrate on military or naval swords. There is a greater profusion of types and styles and many more specimens to choose from, and there is a more obvious separation between enlisted men's and officers' weapons than there had been before.

Some swords continued to be made in America, but no real sword industry ever developed here. What activity there was centered around two great names: Nathan Starr of Middletown, Connecticut, and the Ames Manufacturing Company of Massachusetts. Nathan Starr made the first official swords for the new United States government, the 1798 cavalry sabers (Plate 177A), and he continued to make most of the enlisted men's swords for both the army and navy until 1830. He also produced a few officer's swords and presentation pieces. The Ames brothers, Nathan P. and James T., took over most government contracts after Starr, and it was they who developed the only real large-scale sword manufactory in American history. Their first contract was for a foot artillery sword, copied from the French in the pseudo-Roman form, in 1832 (Plate 177B). Thereafter they continued to make the great bulk of all enlisted men's swords and almost all officers' swords that were manufactured in America before 1900. Although the Ames Company jobbed out some of its work in the very first years, it was soon equipped to do all of the work necessary in the production of a finished sword from the first forging of the blade through the final etching and the fabrication of the scabbard.

While some officers' swords were manufactured in America, the great majority were imported from Europe. Most often they were produced by the famous German swordsmiths of Solingen, but some also came from France, Great Britain and Belgium. These complete swords or sometimes just the blades were usually imported, mounted if necessary by American smiths and then sold by various firms which dealt in the military field. By 1830 two large companies began to handle the bulk of all such trade. These were W. H. Horstmann and Son of Philadelphia and Schuyler Hartley and Graham of New York. Well over half the officers' swords made or sold in the United States after 1830 bore either the Ames mark or the name of one or the other of these concerns. Some enlisted men's swords were also imported directly by the government, particularly during the 1840's and again during the Civil War.

Because of the obvious division between the swords of enlisted men and those of officers, some collectors tend to specialize in one or the other field. Each has its own fascination. The appeal of the enlisted men's swords lies in the fact that they were fighting weapons. Never mere gilded gewgaws fabricated to please an individual's fancy or to indicate a specific rank, these swords were designed for use. The workmanship on them is seldom fine, and sometimes it is crude; but the honesty of purpose behind the strong simple lines creates a character that is lacking in many of the more sophisticated and often more decadent types. Officers' swords, on the other hand, offer far greater variety. At one end of the scale there are officers' swords possessing the same useful and efficient appearance that is characteristic of the enlisted men's swords and enhanced by fine workmanship and esthetic decoration. At the other end are mere trinkets designed for ornamental purposes only.

There are two principal reasons for this great variety among officers' swords. First, there were a sizeable number of ranks, branches and arms of service to be indicated by the sword. Second, and perhaps more important, the patterns for officers' swords for many years were not nearly so rigidly controlled as those for enlisted men. Underlying this lack of control was the fact that officers had to purchase their swords from outside the government. Thus their choice could only be directed through the passing of regulations, some of which were vaguely worded, or controlled only portions of the sword's appearance, so that any one of a number of different swords could qualify under them. Also, there was a tendency among many officers to ignore the regulations and carry a sword of their own choice. This was particularly true of state troops even when serving with regular forces in time of war.

ENLISTED MEN'S SWORDS

American enlisted men's swords of the nineteenth century were influenced largely by those of Great Britain and France. From 1798 until 1840 American cavalry sabers were patterned after British designs. In 1840 a copy of the French light cavalry saber of 1822 was adopted and, with a slight modification at the outbreak of the Civil War, it served for the next seventy-five years (Plate 177D). It was replaced in 1913 by the last official cavalry sword, which was designed by General George S. Patton, Jr., but owed some of its inspiration to British experimentation. In the infantry, only the non-commissioned officers carried swords. Prior to 1840 these were produced under a series of small contracts, and resembled each other only in that they were almost always iron-mounted. In 1840, however, a brass-hilted model was adopted which was based primarily upon types used in the French army but was also reminiscent of some British models (Plate 177E). This sword remained standard until non-commissioned officers ceased wearing swords at the beginning of World War I.

Standardization came to the artillery slightly sooner than to the cavalry and infantry. At first the artillery had carried the same sword as the infantry, though they preferred brass to iron hilts because yellow was the distinctive artillery metal color. In 1832, however, the War Department let contracts for a new and unique sword for the foot artillery. It was a short sword of supposed Roman pattern and was copied from one used in France. The light artillery had originally used cavalry sabers, but in 1840, they received a special saber also based on a French pattern (Plate 177C). Both of these artillery swords continued in use for about fifty years until the enlisted men of the artillery ceased to wear swords.

The Navy, like the Army, started with cutlasses of a British pattern, mounted in iron, but eventually changed to a French type in 1860 (Plate 177F). In the meantime, they had developed a form all their own with the model 1841 which was a clumsy double-edged weapon adapted from the foot artillery sword.

These were the principal types of enlisted men's swords. There were others, those carried by the Marines, by musicians and other small units, but all followed the same general pattern in achieving uniformity.

OFFICERS' SWORDS

Among officers' swords, the study divides itself roughly into two periods with 1840 as the approximate dividing line. Prior to 1840 the regulations were loosely worded, usually specifying only the color of the mountings, the length and general form of the blade. Infantry and cavalry officers were to have swords with white mountings, that is, silver or silver-plated. Artillery, engineer, staff, rifle, and Navy and Marine officers were to have yellow-mounted swords, in other words either brass or gilt hilts and scabbard fittings. Except for cavalry and some mounted officers, blades were usually curved before 1821 and straight afterwards.

This left the individual officer considerable room to gratify his personal tastes, and apparently he did just that. The most popular form of pommel was the eagle head (Plates 178A, 178B), and these came in hundreds of variations. There were also simple convex pommels and some urns. Guards might be simple or covered with lavish cast decorations, and there might also be counter-guards or langets attached to the quillons on the obverse side bearing further decorations of eagles or figures drawn from classical mythology. Up until the middle 1820s the blades were usually blued for about half their length and ornamented with sprays of foliage, military trophies, patriotic symbols and mottoes, and quantities of stars which apparently bore no relation to the number of states in the Union at the time of the sword's manufacture. During the 1820s panels of bright silver etching began to appear in the midst of the blued areas, and by 1830 the new bright etching became almost universally used for the entire blade. Some blades decorated in the older blue and gilt manner continued to be made until 1840, but that date marks just about the end of the practice. During the 1830s and 1840s the etching was lightly done. After 1850 it became deep, and after 1860 the background areas were frequently frosted or gilded.

The beginnings of standardization for officers' swords came as early as 1832, but it was a slow process, taking effect more rapidly in the smaller branches and staff units. By 1840 all branches had their own specific swords and no others were permitted. Except for the general and staff officers, who had adopted a British pattern sword in 1832, most of the models of 1840 were copied from the French. In 1850 there was further standardization when one sword, again based on a French model, was adopted for all foot officers of infantry, artillery and riflemen, and another for all staff and field-grade officers of those units (Plate 178E). In 1860 a light and worthless sword was adopted for staff and field-grade officers (Plate 178F), but was made optional until 1872, when it became mandatory for almost all officers. Despite the protests of many officers that it was useless as a weapon, this sword remained official until it was superseded by a better weapon in 1902, this time for all officers except cavalry. In this way the officers' swords of the Army gradually changed from a confusion of many different types to specific models for each branch of service, and finally to one pattern for all.

The swords of Navy and Marine officers, though controlled by a jurisdiction separate from those of the Army, followed the same general pattern. A standard naval sword for all officers was adopted in 1841 (Plate 178D), and in 1852 it was succeeded by a sword resembling the Army foot officers' sword, and this is still the regulation naval sword today. The Marines adopted their official sword earlier than any other branch or arm of the service. In 1826 they decided on a form of saber with a mameluke hilt to commemorate their activities in North Africa during the Tripolitanian War. During the Civil War the Marines, too, adopted the same swords as the Army, but in 1875 they returned to their distinctive sword, and they still use it today.

PRESENTATION SWORDS

The history of American presentation swords begins with the Revolution, for while that conflict was still in progress the Continental Congress voted that swords should be presented to a number of the officers in recognition of their services to the United States. Thereafter numerous states, cities, towns and organizations joined with the Federal Government in following this traditional practice until it gradually went out of style after World War I.

The student of design finds much of interest in these presentation swords, for they reflect the contemporary tastes in decoration. The presentation swords of the Revolution (Plate 180A) were normally based upon the small sword and were beautifully and delicately ornamented by European artists. The War of 1812 brought a most interesting naval presentation type (Plate 180B) made in America and lacking some of the refinements of the European products. At the same time there were some very fine eagle-pommeled swords made on the order of New York State to present to Army and Navy officers (Plate 180C).

There were a few presentation swords associated with the Mexican War (Plate 180D), but the great deluge of such symbols of admiration came with the Civil War (Plate 180E). Reflecting the gaudy tastes of the times, these swords were massive, heavily ornamented parodies of the fighting blade. Some closely resembled the standard officers' models with heavy mountings of precious metals, often set with gems, while others were given massively sculptured grips in the figures of soldiers or sailors of the period, the goddess of Liberty, or other classical figures, and lost almost all resemblance to the standard swords.

Following the Civil War, the prescribed officers' swords once again began to dominate as models for the presentation swords. The baroque sculpture and decoration disappeared, and the eagle pommel occasionally was seen once more.

GLOSSARY

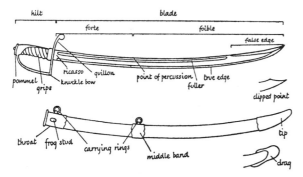

Fig. 1. Terminology of the sword

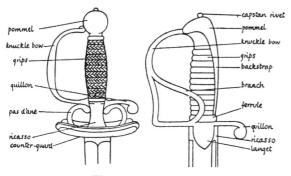

Fig. 2. Terminology of hilt

Colichemarde: *see* small sword.

Counter-guard: comprises those structures in addition to the quillons which are interposed between the hilt and the blade. It may take the form of a solid plate or a network of bars.

Cutlass: a short single-edged cutting sword. Usually it had a full hilt and a sturdy blade which might be either straight or curved. After about 1775 the term came to be applied almost exclusively to the seaman's weapon.

False edge: *see* saber.

Foible: the portion of the blade near the point which is weak from the standpoint of leverage. Usually it comprises from half to two-thirds of the length of the blade.

Forte: the strong portion of the blade, usually about one-third, nearest the hilt.

Frog: a sleeve-like device, normally of leather, used to attach the sword to the belt. Usually the scabbard was thrust through the sleeve and a stud on its throat engaged in a hole in the frog.

Hanger: a much misused term often applied indiscriminately to any short cutting sword not obviously a naval cutlass. Actually it applies more accurately to a hook and chain device used for hanging the sword from the belt during the eighteenth century.

Fig. 3. Sword hanger

Hunting sword: a short, light saber with a straight or very slightly curved blade and usually no knuckle-bow. Originally designed to be worn while hunting, as its name implies, it was often affected by high-ranking officers during the eighteenth century.

Fig. 4. Hunting sword

Obverse: the side toward the viewer when the sword is held in a horizontal position with the hilt to the left and the blade to the right with its edge down. The side away from the viewer is then the reverse.

Point of percussion: the point which divides the forte from the foible, the theoretical spot at which a blow should be struck to achieve its greatest force.

Quillon: one of the branches of the cross-guard of a sword.

Reverse: *see* obverse.

Saber: a sword with a single edge designed primarily for cutting. Usually there is also a short edge along the back near the point which is termed the false edge. Some saber blades are sharply curved and some are only slightly curved or absolutely straight. These straight or only slightly curved blades are frequently called cut-and-thrust blades.

Small sword: a light thrusting weapon popular both with civilians and the military. It developed in the third quarter of the seventeenth century and was widely used until about 1800. Small sword blades were at first double-edged, but after about 1700 a blade triangular in cross-section with three edges became almost universal. Some blades taper evenly from hilt to point; others had a heavy forte and narrowed suddenly to a slender foible. This latter form is often called a colichemarde today.

Fig. 6. Detail of small sword

Fig. 7. Colichemarde

Stirrup guard: a form of knuckle-bow which resembles half of a stirrup.

Tang: the narrow portion of the blade which passes into the hilt.

BOOKS FOR FURTHER READING

ALBAUGH, WILLIAM A.: *Confederate Arms*, Harrisburg, Pennsylvania (1957).

HICKS, JAMES E.: *Nathan Starr, Arms Maker, 1776–1845*, Mt Vernon, New York (1940).

HICKS, JAMES E.: *Notes on U.S. Ordnance*, Mt Vernon, New York (1940), 2 vols. Vol. II reprints some documents related to the purchase of swords during the early nineteenth century.

PETERSON, HAROLD L.: *American Silver-Mounted Swords, 1700–1815*, Washington (1955).

PETERSON, HAROLD L.: *The American Sword, 1775–1945*, New Hope, Pennsylvania (1954).

PETERSON, HAROLD L.: *Arms and Armor in Colonial America, 1526–1783*, Harrisburg, Pennsylvania (1956).

Concise Encyclopedia of Antiques, Vol. I, pp. 188–198. Hawthorn Books, New York (1955).

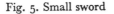

Fig. 5. Small sword

FIREARMS
1650-1865

By HAROLD L. PETERSON

Gun collecting is one of the most popular and certainly one of the most highly organized of collecting activities in the United States. Although gun collectors cannot compete in numbers with philatelists or numismatists, there are probably some 35,000 active collectors of antique firearms in the country today. Almost every state has its own gun collectors' organization; several states have more than one; and there are five national associations. The largest of these is the National Rifle Association, which includes collectors, hunters and marksmen in one organization of almost 300,000 members. Dealing in antique firearms is a large-scale business. Most large cities boast one or more such shops, and a huge bulk of the business is transacted by mail on the basis of published catalogues and lists.

The tendency of the usual collector is toward specialization. The more advanced his collection, the stricter the limits he sets so that he may one day hope to have a complete coverage of his chosen field. Most Americans are interested primarily in American arms, and they tend to place more emphasis on historical importance and mechanical ingenuity than on fine workmanship or beauty of design. The most popular specialties are Colt revolvers, U.S. martial arms, Confederate arms, percussion revolvers and, recently, Colonial and Revolutionary weapons.

THE COLONIAL PERIOD
AND THE REVOLUTION

The first guns used in America were all of European manufacture, and it was many years before a native gun-making industry was established. It is true that gunsmiths and armorers were among the earliest colonists. The remains of one such armorer's shop, which can be dated before 1625, has been excavated at Jamestown, and there are numerous references to them in colonial documents. But these men were occupied more with the repair and maintenance of existing arms than with the manufacture of new ones. It is not until the middle of the seventeenth century that there is definite evidence of a man, James Phips, making complete firearms in America. Not long after that, however, the industry began to take root, and by the beginning of the eighteenth century it was highly developed. Mostly these early American gunsmiths produced firearms to order for individual customers, and they concentrated largely on civilian arms, leaving the strictly military guns to be purchased abroad. Then, in 1748, Hugh Orr of Bridgewater, Massachusetts, contracted to supply the colony with five hundred muskets, and a large-scale arms industry was begun.

Since colonists came to America from many parts of western Europe, there were a number of different influences in the design of guns produced here. In the south and southwest, the Spanish influence was strong, with miquelet locks and characteristic Iberian styles of decoration. The Swedes made a brief appearance along the Delaware River but left nothing permanent. In the Hudson Valley the Dutch occupation was reflected in the heavy butts and raised carving on gun-stocks, the heavy cast brass mountings with deeply incised decorations and the ribbed ramrod thimbles. In this area developed the unique Hudson Valley long fowler (Plate 181A), popular from 1660 to 1770, noted for its extreme length (up to 8 feet) and its Dutch design which persisted well after the English conquered the colony.

In Pennsylvania the Dutch, German and Swiss colonists made a distinct contribution to American firearms with the development of the 'Kentucky', or Pennsylvania, rifle. These people had long used rifles in their native lands, as had most other Europeans, and they set out to adapt them to meet the needs of their new environment. They lengthened the barrel, decreased the caliber, and evolved a style of ornamentation that soon set these American rifles completely apart from their European predecessors. The evolution of the American rifle began early in the eighteenth century (Plate 181B), and its distinctive form was reached possibly by 1740–45. It was a fine, accurate gun in the hands of a man who knew how to use it, but it was slow to load and had no bayonet, so that it was not well adapted for the formal warfare of the period. The early rifles were simple, with straight lines and thick butts. The lavish inlays and sharply dropping butt did not develop until after 1790.

Although the French were active in Louisiana throughout most of the colonial period, their principal influence on American firearms is found in New England. Here, through more than half a century of intermittent warfare, the colonists became familiar with French arms, and they often copied French locks, decorative details such as trigger-guard finials, and also the graceful concave sweep of the underside of the butt.

The predominant influence in American firearms design was, of course, English. Except for the Spanish and French in the south and west, the great bulk of the American colonies quickly came under British control. English arms were brought over by new arrivals or imported by those already established, and the British government supplied the arms for most of the colonial arsenals. Except in Pennsylvania, which clung doggedly to its Germanic forms, the British designs soon predominated, and even in Pennsylvania much that was British was absorbed in firearms other than rifles.

The Revolutionary War brought many changes in American firearms manufacture. There was a sudden demand for muskets (Plate 183A) and pistols at the same time that the normal source of supply was closed. This helped foster the native industry, and several relatively large armories were developed to meet the needs. Notable among these were Hugh Orr in Massachusetts, William Henry in Pennsylvania, James Hunter's Rappahannock Forge and the Fredericksburg Manufactory in Virginia. These and numerous smaller establishments supplied arms first to the local committees or councils of safety and then to the new state governments. In the beginning all their arms were patterned after the standard British 'Brown Bess' musket, but in 1778, after France entered the war on the American side, they began to switch to the French 'Charleville' pattern with its iron furniture, smaller caliber, and banded construction. Very few of these arms were made in America during the war because the alliance with France provided an opportunity to purchase quantities of ready-made arms. In the later years of the war American smiths seem to have spent most of their time repairing arms and building new ones out of various parts reclaimed from broken weapons acquired during the campaigns.

FROM 1800 TO 1865

The early-nineteenth century witnessed a continuing expansion of American arms production. The ever-advancing frontier with its unsettled conditions made firearms a necessity. The *code duello*, the desire for personal pistols, and the popularity of hunting and target shooting as sports provided a market in more firmly established areas. The War of 1812 and the Black Hawk, Seminole and Mexican Wars, along with other minor military activities, fostered a constant demand for military arms.

The rifle: the American rifle reached the height of its development between 1800 and 1810. Thereafter it declined in artistic appeal though remaining an effective and accurate weapon. The numerous silver inlays that characterized the Federal Period disappeared. Pewter and German silver began to compete with brass as popular metals for mountings. The flintlock was to be replaced by the percussion lock soon after 1820, and the full stock gave way to the half-stock. These shorter, half-stocked rifles were often called 'plain' rifles to distinguish them from the finer long rifles with their patch-boxes and other ornamentation. Since this transition coincided with the opening up of the Great Plains area of the United States, modern collectors have corrupted the term to 'plains' rifle in the belief that they were developed especially for use by plainsmen on horseback who could not use the longer guns. Actually, these plain rifles were widely used by such men for just that reason, but it was not this that gave them their name. In contrast to the long rifles whose production centered in the Appalachian region, the center of manufacture for these newer rifles was farther west, some of the most sought-after being made by the Hawken brothers in St. Louis (Plate 182c).

Deringers: it was among the hand guns, however, that America really achieved distinction, and consequently many collectors are attracted to that particular field today. Some fine duelling pistols were made in America (and there were even shops which would rent them—presumably with the rental paid in advance), but most such pistols were imported from England. American smiths devoted most of their attention to arms for less formal modes of self-preservation.

One of the foremost gunsmiths in this field was Henry Deringer of Philadelphia. A fine craftsman, noted for the excellent workmanship on his products, Deringer at first made both rifles and duelling pistols, but shortly after 1825 he began to concentrate on short pocket pistols with large calibers. These little weapons, ranging from 3¾ inches to 9 inches in overall length, had calibers varying from .33 to .51 inches. Thus considerable power was packed into arms that could be carried easily and inconspicuously almost anywhere. They were always fired with percussion-caps

and were almost always rifled. Deringer's pistols quickly became immensely popular, especially in the south and west, and his name became synonymous with the type of pistol he had developed. In fact, often spelled derringer, it was soon applied to any short pocket pistol, even cartridge arms with two or more barrels, and in that connotation it is still in use today. Because of the pistol's popularity, there were many imitators, some of whom put Deringer's name or slight variants such as Beringer on their own products, hoping to fool the unsuspecting. Deringer himself died in 1868, three years after one of his pistols (Plate 188c) had achieved national notoriety in the hands of John Wilkes Booth when he assassinated President Abraham Lincoln.

Pepperboxes: another percussion-cap muzzle-loading pistol which achieved great popularity in America during the 1830s and '40s was the pepperbox. This was by no means an American invention. It had developed gradually for well over a century and a half, but it found a definite market at this period, and Americans were quick to make improvements and alterations in the basic design. Fundamentally, the pepperbox was a series of barrels grouped around a central axis that could be fired one after another by a single hammer. Some were single-action, some double-action. On some the barrels revolved automatically and on others it was necessary to turn them by hand. Normally these pistols had from three to six barrels, but occasionally there were more – eight, ten, twelve and even eighteen. When first developed, they were the fastest-firing guns of their time and they were widely carried as personal arms both by civilians and soldiers. The most prolific maker of American pepperboxes (Plate 188A) was Ethan Allen of Grafton and Worcester, Massachusetts, in partnership with Charles Thurber and later with T. P. Wheelock. Second was the firm of Blunt & Syms of New York City, but there were many others. Even in the cartridge era there were pistols that still qualified as pepperboxes, notably those four-barreled pocket pistols made by Christian Sharps of Philadelphia.

Colt revolvers: the pistol that arose to challenge the pepperbox and eventually to supplant it was the Colt revolver. Samuel Colt, a naturally inventive boy, whittled out the first model of his design for a new revolving firearm in 1830 when he was only sixteen years old. At the time he was a seaman on a voyage to India. After his return to the United States he continued to work on his invention, and in 1835 he was granted patents in both Great Britain and France. His American patent was awarded a year later. Colt's contribution consisted of devising a system of revolving the cylinder of a firearm automatically when the hammer was cocked. As such it was the first practical revolving-cylinder firearm and one of America's greatest contributions to firearms technology.

Despite the importance of Colt's invention, he had considerable difficulty in selling it. His first manufacturing plant was established at Paterson, New Jersey, in 1836, and it produced pistols, rifles, carbines and shotguns, all with revolving cylinders. Orders were slow in coming, however. The venture failed, and the factory was sold. Today the revolvers made at this factory are known as 'Colt Patersons' (Plate 187B) and are much sought after by collectors.

In 1847 Colt finally succeeded in obtaining a government contract for a thousand of his pistols based on an improved design suggested by Capt. Samuel Walker of the Texas Rangers. With this order Colt was able to resume manufacturing his pistols, and soon his fortunes prospered. The Walker Colts (Plate 187C) were huge guns, 15½ inches long, but poorly made. They saw considerable service in the Army, and those specimens that have survived are considered by modern collectors the most valuable of all standard Colt models.

Following the Walker, the trend was to decrease the size of the revolver and improve its construction. There were three subsequent models for dragoons (Plate 188D) and two pocket pistols before the advent of the so-called 1851 Navy revolver (Plate 186D). This well-balanced .36 caliber arm was the most popular of all Colt percussion-cap military revolvers, and it was widely used by both the Army and Navy as well as by civilians from its first production through the Civil War and as long as percussion-cap revolvers were used. In 1860 Colt also developed a .44 caliber revolver for the Army (Plate 188B) which also was widely used during and after the Civil War. In addition to these principal models, Colt also produced numerous others, both pistols and long guns, to meet almost every possible need. Examples of all models were frequently engraved (Plates 185, 188D) and had carved grips of bone, ivory, special woods, or even silver, for presentation purposes. Colt himself died in 1862, well before the company he founded reached its greatest peaks of production.

Other percussion-cap revolvers: like any successful development, the Colt revolver soon had a host of imitators, both before and after the basic patent expired in 1856. The Massachusetts Arms Company was the first to copy Colt's design, but Colt sued them successfully and forced them to abandon their project. The Metropolitan and Manhattan revolvers were exact copies of the Colt, but they were not made until after the patent's expiration. More original designs were embodied in the Butterfield, Pettingill, Savage, Starr, Walch, Whitney and others. Some of these, like the Starr, were double-action, and the Walch even had two hammers and fired either ten or twelve shots, depending upon the model.

The most successful percussion-cap revolver, aside from the Colt, was the Remington. Eliphalet Remington, Jr., of Ilion, New York, had been a gunsmith since his youth. His products had been primarily long arms – flint and percussion-cap rifles for local customers and rifles and carbines for the Army. He produced his first revolver in 1849. It had many defects, however, and it was not until he brought out an improved model in 1856 that the Remington revolver really became popular. These revolvers and several of Remington's subsequent models resembled the Colt but had stronger frames and other mechanical refinements patented by Fordyce Beals. During the Civil War Remington furnished the government with over 128,000 revolvers

(A) 1798 cavalry saber by Nathan Starr. *Coll. of Harry D. Berry, Jr.*

(B) Foot artillery sword, 1832, made by Ames.

(C) Light artillery saber, 1840, in use about fifty years.

(D) Heavy cavalry saber, adopted in 1840 after a French type.

(E) Infantry non-commissioned officer's sword, 1840.

(F) Naval cutlass; a French type adopted in 1860.

PLATE 177

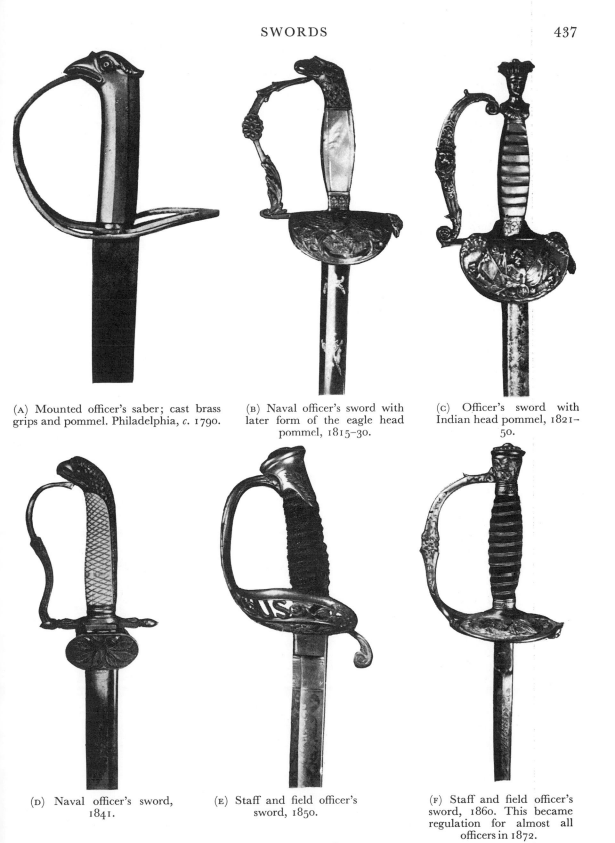

(A) Mounted officer's saber; cast brass grips and pommel. Philadelphia, c. 1790.

(B) Naval officer's sword with later form of the eagle head pommel, 1815–30.

(C) Officer's sword with Indian head pommel, 1821–50.

(D) Naval officer's sword, 1841.

(E) Staff and field officer's sword, 1850.

(F) Staff and field officer's sword, 1860. This became regulation for almost all officers in 1872.

PLATE 178

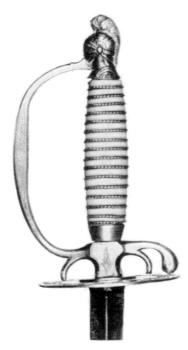

(A) Silver mounted small sword by Timothy Bontecou, Jr., of New Haven, Connecticut, c. 1750. *Coll. of Hermann W. Williams.*

(B) Silver mounted small sword by Joseph Draper of Wilmington, Delaware, c. 1815. *Coll. of Hermann W. Williams.*

(C) Silver mounted hunting sword by John Bailey of Fishkill, New York, which belonged to George Washington. *U.S. National Museum.*

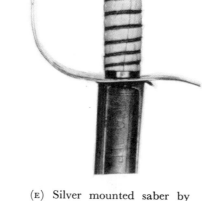

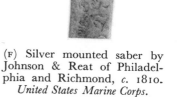

(D) Silver mounted hunting sword by William Gilbert of New York City, c. 1770. *The Farmington Museum.*

(E) Silver mounted saber by William Ball, Jr., of Baltimore, c. 1790. *Coll. of Charles West.*

(F) Silver mounted saber by Johnson & Reat of Philadelphia and Richmond, c. 1810. *United States Marine Corps.*

PLATE 179

(A) Congressional presentation sword of the Revolution. *United States National Museum.*

(B) Congressional naval presentation sword of the War of 1812. *United States Naval Academy Museum.*

(C) New York State presentation sword of the War of 1812. *United States National Museum.*

(D) Presentation sword of the Mexican War. *United States National Museum.*

(E) Presentation sword of the Civil War. *United States National Museum.*

(F) Presentation sword of 1887. *United States National Museum.*

PLATE 180

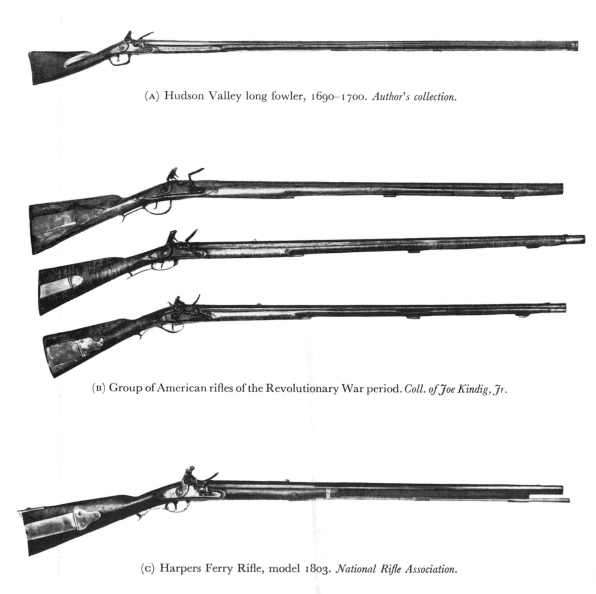

(A) Hudson Valley long fowler, 1690–1700. *Author's collection.*

(B) Group of American rifles of the Revolutionary War period. *Coll. of Joe Kindig, Jr.*

(C) Harpers Ferry Rifle, model 1803. *National Rifle Association.*

PLATE 181

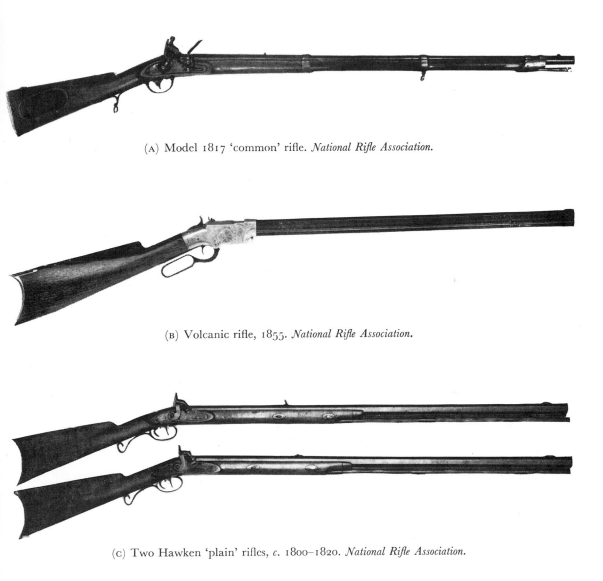

(A) Model 1817 'common' rifle. *National Rifle Association.*

(B) Volcanic rifle, 1855. *National Rifle Association.*

(C) Two Hawken 'plain' rifles, *c.* 1800–1820. *National Rifle Association.*

(D) Spencer rifle with breech open and tubular magazine lying below. *National Rifle Association.*

PLATE 182

(A) Maryland Committee of Safety musket, 1775–76. *Author's collection.*

(B) United States musket, model 1795. *National Rifle Association.*

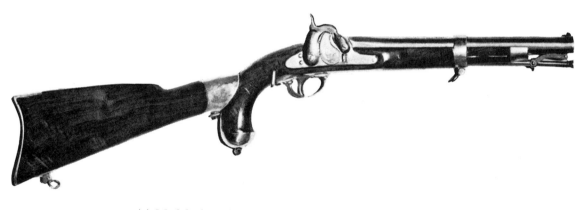

(C) Model 1855 pistol carbine. *United States National Museum.*

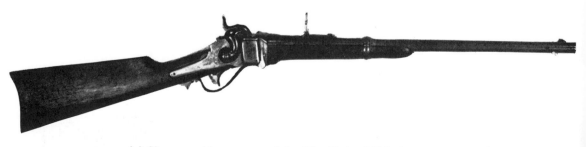

(D) Sharps carbine, new model, 1863. *National Rifle Association.*

PLATE 183

Pair of American 'Kentucky' pistols, c. 1775–83. Coll. of Joe Kindig, Jr.

PLATE 184

Pair of fully engraved 1860 Army Colt revolvers with cast bronze grips. *United States National Museum.*

PLATE 185

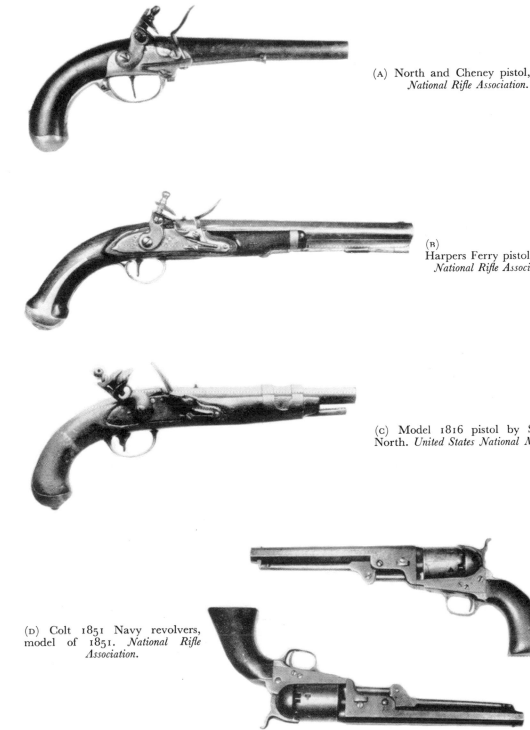

(A) North and Cheney pistol, 1799.
National Rifle Association.

(B) Harpers Ferry pistol, 1807.
National Rifle Association.

(C) Model 1816 pistol by Simeon
North. *United States National Museum.*

(D) Colt 1851 Navy revolvers,
model of 1851. *National Rifle
Association.*

PLATE 186

(A) The Volcanic pistol of 1854.
National Rifle Association.

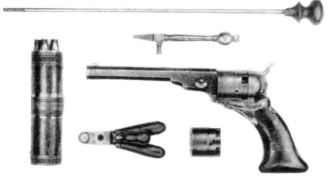

(B) Colt Paterson with accessories, 1836. *National Rifle Association.*

(C) Colt Walker revolver, 1848.
National Rifle Association.

PLATE 187

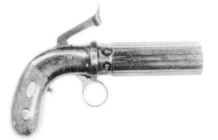

(A) Patent model of the Allen pepperbox. *United States National Museum.*

(B) Colt 1860 Army model revolver. *National Rifle Association.*

(C) Deringer used by John Wilkes Booth to assassinate Abraham Lincoln. *National Park Service.*

(D) Dragoon third model. Cut for shoulder stock and fully presentation engraved. *National Rifle Association.*

(E) Model 1842 pistol. *United States National Museum.*

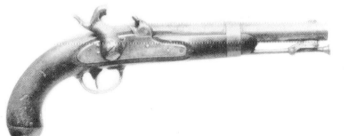

PLATE 188

(A) Samuel Bispham, Philadelphia, c. 1695. One of the earliest American clocks. *Coll. of Vincent D. Andrus.*

(B) Benjamin Chandlee, Nottingham, Maryland, c. 1720. Ht 81½ ins. *Coll. of W. Blakeley Chandlee.*

(C) Benjamin Chandlee, Jr., Nottingham, Md., c. 1750–60. *Coll. of Mrs Chandlee Archer.*

(D) Benjamin Chandlee, Jr., c. 1750; walnut Queen Anne case. *Coll. of Edward E. Chandlee.*

PLATE 189

(A) Benjamin Cheney, East Hartford, Connecticut, *c.* 1750–60. Ht 92 ins. Brass covered wood dial. 30-hour wood movement. *Old Sturbridge Village, Sturbridge, Massachusetts.*

(B) Gawen Brown, Boston, *c.* 1760. Ht 90 ins. One of New England's earliest tall clocks. *Old Sturbridge Village.*

(C) David Rittenhouse, Philadelphia, *c.* 1770. Ht 108 ins. Considered his finest. *Drexel Institute of Technology, Philadelphia.*

PLATE 190

(A) David Blaisdell, Amesbury, Massachusetts, 1744; wag-on-the-wall with only one hand; brass dial with pewter chapter ring. *Coll. of Dr Charles Mixter. Photo N. Tilley.*

(B) Preserved Clapp, Amherst, Massachusetts, *c.* 1750–60, 8 by 11 ins. Probably originally a wag-on-the-wall; now in primitive tall case. Wood dial with pewter chapter ring; brass spandrels. *Author's collection. Photo R. Coffin.*

(C) Wall clock, forerunner of banjo; Simon Willard, Grafton, Massachusetts, *c.* 1775. Ht 26½ ins. *Old Sturbridge Village, Sturbridge, Massachusetts.*

(D) Simon Willard, Roxbury, *c.* 1805. Ht 33 ins. The banjo, called by Willard his 'patented timepiece' (1802). *Old Sturbridge Village, Sturbridge, Massachusetts.*

C

D

PLATE 191

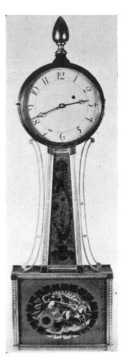

(A) Aaron Willard banjo clock, Boston, *c.* 1820. *Owner unknown.*

(B) Aaron Willard, Jr., Boston, *c.* 1825; Arabic numerals unusual. *Coll. of Edwin B. Burt.*

(C) Unknown maker, *c.* 1825. Tablet with Constitution and Guerriere. *Author's collection.*

(D) 'Girandole' wall clock by Lemuel Curtis, Massachusetts, *c.* 1815. Ht 45 ins. *Old Sturbridge Village, Sturbridge, Mass.*

(E) Lyre clock with a striking movement; Abiel Chandler, Concord, New Hampshire, *c.* 1830. *Coll. of Edwin B. Burt.*

(F) Lyre clock; carved mahogany case; William Grant, Boston, *c.* 1830. Ht 37 ins. *Author's collection.*

D   E   F

PLATE 192

(A) Riley Whiting, Winchester (now Winsted), Connecticut, *c.* 1815; 30 hour wooden movement used as wag-on-the-wall; usually found in simple grandfather cases. *Author's collection.*

(B) Ellis Chandlee, Nottingham, Maryland, *c.* 1800; moon phases in arch. *Coll. of Dr Everett P. Barnard.*

(C) Joshua Wilder, Hingham, Massachusetts, *c.* 1810. Ht 55 ins. Grandmother clock. *Coll. of Donald K. Packard.*

(D) Benjamin Morrill, Boscawen, New Hampshire, *c.* 1825. Finely decorated mirror clock. *Coll. of Edwin B. Burt.*

C   D

PLATE 193

(A) Elnathan Taber, Roxbury, *c.* 1800. Apprentice of Simon Willard. *Coll. of Edwin B. Burt.*

(B) Aaron Willard, Boston, *c.* 1805. Ht 93½ ins; mahogany case; rocking ship in arch of dial. *Old Sturbridge Village, Sturbridge, Massachusetts.*

(C) Simon Willard, Roxbury, *c.* 1810. Ht 102 ins. Inlaid mahogany case of 'Roxbury' type. *Old Sturbridge Village, Sturbridge, Massachusetts.*

(D) Ellis Chandlee, Nottingham, Maryland, *c.* 1800; walnut case, moon phase in arch. *Coll. of Dr Everett P. Barnard.*

PLATE 194

(A) Early Massachusetts shelf clock by Simon Willard, Grafton, *c.* 1780. Ht 32½ ins. *Old Sturbridge Village, Sturbridge, Massachusetts.*

(B) Joshua Wilder, Hingham, *c.* 1820; Massachusetts shelf clock with kidney dial. *Coll. of Donald K. Packhard.*

A

B

(C) Aaron Willard is known for this type of Massachusetts shelf clock; Boston, *c.* 1820. *Author's collection.*

(D) John Sawin, Boston, *c.* 1830; has both hour strike and alarm. *Coll. of Donald K. Packard.*

C

D

PLATE 195

(A) Pillar and scroll clock, escapement in front of dial; 30-hour wooden movement. Eli Terry, Plymouth, Connecticut, *c.* 1817. *Old Sturbridge Village, Sturbridge, Massachusetts.*

(B) Unusual movement having pendulum hung 'off-center' and a second's hand. Seth Thomas, Plymouth, Connecticut, *c.* 1817. *Author's collection.*

(C) Seth Thomas, Plymouth, Connecticut, *c.* 1820. Ht 31 ins. Typical pillar and scroll clock. *Coll. of Edwin B. Burt.*

(D) Early Connecticut shelf clock with 8-day brass movement. Heman Clark, Plymouth, *c.* 1815. Ht 20 ins. *Author's collection.*

PLATE 196

(A) Eli Terry and Sons, Plymouth, Connecticut, *c.* 1820. Ht
35 ins; stenciled posts and splat
with well painted tablet; wooden
movement. *Author's collection.*

(B) Eli Terry, Jr., Plymouth, Connecticut, *c.* 1830; carved case, 30-hour
wooden movement. *Coll. of Fraser
R. Forgie.*

(C) Chauncey Jerome, Bristol, Connecticut, *c.* 1840. Ht 29 ins. 30-hour
movement; weights travel inside
columns. *Author's collection.*

(D) J. C. Brown, Forestville, Connecticut, *c.* 1840. Ogee, with colored
decalcomania on tablet; 8-day brass
movement. *Author's collection.*

PLATE 197

(A) Joseph Ives, New York, New York, c. 1830; 8-day wagon spring movement. *Coll. of Edward M. Mitchell.*

(B) Birge and Fuller, Bristol, Connecticut, c. 1845; 30-hour wagon spring movement in a double steeple case. *Coll. of Walter M. Roberts.*

(C) Has a torsion pendulum and will run a year on a winding. The Year Clock Co., New York, New York, c. 1850. *Coll. of Edward M. Mitchell.*

(D) Wall clock with 30-day wagon spring movement. Atkins, Whiting & Co., Bristol, Connecticut, c. 1850. *Coll. of Edwin B. Burt.*

PLATE 198

(A) Three sizes of gothic or steeple clocks, *c.* 1850–60. Left: C. Jerome, New Haven. Others: Brewster and Ingraham, Bristol. *Author's collection.*

(B) Beehive clock, Forestville Mfg. Co., Forestville, Connecticut. *Coll. of Edward M. Mitchell.*

(C) Shelf clock, New England Clock Co., Bristol, 1850. *Author's collection.*

(D) Beehive clock, J. C. Brown, Bristol, 1850. *Coll. of Edward M. Mitchell.*

PLATE 199

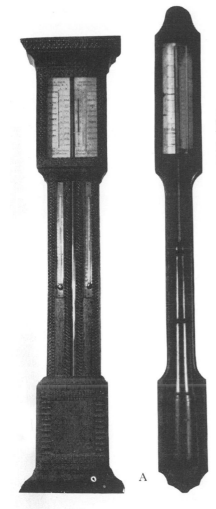

(A) Barometers: H. A. Clum, Rochester, New York. Patented 1860. B. C. Spooner, Boston. Patented 1860. *Coll. of B. W. Brandt.*

(B) Watch, marked *J. Sargeant Springfield, Massachusetts*, and probably made by him, *c.* 1795. *Coll. of Percy L. Small.*

(C) New York Watch Co., Springfield, Massachusetts, 1870. Keywinding and set from back. *Coll. of Hamilton Pease. Photo R. Coffin.*

(D) E. Howard & Co., Boston, 1859. *Coll. of Hamilton Pease. Photo R. Coffin.*

(E) American Waltham Watch Co., *c.* 1878. Chronograph. *Coll. of Hamilton Pease. Photo R. Coffin.*

(F) Benedict & Burnham Co., Waterbury, 1878. First successful cheap watch; has a revolving train seen through the cut-out dial. *Coll. of Hamilton Pease. Photo R. Coffin.*

PLATE 200

(A) De Peyster Boy with Deer. 1720–30. Unknown New York artist. *New-York Historical Society.*

(B) James Badger by Joseph Badger, 1760. *Metropolitan Museum of Art, New York.*

(C) Isaac Winslow by Robert Feke. *Museum of Fine Arts, Boston.*

(D) Mrs William Walton by John Wollaston. *New-York Historical Society.*

PLATE 201

(A) Bishop George Berkeley and his Family by John Smibert, 1729. *Yale University Art Gallery.*

(B) The American School (Benjamin West in his Studio) by Matthew Pratt. *Metropolitan Museum of Art, New York.*

PLATE 202

(A) Unknown Lady by Joseph Blackburn. *Brooklyn Museum.*

(B) Thadeus Burr by J. S. Copley. *City Art Museum, St Louis.*

(C) Mrs James Mackubin by Charles Willson Peale. *Fogg Museum of Art.*

(D) The Rapalje Children by John Durand, 1768. *New-York Historical Society.*

PLATE 203

Daniel Boardman by Ralph Earl. *National Gallery of Art, Washington.*

PLATE 204

(A) Storm in the Wilderness by J. F. Cropsey, 1823–1900. *Cleveland Museum of Art.*

(B) View near Newport by J. F. Kensett, 1819–72. *Cleveland Museum of Art.*

PLATE 205

(A) Owl's Head, Penobscot Bay by Fitz Hugh Lane, 1804–65. *M. and M. Karolik collection, Museum of Fine Arts, Boston.*

(B) Raffling for the Goose by W. S. Mount, 1807–68. *Metropolitan Museum of Art.* (Slightly trimmed top and bottom.)

PLATE 206

(A) Music and Literature by W. M. Harnett, 1848–92. *Albright Art Gallery.*

(B) The Writing Master by Thomas Eakins, 1844–1916. *Metropolitan Museum of Art.*

PLATE 207

Winter Coast by Winslow Homer, 1836–1910. *The J. G. Johnson collection, Philadelphia Museum of Art.*

PLATE 208

in addition to those that were purchased privately by individual soldiers and state organizations.

Smith & Wesson: in the same era, at the middle of the last century, America made one more major contribution to firearms technology through the work of Horace Smith and Daniel B. Wesson. These two young gunsmiths became friends in 1831 and together developed a new repeating pistol and rifle using a new cartridge. The repeating mechanism was an improvement of one devised some time before by Walter Hunt and Lewis Jennings. As strengthened and simplified by Smith and Wesson, it formed the basis for the Volcanic pistols (Plate 187A) and rifles (Plate 182B) of 1855 and, later, with further improvements by B. Tyler Henry, for the famous Henry and Winchester rifles. The cartridge, which contained its own primer and propelling charge, was a distinct advance, but it did not function sufficiently well. The partners continued to study the problem, and in 1854 Wesson patented the first really successful metallic center-fire cartridge. In 1856 Smith & Wesson began the production of the first revolvers designed for metallic rim-fire cartridges, and through their control of a patent covering revolver cylinders with the chambers bored all the way through, they enjoyed practically a monopoly of the manufacture of cartridge revolving arms until the patent expired in 1869.

The Hall rifle: in the field of American long arms there was also an evolution from the muzzle-loaders to breech-loaders and repeaters. The idea of breech-loading and repeating guns was not a nineteenth-century innovation. Actually both had been tried with more or less success ever since the development of firearms. John Pym and John Cookson of Boston and Joseph Belton of Philadelphia had made repeating arms in America during the eighteenth century. It was during the nineteenth century, however, that the first really practical, inexpensive systems were perfected and produced on a large scale.

Among the breech-loaders the first to achieve widespread success was one patented by John H. Hall of Yarmouth, Maine, in 1811. Hall's gun was a flintlock with a section of the breech that could be tipped up to expose the chamber and permit a charge to be inserted. The inventor succeeded in interesting the United States Government in his gun, and in 1819 production was begun at the Harpers Ferry Armory with Hall himself to supervise the work. Thus the Hall rifle became the first breech-loader officially to be adopted as a regulation arm by any army in the world. It also had the distinction of being the first American gun made with completely interchangeable parts. In addition to the Hall rifles, there were also Hall carbines, both flint and percussion-cap, a very few pistols, and sporting rifles produced at the Armory and by private contractors, particularly Simeon North.

Sharps carbines and rifles: despite its relative success, the Hall had several defects. It was clumsy and awkward to use, and there was a considerable leakage of gas at the joint between the breech chamber and the barrel when the gun was discharged. It remained for Christian Sharps of Philadelphia, who had worked under Hall, to develop a really satisfactory system in 1848. In Sharps's guns the breech-block was raised and lowered in a vertical mortise by the action of a lever which usually also served as the trigger-guard. When the breech-block was lowered, the chamber was exposed and a paper or linen cartridge could be inserted. As the breech-block was raised, it sheared off the rear of the cartridge, exposing the powder to the sparks from the priming pellet which was not contained in the cartridge but was fed automatically over the cone by the action of the hammer.

The Sharps action was very strong and tight. It allowed no gas leakage, and it would not bend or crack, even with excessively large charges. The basic Sharps principle, in fact, is still in use today on some heavy arms and small cannon where its strength is needed. At the time, the action was used on both rifles and carbines (Plate 183D), as well as buffalo-guns, pistols and pistol-rifles. The famous abolitionist John Brown used Sharps carbines, and the Sharps guns were the most popular single-shot breech-loading arms used in the Civil War. The famous Sharp Shooters of Hiram Berdan, among other well-known units, were armed with them. After the War, Sharps converted to metallic self-contained cartridges and increased the variety of models using his system. He died in 1874.

Other single-shot breech-loaders: the Sharps was only the first of a whole group of breech-loaders which were produced immediately prior to the beginning of the Civil War and which had completely supplanted the older muzzle-loading arms by the end of that conflict. There were, for instance, the Ballard, Burnside, Cosmopolitan, Gallager, Gibbs, Greene, Jenks, Joslyn, Lee, Lindner, Maynard, Merrill, Palmer, Peabody, Perry, Smith, Starr, Symmes, Warner and Wesson. Most of these were percussion-cap arms, but a few were metallic cartridge guns. All saw service in the Civil War, and, in fact, it was only the war which allowed most of them to get into production. Few of them were good enough to have found a market in peace time.

The Henry rifle: repeating arms also came into their own during the Civil War. Joseph Chambers and Reuben Ellis had made muzzle-loading repeaters for the Federal Government in 1814 and 1828 respectively. As late as 1863 muzzle-loading rifle-muskets firing two charges loaded one ahead of the other were manufactured at the Springfield Armory under a patent granted to John P. Lindsay.

The really successful repeaters, however, were breech-loaders using metallic cartridges. The first of these began with Walter Hunt's invention of 1849 referred to above in the section on Smith & Wesson. Hunt's gun had a tubular magazine under the barrel and a lever action, but it was a complicated mechanism. Lewis Jennings refined and simplified it, and in 1850 5,000 rifles were produced. Horace Smith of Smith & Wesson fame improved the gun further in 1851. B. Tyler Henry added still further improvements in 1860, and 10,000 of these new 12-shot Henry rifles manufactured by the New Haven Arms Company saw service in the Civil War. In 1866 Oliver F. Winchester reorganized the New Haven Arms Company as the Winchester Repeating Arms Company, and the Henry rifle became known as the Winchester.

The Spencer rifle and carbine: the chief competitor of the Henry was the Spencer (Plate 182D). Christopher M. Spencer patented his new gun March 6, 1860, just a year before the outbreak of the Civil War. It was an excellent gun with a tubular magazine for seven metallic cartridges in the butt. It was sturdy, did not get out of order easily, and was a great favorite with troops during the war. Some 12,471 rifles and 94,000 carbines were purchased by the Army, and they played an important part in many battles. In addition, a great many more Spencers were purchased by state troops and individual soldiers. After the war the Spencer plant was purchased by Winchester, and manufacture of the rifle and carbine was discontinued.

Other repeaters: in addition to these two excellent breech-loading repeaters, there were also two other types which developed during the Civil War. These were the Ball and the Triplett & Scott carbines. The Ball was patented in 1864, and 1,002 were purchased by the Army. None were delivered, however, until after the end of hostilities. The Triplett & Scott was patented in December 1864, and none was purchased by the Government. Neither was successful after the war.

MARTIAL ARMS

Martial arms have long been a favorite category for collectors. Although true American military arms actually were made during the colonial period, the establishment of the National Armories at Springfield in 1795 and at Harpers Ferry in 1796 mark the beginning dates for most of these collectors. The products of these two armories included muskets, rifles and pistols in quantity as well as pattern pieces for arms made under contract by private smiths. The Harpers Ferry Armory was destroyed by the Confederates in 1861, but the one at Springfield is still active today.

Muskets: throughout the period under consideration American muskets generally followed French patterns. The first official American musket after the ratification of the

Constitution was the model of 1795 (Plate 183B) made at Springfield. It was an exact copy of the French model of 1763 or 'Charle-ville' musket which had been so popular during the later years of the Revolution. Thereafter slight changes were made in 1808, 1812, 1816, 1835 and 1840, but the guns remained flintlocks and French-inspired. In 1842 the first percussion-cap musket was adopted, and in 1855 there was a radical change with the appearance of the first rifle-musket. As mentioned above, rifles using round balls were slow to load: the ball had to be wrapped with a greased patch to fit the bore tightly and take the spin imparted by the spiral grooves of the rifling. This slowness was a liability in a military arm. The 1855 rifle-musket, however, was based on the use of a cylindro-conoidal bullet with a hollow base known as a Minié ball after the French officer who had invented the original. It could be dropped loosely down the barrel and would expand when fired to take the rifling. Its coming marked the end of the era of the smooth-bored musket. The model 1855 also had a patented tape primer invented by Edward Maynard which fed the caps automatically to the cone much in the manner of a modern cap-pistol. It proved impractical, however, and it was omitted in the succeeding models of 1861 and 1863.

Rifles: despite the fact that they were slow to load, the United States Army had had some rifles from the beginning. The first to be made in the national armories was the model 1803 (Plate 181C) produced at Harpers Ferry in time for the use of the famous Lewis and Clark expedition to explore the newly-purchased Louisiana Territory. These rifles followed a strictly American design, but they were closer to British patterns than to French. There were changes in 1814 and 1817 designed to strengthen the guns and make them more serviceable. The model of 1817 (Plate 182A) rifles were made by private contractors, and in order to distinguish them from the Hall breech-loading rifles mentioned above, which were also an official arm, they were called 'common' rifles. Collectors still use the term. In 1841 the first percussion-cap rifle was

adopted, and in 1855 a new model boasted both a tape primer and a bayonet for the first time. Some of the later 1841 model rifles had been adapted for bayonets, it is true, but the model 1855 was the first to be designed for one. Previously only muskets had had them.

Pistols: United States martial pistols, like the muskets, usually followed French patterns. The first official pistol of the new nation, the model of 1799 made by Simeon North and Elisha Cheney of Middletown, Connecticut, was an exact copy of the French model of 1777 (Plate 186A). Only 2,000 were made. Today they are the most highly prized of any standard model firearm, and they bring tremendous prices when they appear on the market. From 1806 until 1808 Harpers Ferry manufactured pistols (Plate 186B) of a purely American design, and in 1818 the Springfield Armory began the production of 1,000 pistols. Almost all other official government flintlock pistols, however, were made under contract by Simeon North, including the so-called models of 1799 (Plate 186A), 1808, 1810, 1813, 1816 (Plate 186C), 1819 and 1826. All of these showed a strong French influence. Some of the 1826 pistols were also made by W. L. Evans of Valley Forge, Pennsylvania, and in 1836 the last official flintlock pistol was made by Robert Johnson of Middletown, Connecticut, and Asa Waters of Milbury, Connecticut. In 1842 a percussion-cap pistol (Plate 188E) was adopted and manufactured by Henry Aston and Ira Johnson, both of Middletown. In 1843 a percussion-cap pistol with the hammer pivoted on the inside of the lock-plate was contracted for by N. P. Ames of Springfield, Massachusetts and Henry Deringer of Philadelphia, and these were the last of the contract pistols.

In 1855 the final percussion-cap pistol was adopted and manufactured at the Springfield Armory (Plate 183C). Like the rifle-musket and rifle of that year, it had a Maynard tape primer. In addition it was equipped with a detachable shoulder-stock so that it could be used as a carbine as well as a pistol. It was a good arm, but it was not popular with the troops, and it was soon supplanted by the percussion-cap revolvers which became universal for cavalrymen during the Civil War.

In addition to the primary arms listed above which were made specifically for the United States Government, both the Army and Navy were given special carbines, musketoons and cadet muskets. They also purchased arms from private companies. These included the Colt and other percussion-cap revolvers, and the various breech-loaders and repeaters of the Civil War era.

CONFEDERATE ARMS

Confederate firearms form another popular collectors' category. Because the Confederacy had few private armories at the beginning of the Civil War and because industrial equipment of all kinds was scarce, it was necessary for them to improvise. As a result, there was considerable variety among Confederate-made arms. Flintlock arms and sporting guns were modernized and converted to military use, and all available spare parts and captured material were utilized.

Usually those arms made completely in the Confederacy followed either the standard United States or British Enfield designs. They can be recognized, however, by the names of the manufacturers, by difference in workmanship caused by the shortages both of machine-tools and of skilled machinists, by the elimination of non-essential features, and by the substitution of different materials. Brass, for instance, was often used instead of iron or steel because it was more easily worked.

Pistols, revolvers, rifles and carbines, all were made in the South. Most revolvers were based on the Colt or Whitney designs, but a few, such as the Cofer and the Shawk & McLanahan, had unusual modifications. The most interesting Confederate revolver, the Le Mat, though invented and patented in America, was manufactured in France. It had nine regular charges in its cylinder and a separate barrel for one load of shot underneath which could be fired by adjusting the nose of the hammer. Most of the rifles and rifle-muskets were copied from the Springfield or the British Enfield. Among the breech-loading carbines, the Sharps pattern prevailed, but here again there were also a few local and unique patterns.

GLOSSARY

Amusette: a heavy military firearm shaped like a normal rifle or musket but designed to be fired from a swivel mount. Such guns were popular in America from the seventeenth through the early-nineteenth centuries.

Fig. 1. A swivel gun or amusette

Back-strap: a metal strap along the outside of back of the grip of a pistol or revolver.

Bands: loops of metal encircling the barrel and stock as a means of fastening these two structures together.

Barrel tang: a metal strap attached to the breech of the barrel and projecting toward the butt. It was used to anchor the barrel more firmly in place.

Battery: that portion of a flintlock which serves as the steel for the flint to strike against and thus produce sparks. In true flintlocks it is made in one piece with the pan cover. It is also often called the steel or, in modern times, the frizzen. During the eighteenth and early-nineteenth centuries it was known as the hammer.

Bayonet: a blade designed to be attached to the muzzle of a gun so that it could be used as a polearm when its ammunition was expended. The predominant form throughout the period in America was a stabbing blade, triangular in cross-section with an offset socket that was slipped over the muzzle of the gun. Some bayonets had sword blades, however, and some were attached permanently to the barrels of pistols and blunderbusses with a hinge and spring device.

Blade sight: an upright elongated front sight.

Blunderbuss: a short firearm with a large bore flaring at the muzzle, designed to scatter shot in a wide pattern and do considerable execution in a confined area. For this reason they were particularly popular as ship's arms for repelling boarders, and for defending streets and staircases. The period of the blunderbuss's greatest popularity in America was the eighteenth century. Although popular myth insists that the Pilgrims were armed with them, very few of these guns were used in this country prior to 1700, and certainly none was used at Plymouth.

Bluing: a chemically induced oxidation used to color iron or steel gun-parts in shades of blue and black.

Bore: the interior of the barrel of a firearm. Also used as a designation of the diameter of the interior of the barrel in terms of the number of spherical lead balls of corresponding diameter in a pound weight. In this connotation it is synonymous with gauge.

Bootleg pistol: peculiar form of percussion-cap pistol made largely in Massachusetts with the hammer underneath the barrel and the grips at a right angle.

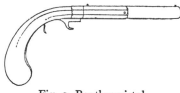

Fig. 2. Bootleg pistol

Breech: the rear of the barrel.

Breech-loader: a firearm receiving its charge at the breech.

Breech plug: a cylindrical plug screwed in at the breech of muzzle-loading firearms to close the bore.

Browning: a process to color the iron or steel parts of a firearm in shades of brown. Sometimes this was done through artificial oxidation, and sometimes a lacquer was used.

Butt: the portion of a long arm which fits against the shoulder, or the terminus of the grip of a pistol.

Butt-cap: a metal covering for the butt of a pistol.

Butt-plate: a metal plate used to cover and protect the extreme end of the butt of a shoulder-arm.

Caliber or calibre: the diameter of the bore of a firearm expressed in hundredths of an inch.

Cap: a small charge of a percussion-igniting compound, usually fulminate of mercury, sealed within a paper or metal container and used to ignite the main charge of a firearm.

Cap-box: a small receptacle in the butt of a percussion-cap pistol, rifle or even a fowling-piece, designed to hold a supply of percussion-caps.

Fig. 3. Rifle cap-box

Carbine: a short shoulder-arm intended for the use of mounted troops (Plate 183D). In the eighteenth century both rifle and smooth-bored arms were often termed carbines, but in the next century the name was used only for rifled arms while the short smooth-bores were called musketoons.

Cartridge: a combination of the ball and powder charge for a gun fastened together in a single container. The earliest cartridges were wrapped in paper or cloth. Later metal cartridges were developed which contained their own detonating charges as well.

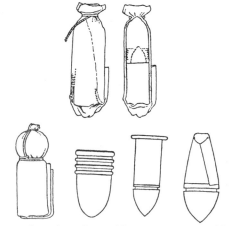

Fig. 4. A series of cartridges; paper cartridge; self-contained; rim fire; combustible.

Chamber: that portion of the bore of a firearm which receives the charge.

Cock: the pivoted arm of a flintlock or snaphaunce mechanism which holds the flint and snaps forward to bring it in contact with the steel in order to produce the spark necessary to ignite the charge.

Cone or nipple: the small tube at the breech of a percussion-cap firearm on which the cap is placed.

Cutlass pistol: a type of single-shot percussion-cap pistol with a heavy cutting blade mounted underneath the barrel, patented by George Elgin in 1837.

Fig. 5. Cutlass pistol

Cylinder: the portion of a revolver which holds the chambers for the charges. It revolves around an axis and presents its loads successively to the breech of the barrel.

Escutcheon plate: a metal plate set in the wrist of either a pistol or shoulder-arm as a place to engrave the name or monogram of the owner or other similar data.

Flintlock: a type of firearm in which the charge is ignited by a spark produced by striking a piece of flint against a steel surface. Modern collectors tend to identify as true flintlocks only those types in which the steel and pan cover are combined in one piece. Those with separate steel and pan cover they call snaphaunces. This is just the reverse of seventeenth century usage in which all flint arms were called snaphaunces.

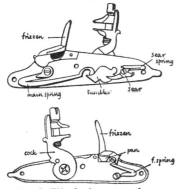

Fig. 6. Flintlock nomenclature

Fore-stock: the portion of a gunstock in front of the trigger guard.

Frizzen: *see* Battery.

Gauge: *see* Bore.

Hammer: in a percussion-cap or cartridge gun the movable arm which strikes the primer and sets it off either directly or through the use of a firing pin. Modern collectors often use the term incorrectly to refer to the cock of a flint arm.

Key: a wedge-shaped device used to fasten the barrel to the stock through corresponding slots in the fore-stock and lugs on the underside of the barrel.

Lands: the uncut portions of the original surface left between the grooves in the bore of a rifled gun.

Lock: the mechanism of a firearm used for igniting the explosive.

Lock-plate: the basic iron or steel plate on which the movable parts of a gun lock are mounted.

Long arm: those small arms designed to be fired from the shoulder. Synonymous with shoulder-arm.

Magazine: a device for holding a number of cartridges together to facilitate loading for successive discharges. Also the part of a repeating firearm containing cartridges for successive discharges.

Minié bullet or Minié ball: a cylindro-conoidal projectile with a cavity in its base which expanded when the powder charge was fired and caused the bullet to fit the bore tightly and thus take the spin imparted by the rifling. It was named after Captain C.E. Minié of the French Army who originally developed the principle on which it functioned. Because this type of bullet allowed a muzzle-loading rifle to be loaded as rapidly as a musket, it ended the supremacy of the musket as a military arm.

Miquelet lock: a form of flintlock developed in Spain and Italy about the middle of the sixteenth century and used well into the nineteenth.

Musket: a military firearm with a smooth bore designed to be fired from the shoulder.

Musketoon: a short musket. *See* Carbine.

Muzzle: the distal or front end of the barrel.

Nipple: *see* Cone.

Pan: the receptacle on the outside of the barrel or lock plate used to hold the priming powder. Sometimes called the flash pan or priming pan.

Patch-box: a receptacle in the side of a rifle butt designed to hold greased patches or small pieces of equipment.

Fig. 7. Rifle patch-box

Percussion lock: a system of ignition in which a blow from the hammer detonates a small charge of fulminate and thus produces the sparks which set off the main charge.

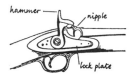

Fig. 8. Percussion lock

Pistol: a firearm designed to be fired while grasped in one hand.

Ramrod: a rod of wood or metal used to force home the charge in a muzzle-loading firearm.

Ramrod thimbles: the metal tubes on the underside of a muzzle-loading firearm which hold the ramrod.

Revolver: a pistol with a revolving cylinder containing charges which it presents successively to the breech of the barrel. Some long arms are also made with revolving cylinders, but they are not normally designated revolvers. The term has also been applied to pepperbox pistols, but this is an uncommon usage.

Rifle: a shoulder-arm with a bore which has been cut with spiral grooves or rifling to impart a spin to the projectile when it is fired.

Rifle-musket: a term used during the nineteenth century to designate a firearm of musket size with a rifled bore.

Rifling: the grooves cut into the sides of the bore which impart the spin to the projectile. Also the act of cutting these grooves.

Screw plate: an elongated plate opposite the lock of a firearm which acts as a washer for the screws holding the lock in position. Sometimes also called the side plate or key plate.

Short arms: a classification name often applied to pistols of all kinds.

Side plate: *see* Screw plate.

Small arms: a military term applying to all arms carried on the person and designed to be fired without a support.

Smoothbore: any firearm without rifling.

Snaphaunce: *see* Flintlock.

Stock: the wood or metal structure of a firearm used to hold the barrel and lock together in proper position and to provide a suitable means of holding the arm.

Tang: *see* Barrel tang.

Touch-hole: a small hole or channel used to convey the sparks from the priming charge outside the barrel to the propelling charge inside the barrel.

Trigger: the lever which activates the lock mechanism of a firearm and sets off the discharge.

Wheel lock: an early ignition system in which the priming charge was set off by bringing a piece of iron pyrite in contact with a revolving, rough-edged wheel.

Wrist: the slender portion of the butt stock immediately behind the lock.

BOOKS FOR
FURTHER READING

There is a vast literature relating to American firearms. The following are only some of the more general references. For other firearms books published before

1951, students would do well to consult Ray Riling, *Guns and Shooting, a Selected Chronological Bibliography*, New York (1951).

CHAPEL, CHARLES E.: *The Gun Collector's Handbook of Values* (New York). Revised editions are published regularly every few years.

DILLIN, JOHN G. W.: *The Kentucky Rifle*, New York (3rd edition, 1946).

FULLER, CLAUD, AND STEUART, RICHARD D.: *Firearms of the Confederacy*, Huntington, West Virginia (1944).

GLUCKMAN, ARCADI: *United States Martial Pistols*, Buffalo (1939).

GLUCKMAN, ARCADI: *United States Muskets, Rifles and Carbines*, Buffalo (1948).

GLUCKMAN, ARCADI, AND SATTERLEE, L. D.: *American Gun Makers*, Harrisburg (2nd edition, 1953).

HATCH, ALDEN: *Remington Arms*, New York (1956).

KAUFFMAN, HENRY J.: *Early American Gunsmiths, 1650–1850*, Harrisburg (1952).

McHENRY, ROY C., AND ROPER, WALTER F.: *Smith and Wesson Hand Guns*, Huntington, West Virginia (1945).

PARSONS, JOHN: *Henry Deringer's Pocket Pistol*, New York (1952).

PETERSON, HAROLD L.: *Arms and Armor in Colonial America, 1526–1783*, Harrisburg (1956).

ROBERTS, NED H.: *The Muzzle-loading Cap Lock Rifle*, Harrisburg (2nd edition, 1952).

SERVEN, JAMES E.: *Colt Firearms*, Santa Ana (1954).

SMITH, WINSTON O.: *The Sharps Rifle*, New York (1943).

WILLIAMSON, HAROLD F.: *Winchester*, Washington (1952).

WINANT, LEWIS: *Pepperbox Firearms*, New York (1952).

Concise Encyclopedia of Antiques, Vol. I, pp. 188–198, Hawthorn Books, New York (1955).

CLOCKS AND WATCHES

By AMOS G. AVERY

THE production of American timepieces in any quantity extends back little more than two hundred years, as compared to more than twice that in Europe. There is evidence that mechanical clocks were in use in the Far East as early as the eleventh century. However, the American clock and watchmakers have surpassed those of the older countries in the variety of styles created, the mechanical ingenuity displayed and the new methods of manufacturing originated. A complete history of American clock- or watchmaking cannot be attempted here. The few glimpses into the beginnings of the craft, the growth of the small shops and the development of the craft into a large industry may help to kindle the interests of beginning collectors and to serve as a guide to those only casually interested in timepieces.

CLOCKS

Time has so obscured the records that it is now impossible to say positively who was the first clockmaker in America. During the first hundred years after the settlement of the original colonists a few pioneer clockmakers were at work; and although the products of these early craftsmen are practically extinct, to these men, mostly unknown, goes the credit of having been America's first clockmakers. Evidence of the presence of early clockmakers may be obtained from old town or court records and from inventories of estates. In 1638 THOMAS NASH was one of the early settlers of New Haven, Connecticut. That Nash was a clockmaker is indicated by the inventory of his estate in 1658. Among his tools is listed: 'one round plate for making clocks'. No clocks are known which can be attributed to him, nor is it certain that he

actually made any clocks, but the fact that he had tools for 'making clocks' is evidence that he was actually a clockmaker rather than a repairer.

It is well established from inventories of their estates that many of the wealthier early colonists had clocks. It may be assumed that most of these had been brought over as original household equipment or had been imported later. These early clocks were probably wall or bracket clocks, and had weights and a foliot balance or later a short bob pendulum. Some spring-driven table clocks were also undoubtedly in use in the colonies. These early clocks probably had only an hour hand and the spaces between the hours were divided into quarter-hours. In addition, some of the larger towns had one or more public clocks quite early. Whether these large tower clocks were also imported, or whether they were made by now forgotten colonial clockmakers is unknown. Boston had a tower clock as early as 1657, for in November of that year RICHARD TAYLOR, probably not actually a 'clock maker', was allowed 30 shillings for repairing it. Undoubtedly the oldest American-made tower clock now in existence is one in Guilford, Connecticut, which was installed in the meeting-house there in 1726 by EBENEZER PARMELE.

There are other men of whom some scant records exist of clockmaking activities before 1700. Among these are: JOHN MOLL (Delaware c. 1680), WILLIAM DAVIS (Boston 1683), ABEL COTTEY (Philadelphia c.1690), SAMUEL BISPHAM (Philadelphia c. 1695: Plate 189A) and EVERARDUS BOGARDUS (New York 1698). But for two or three exceptions, no clocks by these early makers are known to be in existance today. It is extremely doubtful that any now unknown seventeenth-century clocks will ever be found.

From about 1715 there were a number of clockmakers to whom existing clocks can certainly be attributed. Most of the men working in this period had come to America as young men after having learned clockmaking from master craftsmen in England. A few learned their craft from earlier clockmakers already in the colonies. BENJAMIN CHANDLEE (Plate 189B), first of a numerous family of clockmakers, was from Ireland. He came to Philadelphia in 1702 and was apprenticed to Abel Cottey, the first established clockmaker of Philadelphia. PETER STRETCH, who was born in England and there learned his trade under English masters, came to Philadelphia in 1702 and became a community leader as well as a prosperous clockmaker. BENJAMIN BAGNALL, perhaps Boston's first clockmaker, was born in England and there, or in Philadelphia, learned his craft and appeared in Boston as a clockmaker about 1710. WILLIAM CLAGGETT, born in Wales, advertised as a clockmaker when first appearing in Boston about 1715. Claggett soon went to Newport, Rhode Island, and became established there as a clockmaker of repute and also as a maker of musical instruments. ISAAC PEARSON, silver- and goldsmith as well as a clockmaker, had a clockshop in Burlington, New Jersey, about 1730. Slightly later than these were GAWEN BROWN (Plate 190B) who was in Boston before 1750; and DAVID BLAISDELL (Plate 191A), one of a family of clockmakers who was in Amesbury, Massachusetts, by 1740. SETH YOUNGS, possibly an apprentice of Ebenezer Parmele, was at work in Hartford, Connecticut, before 1740.

To these men, and others, who were at work during the first half of the eighteenth century, may be credited the making of some of the classical examples of American clocks. If a collector is seeking to acquire specimens of the earliest possible American clocks, he will probably need to be content with examples by any of the makers in this period. Authentic examples of any American clocks made before 1750 are very rare and many of those known have already been acquired by museums.

By 1750 a number of skilled clockmakers were at work in Philadelphia and surrounding areas. While in most cases only a few clocks were produced by any of these makers, their products are often examples of the finest craftsmanship of the American clockmakers. The most famous of the Philadelphia group was DAVID RITTENHOUSE (at work c. 1750–1790), scientist, mathematician, astronomer, and a President (1791) of the American Philosophical Society. A large grandfather clock by Rittenhouse, now in the Drexel Institute of Technology, Philadelphia, is a superb example of the finest in American clocks (Plate 190C).

In other American colonies, in addition to those mentioned, there were a few clockmakers at work in the eighteenth century. These men produced relatively few clocks and had little, if any, influence on the development of clockmaking as an American industry.

The clocks made by the eighteenth-century clockmakers were mostly of the grandfather type. Each clock was individually made by hand and fitted to the case which had also been made in the same shop or by a local cabinetmaker. Probably in most instances the clock had been built on order of a particular customer and had been designed to his specifications. It was not until toward the end of the century that clockmakers were making unordered clocks in quantity. These early tall clocks usually had brass eight-day movements, although a few thirty-hour movements are found. The dials were usually of brass with cast brass spandrels. A few small and simple hang-up, or wag-on-the-wall, clocks were made for the less wealthy customers or by less skilled craftsmen. Members of the Blaisdell family of Massachusetts made a number of such quaint little clocks, examples of which may be rarely found (Plate 191A, B).

These early clockmakers were craftsmen in the full sense of the word. Working in small home shops alone, or with an apprentice or two, they produced finished clocks from raw material. Plates, rough blanks for wheels, and other parts, were cast of brass in sand molds. These were hammered to harden the brass and the wheels were turned and the teeth cut and shaped with only the simplest of hand tools. In addition many craftsmen doubled as cabinetmakers, making the cases for their clocks. It was natural that these men, skilled in several fields, should use their abilities for more than clockmaking; many advertised as gold- or silversmiths, engravers or instrument makers; others qualified as lock- or gunsmiths, and many turned to surveying, for which there was a great need. Thus, in many ways, these skilled craftsmen took a very important part in the general economy of the colonies. These other services were probably of more general usefulness and benefit to their neighbors than the few clocks which they were able to produce.

From 1750 to 1800 clocks, principally tall or grandfather, were made in increasing numbers. Before this period the only families who were able to afford a clock were the wealthy ones. As the young country prospered more people became able to enjoy finer things and thus a market developed for articles which had formerly been luxuries. Clockmakers throughout the colonies, but especially in New England, were endeavoring to meet the increased demand for clocks. More individuals were learning the craft, and methods were being found to increase the output of the small shops and to reduce the cost of the finished product. About the middle of the eighteenth century a few clockmakers in Connecticut were making innovations which ultimately were to result in making Connecticut the center of the clockmaking industry of America. The most revolutionary of these new ideas was the use of wood in movements to replace brass, which was both expensive and difficult to obtain. Authorities do not agree as to the American origin of the wooden movement. It is generally agreed that some of the simple clocks made in central Europe during the seventeenth century were of wood. The Connecticut clockmakers undoubtedly knew these older European wooden clocks and probably obtained some ideas from them.

BENJAMIN CHENEY (Plate 190A) and his younger brother TIMOTHY of East Hartford, Connecticut, are usually credited with making, about 1745, the earliest of the existing Connecticut wooden movements. Benjamin had probably been an apprentice of Seth Youngs of Hartford. Others in central Con-

necticut were also making wooden clocks about this time, but the Cheneys were apparently the most successful and are especially important because of their influence as teachers of the craft.

These early Connecticut wooden clocks were clumsy, thirty-hour grandfather clocks which were wound by pulling down on cords. They usually had brass dials, or brass-covered wood dials and often were in nice cases. Although crudely made, they were satisfactory timekeepers and in comparison with the fine contemporary brass clocks were inexpensive. These earliest wooden clocks by the Cheneys, GIDEON ROBERTS, JOHN RICH and others of Connecticut are now rare and keenly sought by collectors.

The influence of these craftsmen of central Connecticut spread to Massachusetts as well as throughout Connecticut. BENJAMIN WILLARD was born in 1743 in Grafton, Massachusetts. About 1760 he went to East Hartford as an apprentice of Benjamin Cheney. He undoubtedly also visited and knew something of the work of other nearby Connecticut clockmakers. After completing his apprenticeship with Cheney he returned to Grafton and opened (c. 1765) a clock-shop at the old family home. At the time Benjamin Willard opened his shop his three younger brothers, SIMON, EPHRAIM and AARON, were twelve, ten, and eight years old respectively. These three, each of whom was to become a noted clockmaker, first learned of the clockmaking craft from Benjamin. From Grafton the four brothers moved to Roxbury, Lexington, and Boston and independently established profitable clockmaking businesses. From these Willard brothers, from apprentices of each, and from contemporary craftsmen who borrowed their designs and used their methods, there developed an extensive clockmaking industry in eastern Massachusetts, southern New Hampshire and Rhode Island. Clockmakers of this 'Willard' or 'Boston' school made clocks of the highest quality. Many types – tower, grandfather, banjo, lyre, lighthouse, girandole, and shelf – some of which were new designs, were made by them. Little attempt was made to produce an inexpensive clock, as was the trend in Connecticut. No wooden movements were produced by any of these men. In Ashby, Massachusetts, two distantly related Willard brothers, ALEXANDER and PHILANDER, made (c. 1800–30) wooden movements in the Connecticut manner.

Simon is the most famous of the four brothers on account of his patented (1802) timepiece which is now known as the banjo clock (Plate 191C, D). He was probably the most mechanically gifted of the four, having other inventions besides clocks to his credit. He worked first at Grafton (1774–80), and from 1780 to 1839 in Roxbury. Among his many apprentices who became prominent clockmakers were: ABEL and LEVI HUTCHINS, ELNATHAN TABER (Plate 194A), and DANIEL MUNROE, besides his sons, SIMON, JR., and BENJAMIN.

Ephraim worked in Medford, Roxbury, and Boston but produced only a few clocks – grandfather clocks only. He abandoned clockmaking, turned to merchandising, and is presumed to have removed to the city of New York.

Aaron produced large quantities of clocks and is particularly noted for developing the Massachusetts shelf clock (Plate 195C). He opened a shop near Simon's in Roxbury about 1780 and later moved to Boston where he established a small factory. He retired in 1823 with a considerable fortune and was succeeded by his sons, AARON, JR., and HENRY, who continued the extensive clockmaking business. Aaron, Jr., is often credited with originating the lyre clock (Plate 192E, F).

The several members of the Willard family had a very great influence on the development of clockmaking in Massachusetts, and for this, as well as for the fine clocks which they actually produced, are generally thought of as the most noted family of American clockmakers. The earliest clocks made by Benjamin, Simon, or Aaron are exceedingly rare. An excellent history of the Willard family is given in: *A History of Simon Willard, Clockmaker and Inventor*, by John Ware Willard.

Two other clockmakers at work in Connecticut during the last part of the eighteenth century deserve special notice on account of the quantity and variety of their work, and particularly because of their influence on the beginnings of clockmaking as a great industry. THOMAS HARLAND, a skilled clockmaker from England, settled in Norwich in 1773. He had a large shop with numerous apprentices and produced a relatively large output of clocks, jewelry, and related products. DANIEL BURNAP, the most noted of Harland's apprentices, opened his own shop in East Windsor about 1780, and ultimately surpassed his master as a craftsman. Harland and Burnap made fine clocks with brass movements, some with musical attachments. Burnap was a very skilful engraver and many of his brass dials show this special talent. Clocks by either of these makers are rare and choice. Soon after Burnap opened his shop at East Windsor, he took as an apprentice ELI TERRY, born in 1772, the son of a neighboring farmer. There is evidence that Terry also had some woodworking training with one of the Cheneys of East Hartford. After completing his apprenticeship with Burnap, Eli Terry opened his own shop in 1793, for clockmaking and watch repairing in Plymouth, Connecticut. The first clocks that Terry made following his training under Burnap were brass movements for tall clocks. However, he soon turned his attention to producing wooden clocks, using small hand-tools and a foot-lathe for turning. About 1803 Terry erected a small building on a stream and began to use water power to turn his machines. In 1806 he accepted an order for four thousand clocks. To meet the demands for such numbers he devised methods to greatly reduce the amount of hand labor needed. The most important innovation was the use of standardized or interchangeable parts. Instead of making all the parts for one clock before starting the next, he now made large numbers of identical parts which went to an assembling line where the complete clocks were put together. This was the first application of the modern manufacturing methods to clock production and as such, was the beginning of the highly specialized and extensive clock industry in Connecticut.

These early wooden clocks of Eli Terry were thirty-hour movements intended for grandfather cases. In most instances they were sold without cases and the buyer had a case made to his own specification, or the movement could be used as a wag-on-the-wall (Plate 193A). These movements with the weights and pendulum sold for about fifteen dollars and the cases cost from five to thirty dollars, depending on material and workmanship. These wooden clocks were so popular that many others began to copy Terry's methods and to manufacture similar ones. By 1815 the making of wooden clocks was an important industry chiefly in central and western Connecticut and to a less extent in parts of Massachusetts and New Hampshire. Some names most frequently seen on wood-movement tall clocks (c. 1810–25) are RILEY WHITING, SILAS HOADLEY and SETH THOMAS of Connecticut; ABRAHAM and CALVIN EDWARDS, ALEXANDER and PHILANDER WILLARD of Ashby, Massachusetts; JOHN PERKINS and JESSE EMORY of New Hampshire. A great many clocks of this period are found with no indication of the maker and, unless in a particularly nice case, are not especially valuable.

While producing wood-movement tall clocks in quantity Eli Terry was endeavoring to invent a satisfactory movement for a shelf clock. His first model, a modification of the tall clock movement, was made about 1814. Terry's efforts resulted in the production of some seven or more known models, climaxed about 1818 by a design which proved so successful that it was made in large numbers by Terry and his sons and was extensively copied and produced by many other makers (Plate 197A, B) until about 1840, when the introduction of an inexpensive brass movement brought all production of wood-movements to an end. Some of the early models were enclosed in simple box-like cases. Probably in 1817 the first of the graceful and popular case, now called the pillar and scroll, was produced. Some of these first models are recognized by having the escape wheel and pendulum in front of the dial (Plate 196A). All of these early models are very rare.

These complete shelf clocks were produced to sell for about the same price as the wood-movement tall clock, fifteen dollars. Being cheaper than a complete tall clock, smaller and more portable, the new wood-movement shelf clock soon became popular and

the production of tall clock movements ceased about 1825. By 1830 literally dozens of small shops in western Connecticut were producing wooden shelf clocks. By then the cases had been simplified by CHAUNCEY JEROME and others to a much plainer form. While the movement perfected by Terry was most commonly used, other clockmakers had meanwhile invented perhaps fifty other variations of wood movements. Many of these are rare. A few eight-day wood movements were made, but these were rather unsatisfactory on account of the extra heavy weights needed, which often caused broken wheels. To compete with the eight-day brass clocks being made by the Massachusetts clockmakers certain Connecticut makers were producing a few shelf clocks with eight-day brass movements. HEMAN CLARK of Plymouth (Plate 196D), several makers of Salem Bridge (now Naugatuck), and the brothers CHAUNCEY and LAWSON IVES and others of Bristol and nearby towns were specializing in eight-day brass shelf clocks during the time (1815–38) that the thirty-hour wooden movement was the major product of the Connecticut clock factories.

In 1838 NOBLE JEROME, at the suggestion of his brother, Chauncey, devised a simple thirty-hour weight movement of rolled brass, which up to then had only been used for more expensive eight-day clocks. This type of clock almost immediately forced all wooden clocks out of production, for it was cheaper and better in every way. The brass movements were not affected by dampness and were much more rugged than wooden ones. No wood-movement clocks were in commercial production after about 1842. Eight-day weight clocks were also manufactured, but in smaller numbers than the thirty-hour. The simple ogee case, which had occasionally been used with wooden movements before 1838, now became the predominant style (Plate 197D). It was simple and cheap to manufacture, which was an important factor in making it possible for the manufacturers to reduce the cost of a complete clock to the minimum. It was now found profitable to export large numbers of these cheap clocks to England and other countries.

Factory-produced inexpensive steel springs first became available in this country soon after 1840. The use of coiled springs for power made it possible to design smaller cases, since it was no longer necessary to provide space for the up and down travel of the weights. Small clocks of many types began to appear before 1850 and were produced in increasing numbers thereafter (Plate 199A, D). By the mid-1850s brass movement shelf clocks, both weight- and spring-powered, were produced in Connecticut in huge quantities by a few large factories which replaced the many small shops which had made wooden movements. It has been estimated that in the year 1855 four of the largest companies produced more than 400,000 clocks. This period of mass production of inexpensive clocks yielded very few items which may now be considered desirable from the collector's standpoint. Exceptions to this are a few unusual or novelty items made in small numbers.

Clocks are usually acquired by others than collectors for decorative purposes in addition to their use as timekeepers. In 1933 Wallace Nutting wrote: 'The clock and the case, when both are fine and harmonious, still constitute the most beautiful decoration for an American home.' Fine old clocks thus become important items of decorative furniture as well as useful timekeepers. When restored to proper mechanical condition, such clocks will keep time with all the accuracy required by exacting modern schedules.

Few antique clocks can now be found which do not need some restoration. This is partly due to the constant use and handling to which they have been subjected as well as to the nature of the materials of which they are made. The large panels of thin glass in many styles of clocks are easily broken. Many cases are of veneered wood, which may be chipped in handling. The restoration of such damage to fine clocks should only be entrusted to qualified craftsmen.

Of all the kinds of collectable American antiques, clocks and watches are the least stabilized as to value or price. While other antiques such as coins, stamps, guns etc. have had approximate values established by published price lists, the prices of clocks and watches vary greatly from area to area or from dealer to dealer. A signed item usually commands a higher price than a similar one not signed, and one signed by a famous maker even higher. There are many fine unsigned clocks available which in beauty and mechanical quality are equal to any by famous makers, and which may be acquired at much lower prices.

WATCHES

A fine antique clock is usually acquired as a decorative as well as a useful household item. While several clocks may be assembled for such purposes, old watches, on the other hand, have little decorative or practical use. The watch collector must be a true specialist; he must be informed on the complex history of American watch-making; he must also be familiar with the fine mechanical characteristics of the many types of watches. Within the field of watch collecting an even narrower specialization will probably be made by the serious collector. He may try to collect watches by early makers, watches by extinct companies, or mechanically unusual ones. He will need to examine carefully every old watch to make sure that no important example is overlooked. American-made watches dating before 1800 are practically non-existent and those before 1850 are rare. All of these old watches are key-winders and are usually of large size.

Many of the early American clockmakers also advertised as watchmakers. The few watches which they produced were entirely hand-made. The watchmaker doubtless used imported parts – springs, jewels, balances, etc. when available. Most examples of watches made before 1815 and signed with American names are so similar to contemporary English pieces that it is generally assumed that they were English imports or assembled from imported parts (Plate 200B). These, therefore, cannot be considered as being completely American-made. However, they are all very rare.

It is impossible to state who made the first complete American watch. In 1809 LUTHER GODDARD opened a small shop in Shrewsbury, Massachusetts, for the production of watches. It is not certain what proportion of the watch was imported and what was locally made. However, Goddard is usually credited with the first manufacture of watches in quantity in this country. By 1817 when production ceased, about five hundred watches had been made.

Probably the first manufacture of an all-American watch was begun in Hartford, Connecticut, in 1837 by the brothers, HENRY and JAMES PITKIN. The Pitkins had also designed and made the crude machinery with which the watches were manufactured. In 1841 they moved to New York, N.Y. Due partly to competition from the lower-priced Swiss watches the company ceased operations about 1845, when somewhat fewer than a thousand watches had been produced.

In 1843 JACOB CUSTER of Norristown, Pennsylvania, was granted a patent for watches. Custer is only one of many such craftsmen who, about the middle of the nineteenth century, constructed a few watches of their own design. Watches made by these makers often have unusual features and any examples are extremely rare.

The modern American methods of watch manufacturing had their origin in the shop of EDWARD HOWARD (a clockmaker) and AARON DENNISON of Boston about 1850. From this small beginning grew the great Waltham Watch Company. The first model, an eight-day watch, was produced in 1850. The firm was first known as The American Horologe Company, later changed to Boston Clock Co., and in 1859 to American Watch Company (Plate 200D). For making watch parts, Howard and Dennison invented machines which, with only minor changes, are used in modern watch factories. In 1885 the company became the American Waltham Watch Co. Some of the finest watches ever made – repeaters, stop-watches, and chronographs (Plate 200E) – have been made by the Waltham Company.

In 1864 DON J. MOZART was making, in Providence, Rhode Island, a very unusual watch with what he called a 'Chronometer lever escapement'. In 1867 he moved to Springfield, Massachusetts, and with others formed the New York Watch Co. (Plate 200C), which in 1877 became the Hampden Watch Co., later moving to Canton, Ohio, as the Dueber-Hampden Watch Co., at one time one of the largest makers of watches in the country. The early watches by Mozart are very rare.

The inexpensive ('Dollar') watch of 1890–1920 had its beginning with the invention in 1877 by D. A. A. BUCK in Worcester, Massachusetts, of a watch which could be manufactured to sell for four dollars. These were first manufactured in Connecticut by BENEDICT & BURNHAM (Plate 200F), later The Waterbury Watch Co. Early examples of these simple watches are now quite rare. Inexpensive watches were also later made by the Ingersoll Co., New Haven Watch Co., and others.

A great many mechanical innovations in watch movements have been designed by American makers. In the design of escapements used there is great variation. Some of the types of escapements found on American watches are: verge and crown wheel (Goddard), English sharp-tooth lever (Pitkin), club-tooth (Howard), duplex (Waterbury) and others, most of which have been replaced in later watches by the simple lever escapement.

From 1850 to 1885 more than fifty independent companies were organized for the manufacture of watches. Most of these survived only a short time. It has been the usual custom for watchmakers and watch companies to sign and number watch movements. From these numbers the age of the watch can be ascertained. *The Book of American Clocks* lists by years the serial numbers used by some of the American watchmakers.

COLLECTIONS

While many of the larger public museums may have one or more outstanding clocks in their collection, there are only a few museums which have any extensive collection of American clocks or watches on display. Notable collections are in the following museums: Boston Museum of Fine Arts, Boston, Massachusetts; Bristol Clock Museum, Bristol, Connecticut; California Academy of Sciences, San Francisco, California; Essex Institute,

Salem, Massachusetts; Metropolitan Museum of Art, New York; Newark Public Library, Newark, New York; New York University (the James Arthur Collection), New York; Old Sturbridge Village, Sturbridge, Massachusetts; Pennsylvania Historical Society, Philadelphia, Pennsylvania; Smithsonian Institution, U.S. National Museum, Washington, D.C.

There are also many large private collections of clocks and watches. Although these are not generally open to the public, most of the owners are glad to show their collections to especially interested persons or groups, but arrangements should be made in advance for the privilege. Most collectors of clocks and watches are members of the National Association of Watch and Clock Collectors, Inc. This organization, formed in 1943, publishes a *Bulletin* which contains articles of general interest to collectors of horological objects and material.

BAROMETERS

The ornamental mercurial barometer, though frequent in England and on the Continent, has never been in general use in America and the majority of examples found have been imported. This is true even of many fine barometers bearing names with Boston, New York, or Philadelphia addresses. Such names are nearly always those of dealers or importers.

There were a few, relatively plain barometers made in America during the nineteenth century. Among those to whom patents were granted are: WILLIAM HOPKINS, Geneva, New York (1841); TIMBY (1857); H. A. CLUM (Plate 200A), Rochester, New York (1860); WOODRUFF (1860); B. C. SPOONER (Plate 200A), Boston, Massachusetts (1860); C. WILDER, Peterborough, New Hampshire (1860).

The American makers have stressed the utilitarian rather than the decorative use of barometers. Thus, Clum and King of Clifton Springs, New York, advertised an 'Agricultural Barometer' about 1860. Even though American-made barometers are rarely over a hundred years old, they deserve the attention of collectors.

GLOSSARY

Acorn clock: a type of Connecticut shelf clock, in shape suggesting an acorn. *C.* 1850. Rare.

Alarm: a mechanical attachment which, at a predetermined time, rings a bell or activates some other alarm. Found on many types of American clocks, but least commonly on tall clocks. The time for the release of the alarm is usually determined, or 'set', by a brass disk numbered 1–12, or by a third hand.

Arbor: the shaft or axle to which pinions and wheels are attached. (Fig. 1A.)

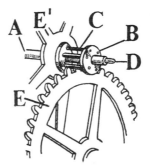

Fig. 1. A. Arbor, B. Collet, C. Pinion, D. Pivot, E, E¹. Wheels.

Balance staff: the arbor or shaft which carries the balance wheel.

Balance or balance wheel: an oscillating wheel which, controlled by the balance (hair) spring, regulates the rate of a watch or certain small clocks.

Banjo clock: the recent term applied to various wall clocks somewhat resembling a banjo in shape. The earliest American example was the 'Improved Timepiece' produced by SIMON WILLARD before 1800 and patented by him in 1802. Developed by the Willards and others in eastern Massachusetts and Rhode Island, it became one of the most popular types of clocks. Others copied and modified the original design in so many ways that an almost endless number of varieties resulted.

The banjo, in its best form, is a finely made piece. The movements used, although varying in details, were ordinarily brass, weight-driven eight-day timepieces, with a pendulum about

20–26 inches long. A few striking, as well as alarm, movements were also used. A very few Connecticut wall clocks, somewhat resembling the true banjo, were made using the 30-hour wooden movement.

Since 1800, there probably has not been a single decade when banjos have not been manufactured, so popular have they been. The clocks produced by the Willards, their apprentices, and other contemporaries until about 1830 are the most pleasing in design. Later plainer, and not so perfectly made banjos were sold in large numbers. After about 1845, EDWARD HOWARD in Boston, alone and with others under various company names, manufactured large numbers of simple banjos in several sizes.

Because of the popularity of the banjo clock and the rarity of the best examples, a great many reproductions and rebuilt pieces have appeared. It is probably a fact that more deliberate faking has been attempted in 'making' old banjos than any other type of clock. Many old banjos have been 'improved' by adding the name of a famous maker. Such imitations or fakes are sometimes very difficult to detect. There are no consistent and positive characteristics by which genuine banjos by the Willards or other famous makers can always be identified (Plates 191D, 192A, B, C).

Banking pins: two fixed pins which limit the motion of the lever of a lever escapement.

Barrel: a cylindrical box containing the mainspring; usual in watches. Most American spring-powered clocks made before 1900 have unenclosed springs.

Battery clock: any clock using electrical energy from batteries. It may either be: (*a*) electrically driven or (*b*) electrically wound. In the latter case the clock mechanism may be a standard weight or spring movement which, when partially run down, may activate a magnet or electric motor which again winds it – such clocks are called self-winding. Various types of battery clocks were made in small numbers during the latter part of the nineteenth century and up to nearly 1920 when the small synchronous clock motor was perfected. Most types are now rare, and are of interest historically and mechanically.

Beat: the sound made by the action of the escapement – the 'tick-tock'. A timepiece is 'in beat' when the intervals between beats are even.

Beehive clock: a form of small Connecticut shelf clock, also called 'flatiron' clock; so named because of the resemblance of the shape to an old-time beehive or flatiron. *c.* 1850–60. Common. (Plate 199B, D).

Bezel: the circular frame, metal or wood, into which a clock or watch glass is fitted.

Blinking-eye clocks: novelty clocks with cast-iron cases representing various figures. Painted in natural colors; with pivoted eyes that 'blink' with the motion of the clock mechanism. Interesting as novelties. *c.* 1860. Rare.

Bob: the weight at the lower end of the pendulum, also called the pendulum ball. The form varies from spherical or cylindrical to lenticular or disk-shaped. Some American clocks have bobs of unusual forms, as swinging dolls, flying eagles, etc. (Fig. 5G.)

Bob wire: the wire loop which passes through the bob of many American clocks. One end is threaded for the regulating nut (Fig. 5H).

Bushings: extra material, usually metal, inserted in the plates and serving as bearings for the pivots. The removal of worn bushings and replacement with new is called 'rebushing'.

Calendar clock: in general, any clock with attachments to indicate days, months or years. Used specifically for many forms of wall or shelf clocks (after 1845) in which the calendar dials or indicators are prominent features. These occur in a wide variety of sizes and styles. Some are interesting and highly desirable.

Calendar, perpetual: a calendar mechanism so constructed that months with varying numbers of days and even leap years are provided for.

Case: that which contains the clock or watch movement. Any solid material as metal, stone or wood may be used. American clocks are usually in wooden cases. The variety of designs, selection of woods and the quality of cabinet work contribute to the fascination of clocks to the collector.

Case-on-case clock: *see* Massachusetts shelf clock.

Center seconds, or sweep seconds hand: an arrangement by which the second hand is placed concentric with the minute and hour hands. Found on some watches, rare on clocks, but occasionally on tall clocks, especially those by Pennsylvania makers.

Chapter ring: the part of a dial on which the hours are marked. On clocks made before about 1770 it is often a separate metal ring (brass, pewter or silvered) applied to the dial-plate.

Chronograph: a watch, stop-watch, the hands of which can be started, stopped and returned to zero without stopping its motion (Plate 200E).

Chronometer: an especially accurate portable timepiece, as a marine chronometer.

Chronometer escapement: a special type of escapement used in chronometers, also called a *detent escapement*.

Click: the pawl that works against the ratchet wheel of the winding drum; its action causes the clicking when a timepiece is wound.

Collet: an extra flange or collar strengthening or holding a wheel or pinion on an arbor; also the split ring holding the hairspring to the balance staff (Fig. 1B).

Compensating pendulum, or balance: a pendulum or balance, usually of two different metals so constructed that the effect of temperature changes is compensated for.

Conical pendulum: a pendulum, the bob of which, instead of vibrating to and fro, swings in a complete circle. Not found on American clocks with the exception of certain novelties. The 'Briggs' conical pendulum or rotary clock (patented 1855 by John C. Briggs and made in Connecticut, *c.* 1860–70) is the best known example.

Cottage clocks: name now given to many small Connecticut spring clocks in wood cases. *c.* 1850–1900. Common (Plate 199C).

Count wheel: a wheel, or a plate attached to a wheel of the strike train, with notches or holes at increasing intervals around its rim, controlling the number of blows struck on the bell or gong. Commonly found on Connecticut shelf clocks.

Crown wheel: the type of escape wheel used with the verge escapement of the earliest European mechanical clocks. Probably never used in America, an exception being the Columbus clock (marked 1492) made as a souvenir for the 1893 Columbian Exposition at Chicago; now of some interest in that it demonstrates an early clock mechanism.

Crutch: that part of a clock mechanism which is attached to the pallet arbor (or to the verge) and which transmits the impulses to the independently hung pendulum. Ordinarily the pendulum rod passes through a loop or fork of the crutch (Fig. 5D).

Cylinder escapement: a type of watch escapement in which the teeth of the escape wheel work on a cut-away cylinder attached to the balance.

Dial: the 'face' of a timepiece on which may be marked the hours, minutes or seconds. Dials may be of several shapes – round, square, arched, kidney-shaped, etc.; flat, convex, concave or 'dished'.

The dials of the earliest American grandfather clocks were of brass, pewter, or sometimes of wood with pewter or brass chapter rings. Dials of tall clocks made from about 1750 to 1790 were usually brass, often silvered and usually with considerable etching. The painted iron dial appeared about 1785 and soon was used almost exclusively. Many of these iron dials were imported from England and many have the imprinted name of an English iron foundry on the reverse side. Two such foundries, Osborne and Wilson, both of Birmingham, supplied great numbers of these dials to American clockmakers, as these names are most common. The presence of such English names on otherwise unsigned American clocks has been the cause of much confusion to collectors who may assume that a particular clock so marked is of English origin. It should be remembered that such names of English foundries are found only as stampings or castings on the reverse side of brass or iron dial components.

The dials of practically all wooden movement clocks were of wood, hand-painted and decorated. Dials of the better clocks such as banjos, lyres, Massachusetts shelf clocks and the like were of painted iron. About 1840 the painted thin zinc dial appeared on Connecticut clocks.

Dial, or motion wheels: the wheels that cause the hour hand to turn twelve times slower than the minute hand.

Drum: the spool on to which the cord to the weight is wound.

Duplex escapement: a watch escapement in which the escape wheel has two sets of teeth.

Equation of time: the difference between mean time (shown by the usual clock) and solar time (indicated by the sundial). The mean day is exactly twenty-four hours long, whereas the length of the solar day varies daily.

Escapement: the means, or device, by which the power of a timepiece is allowed to escape, and is transmitted to the pendulum or balance. Hundreds of types have been in-

Fig. 2. Anchor or recoil escapement.

vented, but only a very few are in general use. The anchor or recoil escapement (Fig. 2) and the dead beat (Fig 3) are types used in the majority of American pendulum clocks; the lever escapement (Fig. 4), the cylinder, duplex and other types were used in watches. Great mech-

Fig. 3. Dead beat escapement.

anical ingenuity has been shown by American inventors in designing escapements. These technical features are of special importance in the study of watches.

Escape wheel: the final wheel of the time train of a clock or watch which gives impulse to the pendulum or balance. Often shortened to 'scape wheel (Fig. 5A).

Fan, or fly: a rapidly turning vane on the final arbor of the strike train which slows and governs the rate of striking.

Finials: the turned, carved or molded ornaments, usually brass or wood at the top of various types of clocks.

Foliot: a form of crude balance used before 1660 with verge escapement to regulate the running of clocks or watches. Not known to have been used in America; *see* Crown wheel.

Franklin clock: a type of wooden movement shelf clock made (1825–30) by SILAS HOADLEY of Plymouth, Connecticut, and called by him 'Franklin'. It is perhaps the earliest instance that a clock was given a specific (model) name by a maker. This movement is characterized by being practically an inverted form of the movement then being made by TERRY and others.

Fusee: a conically-shaped and spirally-grooved pulley which equalizes the pull of the mainspring on the train. Used on a few shelf clocks about 1840–60 to compensate for the poor quality of springs then available.

Gathering pallet: a pin, or pawl fixed to one arbor of the striking train which, in revolving, gathers up one tooth of the rack at each revolution. In many clocks it also stops the striking motion at the end of the proper number of blows.

Girandole: a type of wall clock designed by LEMUEL CURTIS. Considered by many to be the most beautiful American clock. *c.* 1820. Very rare (Plate 192D).

Gong: a spirally wound steel wire on which the hours are struck. Used instead of a bell on most shelf clocks after 1835.

Gothic clocks: pointed-topped Connecticut shelf clocks introduced about 1845; many sizes and varieties. The most popular were called 'sharp gothic'; now commonly known as steeple clocks. Including round and sharp topped gothics, variations in style and size of cases, and variations in types of movements, there are probably over a hundred different forms. Most are attractive and deserve the interest of the advanced collector as well as the beginner (Plate 199A).

Grandfather clock: common American name for hall or long-case clocks. Small examples are called miniature grandfather clocks or grandmother clocks.

Grandmother clock: a small hall clock about five feet or less in height. There is no exact point where a distinction between grandfather or grandmother clocks can be made (Plate 193C).

Gravity escapement: an especially accurate escapement often used in tower clocks or regulators. Impulse is given to the pendulum by two weighted arms which are raised by the clock mechanism.

Hairspring: the fine spring which regulates the motion of the balance wheel.

Hands: the pointers of a clock or watch. There are many designs of hands used on American clocks. Many on eighteenth-century clocks, especially those on tall clocks, are similar to those found on English clocks of the period and were undoubtedly imported with other metal parts. On wood-movement tall clocks and on the earliest wood-movement shelf clocks the hands were usually of pewter. On the better-quality clocks of the 1790–1825 period the wide variety of hands are of steel and usually nicely designed and cut. An excellent study of clock hands with drawings is given in Volume III of Nutting's *Furniture Treasury* (1933).

Hollow column clocks: weight-powered shelf clocks with free standing hollow columns as part of the case decoration within which the weights travel. *c.* 1830–40. Rare (Plate 197C).

Hourglass: a sandglass which measures an hour; *see* Sandglass.

Hourglass clock: any of several styles of Connecticut clocks in the general shape of an hourglass. *c.* 1850. Rare.

Jewels: synthetic or semi-precious stones used as bearings for the pivots of many watches and some especially fine clocks.

Iron-front clocks: small Connecticut shelf clocks with fronts of cast iron in many forms, painted and often decorated with shell inlays. *c.* 1860. Common, but interesting.

Labels: engraved, lithographed or printed papers found inside many clocks. The use of such labels in clocks may have been suggested by the somewhat similar use of labels that certain master cabinetmakers occasionally placed in their furniture. Cabinetmakers' labels, as well as those of clockmakers, are found in a few tall clock cases made about 1800 or earlier. Clock labels became a usual feature of shelf clocks from their very earliest production (*c.* 1815). These labels give the maker's name and place of business and usually the directions for setting up, regulating and caring for the clock. Occasionally some additional useful knowledge may be given as the equation of time, postal rates or census figures. Such papers are of the greatest importance in identifying and valuing any clock. The latest published list of American makers, *The Book of American Clocks*, by Brooks Palmer contains some six thousand names.

Lantern clock: an English type of bracket clock (*c.* 1625–1725). Not known to have been made in America, but certainly imported and used.

Lever escapement: an escapement in which the impulse is transmitted from the escape wheel to the balance by a detached lever.

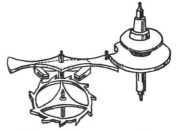

Fig 4. Lever escapement.

Lighthouse clock: (*a*) a clock made in small numbers by SIMON WILLARD and suggesting a lighthouse in form. *c.* 1820. Very rare; (*b*) any of several later novelty clocks resembling a lighthouse.

Long-case clock: any free-standing floor clock, now commonly called hall, tall or grandfather.

Lyre clock: wall or shelf clocks with cases in the general shape of a lyre; the original design is attributed to AARON WILLARD, JR. Many variations in detail of cases. All of excellent quality; eight-day movements; mostly by Massachusetts makers. *c.* 1820–40. Rare (Plate 192E, F).

Mainspring: a long coiled ribbon, usually of steel, which provides power. Steel springs were not successfully manufactured in America for use in clocks until about 1840. Brass springs are occasionally found in small Connecticut clocks of 1840–55.

Maintaining power: temporary power activated by any of several methods to keep a clock running while it is being wound. Rarely used on American clocks except tower clocks and some especially accurate timepieces.

Main wheel: the first, and largest, wheel of the train; the one which first receives the power from the mainspring or weight. Also called the great wheel.

Mantel clock: nearly synonymous with shelf clock, but used mostly in reference to modern clocks.

Massachusetts shelf clock: a type made by the WILLARDS and others, chiefly of Massachusetts. Also called half-clock, box-on-box, or case-on-case. Eight-day brass movements, timepieces or occasionally striking clocks. *c.* 1800–30. Rare (Plate 195A, B, C, D).

Mirror, or looking-glass clock: any clock having a mirror as a prominent part of the case. In 1825 CHAUNCEY JEROME (Bristol, Connecticut) invented the 'looking-glass' clock to compete with the pillar and scroll case then being made by other manufacturers.

New Hampshire mirror clock: as now used refers to a distinct type of rectangular wall clock produced by several makers, mostly of New Hampshire. These usually are about 28–36 inches tall, 14–16 inches wide and about 4 inches deep. The cases may be plain or with a scroll at top, or top and bottom; sometimes partly gilded; and usually have a square decorated glass over the dial. Weight-powered, eight-day brass movements. *c.* 1820–40. Rare (Plate 193D).

Moon dial: a moving disk on which the phases of the moon are represented pictorially. Found on some grandfather clocks, rare on other types (Plate 193B).

Movement: the mechanism, or the 'works' of a timepiece. Usually principally brass with steel or iron parts. Wood was used to replace brass in clock movements by many makers in New England, especially in Connecticut, from about 1790 to 1840. To the mechanically-minded the study of movements offers a wide and interesting field.

Novelty clock: any of many types which, in addition to indicating time, has some unusual feature or that indicates time in a peculiar way. Most clocks in this group were made after 1850; many are now rare and are of interest to collectors for their peculiar features. Most were inexpensive when originally manufactured; some were made to be sold as souvenirs, or to be used for advertising purposes and might be made in the shape of flowers, animals or globes. Many sorts of novelty alarm clocks were made – some that lighted a lamp or fired a powder charge at the preset time. Other novelties had the conventional pendulum replaced by swinging figures or flying balls.

Off-center pendulum: a pendulum which is not hung in the center. Specifically used in reference to certain early shelf clocks with wood movements by ELI TERRY or SETH THOMAS (Plate 196B).

Oil sink: a shallow cup cut in the outside of a clock or watch plate concentric with a pivot hole, to retain oil.

Ogee, or O. G. clock: technically a molding with a reverse curve like the letter S. Used to designate the plain rectangular clocks with such an ogee molding on the front. Probably originated in Connecticut about 1830 and made in great numbers until the first of the twentieth century. The design was simple, inexpensive to make, easy to ship and attractive. Made in numerous sizes ranging from less than a foot to over four feet in height. Many types of movements, wood or brass eight-day or thirty-hour, weight- or spring-powered, were used in these cases. They were primarily shelf clocks but could be hung as wall clocks. Probably more O.G. clocks have been produced in Connecticut than any other type. Some are desirable on account of rare movements or other features (Plate 197D).

Pallets: the parts of the escapement against which the teeth of the escape wheel push and by which it gives impulse to the pendulum or balance (Fig. 5C).

Paperweight clocks: small (4–6 inch) clocks with cases of molded glass in several shapes, sizes and colors. *c.* 1880–1910. Occasional.

Papier-mâché clocks: usually small shelf clocks, the cases of which are molded of papier-mâché; of many forms – some with shell inlays. Connecticut. *c.* 1860. Occasional.

Pendulum: a weighted body so suspended that it can freely swing to and fro as a result of the forces of gravity and momentum. Theoretically a simple pendulum is a weight suspended by a weightless thread. A complete clock pendulum usually consists of a suspension spring, a pendulum ball or bob and a rod which at its lower end has a threaded section with a regulating nut (Fig. 5). CHRISTIAN HUYGENS of Holland is generally considered to have been the first (*c.* 1660) to use the swinging pendulum to regulate a clock. Previously the inaccurate foliot balance was used. The great advantage of the pendulum

for accurate time-keeping was immediately apparent. Within a few years all new clocks were made with pendulums. Many clocks with a foliot balance were converted to use a pendulum. Some of the early clockmakers or repairers advertised about 1700 to convert the older clocks 'in the most modern manner'.

The rate of oscillation (the time needed to swing from one extreme to the other) of a pendulum is determined by its length and is approximately constant at any given place.

The rate will vary with any change in gravitational pull that may be caused by a change in altitude or latitude. Many methods and devices have been developed to reduce the effects which temperature changes have on the length of a pendulum and thereby disturb its rate (*see* Compensating pendulum). Much has been written concerning the theoretical action of the pendulum.

The effective length of a pendulum is the distance from the

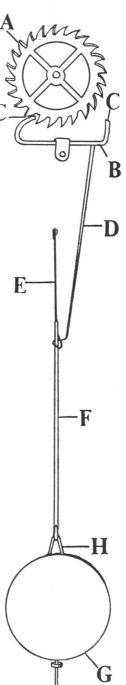

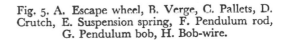

Fig. 5. A. Escape wheel, B. Verge, C. Pallets, D. Crutch, E. Suspension spring, F. Pendulum rod, G. Pendulum bob, H. Bob-wire.

point of suspension to the center of oscillation of the whole pendulum. This point is near, or slightly below, the center of gravity of the pendulum. The following is a simple rule for finding the length of a pendulum required for any given number of vibrations (one way swing) per minute:

If V = vibrations per minute;
L = unknown length in inches;

then

$$L = (375.4 \div V)^2.$$

Some frequently used pendulums are:

Length in inches	Rate of oscillation
2.45	$\frac{1}{4}$ second
9.78	$\frac{1}{2}$,,
22.01	$\frac{3}{4}$,,
39.14	1 ,,
61.15	$1\frac{1}{4}$,,
88.07	$1\frac{1}{2}$,,
156.56	2 ,,

Pillar and scroll: the modern name given to a style of shelf clock having delicate feet, slender pillars, and a broken arch or double scroll at the top. The design was probably an adaptation from eighteenth-century styles. Sometimes called 'Terry-type' clocks as ELI TERRY (c. 1816) was the first to manufacture them in large quantities. Large numbers and several variations were made by Terry, SETH THOMAS, SILAS HOADLEY and other Connecticut makers until about 1830.

Thirty-hour wood movements of several types were usually used, although some fine examples are found with eight-day weight brass movements. The pillar and scroll clock was the first successfully mass-produced shelf clock in America. Similar clocks are found with labels of makers working (1825–40) in Pennsylvania, Massachusetts and Nova Scotia. In addition to being so historically important, these are, perhaps, the most pleasing in appearance of all shelf clocks. Rare (Plate 196A, B, C).

Pinions: the small gears which are driven by the larger wheels. Pinions are of two sorts: (a) those which are cut from the same stock as the arbor; (b) lantern pinions which are built up of two disks or collars joined by short lengths of wire (or wood, as in some wood-movement clocks) which may be rigid or free to roll as the arbor turns (Fig. 1C). Lantern pinions are usual in Connecticut shelf clocks; cut pinions are regularly found in brass-movement tall clocks, banjos, lyres and the like, as well as in most wood movements.

Pinwheel escapement: a form of escapement in which the impulse is given by pins located near the rim of the escape wheel. Rare on American clocks.

Pivots: the small ends of the arbors which turn in holes (pivot holes) of the plates. (Fig. 1D).

Plates: the front and back (or top and bottom) supporting elements of a movement between which the wheels are arranged.

Position error: the change in rate of a watch when run in different positions.

Rack and snail striking: a method of controling the number of blows struck for the hours. Permits the strike to be repeated, also the number of blows will always agree with the hour indicated by the hour hand. The snail is a graduated or snail-shaped cam usually concentric with the hour wheel. The rack is an arm with a series of notches, which in conjunction with the snail determine the number of blows struck for each hour. Usual on brass-movement tall clocks, rare on Connecticut-type shelf clocks and extremely rare on wood-movement clocks.

Rate: a measure of the performance of a timepiece; sometimes the amount of time gained or lost in 24 hours.

Regulator: an accurate timepiece used as a standard. Now used to designate any large pendulum wall clock designed especially for accurate timekeeping.

Repeater: a striking clock or watch on which the hours or smaller units of time can be struck and repeated at will.

Ripple or piecrust trim: wavy wood trim occasionally used to decorate the fronts of some small Connecticut clocks. Occasional (Plate 199B).

Saddle or seatboard: the wooden platform to which the movement of a tall clock is fastened. Also found in certain smaller clocks.

Sandglass or hourglass: an early device for measuring time consisting of two glass globes one over the other, containing fine sand which may pass from one to the other through a small opening. Supporting frames of wood or metal. Made in several sizes.

Sandglasses and sundials were the principal time-measuring devices of colonial America. Seventeenth-century inventories, as well as town, church and court records mention hourglasses. In newspapers of the early-eighteenth century are found advertisements for the making or repair of hourglasses. They were in general use on shipboard until about 1800.

Sandglasses are easily and frequently reproduced, and these are often difficult to distinguish from the antique. Original examples are rare and seldom is one found with the maker's name.

Seconds dial: the small circle on the dial within which the second hand turns.

Self-winding watch: one that is wound by the motion of being carried; some early inventions toward this end are of interest to the advanced collector.

Shelf clock: a clock, either weight- or spring-powered, designed to be placed on a shelf.

Spandrels: the separate decorative corner-pieces often found on eighteenth-century clock dials; also used for the painted corners of more recent dials.

Splat: the decorative panel, painted, veneered or carved, placed at the top of many clocks.

Steeple clocks: *see* Gothic clocks.

Stenciled clocks: name now given to many shelf clocks which have painted and stenciled columns and splats. Also called 'Hitchcock' on account of the similarity of the decoration to that on Hitchcock chairs. Usually with wooden movements. Desirability depends on maker, type of movement, and condition of tablet and stenciling. *c.* 1825–40. Common (Plate 197A, B).

Strike-silent: a device by which the striking or chiming of a clock may be prevented at will. Rare on American clocks.

Sundial: an early device to show the time of day by the shadow of a gnomon, or standard, on a base. Sundials were in common use in the colonies from the first. Small portable dials, combined with a compass, were probably the most useful 'pocket timepieces' available. Most of the early sundials were imported; original sundials signed by American makers (usually silversmiths or pewterers) are very rare. It is said that THOMAS JEFFERSON and BENJAMIN FRANKLIN made sundials.

Suspension: any method by which the pendulum of a clock is supported. On most clocks it is a thin, flexible spring called the suspension spring. (Fig. 5E).

Tablet: the painted or otherwise decorated glass panel found in many American shelf and wall clocks. In clocks made to about 1830–5 the designs were hand-painted on the back of glasses. Scenic designs with gilt or gold-leaf borders were most common, while floral or conventional designs were also used. Most of the scenes appear to have been drawn as synthetic compositions and not from real life. Original tablets in fine condition are scarce and add much to the value of a clock. The restoration and reproduction of these reverse paintings is a specialized art and few artists are now able to duplicate the appearance of original glasses.

The tablets in clocks since 1840 are usually printed decalcomanias, plain or colored. Etched glasses or stenciled designs are also found in clocks of this period.

T-bridge: a type of pendulum support particularly used by SIMON WILLARD in his banjo clocks. The suspension spring is pinned to a T-shaped unit which fits into and is held by a support on the clock movement.

Three-tier or three-decker clock: a variety of large weight-driven Connecticut shelf clock, the front of which usually consists of an upper and a lower door with a fixed panel between. *c.* 1828–50. Occasional.

Time, measurement of: there are several systems for the measurement of time, only three of which need be mentioned and only one is in ordinary use. *Mean time* is calculated on the basis of exactly 24 hours in a day and is the time shown by all ordinary clocks. *Solar time* is calculated from the passage of the sun across the meridian; is shown by a sundial and varies daily. The difference between solar and mean time is known as the equation of time. *Sidereal time* is calculated from successive passages of a particular star across the meridian. A sidereal day is approximately 23 hours, 56 minutes and 3.5 seconds of mean or clock time. Sidereal time is used only by astronomers.

Tin-plate movement: a clock movement the plates of which are of tinned iron. Invented (patented 1859) in an attempt to save brass and reduce the cost of clocks. Small Connecticut clocks. Rare.

Torsion pendulum: a pendulum in which the bob rotates by the twisting and untwisting of a long suspension spring. Usually found on clocks designed to run a long time on one winding, as year clocks. Clocks with torsion pendulums were not generally made in America. A few eight-day, thirty-day and year clocks with torsion pendulums were produced under one or more patents to AARON CRANE of Newark, New Jersey and Boston, Massachusetts. *c.* 1840–60. Several styles, all rare (Plate 198c).

Tower clock: a large clock as used in the towers of churches and other public buildings; often with two, three or four dials. Probably the first clocks made in America were of this sort. Some in New England were made with wood movements.

Train: the series of wheels and pinions which transmits power from the weight or mainspring to the escapement or striking mechanism. A striking clock has two trains, a chiming clock may have three, whereas a timepiece has only one.

Verge: commonly used to designate the unit including the two pallets of the escape-

ment; it is fixed to an arbor or directly to the crutch (Fig. 5B).

Visible escapement: an escapement which is visible or directly in front of the dial. Certain experimental models or shelf clocks by ELI TERRY are rare examples (Plate 196A).

Wagon-springs: flat-leaved springs used to power certain Connecticut shelf and wall clocks. Invented by JOSEPH IVES, also made by ATKINS, BIRGE and FULLER and others. *c.* 1825–55. Rare (Plate 198A, B, D).

Wag-on-the-wall: any wall clock in which the weights and pendulum are not enclosed in a case. Some of the earliest American clocks were of this sort. Many of the Connecticut wooden movements intended for tall clocks (*c.* 1800–25) were sold without cases and often used as wall clocks until a case might be provided. Some used in this way were provided with simple hoods to protect them from dust (Plates 191A, 193A).

Warning: the partial release or unlocking of the striking train a short time before striking; often heard as a faint click a minute or more before the actual striking.

Watch-paper: originally small pieces of cloth inserted to keep the two cases of the double-cased watches from rubbing together. Later (before 1800) these became finely embroidered with delicate designs and tender sayings. The engraved or printed watch-paper (*c.* 1800) served as an advertisement of the watchmaker.

Weights: most American clocks made before 1840 used weights for power. These were of many shapes, sizes and materials. Weights cast of iron in various forms are the most common. Lead was often used and occasionally original weights of natural stone are found. Weights of many grandfather clocks, especially those with wooden movements, were often cylinders of thin sheet iron (tin) filled with scrap iron or any other heavy material. These latter are called 'tin-can' weights.

BOOKS FOR FURTHER READING

BRITTEN, F. J.: *Old Clocks and Watches and their Makers*, 7th edition, by BAILLIE, G. H., CLUTTON, C., and ILBERT, C. A., New York, E. P. Dutton & Co. (1956).

CHANDLEE, EDWARD E.: *Six Quaker Clockmakers*, Philadelphia, Historical Society of Pennsylvania (1943).

DREPPERD, CARL W.: *American Clocks and Clockmakers*, Garden City, New York, Doubleday (1947).

ECKHARDT, GEORGE H.: *Pennsylvania Clocks and Clockmakers*, New York, The Devin-Adair Co. (1955).

HOOPES, PENROSE R.: *Connecticut Clockmakers of the Eighteenth Century*, Hartford, Conn., E. V. Mitchell; New York, Dodd, Mead & Co. (1930).

JAMES, ARTHUR: *Chester County Clocks and their Makers*, West Chester, Penn., Author (1947).

MILHAM, WILLIS I.: *Time and Timekeepers*, New York, Macmillan (1941).

MILLER, EDGAR G., JR.: *American Antique Furniture*, Baltimore, Maryland, M. S. Watkins (1937).

MOORE, N. HUDSON: *The Old Clock Book*, 2nd edition, New York, Tudor Publishing Co. (1936).

NUTTING, WALLACE: *The Clock Book*, 2nd edition, New York, Garden City Publishing Co. (1935).

NUTTING, WALLACE: *The Furniture Treasury*, 2nd edition, New York, Macmillan (1949), 3 vols.

PALMER, BROOKS: *The Book of American Clocks*, New York, Macmillan (1950).

WILLARD, JOHN WARE: *A History of Simon Willard, Inventor and Clockmaker*, Boston, G. W. Humphrey (1911).

Bulletins of the National Association of Watch and Clock Collectors, Inc. (1943 to present date).

Concise Encyclopedia of Antiques, Vol. I, pp. 173–186, Hawthorn Books, New York (1955).

EARLY
PORTRAIT PAINTING

By HELEN COMSTOCK

(Revised from 'American Painting in the Eighteenth Century', *The Connoisseur*, Vol. CXXXIV, No. 542.)

So many seventeenth-century American portraits have gravitated to historical societies and museums, or remain cherished among family heirlooms, that the opportunity to acquire examples seldom presents itself to the private collector. The Massachusetts Historical Society in Boston, the American Antiquarian Society in Worcester, Pilgrim Hall in Plymouth, the New-York Historical Society, and the Virginia Historical Society in Richmond should be visited to gain a fair impression of what American portrait painting was like in the period of its origins. In 1935 an important exhibition was held at the Worcester Art Museum in order to study New England portraiture of the seventeenth century. Although highly instructive, it left students unable to identify many of the painters by name. However, it brought together certain works as coming from the same hand, such as the Freake and Gibbs family portraits. Not only has it been difficult to discover the names of our first portrait painters, but it is also in many cases difficult to differentiate between the work done in the colonies and in Europe. The portraits brought over among family possessions, or of colonials who had their portraits painted on a visit to Europe, as did Increase Mather in London in 1688, tend to form a homogeneous group with subjects painted in America. Some of the portraits which are considered probably of American origin include those of Elizabeth Paddy Wensley at Pilgrim Hall; of Captain George Cur-

win (*c.* 1681) at the Essex Institute, Salem; of John Davenport (died 1670) at Yale University; of Alice Mason, belonging to the Adams Family Memorial Society of Quincy, Massachusetts.

While the English style dominated early portrait painting, Dutch influence was strong, not only as a distant echo in seventeenth-century English painting, but because of the actual presence of a large Dutch element in the population. In the Hudson River Valley a number of anonymous Dutch-descended painters have left portraits of the wealthy Dutch families, the de Peysters (Plate 201 A), Van Cortlandts, Van Rensselaers and others of the patroons. The DUYCKINCK family of artists came from Holland (EVERT I arrived in 1638), and PIETER VANDELYN (1687–1778), the oustanding painter of the Colonial Dutch School in America, who worked chiefly in Kingston, New York, was born in Holland.

NATHANIEL EMMONS, the first painter of recorded American birth, worked in Boston in the first quarter of the eighteenth century. His somewhat stiff portraits in the manner of engravings were contemporary with the work of JOHN WATSON (born in Edinburgh) in New Jersey and New York, almost equally stiff and lifeless but of historical importance. The work of the German JUSTUS ENGLEHARDT KÜHN (1708) and the Swedish GUSTAVUS HESSELIUS (1712) in Maryland, in portraits of the Calvert and Darnall children showing them in elaborate architectural settings and rich costumes, brings the baroque style to America.

Most influential of the English-born painters was JOHN SMIBERT (Plate 202 A) who had made a modest reputation in London before he accompanied Bishop Berkeley to America. His friend, George Vertue, admitted him to the second rank of English painters, and Walpole spoke of him with mild approbation in his *Anecdotes of Painting*. It is not fair to Smibert to say that he brought little more than the mannerisms of the school of Kneller to America. He was not without force in his characterizations and there is an earnestness in his work which made him an admirable recorder of Boston worthies. His work falls between 1730 and 1747, when he ceased to be active. Smibert was studied with great profit by ROBERT FEKE when the latter was in Boston about 1741.

CHARLES BRIDGES was one of the more important visitors from England to Virginia, arriving in 1735 and introducing there the style of Kneller about the same time that Smibert was working in Boston. He had more grace than Smibert, and he was not bound to tradition. He introduced suggestions of the new environment, as seen in the cardinal bird, with its red plumage, in his delightful portrait of Evelyn Byrd now in the Governor's Palace in Williamsburg. His portrait of her father, William Byrd of Westover, has a dashing air well suited to please Virginian aristocrats, and is also quite in keeping with the impression of Byrd given by the latter's *Diary*. By contrast with Bridges, the Swiss JEREMIAH THEÜS in Charleston in 1739 painted an unflattering, stiff presentation of Gabriel Manigault and his wife, now in the Metropolitan Museum. Theüs remained in South Carolina for over thirty years and painted in most of the leading families.

ROBERT FEKE (*c.* 1705 – *c.* 1748) is considered a native of the American continent although his origin has never been proved. Whether born on Long Island, in the West Indies, or elsewhere, it is reasonably sure that he did not come from England, and it is apparently certain that he was self-taught in that he did not have any formal instruction. He painted a self-portrait at an early age which shows that he must have known Smibert's self-portrait in the Berkeley family group (Plate 202 A) and this same group has obviously influenced his own group portrait of the family of Isaac Royall. His portrait of the Loyalist, Isaac Winslow (Plate 201 C), is one of his best. The pose is traditional in English portrait painting, but the manner has something new, a kind of hard, plastic quality, firm, uncompromising and possessing a lively vigor.

Local styles were to some extent harmonized and brought into the English pattern by JOHN WOLLASTON (Plate 201 D), a mediocre English painter whose treatment of costumes suggests that he was probably a drapery painter in England. But he had the initiative (well rewarded) to travel extensively along the Atlantic coast before returning to England. He worked in America for a little more than fifteen years, starting in New York about 1751, Philadelphia, 1754; Maryland, 1754–5; Annapolis, 1755; then to Virginia where he painted in many Tidewater families. Finally, in the 1760s, he went to Charleston. His almond-eyed ladies in gleaming satins represent members of the leading families of North and South. A similar success was enjoyed by JOSEPH BLACKBURN in New England: he introduced even more artificial poses in portraits of ladies with shepherds' crooks. His series of portraits from Boston and Portsmouth, New Hampshire, ended in 1763, when he disappeared from view (Plate 203A).

Americans in search of European art at first hand were led by BENJAMIN WEST, who left his native country at the age of twenty-two, never to return. He first studied in Italy and then went to London, where he remained until his death in 1820. In spite of declining recognition, his part in establishing a realistic type of historical painting through his *Death of Wolfe* cannot be overlooked, while his role of instructor to three generations of American painters in London gave him unique influence in American art. He helped Copley show his first works in London in advance of the Bostonian's coming to England; he received MATTHEW PRATT (Plate 202 B), GILBERT STUART, CHARLES WILLSON PEALE, JOHN TRUMBULL into his studio, and, in the nineteenth century, THOMAS SULLY and S. F. B. MORSE.

JOHN SINGLETON COPLEY (1737–1815), the stepson of the English-born engraver and painter, Peter Pelham, had more formal instruction than Feke, but little enough, and his greatest asset was an inquiring mind. He was gratified to find some contact with the great European schools of painting in the copies which Smibert had brought to Boston. An impassioned dream led him to quit America to perfect himself, but unfortunately his contact with European art did not develop his individual gifts. 'Copley cannot paint like that now,' said Reynolds when shown some of Copley's American work after Copley had been painting in London.

In his American period, Copley carried portrait painting to a height it had never reached before and he possibly deserves to be considered our greatest portrait painter (Plate 203B). Although one sees in his style the conventions of Wollaston and Blackburn, he completely transformed them, while in his delineation of character he has given us a vivid, living impression of the wealthy merchants and their wives of Boston, New York and Philadelphia just prior to the Revolution.

CHARLES WILLSON PEALE arrived in West's studio in London in 1767 when the latter was thirty and the pupil twenty-seven. Peale remained for two and a half years, supporting himself to some extent with portrait commissions. Such work may have prevented him from absorbing as much of the English atmosphere as Gilbert Stuart did a few years later, or it may have been the result of his own temperament. Peale remained an American painter and his work continued in the direction marked out by Feke and Copley. He was a man of many interests, tried his hand at many crafts including metalwork, engraving, silversmithing, and was deeply interested in natural science. There remains something of the self-taught artist throughout his work, but because of his excellent drawing, firm modeling, and his unaffected simplicity his portraits (Plate 203 C) frequently rise to the level of Copley's although they do not have the latter's elegance.

The self-taught artist is well represented by JOHN DURAND (Plate 203D) who left Connecticut to lead the role of an itinerant portrait painter in New York and Virginia (1767–82). He has a feeling for pattern, for strong outlines and flat masses of color, all attributes that distinguished the self-trained, gifted provincial painter who appears so often in American art. He is mentioned here as representative of a class which included Winthrop Chandler, Reuben Moulthrop, Richard Jennys and others.

GILBERT STUART (1755–1828), on the other hand, represents the American artist who formed himself on the European pattern. After remaining in West's studio for five years, during which time he acted as West's assistant, he finally set up his own studio in London. He married an Englishwoman, and had he been more prudent in his finances would probably have remained in England. But his many debts caused him to make a painting trip to Ireland in which he was so successful that he remained until 1792. He returned to America far more of an English painter than any of his compatriots and he remained one, as is evident in the later portraits in New York, Philadelphia, Washington and Boston. However, he was no lifeless imitator of Gainsborough and Reynolds but vied with them in urbane grace and technical skill. His portraits of George Washington have undoubtedly impressed themselves on the national consciousness as no others have done, although Washington himself is said to have preferred his portrait by Joseph Wright. Stuart's portraits of Jefferson, Jay, Hamilton, Knox, and many others of the day show him to have been a great draughtsman, a master of the brush, able to portray his sitter livingly against a severely empty background, with none of the accessories on which the earlier painters depended for effect. Our most sophisticated portrait painter, he was also the most direct.

After Stuart, it is natural to think of another portrait painter who remained long enough in London to have made a place for himself there, RALPH EARL (1751–1801) of Connecticut (Plate 204). He had worked as a portrait painter, even as Stuart had done, before going to London, but he had shown more originality in presenting his sitters in the background in which they lived, as in his portrait of Roger Sherman at the Yale University Art Gallery. In London, where he was studying with West in 1779, he, like Stuart, absorbed much from the art he saw practised around him, as two portraits of his English period now at the Worcester Art Museum prove. He exhibited at the Royal Academy in 1783 and remained in England until 1785. Just why he discarded his acquired accomplishments on his return, when he was painting portraits in Connecticut families, would be difficult to say. He again became a 'primitive', but naturally so, without affectation, and allowed his feeling for design and color full rein. His figures tend to be wooden and expressionless, but as he paints his subjects on country estates or in their best parlors, with a view of a distant landscape from the window, the results satisfy us. Here are portrayals, not of character, but of a period in American life. In Earl the native style comes further into expression. It has something which West had called a 'liny'

quality, in writing a criticism of Copley's work to that artist. It is 'liny' and somewhat sharp, but by no means lifeless, for the forms are boldy projected. With Earl's death in 1801 the early period comes to a close, and other fields of expression, notably landscape, also still-life and genre, absorb the attention of the painter.

BOOKS FOR
FURTHER READING

BURROUGHS, ALAN: *Limners and Likenesses; Three Centuries of American Painting* (Cambridge, Massachusetts).

DRESSER, LOUISA: *Seventeenth-century Painting in New England*, Worcester Art Museum (1935).

FLEXNER, J. T.: *America's Old Masters*, New York (1939); *First Flowers of our Wilderness, American Painting*, Boston (1947); *The Light of Distant Skies, 1760–1835*, New York (1954).

FOOTE, H. W.: *Robert Feke*, Cambridge, Massachusetts (1930); *John Smibert*, Cambridge, Massachusetts (1950).

PARKER, B. N., AND WHEELER, A. B.: *John Singleton Copley*, Boston (1938).

SELLERS, C. C.: *Charles Willson Peale*, Philadelphia (1947), 2 vols.; *Portraits and Miniatures by Charles Willson Peale*, Philadelphia (1952).

PAINTING IN THE NINETEENTH CENTURY

By JOHN I. H. BAUR

(Reprinted from *American Painting in the Nineteenth Century: Main Trends and Movements* (Frederick A. Praeger, Inc., New York, 1953), out of print.)

Romantic realism; the early portrait tradition and the Hudson River School: at the opening of the nineteenth century portrait painting was still the major branch of art in the United States, as it had been since the arrival of the first settlers. By 1800 the dominant trend was clearly that established by GILBERT STUART in the late-eighteenth century and carried by him well into the nineteenth. Stuart's bravura style of deft brushwork, high key and forceful characterization was closely related to contemporary English work but went beyond its sources to the verges of impressionism. This blend of romantic handling with a generally realistic approach had an immense and persistent influence on American portrait painters up to the time of the Civil War. In many personal variations it was the style of THOMAS SULLY, SAMUEL F. B. MORSE, HENRY INMAN, JOHN NEAGLE and a host of lesser figures through two generations.

A somewhat similar fusion of realism and romanticism marked the work of the HUDSON RIVER SCHOOL, America's first widespread landscape painting movement. Earlier artists had largely neglected the subject, but by the 1820s a new appreciation of the country's wild and picturesque beauties began to spread through all levels of society. Under the leadership of THOMAS COLE, the men of the Hudson River School broke away from the topo-graphical handling of the eighteenth century and approached nature with a more romantic eye. Many of them had studied abroad – generally in Düsseldorf, Rome or Paris – and they drew freely on both contemporary European work and on old masters like Salvator Rosa and Claude Lorrain. From these sources came, in large part, the romantic paraphernalia of blasted trees, crags, boulders, precipices and panoramic views which appear so often in their work.

Yet, much as they owed to Europe, the American wilderness presented new problems for which there was no precedent and aroused feelings that were deeper than any they had experienced abroad. Many, like WORTH-INGTON WHITTREDGE, were in despair as they faced for the first time 'a mass of decaying logs and tangled brush. ... no well ordered forest, nothing but the primitive woods with their solemn silence reigning everywhere'. At the same time the challenge, excitement and genuine love which their country inspired lent a freshness of discovery to their spacious images, and led them in widening circles of exploration from the Catskills to the Rockies. By the middle of the century landscape painting had, as Jarves* remarked, surpassed all other kinds in popular favor.

It has long been apparent that there was a

* James Jackson Jarves, mid-nineteenth-century collector, author of *The Art Idea, Art Studies*, etc—*Editor.*

close link between the work of the whole group and the extensive nature poetry of the day. A strong religious current ran through both, a belief that God's presence is manifest in mountain, lake and waterfall and that the artist's chief function is its revelation. It was logical, then, to argue – as many did – that the painter should romanticize nature only to the extent of heightening its God-given aspects. This moral conviction was probably the principal force in determining the degree of romanticism permitted within a generally realist approach. The degree varied somewhat with individual artists, being considerable in the case of Cole and his pupil FREDERICK E. CHURCH, much less with men like WORTHINGTON WHITTREDGE and JOHN F. KENSETT (Plate 205B). Other factors doubtless contributed to establishing the current romantic-realist blend.

Thus the painter's sense of dedication to the portrayal of his country imposed its own restrictions on the liberties which he could take, while at the same time Emersonian idealism encouraged romanticizing within these limits to give mankind 'the suggestion of a fairer creation than we know'.

The Tonalists: for many years the fame of the Hudson River School obscured the work of a smaller group of contemporary landscape painters who worked in a more precisely realist vein, avoiding the obviously romantic or picturesque and seeking, in general, a serene and poetic interpretation of nature through subtle gradations of tone and light. The tentative beginnings of the movement can be seen in the work of two English born and trained artists, ROBERT SALMON and GEORGE HARVEY. Indeed, the latter was so greatly impressed by the unique quality of American light that he projected a series of water colors called 'Atmospheric Landscapes of North America'.

The movement culminated about the middle of the century in the work of two men, MARTIN J. HEADE and FITZ HUGH LANE (Plate 206A), both virtually forgotten until their rediscovery a few years ago. While there is no indication that they knew each other, their painting is similar in many respects, just as it is also related to the style of several other still obscure artists like JOSEPH RUSLING MEEKER and GEORGE TIRREL. Using a tightly descriptive realism, Heade and Lane sought to capture with mirror-like clarity effects of sunlight and atmosphere that the Hudson River School had almost totally ignored. Heade even did a series of haystack views under changing conditions of mist and rain and sunshine, much as Monet was to do later. Thus, in a sense, these men forecast the impressionism of Homer and others at the end of the century. There was, of course, no hint of impressionist technique in their enameled surfaces, but their lyrical feeling for American light with all its brilliance and sudden changes was an important discovery for those who came after.

Quite apart from their atmospheric studies they are also notable for transforming realism into a poetic instrument that depends relatively little on the usual expressive elements of design and color. This quality in their work is difficult to define. It is a kind of intensity of feeling which is imparted to the spectator by the equal intensity of the artist's observation, the infinite care with which every aspect of his scene has been analysed and affectionately preserved. Such paintings, at their best, suggest an almost mystical identification of the artist with his subject, a losing of self in the enveloping moods of nature. They are hypnotic, trance-like – a moment of poetic insight immaculately preserved.

Genre painting: at about the same time that American artists were discovering their native landscape, another group, led by WILLIAM SIDNEY MOUNT (Plate 206B), began to paint the daily life of the young democracy. There had been earlier attempts at scattered intervals, like the charming scenes of social gatherings by HENRY SARGENT, but such pictures had little influence on the school which followed, being more closely related to the formal elegance of the portrait painters. Mount, on the other hand, distrusted 'ideality and the grand style' and professed that his aim was 'to copy nature ... with truth and soberness'. For this purpose

(A) Dr Smith, Mount Vernon, New Hampshire. Signed 'E. Woolson, Pinxt., May 1842.' *Old Sturbridge Village, Sturbridge, Massachusetts.*

(B) Mrs J. B. Sheldon, Unionville, Ohio. Artist unknown, *c.* 1825. *Garbisch collection, National Gallery of Art, Washington, D.C.*

(C) Truman Holmes, Jr., New Orleans, Louisiana. Signed 'Bahin, 1864.' *Abby Aldrich Rockefeller Folk Art Collection, Williamsburg, Virginia.*

(D) Washington and Liberty. Artist unknown, *c.* 1810. *New York State Historical Association, Cooperstown, New York.*

PLATE 209

(A) A View of Mr. Joshua Winsor's House, Duxbury, Massachusetts by Dr Rufus Hatheway, *c.* 1795. *On loan to The Society for the Preservation of New England Antiquities, Boston, Massachusetts.*

(B) A. Dickson Entering Bristol, 1819. Pennsylvania. Signed 'Alexandr Boudrou, Painter, 1851.' *Abby Aldrich Rockefeller Folk Art Collection, Williamsburg, Virginia.*

PLATE 210

(A) Nathan Hawley and Family, Albany, New York. Dated November 3, 1801. Artist unknown. *Albany Institute of History and Art, Albany, New York.*

(B) Fishing with Waterfall. Artist unknown, *c.* 1845. *American Heritage collection, Colby College, Waterville, Maine.*

PLATE 211

(A) Naomi and Ruth. Artist unknown, *c.* 1830. *Author's collection.*

(B) Mourning Picture by Maria S. Perley, Lempster, New Hampshire, *c.* 1830. *Author's collection.*

PLATE 212

(A) Mrs John Melville (Deborah Scollay), by J. S. Copley. *Worcester Art Museum.*

(B) Mrs John Pintard (Elizabeth Brasher), by John Ramage. *New-York Historical Society.*

(C) Mrs John Williamson (Elizabeth Ann Timothée), by Henry Benbridge. *Metropolitan Museum of Art, New York.*

(D) Miss Ross, by James Peale. *Metropolitan Museum of Art, New York.*

(E) Mrs Charles Bulfinch (Hannah Apthorp), by Joseph Dunkerley. *Museum of Fine Arts, Boston.*

(F) Major General Nathanael Greene, by C. W. Peale. *Metropolitan Museum of Art, New York*

PLATE 213

(A) Thomas Jefferson, by John Trumbull. *Metropolitan Museum of Art, New York.*

(B) Portrait of an unknown young man, by Raphaelle Peale. *Department of Fine Arts, Carnegie Institute.*

(G) **Portrait of the Artist, by Charles Fraser.** *Gibbes Art Gallery, Charleston, South Carolina.*

(D) Elizabeth Sarah Faber, by Charles Fraser. *Walters Art Gallery.*

PLATE 214

(A) Mrs James Lowndes (Catherine Osborn), by E. G. Malbone. *Metropolitan Museum of Art, New York*

(B) Sarah Louisa Jenkins, by R. Field. *Metropolitan Museum of Art, New York.*

(C) Benjamin Kintzing, by Benjamin Trott. *Metropolitan Museum of Art, New York*

(D) Edward Livingston, by Anson Dickinson. *Metropolitan Museum of Art, New York.*

(E) Mrs Manigault Heyward (Susan Hayne Simmons), by Robert Fulton. *Metropolitan Museum of Art, New York.*

(F) Joel Roberts Poinsett, by E. G. Malbone. *Metropolitan Museum of Art, New York.*

PLATE 215

(A) James Bogert, Jr., by Henry Inman. *Metropolitan Museum of Art, New York.*

(B) Mr Cook, by J. W. Jarvis. *Metropolitan Museum of Art, New York.*

(C) Portrait of the artist at the age of 42, by Sarah Goodridge. *Museum of Fine Arts, Boston.*

(D) The Bracelet; Jane Cook, the artists's wife, by T. S. Cummings. *Metropolitan Museum of Art, New York.*

(E) Mrs Thomas Sully (Sarah Annis), by Thomas Sully. *Metropolitan Museum of Art, New York.*

PLATE 216

(A) Portrait of Rev. Jonathan Mayhew by Paul Revere. Line engraving. *Prints Division, The New York Public Library.*

(B) Portrait of John Jay by Cornelius Tiebout. Stipple engraving. *Prints Division, The New York Public Library.*

(C) The Country Store by Alexander Anderson. Wood engraving. *Prints Division, The New York Public Library.*

PLATE 217

(A) A North-West Prospect of Nassau-Hall (Princeton) with a Front View of the President's House in New Jersey by Henry Dawkins. *The Old Print Shop, Harry Shaw Newman.*

(B) Library and Surgeons Hall, Philadelphia by William Birch. 1800, line engraving. *The Old Print Shop, Harry Shaw Newman.*

PLATE 218

(A) View of the Battle at Concord, Massachusetts, 1775. by Amos Doolittle. Colored line engraving after Ralph Earl. *Prints Division, The New York Public Library.*

(B) Newburgh. Colored aquatint from the *Hudson River Portfolio,* after W. G. Wall, by John Hill. *The Old Print Shop, Harry Shaw Newman.*

PLATE 219

(A) Buffalo from Lake Erie, 1836, by William J. Bennett. Colored aquatint after a sketch by J. W. Hill. One of the series, *Views of American Cities. The Old Print Shop, Harry Shaw Newman.*

(B) City Hall (New York) by John Hill. Colored aquatint after W. G. Wall. Published 1826. *The Old Print Shop, Harry Shaw Newman.*

PLATE 220

Original silhouette of an unknown man, by William H. Brown, 1808–82. The subject is shown against a background drawn in crayon. *Coll. of C. F. O'Connor, New York.*

PLATE 221

(A) The Town Crier and John Bowen of Barnstable by William James Hubard. *Valentine Museum, Richmond, Virginia.*

(B) Dr E. A. Holyoke of Salem, 1728–1829, by Master Hankes. *Essex Institute, Salem, Massachusetts.*

(C) Equestrian subject by William James Hubard. *Valentine Museum, Richmond, Virginia.*

PLATE 222

(A) Painted silhouette of Robert Bolling, Petersberg, Virginia, 1781, signed Chapman. *Coll. of Mrs Francis Hartman Markoe, née Rebecca Bolling.*

(B) Silhouette of Titian R. Peale, Philadelphia, against a lithographic background, by Édouart, 1842. *The Old Print Shop, Harry Shaw Newman.*

PLATE 223

(A) David Wadsworth by William Bache. *Wadsworth Atheneum, Hartford.*

(B) Painted and shaded profile signed by Bache. *Essex Institute, Salem, Massachusetts.*

(C) Hollow-cut Peale silhouette with the rare *Peale* stamp. *Library of Congress.*

(D) A Peale head, the curls delicately executed; hollow-cut. *Library of Congress.*

PLATE 224

he developed a rather hard, meticulously realistic style, somewhat akin to that of the tonalists, particularly in his many outdoor scenes. With it he told rural anecdotes and recorded the humorous events of country life around his home on Long Island, preferring to overlook its harsher aspects or the industrial life of the nearby city, which was already beginning to make his farm subjects seem like nostalgic memories of an older and happier way of life. Yet in his earthiness, his high spirits and canny regard for popular taste, Mount reflected accurately the bustling optimism of Jacksonian democracy. Much the same qualities are found in the work of RICHARD CATON WOODVILLE, THOMAS LE CLEAR and the host of Eastern genre painters who followed him, creating by mid-century a whole school of anecdotal art in realist vein.

The same movement spread rapidly to the West, but there the different conditions of life produced their own distinctive forms. A number of painters, including GEORGE CATLIN, ALFRED JACOB MILLER and CHARLES DEAS, were fascinated by the American Indian, as Cooper and Parkman and so many other writers were at the same time. This was partly a romantic interest, like that of French artists in the Near East, and it lent romantic color to much of their work. But Catlin, and the rest to a lesser extent, also viewed their mission as scientific, an obligation to record for posterity a vanishing culture and race. This soberer aim tempered their romanticism and kept them largely within the realist camp.

Western genre was not entirely devoted to Indians. It culminated in the scenes of Mississippi River life painted by the most gifted of the group, GEORGE CALEB BINGHAM, who was close to Mount both in his humor and the sharp clarity of his style. To these qualities Bingham added an unusual color sense, apparent in his consciously arranged sequences of muted browns, blues and reds that combine like chords in the ragged costumes of his figures. He also had an exceptional ability to compose his often crowded scenes in classically balanced, almost Poussin-like designs which still preserved, miraculously, a natural and uncontrived appearance. It is one of the paradoxes of American art that this clarity and order came out of the turbulent life of the frontier.

Still-life painting: like genre and the landscapes of the tonalists, still-life painting followed a predominantly realist vein throughout the century, although it seems to have been more strongly influenced at the beginning by European conventions, particularly those of Dutch art. RAPHAELLE PEALE, who emerges as the most interesting of our early specialists in the field, used many Dutch devices such as a generally dark tonality, a plain background enlivened by arbitrary shading and a table-top setting with the table edge a straight band across the bottom of the picture. Nevertheless, he departed from tradition in the extreme simplicity of his designs and in his preference for humble objects such as a cup-cake and a few raisins, a handful of carrots and a tomato or a sprig of blackberries in an ordinary china dish. The quality of Peale's work is not to be found so much in his subjects or designs, however, as it is in that same intensity of vision which the best of the tonalists and a few of the genre painters also possessed. Peale had an advantage over both groups in that he was working with small, inanimate objects on which he could focus with a microscopic concentration impossible in landscape or genre. His leaves curl through space with the utmost exactitude; every texture and form is completely stated; even air, light and shadow seem palpable. In some mysterious way this kind of realism gives the simplest things a heightened significance beyond that of common association. They are miracles of being, sensed for the first time.

For many years the tradition established by Raphaelle and his uncle JAMES PEALE continued to dominate American still life painting. In the last quarter of the century, however, a somewhat different school emerged, led by WILLIAM M. HARNETT (Plate 207A). Working in a style of *trompe l'oeil* (meaning literally 'fool the eye') realism, Harnett and his circle delighted even more than Peale in the exact imitation of the look and feel of things. A burnt match, a piece of string hanging down over the frame, appear so real that the spectator is irresistibly moved to pick them off the surface. Harnett, himself, was also a master of subdued color and intricately balanced design. His mugs and pipes and musical instruments glow with soft hues and their apparently casual arrangement is, in fact, a carefully wrought structure with every object playing its part. The beauty of his pictures, to modern eyes, is almost abstract.

Oddly enough, the realism of the *trompe l'oeil* group, while far surpassing that of Peale, missed entirely the latter's symbolic quality. The objects of Harnett and his followers are neither more nor less significant than in daily life and the wonder they evoke is not of a miraculous creation revealed but rather an astonishment at the artist's supreme technical skill. The reason for the difference is hard to explain. Perhaps it lies quite simply in the fact that Peale was genuinely moved by the beauty of his subjects while the later men were more concerned with the effects they were producing. Today it is Harnett's color and design, almost totally ignored in his own lifetime, that have lifted him to the equal of Peale in critical opinion. And, to balance the score, it is Peale's less spectacular but more penetrating vision that seems the finer expression of American realism.

Late portrait and figure painters: while genre painting continued to flourish throughout the century, it became more artificial and sentimental with the passage of time. The freshness and vigor as well as the naïveté of the early men yielded to J. G. BROWN's coy bootblacks, E. L. HENRY's nostalgic costume pieces and eventually to much worse levels of bathos. The true inheritors of the mid-century school were several figure painters who scarcely formed a homogeneous group but who recorded with a sober and more sophisticated realism the much-changed aspects of American life.

In the work of THOMAS EAKINS the American realist tradition reached its culmination and perhaps its fullest expression (Plate 207B). Eakin's rowing, sailing and hunting scenes, his old men playing chess or zithers, his family gatherings around the piano grew out of the earlier genre school and are an even more faithful record of middle-class life, now in an urban and Victorian setting. But, unlike the work of Mount or Bingham, his paintings are conceived in an analytical spirit, with a passionate concern for accuracy of anatomy and perspective, above all with a seriousness of purpose which removes them far from anecdote and sentiment. In his later life the artist painted portraits almost exclusively. To the literal description of form and action he now added that most difficult quality, the penetrating analysis of character. Never flattering, his likenesses tend to be awkward and graceless in a conventional sense, but they reveal the bare humanity of his subjects with warmth, with insight and often with sadness. They are memorable images of men and women who have worked and suffered. To a greater degree than any of his predecessors Eakins made realism a style with its own esthetic justification, a tool for communicating with uncompromising honesty his understanding of life.

While doubtless the greatest, he was not entirely alone in this. By the time of the Civil War the old, remarkably persistent portrait tradition of Gilbert Stuart had finally vanished and for a time the daguerreotype's mounting influence threatened to turn this branch of art into a drably unselective rendering of features. It was rescued, not only by Eakins, but by several other painters such as WILLIAM PAGE and WILLIAM MORRIS HUNT, who succeeded in preserving the realist approach without becoming photographic and who resisted, at the opposite extreme, a growing trend toward the facile brushwork of John Singer Sargent and the fashionable society painters.

Painters of the inner eye: while realism, though sometimes tinged with romantic feeling, was the dominant trend in nineteenth-century American painting, individual artists throughout the period explored other directions and added the leaven of mysticism, fantasy and satire to the more sober work of their contemporaries. They established no schools and were unrelated to each other except in their general attitude. A few – notably

WASHINGTON ALLSTON and ROBERT L. NEWMAN – were deeply influenced by European art, but the majority did not study abroad and developed their individual styles in relative isolation. With one or two exceptions, they were unsuccessful during their own lives, paying a high price of neglect and hostile criticism for their non-conformity to the esthetic standards of the age. 'His horse is not a horse,' wrote one critic of a painting by John Quidor, '... being unlike to anything in the heavens above, the earth beneath, or the waters under the earth.'

Allston was probably the first true romantic in our art history. His style was formed, conventionally enough, by long study of the Venetian masters of the Renaissance, but his sensitive imagination dwelt often on supernatural themes from the Bible, on Lazarus rising from the dead, Elisha fed by the ravens, on the hand that warned Belshazzar or the terrible desolation wrought by the Flood. These he translated to canvas, sometimes a little theatrically, but at best with grandeur, originality and a compelling romantic sweep. Allston's kind of mysticism vanished from American art with his death. It was followed in the mid-century by the earthier romanticism of JOHN QUIDOR and DAVID BLYTHE who were, however, quite different in other respects. Quidor's inventive brush embroidered subjects drawn from the tales of Irving and Cooper with a wealth of fantastic detail, his figures contorted in baroque exuberance but never quite slipping into caricature. Blythe's distortions, on the other hand, were frankly satirical, sometimes good-humored, more often sharp and bitter.

Then, at the end of the century, during one of America's most materialistic ages, mysticism of various kinds became once more the refuge of the non-conformists. With Newman, as with Allston, it was religious or at least Biblical in inspiration. With RALPH BLAKELOCK it was night and the moods of primitive nature, recalled from a youthful trip to the West, that fired his imagination. Over and over until his final insanity he painted visionary glades and Indians engulfed in moonlit landscapes. With ALBERT RYDER, the greatest of them all, it was a deeper and more ample mysticism, embracing everything miraculous in nature and in myth, both divine and demonic. Living the life of a hermit in his New York studio, he drew on childhood memories of the sea to paint his nocturnal marines with their strange arabesques of cloud shapes and their lonely boats. Even such prosaic events as the suicide of a waiter, who had lost his money on a horse race, haunted his mind until he had given it form and supernatural meaning in *The Race Track*. But above all it was poetry and legend that moved him, the stories of Jonah and the Flying Dutchman, of Siegfried, Macbeth and the dead Christ's re-appearance on earth. Under his hesitant brush, beset by endless doubts and changes, these grew slowly into the majestic patterns that evoke so fully the mystery of each theme.

Despite wide differences separating these men, they were akin in their awareness of spiritual forces and in their search for styles adequate to express their romantic perceptions.

Visual realism; the beginnings of Impressionism: the Civil War was scarcely over in 1865 when a new trend appeared in American art. This was a movement away from the tightly descriptive realism of the mid-century toward a purely visual realism that rendered objects as the eye alone perceived them, greatly modified by light, shadow and atmosphere. With it came a freer handling of paint, a livelier surface, often a delight in brushwork for its own spontaneous effects. Contours were deliberately broken, form suggested rather than analysed, detail blurred by strong sunlight or lost in shade. Tone rather than design became the prevalent means of unifying a picture.

This was, of course, a common trend in Europe also, from the early work of the Barbizon men through that of the Impressionists, and many of its American forms are traceable to European influence. JAMES HAMILTON studied Turner's work in England, as Monet was to do later. WILLIAM MORRIS HUNT painted with Millet at Barbizon, W. ALLAN GAY with Troyon, while GEORGE INNESS, more than either, adapted the atmospheric style of the Barbizon School to American landscape. At about the same time a quite different kind of impressionism was discovered by FRANK DUVENECK in Munich, where the influence of Courbet and of old masters like Frans Hals had united to produce a movement of dark tonality, slashing brushwork and rapid, *alla prima* technique. Under Duveneck's leadership a whole generation of American art students went to Germany or absorbed the new approach from Munich-trained teachers like WILLIAM M. CHASE. Still another kind of impressionism, modified by Oriental design, reached this country with the paintings of JAMES McNEILL WHISTLER, who had lived for some time in Paris before settling as a permanent expatriate in England. And Whistler's shadowy *Nocturnes* with their novel range of twilight and night effects attracted many followers in America at the century's end.

While one must not underestimate the great effect which these European trends had on our art, it is still apparent that the new way of seeing and the freer way of painting were appearing spontaneously everywhere and would probably have done so here regardless of developments abroad. Indeed, one of the most vigorous forms of American impressionism was purely native in origin, growing logically out of the landscapes of the mid-century tonalists and culminating in the broad naturalism of WINSLOW HOMER (Plate 208). The transition from the enameled surfaces of the earlier men to Homer's painterly style can be traced in the work of several artists. A clear instance is EASTMAN JOHNSON, who was trained in the meticulous realism of the Düsseldorf School and whose early canvases are tightly descriptive. Yet soon after the Civil War Johnson's brushwork began to grow freer, his effects of outdoor light richer and crisper until, by the mid-seventies, he was painting his Maine and Nantucket genre scenes with a broad touch which suggests, though still a little timidly, the palpable radiance of sun on beach and meadow.

Homer, himself, went through an exactly parallel development in the same years, but he carried native impressionism much farther than Johnson or any of the other transitional figures. Virtually unaffected by his two brief trips to Europe, he developed in his isolated studio on the Maine coast an art that miraculously preserved the big forms and structure of nature at the same time that it captured the full brilliance of American light and its elusive changes at different seasons or times of day. Unlike the French Impressionists, Homer never permitted atmosphere and light to consume form. His feeling for the solid reality of nature was too deeply rooted in the long tradition of American landscape painting. Rather, his great accomplishment was wedding that tradition to the new vision in a way that seemed, like all good art, inevitable. More fully than any predecessor, he realized the nineteenth century's long dream of revealing, through perfectly appropriate means, the rugged beauty of his native land.

BOOKS FOR FURTHER READING

BARKER, VIRGIL: *American Painting*, New York (1950).

BURROUGHS, ALAN: *A History of American Landscape Painting*, New York (1942).

FRANKENSTEIN, ALFRED: *After the Hunt: William Harnett and Other American Still Life Painters*, University of California Press (1953).

GOODRICH, LLOYD: *Winslow Homer*, New York (1944).

ISHAM, SAMUEL: *The History of American Painting*, New York (revised 1927).

LARKIN, OLIVER W.: *Art and Life in America*, New York (1949).

RICHARDSON, E. P.: *Painting in America*, New York (1956).

TUCKERMAN, HENRY T.: *Book of the Artists: American Artist Life*, New York (1867).

FOLK PAINTING

By NINA FLETCHER LITTLE

FOLK art was the tangible expression of the average man's creative impulse. It was sometimes untrained, frequently anonymous, but at its best always vigorous and forthright. Fine art, on the other hand, was produced for the esthetic enjoyment of his patron by a craftsman trained in an accepted artistic tradition. The true folk painter was not a clumsy imitator of conventional styles. He was intrinsically unsophisticated, sincere in his efforts, and essentially uninhibited by the academic precepts of his time.

Confusion regarding terminology has arisen over the years with reference to American folk painting, *popular, primitive, pioneer* and *provincial* being among the many designations in current use. Each has its merits, but the term *folk art* more nearly approximates the dictionary definition of the art 'of, or pertaining to, the folk, or used among the common people'. European folk arts and crafts followed an inherited pattern, passed down from one generation to another. In America personal initiative was inherent in the new environment, traditional forms took on added individuality, and the word *folk* assumed a new connotation.

The work of two groups, professional and amateur, is included in the United States under the generic title of folk art. Although their training and technique differed widely, these people possessed in common a fresh and spontaneous approach which rendered their best efforts dynamic, even when lacking in technical proficiency.

Most of the professionals were men who earned at least a part of their living through the painting trade. In the early-nineteenth century citizens of the average country town engaged in various seasonal occupations. Some of them taught school in the winter and painted in the summer when it was feasible to travel from place to place. Many boys began their careers by apprenticeship to master craftsmen who taught them coach, sign and ship painting, along with gilding, lettering and general decorating. A few worked for short lengths of time in the studios of recognized artists and eventually achieved distinction as landscape or 'face-painters', but the majority remained artisans rather than artists. Their work reflected the traditions of their trade, listed in contemporary city directories as House, Sign and Fancy Painters.

Few small communities could provide year-round support for a limner, but many remote families were potential patrons if he could present himself at their doors. To satisfy this desire for commodities which were otherwise unobtainable, numerous itinerants of all types roamed the countryside during the first half of the nineteenth century. Furniture makers, tin-peddlers, cobblers, and weavers were only a few of the many 'travelers' who went from house to house and were eagerly welcomed by rural housewives.

The itinerant painter usually traveled on foot or, if he was sufficiently affluent, with a hand-cart or wagon in which to carry his canvases and equipment. Some of these men covered long distances annually, traveling through the South or penetrating into upper New York State and out into the Western Reserve. Most of them counted on receiving board and lodging in the homes of their clients. Such accommodation might stretch out for a number of weeks if many commissions were secured in one family or neighborhood. Other artists hired a room in a town where they had been previously successful or believed the prospects to be good, and announced their presence by means of posted handbills or notices inserted in the local press. Still others were entertained by the landlord of the nearby tavern in return for decorating the ballroom or other apartments with stenciled or scenic designs.

Prices charged for portraits frequently varied from three to twenty-five dollars according to the locality and the reputation of the artist. Profiles and small pictures of children were advertised from twenty cents to one dollar.

Portraits in oil, painted on canvas or wood, formed the larger part of the output of professional folk artists. In their pictures they frequently included accessories to denote the characteristics or occupations of their sitters. Dr Smith of Mount Vernon, New Hampshire, is portrayed (Plate 209A) with the vials and scalpels of his profession spread out on the table beside him. His house and doctor's buggy may be seen through an adjacent window. Mrs J. B. Sheldon of Unionville, Ohio, painted by an unknown artist about 1825, holds her ear trumpet without visible embarrassment (Plate 209B). Here one recognizes the realistic approach of folk art in contrast to the conventional poses employed by the academicians. A different type of portrait which is signed by Louis Joseph Bahin, represents a little-known French artist to whom reference has been found during the 1850s in Mississippi and Louisiana. New Orleans, home of the subject, Truman Holmes, Jr, has been subtly suggested by including a river steamboat in the background (Plate 209C).

It has been frequently stated that the majority of traveling artists carried with them previously painted stock figures to which they subsequently added the heads of their respective sitters. Although this may occasionally have been done, pictures of headless torsos have never come to light to support the contention that it was a general practise. Moreover, the care required to transport partially completed likenesses would have presented far greater problems to the itinerant than the carrying of unused canvases. Occasional duplication of poses, costumes, and accessories by individual painters indicates that repetition of familiar details was the easiest solution for the artist of limited experience.

Landscapes, real or imaginery, were painted to special order. A view of the home of Joshua Winsor, a prominent merchant of Duxbury, Massachusetts, was executed by Dr Rufus Hatheway in the late-eighteenth century (Plate 210A). Hatheway began his career as a traveling artist but exchanged the uncertainties of limning for the more stable profession of medicine after his marriage to Judith Winsor in 1795. In the right foreground Mr Winsor may be seen with keys in hand, making his way toward the wharves and warehouses which were the center of his prosperous fishing business. A man (entirely out of proportion) stands on the forward deck of the two-masted vessel at right center. He is firing a double-barreled shotgun with results observable in the flight of ducks above.

Perspective was never of paramount importance to the folk artist and this element has been happily disregarded in Alexandr [sic] Boudrou's view of A. Dickson entering Bristol, Pennsylvania, in 1819 (Plate 210B). Here the subject, astride his white horse, has been featured in the center of the scene. Far below, however, viewed by the artist from a different vantage point, several small buildings and a group of trade symbols have been painted in the manner of a pasteboard collage.

Genre, or scenes of everyday life, are not prevalent, but when the folk artist looked about him his pictorial observations were usually noteworthy. Apart from esthetic considerations folk pictures may be desirable for their documentary content, and domestic scenes are eagerly sought and carefully studied. The representation of the Nathan Hawley family painted in their Albany home on November 3, 1801, records a wealth of detail invaluable both to the antiquarian and the social historian. The combined elements of costumes, furniture, pictures, floor-covering, and window treatment make this interior worthy of special note (Plate 211A).

Historical scenes frequently depicted events at which the artist was obviously not present. In such cases details were supplied by participants or by his own imagination. The early-nineteenth century witnessed the appearance of combinations of patriotic emblems such as those (Plate 209D) which symbolized the national pride of the young Republic.

In addition to portraits and subject pieces some itinerants specialized in ornamental interior painting. Before the Revolution architectural trim painted to simulate marble or handsomely grained woods was fashionable, following European custom. Paneled chimney-breasts embellished with decorative landscapes were to be seen in many houses in New England and the South between 1750 and 1800. After the turn of the century plaster walls, decorated with stenciled and freehand patterns or scenic panoramas, were encountered also in upper New York, Kentucky, Ohio, and as far west as Indiana. At a period when wall-paper was scarce and expensive the traveling decorator was able to offer painted substitutes which provided a variety of patterns applied at minimum expense.

Wall designs were usually repeat-patterns utilizing geometric and floral motifs, or scenes chosen for their decorative quality. However, artists occasionally elected to use a topical subject of local interest, such as the unusual event illustrated in a partially ruined house in Deansboro, Oneida County, New York, and now preserved in the Shelburne [Vermont] Museum. This shows a man leaping over a waterfall, and is believed to represent Sam Patch, who traveled in New York State, making exhibition jumps in the 1820s. A broadside dated October 12, 1829, advertises one of his spectacular leaps into Niagara Falls. His traditional procedure was to shed his coat and shoes, then to stand erect and jump feet first with great precision as he is shown doing here. He eventually lost his life in an unsuccessful leap into the Genesee Falls.

Amateur folk artists were motivated by social and educational requirements rather than by a desire for financial recompense. Included among the amateurs were men, women, and children, but the majority who painted for pleasure were young ladies who learned the rudiments of art as a requisite of a genteel education. Lessons in drawing and painting were given in academies and independent drawing schools, as well as through the medium of individual instruction books, of which many were available for home use.

During the second half of the eighteenth century decorative embroidered pictures,

worked from patterns based on European engravings, were executed by young girls at home or in school. Toward the end of the century watercolor was combined with needlework, and ultimately painting superseded stitchery as a pictorial medium. Watercolor on paper or fabric (such as silk, satin or velvet) characterized ladies' work, although pastel and oil on canvas were also used. Small portraits were done at home for family or friends. Landscapes were often charmingly unrealistic views of picturesque scenery. Episodes from the popular romantic novel, *Paul et Virginie*, first published in Paris in 1788, and widely translated and reissued, served as inspiration for many schoolgirl pictures (Plate 211B). A carry-over of the influence of needlework technique may be recognized in many of these 'fancy' pieces where the foliage is cleverly painted to simulate different types of embroidery stitches.

Much amateur work was accomplished with the aid of stencils which were also referred to as *theorems* in the early instruction books. These units were hollow-cut patterns fashioned out of paper which, when laid on a flat surface, allowed the paint to penetrate through the aperture to the object below. A picture composed with stencils may be recognized by the distinct outline of each element which never blend with one another in the manner of a composition painted 'freehand'.

Still-life compositions – vases of flowers, baskets of fruit, and handsome arrangements which combined the two – were typical of the amateur repertoire. They were usually accomplished by the use of individual stencils which were adaptable to many combinations according to the ability of the artist. White cotton velvet was a favorite medium for this type of picture during the years from 1810 to 1840. The textured surface imparted a rich background for brilliant colors which were specifically designated in the instruction books for the painting of fruit and flowers. One set of contemporary instructions for velvet painting called for a base of gum tragacanth dissolved in boiling water and mixed with powdered colors and lemon juice.

Religious scenes inspired by illustrations in family Bibles were considered particularly suitable subjects for young amateurs, and included such popular favorites as the *Prodigal Son*, the *Good Samaritan*, *Jephthah's Return*, and *Moses in the Bulrushes*. Two scenes have been found picturing different incidents in the story of Ruth and Naomi. One of these is illustrated (Plate 212A). These were apparently painted in pairs, as several examples by different artists have been found.

Akin to these subjects were the mourning pictures which suggested the preoccupation with death which was widespread in the nineteenth century. Family mortuary pieces reflecting these sentiments followed an accepted pattern and were painted by countless young girls during the first half of the century. The tombs, the river, the weeping willows, churches and mourners were not intended to be literal representations. They were conventional symbols expressing the universality of death while suggesting a belief in immortality which triumphs beyond the grave. Names of parents, grandparents, and other deceased relatives were placed on these memorials, or they were occasionally left blank according to the fancy of the artist. Illustrated here is a stylized version painted in monochrome (Plate 212B), which nevertheless includes the usual elements. The handsome gothic church, and hearse-house with conventional black doors, are features of unusual interest.

Glass painting was a technique employed by both the professional and the amateur. In the eighteenth century engraved designs were utilized by laying a mezzotint, which had been soaked in water, on the reverse of a glass that had been previously coated by a sticky substance such as Venice turpentine. After smoothing, the print was again moistened until it was capable of removal by the gentle rubbing of a sponge. By this process the outlines of the engraving were transferred to the reverse of the glass, and the resulting design was then ready to be filled in with color. By the nineteenth century such painting was being done freehand without mechanical aid, and many decorative designs appeared for clock panels, mirror tops, and other utilitarian purposes.

While some folk artists were able to paint creatively, manyothers derived their inspiration from basic sources of design. Copying well-known works of art was an accepted method of instruction at a time when originality was not stressed as it is today. One of the most comprehensive collections of pictorial source material was to be found in the many illustrated art instruction books which were imported from England in the late-eighteenth century. Numerous American editions followed which contained illustrations based on English originals. This accounts for the appearance of rustic cottages and picturesque castles, in early schoolgirl art, which are hardly indigenous to the American scene. The lithographs of Currier and Ives, pictures in *Gleason's Pictorial* and *Godey's Lady's Book*, and illustrations such as the Bartlett views in Willis's *American Scenery*, all provided good copy material. If the resulting reproduction was a free and imaginative adaptation, a significant example of folk painting might ensue despite its basic lack of originality.

Folk art has appeared at different periods in many parts of the United States but the two territories which have produced the most regionally diversified material are New England and Pennsylvania. In New England the professional artists were predominantly of English stock, and American portraits of the seventeenth century reflect the style of provincial English painting of the sixteenth and seventeenth centuries. During the mid-eighteenth century numerous English mezzotints were imported into this country and provided models for aspiring colonial painters whose skill was unable to match the exacting requirements of their aristocratic subjects. Poses and costumes were copied with painstaking fidelity, but backgrounds and accessories were simplified according to fancy and the faces were the only personal insertions. At this period there was little demand for the genuine but unflattering likenesses of the folk artist, and it was not until immediately after the Revolution that face-painting from life, minus artificiality, became generally acceptable to the average citizen.

As fresh territory was opened up toward the West many New Englanders traveled out to settle on the newly expanding frontier. A few carried their family portraits with them, but the majority were happy to patronize the traveling artists who followed in the wake of the pioneers. Folk painters from New England also journeyed through the South but they encountered competition from the foreign-born artists who emigrated to Philadelphia, Baltimore, Charleston and New Orleans. This circumstance, with the factors of climate, exigencies of war, and an economy based on slave labor, accounts in part for the apparent scarcity of southern folk painting.

Differing entirely from the pictorial folk art of the northeastern states were certain traditional forms brought from the Rhineland by Protestant refugees. These people, encouraged by William Penn and his agents, began their migration to the counties of southeastern Pennsylvania in the late-seventeenth century and continued to settle until the American Revolution. Illuminated family documents – birth and baptismal certificates, religious texts and rewards of merit – are known as *Fraktur* because of a similarity of lettering to the sixteenth-century type-face of that name. Gay watercolor borders, frequently incorporating stylized birds, angels, animals or flowers, surrounded the hand-lettered texts. Most of these documents were executed by local ministers, school-masters, or itinerant penmen. (*See also* Pennsylvania-German Folk Art by Frances Lichten, Vol. II.)

The decline of folk art in America commenced about the middle of the nineteenth century. Mechanical inventions made multiple reproductions possible and thereby obviated the need for the individual craftsman. Inexpensive lithographs were widely distributed for home consumption, and these gradually replaced the work of the schoolgirls and the hand-lettered texts of the *Frakturschriften*. The invention of the daguerreotype in 1839 was a decisive step toward modern photography whose speed and accuracy were destined eventually to supplant the traditional methods of the folk painter.

BOOKS FOR FURTHER READING

DREPPERD, CARL: *American Pioneer Arts and Artists*, Springfield, Mass. (1942).

FORD, ALICE: *Edward Hicks, Painter of the Peaceable Kingdom*, Philadelphia (1952), *Pictorial Folk Art*, New York (1949).

LIPMAN, JEAN: *American Primitive Painting*, New York (1942).

LIPMAN, JEAN, AND WINCHESTER, ALICE: *Primitive Painting in America, 1750–1950, An Anthology*, New York (1950).

LITTLE, NINA FLETCHER: *American Decorative Wall Painting*, Old Sturbridge Village, Massachusetts (1952), *The Abby Aldrich Rockefeller Folk Art Collection*, Colonial Williamsburg (1957).

MINIATURE PAINTING

By JOSEPHINE L. ALLEN

MINIATURES have always served a personal need – as a gift to a loved one, an exchange at the time of marriage, a precious reminder of persons away from home. Though the cost to the patron of having a miniature painted was usually small, the art flourished only in times of prosperity and tranquil living. The American settlers were too busy finding and creating the necessities of life to think about the fancy trimmings until the eighteenth century.

Miniature painting in America followed fairly closely the English and European pattern, allowing for a certain time lag for ideas and fashions to cross the Atlantic. The men and women portrayed, however, have a recognizably American appearance, due probably to our more rugged life and more simple society, especially where Puritans and Quakers held sway. Little is known of any miniatures done in the first half of the eighteenth century, but the earliest painter usually listed is JOHN WATSON of East Jersey, whose self-portrait in 1720 is actually a small grey wash drawing and not a miniature. Charleston was the home of JEREMIAH THEÜS, the first painter who worked in full color on ivory. His paint is neat and opaque, a reduced formula of his life-sized oil portraits. In Philadelphia JAMES CLAYPOOLE and MATTHEW PRATT were working similarly in techniques adapted from oil portraits, if the identification of their miniatures is correct. BENJAMIN WEST'S self-portrait at eighteen is a sallow work, but more in the manner of true miniatures. He left for Rome and London a few years later and devoted himself to large historical projects. His home and advice were sought by all visiting American artists for sixty years.

The first real flowering of the art of miniature painting came in Boston with Copley, Pelham and Dunkerley, in Philadelphia with the Peale family and in New York with Ramage and Fulton. JOHN SINGLETON COPLEY was the foremost portrait painter of the pre-Revolutionary period. He worked in oils, pastel and in miniature, and with each method he expressed admirably the sober integrity of his sitters. His miniatures are done on ivory, copper or wood and show with great clarity and simplicity the essential traits of his subjects. This can be seen in his portraits of Mrs John Melville (Plate 213A) and Samuel Carey and his wife. At the beginning of the war he left for England and did not return. Apparently he painted no miniatures in London. Copley taught his younger half-brother HENRY PELHAM what he knew of miniature painting. The few American examples identified as works of Pelham are forceful, showing a decided stipple. He too left America soon after the war started. Other New England artists were JOSEPH DUNKERLEY and NATHANIEL HANCOCK. Dunkerley's little elongated ovals are finely drawn and pale (Plate 213E). Hancock, with less skill but in similar vein, gave his sitters a thin, wispy look. In Connecticut a vigorous painter, JOHN TRUMBULL, was working out large historical paintings of the Declaration of Independence and various American battles. The series was begun in London under the guidance of Benjamin West. In the process Trumbull (Plate 214A) painted some remarkably fine portraits in oils of officers and individuals whose heads he needed to use in the large compositions.

Returning to Philadelphia, we find CHARLES WILLSON PEALE in the 1760s painting portraits in oil and in miniature. He had spent two years in London where he had expected to specialize in miniatures. He found, however, that he was equally successful in the larger-sized paintings. His miniatures are on small oval slices of ivory in which the heads fill most of the space. His colors are bright and pleasing, and his sitters are shown with sweet, gentle expressions (Plate 213F). Peale established a museum in Philadelphia for which he collected natural specimens and painted portraits of distinguished personalities. During the war he was able to take his miniature kit along and painted as many as forty portraits of such officers as George Washington, Nathanial Greene and Arthur St Clair. Having the support of his large family much on his mind Peale taught most of them to paint in one form or another, and in 1786 he left the field of miniature painting in Philadelphia to his younger brother James, who came to surpass him in this branch.

JAMES PEALE'S miniatures (Plate 213D) are better composed than his brother's, showing more of the sitter's figure. The size is larger, two and a half to three inches compared with Charles Willson's one and a half inches. His brush work in clear harmonious color combines little lines and stipple. His earlier miniatures may be confused with his brother's, but from 1788 on James signed his work with an elongated IP and the date.

After doing his share of the chores around the Peale Museum such as mounting exhibits and copying portraits, RAPHAELLE PEALE, son of Charles Willson, started to paint miniatures in his turn. His work is somewhat similar to James's but a bit larger and more open in manner (Plate 214B).

A native of Philadelphia, HENRY BENBRIDGE (Plate 213C) had five years' training in Rome under Mengs and Batoni, and in London where he was befriended by Benjamin West. His oil portraits and miniatures, smoothly painted in rich color, are occasionally mistaken for Copleys. Much of his work is found in Charleston.

Another Pennsylvania artist, ROBERT FULTON (Plate 215E), may have been a pupil of James Peale, his early works showing Peale's influence. At twenty-one, however, he

went to England and stayed twenty years, taking on more English mannerisms than any other native-born American who studied abroad. On his return his miniatures of New York ladies have the appearance of fancy portraits with flying locks and pseudo-Greek costume in the Angelica Kauffman manner, though a good deal more vigorous. His time, however, was soon taken up with researches on the steamboat.

The colonies and young republic attracted a number of excellent foreign artists. The earliest of these was an Irishman named JOHN RAMAGE (Plate 213B) who started to work in Boston just before the Revolution. In 1776 he went with other British loyalists to Halifax. As a result of marital troubles he soon left Nova Scotia for New York, where he settled down to a flourishing business painting the best families of New York such as the Pintards, the Ludlows and the Van Cortlandts. His miniatures are small and exquisite. The women have delicate features and masses of dark hair; the men, wearing elegant clothes, are smoothly painted. Ramage was a goldsmith as well as a painter and made his own frames. Some are lozenge-shaped and others oval; the frames have narrow engraved rims and in most a scalloped gold border lies inside the frame under the crystal.

Two Scots, ARCHIBALD and ALEXANDER ROBERTSON, settled in New York in the 1790s. They opened a school called the Columbian Academy of Painting, at which they were fairly successful. A portrait of Washington painted by Archibald on a slab of marble is in the collection of the New-York Historical Society. Another artist of the same name but not related to the first two, WALTER ROBERTSON, came from Ireland on the same boat that brought Gilbert Stuart back to America in 1793. Robertson painted General Washington, in uniform, and Mrs Washington. There are only a few of his elegant and sophisticated miniatures in America. He left for India a few years later. WILLIAM BIRCH arrived from England in 1794 and set himself up in Philadelphia as an enamel painter, remaining there the rest of his life. He made original portraits of Lafayette and Washington, and also copied Stuart's

Washington about sixty times. The portrait of his daughter Priscilla, looking coyly through a lace veil is especially charming. Birch is the only enameler of note in America.

The most distinguished visitor from England in the last decade of the eighteenth century was ROBERT FIELD. His beautiful, luminous miniatures celebrated the beaux and belles from Boston to Washington during the fourteen years of his stay in America (Plate 215B). While visiting in Georgetown, Field painted seven copies of Stuart's portrait of Washington for Mrs Washington and friends of the President. They have been considered the best copies ever painted. Incidentally, GILBERT STUART'S name comes up every now and then in connection with miniatures. Except for demonstrating that he could paint them Stuart does not appear to have enjoyed working in the small size. He was kept more than busy with the life-size oil portraits at which he excelled. On the other hand, it is known that many of his portraits were copied in miniature by Field and other good artists.

Good as were the products of English painters in America, the works of the native-born American, EDWARD GREENE MALBONE surpassed them in beauty, charm and delicacy. He made full use of the luminosity of his ivory and blended and varied his color to suit each sitter, enhancing the loveliness of the women and showing the strength and character of the men. His portrait of Mrs James Lowndes is a good example of a sweet, assured Charleston beauty (Plate 215A & 215F). Unfortunately, Malbone's life was tragically short. He taught himself to paint by copying engravings and helping a scene painter in the local theatre. At seventeen he went to Providence to make his living as a miniature painter. An early work now in the Providence Athenaeum shows that he had mastered the skill of producing a likeness. In two years he moved on to Boston where he had a wider field and was able to meet a number of artists including Washington Allston. Like many other painters, Malbone made the circuit of Boston, New York, Philadelphia and Charleston, finding patrons everywhere. In 1801 he went to England with Allston for a

few months and was especially impressed by the portraits of Lawrence, and the miniatures of Cosway and Shelley. He must have learned a good deal from the last two, for his work most nearly resembled theirs. After a few more years of work in America he died of tuberculosis, not quite thirty years old.

Another fine painter, CHARLES FRASER, who was a contemporary and friend of Malbone, spent most of a long life in Charleston. He had been prepared for the law and practised until he was thirty-five, but his natural bent for art was early stimulated by a boyhood friendship with Thomas Sully and the visits in Charleston of Malbone and Allston, who encouraged him to spend his whole time in painting. His perception of character shows in each miniature, accurately and sympathetically put down in well-blended color against gray stippled backgrounds (Plate 214C & 214D). During a visit of Lafayette to Charleston in 1825, Fraser was commissioned by the City Council to paint a portrait of the great man to commemorate his visit, and a second portrait of Francis Kinlock Huger as a gift to Lafayette. Huger had taken part in an attempt to free the General from imprisonment in an Austrian fortress thirty years earlier and had himself been caught and imprisoned. This miniature is now in the Metropolitan Museum.

THOMAS SULLY was brought to Charleston from England as a boy of nine. His family were actors and rather hoped that he would succeed in a business career. However, Thomas had a decided leaning toward painting and, although he disagreed violently with his first teacher, he persisted and at eighteen decided to go into the business of miniature painting (Plate 216E) with his older brother Lawrence in Norfolk. Lawrence was not able to teach him a great deal, being an indifferent painter himself, and Thomas moved on to New York and Boston where he received help from Jarvis and Stuart, and eventually went on to London. He finally settled in Philadelphia. The greater part of his work is in oil portraits, which have a smooth loveliness reminiscent of Thomas Lawrence.

BENJAMIN TROTT comes to mind as making a third fine artist with Malbone and

Fraser. His miniatures were neither as fine nor as consistently good as theirs, but he did paint some remarkably fresh and lovely portraits (Plate 215 c). He turned out many a romantic young man with wind-tossed locks in the Byronic manner, painted on a lightly washed or almost bare ivory background. He worked in both New York and Philadelphia, made frequent trips to the south and spent one year in a horseback journey to the west.

Although New York had played host to a number of traveling artists, it was not until the beginning of the nineteenth century that she had a resident group of her own. JOHN WESLEY JARVIS was brought by his father from England to Philadelphia at the age of five. He was apprenticed to Edward Savage, an engraver, and at the end of his time in 1802 he went to New York to set up as an engraver. Not long after he joined with a young man from upstate New York, JOSEPH WOOD, to open a studio. From all accounts they were a gay and boisterous pair. For a time they painted silhouettes, then commissions for miniatures came in, and some work in oils. Wood's miniatures are delicate with subdued color and an olive tone in the backgrounds. Jarvis, who also painted in oils, had a stronger, more juicy, brush stroke, especially vigorous in portraits of men (Plate 216 B). In portraying women his color is more gentle and charming. After he broke his partnership Jarvis made several trips to the south during the winters, going as far as New Orleans. With him went a young apprentice, Henry Inman, who later became the most important portrait painter in New York. Joseph Wood stayed on in New York, taking on NATHANIEL ROGERS as apprentice. In 1813 Wood left for Philadelphia, while Rogers became a fashionable miniature painter in New York. His best work is smooth with well-blended color; early examples are faulty in drawing.

HENRY INMAN settled down to marriage at twenty-one and serious work in New York after his wanderings with Jarvis. He took on THOMAS SEIR CUMMINGS as a pupil, though there was only three years' difference in their ages. Both became prominent in the social and intellectual life of New York and held offices in the newly-founded National Academy of Design. Inman's portraits are clearly seen and solidly painted; the character of the sitters is skilfully presented (Plate 216 A). His miniatures are rather cool in color and delicately painted. His portrait of Mrs Alexander Hamilton at the age of sixty-eight is a beautifully sympathetic rendering of an ageing gentlewoman. About 1827 Inman gave up miniature painting to concentrate on his oil portraits, and Cummings continued this side of the business. Cummings's miniatures are warmer in color and more lively in expression. The Metropolitan Museum has two family mementoes: a portrait of his young wife in a golden-brown dress (Plate 216D) and a charming necklace of portraits in graduated sizes of his nine children. Two English artists continued after Cummings in painting lovely women with grace and beauty: RICHARD M. STAIGG worked in Boston and finally settled in Newport, and GEORGE L. SAUNDERS visited America twice and painted largely in Baltimore, but worked also in Boston and Philadelphia.

As the art of miniature painting approached its deadline in the invention of the daguerreotype, portraits became more and more realistic. Their main attraction was in the smooth bright colors, and the meticulously painted details of hair and dress. SARAH GOODRIDGE stands out among these artists. She had instruction from Gilbert Stuart and made her way in Boston under his patronage. Her self-portrait shows a strong character in unflattering terms (Plate 216 c). Collections of European miniatures are most frequently made even in America, but portraits of our own forebears are equally rewarding and well worth searching for. Many miniatures have remained in the families for whom they were painted. Identification of the author can often be made by reference to the location of the sitter. Whereas certain artists were known to have moved up and down the Atlantic seaboard, others kept to established centers. The patrons were more apt to have the leisure for sittings when at home.

GLOSSARY

Miniature painters arranged alphabetically, with life dates or activity and the location of their activity.   * Asterisk indicates artists discussed in the text.

Ames, Ezra, 1768–1836; New York State.

*****Benbridge, Henry,** 1744–1812; Philadelphia and South.

*****Birch, William,** 1755–1834; Philadelphia.

Blanchard, Washington, active 1831–43; Boston.

Bounetheau, Henry Brintnell, 1797–1877; Charleston.

Bridport, Hugh, 1794–c. 1868; Philadelphia.

Brown, John Henry, 1818–91; Pennsylvania.

Carlin, John, 1813–91; New York.

Catlin, George, 1796–1872; New York.

Clark, Alvan, 1804–87; Boston.

*****Claypoole, James,** 1720–c. 1796; Philadelphia.

*****Copley, John Singleton,** 1737–1815; Boston, New York and Philadelphia.

*****Cummings, Thomas Seir,** 1804–94; New York and New Jersey.

Cushman, George Hewitt, 1814–76; Philadelphia.

Dickinson, Anson, 1779–1852; New York State and Connecticut (Plate 215D).

Dickinson, Daniel, 1795–after 1840; Philadelphia.

Dodge, John Wood, 1807–93; New York.

Doyle, William M. S., 1769–1828; Massachusetts.

Dubourjal, Savinien Edmé, 1795–1853; New York.

*****Dunkerley, Joseph,** active 1783–7; Boston.

Dunlap, William, 1766–1839; New York.

Durand, Asher Brown, 1796–1886; New York.

Eichholtz, Jacob, 1776–1842; Philadelphia.

Ellsworth, James Sanford, 1802–73; Connecticut.

Elouis, Jean Pierre Henri, 1755–1840; Philadelphia and Annapolis.

*****Field, Robert,** c. 1770–1819; Philadelphia, Baltimore and Boston.

Franks, William, active 1795–8; New York.

*****Fraser, Charles,** 1782–1860; Charleston.

Freeman, George, 1789–1868; Connecticut and Philadelphia.

*****Fulton, Robert,** 1765–1815; Philadelphia and New York.

Gimbrede, Thomas, 1781–1832; New York.

*****Goodridge, Sarah,** 1788–1853; Boston.

Hall, Ann, 1792–1863; New York.

*****Hancock, Nathaniel,** active 1792–1809; Massachusetts.

Harvey, George, c. 1800–78; New York and Boston.

Hill, Pamela E., 1803–60; Boston.

*****Inman, Henry,** 1801–46; New York and Philadelphia.

*****Jarvis, John Wesley,** 1780–1839; New York and South.

Jouett, Matthew Harris, 1787–1827; Kentucky.

Lambdin, James Reid, 1807–89; Pennsylvania and South.

McDougal, John Alexander, 1810 or 1811–94; New York, New Jersey and South.

*****Malbone, Edward Greene,** 1777–1807; New England, New York and South.

Metcalf, Eliab, 1785–1834; New York.

Miles, Edward, 1752–1828; Philadelphia.

Peale, Anna Claypoole, 1791–1878; New York, Philadelphia and Baltimore.

*****Peale, Charles Willson,** 1741–1827; Philadelphia, New York and South.

*****Peale, James,** 1749–1831; Philadelphia.

*****Peale, Raphaelle,** 1774–1825; Philadelphia, Baltimore and South.

Peale, Rembrandt, 1778–1860; Baltimore, Philadelphia and New York.

*****Pelham, Henry,** 1749–1806; New England.

Peticolas, Edward, 1793–c. 1853; Richmond.

Peticolas, Philippe A., 1760–1841; Pennsylvania and Richmond.

Picot de Limoelan de Clorivière, Joseph Pierre, 1768–1826; South.

*****Pratt, Matthew,** 1734–1805; Philadelphia and New York.

*****Ramage, John,** active 1763–1802; Boston and New York.

*****Robertson, Alexander,** 1772–1841; New York.

*****Robertson, Archibald,** 1765–1835; New York.

*****Robertson, Walter,** active 1765–1802; Philadelphia and New York.

Robinson, John, active 1817–29; Philadelphia.

*Rogers, Nathaniel, 1788–1844; New York.

*Saunders, George Lethbridge, 1807–63; Baltimore, Boston and Philadelphia.

Savage, Edward, 1761–1817; Philadelphia and New York.

Shumway, Henry Cotton, 1807–84; New York.

Smith, James P., 1803–88; Philadelphia.

Smith, John Rubens, 1775–1849; New York.

*Staigg, Richard Morrell, 1817–81; New England and New York.

*Sully, Lawrence, 1769–1804; South.

*Sully, Thomas, 1783–1872; South and Philadelphia.

*Theüs, Jeremiah, 1719–74; Charleston.

*Trott, Benjamin, *c.* 1770–after 1841; Philadelphia, New York and Baltimore.

*Trumbull, John, 1756–1843; New York and Connecticut.

Vallée, Jean François de la, active 1785–1815; Charleston.

Verstile, William, *c.* 1755–1803; Massachusetts, New York and Philadelphia.

Waldo, Samuel Lovett, 1783–1861; New York.

*Watson, John, 1685–1768; New Jersey.

Wertmüller, Adolph Ulric, 1751–1811; Philadelphia.

*West, Benjamin, 1738–1820; New York and Philadelphia.

Williams, Henry, 1787–1830; Boston.

*Wood, Joseph, *c.* 1778–*c.* 1832; New York, Philadelphia and South.

BOOKS FOR FURTHER READING

BOLTON, THEODORE: *Early American Portrait Painters in Miniature*, New York (1921). A dictionary of artists with check list of their works. Illustrated.

PARKER, BARBARA NEVILLE, AND WHEELER, ANNE BOLLING: *John Singleton Copley: American Portraits in Oil, Pastel and Miniature*, Boston (1938). Illustrated.

SELLERS, CHARLES COLEMAN: *Portraits and Miniatures by Charles Willson Peale*, Philadelphia (1952). Includes catalogue of works. Illustrated.

TOLMAN, RUEL P.: *The Life and Work of Edward Greene Malbone, 1777–1807*, New York (1957). Illustrated.

WEHLE, HARRY B.: *American Miniatures, 1730–1850*, New York (1927). Illustrated.

Concise Encyclopedia of Antiques, Vol. I, pp. 228–238, Hawthorn Books, New York (1955).

ENGRAVINGS

By ELIZABETH E. ROTH

For the collector, American prints in the wider sense of the word begin with the views of the second half of the sixteenth century, engraved and published in Europe by Theodore de Bry from 1590 onwards; while in the narrower sense they are restricted to prints produced in America, beginning in the middle of the seventeenth century. John Foster of Boston illustrated the books he printed with woodcuts which are the first American prints to which a maker's name can be attached; they hardly merit the word artistic. However, his name stands out in the anonymity of seventeenth-century American engravings, surrounded, as it were, by a number of crude productions by unknown craftsmen who were most likely printers or silversmiths working with simple tools and having little or no training.

Among European prints of the American scene a few of the many topographical works containing views or pictorial descriptions should be noted. Theodore de Bry, a Flemish engraver and copperplate publisher who resided in Frankfurt, Germany, from 1588 until his death in 1598, engraved for his collection of *Great Voyages* the first views and pictorial accounts of the North American mainland with its native inhabitants, their tribal customs, their villages and the flora and fauna of the newly discovered country. Some of the engravings were made after the paintings by Jacques Le Moyne de Morgue, the French explorer who had journeyed to Florida with the Huguenots under René de Laudonnière in 1564. Twenty years later Le Moyne wrote a narrative of his explorations and illustrated his account, entitled *Brevis Narratio*, with forty-three sketches which de Bry engraved and published in 1591. A year earlier de Bry had engraved the drawings by John White, the artist who had accompanied Sir Walter Raleigh on his unsuccessful expedition to Virginia in 1585, and a second time as 'Governor of the Colonie' in 1587. Of the seventy-five watercolors by John White – the 'first' English watercolors – de Bry engraved twenty-three to illustrate Thomas Hariot's account, *A Briefe and True Report of the New Found Land of Virginia*, for his Virginia volume of the *Great Voyages*, and later two others for the work on Florida. The twenty-three watercolors by John White are now preserved in the British Museum, while of Jacques Le Moyne's small paintings only one is known to exist, in the possession of an American collector; the others are presumed lost. De Bry's collection of *Great Voyages* was issued in a number of editions and translations. Some of the later publications based their illustrations on those which appeared in de Bry's work but, in addition to these, other travel books written by European explorers and travelers were illustrated with new pictorial material. In Sir Francis Drake's *Expeditio* of 1588 appears the first view of a town within today's limits of the United States, the town of St Augustine in Florida; while the earliest known engraved view of New York, the so-called Hartger's view, was issued with the small book entitled *Beschrijvinghe van Virginia, Nieuw Nederlandt, Nieuw Engelandt ...* published in Amsterdam in 1651. John Ogilby's *America* (London, 1671) contains views of a number of ports in this hemisphere, and in Father Louis Hennepin's *New Discovery of a Vast Country* (London, 1698) there is possibly the earliest view of Niagara Falls. Not only do the early views appear in books, but also as insets on handsome maps like the important maps of the Visscher series published in the middle of the seventeenth century.

Parallel, although on a very different level artistically, was the production of illustrated books in colonial America. The crudity of the early cuts, either wood or type-metal, is more than made up for by their historical importance in the development of the American graphic arts. Their naïve charm somewhat compensates for their lack of artistic quality. It is John Foster of Boston, who established his printing shop in 1675, to whom goes the credit for being the first American-born 'artist' to have made engravings in this country. His woodcut portrait of Richard Mather, the Massachusetts clergyman (1670), is known in only five impressions, the latest acquisition having been made by Princeton University in January 1957. Almost as rare are his other woodcuts, a seal for the Massachusetts Bay Colony in 1675 and a map of New England which appeared in William Hubbard's *Narrative of the Troubles with the Indians* (1677).

It was not until the beginning of the eighteenth century that single prints were published, apart from book illustration. Again the earliest were published in Europe, although drawn in America and advertised for sale in the colonial newspapers. William Burgis was the first to supply large single views of American cities. Very few copies of these views, however, are known to exist, either in first states or in later, second, states, but they can be studied in public collections which are fortunate enough to own them. William Burgis's panoramic views of New York (1719) and Boston (1722) were engraved by John Harris of London and published there, copied and plagiarized by later engravers, no doubt to satisfy the great demand of a curious public eager to know what the new country looked like. In studying these early views we find that some are fairly accurate renderings, others slightly fictitious, while still others, like the colorful *vues d'optique*, show a remarkable fantasy and lack of knowledge of conditions in a pioneering country. These handcolored – amusing rather than puzzling – peepshow prints, with reversed lettering in the top margin, and the text often in both German and French, were published in the second half of the eighteenth century

in Augsburg and Paris to be used in mirrored boxes and carried around by itinerant showmen.

Not more than about a dozen engravers were working in colonial America in the eighteenth century, and these were primarily engaged in illustrating books, including several Bibles and periodicals; but they probably earned their daily bread and butter with commercial work like bill-heads, advertisements and broadsides. It was from Europe that the colonists received their large prints to be hung on the walls of their homes, or in some few cases, kept in portfolios. These prints were either ordered directly from London or purchased from the local printsellers known to have been well established in larger towns of colonial America.

The post-Revolutionary period brought a radical change in the conditions in the field of printmaking in this country. Professionally trained painters and engravers arrived in increasing numbers from England and Scotland and settled in Boston, New York or Philadelphia, where publishers were ready to employ them. Among these was John Hill (Plate 219B). The English artists brought with them the knowledge and techniques of the highly developed art of watercoloring, which had such a vogue in eighteenth-century England, while the engravers were equipped to handle the aquatint process, so well suited to reproduce the watercolors. The beginning of the nineteenth century saw an increased production in the numbers of town and local views and, due to their artistic and picturesque quality, these views are among the most attractive to today's collector. The aquatints were colored, either by hand or printed from several plates, limiting the use of the process usually to topographical work – to the picturesque rather than mere landscape. Very few attempts were made to use this technique for portraits, which are more suitably engraved in either stipple or mezzotint.

The growing periodical literature gave increasing opportunity for employment to engravers. This had already been done by American editions of British encyclopedias published in Philadelphia (Dobson's edition of Rees's *Encyclopaedia*, 1794–1803, and the

Philadelphia edition of the Edinburgh *Encyclopaedia*, 1806–13), although there was little chance given for artistic development and imagination. Bank-note engraving was another field for many excellent engravers, who had to meet the high standards of workmanship required for such meticulous work. The first half of the nineteenth century has been called the 'Golden Age of Engraving', brought to a close by the activities of a number of art societies which sponsored annual distribution of large engravings to their membership, the most prominent being the Apollo Association, later called the American Art Union, 1839–51. Unfortunately the invention of a number of mechanical ruling devices for use in engraving began to spoil the artistic quality of many of the prints produced toward the middle of the century, which deteriorated to mere hack work. Finally the photomechanical processes liberated the engravers from mere reproductive work and gave the field of print-making a new lease of life.

Views: the earliest views of American towns appeared in books published in Europe, but they can often be found as separates, either with or without the accompanying text. Single prints of American scenery were not published till the early-eighteenth century, and among the earliest are the very rare Burgis views of New York (1719) and Boston (1722), the Boston Lighthouse and the view of the New Dutch Church in New York, dedicated to Governor Rip van Dam. Of equal importance are the panoramic views of Charleston, South Carolina, by B. Roberts (1739) and the Scull-Heap view of Philadelphia (1754). London publishers re-issued some of these views with alterations in the lettering, while other engravers copied some of them for which they found a ready market. The Carwitham views of Boston, New York and Philadelphia, published for Carington Bowles of London some time after 1764, are based chiefly on earlier views, although with a character of their own. These colored line engravings, signed by John Carwitham, are among the most attractive, although very scarce; later states with alterations exist: however, they are not as valuable.

In 1734 the earliest view of Savannah was engraved by Pierre Fourdrinier after a drawing by Peter Gordon, a bird's-eye view, showing the newly settled town with its straight streets and large squares for markets amidst a wilderness. The view of Philadelphia depicting the House of Employment, Alms House and Pennsylvania Hospital, about 1767, was engraved by John Hulett after a drawing by Nicholas Garrison, and is another of the important early views of an American city.

One of the handsomest of large collections of topographical prints of North America and the West Indies in the middle of the eighteenth century is the *Scenographia Americana*. This collection, which was published in London in 1768, contains twenty-eight engraved plates. In some cases it has been augmented to include as many as seventy-four, reproducing the drawings made by British army and navy officers. Matching in importance the *Scenographia Americana* is another set of views, the *Atlantic Neptune*, a collection of as many as 275 maps, charts and views brought together for the British Admiralty by J. F. W. Des Barres during the years 1763 to 1784. This publication includes aquatinted views of American ports.

Following the Revolution a number of very beautiful views were executed by newcomers to America, some using the relatively new aquatint process for reproducing watercolors. Saint-Mémin, in addition to his prolific output of profile portraits, made two charming etchings of New York in 1796. The well-known London aquatinter Francis Jukes reproduced four watercolors by Alexander Robertson, the Scottish artist who had come to New York around 1794 and opened the Columbian Drawing Academy together with his brother Archibald. Included in this set of four views are *New York from Hobuck Ferry* and *Mount Vernon* in 1799.

At the turn of the century William and Thomas Birch, father and son, drew, engraved and published a set of twenty-eight line engravings entitled: *The City of Philadelphia as it appeared in 1800* (Plate 218B). Dates on individual plates range from 1798 to 1800. A later edition was published by Birch in 1806 and re-issued by Desilver in 1841. The aquatints by J. Cartwright in the

Atkins and Nightingale series of American views are all very rare. They were made after the paintings by George Beck of Philadelphia and published in London between 1800 and 1810. A decade later W. G. Wall executed his watercolors for the justly famous *Hudson River Portfolio* (Plate 219B), a series of twenty aquatinted views engraved by John Hill and published by Henry J. Megarey in New York about 1825. Together with William J. Bennett's nineteen views of American cities (Plate 220A) published in the 1830s, they make up the finest and most desirable group of colored aquatints in America. In a different style altogether are two other publications containing views of the city of New York. These are the small, well-executed engravings of the Bourne *Views of New York City* (1831) and the Peabody *Views of New York and Environs* (1831–4). Both series contain double plates with accompanying text and were issued in parts.

Among the last aquatinters in this country who engraved views of American scenery were Robert Havell, Jr., who had come to New York after completing the engravings of Audubon's *Birds of America* in London. Havell made two panoramic views of New York, one from the North River (1840), the other from the East River (1844); a view of Hartford, Connecticut, and a view of Niagara Falls. Another was Henry Papprill, who engraved the Catherwood view of *New York from Governor's Island* in 1846, and in 1849 his bird's-eye view of New York from the steeple of St Paul's Church, after a drawing by John W. Hill, published by Henry J. Megarey. Modern impressions, or re-strikes, exist of many of the listed views, and in some cases the original copperplates have been preserved and are owned by public institutions. It is, therefore, advisable for collectors to study the literature on these prints before purchasing any of them. Sidney L. Smith re-engraved a number of rare American views, but these are all clearly signed and identified; in themselves they are very attractive and in some instances also rare.

Woodcuts and Wood-engravings: although not really within the scope of an

account of American engraving, mention may be made of the extremely rare, crude, anonymous German woodcut of about 1505 which depicts the Indians of the northern shores of South America and is 'the first pictorial representation of any part of the mainland of the western hemisphere'. This cut is known in two states and shows the Indians with fearful evidence of cannibalistic habits.

It was not until the middle of the seventeenth century that woodcuts were first printed in colonial America by the before-mentioned John Foster of Boston, who is credited with producing the first woodcuts of known authorship. Many other relief cuts, either wood or type-metal, remain anonymous, but were most likely executed by printers who used them on bill-heads, trade-cards, broadsides and in books. Not till the eighteenth century, and well into the middle of it, did the artistic quality of the woodcuts improve, decorating pages of farmers' almanacs and broadsides describing cruel deeds and crimes or advertising traveling entertainers. Crude as they are, these cuts have a quaint charm and may attract the collectors of folk art as well as the social historian. James Franklin of Boston and his younger brother Benjamin in Philadelphia are both credited with having made some woodcuts and metal-cuts in their printing shops. The Revolution inspired broadsides in the nature of political caricatures while the post-Revolutionary period created pictorial evidence of the growing national strength and geographical expansion. At the turn of the century Alexander Anderson, a New Yorker, introduced to this country Thomas Bewick's white line technique of cutting the design on the end-grain of the woodblock instead of on the plank. In this manner Anderson executed nearly ten thousand cuts during his lifetime, for books, periodicals and commercial ephemera; even if not of great artistic quality, they reflect a certain high standard of craftsmanship (Plate 217C). Among the few other known wood engravers of the first half of the nineteenth century is Abel Bowen, who is known for his large historical woodcut in three sections, *View of Colonel Johnson's Engagement near the Moravian Town*, October 5, 1812, as well as for some cuts for book illustration. Other wood engravers active in the second quarter of the century, supplying illustrations for books and magazines, were Alfred A. Lansing, John H. Hall, Abraham J. Mason, Joseph Alexander Adams and Benson J. Lossing.

Historical subjects: the first historical print produced in America was Samuel Blodget's *Battle of Lake George*, September 8, 1755, which was published in Boston, December 22 of that year. An English copy was published a year later in London and like the American edition was accompanied by a pamphlet describing this battle of the French and Indian War. Henry Dawkins's *Paxton Expedition* in Philadelphia in 1764 records an historical event in which Benjamin Franklin played an important part. It is also the earliest known street view of this city. Paul Revere's engravings of the British ships landing their troops in Boston Harbor, 1768, and his print of the 'Bloody Massacre' in Boston on March 5, 1770, are foundation stones of American historical engraving. The original copperplate of Revere's *Boston Massacre* is still preserved in the office of the State Treasurer of Massachusetts.

During the Revolution a set of four crude, but highly important historical prints were engraved by Amos Doolittle, showing the *Battles of Lexington and Concord* in 1775 (Plate 219A) after paintings by Ralph Earl, later known as a portrait painter. Doolittle also engraved a view of the façade of Federal Hall in New York City after a drawing by Peter Lacour, depicting George Washington's first inauguration in 1789 on its balcony. Another print of the Revolutionary period was made by Bernard Romans, whose *Exact View of the Late Battle of Charlestown* (Bunker Hill), 1775, was re-engraved by Robert Aitkin on a reduced scale and published in the latter's *Pennsylvania Magazine* for September 1775 (issued probably in October of that year) and called a *Correct View...* Robert Edge Pine's painting of *Congress Voting Independence* exists in an unfinished line and stipple engraving by Edward Savage, c. 1794.

The War of 1812 produced the following prints: *The Capture of the City of Washington by the British Forces*, Aug. 24, 1814, a line en-graving by an unknown engraver published by John Ryland; John Bower's rather crude prints of the *Battle of Patapsco Neck*, Sept. 12, 1814 and the *Bombardment of Fort McHenry near Baltimore*, on Sept. 13, 1814; a pair of aquatints by Robert Havell, Sr., of the *Attack on Fort Oswego, Lake Ontario*, May 6, 1814 and *Storming of Fort Oswego*, published in 1815; *The Battle of New Orleans, 1815 and Death of Major General Packenham*, a line engraving by Joseph Yeager of Philadelphia. Historical prints of the Mexican War were executed almost entirely in lithography. (*See* 'Marine Paintings and Prints' by Harold S. Sniffen, p. 456).

College views: among the earliest college views is the Burgis view of Harvard, *Prospect of the Colledges in Cambridge in New England*, in 1726; another early Harvard view was engraved by Paul Revere in 1768. *William and Mary*, c. 1740, the second oldest college view in America, was engraved after a drawing possibly made by the colonial botanist John Bartram. The earliest view of Princeton appears in the New American Magazine for 1760 entitled *Auld Nassovica*, while the second oldest view of this college (Plate 218A) was engraved by Henry Dawkins (*North-West Prospect of Nassau-Hall*) published as a frontispiece to *An Account of the College of New Jersey* (Woodbridge, N.J., 1764). Yale College is first shown in an engraving by Thomas Johnston from a drawing by John Greenwood and published by James Buck, c. 1749. King's College (Columbia) is shown prominently in a view of New York from the collection of the *Scenographia Americana* (1768). One of the last college views in the eighteenth century appeared in the *Massachusetts Magazine* for February 1793; this is a view of Dartmouth College in New Hampshire. Beginning with the nineteenth century, the number of college views increases rapidly. Alvan Fisher drew a 'North East View' of Harvard as well as a 'South View', which were engraved and published in 1823. The University of Virginia appears as an inset on a map of the state published in 1825 and engraved by B. Tanner. J. H. Hinton, in his *History and Topography of the United States* (1830-1), included views of Amherst College, Massachusetts, and Kenyon

College, Ohio. William Henry Bartlett drew a view of Yale College in 1839 which was engraved and issued in N. P. Willis's *American Scenery* (1840). J. W. Barber's view of *New Haven Green with Buildings of Yale College* is much sought after by collectors, as is the view of Dartmouth College by Christian Meadows, 1851.

Portraits: from among the great number of portraits executed in America in the period under discussion a few may be mentioned here either for their historical importance or for their artistic merit. The first woodcut portrait produced in this country was made by John Foster, the Boston printer, in 1670. This is the portrait of Richard Mather, the New England clergyman and grandfather of Cotton Mather, whose portrait was engraved in mezzotint by Peter Pelham, a London-trained engraver who had come to America and executed a series of mezzotint portraits of clergymen about 1727. Paul Revere engraved the portraits of Samuel Adams, Benjamin Church, John Hancock, Jonathan Mayhew (Plate 217A) and others. Amos Doolittle, the engraver of four important battle scenes of the Revolution, also engraved a number of small portraits. Late in the eighteenth century Charles Willson Peale made a few and very rare mezzotint portraits of Benjamin Franklin, Lafayette, William Pitt, and George and Martha Washington. John Norman is credited with having made the first engraved portrait of George Washington in 1779 as well as a series of other historical portraits. H. Houston of Philadelphia did some meritorious portrait engravings in stipple, as did Edward Savage, a native American engraver who had studied in London. His important portraits are those of John Adams, Benjamin Franklin and George Washington. Cornelius Tiebout is called the first American-born engraver of any artistic talent. He engraved portraits of George Washington, John Jay (Plate 217B) after Gilbert Stuart and the generals of the American Revolution. Charles B. J. Févret de Saint-Mémin, a French nobleman who, while earning his living in New York and Philadelphia by making profile crayon drawings with the aid of the *physionotrace* and reducing them with a pantograph

on to the copperplate which he then etched and aquatinted, executed about eight hundred portraits of distinguished American ladies and gentlemen. Another engraver who used the aquatint process for portrait work was William Strickland. David Edwin was an excellent and prolific engraver of stipple portraits and has been called 'the American Bartolozzi' by Stauffer. James Barton Longacre executed some very fine stipple portraits, among them one of Andrew Jackson after a painting by Thomas Sully (1820). Longacre is also responsible for many of the plates in the *National Portrait Gallery* (1834–9), in four volumes, which he published together with the painter James Herring. Asher Brown Durand, before becoming known as the father of American landscape painting, was a very fine engraver of portraits in line, which are described in the catalogue issued by the Grolier Club of New York in 1895. J. F. E. Prud'homme did fine portrait work in stipple, while John Rubens Smith used both stipple and mezzotint for his many portrait engravings.

No other person in America has been so much portrayed as George Washington. Hart, in his catalogue of the engraved portraits of George Washington, lists eight hundred and eighty entries with several states adding up to a number close to fifteen hundred. The largest number of these are engravings after the paintings by Gilbert Stuart.

GLOSSARY

(See conclusion for technical terms)

Aitken, Robert: 1734–1802. Printer and publisher, originally from Scotland, who issued the *Pennsylvania Magazine* 1775–6. He supposedly re-engraved on a reduced scale the view by Bernard Romans of the Battle of Bunker Hill: *A Correct View of the Late Battle at Charlestown*, June 17th, 1775, which appeared in the *Pennsylvania Magazine* for September 1775.

Allen, Luther: 1780–1821. Engraved *A South West View of Newport, R.I.*, after a drawing by S. King, 1795.

Anderson, Alexander: 1775–1870. Wood engraver, born in New York of Scottish parents, studied medicine but turned to wood engraving, introducing to this country the 'white line' technique of Thomas Bewick. He made about 10,000 cuts for books, periodicals, bill-heads, advertisements, etc. (Plate 217C).

Atlantic Neptune: a large collection of about 275 views, maps, charts, etc. of ports in North America, published for the British Admiralty under the direction of Joseph F. W. Des Barres during the period 1763–84.

Audubon, John James: 1785–1851. American ornithologist and artist whose water-color drawings for the double elephant folio *The Birds of America* were engraved by Robert Havell, father and son, in London, 1827–38. There are four volumes of 435 plates which are a combination of aquatint, etching and line engraving on dated Whatman paper. W. H. Lizars of Edinburgh engraved the first ten plates, later retouched by Havell. Some plates were re-issued, noting changes of address of the engravers.

Bakewell, Thomas: London publisher of the 2nd state of the famous Burgis view of New York, called the Bakewell re-issue of 1746.

Barber, John Warner: 1798–1885. Engraver and publisher of New Haven, Conn., whose interest in history led him to illustrate and publish the following books: *History and Antiquities of New Haven* (1831); *Connecticut Historical Collections* (1836); *Views in New Haven and Vicinity* (1825). Very much sought after by collectors is his view of New Haven Green with the buildings of Yale College.

Barralet, John James: 1747?–1815. Philadelphia painter and engraver; chiefly a designer of views engraved by others. Came to America in 1795 from Ireland.

Bartlett, William Henry: 1809–54. Artist, whose numerous sepia drawings were engraved by others for books such as N. R. Willis's *American Scenery* (1840), which was issued in parts.

Beck, George: landscape painter, located in Philadelphia from 1798 to 1807, drew the views of American scenes published by Atkins & Nightingale in London, *c.* 1801–9.

Bennett, William James: 1787–1844. Painter and engraver of aquatints, born in England. A pupil of the Royal Academy and of Westall, he came to America in 1816. Known for his series of *Views of American Cities* (Plate 220A), the finest color aquatints in this field; also for the three *Street Views in the City of New York* published by H. J. Megarey in New York in 1834; two views of the Great Fire of New York in December 1835 (after N. V. Calyo), and *The Seasons* after George Harvey (1841).

Bingham, George Caleb: 1811–79. Portrait and genre painter whose paintings were engraved by John Sartain, Gautier and Thomas Doney and widely distributed, especially to the members of the American Art Union.

Birch, Thomas: 1779–1851. Landscape and marine painter, son of William (q.v.), with whom he worked. Later became known for naval subjects of the War of 1812 which were engraved by Tiebout, Tanner and Lawson.

Birch, William: 1755–1834. Born in England, active as an enamel painter, engraver and print publisher. He came to Philadelphia in 1794. His earlier engraved work was done in stipple. Drew and engraved, together with his son, a series of twenty-eight views of the City of Philadelphia (Plate 218B), issued in 1800, either plain or colored; also a series of small views of the *Country Seats of the United States* (1808).

Blodget, Samuel: first American-born artist to draw an eye-witness account of an historic event, the view of the *Battle of Lake George*, engraved by Thomas Johnston, Boston, 1755, also published by Thomas Jefferys in London, 1756. This is the first historical print engraved in America. Both the English and American issues were accompanied by a pamphlet describing the battle.

Bourne, George M.: publisher of the so-called Bourne *Views of New York City*, 1831. There are nineteen double plates, all but the first six copyrighted in 1831. Charles Burton drew most of these views, while James Smillie engraved the greater number of the plates.

The New-York Historical Society owns original drawings of eighteen of the views, while fifteen of the remaining twenty are in the Smillie Collection of the New York Public Library. The New-York Historical Society owns all but three of the copperplates.

Bowen, Abel: 1790–1850. Copper and wood engraver, known for his line and stipple engravings of public buildings in Boston for Snow's *History of Boston* (1825) and for a woodcut in three sections of the *View of Colonel Johnson's Engagement with the Savages near the Moravian Town*, Oct. 5, 1812. Publisher of the *Naval Monument*, partly illustrated by him.

Bower, John: fl. 1809–19. Philadelphia engraver who executed two important battle scenes of the War of 1812: *The Battle of Patapsco Neck*, Sept. 12, 1814, and *The Bombardment of Fort McHenry near Baltimore*, Sept. 13, 1814.

Bry, Theodore de: 1528–98. Flemish engraver and publisher of the earliest prints depicting North American Indians, their villages and customs, appearing as part of his collection of *Great Voyages* published in 1590 and 1591.

Buck, James: Boston publisher of the first view of Yale College in 1749, engraved by Thomas Johnston after a drawing by John Greenwood.

Burgis, William: early eighteenth-century publisher of maps; an artist whose panoramic views of New York and Boston were engraved by John Harris of London and published in 1719 and 1722 respectively. He also drew a view of Harvard College, issued in 1726, a view of the Boston Lighthouse and the New Dutch Church in New York. These views are among the most sought after by collectors; only a few recorded impressions are known.

Burt, Charles: 1823–92. Engraver, born in Edinburgh, came to New York in 1836. Engraved portraits and illustrations for books, some large 'framing' prints for the American Art Union; after 1850 worked almost exclusively on banknote engraving.

Calyo, Nicolino V.: 1790–1884. Painter who came to New York from Italy and is known for two aquatint views of the Great Fire in New York in 1835 engraved by William J. Bennett; also for a series of Street Cries of New York (now at the Museum of the City of New York.)

Cartwright, John: English engraver of the aquatint series of American scenes by George Beck of Philadelphia, published by Atkins & Nightingale of London from 1801–9. (Not to be confused with T. Cartwright.)

Carwitham, John: active 1723–64. London engraver for Carington Bowles: his name appears on three important and attractive views of New York, Boston and Philadelphia. His name appears on the second states only of these prints which were issued after 1764, although the three cities are depicted between 1731 and 1755. The Boston view is probably based on the Burgis view of 1722, while the Philadelphia view seems to copy the Scull-Heap view of *c.* 1754.

Casilear, John W.: 1811–93. A good line engraver who turned to painting of landscapes.

Catesby, Mark: 1679–1749. English naturalist and engraver of birds and flowers of America and the West Indies who drew and etched the 220 colored plates for the two-volume work entitled: *Natural History of Carolina, Florida and the Bahama Islands* (London, 1731–43).

Catherwood, Frederick: 1799–1854. English artist, architect and engineer, known for his views of Central America and his view of *New York from Governor's Island*, 1846, which was engraved in aquatint by H. Papprill.

Charles, William: engraver and etcher who came to America from Scotland in 1801 and died in Philadelphia about 1820. Known for his caricatures of the War of 1812.

Childs, Cephas G.: 1793–1871. Philadelphia engraver in line and stipple of portraits, landscapes and city views, especially of Philadelphia; later worked in lithography.

Clover, Lewis P.: New York publisher of William J. Bennett's aquatints, 1834–8.

Cooke, George: 1793–1849. Maryland artist, known for the four views in the Bennett series of American Cities: Charleston, S.C., Richmond, Washington and West Point.

Copley, John Singleton: 1737–1815. Painter (stepson of Peter Pelham), who is known to have made only one mezzotint, the portrait of the Rev. William Welsteed of Boston, 1753.

Davis, Alexander Jackson: 1803–92. New York architect whose drawings of private homes, towns and colleges, from 1820 to 1850 were engraved by a number of different engravers.

Dawkins, Henry: active in New York by 1754, also in Philadelphia, as an engraver of bill-heads, maps, caricatures, but known chiefly for his *View of Nassau-Hall* (Princeton College) which appeared as a frontispiece in Blair's *An Account of the College in New Jersey* (Woodbridge, N.J., 1764). Dawkins died probably in 1786 (Plate 218A).

Des Barres, J. F. W.: English cartographer and artist who prepared the *Atlantic Neptune* for the British Admiralty, 1763–84.

Dewing, Francis: English engraver and printer in Boston who engraved and printed the earliest and most important plan of Boston, the *Bonner Map* of 1722, known in five states and republished three times: in 1733, 1743, 1769.

Doney, Thomas: New York mezzotint engraver whose print after Bingham's *Jolly Flatboatmen* was distributed by the American Art Union to its members in 1845. Contributed mezzotints to periodicals.

Doolittle, Amos: 1754–1832. Engraver of New Haven, Connecticut, known for his crude but important set of four views of the Battles of Lexington and Concord (Plate 219A) in 1775 after Ralph Earl, as well as a view of Federal Hall in New York, after a drawing by Peter Lacour, showing George Washington's first inaugural ceremony on its balcony, April 1789.

Durand, Asher Brown: 1796–1886. Engraver of portraits, subjects (John Trumbull's *Declaration of Independence*, 1820) and banknotes. In 1836 he turned to painting and came to be known as the 'Father of American Landscape Painting'.

Earl, Ralph: 1751–1801. American portrait painter whose original drawings of the Battles of Lexington and Concord, 1775, were engraved by Amos Doolittle.

Edwin, David: 1776–1841. Engraver, born in England, came to Philadelphia in 1797. Excellent engraver of portraits in stipple, including portraits of generals.

Fay, Theodore Sedgwick: 1807–98. Editor of *Views in New York and its Environs* published by Peabody & Co., New York, 1831–4, a collection of thirty-eight engraved views on sixteen plates, including a map and descriptive text, issued in parts (only eight of the proposed ten were published) after drawings by J. H. Dakin, A. J. Davis and others, and engraved by A. Dick, among others.

Févret de Saint-Mémin, Charles Balthazar Julien: *see* Saint-Mémin, C. B. J. Févret de.

Foster, John: 1648–81. Boston printer and engraver, credited with the first signed portrait in colonial America, the portrait of Rev. Richard Mather; also a seal of the Massachusetts Bay Colony and a map of New England which served as a frontispiece for William Hubbard's *A Narrative of the Troubles with the Indians in New England ...* Boston, printed by John Foster, 1677. These are woodcuts.

Greenwood, John: 1727–92. American-born artist who did etchings and mezzotints in eighteenth-century Europe. There is no record of his having made prints in America. Born in Boston, he worked in Holland and England.

Harris, John: London engraver of the William Burgis views of New York and Boston.

Harvey, George: c. 1800–c. 1877. English painter who resided in America between 1820 and c. 1842. Known for his *Atmospheric Views of North America* in watercolors, of which only four were engraved in aquatint by William J. Bennett and published under the title: *Primitive Forest in America, at the four seasons of the year*, London, 1841.

Havell, Robert, Jr.: 1793–1878. English engraver who came to America after completing Audubon's *Birds of America* published in London. He engraved in aquatint a number of desirable views of American cities, among them two panoramic views of New York, one of Hartford, Conn., Boston and Niagara Falls in 1845.

Heap, George: map-maker, map-seller and surveyor who drew one of the most important early views of Philadelphia, the so-called Scull-Heap view of 1754.

Hill, John: 1770–1850. London-born artist who came to New York in 1816. Known for the aquatint plates in the *Hudson River Portfolio* (Plate 219B) after the paintings by W. G. Wall, published by Megarey, New York, c. 1825; also engraved Joshua Shaw's *Picturesque Views of American Scenery* (Philadelphia, 1819) and seventeen aquatints for *Lucas' Progressive Drawing Book* (Baltimore, c. 1827).

Hill, John William: 1812–79. Son of John Hill; made some aquatints, but known chiefly for the views which were engraved by others.

Hill, Samuel: Boston engraver of portraits and views for the *Massachusetts Magazine* between 1789 and 1796.

Hornor, Thomas: English watercolor artist and engraver who came to New York in 1828. *Broadway, New York* (c. 1834) was drawn and etched by this artist, but aquatinted by John Hill. An unfinished etching of a panoramic view of New York from Brooklyn, c. 1837, and an unfinished wash drawing of a bird's-eye view of City Hall Park, are in the collection of the New York Public Library.

Hudson River portfolio: a series of twenty views drawn by W. G. Wall and engraved by John Hill (Plate 219B). Four of the first issued views were engraved by J. R. Smith. Published by Henry J. Megarey, New York, c. 1825. 'The finest collection of New York State views'; originally planned to include twenty-four plates, issued in six numbers of four views each. Only five numbers with a total of twenty views were actually published.

Johnston, Thomas: 1708–67. Boston engraver of the *Prospect of Yale College*, 1749, after a drawing by John Greenwood, published by J. Buck; also of *The Battle Fought near Lake George*, 1755; *Plan of Boston* after Wm. Burgis, and a *View of Quebec*, 1759.

Jones, Alfred: 1819–1900. English-born engraver who worked in New York, known for some large engravings distributed by the Apollo Association, among them Mount's *Farmers Nooning*, engraved in 1836, distributed in 1843.

Jukes, Francis: 1747–1812. London aquatint engraver, specializing in views and marine scenes. Engraved Henry Pelham's *Plan of Boston*, 1777; four aquatints after watercolors by Alexander Robertson, including the views of *New York from Hobuck Ferry* and *Mount Vernon*, 1799.

Krimmel, John Lewis: 1787–1821. Philadelphia artist, whose *Election Day at the State House, Philadelphia*, 1815, was engraved, but left unfinished, by A. Lawson. Joseph Yeager made an aquatint after his *Procession of Victuallers of Philadelphia*, 1821.

Lawson, Alexander: 1773–1846. Born in Scotland, came to Philadelphia in 1793. Engraved plates for A. Wilson's *Ornithology* and a number of periodicals; *Perry's Victory on Lake Erie*, 1813, after a painting by T. Birch; *Election Scene at the State House, Philadelphia*, 1815, after J. L. Krimmel (unfinished plate).

Lehman, George: Philadelphia engraver and painter who did a number of very attractive views of towns in Pennsylvania; he also worked in lithography. He died in 1870.

Longacre, James Barton: 1794–1869. Engraver specializing in stipple portraits. Noteworthy among these is the portrait of Andrew Jackson after the painting by T. Sully, 1820. Together with James Herring, a portrait painter, published the *National Portrait Gallery of Distinguished Americans*, 4 vols., 1834–9.

Maverick, Peter: 1780–1831. Son and pupil of Peter Rushton Maverick, 1755–1811. Conducted a large engraving and publishing business in New York, turning to lithography about 1824. Best known for his view of Wall Street (lithograph) after Hugh Reinagle.

Meadows, Christian: New England engraver and apparently a counterfeiter, active about 1840–59; known for one of the most desirable college views, the Meadows's View of Dartmouth College, Hanover, N.H., 1851.

Megarey, Henry J.: New York publisher of *The Hudson River Portfolio* (Plate 219B), a set of twenty aquatint views engraved by J. R. Smith and John Hill after the watercolors by W. G. Wall, 1821–5; Street Views in the City of New York (Fulton Street and Market, South Street from Maiden Lane, Broadway from Bowling Green), a series of three views engraved by W. J. Bennett, *c.* 1834.

Mount, William Sidney: 1807–68. America's first genre painter whose paintings were reproduced by a number of engravers as well as lithographers and widely distributed in this country and in Europe.

Norman, John: 1748–1817. Architect and landscape engraver from London who worked in Philadelphia and Boston. Engraved portraits of heroes of the Revolution and a portrait of George Washington in 1779. Worked also for New York publishers.

Okey, Samuel: mezzotint engraver from London who worked in Newport, R.I., 1773–5; is known for having been America's first engraver to reproduce old master paintings.

Papprill, Henry: aquatint engraver who worked in New York in the 1840s. He engraved two large views of New York, one after F. Catherwood called *New York from Governor's Island*, 1846 (the Papprill-Catherwood view) and *New York from the Steeple of St. Paul's Church*, after a drawing by J. W. Hill, 1849, re-issued in 1855.

Parkyns, George Isham: *c.* 1749/50 – after 1820. English artist and aquatint engraver who came to Philadelphia in 1795, planning a series of twenty aquatint views, of which, however, only four were executed. These are: *View of Mount Vernon, Annapolis, Md.* and two views of *Washington*. Parkyns is also the author of *Monastic and Baronial Remains*, 1816.

Peale, Charles Willson: 1741–1827. Painter and founder of a museum in Philadelphia; he engraved a few, rare, mezzotint portraits.

Pelham, Peter: *c.* 1684–1751. Earliest engraver in America; came from England to Boston in 1726 as an experienced mezzotint engraver; did a series of portraits of American clergymen, among them the portrait of Cotton Mather, 1727. Stepfather of John Singleton Copley.

Prud'homme, John Francis Eugène: 1800–92. Engraver of stipple portraits, and plates for periodicals and banknotes for the U.S. Treasury Dept. in Washington.

Revere, Paul: 1735–1818. Boston's most famous silversmith and a patriot who was also an engraver of three important historical prints. These are: *The Landing of the British Troops in Boston* (1768) issued in 1770; the so-called *Boston Massacre* in 1770, a *View of Harvard College* in 1768. He also engraved a number of plates for the *Royal American Magazine*, 1774–5; the Massachusetts paper currency, 1775–6 and some portraits (Plate 217A) and political caricatures.

Roberts, Bishop: English artist who drew the most important early view of Charleston, South Carolina, in 1739, which was engraved by Wm. H. Toms and published in London. Roberts died in October 1739.

Robertson, Alexander: 1772–1841. Scottish artist who established, together with his brother Archibald, the Columbian Drawing Academy in New York, *c.* 1795. Four of his watercolor views were engraved in aquatint by Francis Jukes of London.

Robertson, Archibald: 1765–1835. Painter and etcher, born near Aberdeen, Scotland. Studied in Edinburgh and London from 1782 to 1791 when he came to New York. Painted a portrait of George Washington at the request of the Earl of Buchan. From 1792 to 1821 he worked in New York as a painter, chiefly in watercolor, and as a teacher of drawing. Established the Columbian Drawing Academy in New York, *c.* 1795.

Robertson, Archibald: *c.* 1745–1813. British naval officer during the Revolutionary period, who, like several fellow officers, made sketches of American ports and naval engagements. The Spencer Collection of the New York Public Library owns a large part of these original drawings. He is not to be confused with the aforementioned artist.

Rollinson, William: 1762–1842. English-born engraver of stipple portraits for magazines, who became interested in banknote engraving, inventing a mechanical ruling device. Best known for his portrait of Alexander Hamilton, published in 1804, after a painting by Archibald Robertson; and for his aquatint view of New York, 1801, which was printed in colors.

Romans, Bernard: 1720–84. Engraver, engineer and cartographer from Holland whose eye-witness view of the Battle of Bunker Hill, Boston (*Exact View of the Late Battle at Charlestown, June 17th, 1775*) was published in America in 1775; an almost identical engraved plate was published in London in 1776; a reduced re-engraving was made by Robert Aitkin for the *Pennsylvania Magazine* for September 1775.

Saint-Mémin, Charles Balthazar Julien Févret de: 1770–1852. French émigré who came to the United States in 1793, staying in New York and Philadelphia, earning a living by making crayon profile drawings with the aid of the *physionotrace* and reducing them with the pantograph to fit a circle of about two inches in diameter on to a copperplate which he then etched and finished in aquatint and some roulette work. In this manner he made about 800 portraits of distinguished Americans; he is also known for two views of New York. Returned to France, where he became the director of the Museum of Dijon in 1817.

Sartain, John: 1808–97. Prolific engraver in mezzotint who came to America from England in 1830 and settled in Philadelphia where he died in 1897. He was also a publisher of several illustrated magazines. His larger plates are in line, among them the engraving after Bingham's *County Election* and *Martial Law* (Order No. 11).

Savage, Edward: 1761–1817. Painter and engraver, generally credited with the first aquatint made in America: *Action between the Constellation and L'Insurgent*, 1798, published 1799. Originally a goldsmith, he learned to engrave portraits in stipple and in mezzotint in London. Known for his portraits of George Washington and an unfinished engraving of the *Congress Voting Independence* after a painting begun by Robert E. Pine.

Scenographia Americana: a collection of views in North America and the West Indies, engraved by Sandby, Grignion, Rooker, Canot, Elliot and others from drawings taken on the spot by several officers of the British Navy and Army. Printed in London for John Bowles, Robert Sayer, Carington Bowles, Henry Parker, 1768. This collection contained originally twenty-eight plates, but was in some cases augmented to as many as seventy-four plates.

Scull, Nicholas: d. 1762. A native of Pennsylvania who became a cartographer and Surveyor-General of the Province of Pennsylvania in 1748, under whose direction the so-called Scull-Heap *East Prospect of the City of Philadelphia*, 1754, was made.

Seymour, Samuel: Philadelphia engraver, active 1797–1820, who engraved portraits and views after the paintings by Thomas and William Birch, among them views of Philadelphia, New York and Mount Vernon.

Shaw, Joshua: 1776–1860. Landscape painter who came to America in 1817 and drew the originals for *Picturesque Views of America* which were engraved in aquatint by John Hill (Philadelphia, 1819–20) and published by Moses Thomas and M. Carey & Son.

Smillie, James: 1807–85. Born in Scotland, came to New York in 1828. Engraved a great number of fine landscapes, largely after his own drawings; a series of four allegorical prints of the *Voyage of Life* after Thomas Cole. From 1861 he worked almost exclusively on banknote engraving. Some of his large plates were issued as membership prints by the American Art Union.

Smith, John Rubens: 1775–1849. Born in England, son of the engraver John Raphael Smith, 1752–1812. Worked first in Boston and then in New York where he painted, engraved and directed a drawing school. For a while he worked also in Philadelphia. He engraved portraits in stipple and mezzotint and did some views in aquatint for the Hudson River Portfolio, as well as naval subjects.

Strickland, William: 1788–1854. Philadelphia engraver and architect who was one of the first to engrave in aquatint in America; executed some small views and a few portraits. Although unsigned, except for the vignette on the title page, Strickland did the ten plates for *The Art of Colouring and Painting Landscapes in Water Colours*, published by F. Lucas, in Baltimore, 1815.

Tanner, Benjamin: 1775–1848. Engraver in both line and stipple; publisher in Baltimore. He engraved some large plates of portraits and naval subjects relating to the Revolution and the War of 1812. Among these are *Macdonough's Victory on Lake Champlain*, *Perry's Victory on Lake Erie*, published January 1, 1815.

Tennant, William: Princeton graduate, class of 1758, who drew the view of *Nassau Hall* (Princeton) 1764, which was engraved by Henry Dawkins.

Tiebout, Cornelius: c. 1773–1832. The first American-born engraver who produced good stipple portraits; also some small landscape prints for the *New York Magazine*. (Plate 217B).

Toms, William Henry: c. 1700 – c. 1750. London engraver of the important Roberts's view of Charleston, S.C., published in 1739.

Trenchard, James: engraver, active in Philadelphia in the 1770s, who did some portraits and views, among them a view of the State House in Philadelphia after a drawing by Charles Willson Peale, 1778, as well as illustrations for the *Columbian Magazine*.

Trumbull, John: 1756–1843. Painter of historical subjects, among them the *Declaration of Independence* which he commissioned A. B. Durand to engrave in 1820. Trumbull is credited with engraving a caricature depicting the Loyalists, published in New York in 1795. Elkanah Tisdale engraved nine satirical copperplates for Trumbull's *M'Fingal, a modern epic poem in four cantos* (New York, printed by John Buel, 1795).

Turner, James: engraver who moved from Boston to Philadelphia, where he died in 1759. Engraved portraits and views for books and magazines and is known for his maps of Boston, the Middle Colonies (1755) and Philadelphia.

Wall, William Guy: 1792 – after 1862. Dublin-born landscape artist who resided in New York from 1818 till 1836, returning once more in 1856. In the 1820s he painted the watercolors which were engraved for Megarey's *Hudson River Portfolio*; also known for views of New York: *New York from Weehawk*, and *New York from Brooklyn Heights* 1823, *City Hall*, 1826 (Plate 220B).

Wilson, Alexander: 1766–1813. Ornithologist, native of Paisley, Scotland, emigrated to the United States in 1794. Author and artist of *American Ornithology*, 1808–14, 9 vols. of engravings by A. Lawson, preceding Audubon's work by about twenty years.

Yeager, Joseph: c. 1792–1859. Engraver in Philadelphia from 1816 to 1845, who worked for Philadelphia publishers. Known for his aquatint of the *Procession of Victuallers of Philadelphia*, 1821, and his line engraving of the *Battle of New Orleans and Death of Major General Packenham*, 1815. Together with William H. Morgan published many children's books.

TECHNICAL TERMS

Aquatint: a print with a grainy tone effect, achieved by dusting powdered resin on to the metal plate and regulating the biting of acid for gradations of tone. Coarseness or fineness of the grain is obtained according to the quantity of resin used. Best suited for reproducing watercolors, and used particularly from 1775 to 1830.

Color prints: (*a*) colored from single plate, which necessitates painting between each printing; (*b*) colored from several plates, which permits greater uniformity in the impression.

Cum privilegio: with the privilege to publish, corresponding to modern copyright.

Del., delin., delineavit: drew.

Engraving: a print obtained by a process of incising lines into a metal plate with a burin or graver.

Etching: a process by which the lines are made by an etching needle on a grounded plate, exposing the metal below, which then is bitten by the use of acid.

Exc., excud., excudit: published, also printed.

F., fec., fecit: made, also etched, occasionally for engraved.

Imp., imprimavit: printed.

Impression: a term applied to any print made from a metal plate, wood block or stone.

Inc., incid., incidit: engraved.

Inv., invenit: designed, invented.

Mezzotint: a velvety tone process, rather than pure line, achieved with the aid of a rocker and roulette. The design is then worked on the roughened surface with scraper and burnisher. Best suited for portrait work; but few good impressions can be pulled from the plate.

Pinx., pinxt., pinxit: painted.

Proof before letters: a print before the title, dedication, publisher's name and address have been added in the margin of the print.

Sc., sculp., sculpsit: engraved.

State: a term applied to differences in the stages of development of a print, including the lettering; hence, any changes in the work of a print, or alterations.

Stipple: a mixture of dots and short strokes (flicks) obtained with the point of the stipple graver on a plate covered with a wax ground which then is bitten with acid. Stipple is coarser than mezzotint and often combined with line engraving, or aquatint.

Woodcut: a relief process, or black line process, obtained by cutting the plank of the wood with a knife.

Wood engraving: a white line method on the end-grain of the wood, which has a harder texture and is fit for more delicate work. The graver, or burin, is used on the end-grain.

BOOKS FOR FURTHER READING

BRIGHAM, CLARENCE S.: *Paul Revere's Engravings*, Worcester, Mass., American Antiquarian Society (1954).

BROWN, H. GLENN, AND BROWN, MAUDE O.: *A Directory of the Book-Arts and Book Trade in Philadelphia to 1820, Including Painters and Engravers*, New York, The New York Public Library (1950).

DREPPERD, CARL WILLIAM: *Early American Prints*, New York, The Century Co. (1930).

FIELDING, MANTLE: *American Engravers upon Copper and Steel*, a supplement to David McNeely Stauffer's *American Engravers*, Philadelphia (1917).

GROCE, GEORGE C., AND WALLACE, DAVID H.: *The New-York Historical Society's Dictionary of Artists in America, 1564–1860*, New Haven, Yale University Press (1957).

JOHNSON, UNA E.: *American Woodcuts, 1670–1950; a Survey of Woodcuts and Wood-Engravings in the United States*, Brooklyn, New York, Brooklyn Museum (1950).

MCKAY, GEORGE LESLIE: *A register of artists, engravers, booksellers, bookbinders, printers and publishers in New York City, 1633–1820*, New York, The New York Public Library (1942).

STOKES, I. N. PHELPS: *The Iconography of Manhattan Island, 1498–1909*, New York, R. H. Dodd (1915–1928), 6 vols.

STOKES, N. PHELPS, AND HASKELL, DANIEL C.: *American Historical Prints, Early Views of American Cities, etc.*, from the Phelps Stokes and other collections, New York, The New York Public Library (1932 and 1933).

STAUFFER, DAVID MCNEELY: *American Engravers upon Copper and Steel*, New York, The Grolier Club of the City of New York (1907), 2 vols.

WEISS, HARRY BISCHOFF: *The Number of Persons and Firms Connected with the Graphic Arts in New York City 1633–1820*, New York, The New York Public Library (1946).

WEITENKAMPF, FRANK: *American Graphic Art*, new edition revised and enlarged, New York, The Macmillan Co. (1924).

WROTH, LAWRENCE C., AND ADAMS, MARION W.: *American Woodcuts and Engravings, 1670–1800* Providence, Associates of the John Carter Brown Library (1946). (Catalogue of an exhibition.)

Concise Encyclopedia of Antiques, Vol. III, Hawthorn Books, New York (1957).

One Hundred Notable American Engravers, 1683–1850, annotated list of prints on exhibition, New York, The New York Public Library (1928).

SILHOUETTES

By M. L. D'OTRANGE-MASTAI

IN 1767, Benjamin Franklin wrote home from London: 'I send you the little shade that was copied from the great one.' This 'great' shade – presumably life-size – was a silhouette of Franklin, now lost, made by Patience Wright, the New Jersey Quakeress then established in England. Patience was chiefly renowned for her wax models, but occasionally dabbled in silhouette. However, the earliest mention of silhouette work done in America is found in a letter written in 1799 by Harriet Pinckney, a South Carolina belle, in which she mentions her 'shade' by Thomas Wollaston. The whereabouts of the profile are unknown; it is probable that the artist was an amateur.

Silhouette was then chiefly a new and intriguing pastime for amateurs with artistic inclinations, much as it had been somewhat earlier in Europe. It is the peculiarity of the medium that the dramatic contrast of black and white and the necessary precision of outline are able to endow even a commonplace delineation with unexpected merit. Foremost among the notables of the period, George and Martha Washington were innumerably portrayed by amateur silhouettists, among whom were their granddaughter Nelly Custis, Samuel Powell, Mayor of Philadelphia, and Miss Sarah de Hart, of Elizabethtown, New Jersey. The work of Major André – his own self-portrait, his studies of General Burgoyne, Major Stanley, 'Becky' Stedman – is naturally of high historical interest. Such 'shades' when encountered speak for themselves eloquently enough. An eighteenth-century silhouette signed CHAPMAN, 1781, showing a Virginia subject Robert Bolling of Petersburg, Virginia, still in the possession of the family, is illustrated (Plate 223A).

However, with the advent of the nineteenth century, the growing popularity of silhouette soon created a real demand, and the sporadic manifestations of amateurs were supplemented by the steady production of a group of professionals. One of the earliest among these was MOSES CHAPMAN of Salem, Massachusetts (c. 1780–1821), no relation to Chapman of Virginia so far as is known. The Salem silhouettist was not a particularly gifted artist; his work is correct but undistinguished. But he was an innovator in the sense that he made use not of the silhouette proper but the outer contour usually discarded by the cutter. This, placed on a black ground, paper, silk, or any other material, furnished a striking effect. Chapman employed the tracing and cutting machine invented by Chrétien in France, the 'physionotrace', but occasionally still cut freehand.

The possibilities of silhouette work by this 'hollow-cut' process were to be fully realized by CHARLES WILLSON PEALE (Plates 224C and 224D) (1741–1827), the extreme example of Yankee ingenuity and business sense, who resolved to bring about the mass production of silhouettes. He actually achieved this by means of the 'physionotrace', complemented by an ingenious stencil machine (invented by his assistant ISAAC HAWKINS) which is described as enabling 'any steady hand in a few moments' to 'produce a correct indented outline'. Peale was eminently successful financially, but it is obvious that the works executed entirely by this means are almost devoid of artistic value. The work of Peale himself must, at least in some cases, be excepted. Alice van Leer Carrick has noted that she was able to discern in a number of Peale silhouettes 'the faint lines made by the pantograph in tracing the reduced shadelines that Peale apparently

545

ignored, for each profile is cut well within the indication. He may have decided that his scissors could improve upon the machine.' And well he might, for Peale was a serious, really excellent artist and craftsman, having been in succession, though more often simultaneously, a saddler, clock-maker, silversmith, taxidermist, soldier, legislator, educator and scientist (naturalist and archeologist). He established his own museum in Philadelphia, largely devoted to natural history. Of the three stamps he used on silhouettes, *Museum* is the most usual; *Peale's Museum* comes next, and rarest is the plain mark, *Peale*; all three are embossed in Roman Capitals.

One of his sons, REMBRANDT PEALE (1778–1860) attempted to follow in his father's footsteps, both as an artist – he studied one year with West, in England – and in establishing his own museum (in Baltimore). But he lacked the dash and bravura of his father. He may have done some silhouette work. It is reported that he spent 'much time and ingenuity in devising mechanical means wherewith to speed the production of shadow portraits'.

Peale's nephew, CHARLES PEALE POLK (1767–1822) made profiles on gold background, the rarest type of American silhouettes.

Not on a level with Peale, the elder, but something more than an amateur was SAMUEL FOLWELL (1765–1813), whose first avocation had been the engraving of bookplates in New Hampshire. Having moved to Philadelphia, then the metropolis of the arts in America, Folwell, in order to meet active competition, turned to various occupations, among them miniaturist, profilist, worker in hair (as were most profilists) and, in his spare time, school teacher. His most famous work, the profile of George Washington, is firm and delicately chiseled. A Folwell silhouette is *rarissima avis*.

WILLIAM DOYLE was born in Boston in 1769, the son of a British soldier. He divided his admiration equally between Peale and Miers. To Miers he paid artistic homage, and he strove to emulate him, but never attained to the subtle effects of the English artist. He did rival Peale, if not as an artist, at least as

a museum founder. His business enterprises, in co-operation with another silhouettist, DAVID BOWEN (whose only date, 1791, is found on a portrait, *George Washington and his lady*), were quite successful, in spite of disaster by fire. Doyle generally copied the Miers bust curve but interrupted it half-way with an odd little nick that is extremely characteristic. He was known to have done some works on plaster, but none was thought to exist until a unique discovery of such a profile on 'composition'. He signed in careful script, but never stamped.

HENRY WILLIAMS (Boston, 1787–1830) was fully as versatile as any of his colleagues, and in addition was a professor of electricity and a modeler in wax. His method was the usual hollow-cut technique, and his advertisements offered '16 different sizes down to a quarter of an inch', this last no doubt intended for setting in jewelry. His work is very rare.

'TODD' must remain just that; his first name is not known. He was approximately a contemporary of Doyle and Williams, and an album with about two thousand examples of his work is in the collection of the Boston Athenaeum. It provides a delightful and lively record of costumes and types, in an unpretentious and effective clean-cut style without any pen flourishes. The stamp *Todd's Patent* is the only signature. Most valuable perhaps, Todd kept a meticulous record of his sitters' names, with dates of posing.

WILLIAM KING (active 1785–1805) wielded his magic 'Patent Delineating Pencil' in Salem and vicinity. Possibly it may have been his own invention; he is spoken of as 'an ingenious mechanic but full of projects & what he gains in one he loses in the other'. He was also a carpenter and a turner and, Alice van Leer Carrick adds, somewhat affectionately, 'a scamp'. In spite of a long line of Puritan ancestry the atmosphere of Salem proved too much for this true Bohemian, who 'disappeared' in 1809, leaving wife and children behind. As Bentley's *Diary* puts it: 'the father is now upon his pilgrimages'. How extensive these were we may judge by the fact that his son was sent to 'Martinico', perhaps to rejoin him or to establish a branch there. In an advertisement published in 1806, King claimed to have executed upwards of twenty thousand silhouettes. Yet today it is rare to find even one.

King was a serious and steady character by comparison with his colleague, J. WESLEY JARVIS (born in England 1789, died New York 1839). Jarvis, together with his partner JOSEPH WOOD (born in Clarkstown, Orange County, New York), engaged as a hobby in 'mysterious marriages'. Jarvis was disreputable but undeniably charming and brilliant, and these qualities must have been reflected in his work. His evil ways were punished, for none of it survives. Yet he was highly successful in his lifetime, netting as much as one hundred dollars a day. This was due in great part to his invention of a machine for drawing profiles on glass: one imagines it must have been a pantograph of some sort with a diamond-tipped stylus. Jarvis painted miniatures and also portraits in oil.

In perfect contrast to King was the serious and honest WILLIAM BACHE, who was to raise hollow-cutting (Plates 224A, 224B) to the level of art. Born on December 22, 1771 (at Bromsgrove in Worcestershire, England), Bache emigrated to Philadelphia when he was twenty-two years old. His career as a profilist took him far and wide through the south, particularly Louisiana where he did some excellent work, and later to the West Indies. In 1812 he became one of the first pioneers of western Pennsylvania, and embarked on a successful career as a merchant. Silhouette work, which had become only a hobby, was definitely put to an end by an accident in which he lost his right arm. He seems to have resigned himself easily to this, particularly since he had been financially successful in his other undertakings. In his short career as a profilist he produced much and created a new style, being the first hollow-cutter to paint on his paper backings details of dress such as the transparent collar ruffle worn by the lady in Plate 224B. At his hands, hollow-cutting lost rigidity and coldness. A true artist, he was equally skillful in cut-and-pasted work and in painted silhouettes.

Bache had a partner, T. NIXON, who provided colored profiles for his clients. These are extremely rare, not too high in quality, and do not concern us here, as they are not true silhouettes.

The last days of silhouette, before the advent of daguerreotype sounded its doom, saw its richest flowering. Among a host of lesser lights, which limitations of space preclude mentioning, there emerges WILLIAM HENRY BROWN, who was born in Charleston, South Carolina in 1808, died there in 1883. Brown[1] was something of a prodigy; his first silhouette, of Lafayette, was executed at the age of sixteen. In contrast to the usual American practice, Brown was a free-hand cutter. His style is pure and severe, without extraneous embellishments of gold or color. This is silhouette in the finest sense of the word, which implies denudation to the point of artistic asceticism. The characterization of subjects is superb but is always rightly held subservient to the artistic conception. Brown was an artist, and social observer, and, as a result of this, has given us a more enduring record of his age than the most slavish hollow-cutter.

Brown's greatest accomplishment was the compilation of the *Portrait Gallery of Distinguished American Citizens*, published at Hartford, Connecticut, in 1846. To this album of lithographs he furnished both text (biographical notes) and illustrations, the subjects being shown against backgrounds which he did not execute himself, but must have supervised and in many cases suggested. These are of great historical interest. Almost the entire edition of the *Portrait Gallery* was destroyed by fire shortly after publication, so that copies are of the utmost rarity (Plate 221).

The prestige of free-hand cutting quite did away with the hollow-cutting by machine that had satisfied earlier: silhouettists now were 'scissorgraphists'. WILLIAM JAMES HUBARD ('Master Hubard', born in England in 1807, died 1862) was advertised as a child prodigy, starting on his career at the age of twelve. There is skepticism on this point now, and it is thought, on good grounds, that he may actually have been fifteen at his debut.

[1] Original works by Brown (Plate 221) are also scarce. Among them is his silhouette of the first run of the Mohawk and Hudson Railroad, 1831, now owned by the Connecticut Historical Society.

(A) Washington by Rembrandt Peale. Pendleton Lithograph. *Library of Congress; Culver Service photograph.*

(B) Passed midshipman, U.S. Navy. *U.S. Military Magazine. P. S. Duval lith. Phila. The Old Print Shop, Harry Shaw Newman.*

(C) Osceola. Drawn and on stone by George Catlin, 1838. The greatest life portrait of an Indian. *The Old Print Shop, Harry Shaw Newman.*

PLATE 225

(A) Wall Street from Trinity Church, New York, 1834. Lithograph by Peter Maverick after Hugh Reinagle. *New-York Historical Society*.

(B) Great Fire, New York, 1835. One of the first 'disaster' prints. Published by H. R. Robinson, New York. *Photograph courtesy of Antiques*.

PLATE 226

(A) Castle Garden, *c.* 1825. Early lithograph of Imbert & Co., New York. Drawn by A. J. Davis.
New-York Historical Society.

(B) Preparing for Market. After L. Maurer. Lithograph N. Currier, 1856. *The Old Print Shop,*
Harry Shaw Newman.

PLATE 227

(A) East View of Faneuil Hall Market. Boston 1827. Early Pendleton lithograph; drawn by J. Andrews. *New England Historical Art Society.*

(B) National Lancers with the Reviewing Officers on Boston Common, 1837. Moore's Lithography, Boston. On stone by F. H. Lane after C. Hubbard. *Library of Congress.*

PLATE 228

(A) *De Witt Clinton* (Mohawk & Hudson). Lithograph by Leggo & Co., Montreal, Canada, 1869, from Brown's silhouette of 1832 in the Connecticut Historical Society. *The Old Print Shop, Harry Shaw Newman.*

(B) Ellicott's Mills; end of first section of Baltimore & Ohio Railroad. Drawn and lithographed by Ed. Weber, Baltimore, *c.* 1837. *The Old Print Shop, Harry Shaw Newman.*

PLATE 229

(A) Twentyfive Ton Passenger Engine. Made by Lawrence Machine Shop, Lawrence, Massachusetts. Drawn by A. Lederle; lithograph, S. W. Chandler, Boston, 1853. *Coll. of C. L. Winey.*

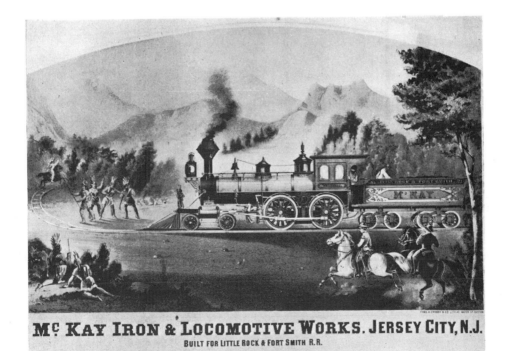

(B) *The Arkansas:* built by McKay Iron & Locomotive Works, Jersey City. Lithograph, Charles H. Crosby & Co., Boston. No date. *Coll. of C. L. Winey.*

PLATE 230

(A) Carrolton Viaduct. Drawn on stone by Moses Swett. Lithograph, Endicott & Swett, *c.* 1831. *Kennedy Galleries.*

(B) Portage Bridge. Lithograph, Compton & Co., Buffalo, New York, from drawing by J. Stilson, *c.* 1865. *Kennedy Galleries.*

PLATE 231

(A) *American Autumn*. Starucca Valley viaduct, Erie Railroad. Painted by Jasper Cropsey; chromolithograph, T. Sinclair, Philadelphia, 1865. *Kennedy Galleries*.

(B) *Across The Continent, Westward The Course of Empire Takes Its Way*. Drawn by F. Palmer after J. M. Ives; large folio; Currier & Ives, 1868. *Coll. of C. L. Winey*.

PLATE 232

(A) Snipe shooting, Norfolk County, Massachusetts, 1840, by Thomas Hewes Hinckley. *Coll. of Harry T. Peters, Jr.*

(B) *Shooting for the Beef,* by George Caleb Bingham, 1811–79. *Brooklyn Museum.*

PLATE 233

(A) The undefeated Asteroid with jockey and trainer by Edward Troye, 1808–74. *Courtesy of E. J. Rousuck.*

(B) *Eel spearing at Setauket,* by William Sidney Mount, 1807–58. *New York State Historical Association, Cooperstown.*

PLATE 234

(A) *Striped bass fishing*, by A. F. Tait, 1819–1905. *Coll. of Harry T. Peters, Jr. Photo: Frick Art Reference Library.*

(B) *Max Schmitt in a single-scull*, by Thomas Eakins, 1844–1916. *Metropolitan Museum of Art.*

PLATE 235

(A) William Fuller. Engraved by A. B. Durand after C. C. Ingham, *c.* 1828. *Author's collection.*

(B) *The lower lake, Central Park,* 1865, by J. M. Culverhouse. *Museum of the City of New York.*

(C) *Croquet scene,* by Winslow Homer, 1836–1910. *Art Institute of Chicago.*

PLATE 236

(A) *Colonists on the Red River*, 1825, by Peter Rindisbacher. *Public Archives of Canada.*

(B) *Interior of a Mandan Hut.* Lithograph after Karl Bodmer. *New-York Historical Society.*

PLATE 237

(A) *A Sioux village,* by George Catlin. *Museum of Natural History, New York.*

(B) *The Buffalo Dance,* by Charles Wimar. *City Art Museum, St Louis.*

PLATE 238

(A) *The Judith Round-up at Sage Creek*, by Charles M. Russell. *M. Knoedler & Co.*

(B) *The Attack on the Supply Train*, by Frederic Remington.

PLATE 239

(B) *The Bronco Buster.* Bronze by Frederic Remington.

(A) *Indian Telegraph,* 1869, by John Mix Stanley. *Detroit Institute of Arts.*

PLATE 240

He later became a pupil of Sully and a competent portrait painter in his own right. His highest success was won in Charleston, and he finally settled in the south. During the Civil War, he espoused the Confederate cause and put to its service unexpected talent as a scientist. He was the inventor of a new explosive, but was killed by the accidental bursting of a shell he was filling with his own compound. The Valentine Museum in Richmond, Virginia, has a collection of his work (Plates 222A, 222C).

A successor, MASTER HANKES, was also born in England. Hankes's career started in Salem, Massachusetts, in 1828. He may have been an early anonymous associate of Master Hubard, helping to satisfy the press of business. When he appeared under his own name, he was only moderately successful, doing best of all in Baltimore. Returning to New England after this tour, Master Hankes disappears from view. His talent, however, was not mean, as seen in the portrait of Dr Holyoke (Plate 222B).

Phenomenal also, but far inferior artistically, were MISS HONEYWELL and MASTER NELLIS. The first, born without arms, contrived to cut with scissors held in her mouth. Her work may have fully satisfied many, but it is probable that most of her patronage was due mainly to compassionate interest. Mrs Nevill Jackson has justly remarked that 'it is naturally clumsy, but marvellous that it could be done at all'. Little of it has survived.

Of Sanders K. G. Nellis we know nothing but his name from an advertisement. Also armless, he made use of his toes in place of fingers. Mention is made merely on the chance that some vestige of his pathetic industry might turn up at some future date.

AUGUSTUS DAY (active c. 1833–4) did a certain amount of hollow-cutting in Philadelphia and vicinity, but is best known for his painted profiles, generally in olive green touched with gold. Examples in black are rare.

SAMUEL METFORD (1810–90), an English Quaker, came to America in 1834 and became a naturalized citizen. However, he returned to England in 1844 and remained there the rest of his life, except for a two years' visit to his adopted country. Much of his work is to be found in Scotland. It is delicate in feeling and technique, and generally consists of full-lengths mounted against lithographed backgrounds. He was almost the last of the silhouettists in America. His departure coincides with the rise of the daguerreotype.

A history of silhouette in America must necessarily include mention of the work of visiting artists from abroad, whose works represent a documentary study of national interest.

CHARLES BALTHAZAR JULIEN FÉVRET DE SAINT-MÉMIN (born in Dijon in 1770, died 1852) was a French émigré originally destined to a military career. A gifted amateur artist in happier days, he developed under pressure of financial necessity into a masterly professional. Although he undertook to furnish the American market with silhouettes, his most important work was in the related form of colored profiles in life size, and engravings, of which he executed a large number during his stay. In style, he combines eighteenth-century grace and the cold intensity of Davidesque neo-classicism. Much of this is reflected in his silhouettes which have purity of line and a very special flavor of French elegance.

It is not possible to attempt here even a sketch of the long and extraordinary career of AUGUSTIN AMANT CONSTANT FIDÈLE ÉDOUART (1789–1861). He was the universal silhouettist – his subjects ranging all the way from dignified historical portraits to humorous genre scenes. In addition to his huge European output, his ten years' stay in America resulted in a unique and priceless record totaling upwards of ten thousand silhouettes. Much of this was lost in a shipwreck, that is, the careful record of duplicates kept by the artist; many of the originals have survived. But Mrs Nevill Jackson was still able to refer to her photographic files of the remaining thirty-eight hundred American Édouart silhouettes as 'in such number as no other nation possesses'. His portrait of Titian Peale, son of Charles Willson Peale, is illustrated (Plate 223B).

Édouart's style was that of a purist of genius: no adornments, no shading of any sort, gold or otherwise. Edouart allowed himself at most a slit of white for the gentlemen's neckcloths but within the bounds of this self-imposed economy achieved extraordinary linear expressiveness.

GLOSSARY

(A condensed list of silhouettists *not mentioned* in text)

Andrews, Mrs M.: died 1831. Illustrated reminiscences of Washington, D.C.

Banton, T. S.: early-nineteenth century, New England.

Bascom, Ruth: 1772–1848, Gill, Massachusetts. Her silhouettes are frequently adorned with details of metal foil.

Brooks, Samuel: Boston, 1790.

Brown, J.: *c.* 1812–20, Salem, Massachusetts.

Chamberlain, William: *c.* 1824, New England.

Colles, J.: *c.* 1778, New York.

Cottu, M.: *c.* 1811, a French *émigré*.

Cummings, Rufus: *c.* 1840s, Boston.

Doolittle, A. B.: *c.* 1807. Son of Amos Doolittle, the engraver.

Doolittle, S. C.: *c.* 1810–20. Worked in South Carolina.

Edwards, Thomas: 1822–56, Boston.

Ellsworth, James: *c.* 1833. Worked in Connecticut.

Griffing, Martin: 1784–1859. Cripple, itinerant. New England.

Harrison, A. H.: 1916, St. Louis, Missouri.

Howard, Everet: *c.* 1820.

Jones, F. P.: early-nineteenth century, New England.

Joye, John?: born Salem March 14, 1790. Active, Salem 1812.

Letton, R.: *c.* 1808. Showman and silhouettist.

Lord, Philip: 1814–40. Born in Newburyport, Massachusetts. Active 1830–40. Made use of silver and gold in shading.

Metcalf, Elias: 1785–1834, New York. Traveled in Guadeloupe, Canada, New Orleans and West Indies.

Mitchell, Judith: born 1793, married 1837. Quakeress, Nantucket, Massachusetts.

Perkins, George: *c.* 1850–55, Salem. Did some original work and numerous replicas of the silhouettes of William Henry Brown. Often confused with the originals.

Rogers, Sally: armless cutter. Active, New York, 1807.

Rossiter: active 1810–11. Hanover, N.H.

Seager: *c.* 1834. Cutter, New Bedford, Massachusetts. Halifax, Nova Scotia, 1840, Boston, 1845–50.

Stewart, Rev. Joseph: active 1806. Hartford, Connecticut.

Valdenuit, M. de: assistant to Saint-Mémin. Silhouette work is often signed *Vnt & S. M.* or *Drawn by Valdenuit and Engraved by St. Mémin.*

Vallée, Jean-François de la: 1785–1815. Portrayed Washington. Active Virginia, Philadelphia, New Orleans.

Waugh: active 1835. North Carolina.

Way, Mary: active 1811. New London, Connecticut.

Williams, Henry: 1787–1830. Boston.

BOOKS FOR FURTHER READING

BOLTON, ETHEL STANWOOD: *Wax Portraits and Silhouettes*, Boston (1914).

CARRICK, ALICE VAN LEER: *Shades of our Ancestors*, Little, Brown & Company, Boston (1928).

JACKSON, MRS E. NEVILL: *A History of Silhouette*, The Connoisseur, London (1911). *Ancestors in Silhouette* New York (1921). *Silhouette – Notes and Dictionary* (1938).

LITHOGRAPHS

By FRANK WEITENKAMPF

LITHOGRAPHY, invented by ALOIS SE-NEFELDER in 1796, brought a new, and both artistically and profitably valuable, reproductive process to the graphic arts. The artist could put his drawing directly on the lithographic stone, from which it was printed without the intervention of an engraver. The result is a direct facsimile, giving the artist's individual touch.

This supple medium, with a wide range of possible effects, began to be used in the United States soon after the painter BASS OTIS did two drawings on stone in 1819-20. Otis apparently had no idea of the possibilities of lithography, but they were soon realized and utilized in our land. Only about seven years later REMBRANDT PEALE, in his copy of his own painted portrait of Washington, showed real understanding of what could be done by this new process (Plate 225A).

From then on there was increasing employment of lithography, somewhat as a means of expression for artists, but particularly with commercial purpose and activity. However, in that, too, there was often artistic proficiency. In the development of the technique of the art there was some French influence, and later artists and printer-publishers of German origin were also notably active.

That the new process had importance through possible service to business appeared from the start. What concerns us here is that this exploitation for profit has given us a very large storehouse of documentary material. And historical documentation is an important function of antiques.

It is an impressive, many-sided picture of American life and its rural and urban setting that is presented in this mass of publications serving popular interest and demand.

Portraits there are in large number, including many good ones. Among those who signed them were HENRY INMAN, ALBERT NEWSAM, CHARLES FENDERICH, F. D'AVIGNON (who did a series of drawings in delicate, silvery gray, after daguerreotypes by Brady), L. GROZELIER, C. G. CREHEN (portrait of the painter W. S. Mount) and FABRONIUS. There are also the numerous portraits of North American Indians by J. O. LEWIS, KING and CATLIN (Plate 225C).

Views of natural scenery were done by CHARLES GILDEMEISTER, E. WHITE-FIELD, MRS FRANCES F. PALMER (who drew a number of country scenes for Currier & Ives), CHARLES PARSONS and others. Pictures of rural life were offered by various artists, among them LOUIS MAURER (his *Preparing for Market*, 1856 (Plate 227B), is full of detail in picturing farmyard appearance, wagon construction, harness). In these the life of the gentleman farmer is often accentuated, and they present also an interesting record of suburban architecture. One feels the spirit of the countryside in all this.

City views were numerous, naturally, giving expression to local pride in urban development. Avoiding a catalogue, here are a few names: MAVERICK (Plate 226A, view of Wall St., New York), A. J. DAVIS the architect (Plate 227A), C.W. BURTON (panoramic view of New York), MAX ROSENTHAL (Independence Hall, Philadelphia, 1846, printed in colors by L. N. ROSENTHAL). Interest in the city and its life brought also pictures of city types, including such valuable items as the series on New York's volunteer firemen, by Louis Maurer. Other human figures thus preserved for us are the 'Bowery B'hoy', and people skating on ponds in parks and elsewhere, with a show of changing fashions in dress. Dress brings to mind the uniforms of military companies, of which there is a notable array in drawings such as those by A. HOFFY and F. J. FRITSCH. (The latter's large prints of the 38th Regiment, Jefferson Guards, 1843, and the First Division, 1844, have been collected as highly interesting New York views.) To this record of military dress are to be added the many illustrated sheet-music covers of marches dedicated to various military companies, many of them grenadier guards wearing the French high bearskin shako. These covers usually show uniformed members of the company in question, and they give us a valuable record of militia uniforms that is scattered and apparently cannot be found in any collected form. Here is one of the many opportunities to collect lithographs on a given topic. And, by the way, sheet-music covers form a subject of their own, which is of decided interest from more than one standpoint.

Transportation is another specialty dealt with in lithographs. Railway prints are numerous; Gen. Wm. Barclay Parsons brought together a considerable number of them. Sailing vessels were portrayed by CHARLES PARSONS and others in good number.

Sports were also much pictured. Hunting and fishing scenes, ably done by A. F. TAIT and LOUIS MAURER, bear the stamp of actual experience and interest and add their part to the colorful panorama of our social life. Horse races were naturally a popular subject. Pictures of trotting races and trotters show changes in the form of vehicle used; there was also at least one early one in which there was no sulky at all, the man being mounted in the saddle. The numerous portraits of individual horses, running and trotting, included one of *Hambletonian*, the famous sire of trotting horses, shown with his owner at Chester, New York.

There were also the separately published political caricatures (1155 of them listed and described in the present writer's *Political Caricature in the United States*, 1953) of obvious importance to the historian. Large collections of these may be seen in the New-York Historical Society, the American Antiquarian

Society, Worcester, the New York Public Library, the Library of Congress, and other institutions.

Theater posters illustrate still another phase of our social life. Designed by MATT MORGAN, H. A. OGDEN and H. F. FARNY, among others, and printed by various firms such as the Strobridge Lithographic Co., many of these productions are so large as to make preservation a problem. However, they have been collected, and toward the end of the nineteenth century there came a vogue, almost a craze, which resulted in numerous articles and books, exhibitions, and much collecting activity. Advertising art also made use of lithography, and examples of this are finding their way into collections of industrial subjects. Still other specialties come to mind, for instance Christmas cards, for the designing of which Louis Prang enlisted the services of well-known artists.

All this pictorial material evidently had its appeal, to which the public made a response that is reflected in the productiveness of the many lithographic printing firms. The name of Currier & Ives is apt to come first and most easily to mind, but there were plenty of others competing with them and, indeed, in business long before Nathaniel Currier started on his career. Childs & Inman, Childs & Lehman, P. S. Duval & Co., W. Sharp, B. W. Thayer & Co., Pendleton, T. Moore, Lehman & Duval, Imbert, J. T. Bowen, J. H. Bufford, T. Sinclair, L. N. Rosenthal, Nagel & Weingaertner, D. W. Kellogg, T. Kelly, Sarony & Major, Heppenheimer & Maurer, Louis Prang, Julius Bien, and plenty of others, were located in New York, Boston, Philadelphia, Hartford, and other places. Their story is told with much detail in three quarto books by Harry T. Peters: *Currier & Ives*, *America on Stone*, *California on Stone*. There are public collections of prints where much of their work may be seen, studied and enjoyed – the New York Public Library, Library of Congress, American Antiquarian Society, Museum of the City of New York, New-York Historical Society and many more.

In the enormous mass of material here hinted at there is very much of great interest and value to collectors and historians, and in fact to anyone interested in the development of our country's social and political life. It is to be noted also that from the 'forties and 'fifties drawings of similar subjects and interest, engraved on wood, were appearing in illustrated weeklies and comic papers.

Quite naturally he who collects as well as he who writes history should carefully examine this output of the nineteenth century before choosing. For instance, the sentimental bits relating to domestic life have no great interest save in showing what the public bought. The Civil War battle scenes put out by Currier & Ives are quite negligible (compare them with the *Campaign Sketches* by WINSLOW HOMER, issued by Prang). But when the same firm issued pictures based on actual contact of the artist with the scene depicted, as in the pictures of New York City's volunteer firemen, or hunting subjects, or country life, we were given valuable pictorial illustration of social history.

Here, then, is a rich field to delve into. Critical discrimination in choice will still leave a full storehouse, a crowded one, of pleasure and profit.

GLOSSARY

Autenrieth, C.: name appears on a set of lithographs of New York views in decorative borders published by Henry Hoff, New York, 1850.

Barnet & Doolittle, New York: first American lithographic firm, 1821–2.

Beyer, Edward: 1820–65. Drew originals for Beyer's *Album of Virginia*, a desirable set of views containing representations of the fashionable spas of the ante-bellum South, drawn in America but lithographed Berlin, Dresden, 1858.

Bien, J.: New York lithographer, active 1850–68. In 1860 issued Audubon's *Birds of America*, elephant folio, in chromolithography.

Bowen, J. T.: lithographer, New York, 1835–8. Moved to Philadelphia, 1838–44; issued a good series of twenty views of Philadelphia after J. C. Wild.

Britten & Rey: San Francisco lithographic firm, *c.* 1849–*c.* 1880; of great importance for scenes of the Gold Rush.

Brown's Portrait Gallery of Distinguished American Citizens: lithographs from twenty-six silhouettes cut by W. H. Brown, published with decorative backgrounds by Kellogg, Hartford, 1845. Most of original edition destroyed by fire; has been published in facsimile about 1930.

Burton, C.: artist, active 1830–50, New York. Did work for Sarony & Major, Pendleton, Michelin.

Buttersworth, James: marine painter whose subjects were lithographed by Currier & Ives.

Cameron, John: lithographer and artist, active 1852–62, New York; best known for horse subjects done for Currier & Ives, but did work independently, or with other lithographers.

Castelnau, Francis: French traveler in America, 1838–40; published *Vues de l'Amérique du Nord*, Paris, 1842; illustrated in lithography.

Catlin, George: 1796–1872, artist and lithographer, traveler in Far West in the 1830s. Best known for *North American Indian Portfolio*, folio, with lithographs (London, England, published by the author, 1844); later published in America.

Childs, Cephas G.: Philadelphia lithographer, active 1823–58; associated at various times with Pendleton, Kearny, Inman and Lehman.

Currier & Ives: the leading American lithographic firm, founded by Nathaniel Currier in New York in 1833. James M. Ives became a partner in 1857. The firm was in existence until 1906. Publishers of popular subjects including sporting subjects, genre, comics, etc., and employing such artists as Louis Maurer, A. F. Tait, Fanny Palmer, Charles Parsons, Thomas Worth and James Buttersworth.

Durrie, George H.: 1820–63, painter, born and worked in Connecticut. Did the originals of the best known farm and winter scenes published by Currier & Ives.

Duval, Peter S.: Philadelphia lithographer, active 1831–79; associated at times with Lehman, Huddy, Prang and others.

Endicott: an important name in American lithography. Firm began as Endicott & Swett in Baltimore, 1828, and moved to New York 1830; active under various names until 1896.

Hoff, Henry: New York lithographer, active 1850.

Hoffy, Alfred: Philadelphia artist and lithographer, active 1840–60; best known for his drawings of military costume in Huddy & Duval's *U.S. Military Magazine.*

Huddy & Duval: Philadelphia lithographers, 1839–41; published *U.S. Military Magazine*, 3 vols., prized for costume plates.

Imbert, Anthony: active 1825–35 as pioneer lithographer, New York. His work for Colden's *Erie Canal Memoir*, 1826, the first outstanding American work.

Inman, Henry: 1801–46, painter; member of Philadelphia lithographic firm, Childs & Inman, 1831–33.

Jevne & Almini: leading Chicago lithographic firm, established about 1866. Publishers of *Chicago Illustrated 1830.*

Kearny, Francis: Philadelphia engraver and lithographer; member of the firm of Pendleton, Kearny & Childs, *c.* 1829–30.

Kellogg, D. W., later **E. B. & E. C. Kellogg:** lithographic firm of Hartford, also in New York and Buffalo; the most prolific firm after Currier & Ives; established 1833; subjects included sentimentals, portraits, book illustrations.

Klauprech & Menzel: one of the best Cincinnati lithographic firms; active 1840–59; views of Ohio a specialty.

Koellner, August: 1813–*c.* 1878, artist and lithographer, best known for fifty-four well-drawn views of American cities lithographed by Deroy, Paris, published by Goupil, Vibert, 1848–51.

Lane, Fitz Hugh: 1804–65, marine artist, born in Gloucester, Massachusetts. Did

originals of town views; having worked at the lithographic firm of Pendleton in Boston, he put some of his own work on stone (Plate 228B).

Lehman, George: *c.* 1800–70, painter, engraver in aquatint, lithographer; worked in Philadelphia with Duval and also with Childs.

Leighton, Scott: painter of horses for Currier & Ives.

Mathews, A. E.: artist, known for *Pencil Sketches of Colorado*, 1865, lithographs by J. Bien, New York, and *Pencil Sketches of Montana.*

Maurer, Louis: one of the Currier & Ives artists, whose specialty was sporting subjects including field sports, represented by *Deer Shooting, On the Shattagee*, and horse subjects, such as *Trotting Cracks on the Snow.*

Maverick, Peter: 1780–1831, engraver in New York who turned to lithography about 1824; most famous is his *View of Wall Street from Trinity Church* from a drawing by Hugh Reinagle (Plate 226A).

Michelin, Francis: lithographer, Boston 1840; moved to New York 1844; worked to 1859.

Milbert, J.: French artist, in America 1815–23. Author of the *Itinéraire Pittoresque du Fleuve Hudson* ... issued in Paris in thirteen parts beginning 1826 and containing fifty-three numbered views in lithograph.

Nagel, Louis: lithographer, in New York 1844; Nagel & Weingaertner, 1849–57. Went to San Francisco in 1862, where he was associated with Fishbourne & Kuchel.

North American Indian Portfolio, 1844: lithographed in England by Daye & Haghe, after George Catlin (*q.v.*).

Otis, Bass: made the first American lithograph, Philadelphia, 1818–19.

Pendleton: important lithographic firm, Boston, New York, Philadelphia, 1825–*c.* 1866.

Robinson, H. R.: New York lithographer, active 1832–51. Showed the news value of the lithograph with his view of the New York Fire, 1835 (Plate 226B), issued a few weeks later; also the arrival of the steamship *Great Western* in New York harbor, 1838; his *Peytona and Fashion* was the first print of an American horse race, 1842 (also issued by N. Currier).

Sarony, Napoleon: 1821–96, expert lithographer and artist working in New York alone and with others, as Sarony & Major, also Sarony, Major & Knapp; withdrew from lithography about 1867.

Tait, A. F.: 1819–1905, leading sporting painter of the nineteenth century; not a staff artist of Currier & Ives, but many of his scenes of field sports were issued in lithograph by them.

Walton, Henry: English artist known for attractive town views in New York State, such as Ithaca, Elmira, Binghampton and Watkins Glen; was in Ithaca 1836–46. Work issued in lithograph by Bufford and others.

Whitefield, Edwin: active 1854–5, artist and publisher of largest series of American city views in lithograph, printed by F. Michelin, Endicott & Co., Lewis & Brown.

Wild, J. C.: artist, came to Philadelphia in 1838. The firm of Wild & Chevalier issued lithographs of Philadelphia. Later Wild went to Ohio, St. Louis and Davenport, Iowa, where he died in 1845. Wild drew originals for *The Valley of the Mississippi*, published 1840 by Chambers & Knapp, St. Louis.

Worth, Thomas: artist, worked for Currier & Ives; best known for horse subjects, such as *Trotting Cracks at the Forge*; also comics.

BOOKS FOR FURTHER READING

COMSTOCK, HELEN: *American Lithographs*, New York (1950).

PETERS, HARRY T.: *America on Stone*, New York (1931). *California on Stone*, New York (1935). *Currier and Ives: Printmakers to the American People*, New York, Vol. I (1929); Vol. II (1931).

WEITENKAMPF, FRANK: *American Graphic Art*, New York (2nd ed., 1924).

American Historical Prints, Stokes and Haskell, New York (1933).

Concise Encyclopedia of Antiques, Vol. III, pp. 135–141, Hawthorn Books, New York (1957).

EARLY RAILROAD PRINTS

By RUDOLPH WUNDERLICH

The beginnings: the first incorporated railroad to perform transportation service in the United States was the Granite Railway, organized in Quincy, Massachusetts, in 1826: it was horse-drawn. The first full-sized steam locomotive to operate on rails here was the *Stourbridge Lion*, brought from England in 1829. As early as 1825 Colonel John Stevens demonstrated a steam railway in Hoboken, New Jersey. The *American Railway Journal*, which began publication in 1832, carried a wood engraving of the *Stourbridge Lion* on its mast for several years. Otherwise there are no contemporary prints of these interesting 'firsts'.

The *De Witt Clinton* was the first practical American steam locomotive to operate. It ran from Albany to Schenectady, beginning July 31, 1832. On that day a dextrous observer, WILLIAM H. BROWN, cut a silhouette of the train. In 1869, LEGGO & COMPANY of Montreal made a lithograph (Plate 229A) from the silhouette. Although not contemporary, the lithograph gives a clear picture of the first locomotive of the New York Central.

Equally important is the lithograph by ED. WEBER of a view of Ellicott's Mills (Plate 229B), the first stopping place of the Baltimore & Ohio Railroad. Begun in 1828, the road was used as horse-drawn means for carting granite blocks from which, incidentally, the Carrollton Viaduct was built. A print of this viaduct shows one of Ross Winans's locomotives with steam up and two cars attached, ready to leave for Baltimore. The print dates from about 1837.

With the full development of lithography in the United States, railway prints came into their own. It is interesting that this process, easier and cheaper than the etching and en-graving processes favored in Europe, formed the bulk of American railroad prints. A list of known early American railway prints was published by the Railway and Locomotive Historical Society in 1934. 326 items are listed. By far the greater number are lithographs, only fifteen having been executed in other techniques.

Locomotive prints: among the most prized items on the lists of collectors of railroad subjects are prints of early locomotives. They are actual portraits of the engines themselves. They were engineer scale-drawings transferred to the lithographic stone and include a mass of detail often showing even the decorative panels which had been painted on the engine and tender. The prints were large and bright and bold in coloring, but the engine is not shown in motion. They were used as advertisements by the builders and were circulated among their agents and railroad companies (Plates 230A, 230B).

One hundred and fifty of these locomotive prints are included in the Railway and Locomotive Historical Society list. Forty-four builders are listed. Often the same lithographer was employed over a period of years by a firm, and we find the same print-maker's name appearing again and again. J. H. BUFFORD is one of these. He lithographed the *Auburn, Amoskeag, Ontario, Gazelle, Jervis* and *Saturn* for the Amoskeag Manufacturing Company. For the Boston Locomotive Works he did the *Buffalo, Norwalk, Lisle, Rapid, Sacramento, Boston, Fashion, Ysabel* and *Marquette*. For other manufacturers he did the *Express, Janus, State of Maine, Forest State, Shelburne, Minnehaha, Rough and Ready, Calumet and Tender, President and Tender, New Englander and Tender,* and *Northener* [sic].

JULIUS BIEN did the following lithographs for M. W. Baldwin: *Locomotives 4-4-0, 4-6-0 and 0-8-0, Baldwin & Co. Locomotives, Baldwin's Coal Burning Boiler, Baldwin Engines Types C, D, and E, Thomas Rogers.* Bien's partner, STERNER, did *Baltic, Young America,* and *Superior* for Breese & Knowland. Richard Norris & Son, locomotive builders in Philadelphia, hired L. N. ROSENTHAL and A. BRETT to portray the *Auburn, Meredith, Sagua la Grande, Wyoming, Union,* and at least four others.

THOMAS S. SINCLAIR lithographed the *Massachusetts* for Hinkley & Drury of Boston; the *John C. Breckenridge and Tender,* for the Lancaster Locomotive Works; the *Assanpink* for the Trenton Locomotive Works; and a miscellaneous lithograph called *Track Across the Susquehannah River.* The lithography firm of TAPPAN & BRADFORD published some of the finest examples of the locomotive print: *General Stark* for the Amoskeag Manufacturing Company; *Columbia, Mercury* and *Ariel* for other manufacturers. CHARLES H. CROSBY and also Tappan & Bradford worked on the stone for William Mason, the builder in Taunton, Massachusetts, and brought out the *Armstrong, Phantom, Highland Light* and *Janus.* JOHN SARTAIN, probably the leading mezzotint engraver in the United States in his time, scraped *Three Locomotives with Baldwin Plant in Background; The Baldwin Works;* and *Certificate of the Franklin Institute* which is, technically, a railroad print.

Donald McKay built the *Arkansas* and C. H. CROSBY's lithograph of this engine is a gem (Plate 230B). The *Arkansas* is shown in the Far West. Two U.S. troopers appear lower right. Indians, of which there are seven, are in a state of agitation occasioned by this, their first view of a locomotive. The most remarkable figure in the piece is the fireman, who is wearing a pigtail and Chinese dress. He is one of the thousands of Chinese who were encouraged to emigrate to the United States, where they played an important part in the construction of the railroads in the West.

No doubt the very popularity of these gay and decorative prints accounts for their scarcity today. Cheaply framed, if at all, they were hung in railroad stations, offices, barns, bedrooms, and bagnios, where they were thrown away when damaged. Those kept in the files of the manufacturing firms were discarded as their prototypes were replaced by newer and better models.

Viaducts and bridges: when the road-beds were laid out it was necessary to provide a place for the rails that was much less up-hill and down-dale than the country roads. Bridges and viaducts were required. They were viewed as wonders at the time of their building and shared some of the enthusiasm accorded the locomotives. The type of construction varied according to the materials available locally. There is a peculiar satisfaction in contemplating the old prints and reflecting that our ancestors' ingenuity served them well in overcoming obstacles to their progress.

In the vignette of *The Carrollton Viaduct* (Plate 231A) published by ENDICOTT & SWETT in 1831, we see the solidly constructed viaduct straddling the glen, its beautiful arch and well-built buttressed walls made of granite from the quarry at nearby Ellicott's Mills. The horse-drawn railway coach is practically bursting with passengers as it proceeds majestically across the glen.

Thirty years later we find a larger print lithographed by COMPTON & COMPANY after a drawing by J. STILSON. It is called *Portage Bridge* (Plate 231B) and represents a bridge of the Erie Railroad in Western New York. Of timber construction, it had a cross walk from which pedestrians could contemplate the waterfalls below. The legend on the print states that 1,602,000 feet of timber and 108,862 pounds of iron were used in its construction. In the picture a steam locomotive chugs across this wonder of engineering, pulling two freight and five passenger cars.

CURRIER & IVES's *Railroad Suspension Bridge near Niagara Falls* appeared at the same time as the *Portage Bridge.* Lithographed from a painting by CHARLES PARSONS, it designates as engineer John A. Roebling, whose name was to become a household word in America after the building of Brooklyn Bridge. Across the Niagara Bridge, suspended by cables from the huge stone towers, goes the train, while below, on the underpath, horse-drawn carriages proceed.

A beautiful chromolithograph done in 1865 by THOMAS SINCLAIR is entitled *American Autumn* (Plate 232 A). It shows the Starucca Valley Viaduct on the Erie Railroad which was said to be the longest viaduct in the country at that time. JASPER CROPSEY, a first-rate artist of the Hudson River School, was commissioned to do the original painting. Cropsey had been trained as an architect and was well qualified to do justice to the architectural features and incorporate them and a railroad train into a fine landscape painting.

Railroad accident prints: lithography lent itself well to tabloid reporting, and JOHN COLLINS published *Accident on the Camden and Amboy Railroad near Burlington, New Jersey, August 29, 1855*, shortly after the disaster. *The Abolition Catastrophe*, a political cartoon published by BROMLEY & COMPANY is another story. HULLMANDEL & WALTON published *Accident on the Baltimore and Ohio Railroad* in 1853. JOHN L. MAGEE published *The Dreadful Accident of the North Pennsylvania Railroad, 14 Minutes from Philadelphia*, July 17, 1856. One can imagine that these prints made our ancestors reflect on the dangers of railroad travel in much the same way we ponder the perils of travel by air.

Prints with historical significance: CHARLES PARSONS'S *Panama Railroad – View of the Culebra or the Summit* shows the first railroad which operated between the Atlantic and Pacific Oceans. It is dated 1854. CURRIER & IVES's *Across the Continent* (Plate 232B) commemorates the completion of the railway across the North American Continent. SCHILE & COMPANY also issued no less than three colored lithographs under this title. Be it said that these prints are more noted for dash than accuracy.

Railroad scenes of the Civil War include: *The Invasion of Pennsylvania*, a colored woodcut by BERGHAUS; *Volunteer Refreshment Saloon, Supported Gratuitously by the Citizens of Philadelphia, Pa.*, published by B. S. BROWN and printed in color by W. BOELL; *Lookout Mountain near Chattanooga, Tennessee*, by DONALDSON & ELMES; *Military Post, Cowan, Tennessee*, by HENRY ENO; *Tracy City, Tennessee*, also by Eno; *Away to the Front*, by MacCLURE, MacDONALD & MacGREGOR; and *Camp at Melville, Md.*, by SACHSE & COMPANY.

Western print makers of railroad items: information concerning Western print makers is small and examples of their work are much appreciated by collectors. A few titles are: *The Way Not to Build the S.P. Railroad* – anonymous and with no date; *What we want in California. From New York Direct, Family and Fireside*, by BRITTON & REY; *San Diego, Cal.*, by GEORGE H. BAKER. This is an interesting field for collectors with pioneer instincts.

The place of Currier & Ives: it may seem surprising that so little space has been devoted to Currier & Ives thus far. To the American public their names are almost synonymous with the word 'antiques'. This energetic firm published lithographs of most of the important events of American history of the eighteenth and nineteenth centuries and provided a social record of the United States all during their extremely productive career, which dates from the founding of the firm by NATHANIEL CURRIER in 1834 until the turn of the century. Its success was the result of a combination of circumstances, not the least of which was the simultaneous development of lithography, the country's rapid growth, and the development of power inventions and means of production, with the consequent growth of the national wealth.

Strangely enough, early railroad prints before 1860 were comparatively few among the Currier & Ives's productions. The first railroad print issued by Nathaniel Currier is a small folio entitled *The Express Train*, and was taken from a banknote of the Fort Jervis Institution. Undated, it shows the engine before the addition of a headlight. *The American Express Train*, after Charles Parsons, published in 1855, is a large folio. It was reissued with an overprint in the sky, *Adams Express Co.*, with that company's advertising legend in the margin. The large *Express Train*, published in 1859 after a painting by Parsons, is almost a duplicate of the former, but in reverse. All of these prints show entire trains in motion with smoke issuing from the stack, and with landscape backgrounds.

The most important railroad prints done by Currier & Ives, however, were those issued toward the end of or shortly after the Civil War. These are imaginative to the point of being theatrical, are not accurate as to detail, are well drawn and highly-colored, and seek to dramatize some important railroad incident. We find such titles as *The Lightning Express Trains Leaving the Junction; Night Scene at an American Railway Junction; The Great West; American Railroad Scene, Snow Bound; Through to the Pacific; Prairie Fires of the Great West;* and *Across the Continent, Westward the Course of Empire Takes its Way* (Plate 232B). The Currier & Ives's productions are among the most charming of the railroad prints.

Mention should be made of the long series of 'comics' issued by Currier & Ives, those caricaturing new railroad conveniences such as the 'accommodation train', stops for refreshments at the station, entanglements with cattle, and so on plus the amusing group of *Darktown* prints.

Music sheets, banknotes and stock certificates: any event which kindles public interest and enthusiasm is usually a theme of popular poetry and song. Railroading was no exception. One finds numerous titles referring to this industry and most have lithographed representations of railroads on their covers. Perhaps the earliest in this field are the marches dedicated, at the time of the inception of the Baltimore and Ohio Railroad, to Charles Carroll of Carrollton, the last surviving Signer of the Declaration of Independence. The marches were dedicated to him and the other directors of the company. The event took place on the Fourth of July 1828 and *The Carrollton March* and *The Baltimore and Ohio March* were sold on the streets on that momentous day. *The Lion Quickstep* was played for the first time at the opening of the railroad to Westborough (Boston), November 15, 1834. *The New Orleans and Great Northern Railroad Polka* was published in 1854. The galops, polkas, quicksteps, and even 'steam galops' generally bore names at least as exuberant as the pictures on their

covers. Amusing collectors' items, they yet offer important sources for certain elusive railroad data.

Banknotes and stock certificates of the early period utilized railroad material for decoration. On its notes of 1833 the Bank of Tecumseh, Michigan, used a picture of a railroad train with a sharp-pronged cowcatcher on little wheels. This device was actually used by Isaac Dripps of the Camden and Amboy Railroad in 1832. The engraving also shows the iron bonnet on the smokestack devised to arrest the burning embers belched forth from the engine. The first trip of the *De Witt Clinton* and the near incineration of the passengers had made the necessity for such an invention obvious. There is no doubt that the engravers of the notes, RAWDON, WRIGHT & HATCH of New York, had actually seen this train in operation and have left us an accurate picture of it.

Catalogues of railroad subjects offered for sale often list old stock certificates which have a current value only because of the railroad items engraved on them. These vignettes have a charm of their own which comes from the fact that the spectator generally holds them and looks at them close up. The New York Public Library has a fine collection of vignettes, many of which portray railroads.

WELL-KNOWN MAKERS OF RAILROAD PRINTS

Bien, Julius: active New York 1850–68.

Brett, Alphonse: active Philadelphia and New York 1852–64.

Bufford, John H.: active Boston and New York 1835–1870s.

Crosby, Charles H.: active Boston 1852–72.

Currier & Ives: active New York 1834–1907.

Duval, Peter S.: active Philadelphia 1831–93.

The Endicotts: active New York 1830–96.

Rosenthal, Louis N. & family: active Philadelphia 1852–70.

Sartain, J.: born 1808 and died 1897.

Sinclair, Thomas: active Philadelphia 1839–89.

Swett, Moses: active New York, Boston and Washington 1830–7.

Tappan & Bradford: active Boston 1848–53.

BOOKS FOR FURTHER READING

BROWN, WILLIAM H.: *History of the First Locomotives in America*, Appleton, New York (1871).

COMSTOCK, HELEN: *American Lithographs of the 19th Century*, Barrows, New York (1950). (Collectors' L ittle Book Library.)

FISHER, CHARLES E.: 'Early Railroad Items' in *Bulletin No. 35* of The Railroad and Locomotive Historical Society, Baker Library, Harvard Business School, Boston, Massachusetts (1934).

PETERS, HARRY T.: *America on Stone*, Doubleday, Doran, New York (1931); *Currier & Ives, Printmakers to the American People* (1929); *California on Stone*, Doubleday, Doran, New York (1935).

Appleton's Cyclopaedia of American Biography, D. Appleton and Co., New York (1894).

The William Barclay Parsons Railroad Prints, Columbia University Library (1935).

Concise Encyclopedia of Antiques, Vol. III, pp. 135–141, Hawthorn Books, New York (1957).

SPORT IN ART

By PAUL MAGRIEL

COLONIAL America was not a sporting country. The Puritans who came to Massachusetts and the other colonies of the new England brought with them firm convictions. Local ordinances forbade their playing at bowls, quoits, ninepins, cards or any other 'unlawful game in house, yard, garden or backside', and constables were ordered to 'search after all manner of gameing, singing and dancing'. Throughout the new country the teachings of John Knox and Calvin were adhered to more strictly than they had been in the homeland. In England, King James had in 1618 issued a famous declaration, known as the *Book of Sports*, which stated that the royal pleasure would have it, 'that our good people be not disturbed, letted, or discouraged from any lawfull Recreation; such as dauncing, either men or women, archeries for men, leaping, vaulting, or other harmless Recreation. ...' But in Puritan America the people's pleasure was the exercise of conscience. One day in 1621 Governor Bradford was shocked to discover a group of newcomers to his godly community 'in the streets at play, openly; some pitching the barr and some at stoole ball, and such like sports'. The good Governor promptly took away their 'implements', telling them they were playing against his conscience.

Not only were sports prohibited because of the Calvinist temper prevailing in the colonies at this time: such pastimes were made difficult by the economic circumstances of the people. But with developing economic security there came a pronounced need for recreation, and the inherent and traditional English love of sports and games reasserted itself. Hunting and fishing became the chief diversions, with games of skill such as quoits, skittles and bowls, and ball games of various types also being played.

In the South particularly, hunting on horseback became a favorite sport. The plantation owners were ardent riders and huntsmen, who chose their horses with discernment and knowledge, their fowling pieces, their hounds and their riding accessories with taste and pride. They rode almost daily, and it is interesting to note that an eminent Virginia squire named George Washington records in his *Diary*, February, 1769, that he rode to hounds fifteen times that month, six times in one week. One of the earliest and certainly one of the most interesting representations of this sporting activity is the painting titled *The End of the Fox Hunt*, painted in 1780. It was in all probability painted for a Southern gentleman and depicts the traditional hunt with its numerous hounds and the properly costumed gentlemen riders in pursuit of the elusive fox. The naive charm and primitive freshness of this over-mantle painting are unmatched in American sporting iconography. This painting is illustrated in the catalogue of the *Life in America* exhibition, Metropolitan Museum of Art, 1939, No. 115.

The sport that drew the most spectators was horse racing, and in some communities in the North and many in the South, racing meets were held which were attended by large throngs of enthusiastic partisans, come to cheer their favorites. Some first-class native horses were bred, though the best were still brought over from England. The largest single group of paintings dealing with sport were those depicting horses.

EDWARD TROYE, working in the tradition of the English artists Wootton, Stubbs and Ben Marshall, painted with extraordinary skill a great gallery of portraits of the equine racers of his time. Most of them were commissioned, for fees of under a hundred dollars, by the horse breeders of Charleston, New

Orleans, Baltimore, Richmond and those of Kentucky. Among the most notable of Troye's portraits which number into the hundreds are paintings of the champion *American Eclipse*, undefeated in his entire racing career; the dark chestnut *Sir Henry* from North Carolina; and the beautiful bays *Asteroid* (Plate 234A) and *Richard Singleton* from the Kentucky blue grass country. Most of the paintings are faithful individual renderings of the animals – sometimes in solitary calm, as in that of the beautifully proportioned gray mare *Reel* in her stall, more often in the fields, grooms and jockey attending. Edward Troye loved horses, and painted himself in his buggy, drawn by a white horse, observing another one of his beloved racers – a revealing self-portrait of a painter who devoted his entire artistic life to this subject.

The thoroughbred horse was also a subject of interest to other painters. ALVAN FISHER painted many of the Southern pedigreed stock, and in 1824 also produced a painting of the renowned *American Eclipse*. Some years later HENRI DELATTRE, a visiting French artist, made a number of paintings of outstanding horses, one of the most successful of which is titled *Zachary Taylor and Mac*, and depicts these two champions racing at full gallop, their jockeys up and dressed in the brilliant colors of their stables. This is shown in a lithograph by N. Currier of 1851.

Horse racing was the most popular sport with spectators, but it was hunting, shooting and fishing at which most men spent their leisure. America was rich in all kinds of game – deer, bear, rabbits and numerous varieties of fowl. The early forms of fowling pieces imported from abroad were soon replaced by new American types designed for use in the almost virgin forests. Hunting in the early days was both a business and a pastime, and almost every American man and boy owned a gun.

Shooting matches were very popular in many parts of the country. Usually held on Saturdays, they were well attended by the local people who came to see their townsmen vie for both a monetary prize and the important title of 'best shot'. A number of paintings were done of these shooting matches which

graphically illustrate their flavor, in both its seriousness and humor. One of the most striking and charming of them is *The Turkey Shoot*, by CHARLES DEAS.

Born in Philadelphia, Deas spent some time at the Pennsylvania Academy and then moved to the Hudson River Valley, where he spent as much time hunting and fishing as he did in sketching. *The Turkey Shoot* was painted in 1836 when he was only eighteen years old. Shown at the Metropolitan Museum of Art in the 1939 *Life in America* exhibition, this work by Deas aroused great interest in this little-known American artist who gave us one of the most individual examples of American sporting art.

The best-known and most interesting of the paintings in this genre is *Shooting for the Beef* by GEORGE CALEB BINGHAM (Plate 233B). Bingham was a boy of eight when his family left Virginia and went to settle in Missouri. He grew up in that frontier country and set up a studio at Columbia, but his love was for the out-of-doors. Traveling up and down the Mississippi, he produced a series of memorable paintings of the men who made a livelihood on the river. *Shooting for the Beef* was painted in 1850. It illustrates a typical scene of the period – the log cabin at the crossroads, the eager intense marksmen in frontier attire, and the fat ox, which is to be the winner's prize, chained at the side. The painting shows Bingham's great skill in the placing of the figures and in the masterly ordering of light and shade. Bingham stated his credo as an artist to be, to 'assure us that our political and social characteristics will not be lost in the lapse of time for want of an art record to know life on the great western rivers', and in this painting and others he fulfilled this aim.

Subjects relating to the hunt and other out-of-door sports were naturally of interest to many of our artists. For them, such subjects provided a point of departure from the more formal art of portraiture and historical painting, and enabled them to focus on the leisure-time pursuits and interests of the average American. Though the average man could not afford to own original works by these anecdotal painters, he could have reproductions of them and often his home had more than one such reminder of the pleasures of life in the open with gun, rod and reel.

ARTHUR FITZWILLIAM TAIT was thirty-one when he came to the United States from England, where he had studied painting and had produced works in the current Victorian narrative manner. However, Tait saw the new American scene with a fresh eye, and he began to turn out a large number of extremely popular sporting pictures. His original works were eagerly sought after, but also he contracted with the enterprising printing firm of Currier & Ives to publish his work, so that reproductions of his most popular pictures were seen literally everywhere. It was through such reproductions that A. F. Tait became one of the most widely known artists of his time. Some of the favorites were published in series with titles such as *American Frontier Life, Brook Trout Fishing, American Hunting Scenes,* and others (Plate 235A). Currier & Ives did their work well: one of their advertisements, 'Pictures have become a Necessity', brought Tait's sporting scenes into thousands of American homes. It was the first time in our history that a mass market for 'works of art' came into existence.

Numerous mid-nineteenth century paintings dealt with familiar and pleasurable aspects of the American scene as Tait's did. WILLIAM SIDNEY MOUNT's *Eel Spearing at Setauket* (Plate 234B), painted in 1845 in his native Long Island, is a work of high quality, without the cloying sentimentality of so many genre pictures. Mount's simple, natural style makes his anecdotal subject moving and lucid. There is no sentimentality in Bingham's *Fishing in the Mississippi* either – it is a superior example of American sporting painting done in 1851 when Bingham was at the peak of his talent. Among others which rank with our best as documentary representations of rural sports as well as interesting pictures are *Shooting Flamingoes,* by GEORGE CATLIN; *Night Fishing,* by ALBERT BIERSTADT; *The Fishing Hole,* by E. L. HENRY; and THOMAS DOUGHTY's *The Fisherman.* Others which illustrate American leisure-time pursuits are the series of paintings of rail shooting by THOMAS EAKINS, and the superb group of watercolors and paintings by WINSLOW

HOMER. Taken as a whole, this group of paintings of hunting and fishing, pastimes which have been perennial favorites in this country for more than two centuries, constitutes an unsurpassed artistic record of our American sporting heritage.

Curiously enough, the games played with a ball, such as golf, cricket, croquet, lacrosse, bowls, and tennis, as well as baseball and football, did not seem to be of special interest to our artists. There are, of course, a small number of paintings that deal with them. CHARLES DEAS painted a violent and exciting picture of Indians playing lacrosse, a subject that was also vividly presented by SETH EASTMAN in his *Lacrosse playing among the Indians.* ALFRED JACOB MILLER and GEORGE CATLIN, admirable reporters of the Western scene, have also given us graphic illustrations of Indians playing this vigorous game.

Croquet was more than a game, it was a social activity, providing an opportunity for both sexes to indulge in the mildest of physical exercise. It was played a great deal by the fashionable set in the East, where it was at one time so popular that manufacturers made sets with candle-sockets for play at night. The lovely canvas by GEORGE INNESS titled *Croquet, Conway, New Hampshire* is an ideal evocation of this tranquil game. HOMER, who loved so many sports, has also given us two beautiful paintings of this subject (Plate 236C).

Baseball and football, now our most popular spectator sports, were just being developed in the mid-nineteenth century. The iconography depicting them is meager. HOMER executed some drawings for *Harper's* in 1857 which included one of a football match. Of the game of baseball EAKINS made a watercolor, *Baseball Players Practising.* Currier & Ives along with other publishers produced a number of prints of the national pastime. Before the turn of the century A. B. FROST became the chronicler of American sports, and his production included drawings of the games of golf and tennis.

As for water sports, the poetic figure pieces of WILLIAM MORRIS HUNT and THOMAS EAKINS depict the joys of swimming, and the pleasures of the beach were also amusingly rendered in the painting *Bathing Beauties* by JAMES O'BRIEN INMAN. JAMES BUTTERSWORTH'S paintings of yachts are as faithful as Troye's of thoroughbred horses. And Eakins also produced a great group of oils and watercolors of sculling, unmatched in American art for their rendering of the sport which this painter so dearly loved (Plate 235B).

The pleasures of boyhood were handsomely depicted in HENRY INMAN's *Mumble the Peg*, and in WINSLOW HOMER's *Snap the Whip* we have a superb example of American genre painting. A watercolor by Homer, *Skating in Central Park, New York*, and an admirable oil by THOMAS BIRCH titled *Skating*, also rank with our most interesting examples of the sporting scene. Another nostalgic vision of this delightful winter pastime is JOHANN CULVERHOUSE's painting *Skating on the Wissahickon* (Plate 236B).

Though prize fighting was outlawed in America, notices of boxing matches appeared in the press in the eighteenth century and as early as 1810 the American Negro Tom Molineaux challenged and fought the great British champion Tom Cribb. The sporting bloods of this country went to extraordinary lengths to arrange illegal boxing matches. One of the earliest graphic evidences that the prize ring was in existence was a painting done of William Fuller, who settled here in 1820. Executed in the manner of the formal studied British boxing pose by CHARLES CROMWELL INGHAM in 1828, it was shortly afterwards made into an engraving by ASHER

B. DURAND (Plate 236A). It is an excellent portrait study, and the forebear of a whole series of prints depicting individual fighters and matches which became standard features of bar-room decoration.

The gallery of sport by American artists is thus numerous and, taken as a whole, this work is unique. In it the customs, pastimes and pleasurable pursuits of the people are reflected more fully and vividly than in any other form of artistic expression. In the works of such artists as Winslow Homer and Thomas Eakins, Thomas Birch, William Sidney Mount, and others, we have a sporting art which represents an important and vital aspect of our culture.

BOOKS FOR FURTHER READING

DULLES, FOSTER RHEA: *America Learns to Play – A history of popular recreation, 1607–1940*, Appleton-Century Co., New York (1940).

HOLLIMAN, JENNIE: *American Sports, 1785–1835*, The Seeman Press, Durham, North Carolina (1931).

MAGRIEL, PAUL: 'American Prize-fight Prints' in *Antiques* (November 1949).

The Ring and the Glove, Catalogue of an exhibition, Museum of the City of New York (1947).

Sport in American Art, Catalogue of an exhibition, Museum of Fine Arts, Boston (1944).

Highlights of the Turf, Catalogue of an exhibition (April–May 1948, M. Knoedler & Co.). Illustrated.

Sport in Art, from American collections assembled for an Olympic year, *Sports Illustrated*, New York (1956). Illustrated.

Sport in Nineteenth Century American Painting, Panorama, Harry Shaw Newman Gallery, New York (February 1948). Illustrated.

Sports and Adventure in American Art, Catalogue of an exhibition, Milwaukee Art Institute (February–March 1947). Mimeographed.

Sport in Art, Catalogue of an exhibition, Albright Art Gallery, Buffalo (February 1948).

THE OLD WEST

By Dr HAROLD McCRACKEN

FROM the days of the earliest European explorers until the last Indian war-whoop was permanently silenced, the sprawling territory that stretches westward from the Mississippi River to the Pacific has provided history with one of its most dramatic and colorful epochs. Its long cavalcade of wilderness strife and struggle has involved the nations of Spain, Portugal, France, England, the United States, and others to a lesser extent. It produced a number of clear-cut types strictly indigenous to the land and the period which created them – the *conquistadores*, *coureurs de bois*, frontier scout, mountain man, squawman, cowboy, Indian warrior, cattleman and 'tenderfoot'. A documentation of the characteristics of these types in their contemporary environment is the broad subject of the artists of the Old West. The value of their work depends on its objectivity. Sometimes there is a happy union with purely artistic virtues.

We are entirely dependent upon the artist-explorer for the pictorial record of the transformation of the wilderness, except for the last brief phase, which was late enough for portrayal by photography. It is unfortunate that prior to the 1820s there exists little more than the infrequent drawings of illustrators who relied largely upon hearsay and imagination when illustrating journals of explorers and works of historians. However, the most important phase of the development of the West took place during the nineteenth century, and we have a comprehensive report from artists regarding a large part of that development.

The Spanish contributed practically nothing in the way of a pictorial record of their early explorations, beyond an influence upon the religious folk art developed among the Indians in the Southwest. These are the *santos* (images of the saints), *santos de bulto* (figures of saints in the round) and *santos retablos* (painted panels of saints), which were painted to imitate the religious adornments brought to decorate the frontier churches. The early French and English, who began pushing westward across North America from the north-east in the middle of the seventeenth century and contributed considerably more to the exploration and settlement of the continent, did not supply any amount of realistic pictorial material to supplement their journals.

The West of the early part of the nineteenth century offered the adventurous artist everything he could desire in the way of inspiration and incentive. Here was history in the making, against a backdrop of rolling prairies, arid deserts, giant forests and mountain grandeur. Millions of shaggy buffalo roamed the plains, and there were scores of Indian tribes distinguished by their own picturesque styles of dress. Here could be seen Indians on the warpath and in the scalp dance; the pageantry of migration; and the recklessness of unexcelled bareback horsemanship in warfare and pursuit of dangerous game.

Among the earliest artists, if not the first, afforded the opportunity of documenting this era as an eye-witness was SAMUEL SEYMOUR, who accompanied the official United States Government expedition of 1819–20 under the direction of Major Stephen H. Long, U.S. Engineers. They traveled up the Missouri River to the Yellowstone, then swung southward along the edge of the Rocky Mountains. Seymour painted one hundred and fifty landscapes and other pictures, eight of which were reproduced in an atlas to accompany the published journal of the expedition in 1823. His *View of the Rocky Mountains* was the first authentic portrayal of its kind.

Following closely after Seymour came

PETER RINDISBACHER. As a fifteen-year-old Swiss immigrant he came to America with his parents in 1821, in a party of one hundred and fifty-seven settlers recruited to join Lord Selkirk's doomed Red River colony in the vicinity of Fort Douglas, near the present site of Winnipeg, Manitoba. They were brought by ship into icy Hudson's Bay, from whence they had to make a six-hundred-mile overland journey through the wilderness. The youthful Peter Rindisbacher made an exceptional series of watercolor paintings of the whole journey, and they were supplemented with numerous other scenes of the country in which the family settled. These are the earliest known genre works of any artist in the interior of North America. Forty of this artist's early portrayals of the Red River colony, the Indians, buffalo hunts and other subjects are today in the Public Archives of Canada (Plate 237A).

In 1826, after a disastrous experience, the Rindisbacher family and other settlers abandoned Red River and migrated into the United States. Peter went to St Louis in 1829, where he set up a studio and worked successfully as an artist until his death in August, 1834, at the early age of twenty-eight. Ten of his pictures appeared in the *American Turf and Sporting Magazine*. A portfolio of six others, entitled *Views in Hudson's Bay*, was issued in London before his death. Another of his pictures, *War Dance of the Sauks and Foxes*, was selected to be the frontispiece of Volume I of McKenney and Hall's *Indian Tribes of North America* (1836-44).

A third artist who enjoyed an unusual opportunity to become one of the early artists of the West was JAMES OTTO LEWIS. During the years 1825 to 1828 he was commissioned by the United States Indian Department to attend the different Indian councils, for the purpose of making portraits of the distinguished chiefs and depicting the various events surrounding those historic conclaves during which treaties were made and the United States Government negotiated the purchase of millions of acres of rich agricultural land. The Indians who gathered for these big council meetings provided a colorful spectacle. Lewis also wrote the text which ac-

companied his extensive *Aboriginal Portfolio*, published in 1839. This set a pattern for the future, by which artists were sent along with most of the Government expeditions to document the Indian council meetings, explorations and surveys. Here the school of western American art had a serious beginning.

The first artist of real stature to go into the West for the express purpose of making a documentary record of all the Indian tribes was GEORGE CATLIN (1796-1872). He covered more territory and visited more tribes, while they were still in their unspoiled primitive state, than any other artist. Furthermore, he accompanied his pictures with comprehensive text in his great opus, *Illustrations of the Manners, Customs and Conditions of the North American Indians* (1841).

Catlin began his career in 1830-1, when he attended several of the important council meetings with the tribes along the Mississippi River, the eastern margin of the wilderness. In 1832 he made a two-thousand-mile journey up the Missouri River to remote Fort Union, where he began his real work among the northern Plains Indians. He made numerous trips by canoe, up and down the rivers and overland to the homes of the various tribesmen. He usually traveled alone and had remarkable success in gaining the friendship even of the scalp-hunters. His hundreds of

Fig. 1. Catlin Sketchbook, 1852
Newberry Library, Chicago

sketches and paintings were supplemented by voluminous notes on everything he saw and learned. This pattern of work was carried on year after year and eventually took this remarkable pioneer across the vast wilderness from north to south and to the Pacific coast. Probably no other artist in history has ever made a greater contribution to the pictorial record of a human race. He even extended his work to South America.

In the fall of 1836 Catlin transported all his Indian paintings and large collection of Indian paraphernalia to New York, where he held an exhibition and gave lectures. In 1837 he held similar exhibitions in other eastern cities. One of the most important results of this was the direct inspiration which it gave to a number of other artists to devote their talents and energies to a similar career. In 1839 he took his collection to London, where he leased Egyptian Hall, Piccadilly, for three years of display and lectures. In 1845 he moved to Paris, where the French uprisings and riots of February, 1848, brought sudden disaster to him. Escaping with his precious collection to London, his career ended in bankruptcy and the total loss of his lifetime's efforts. He finally died in the United States, virtually destitute, but leaving a work of undying influence. Many of his paintings and sketches are preserved today in the Smithsonian Institution, Washington, D.C., and in the Museum of Natural History, New York (Plate 238A).

The artists who followed the inspiration of George Catlin are numerous. Many of them were accomplished craftsmen and sincere in their devotion to realism. A number of them have remained in virtual oblivion until quite recently, when students have become increasingly aware of the vital importance of their work. Among the more noteworthy of these men is SETH EASTMAN (1808–75). One of the self-taught artists, he produced some highly creditable canvases. A graduate of West Point, Eastman spent most of his life in the West as a military man. He was stationed at Fort Crawford on the upper Mississippi River as early as 1829 and from 1830 at the big military supply base at Fort Snelling, near the present city of Minneapolis. Not only did he make an extensive series of pictures of frontier and Indian life executed during the seven years he was stationed there, but he also painted a series of military fortifications throughout the West which today hangs in the Capitol in Washington, D.C. His unusually accomplished wife, Mary Henderson Eastman, was the author of several books, which contained reproductions of her husband's paintings. Her *Dakotah: Life and Legends of the Sioux* and the accompanying plates was a principal source of inspiration and information for Longfellow's poem *The Song of Hiawatha*.

Probably the most accomplished early artist whose work became a part of this school was the Swiss, KARL BODMER, who accompanied Alexander Philip Maximilian, Prince of Weid-Neuweid, up the Missouri River in the spring of 1833. They returned to St Louis in the early summer of the following year. Later, Bodmer took up permanent residence with the Barbizon colony at Fontainebleau in France. Here he worked into finished paintings eighty-one pictures which were reproduced to form the handsome folio atlas accompanying the two-volume narrative of Maximilian's North American journey, published in 1839. The lithographs from these pictures are considered by many to be the finest of all works in this field (Plate 237B).

ALFRED JACOB MILLER (1816–74) of Baltimore came into rather sudden prominence about a decade ago. He accompanied the Scottish explorer, Sir William Drummond Stewart, in 1837–8 as official artist when the latter made a trip to the Far West. Miller's pictures of the fur-trading posts and rendezvous of the Rocky Mountain trappers show the influence of his European training and do not have the vigor of the work of Catlin. Much of his work is in the possession of the Walters Art Gallery in Baltimore.

Among those who deserve greater recognition than students have so far bestowed is JOHN MIX STANLEY (1814–72). He began his extensive travels in 1842 for the express purpose of delineating the Indian tribes and council meetings of the eastern Great Plains region. In 1846 he accompanied the famous Magoffin expedition over the Santa Fe Trail to the south-west. Later, he went on to California with Colonel H. W. Emory, who was head of a United States exploring expedition. The famous Kit Carson was official guide. In 1853 he was the artist on the government expedition sent out to explore and survey the first route for a railroad across the north-west to the Pacific coast. The paintings by John Mix Stanley of the numerous Indian tribes and historic events throughout the West place him well in the forefront of western artists (Plate 240A).

The decades before and after the middle of the nineteenth century saw a number of artists devoting their talents and efforts to a serious documentation of the Old West. Among the most important were the Canadian PAUL KANE (1810–71); the eccentric Academician CHARLES DEAS (1818–67); CHARLES WIMAR (1828–62), whose work is illustrated here (Plate 238B); the Swiss FREDERICK KURZ (active 1851); the Californian ERNEST NARJOT (active 1865); the German BALDOUIN MÖLLHAUSEN (active 1824–57); WILLIAM RANNEY (1813–72); and the illustrator F. O. C. DARLEY (1822–8).

The Gold Rush to California, which began in 1849, developed into one of the most potent influences upon the course of American history and provided a tremendous impetus to western art. The experiences of the men and women in the covered wagon trains that moved across the Great Plains and Rocky Mountains, as well as the fortune-crazy life at the end of the journey, which was richly spiced with melodrama, completely captured public imagination. The demands of the market led to the production of a great number of lithographs by Currier & Ives in New York, Britten & Rey, Nagel & Weingartner and others in San Francisco.

As the West became settled and the vast wilderness was transformed, it attracted an ever increasing number of artists. Some of these drifted away from the realism of documentation, adding a strong romantic flavor to their work, as seen in the paintings of the Rocky Mountains by ALBERT BIERSTADT (1830–1902) and THOMAS MORAN (1837–1926); later by GEORGE DE FOREST BRUSH (1855–1941).

As the old West faded into the limbo of things forgotten, there were a few delineators who became intensely interested in perpetuating its final aspect. Two of these stand pre-eminently above the rest. Both were self-taught; both went west in 1880; and both devoted their whole careers to the subject of the frontier. They were FREDERIC REMINGTON (1861–1909) and CHARLES M. RUSSELL (1864–1926.) They contributed more to western art than any of the others with the possible exception of George Catlin. In addition to being accomplished painters, they were equally proficient as sculptors and writers.

CHARLES M. RUSSELL, who was raised in a prosperous St Louis home, went west to Montana Territory and became a rough-riding cowboy when still in his 'teens. He led a rough and rather vagabond life, becoming known as 'the cowboy artist' around the cattle round-up camps long before he gained recognition of any consequence. After about fifteen years as a *bona fide* cowboy he married and settled down to the serious profession of an artist, in a log studio. He became eminently successful during a colorful lifetime, and the scope of his work was almost entirely restricted to cowboy and Indian life of Montana (Plate 239A). He never quite ceased to be a cowboy at heart and in temperament.

FREDERIC REMINGTON was raised in a prosperous family of Ogdensburg, New York. He attended private school and was a football star at Yale. He too went west at an early age in search of adventure and fortune. After four years of wandering from Canada to Mexico, riding horseback over hundreds of miles of wild trails, working as a cowboy, prospector, rancher and saloon proprietor, he gradually turned to the career of a documentary artist. Returning to New York he rose to fame as an illustrator in a remarkably brief time and later as a painter and sculptor. He maintained an elaborate studio and country estate, although he continued to spend a considerable part of practically every year in some part of the West. The scope of Remington's work covered the whole story of the West, both geographically and historically – the most comprehensive of any artist. One of his works in sculpture, the *Bronco Buster* (Plate 240B), is probably the best known bronze by any American artist. Also a prolific writer, one of his books, *John Ermine of the Yellowstone*, was produced as a play on Broadway. Well over a hundred of his western paintings were reproduced as color prints, and thousands of these were widely distributed. These are still popular, almost fifty years after his death at the untimely age of only forty-eight, while his original sketches and paintings (Plate 239B) find increasing appreciation among collectors. A memorial gallery of his works is in his native Ogdensburg.

BOOKS FOR FURTHER READING

McCracken, Harold: *Frederic Remington*, Philadelphia (1947).

McCracken, Harold: *Portrait of the Old West*, New York (1952).

McCracken, Harold: *The Charles M. Russell Book*, New York (1957).

Ross, Marvin C.: *The West of Alfred Jacob Miller*, University of Oklahoma Press (1951).

Taft, Robert: *Artists and Illustrators of the Old West, 1850-1900*, New York (1953).

Westward the Way, Catalogue of an exhibition at the City Art Museum, St Louis (1954).

FOLK SCULPTURE

By ERWIN O. CHRISTENSEN

THE term 'folk art' as used in Europe is often synonymous with peasant art. In the United States the term is apt to be less specific; it often refers to primitive or untutored art. When the early settlers came to America they brought with them their own folk heritage, which was at times modified by the changing conditions of the new country. This was true of wood carving, perhaps the most widely distributed American folk art. The ready supply of wood and the ease with which it was possible to acquire some elementary skill must have contributed historically to the continuity and geographically to the wide distribution of wood carving.

Though practised in many places, wood carving is individual; it cannot be made from a mold like china or pressed glass, and the collector finds relatively few examples. Much that has been preserved is already in collections. Wood carvings are of the eighteenth century and, to a larger extent, of the nineteenth. As carvers did not sign their works, they are mostly anonymous. But the discerning student of wood carving can differentiate between the professional and the amateur carver. The professional artist in shop, studio or art school absorbs the traditions of his period and acquires techniques above the level of the untrained amateur. Since folk art may include both the amateur and the professional, well-known carvers are here represented only by those works which are closer to folk than to academic art. Early American wood sculpture was usually painted or gilded. White was used in imitation of stone, or various colors to represent costume and flesh tints.

Rush, McIntire and the Skillin brothers: WILLIAM RUSH (1756–1833) of Philadelphia, who is rightly claimed as the first American sculptor, was trained in the European tradition. Though much of his work has not been identified or has disappeared, his known works indicate that he transcends the limits of folk art. His signed bust of Samuel Morris (1812) conveys a definite personality in a style which shows that Rush had an easy command of the tradition of sculpture. An eagle in the Philadelphia Museum of Art, carved for a volunteer fire company and attributed to him, could perhaps be classified as folk art. Even here the composition and vigor of carving suggest the academic background fused with a personal style.

Whereas Rush was largely a figure carver, SAMUEL MCINTIRE (1757–1811) of Salem, Massachusetts, was an architectural carver who occasionally carved figures. Like Rush, he began in the eighteenth-century tradition and developed a style of his own. Though he was a master craftsman of interior woodwork of houses, McIntire is close to folk art in his busts, *Voltaire* (Plate 241) and *Governor John Winthrop,* painted to suggest stone. His emphasis on meticulous detail may be as much due to his decorative bent as to his lack of experience with the living figure. For the *Voltaire* bust McIntire must have depended on some model, as he never saw Voltaire. McIntire's carved relief of Washington, oval-shaped and medallion-like (Peabody Museum, Salem) follows a drypoint etching by Joseph Hiller, Jr., which was derived from a similar profile etching by Joseph Wright. Here the accomplished craftsman is more in evidence than the self-trained folk artist. A full-length figurehead of a woman holding a medallion (Peabody Museum, Salem) has been attributed to him and may be placed with folk art.

Well-known among the carvers of the late-eighteenth and early-nineteenth centuries were the SKILLIN brothers of Boston, JOHN (1746–1800) and SIMEON (1756–1806). Mabel M. Swan has identified the Skillin style on the basis of three small figures on a chest in the Garvan Collection at Yale University. The style is characterized by a heavy neck, sturdy arms and an ornamental treatment of drapery, hair and other details. The figures of *Justice* and *Hope*, and a gilt *Justice* in the Worcester, Massachusetts, Historical Society may be attributed to the Skillins on stylistic grounds. The figures of *Justice* and *Hope* were used architecturally in niches, and a flying *Mercury*, attributed to the Skillins, stood over the door of the Boston Post Office on State Street. Two painted busts (New York State Historical Association, Cooperstown) show Skillin characteristics, an easy naturalism and details of an ornamental linear character. The busts, about two feet high, represent *Ceres* (Plate 242A) and *Apollo*. Several garden figures have also been attributed to the Skillins. After the death of the younger Skillin the shop was taken over by Isaac Fowle and Edmund Raymond.

Early figures and busts: other examples of carving of this period survive; sometimes the original location and carver are known. A small figure of *Justice* by JOHN FISHER, privately owned, was in a courtroom in Pennsylvania at the time of the Revolution. The head of a statue of *Minerva* (Historical and Philosophical Society of Ohio, University of Cincinnati), carved in 1822 by one Schafer (anglicized to Shepherd) of Cincinnati, is in the traditional eighteenth-century classical manner. JOSEPH WILSON, a carver of Newburyport, Massachusetts, around 1810 may have carved two near-life-size reclining female figures, *Peace* and *Plenty* (for 'Lord' Timothy Dexter). They appear to have been used one on either side of some central feature. In these figures, privately owned, a traditional style has received a vigorous expression. The Royall house in Medford, Massachusetts, had a weathervane of which a fragment of a flying *Mercury* has been preserved.

A garden figure in the Rhode Island School of Design reveals the touch of the figurehead carver. The standing figure (purchased in Philadelphia) holds a bouquet in her right hand; feet and pedestal are missing. A garden figure of a girl, half nude and caressing a bird, reveals a dependence on academic art. A large painted wooden statue of George Washington in uniform, said to be by WILLIAM SULLIVAN, stood on Bowling Green in New York City from 1792 to 1843. It subsequently served in three different locations as a shop figure before it was acquired for the Delaware Historical Society.

A trend toward carved life-size wooden statues continued into the second half of the nineteenth century. DAVID G. BLYTHE (1815–65) of East Liverpool, Ohio, is known to have carved the figure of General Lafayette in walnut, eight feet high; HERMAN D. A. HENNING of Baltimore (*c.* 1875) carved the four-foot figure of the Civil War General of the Union forces John A. Dix. A bust of Franklin in the post office of Newport, Rhode Island, was carved by ALEXANDER SWASEY (1784–1864) in the manner of marble sculpture. Carved portrait busts parallel portrait busts in painting. More like a realistic portrait painting is the painted head of a boy by ALEXANDER AMES (d. 1847) in the New York State Historical Association (Plate 242B). The carver probably had little if any academic training, as is indicated by the lack of correct anatomy, even though he achieved a general semblance of the structure of the head. Definitely in the folk art manner (Plate 245C) is a twelve-and-a-half-inch figure of a seated woman (Colonial Williamsburg). The motif of the raised arms is a device to suggest animation; the skirt, left in the cubical shape of the block, suggests the folk carver; the dress with its rickrack braid suggests the nineteenth century. It was found near Ephrata, Pennsylvania, and is Pennsylvania-German.

Figureheads and ship carvings: the figurehead was a carved and painted decoration placed under the bowsprit of the old sailing vessels. It was the most important part of ship carving. During the early period of the newly-formed republic figurehead carving took on a native expression. There are several characteristic American contributions to ship figurehead design. The typical American full-length, life-size figurehead is slightly detached from the hull and stands with head erect, as if peering into the distance. Another American characteristic is the variety of subjects chosen. American carvers selected motifs from contemporary life, and used as models the ship owner, his wife and daughter, figures from history and literature, and American generals and admirals, as well as figures of *Liberty*. In addition to the full-length figure, busts, heads, and half and three-quarter-length figures were used, as well as eagles and occasionally animals, like serpents' heads. Where individuals were represented the intent was to achieve a portrait-like character in the head, as in those of George Washington, Benjamin Franklin, and Andrew Jackson. The classic influence produced *Hercules*, *Julius Caesar*, and *Galatea*; an American Indian contribution is noted in *Tamanend*, *Minnehaha* and Indian chiefs and princesses. Of celebrated contemporaries we have portraits of Jenny Lind, the singer, and ship builders like Donald McKay. Figureheads still show a relationship to academic art, and a realistic trend is indicated in the use of contemporary costume. Figureheads vary stylistically, but individual expression in the features is ordinarily not attempted, even where a general resemblance has been achieved in the case of portraits. But there are exceptions; some heads have jovial expressions and smiling faces. A bust-length figurehead in the Abby Aldrich Rockefeller Collection, Williamsburg, Virginia, shows a young woman with engaging features in a style that recalls the Gothic or early Greek sculpture at the transition of the archaic to the classic period (Plate 242D).

A unique ship carving (Plate 246c) in a vigorously naturalistic style is a figure from the American Civil War, a Negro mascot of the Union Army (City Art Museum, St Louis). It was dredged from the Missouri River in the early 1870s. A figurehead about contemporary with the Negro mascot, carved in Boston for *The Highlander* (built in 1868), shows a Scot in native dress (Peabody Museum, Salem, Massachusetts). The timidity of the carving, lacking the skill of the earlier work, suggests that in this late period some

work was also entrusted to less competent carvers. Even so, excellent work was still being done as shown by the *Cassandra Adams* figurehead carved about 1876 (Plate 243A).

Where subject permitted, drapery from classic sculpture played a part. The carved drapery often retains something of the pliability of cloth with overlapping folds, or it may be expressed by a near-abstract linear pattern of sharp curves and spirals gouged out of the wood. Arms may be held freely above the head or they may cling to the figure; the feet in figures of women are occasionally revealed fully and carved with the skill of a sculptor versed in anatomy, but in others they are concealed or given less emphasis. The extent to which the figure makes itself felt beneath the drapery or costume places the carver nearer the academic or the folk art level.

The smaller vessels used busts as figureheads, growing out of scroll and leaf carving, or resting on scrolled shelf-like supports. Billet-heads consisted of voluted scrolls gilded and painted. This particular type is close to the architectural carving of the classic and baroque periods.

Eagles used on whalers show variety in the carved details. Where the neck of the eagle terminates, scroll work or leaf carving finishes the decoration. The length of the neck, the shape of the beak and the carving of the eye and of the feathers differentiate the work of one carver from another. Eagles were gilt or painted to set off eye and beak against the color of the feathers. Eagles on pilot houses of tugboats, river craft or other steamers have been preserved. They were carved in the round, at times with a wingspread of several feet. The wings may be spread horizontally or lifted to a vertical position; they were carved separately to fit into grooves. Examples are preserved in the Museum of the City of New York (tugboat eagle) and the Public Museum of Davenport, Iowa. The latter eagle was carved in 1845 for a Mississippi River boat. Another for a Great Lakes steamer is in the Grand Haven, Michigan, Historical Society. Such eagles are usually poised on a globe-and-rope base. Small eagles cut board-like from the same pattern and used originally on ships were carved by JOHN BELLAMY of Maine, the well-known ship carver, to be given away to his friends (Plate 244B). They were painted red, white and blue, and have been imitated. The template he used has been preserved by Joseph W. P. Frost, a descendant.

Carved eagles, gilt and painted and combined with flags, shields and scrolls in the manner of ship carving, were also used architecturally in pediments over doorways (Library, Goshen, Connecticut) or as finials on flagpoles and fence posts. The boom, used on sailing vessels as a derrick for the raising of the anchor, at times terminated in a carved cat's head.

Ship carvings included sternboards, mast-sheaths and some interior decoration. A sternboard might bear the ship's name, a portrait of the owner, or scrolls, eagles and shields with stars and stripes. As the stern changed with the development of the hull, the carved sternboard decorations had to be changed accordingly. Toward the latter part of the ship-carving period (1850–80) sternboard design was developed around the American eagle holding the shield. The horizontal extension of the stern favored a spread-eagle type of design, such as the shield with stars and stripes, sunbursts and banderoles with *E Pluribus Unum*. No single type was preferred; the design was left to the carver. Of mast-sheaths and gang-boards fewer are available, although examples are to be seen in the Chicago, Illinois, Historical Society, and in the Portsmouth, New Hampshire, Historical Society. A mast-sheath is owned by the Old Dartmouth Whaling Museum in New Bedford, Massachusetts.

Figureheads have been documented by Pauline Pinckney in *American Figureheads and Their Carvers* (1940). Over seven hundred names of ship carvers are known and in some instances carvings have been related to particular artists. Among those whose work is known are CHARLES A. L. SAMPSON of Bath, Maine (d. 1881), who carved the figurehead for the *Belle of Oregon*; and JOHN HALEY BELLAMY (1836–1914) of Kittery Point, Maine, Portsmouth, New Hampshire, and Boston, especially known for his great

eagle with a wing-spread of eighteen feet, carved as a figurehead for the U.S.S. *Lancaster* (Mariners' Museum, Newport News, Virginia). Other carvers were WILLIAM S. GLEASON & SONS of Boston (clipper *Minnehaha*); WILLIAM LUKE of Portsmouth, Virginia (*Tamanend* bust, U.S. Naval Academy); LABAN S. BEECHER of Boston (*Jackson* figurehead of the frigate *Constitution*); DODGE & SON of New York, carvers of a later *Jackson* figurehead; WOODBURY GERRISH of Portsmouth, New Hampshire (*Franklin*); JACOB S. ANDERSON of New York City (*David Crockett*); HASTINGS & GLEASON of Boston (*Indian Chief*); EMERY JONES of Freeport, Maine (*Samuel Skolfield*); WILLIAM SOUTHWORTH of Portland, Maine; J. E. VERRILL of Rockland, Maine; and JOHN W. MASON of Damariscotta, Maine. Ship carvings today are in historical and marine museums, in private collections, and in gardens of private estates. Although figureheads belong to sculpture, few are in art museums.

EDBURY HATCH (1849–1935), one of the later ship carvers of Newcastle, Maine, continued to carve after ship carving as a craft had come to an end. From his later years are a number of his carvings of fine quality now privately owned around Wiscasset, Damariscotta and Newcastle, Maine. He embellished his house with wood carvings and carved a fine coat-of-arms of the state of Maine (Plate 244A), privately owned (1949). His style is characterized by boldness and simplicity, as yet without the self-conscious stylization of our own day.

Shop figures and tavern signs: an earlier type of shop figure and tavern sign existed during the eighteenth century and the tradition was continued into the nineteenth. Such shop signs as wood-carved boots and gloves, mortars and pestles, spectacles, razors, clocks, and other forms continued almost to our own day; the striped barber pole is a remnant of this tradition. The eighteenth-century shop sign is represented by a man in uniform (Plate 247B) in a style which for ease and competence is above the usual level of the later cigar-store Indians. The date *1720* on his belt probably refers to the year in which the business, tailor shop or tavern, was established.

A well-known figure (Old State House, Boston), the so-called *Little Admiral* with *1770* on the base, served as a sign for William Williams, a mathematical instrument maker in Boston. The same date appears on an early tobacconist's figure in an eighteenth-century costume for Demuth's Tobacco Shop in Lancaster, Pennsylvania.

A figure in naval uniform (Plate 247C) with a stovepipe hat, holding a sextant (Whaling Museum, New Bedford, Massachusetts), belonged to James Fales's nautical instrument maker's shop, New Bedford. It was made between 1830 and 1870, the period during which the Fales shop is known to have been in business. Carver and place of origin are unknown. Its well-defined style suggests that it belongs to an established, presumably English, tradition and is the work of an experienced carver. Dickens, in *Dombey and Son*, writes of a shop sign which was 'a little ... timber midshipman with an offensively disproportionate piece of machinery'.

Several tavern figures carved in a bold manner with dramatic expression suggest a European tradition. Well known is the *Bacchus* of the Windham, Connecticut, Library, the work of JOHN RUSSELL, an English ship carver who, with his assistants, was held prisoner during the Revolutionary War. The same lusty naturalism pointing to the experienced carver who worked in the English tradition is shown in two tavern busts of a man (Plate 242C) and woman, in the Waters Collection (1936) in Grand Rapids, Michigan. Derived from the Hogarthian tradition, both could have been imported, or carved in this country. Such bold characterization, showing massive features with broad grins bordering on the grotesque, represent a mature art. Wherever such carvings may have been produced culturally they are European in tradition and not the unaided products of the colonies, just as the finest Philadelphia furniture before the Revolution cannot be divorced from the English heritage.

A ship-chandler's figure in the New York State Historical Association belongs to a tradition that existed before the appearance of the cigar-store Indian. Other shop figures of the same tradition had their individual motifs.

An interesting shop sign is one carved in 1835 for a Fairhaven, Massachusetts, slaughterhouse. It represents a man driving a pig, both placed on top of a huge butcher's knife (New Bedford Whaling Museum). A drug store in Salem, Massachusetts, had a bust of *Paracelsus*, the sixteenth-century Swiss physician, in which a classicizing style shows the influence of sculpture. A coachman over two feet high (privately owned, 1938) with extended arms to hold the reins, and dressed in a blue coat, yellow trousers, high boots and a three-cornered hat, may have been an early shop sign. Horses' heads carved in the round were placed over entrances to livery stables, and large wooden horses stood in show windows of saddlers. A figure of a Negro porter carved about 1850 (arm restored) stood for years in the Old Trenton, New Jersey, Hotel. The ingratiating porter about to welcome his guests is vividly expressed in pose and facial expression. A life-size figure of a Negro holding a wooden pestle in a large tin mortar from New Orleans (Louisiana State Museum), of about 1850, is calm in features and quiet in pose, but looks alive. This life-like quality which is usually absent in shop figures is felt in another figure of a Negro. This one belonged to an early-nineteenth-century traveling medicine show that used carved figures representing various ailments. The carving is remarkably vigorous; the figure (New-York Historical Society), freely posed, has his right arm pressed against his forehead to illustrate 'headache'. In its forceful, convincing realism the figure is exceptional and suggests another, in the New York State Historical Association, the so-called *Dancing Negro*. This posture also recalls the bowing and scraping hotel porter.

A figure of *Colonel Sellers*, late-nineteenth century, was suggested by a character in Mark Twain's novel *The Gilded Age*. The strained pose of the raised arm, the doll-like head and emphasis on simplified form is folk art style of the untutored variety. Two shop figures used for display on the counters of tailoring shops are from rural Pennsylvania and are likewise closer to the amateur level. They represent *George Washington* and *Thomas Jefferson* (privately owned) and are about twenty-six inches high.

An early-nineteenth-century sign was made for a Boston hardware dealer by the figurehead carver ISAAC FOWLE. Out of a single semi-circular panel to fit in an arched opening, Fowle carved a collection of carpenter's tools. Saws and planes are skilfully arranged within the available space. Another board-like sign, also belonging to this relief-carved group, shows a sheaf of wheat carved by CLARKE NOBLE around 1900 for a bakery building (Newport, Rhode Island).

Cigar-store Indians: as sailing ships were replaced by steam ships and iron supplanted wood, figureheads disappeared. Some of the figurehead carvers turned to the growing craft of tobacconists' figures. THOMAS W. BROOKS of New York was a ship carver who carved and sold cigar-store Indians for at least thirty-five years. A relation to ship carving is occasionally suggested in a tobacconist figure in its posture with raised head and chunky modeling. As a group, the tobacconist figures appear to be independent of an earlier traditional shop-figure type carried over from the eighteenth century. Though an English custom of using small counter figures preceded the use of the American life-size tobacconist figures, the latter bear no stylistic relation to the English counter figures.

The man credited with having introduced tobacconist figures into New York after 1850 was named CHICHESTER. Today cigar-store figures have disappeared from our sidewalks, but many are still in existence, owned by dealers, collectors, or by descendants of the original owners. In 1937, five hundred and eighty-five were counted in forty-two states. Of the carvers, few names are known; but occasionally a figure is known to have been carved by a professional sculptor, like HERMAN MATZEN of Cleveland or JULIUS THEODORE MELCHERS of Detroit, who carved the figure of a Scot (about 1868) for Tom Dick's saloon in Detroit. The figure was owned (1937) by the St Andrew's Society of Detroit. S. A. ROBB of New York, who after nearly twenty-six years of activity was still in business in the city toward the end of the last century, is believed to have had some art school training. HERMAN KRUSKE is reported to have carved the Indian, *Sitting Bull,* for Bob Parson's tobacco shop in Ashland, Wisconsin, and CASPARI opened a workshop in Baltimore in 1864 according to Kate Sanborn's *Hunting Indians in a Taxicab.*

With exceptions, cigar-store figure carving was a business geared to mass production. In place of a master craftsman taking commissions for individual figureheads, the owner of the business hired carvers to produce figures for sale. The cigar-store Indian carving was divided among half a dozen firms which are said to have produced from two hundred to three hundred wooden Indians a year. When eventually an old figure was replaced by a new one, the old figure might be repaired, repainted, and sold.

The life-size cigar-store Indian (Plate 245B) suggests the hand of the less skilled artisan; repetitions of a few typical poses are characteristic, but occasionally we see academic influences, particularly from well-known classic sculpture. This influence resulted in freer movement and a more individual style in the exceptional figure. In the usual cigar-store Indians there are perhaps half a dozen standard postures; the simplest of these consists of a flat profile sawed out of a thick board. In the fully-developed figure the right arm may be raised to the forehead in Indian salute. Extended arms were carved separately and doweled in. There was no intention to imitate the Indian of the plains in realistic fashion, either in dress or physiognomy. Cigar-store Indians were white man's creations, excepting those instances where a specific Indian chief was carved in a portrait-like manner.

Cigar-store Indians, as an art form, have received little attention. Though, as a group, they offer less variety than figureheads, there are nevertheless differences as to artistic quality. Collectors today, judging from the recent sale of the Haffenreffer Collection (April 1956), compete for rarity.

Four groups of tobacconists' figures may be distinguished: Chiefs; Squaws or figures of Pocahontas; Blackamoors or Pompeys; and White Men. This last group includes historical figures, like *Sir Walter Raleigh, Uncle Sam,* the *Policeman,* the *Scottish Highlander* in kilts (snuff), the *Turk* with turban, baggy trousers and a long pipe (Turkish tobacco) and a silk-robed Chinese figure (tea stores).

The group of White Men appears to have been the work of better trained carvers. The before-mentioned Julius Melchers probably carved also a *Sir Walter Raleigh* similar in style to his *Scot*. A relationship to England is indicated in the case of a figure of *Punch*, now in the Bucks County Historical Society (Doylestown, Pennsylvania). This figure, fifty-four inches high, is reported to have been brought from England in 1857. Others of the same type were presumably carved in the United States. Such figures as *Mr Pickwick* (Buffalo Historical Society) (Plate 246B), *Dude* and *Man of Fashion* indicate a search for novelty to attract business. Though postures are free and each figure is individualized, with all their ease and competence, the White Men are also advertising dummies.

Circus and carrousel carvings: a third category of figures, carved in relief as well as in the round, consists of decorations for circus wagons. The trap-wagons, used to carry the equipment, were disguised and enriched through carved, gilded or painted figures. Comparatively few circus carvings are known today, perhaps because the wagons were eventually abandoned and allowed to disintegrate. The circus equipment was periodically reconditioned, and old figures put to new uses. What circus carvings remain go back to the late-nineteenth century and reflect the eclectic character of American academic art of the period.

Circus carving does not stand out as a unit with a character of its own, as is the case with ship carving and shop figures. The carver appears to have worked from blueprints furnished him by a designer, who in turn depended upon available pictorial material. In one instance the inspiration might have come from Greek sculpture, and in another from the medieval or Renaissance period. For dragons carved in the round on top of a circus wagon inscribed *The Age of Chivalry*, Mantegna's engravings were used. A lion carved in the round is based on a study of lions in illustrations or of real lions in the zoological garden (Plate 248B). American circus carving appeared late in history; unlike European folk art, it was not limited to a few

traditional types that were repeated generation after generation. Existing examples are found in a few private and public collections and are reflected in the *Index of American Design*.

Figures and carved scrolls were applied to the sides of the wagon, in the round and in relief. Even the small number of figures available for study present several styles. One group, carved perhaps by SAMUEL ROBB, who worked for the Sebastian Wagon Company of New York, presents a decorative style of its own (collection of William Warren, Litchfield, Connecticut). In a figure with a lyre (Plate 243B) drapery motifs are adjusted to each other, but not to bodily structure. In spite of a lack of correct anatomy, the total effect is attractive. In one figure the pose may be an adaptation of the *Wounded Amazon* type of Greek sculpture. From the point of view of academic art such carving may look like haphazard, slovenly work. Seen through the spectacles of contemporary art these arms and legs, so out of joint, look like forerunners of modernism, but individual passages are consistent and can be enjoyed.

Closely related to circus carvings were carrousel carvings. Dancers and musicians were carved as free-standing figures to occupy a place in front of the carrousel's steam organ or calliope. The carrousel animals are of European ancestry; English carrousel horses are not very different from those made in this country, where the carrousel with rotating platform originated in North Tonowanda, New York, in 1879. Carrousel horses with their elaborate trappings adhere to the ornate pageantry of the Renaissance. Circus carvings were made in Abilene, Kansas, around 1890 by the Parker Carnival Supply Company; others were made in New York, Chicago, Milwaukee, and perhaps elsewhere. Names of carvers are usually unknown, though certain carrousel animals from the period of 1880–88 have been attributed to a CHARLES LOUFF and related to Riverside, Rhode Island, a site once occupied by a late-nineteenth-century amusement park. Louff's horses are vigorous; they show lively postures with a good deal of movement in the carving of the mane, the placing of the feet and the elaboration of the trappings. The Louff type of carrousel horse represents a developed style, but there are variations that are less extravagant and even primitive. Carrousels experimented with goats, deer, tigers, bears, panthers, pigs, giraffes, and even dogs; but these animals never became popular, and the carvers returned to the horse, which has continued the favorite to our own day.

Puppets and marionettes: puppets and marionettes represent another group of wood carving. Puppets are worked over the hand, glove-like; marionettes are suspended from strings attached to the operator's fingers. The heads were carved of wood, painted and dressed like dolls. Puppetry is world-wide, and the American variety carried on English and Continental traditions. A few collections have become known, particularly those made (after 1825) by the several members of the LANO family, who were originally from Milan, Italy; by JOHN DIFENDERFER, and by MEADER of San Francisco (around 1880). Each puppet or marionette head is caricatured according to the type of character used in slapstick comedies, like *Punch* and his wife *Judy*, his sweetheart *Sally*, and others. Facial expression is accentuated by paint. *Punch* has a hooked nose, *Judy* a broad grin, and DIFENDERFER'S *Policeman* of the period 1888–90 looks like Charlie Chaplin. A novel American contribution was introduced in the puppet of the well-known Indian, *Rain-in-the-Face*.

Butter molds: the greatest variety of wood carvings is to be found in household articles and small carvings related to the home. Carvings in intaglio include butter molds and molds for marzipan boards, molds used by tailors for the steaming of cloth, and occasionally stamps used for burlap bags for grain, as well as relief-carved maple sugar molds.

Butter molds, known in England and on the continent of Europe, were turned out on a lathe, knob and carved disc in one piece (Bucks County Historical Society, Doylestown, Pennsylvania). Circular bell-shaped covers (plunger type) used to cut and shape the butter have occasionally been preserved. The bell-shaped 'skirt' represents the mold.

The design which printed the butter was also carved on a separate disc or stamp, to which a handle was attached which worked plunger-like within the 'skirt'. The flat or slightly concave disc was chip-carved with a symmetrical and compact design of tulips, hearts, cows and other motifs (Pennsylvania-German type), or with floral and animal motifs in a more open style (New England type). The former point to a German Swiss, the latter to an English, origin. Some of these butter stamps may have been originally combined with a skirt, and were a part of the plunger type.

In a box-mold type the mold consists of a box with hinged sides so that it could be opened. The design was carved on a removable bottom. There are even hollow cylinder molds made from six strips of wood fastened together so that they could be opened and cleaned. The inside was hexagonal and removable stamps were fitted into each end. This mold produced a six-sided column six inches high with designs impressed on the ends. These various types have been published by Peter Larsen.

Marzipan boards: marzipan molds are rectangular intaglio-carved mahogany boards, from fourteen to thirty inches long. They were used for large cakes baked for special celebrations or in memory of historical events; Lafayette's visit to this country in 1824 and the defeat of Cornwallis in 1781 are examples. Lafayette is shown on horseback, surrounded by an inscription and an ornamental wreath and with ivy sprays and roses. According to an incised inscription this board was carved in 1824 by H. F. COX. Cake and cookie molds are known in European countries, and no doubt these American molds are a continuation of the European practice. For excellence in design and craftsmanship the marzipan molds are of the best. They are known from a collection in the New-York Historical Society.

In certain types of German cookie molds (*springerle* boards), the German style was continued practically unchanged. CARL LINNS was a Missouri carver of such molds, around 1835. He was also a school teacher, farmer and bed- and spinning-wheel maker.

Schimmel eagles: carvings in the round include Pennsylvania-German eagles and other birds, toys, dolls, pipe-heads, walking-sticks, chains and 'balls-in-a-cage', decoys, also weathervanes and whirligigs. They were carved by amateurs and professionals, some by local carvers, others by sailors and migratory workers. WILLIAM SCHIMMEL (around 1865) and AARON MOUNTS are well-known Pennsylvania wood carvers of eagles, squirrels, owls, dogs, and perhaps other animals. Schimmel eagles with detachable wings, painted black and touched up with yellow, are represented in the American Wing of the Metropolitan Museum of Art, in the New-York Historical Society, in the Winterthur Museum, Delaware, Sturbridge Village, Massachusetts (Plate 247A), and elsewhere. Schimmel is also said to have carved smaller parrots and roosters on which he painted the feathers. Schimmel's impetuous style is individual, and his eagles differ in style from the nautical eagles of the ship carvers or the official eagles derived from the design of the Great Seal. Schimmel seems to have been a migratory worker by choice, unlike the European journeyman who sought employment in different shops until he could settle down as a master in his own right. His pupil, Aaron Mounts, also carved eagles and other types like owls and dogs, in a more meticulous style. There were other wood carvers among the Pennsylvania Germans. Frances Lichten has called attention to NOAH WEIS (1842–1907), an innkeeper and wood carver of Lehigh County.

Toys: home-made hobby-horses were carved out of solid wood with legs made separately and attached. Small toy horses on platforms with wheels were made commercially, but others of a Pennsylvania-German type have a less professional, folk art look, and were probably made by wood carvers as a hobby.

Dolls of various types have found favor with collectors and some dolls were carved of wood. An early example, about thirteen inches high, in the Philadelphia Museum of Art, shows a little girl in hoop skirt and tight bodice. She was carved in 1776 in Philadelphia. A heavy bulky style suggests the ship carver was used to working in a large scale, and may have been intended as an ornament for the mantel rather than a doll to play with. According to tradition, this figure was carved for Sarah Horn when she was seven years old.

Wooden dolls were carved regionally, as in New England and the Southern Highlands; others achieved a general vogue and were carved in many places. A primitive type of doll with a wooden head and kid hands may go back to colonial days, and is believed to be from the mountains of western Virginia. The round head shows a minimum of detail, a peg nose in a head that otherwise depends on painting and a cloth dress.

A group of Swiss settlers in New Hampshire carved dolls about six to twelve inches high in solid pine. They were not painted, but were left in the natural wood. These New Hampshire dolls are carved from head to foot (Plate 245A). Dress, shoes and costumes are carved in the wood, and hands and features are individually expressed; no special emphasis is given the head. The carving is a little wooden figure, fully rounded, as only a trained wood carver would attempt. The forms are simplified; realism is modified by an insistence on near-cylindrical and spherical volumes.

There are other more individually conceived dolls like two named *Emma* and *Jim* which JAMES RICH of Bedford, Ohio, carved for his daughter in 1859. They conform to the type that emphasizes the head and allows the dress to conceal the body. In contrast to this type carved by a father for his children is the so-called 'Dutch' doll or 'penny wooden'. It came originally from Germany and Switzerland, but was imitated in the United States and exists in many examples. 'Penny woodens' are jointed dolls, arms and legs are pegs. They are made movable by having wood joints which connect arms and legs to a torso and head carved in one piece. The egg-shaped head has a peg nose and painted hair and features. 'Penny woodens' are still being made today.

Small carvings: the carving of 'chains' and 'balls-in-a-cage' is known in various countries, including the United States. Pipe-heads and walking-sticks continue European or native western traditions and at times are traceable to inmates of prisons. An eighteenth-century German type of vase, called *Maikrüge*, may have furnished inspiration for a few decorative carvings from Utah. A South German (Swabian) naturalistic style became stylized in these unpainted wood-carved flowers fitted into stone vases (1899). Wooden birds, often left in the natural wood, are linked to the interest of the naturalist, and were produced by specialists. They are being carved for collectors today. A Pennsylvania type of ornamental bird was painted.

Decoys and weathervanes: the carving of decoys and wild fowl, ducks (Plate 246A), geese and other water-birds out of solid blocks of wood, goes back to the colonial period and reached its maturity at the time of the Civil War. Decoys (New York State Historical Association) were painted and set with glass eyes; at times the heads were carved separately. They are still available for collectors. A flat stick-up type shows the profile only. The bird is attached to a stick which is stuck in the grassy marsh to attract the wild fowl.

Roosters, horses (Plate 248A), and cows were favored by weathervane carvers, but they also carved more unusual subjects such as serpents, dragons, grasshoppers and fish. This variety appears to have been an indigenous American development which was continued in metal weathervanes. The usual type of wooden weathervane sawed out of a board is to be differentiated from the more elegantly carved weathervane that served as a pattern for a metal vane. Examples of this type, a cow, and a figure of *Columbia* holding a flag, are in the New York State Historical Association.

Whirligigs from two to over four feet high come from Pennsylvania. They are figures with paddle-like arms that rotate with the wind, a revolving rod being set through arms and shoulders. The cylindrical figure is slightly shaped to differentiate the coat-tailed upper part from the legs fitted with knee-high boots. A uniform is indicated largely by painting. Whirligigs as toys have an old European ancestry, to which these Pennsylvania-made examples may also be linked.

Religious carvings: the regions important for religious wood carving, particularly in the southwestern states, are those once held by Catholic France and Spain. The southwest may be divided into two parts: New Mexico (including Arizona) with a background of two and a half centuries of Spanish-Mexican rule; and California, where white settlement did not begin until 1769. In California wood carving is largely confined to church furnishings. (*See section, Arts of the South-west*, page 518, by E. Boyd.)

New Mexico has produced the largest number of wood-carved saints or *bultos*, dating back as early as 1750. The early religious carvings, *santos*, were made by priests; they show lively gestures and expressive features. As the native craftsman became independent during the early decades of the nineteenth century he developed a folk art or *santero* style of his own which, however, perpetuated a Mediterranean tradition. These statuettes of patron saints, usually under two feet high, are serious and dignified with an emphasis on simplicity. They are in private and museum collections in Santa Fe, Denver, Colorado Springs, and elsewhere. The *bultos* are carved of cottonwood and painted in tempera over a gesso ground. The upper part of a *bulto* may be solid and the lower part made up of a hollow framework of an armature of sticks covered with cloth dipped in gesso and painted.

The stylistic analysis of the *bultos* has progressed in recent years, particularly at Santa Fe, New Mexico, through the research of E. Boyd. Several groups with common characteristics have been identified, each group perhaps representing the work of one *santero*. Santa Cruz is believed to be a point of origin for a type of tall, lean figure. Another group is related to a *santero*, MIGUEL ARAGON, and to an unidentified carver who sought expression in the head. A 'classic' *santero* type, with delicately carved features and hands, has been differentiated from a more provincial type found in Mora and western Miguel counties. The latter is characterized by stylization and fine black dots on the painted eyebrows and lashes, and small hoof-like feet or boots. A special group of nearly life-size figures was related to the rites of the Brotherhood of Penitents, members of which re-enacted the Passion of Christ as an act of penance during Holy Week. The figures include *Death with Bow and Arrow Seated on a Cart* and *Christ Crucified and Entombed*.

A different type of wood carving of nearly life-size figures shows the influence of French Canada. Examples (mostly privately owned) have been found in Illinois and Wisconsin. A *Virgin and Child* from Sullivan, Wisconsin, shows a Gothic element in the posture and the backward tilt of the figure. Another *Virgin Mary*, under three feet high, carved out of a heavy plank over a foot wide in the manner of a relief, is attributed to an Irish barber, JOHN BEREMAN, also of Sullivan. A figure of *St Joseph*, about four feet high and seven inches thick, shows a slight backward tilt due to the contour of the board. This figure has also been related to Sullivan; the date is uncertain.

Valuation of wood carvings in terms of dollars and cents is determined by scarcity and by collectors' preferences, as is true of other collectables. The student or collector desiring further information on American wood carving will find it in the files of the magazine *Antiques* and the bibliography of *Early American Wood Carving*, by the author (World Publishing Company, 1952). This book also gives the *Index of American Design* numbers of all wood carvings mentioned, but not included among the sixty-three illustrations, and lists the approximate numbers and kinds of wood carvings owned by twenty-nine museums in fifteen states. The renderings of the Index of American Design at the National Gallery of Art include a representative collection of wood carvings.

BOOKS FOR
FURTHER READING

BARBER, JOEL D.: *Wild Fowl Decoys*, Windward House (1934).

BOYD, E.: *Saints and Saint Makers*, Laboratory of Anthropology, Santa Fe, New Mexico (1946).

CAHILL, HOLGER: 'American Folk Sculpture' in *Newark Museum Catalog* (October 1931–January 1932).

CHRISTENSEN, ERWIN O.: *Popular Art in the United States*, Penguin Books, London (1948).

CHRISTENSEN, ERWIN O.: *The Index of American Design*, The Macmillan Company, New York (1950).

FLOWER, MILTON E.: 'Schimmel the Woodcarver' in *Antiques* (October 1943).

IIYNSON, GARRET, AND NASH, SUSAN HIGGINSON: 'Design in Yankee Butter Molds' in *Antiques* (February 1942).

KIMBALL, FISKE: *Mr. Samuel McIntire, Carver, the Architect of Salem.* The Southworth Anthoesen Press, Portland, Me. (1940).

LICHTEN, FRANCES: *Folk Art of Rural Pennsylvania*, Charles Scribner's Sons, New York (1946).

LIPMAN, JEAN: *American Folk Art in Wood, Metal and Stone*, Pantheon, New York (1948).

MARCEAU, HENRI: 'William Rush' in *Philadelphia Museum Catalog* (1937).

MORRISON, J. L.: 'Passing of the Wooden Indian' in *Scribners Magazine* (October 1928).

PINKNEY, PAULINE A.: *American Figureheads and Their Carvers*, W. W. Norton & Company, New York (1940).

SANBORN, KATE: *Hunting Indians in a Taxicab*, Gorham Press, Boston (1911).

STAFFORD, VICTOR: 'John Haley Bellamy' in *Antiques* (March 1935).

SWAN, MABEL M.: articles in *Antiques* (December 1931, March 1948). 'What is American Folk Art? A Symposium' in *Antiques* (May 1950).

WILDER, MITCHELL A., AND BREITENBACH, EDGAR: *Santos, The Religious Folk Art of New Mexico*, The Taylor Museum, Colorado Springs Fine Arts Center, Colorado (1943).

Voltaire by Samuel McIntire, 1757–1811. Ht 15½ ins. *American Antiquarian Society, Worcester, Massachusetts. (Index of American Design.)* (The word *Index* with the following illustrations indicates renderings by the artists of the Index of American Design, National Gallery of Art, Washington, D.C.)

PLATE 241

(A) Ceres, by Simeon Skillin, 1756–1806. Ht 24 ins. *New York State Historical Association, Cooperstown, New York.*

(B) Head of a Boy, dated 1845, by Alexander Ames. *New York State Historical Association, Cooperstown, New York.*

(C) Tavern Bust. Ht 19 ins. *Coll. of Mrs Dudley E. Waters, 1936 (Index).*

(D) Ship Figurehead; about 1825. Ht 27½ ins. *Abby Aldrich Rockefeller Folk Art collection, Williamsburg, Virginia.*

PLATE 242

MUSE WITH A LYRE

(A) Figurehead of Ship *Cassandra Adams*, built 1876; from Port Townsend, Washington. *Private collection*, 1937 (*Index*).

(B) From a Barnum & Bailey Circus Wagon; designed by Sebastian Wagon Co., New York. Ht. 48½ ins, *c.* 1880. *Coll. of Warren L. Warren* (*Index*).

PLATE 243

(A) State of Maine Seal, by Edbury Hatch. *Private collection (Index).*

(B) Eagle, by John Haley Bellamy, 1836–1914. W. 18 ins (*Index*).

PLATE 244

(A) Doll; cut from pine; Swiss in New Hampshire; *c.* 1790. Ht 12 ins. *South County Museum, North Kingston, Rhode Island (Index).*

(C) Seated Woman, *c.* 1875. Ht 12 ins. *Abby Aldrich Rocke-feller Folk Art collection, Williams-burg, Virginia (Index).*

(B) Cigar store Indian Chief. Ht 5 ft 11 ins. *Formerly Waters and Haffenreffer collections (Index).*

PLATE 245

(A) Decoy Duck. L. 12¾ ins. Nineteenth century (*Index*).

(B) Mr Pickwick. Cigar Store Figure. Ht 6 ft 2 ins, inc. base. *Buffalo Historical Society* (*Index*).

(C) Negro Mascot. Union Army collection. *Capt. B. J. Carragher, City Art Museum. St Louis, Missouri.*

PLATE 246

(A) Eagle by William Schim-
mel, *fl.* 1860–90. Ht 13 ins. *Old
Sturbridge   Village,   Sturbridge,
Massachusetts (Index).*

(B) Shop or Tavern Figure.
After 1720. Ht 20 ins. *Private
collection, 1938 (Index).*

(C) Navigator. Shop Sign of James
Fales. *Old Dartmouth Historical
Society Whaling Museum, New Bed-
ford, Massachusetts (Index).*

PLATE 247

(A) Weathervane; wood. Nineteenth century. *Private collection*, 1939 (*Index*).

(B) Lion; circus figure. Nineteenth century (*Index*).

PLATE 248

(A) Painted chest, 1786, with sunken panels separated by channeled pilasters; stippled framework. Chests of this type were made by cabinetmakers, not carpenters. *Coll. of Florence Maine.*

(B) Dower chest, 1788, decorated and signed by Christian Seltzer and Johann Rank. *Reading Public Museum and Art Gallery.*

PLATE 249

(A) Birth Certificate; for Margaret Yerger, *b.* 1810, West Hanover Township, Dauphin Co.; in pen and wash. *Coll. of Ross Trump.*

(B) *Fractur* dated February 19, 1799; a pious admonition to a child. *Coll. of Arthur J. Sussel.*

PLATE 250

(A) Birth and baptismal certificate, 1855;
characteristic of Francis Portzline of Union
Co., d. 1858. *Coll. of Henry S. Borneman, The
Free Library of Philadelphia.*

(B) Hasp for Conestoga Wagon Tool-box;
eighteenth century. *Coll. of Titus Geesey,
Philadelphia Museum of Art.*

(C) Buttermolds carved with tulip, heart,
eagle and six-pointed stars. *Coll. of Titus
Geesey, Philadelphia Museum of Art.*

PLATE 251

(A) Painted salt box, made for Anne Leterman, signed 'John Drissell his hand May 22nd 1797'. *Index of American Design.*

(B) Wardrobe (*Scl.rank*), 1794, inscribed 'Martin Wisenhauer'; painted blue, red and ivory with some areas stippled. *Philadelphia Museum of Art.*

(C) Hooked rug with border of hearts and birds. *Coll. of Norman Smith.*

PLATE 252

(A) Appliquéd bedspread with tulip, eagle and heart motifs; nineteenth century. *Coll. of Titus Geesey, Philadelphia Museum of Art.*

(B) Slipware: twin covered pots, an unusual form. *Coll. of Titus Geesey, Philadelphia Museum of Art.*

PLATE 253

(A) Appliquéd quilt in red, orange and green; Lancaster Co. *Coll. of Ross Trump.*

(B) Wool-on-wool rug; bright polychrome on black ground, *c.* 1860; pattern taken from a dower chest. *Coll. of Norman Smith.*

PLATE 254

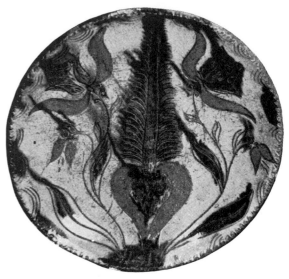

(A) Sgraffito earthenware plate, religious symbols in unusual design. *Bucks County Historical Society, Doylestown, Pennsylvania.*

(B) Sgraffito; marked 'JR' probably for John Richline who worked with Henry Roudebush. *Pennsylvania Historical and Museum Commission.*

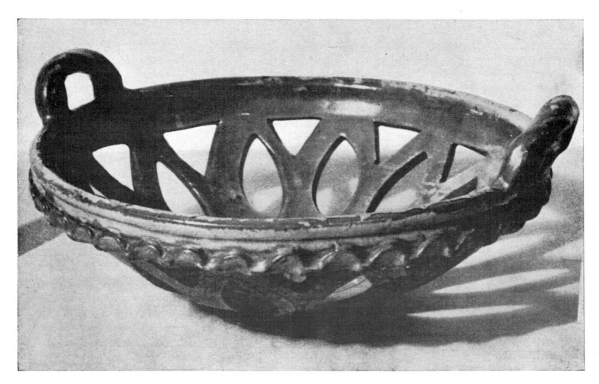

(c) Pierced red earthenware bowl with thumb-print border and rope-twist handles. *Philadelphia Museum of Art.*

PLATE 255

Sgraffito plate signed 'HR 1804'; probably Henry Roudebush; execution characteristic but forms unusual.
Coll. of Arthur J. Sussel.

PLATE 256

PENNSYLVANIA-GERMAN
FOLK ART

By FRANCES LICHTEN

THE early colonists in Pennsylvania were more fortunate than most pioneers in establishing themselves. Pennsylvania provided so fertile a soil, both for physical as well as spiritual needs that, when certain groups of Rhineland Germans and Swiss, harassed by war and persecution, emigrated to the land granted to William Penn by Charles I, they could carry on the ways of their forefathers in an almost identical fashion. After the original colony was established in Germantown in 1683, wave after wave of settlers entered the port of Philadelphia until the time of the American Revolution.

Hard-working, peace-loving, thrifty and pious, these folk and their descendants are known to the scholar as Pennsylvania Germans, though they refer to themselves as 'Pennsylvania Dutch', *Dutch* being a corruption of *Deutsch* or German. While their first contributions to American life were chiefly agricultural, these newcomers also developed a genuine folk art unique in America.

As pioneers they were especially fortunate, for they had taken land in a region which provided them with all the basic elements necessary to life. Field stone for building and clay for roof tiles and earthenware utensils were at hand. Iron lay just below the surface of the earth, waiting to be turned into nails, hardware, cooking pots and stoves. Wood for fuel and furniture was almost too abundant. Flax, hemp and wool for clothing were raised as field after field was hacked out of the omnipresent woodland, the woodland after which Pennsylvania (Penn's Woods) was named.

As they knew no language but their own, a Rhenish dialect, for mutual convenience the German immigrants set up their own communities. Thus isolated by a language barrier from the English, for Pennsylvania was governed by English laws and customs, they could pursue their own way of life – a way which was markedly different from that of the neighboring Quakers and one noted by every traveler. In the 1780s a visiting German naturalist remarked: 'These country towns have for the most part quite the look of our German market towns; the houses, according to the taste of the inmates, are painted divers colors, and the interior arrangement is very like the German, for most of the inhabitants are German.'

In European rural districts throughout the decades the art of the folk underwent modifications; the country craftsman, living in a village as did all peasants, could not remain wholly untouched by the dictates of fashion, with the result that in the eighteenth century his ornamented pieces, even in the simple forms ordered by his rustic patrons, reflected the prevailing taste for the baroque. During the same period in German Pennsylvania the artisan was so isolated by existing circumstances that no trace of fashion ever filtered in to alter his traditional conceptions of what constituted decoration. Indeed, until after 1750, he made no use of his ideas, for he had found no time earlier to devote himself to the finer aspects of his craft. But from then on, and for about the next one hundred years, from his hands came those distinctive pieces which have given him his place in the history of American decorative arts.

The finest work seems to have been produced in the decades immediately following

612

the Revolution, a period when the Pennsylvania farmer was well-to-do and could place orders for the best with the various craftsmen. Each of the latter, summoning up his memories of the most ornamental phases of his craft, began to adapt them to pieces made for dowries, or for gifts. Perhaps the image in the craftsman's mind was slightly blurred, so that the decoration he placed on dower chest or earthenware platter was not quite so surely executed as was the prototype. Perhaps he translated a motif formerly carved on an oaken chest into a like form executed with paint on one of pine. Perhaps, if a worker in metal, he had to use tin instead of pewter. Such changes were primarily the outcome of lack of actual contact with European models, for the settlers, arriving on small over-crowded ships, brought with them only tools and household necessities of the most practical nature. Other differences can be attributed to insufficient skill or lack of particular tools. The pressure of life, too, also accounted for the non-use of certain techniques. In Pennsylvania-German household gear we will not find the elaborately carved cheese presses or milkpails on which the European peasant lavished his skill, for carving is an occupation which requires leisure.

Unlike the formally trained artist who uses his talent to picture his environment, the folk artist expresses himself in ornament which he applies to articles of daily use. He is artistically sound only when he closely follows tradition, and, since he adheres to motifs which his forbears have used for centuries, his decoration has an ageless quality. Although the motifs found in the Pennsylvania-German folk arts bear a casual resemblance to those of other countries, there is a certain individuality imparted to them by the manner in which they are presented. This factor might be said to be an artless approach to the problems of design, and a primitiveness in execution.

The motifs used in decoration were practically standardized, and all types of craftsmen dipped into this well of traditional patterns. On birth and baptismal certificates (Plates 250, 251A), on house blessings, on dower chests (Plates 249A, 249B), ceramics, butter-

molds (Plate 251C) and stove-plates, the same devices are discovered. They appear, too, carved on tombstones and painted on barns, the latter decorations restricted to certain geometrical forms. Woven into the folk artist's balanced arrangements are stylized tulips and other floral forms, the tree of life, confrontal and solitary birds, doves, urns, parrots, peacocks, hearts unadorned and hearts with tulips springing from the cleft, and endless variations of six-pointed and other geometrically divided star forms. In addition to these, the decorator's stock-in-trade included heraldic devices such as the crown, and lion and unicorn; medieval symbols such as the cock, mermaid, stag, pelican, fish, and double-headed eagle.

Beyond an occasional angel and winged cherub head, however, there are none of the religious symbols commonly used by European Catholic folk artists. These immigrants were Protestants of various denominations, among whom were certain groups – members of pietistic sects – who had revolted against the established church. Led by mystics, they hoped to find a spiritual rebirth in this land of Penn's 'Holy Experiment'. Examination of the text of their hymnals provides some reason to believe that the motifs preferred by the pietists were symbols capable of a mystical interpretation.

Custom dictated that the dowry of the peasant maiden comprise certain articles and pieces of furniture; these included wardrobe (Plate 252B), chest, table, bed, with a stated number of quilts and household linens spun and woven by the bride. Such were the foundation pieces of country housekeeping, and decorated pieces that have survived to this day are greatly sought.

The elaborately painted chests (Plates 249A, 249B) of the Pennsylvania Germans are noteworthy examples of folk art, differing only from their European prototypes in being simplifications in construction and detail. Since the local artisan painted with no guide but memory, and was often less trained than his fellow craftsman overseas, his work had a certain crude but charming individuality.

Although the rural decorators for the most

part remained anonymous, nevertheless the work of different persons can be distinguished through the craftsman's own treatment of space and form and his preference for certain motifs. Although the maker's signature was omitted, that of the owner was frequently given great prominence; in fact, its placement on chests was important to the decorative scheme. Dower chests were marked with the owner's name or initials and the date in Roman characters. The amount of decoration on chests varied. Besides the usual ornamental front panels, the more elaborate carried panels on the ends and top. The surface surrounding the panels was often enriched with mottled or stippled texturing, a peasant technique which was also employed on other painted pieces such as wardrobes and cupboards.

The favorite background color for chests was a medium blue, but dark green, brown, and black were also used. A bright contrasting color on the moldings added liveliness to the gayety already achieved by the boldly painted decorations in the panels on which comparatively few colors were used to give the effect. These cheerful painted pieces probably provided the only touch of color and beauty in the farmhouses of the time, and then only in well-to-do establishments. The less affluent restricted themselves to one pigment – barn red – which they daubed over all their few possessions.

While most Pennsylvania-German pieces continued to be made of familiar woods and along accustomed Germanic lines, an occasional cabinetmaker working for a substantial client would adopt ideas from the furniture of his English fellow-craftsmen. But it must be admitted that he adhered to these alien ideas none too slavishly, for he produced some piquant results in the process of grafting motifs from late-eighteenth-century English culture on to those of his own.

All through the handcraft era the settler depended on the potter – an indispensable craftsman in every community – to furnish him with earthenware utensils (Plate 253B). These were made of the local red clay which was covered with transparent lead glaze. From his skilled hands came all the ceramic pieces any household needed: bowls, milk

pans, dishes, pots, jugs, crocks, lamps, candlesticks, even toys. For everyday use this redware bore no ornament except a few wavy yellow lines or incised markings. When the potter wished to demonstrate his abilities, he turned to ornamental pieces, using techniques learned in the Rhine Valley where the vogue for decorated earthenware was at its height in the seventeenth and eighteenth centuries. Although redware of a rather plain variety was produced elsewhere in colonial America, the Pennsylvania-German potters turned out the finest examples of ceramics in the folk tradition (Plates 255A, 255B and 255C).

Salt-glaze stoneware, a much harder pottery made from a fine-textured gray clay, eventually supplanted the frangible redware. Since it was used chiefly for food containers, little attempt was made to adorn its pebbly gray surface except with small decorations dashed on with cobalt. For a long period in the nineteenth century, stoneware was turned out by many potteries in the eastern United States and, despite the onslaught of the Industrial Age, a certain amount retained a modicum of the folk art quality.

In every group assembled for colonizing the blacksmith was a vital unit, for the settlers looked to this skilled craftsman to supply them with all the tools and implements which had to be wrought of iron. And since ductility was a characteristic of red-hot iron, even the most utilitarian of articles frequently left the anvils with a slight touch of ornament – a graceful tip to the end of a kitchen implement or a crude tulip on the piece intended for a gift. Hardware (Plate 251B), hinges for chests, cupboards and doors were often finished with more scrollery than was necessary, a pleasant gesture on the part of the busy smith toward the high ornamental standards set for his craft by his overseas predecessors.

In the section of Pennsylvania first settled the manufacture of iron was one of the chief industries. The first forge began operating in 1716, and in 1728 the English ironmasters manufactured the first cast-iron heating stove in America. Known as a 'Dutch stove', this was a simple iron box made to fill a demand of the Pennsylvania Germans who were accustomed to such stoves in their homelands.

Though the English settlers disdained them and remained faithful to the fireplace, these unique box stoves never failed to attract the attention of early travelers because of their practicality. (*See* Period Stoves, Vol. 1, by Josephine H. Peirce, page 122.)

During the time America still held colonial status tinware was a rarity. The little used here was imported from England, who saw to it, by means of restrictive laws, that it was cheaper to buy the finished article than to manufacture it here. Lacquered tin canisters, teapots, and tea caddies were made to catch the eye of the country housewife. Recently, antique dealers, finding pieces of this gay ware in Pennsylvania cupboards, concluded that it had been made locally and called it 'Pennsylvania Dutch', a claim difficult to support since the motifs as well as the techniques suggest those of New England and New York. In the nineteenth century, when tin became cheaper, a few local tinsmiths did produce tinware that was unmistakably their own, both in motif and technique. As usual, they reverted to old European methods of ornamenting, such as wriggled or pierced work, as well as their own punched work.

One of the outstanding forms of artistic expression among the Pennsylvania Germans was *Frakturschriften* (Plates 250A, 250B and 251A), the last notable practice of medieval manuscript writing and illumination. By the time of the migrations from Europe printing had already supplanted the art of the calligrapher, except among those simple folk who clung firmly to ancestral custom. Among such persons the calligrapher still found employment. Since German law demanded that vital statistics be recorded, it was general practice to have data concerning birth (Plates 250A, 251B), baptism and marriage inscribed on documents in a species of freely drawn Gothic lettering known as fractur. Such papers, being memorials of important religious events, were enhanced with as much embellishment as the abilities of the scribe allowed. In Pennsylvania the Germanic settlers followed this observance without change, and developed what had been a moribund tradition into something vigorous and undoubtedly decorative. Indeed, the transplanting of this medieval art to virgin soil prolonged its existence, for it managed to survive (though in gradually weakened forms) concurrently with the products of the printing press until the twentieth century.

The feminine contribution to local folk art consisted of practical forms of needlework: quilts (Plates 253A, 254A), hooked rugs (Plates 252C, 254B), and a few types of household linen, such as the show-towel. In quilt-making, a field of needlework shared by most nineteenth-century women, none surpassed the Pennsylvania Germans in boldness of design. And, since they were not controlled by standards of taste held elsewhere, they pleased themselves and selected color combinations so unorthodox that they shocked those of conventional taste.

The hooked rug never assumed the importance here that it did in other sections of the Atlantic seaboard. Neither large nor formal in design, it was completely free of French or English inspiration. Existing specimens display farm animals and time-honored ornament mingling in great informality.

About 1850 the handcraft era was extinguished everywhere by the surge of the Industrial Age, but before its final expiration the folk art spirit had one last expression. This manifested itself in the form of enormous circular decorations painted on the walls of the huge barns which dominated every farm. Before the middle of the nineteenth century such buildings were left unpainted. But when paint became less costly even the thriftiest of farmers covered these great structures with Venetian red, and then could not resist the urge to decorate this inviting flat surface – an urge which resulted in a varying number of compass-drawn ornaments colored in white, black, red, yellow and green. To this day in certain counties one can still see many of these strikingly decorated barns, a charming custom maintained in the modern age to gratify what vestiges remain of the folk art spirit in Pennsylvania.

GLOSSARY

Amish: *see* Pietistic sects.

Bag stamp: ornamentally carved wooden

block used to mark owner's name on grain sacks for identification at the mill.

Bandbox: *see* Bride box.

Barn: *see* Swiss bank barns.

Barn decorations (so-called hex signs): large, geometrically-divided circular ornaments painted on barn in numbers from two to seven. The term *hex sign* (*hex* meaning witch) is today discredited, though popular belief once had it that the colorful circles were supposed to protect barn and stock from the machinations of witches. This superstition may formerly have had some foundation as the compass-drawn stars were an ancient symbol of the Sun Cult.

Fig. 1. Barn decorations

Fig. 2. Barn decorations

Fig. 3. Barn decorations

Barn red: *see* Venetian red.

Basket, rye straw (German *Strohkorbe*: 'Pennsylvania-Dutch' *shtrow-korab*)*;* heavy coils of rye straw bound with splint were transformed into large, lidded, storage hampers, beehives, mats, cradles, and the circular baskets in which rye bread was set to rise.

Baumann, Johannes; Baumann, Joseph: operated press at Ephrata, where they printed birth certificates in the early 1800s.

Bird whistle: *see* Water whistle.

Birth-and-baptismal certificate (*Geburts-und-Taufschein*)*:* a highly embellished document recording these events. In Germany such documents were required by law; the custom was followed here. The data comprised the names of parents, mother's name before marriage, date, hour, and place of birth, also name of pastor and sponsors. In the nineteenth century certificates printed from woodblocks, colored and filled in by hand, supplanted the earlier hand-drawn type. Used only by the sects that believed in infant baptism, chiefly the Lutheran and Reformed churches (Plates 250, 251A).

Boi-schissel: *see* Pie plate.

Bookplate: fractur painting filling end sheets of songbook, Bible, hymnal or schoolbook. It bore owner's name, date, and often donor's pious admonition.

Bride box (so-called Pennsylvania-German): oval splint box, decorated with human figures and German mottoes, the work of professional decorators in Berchtesgaden, Bavaria. They were brought here by colonists.

Broadside, *Adam and Eve:* popular subject featuring Adam and Eve as illustration to verses about the Fall of Man. Many editions printed by Otto, Baumann, and other local presses from woodcuts; hand-colored. Often embellished with additional fractur decorations. *c.* 1800–12.

Bucket bench (water-bench): a functional farm piece of pine or poplar with two or three shelves over cupboard base, to hold pails and dippers.

Bulb jar (Swiss *bollekessi*): glazed, pierced earthenware vessel planned to hold onions which soon sprouted through the apertures, and in winter furnished a taste of spring greens.

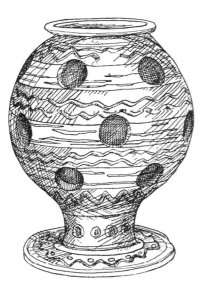

Fig. 4. Bulb jar

Buttermold: carved wooden artifact which facilitated the handling of butter and provided decoration at the same time. Executed with pocket-knife in a crude form of chip-carving, buttermolds, though not so finely worked as European types, display an infinite variety of well-designed conceptions of tulip and heart, eagles, doves and geometric designs (Plate 251C).

Cabinet, hanging wall: small hanging cabinet, with raised-panel door, occasionally with drawers or open shelf. Medieval in aspect with wrought-iron hardware. Rarely decorated.

Ceramics, Pennsylvania-German: a whole category of peasant earthenware (Plates 253B, 255A, B, C, 256), the decorated examples distinguished by their vigorous presentation of devices familiar to the potters' forbears overseas. In addition to decorative motifs, eighteenth-century pieces carried mottoes, bits of hymns, also humorous or vulgar inscriptions in the dialect inscribed on the rims of plates. Colors are the red of clay, the golden hue of glazed white slip, and green (copper oxide) applied as dashes and dapplings. Black, when desired, was obtained from manganese. *See also* Bulb jar, Coin bank, Fat-lamp, Pie plate, Sgraffito decoration, Slipware, Water whistle.

Chest decorators: as rural artisans almost never signed their work, they are practically unknown. The exception is the Seltzer-Rank family (Plate 249B) of Jonestown, Lebanon County, who scratched their signatures into the freshly painted vases holding their typical decorations of tulips and other stylized forms. One Jacob Schelli marked a few chests with his own as well as the owner's name.

Chest, dower (G. *Kiste;* P.-G. *Kischt*): a simple, dovetailed box, about four feet long, of pine, poplar, or walnut. Base and lid finished with molding. Usually mounted on supports which may be bracket-shaped, ball-footed, ogee-molded, or trestles. Wrought-iron keyplate, handles, and inside strap-hinges. When of pine, the chest was gayly decorated with paint; of walnut, it was adorned with simple inlays. Shapes and arrangement of panels in which decoration was placed varied. Best examples were made in the late eighteenth century (Plate 249A, B). Many chests carry owner's name terminating with the German feminine ending (i.e. *Kern,* m. *Kernin,* f.) and also the date. A few display names of males, as they also received dowry pieces if they set up their own establishments.

Chip carving: peasant technique, widely used for surface ornamentation; used locally on buttermolds. Achieved by diagonally opposed cuts of knife or chisel (Plate 251C).

Coin bank: earthenware coin bank, vase-shaped and topped with a bird or birds was a time-honored conceit of the peasant potter from England to Moravia.

Conestoga wagon tool-box: the Conestoga wagon, carrier for freight before the days of railroads, was equipped with a tool-box, the hasp (Plate 251B) and hinges of which were often exceptional examples of the blacksmith's craft.

Cookie cutter: kitchen implement of tin, for cutting out small cakes from thinly rolled dough. Outlines of cookies were reduced to fundamentals: the subjects were chiefly animals, naïvely drawn human figures, stars, hearts and birds. The cutter of tin was a makeshift for the handsome wooden molds used to shape the gingerbread figures of tradition which were carved by European professionals.

Corner cupboard (G. *Eckschrank;* P.-G. *Eckshank*): usually movable, a tall triangular piece, fitting corner. Upper section with solid or small-paned glass doors and shelves; lower half closed with doors. When made of soft woods, often painted red, rarely decorated. The finer hardwood pieces follow Georgian models with the rural joiner adding amusing details of his own.

Corner cupboard, hanging: smaller suspended type of cupboard with closed paneled door.

Cottage-cheese mold: utensil of tin, perforated in decorative fashion, shaped as heart or other simple form, which served as colander to drain sour milk and as mold to form and ornament the resultant cottage cheese.

Coverlet: from about 1820 to 1860 heavy coverlets, woven on hand-looms improved with Jacquard's mechanical device, were a noteworthy product of the Pennsylvania-German professional weaver. The coverlets, made of wool and linen or wool and cotton, featured the usual motifs in brilliant, even clashing, hues, in sharp contrast to the earlier geometric weaving in indigo and white. Made as stock pieces as well as to order, the latter type often had the customer's and weaver's names plus that of the latter's village and date woven in the corner.

Cupboard: *see* Dresser.

Cut-work on paper: a transplanted peasant art, that of cutting openwork designs in paper (*see* Valentines, by Ruth Webb Lee, page 494). Used for valentines and as a substitute for fractur on birth certificates and *Haussegen,* often enhanced with brightly painted areas. Mounted, framed, and used as wall decorations.

Date stone: marker of wood or stone inserted in wall of house. Incised with owners' names or initials and date of erection. Local date stones are sometimes adorned with familiar motifs and a house blessing, an ancient Rhenish custom. Such markers are also found on barns, mills and churches.

Distelfink: the German for goldfinch. In the A B C books used by Pennsylvania-German children, D stood for *Distelfink.* Today those bent on commercial gain have taken advantage of the present interest in things 'Pennsylvania-Dutch' and have concocted symbolic meanings, folklore tales, and rainbow colorings for the small yellow bird and apply the term *Distelfink* to all the nondescript birds of local folk art.

Document box: a small, wooden, oblong box with sliding lid, used also for trinkets. Painted and elaborately decorated. Probably a gift piece, as some examples bear dates and names of owners.

Door lintel: a wooden panel on which is incised a prayer or blessing in Roman lettering, with date, following a custom of Switzerland and the Palatinate. Extremely uncommon; existing examples are dated between 1740 and 1760.

Door panel: *see* Show-towel.

Dough trough or Dough tray: a rectangular dovetailed box, lidded, with sides sloping slightly outward, in which bread was mixed. When inverted the lid served as kneading table. Often mounted on turned or plain legs or, if not, equipped with handgrips for portability. A utilitarian piece which was never decorated.

Dresser: large piece on lines of Welsh oaken dresser, composed of two sections, the upper divided with shelves supported by scrolled sides, the lower spaced out in drawers and cupboards. Shelves often notched to hold spoons. An important piece if made of walnut; of pine or poplar, it was a necessary article of furnishing in the kitchen.

Drissell, John: a decorator in Bucks County of small wooden objects; salt boxes (Plate 252A), tape looms, document boxes. Working about 1794–7, he marked his work in a mixture of English and German with his and the owner's name.

Dunkard: *see* Pietistic sects.

Eagle: the double-headed eagle, emblem of the Teutonic Empire, was a favorite of eighteenth-century local potters. Gradually it gave way to the Bird of Freedom. Pictured with heart-shaped breastplate or shield, the American eagle was incised on buttermolds, painted on fractur sometimes clutching a tulip instead of an olive branch, blazoned on quilts, woven in coverlets, and painted on chests, as well as limned on gift plates.

Eckschrank: *see* Corner cupboard.

Eggs, decorated: so prevalent an Old World custom as decorating eggs at Easter was not overlooked by the Germans in Pennsylvania. Eggs were dyed brown with onion skin, then ornamented with tulips, birds, etc. delicately engraved with a fine-pointed tool. Another Old World tradition – that of hanging blown eggs on a bush or small tree – was continued sporadically in remote rural districts until the turn of the century or even later.

Ephrata: a town in Lancaster County, site of settlement of an early religious experiment in communal living, founded in 1732 by Conrad Beissel. The founder's ideas, which stressed celibacy and asceticism, governed this self-sustaining colony of men and women. In colonial America the productions of the Ephrata press were noteworthy, and the hundreds of hand-written and illuminated volumes of music made by the Protestant nuns were superb specimens of fractur. Some of the colony's medieval Germanic buildings may still be seen, as may examples of the large fractur writings of Biblical texts which adorned their monastic walls. This sect, always small, scarcely survived the eighteenth century.

Fat-lamp, earthenware: handled lamp of candlestick type with wick laid sidewise in lard or grease (*Fett:* fat) contained in lipped, open reservoir. The form is an ancient one.

Fig. 5.   Fat-lamp

Fat-lamp, metal: hanging lard-lamp of wrought-iron with brass or iron cover, equipped with hook for suspension or carrying. Called '*Schmutzamsel*' or 'dirty blackbird' because of smoke it emitted when carried about.

Fractur: a contraction of *Frakturschrift*, is the term used by the Pennsylvania Germans for the entire field of their hand-lettered, illuminated manuscripts and decorative drawings (Plates 250, 251A). The official practitioners of fractur were the 'educated men': the clergymen and schoolmasters; but this did not preclude children and adults from trying their hand at the gayly-colored pen and brush work. *See also* Birth-and-baptismal certificate, Broadside, Bookplate, Frakturschrift, Haussegen, Reward of merit, Vorschrift.

Frakturschrift: German term for a style of decorative calligraphy named after a sixteenth-century German type-face called *fraktur*, which was in itself an imitation of the lettering of the manuscript writer. Its rounder, more cursive forms were a departure from the rigidity of German Gothic or black-letter.

Fractur-scriveners: although most are unknown, among the early practitioners who signed their work were schoolmasters CHRISTIAN STRENGE, working in the 1790s, MARTIN BRECHALL, *c.* 1793–1823, FRANCIS PORTZLINE (Plate 251A), *c.* 1800–40. At Ephrata the OTTO and BAUMANN families turned out printed forms, as did F. KREBS at Reading, FRIEDERICH SPEYER and others. Itinerant *Taufschein* writers purchased the forms, and added color and decoration and vital statistics. In the nineteenth century they often signed them in addition.

Geburts-und-Taufschein: *see* Birth-and-baptismal certificate.

Haussegen (House-blessing): religious quotation, often from the Psalms, executed in fractur, to be recited daily as a pious invocation. Hung on the wall as a decoration.

Hex sign: *see* Barn decorations.

House-blessing: *see* Haussegen.

Knife-box: to hold cutlery, of walnut or other wood, sometimes painted and decorated. Made in two styles, portable or hanging, the latter sometimes combined with compartments for spices.

Lehn, Joseph: *see* Lehn ware.

Lehn ware: small turned wooden egg-cups, spice-boxes, lidded sugar-pails made by JOSEPH LONG LEHN, 1798–1892, of Lancaster County. In addition to these kitchen pieces, decorated free-hand in individual colors and style, this retired farmer ornamented chairs and other pieces, c. 1850. In later life he used decalcomania.

Fig. 6. Lehn ware

Mahantongo Valley furniture: a distinctive group of furniture made by the 'Consortia' or 'Brotherhood' of cabinet-makers working in the Mahantongo Valley, Schuylkill County, 1820–40. Characterized by borders of stenciled rosettes on the stiles, combined with well-designed traditional motifs of birds, tulips, and geometric forms on drawers and chest fronts. Desks, chests, cupboards and chests of drawers have turned supports and painted details which seem inspired by Sheraton inlays. A few signed pieces bear name of JACOB MASER. Other known members of the guild were GEORGE and JACOB BRAUN and JOHN MOYER.

Marzipan (known as *marchpane* in English): a traditional confection of ground almonds and sugar, shaped in decoratively incised flat wooden molds. The sweetmeat was sometimes touched up with color and hung on Christmas tree.

Maser, Jacob: *see* Mahantongo Valley furniture.

Mennonites: *see* Pietistic sects.

Molds: were used to shape and decorate marzipan, butter (Plate 251C), cottage cheese and cookies. *See* individual listings.

Otto (Johann) Heinrich: an outstanding designer who often signed his fractur pieces. Earliest examples, c. 1772, are wholly free-hand work. In the 1780s he printed birth certificates from woodblocks on a press he operated at Ephrata, and colored them by hand. Some pieces are signed JACOB OTTO. Extant are several chests decorated, though not signed, by this skilled craftsman.

Pie plate (*boi-schissel*): of red earthenware, usually decorated with a few yellow swirls applied with slip-cup. A rather flat dish with curved bottom, without rim or base, made over mold. An unusual shape from which pies slipped out easily.

Pierced ware, ceramic: glazed dark brown ware which depended on pierced geometric decoration for its sole ornamentation. Small objects such as tobacco-jars and sugar-bowls were given an inner lining. A transplanted German technique which required precision to execute (Plate 255C).

Pietistic sects: include the Mennonites, Amish and Dunkards, groups believing in non-resistance. Originating in Switzerland in 1525 and known as the 'Plain People', the sects still wear their distinctive garb, a survival of the seventeenth century: men with broad-brimmed hats and beards, all females with lawn cap and bonnet. Plainness (austerity) is their guide in life. Farmers primarily, they constitute today but a small fraction of the Pennsylvania-German population.

Plank-bottom chair: made in sets of six, an essential part of mid-nineteenth century country furnishing. Painted, with rails and splat carrying stenciled or free-hand embellishments in bright colors. The decorations reveal the rural artisan's attempts to attain a fashionable Victorian effect.

Punched work: decoration wrought in closely-set repoussé dots on tin coffee-pots, small boxes, etc. of usual motifs, made from 1830–60 by local tinsmiths, some of whom stamped their names on articles. Tin was left in the natural state. *See* Tinsmiths.

Reward of merit: a colored drawing of bird and stylized flower made by schoolmaster and presented for meritorious work.

Safe (pie cupboard): movable closet of wood, usually footed, with panels in doors and sides filled with tin perforated in designs. Used to store cooked food. Supposed to have originated in Pennsylvania and been carried elsewhere. Many of the pierced designs support claim of local origin.

Salt box: dovetailed box with hinged lid and back extended as support for hanging on wall (Plate 252A). Often decorated when made as gift, but with much less elaboration than on Old World examples.

Schrank: *see* Wardrobe (Plate 252B).

Seltzer-Rank family: *see* Chest decorators (Plate 249B).

Sgraffito ware: red earthenware decorated by the sgraffito process (from Italian *sgraffiare*, to scratch): inscribing a design on clay with a dull-pointed tool (Plates 255A, 255B, 256). The object to be ornamented was first given a coat of pale clay, the design scratched through this layer to disclose the red base, then glazed. Made only as gift or show pieces, as the indentations made by the tool rendered surface impractical for use. As the technique was under complete control, potters preferred it to the more difficult method of slip-decoration. *See* Ceramics, Pennsylvania-German.

Show-towel: a long narrow panel of linen embroidered in cross-stitch or in a form of darned lace, to be hung on a door. Worked as part of dowry linens, it bore maker's name and date. Common to all European nationalities as well.

Slip-decoration: ornament attained on earthenware with slip, a light-hued clay thinned with water, applied by trickling the mixture through a quill attached to small cup on to unfired ware before glazing (Plate 253B). Although this technique was used elsewhere in the colonies, it seems to have originated in the Rhine Valley and the Pennsylvania Germans produced the most distinctive examples. To execute an elaborate piece required considerable dexterity. *See* Ceramics, Pennsylvania-German; Pie plate.

Slipware: earthenware jars, dishes, plates, adorned with slip-decoration of familiar motifs and inscriptions, made as ornamental pieces.

Stove, German box: unventilated cast-iron box made of five plates, open side communicating through wall with fireplace in adjoining room, from whence coals were fed into it. Known as 'Dutch' or 'carved stove' by the English ironmasters. Castings were highly decorative, featuring scenes from Bible stories, religious texts, name of forge, master and date, executed in style of German Renaissance.

Swastika, whirling: most ancient of Aryan symbols, associated with sun worship. An emblem of good fortune favored by the Pennsylvania Germans who used it on barns, chests, embroidered it, cut it on buttermolds, worked it on tinware and drew it on fractur.

Fig. 7. Whirling Swastika

Swiss bank barns: very large local type of barn, built into rise of ground so that main entrance leads into upper story. The upper story extending about six feet over barnyard, protects entrances into stalls. Usually painted red and decorated with great wheels of ornament and white bands outlining non-existent arches. *See* Barn decorations.

German tinsmiths bear the names of E. Angstad, D. Gilbert, John Shade, Ketterer, M. Eubele. *See* Punched work.

Tulip motif: stylized form resembling tulip in profile, ubiquitous in Pennsylvania-German folk arts, and common in that of other countries as well.

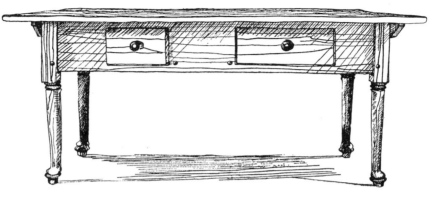

Fig. 8.   European-type table

Table: early type was X-shape medieval trestle, with heavy stretchers and removable top. Placed in corner of room as in Old World farmhouse, flanked with benches. Later model had turned legs and stretchers or else followed another European type which had free-standing legs and two drawers for linen and cutlery (Fig. 8).

Taufschein: *see* Birth-and-baptismal certificate.

Tile, roofing: oblong, flat, clay tile, indented with curving channels. Projection on back for suspension on cross-bars. Medieval type, used here in early days as fireproof roofing. Can still be seen in Berks County on small outbuildings.

Tin, pierced: perforations of dots and small slits on tin objects in certain categories were arranged ornamentally to serve functional as well as esthetic purposes. *See also* Cottage-cheese mold; Safe.

Tinsmiths: marked examples of unpainted but decorated punched work of Pennsylvania-

Fig. 9.   Tulip motif

Venetian red: a red oxide of iron, which when mixed with linseed oil forms the red paint used on barns, the background for the striking decorations worked in red, yellow, green, black and white. *See also* Barn decorations, Swiss bank barns.

Vorschrift: a writing model, the forerunner of the nineteenth-century copybook, prepared by the schoolmaster. Often presented as a gift and highly valued by the pupil, who learned to write by copying its German script alphabets and numerals. Chief feature was a religious precept or quotation in impressive lettering with an even larger highly embellished capital letter, the sentence occupying the major part of a fractur sheet.

Wardrobe (*Schrank*): a towering Germanic piece with closet and drawers, resting on varying types of support, made in sections for ease of handling (Plate 252B). Soft-wood examples were painted in light hues, then covered with streaking or mottling. Examples in walnut were show pieces of cabinetmaking, with heavy molded cornices, iron rat-tail hinges, drawers with brass handles, and sometimes ornamentation of applied carving or inlay.

Water bench: *see* Bucket bench.

Water whistle (*Wasserpfeife*): glazed pottery toy shaped like a bird, duplicating European prototype. Water was put into body and user applied mouth to beak to produce sound.

Wriggle work: a surface ornamentation on tinware, adopted from Old World technique used to ornament pewter. Wriggled ornament was obtained by tapping a chisel with a hammer; under the tapping the chisel, moving slowly forward, engraved a series of closely-set zigzag lines.

BOOKS FOR FURTHER READING

BARBER, EDWIN ATLEE: *Tulip Ware of the Pennsylvania-German Potters*, Patterson, Philadelphia (1903).

BORNEMAN, HENRY S.: *Pennsylvania German Bookplates*, Pennsylvania German Society, Philadelphia (1953).

BORNEMAN, HENRY S.: *Pennsylvania German Illuminated Manuscripts*, Pennsylvania German Society, Norristown, Pa. (1937).

KLEES, FREDRIC: *The Pennsylvania Dutch*, Macmillan, New York (1951).

LICHTEN, FRANCES: *Folk Art of Rural Pennsylvania*, Scribner, New York (1946).

LICHTEN, FRANCES: *Folk Art Motifs of Pennsylvania*, Hastings House, New York (1954).

MERCER, HENRY CHAPMAN: *The Bible in Iron*, Bucks County Historical Society, Doylestown, Pa. (1914).

ROBACKER, EARL F.: *Pennsylvania Dutch Stuff*, University of Pennsylvania Press, Philadelphia (1944).

SONN, ALBERT: *Early American Wrought Iron*, Scribner, New York (1928).

WEYGANDT, CORNELIUS: *The Blue Hills*, Holt, New York (1936).

WEYGANDT, CORNELIUS: *The Dutch Country*, Appleton-Century, New York (1939).

DOLLS AND TOY MINIATURES

By JANET PINNEY

Toys are in reality modified replicas of the adult world, and therefore depict the era in which they were made. Through the ages children have played with small reproductions of the objects around them and in their own way mimicked the grown-ups. Their toys have now found their way into museums and into the hands of collectors as evidence of an earlier way of life.

In the collecting of American antique toys there are certain facts to be borne in mind: that the United States is young in comparison with European countries and that, therefore, what is considered old and unusual in America will not seem so to Europeans; that our seventeenth- and early-eighteenth-century toys were not mass manufactured, and are therefore extremely rare; that our dolls do not have regional dress, although occasionally there is one dressed in Quaker or Shaker clothes. Naturally enough, there is a regional differentiation in certain types of toys. A farm child might have a doll made from corn husk, or crudely carved farm animals, while the city child might have a doll dressed in bits of her mother's brocade dress, or a wooden sleigh similar to the ones she saw on the city streets; a country child would have been delighted with a peddler's wagon (Plate 257 A) looking like the itinerant peddler with his wares making his rounds through the countryside.

The collecting of dolls and toys has become extremely popular in the United States, but because so many children in this country received imported toys it is sometimes difficult to isolate the strictly American examples of the eighteenth and nineteenth centuries (Plates 257B).

The early dolls were usually of very crude home-made type with painted faces, sometimes referred to as bedpost dolls, because of their similarity to a post of the four-poster bed. These dolls naturally varied in size from the small penny ones to those of larger size, just as they did in England. Strictly American is the wishbone doll. Taking the Thanksgiving Day turkey wishbone and dipping its joined end in sealing wax, the doll's head was made. The bones were wrapped with cloth, and these became the doll's body and legs and the cloth arms were sewn on to the dress. How long such a doll lasted would depend upon its treatment, but it is understandable that there are not many around. Rag dolls (Plate 260B), made completely of cloth or with a stick or clothespin as part of the body, may also be found.

Patented dolls: it was not until 1858 that the first American patent was issued to a doll maker, Ludwig Greiner, a German toy maker who settled in Philadelphia in the 1840s. Though his dolls are regarded by many as typical American dolls, he was undoubtedly creating the same type of heads he made in his homeland. His labels, placed between the shoulder blades, read *Greiner's improved Patent Heads. Pat. March 30, '58*, or *Greiner's Patent Doll Heads. Pat. March 30, '58 Ext. '72*. Size numbers sometimes appear on these *papier-mâché* heads. The bodies were usually made by the customer, and for that reason the collector may find a wide variety of Greiner dolls, some with kid arms, others with carved wooden arms or plain cloth. The important thing to look for is the Greiner patent label, and then from the hairstyle the exact date of the doll can be calculated, for the hair was molded as a part of the head.

Charles Goodyear, with his invention of hard rubber, brought a new medium into the toy world in 1850, and dolls marked *I.R.C. Co.* or *India Rubber Comb Co. – Goodyear Pat. March 28, 1854–68* or *Goodyear Pat. May 6, 1851 – Ext. 1865*, have sometimes withstood the hardships of time and have found their way to museums or into collectors' hands.

By 1850 the making of toys as an industry was well on its way in America, and following the Civil War many doll manufacturers applied for patents and marked their doll heads and bodies. Among these were Lerch & Klagg, Philadelphia, and a Covington, Kentucky, firm run by Philip Goldsmith, who in 1875 was selling dolls. A problem arises here, for it is not certain whether Goldsmith imported the wax, porcelain and composition heads or whether they were designed by a German worker and made in his factory. Records were not kept by the manufacturers, nor did these firms or shops keep samples of their products. Had they done so the work of the collector or museum curator would have been greatly simplified.

In New England Joel Ellis took out a patent in 1873 for a jointed wooden doll (Plate 259B), which had a hard-wood head and lathe-turned body with small flat joints. These were evidently easily broken by the young of the day, and Ellis gave up manufacturing them at the end of one year. In 1879 F. D. Martin of Vermont, took out a patent for the same type of doll but with sturdier ball joints. The next year another Vermont man, George W. Sanders of Springfield, patented such a doll with a 'new and improved shoulder, elbow and knee joint'. Henry H. Mason and Luke Taylor improved these joints in 1881 and made a revolving head of composition. When in 1881 M. C. Lefferts and W. B. Carpenter, as the Celluloid Manufacturing Company of New York, took out a patent, even celluloid dolls became popular.

As always, though, the child was anxious for greater realism, or so the adult thought.

There should be motion and speech, and so the manufacturer turned his mind to the creation of the walking doll (Plate 260A). In 1862 the government granted a patent to a manufacturer who neglected to attach his name to his product. It was a walking doll with a *papier-mâché* head, machinery to be wound up, and metal feet that moved, protruding from its circular cardboard base. Fortunately the fashion of the day decreed hoop skirts, so that all the ugly machinery was hidden by the doll's skirt, and as she moved across the floor the gliding motion was most natural.

From walking dolls the manufacturer went to a talking and crying doll, patented by W.A. Harwood in 1877; in 1881 the Webber singing doll was patented. In the latter case each doll's body was marked with the name of the song she could sing. Her body was of the finest kid, her face of wax with long hair. In 1888 the Edison Phonograph doll was brought on the market. This was a French doll reciting in a childish voice one of a number of well-known nursery rhymes. It is assumed that Mr Edison took part in developing the record for this doll.

Rag dolls: perhaps the most loved dolls have been the soft cuddly rag dolls, and America was filled with them. In the south the colored Mammy doll (Plate 260B) with her shoe button eyes was an extremely popular one. Most rag dolls were home-made, but among the first rag doll manufacturers was Mrs Izannah Walker of Central Falls, Rhode Island. Very few of her dolls remain. Another type of manufactured rag doll was the one that was stamped on a piece of cloth, the pattern showing the front and back of the doll and sometimes the feet. The doll design could be cut out and sewn and stuffed at home. In the 1890s there were two women who were manufacturing much the same type of doll. They painted the features of their cloth dolls with oil paints, thus giving them a life-like appearance. Emma E. Andrews called hers the Columbian doll, because it was exhibited at the Columbian Exposition, while Martha Chase's doll, which was inspired by her childhood love for one of Mrs Izannah Walker's, is known to collectors as the Chase doll. In both cases the women started making dolls for their own children, then their children's friends, and eventually found themselves in business.

Paper dolls: this category presents two types, the manufactured dolls that came either in booklet or sheet form and could be cut out, or the definitely hand-made painted examples. Anson D. F. Randolph of New York published a book in 1857: *Paper Dolls and How to Make them – A Book for Little Girls*, and C. B. Allair wrote what is almost a companion to it, *Paper Dolls' Furniture and How to Make It – or How to Spend a Cheerful Rainy Day*. But the doll that is most often considered to be the first American paper doll was published in the November 1859 issue of *Godey's Lady's Book*. Six figures of boys and girls cover one page, and a second page follows with a costume for each child, done in crude colors. The 1860s saw three important paper doll manufacturers producing popular sets: Chandler, whose dolls were published by Brown, Taggard & Chase, of Boston; Clark Austin & Smith, and McLoughlin Brothers of New York. All the dolls had many items in their wardrobes; all bore names fashionable in the period: *Charley, Emma, Little Fairy Lightfoot, Goody Two Shoes, Miss Florence*, even *Tom Thumb* and *Lavinia Warren* (his wife). Kimmel & Forster, New York lithographers, brought out a boxed set in 1866: *The American Lady and her Children in a Variety of the Latest Beautiful Costumes*. A collector's trials can sometimes be greater in this field than in any other in doll collecting, for often a particular doll will have all but one known dress of a set, the original owner having exchanged wardrobes with a young friend. Then comes the challenge to see if it is possible to locate the missing dress and complete the set.

Dolls' houses: another fascinating field for collectors is that of dolls' houses and dolls'-house furniture. In America they were definitely considered children's toys, unlike the elaborate dolls' houses in many European museums, which were not made for play. While in many cases the furniture and accessories for the American examples may have

been imported, the houses or rooms were made here. Because of the fragility of the tiny furniture that filled these houses it is understandable that original pieces have often vanished (Plate 258B). In some cases dolls' houses have been sold and their histories lost or misinterpreted. The oldest known dolls' house on view to the public is in the Van Cortlandt Mansion in the city of New York and was made for a child of the Homan family of Boston in 1744. It is a two-storied house with a high hipped roof, a center chimney and a toy storage drawer below. With a room across each side on the two floors the young owner had four rooms with which to play.

In every case the early dolls' house, before the manufacturer entered the field, was a replica to some extent of the child's family home and was made either by parents or the family carpenter. We therefore find palatial summer residences, Federal and later Victorian houses, country homes or the city mansion with its private garden and stables. In the Museum of the City of New York is an 1846 doll's house – a brownstone with a high stoop, basement and three floors. It is in reality a modified replica of 890 Broadway, where the children were living with their recently widowed mother and her brother, Peter Goelet. For houses such as these the furniture bears no manufacturer's marks, rather the importer's label, so that it is extremely difficult to ascertain whether or not there was a real industry producing such furniture in America. Certain of the living-room sets with their simulated carvings and stenciled work give the impression of New York's outstanding Victorian cabinetmaker, John Belter, while others are reminiscent of the Empire style and recall Duncan Phyfe.

China and household articles are difficult to identify as to origin, unless they fall into the category of tinware. While the first tinsmiths established themselves in New England in the middle of the eighteenth century they apparently did not make toys for another hundred years. Then they began producing dolls' furniture, toy kitchens, plates and cups, cutlery and trays. The latter were very often stenciled in patterns similar to the larger ones. On these and in the toy kitchens regional designs sometimes occur, such as those from the Pennsylvania-German section.

Furniture miniatures: there is still another subject for the collector, and that is doll-size furniture. In the early days they were simple pieces made by the father or grandfather of the little girl; four-poster eighteenth-century beds (Plate 259A), some with *toile de Jouy* canopies and appliquéd spreads, or straight chairs with rush seats. One young officer setting off for the Revolutionary War made a collapsible field bed with posts and a canopy so that his daughter could put her doll to bed in one similar to his. Another in the Civil War used the bits of wood from the bureau of his sunken ship to make a bureau, sofa and chair for his child (Plate 260C). When spool beds came in they too were copied, if not by a toy-maker in great numbers, at least by a cabinetmaker, for members of his family, using bits of wood which might otherwise have been wasted. The same holds true for the marble-topped Victorian bureaus and washstands. With spinets and pianos the center of attraction in the homes of the day, it was most natural to find Joel Ellis manufacturing them for dolls' houses in the 1860s; then, much later, Schoenut producing them in Philadelphia.

Perhaps the most amusing of all dolls' furniture is the cast-iron stove (Plate 260B), with accompanying pots, saucepans, coal-scuttles and shovels, boilers for the clothes, flat-irons and stands that made the child's world seem so real. There are many types of stoves, and all workable, some with revolving tops so that the food could be placed over the hottest part of the fire; some with the section for keeping water hot; some with a place to keep the plates warm; some with extra stovepipes, so that the room would not become smoky.

Collections: the United States is fortunate in having toys exhibited in many sections of the country. If they are not to be found in the art museums they may be seen in historical societies or historic houses open to the public. Among the well-known museum toy exhibits are those of the Lyman Allyn Museum, New London, Connecticut; the Vaughan Doll and Toy House of the Essex Institute, Salem, Mas-

sachusetts; Shelburne Museum, Shelburne, Vermont; Wenham Historical Society, Wenham, Massachusetts; Goyette Museum of Americana, Peterborough, New Hampshire; The Henry Francis du Pont Winterthur Museum, Winterthur, Delaware; Henry Ford Museum, Dearborn, Michigan; Newark Museum, Newark, New Jersey; New-York Historical Society; Van Cortlandt Mansion, New York, N.Y.; Museum of the City of New York.

Games: it is interesting to a collector to note the evolution of the types of games that have been manufactured for children through the years and to see how they reflect the adult philosophy of the era. In 1860 Crandall, a leading game manufacturer in the United States, brought out a wooden toy *Crandall's District School*. Flat wooden figures of the schoolmaster, the students, the dunce, Mary and her little lamb could all be set up on wooden blocks to recreate the schoolroom scene. Twenty years earlier, W. & S. B. Ives of Salem, Massachusetts, had patented *The Game of Pope and Pagan, or the Siege of the Stronghold of Satan by the Christian Army*. In the 1860s they issued *The Mansion of Happiness. An Instructive Moral and Entertaining Amusement*. This was a parchesi-like game with moves designated 'The Pillory', 'A Cheat', 'Industry', 'Justice', to mention a few before reaching the 'Mansion of Happiness'.

Carvings of Noah's Ark (Plate 258A) have been popular down through the years. While those exhibited in American museums bear no manufacturers' labels, they have definite American characteristics, and although they may not have included all the animals reputed to have been in the Ark, there were always two of a kind.

Indian dolls: the early dolls of the American Indian are so rare they exist only in museums, but there one can see clay dolls from our southwest, to be dated as early as 800 B.C. Wooden dolls are also found, but these are more difficult to date, and as for cloth dolls, they came in very much later. It is understandable, yet regrettable, that our early settlers did not preserve these toys, and it has remained for the archeologist to rediscover them.

The collection of toys and miniatures has the advantage of not taking up too much space in relatively small quarters. After considering all phases of the subject and deciding upon the type of collection desired, the collector will find great satisfaction in the pursuit. In the gathering of a collection the beginner is bound to make mistakes, but in the making learn. The persistent collector develops through knowledge an inner sense, which helps him recognize periods and discriminate between the real and the sham.

BOOKS FOR FURTHER READING

FAWCETT, CLARA HALLARD: *Dolls, a Guide for Collectors*, H. L. Lindquist Publications, New York (1947.)

FAWCETT, CLARA HALLARD: *Paper Dolls, a Guide to Costume*, H. L. Lindquist Publications, New York (1951).

HERTZ, LOUIS H.: *Handbook of Old American Toys*, Mark Haber & Co., Wethersfield, Conn. (1947).

JACOBS, FLORA GILL: *A History of Doll Houses*, Charles Scribner's Sons, New York (1953).

JOHL, JANET PAYTER: *More About Dolls*, H. L. Lindquist Publications, New York (1946).

ST GEORGE, ELEANOR: *The Dolls of Yesterday*, Charles Scribner's Sons, New York (1948).

Concise Encyclopedia of Antiques, Vol. II, pp. 244-9, Hawthorn Books, New York (1956).

MECHANICAL TOYS

By LOUIS H. HERTZ

THE collecting of old American toys, particularly in certain favored mechanical categories, has witnessed an amazing and continuing expansion of interest and activity in recent years. That this expansion has been accompanied by a certain disproportionate lack of publicity is probably due to the fact that the range of dates of acceptable and desirable collectors' items in the toy field, as well as other standards and customs, differs materially from those generally obtaining in the area of antiques collecting as a whole. Many of the highest prices recorded, prices which would be widely and immediately publicized if paid for eighteenth-century clocks or chairs, have been paid for fine toys manufactured not only in the nineteenth but even in the twentieth century.

On the other hand, the standards and customs applying in the field of old American toys, different as they may be from those in many other branches of collecting, have done much to enhance the popularity of this field, particularly among men, and to provide a considerable stability of values. Interest in gathering and preserving these toys results in a collecting activity more akin to stamp or coin collecting than the mere acquisition of occasional or selected specimens for their decorative value, although this element still plays a part in certain spheres of interest.

While virtually every type of toy has been manufactured in the United States, the chief collecting interest centers in certain groups: tin toys, cast-iron toys, clockwork toys, steam toys, mechanical banks, animated cap pistols, bell toys, and toy trains. The common denominator here is that all of these toys are either in some measure mechanical – that is, capable of movement or operation – or are replicas of objects in life that possess these attributes. In the literal sense, a 'mechanical' toy is a clockwork-operated toy.

The inherent and in some cases distinct principles of toy collecting, as generally recognized, are these :

(1) There is no limitation of date which in any way arbitrarily affects value and interest; some of the most desired toy trains and mechanical banks were manufactured in the 1920s and even the 1930s!

(2) Only commercially manufactured toys are sought (together with occasional surviving samples or patterns from the factories). Individually-made toys or models, regardless of the calibre of design or workmanship, are not sought by toy collectors.

(3) Restoration and refinishing, or any repairs or replacements that do not make use of authentic original parts are frowned upon, and materially reduce the value of an item. Many collectors will not accept any refinished toys; the over-all result is that most toy collections are 'purer' and maintain a higher standard of originality than many other fields.

Old American toys are attractive not only for their nostalgic interest, but perhaps even more because of the amazing ingenuity and workmanship these toys display. They are interesting not only in themselves but as representing objects of daily life – trains, wagons, steam engines, etc. – of America's growing commercial and mechanical progress over the years.

Research has long since established the fact that the United States possessed a great and flourishing toy manufacturing industry from the 1830s onward, producing a vast quantity of fine toys, many of them unexcelled in ingenuity, durability, and workmanship anywhere in the world. Many of these toys were later copied in cheaper form by European toy manufacturers, and imported into the United States, giving rise to the fallacious tradition that Europe was the home of most toys prior to the first World War, a legend that was encouraged by certain later American producers who sought tariff protection for the supposedly 'new' industry that had come to the fore during the period of that conflict.

In certain fields of American toy collecting where the entire range of productions is by now fairly well known, whether in terms of dozens or of hundreds of types, such as mechanical banks, track trains, and animated cap pistols, the parallels to stamp collecting become very close. A certain number of types must be obtained for a 'complete' collection (although, of course, no literally complete collection in any category has been or is likely to be formed). Also, as in stamp collecting, there is a standardization and acceptance of a scale of values based on the two essential factors of rarity and desirability. This has led to the contention at times that American toy collectors are more interested in rarity than in esthetic or artistic values. Were rarity alone the determining factor in values, there might be some measure of truth in this charge. However, American toy collectors have always also accepted the equal importance of desirability, and this factor is based on design, mechanical ingenuity, workmanship, appearance and finish, and other often less tangible attributes. In any mass-produced article, the degree of artistry and originality displayed depends on the manufacturer and his staff, both in establishing the specifications for the original design, and in maintaining standards of production, whether ten or ten thousand are produced. The machine does not necessarily destroy the individuality of the creative artist; it merely places him one step removed from the finished product, and multiplies that product.

The collector therefore accepts, and often specifically seeks, certain particular manufacturers' names as hallmarks of standards of design and workmanship, or of certain characteristic techniques of design and production.

Of all the names notable in this manner, none is more important in the field of collected American toys that that of the Ives Company, of Bridgeport, Connecticut (1868–1932), whose productions included almost the entire range of the most sought toys today and were especially extensive in the fields of clockwork toys, cast-iron toys, animated cap pistols, trackless trains, clockwork track trains, and electric trains. Ives was the great pioneer and producer, and their toy creations are among the most widely sought and highly prized. Other outstanding names in some of the more interesting categories include those of Secor in clockwork toys; Beggs and Weeden in steam toys; Stevens in mechanical banks; and Carpenter, Wilkins, Kenton, and Hubley in cast-iron toys. But this is merely to designate a few out of the many worthy of mention. Similarly, the following brief discussions of eight categories, while covering what are unquestionably the most widely sought and collected groups must necessarily omit mention of many lesser groups in which there exists a varying degree of interest, and which may attain greater proportionate popularity in the future.

Very few of the earlier toys carry the name of their maker. Definite identification as to make is often a somewhat complex process. There is a considerable and ever-expanding body of research data based on detailed studies of designs, materials, manufacturing techniques, and of patent specifications. Much has been contributed by catalogues and other trade literature. Catalogues are much sought and greatly valued, both for their interest in themselves and their research value. The most prized are the manufacturers' own issues; next, those of jobbers, and, finally, retail and mail order catalogues. These catalogues may be devoted exclusively to toys, or may merely include toys with varying other types of merchandise. Twentieth-century toys more frequently carry the manufacturer's name. This is particularly true in the case of trains and related equipment. Many of the later iron toys, however, can be identified only through the same process of study and comparison as obtains with the older models.

Tin toys: the tin toys sought by collectors

are generally of the japanned (painted) type, the product of a flourishing industry in several states between about 1840 and 1900. The lithographed (tin printed) tin toys of later years (except for train equipment which is much sought) attracts substantially less interest. Many of the early tin toys which are scarce or rare today were produced in enormous quantities. A single factory in the 1870s is known to have made over forty million tin toys annually! Countless types of toys were fabricated in tin: rattles, dolls' furniture, animals, boats, trains, banks, and every conceivable type of horse-drawn vehicle (Plate 261D, E). The wheels of these toys were generally of cast iron, and the lettering and final detailed decoration of the toys usually rendered through a stencil process, or lined in by hand.

Speaking broadly, size is the criterion of value and rarity; the larger the toy the finer the detail and workmanship and the smaller the comparative quantity manufactured. Tin toys with bells (Plate 261F), or some form of animation, particularly those incorporating clockwork mechanisms, are particularly sought (Plate 261D, E).

Iron toys: cast iron was by no means unknown in the American toy industry prior to 1880, and was extensively used for banks, cap pistols, cannon, certain minor types of toys, and for wheels and other parts. However, the great range of miniature iron vehicles of all types (Plate 263), including wagons, fire engines, and trains, did not come into being until the 1880s, and these lines were extensively developed in that decade and the 1890s. Iron toy manufacture flourished through the first two decades of the twentieth century, although in the main both quality and size decreased, particularly after the first World War. Automotive designs gradually replaced horse-drawn types, although a few of the latter models were still manufactured, or re-introduced, even following the second World War.

There were a substantial number of manufacturers of iron toys, and quite a few of these at one time or another produced outstandingly large or fine models. The most sought-after iron toys are those made by Ives, roughly from 1880 to 1912, followed by the distinctive

early Carpenter and Wilkins models. Aside from these three makes, value in iron toys is chiefly determined by size, fineness of finish, and intricacy of casting design, as well as certain particularly-sought types such as passenger vehicles (brakes, hansom cabs, etc.), circus equipment, trains, and the always popular fire departments. Iron toys with clockwork mechanisms are, of course, particularly valued.

Clockwork toys: probably no range of toys is more interesting and more representative of a variety of ingenious concepts than the fine clockwork toys made in the United States during the nineteenth century. The industry originated about 1845, but reached its peak in the twenty-five years following the Civil War. There are two main general categories of these toys: (1) Dressed figures, usually mounted on wooden bases containing the clockwork mechanism, which perform a variety of actions such as playing musical instruments, dancing, preaching, and so on, and including various walking dolls and figures with self-contained clockworks (Plate 261G–I,) and, (2) locomotives, steamboats, horse-drawn vehicles (Plate 261D, E or 264A), and similar vehicles, usually of tin and sometimes including animated figures. A few clockwork iron toys were also manufactured in the 1880s, 1890s, and early 1900s.

Virtually all of these toys are of outstanding design and avidly sought. The number of types seems almost endless. Those manufactured by Ives and by Secor are particularly valued, but the products of other factories such as Althof, Bergmann & Co. and George W. Brown & Co. are, for the most part, of only slightly less interest. There is also now a considerable interest in the numerous types of steel clockwork automotive toys, dating from the early 1900s (Plate 264F).

Steam toys: live steam-operated toys were extensively manufactured in a wide range of types and qualities, especially between about 1880 and 1910, although production continued many years thereafter, and there were some lines made earlier. These toys include stationary steam engines, steam locomotives

(Plate 264B), steamboats, steam fire engines (Plate 264E), and various other devices: pumps, derricks, pile drivers, etc. The most extensive line was that of the Weeden Manufacturing Company of New Bedford, Massachusetts, which included many items that are now prized by collectors. However, broadly speaking, many of the most sought-after models are of somewhat earlier makes. The steam locomotives made by Beggs and Garlick are especially prized. Steam toys are fine collectors' shelf items. However, extreme caution should be observed in attempting to operate any old model of this category. Indeed, both for the safety of the operator and the continuing preservation of the toy, it is probably best to observe a firm rule of *admire, but do not try to operate!*

Mechanical banks: this class of old toys has probably, to date, attracted more interest than any other, with the exception of trains. Mechanical banks are those in which the depositing of a coin is accomplished by, accompanied by, or followed by, some action, usually of an animated figure (Plate 262C–F). In most cases the action is through the release of a simple spring; few have actual clockwork mechanisms. For the most part they are of cast iron, and flourished from about 1870 to 1910, although a number of types, including some of considerable interest, were manufactured in the late 1920s and even later. There is a wide range of subjects: *William Tell, Jonah and the Whale, Punch and Judy*, animals, bank buildings with moving cashiers, and so on. The J. & E. Stevens Company of Cromwell, Connecticut, produced the most extensive line, although there were a number of other important makers. Mechanical banks should not be confused with registering banks, which often incorporate elaborate internal mechanisms but lack the animated figures, or still banks, in which there is no movement. Mechanical bank collecting is a highly specialized field. Some banks command very high prices. There were approximately 250 major types, each of which has a fairly definitely established scale of comparative rarity and desirability. It is impossible to generalize here as to which are the most sought-after types. The

reader is referred to the gradation list included in *The Handbook of Old American Toys*.

Animated cap pistols: this is a comparatively small group of toys, mainly of the 1880s and 1890s, although a few types originating in the period of the first World War have attracted considerable interest, probably due to their similarity of action to mechanical banks. Animated cap pistols incorporate figures, often comical, which move when the trigger is pulled and the cap is fired. Most of them were made by Ives. There are probably less than twenty-five major types in all, as distinct from the hundreds of types of ordinary cap pistols which are of far less interest to collectors. Closely allied to the animated cap pistols are the small 'bombs', often in the shape of a head such as *Admiral Dewey* or the *Yellow Kid*, which exploded a cap when dropped on the sidewalk by a string.

Bell toys: bell toys comprise a field of somewhat lesser interest than most of those discussed here, but some of the more elaborate models, or those of historical design are greatly sought. A bell toy is a device, whether a simple chime between a pair of wheels, or an elaborate and ornate cast-iron design, that sounds a bell as it is pushed or pulled along. There are three main types: (1) the earliest group of japanned tin (Plate 261F); (2) an intermediate group of cast iron in designs rendered in techniques similar to the mechanical banks; and (3) a later type in which iron is used mainly for the figures, and the framework of the toy is of strip steel.

Trains: in the collecting of miniature trains (Plate 264A–D) of all types (including early items already mentioned under previous headings) is to be found perhaps the most extensive and rapidly-growing phase of toy collecting. The introduction and continuing manufacture of electric and clockwork-propelled toy trains operating on track which enabled extensive model railroad systems to be constructed has brought the collector a wealth of differing types of locomotives, freight and passenger cars, stations, signals, power supply units, track parts, etc., the collecting of which on either a general or a specialized basis presents an extraordinary fascination. Comparative values are firmly established on an elaborate and generally recognized basis of rarity and desirability. Unlike mechanical banks, however, where the number of types is fairly limited, so many different train items were manufactured that the field offers seemingly limitless possibilities for assembling extensive and worth-while collections at widely varying costs. There are both common and rare items from almost every period and it is interesting to observe that some of the most valuable models are of comparatively recent date, the late 1920s and even the 1930s.

It is not possible to generalize as to the most desirable types, although it may be noted that here again the name Ives looms large, and this make is unquestionably the most generally sought, and the subject of the greatest number of specialized collections. Track trains are classified according to the width or gauge of the track, the gauge being the distance between the inside edges of the running rails. The chief gauges used for track trains manufactured in the United States prior to the second World War are: o ($1\frac{1}{4}$-inch), No. 1 ($1\frac{3}{4}$-inch), Beggs' ($1\frac{7}{8}$-inch), No. 2 (2-inch), and Standard ($2\frac{1}{8}$-inch), as well as a few models in narrower or wider gauges.

BOOKS FOR
FURTHER READING

HERTZ, LOUIS H.: *Collecting Model Trains*, Simmons-Boardman Pub. Corp., New York (1956).

HERTZ, LOUIS H.: *The Handbook of Old American Toys*, Mark Haber & Co., Wethersfield, Conn. (1947).

HERTZ, LOUIS H.: *Messrs Ives of Bridgeport, The Saga of America's Greatest Toymakers*, Mark Haber & Co., Wethersfield, Conn. (1950).

HERTZ, LOUIS H.: *Mechanical Toy Banks*, Mark Haber and Co., Wethersfield, Conn. (1947).

HERTZ, LOUIS H.: *Riding the Tinplate Rails*, Mark Haber & Co., Wethersfield, Conn. (1944).

MEYER, JOHN D.: *A Handbook of Old Mechanical Penny Banks*, John D. Meyer, Tyrone, Pa. (1948).

COINS AND MEDALS

By SYDNEY P. NOE

THE collector of United States coins has usually started by trying to obtain a specimen of one denomination for each year. Once such an objective is completed there is a turning to specialization in any of the fields to which there is a personal attraction. Forming a cabinet of types is likely to prove much more ambitious than it seems at first. In what follows an effort is made to show the attractiveness of the respective branches or groups, with any commercial criterion eliminated. It is hardly possible for a collector of Americana to go far without learning much about his country's history, and coins often bring home the significance of events unknown before or previously disregarded. The coins illustrated show some of the most interesting of such connections. The coinage of Canada is not included, for reasons of space; that of Mexico is omitted for like cause. Both are rightly to be considered American, and both of them boast their enthusiastic students.

Colonial coinage of Massachusetts: advantage was never taken of the right of coinage granted in the charter of Virginia, until 1773. No such grant was made in the charter of the Massachusetts Bay Colony. The coinage struck at Boston between 1652 and 1683 is perhaps the most interesting in our history. The shortage of small change was one of the most serious handicaps which the colonists had to face. Petitions to Charles I for a colonial mint had proved fruitless. A like inadequacy of the coinage prevailed in England at this time. Granting the right to coin money was a prerogative of the king. Within a few years after the death of Charles I, whether with or without the consent of the Commonwealth is not known, a mint was set up in Boston. John Hull was placed in charge along with his partner, Robert Sanderson, both silversmiths. The earliest pieces bear merely the initial letters *NE* in script capitals (for New England) on the one side and the value in Roman numerals on the other (Plate 265A & B). With but one exception, all the subsequent coins bear the date 1652. With the return of Charles II to the throne in 1660, the colonists were in a serious predicament, and the charge of having infringed the royal prerogative was one of those alleged as a cause for the withdrawal of the charter in 1683.

Because the NE pieces had a large part of their field blank, it was realized that this would offer opportunity for clipping, so a design which would fill the field was ordered, namely 'a tree'. This tree-type has three forms. The first of them, and the crudest, has since been dubbed a *Willow Tree* (Plate 265C & D), to which it has but slight resemblance. Many of the *Willow Tree* pieces have been double-struck, with the traces of the first striking interfering with the other. Their crudity must have been one of the reasons why this type is the rarest of the tree forms.

A marked improvement characterizes the succeeding type, the *Oak Tree* (Plate 265E & F), to which the design does bear some resemblance. To explain this improvement it has been suggested that some mechanical device must have been procured; color is lent to this suggestion in that years later 'an engine for coining with all the utensils belonging thereto' is listed in the inventory of the estate of John Coney, a one-time apprentice to the mint-master John Hull. If this surmise is correct and this 'engine' was a coining press of the screw type, we should have an adequate explanation for the improvement in the Oak Tree over the Willow Tree issues. In 1662 an *oak tree twopence* was added to the three previous denominations, and this bears the date of its authorization; it is the only issue with a date other than 1652.

The *Pine Tree* (Plate 265 G & H) type is the latest of the three. At its initiation it is on the same-sized flan as its predecessors, but about half of the known dies are constricted, from 30 to 25 mm. All of these tree forms were engraved in the die and resemble line drawings rather than modeled reliefs. This is less noticeable in the inscriptions which are marked by interesting letter forms and variations. The spelling *Masathusets* continues unchanged (with one exception – the H omitted), and this gives that spelling some title to having been considered official.

Despite long-drawn-out efforts to overcome opposition, it became apparent that the colony's charter was about to be rescinded, and since the coining of money was one of the offences charged, and because any minimizing of the offence was impossible, the production seems to have been increased, for we find more than the usual number of dies being used at the same time. A realization must have been reached that, since nothing they could do would lessen the punishment they were bound to receive, they might as well make the most of the situation. The thinness of these pieces permitted bending, from which one very interesting phenomenon resulted, for they were believed a protection from witches and were worn (bent or pierced) on the person for this purpose.

Perhaps the rarest of the Massachusetts issues, and the most ambitious artistically, is the *Good Samaritan shilling*, with the two figures of that parable on its obverse. It was struck from dies, but in the placing and form of the inscription it differs from all previous forms. The occasion for its production, probably unofficial, has not been discovered.

Maryland, New Jersey, Connecticut: a coinage for Maryland dated 1658 was struck in England by the Proprietor, Cecil Calvert, Lord Baltimore, whose bust occupies the obverse. The reverse bears the family coat-of-arms. There were three silver denominations –the *shilling* (Plate 265 I & J), *sixpence* and *groat* (four pence) as well as a copper *penny* (Plate

265K & L), which has a crown with two pennants for its reverse type. The coinage was not an extensive one; it resulted in serious difficulties with the authorities for the Lord Proprietor.

In 1682, in order to relieve the shortage of small change, the General Assembly of the Province of New Jersey authorized the circulation of *halfpence* and *farthings*, which are believed to have been issued in Dublin and brought to the colony by MARK NEWBY the preceding year (Plate 265 M & N). Because of the type, St. Patrick in ecclesiastical robes, these pieces are known by both names. The supply must have been fairly considerable, to judge from the number of dies known.

The patent granted to William Wood for making *copper tokens* for Ireland and the American colonies resulted in two types. Both bore on the obverse the head of George I. The former has for its reverse a beautifully conventionalized rose, and for inscription ROSA AMERICANA and UTILE DULCI (Plate 265 O & P) with the date for all but the first issue. The denominations are *twopence*, *penny* and *halfpenny*; the dates are 1722, 1723, 1724, 1733 (this last for a pattern twopence only). The issue for Ireland had for its reverse a seated woman with a harp; the dates are 1722–4. When these pieces proved unpopular in Ireland, they were sent to America. The denominations were halfpenny and farthing only.

A small group of coppers having a connection with Connecticut is known as the 'Higley Coppers' (Plate 265 Q & R). Their producer, John Higley, controlled a small copper mine near Granby from which came the metal for these coins. The earliest pieces had for type a stag to left with the inscription *Value of Three Pence*. When refused for this equivalent in circulation a second die was prepared with the words *Value me as you please*. Later there was a second reverse die having a hatchet for its type and for legend *I cut my way through*. This last and another type (a wheel) are undated; the others show the date 1737.

There would probably be more New England and Maryland coins today if there had been conditions which brought about hoarding. Hoarding was common in Europe and classical lands in times of war, resulting in the secreting of savings to which the owner was prevented from returning. Two hoards of silver coins are recorded. One was found at Castine, Maine, and the other in Roxbury, Massachusetts. It is not too much to believe that their number may even yet be increased, although most of the New England garrets must have been ransacked by this time. There is also another possibility. Spanish galleons returning from Mexico laden with silver and gold are known to have been wrecked on the Florida coast. Gold pieces have washed ashore there, and deep-sea diving may some day result in their recovery.

Latin America: the abundance of coined silver in Latin America explains why some collectors have been turning to the coinages of the Spanish mints in the New World. It is from these that much of the silver which circulated here came after the coining in Boston was stopped. It is these *Spanish milled dollars*, in which payment was promised on the Continental Congress's *paper notes* (Plate 265 s & T) which helped to finance the Revolution. The paper notes of the Continental Congress were printed in large numbers and so soon counterfeited that they quickly depreciated, becoming 'not worth a Continental'. Besides Mexico City, Santa Fe de Bogota in Columbia and Potosi and Lima, then both in Peru, were the most prolific mints for the 'pieces of eight' with which Stevenson's *Treasure Island* has made us familiar. Some of the gold in circulation came from Brazilian sources, possibly by way of Jamaica. They were known as '*Joes*' and '*half-Joes*' because they bore the Latin form of the name of the Portuguese king (Johannes). The New Englanders brought their salted codfish to the West Indies, exchanging it there for other desirables, including hard cash. A little later, when coins in small denominations became very scarce in the West Indies, they resorted to an interesting substitute which has intrigued many collectors. The Spanish mainland coins were cut into segments or lowered in weight by having a portion cut away. Some perversions consist in having cut the 'piece of eight' into five 'quarters', with the shortage so slight that it would escape the observation of the unwary. Gold pieces were sometimes plugged with added metal to raise them to a standard required by local legislation.

Other pre-Revolutionary coinage: shortly before the outbreak of the American Revolution Virginia took advantage of permission given in her charter to have an issue of *halfpennies* (Plate 266 A & B) struck in England. These bear the date 1773, but the shipment did not reach its destination until 1774, and since the obverse shows the head of George III, they can scarcely have become popular.

A few specimens of a *dollar* bearing the date 1776 and the inscription *Continental Currency* are known. There are strikings in pewter and brass as well as in silver, and this seems an indication that it never got beyond the pattern or trial-piece stage. The interval between the signing of the Treaty of Peace in 1783 and the ratification of the Federal Constitution in 1788 found several of the states authorizing the coinage of *cents*, and one of these issues was by provision of the Continental Congress and bears the dates 1787 and 1788. The design (Plate 266 O & P), a sun-dial and the word FUGIO, had for reverse a chain of thirteen links – one for each state – a device which had been used for the earlier *Continental dollar*, which is thought to have been supplied by Franklin.

The devices used on issues authorized to relieve the currency shortage by the several states display wide variety and some ingenuity. One of the first to appear, that of Vermont (Plate 266 C & D), came from a state not among the first thirteen to ratify. Massachusetts issued a *half cent*. New York and New Jersey (Plate 266 K & L) latinized their names. The coinage for Connecticut was one of the heaviest. There is an unofficial issue (1783–6) with the inscription NOVA CONSTELLATIO (Plate 266 M & N). Unofficial coinings often bear the head of Washington. The absence of specific laws prohibiting such coins was taken advantage of by several goldsmiths or jewellers, such as Ephraim Brasher in New York, who fathered a very well designed *doubloon* (gold) on which he counterstamped his initials EB. In Maryland, I. Chalmers of Annapolis struck silver *shillings*, *sixpences* and *threepences* dated 1783, and in 1790 in Baltimore Standish Barry produced a silver *three-*

pence bearing his name. The federal mint did not come into operation until 1792.

Federal mint established: the initial coinings at the mint set up in Philadelphia are an indication of the great need for the smaller denominations. A few pieces were struck in 1792 – the *disme* and its half (Plate 267A & B)–traditionally believed to have been struck from silver plate supplied by Washington. These were obviously patterns, as were designs for *cents* prepared by Thomas Birch. By 1793 *cents* and *half cents* had been put into circulation, the former in several varieties— chain type (Plate 267E & F), wreath, Liberty head (Plate 267M & N). By 1796 a type with a draped bust had become established. In 1794 *dollars* as well as *half dollars* and *half dimes* (Plate 267C & D) were issued. 1795 saw the striking of gold; the *half eagle* ($5.00) preceded the *eagle* (Plate 267 O & P). Not until 1796 were *quarter eagles* minted ($2.50); the *quarter dollars* of this date were without indication of their value, and further strikings did not occur until 1804. Pieces of these early dates in prime condition are eagerly sought today, but it is impossible even to list here the many varieties. Sometimes changes are very considerable, such as that in the diameter of the cents in 1857, when the *flying eagle* type appeared officially. Pieces of this type bearing the date 1856 are considered patterns; only one thousand are believed to have been struck. Other patterns are known to have been considered but never sanctioned. Among these is the gold *stella* of 1879 and 1880, with a gold value of four dollars, but patterns were also struck in other metals. *Three dollar* pieces in gold were struck between 1854 and 1889 (Plate 267 I & J).

Controversy has long been waged as to whether any dollars dated 1804 were coined in that year. Re-strikes at the mint are believed to have been struck in 1833, 1858 and 1866. Since many of these rarities differ only in date from the issues which preceded or followed them, there is little to be learned from them. The *Confederate half dollar* (Plate 267V & W), however, is in another class. When the mint at New Orleans fell into the hands of the Southerners they found dies there for half-dollars bearing the date 1861. A reverse die with the inscription *Confederate States of America* was cut, and a small number (four?) of specimens were struck. One of the coins and both dies were found in the possession of a citizen of New Orleans in 1879 and later acquired by a New York coin dealer. He obtained five hundred half-dollars of the New Orleans mint for 1861, planed off their reverses and re-struck them from the Confederate die. A die for a *cent* was ordered but never delivered. It was used later for re-strikes by the dealer who acquired the die.

Territorial gold coins: the private or territorial gold coins constitute a series from which considerable American history may be learned. Prior to the California Gold Rush of 1849 the supply of gold came from two southern states, Georgia and North Carolina. Local assayers were responsible for pieces of honest weight, and these circulated without government prohibition. The first, struck by Templeton Reid, bore the words 'Georgia Gold', his name and the date 1830, along with indication of their value – *ten, five* and *two and a half dollars*. Later (1849) pieces having the value of ten and twenty-five dollars bear his name, but it is accompanied by *California Gold*. He must have gone to the west in the interval.

In Rutherford County of North Carolina a family of German metallurgists named Bechtler coined *one, two and a half* and *five dollar gold pieces* (Plate 267K & L) over a period of twenty-two years. These too were without type or symbol, merely giving name, date and denomination.

The exigencies of the Gold Rush to California are brought out by the pieces struck there by accredited assayers while that state was still a territory, and both before and after Augustus Humbert had set up as United States assayer. The earliest of the *fifty-dollar slugs* (Plate 266Q & R) coined by him are dated 1851, and previous issues of smaller size were discredited with a very inconvenient shortage of small change resulting. Authority for *ten-* and *twenty-dollar* coins were finally accorded in February of 1852. By 1854 *eagles* and *double eagles* were being struck by the San Francisco branch mint. A state assay office provided by law in 1850 seems to have been discontinued as soon as the United States assay office was established. Bars and ingots, stamped with their intrinsic value and the name of the assayer, circulated as late as 1860 and are collected by some enthusiasts although they can scarcely be classed as coins.

Five- and *ten-dollar* pieces struck by the Oregon Exchange Company have a beaver as type and are dated 1849. The Mormons in Salt Lake City struck pieces in 1849 with the inscription *Holiness to the Lord* and with clasped hands on the reverse. In Colorado several firms, among which that of Clark, Gruber & Company were prominent, struck gold coins dated 1860 and 1861, the largest denomination being twenty dollars. Many of these bars and slugs must have gone into the melting-pot when the stabilized price for gold was less than their pure content.

Tokens: in two periods of our history tokens played a part which entitle them to the attention of collectors. Shortly after 1837, during the presidencies of Jackson and Van Buren, a period of widespread depression, there was a considerable striking of these unofficial coins which are now called '*Hard Times Tokens*'. Many are of a satirical nature and reflect the economic situation. More than a hundred varieties are recorded, chiefly in the *large cent* size.

A second period of coinage stringency occurred during the War between the States. The mint did not strike *cents* in sufficient quantity to meet the needs of circulation, and substitutes were put out by commercial firms, redeemable at their establishments, to overcome the shortage. Many have a local interest because they bear the names of issuers no longer in existence. These little tokens were of the size of the small cents introduced in 1857 and were usually in bronze. The varieties run into thousands.

New designs: during the presidency of Theodore Roosevelt, and with his enthusiastic encouragement, an effort was made to improve the artistic standard of the coinage. Augustus Saint Gaudens (and his pupils) were entrusted with the making of new designs. His design for the twenty-dollar gold piece was of great beauty, but by the time the mint officials had modified it to meet the requirements of minting and circulation it had lost much of its initial attractiveness. The half-dollar and the dime were designed by A. A. Weinmann, the quarter by H. A. MacNeil and the five-cent piece (perhaps the most characteristically American of the types) by James E. Fraser. The Lincoln cent was the work of V. D. Brenner. In 1921 a *Peace Dollar* was authorized; the design, selected from a competition in which eight invited sculptors participated, was by Anthony de Francisci.

Medals: until the mint was established in 1792 facilities for preparing medals were almost entirely lacking, and it was necessary to rely on English or French artists. The direct cutting of steel dies was arduous, and there were few in the colonies with experience for doing this. Later, hubs, modeled in relief, were used for portrait medals. Not until a reducing machine had been imported well after the mid-nineteenth century were medals produced in any considerable number. There is one outstanding exception to this statement, however: the *Indian Peace Medals*, which have exceptional antiquarian interest. Intended as marks of favor to prominent chiefs, whose aid, along with that of their tribe, it was desirable to enlist, they had been used with considerable effect by the French in Canada, later by the English also. Possession of one of these medals was a fairly clear indication, and this was sometimes needed, of the side to which the wearer belonged. Indeed, several of the French medals are known with the LUDO-VICUS of their inscription erased and GEOR-GIUS (in one case GORGIUS) substituted to indicate a change of front on the part of the owner. In consequence the Congress was early faced with the necessity for attracting Indians they wished to draw away from their allegiance to the English forces in the north. How could this be done when no equipment for striking medals was available? During Washington's administration the situation was met by presenting large oval plaques of silver with the design engraved (Plate 268A). As these were considerably larger than the struck English medals, they seem to have made a deeper impression and to have been more highly prized. An early recipient was the famous and rightfully distinguished leader, Red Jacket, who received the largest of the three sizes distributed; and it is by his name that these engraved medals are sometimes known. The preparation of an engraved medal was possible much more quickly than would have been the case had dies been made, and their popularity with the red warriors satisfied both parties. Such engraved medals with the dates 1789, 1792, 1793 and 1795 are known and are assumed to indicate that they were awarded during the visit of a formal nature to the capital in those years. The designs are in some instances signed with the initials *JR*, probably to be identified as those of Joseph Richardson of Philadelphia. Another countermark, *JL* or *IL* is less certain.

A group of three *Seasons Medals*, 45 mm. in diameter, were ordered in England by Rufus King, the American minister. They are dated 1796, and their design was entrusted to the painter John Trumbull, at that time an art student in England. His designs were rather fanciful and intended to persuade the Indians of the advantages of the pursuits of peace, such as cattle raising and agriculture. These medals in silver and copper were not received until 1798. Under Thomas Jefferson and most of the succeeding presidents, struck medals were prepared at the mint; a common reverse displayed clasped hands and the words PEACE AND FRIENDSHIP (Plate 268B). There are three sizes for the medals of Jefferson, just as

there had been three grades of the engraved pieces, and there are further variations in size or method of manufacture. A supply of Jefferson medals is known to have been taken by Lewis and Clark on their expedition to the north-west. The most important collection of Indian Peace Medals is in the Museum of the American Numismatic Society in New York. A supplementary group consists of medals given by the American Fur Company to its Indian trappers. One, in silver, bearing the portrait of John Jacob Astor and PRESIDENT OF THE AMERICAN FUR COMPANY, is to be dated about 1834. The second (in pewter) is that of Pierre Chouteau, Jr. Both bore the customary clasped hands on the reverse; the latter is dated 1843. The privilege of distributing such medals was withdrawn by the Secretary of War in 1843.

An excellent selection of recent medals of which one is illustrated (Plate 268c) will be found in the Museum of the American Numismatic Society.

BOOKS FOR FURTHER READING

BELDEN, B. L.: *Indian Peace Medals Issued in the United States*, American Numismatic Society, New York (1927).

CAROTHERS, NEIL: *Fractional Currency*, New York (1930).

CROSBY, S. S.: *Early Coins of America* (reprinted photostatically 1946).

MILLER, H. C. et al.: *State Coinages of New England*, American Numismatic Society, New York (1920).

Concise Encyclopedia of Antiques, Vol. I, pp. 199-209, Hawthorn Books, New York (1955).

RARE BOOKS

By JOHN COOK WYLLIE

THE passion for collecting books without regard to their usefulness or textual merit is so recent a phenomenon in America as to have required a formal defense before the American Library Association in 1948. Scarcely a century ago the country was poor in public and destitute of private collections of rare books. Gentlemen's libraries consisted of works for reading purposes and reference only. So outstanding an American book collector as Thomas Jefferson preferred the 'latest and best edition' of a work, and even his collections of books on the fine arts were those of a practising, if amateur, architect. Jefferson was never what the French call an *amateur* of the book, an expression in which the meaning of the word 'amateur' runs strongly to its root of 'love'.

Only Thomas Prince of Boston and William Byrd II of Westover, Virginia, may be said to have ante-dated Jefferson among the giants in American book collecting, but colonial American libraries, without a recorded exception, were utilitarian in character for their century and a half. These libraries reflected striking regional differences, but the how-to-do-it nature of their contents was inescapable: they inclined to divinity and commerce in the north; to politics and agriculture in the south. As the west opened, the story was repeated, and (not forgetting Bancroft and Draper) it is only within the memory of people now living that collections such as Huntington's have been formed in the west.

To argue the youth of a phenomenon is not, however, to question its vitality. Book collecting in America is young, but whereas Europe today brings to mind a single collector of the stature of Martin Bodmer, collecting in America recalls names like Waller Barrett, the Berg brothers, J. K. Lilly, Carl Pforz-

heimer, Louis Rabinowitz, and Lessing Rosenwald, to mention only an even half-dozen of the foremost American names known in every book capital in the world.

No generalization about the national character of book collectors can ever give much satisfaction, but if it is true that the French collector values books chiefly for their physical beauty, then it is true that the American collector has seized upon, developed, and made his own, the fetish of firstness.

A first edition, even where there has never been a second, would seem to the American collector of some value *per se*. The first published work of an author, the first book ever printed, the first book printed in the New World, the first book printed in British America, the first book of poetry by America's first professional poet, the first folio of Shakespeare, the first printing of the Declaration of Independence, the first woodcut made in America – these are among the greatest items to appear in the auction rooms by American collecting criteria.

And with the unblushing immodesty of youth, the first of all firsts to the American are those of the 'first country of the world', namely his own. Hence the chauvinistic fanaticism over Americana.

Among the pioneer American collectors, besides Prince, Byrd, and Jefferson, were Isaiah Thomas, Peter Force, John Carter Brown, and James Lenox.

In more modern times the names of Clements, Coe, McGregor, Wren, or (among the living specialists) of Arents, Bell, Feinberg, Graff, Houghton, Wilmarth Lewis, Mrs. Hunt, the Hydes, Streeter, Henry C. Taylor, suggest a few who could have been serious competitors to the generalized interests of a Huntington or a Morgan, both of whom collected massively in Americana at the same time that they competed sharply with Folger in English literature.

Booksellers and institutional libraries have always been the backbone of the collecting interests of Americans. The tradition among American booksellers is great, from Henry Stevens of Vermont down to John Fleming, H. P. Kraus, Kohn, and Papantonio of our own day. No casual list can do them justice, but among the greatest have been the Eberstadts, the Goodspeeds, Lathrop Harper, Dr. A. S. W. Rosenbach, and George Smith. The most important manuscripts have generally been handled by the book dealers, but there have been manuscript specialists from Madigan to Forrest Sweet and Charles Hamilton. Such specialization has in latter days, however, drifted to the distaff side of the business, with Mary Benjamin and Emily Driscoll among the quick.

The chief American auction houses have been Henkels, American Art Association, Anderson Galleries, and (among the living) the Parke-Bernet Galleries. Minor American auction houses are less interesting to the big-time American collector than the sales of Sotheby in London.

Among the outstanding figures in institutional libraries, where tax-exempting gifts have built some of the greatest book collections in the world, the past is rich with names like those of Wilberforce Eames of the New York Public, Justin Winsor of Cambridge, Belle Greene of the Morgan, and Randolph Adams of the Clements. But the present is if anything richer, with names like Clarence Brigham of Worcester, Lawrence Wroth of the John Carter Brown, William H. Jackson of Harvard, James Babb of Yale, Frederick Adams of the Morgan, John Gordan of the Berg, Lawrence Powell of California, Edwin Wolf of Philadelphia, and David Randall of Indiana.

Book collecting is, then, the oldest of the collecting arts of the New World, and has about finished with the diseases of infancy. There are signs that the youthful frontiers of book collecting have already moved from California to Argentina and Australia, but Americans, having come partly into their in-heritance of the European tradition of book collecting, show every sign of enjoying for some decades to come the role of head of the family.

ABBREVIATIONS

For fuller lists of abbreviations see: *The Bookman's Concise Dictionary*, F. C. Avis, London (1956). R. R. BOWKER CO., *The Bookman's Glossary*, Bowker (1951): the first two editions, of 1925 and 1931, were published under John A. Holden's name; (it is the 3rd revision that is referred to here). JOHN CARTER, *ABC for Book-Collectors*, Knopf (1952).

A.d. and **a.d.s.:** autograph document, and autograph document signed, as distinguished from an a.l. or a.l.s., is likely to have relatively less collector's value; thus ship's papers, commissions, and land grants made out to or signed by famous men would be described as a.d. or a.d.s.

A.l. and **a.l.s.:** autograph letter, and autograph letter signed; these, as opposed to l.s. and t.l.s., mean that the letter, in the one case without, in the other with, a signature, is in the hand of the writer, that the letter is not typed, not a copy (unless the writer's own), and not in the hand of a secretary.

A.n. or **a.n.s.:** autograph note or autograph note signed. The expression refers to ms. memoranda, fragments, etc.

Ad. or **adv.** or **advt.:** advertisement or advertisements. See Glossary under this heading.

Anon.: anonymous; i.e. published without the name of the author.

B.M.: a reference, generally, to one of the British Museum's printed catalogues of books. 'Not in B.M.' is a loose expression of American dealers meaning the book is probably English and may also be rare.

Bds.: boards. Etymologically, as with most American-bound books before 1800, this may have meant that the leather of the binding covered a piece of wood, but in a dealer's catalogue today, all it means is that the book is hardbound rather than paperbacked. *See* Wraps.

c.: used indiscriminately to mean copyright or *circa*. When anyone wants to be sure of not being misunderstood, the 'c' for 'copyright' is raised and 'ca' is used for '*circa*'.

C.w.o.: check or cash with order. Dealers often advertise that they will send books post-free to collectors sending c.w.o. This is the book dealers' inversion of the abbr. c.o.d., which means 'cash on delivery'.

Cf.: calf. Used for any smooth-finish leather on a binding. *See also* Hf. Cf.

Cl.: cloth. Refers to the cloth covering the binder's boards on books.

Cont.: contemporary. As in Cont. cf., meaning that the leather binding is contemporary with the printing of the book.

Cr. or **Cr. 8vo:** crown octavo. *See* Book Sizes.

D.e.: deckle edges. This is the rough frame-edge of mold-made paper, simulated in machine-made paper to evoke a nostalgia for the antique.

D.j.: *see* D.w.

D.s.: *see* A.d.s.

D.w. or **d.j.:** the book's printed or unprinted 'jacket', as it is generally called in America, though the unhyphenated expressions book jacket, dust cover, dust jacket, and dust wrapper, are all also widely used.

12mo (duodecimo or twelvemo): *see* Book Sizes.

Engr.: engraved; that is, printed from the indentations in a plate, as opposed to lithographed (from a flat surface) or letterpressed (from a raised surface).

Evans: a reference to Charles Evans's *American Bibliography*, which lists all books printed before 1800 within the bounds of the present U.S. 'Not in Evans' means that the work is listed in one of the supplements to Evans.

FC.: the file copy of an a.l.s., as opposed to the RC.

Facs.: facsimile.

Fcap or **fcp.:** foolscap. A size and quality of writing paper which, when folded once, measures about 13 × 8 inches, or a little larger than what would in America be called 'legal size'; formerly identified by its watermark of a fool's cap and bells.

Fl.: flourished. When an author's dates of birth and death are unknown, it is common in America to distinguish him from others of the same name by saying that he flourished on the date of the publication of his book or books. Thus the author of *Cytherea*, identified in England as John Smith of Snenton, is in America identified as John Smith, fl. 1677.

Fol. or **fo.** or **f.:** folio. *See* Book Sizes.

Frontis. or **front.:** frontispiece.

g. or **glt.** or **gt.:** gilt; especially in the combinations g.e. for gilt edges, and g.t. for gilt top.

Gesamtkatalog: a reference to the *Gesamtkatalog der Wiegendrucke*, an alphabetical listing of incunabula, interrupted at the letter E by World War II and never resumed.

Haebler: a reference to one of Konrad Haebler's works on incunabula, most likely his *Typenrepertorium der Wiegendrucke*.

Hain: a reference to L. Hain's *Repertorium Bibliographicum*, a list of incunabula.

Harrisse: a reference to Henry Harrisse's *Bibliotheca Americana Vetustissima*, which describes Americana of the period 1492 to 1551.

Hf.: half; especially in the expressions hf. cf. for half calf, hf. mor. for half morocco. *See* Binding.

Inscr.: inscribed.

L. or **ll.:** leaf or leaves; not often used in America because of the prevalence of the typewriter, which fails to distinguish between the letter l and an Arabic numeral one.

L.C.: a reference, generally, to one of the printed bibliographical tools of the Library of Congress based on their printed catalogue cards. 'Not in LC' is a phenomenon so common with very rare books as to have little meaning.

L.s.: *see* A.l.s. When the A is omitted, the letter is probably in a clerk's hand, with the signature only being the writer's.

Lev.: Levant morocco; a high-quality coarse-grained goatskin, used in binding books; distinguished, for example, from another goatskin, Niger, which has a finer grain.

M.e.: marbled edges; i.e., a marble-veined multi-coloring of the fore-edge and perhaps one or more of the other edges of the book.

Mor.: Morocco. A goatskin used for binding. Among the kinds are Levant, Niger, Turkey.

Ms. or **mss.:** manuscript or manuscripts. The expression is used arbitrarily about most documents other than letters, but may also refer to these. Thus the mss. of an author would include, say, the ms. of one of his novels, besides numerous a.d.s., a.l.s., t.l.s., etc. The ms. abbreviation is peculiarly confusing to autograph collectors having to do with German catalogues, since in German 'MS' (for *Maschinenschrift*) is used to indicate that the ms. is not ms., but rather is typewritten. The German refers to the ms. proper as an 'HS' (for *Handschrift*) when it is handwritten.

N.d.: no date on the title page.

N.p.: no place of publication (or perhaps publisher's or printer's name), given on the title page. The abbreviation is also used by professional cataloguers to mean a book for which there is no prospect of getting a Library of Congress card.

O.p.: out of print.

8vo (octavo): see Book Sizes.

P. or **pp.:** page or pages. The American usage of p. for both singular and plural is logically superseding the inexplicable 'pp', especially as the latter is widely understood in context to mean, more logically, past participle, pluperfect, pianissimo, parcel post, page proofs, parish priest, and postpaid.

Phillips: a reference, usually, to P. Lee Phillips's *A List of Geographical Atlases in the Library of Congress*, but sometimes instead to the same author's *A List of Maps of America*.

Pl. or **plts.:** plates.

PoC: polygraph copy. Thus, with Jefferson letters dated 1804 or after, of two nearly identical specimens, both would be a.l.s., but one would be a PoC, and the chances are that the PoC would be the FC, the one written by the pen held in the author's hand, the RC.

PrC: press copy. An offset impression, made under pressure on a damp tissue from the original. The FC of a Jefferson a.l.s., before Jefferson started using PoC's in 1804, is likely to have been a PrC. Letterpress copies were used for file purpose well into the present century.

Prelims or **p.l.:** preliminary leaves.

Priv. pr.: privately printed.

Proctor: a reference to R. Proctor's *Index to the Early Printed Books in the British Museum*.

Pseud.: pseudonym; an assumed name, as Mark Twain or O. Henry.

4to (quarto): *see* Book Sizes.

RC: recipient's copy of an a.l.s., opposed to the FC.

Rect. or **r°:** recto. The top surface of a right-hand page. *See* Vso.

S.a., s.d., s.l., s.n.: the abbreviations beginning 'sans' or 'sine' for no year (anno), date, place (loco or lieu), or name (nomine) are seldom used in America, and then only from snobbishness or affectation. *See* n.d., n.p.

STC: a reference either to the *Pollard and Redgrave Short-Title Catalogue* (1475–1640) or to *Wing's Short-Title Catalogue* (1641–1700). In either case, the books referred to are English. The date will show which STC is meant, and if the numerical citation is without a preliminary letter, then the reference is to the earlier work. The later one is generally cited as 'Wing' or 'Wing STC'. 'Not in STC' or 'Not in Wing' generally means that the dealer supposes the work to be of extreme rarity because he has not found how one of the STCs listed it.

Sabin: a reference to Joseph Sabin's *Dictionary of Books Relating to America*. 'Not in Sabin' generally means that Sabin thought the work of too little American interest to list.

Sig.: signature. This is one of the common words in America for gathering, or section, or quire. The common verbs, some with different meanings, derive from these nouns of identical meaning: e.g., 'signed' in Roman numerals, 'gathered' or 'quired' in eights.

(A) Peddler's cart and horses, inscribed on front 'Toys 1884 Linens Skins Bought'. *New-York Historical Society.*

(B) Painted wooden horse, early-nineteenth century. *Henry Francis du Pont Winterthur Museum.*

PLATE 257

(A) Noah's Ark with birds and animals marching in pairs. *Essex Institute, Salem, Massachusetts.*

(B) Highboy, early-nineteenth century; cradle made by British prisoner-of-war, 1812; doll, 1809. *Essex Institute, Salem, Massachusetts.*

PLATE 258

(A) Doll's ironwood bedstead, toile de Jouy canopy, made by Mr and Mrs Thomas Ellison for their granddaughter, Anna Hearn, 1785. *Museum of the City of New York.*

(B) Jointed wooden dolls, patented by Joel Ellis of Springfield, Vermont, in 1873. *Lyman Allyn Museum, New London, Connecticut.*

PLATE 259

(A) Walking doll, 'autoperipatetikos', patented 1862 by O. B. Gray, India Rubber Company; walking doll, right, with baby carriage; by W. F. Goodwin, 1865. *Lyman Allyn Museum, New London, Connecticut.*

(C) Doll's sofa of mahogany inlaid with fruit wood, covered with rose satin; chair covered with a bit of his wife's bonnet ribbon, made by Captain John Watters, 1860s. *Museum of the City of New York.*

(B) Mammy rag doll with shoe button eyes, 1880s; French cooking stove with copper pots, 1870s. *Museum of the City of New York.*

PLATE 260

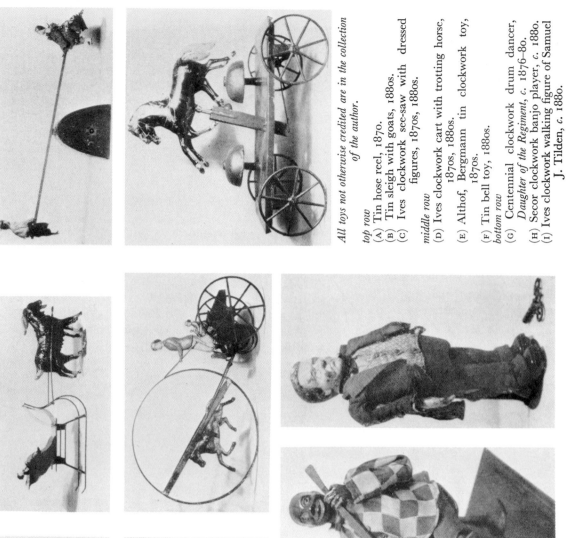

All toys not otherwise credited are in the collection of the author.

top row
(A) Tin hose reel, 1870.
(B) Tin sleigh with goats, 1880s.
(C) Ives clockwork see-saw with dressed figures, 1870s, 1880s.

middle row
(D) Ives clockwork cart with trotting horse, 1870s, 1880s.
(E) Althof, Bergmann tin clockwork toy, 1870s.
(F) Tin bell toy, 1880s.

bottom row
(G) Centennial clockwork drum dancer, *Daughter of the Regiment, c.* 1876–80.
(H) Secor clockwork banjo player, *c.* 1880.
(I) Ives clockwork walking figure of Samuel J. Tilden, *c.* 1880.

PLATE 261

(A) Tin double-deck horse car, 1880s.

(B) Tin bus, 1880s. *New-York Historical Society.*

(C) Roller-skating mechanical bank, 1880s.

(D) Clown and Harlequin mechanical bank, *c.* 1908.

(E) Mikado mechanical bank, 1880s.

(F) Jumping-rope mechanical bank, 1890s.

All banks on this page from the collection of Mr and Mrs William C. Roup.

PLATE 262

(A) Ives iron walking horse and sleigh, 1880s.
Coll. of A. J. Koveleski.

(B) Wilkins iron dray, 1880s.
Coll. of A. J. Kovelski.

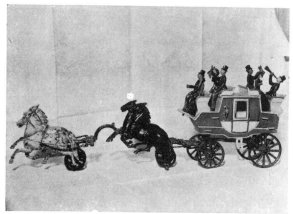

(C) Carpenter iron brake, 1890s.
Coll. of Mr and Mrs William C. Roup.

(D) Wilkins iron water tower, c. 1900.
Coll. of Mr and Mrs William C. Roup.

(E) Hubley circus band wagon, c. 1905–20.
Coll. of Mr and Mrs William C. Roup.

(F) Hubley iron circus parade wagon, c. 1905–20.
Coll. of Mr and Mrs William C. Roup.

PLATE 263

(B) Beggs 1⅞-in gauge live steam locomotive, 1890s.
Passaic County Historical Society. Photo, W. A. Lucas.

(A) Ives trackless tin clockwork locomotive, 1870s,
1880s.

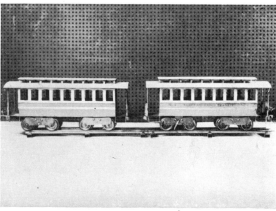

(C) Howard 2-in gauge electric locomotive, c. 1908.

(D) Lionel 2⅛-in gauge electric street car and
trailer, c. 1908.
Coll. of A. J. Koveleski.

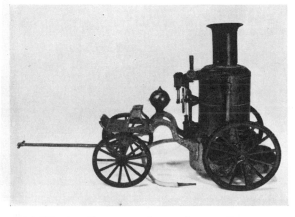

(E) Weeden live steam fire engine, c. 1890–1910.

(F) Hafner clockwork automobile, c. 1903.
Coll. of A. J. Koveleski.

PLATE 264

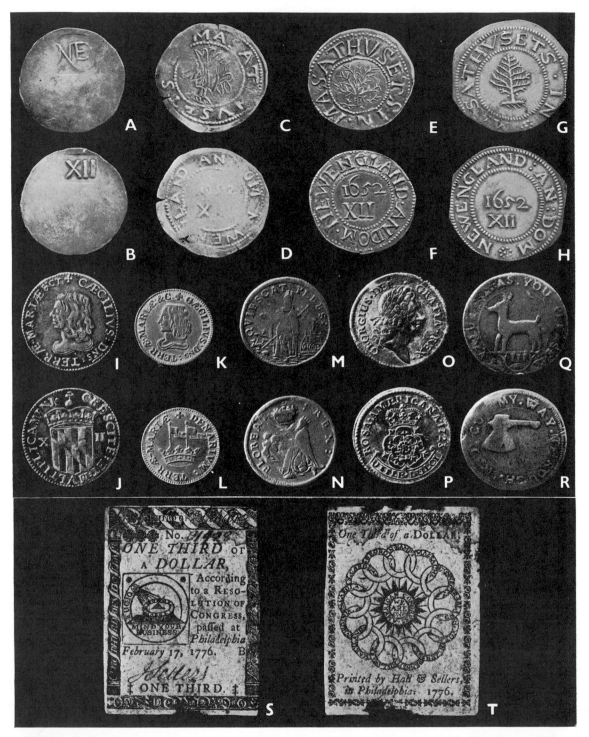

(A) New England shilling, (B) reverse; (C) Willow Tree shilling, (D) reverse; (E) Oak Tree shilling, (F) reverse; (G) Pine Tree shilling, (H) reverse; (I) Lord Baltimore shilling, (J) reverse; (K) Lord Baltimore penny, (L) reverse; (M) Mark Newby halfpenny, (N) reverse; (O) Rosa Americana halfpenny, (P) reverse; (Q) Higley copper (III-pence), (R) reverse; (S) Continental three-shilling note, (T) reverse.

PLATE 265

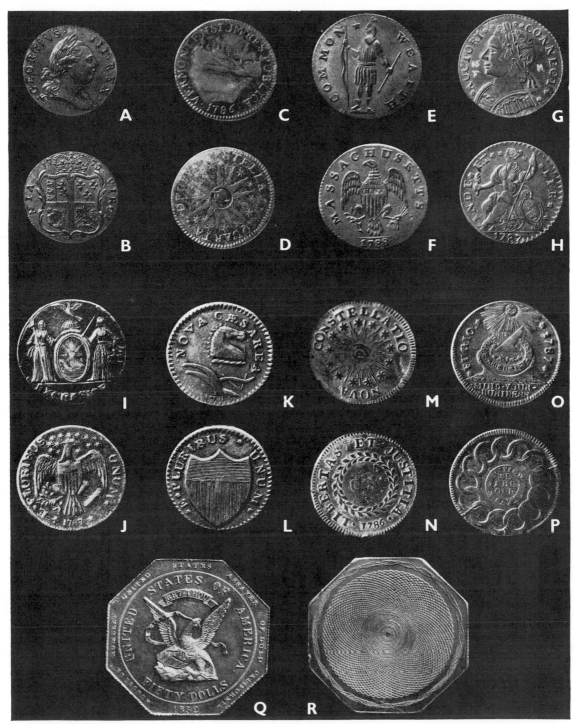

(A) Virginia halfpenny, 1773, (B) reverse; (C) Vermont cent, 1786, (D) reverse; (E) Massachusetts cent, 1788, (F) reverse; (G) Connecticut cent, 1787, (H) reverse; (I) New York cent, 1787, (J) reverse; (K) New Jersey cent, 1786, (L) reverse; (M) Nova Constellatio, 1786, (N) reverse; (O) Fugio cent, 1787, (P) reverse; (Q) Fifty dollar gold slug, 1852, (R) reverse.

PLATE 266

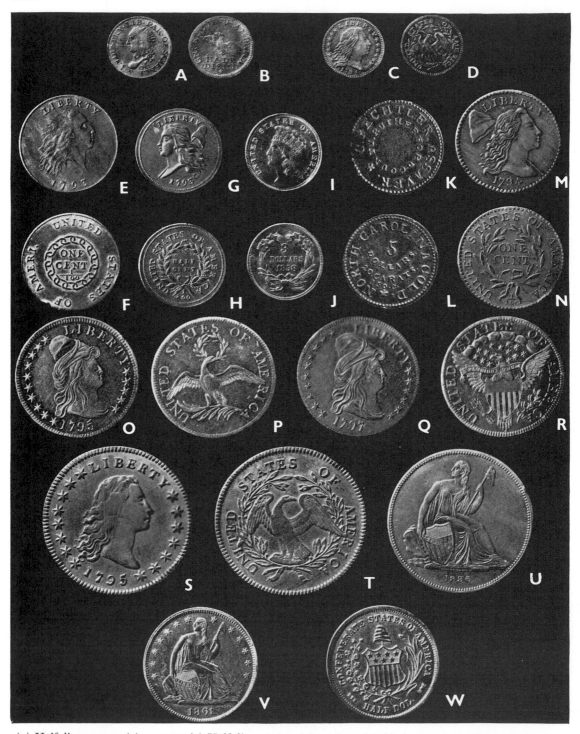

(A) Half disme 1792, (B) reverse; (C) Half dime, 1794, (D) reverse; (E) Chain type cent, 1793, (F) reverse; (G) Half cent, 1793, (H) reverse; (I) Three dollars, gold, 1858, (J) reverse; (K) Bechtler five dollars, gold, (L) reverse; (M) Liberty Cap cent, 1794, (N) reverse; (O) Eagle 1795 type ($10 gold), (P) reverse; (Q) Eagle 1797 type ($10 gold), (R) reverse; (S) Silver dollar, 1795, (T) reverse; (U) Gobrecht silver dollar, 1836, (V) Confederate half dollar, 1861, (W) reverse.

PLATE 267

(A) Washington oval Indian Peace Medal, obverse and reverse.

(B) Jefferson Indian Peace Medal.

(C) Saltus Medal, American Numismatic
Society, Weinmann.

*All illustrations by courtesy of the American
Numismatic Society.*

PLATE 268

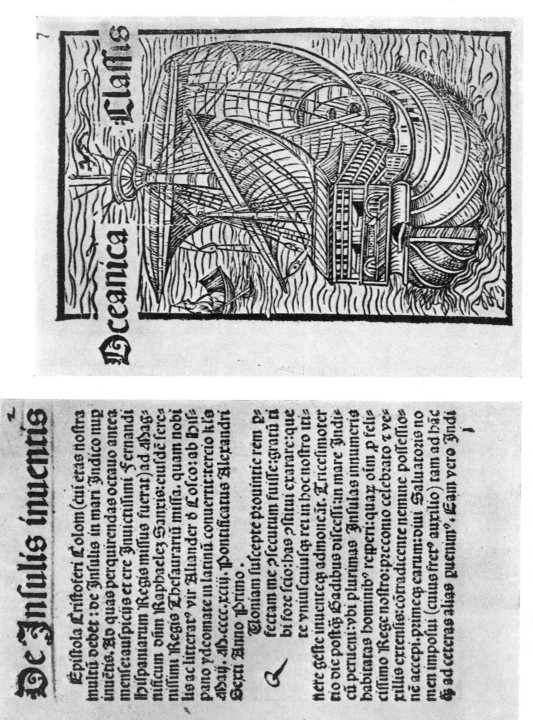

First illustrated edition of the Columbus letter, 1493, Basel. *Lenox collection, New York Public Library.*

PLATE 269

Title-page of the *Dotrina breve* of Bishop Juan Zumarraga, among the earliest printed books of the New World; Juan Croberger, Mexico, 1543 (1544). *In the Library of the Hispanic Society of America, New York.*

PLATE 270

A John Ratcliff binding, done in Massachusetts about 1680; the volume is Increase Mather's *A Call from Heaven*, 1679. *Mather collection, University of Virginia Library.*

PLATE 271

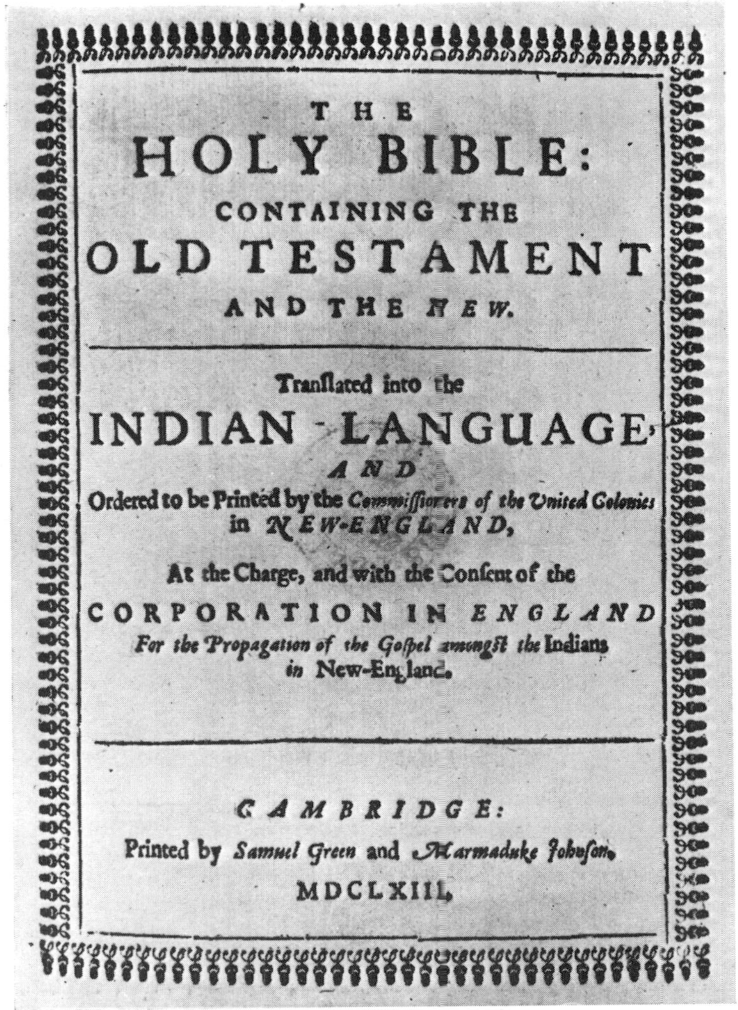

THE
HOLY BIBLE:
CONTAINING THE
OLD TESTAMENT
AND THE NEW.
Translated into the
INDIAN LANGUAGE,
AND
Ordered to be Printed by the Commissioners of the United Colonies
in NEW-ENGLAND,
At the Charge, and with the Consent of the
CORPORATION IN ENGLAND
For the Propagation of the Gospel amongst the Indians
in New-England.
CAMBRIDGE:
Printed by Samuel Green and Marmaduke Johnson.
MDCLXIII.

(A) The first Bible printed in America, the John Eliot Indian Bible, Cambridge, 1663. *McGregor Library, University of Virginia.*

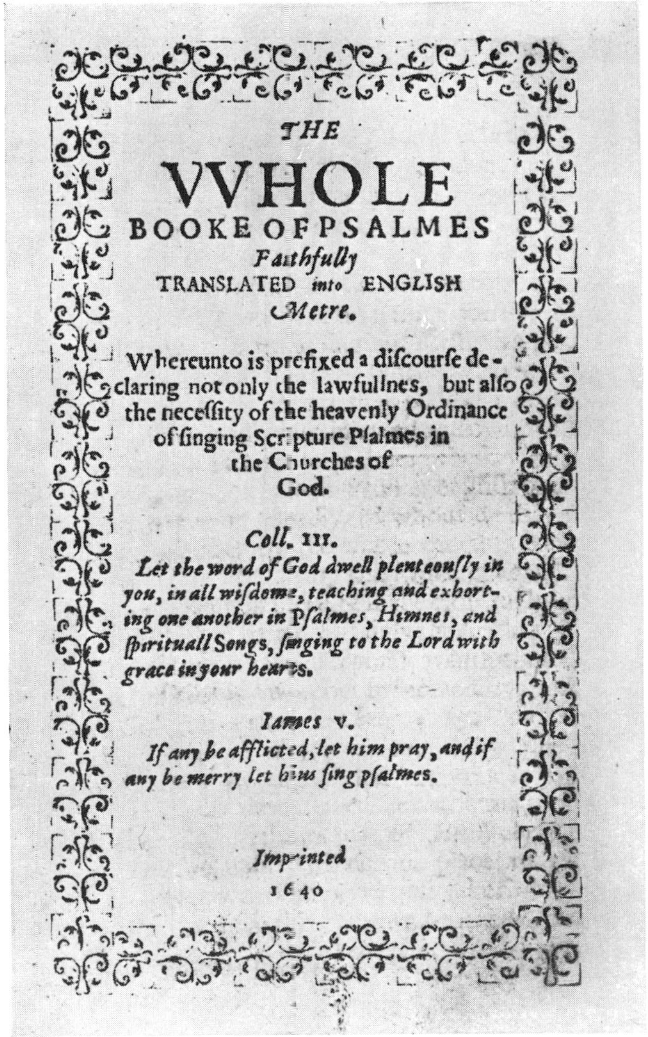

THE
VVHOLE
BOOKE OF PSALMES
Faithfully
TRANSLATED into ENGLISH
Metre.
Whereunto is prefixed a discourse declaring not only the lawfullnes, but also the necessity of the heavenly Ordinance of singing Scripture Psalmes in the Churches of God.
Coll. III.
Let the word of God dwell plenteously in you, in all wisdome, teaching and exhorting one another in Psalmes, Himnes, and spirituall Songs, singing to the Lord with grace in your hearts.
Iames V.
If any be afflicted, let him pray, and if any be merry let him sing psalmes.
Imprinted
1640

(B) The Bay Psalms, first book printed in what is now the United States of America; 1640, Cambridge. *Yale University Library.*

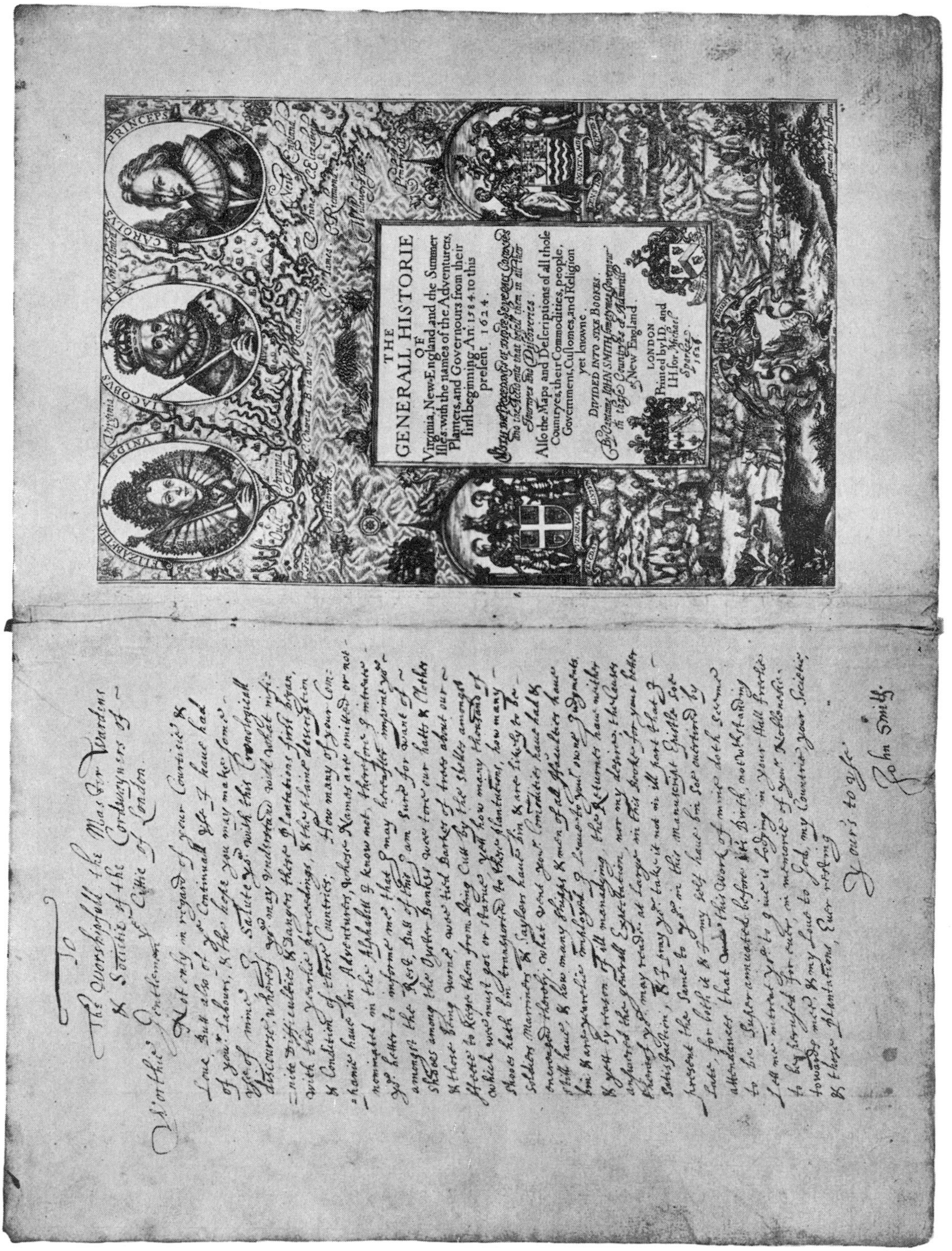

First edition of John Smith's *Generall Historie of Virginia* ... , London, 1624, inscribed to the Company of Cordwainers, London. *Henry E. Huntington Library, San Marino, California.*

PLATE 273

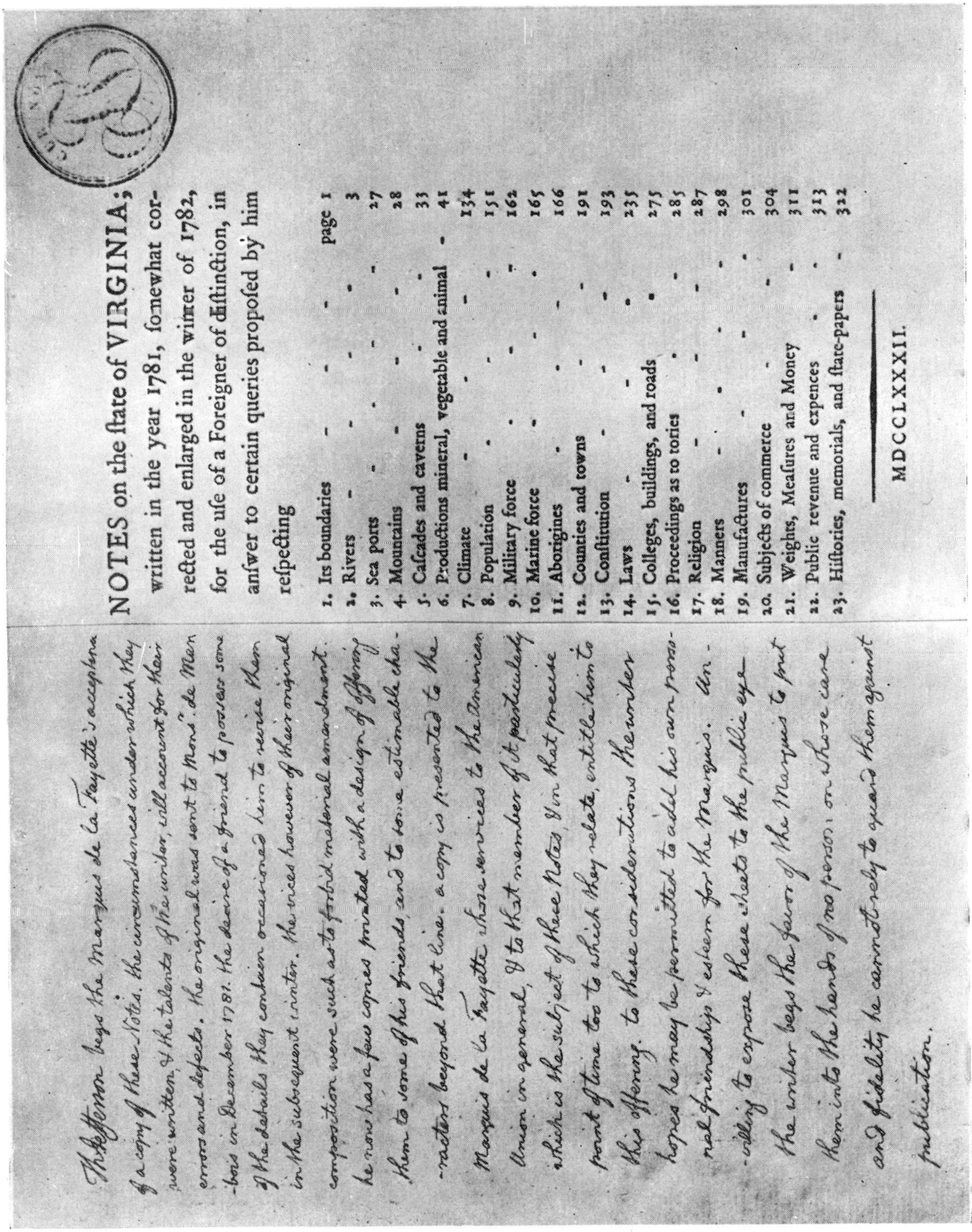

Th: Jefferson begs the Marquis de la Fayette's acceptance of a copy of these Notes. the circumstances under which they were written, & the talents of the writer, will account for their errors and defects. the original was sent to Mons.r de Marbois in December 1781. the desire of a friend to possess some of the details they contain occasioned him to revise them in the subsequent winter. the vices however of their original composition were such as to forbid material amendment. he now has a few copies printed with a design of offering them to some of his friends, and to some estimable characters beyond that line. a copy is presented to the Marquis de la Fayette whose services to the American Union in general, & to that member of it particularly which is the subject of these Notes, & in that precise point of time too to which they relate, entitle him to this offering. to these considerations the writer hopes he may be permitted to add his own personal friendship & esteem for the Marquis. unwilling to expose these sheets to the public eye the writer begs the favor of the Marquis to put them into the hands of no person on whose care and fidelity he cannot rely to guard them against publication.

NOTES on the ſtate of VIRGINIA; written in the year 1781, ſomewhat corrected and enlarged in the winter of 1782, for the uſe of a Foreigner of diſtinction, in anſwer to certain queries propoſed by him reſpecting

MDCCLXXXII.

First edition of Jefferson's *Notes on the State of Virginia*, 1784, inscribed by him to Lafayette. *McGregor Library, University of Virginia.*

PLATE 274

IN CONGRESS, JULY 4, 1776.

A DECLARATION

BY THE REPRESENTATIVES OF THE

UNITED STATES OF AMERICA,

IN GENERAL CONGRESS ASSEMBLED.

WHEN in the Course of human Events, it becomes neceſſary for one People to diſſolve the Political Bands which have connected them with another, and to aſſume among the Powers of the Earth, the ſeparate and equal Station to which the Laws of Nature and of Nature's God entitle them, a decent Reſpect to the Opinions of Mankind requires that they ſhould declare the cauſes which impel them to the Separation.

WE hold theſe Truths to be ſelf-evident, that all Men are created equal, that they are endowed by their Creator with certain unalienable Rights, that among theſe are Life, Liberty, and the Purſuit of Happineſs—That to ſecure theſe Rights, Governments are inſtituted among Men, deriving their juſt Powers from the Conſent of the Governed, that whenever any Form of Government becomes deſtructive of theſe Ends, it is the Right of the People to alter or to aboliſh it, and to inſtitute new Government, laying its Foundation on ſuch Principles, and organizing its Powers in ſuch Form, as to them ſhall ſeem moſt likely to effect their Safety and Happineſs. Prudence, indeed, will dictate that Governments long eſtabliſhed ſhould not be changed for light and tranſient Cauſes; and accordingly all Experience hath ſhewn, that Mankind are more diſpoſed to ſuffer, while Evils are ſufferable, than to right themſelves by aboliſhing the Forms to which they are accuſtomed. But when a long Train of Abuſes and Uſurpations, purſuing invariably the ſame Object, evinces a Deſign to reduce them under abſolute Deſpotiſm, it is their Right, it is their Duty, to throw off ſuch Government, and to provide new Guards for their future Security. Such has been the patient Sufferance of theſe Colonies; and ſuch is now the Neceſſity which conſtrains them to alter their former Syſtems of Government. The Hiſtory of the preſent King of Great-Britain is a Hiſtory of repeated Injuries and Uſurpations, all having in direct Object the Eſtabliſhment of an abſolute Tyranny over theſe States. To prove this, let Facts be ſubmitted to a candid World.

HE has refuſed his Aſſent to Laws, the moſt wholeſome and neceſſary for the public Good.

HE has forbidden his Governors to paſs Laws of immediate and preſſing Importance, unleſs ſuſpended in their Operation till his Aſſent ſhould be obtained; and when ſo ſuſpended, he has utterly neglected to attend to them.

HE has refuſed to paſs other Laws for the Accommodation of large Diſtricts of People, unleſs thoſe People would relinquiſh the Right of Repreſentation in the Legiſlature, a Right ineſtimable to them, and formidable to Tyrants only.

HE has called together Legiſlative Bodies at Places unuſual, uncomfortable, and diſtant from the Depoſitory of their public Records, for the ſole Purpoſe of fatiguing them into Compliance with his Meaſures.

HE has diſſolved Repreſentative Houſes repeatedly, for oppoſing with manly Firmneſs his Invaſions on the Rights of the People.

HE has refuſed for a long Time, after ſuch Diſſolutions, to cauſe others to be elected; whereby the Legiſlative Powers, incapable of Annihilation, have returned to the People at large for their exerciſe; the State remaining in the mean time expoſed to all the Dangers of Invaſion from without, and Convulſions within.

HE has endeavoured to prevent the Population of theſe States; for that Purpoſe obſtructing the Laws for Naturalization of Foreigners; refuſing to paſs others to encourage their Migrations hither, and raiſing the Conditions of new Appropriations of Lands.

HE has obſtructed the Adminiſtration of Juſtice, by refuſing his Aſſent to Laws for eſtabliſhing Judiciary Powers.

HE has made Judges dependent on his Will alone, for the Tenure of their Offices, and the Amount and Payment of their Salaries.

HE has erected a Multitude of new Offices, and ſent hither Swarms of Officers to harraſs our People, and eat out their Subſtance.

HE has kept among us, in Times of Peace, Standing Armies, without the conſent of our Legiſlatures.

HE has affected to render the Military independent of and ſuperior to the Civil Power.

HE has combined with others to ſubject us to a Juriſdiction foreign to our Conſtitution, and unacknowledged by our Laws; giving his Aſſent to their Acts of pretended Legiſlation:

FOR quartering large Bodies of Armed Troops among us:

FOR protecting them, by a mock Trial, from Puniſhment for any Murders which they ſhould commit on the Inhabitants of theſe States:

FOR cutting off our Trade with all Parts of the World:

FOR impoſing Taxes on us without our Conſent:

FOR depriving us, in many Caſes, of the Benefits of Trial by Jury:

FOR tranſporting us beyond Seas to be tried for pretended Offences:

FOR aboliſhing the free Syſtem of Engliſh Laws in a neighbouring Province, eſtabliſhing therein an arbitrary Government, and enlarging its Boundaries, ſo as to render it at once an Example and fit Inſtrument for introducing the ſame abſolute Rule into theſe Colonies:

FOR taking away our Charters, aboliſhing our moſt valuable Laws, and altering fundamentally the Forms of our Governments:

FOR ſuſpending our own Legiſlatures, and declaring us out of his Protection and waging War againſt us.

HE has abdicated Government here, by declaring us out of his Protection and waging War againſt us.

HE has plundered our Seas, ravaged our Coaſts, burnt our Towns, and deſtroyed the Lives of our People.

HE is, at this Time, tranſporting large Armies of foreign Mercenaries to compleat the Works of Death, Deſolation, and Tyranny, already begun with circumſtances of Cruelty and Perfidy, ſcarcely paralleled in the moſt barbarous Ages, and totally unworthy the Head of a civilized Nation.

HE has conſtrained our fellow Citizens taken Captive on the high Seas to bear Arms againſt their Country, to become the Executioners of their Friends and Brethren, or to fall themſelves by their Hands.

HE has excited domeſtic Inſurrections amongſt us, and has endeavoured to bring on the Inhabitants of our Frontiers, the mercileſs Indian Savages, whoſe known Rule of Warfare, is an undiſtinguiſhed Deſtruction, of all Ages, Sexes and Conditions.

IN every ſtage of theſe Oppreſſions we have Petitioned for Redreſs in the moſt humble Terms: Our repeated Petitions have been anſwered only by repeated Injury. A Prince, whoſe Character is thus marked by every act which may define a Tyrant, is unfit to be the Ruler of a free People.

NOR have we been wanting in Attentions to our Britiſh Brethren. We have warned them from Time to Time of Attempts by their Legiſlature to extend an unwarrantable Juriſdiction over us. We have reminded them of the Circumſtances of our Emigration and Settlement here. We have appealed to their native Juſtice and Magnanimity, and we have conjured them by the Ties of our common Kindred to diſavow theſe Uſurpations, which, would inevitably interrupt our Connections and Correſpondence. They too have been deaf to the Voice of Juſtice and of Conſanguinity. We muſt, therefore, acquieſce in the Neceſſity, which denounces our Separation, and hold them, as we hold the reſt of Mankind, Enemies in War, in Peace, Friends.

WE, therefore, the Repreſentatives of the UNITED STATES OF AMERICA, in GENERAL CONGRESS, Aſſembled, appealing to the Supreme Judge of the World for the Rectitude of our Intentions, do, in the Name, and by Authority of the good People of theſe Colonies, ſolemnly Publiſh and Declare, That theſe United Colonies are, and of Right ought to be, FREE AND INDEPENDENT STATES; that they are abſolved from all Allegiance to the Britiſh Crown, and that all political Connection between them and the State of Great-Britain, is and ought to be totally diſſolved; and that as FREE AND INDEPENDENT STATES, they have full Power to levy War, conclude Peace, contract Alliances, eſtabliſh Commerce, and to do all other Acts and Things which INDEPENDENT STATES may of right do. And for the ſupport of this Declaration, with a firm Reliance on the Protection of divine Providence, we mutually pledge to each other our Lives, our Fortunes, and our ſacred Honor.

Signed by ORDER and in BEHALF of the CONGRESS,

JOHN HANCOCK, PRESIDENT.

ATTEST.
CHARLES THOMSON, SECRETARY.

PHILADELPHIA: PRINTED BY JOHN DUNLAP.

The first printing and the only authoritative text of the American Declaration of Independence; printed by John Dunlap, Philadelphia. *Harvard University Library.*

PLATE 275

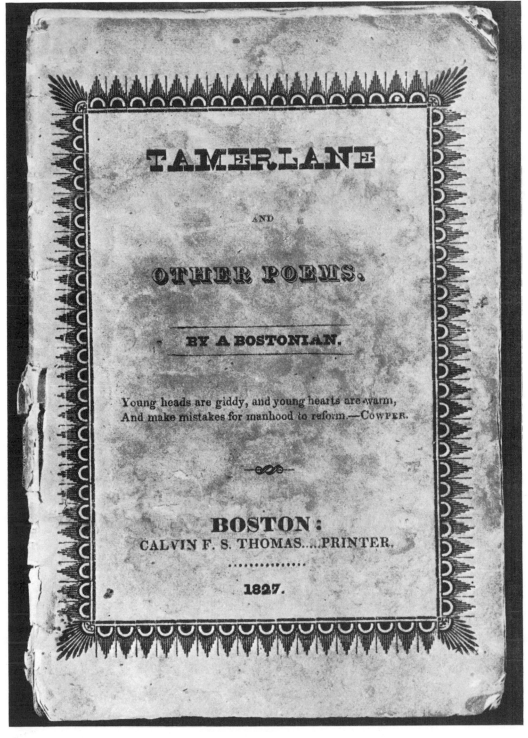

Front cover of Poe's first book of poetry, *Tamerlane*, Boston, 1827. *Barrett collection, University of Virginia Library.*

PLATE 276

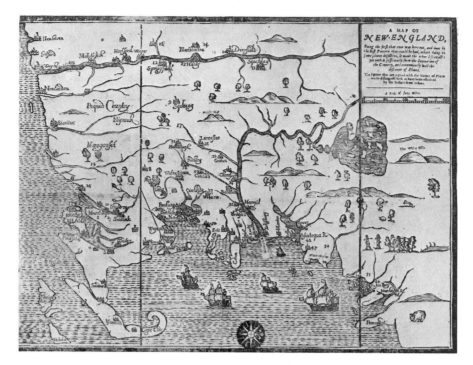

(A) New England. The first American printed map. Boston, John Foster (?), 1677.
The John Carter Brown Library, Providence.

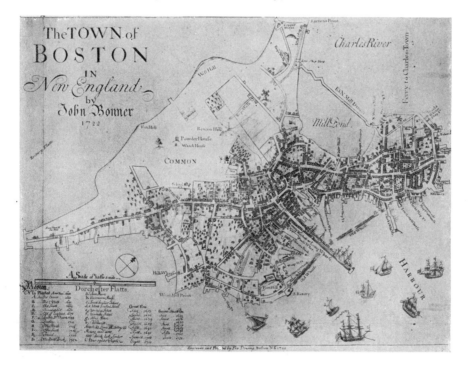

(B) Captain John Bonner's map of Boston, engraved by Francis Dewing, Boston,
1722. *Coll. of I. N. Phelps Stokes, New York Public Library.*

PLATE 277

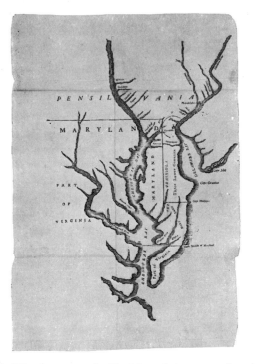

(A) Woodcut map in 'Articles of Agreement' ...
Philadelphia, B. Franklin, 1733. *The John Carter
Brown Library, Providence.*

(B) Thomas Johnston's plan of the Kennebeck
region of Maine. Boston, 1753. *Map collection, Yale
University Library, New Haven.*

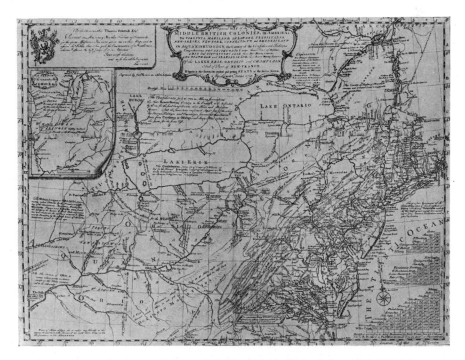

(C) James Turner's map of the ... 'Middle British Colonies' ... Philadelphia, 1755.
The Old Print Shop, Harry Shaw Newman.

PLATE 278

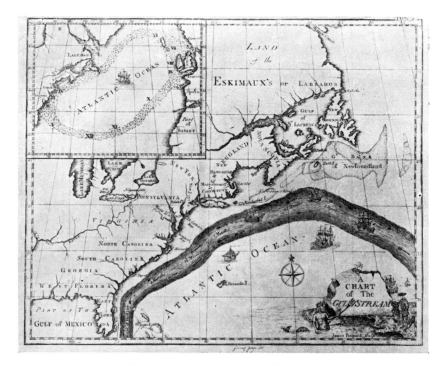

(A) James Poupard's 'Chart of the Gulf Stream', Philadelphia, 1786.
The Old Print Shop, Harry Shaw Newman.

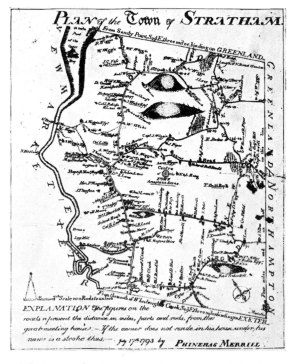

(B) John Churchman's map of the ... 'Peninsula
Between Delaware and Chesopeak Bays' ...
Philadelphia, *c.* 1786. *The Old Print Shop, Harry
Shaw Newman.*

(C) Phineas Merrill's map of the ... Town of Stratham,
New Hampshire, 1793. *Map collection, Yale University
Library, New Haven.*

PLATE 279

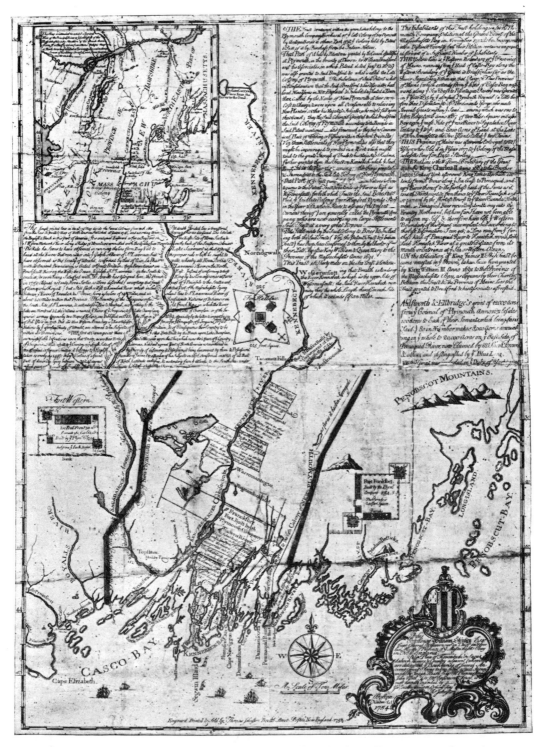

Thomas Johnston's map of Kennebeck and Sagadohock Rivers. Boston, 1754. *Connecticut Historical Society, Hartford.*

PLATE 280

Major Sebastien Bauman's map of the siege of Yorktown, Virginia, engraved by Robert Scot, Philadelphia, 1782. *Map collection, Yale University Library, New Haven.*

PLATE 281

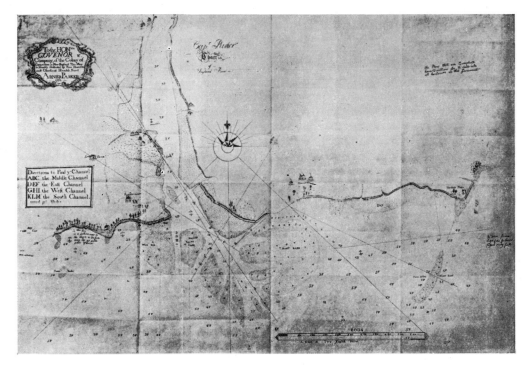

(A) Captain Abner Parker's ... 'Chart of Saybrook Barr', engraved by Abel Buell, New Haven, *c.* 1773. *Connecticut Historical Society, Hartford.*

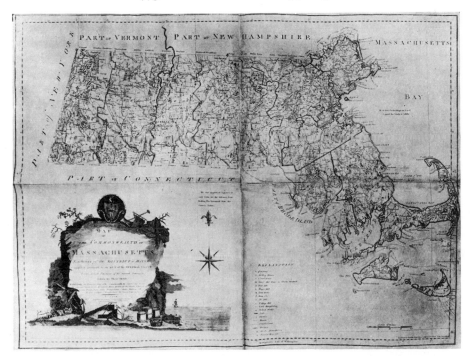

(B) John Norman and Osgood Carleton's map of the 'Commonwealth of Massachusetts.' Boston, *c.* 1800. *The Old Print Shop, Harry Shaw Newman.*

PLATE 282

(A) Believed to be the oldest American ship model; unidentified miniature attributed to the mid-eighteenth century. *Peabody Museum, Salem, Massachusetts.*

(B) Ship *Friendship* of Salem; made by the ship's carpenter during a voyage to Sumatra for the captain's son. Acquired 1803. *Peabody Museum, Salem, Massachusetts.*

PLATE 283

(A) Built-up model of the United States Brig *Lexington* of the Revolutionary War; by August F. Crabtree. Some planking and decking left off to show construction. *The Mariners Museum, Newport News, Virginia.*

(B) Half model of the schooner yacht *America* built in 1851, New York. This model made as a presentation to Queen Victoria. The donor and designer of the vessel, George Steers, died before the presentation could be made. *The Mariners Museum, Newport News, Virginia.*

PLATE 284

(A) Five-foot rigged model of the U.S. Frigate *Constitution* made prior to July, 1813, when it was presented to the Salem East India Marine Society. *Peabody Museum, Salem, Massachusetts.*

(B) Miniature model of clipper ship *Flying Cloud* 8½ ins. in overall length; made by A. G. Law. *The Mariners Museum, Newport News, Virginia.*

PLATE 285

(A) Sailor-made model of a full-rigged ship. A waterline model mounted on a board the surface of which has been carved and painted to represent the sea. Sails made of paper and bellied as under pressure of the wind. *The Mariners Museum, Newport News, Virginia.*

(B) Framed-hull model identified as the *Cradle of Commerce*. Built in 1825 for instruction.

(C) Sterling silver and gold plated model of the Long Island Sound steamer *Commonwealth*. Mounted on a music-box mechanism which activates paddle wheels and walking beam. Model built about 1864. *The Mariners Museum, Newport News, Virginia.*

PLATE 286

(A) *Capturing a Sperm Whale*. After a sketch by C. B. Hulsart. Aquatint by John Hill. Published by Hulsart, New York, *c.* 1835. *The Old Print Shop, Harry Shaw Newman.*

(B) *The Whale Fishery*. Attacking a Sperm Whale and 'Cutting In'. First state, before change of title to Attacking a Right Whale. Currier & Ives, undated; large folio. *The Old Print Shop, Harry Shaw Newman.*

PLATE 287

(A) Sperm Whaling No. 1 – *The Chase*. After A. van Beest and R. S. Gifford; corrected by Benjamin Russell. Endicott lithograph, New York, 1859. *The Old Print Shop, Harry Shaw Newman.*

(B) Whaleship *Kutusoff* of New Bedford; cutting in her last right whale on the northwest coast. Porpoise tail on bowsprit indicates 'homeward bound'. After Benjamin Russell. Lith. A. Mayer, Paris.

(C) *The Sperm Whale 'in a Flurry'*. N. Currier, New York; small folio, lithograph, 1852. *The Old Print Shop, Harry Shaw Newman.*

PLATE 288

Spr.: sprinkled. If the edges are sprinkled, they have been brush-spattered with color. If the leather of the binding has been sprinkled, it has been with a liquid such as copperas to give it a characteristic speckled or mottled appearance. Thus Spr. cf.

T.e.g.: top edge gilt. This refers to the gilding by the binder of the trimmed top edges of the folded sheets.

T.l.s.: typed letter signed. *Cf.* A.l.s. This abbreviation is not to be confused with the British T.L.S. abbreviation for *The Times Literary Supplement*.

T.p.: title page. Americans eschew the hyphen except in adjectival use: thus, 'Ornaments on the title page' and 'Title-page ornaments'.

Tr.: transcript. Used indiscriminately of manuscript copies without regard to the period of transcription unless specified.

12mo (twelvemo): *see* Book Sizes.

Unct. or **unc.:** uncut. As distinguished from unopened, this means that the binder did not trim the book. A reader with a paper opener can open the leaves in a book, but only a binder can leave them uncut. Thus an 'unopened' book is certain also to be 'uncut', but even after an 'unopened' book is opened, it is still 'uncut'.

V.d., v.p., v.y.: various dates, various places, various years. The 'v.y.' effort to replace an abbreviation commonly also used for 'venereal disease' has not been wholly successful in America.

Vso.: verso. The top surface of a left-hand page. *See* Recto.

W.a.f.: with all faults; i.e., the dealer or auction house will not refund the money if there are additional defects not described. Not to be confused with w.f., which means 'wrong font', or, in England, 'wrong fount'.

Wraps.: wrappers. These are an important part of paperbound books that are generally removed by binders, to the detriment of the value of a book. Not to be confused with d.j. *See* Bds.

GLOSSARY

Advertisements: separately quired advertisements edition-bound into the end of books were once used as bibliographical evidence of priority of issue, but for this purpose they have as little value as dust jackets.

Bibliography: there are three meanings. The bibliography of a subject may be a reading list for a special audience or a reference list (whether highly selective or completely exhaustive) for experts. The bibliography of an author (or of kinds of books, as color-plate books, or of some subjects, as fox-hunting) may be a list of books in their first or important editions, prepared for collectors. A bibliography that is analytical (besides being accidentally enumerative or physically descriptive) is, on the other hand, the product of the application to textual study of scholarly techniques developed through a knowledge of the production of books as physical objects.

Most bibliographies fall between the three stools. Most Americana collectors have on their shelves McKerrow's *Introduction to Bibliography* and Bowers's *Principles of Bibliographical Description*, but these books are seldom used, whereas Merle Johnson's *American First Editions* and Lyle Wright's *Early American Fiction* are thumbed daily by active collectors in their respective fields.

Bindings: American collectors today so uniformly insist on the original or a contemporary binding of a work that the art of hand bookbinding has fallen in America almost into desuetude. Only Tribolet of Lakeside and MacDonald of New York in this country are widely known and used by discriminating collectors, though there are a few other competent workmen available and some others whose services have been entirely pre-empted by single employers. Thus much of the binding done for American collectors is still done in England or France.

The amateur, unless he be a collector of bindings, might satisfactorily rest his information about binding on Cockerell's *Bookbinding and the Care of Books*, Zaehnsdorf's *The Art of Bookbinding*, or the more recent Edith Diehl's *Bookbinding, Its Background and Technique*.

But most American collectors will accumulate a small body of binding information in which these facts will be essential and characteristic:

Cloth edition bindings were introduced in the first quarter of the nineteenth century and have been common since 1850. Today they are universal only in the sense that cloth and paper are no longer distinguishable to the untrained eye.

The first American binder was Ratcliff (Plate 271).

Vellum bindings (the limp ones were most common in Italian binding of the sixteenth and seventeenth centuries) warp and cockle in American heated homes. Vellum on boards will tear itself loose unless kept in a reasonable approximation of the uncomfortable atmosphere of the European home, namely, at not over 65° Fahrenheit, with a relative humidity between 55 and 60 percent.

Dust jackets as early as the first half of the nineteenth century are known, but they are museum pieces. After World War I they were common, and any collector of a modern author whose books post-date the 1920s might properly consider incomplete any volume lacking a dust jacket.

Marbled endpapers were introduced in the late seventeenth century, but until the last quarter of the eighteenth century were as uncommon as they have again become in the twentieth century.

A fore-edge painting is a painting on the fanned-out edges of a book. Gilding on the trimmed edge conceals the painting until the leaves are fanned out.

American amateurs should know how to distinguish certain types of leathers used in binding (see Leathers), but only the expert or the specialist would be exposed to the vocabulary of the tooling styles: Grolier, Maioli, Harleian, Cottage, etc.

Book sizes and formats: the size of a book depends upon the size of the sheet it was printed on and the way the sheet was folded. A book's format, in turn, depends upon how its sheets were folded and then how these sheets were gathered into quires.

Since the two terminologies overlap and are used by the professionals in their variant meanings with precision, it is well for the amateur to understand these matters from the beginning.

For sheet sizes in detail, see Labarre's *Dictionary and Encyclopaedia of Paper and Papermaking*, pp. 251–72; but here are the most common sizes that clutter up the terminology, each of these commonly subdivided into large and small:

Foolscap	$13\frac{1}{2}$ ×	17 inches
Post	15 ×	19 inches
Crown	15 ×	20 inches
Demy	$17\frac{1}{2}$ ×	$22\frac{1}{2}$ inches
Medium	18 ×	23 inches
Royal	20 ×	25 inches
Imperial	22 ×	30 inches

If the printed sheets are each folded once (to make 2 leaves or 4 pages), then the book is a folio. The Hakluyt folios (printed on sheets of about foolscap size) stand about 13 inches high by about 8 inches wide. But it will be noted from the above table that an Imperial folio (such as the Mark Catesbys) would be nearly twice this size. Folios other than chart books are typically gathered into 6 leaves or 3 sheets of 12 pages per quire. Thus, in the bibliographer's annotation, a book described as 'fo. A–D⁶' would be made up of four quires (A to D) each made up of 6 leaves or 3 sheets, with A1ʳ: p.1, A1ᵛ: p.2, A6ʳ: p.11, A6ᵛ: p.12. The conjugate pairs of full sheets in the A signature would be A1 and A6, A2 and A5, A3 and A4; and the outer and inner formes would be in the pattern of outer: p.1 and 12, inner: p.2 and 11.

If the printed sheet is folded twice, into four leaves of 8 pages, the book is a quarto.

Folded once again, into 8 leaves or 16 pages, the book is an octavo. It should now be clear why a Crown Octavo is $7\frac{1}{2}$ × 5 inches, whereas a Royal Octavo is $10 × 6\frac{1}{4}$ inches.

There are several ways of imposing 12mos, for which see McKerrow's *Introduction to Bibliography*, pp. 325–8, but the most common is a four-leaf cut-off from the top of the sheet inserted into an eight-leaf fold.

By the time one reaches the 16mo fold, the book is small enough to be uncommon, and the folds so numerous that half-sheet imposition is likely. The quiring in half-sheets of 32mos would be normal.

Publishers' Weekly in recent years has established an arbitrary standard for size-indication in its *Weekly Record of Books Published*, and this, for the most common sizes, is given below in juxtaposition with the measurements that might be taken as normal for the antiquarian book trade. The discrepancy between the two columns arises from *Publishers' Weekly*'s measurement of bindings rather than of sheets, and from *Publishers' Weekly*'s adhering to a theoretical standard for sheets; even though, as a practical matter, printers tend to vary the sheet size inversely with the height of the finished book.

Format	PW	Antiquarian
Fo	over 30 cm.	13 inches
4to	30 cm.	9 inches
8vo	25 cm.	8 inches
12mo	20 cm.	5 inches

Care of books: no American collector should omit at least one reading of the Archer-Lydenberg *Care and Repair of Books*. Leather dressings (not saddlesoap) should be applied to leather bindings once in five years in most American climates, and places where books are kept should be underheated by American living standards. If a 55 percent relative humidity can be maintained without substantial fluctuation, little damage will be done to books of any sort within the normal range of American temperatures.

Extra-illustrated: an extra-illustrated or Grangerized book is one whose pictures have been inversely Bowdlerized; that is, instead of removing things that ought to be there, things have been stuck in that ought not to be there, and there is no health in us miserable offenders.

Incunabula: books printed before 1501, 'in the cradle' of printing. By extension, the word has come to mean the first fifty years of printing in any specified geographical area.

Leathers: the amateur can without difficulty learn, and generally does learn quickly, the difference between the binding skins of goat, calf, pig, and sheep. Goatskins are the most usual on the finest bindings, and in America are almost indiscriminately called Morocco, with no more reference to material or place of origin than an American would have in using the word 'hamburger'.

In texture, the largest and least regular of the grains is the goatskin. Calf (a special cowhide is called Russia) is smooth, as on the usual shoe. Untanned calf, with a parchment look, is called vellum. Tanned pigskin is almost indistinguishable from tanned human skin, though it is slightly coarser in texture. Footballs are not really made of pigskin. The pebbled surface on the football 'pigskin' is stamped there without much attention to the real appearance of the skin of a pig, which is made up in fact of irregularly dispersed pore-holes, on a surface in which the visual attention is drawn more to the holes of the pores than to the raised pebbling around them. Sheepskins on bindings have a buckskin or suède look; they shred off easily, and are sometimes called Roan.

Many other skins have, of course, been used in binding (reindeer skin, still used in Iceland, looks a little like sheep), but the chief fine bindings are done in goatskins, and these Moroccos are identifiable by the relative size of grain, in descending order of fineness, as Levant, Turkey, French, Oasis (generally in England called Niger), and Persian.

What happens to a leather after it is tanned makes a further subdivision of a binder's vocabulary. The Levant, being large-grained, frequently has its surface mechanically depressed and polished; hence the term Crushed Levant. Persian, on the other hand, is likely to be a Straight-grained Morocco; that is, uncrushed. Sprinkled or Tree Calf is the result of a treatment that yields a bark- or tree-like design on the finished leather. The amount of inlaying or gold-tooling on a binding produces such terms as Morocco Extra, which means extra-tooled, or extra-inlaid, or extra-special something.

See also Care of Books.

Provenance: the ownership pedigree of a book.

BOOKS FOR
FURTHER READING

CANNON, CARL L.: *American Book Collectors and Collecting*, Wilson (1941).

CARTER, JOHN: *Books and Book-Collectors*, Hart-Davis, London (1956).

CARTER, JOHN: *Taste and Technique in Book-Collecting*, Bowker (1948).

CARTER, JOHN, WINTERICH, JOHN T., MUIR, P. H. AND OTHERS: *New Paths in Book Collecting*, Constable, London (1934).

CHAPMAN, R. W., HAYWARD, JOHN, CARTER, JOHN, AND SADLEIR, MICHAEL: *Book Collecting*, Bowes & Bowes, Cambridge (1950).

CURLE, RICHARD: *Collecting American First Editions*, Bobbs-Merrill (1930).

GOODSPEED, CHARLES ELIOT: *Yankee Bookseller*, Houghton Mifflin (1937).

JACKSON, HOLBROOK: *The Anatomy of Bibliomania*, Farrar (1950). The work was originally published in London in 1930.

LEHMANN-HAUPT, HELLMUT, WROTH, LAWRENCE C. AND SILVER, ROLLO G.: *The Book in America*, Bowker (1951). (Originally published in 1939, this is the 2nd edition referred to here.)

LEWIS, WILMARTH S.: *Collector's Progress*, Knopf (1951).

MCMURTRIE, DOUGLAS C.: *The Book*, Covici Friede (1937).

MUIR, PERCY H.: *Book-Collecting as a Hobby*, Chesham, Gramol, London (1944).

MUIR, PERCY H.: *Talks on Book-Collecting*, Cassell, London (1952).

NEWTON, A. EDWARD: *The Amenities of Book-Collecting*, Little, Brown (1918).

NEWTON, A. EDWARD: *The Book-Collecting Game*, Little, Brown (1928).

NEWTON, A. EDWARD: *End Papers*, Little, Brown (1933).

NEWTON, A. EDWARD: *A Magnificent Farce and Other Diversions of a Book-Collector*, Little, Brown (1921).

OSWALD, JOHN CLYDE: *Printing in the Americas*, Gregg (1937).

ROSENBACH, A. S. W.: *A Book Hunter's Holiday*, Houghton Mifflin (1929).

ROSENBACH, A. S. W.: *Books and Bidders*, Little, Brown (1927).

STILLWELL, MARGARET BINGHAM: *Incunabula and Americana*, Columbia (1931).

STORM, COLTON, AND PECKHAM, HOWARD: *Invitation to Book Collecting*, Bowker (1947).

TARG, WILLIAM: *Bouillabaisse for Bibliophiles*, World (1955).

WALDMAN, MILTON: *Americana*, Holt (1925).

WINTERICH, JOHN T.: *Collector's Choice*, Greenberg (1928).

WINTERICH, JOHN T. AND RANDALL, DAVID A.: *A Primer of Book-Collecting*, Greenberg (1946). The work, without Randall's collaboration, was originally published in 1926; the edition referred to here was extremely revised.

WROTH, LAWRENCE C.: *The Colonial Printer*, Southworth (1938). First published in 1931, this is the 2nd edition referred to here.

PRINTED MAPS

By ALEXANDER O. VIETOR

THE development of the map in America, or more properly for this essay, English-speaking North America, runs roughly parallel, as would be expected, to the growth and development of maps in the rest of the civilized world and in particular as the result of discovery, exploration and settlement in a new hemisphere. Maps have a tall and honorable family tree whose roots are buried in the dawn soil of historical man. From the first clay and stone tablet of Mesopotamia to the precise survey of modern times, one can trace maps as a direct function of man's interest in his local environment and the globe as a whole and as a graphic method of picturing these features. Maps are a fascinating hybrid – a cross between a picture and a diagram.

It was the age of discovery, however, that finally brought map-making out of the theologians' cells back to the concepts of the classical Alexandrine geographers and pointed up the vital necessity of scientific accuracy if a map was to be worth the paper or parchment on which it was recorded. For an explorer a map became not only a philosophical exercise and speculation, but also a life and death matter. Most, if not all, of the early voyagers were map-makers – Columbus, Verrazano, Vespucci, Hudson, Block and the like. None of their maps are American in the sense of this article, but they were the direct ancestors of what later would become native products.

Over the years preceding the actual settlement in America, several techniques for producing maps in multiple copies had been worked out to circumvent the limitations of the hand-drawn manuscript map and chart of earlier days. These techniques, all dependent on the art of printing, were refinements of this art as applied to pictorial matter.

They were the woodcut and the copper-plate engraving, the former primarily a product of northern Europe and the latter an Italian development via the goldsmith's *niello*. Through these two methods maps could be produced in some quantity, and it was these procedures that were finally imported into the western hemisphere.

To undertake any study of maps in America it is important that attention be paid to the various phases of map reproduction: that is to the relationships of cartographer, engraver, printer and publisher. At times all of these functions were combined in one person, at other times they were separated into several individuals or other combinations.

Colonial period: like the famous Bay Psalm Book, the first American printed map was a New England affair and appeared as an illustration bound in William Hubbard's *A Narrative of the Troubles with the Indians in New-England* published in 1677 by the colonial printer JOHN FOSTER at Boston. Entitled *A Map of New-England, Being the first that ever was here cut* ... (Plate 277A), this cornerstone of American map-making is generally conceded to have come from Foster's own hand, although there is no specific indication of this on the map itself. Known as the 'White Hills' map to distinguish it from the English edition which is identified by the misprint 'Wine Hills', the area shown extends from Maine to the Connecticut River and serves to illustrate the Indian depredations on the colonial towns. Printed from a woodcut block, the map is the first essay into this technique in the colonies. Wood-cut maps were soon displaced by copper-plate engraving, and possibly the only other early wood-cut map of note is that issued by BENJAMIN

FRANKLIN to illustrate the location of the boundaries between Maryland and Pennsylvania in Franklin's printing of the agreement between Lord Baltimore and the Penns in 1733 (Plate 278A). This is thought by some to have come from Franklin's hand, and it is the first map printed in the English colonies south of New York.

It was not until after the emigration of FRANCIS DEWING from England to Boston that the first copper-engraved map appeared in America. *A New Chart of the English Empire in North America* ... it was engraved by Dewing for Captain Cyprian Southack in 1717 at Boston. Southack was a doughty Massachusetts mariner who commanded, for part of his career, the colony's *Province Galley*, in which he chased pirates and patrolled the coast. At one point he was awarded a sum of money by the British Crown with which to purchase a gold chain as a reward for his efforts in producing a survey of the St Lawrence River, and he was also responsible for a series of charts of the American coast published abroad.

It was only a step from regions to localities and Dewing was again employed by another seafaring gentleman of Boston to engrave a map of that town in 1722 (Plate 277B). CAPTAIN JOHN BONNER, by whom the map was published, appears also to have been a respected mariner of Boston and his plan of that place was so popular that it was re-issued in varying editions in 1729, 1733 (as re-engraved by Thomas Johnston), 1739, 1743 and 1769! The map's only competition was a similar plan showing the city on a smaller scale, drawn by WILLIAM BURGIS, engraved by Thomas Johnston in 1728 and dedicated to Governor William Burnet. It obviously did not capture the public's fancy, as only one edition is known.

New York was not far behind Boston with its own map of the streets, wharves and important buildings, for around 1735 WILLIAM BRADFORD, the first printer of New York, issued such a map from a survey by JAMES LYNE and an unknown engraver. This is one of the rarest maps of the colonial towns; a copy is in the New-York Historical Society.

The art of copper-plate engraving, which is so intimately connected with map-making, received an infusion of new blood with the establishment of additional professional engravers in the colonies. Listed among these are PETER PELHAM,[1] LAWRENCE HEBERT and JAMES TURNER. All three were trained abroad.

The first, Peter Pelham, has left for posterity *A Plan of the City and Fortress of Louisbourg with a small Plan of the Harbour* ... after a drawing by RICHARD GRIDLEY in 1745. Pelham's mezzotint, a departure from the usual line engraving, was sold by the painter John Smibert at Boston in 1746 and is the only map product that we know from Pelham's hand. Copies are in the John Carter Brown Library at Providence and the Massachusetts Historical Society.

Lawrence Hebert lived, it is believed, at least three years in Philadelphia, during which he engraved for LEWIS EVANS, friend of Franklin's, *A Map of Pensilvania, New Jersey, New-York, and the Three Delaware Counties*. ... This was issued in 1749 and was the precursor of Evans's well-known work on the middle British colonies.

Hebert also engraved a most interesting map ... *of Philadelphia, and Parts adjacent. With a Perspective View of the State House. By N. Scull and G. Heap*. ... Issued around 1752, the representation of the State House at the top center of the map is particularly important.

James Turner, the third professional mentioned above, was concerned to a considerable degree with map engraving. At first he was a resident of Boston where he cut, in 1747, three maps of sections of New Jersey in the vicinity of Elizabeth Town, as illustrations for a lawsuit against the people of that place by the Proprietors of East Jersey. Following this he engraved a chart in 1750 ... *of the Coasts of Nova-Scotia and Parts adjacent* ... dedicated to Governor Edward Cornwallis of that province.

Turner's most popular work, however, was his engraving of the famous *A general Map of the Middle British Colonies, in America. ... By Lewis Evans ...* in 1755 at Philadelphia (Plate 278C). It was issued originally as part of Evans's *Geographical, Historical ... Essays* printed by Benjamin Franklin and D. Hall the same year. This important map was the result of the interesting relationship of Franklin, Evans and Turner, and was the prototype for eighteen editions and issues printed abroad until 1814.

Turner likewise cut in copper JOSHUA FISHER's large chart of Delaware Bay in 1756 which was dedicated to the *Merchants* and *Insurers* of Philadelphia and printed by JOHN DAVIS at that city. Known by only two recorded copies, this chart evidently was suppressed by authority due to the aid it might have given a French enemy fleet in entering the Delaware in this period. The chart was re-issued in Philadelphia possibly as early as 1766 and was re-engraved in London in 1776.

In 1759 Turner engraved what has been called by Lawrence C. Wroth 'the most ambitious cartographical work to come from an American source before ... 1775'. This was the *Map of the improved Part of the Province of Pennsylvania* drawn by NICHOLAS SCULL and printed in six sheets by John Davis at Philadelphia.

THOMAS JOHNSTON of Boston, mentioned above, was quick to benefit from the influence of the French and Indian War on the public's appetite for maps. He engraved S. BLODGET's rare and important *A Prospective Plan of the Battle fought near Lake George on the 8th of September 1755* ... which, although strictly not a map, is mentioned for its map-like quality. This has been called the first historical print engraved in America.

Johnston also was responsible for engraving in 1756 the scarce ... *Plan of Hudsons Riv^r from Albany to ... Crown Point* by the Haverhill surveyor, TIMOTHY CLEMENT, which further set forth the areas of the French conflict.

In 1753, several years before the above, Johnston engraved a plan of the Kennebeck region of Maine to accompany a broadside setting forth the claims of the Brunswick proprietors of the area (Plate 278B). It is printed on one sheet with the broadside and has an amusing cartouche displaying two Indians with cartoon-like balloons coming from their mouths, the one stating that 'God hath Planted us here' and the other that

'God Decreed this Land to us'. The Plymouth Company, with conflicting claims, decided to fight fire with fire, so to speak, and likewise hired Johnston to engrave for them a full-dress map of the same area, in greater detail and with an inset of New England, to serve to illustrate their rebuttal of the Brunswick claims (Plate 280). Although Johnston entered upon the preliminaries of this work, it is suggested[2] that the map was completed on his own account and published by him with a dedication to Governor William Shirley in 1754. Engraved on two plates, this map measures $31\frac{1}{2} \times 22$ inches and is known by copies in the Massachusetts and Connecticut historical societies.

In 1765 an interesting map, *A General Map of the Country on the Ohio and Muskingham ...* was drawn and issued by THOMAS HUTCHINS, Assistant Engineer in the expedition led by Henry Bouquet against the Indians on the Ohio. It has been suggested by Wroth[3] that this was the work of HENRY DAWKINS, a Philadelphia engraver, due to similarities in style with his known work. Among the charming features are two scenes illustrating an Indian encampment and treaty.

Dawkins likewise engraved a map of the ... *Province of Pennsylvania ...* dedicated by its author, W. Scull, to Thomas and Richard Penn and printed by JAMES NEVIL at Philadelphia in 1770. This shows the final Mason and Dixon line run in 1763–7 between Pennsylvania and Maryland.

During the exciting pre-Revolutionary-war period, maps from native map-makers and engravers are scarce. Possibly many of the professional engravers of English background found sympathy with the Royal cause, or more probably the climate of increasing tension with England restricted the issue of maps that might be interpreted as having military significance. Certainly the majority of maps of this period and that of the war itself were dominated by manuscript military fort plans and surveys for army intelligence and use issued by the officers and engineers of the British and French armies.

A few special-purpose maps did see the light of day just prior to the outbreak of hostilities and one of these was CAPTAIN ABNER

PARKER'S ... *Chart of Saybrook Barr* (Plate 282A) cut by Connecticut's first engraver and jack-of-all-trades, ABEL BUELL.[4] Known by a single copy at the Connecticut Historical Society, this superlatively rare chart was issued in response to the desperate need by shipping interests for such a guide across the shoals at the entrance to the Connecticut River. Published around 1773 in New Haven, the chart came into being as the direct result of a lottery authorized in 1770 by the General Assembly. The current scarcity of this chart may be attributed to the fact that its fate could have been similar to Joshua Fisher's chart of the Delaware of 1756 which was suppressed, in all probability, due to the assistance it could have given the French. For the same reason the Parker chart may have been withdrawn so as not to have allowed the British forces knowledge about the entrance to the river.

Later Abel Buell also 'compiled, engraved and finished' at New Haven in March 1784 a large map of the United States[5] dedicated to the 'Governor and Company of the State of Connecticut'. Presumably the first map of the United States done in this country after the official treaty of peace with Great Britain, it bears in its cartouche one of the earliest representations of the newly-adopted American flag.

In a similar vein and also the product of a most colorful figure, was the mammoth chart in two sheets engraved for and published in 1775 by BERNARD ROMANS covering the Atlantic and Gulf coasts of East and West Florida and part of the Bahamas. Dedicated to the Marine Society of the city of New York, this endeavor is particularly appealing due to the speculations carried on as to its engraver. According to Clarence S. Brigham,[6] the chart itself was a product of PAUL REVERE's hand, while the decorative cartouches were cut by Romans. If true, this would represent the only map work of the famous patriot.

Romans[7] was intimately familiar with Florida due to his activity there as a surveyor under DeBrahm and Mulcaster, and as a result of his knowledge published *A Concise Natural History of East and West Florida*, a vol-ume that contained, along with the text, three small charts of harbor entrances on the Florida coast.

Of the local scene, this enterprising character from Holland engraved an important and extremely rare map of *Connecticut and parts adjacent* issued at New Haven in 1777. As a companion piece, Romans published *A Chorographical Map of the Northern Department of North America* ... issued also at New Haven in 1778. This was a northward extension of the Connecticut map. A similarly styled map of the ... *Country round Philadelphia* was issued by Romans the same year and a ... *Map of the Seat of Civil War in America* ... came out earlier in 1775 with no place of publication.

The Revolution kept men too busy to be concerned with map engraving, but its end was signalized by MAJOR SEBASTIEN BAUMAN's handsome map of the Yorktown siege dedicated to General Washington and engraved in 1782 by ROBERT SCOT of Philadelphia. This truly important map, depicting the last great campaign of the Revolutionary War, shows in its every line the European map training received by Bauman before his emigration to America and officership in the Continental Army. As far as is known, although there are many manuscript plans of the siege from various sources, the Bauman map is the only one drawn and engraved in America contemporaneously with the event (Plate 281).

In ending the colonial period it must be stressed once again that many other maps of American areas were engraved and printed abroad. Also there are extant many manuscript maps of vast importance and significance. Again, there may be other American printed maps not yet discovered as well as a number overlooked in printed volumes such as the *Map of Parts of Pennsylvania, Maryland, and Delaware* ... engraved by J. SMITHER and published as an accompanying illustration to an article on improving the inland navigation of Pennsylvania and Maryland in volume one of the *Transactions of the American Philosophical Society* in 1771. Printed maps can be most elusive and new ones are uncovered periodically.

Post-Revolutionary period: after the war America's eyes turned westward and seaward and map-makers soon began to reflect the public demands of the expanding young nation. Nine months after Buell's map of 1784 mentioned above, WILLIAM M'MURRAY,[8] 'Assistant Geographer to the United States', issued a map entitled ... *The United States according to the Definitive Treaty of Peace* ... engraved by Robert Scot at Philadelphia in the same year.

With the development of the western lands and grants to war veterans of the Revolution, came such works as HENRY D. PURSELL'S engraving of the ... *Map of Kentucke* ... drawn by JOHN FILSON and dedicated to Washington. Printed by T. Rook, it was issued in 1784 to illustrate Filson's book *Discovery Settlement and Present State of Kentucke.*

In 1785 'Poor JOHN FITCH' struggled to bring forth his ... *Map of the north-west parts of the United States of America* ... *Engraved & Printed by the Author,*[9] which he sold to settlers in the region in order to raise money for the development of his steamboat. This crude but highly significant piece of work shows the boundaries and new names for the old northwest as proposed by Thomas Jefferson in his ordinance of 1784. In this case surveyor, engraver, publisher and printer were all one man.

Of considerable interest in this period is the ... *Map of the Peninsula between Delaware & Chesopeak Bays* ... by JOHN CHURCHMAN and an unknown engraver. This was issued in Philadelphia around 1786 (Plate 279B).

Engravers became more numerous and surveyors and cartographers more active with the many demands of land controversies that followed the Revolutionary War. Some of the state boundaries were still in a state of flux, and western land claims bred the need for men with transit and chain line who could untangle the difficulties that continually arose. It is no longer possible to single out the great majority of specific maps for citation. City plans were engraved from New Orleans to Maine and engravers were kept busy with map orders. Some of these were JAMES POUPARD, JOHN and WILLIAM NORMAN, JOSEPH SEYMOUR and others.

James Poupard is remembered for his fine map of Baltimore engraved after a drawing by A. P. FOLIE in 1792 and also for his delightful ... *Chart of the Gulf Stream* ... (Plate 279A) in the 1786 *Transactions* of the American Philosophical Society illustrating Benjamin Franklin's article on the subject and showing Dr Franklin conversing with Father Neptune in the cartouche.

The two Normans, John (Plate 282B) and William, along with Joseph Seymour, were responsible for engraving charts for MATTHEW CLARK'S *A Compleat Chart of the Coast of America* published in atlas form at Boston in 1789, the first totally American pilot or book of charts. This was followed by the first edition of the *American Pilot* by John Norman in 1791 and the *Pilot for the West-Indies* by William Norman in 1795. These new publications began to supplant the previous English-made charts on board the ships of the new republic and[10] 'were, perhaps, the most important practical contributions to American life made up to that time by American engravers'.

Along this line was the local work of CAPTAIN PAUL PINKHAM of Nantucket, who was responsible for a survey of the Nantucket shoals published by Norman in his *Pilot* and who also produced the first accurate survey ... *of George's Bank including Cape Cod, Nantucket and the Shoals lying on their Coast.* ... *Engraved by Amos Doolittle, Newhaven, 1797.* This separate chart *Engraved and Printed for Edmund M. Blunt, Proprietor of American Coast Pilot 1797* was probably initiated by that energetic publisher of what was to become the sailor's most valued handbook on the American and West Indian coasts. Pinkham states on the chart with justifiable pride that '... you now have before you a New Chart which will enable the Mariner to shun those dangers which await him, actually surveyed and drawn by Paul Pinkham, Nantucket 1796'.

It is soon apparent that the tremendous stimulation to map making by the new enterprises and commercial development of the United States began to result in a flood of cartographical productions. The prolific burin of AMOS DOOLITTLE, the engraver of the chart mentioned above, was hard at work turning out maps of the four corners of the globe for the new gazetteers and geographies of JEDIDIAH MORSE, MATTHEW CAREY and others. In 1789 CHRISTOPHER COLLES anticipated the modern road-map with a volume of strip engravings showing the route of the post roads along the Atlantic seaboard. A large general map of the same subject was issued by ABRAHAM BRADLEY in 1796 and at intervals thereafter.

State maps began to appear in increasing quantity during the first part of the nineteenth century and land surveys, such as that made by SETH PEASE in his ... *Map of the Connecticut Western Reserve, from actual Survey* ... engraved by Doolittle in 1798, kept before the public the magnet of rich lands to the westward, and the depopulation of the rocky New England hills began in earnest.

Western expeditions such as that of Lewis and Clark resulted in a spate of new mapping and in 1807 the United States Coast Survey was founded to systematize charts of the coastline.

Broadly speaking, map making developed in the nineteenth century along two lines – private and public. The former was characterized by individual business ventures such as Reid's and Carey's atlases, the latter publishing the first general United States atlas in 1794 at Philadelphia. The public map making was in the hands of the government as a result of the western land development and the great transcontinental surveys of the latter part of the century. The period from 1820 to 1840 has been referred to as the golden age of American cartography and resulted in a vast outpouring of atlases and map materials of all sorts.

The first American globes were made around 1811 by a self-taught engraver, JAMES WILSON of Bradford, Vermont, who later moved his establishment to Albany.

The newly developing techniques of lithography, and later wax engraving, reduced the cost of multiplying maps by permitting a far greater run from one stone or plate. Wax engraving was invented by SIDNEY E. MORSE, brother of the inventor of the telegraph, and the first 'cereographic' atlas using

this method was published in 1841. Steel engravings and the use of electroplated copies from copper and steel plates allowed for an almost unlimited supply of impressions of new maps, far above the restrictions placed by wear on the copper-plate printing of earlier days.

County atlases and town plans made their appearance in the second quarter of the nineteenth century and are familiar to most as the first general run of maps to show houses with their owners' names, although this method was used as early as 1793 by PHINEAS MERRILL on his engraved map ... *of the Town of Stratham* in New Hampshire (Plate 279C).

The final spanning of the continent was achieved by the four elaborate western surveys of KING, WHEELER, POWELL and HAYDEN, and in 1878 the formation of the United States Geological Survey spelled the true beginning of organized land-mapping of the country as a whole. As yet this object has not been achieved, and almost two-thirds of the United States is still to be mapped accurately.

From that time through the present, map making in America has been dominated by the development of newer and faster processes for getting a survey down on paper. Airplane photographs and gigantic projection and drafting machines make it now possible to construct an accurate contour map of an area directly from overlapping air views in a fraction of the time formerly taken by ground surveyors.

The 1950s have seen this technological improvement continue apace, due to the stimulation of World War II and the great need for strategic and operational maps of all quarters of the globe. The formation of the Army Map Service and allied agencies has removed map making from a rather haphazard discipline to an accurate, vital and necessary science – an integral part of the world of today.

[1] L. C. Wroth and Marion W. Adams, *American Woodcuts and Engravings 1670-1800*. Providence, The Associates of the John Carter Brown Library (1946).
[2] L. C. Wroth, *The Thomas Johnston Maps of the Kennebeck Purchase* in *In Tribute to Fred Anthoensen Master Printer*, Portland, Maine (1952).

[3] L. C. Wroth and Marion W. Adams, *op. cit.*, no. 22.

[4] L. C. Wroth, *Abel Buell of Connecticut.* ... Acorn Club (1926).

[5] Ibid.

[6] Clarence S. Brigham, *Paul Revere's Engravings*, American Antiquarian Society, Worcester, Massachusetts (1954).

[7] P. Lee Phillips, *Notes on the Life and Works of Bernard Romans,* The Florida State Historical Society, Deland, Florida (1924).

[8] L. C. Wroth, *Abel Buell of Connecticut (cit.)*

[9] P. Lee Phillips, *The Rare Map of the Northwest 1785, by John Fitch.* ... W. H. Lowdermilk & Co., Washington (1916).

[10] L. C. Wroth, *Some American Contributions to the Art of Navigation,* Providence, The Associations of the John Carter Brown Library (1947).

BOOKS FOR
FURTHER READING

FITE, EMERSON D. AND FREEMAN, A.: *A Book of Old Maps Delineating American History from the Earliest Days Down to the Close of the Revolutionary War,* Cambridge, Harvard University Press (1926).

KARPINSKI, LOUIS C.: *Bibliography of The Printed Maps of Michigan, 1804–1880,* Lansing, Michigan, Michigan Historical Commission (1931).

KENDALL, HENRY P.: *Early Maps of Carolina and Adjoining Regions,* Second Edition Prepared by Louis C. Karpinski, privately printed (1937).

PHILLIPS, P. LEE: *A Descriptive List of Maps and Views of Philadelphia,* Philadelphia, Geographical Society of Philadelphia (1926).

PHILLIPS, P. LEE: *A List of Maps of America in the Library of Congress,* Washington, The Library of Congress, Division of Maps and Charts (1901).

RAISZ, ERWIN: *General Cartography,* New York and London, McGraw-Hill Book Company, Inc. (1938).

STEVENS, HENRY N.: *Lewis Evans. His Map of the Middle British Colonies,* Second Edition, Henry Stevens, Son, and Stiles, London (1920).

THOMPSON, EDMUND: *Maps of Connecticut Before the Year 1800,* Hawthorn House, Windham, Connecticut (1940).

THOMPSON, EDMUND: *Maps of Connecticut for the Years of Industrial Revolution, 1801–1860,* Hawthorn House, Windham, Connecticut (1942).

TOOLEY, R. V.: *Maps and Map-Makers,* B. T. Batsford, Ltd., London, New York, etc. (1949).

WINSOR, JUSTIN (Ed.): *A Narrative and Critical History of America,* Boston (1889).

Concise Encyclopedia of Antiques, Vol. III, pp. 227–37, Hawthorn Books, New York (1957).

SHIP MODELS

By ROBERT H. BURGESS

SINCE pre-Revolutionary days ship models have played a decorative role in many homes of this country. Most of these were apparently made by American seamen or ships' carpenters, particularly of the favorite ships on which they sailed. Some of the existing early models of American ships have been authenticated as having been made by seamen. This fact is also evident in the workmanship of the few remaining contemporary American ship models. Generally referred to as 'sailor-made', these models are usually on the crude side due to lack of use of proper tools. A jackknife sufficed to carve the hull; an awl, needle and file produced the fittings. But, even though the seaman has fallen short in making a model with finesse according to present-day standards, he is almost certain to have rigged it properly.

What is believed to be the oldest American sailing ship model (Plate 283A) in existence appears to have been 'sailor-made'. This is a model in the collection of the Peabody Museum, Salem, Massachusetts, and is attributed to the mid-eighteenth century. Although unidentified and damaged in the rigging, it serves as an interesting example of early American ship model-making.

Two other models dating back to the eighteenth century are also preserved at Peabody. The *Friendship* (Plate 283B) is one of the largest and finest in that museum's collection. This was made for the son of the vessel's commander, Captain William Story of Salem, by the ship's carpenter, Thomas Russell, during a voyage to Sumatra. Nine feet in length, the model proved to be too large for the captain's house, so was given to the East India Marine Society in 1803. The other model, recently acquired, was built in 1768 by a ship's carpenter named John Brett.

Since it came directly from the family its entire history can be authenticated by documents.

Also at the Peabody Museum is a model of the United States Frigate *Constitution* (Plate 285A) made before July 1813, when it was given to the East India Marine Society by Captain Isaac Hull, one of the vessel's commanders. This is the only accurate contemporary model of the ship known and was used by authorities of the United States Navy when the *Constitution* was restored at Boston in 1907.

Seamen enjoyed making models of their ships during the long passages at sea and would use any material at hand. A familiar type of model in the nineteenth century was the waterline model placed on a painted sea of putty or similar substance. The whole was placed on a board base; or the model itself (Plate 286A) might be mounted on a board, the surface of which had been flecked with chips raised by a chisel and painted to simulate the sea. Such models were usually rigged with sails set at the proper angle and bellied as under pressure of the wind. In some instances paper was used for the sails, but often these were carved from wood and rounded as though they were billowing.

Similar to this was the rigged half-model secured to a backboard. Just half of the ship lengthwise was constructed and on this were mounted the masts. The yards protruded horizontally out of the backboard and usually had wooden sails attached to them. These more primitive models seldom appeal to the more seasoned ship model collector, who is a stickler for details, but there is a certain charm attached to them.

The oldest American ship model in the collection of The Mariners Museum, New-

687

port News, Virginia, is a unique framed-hull model (Plate 286B) identified as the *Cradle of Commerce*. Attached to the keel is a brass plate inscribed: *William Ballard, Boston*, 1825. Bluff of bow and with a deep draft for its length, this is a model characteristic of a ship of that period. Devoid of planking and decking, but otherwise complete as far as constructional timbers are concerned, it is believed this model was used for instruction purposes. The frames and other timbers used in its make-up are alphabetized and marked with numerals for identification. Made of mahogany, the model reveals the vast amount of jointing and scarfing required in the construction of a large wooden ship.

Although rigged full-models have been the most sought after by the collector, there is still another type of model which has long been popular. This is the half-model or builder's model, used in conjunction with the actual construction of a ship. Usually mounted on a backboard, a model of this type reveals the entire length of one side of a ship. The graceful underwater lines and curves are shown to the best advantage. Of particular interest and value to museums, since they are scaled down replicas of ships actually built, half-models also make handsome decorative pieces.

A classic example of a half-model of America's most famous yacht (Plate 284B), the schooner *America*, is in the collection of The Mariners Museum. This vessel was designed and built by George Steers at New York in 1851 to compete with a group of British yachts in a race around the Isle of Wight. Winning that event the *America* was presented with a trophy which was to become known as the *America's* Cup, defended successfully ever since by American yachtsmen.

Steers built this half-model, $4\frac{1}{2}$ feet in length and mounted on a mahogany plaque, expressly as a gift for Queen Victoria. A silver plate attached to the plaque is inscribed to that effect. However, Steers died before the presentation could be made and his widow kept the model and later gave it to friends of the family. They kept it in their possession for ninety-three years before placing it in the museum.

Most shipyards in years past had quantities of half-models hanging in their lofts or offices. Very little value was placed upon them by the shipyards after they had served their purpose, and many were disposed of or permitted to fall into a state of deterioration. Their technical value was appreciated by museums and historians who made efforts to obtain them for preservation. Individual collectors also tried to obtain these models. Sensing their antique and decorative qualities, dealers ferreted many of these models out of old shipyards or homes of descendants of the ships' owners or builders. Today the most likely place to find available half-models is dealers' shops, particularly in the New England area, which was the major American shipbuilding center of years past.

Before purchasing a model a collector should select a model of an actual ship. Too often one finds a model of a ship not listed in any directory but named after the wife, daughter, or sweetheart of the model-maker, a composite of features of many vessels. Such models have little other value than as a form of folk art. But with a known ship it is possible to trace its history in museums, libraries, or customs houses, which adds considerably to the interest and value of the model.

Perfection should be the chief requisite in a model if one sets out to make a collection. There are too many likenesses of ships available which are inaccurate in hull and rigging. Few are those who can determine what is right or wrong on a model, especially on those of an early period.

To verify the accuracy of a model it is recommended that a marine museum, expert model-maker, or marine historian be consulted. Books, plans and contemporary prints and paintings can be of assistance in pointing out inaccuracies which affect the historical value of a model; and that should be stressed above its decorative value. In most instances the older models have some damage to their rigging. Repairs should be undertaken only by expert model-makers and should be in keeping with the period of the ship.

If a model of a certain type or period is desired, a reputable model-maker can be commissioned to build one. Marine museums can recommend reliable and skilful model-makers, and there are numerous ship model societies situated in principal cities. One of the most outstanding in this field is the Nautical Research Guild, an international marine historical organization whose membership is composed of leading model-makers in America.

Perhaps the most outstanding model-maker in America today is August F. Crabtree of Hampton, Virginia, who specializes in the built-up ship model (Plate 284A). His models are framed and planked just as the actual ships were constructed. Ships of the period when lavish wood carvings embellished their bows and sterns are his favorite subjects: the carvings on his models are reproduced to the most exacting detail. But ships of any period, sail or steam, are faithfully constructed by this artisan.

For suitable materials Mr Crabtree has selected woods not normally used by model-makers. His requirements call for close-grained hard woods to make possible the diminutive carvings. He makes his own carving tools from cast-off dental and surgical instruments in order to bring out the smallest details in the minute figures. His series of ship models depicting maritime progress from 1480 B.C. to A.D. 1840 is on display at The Mariners Museum.

Some collectors of models are limited in their pursuit by lack of display-space in their homes. This calls for concentration on small models which retain accuracy and detail. This problem has been solved by the New Jersey model-maker, A. G. Law, who specializes in miniature ship models. His model (Plate 285B) of the clipper-ship *Flying Cloud* measures 8½ inches in length and 5 inches in height. Yet this jewel-like miniature would satisfy the most severe seaman-critic. Fittings like deadeyes, blocks and other items are simplified in their make-up on these models, but are very effective.

Occasionally there is an opportunity to acquire an exceptionally rare example of a ship model. The Mariners Museum acquired at an auction such a model (Plate 286C) in the form of the sterling silver and gold-plated steamboat *Commonwealth*, 27½ inches

in length. The actual vessel was built at Greenpoint, New York, in 1855. The model is mounted on a music box which when played actuates the side-wheels and walking beam of the steamboat. Ten different songs make up the musical selections. The model is a fine example of the silversmith's art and, at the same time, of skilful model-making. This was made especially for the captain of the steamer and presented to him by friends. No maker's name can be found on the model, but close examination of its components revealed that the hubs of the side-wheels are American pennies dated 1864. This accurately dates the construction of the model just before the loss of the actual ship by fire in 1865.

If a collector concentrates on collecting old models of American ships made in this country his field is somewhat limited. This is due to the youth of our nation as compared with the European countries which have had a lead of centuries in producing ship models. But restricting the field to American ship models can still produce satisfying results if the collector is persistent in his search.

GLOSSARY

Aft: towards the stern or back end of the ship.

Amidships: approximately midway between the bow and stern.

Athwartship: across the ship.

Backstays: ropes or cables forming part of the standing rigging leading from the top of a mast to aft of the mast to support the mast against a forward pull.

Bark: a sailing vessel of three or more masts being square-rigged on all masts except the after mast, or jigger, which is fore-and-aft rigged.

Barkentine: a sailing vessel of three or more masts being square-rigged on the foremast and fore-and-aft rigged on all other masts.

Belaying pin: an iron, brass, or wooden pin on which a rope is belayed or secured.

Bitt: an iron or wooden post, usually in pairs on a ship's deck or dock, to which are fastened mooring lines, anchor cables or ropes.

Boom: a spar at the foot of a fore-and-aft sail.

Bow: the forward part of the ship where its sides converge toward the stem.

Bowsprit: a spar which projects from the forward end of a sailing ship.

Braces: ropes controlling the horizontal motion of yards of a square-rigged ship.

Brig: a two-masted square-rigged sailing ship.

Brigantine: a two-masted vessel with square-rig on the foremast and fore-and-aft rig on the mainmast.

Bull's-eye: a round, flattened piece of hardwood pierced by a hole through which a line passes.

Bulkhead: a partition placed fore-and-aft or athwartships to separate compartments.

Bulwarks: an extension of a vessel's side above the weather deck to keep the deck free of water.

Capstan: a drum-like machine mounted vertically on a ship's deck. Revolved by hand power by means of long wooden bars inserted in its head or by auxiliary power.

Cat-head: a short timber or iron piece projecting from each bow at the forecastle deck and used in hoisting the anchor.

Chain plate: a strap of iron secured vertically to a ship's side to which the lower deadeyes, backstays, or shrouds are secured.

Chock: a heavy wooden or metal fitting open at the top and with rounded edges and horn-like projections through which lines are passed; secured to a ship's deck or dock.

Clew: either of the lower corners of a square sail or lower aftermost extremity of a fore-and-aft sail.

Clipper bow: a ship's bow in which the stem forms a concave curve which projects outward above the waterline.

Clipper-ship: a square-rigged sailing vessel with a sharp hull and large sail area built expressly for fast sailing from the 1840s through 1860.

Counter: the underside of the overhanging portion of a ship's stern above the water.

Course: a sail bent to the lower yard of a square-rigged vessel.

Crossjack: square sail spread by the yard of the same name or the lowest yard on the aftermost mast in a full-rigged ship.

Crosstrees: timbers laid on and across the trestletrees of a mast to spread the rigging of the topmast or topgallant mast.

Crow's nest: a lookout platform or enclosure mounted atop a mast.

Cutwater: forward edge of the stem at the waterline.

Davit: arched metal tubular crane, usually in pairs, used for hoisting and lowering boats. Earlier ones made of wood.

Deadeye: a flat rounded piece of hard wood, strapped with rope or iron and bearing holes through which are passed lanyards. Found at the ends of stays and shrouds for setting up or tightening purposes.

Dolphin striker: a short wooden or iron spar suspended under the bowsprit cap to spread the martingale stays.

Draft: the depth of the lowest part of a vessel below the waterline.

Figurehead: ornamental carving mounted on the upper portion of the cutwater just beneath the bowsprit.

Fore-and-aft sail: a sail which pivots at its forward edge and slides on a stay or is hoisted up a mast by means of hoops or track.

Forecastle: the upper deck of a vessel forward of the foremast. The forward compartment where the crew of sailing ships was generally housed.

Full-model: a ship model with complete hull and rigged.

Half-model: half of the hull form of a ship made of a solid wooden block cut along its central vertical fore-and-aft plane.

Halyards: ropes to hoist or lower sails, yards or spars.

Hatch: an opening in a ship's deck serving as access to the hold for cargo.

Hawse pipe: holes in the ship's bows through which the anchor cables pass.

Jib: a triangular fore-and-aft sail extended upon a stay between the jib-boom, bowsprit and foremast.

Jib-boom: a spar extending out beyond the bowsprit.

Keel: principal piece of timber in a ship extending longitudinally along the bottom of the ship from stem to sternpost.

Lanyards: ropes rove through the upper and lower deadeyes to set up or tighten the shrouds.

Martingale: a stay under the jib-boom to sustain the strain of the head stays. Fastened to or rove through the dolphin striker to the cutwater.

Poop deck: the after part of the main deck at the stern.

Ratlines: small lines crossing the shrouds and serving as a ladder for seamen climbing aloft.

Rudder: a flat piece of wood or metal mounted vertically at the immersed portion of the ship's stern which serves as a means of directing the course of the ship.

Running rigging: the movable ropes hauled upon to brace yards and make or take in sail.

Scuppers: drains set in the waterways at the junction of the deck and bulwarks to carry off water.

Sheer: the longitudinal curvature of the ship's deck between stem and stern.

Sheets: ropes or chains fastened to the after end of yards or booms or to the after lower corner of a fore-and-aft sail.

Shrouds: ropes or cables extending from the masthead to the ship's sides to laterally support the mast.

Square-sail: rectangular sails set from yards which pivot at their middle.

Standing rigging: rigging which acts chiefly to support the masts.

Stem: the forward edge of a ship's hull.

Stern: the afterpart of a vessel.

Studding sails: light sails set from studding sail booms, portable extensions of yardarms on the fore and main masts of a square-rigged ship.

Taffrail: railing about a ship's stern.

Trestletrees: two fore-and-aft pieces of wood, one on each side of the mast, supporting the weight of the crosstrees.

Waterline model: a model showing a ship from the waterline up, not revealing any of the underwater sections.

Yard: a long, nearly cylindrical spar tapering towards the ends used to support and extend a square sail.

BOOKS FOR FURTHER READING

(Not all of these volumes deal with ship models, but are helpful in giving an account of shipping, particularly in regard to sailing vessels.)

CHAPELLE, HOWARD I.: *The History of American Sailing Ships*, W. W. Norton & Company, New York (1935). *American Sailing Craft, The American Sailing Navy, The Baltimore Clipper.*

CULVER, HENRY B.: *Books of Old Ships*, New York (1926).

CULVER, HENRY B. AND GRANT, GORDON: *Forty Famous Ships.*

CUTLER, CARL C.: *Greyhounds of the Sea*, New York and London (1930).

DAVIS, CHARLES G.: *Ship Models – How to Build Them*, E. W. Sweetman, New York (1946). *Ship Model Builder's Assistant, Ships of the Past.*

HOWE, OCTAVIUS T. AND MATTHEWS, F. C.: *American Clipper Ships.*

LA GRANGE, HELEN: *Clipper Ships.*

MAGOUN, F. ALEXANDER: *The Frigate 'Constitution' and Other Historic Ships*, Salem, Massachusetts, Marine Research Society (1928).

MATTHEWS, F. C.: *American Merchant Ships.*

MITMAN, CARL F.: *Catalogue of the Watercraft Collection in the U.S. National Museum*, Washington, Government Printing office (1923).

The Marine Room of the Peabody Museum of Salem: *Catalogue.*

Concise Encyclopedia of Antiques, Vol. II, pp. 250–4, Hawthorn Books, New York (1956).

WHALING COLLECTIONS

By EDOUARD A. STACKPOLE

PRINTS OF WHALESHIPS

THE American whalefishery a century ago, the most extensive and lucrative phase of that industry in the world, was just past its peak. As a theme for adventure in industry, whaling had few peers; as a nursery for seamen it has been unrivaled, and yet it was one of the hardest and most brutal seafaring activities ever known. Although whaling alongshore in Norway and other northern European countries was traditional, the Basque fishermen were the first to make it an industry in systematic and extensive pursuit. The tenth century found these bold mariners sailing as far north as Iceland. The search for a northeast and northwest route to India brought knowledge of the vast numbers of whales in Arctic seas, and the Dutch and English led the way in taking advantage of this knowledge. Early in the seventeenth century voyages of small whaling fleets to Spitzbergen and Greenland were organized, and for the next century the English, Dutch, German (Hamburg), French and Spanish divided the northern seas into whaling grounds. The economically-minded Dutch were at first the most successful and led the world until the English, stimulated by government bounties, opened a new era in the mid-eighteenth century, and before the American Revolution a whaling fleet of some sixty vessels annually visited the Greenland seas from English ports.

The American colonies had evinced an interest in the whaling industry from the earliest settlement. At first whales were taken near shore, with Long Islanders at East Hampton originating the practice of organized boat crews. Small sloops were fitted out for cruising and Cape Cod, Salem, Boston and Nantucket in Massachusetts, and New-

port in Rhode Island, were soon fitting out several whaling craft. In 1716 Captain Christopher Hussey, of Nantucket, sighted and killed a sperm whale at sea off that island, thus beginning one of the most exciting chapters in American maritime history. The Nantucketers, 'issuing' (as Melville wrote) 'from their ant-hill in the sea' literally chased the sperm whale all over the watery world, and for a century and a half this island-town was the greatest deep-sea whaling port in the world. During the first few decades of the nineteenth century Nantucket and New Bedford, Massachusetts, Sag Harbor, New York (Long Island), Stonington and New London in Connecticut, and Bristol, Warren and Newport in Rhode Island, rapidly developed the industry, with New Bedford emerging as the leader. In 1846 that port had a fleet numbering more than half the total whaleship fleets of America. The business naturally divided itself between sperm and right whaling, with the latter including the taking of baleen or whalebone used for making stays for ladies' corsets, buggy whips, canes, umbrella ribs. The oil was used for lighting, lubrication and tanning hides. Sperm oil was chiefly used for lighting, while the spermaceti wax was processed into candles which provided the finest light known to man at that time. Not only did whaling give America a strong and vitally important industry, but its attendant industries of barrel-making, cordage, shipbuilding, block-making, candle-making and oil-refining gave impetus to coastwise trade as well as providing products for export trade with Europe and South America. The discovery of 'rock-oil' (kerosene from petroleum) brought serious competition to whale-oil for lighting, with the raids on whaleships by Confederate raiders during the Civil War and the disasters to the Arctic fleet trapped in Arctic ice (notably in 1871) contributing to the ending of the industry in America. The fleet dwindled from seven hundred ships in 1846 to a half a dozen vessels in 1912.

Despite its wide range of incidents in whaling, with shipwrecks, fighting whales, mutinies, pirates and voyaging in every ocean, only a few of the great marine painters found inspiration in this subject. The most renowned name was that of J. M. W. TURNER, whose painting of whalers became a fine engraving by BRANDARD, while THOMAS BIRCH, who lived in Philadelphia, contributed an excellent painting, *Shoal of Sperm Whales off the Island of Harwaii* [sic], which was engraved by JOHN HILL.

The earliest engravings were used as book illustrations and were quaint and curious, such as those in Barentz's *Voyages*, published at Venice in 1699, and in Hans Egede's *Beschryving van Oud-Groenland* re-engraved for Churchill's *Voyages*, London, 1745. These reveal the type of whaleship and whaleboat, and some of the implements used in killing the whale and cutting him up. The engravings for Martens's *Voyage into Spitzbergen and Greenland*, London, 1711, show harpooners striking the whale and depict other details. Other noteworthy engravings are by C. MOY in J. A. Van Oelen's work on whaling, published in Leyden in 1684, and the series printed by Carington Bowles, map- and print-maker of London, now in the famous Macpherson Collection.

ROBERT DODD, the English painter, had two aquatints (engraved by himself and FRAN. AMBROSI) depicting the Davis Straits and Greenland whale-fishery, published by Boydell of London in 1789. These were entitled *The Northwest or Davis Streights Whale Fishery*, and *The Greenland Whale Fishery*. Of considerable interest are the engravings of T. SUTHERLAND and E. DUNCAN, after paintings by W. I. HUGGINS, published by Huggins in London in 1825. These two, titled *The South Sea Whale Fishery* and *Northern Whale Fishery*, show much valuable detail and provide students of whaling with a considerable study. The first of these two

prints represents the English whalers *Amelia*, *Wilson* and *Castor* off the Island of Bouro (East Indies), with the boats lowered and engaged in the several phases of attacking and killing sperm whales. In the center foreground a boat has been 'stove' by the whale's powerful flukes (tail) while to the left the head of a large bull sperm is depicted 'in the agonies of death', at the same time revealing the dangerous lower jaw with its row of teeth so hazardous to boat and men attackers. The ship in the center, 'cutting in', is bringing aboard a blanket-piece of blubber preparatory to boiling and trying out the oil. The *Amelia* was the first whaleship to round Cape Horn in 1788. American copies of these paintings were published by James S. Baillie in New York and these are thought to have been painted by EDWARD W. CLAY, who was a marine artist. They appeared in America some fifteen years after Huggins issued them in London, and were sold by Soule & Shaw of New Bedford and Boston. N. Currier also engraved and published a variant of another Huggins print, *Northern Whale Fishery*, which he called *North Sea Whale Fishery*.

Another Huggins painting which inspired American copyists was *South Sea Whale Fishery*, engraved by E. DUNCAN and published by Huggins in London in 1834. The sub-title reads, *A Representation of Boats Attacking a Sperm Whale from descriptions given by experienced Masters and officers of the South Sea Fishery*. Two decades later, Charles Taber, a New Bedford bookseller, commissioned a Dutch painter, ALBERT VAN BEEST, to do a series of three paintings – *The Chase*, *The Conflict* and *The Capture*, of which the last is a copy of the print noted above. The subjects in *The Capture* and *South Sea Whale Fishery* are similar in both. A great sperm whale is depicted half out of water on his back, his jaw open and his flukes raised. One whaleboat has been tossed aside by his body and one man is falling out of the bow; a second whaleboat is coming up from the left, with the third directly in the foreground 'going on' to the whale with the mate braced in the bow with his lance poised for plunging toward a vital spot. Van Beest's painting gave vigor to the original

Huggins print. *The Capture*, issued in 1862, has been a favorite ever since. It is easily the most dramatic of American whaling prints, and was a companion piece to *The Chase* and *The Conflict*, issued in 1859.

The first two Taber prints (in this series of three folio lithographs called *Sperm Whaling*) were: *No. 1 – The Chase, No. 2 – The Conflict*, with *No. 2* [*sic*] – *The Capture*, actually the third, as noted above. *The Chase* is a strong print (Plate 288A) painted by Van Beest assisted by ROBERT SWAIN GIFFORD and WILLIAM BRADFORD, two young New Bedford artists, with BENJAMIN RUSSELL (who will be noted later) as the technical adviser. It shows two boats approaching a sperm whale from both sides, the one in the foreground coming down under sail with the harpooner ready; the other, having no sail, being closer, with oarsmen pulling and harpooner ready to throw his 'iron'. Three whaleships are to be seen, with the island of Hawaii in the background. The second issue, *No. 2 – The Conflict* is a dramatic scene, with a boat being tossed in the air by a whale's flukes. The men are desperately hanging on to thwarts and gunwales as the boat, its sail in the water, is practically capsized on the 'small' of the whale's back. The action in the print helps relieve the disproportions of sea and whale. Endicott of Boston was the lithographer. *The Chase* and *The Capture* deserved their wide popularity. Prang & Meyer of Boston did the lithography on *No. 2 – The Conflict* in 1859, and J. Cole added some touches to the Van Beest painting.

Whaling as a subject for American artists had lagged until the third decade of the nineteenth century, when CORNELIUS B. HULSART published a print, *Capturing a Sperm Whale* (probably 1835), followed by *A Shoal of Sperm Whale off the Island of Harwaii* already noted. These are excellent for detail. Hulsart, a whaleman who had lost an arm during his voyage on the ship *Superior* of New London, developed a business sense for the marketing of these prints, dedicating the first to his former employers, Messrs N. & W. Billings of New London, and the second to the merchants, captains, and officers and crews engaged in whaling. The prints are notable for fine action as well as detail (Plate 287A).

Capturing a Sperm Whale was engraved in aquatint by JOHN HILL, an English engraver who came to the United States in 1816 and is best known for his work on the important set of New York views, the *Hudson River Portfolio*. Hulsart did the original sketch for *Capturing a Sperm Whale*, but WILLIAM PAGE was the painter of the finished canvas. Page was a portrait artist who at one time studied under Samuel F. B. Morse. Depicting the attack of whaleboats on a gigantic sperm whale, the print suffers from the extraordinary position of the whale almost completely out of water. Action in the boats is good, the oarsmen in one holding it close up to allow the officer with the lance to get in a lethal plunge. The second boat is 'stove', knocked high by the whale's flukes with the crew falling into the water. Highly-colored, it created an impression from its first appearance. A smaller lithograph of this print was used as an advertisement by Mitchell & Croasdale, whale-oil merchants of Philadelphia. The reproduction was much smaller than the original and was lithographed by W. H. Rease of Philadelphia and printed by Wagner & McGuigan.

The Thomas Birch painting *A Shoal of Sperm Whale off the Island of Harwaii* resulted in what is without doubt one of the best of the whaling prints. The sub-title identified the ships as the *Enterprise, Wm. Roach, Pocahontas* and *Houqua*, and the date as December 10, 1833. Hulsart also stated here that he had lost an arm on board the ship *Superior* and was on board the *Enterprise* at the time he made the original sketch. Little can be learned of Hulsart, but to have his sketch serve as a basis for a painting by the renowned Thomas Birch speaks well for him. JOHN HILL was the engraver and also colored the print, with Hulsart the publisher in 1838. The various whaling scenes are carefully handled with far better proportions than in most prints, and the coloring is excellent. The skill of the painter is matched by the engraver and the whole is an authentic reproduction of an actual scene which ranks high. Even the curious spelling of 'Harwaii' adds an extra touch to the title.

The group of lithographs issued by N. Currier, and later Currier & Ives, were important in popularizing whaling. Their appeal is in dramatic content rather than artistic quality. The prints appeared from 1852 through 1860, and altogether a series of fifteen were issued. The first three: *The Whale Fishery – Laying On*; *– Capturing the Whale* and *– In a Flurry* (Plate 288c) are N. Currier publications of 1852, and reveal in exciting sequence these important stages of pursuit and attack. Two boats approach a right whale in the first print; the whaleboats come up to the whale for lancing in the second, with a gigantic iceberg towering in the background; and the third print reveals a boat caught in a sperm whale's jaw, with a second boat near at hand and a third making its way to the scene.

Even before these appeared J. Chardon & Son of Paris in 1850 published *Dépècement d'une Baleine* (cutting-in a whale) from a painting by M. BOUQUET and engraved by ROUARGUE. This showed a whale alongside a ship being stripped of its blubber, the tryworks going and the French whalers with stocking hats and caps. A short time before this appeared AMBROISE LOUIS GARNERAY painted some whaling scenes, *Pêche de La Cachalot* and *La Baleine*, which were made into aquatints by MARTENS. No less an authority than Herman Melville praised these highly. Earlier still (1835) Garneray had a painting, *South Sea Whale Fishery*, engraved by Duncan and published in London by Rudolph Ackermann. Another good Garneray print is his *Spouter Fishing in the Zanzibar Channel*, engraved by JAZET in 1859.

Currier & Ives copied Garneray in issuing a pair of folio-sized colored lithographs known as *The Whale Fishery – Attacking a Right Whale and Cutting In* and *– The Sperm Whale in a Flurry*. The first, a superior print, is shown here in the first state (Plate 287B). The latter is a poor copy of an excellent original.

In the early 1840s D. W. Kellogg of Hartford, Connecticut, issued a set of whaling prints; *Dangers of the Whale Fishery* and *Dangers of the Cachelot Fishery* are two of these curious renderings.

Ranking foremost in American whaling prints for both artistic and technical quality is the series issued by J. H. Bufford of Boston after the paintings of BENJAMIN RUSSELL

of New Bedford. Russell had made a whaling voyage and was familiar with the technique of the trade as well as with the rigging and gear of the ships and small boats. Russell recognized the need for capturing authentic phases of the gradually dying industry, as in his portrayal of the Kutusoff of New Bedford (Plate 288B). His pair entitled *Sperm Whaling and Its Varieties* and *Right Whaling in Behring Straits, with Its Varieties*, published in 1871, is full of important detail. Russell's outstanding contribution was the series of five prints depicting *The Abandonment of the Whalers in the Arctic Ocean, Sept. 1871*. These record the tragic circumstances when some thirty whaleships were crushed in the Arctic ice pack. Another graphic illustration of a page in American whaling history was his *View of the Stone Fleet*, when a fleet of old whaleships was loaded with paving stone and rock at New Bedford and dispatched to be sunk in the channel entrances of southern ports.

In the mid-1850s there appeared in Paris *Pêche à la Baleine dans Les Mers du Sud*, published by Lemercier from a painting by L. LE BRETON. It shows a whale smashing two whaleboats and a whaleship 'cutting-in', and has an animated background. Le Breton also painted *Whale Fishery off the Cape of Good Hope*, published by Lemercier, showing three ships, one of which is the American whaler *Uncas*, and a British whaler. Boats are down approaching a sperm whale whose flukes unfortunately resemble those of a fish, thus detracting from an otherwise excellent study.

Some Japanese prints issued by the Taiju Fishing Company, Ltd., from an original picture scroll of 1773, and published as gifts to delegates at the International Whaling Conference in 1952, are quite fine in composition, drawing and color.

The dangers of a whaling voyage are well captured by these varied prints. That type of whaling no longer exists, with the possible exception of open-boat whaling by the Portuguese in the Azores, and so the value of these prints is in their record of the perils and picturesque methods of the whaling past and their graphic presentation of those adventuresome days. Through their presentation of a hazardous calling, whaling prints have played their part in a cultural sense. However, it should be noted that the less known side of the whaleman's life was considered too prosaic as a subject for study by artists. There are no contemporary records in prints or paintings of life on board ship in the crowded forecastles, activities on deck during 'cutting-in' and boiling oil, standing watch, working on scrimshaw, visiting exotic South Sea Islands or the icebound shores of Antarctic and Arctic Islands. In view of what was recorded through published prints, it appears that much of our basic whaling history was lost while the spectacular features were preserved.

SCRIMSHAW

This is an American whaling folk art, developed by New England whalemen early in the nineteenth century. The term denotes the object created and also the process of etching or carving on whale's teeth or whalebone by the whalers. Where the art first originated remains in doubt. Some writers refer to the influence of Eskimo culture on New England whalers; others to contacts of the whalemen with South Sea Islanders. There are those who consider it strictly an authentic American seafaring art, indigenous to America. But carving in ivory on elephant and walrus tusks was known as early as the eleventh century, and so it may be said that scrimshaw was the American whalemen's contribution to an ancient folk art – an adaptation of the older form which became peculiarly American. It is probable that when the Nantucket whalemen used Dunkirk in France as a whaling port in 1785 they had contact with the French ivory workers of Normandy who for over two centuries had worked on elephant tusks brought from the African coast. Even before that the tusks of the 'morse' or walrus were brought into Europe for carving, and many examples of this art exist.

The name scrimshaw is a derivative of early terms – 'skrimshander', 'scrimshonter' and 'scrimshorn'. Early whalebooks refer to it as 'scrimshonting' (1826, log book of the *By Chance* of Dartmouth); while Cheever in *The Whale and his Captors* (1850) wrote it as 'scrimshander' and Melville in *Moby Dick* (also 1850) referred to 'skrimshander articles'. The origin of the term appears to suggest indulgence in too much leisure, or a 'lazy fellow', thus easily transferred to those whiling away time aboard ship.

In their long voyages (often three years in duration), the whaleman had plenty of time to indulge his fancy by engraving or etching varied designs or pictures on the ivory teeth of the sperm whale or the whalebone from both right and sperm whales. For years the whaler's jackknife had been used to carve in wood many practical keepsakes for the sweethearts, wives, mothers and sisters at home. As early as 1782, Hector St John de Crèvecoeur had noted the Nantucket whaleman's proclivity toward fashioning ditty-boxes, bowls, 'and a variety of boxes and pretty toys, in wood ... executed cooper-wise, with the greatest neatness and elegance'. Inlay with mother-of-pearl and tortoise shell was followed by the use of bits of ivory. Finally the sperm whale's teeth were used for etching familiar scenes of ships and whales. One of the earliest known dated pieces of scrimshaw is a sperm whale's tooth done on board the *Susan* of Nantucket in 1828, but an earlier piece is dated 1827 and shows a slave ship and a slave. Later the whaleman etched flags, eagles and whaling scenes, followed by figures of ladies and gentlemen. Sometimes the designs were transferred by etching over the picture itself pasted to the tooth or bone.

Perhaps two of the most common types of scrimshaw are the busk and jagging or crimping wheel. The busk, made of whalebone, was the bodice stay in the corsets of the ladies of the time, and many a whaler etched elaborate patterns and designs on his gift for his lady-love. Jagging or crimping wheels were of various patterns, some had plain handles for the little wheel intended for laying a design along the edge of a pie; others had a fork at one end and the wheel on the other; still others with serpents' or horses' heads or whales provided further interest of design.

Among the extensive variety of scrimshaw articles were the 'swifts' of whalebone, used to wind yarn; workboxes, ranging from those entirely of bone to wooden boxes with ivory inlay; rolling pins, often with only the handles of sperm ivory; cocoanut dippers with bone handles; napkin rings and spool holders; canes of great variety; wick-pickers for whale-oil lamps and bodkins for sewing; knitting needles, clothespins and coat racks. The ingenuity of the whaleman-artisan was amazing. Whether he was fashioning a bird cage or work basket of whalebone, or a jagging wheel of pure ivory, his work need not be hurried as time was a dependable commodity.

For his own use, the whaleman made scrimshaw needle cases, yardsticks, scribers and seam rubbers for the sail-maker; belaying pins and fids and oil-cask measures for the deck; small blocks and cleats for the whaleboat sail and mast, and cribbage boards, checkers and chess sets and jackstraws for fo'c's'le games. The master-carver would attempt brooches, earrings, buttons, combs, beads, pins and even necklaces and fans.

It was in his choice of design as well as of object that the whaleman evolved an art peculiar to his trade and thus developed scrimshaw as a special folk art. His carved sperm teeth were like trophies of the successful hunt; his carefully etched busk a tribute to his wife or sweetheart; his strongly cut clothespins a son's gift to his mother, with an ivory-headed cane a thoughtful present for father or grandfather. Each was a symbol of his faith in the ship and the loved ones at home. The use of time in these painstaking tasks was welcomed to break the monotony. As Captain William Reynard stated in his log of the New Bedford whaler *Abigail* in 1836: 'An idle head is the work shop for the devil. Employed scrimshon.'

The technique of scrimshaw found the whaleman developing his own tools. First, no doubt, was the omnipotent jackknife, ground to a fine point on the whetstone, but the most versatile tools were the sailor's needles for pricking and scraping out the design. Herman Melville remarked: 'Some of them have boxes of dentistical looking implements especially intended for the skrimshandering business, but in general they toil with jackknives alone.' Files, awls and gimlets were used in boring holes and piercing bone. Many of the handles

for these tools were whalebone or wood tipped with ivory and the skill of the cooper was often borrowed. As the log of the *Abigail* reported: 'Times are dull ... The cooper is going ahead making tools for scrimshon ...'

Preparing the ribbed sperm (ivory) tooth or the tough right whale bone consisted of scraping and cutting and polishing. The fresh material was scraped with broad-bladed knife, ground to a smooth surface with file and sharkskin sandpaper, and buffed with ashes from the tryworks before it was ready for its design. Sometimes pumice and whiting were used to further prepare the surface. Softening agents ran the gamut from soaking the teeth or bone in brine to the use of plain hot soapy water. In later years, a small lathe was used for turning and buffing. There is a fine example of one at Mystic Seaport, Connecticut.

Usually, the design was first outlined or scratched upon the surface. Often a picture from a book or periodical was pasted on the tooth or piece of bone and the detail transferred to the surface by pricking in the outlines. Patience was the key to the next step which was the actual engraving. The use of inks to complete the job was customary. Often India ink was not available and so paint, lamp-black, tar and even soot were utilized. Colored inks provided excellent touches for the design, with scrolls and elaborations introduced for effect. Painstaking efforts many times produced outstanding pieces, although the earlier examples are invariably crude. Some whalers revealed an artistic insight which has made their scrimshaw handiwork collectors' items. A number of professional engravers have tried their hand at this art but their product, while finely executed, lacks the value of the authentic scrimshaw. During the past two decades many spurious pieces have appeared, the work of people who deliberately seek to trick the collector and student. In a number of instances they have employed clever means to produce imitations which put the collector on guard.

BOOKS FOR
FURTHER READING

ASHLEY, CLIFFORD: *The Yankee Whaler*, New York (1932).

BARBEAU, MARIUS: 'All Hands Aboard Scrimshawing' in *American Neptune* (October 1950).

BREWINGTON, M. V.: *A Check List of the Paintings, Drawings and Prints at the Kendall Whaling Museum*, Sharon, Massachusetts (1957).

CHILDS, CHARLES D.: 'Thar She Blows' in *Antiques* (July 1941).

DALAND, EDWARD L.: 'Engraved Types of Scrimshaw' in *Antiques* (October 1935).

DOW, GEORGE FRANCIS: *Whale Ships and Whaling, a Pictorial History of Whaling During Three Centuries*, Marine Research Society, Salem, Massachusetts (1925).

LOTHROP, FRANCIS B.: *A Check List of an Exhibition of Whaling Pictures*, Salem (1955).

STACKPOLE, E. A.: *The Sea-Hunters*, Lippincott, Philadelphia (1953).

THOMAS, STEPHEN: 'Dutch Painter of the Sea – the American Career of Albert van Beest' in *Antiques* (January 1936).

WATSON, ARTHUR C.: *The Long Harpoon*, New Bedford (1929).

The Forbes Collection of Whaling Prints, Massachusetts Institute of Technology, Cambridge (1941).

Whale Ships and Whaling Scenes, State Street Trust Co., Boston (1955).

MARINE PAINTINGS
AND PRINTS

Part I. The United States Navy 1776-1865

By HAROLD S. SNIFFEN

NAVAL pictorial art emerged in America as soon as national pride demanded it. It was not until the country became a nation on its own, with a navy of its own, that pictures of naval and maritime accomplishments were created. American primitive art had started in colonial days, but its subjects were those close to the hearts of the people and their everyday life.

The task of recording pictorially the history of the country from its colonial days until after its independence from England fell upon artists and engravers of foreign lands. There was a dearth of material produced even in the mother country.

By the early-eighteenth century engravings printed in London appeared, showing the cities of the New World. Although such views are not the subject of this article, they deserve mention since the colonial cities most often depicted – Boston, New York, Philadelphia and Charleston – were all ports, and, therefore, show shipping. Some naval vessels appear in these prints but, of course, these ships were under the British or other flags.

The Revolutionary War: it was not until the outbreak of the Revolutionary War that an American warship sailed the seas, and it was later before there appeared an American picture of an American ship. The people were too busy fighting the war to have time to paint or engrave its events. It fell upon well-established British and French artists and engravers to be the 'combat artists' of the American Revolution.

JOSEPH F. W. DES BARRES of London published *The Atlantic Neptune* in 1777, a book of charts 'for the use of the Royal Navy of Great Britain'. Among the charts appeared sketches of landfalls and port views. One of the most handsome of these aquatints shows *The "Phœnix" and the "Rose" Engaged by the Enemy's Fire Ships and Galleys on the 16 August, 1776*. This naval action was the first important one of the American Revolution, and the print the first view of the War to be published.

Naval historians consider the Battle of Lake Champlain in October 1776, early in the War, to rank in importance with Admiral De Grasse's fleet action off Chesapeake Bay at the War's end. Although lost by the Americans, the Lake Champlain action was important because it delayed the advance of British troops until winter set in. Contemporary engravings published in London by ROBERT SAYRE and JOHN BENNETT record this battle.

Naturally enough these prints published in England generally record British victories. Other examples are two prints which appeared in *The Naval Chronicle* in 1814 showing the disembarkation of British troops on Long Island on August 22, 1776, and Sir George Collier's victory over a small Continental fleet in Penobscot Bay, August 13, 1779. A map, engraved by WILLIAM FADEN, London, 1778, is illuminated with drawings of warships which took part in the action off Mud Fort in the Delaware River on October 22, 1777. LIEUTENANT W. ELLIOTT, Royal Navy, also produced an aquatint of this attack, an action not entirely favorable to the British. Another British naval officer painted a view of the explosion of H.M.S. *Augusta*, 64 guns, in the Delaware River, October 23, 1777, which is in the Historical Society of Pennsylvania.

Pictures of naval engagements of the Revolutionary War were few, indicative, perhaps, of the lack of importance which the British placed upon the War. There was one engagement, however, which is generously depicted, the battle between the *Bon Homme Richard* and the *Serapis*, off the coast of England on September 23, 1779. Although it was a victory for Captain John Paul Jones, it is also remembered with pride in England because the *Serapis*, although sunk, achieved its purpose of protecting a convoy of merchant ships, and because of the gallantry of the British commander, Captain Richard Pearson. British artists produced pictures of the battle, the most notable of which is the line engraving published by JOHN BOYDELL after a painting by RICHARD PATON. THOMAS BUTTERSWORTH and ROBERT DODD are other English painters who immortalized this battle.

The Quasi-War with France: it was not until the Quasi-War with France, 1799–1801, that the first completely American prints appeared. EDWARD SAVAGE, an American-born engraver of Philadelphia, brought out a pair of aquatints in 1799 depicting the action between the *Constellation* and the *Insurgent* (Plate 291A), the principal engagement in this naval war to protect American commerce in the Atlantic and to establish respect for the fledgling nation.

The War with Tripoli: several naval subjects appeared at the time of the romantic War with Tripoli (1801–5). This war was the result of attacks by the Barbary pirates on American shipping in the Mediterranean, and in it the United States managed to convince the Barbary States that she was an established nation. There were incidents in the Tripolitan War which captured the imaginations of Americans interested in the fortunes of their young Navy. Print-makers were ready with depictions of Stephen Decatur's bold destruction of the captured frigate *Philadelphia*, and of the unfortunate explosion of the fireship *Intrepid* before she was able to destroy enemy ships in the harbor of Tripoli. The former is recorded in an aquatint by FRANCIS KEARNY,

published in New York in 1808. An illustration of the *Intrepid* incident appears in *The Port Folio* in 1810. MICHÈLE CORNÉ, an Italian-born artist who came to America, created, both in oils and watercolors, views of the Battle of Tripoli. CHARLES DENOON drew interesting views of the loss to the Tripolitans of the *Philadelphia*, and Preble's bombardment of Tripoli.

The War of 1812: the War of 1812 was a trade war, resulting from American indignation over the British practice of impressing American sailors. The slogan was, 'Free trade and sailors' rights', both of which the United States achieved in the end. By 1815 the country's independence of Great Britain was fully acknowledged.

This was principally a naval war and from the pages of its history emerge names of naval engagements which have been pointed to with pride by Americans ever since. Artists and print makers have not been the least among the naval historians to make these battles famous.

The city of Philadelphia was the center of artists and engravers of naval pictures at the time of the War of 1812. THOMAS BIRCH (1779–1851), who had taken up marine painting in 1807, was the artist of many well-known engagements of the war: the *Constitution* and the *Guerrière*, August 1812; the *Wasp* and the *Frolic*, October 1812; the *United States* and the *Macedonian*, October 1812; the Battle of Lake Erie, September 1813; the *Peacock* and the *Epervier*, April 1814; and the *Constitution* versus the *Cyane* and the *Levant*, February 1815; all American victories.

Engravers of these Birch views were CORNELIUS TIEBOUT, FRANCIS KEARNY, DENISON KIMBERLY, SAMUEL SEYMOUR, BENJAMIN TANNER, ALEXANDER LAWSON, WILLIAM STRICKLAND, P. S. DUVAL, and ABEL BOWEN, most of them of Philadelphia, and all of them well known in the world of print makers.

The battles named above were also painted by J. J. BARRALET, MICHÈLE CORNÉ, THOMAS SULLY, THOMAS CHAMBERS, W. A. K. MARTIN, and GEORGE THRESHER. Prints were published by FREEMAN AND PIERCE, WILLIAM KNEASS, J. R. SMITH,

SAMUEL WALKER, WILLIAM SMITH, JOSEPH DELAPLAINE, H. QUIG, J. BAILLIE, D. W. KELLOGG and CAMMEYER & ACOCK.

Other well-remembered American victories have been recorded in prints and paintings, such as the engagement between the *Constitution* and the *Java*, December 1812; the *Hornet* and the *Peacock*, February 1813; the *General Pike* and the *Wolf*, September 1813; the *Enterprise* and the *Boxer*, September 1813; Macdonough's victory on Lake Champlain, September 1813; the bombardment of Fort McHenry, September 1814; and the battle of Lake Borgne, Louisiana, December 1814. Outstanding among the pictures of these battles is an engraving by BENJAMIN TANNER after a painting by HUGH REINAGLE of Macdonough's victory; a lithograph by H. R. ROBINSON of the victory of the *Enterprise*, and an aquatint of Fort McHenry (Plate 291B) by J. BOWER showing 'the bombs bursting in air', as seen on that occasion by the writer of the *Star Spangled Banner*, Francis Scott Key.

GEORGE THRESHER was a primitive painter of New York and Philadelphia. He painted in watercolors the battles between the *United States* and the *Macedonian*, the *Constitution* and the *Guerrière*, and 'Old Ironsides's' fight with the *Java*. As far as is known, his pictures were not reproduced as prints. Besides Thresher, GEORGE ROPES seems to have been one of the few contemporary American painters of the *Constitution-Java* battle, although British and French print makers covered it well.

It is pertinent to add that there were other battles of the War of 1812 better known in England than in the United States because they were British victories. These include the engagements between the *Pelican* and *Argus*, the escape of the *Hornet* from the *Cornwallis*, the *Endymion* versus the *President*, the attack on Fort Oswego, and the famous *Shannon* and *Chesapeake* battle. Scarcely an American print appeared to immortalize these actions, whereas they are generously recorded by the English artists and engravers. An exception is a painting by the American artist, GEORGE ROPES, of the British capture of the frigate *Essex* by H.M.S. *Phoebe* and *Cherub* at Valparaiso, Chile, 1814. The opportunity must not be passed of mentioning the set of four fine lithographs of the capture of the *Chesapeake*, drawn on stone by L. HAGHE of London, after paintings by J. C. SHETKEY.

A number of naval prints originated in periodicals contemporary with the War of 1812. *The Naval Monument* was one of these. Most of the engravings are by ABEL BOWEN, W. HOOGLAND, W. B. ANNIN, and WIGHTMAN after originals by MICHÈLE CORNÉ. Works of Corné are also reproduced in *The Naval Temple*. THOMAS BIRCH drew for another periodical, *The Port Folio*, and SAMUEL SEYMOUR did the engraving. Printed later (1840) was the *United States Military Magazine*, which carried lithographs by J. QUEEN after J. EVANS and THOMAS BIRCH. This magazine specialized in pictures of uniforms. Portraits of naval officers are reproduced in the *Analectic Magazine* appearing in 1813.

The Mariners Museum owns a remarkable collection of 254 watercolors of naval battles. The artist is unknown, although they have been attributed to CHARLES T. WARREN and/or his son, ALFRED W. WARREN. It seems improbable that the pictures are contemporary with the scenes shown. They embrace naval actions from the American Revolution through and beyond the War of 1812. Possibly they were painted for use in an unpublished naval history. They are of interest particularly because they depict less-known engagements as well as the famous ones. They appeared among the possessions of Charles Kingsley Bailey in England. The Parker Gallery, London, owns one or more watercolors of engagements other than American, which leads to the conjecture that the collection was more extensive.

The United States Naval Academy owns a collection of twenty watercolors by R. CLAUDUS of naval engagements of the War of 1812. The Academy also has the *Thirteen Historical Marine Paintings* by EDWARD MORAN (1829–1901) which embrace four subjects which should be mentioned here: *The First Recognition of the American Flag by a Foreign Government, in the Harbor of Quiberon, France, February 14, 1778*; *The Burning of the*

Frigate PHILADELPHIA, in the Harbor of Tripoli, February 16, 1804; *The Brig ARM-STRONG Engaging the British Fleet, in the Harbor of Fayal, September 26, 1814*; and *The Sinking of the CUMBERLAND by the MERRI-MAC, in Hampton Roads, March 8, 1862.*

The War with Algiers: the fifth war fought by the United States Navy was brief and almost bloodless. Algiers attempted extraction of tribute money from American ships, as had her neighbor, Tripoli. She had a free hand in such practice until the war with England ended. In June 1815, however, squadrons under Decatur and Bainbridge appeared off Algiers, as the result of which threat the Dey released American prisoners and signed a treaty. This short chapter in our naval history is illustrated with several small prints, principally appearing in magazines of the day. One of the best shows *The U.S. Squadron, under the Command of Com. Decatur at anchor off the City of Algiers, June 30th, 1815*, published in New Haven by N. JOCELIN and G. MUNGER.

Portraits of naval ships: a classification of naval picture, different from the 'naval action picture', is the ship 'portrait' which shows the likeness of a ship when not engaged in battle.

The best known and most frequently painted ship of the United States Navy is the *Constitution*. She was one of a group of frigates to be built by the Congress when the infant republic first realized the need for a regular navy, and she remains afloat today, 160 years after her launching. Her celebrated engagements with the *Guerrière* and the *Java* have been mentioned.

One of the earliest portraits of the *Constitution* is an engraving by ABEL BOWEN (1790–1850) of Boston, the publisher of *The Naval Monument*. The artist was WILLIAM LYNN. The SENEFELDER LITHOGRAPHIC COMPANY produced another portrait of 'Old Ironsides' about 1830 after a drawing by WILLIAM MARSH, JR., copied on stone by JAMES KIDDER. The same print appeared later under the name of WILLIAM S. PENDLETON who took over the Senefelder presses after 1831. Other portraits of this famous ship are: lithographs by J. BAILLIE,

three by P. S. DUVAL after J. EVANS, 1840; engravings by J. THACKARA; a drawing by O. E. LINTON; paintings by ROBERT SALMON and foreign artists including NICHOLAS CAMMILLIERI; and more modern portraits, including GORDON GRANT'S painting which helped to inspire gifts of pennies from school children to finance restoration of the frigate.

Just as there was a surge of shipbuilding activity a few years after the Revolutionary War which added famous frigates to our Navy, so was the War of 1812 followed by the creation of great ships-of-the-line. Four of these, the *Washington, Independence, Franklin* and *Columbus*, were built in the last years of the War. The names of later ones indicate the start of the practice of naming battleships after states. They were the *North Carolina*, launched in 1820; *Delaware*, 1820; *Ohio*, 1821; *Pennsylvania*, laid down in 1822 but not launched until 1837 (Plate 292), and *Vermont*, launched in 1845 after 27 years' building.

These impressive ships were popular subjects with artists, engravers and lithographers. The *Delaware* seems to have been the most popular of all. J. HILL shows her on the stocks at Gosport (now Norfolk), Virginia. A pair of lithographs published by CHILDS & INMAN after J. G. BRUFF show her entering America's first dry dock (still in use) at Gosport Navy Yard in 1836. There are three oil paintings by JAMES C. EVANS and an ENDICOTT lithograph after an EVANS painting. A tempera in the Roosevelt Collection shows the *Delaware* off Naples. N. CURRIER produced a small folio print. A lithograph by F. W. MOORE seems to be after an ANTOINE ROUX painting. Another foreign artist, NICHOLAS CAMMILLIERI, also painted a portrait of the *Delaware*.

The *Ohio* was lithographed by J. C. SHARP, ENDICOTT & CO., and N. CURRIER. A view of the launching of the *Pennsylvania* appears as a lithograph published by LEHMAN & DUVAL and there are portraits by GIBBS & CO. and N. CURRIER. Currier, in fact, published prints of all these ships-of-the-line. A spirited view of the *Pennsylvania* (Plate 292) in a storm is in an aquatint by W. J. BENNETT after J. PRINGLE. The

North Carolina was painted by HENRY WALKE and CAMMILLIERI. She was lithographed by ENSIGN & THAYER and appears on a sheet-music cover. Anonymous artists have done numerous pictures of these vessels.

Portraits of these few vessels have been mentioned as examples of portraits of naval ships. The catalogue could be extended through most of the roster of United States naval vessels.

The peacetime Navy: during some eleven years scattered throughout the country's first forty years, the American people had been at war. The period of quiet which followed gave the nation three decades in which to build up its economy. The Navy was active during these years, playing its part in the protection of merchant marine and the expansion of American trade.

One phase of this period had to do with the opening of the Far East to American trade. In 1842 Commodore Lawrence Kearny sailed to China to protect interests of the United States in incidents connected with the British-Chinese Opium War. Kearny's work extended further and before he was through he had done much to increase China's trade with America. A formal trade treaty was made the following year by Caleb Cushing who sailed for China in the steam frigate *Missouri*. A pair of lithographs published by DAY & HAGHE, London, and one by N. CURRIER, show the untimely end of the *Missouri* by fire at Gibraltar while on the way to China. Cushing continued his voyage in the frigate *Brandywine*.

The treaty which Cushing brought back was ratified by Congress and was returned to the Chinese Government by Commodore Biddle in the ship-of-the-line *Columbus* in company with the sloop-of-war *Vincennes*. Before returning to the United States, Biddle made the first attempt to open the fast-closed trade door to Japan. A lithograph by WAGNER & McGUIGAN after drawings by JOHN EASTLEY shows the *Columbus* and *Vincennes* in the Bay of Jeddo (Tokyo), surrounded by hundreds of Japanese craft. These boats finally helped to tow the American ships out of the Bay, 'rejoicing', as the title puts it, 'that they

had rid themselves so easily of such a number of Barbarians'.

Although Biddle's visit to Japan failed, he learned customs and protocol which were valuable to Commodore Matthew C. Perry in his successful venture on the same mission in 1853. Lithographs by SARONY & COMPANY (Plate 294A) and by HATCH and SEVERIN show Perry's imposing squadron at Jeddo and details of the theatrical pomp which the astute Perry knew would appeal to the Japanese. Perry's official report, a two-volume publication, is generously illustrated with lithographs by SARONY & COMPANY. The Chicago Historical Society has a painting by J. EVANS with the curious title *Commodore Perry carrying the Gospel of God to the Heathen, 1853*.

Two prints, one by J. L. KEFFER and one by J. H. BUFFORD, Boston, bring to mind one other incident which occurred in this period when the door to the Orient was being opened. Commander A. H. Foote with the sloops-of-war *Portsmouth* and *Levant* was attempting to withdraw American neutrals from Whampoa lest they become involved in British-Chinese hostilities in 1856. Despite an understanding with Chinese authorities, the American ships were fired upon and denied passage beyond the 'barrier forts'. The prints show the exchange of fire and the landing of a force of Americans to attack the forts from land.

Captain Ingraham Vindicating American Honor is the title of a lithograph by ENDICOTT & COMPANY recalling an incident which took place in the harbor of Smyrna in July 1853. Martin Koszta, a naturalized American citizen, was arrested by Austrian officials and held aboard a warship in the harbor. Commander Ingraham, of the sloop-of-war *St. Louis*, took the initiative in the situation, anchored abreast of the Austrian warship and, with loaded guns, demanded Koszta's release. As a result the man was placed in neutral hands ashore.

Two other examples should suffice to illustrate the type of activity of the peacetime Navy which appealed to the artist and printmaker.

The Boston lithographers, LANE & SCOTT,

brought out a print of the departure from Boston of the sloop-of-war *Jamestown* for Ireland, laden with food for the relief of victims of the Irish famine. The Irish people replied with a lithograph (published by W. SCRAGGS) of the *Jamestown* entering the Cove of Cork, April 13, 1847. The caption states the print to be 'commemorative of the splendid generosity of the American government in dismantling a ship of war for a Mission of Peace and Charity'.

A handsome lithograph was published in England at the time of the joint British-United States venture of laying the Atlantic telegraph cable in 1856. This print, published by W. FOSTER, London, shows the U.S. Steam Frigate *Niagara* together with H.M.S. *Agamemnon* laying the cable. The collection at India House, New York, contains an oil painting attributed to JAMES E. BUTTERSWORTH of the *Niagara* occupied in cable laying. There are also anonymous paintings on the subject.

The Mexican War: in 1846 the controversial Mexican War broke out over the disputed Texan frontier and ended in the annexation of the territories of Texas, New Mexico and California, and the establishment of the Rio Grande River as the United States-Mexican border. The U.S. Navy's principal part in this war was to transport General Wingfield Scott's army to Vera Cruz, whence it could move on Mexico City, carrying the War to the heart of Mexico.

LIEUTENANT H. WALKE, U.S.N., served aboard the bomb-brig *Vesuvius* in the naval operations against Mexico. Possessed of artistic talents, he made paintings of the movements of the ships in this expedition. Eight of his views were produced as lithographs by SARONY & MAJOR under the title *Naval Scenes of the Mexican War* (Plate 293).

Another U.S. Navy lieutenant, CHARLES C. BARTON, drew Mexican War scenes of the landing of General Scott's army which P. S. DUVAL, Philadelphia lithographer, reproduced on stone. In Frost's *Pictorial History of the Mexican War* appeared a spirited picture of the Vera Cruz landing, lithographed by Wagner & McGuigan. Nathaniel Currier, alert as ever for news pictures,

secured from a midshipman a sketch for his lithograph, *Attack of the Gun Boats upon the City and Castle of San Juan de Ulloa* (Vera Cruz). A rare oil painting, signed by J. EVANS, recently turned up, showing the bombardment of the Castle on March 26, 1842, in spite of a raging hurricane. United States Naval ships ride out the storm, each with more than one anchor out.

Civil War: the story of the navies of the Civil War is one of blockade and blockade running, a few engagements between individual ships, river warfare, some 'amphibious' operations, and attacks from the sea on near-impregnable forts.

When President Lincoln ordered the blockade of southern ports the Union Navy consisted of scarcely twenty-five vessels. Yet, years later, the naval historian, Alfred T. Mahan, said, 'Never did sea power play a greater or more decisive part than in the Civil War'. Mahan was referring principally to the effectiveness of the blockade, one of the greatest factors in the outcome of the War.

The New York lithographers, ENDICOTT & COMPANY, have left a telling record of the Union Navy's answer to Lincoln's order for the blockade. With what soon amounted to monotony, the Endicott lithographic stones rolled out print after print of newly-constructed gunboats. The portraits themselves vary little, and the names even were similar, being of Indian origin: *Winooski, Ascutney, Lenape, Mackinaw,* to mention but a few, with *Grand Gulf* and *Fulton* added for variety.

The answer of the Confederates to the blockade was the 'blockade runner', which dashed through the blockade with greater speed than the Federal guard ships could muster, to bring the South imports necessary to carry on the war. Unfortunately there were few artists to record these craft and their existing exploits. A watercolor by 'the EARL OF DUNMORE' entitled, *Blockade Running on Board the Confederate S.S. Nashville, Morning of April, 1862,* is one of the few.

Some Confederate vessels acted as privateers. The U.S. Revenue Cutter *Aiken*, seized in Charleston at the outbreak of the War, was converted to the privateer schooner

Petrel. On her first cruise she was chased by the U.S. Frigate *St. Lawrence*. After a brief action the schooner sank. The Philadelphia lithographer, L. HAUGG, published a handsome print to commemorate this incident (Plate 294B).

One of the most notable exploits of the War was the cruise of the Confederate Raider *Alabama* under Raphael Semmes. During this eleven-month cruise the *Alabama* captured sixty-nine prizes. The successful voyage was brought to an abrupt end in June 1864, when the raider was cornered in Cherbourg harbor by the U.S. Sloop-of-War *Kearsarge*. The Confederate ship unhesitatingly went forth to meet her opponent, but after a battle of less than two hours, she struck her colors and sank. This, one of the few duels of the War, was popular in story, song, and picture. An artist named XANTHUS SMITH, an enlisted man in the U.S. Navy, has left several paintings of the engagement and W. F. MITCHELL and C. OLIVER did watercolor drawings of it. Prints include French lithographs, a pair of small folios by CURRIER & IVES, a chromolithograph by L. PRANG & CO., and a sheet-music cover by L. R. ROSENTHAL.

The renowned battle between the first ironclads, the *Virginia* (ex-*Merrimac*) and the *Monitor*, was a popular subject for prints and paintings. The *Merrimac*, as a steam frigate before conversion by the Confederates, appears in a portrait lithographed by L. H. BRADFORD & COMPANY. CURRIER & IVES have pictured her on her first appearance as the ironclad ram *Virginia*, sinking the frigate *Cumberland*. XANTHUS SMITH painted a handsome oil of the sinking of the *Congress* by the *Virginia*.

The fight of the *Virginia* and *Monitor*, which revolutionized naval history, took place on March 9, 1862. Among the many contemporary pictures it inspired are lithographs by CASIMIR BOHN, HENRY BILL, ENDICOTT, HATCH, and CURRIER & IVES. The battle, though not in itself a decisive one, was ostensibly a victory for the *Monitor*. The *Virginia*, confined in the waters of the Elizabeth River both by the *Monitor* and by her own excessive draft, was incapable of rendering further

assistance to the Confederate cause, and had to be destroyed by the Confederates. A lurid print published by CURRIER & IVES shows *The Destruction of the Rebel Monster MERRIMAC off Craney Island, May 11, 1862*.

There followed the construction or conversion of ships of the types of both of these vessels. The rams, similar in appearance to the *Virginia*, were later seen particularly on the Mississippi River and are recorded especially in lithographs by Currier & Ives. Vessels of the design of the *Monitor* were built in numbers by the Federal Navy. Endicott published a series of lithographs, over a dozen, of monitors also having Indian names, as *Manhattan*, *Weehawken*, *Monadnock* and *Wassuc*.

The firm of Currier & Ives, lithographers, was in its prime at the time of the Civil War. The six thousand-odd titles published by these prolific print-makers cover a wide range of subjects. Many had to do with current events and were, in effect, forerunners of the present-day newspaper pictures. In consequence we find the firm furnishing its 'readers' with views of the latest developments at the 'front', including the naval 'front'. Thus a list of Currier & Ives naval prints, in order of publication, becomes a chronology of the naval war.

The Mississippi River was the Confederate front in the west. Important naval operations took place on the river and its tributaries. One of the key points first to be won with the aid of Commodore Foote's fleet of Union gunboats was Fort Henry, Tennessee, on February 6, 1862. This action is recalled in a Currier & Ives print, as is the Battle of Shiloh, April 6, 1862. MIDDLETON, STROBRIDGE & COMPANY, lithographers of Cincinnati, who produced a series of Civil War battle scenes, also depicted this battle. Proceeding southward, the fleet engaged in *The Bombardment and Capture of Island Number Ten, April 7, 1862, by the Gunboat and Mortar Fleet*, another Currier & Ives title. A Union commander describes how the rams in the fleets off Memphis 'rushed upon each other like wild beasts in deadly conflict', resulting in the destruction of a Confederate fleet.

Meanwhile a fleet under Admiral Farragut

entered the mouth of the Mississippi. A wood-cut published by HOWARD BROWN after a drawing by WILLIAM WAUD records the *Bombardment of Forts Jackson and St Philip.* A drawing by WILLIAM McMURTRIE shows the fleet lying before New Orleans, before proceeding northward to 'engage the Rebel Batteries at Port Hudson (Louisiana) March 14th, 1863', as the Currier & Ives title reads. A dramatic chromolithograph by L. PRANG shows the Union fleet as from a Confederate battery near Port Hudson. The last major engagement on the Mississippi was the Battle of Vicksburg in which the Naval forces took part, as is evidenced by the title, *Admiral Porter's Fleet Running the Rebel Blockade of the Mississippi at Vicksburg, April 16th, 1863.* Other naval operations followed, but with the River opened and the Confederacy divided, the Navy had done most of its work in the West.

A 'combat artist' of the Civil War, worthy of special mention, was ALFRED WAUD. He was employed by *Harper's Weekly* as a 'war correspondent'. Most of Waud's pencil sketches had to do with the operation of the Army, but there were many drawings of naval activity done in his admirable style. The Library of Congress owns most of his work.

It was difficult to blockade the coast off Hatteras, North Carolina, due to generally unfavorable weather, so the Federals decided early in the War to get a foothold on shore in order to prevent blockade runners from bringing supplies in at this point. Currier & Ives recorded this operation in a print entitled *The Bombardment and Capture of the Forts Hatteras and Clark at Hatteras Inlet, N.C., by the U.S. Fleet under Commodore Stringham and the Forces under Genl. Butler, August 27th, 1861.*

The Victorious Bombardment of Port Royal, S.C., November 7, 1861, by the United States Fleet under the Command of Commodore Dupont, a Currier & Ives print, depicts the action which gave the South Atlantic Blockading Squadron a much-needed base of operations at a point between Charleston and Savannah.

The Savannah River was closed to Confederate use after *The Bombardment of Fort Pulaski, Cockspur Island, Georgia, 10th and 11th of April 1862,* as the title of the Currier & Ives lithograph puts it.

We turn to prints by Endicott and W. H. REASE to give a prelude to the siege of Charleston. These lithographs show the monitor *Weehawken* fighting rough weather on the way south to attack, with other monitors, the invulnerable Fort Sumter. The action was disastrous to the Union naval forces and proved an unfounded reliance on this new type of vessel.

Fort Sumter proved a stronghold hard to silence. Other Currier & Ives prints show that it was 'bombarded' frequently. The print, *The Siege of Charleston, Bombardment of Fort Sumter and Batteries Wagner and Trigg ... August 1863* depicts the climax of the naval war at Charleston and the silencing of Sumter, though the town was not abandoned until General Sherman's arrival by land.

Wilmington, North Carolina, was one of the last important strongholds on the coast to be captured. A fleet, comprising over 150 warships and transports, was assembled for the amphibious assault which the Currier & Ives print, *The Bombardment and Capture of Fort Fisher, N.C., January 15, 1865,* depicts. Endicott & Company also produced a print of this battle which took place three months before the Confederate surrender at Appomattox.

Part II: Merchant Sail and Steam

Merchant sail; post-Revolutionary War period: in colonial days, England had confined American ships principally to trade with the West Indies. After the colonies won their independence American ships theoretically were free to trade where they pleased. Actually, with England hostile and Europe cool, the American merchants found their trade still controlled. This state of affairs led enterprising merchants to decide to try their luck in the 'China Trade'.

One of the first ships to trade with the Orient was the *Grand Turk* of Salem in 1785. Her likeness appears on a 'Chinese Lowestoft' bowl (*see* China-Trade Porcelain, by Alice Winchester, page 126). This is the first pictorial document of an American merchant ship. ROBERT HASWELL, mate of the ship *Columbia*, painted the likeness of his ship in 1787 when she was en route to China with a cargo of furs from the Pacific Northwest. The *Columbia*, returning westward with tea, was the first American ship to circumnavigate the globe.

Fur proved a successful export and soon another profitable import was discovered. Ships came home loaded with pepper and spices, which commodities, having come through the British before but now being denied, were much in demand. Trade with the Orient helped to tide the country over the lean years. As the turn of the century approached, America began to find her place in other world markets, in spite of continuing British and French opposition.

There were a number of marine artists at work during these early years of the American merchant marine. Outstanding was MICHÈLE FÉLICE CORNÉ, who came from Italy in 1799 on the *Mount Vernon*. He painted this ship as well as many others of Salem, where he settled. Typical of his style is the painting (1799) of the *America* (Plate 296). This vessel, Salem's largest at that time, was purchased by its owner from the French

Navy. Other Corné portraits of the period include the *Belisarius, Fanny, John, Margaret, Ulysses, Volusia* and *Two Brothers* (Plate 295A).

GEORGE ROPES was a deaf and dumb sign and carriage painter whose field was broadened into marine painting through instruction received from Corné. At least nine of his oil paintings have been preserved, all of ships of Salem or Boston. One of documentary value depicts the launching of the *Fame* at Salem in 1802. He also showed the *Fame* with the *America* at Crowninshield's Wharf, Salem (Plate 295B). It is possible that Corné may have influenced other artists of the day, among whom were C. F. DANENBERG, WILLIAM WARD, and JON PHIPPEN.

Privateers in the War of 1812: the expanding prosperity of American trade was interrupted in its youth by the War of 1812. The United States had become an unfortunate neutral caught between the pincers of France and England, at war with one another, yet mutually unhappy over the intrusion of the upstart nation in world trade. Both nations interfered with American shipping. In answer, the country went to war. The merchant marine turned to privateering, a profitable occupation at which it was adept because of the speed of American-designed ships.

An example of a ship converted for privateering was another *America*, painted by THOMAS BIRCH. By removing her upper deck her tonnage was reduced from 473 to 331 which, with a probable increase of sail area, changed her into the swift privateer which captured six vessels off the very coast of England. George Ropes painted her chasing H.B.M. Packet *Princess Elizabeth*.

The pre-packet period: the recovery of American seafaring merchants was rapid following the War of 1812. That war, in contrast to the Revolution, had been fought

(B) Whalebone ditty or workbox. *c.* 1845, showing a cooper's influence; fastened with copper and brass pins. *Mystic Seaport.*

(A) Busk, *c.* 1840. *Mystic Seaport, Marine Historical Association, Mystic, Connecticut.*

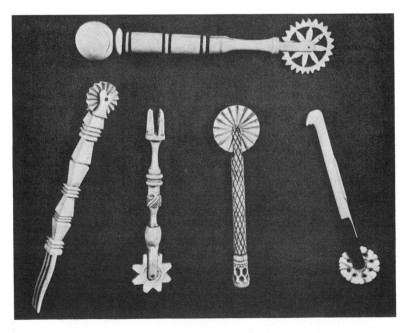

(C) Pie crimpers or jagging wheels. *Mystic Seaport.*

PLATE 289

(B) Whalebone cane and wooden cane with whalebone head, *c.* 1860. *Mystic Seaport.*

(A) Walrus tusks traded by Alaskan Eskimos to the whalemen, *c.* 1855. *Mystic Seaport.*

(C) Sperm whale tooth, *c.* 1850. *Kynett collection, Mystic Seaport.*

PLATE 290

CONSTELLATION & L'INSURGENT - the CHACE.

(A) The *Constellation* and *Insurgent*, February 9, 1799. One of two aquatints by Edward Savage, among the earliest American naval prints. *Coll. of Irving S. Olds, New York.*

A VIEW of the BOMBARDMENT of Fort McHenry, near Baltimore, by the British fleet, taken from the Observatory where the Commanc of Admiral Cochrane & Cockburn on the morning of the 13.of Sep.1814 which lasted 24 hours, & thrown from 1500 to 1800 shells in the Night attempted to land by forcing a passage up the ferry branch but were repulsed with great loss.

(B) Bombardment of Fort McHenry, September 13, 1814. Aquatint by S. Bower, Philadelphia. *The Peale Museum, Baltimore, Maryland.*

PLATE 291

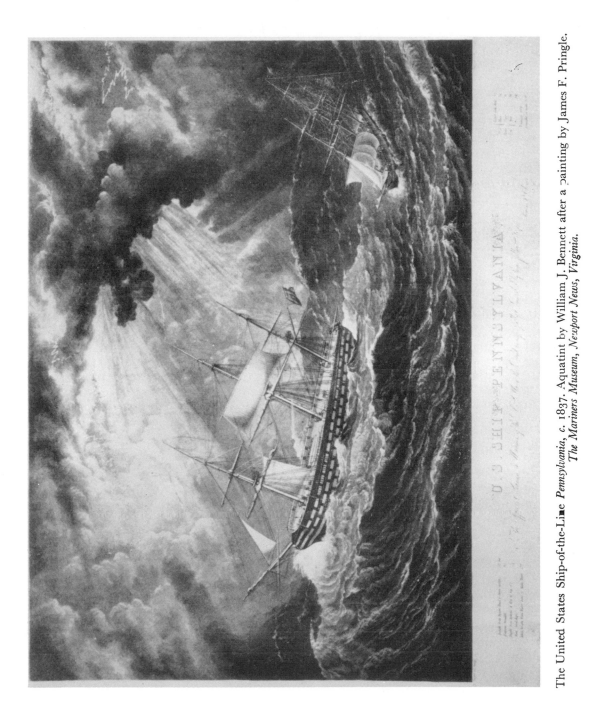

The United States Ship-of-the-Line *Pennsylvania*, c. 1837. Aquatint by William J. Bennett after a painting by James F. Pringle. *The Mariners Museum, Newport News, Virginia.*

PLATE 292

Attack on the city of Tabasco, June 15, 1847, during the Mexican War. Lithographed by Sarony & Major after a painting by Lieutenant Henry Walke, U.S.N. *U.S. Naval Academy Museum, Annapolis, Maryland.*

PLATE 293

(A) *Passing the Rubicon*. Commodore Perry in Japan, 1853. Lithograph by Sarony & Co. *The Mariners Museum, Newport News, Virginia*.

(D) The Confederate Privateer Schooner *Petrel* being attacked by the U.S. Frigate *St. Lawrence*, in the Civil War, July 28, 1861. Lithograph by L. Haugg after Sergeant A. Kaercher. *The Mariners Museum, Newport News, Virginia*.

PLATE 294

(A) Ship *Two Brothers* of Salem. Watercolor by Michèle Félice Corné. *Peabody Museum, Salem, Massachusetts.*

(B) Crowninshield's Wharf, Salem. By George Ropes. Shows the *Fame* and *America*. *Peabody Museum, Salem.*

PLATE 295

The ship *America* of Salem. Watercolor drawing by Michèle Félice Corné, 1799. *Peabody Museum, Salem.*

PLATE 296

Ship *Courier*, built in 1822. Oil portrait by J. T. Evans, painted about 1847. *India House, New York.*

PLATE 297

(A) Clipper ship *Dreadnought*, off Tuskar Light. After McFarlane, N. Currier, lithograph 1856. *The Mariners Museum.*

(B) Original stone of the *Dreadnought*, off Tuskar Light, a rare instance of the survival of a lithographic stone with a mid-nineteenth-century subject. *The Mariners Museum.*

PLATE 298

STEAM SHIP UNITED STATES.

Burthen 2000 Tons.

Built for Charles H. Marshall and Associates by Wᵐ H Webb Esq - Engines by T. F. Secor & Cº

(A) The steamship *United States*, built in 1848, one of America's first transatlantic liners. G. & W. Endicott lithograph. *Eldredge collection. The Mariners Museum.*

(B) The Collins Line steamship *Baltic*. American steamer which won the Blue Ribbon of the Atlantic, 1850. Lithograph by Charles Parsons, published by Endicott & Co. *The Mariners Museum.*

PLATE 299

(A) Towboat *Peter Crary*, built in 1852. Oil painting by James Bard, 1858. *Eldredge collection. The Mariners Museum.*

(B) The steamboat *Mary Powell*, which was built in 1861 and ran on the Hudson River for 62 years. Lithograph by Endicott & Co. *The Old Print Shop, Harry Shaw Newman.*

PLATE 300

(B) Annapolis, Maryland, 5c carmine red impression on white envelope, Scott 2XU1. One of two existing examples and the rarest stamped envelope in the world. Realized $11,000 at Caspary Sale One.

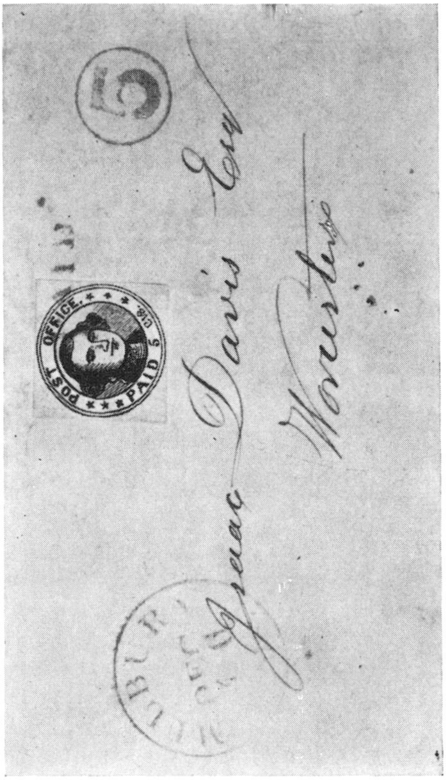

(D) Provisional of Millbury, Massachusetts, illustrating portrait of George Washington.

(A) Baltimore 'Buchanan' 10c black on bluish paper on folded letter. Only two copies of the stamp exist, one off cover and this unique cover. Realized $14,000 at Caspary Sale One.

All illustrations in this section, courtesy of H. R. Harmer, Inc., New York.

(c) This 'Beckman's City Post' cover was sold for a record $11,000 in the Caspary Carriers and Locals auction.

PLATE 301

(A and B) Examples of the first two stamps issued by the United States in 1847.

(c) The same 1847 10c in a marginal strip of four on cover. This realized $7,250 at Caspary Sale Two as against about $75 for an ordinary used single of the same stamp.

(E) The 1875 Official imitations of the 1847 issue (A and B, above) made by the Bureau of Engraving and Printing by order of the Post Office Department for display at the Centennial Exposition of 1876.

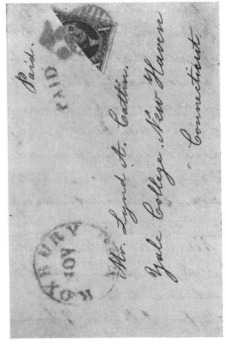

(d) The 1847 10c bisected and used for 5c, due to temporary shortage of 5c value at a particular post office.

PLATE 302

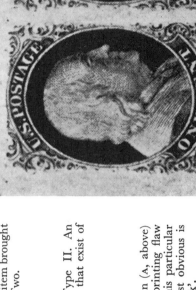

(A) An example of a pair of the 1851–57 imperforate 1c Franklin. Due to different 'Types' and the re-engraving of plates that had worn, this and other values of this set are extensively collected by philatelists.

(B) A phenomenal horizontal pair of the 1851–57 5c red brown with the sheet margin at bottom, superbly used on cover. An average single used copy is worth $35; this item brought $6,000 at Caspary Sale Two.

(C) 1851–57 imperforate 10c Type II. An example of one of the four types that exist of this stamp.

(D) A mint pair, of the 1c Franklin (A, above) the right-hand copy showing a printing flaw caused by the plate cracking. This particular crack in the plate being the most obvious is known as 'The Big Crack'.

PLATE 303

(B) 1851–57 imperforate
12c value. A strip of two
and a half stamps used for
30c postage to England.
This value was both
bisected and used as 6c
and quartered for use
as 3c.

(C) 1357–61 perforated issue. An
important cover bearing a 5c, 10c
and 50c of this issue paying $1.05
postage for a quintuple rate (due
to weight) to Spain. One of
the great entires of U.S. stamps.
Realized $10,000 at Caspary Sale
Two.

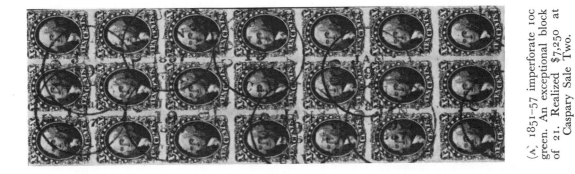

(A) 1851–57 imperforate 10c
green. An exceptional block
of 21. Realized $7,250 at
Caspary Sale Two.

PLATE 304

(B) Grove Hill, Alabama. A crudely prepared 5c stamp of which only two or three on covers are believed to exist. Realized $7,000 at Caspary Sale Three.

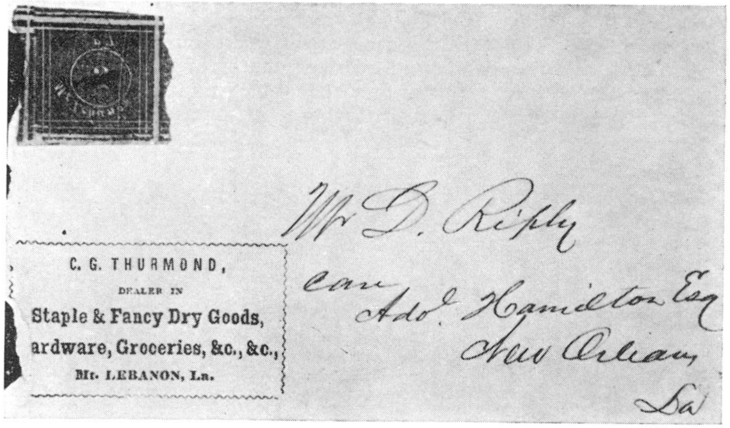

(D) Mt Lebanon, Louisiana. A stamp, hand engraved on wood backwards! The local Postmaster took a small block of wood, impressed with a metal die the '2' and then engraved out by hand a circle, 'Mt Lebanon, La.' around the circle and some frame lines. He omitted to remember that if he engraved the lettering in the normal manner it would print reversed or mirror fashion. Unique. Realized $5,500 at Caspary Sale Three.

(A) Livingston, Alabama. The only known pair of the provisional 5c: used on an envelope. Generally considered the most outstanding and valuable Confederate item in existence. Realized $14,000 at Caspary Sale Three.

(c) Another unique item, this time from Hallettsville, Texas, which has not attained popularity and which brought only $800 in the same auction. Very probably if a further example of this stamp was found it would be more readily acceptable and would increase in value, although no longer unique.

PLATE 305

(B) Hawaiian Islands, 1851–52, so-called Missionary stamp. The very rare 2c used with a 5c on a cover to New York which also bears two U.S. 3c stamps to cover American postage. Considered the greatest Hawaiian Islands item in existence. Realized $25,000 at Caspary Sale Ten.

(C and D) Examples of the two 13c Hawaiian Missionaries, right reading 'Hawaiian Postage', and the left reading 'H.I. & U.S. Postage'.

(A) An Air Post classic error. The famous 1918 24c airpost stamp with the airplane printed inverted. One sheet of 100 distributed.

PLATE 306

Park Theater, New York, 1822, with the English comedian Charles Matthews in *Monsieur Tonson*.
Watercolor by John Searle. Shows portraits of Robert G. L. de Peyster, Dr John W. Francis, Mrs
Dewitt Clinton, William Bayard and Henry Brevoort. *New-York Historical Society*.

PLATE 307

Playbill, 1792, John Street Theater; New York's leading eighteenth-century theater until the Park was opened in 1798. *New-York Historical Society.*

PLATE 308

PARK THEATRE & PART OF PARK ROW.

(A) Park Theater and part of Park Row. Junius Brutus Booth played here in 1821, Fanny Kemble in 1832, and the 'Boz Ball' in honor of Dickens was held here in 1842. From Valentine's *Manual*, 1855. *The Old Print Shop, Harry Shaw Newman.*

(B) Astor Place Opera House, scene of the riots of 1849 centering around Macready playing at the Astor, and Forrest at Wallack's, both in *Macbeth*. From Hoff's 'Views of New York'. *New-York Historical Society.*

PLATE 309

(A) Junius Brutus Booth as Sir Giles Overreach. Booth played in America 1821–5, 1827–36, and 1837–51. Published London, 1817. *Museum of the City of New York.*

(B) William Macready as Iago. Macready had the sympathy of the better element in New York during the Astor Place Riots of 1849. *Museum of the City of New York.*

(C) Fanny Elssler in *The Gypsy*; the Viennese dancer appeared in New York in 1840. Lithograph by Endicott. *The Old Print Shop, Harry Shaw Newman.*

PLATE 310

(A) Lola Montez. By David Claypoole Johnston, the 'American Cruikshank'. Lola appeared at the Broadway Theater, New York in 1851 and toured the country. *The Old Print Shop, Harry Shaw Newman.*

(B) The Flower Dance, by the Vienna Children. 1846. Lithograph by N. Currier. *The Old Print Shop, Harry Shaw Newman.*

PLATE 311

Circus poster; can be dated by its reference to the 'portrait of President John Quincy Adams', *c.* 1825.
New-York Historical Society.

PLATE 312

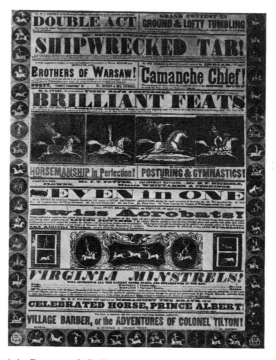

(A) Poster of J. T. Potter's Circus advertising
'Virginia Minstrels'. Noteworthy for its woodcuts;
early-nineteenth century. *The Old Print Shop,
Harry Shaw Newman.*

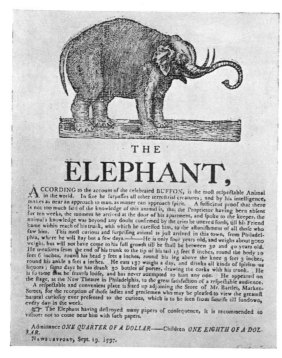

(B) Probably the first elephant in America, brought
from Bengal to New York in 1796 by Captain Jacob
Crowninshield and sold for $10,000. *New-York
Historical Society.*

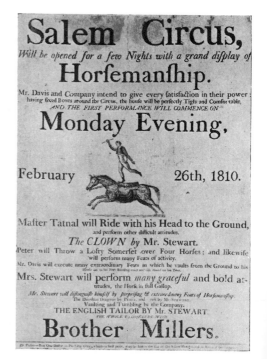

(C) Handbill, Salem Circus, dated February
26, 1810; to be distributed in the streets.
B. True, printer, Boston. *The Old Print Shop,
Harry Shaw Newman.*

PLATE 313

(A) Sheet Music showing Jackson at Battle of New Orleans, lithograph issued when Pendleton was at 9 Wall Street, New York, 1832—3; this was published in honor of Jackson's second election. *Cincinnati Public Library; photograph courtesy of Antiques.*

(B) Sheet Music, Cochituate Grand Quick Step; in honor of Boston's new water supply system, 1848. Lithograph by J. H. Bufford. *Antiques*, March, 1933.

PLATE 314

(A) Paper taken from Buckingham House, Old Saybrook, Connecticut; believed to be English, *c.* 1765, now at Mystic Seaport, Mystic, Connecticut. *Courtesy Jones & Erwin.*

(B) American copy of Buckingham House paper with 'arches' motif; by Zechariah Mills, Hartford, Connecticut, *c.* 1794; the back shows his stamp. *Jones & Erwin.*

(C) Label on reverse.

PLATE 315

(A) Commemorating General Nathaniel Greene, 1742–86, of Washington's staff; from the Old Shute House, South Hingham, Massachusetts; grays and black; may be English or French, late-eighteenth century. *Nancy McClelland*.

(B) English paper with tax stamp, *c.* 1765. Gray with rose and green; from the Clapp House, Dorchester, Vermont. *Courtesy of Mrs. Dorothy S. Waterhouse*.

(C) Original English Flock paper, dark red; hung in 1781 *Webb House, Wethersfield, Connecticut*.

PLATE 316

(A) French 'mock India' paper imitating designs on chintz; reds and blues on a white ground; imported *c.* 1800. *Cooper Union Museum, New York.*

(c) French paper showing portrait of Commodore Isaac Hull and engagement of the *Constitution* and *Guerrière*, *c.* 1815. Printed from woodblocks on blue ground. *Cooper Union Museum.*

(B) French 'moiré' design printed from woodblocks, *c.* 1800; pink vertical bands with black sprig-work, alternating with dark green bands with bright green sprig-work. *Cooper Union Museum.*

PLATE 317

(B) American eagle design printed for a band-box 1800–10. *Cooper Union Museum.*

(A) American festoon border, 1805–20; wood-block on joined sheets of paper. *Cooper Union Museum.*

(C) American paper printed from woodblocks in oil and distemper colors, *c.* 1820. *Cooper Union Museum.*

PLATE 318

(A) 'The Voyages of Antenor', French, printed by Dufour, Paris, 1830; hung in early-nineteenth century at The Lindens, originally in Danvers, Massachusetts, now moved to Washington, D.C. *Courtesy of Mrs George Maurice Morris.*

(B) Mexican War Scene; vignette possibly printed by an American manufacturer over French paper, *c.* 1847; the view shows the 'Battle of Chapultepec', September 12–13, 1847; gray ground with maroon scrolls touched with white; uniforms blue and gray with touches of white and maroon. Reproduced from *Antiques*, October, 1941; article by Esther Lewitte on Mexican War Designs.

PLATE 319

(A) French geometric paper, 1800–10, printed from woodblocks on joined sheets of paper. *Cooper Union Museum.*

(B) American geometric paper in gray taupe, black and white *c.* 1800. Found near Henniker, New Hampshire. *William J. Galligan, Document collection.*

(C) American version of *chinoiserie* design; a roll found near Hartford, Connecticut; bright dark blue ground with Chinese red and white. *William J. Galligan, Document collection.*

(D) American hat-box paper found in Kennebunk, Maine, *c.* 1800; orange and red, green and gold. *William J. Galligan, Document collection.*

PLATE 320

principally at sea. The part played by privateersmen had left experienced seamen who unloaded guns, loaded cargo, and were off to sea again. Among such ships returning to trade from privateering might have been the *Hazard*, *New Hazard*, *Fame*, *Packet* and *Glide* depicted by George Ropes. American shipyards also were soon busy launching ships to replace the many lost in the War.

One of the better painters of this time was ROBERT SALMON. His picture of the American ship *Aristides* was painted in English waters before he came from Scotland in 1828. His views of Boston harbor are notable, as are his portraits, which include the *Liverpool*, and the brig *Oriental* entering a crowded harbor in a stiff breeze. He also painted whaling scenes.

Among the other painters of portraits of miscellaneous ships of the first half of the nineteenth century was BENJAMIN F. WEST (1818–54), a self-taught artist. He was one of the more prolific of the Salem artists. Eight or more of his paintings are preserved at Peabody Museum. WILLIAM H. LUSCOMB (1805–66) and GEORGE SOUTHWARD (1803–76) were also Salem painters. Others of the Boston area were J. V. DODGE, CLEMENT DREW, WILLIAM HARE, C. W. NORTON, J. PENN, and C. S. RALEIGH.

JAMES T. EVANS was a marine artist of New Orleans. His ships were always drawn with care, as was the picture reproduced here of the *Courier* (Plate 297). A drawing, signed *Evans, N. Orleans, 1845*, is of the *Emperor* and another shows the *Barque MARTHA ... entering Mobile 1845*. An oil of the ship *Warren Hastings*, 'in the Hurricane of the 21st of October', shows his inclination for painting boisterous seas.

The packet period: speed and regularity were the principal elements beginning to develop in shipping during the first quarter of the nineteenth century. Although Americans can be charged with an inordinate pride in speed for itself, the motivating force behind the fever was economic. A ready market and a good profit came from goods quickly delivered at a specified time. Capacity cargoes went to ships departing on schedule. These were reasons for the advent of the packet ship, called by the maritime historian, Robert G. Albion, 'Square-riggers on Schedule'.

The best-known packet ship company was the Black Ball Line, which started operations in 1817 with four ships. In 1848, the climax of the packet era, the company operated ten vessels. During the sixty years the line was in existence thirty-nine ships sailed under the Black Ball house flag.

Among the American painters of Black Ball ships was ROBERT SALMON, already mentioned, who painted the first packet named *New York*, which operated from 1822 to 1834. The *Isaac Webb* (1850–78) was painted by L. A. BRIGGS, the *Webb* and the *Harvest Queen* (1854–75) were painted by J. HUGHES. Dramatic is the engraving of the wreck of the *Albion* in 1822 after a painting by THOMAS BIRCH.

Many packet ship lines were formed on the pattern of the Black Ball Company. Most of them, like the older line, ran between New York and Liverpool. Others served London and Le Havre. Coastal packet lines between New York and Charleston, Savannah, Mobile and New Orleans also came into being.

American marine artists have recorded vessels of most of these lines. WILLIAM BRADFORD painted the *Meteor* of the Red Star Line; JAMES PRINGLE, the *Corinthian* of the Blue Swallowtail Line; W. MARSH, the *Henry Clay*, also of the same line (lithographed by F. PALMER); DANIEL McFARLANE, the *Ellen Austin* of the Dramatic Line, and also the *Southampton* and *Mediator* of the Black X Line; JOSEPH DE SILVA, the *Devonshire*, also of the Black X; and GEORGE DELL, the *America Congress* of the Red Swallowtail line. Coastal packets are represented in paintings: the *Emperor* by J. EVANS; the *Baltimore* by J. F. HUGE; the *Nashville* by DANIEL McFARLANE; and the *Tybee* by an artist named AUGUSTUS D. ROGERS of Salem. N. CURRIER also published prints of packets, including one of the wreck of the New Orleans Line packet, *John Minturn*, on the New Jersey coast, February 15, 1846.

The clipper ship period: the 'Golden Age of Sail' reached its climax about 1850 with the advent of the clipper ship. Ship designers lengthened and narrowed the hull, reached forward with the graceful 'clipper bow', raked the masts, and reached upward for more driving power. Masters drove these creations and their crews mercilessly. This was merchant sail's attempt to carry goods even faster; to bring fresher tea and spices, and more silks from the Orient; to rush gold hunters and their needs to California; and particularly to try to answer the challenge of the inevitable coming of steam.

The spirit of competition was an element which then, as ever, appealed to the imagination, creating a demand for pictures of these 'Sovereigns of the Sea'. Not only did the wealthy owners and masters want to be able to point with pride to oil portraits of their ships, but the 'man in the street' was asking for their likenesses. This demand was answered by Currier & Ives, who published a generous choice of subjects in large or small folio to suit the pocketbooks of their clients. A list of the twenty-odd named clipper ships has a poetic sound appropriate to the beauty and dash of the ships themselves. There were the *Sea Witch, Golden Light, Hurricane, Queen of the Clippers, Antarctic, Challenge, Witch of the Wave, Dreadnought, Comet, Contest, Flying Cloud, Great Republic, Lightning, Nightingale, Ocean Express, Racer, Red Jacket, Young America, Three Brothers, Adelaide* and *Sovereign of the Seas*. The first six of these N. Currier or Currier & Ives subjects were available in small folio only.

DANIEL MCFARLANE was one of the artists hired by Nathaniel Currier to paint originals for copying on stone. Of such was his *"Dreadnought" off Tuskar Light* (Plate 298A, B). A McFarlane original of the *Sweepstakes* has been preserved, as have about seven others of his pictures of ships not truly in the clipper ship classification.

JAMES E. BUTTERSWORTH was an active worker for Currier, though credited with but two prints, the *Great Republic* and *Antarctic*. There are also Buttersworth paintings of the clipper *Racer* and the vessels *Union, Highflyer, Architect, Kennebec,* and many yachting pictures.

J. B. SMITH & SON were painters of Brooklyn. The father painted the ships, and the son the water. Four Currier & Ives prints were their work, and paintings of the *Young America, Golden West, Empress of the Seas* and the post-clipper *Mahlon Williamson* were also probably done by them.

FANNY PALMER, ELIPHALET BROWN, JR., and JOHN CAMERON were other workers for the Currier firm, and mention must be made of CHARLES PARSONS, who did original lithographic work as well as transferring to stone so many of the paintings mentioned above.

It is strange that other lithographers seem not to have published prints of ships in numbers proportionate to Currier & Ives' output. NAGEL & WEINGARTNER and LOUIS MENGER of New York, and WAGNER & MCGUIGAN of Philadelphia produced a few. Their artists were J. HANSEN, W. H. REASE, and ELIPHALET BROWN, JR.

By no means did all the painters of clipper ships become associated with Currier & Ives. There was, for instance, FITZ HUGH LANE, a New England artist whose work approaches the fine arts classification. To his credit are likenesses of the *Northern Light, Radiant* and *Golden Rule*, as well as his handsome harbor views. Other painters not to be neglected include THOMAS PITTMAN, WILLIAM B. EATON, CHARLES A. NISSEN, WILLIAM F. HALSALL and J. W. STANCLIFFE.

By 1865 'sail' was ready to admit that 'steam' had won the seas in the task of carrying cargoes to be delivered quickly. But 'sail' had many more useful years ahead and its devotees consider its last years, when its ships became more full-bodied and functional, to be looked upon with as much nostalgia as the feverish days of the 'fifties.

Steam: a French artist of note, CHARLES BALTHAZAR JULIEN FÉVRET DE SAINT-MÉMIN, drew in 1810 the only known contemporary view of Fulton's first steamboat, the *Clermont*, while 'Poor John Fitch's' steamboat, which was really America's first one to succeed, was recorded only by an obscure wood engraver, BAXTER HARLEY. The name of Fitch's 1778 invention was the *Phila-*

delphia. Fitch took his own life in bitter disappointment, while Robert Fulton received acclaim and lived to build a number of steamboats.

One of the earliest lithographs to be published in America depicts the last one of Fulton's steamboats, the *Chancellor Livingston,* named after Fulton's business partner. This print came from a stone of W. S. PENDLETON, pioneer American lithographer. The print is important to the steamboat historian and the graphic arts historian alike.

Transatlantic steamships: the American merchant marine, which had bested other nations in the perfection and operation of the sailing vessel, was slow in the development of transoceanic steam navigation. To be sure, the *Savannah* had been the first to cross the ocean in 1819, but it crossed only partially under steam. For years the titles of 'first' and 'fastest' were to be won by the British.

HENRY R. ROBINSON, a lithographer with a good sense of news, brought out a print of the British steamship *Sirius* arriving in New York on April 22, 1838, only a few hours ahead of her British rival, the *Great Western,* the first vessels to cross the ocean entirely under steam power.

America's first answer to these and other British steamers came in 1847 and 1848 with the *Washington, Hermann* and *United States* (Plate 299A), whose portraits were published by N. Currier and G. & W. Endicott. The success of these ships was only fair. It still remained for energetic E. K. Collins to wrest the prize for speed in the Atlantic temporarily from the Cunard Line in 1850 with the *Baltic* (Plate 299B). American reaction to the success of the Collins Line is evidenced by the thirty or more prints and paintings which appeared of the company's vessels. Currier & Ives alone were responsible for sixteen of these, the Endicotts, L. A. Menger and Sarony & Major for others. There are several oil paintings, some of them anonymous. Also several British prints and paintings were made.

Other American wooden-hulled steamships of the pre–1865 period included the *Franklin* (1850), *Humboldt* (1851), *Arago* (1855) and *Fulton* (1856) of the New York and Le Havre Steam Navigation Company; and the *North Star* (1852), *Ariel* (1855) and *Vanderbilt* (1857) of the Vanderbilt European Line, all of which have been documented in prints by Endicott and N. Currier.

Coastal, sound and river steamers: although America's transoceanic steamship achievements left much to be desired, the country was not backward in developing steam power in her coastal, sound and river areas.

The metropolis of New York was fed by steamboat lines on the Hudson, linked by the Erie Canal with the Great Lakes. Lakes George and Champlain connected Canada with the system. Lines through Long Island Sound, with branches up the rivers of Connecticut, went to Fall River and other ports where rail connections reached Boston. Coastal lines from 'Down East' Maine fed Boston. Steamboats went southward from New York to New Brunswick to connect, by stage coach or later canal and railroad across the narrow waist of New Jersey, with steamers on the Delaware River to Philadelphia. The Delaware almost reached the upper branches of Chesapeake Bay which extended southward to Hampton Roads. Norfolk, Charleston and Savannah were connected with the system by coastal lines. Lines to New Orleans joined the whole with the Mississippi waterways. And finally the Far West was included. Hundreds of steamship lines made up this network on which thousands of steamers operated.

New York and New England: the most cosmopolitan of the pictorial recorders of many of these steamboats were the Endicotts of New York. The Mariners Museum alone has over two hundred and fifty Endicott lithographs, most of which are in the steamship classification. Over a hundred of these are of ships built before 1865. They represent vessels of the Hudson River (Plate 300B), Long Island Sound, New England, most of the coastwise lines, the Delaware River and Chesapeake Bay.

The Endicotts are being stressed over Currier & Ives because of their emphasis upon the steamship. Actually Currier published over two hundred steamship prints. Half of these are of foreign vessels, however, and of the hundred American steamers about sixty represent vessels of the pre–1865 period. Most of the twenty-odd transatlantic steamers have been referred to, especially the Collins Line group. The balance are divided between Hudson River, Mississippi River, Long Island Sound, coastwise and Great Lakes. Mention must be made of one classification of print typical of Currier & Ives' eye for the news. These are 'disaster' prints, twelve of which depict disasters before 1865.

Artists working for the Endicotts during these early years include SIMEON HALL, THEODORE BERGNER, S. COLMAN, C. F. DAVIS and FRED PANSING. The most prolific, however, was CHARLES PARSONS (1821–1910), who was apprenticed to George Endicott when he was twelve, lived in the Endicott home, and later became a partner in the firm. Over a hundred and forty prints in the collection at The Mariners Museum are credited to Parsons, and many more Endicott and Currier prints are his work. The time which such an output of work on stone must have taken probably accounts for a scarcity of original work on paper or canvas. Steamers were his specialty, and he drew them masterfully.

A less sophisticated artist of the steamboat of New York was JAMES BARD (1815–97), from whose brush came portraits not only of the grander steamers of his day, but of the more humble steamboats and workboats (Plate 300A) as well. Bard produced a remarkable volume of work, over three hundred paintings or drawings having been recorded.

Being a self-taught artist, his style in painting backgrounds and human figures was primitive, but his vessels were drawn with painstaking care. Thus in Bard we find a charming contribution to American folk art combined with a major contribution to maritime history.

Another primitive artist, comparable with James Bard in style, though by no means in volume, was J. FREDERICK HUGE of Bridgeport. The names of some of the steamers he painted, the *New Haven* (1835),

the *Connecticut* (1848), the *Ansonia* (1848) and the *Bridgeport* (1857) indicate the provincial scope of Huge's work.

Three Boston lithographers made significant recordings of the Massachusetts steam vessels. WILLIAM S. PENDLETON, the father of American lithography, produced a portrait of the 1834 steamer *Portland*, the first vessel of the Portland Steam Packet Company. JOHN H. BUFFORD'S contribution of a dozen or more prints of Boston ships was more significant, and his New England port views carry likenesses of other steamers. Important also were two Bufford prints showing the wreck of the steamship *Union* on the coast of Lower California, July 5, 1851 – a wreck resulting from too much Fourth of July celebration. Bufford's artists were FITZ HUGH LANE, F. CROW, EDWIN MOODY and J. P. NEWELL. WILLIAM H. FORBES & Co. were just getting established as Boston lithographers at the close of the period with which this article deals. The steamboat *Linda* of the Yarmouth & Boston Line was pictured by Forbes.

The Delaware River: in 1808 a New Jersey inventor, John Stevens, Jr. tried to break the monopoly which Fulton and Livingston held on steamboating in New York waters. Failing in this, he took his steamboat, the *Phoenix*, around to the Delaware River, thus securing for it distinction as the first steamboat to navigate the ocean. Another 'first' is associated with this steamer, for CHARLES B. LAWRENCE'S paintings of the *Phoenix* and *Philadelphia*, at The Mariners Museum, are the first oil paintings on record of American steamboats. These vessels opened the Philadelphia to Trenton steamboat service. Another Delaware River steamer, the *Trenton* (1825) is portrayed in a charming lithograph by P. S. DUVAL after D. S. QUINTON.

Coastwise traffic between Philadelphia and New York was carried by steamships including the *Penobscot* and *Kennebec* (1844), the *Delaware* (1852), and the *Menemon Sanford* (1854), the latter named after the founder of the line. These vessels are recorded pictorially by James Bard, Endicott & Co., and the New York lithographers, Nagel & Weingartner.

Connections between Philadelphia and Boston were possible in 1851 on the *William Penn* and *Benjamin Franklin*, two of the earliest screw steamers in America. Their importance seems indicated by the several contemporary portraits that appeared. A print by E. HILLEN introduces the name of an obscure Philadelphia lithographer into this index. Better known was THOMAS S. SINCLAIR, also of Philadelphia, who published two prints of the *Penn*. A pastel drawing by WILLIAM H. REASE in the extensive Eldredge Collection at The Mariners Museum is the original from which one of these Sinclair prints was made.

The Chesapeake Bay: pictorial likenesses of steamboats seem to decrease in numbers in proportion to the increase in distance of their area of operations from New York, the center of the lithography business. This may account for the scarcity of portraits of Chesapeake Bay steamers. Maryland and Virginia waters now float vessels of the oldest steamboat company still in operation, the Old Bay Line. Only about five of the seventeen steamers owned by this line between its incorporation and 1865 have been individually depicted. Three of these are by unknown draughtsmen, leaving only two views by Endicott & Co. of the *Louisiana* and *Adelaide* (1864), to represent the Old Bay Line, except for steamers which appear incidentally in port prints by E. WHITEFIELD and E. SACHSE. Endicott also published a print of the *George Leary* (1864), owned by one of the Old Bay Line's competitors.

The Mississippi River: if proof of the popular appeal of the Mississippi River steamboat is needed, we have only to mention that the publishers, Currier & Ives, with their fingers on the pulse of the public, readily sensed it. From their stones came over thirty lithographs of Mississippi views, many before 1865. Such masterpieces as *The Mississippi in Time of War and in Time of Peace*, *Through the Bayou by Torchlight*, the *Steamboat PRINCESS 'Wooding Up'*, or *A Midnight Race on the Mississippi* need only be mentioned to bring the romance of the River to mind.

A. WEINGARTNER and THOMAS KELLY

of New York published views of the celebrated race between the *Baltic* and *Diana*. FORBES & Co. of Boston depicted the ornate steamboat *Grand Republic*. A New Orleans firm, FISHBOURNE LITHOGRAPHY CO., published a portrait of the *Grand Turk*, as did HENRY LEWIS in *Das Illustrierte Mississippithal* in 1854. Besides these printmakers there were artists who gave steamboats more or less prominence in their works. C. E. BIGOT painted the *Sultana*, *c.* 1840; FRIEDRICH KURZ, the *St Ange*, 1851; HIPPOLYTE SEBRON, *Giant Steamboats at New Orleans* in 1853; and steamboats appear in the works of the better-known artists, GEORGE CATLIN and GEORGE CALEB BINGHAM.

The Great Lakes: a print by CORRIE'S DETROIT LITHOGRAPHIC OFFICE entitled *Detroit in 1820* shows a curious paddle-wheel steamboat called the *Walk-in-the-Water*. This portrait of the first steamboat on the Great Lakes is attributed to an artist named GEORGE W. WHISTLER. Pictures of other early Lakes vessels are plentiful. Six wood-cuts by JOHN ORR of Buffalo depict vessels between 1835 and 1838. Henry Robinson and Nathaniel Currier each produced a view of the burning of the steamboat *Erie*, August 9, 1841, 'when over 200 human beings perished in the dreadful conflagration'. Other Great Lakes prints were published by Napoleon Sarony, the Endicotts, J. Sage & Sons, Buffalo, Charles Hart, I. C. Miller, T. Sinclair, and curiously there is a painting of the *Bunker Hill* by the Bridgeport, Connecticut, painter, J. FREDERICK HUGE.

The Far West: in conclusion mention should be made of the Pacific Mail Steamship Company, a line which operated for almost a hundred years and attained a reputation comparable with that of any steamship company in the world. When its first steamer, the *California*, sailed from New York its owners little knew that gold would be discovered before the ship reached California, a stroke of luck which was to launch the Pacific Mail Line into immediate success. Artists and publishers, including JAMES BARD, WILLIAM MARSH, ENDICOTT, PALMER & COMPANY, G. F. NESBITT &

COMPANY, SARONY & MAJOR, P.S. DUVAL and BRITTON & REY were to produce pictures of eighteen vessels owned or operated by the company before 1865, which is in itself no mean indication of the success of the line.

BOOKS FOR
FURTHER READING

NAVAL

MILHOLLEN, KAPLAN AND STUART: *Divided We Fought*, Macmillan Co., New York (1952).

OLDS, IRVING S.: *Bits and Pieces of American History*, New York (1951).

POSCOE, THEODORE, AND FREEMAN, FRED: *Picture History of the U.S. Navy*, Charles Scribner's Sons, New York (1956).

An Album of American Battle Art, 1755–1918, The Library of Congress U.S. Government Printing Office (1947).

American Battle Painting, 1776–1918, National Gallery of Art and The Museum of Modern Art (1944).

The Beverley R. Robinson Collection of Naval Battle Prints, U.S. Naval Academy Museum, U.S. Government Printing Office (1942).

Naval Actions in the American Revolution, The Bailey Collection of Water Colours, Reprint from *U.S. Naval Institute Proceedings*, The Mariners Museum (1856).

The United States Navy, 1776–1815, The Grolier Club, New York (1942).

U.S.S. Constitution. A Sesquicentennial Exhibition, The Mariners Museum (1947).

SAIL

HALL, W. S.: *Currier & Ives Prints – Clipper Ships*, William E. Rudge, New York (1932).

JENKINS, LAWRENCE W.: *Catalogue of the Charles H. Taylor Collection of Ship Portraits*, The Peabody Museum, Salem (1949).

PETERS, FRED J.: *Clipper Ship Prints by N. Currier and Currier & Ives*, Antique Bulletin Publishing Co., New York (1930).

ROBINSON, JOHN, AND DOW, GEORGE F.: *Sailing Ships of England 1607-1907.* (Three series), Marine Research Society, Salem (1922, 1924, 1928).

American Merchant Sailing Vessels of the Nineteenth Century, The Mariners Museum (1951).

The Marine Room of the Peabody Museum of Salem, The Peabody Museum, Salem (1921).

STEAM

BROWN, ALEXANDER C.: *The Old Bay Line*, The Dietz Press, Richmond (1940).

HALL, W. S.: *Currier & Ives Prints – Early Steamships*, The Studio Publications, New York (1933).

LANE, Carl D.: *American Paddle Steamboats*, Coward-McCann, Inc. (1943).

SNIFFEN, HAROLD S. AND BROWN, ALEXANDER C.: *James and John Bard, Painters of Steamboat Portraits*, Reprint from *Art in America*, The Mariners Museum, (1949).

Mississippi Panorama, Catalogue of an Exhibition at the City Art Museum of St Louis (1949).

Ships of the Great Lakes, A catalogue of selections from the Marine Collection of the Canadian Steamship Lines and The Mariners Museum (1943).

GENERAL

DURANT, JOHN AND ALICE: *Pictorial History of American Ships*, A. S. Barnes and Co., New York (1953).

PETERS, HARRY T.: *American On Stone*, Doubleday, Doran & Co., New York (1931).

PETERS, HARRY T.: *Currier & Ives, Printmakers to the American People*, Doubleday, Doran & Co., New York, (1942).

PHELPS STOKES, I. N., AND HASKELL, DANIEL C.: *American Historical Prints from the Phelps Stokes and Other Collections*, New York Public Library (1933).

A Descriptive Catalogue of the Marine Collection at India House, Sign of the Gosden Head, New York (1935).

The Old Print Shop Portfolio and *Panorama* – Harry Shaw Newman Gallery, New York (1942–57).

STAMPS

By KENT B. STILES and GEORGE B. SLOANE

AN introduction to the subject of postal antiques in the United States may be obtained from a study of the Caspary collection, dispersed 1955–1958. It will be many years before another collection such as his will be on the market.

Alfred H. Caspary, 1877–1955, New York financier and collector in many fields, was an ardent stamp connoisseur who traveled widely – several times to England and to Continental Europe – to do bidding in person for American rarities which he knew were reposing in the famous European albums. He provided in his will that his postal classics, estimated to have an aggregate value approximating three million dollars, should be dispersed through public sales. A series of Caspary auctions was inaugurated late in 1955, the final ones (of sixteen) scheduled for 1958, by H. R. Harmer, Inc., New York office of the London stamp auctioneering firm of H. R. Harmer, Ltd.

The sales came at a time when American postal antiques were beginning to enjoy virtually unprecedented popularity. By 1955 the number of adult philatelists (not in the United States alone) with money to finance purchases had expanded amazingly; thus this Caspary 'cream of the crop' came on the market at a propitious time, for new collections were being assembled by men of wealth. And it is because the Caspary offerings included so many 'only surviving' examples that prices in many instances sky-rocketed above what had been considered normal catalogue values.

Postmasters' provisionals: here is a striking example, based on bidding at a recent Caspary sale, of how scarcity is influencing the price trend. The piece involved, a cover with a postmaster's provisional stamp, is typi-

cal of the complex picture that existed in the United States in the era when stamp-producing was in its infancy. Early in January of 1845 (two years before the use of Government-provided postage stamps was authorized by Congress) James Madison Buchanan was the postmaster at Baltimore, Maryland. He prepared provisional stamps, oblong-shaped, the design being a facsimile of his autograph above the denomination, either 5 cents or 10 cents; color, black on bluish paper. These stamps he sold to Baltimore people, who placed them on letters (Plate 301A).

Of the 10-cent value, only two used on covers are known to have survived. One moved from Baltimore to Annapolis, Maryland. Eventually this cover was acquired by the late Arthur Hind, Utica, New York, who owned one of the leading collections of all time; his foreign stamps were auctioned in London after his death. The United States stamps were sold in New York and at this sale in 1934 Mr Caspary was the successful bidder, paying $10,500 for the Baltimore cover. In a Caspary collection catalogue, the Buchanan piece is called a 'fabulous rarity'. This judgment was more than amply sustained when an unidentified collector paid $14,000, or $3,500 better than the sum Caspary paid.

The United States was comparatively slow in issuing stamps (Plate 302A & B). A 5-cent brown with portrait of Benjamin Franklin and a 10-cent black with head of George Washington appeared in 1847. The situation may be summarized as follows: Great Britain had issued two denominations, 1-penny and 2-pence, in 1840, and was soon followed by Brazil, in 1843, and by Switzerland with various 'Cantonal' issues in 1843–5. Meanwhile, in the United States, the lack of adhesive postage stamps, as evidence of prepayment of postal fees, was due to indifference, indecision and ineptitude on the part of the Post Office Department, and was a source of great inconvenience to the general public. While the Department dallied and deliberated whether to adopt official postage stamps, some stamps actually did go into use. In New York, in 1842, a private citizen named Alexander M. Greig organized his 'City Dispatch Post'; he provided a stamp, 3-cent black on grayish paper, for this post, which he conducted solely for handling letters within the city. His principal office was at 46 William Street, and he had branches and letter boxes installed throughout the city – 'in conspicuous places', as he advertised. The merits of this impressed John Lorimer Graham, the Postmaster, and the Government purchased the enterprise, hiring Greig as superintendent. But within a few years the Government disposed of the post to private ownership.

Individual postmasters in several large cities began issuing 'provisional' stamps – devised and designed according to their whims – to meet growing public necessity. Cost of these productions came out of their own personal funds, while the Post Office Department, accepting receipts of sales, observed the undertakings as experiments. Robert H. Morris, New York's postmaster in 1845, was the first municipal postmaster to issue such a provisional – distinguished from Greig's postal pieces in that it was for use on mail throughout the United States. Morris's, printed in black and illustrating a Gilbert Stuart portrait of George Washington, was sold for 5 cents. One stamp alone would prepay postage (on a single letter not over a half-ounce in weight) for a distance not exceeding 300 miles. Morris sent samples of this stamp to the postmasters of Albany, Boston, Philadelphia and Washington, and later to other postmasters, to acquaint them with his 'newly adopted stamp', which he hoped would encourage prepayment of postage. (In that period prepayment was optional with the sender; most of the mail in transit was on a 'collect' basis.) The Morris idea of a prepaid postage stamp was copied by postmasters elsewhere – in Alexandria, Virginia, Annapolis (Plate 301B) and Baltimore, Maryland, Brattleboro, Vermont, Millbury, Massachusetts (Plate 301D), New Haven, Connecticut, Providence, Rhode Island, and St. Louis, Missouri. Some postmasters made provisional stamps; others provided envelopes handstamped by the postmasters and sometimes bearing their own or facsimile autographs as marks of authenticity.

These postmasters' provisionals are regarded by collectors as the 'primitives', and most of them are great rarities. Many such classics were in the Caspary collection. Two of the Alexandrias, each on original cover, sold for $7,400 and $9,250 respectively; and a third, the only one known on blue paper, brought $10,000. At the same auction, $11,000 was paid for the Annapolis postmaster's 1845 provisional 5-cent in red on a white envelope. This was the same sale at which $14,000 was recorded for the Baltimore cover already described. Other postmasters' provisionals, such as New Haven and St. Louis, brought high sums.

In the early days, mailing and receipt of letters were achieved through personal visits to post offices, which were sometimes at a distance. There was seldom a letter box in the sender's neighborhood, and there was almost no carrier service for deliveries.

These conditions brought into business various *Local Posts* and the somewhat related *Semi-Official Carrier* service, which furnished delivery conveniences at nominal service fees. The independently owned local posts installed their own boxes throughout the city for reception of mail; and usually for a 1-cent fee carried the letter to the post office. If required they advanced the Government's postal charges when unpaid and made door delivery, collecting the combined charges. Deliveries by the local posts were outside the Government mail, and the services were in much demand for distribution of valentines and notices essential in everyday life. Often they were employed to deliver wedding announcements because their private messengers gave to the deliveries an aura of social distinction. It was an era of expensive postal rates, and much mail was transmitted postage-unpaid. The business man who sent a clerk for the routine pick-up of mail daily paid out considerable sums in postage due, the latter based on distances which the mail was carried by the Post Office Department. In consequence, there was much 'boot-legging' of mail to save on postage; thousands of letters were, as a matter of course, carried 'outside the mails' by travelers, stage-drivers, railroad and steamship employees and others. Much mail from distant places was slipped into post offices for delivery by the postal service at the cheaper 'drop letter' rate. It was customary for business men when making trips to other cities to take along friends' letters, thus depriving the post office of considerable revenue in postage fees charged for long hauls.

In addition to the local posts there were some *Independent Mail Routes*, such as the American Letter Mail Company, Hale & Company, Letter Express, and Pomeroy's. Early in the 1840s such firms were carrying enormous quantities of mail interstate throughout the east and into the middle west, at rates much below those charged by the Post Office Department, and with speedier and more reliable dispatch. At one time it appeared that these companies, if allowed to continue, would soon be handling more mail than the Government, and more efficiently. They often divided territories and had working agreements among themselves to handle letters addressed to points off their own routes.

It is recorded that Henry Wells (then a principal partner in Letter Express and later one of the founders of Wells Fargo) proposed to Charles A. Wickliffe, Postmaster-General under President Tyler, that Wells take over and operate the entire postal service of the United States, at a lower rate of postage than the Government contended was necessary. This confronted Wickliffe with an alarming prospect of what could happen to 16,000 postmasters. The Post Office Department pleaded to Congress for legislation to suppress such practices; and there has since been a long record of Federal Acts, known as the Private Express Statutes, restricting transport of letters. Some one hundred and fifty private local posts and independent mail companies have at one time or another operated in the United States. Competition, even among themselves, for public patronage was formidable, often

suicidal; so that besides harassment by the Government through ceaseless legal action, their mortality was high, although some successfully fought off the Post Office Department for nearly forty years, well into the 1880s, before conceding final defeat.

The *Semi-Official Carrier* services were usually operated by post office employees or others, who, with the postmaster's permission, performed delivery service at approximately the same fees set by local posts. Their activity roughly spanned the period from 1842 to the late 1850s, but they differed from the private local posts in one important way; they had the approval of the Post Office Department.

Among the semi-official carrier stamps are many philatelic rarities which, present in the Caspary collection, included (as probably the scarcest) a tiny 2-cent in a simple type-set design (Plate 301C). This was used by John C. Beckman, who once made his rounds in the streets of Charleston, South Carolina (and later served as assistant postmaster). The Caspary copy is the only Beckman stamp known to have survived. This one was used on a letter with a Government 3-cent perforated stamp of 1857; the two were neatly postmarked at Charleston in June, 1860. The letter was addressed to Brunswick, Georgia. Beckman's stamp represented his fee for transporting the letter to the Charleston post office; the 3-cent stamp prepaid the Government's postage to Brunswick. This item brought the spectacular price of $11,000 at a Caspary auction – by far the highest figure ever paid for a carrier stamp. For it Mr Caspary had paid only $515.

Private local post and carrier stamps have always enjoyed popularity. The Caspary collection of such issues was acknowledged to be the finest extant, with rarities that readily sold into the hundreds and thousands of dollars apiece. The combined lots realized more than $165,000 in a four-day sale.

Confederate provisionals: postmasters' provisionals returned to the American postal scene when the Civil War broke out in 1861 (Plate 305). Both in North and South the people approached the war with an attitude that was somewhat naïve, and apparently with no understanding or foreboding as to what the tragic conflict was to involve. Even the newly-appointed officials of the Confederate Government proceeded on a basis of 'business as usual', evidently expecting that they would continue to obtain needed essentials from the North. The Confederate Post Office Department, as a matter of fact, was arranging in 1861 a contract with New York banknote engravers to supply Confederate postage stamps (and currency), but the negotiations collapsed when the United States Post Office Department suspended mail service between the enemy areas. The Federal Government shortly thereafter blockaded all Southern ports, the aim being to strangle Confederate commerce with Europe.

The Civil War offers much in postal history as well as in philatelic material which today is highly regarded by collectors. At the top of the list are the postmasters' provisionals, improvised through the South while the postmasters were waiting for the Confederate States to provide newly-designed stamps. Some postmasters converted postmarking handstamps to show the names of the towns and *Paid 5c* or *10c*, etc., which they impressed on the envelopes. Others devised their own crude designs on adhesives, or were able to have better ones made in convenient print shops. When lacking postal stationery, some postmasters reached into their stocks of United States embossed stamped envelopes, then invalid for postage in the South. They crossed out the *United States* inscription and handstamped the envelopes for use within the Confederacy. Most of the adhesive stamps provisionally issued by the Confederate postmasters are valuable; some run into the hundreds or thousands of dollars each. One of the rarest is the attractively designed 5-cent blue issued by the postmaster of Livingston, Alabama. The only known pair of these, on original cover, is considered the most famous Confederate piece in existence; it brought $14,000 at a Caspary auction. A single used-on-letter copy realized $4,200. Others of these Southern provisionals sold for $1,000 each and upward. More than one hundred Confederate postmasters resorted to provisionals of one kind or another in 1861. It was not until late in that year that the South's Post Office Department began to supply adhesives which had been lithographed by qualified firms safely below the Mason-Dixon line. The war lasted four years, and today's collector finds many things of philatelic interest from that period. There are, for instance, the *Blockade Letters* carried in the early days of the war. The Adams Express Company made a specialty of this mail. The firm transported letters between North and South for 25 cents each (Government postage had been 3 cents prior to hostilities). Adams used certain offices, at Nashville, Tennessee, and Louisville, Kentucky, as clearing points for transfer of mail from one side to the other. Though warned by the Government the company persisted, and the traffic continued for about two months, notwithstanding the fact that President Abraham Lincoln had declared the business unlawful. The traffic ceased when the incensed Lincoln issued (August 26, 1861) an order directing the arrest of persons engaging in this means of communication. These letters are scarce and usually bear handstamps with the names of the companies which carried them.

Patriotic envelopes are widely collected and generally are not in the high-price bracket. In the war fever of 1861 people found an outlet for their feelings in the use of these vividly-colored envelopes, manufactured by many stationers, with pictures of Lincoln, flags and other patriotic subjects, and often the favorite, Colonel Ellsworth, the first Union officer killed in the war. There were many which caricatured Jefferson Davis and the aims of the South. Within two weeks after Lincoln's Proclamation of War thousands of such envelopes were seen in the mails. Southerners also used them in quantity, glorifying Davis and other prominent figures in the Confederacy and ridiculing Northern sentiment.

The *Prisoner of War* covers are popular today and rate well in value. Prisoners confined in North or South were permitted to correspond with their folks at home under certain regulations and censorship. These covers are usually identified by a handstamped marking, *Prisoner's Letter* with the name or location of the prison, and sometimes with the word *Ex-*

amined or *Approved*. In the category of prisoners' letters there are also the *Flag of Truce* letters, so marked in penmanship by the writers. This historically interesting mail was passed between the lines through Fortress Monroe in Virginia and taken up the James River on a Flag of Truce boat, the *New York*, to Aiken's Landing, where mail exchanges were made by representatives of the opposing forces.

There are other Civil War philatelic mementoes in collectors' albums. These include envelopes which, used in the South, were made of wallpaper; various kinds of printed forms shaped into envelopes; and envelopes which were twice used; the second time when the envelope was refolded, inside out, and used again, because paper of all grades became scarce as the Union blockade gradually became effective. The experienced collector of today, when shown an envelope that transmitted Confederate mails, eagerly peers inside it, and often is rewarded by discovery of a better item carefully preserved through the years because its original recipient was by circumstances forced to make second use of the envelope to carry on his correspondence.

Airpost: although the transporting of mails in airplanes operating on regular schedules is modern – this development came in the second decade of the twentieth century – the earliest stamps printed specifically for the new service must fall within the American antiques classification. Aero-philatelists like to consider the United States' pioneer airpost issue an old-timer, notwithstanding its relatively brief span of use. This particular 'antique', a 24-cent red, white and blue adhesive which appeared in 1918, has a history rich with drama and color not possessed by earlier United States postal covers and stamps which were nearly contemporary with Great Britain's 'penny black' of 1840, the great classic for the philatelist of all countries. One hundred copies (one full sheet) of the United States 24-cents airmail item became each in itself a classic which outranks in commercial value, although not in philatelic interest, the British pioneer. All the British 'penny blacks' were printed with the portrait of the youthful Queen Victoria in the appropriate position intended. But two full sheets of the American airpost 24-cent came off the presses with the design, an airplane, upside-down (Plate 306A). One sheet was detected and destroyed at Washington, but the other sheet, comprising one hundred inverts, escaped scrutiny by official inspectors both in the Bureau of Engraving and Printing and the Post Office Department. An alert philatelist paid $24 for this sheet at a post office window. Of the hundred inverts, eighty-five are known to have survived. The precise whereabouts of the other fifteen, if they still exist, has not been traced.

Several years ago a 24-cent invert brought $4,100 at auction and this price was duplicated by an exceptionally fine copy sold in June, 1957, at Harmer, Rooke & Company, New York. At this same auction a copy of a Honduras airmail stamp of 1925, the '10-cent dark blue', over-printed '25-cents', listed in the Scott catalogue at $10,000, realized $11,000, the highest figure recorded up to that date for any single airmail stamp. The stamp sold is the only copy known to collectors.

The authoritative historian of the United States 24-cent airpost stamp is Henry M. Goodkind of the Collectors Club, New York. Mr Goodkind has identified the known owners of the eighty-five surviving copies, and he is trying to solve the mystery of the disappearance of the other fifteen. Separating fact from fantasy, Mr. Goodkind has set down in a book, published by the Collectors Club, information based on Government records, on personal interviews with owners of the inverts, and has given auction prices across the intervening years.

Historical subjects: recognition of the past is to be seen in designs in the postage series in use in 1957. These vignettes include:

On 1½-cent brown-carmine, Mount Vernon, the Virginia estate which the first President, George Washington, acquired in 1752 and where he was buried in 1799.

On 20-cent ultramarine, Monticello, the Charlottesville, Virginia, home built by Thomas Jefferson, to which he retired in 1808.

On 10-cent rose-lake, Philadelphia's Independence Hall, where the Declaration of Independence was signed in 1776.

On 9-cent rose-lilac, the historic Alamo which was besieged by the Mexicans at San Antonio, Texas, in 1836.

These and other national shrines are linked intimately with the nation's history and heritage.

No review of American stamps and their relation to antiquities would be complete without allusion to Federal legislation which became effective in 1906, when President Theodore Roosevelt signed a Congressional Act for the Preservation of American Antiquities, approximately eight-five scientific historic and semi-historic sites and landmarks. Under this law the United States Department of the Interior now protects one of the world's oldest antiquities – a volcanic tower which geologists have estimated to date back perhaps fifty million years. The philatelic connection is that this tower is illustrated on a commemorative 3-cent violet stamp which Postmaster-General Summerfield issued in 1956 to mark the fiftieth anniversary of President Roosevelt's official order proclaiming the volcanic formation the first American antiquity to be assured such safeguarding under the Preservation Act. The natural monument pictured on the stamp is Devil's Tower, which rises 1,280 feet from the bed of the Belle Fourche River amid rolling grasslands and pine forests in the north-east corner of Wyoming.

BOOKS FOR FURTHER READING

ASHBROOK, STANLEY B.: *The Ten-cent Stamp of 1855-57* (Lindquist Publications, New York City).

BROOKMAN, LESTER G.: *United States Stamps of the Nineteenth Century* (Lindquist Publications, New York City).

CHASE, DR CARROLL: *United States Three-Cent of 1851* (privately printed).

DIETZ, AUGUST: *The Confederate States Post Office Department. Its Stamps and Stationery* (Dietz Press, Inc., Richmond, Va.).

GOODKIND, HENRY M.: *The 24c Air Mail Inverted Center of 1918* (The Collectors Club, New York City).

KONWISER, HARRY M.: *United States Stampless Catalog* (Van Dahl Publications, Inc., Albany, Ore.).

LUFF, JOHN N., AND CLARK, HUGH M.: *The Postage Stamps of the United States* (Scott Publications, Inc., New York City).

MACBRIDE, VAN DYCK: *Confederate 'Paid' Handstamps* (included in foregoing book by Harry M. Konwiser).

MALPASS, GEORGE N.: *The Jefferson Davis Postage Stamp Issues of the Confederacy* (Stephen G. Rich, Verona, N.J.).

Concise Encyclopedia of Antiques, Vol. II, pp. 185–94, Hawthorn Books, New York (1956).

THEATER, CIRCUS AND BALLET

By PAUL MYERS

THEATER collecting has an aura of glamour that few other subjects can approach. The introduction to *Theatre Collections in Libraries and Museums*, written by Rosamond Gilder with George Freedley, expresses this admirably: 'The snows of yesteryear or even of this are not more evanescent than the creation of the actor's art – which in its full perfection blossoms only to die ... Every relic of such a moment is therefore infinitely precious ... Few who have worked in the theater, and loved the theater, few who have been caught as audience or actor by the inescapable lure of its protean art, can resist these husks and shards, these printed, engraved or written relics of a remembered or a fabulous past.'

In spite of the survival of a certain number of these 'husks and shards', the theater has been very poorly documented. Students of the art are constantly faced with the fact that it is not possible to say that at this theater on that date a certain theatrical event took place. Prof. George C. D. Odell, whose monumental *Annals of the New York Stage* chronicle so much of the theater of that city, begins the first of the volumes in the series of fifteen with the statement that, 'he would be indeed a brave and learned soul who would venture a statement as to when a performance more or less dramatic in intent was first seen in New York City; braver even who would dare set the earliest date for such activity on the continent of North America, or in the Western hemisphere'.

Professor Odell goes on to relate that H. H. Bancroft in his history of Mexico records the production of sacred plays at Tlaxcala in 1538. The same historian's *History of Arizona* informs us that on April 20th, 1598, Onate reached the Rio Grande and took possession of New Mexico and all adjoining provinces. A part of the celebration was 'in the evening, the performance of an original comedy, written by Captain Farfan, on a subject connected with the conquest of Mexico'.

We know that one year before the settlement of Jamestown, Virginia, or in 1606, a pageant was presented at Port Royal in Canada, to mark the return of the Sieur de Poutrincourt from a cruise along the New England coast. Court evidence exists to show that in 1665, three young men of Accomac County, Virginia, were haled into court and accused of having acted a play. They were acquitted after being found 'not guilty of fault'.

Glenn Hughes, in his *A History of the American Theatre*, records: 'Down in Virginia it is chronicled that one William Levingston, a merchant of Williamsburg, entered into a contract with Charles and Mary Stagg, actors, to build a theater for them in that city. The contract was dated July 11, 1716. And in November of that year it is further recorded that Levingston purchased three half-acre lots, on which he laid out a bowling green and erected, among other buildings, a theater.'

The Harvard Theatre Collection, Cambridge, Massachusetts, owns a copy of the earliest known American playbill. It was printed for a production at the Nassau Street Theatre, New York, March 26, 1750, of Otway's *The Orphan* followed by a farce, *The Beau in the Sudds*. The same collection has a 1752 playbill:

'For the Benefit of Mrs. Upton (being the last night of playing) By his Excellency's Permission, At the

Theatre in Nassau-Street, on Thursday the 20th of February, will be acted, *A Tragedy* (never played here) called, *Venice Preserv'd, or A Plot Discover'd*.'

After the distribution of roles, there follows:

'Several select Pieces of Musick between the Acts; particularly, a Solo on the German Flute. A Song by Mrs. Upton called *Jockey*. To which will be added, *Miss in her Teens*.

'If thro' Ignorance, Mrs. Upton, as being a Stranger, shou'd neglect applying to any Gentlemen or Ladies, she hopes they'll excuse it.

To begin precisely at 6 o'Clock.
Box, 5f. Pitt 4f. Gallery 2f.

Tickets to be had at the Crown and Thistle, and at Mr. Evout's, Hatter near the Dock.

N.B. Those who please to favour her with their Company, may depend on seeing the Play decently perform'd, at least perfect, and that all or more than included in the Bills will be done.'

New York's most important eighteenth-century theater, attended by Washington while the city was the capital of the nation, was the John Street, while its most historic nineteenth-century theater was the Park (Plates 307 and 309A).

The collecting of programmes and playbills (Plate 308) is a field that interests almost all theater-goers. Most, however, amass only a collection of programmes that will constitute a record of their personal theater-going. Some try to build up a collection of playbills of the productions of a particular dramatist (a Shakespeare collection, or Shaviana) or of the appearances of a certain player.

It is thought that the largest collection of playbills is the Robert Gould Shaw Collection at Harvard. When Evert Jansen Wendell died, in 1917, his collection also went to Harvard. It took workers there two years to sort the Wendell bequest. The duplicates were sold in New York and brought $40,000.

The largest sale of playbills took place in Boston in the summer of 1898. One hundred and eighty thousand playbills collected by James H. Brown of Malden, Massachusetts, were dispersed at auction. The catalogue of this sale advises:

'He (Brown) had a remarkable faculty for ferreting out old bills. Did one want, for example, a genuine bill of the night of Lincoln's assassination (not the bogus one so often reproduced in magazines, and hung in clubs and theatres), he would find a copy where others failed .... A large number of the playbills which adorn the home of the Players in New York, presented by Edwin Booth, were purchased by that actor from Mr. Brown .... These playbills will call up many pleasant recollections of the old theatre before the "Bill of the Play" had degenerated into an advertising pamphlet.'

Among the great of the American theater listed by Brown were Edwin Booth, Junius Brutus Booth (Plate 310A), Edwin Forrest, John McCullough, Matilda Heron, Lawrence Barrett, Lester Wallack, Charlotte Cushman, Dion Boucicault, Laura Keene, Henry E. ('Adonis') Dixey, James H. Hackett.

The story of the Booth family and the Lincoln assassination is one of the great tragedies of the American theater. Edwin Booth (1833–93) has been thought by many to be the greatest American actor. He was certainly the first to win a reputation abroad. He had made his début with the company of his father, Junius Brutus Booth (1796–1852). At the age of eighteen he had already played Shakespeare's *King Richard III*. In 1854 he toured with Laura Keene in Australia, and in 1861 played a vastly successful engagement in London (Plate 310A).

From 1863 through 1867, Booth managed the Winter Garden Theatre in New York. It was at this theater, on November 25, 1864, that all three Booth brothers appeared in *Julius Caesar*. The performance was given to raise funds for the erection of a statue of Shakespeare in New York's Central Park. Edwin Booth played *Brutus*, Junius Brutus Booth (the younger) appeared as *Cassius* and John Wilkes Booth was *Antony*. The *Herald* of the following day reported, 'The audience was fairly carried by storm from the first entrance of the three brothers side by side'.

Copies of the playbill for this occasion are in the Theater Collection at the New York Public Library and in other archives. This was the last appearance in New York of John Wilkes Booth. Less than half a year later, on April 14, 1865, at Ford's Theatre in Washington, D.C., he took the life of Abraham Lincoln. After this tragic event Edwin Booth retired from the stage for a time; but although he was to suffer occasional outbursts of feeling against him, he returned to the theatre and occupied a position as America's leading actor. In 1869, he opened his own theater in New York. In the early 1880s he appeared at the Lyceum, London, by invitation of Henry Irving. The two actors played *Othello*, alternating in the roles of Othello and Iago.

In 1888 Booth presented his home at 16 Gramercy Park, New York, to the Players. The Club was founded along the lines of the Garrick Club in London. It was to be a place where the gentlemen of the theater could mingle with leaders of other fields of endeavor. Booth continued to occupy an apartment in the building until his death and his rooms there are still as he left them. The Club also houses a fine theatrical library and collections of playbills, scrapbooks, photographs and other memorabilia of the theater.

Among some playbills and other theater material found recently at Keen's Chop House in New York is an 1856 programme, November 13 of that year. The programme has the headline: '*One Hundred Miles Apart.' John Brougham in POCAHONTAS, a play of his authorship.* The first half of the play was presented at the Bowery Theatre in New York, the second half at the National Amphitheatre in Philadelphia. The price of $10 secured admission to both theatres and ferry fare from New York to New Jersey and train fare from New Jersey to Philadelphia and return.

The circus: somewhat akin to the playbills are the handbills, and there are many examples of these in collections. Some of them were designed to be distributed in the streets as an advertisement such as the one for the Salem Circus shown here (Plate 313C). Others gave details of the production and could serve both as preliminary announcements and as programmes.

For rich, expansive prose nothing could outdo the handbills that were distributed in the communities which were about to be visited by a circus or a minstrel troupe. Those responsible for creating the advertising material combined superlatives with still other superlatives. 'Most colossal' became a rather tame manner of describing the wonders that were to be unfolded.

The great master of ballyhoo was Phineas T. Barnum (1810–91). He coined terms which have become a part of the advertising idiom. Shown here is a copy of an antique poster (Plate 313B), announcing the exhibition of an elephant, which is a product of an earlier showman. This is the style in which Barnum worked. His name is still attached to 'The Greatest Show on Earth'.

In 1841, Barnum became the proprietor of the American Museum in New York at Broadway and Ann Street. Though in actuality a theater, the term 'museum' was attached to this as to many other places of entertainment. It placed the resort in an educational sphere and removed it from the stigma of the theater. On exhibition in the Museum were all manner of curiosities. There were preserved mummies, freaks of all kinds, trained animals and insects, statuary, dioramas, ventriloquists, gypsies, demonstrations of handicrafts (knitting, glass-blowing, modeling), *Punch and Judy* shows, automatons. Attached to the Museum was a 'Lecture Room'. Here famous personalities of the day delivered addresses; concerts and ballets were presented, and dramatic programmes were staged.

The enterprise was vastly successful. On some days the institution became so crowded that the management was forced to curtail the sale of tickets. Barnum soon realized that one of his problems was how to get the public out. Some people came with their lunches and planned to spend the day. Barnum wrote in his *Struggles and Triumphs; or, Forty Years' Recollections* (1878): 'In despair I sauntered upon the stage behind the scenes, biting my lips with vexation, when I happened to see the scene-painter at work and a happy thought struck me: "Here," I exclaimed, "take a piece of canvas four-feet square, and paint on it, as soon as you can, in large letters, TO THE EGRESS." ' Many followed this direction expecting to see some rare curiosity and found themselves outside the Museum on Ann Street.

A great deal of color and interest for collectors of theatrical antiques centers about the old Astor Place Opera House (Plate 309B). This theater opened on November 22, 1847, with the opera *Ernani*. On the following January 28 Adelina Patti's mother made her début in New York as *Romeo* in the operatic setting of Shakespeare's play. The opera season failed to win great support. In the summer of 1848, after an unsuccessful attempt by Edward Fry at running the theater, William Niblo became the proprietor. He offered a varied season of theater, ballet and opera.

The Astor Place Opera House entered upon its phase of chief interest to collectors and historians when the English actor, William Macready (Plate 310B), appeared there on September 4, 1848. The opening bill, under the management of Chippendale and Sefton, was *Macbeth* with Macready in the title role. His engagement closed on September 25 with *The Merchant of Venice*. Some of the feeling which was later to erupt with such violence is related in the diaries of the famous actor, which are available in published form. He noted: 'I have been much annoyed and disgusted with the vulgarity and low, coarse character of the newspapers even during these two days that I have been in the United States .... The complacency, indeed the approbation with which a paper speaks of the "independence" of Mr Forrest (an ignorant, uneducated man, burning with envy and rancour at my success) hissing me in the Edinburgh Theatre, makes me feel that I seek in vain to accommodate myself to such utterly uncongenial natures.'

Macready undertook a tour of the principal theaters of this country. William Niblo and J. H. Hackett announced that the English actor would reappear at the Astor Place Opera House on May 8, 1849. Opposition began to grow and to make itself heard in various parts of the city. Here is the text of one such protest:

'Workingmen, shall Americans or English rule in this city? The crew of the British steamer have threatened all Americans who shall dare to express their opinion this night at the English Autocratic Opera House. We advocate no violence, but a free expression of opinion to all public men. *Washington* forever! Stand by your Lawful Rights! *American Committee.*'

On May 10, 1849, Macready appeared as Macbeth with Mrs Coleman Pope as Lady Macbeth. As the performance went on, feeling became increasingly intense inside the Opera House. Outside, a mob was gathering. Troops were dispatched from the City Hall and, about ten o'clock, two troops of mounted military turned into Astor Place from Broadway. They were greeted with stones and invective. A few minutes later, when troops of the National Guard appeared, the mob was impassable.

The crowd was fired upon and violence broke out. Before order was restored twenty-one persons had been killed and thirty-three wounded. Sixty-three rioters were placed under arrest. On May 11, C. S. Woodhull, Mayor of the City, issued a proclamation urging calmness on the citizenry. On the following day Macready took the train to Boston, where he remained until he sailed for home on May 23. From that day forward the theater was often referred to as 'The Massacre Place Opera House'.

Theater collections: brief mention has been made of the early playbills in the Harvard College Theater Collection. Before 1901 Harvard possessed no original material on the theater. Items of this nature were generally presented to the Boston Public Library. On November 19, 1901, largely through the efforts of the late George Pierce Baker, Harvard was presented with a collection of portraits of David Garrick. This was 'given in commemoration of the late Librarian, Justin Winsor, who devoted many years to the study of the English stage in the days of Garrick'.

In December 1902 Professor Baker and the playwright, Louis Evan Shipman (the latter a student of the famed teacher), acquired for the library the collection of the theatrical bibliographer, Robert W. Lowe. This collection contained approximately 900 books and pamphlets on theater subjects. The collection was purchased and presented to Harvard by the noted actor, John Drew. With this as a nucleus, the collection began to grow through the addition of other important items.

Professor Baker carried on negotiations for two years with Robert Gould Shaw. In the end, he dissuaded him from presenting his notable collection to the Boston Public Library and won it for Harvard. It was this acquisition which, in 1915, finally made it possible for Harvard to open a Theater Collection. Today, the Harvard Theater Collection is the largest in the world and the second in point of age. (The Clara Ziegler Theatre Museum in Munich was established in 1910.) There are over one million playbills in it. In addition to the New York and Boston bills we have mentioned, it has bills covering the early stage histories of Chicago, Charleston,

New Orleans, Philadelphia, St Louis and San Francisco.

Rare books are an important feature of the collection. Among these is a copy of Anthony Aston's *The Fool's Opera; or, The Taste Of The Age.* This work was published in London in 1731 and prefixed to the play is 'a sketch of the author's life'. This 'sketch' clearly indicates that Aston was the first professional to have performed upon the American stage. He mentions having visited New York, East and West Jersey, Maryland, Virginia, North and South Carolina and South Florida. *The Month at Goodspeed's* (Volume VII, number 10) gives this footnote:

'His book is also interesting as a rare burlesque on *The Beggar's Opera*; as the principal source of the biography of one of the most popular of the old English actors; as a brief but lively account of early American travel; and as a humorous note on a military expedition from Carolina to Florida, reported Caesar-like with a *veni, vidi*, but no *vici*.'

It is also noted that the McKee copy, sold in 1900 for $81, was resold in the Wendell sale in 1919 for $300.

Other rare volumes to be found in Cambridge are William Dunlap's annotated copy of his *History of the American Theatre* (the first such history, 1832), and John Hodgkinson's *A Narrative of his Connection with the Old American Company.* This was published in 1797 and contains an account of a theatrical squabble which is the first such printed record. In the Theater Collection of the New York Public Library is an obituary of John Hodgkinson. The item is not sourced and purports to have been published some time in 1806:

'Accounts lately received from America mention the death of Mr John Hodgkinson, formerly of the Bath Theatre. He was one of the most successful performers that ever emigrated to that continent; and had at one period acquired a comfortable independence. He possessed great professional merits; with extraordinary versatility of talents; Tragedy, Comedy, Opera, Farce, and Pantomime, were all familiar with MR HODGKINSON; he encountered every department of the drama, high, low, dignified, or genteel, and succeeded in almost every character he attempted ... as well as being there the leading concert singer. He had long escaped the dreadful malady that has been the scourge of that ill-fated quarter of the globe; but passing casually through Boston, he caught the infection, and was in three days a corpse.'

The great theater collection at the New York Public Library is housed in the library's central building at Fifth Avenue and 42nd Street; this collection is conveniently situated near the theater center of the United States. Opened in 1931, this is a collection of the living theater; files are maintained on all theater activity and personnel, as well as that of the cinema, radio and television, circus, night clubs, magic – almost every phase of entertainment.

There are housed here, too, many items that come into a consideration of American theater antiques. Among these is the George Becks Collection of prompt books, copies of plays which include the stage manager's cues, actors' directions and notes on the technical phases of the production. Becks was an actor who specialized in Shakespearean roles. Born in England in 1835, he came to the United States at the solicitation of Henry J. Wallack to join the stock company at the National Theatre in Boston. He played with Jean Davenport Lander, Maggie Mitchell, Laura Keene, Mrs John Wood and Edwin Forrest.

On July 10, 1904 (Becks died in May of that year), the *New York Herald* published an article on this great collection of prompt books which numbered more than three thousand volumes. Take, for example, the prompt copies of Shakespeare's *Julius Caesar*. On the fly-leaf of one is the following notation:

'Marked from observation and notes taken during the performance of the play *Julius Caesar* at Booth's Theatre, New York, March 27, 1876, with additional notes kindly furnished by my friend, M. E. Mason, who says of the acting of E. L. Davenport as *Brutus*, and Lawrence P. Barrett as *Cassius*, "Worthy companion pictures, somewhat difficult to consider separately, as each performance owes much of its effectiveness to the perfect artistic harmony existing between the actors".'

Another copy of the same play is identified:

'Marked from G. Bennett's copy, November 28, 1850, W. H. Waller, sold 1857 to James Stark, bought 1883 by George Becks.'

There is an acting text, too, of John Philip Kemble's production of the play, 1814. Throughout the books, every detail of stage business is noted: diagrams showing the positions of the actors, costumes and physical appurtenances of the production, indications of the manner in which lines are to be spoken.

For many years dramatizations of Alexander Dumas' *Camille* have been popular. It also served as the libretto for Verdi's *La Traviata*. Items relating to *Camille* are outstanding in the Becks Collection. Jean Davenport (Mrs Lander) adapted Dumas' play into English and was the first actress to play the central role in that language. Mr Becks won the interest of Jean Davenport and, upon her death in 1903, inherited her collection of scripts. Among the texts in the collection is a manuscript copy bearing the signature of J. B. Wright. There is also an E. L. Taylor prompt book (Montreal 1876) of Matilda Heron's adaptation of the play.

Interestingly enough, when the old theater was re-opened in Central City, Colorado, in July 1932, it was *Camille* that held the boards. Miss Lillian Gish played the leading role in this revival and she spent a considerable amount of time at the New York Public Library Theater Collection exploring these prompt books and other material relating to productions of the play. In November 1932, this production came into the Morosco Theatre, New York. Thus, the past is constantly inspiring and refreshing the present, particularly in the theater.

The toy theater: material on the toy theater has become a collector's item. The Museum of the City of New York has an outstanding collection relating to the toy theater, and other institutions and private collections possess a wealth of material in this field. The well-known American actor, Alfred Lunt, is a collector of toy theater items and has done a great amount of research in this field. In 1946, in connection with an exhibition of some of Mr Lunt's toy theater material at the Museum of the City of New York, the museum prepared an interesting account:

'The toy theater originated as a form of theatrical souvenir, and is related closely to the prints known as Penny Plain, Twopence Coloured and Tinsel. Sheets containing prints of prosceniums, orchestras, scenery and characters were published and sold through the nineteenth century in England, France, Germany, Spain and Italy. Today they hold a high place as collector's items, and the ones most sought after are those published by Skelt, Hodgson, West, Green, Webb, Redington and Pollock — the last named still in existence. Great contemporary artists such as William Blake, George and Robert Cruikshank, the Brothers Heath, and Robert Dighton drew famous characters and scenes from popular plays of the period. ...'

Though these artists are British and the fad was most widespread in England, there was interest and activity in the toy theater in the United States during the nineteenth century. *Whittington and His Cat, An Entertainment for the Parlor* was published in New York, in 1883, by McLoughlin Brothers. The booklet contains 'Full stage directions, and hints for costumes and Decorations. ... Carefully prepared by an Old Stage Manager and Suitable for Town or Country.'

This publisher also sponsored a *Little Showman's Series.*

'Each of these little Shows is perfect in itself, and contains descriptive verses. All of them are highly colored, and some have moveable parts, such as see-saws, cradles, etc.'

Ballet: the modern audience is apt to feel that interest in the ballet in the United States is a recent one. It is true that there is increasing ballet activity at the present time and new dance companies appear all over the country. If one goes back, however, to the accounts of the visits of European dancers to these shores in the nineteenth century one will quickly realize how much excitement these visits engendered. One of the most fabulous (a term which can appropriately be applied to this ballerina) was Fanny Elssler (Plate 310C).

Elssler was born in Vienna in 1818. She first visited New York in 1840. A reporter, named 'A Gothamite', wrote some years later for the *New York Clipper*:

'Elssler did not disappoint public anticipation, and, for a long time, the incident of attendance at her first appearance was regarded as a feather in the caps of inveterate playgoers. To obtain admission was almost a matter of favor; for, in those days, speculators in reserved seats were unknown .... Possibly Elssler may have been for the moment overrated; still, she excited an enthusiasm never attained by a subsequent artist of European celebrity, not even by Jenny Lind, Rachel, or Ristori. The evidence of her popularity is palpable from the fact that Henry Inman, the most distinguished of our portrait painters, staked his reputation upon a cabinet-sized full-length portrait of the danseuse, while James Varick Stout, at that time a representative American sculptor, devoted many hours of toil to procure a life-sized statue of her, honors never bestowed upon any other exotic artist.'

It is this final sentence that accounts for the apparent scarcity of theatrical antiquities. The people of the stage – particularly in the United States – had not acquired in the last century the respectability of other artists. Most painters or sculptors would not have considered theatrical portraits worthy of their efforts.

Dance Magazine (November, 1949) reproduced the Inman portrait of Fanny Elssler, now in the Landesmuseum in Eisenstadt, Austria. Lillian Moore, whose notes accompany the reproduction of the picture, gives an interesting account of the work. Inman painted the canvas in Elssler's dressing room in the Park Theatre, New York. It is thought that the ballerina must have taken the painting back to Vienna with her when she returned from her American tour.

'In 1845 she permitted the German lithographer, Kohler, to publish his version, which has popularized the picture and made it familiar to all lovers of ballet history. At Elssler's death, it probably went, along with many other souvenirs of the great dancer's career, directly to the museum at Eisenstadt.'

Another dancer who has been the subject of considerable biographical study is Lola Montez (Plate 311A). Lola's amatory adventures have always eclipsed her stage activities; she was the lady for whom King Ludwig I of Bavaria renounced his throne. On the other hand, so different a person as Walt Whitman was proud to be listed among her admirers.

Lola was Irish in spite of her Latin-sounding stage name. Her reputation preceded her to these shores. She was billed as Madame Lola Montez, Countess of Landsfeld. On December 29, 1851, at the Broadway Theatre in New York, she appeared in *Betley, The Tyrolean*. Though the critics did not unanimously praise her artistry, the ticket-buying public was interested and continued to fill the theater whenever she played.

The following May, Lola appeared in a biographical play, *Lola Montez in Bavaria*. The King and Queen of Bavaria and others of this royal court figured as personages in the play. The 'historical' drama displayed in successive acts: 'Lola Montez the Danseuse, Lola Mon-tez the Politician, Lola Montez the Countess, Lola Montez the Revolutionist and Lola Montez the Fugitive'. George C. D. Odell notes: 'When we ponder sadly on the degeneracy of the stage in our time, we have but to look back at that exhibition in 1852; I sympathize with the group of actresses who were forced to take part in it.'

In the New York Public Library's collection is a handbill for a lecture delivered by the fascinating Lola at Mozart Hall, 663 Broadway in New York, on Thursday evening, December 15, 1859. The title of the discourse for the evening was *John Bull at Home – Containing some pleasant gossip, in which many things are said, more in laughter than in anger*. The lecture boasted five themes: The Comic Side of English Character, English and American Characteristics, The Real Origin of National Roguery, English Philanthropy Unmasked, and A Peep at English Gallantries. One of the topics to be touched upon under the last-named heading, for example, was 'The cash value of innocence in England'. All of this was available for twenty-five cents.

Sheet music: closely allied to collecting in this field is the preserving of sheet music. Many song sheets of the nineteenth century show portraits of theatrical favorites. The earliest titles, those of the eighteenth century, are extremely scarce, but the collector may be able to secure early-nineteenth-century imprints of Von Hagen of Boston, Aitken, Blake and Carr of Philadelphia, or J. Hewitt of New York. The song sheet covers reflect contemporary history, with military and political subjects based on events of the War with Tripoli, the War of 1812, the Mexican and Civil Wars. Confederate items are of greater rarity, and therefore more value, than Northern songs. Especially attractive are the sheet-covers showing the handsome uniforms of the volunteer military companies. Others relate to such subjects as Lafayette's triumphal return to America in 1824, the Gold Rush, and the Harrison-Tyler campaign of 1840 with its *Hard Cider Quick Step*. The view of the Battle of New Orleans which appears on the subject illustrated (Plate 314A) is not contemporary with the battle in 1815 but was issued in 1832 when its hero, Jackson, was re-elected to the presidency. A list of lithographers and artists before 1870 whose names appear on sheet music was given by Edith A. Wright and Josephine A. McDevitt in *Antiques* (March, 1933), and appears in enlarged form in Dichter and Shapiro's definitive *Early American Sheet Music*.

BOOKS FOR
FURTHER READING

DELARUE, ALLISON: 'Ballet Music Titles' in *Antiques* (May 1940).

DICHTER AND SHAPIRO: *Early American Sheet Music*, New York (1941).

DUNLAP, WILLIAM: *A History of the American Theatre*, J. & J. Harper, New York (1932).

GREENWOOD, ISAAC: *The Circus; Its Origin and Growth prior to 1835*, Dunlap Society, New York (1948).

MAGRIEL, PAUL: *Chronicles of the American Dance*, Holt, New York (1948).

MARTIN, JOHN: *American Dancing; Background and Personalities of the Modern Dance*, New York (1936).

ODELL, GEORGE C. D.: *Annals of the New York Stage*, New York (1927).

PALMER, MRS WINTHROP: *Theatrical-Dancing in America*, Ackerman, New York (1945).

SEILHAMMER, G. O.: *History of the American Theatre Before The Revolution, 1749–1774*, Philadelphia (1888).

VAIL, R. W. G.: *The Beginning of The American Circus*, New York (1934).

WALLPAPERS USED IN AMERICA 1700-1850

By HORACE L. HOTCHKISS, Jr.

Eighteenth-century wallpapers: from 1700 to 1850 Americans relied on French, English and occasionally Dutch importations for their better wallpapers. Though wallpapers were sold here as early as 1700 there was no native production until 1739 when Plunkett Fleeson of Philadelphia set up the first American factory of paper hangings as a branch of his upholstery business.

Until the early nineteenth century all wallpapers were printed on relatively small sheets of paper of varying dimensions. In the early-eighteenth century in Boston and New York unjoined sheets of wallpaper, following an earlier custom, were sometimes sold in reams or quires. However, the practice of pasting the sheets together, to make rolls before printing, had already become established. In the early-eighteenth century many wallpapers, whether issued in sheets or rolls, were tacked rather than pasted on the walls.

Wallpapers of British make between 1714 and about 1830 can be identified by tax stamps occurring at fairly close intervals on their reverse sides, as seen on an example from the Cooper Union Museum. These are characterized by a double monogram *G R* surmounted by a crown and usually underlined with notations like the word *Paper* and various numbers, the exact meaning of which is not known. Starting in 1771 French wallpaper manufacturers were required to print their names and addresses at both ends of a roll, an occasionally helpful means of identification.

It is probable that few wallpapers used here before 1750, whether of foreign or American make, are still in existence. In the case of later papers which have come down to us it is often difficult to decide whether they are French or American (Plate 319B). Neither, unlike the English, had tax stamps and American papers are scarcely ever marked with the maker's name.

Beginning in the 1740s American manufacturers boast in newspaper advertisements that they produce wallpapers equal in quality to those of England and France. That a great deal of copying of European designs was done is certain and that this could involve tracing an English original has been established in the case of a late-eighteenth-century Connecticut example by Zechariah Mills of Hartford (Plate 315B), first published by Elmer D. Keith in *Antiques*, September 1952.

Entirely successful printing from woodblocks in tempera colors did not evolve until about 1770. Wallpapers before this date either have their outlines printed from woodblocks and the colors filled in by hand or by stencil, or they are entirely hand-painted, or stenciled and hand-painted in varying proportions. The propensities of tempera colors to run or smudge in wood-block printing led the English to do a certain amount of printing in oil colors in the 1750s. Some wallpapers

English Excise Stamp *c.* 1768. *The Cooper Union Museum.*

engraved from metal plates were at that time printed in England and sold in America.

Many of the early papers imported to America carried fanciful repeating *Chinoiserie* scenes or the ever popular floral bouquets and sprays, both types often used with borders which were placed along chair rail and cornice and often vertically between widths of regular paper to make panels.

Until about 1740 wallpaper was probably rather rarely to be found in American houses. Whitewashed plaster walls were usual in simpler rooms where wood paneling was not to be found. By 1750, however, James Birket, writing of up-to-date houses in Portsmouth, New Hampshire, remarks that 'the rooms are well plastered and many wainscoted or hung with painted paper from England. ...'

In 1757 George Washington wrote to London for 'Paper for five rooms ... also paper of a very good Kind and colour for a Dining Room. ...' He also shortly afterwards ordered twelve chair seats 'of three different colours to suit the paper of three of the bed Chambers (also wrote for in my last)'. This was a period in England, incidentally, when matching blue and white curtains, bedhangings and wallpapers were popular.

A type of wallpaper which seems to have been widely used in New England began to make its appearance in the 1750s. This is a repeating paper of the type illustrated (Plates 315A, 316B,) featuring large arches of heavy stone, through which may be seen receding architectural vistas, or which enframe festoons or bouquets of flowers. They were probably meant to be used in hallways, and are also found in parlors as in the Paul Revere House in Boston. They seemed to have remained in favor until the early-nineteenth century.

Popular starting in the 1760s was wallpaper in plain colors which was used with borders. The parlor of Benjamin Franklin's house in Philadelphia, 1765, was papered in plain blue with a 'gilt border', and in 1771 the Ball Room at the 'Palace' in Williamsburg was hung with a 'plain blue paper' bordered with 'a narrow stripe of Gilt leather. ...'

Several years later, in 1784, George Washington ordered from Philadelphia rolls of plain blue, green and yellow paper, and seventy yards of gilded *papier-mâché* border.

Papier-mâché 'edging', either gilded or 'coloured', was used along the chair rails and cornices of rooms and to border windows, doors and mantelpieces. *Papier-mâché* ornaments to be 'tacked up' on the ceiling, often mentioned in eighteenth-century newspaper advertisements, were also common, although plainer ceilings came into favor in the late 1760s. At the end of the eighteenth century advertisements refer increasingly to 'festoon borders'. These designs undoubtedly featured swags of ribbons and ropes of roses and other flowers. They were either printed on an ordinary band or strip or had curving edges which were meant to be cut before hanging. Increasingly in these borders toward 1800 simulations of textiles appear. They were used with either plain or patterned wallpapers.

By the 1770s the Paris manufacturer, J. B. Réveillon, had brought the printing of wallpapers from wood-blocks in tempera colors to a point of excellence not known before. The paper hung in 1775 in the Dorothy Quincy House, Quincy, Massachusetts, reflects the type of panel decoration based on Pompeian wall motifs for which Réveillon is famous. Arabesques, delicate yet brightly colored, of vases, flowers, birds, drapery and classical figures framed in leafy borders are shown. From this period importations of French wallpapers were on the increase. Although it was only a minor cross-current of taste, the style favored by Horace Walpole and employed occasionally by Chippendale is reflected in an advertisement of 1764 in which Thomas Lee of Boston announces 'in Sheets: a fine Assortment of Gothic Paper Hangings', and an American advertisement of 1791 speaks of wallpapers in the 'Gothick' order of architecture.

Blue seems to have been the most popular eighteenth-century color for plain wallpapers, though all colors, including green, pink and orange, were represented in figured patterns. Mica was sometimes applied to obtain a glittering effect.

Many eighteenth-century papers had a large proportion of their surfaces painted by hand. Notable examples of wallpapers entirely painted in tempera are found in a hall taken from the Van Rensselaer House in Albany and installed in the Metropolitan Museum of Art, New York, and in the hall and two rooms of the Jeremiah Lee mansion, in Marblehead, Massachusetts. All apparently dating from the 1760s, the wallpapers were made to order in London and appear to have been executed by the same unknown fabricant.

Composed principally of large panels in grisaille showing pastoral figures in settings of landscapes with ruins, the subjects are known to have been copied from Italian and French engravings. Imitations of plasterwork in the form of rococo scrolls and trophies ornament the spaces between the panels. These wallpapers are too elaborate to be considered typical of eighteenth-century importations.

Chinese scenic and Chinoiserie wallpapers: few Chinese scenic wallpapers known to have been imported into this country from the Orient or by way of Europe before 1850 are found in American houses or museums. The dearth cannot be entirely accounted for by the usual tolls of fire and destruction through the years, since in the related instance of early-nineteenth-century French scenic wallpapers so many have come down to us. We can assume that compared to England or France the American importation of these artistic and costly wall decorations was small.

Outstanding examples of these hand-painted wallpapers may be cited.

In a house in Dedham, Massachusetts, hangs a Chinese wallpaper imported to this country in 1750. Illustrated in Muensterberg's monograph on *Chinese Art in America*, it shows *The Cultivation of Tea*.

Perhaps the most famous Chinese scenic wallpaper in America is that imported from Canton in the 1770s by Robert Morris for his Philadelphia house, but never used there. In the early-twentieth century a portion was installed at Beauport, the Gloucester, Massachusetts, house of the late Henry D. Sleeper, and the remainder hung in a house in Providence, Rhode Island.

As is usual with these papers, each width or strip is twelve feet high, and this set consists of forty widths. Industries of China are shown, including the raising of rice and tea and the making of pottery.

Another Chinese paper, depicting the history of the tea trade, painted on thin silk applied to rice paper is, or was, in a house in West Manchester, Massachusetts. Dated prior to 1700, it was not sent over to Boston from China until the 1840s, by which time, incidentally, the importation of this type of paper into England and France had virtually ceased.

Related to the Chinese scenic papers were the various European imitations which were seen as early as the seventeenth century.

Thomas Hancock of Boston, in an often-quoted letter to the stationer John Rowe of London in 1738, commissioned a paper-hanging to be specially made up in imitation of a Chinese scenic wallpaper of the tree, flower and bird type. He wanted, among other things, 'Birds flying here and there, with some Landskips at the Bottom. ...'

It is difficult to fathom the exact meaning in each case of American eighteenth-century newspaper references to wallpapers termed variously, 'India pictures', 'India patterns', 'India figures', or 'Mock Chinese' and 'Mock India' patterns. The terms 'India', 'Chinese', and sometimes 'Japan', were used interchangeably in reference to importations of the English East India Company. However, there is a very real difference in the designs of Chinese wallpapers and the tree-of-life and other floral and foliage motifs found on Indian textiles. The term, 'Indian designs' might refer to either imitations of Chinese scenic papers, like the one which Thomas Hancock ordered, or repeating papers using Indian calico motifs. 'Mock India' (Plate 317A) and 'Mock Chinese' might refer to the above types or to playful westernized adaptations of Oriental subject matter known as *Chinoiserie*. An expression of this is seen in a simplified form in a paper doubtless of American origin (Plate 320C) found in Connecticut.

Chinoiserie wallpaper patterns are found in the late-seventeenth century in England and flourished during the eighteenth century both there and in France. Becoming progressively less subtle in design, they continued into the nineteenth century and may be found among imported wallpapers until the mid-nineteenth century.

Flock wallpapers: though the perfecting of wood-block printing of wallpapers went on in England and France until the 1770s, the English manufacture of flock papers had reached a high point of excellence early in the eighteenth century. Flocking was a process whereby dyed chopped wool or silk was spread over paper or canvas which had previously been printed in a gluey substance either from wood-blocks or stencils. Part of the wool or silk adhered to the sticky or printed portions of the ground and the remainder was shaken off, revealing the pattern. Effective imitations of cut velvet, damask and moiré wall hangings could be achieved in this manner.

Many eighteenth-century English country houses had and still have this decoration, and it was used at Hampton Court Palace. Little flock used in this country in the eighteenth century remains, although newspapers advertised it regularly. There is an English flock paper in a large damask design of the mid-eighteenth century in the Governor Wentworth Mansion in Portsmouth, New Hampshire, and a bedroom in the Webb House, Wethersfield, Connecticut, has a deep red flocked paper (Plate 316c) in a design of huge curling leaves and flowers, said to have been hung in 1781 in preparation for the visit of General Washington. It has not yet been examined to determine whether there are English tax stamps on the back.

If 1781 may be accepted as the date of the Webb House paper, it comes at the end of the great period of flock production. Improved methods of printing ordinary wallpapers from wood-blocks probably led to less popular interest in wallpapers of this type.

Flock wallpapers had been most successful when they imitated the broad, rich effects of costly fabrics. Increasingly, however, toward the end of the eighteenth century flock was used in a subsidiary way as part of the design of a regular block-printed paper, where it cannot always be said to function as an imita-

tion of a textile. This is especially true of borders where it often appears as a background to festoons of flowers or, again, the floral portions, flocked, are sometimes placed on a plain ground. Flock imitating cut velvet appeared again in the Victorian era, but usually in somber colors and lacking the sumptuous bold designs of early-eighteenth-century examples.

Leather: gilded, painted and embossed leather hangings, which were popular in the Netherlands and to some extent in England in the seventeenth and early-eighteenth centuries, do not seem to have enjoyed an extensive vogue in this country, probably owing to their costliness. They are mentioned, however, in connection with the Palace at Williamsburg. The *Journal* of the Council contains a proposal of 1710: 'That the great Room in the second story be furnished with gilt leather hangings. 16 chairs of the same.' Matching wall coverings and chair seats of this sort were used at Dyrham Park, Gloucestershire, in the 'Gilt Leather Parlour'.

In 1762 in New York one Roper Dawson advertised that he 'has to sell among other things ... a great variety of Paper Hangings ...' and 'gilt leather for Hangings', and also in New York in 1784 is advertised for sale 'a quantity of Gilt Leather, well calculated for ornamenting a ship's cabbin'.

These references indicate that this form of wall hanging was not entirely unknown in America in the eighteenth century.

Nineteenth-century wallpapers: by 1800 English manufacturers, pressed by taxation, were more and more devoting themselves to the production of cheaper papers. The French manufacturers, on the other hand, having successfully weathered their own Revolution, were entering upon the Napoleonic era with their high standards of workmanship intact. From this time on, in New England especially, more and more French papers were used in American houses. They were often of the panel type, with vertical bands defining each width, and have related dadoes and friezes at bottom and top. Major vignettes of pastoral figures (shepherdesses or cowherds) alternating with a smaller vase or floral motif are common. The ground is usually diapered lightly with floral sprigs.

The Napoleonic era in France also saw the manufacture of elaborate wallpapers simulating drapery. Imitations of satin, lace and damask, 'hung' in heavy folds or swags or sometimes 'stretched', were numerous, and there were also representations of watered silk (Plate 317B). It was a period of remarkable color: bright greens, glowing yellows, violet, strong oranges and reds and blues, contrasting black and white. These were used in striking combinations. Designs, though often spectacular, became more mechanical and the fluid drawing of Réveillon's arabesques begins to pass away. The variety of these early nineteenth-century designs is bewildering. Repeating floral papers, striped papers, geometrical designs, many with architectural decorations, imitations of statuary and marble, and panels featuring trophies of Roman helmets, shields and swords are common.

A charming aspect of this wallpaper is seen in the simple, repeating geometrical (Plate 320A), wreath or sprig designs which were probably found in many American houses. Such papers are seen in the famous Peale *Staircase Group* of 1795. Festoon and other borders were often used with these and with plain papers (Plate 318A). On the example illustrated four widths of border are placed on an ordinary width of wallpaper and were meant to be cut before hanging.

Stenciled and painted wall decorations, especially popular in New England between 1815 and 1840, reflect wallpaper designs of the day. Wall painters and stencilers boasted in newspaper advertisements that their services could be secured for less than it would cost to buy and install wallpaper. Some wallpapers, as in the eighteenth century, continued to be stenciled either wholly or in part.

In early-nineteenth-century paintings of American interiors it is sometimes difficult to decide whether the side walls are papered or painted, but it can be assumed that it is the former in the case of the smaller repeating designs which would have been tedious to apply manually.

Lord Sheffield observed in 1791 that 'factories of paper-hangings are carried on with great spirit in Boston, New Jersey, and Philadelphia'. During the early-nineteenth century the copying of European productions undoubtedly continued side by side with a certain amount of original design. Examples of the latter may be seen in various wallpapers commemorating George Washington, the most famous of which is the *Sacred to Washington* produced by Ebenezer Clough of Boston in 1800.

In one instance, at least, aside from the later notable examples of scenic wallpapers aimed at the American market, the French joined in the production of these patriotic papers. The Cooper Union Museum, New York, preserves a panel paper made in France after 1813 commemorating the victory of Commodore Isaac Hull (Plate 317C) in the famous naval engagement between the *Constitution* and the *Guerrière* in the War of 1812.

The first decade of the nineteenth century saw the innovation of 'endless', or continuous, rolls of wallpaper. The English did not make use of this improvement until 1830. The French and Americans must have adopted it before this time, though many wallpapers continued to be printed on joined sheets in the older fashion for several years longer.

Characteristic of American manufacture in the 1820s are simple flowered designs or imitations of damask in blue, green and yellow which 'grade' into one another.

In 1830 the East Room in the White House was hung with a lemon-yellow wallpaper. Soon after this date Americans were caught up in the wave of eclecticism emanating from abroad. The 'Cathedral Style' in France made itself felt in repeating wallpapers featuring views of church interiors with sharply pointed archways and large leaded windows. At the end of the decade French wallpaper designers were turning nostalgically to the sixteenth century and depicting scenes of the chase, and strolling couples in the parks and gardens of the Valois. The French were developing at that time, too, their suites of panel decorations, more elaborate even than those of the early-nineteenth century. Dadoes, pilasters, side-wall panels, friezes, cornices, could all be applied in varying combinations and adjusted to requirements. Few Americans could afford these expensive productions, though some were imported and undoubtedly influenced American designers.

In the 1840s, when Pugin in London was creating his Gothic wallpaper designs for the Houses of Parliament, domestic interiors shown in popular prints show a high incidence of striped papers or papers featuring broad vertical bands ornamented with foliate and strapwork decoration.

Simple striped designs had been one of the earliest sorts of wallpaper to be produced mechanically in England, and later, from England in 1846, the John Howell factory in Philadelphia imported one of the first machines to print figured wallpapers in six colors by the roller-printing process. Within a few years an American firm had learned how to make these machines and mass production of American paper hangings had commenced.

French scenic wallpapers: it is believed that the emergence of printed scenic wallpapers in France in the early-nineteenth century owed something to the popularity of painted panoramas. Examples of these circular views of foreign capitals and historical events, originating in Scotland in 1789, could soon afterwards be seen in Paris and in American coastal cities where they were placed on public exhibition. Continuous, over-all painted decoration in rooms had been known in Europe for many years and hardly less well known were the Chinese non-repeating papers. Americans, however, seem to have been greatly impressed with the uninterrupted aspect of scenic wallpaper design.

The two great makers of these papers in the nineteenth century were Zuber of Rixheim in Alsace and Dufour of Paris. Some of their productions were issued in many colors, requiring for their printing thousands of wood-blocks. Others, no less well executed, were printed in grisaille or sepia, or sometimes in a soft shade of green.

The height of these papers is usually six feet and wallpaper dadoes imitating balustrades were regularly placed beneath them.

The strips or lengths are numbered on the back to indicate their relative positions when placed on the wall, and in the case of the *Voyages of Captain Cook*, Dufour issued a booklet for the convenience of purchasers in which he explained the episodes depicted, and presented hanging schemes which would prevent their being unduly interrupted by door, window and fireplace openings.

French scenic wallpapers may be divided into several categories, according to subject matter. These are principally scenes showing parks or romantic landscapes; views of countries or cities; scenes from history, conquest or adventure; scenes taken from literature, including mythology; and hunting and racing scenes.

By the middle of the second decade of the nineteenth century Americans were importing scenic papers regularly, and would continue to do so for thirty years. The majority dating from that time are found in New England houses. Dufour's popular *Monuments of Paris* found its way to Richmond, Virginia, however, and the likewise popular *Telemachus* was used in Andrew Jackson's house in Tennessee, and also in a house in Bethany, West Virginia.

The Lindens, built in Danvers, Massachusetts, but in recent years moved to Washington, D.C., is notable for having in its hallways not only *Telemachus*, but also the related *Voyages of Antenor* (Plate 319A) and the bizarre *Incas in Peru*, all by Dufour.

Of greatest historical interest to Americans, perhaps, are two Zuber papers of the 1830s. *Scenic America* shows, among other prospects, *Niagara Falls*, and *The Natural Bridge in Virginia*, as well as *Boston Harbor* and *New York City*, seen from the Jersey banks of the Hudson. A few years later, in *The War of Independence*, Zuber used the same backgrounds and introduced new figures to show events of the American Revolution.

A paper called by tradition *The Venetian Scenes* was issued several times with changes of buildings and figures. It appears to be misnamed, for Rome is unmistakably depicted in one of the views.

French scenic wallpapers were not inexpensive. *The Bay of Naples*, a grisaille paper placed on the walls of the Governor Pierce House in Hillsborough, New Hampshire, in 1824 cost five hundred dollars.

During the first half of the nineteenth century painted imitations of block-printed scenic wallpaper were known. This sort of paper was often imported from France, though a certain amount of native work must have been done. In 1828 the painter Charles Codman was engaged in executing landscape wallpaper at the Elm Tavern in Portland, Maine.

More old French scenics are to be found in their original locations in houses in this country than in France itself. Nancy McClelland has made a list of these in *Historic Wall-Papers*. The last fifty years, moreover, has seen the importation of many old sets from France together with numerous reprints from the original blocks.

Bandboxes: closely related to American wallpaper manufacture in the first half of the nineteenth century was the production of printed or stenciled papers for bandboxes (Plates 318B & 320D). Bandboxes were used for the storage or transportation of clothing and were sometimes sold in 'nests', that is, boxes of diminishing size one inside the other.

In some cases actual wallpaper was pasted to these receptacles, which were made either of cardboard or thin sheets of wood. For the most part special papers, usually about ten inches wide, were printed for this purpose by wallpaper manufacturers. Advertisements of the time reveal that some printers of bandbox papers were also engaged in the application of these papers to the bandboxes themselves. Often, however, the printers sold them to bandbox makers, like Hannah Davis of Jaffrey, New Hampshire, who specialized in bandbox construction and who merely applied the papers.

Some bandbox papers do not seem closely related in printing technique or design to wallpapers of the time. A number show contemporary scenes: the newly opened Erie Canal; a balloon ascent of the 1830s; Castle Garden in New York; contemporary firemen with their apparatus. For this reason they are documents of considerable interest. Other designs showing animals and scenes of the hunt seem to be derived, as Mrs Nina Fletcher Little has suggested in her *American Decorative Wall Painting*, from earlier American needlework pictures in turn derived from English sporting prints. Squirrel and bird designs, in flat stylized renderings similar in feeling to the work of contemporary wall painters and stencilers are particularly effective.

Occasionally diminutive bandboxes, sometimes called ribbon boxes, were made to hold ribbons and other small articles, and were undoubtedly used as playthings by little girls.

Other uses of wallpaper: in America in the first half of the nineteenth century wooden panels, called 'fireboards' or 'chimney boards', were often placed in the openings of fireplaces during the summer months. Some fireboards were painted. Others were covered with wallpaper panels made especially for this purpose by French and American manufacturers. They were actually wallpaper pictures derived from still-life, genre and marine paintings and from engravings. Pots of flowers were a popular subject, harking back to an earlier, and then still current, practice of placing large vases of flowers in unused chimney openings. Regular wallpaper borders including those of the festoon type were applied along the edges of these panels.

A New York advertisement of 1791 speaks of paper hangings for ceilings, and there is in existence, dating from about this time, a French ceiling border imitating the soffits of a cornice. Toward 1850, round panels, sometimes ringed with floral ropes and featuring goddesses and *putti*, were used as ceiling centerpieces. Over-all, lightly patterned ceiling papers became common with the advent of the roller-printing machine in the late 1840s.

A great many early-nineteenth-century French panels, horizontal in shape and of different sizes, are found in museum collections. When not used on fireboards they must have been employed as overmantels and overdoors.

As early as the eighteenth century wallpapers were used for the decoration of folding screens. Sometimes special papers were made for this purpose, though many screens were merely covered with Chinese or ordinary wallpaper, panel, scenic or repeating, skilfully cut and edged with borders.

Wallpapers throughout all periods were used to line cupboards, chests, trunks and boxes. Marbleized and small-figured wallpapers were used as end papers and occasionally as covers for books.

AMERICAN WALLPAPER MANUFACTURERS

(Some manufacturers' dates given below are not comprehensive and refer to isolated wallpaper advertisements in contemporary newspapers.)

Albany

John Howell and John B. Howell (John Howell and Son(s)), 1790. Later removed to New York, then Baltimore, finally Philadelphia.

Lemuel Steel, early-nineteenth century. Took over Howell factory after removal of Howell family to New York.

Baltimore

John Howell, early-nineteenth century.
Asa Smith, 1800–10.
Thomas and Caldcleugh, 1808. Sold wallpaper to Thomas Worthington of Adena, Chillicothe, Ohio, in this year.

Boston

Edward Boriken, 1810.
John Bright, late-eighteenth century.
Josiah Bumstead, 1800.
Ebenezer Clough, 1795–1800: 'The Boston Paper-Staining Manufactory'.
Moses Grant, c. 1790. Bought out John Welsh, Jr., who went bankrupt.
Joseph Hovey, 1788–94. 'Stains papers and prints linens.'
William May, c. 1800.
Prentiss and May, 1790.
Appleton Prentiss (A. Prentiss & Co.), 1791.
John Welsh, Jr., 1786. Scott's Court. Bought out by Moses Grant.

Hartford

A. Janes, 1821.
Mills and Danforth, 1814.
Mills and Webb, 1793.

Zechariah Mills, 1793–9. (Plate 315B.)
Putnam and Roff, 1823–4. 'Paper Hanging & Band Box Manufacr.'
Woodbridge and Putnam, 1816. 'Hartford Paper-Hanging Manufactory.'

New York

John Colles, 1787. '... in the Lower Barracks.'
Grant Cottle, 1793.
Cornelius and John Crygier, 1797–9.
Thomas Day, Jr., c. 1830–5. 'Paper Hangings and Band Box Manufactory.' 'No. 369 Pearl-Street, corner of Hague.'
John Howell, early-nineteenth century. Later removed to Baltimore.
Daniel Leeson, 1780–3. 23 Broad Street.
John Rugar, 1765.
John Scully, 1767.

Philadelphia

Boulu, Charden and John Carnes, 1790.
Burrill and Edward Carnes, 1792. 'The Old Manufactory of Paper Hangings.'
Joseph Dickinson, 1784–8.
Plunkett Fleeson, 1739–83.
John Howell, from second quarter nineteenth century until well into the twentieth. Had previously been located at Albany, New York, Baltimore. First roller-printing machine used in this country imported from England, 1844. Second machine (six colors) imported 1846.
James Huthwaite, 1749. '.... does all Sorts of Paper Hangings after the compleatest manner.'
William Poyntell, 1791.
Ryves and Ashmead, 1783.
Ryves and Fletcher, 1775. 'New American Manufacturers and Paper-Stainers.'
White and Laurence, 1756. Possibly importer rather than manufacturer.

Springfield, New Jersey

Mackay and Dixey, late-eighteenth century.

Steubenville, Ohio

James Cole, 1819–22.

BANDBOX MANUFACTURERS

Hartford

Putnam and Roff (see Wallpaper Manufacturers).

Jaffrey (also East Jaffrey), New Hampshire
Hannah Davis, 1825–50.

New York
Thomas Day, Jr. (*see* Wallpaper Manufacturers).

Philadelphia
Henry Barnes, 1829–44. 'H. Barnes' Bandbox Manufactory.' From 1831 to 1844 his address is given in Philadelphia directories as 33 Jones's Alley.

GLOSSARY

Caffaws or **caffoys:** English eighteenth-century term for flock wallpapers simulating damask.

First account taken: printed notation occurring beneath tax stamp on the back of English wallpapers. Starts late-eighteenth century. Meaning not known.

Flock: see text.

Penciling: English eighteenth-century term for painting with a brush, as 'penciled', rather than 'printed', wallpapers.

Piece: early term for a roll of wallpaper.

Pin grounds: dotted grounds.

Sheets: short lengths of paper which were pasted together to make wallpaper rolls until the invention of 'endless paper' in the early-nineteenth century.

Stamped paper: an early term for wallpaper, lasting into the nineteenth century.

Verditer (*verditure*) **paper:** wallpaper printed in either blue or green. Popular into the nineteenth century.

BOOKS FOR FURTHER READING

CLOUZOT, HENRI: *Tableaux-tentures de Dufour et Leroy*, Calavas, Paris (n.d.).

LITTLE, NINA FLETCHER: *American Decorative Wall Painting*, Brattleboro, Vermont (1952).

McCLELLAND, NANCY: *Historic Wall-papers*, Lippincott, Philadelphia (1924).

OMAN, C. C.: *Catalogue of Wallpapers*, Victoria and Albert Museum, London (1929).

SANBORN, KATE: *Old Time Wallpapers*, The Literary Collector Press, Greenwich, Connecticut (1905).

SUGDEN, ALAN VICTOR, AND EDMONDSON, JOHN LUDLAM: *A History of English Wallpaper, 1504–1914*, Scribner, New York (n.d.).

Chronicle of the Museum for the Arts of Decoration of Cooper Union, Vol. I, No. 4, New York (1938).

Concise Encyclopedia of Antiques, Vol. III, pp. 247–54, Hawthorn Books, New York (1957).

VALENTINES AND CHRISTMAS CARDS

By RUTH WEBB LEE

Valentines: some authorities believe that the word valentine came from the Norman, *galantin*, meaning a gallant or lover. Others believe the name is to be traced to the martyred Saint Valentine, ordered to be executed by Emperor Claudius II of Rome. On the eve of his execution he is said to have written a message to the daughter of his jailor, who had befriended him, and signed it *From Your Valentine*. The saint could never have suspected that his words would be endlessly repeated on the anniversary of his death.

The ancient Roman custom of drawing names for mates on February fourteenth, during the celebration in honor of the goddess, Juno Regina, was introduced into England, where it was carried on for many centuries. It has been said that the early Christian pastors decided to abolish what they termed 'this lewd custom of the heathen'. But knowing it would be impossible to eradicate it immediately, they proceeded to give the custom a Christian character by substituting names of saints for names of girls. Significant is the fact that the old English poet, John Lydgate, who died in 1450, spoke of the 'Customs of Seynte Valentine' as a 'religioun'.

The first written message in an American collection using St Valentine's name is of English origin, signed *Edward Sangon, Tower Hill, London*, and dated October 25, 1684. It is in the collection of Malcolm Stone.

In America the sending of valentines appears to have begun shortly before the middle of the eighteenth century as nearly as it is possible to determine from surviving examples. The early ones (Plate 321A, B)

were often simple, yet artistic in style, and for the most part displayed excellent taste in design. They were laboriously wrought by hand by various processes, watercolor, pen work, 'pinprick', and 'cutouts', often beautifully colored. There were also the rebuses, acrostics and cryptograms. Another highly favored style, eagerly sought by collectors, is known today as a 'fold-up'. An example (Plate 322B) shows front and reverse sides, folded. The puzzle consists in refolding one of these valentines once it has been opened.

Among some of our most distinctive valentines are those which were made by the Pennsylvania Germans. The folk art which emanated from rural Pennsylvania was more creative and colorful than that of Puritan New England. Examples of their valentines embellished with *frakturschriften* are much sought today. This is a highly ornamental style of writing based on the Gothic (*see Pennsylvania-German Folk Art*, by Frances Lichten, Vol. II). Pinprick work is another form of their art; pictures are made by pricking the paper in the desired design, often dipping the pin in color and producing soft hues. Designs consist of flowers, tulips, a prime favorite, birds, hearts, and various symbolic figures, often geometric in character.

The Pennsylvania Germans were exceedingly clever with their scissors in executing the most intricate of cutout work in paper. A number of museums show examples of their valentines dating from the early 1800s. The Metropolitan Museum has one particularly choice example, which is not only vividly colored, but has a border of cutout hearts, each carrying a verse in fractur.

The Museum of the City of New York has a beautiful handmade cutout dated 1790, which is all white, delicately-cut with hearts and birds with outstretched wings. This has a different look about it. It suggests a New England, or possibly a Philadelphia or New York background. The sentiments are written across the birds' wings and through the center, and are numbered so that the recipient may read them in proper order. The numbering of lines, or verses, was in vogue up until about 1850. By continually twisting and turning the valentine about it is possible to decipher the following:

1. February the fourteenth day
2. It's Valentine they say
3. I chose you from among the rest
4. The reason was I loved you best
5. Sure as the grape grows on the vine
6. So sure you are my valentine
7. The rose is red the violet blue
8. Lilies are fair and so are you
9. Round is the ring that has no end, So is my love for you, my friend
10. Again take this in good part
11. Along with it you have my heart

THE
LADY'S OWN

I'd be a butterfly, born in a bower,
Where roses, and lilies, and violets meet.

Valentine Writer.

T. W. STRONG, N. Y.

A similar one is illustrated (Plate 322A).

The creators of hand-made valentines had the assistance of little booklets known as *Valentine Writers*, which contained a selection of appropriate verses from which the writer could take his choice. These booklets were printed quite early in England and were also produced in America as early as 1823. They account not only for the marked similarity of sentiments on handwritten valentines, but for identical verses.

From 1835 another style of valentine became popular, particularly in girls' boarding schools. These were hand-made, sometimes on letter paper, and were known as 'theorem' work, or 'poonah', a form of stencil painting (Plate 323B). This was done by drawing or tracing each element of the design on oil paper. From this a stencil was cut and the pattern painted in watercolor; then mixed gum arabic was applied with a stiff brush which fixed the pattern. The same method, with a series of stencils, was used in making theorem paintings on velvet.

Valentines were not produced to any extent on a commercial basis in America before 1840. This was the beginning of the machine age, and while hand-made valentines were still produced, new styles appeared. While some were engraved or made from woodcuts and aquatints, most were lithographed and colored by hand. These were the forerunners of the embossed or lace-bordered valentines. Among the earliest publishers of valentines were Elton & Company of New York, Turner & Fisher of Philadelphia, and T. W. Strong of New York.

ROBERT ELTON was producing valentines in 1833, and possibly earlier. The American Antiquarian Society has examples of his work in its large collection, including colored lithographs made expressly for children.

A delicate bit of designing may be noted in the TURNER & FISHER lithograph (Plate 324B) dated 1840. During this period printed valentines were often left open, as here, for the sender to pen his message, thus making it more personal. Over the years this company, under various firm names, produced a variety of styles, including comics.

The most prolific publisher of valentines

was T. W. STRONG (Plate 323A). Starting about 1842 at 153 Fulton Street, Strong built up an enormous business. His advertisement in 1848 reads:

'Valentines! Valentines! All varieties of Valentines, imported and domestic, humorous, witty, comic. ... got up in the most superb manner, without regard to expense. Also envelopes and *Valentine Writers*, and everything connected with Valentines, to suit all customers, prices varying from six cents to ten dollars; for sale wholesale and retail at Thomas W. Strong's Great Depot of Valentines, 98 Nassau St.'

Among the earlier Strong valentines are hand-colored lithographs, sometimes printed on paper having an embossed edge. They were usually double sheets, with the scene and verse on the outside page. They varied in size, the usual identification marks being *Strong, N.Y.*, or *T. W. Strong*, 98 *Nassau St., N.Y.*, or simply 98 *Nassau St.*

By 1858 the headquarters of the manufacture of valentines was concentrated among five firms in New York City: P. J. COZZENS; FISHER & BROTHERS; MCLOUGHLIN & BROTHERS; T. W. STRONG; and J. WRIGLEY. There were, besides these, five or six small manufacturers in New York, two in New Hampshire, and Esther Howland in Worcester, Massachusetts.

A history of valentine-making in America would not be complete without mention of ESTHER HOWLAND. A graduate of Mount Holyoke College in 1847, she became interested in valentines after seeing some English lace-paper imports in her father's stationery store. It is said she told him that she felt she could make even prettier ones if he would obtain the materials for her. By the end of 1849 she was firmly launched in the valentine business. This girl in her early twenties was possessed of a rare combination of qualities – artistic ability, business acumen, and unbounded energy. She built up a business with sales of $100,000 annually. The Howland valentines were made from lace papers purchased in England. Many of them may be identified by the *H* stamped on the back, usually in red, or by a tiny white heart marked with a red *H* in the center.

Miss Howland retired from business about 1880, apparently having sold out to GEORGE

C. WHITNEY & Company, large producer of valentines and greeting cards in Worcester. Whitney continued some of her styles, marked with a *W*. With the ever increasing volume of business Mr Whitney decided to avoid importing materials and installed machinery for embossing and making paper lace. Since 1840 the English produced most of the fine paper-lace known to collectors today (Plate 324A). They exported to America both valentines and materials for making them for upwards of forty years before Whitney concluded to make his own. By that time the styles in lace had coarsened to such an extent that it was not long before its use was discontinued.

The waning popularity of paper-lace was in part due to another type of valentine which came into favor during the period of Kate Greenaway. These were produced in Boston by L. PRANG & COMPANY. Prang became interested in the reproduction of famous works of art in Europe through lithographs printed in color. He did not specialize in valentines but published a great many. These were usually plain cards or edged with silk fringe and were not always symbolical of the season. He used sprays of flowers, pictures of pretty little girls, or scenes marked *My Valentine, Think of Me*, or *St Valentine Greets You*.

So far as is known, Prang did not make comics. Neither did George C. Whitney, who had a decided aversion to them. However, comics were exceedingly popular in England, the earliest being caricatures of people, or were directed at various trades, and as such reflected the times. Nearly every large publisher of greeting cards in America turned them out, the oldest being woodcuts.

Christmas Cards: the custom of sending Christmas cards during the Yuletide season is fairly recent. Apparently, the exchange of Christmas cards began in England in a very small way during the 1840s. A controversy exists as to whether a card, now in the British Museum, designed by a talented sixteen-year-old artist under the date of what appears to be 1842, was the first; or whether credit is due Sir Henry Cole for a handcolored lithograph card which was designed for him by J. C. Horsely, R.A., in 1843. Leaving debate

PLATE 321

(A) Cutout valentine with birds, hearts and inscription, probably of New England, New York or Philadelphia origin. *Coll. of Mrs Harry Shaw Newman.*

(B) Front and reverse of an eighteenth-century folded valentine. *American Antiquarian Society, Worcester.*

PLATE 322

(B) Theorem valentine, 1835–40. *Coll. of Mr and Mrs Charles Albert Read.*

PLATE 323

(A) Valentine of embossed lace from England but made in America; center hand-painted. *Author's collection.*

(B) Lithograph valentine colored by hand. Turner & Fisher, Philadelphia, 1840. *American Antiquarian Society, Worcester.*

(C) Christmas card after painting by Robert W. Weir, dated 1846. Card published as a chromolithograph, New York, 1894. Has fringe border. *The Old Print Shop, Harry Shaw Newman Gallery.*

PLATE 324

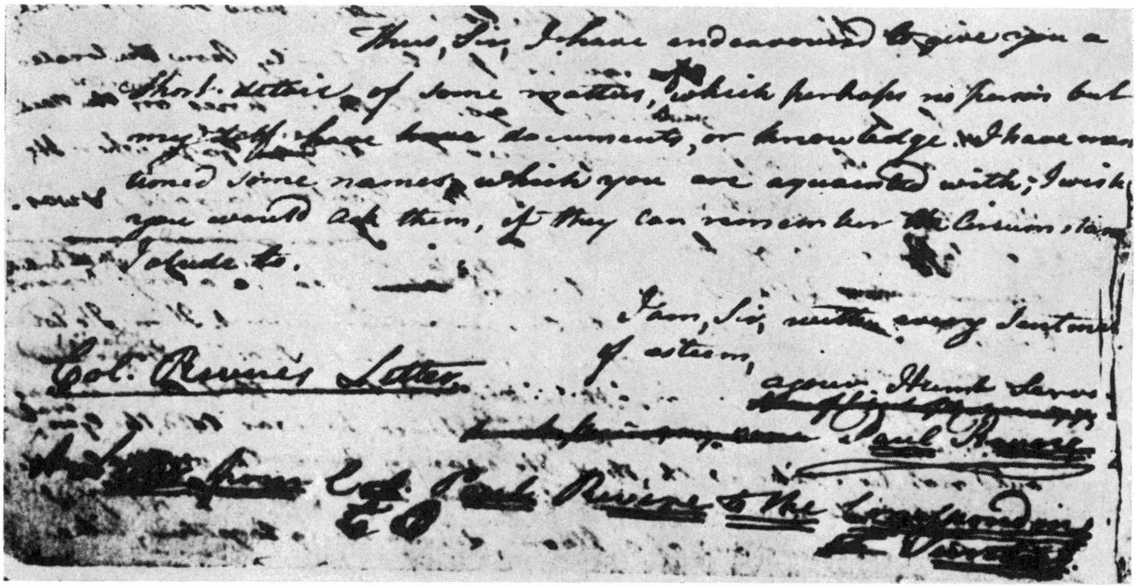
Thus, Sir, I have endeavoured to give you a short detail of some matters, which perhaps no person but myself have documents, or knowledge of. I have mentioned some names which you are aquainted with; I wish you would ask them, if they can remember the circumstance I allude to.

I am, Sir, with every Sentiment of esteem, your Humble Servant

Paul Revere

Col. Revere's Letter

(A) Paul Revere: final page of an eight-page report by Revere of his famous ride warning the countryside of the approach of the British. *Massachusetts Historical Society.*

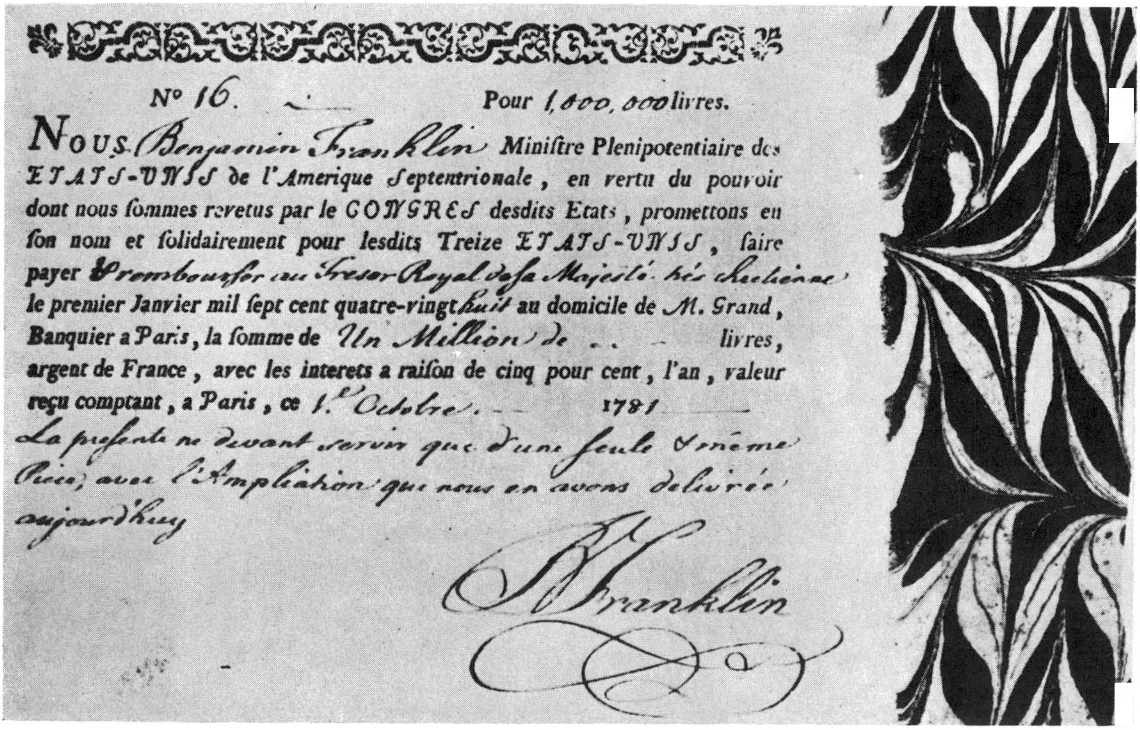
N° 16. Pour 1,000,000 livres.

NOUS Benjamin Franklin Miniſtre Plenipotentiaire des ETATS-UNIS de l'Amerique Septentrionale, en vertu du pouvoir dont nous ſommes revetus par le CONGRES desdits Etats, promettons en ſon nom et ſolidairement pour lesdits Treize ETATS-UNIS, ſaire payer & rembourser au Tresor Royal de sa Majesté très Chretienne le premier Janvier mil ſept cent quatre-vingt huit au domicile de M. Grand, Banquier a Paris, la ſomme de Un Million de livres, argent de France, avec les interets a raiſon de cinq pour cent, l'an, valeur reçu comptant, a Paris, ce 1.er Octobre 1781

La presente ne devant servir que d'une seule & même Piece; avec l'Ampliation que nous en avons delivrée aujourd'huy

B Franklin

(B) Benjamin Franklin: a rare example of printing done on his press at Passy and signed by Franklin while the American Minister to France. *Courtesy of Goodspeed's Book Shop, Boston.*

PLATE 325

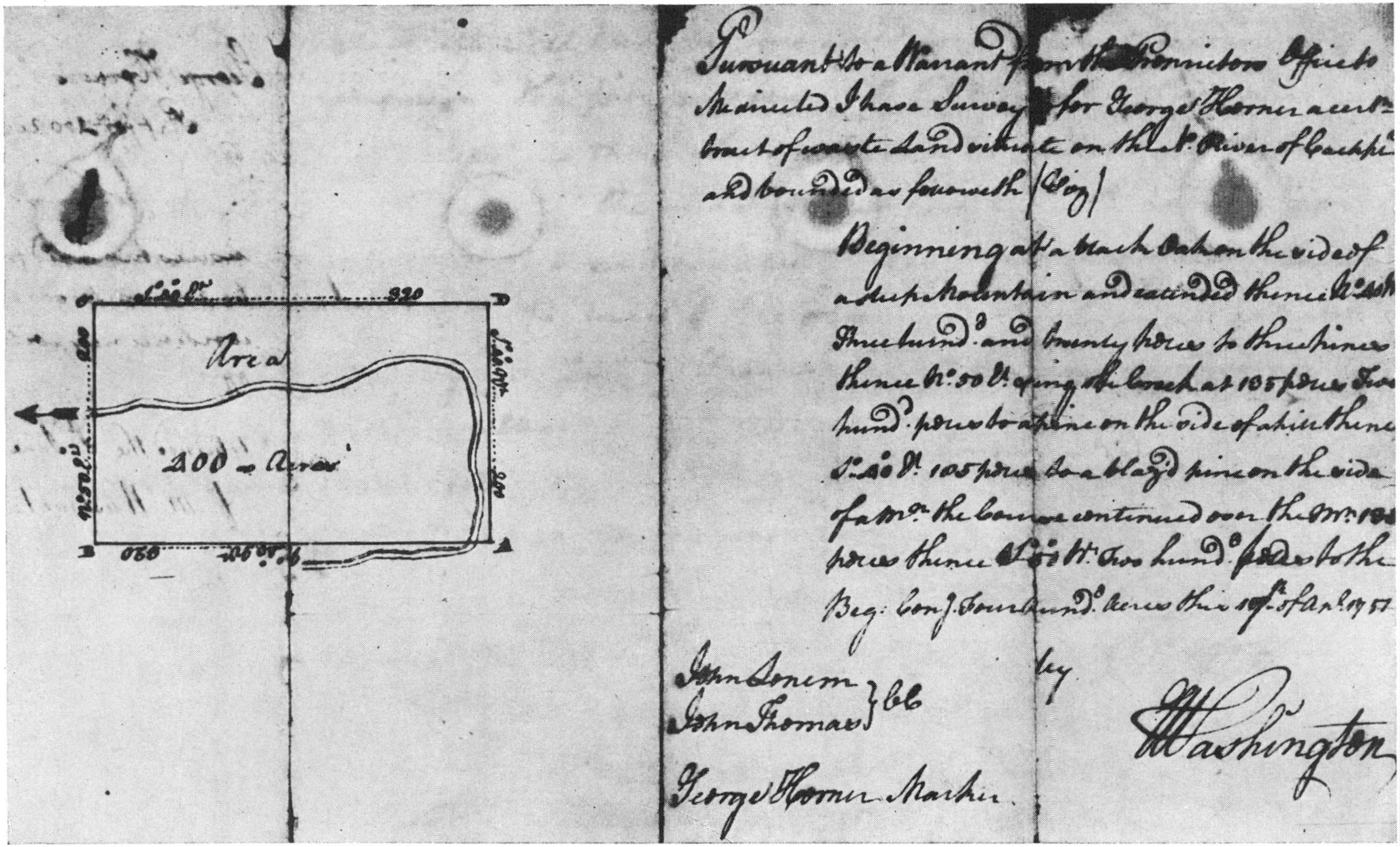

George Washington: survey of land drawn and described by the young surveyor at the age of nineteen. *Courtesy of Goodspeed's Bookshop, Boston.*

PLATE 326

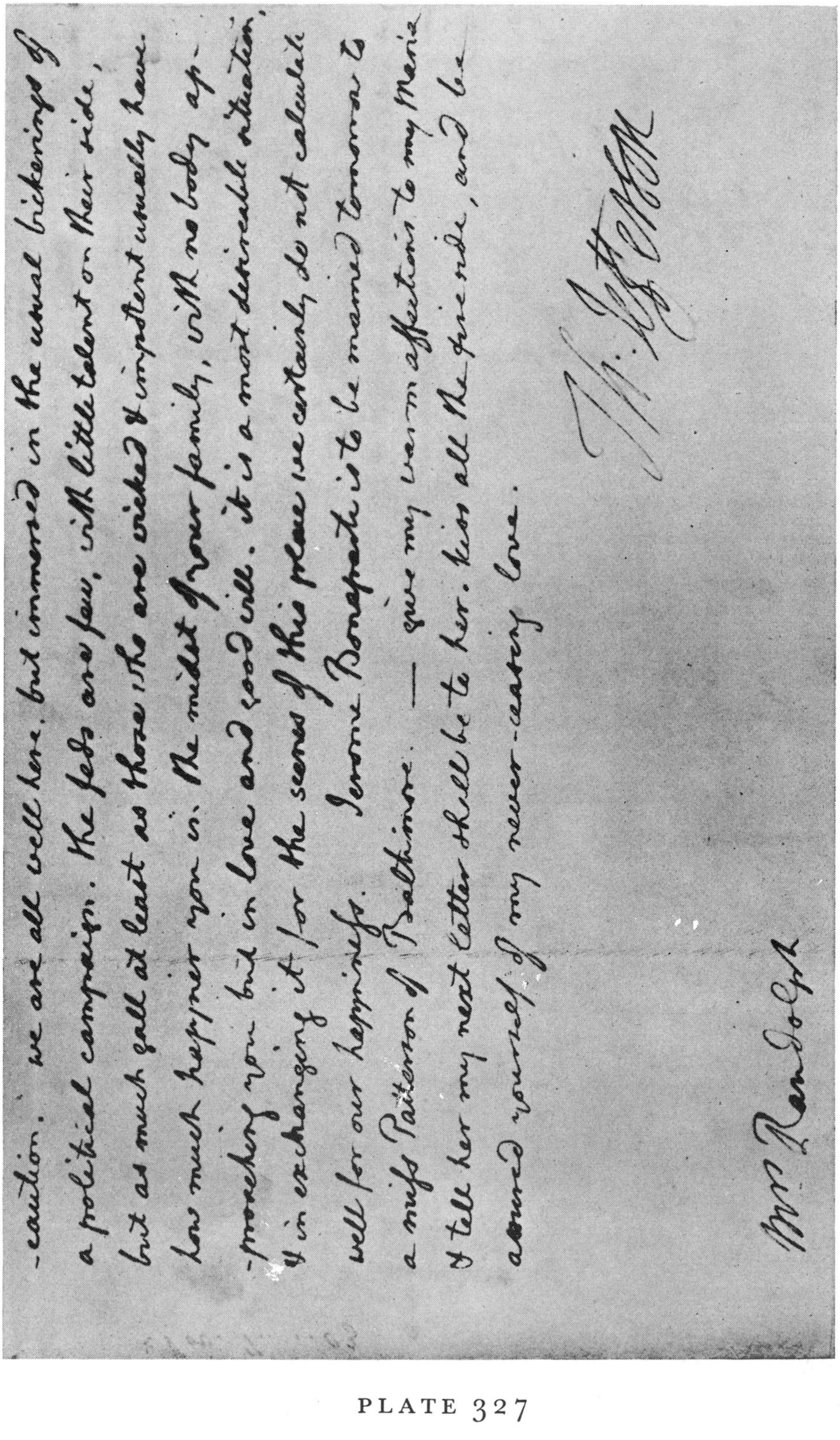

Thomas Jefferson: a letter to his daughter, Mrs Randolph, from Washington, November 7, 1803, while 'immersed in the usual bickerings of a political campaign'. *The Pierpont Morgan Library.*

PLATE 327

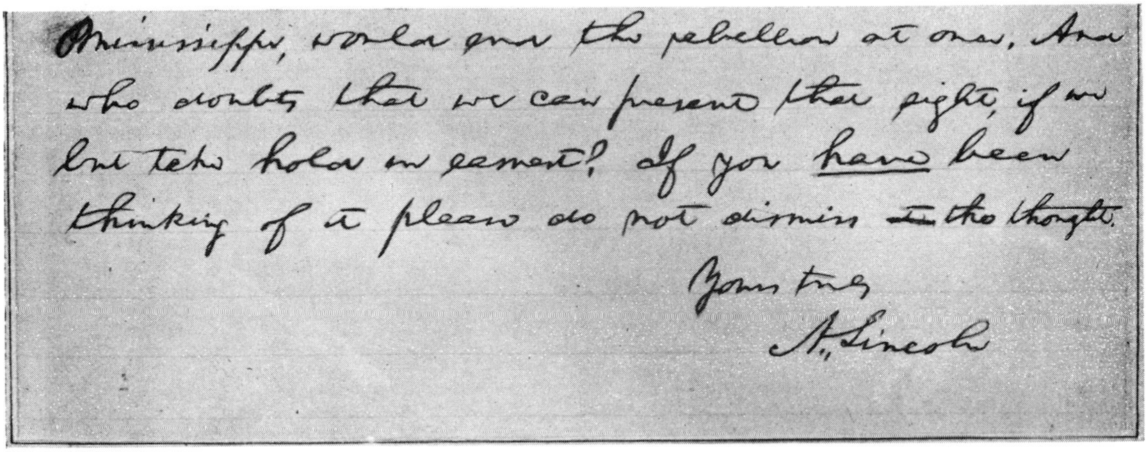

(A) Abraham Lincoln: a letter to Andrew Johnson, March 26, 1863, on the subject of raising Negro troops. *The Pierpont Morgan Library.*

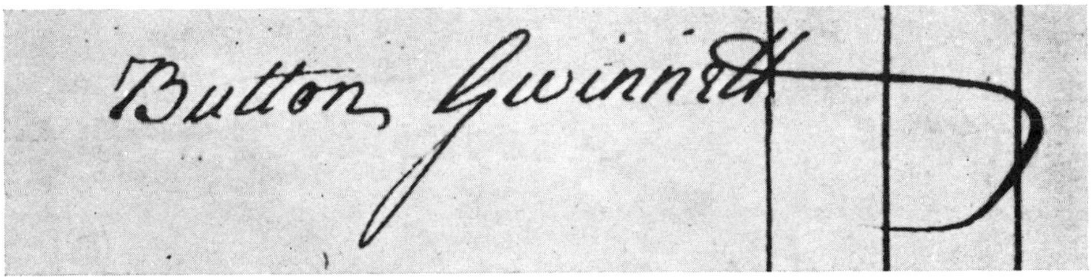

(B) Button Gwinnett: rarest autograph of the Signers of the Declaration of Independence. Gwinnett was killed in a duel with Lochlan McIntosh. *Courtesy of Goodspeed's Bookshop, Boston.*

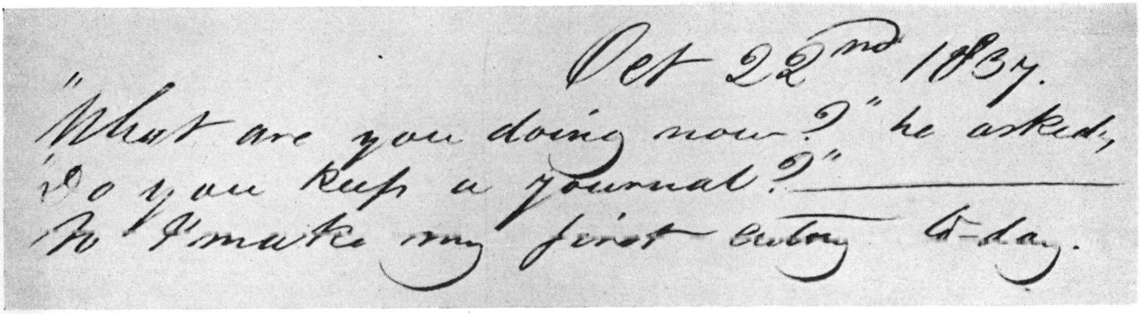

(C) Henry David Thoreau: a page from the Journal, volume III. *The Pierpont Morgan Library.*

PLATE 328

Penmanship Horse. Signed, 'Drawn by James G. Sales under the tuition of J. G. Gray'. *New-York Historical Society.*

PLATE 329

(A) Officer on Horseback. Signed, 'Geo. F. Babbitt'. *Downtown Gallery, New York.*

(B) Andrew Jackson. No provenance. *Kennedy Galleries, New York.*

(C) Mary Newton Her Book. No provenance. *The Old Print Shop, New York.*

(D) Testimonial. Signed, 'Ben F. Brady, 1869'. *New-York Historical Society.*

PLATE 330

(A) The Duke of Orleans. Signed, 'A. F. Davenport', c. 1850. *The Downtown Gallery, New York.*

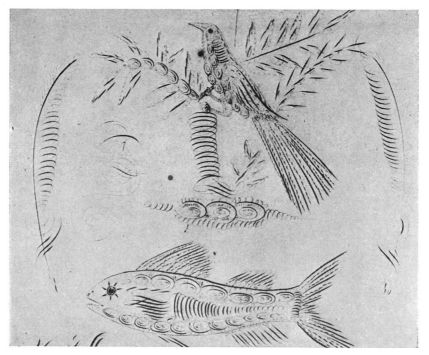

(B) Bird and Fish by A. F. Davenport, c. 1850. *The Downtown Gallery, New York.*

PLATE 331

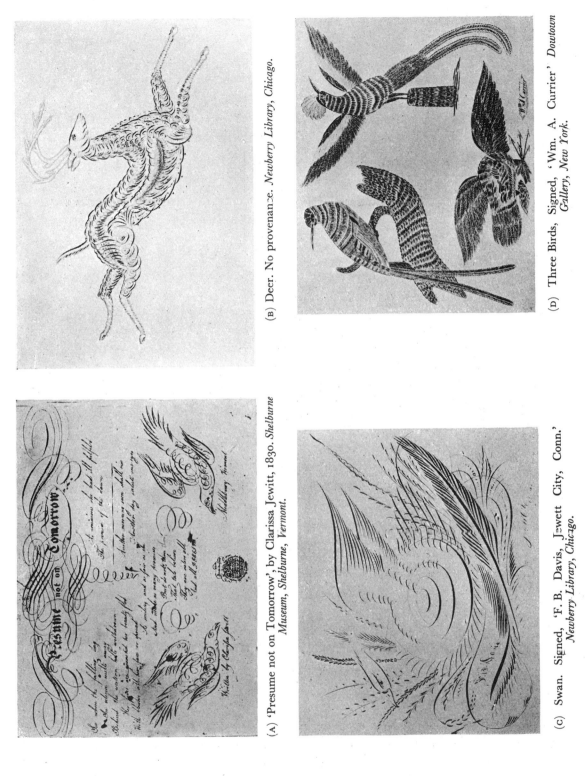

(B) Deer. No provenance. *Newberry Library, Chicago.*

(D) Three Birds, Signed, 'Wm. A. Currier' *Downtown Gallery, New York.*

(A) 'Presume not on Tomorrow', by Clarissa Jewitt, 1830. *Shelburne Museum, Shelburne, Vermont.*

(C) Swan. Signed, 'F. B. Davis, Jewett City, Conn.' *Newberry Library, Chicago.*

PLATE 332

(A) Crown molding plane; blade formed a crown molding 5 ins wide; cross bar at front. The apprentice often looped a rope around this cross bar, pulling the plane while the master guided and pushed it. Length about 17 ins, 1840. *Shelburne Museum, Shelburne, Vermont.*

(B) Wheel plow. *Farmer's Museum, New York State Historical Association, Cooperstown, New York.*

(C) Potter's quern on stand; sagger billets; carrying basket; another type quern. Objects on floor under table are plate molds. *Bucks County Historical Society, Doylestown, Pennsylvania.*

PLATE 333

(A) Spinning by the small or Saxony wheel. *Old Sturbridge Village, Sturbridge, Massachusetts.*

(B) Silversmith raising a silver bowl from a flat sheet of silver; tools of the craft on the walls and over the work bench. *Colonial Williamsburg, Williamsburg, Virginia.*

PLATE 334

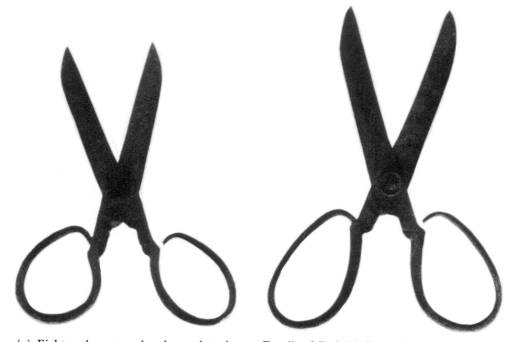

(A) Eighteenth-century handwrought scissors. *Ex-coll. of Frederick Fairchild Sherman; courtesy 'Antiques'.*

(B) Seventeenth-century sickle, broad hoe, pitchfork, rake fragment and mattock; excavated at Jamestown, Virginia. *Museum, Colonial National Historical Park, Jamestown, Virginia.*

PLATE 335

(A) Various types of tin candle molds. *Coll. of E. S. Rushford; courtesy 'Antiques'.*

(B) Tools of the pewterer Samuel Pierce, 1767–1840, of Greenfield, Massachusetts; now installed at the Hall Tavern. *Old Deerfield, Massachusetts.*

PLATE 336

aside, the Cole card might have been forgotten had it not been for the center panel of the design. This depicted a happy family group, each member holding aloft a brimming glass of wine. Beneath was lettered *A Merry Christmas and a Happy New Year to You.* Offering a cheerful toast to personal friends at the holiday season might seem innocent enough, but to temperance groups it represented an open invitation to imbibe. Criticism followed, focusing attention upon the Christmas card. It proved to be good advertising; the idea took hold. In 1881 the Cole card was reproduced by De La Rue and was presumably also copied by American greeting card manufacturers.

With Christmas and New Year cards firmly established in England, American publishers soon added them to their stock. T. W. Strong, Esther Howland, and George C. Whitney all carried them, with Easter cards coming soon after. Outstanding among the producers of Christmas cards was Louis Prang, whose period of greatest prosperity was between 1874, when he published his first Christmas card, and 1890, when cheap foreign imports caused him to abandon the field. His work in multicolor printing was expensive but found a ready sale.

Illustrated is an example of an early Christmas card (Plate 324C) which was based on a painting by Robert W. Weir, drawing master at West Point and father of the artist J. Alden Weir. One of a number of variants of the original, which was painted by Weir in 1837 for his sons, is in the New-York Historical Society. The card, printed by a New York lithographer, is a chromolithograph of a quality which is comparable to the work of Prang.

BOOKS FOR FURTHER READING

HODGSON, MRS WILLOUGHBY: 'Valentines' in *Antiques* (February 1930).

KNITTLE, RHEA MANSFIELD: 'Love and Lace Paper' in *Antiques* (February 1936).

PAUL, FRANCES: 'A Cross Section of Valentineship' in *Antiques* (February 1946).

SMITH, JEROME IRVING: 'Be My Valentine' in *Antiques* (February 1942).

WEBB LEE, RUTH: *A History of Valentines*, New York (1953).

AUTOGRAPHS

By GORDON T. BANKS

As a link with the past, few fields of collecting can compare with the serious gathering together of letters, manuscripts and historic documents relating to the world's notables. One of the happiest phrases coined in the literature of autograph collecting was 'Word shadows of the great'. To the person of high sentiment, the holding in his hands of a manuscript poem of Bobbie Burns or a letter of Abraham Lincoln stirs the emotions. Only a paper-thin barrier separates the collector from the writer. There is a deep emotional transfer. Common to more individuals is the intellectual treat enjoyed by the owner of a Washington letter to one of his commanders in the field, or one of Samuel Johnson's letters to Mrs Thrale, or one of the few Napoleon letters written from exile. Rare but delightful are such intimate letters as Benjamin Franklin's to Deborah, or one of the few letters of Sam Johnson to 'Tetty'. Then there are 'crisis' letters of the sort Charlotte Brontë wrote about her one and late love – or those poured out by Mary Lincoln, under great stress, contesting the limitations set on her during her difficult years by her son Robert.

The individual collector: the great bulk of records both private and public are now housed and cared for by institutions, suggesting that the process of such concentration has lessened the personal side of the acquisition, use and pleasures of autograph collecting. This will never be true, since the very existence of these collections depends, on the one hand, upon years of careful gathering and the final generous giving of one or more individuals. On the other hand, the very maintenance and future welfare of these public collections depend upon personal and individual use and pleasure. This ranges from the youngest school child who visits and admires

a great document to the mature scholar who delves in these primary records and brings back to life a once great personage, now forgotten; or one well remembered, whose earlier biographers have distorted or bowdlerized the true man.

One authority suggests that the word autograph in the modern sense first appeared in the writings of Suetonius the Roman historian. It may even be presumed that he gathered original letters and documents as a background to his noted work, *The Lives of the Caesars*. It is recorded that Ptolemy carried away the original archives of the Athenians, not for destruction but for use; and Nero, the sixth of the Caesars, is reported to have kept a diary. The interest in and the necessities of record keeping predates the ancient days and whether one considers the highly skilled cave paintings or the hieroglyphics on clay and rocks, each was an expression and many were 'collected' and deposited in tomb, jar, or cave against their modern discovery.

The collecting of autographs: as a widespread and personal hobby autograph collecting is very largely a development of the twentieth century. The first departure from collecting solely by persons of great wealth or culture stems from the *Alba Amicorum*, a type of autograph album which flourished near the close of the sixteenth century. Men and women of the period and particularly the students, carried about handsomely bound volumes in which their friends and persons of distinction in their university or area were requested to write brief essays, short poems and other contributions not unlike the familiar Victorian album.

A stimulus to modern widespread collecting came through sales at auction and the general publicity surrounding the breakup of magnificent private collections both here and abroad. One of the most impressive and most valuable of private collections gathered by an English collector was that of Alfred Morrison. In a period of almost unparalleled opportunity he gathered thousands of fine pieces. Among the treasures of the Morrison collection were the correspondence of Lord Nelson with Lady Hamilton, Boswell's pocket notebook in which were perpetuated his conversations with and observations of Johnson, a love letter of George Washington, and a tragic letter of Mary, Queen of Scots, written on the day of her execution.

Nor should Dr Thomas A. Emmett of New York be forgotten; his collection of the Signers of the Declaration of Independence can never be surpassed. Among his four complete sets are magnificent examples, still unique of their type.

Essential to a successful and satisfying collection is an intense interest in at least one area and a willingness to grow with the collection. Those who are uninterested in public affairs and proceed to gather Presidents of the United States or Kings of France, under the advice of a friend, are likely soon to drop their project. Knowledge and enthusiasm linked together has resulted many times in a life-long pursuit in such narrow fields as the original material of a single author, the letters and manuscripts of a single hero, or the gathering of scattered papers from everyone delineating the growth of freedom, the progress of economic thought, or simply the development of the minutiae of life in one's own town, city, or region. Great collectors have found material that has led to an entire change of thought concerning critical periods of history, crucial maneuvers in battle, or the appreciation of economic, social or religious doctrines of a period inadequately covered by the printed book.

Sources of documents and letters: an entire paper could be written describing the ingenuity and concentrated effort of enthusiasts in particular areas. However, barring opportunities to reach original and untouched sources, the common reliance is upon the established dealers of many countries and the great auction houses famous throughout the world. No source of supply will maintain the confidence of any collector of autographs unless prices have an intelligent and rational basis. Experience and frequently re-established prices at auction provide a backlog for realism in pricing any merchandise in this field. There are certain basic established values based on the immutable laws of supply and demand which control the range of prices of ordinary specimens. However, early in the experience of collecting one must learn to judge the value of what is above the signature and realize that the basic signature is the lesser factor in establishing values. Washington signed the discharge papers of every soldier who served honorably in the Revolution, and during civilian life wrote many brief thank-you notes and social responses of trifling interest; these are in the minimum class. On the other hand, should he, in a letter of the same length and general appearance, outline maneuvers before battle and the engagement is historic, the value is enhanced. On up the scale goes the value in proportion to the importance and length of his communication until you reach one of those rare occasions when our first President frankly writes of his discouragement over the progress of his plans, or the attitude of the public toward him. Or, with deep emotion, he eulogizes one of his compatriots, or expresses his great longing to return to Mount Vernon and peace. The peak of Washington values is reached in the rarely found boyhood letter, or to a degree in one of the youthful surveys drawn and written out by the nineteen-year-old surveyor (Plate 326).

Two great pitfalls face the buyer: (1) the impatience that leads to paying too much for a relatively common example (which may be duplicated in kind over and over again), and (2) the failure to grasp the rare opportunity to acquire an extraordinary example, even at a high price. Curbed by reasonable judgment and experience, a collector should always be eager to buy the finest examples and not let price alone rule his purchases.

Care of collection: astonishing carelessness has literally destroyed some of the finest pieces. Autographs of every sort should be kept away from materials that are injurious. Repair work should be done by or under the supervision of those with expert knowledge. Folders, the leaves of bound books, everything that comes in contact with the original, should be as pure (clean—acid free) as possible and seldom, if ever, should be attached in any way to the original. Framing of attractive examples is an adjunct to any collection. It is like the illustrations to a book. It draws attention to the major collection and the finer material, and permits sharing certain pieces with many people. However, it is seldom advisable to frame and hang a piece of major importance. Much satisfaction can be gained from framing minor but attractive letters or documents. Even these should be protected against serious deterioration from direct light. All collections should be safely housed away from extreme heat or dampness. No one method of housing a display has as yet proven ideal and it is a personal problem modified by the usual desire of the collector to share and show his treasures. Most collectors soon learn the undesirability of the direct handling of important pieces; if at all fragile, they are inclined to become more worn or torn. With the best of intentions, guests and friends with moist or sticky fingers will alter the physical beauty of the original. As soon as a collection needs professional housing, gather the opinions of your dealers, librarians, curators, and then simply exercise your judgment.

Symbols and abbreviations: by necessity those cataloguing material for auction or for dealers' catalogues must foreshorten the well-known and constantly repeated phrases. The first symbols to be understood, in the English language, at least, are the *series* of capital letters, each representing a full description: A. for the word autograph, L. for the word letter, S. for the word signed, D. for the word document and Ms. for the word manuscript. Put the first three of these together and you have A.L.S., a common and constantly used phrase to indicate that the letter was both written and signed by the writer. If the original is dictated to a secretary, the symbol is L.S., which is a warning that the author did not write the letter but only signed it. If this proves to be a draft or the signature has been cut off or canceled, one occasionally finds the term A.L., signifying that the person has written the letter but there is no signature. The same series of symbols applies to documents. Occasionally one comes across T.L.S., which is a refinement of L.S., and indicates a typewritten letter signed. Other symbols have had brief or highly specialized use, but these basic symbols will carry almost any collector through the normal dealer or auction catalogue.

The question of size brings in a new terminology which is drawn from the size of books. In the field of autographs, the designations are not as meticulous as with books and are largely used as a warning against an oversized letter. The most common terms are: octavo, which is roughly 5×8 inches or half of the size of a normal letter sheet; and the foolscap or folio sheet, more common to the eighteenth century, which ranges approximately $8\frac{1}{2} \times 14$ or 15 inches. The normal business letterhead is $8\frac{1}{2} \times 11$ inches, or quarto.

Authenticity: every collector must be either prepared to judge for himself or rely upon the opinion of an expert. Experience and specialized knowledge leave but a trifling number of errors due to forgery, facsimile, or incorrect identification. Most of these problems arise from bargain purchases from sources not capable of professional authenticating.

Early American collections: substantial collections of autographs in America prior to 1850 were limited to a few great figures; Robert Gilmor, Isaac Tefft, Rev. William B. Sprague and Louis Cist. GILMOR was a wealthy merchant of Baltimore and his activity spread between the years 1825 and 1851. In 1841 he printed for friends a catalogue of his foreign autographs. TEFFT of Savannah, Georgia, the earliest of American major collectors, apparently began as early as 1815 and was devoted to his hobby until his death in 1861. DR WILLIAM B. SPRAGUE certainly owned the most extensive collection in the United States during his lifetime, and when only twenty-two years of age was privileged to select from the family papers of Lewis

Washington an abundance of letters and documents relating to President Washington and his generals, including extraordinary specimens of Washington's handwriting during his 'teens. Dr Sprague conducted a constant correspondence with other collectors and was unbelievably fortunate in obtaining by gift such things as the correspondence of Samuel Huntington, the Signer, significant portions of the papers of President Monroe, Aaron Burr and Sir William Johnson. For many years he was pastor of the Presbyterian Church in Albany, New York. CIST was a Pennsylvanian who moved into Ohio and collected over a period of approximately fifty years, between 1835 and his death in 1885. He owned letters of Roger Williams, Peter Stuyvesant, Mozart, Beethoven, Schubert and John Paul Jones. Professor E. H. LEFFING-WELL's collection, sold at Boston in 1891, was considered at the time the finest that had been dispersed at auction in the United States. Its great strength was in American historical material, comprising not only the Colonial Governors, but also the Stamp Act Congress, Annapolis Convention, Continental Congress and, of course, Signers of the Declaration of Independence and the American Presidents.

There are more private collectors active at present than during any previous period. There is also a pronounced and healthy trend toward quality in recent years which in turn is producing books, articles, private studies and other evidences of scholarship as against mere ownership. Although great institutions (well financed) may be taking the place of collectors of unlimited means, the cultural benefit of the widespread increase in the number of collectors must not be overlooked.

BOOKS FOR FURTHER READING

BENJAMIN, MARY A.: *Autographs, a Key to Collecting*, New York (1946).

MADIGAN, THOMAS F.: *Word Shadows of the Great*, New York (1930).

For general background: the Catalogue of the collection of Alfred Morrison, 6 vols., illustrated with facsimiles. Morrison, a London merchant of great wealth, formed a collection which ranged over all fields and periods; it was dispersed at auction, London, 1917.

CALLIGRAPHY

By ALEXANDER NESBITT

CALLIGRAPHY is generally considered the basis of a kind of American folk art that was widely practised during the nineteenth century. The term calligraphy is used here with the greatest reservation; no American writing-master called himself a calligrapher; nor was the term used in its present broad, general sense in any of the development of western writing or penmanship from the earliest times to the recent past. It is a sort of euphemism for plain words like writing or penmanship, which, while not disagreeable, are not felt to be distinguished enough by many of the penmen of the present day. The same tendency may be found in many other fields; the advertising copywriter's mentality is usually responsible. To call a station where automobiles are given an oil change and new grease a 'lubritorium' is an example of the same kind of terminology. Certainly the terminology of the history of lettering, penmanship, and writing was confused and difficult enough without the addition of the word calligraphy.

Since the proper genuflection has been made to the magic term, we may now go on to a discussion of the popular art produced by the nineteenth-century American writing-masters and their pupils. It is a bit difficult to apply a generic name to all the collectable items that seem to fall within the scope of this branch of American art. 'Steel-pen drawings' is not the best name for this work, which could only be done with the sharply-pointed, highly flexible spring pen of the nineteenth century. There are many other types of steel pens. It is also quite possible that, especially at the beginning of the century, some of the pens were quills. Although many of the most highly-prized items do have an underlying factor of drawing in them, not all of them may be properly looked upon as drawings – there is much that falls into the writing-master's category of 'command of hand'. These are simply examples of flourishing, based upon rather much-used patterns and traditional figures. Another large class of work is best described as ornamental writing: these are the certificates, diplomas and presentations, testimonials produced by engrossers or writing-masters for various ceremonial functions or for the use of the engraver.

Most of the good examples of writing-masters' drawings, presentations, and *tour-de-force* creations have been found in the north-eastern section of the United States. Pennsylvania, New Jersey, New York, Connecticut, Vermont and Maine have been the source of many of the interesting specimens in this writer's most recent investigation. The middle-western states also produced much work; but it does not appear to be of as creative a quality nor as highly skilled. In the southern states local talent did not develop; they imported most of their art of whatever kind from Europe. One finds practically nothing from the south that fits into our category. Anything that does have this provenance is suspect of being not truly American, but the work of an imported foreign master.

Of course, in any final analysis all writing and penmanship, as it was practised in America from the earliest colonial period until the one with which we are dealing, was based on the styles, traditions, and teaching of European writing-masters. The subject matter of most of the pen drawings came directly from the writing books of Italian, Spanish, Portuguese, French, German, and English penmen. The horse and rider can be found almost exactly in the work of Manoel de Andrade de Figueiredo of Lisbon, *Nova escola para aprender a ler, escrever, e contar*, published in 1722. Indeed, all manner of riders, centaurs, dogs, griffins, and strange creatures are to be seen in the pages of François Desmoulins' writing book, *Le Paranimphe ...* , issued at Lyons in 1625. Edward Cocker's *Pen's Triumph* of 1660 has in it many of the curious figures so dear to the heart of the penman of the next two centuries. This, and other writing books published in London, must have had great effect on the colonies, later to become states. It is clear from just a little study of Europe's seventeenth- and eighteenth-century writing books that most, if not all, of the traditional patterns of the nineteenth-century American penman were derived from them. If they were not directly copied, they were at least remembered; just as the Pennsylvania Germans, in the production of their birth and marriage certificates, remembered the *Bauernkunst* of their homeland.

A little discussion of the illustrations that accompany this chapter on written folk art of the American nineteenth century will indicate to the reader what he may hope to find in this field of collecting. Perhaps the most charming of the examples is the riderless horse (Plate 329). This is in the collection of the New-York Historical Society; it is tinted with watercolor as are many of the specimens that one may see. The rider on the rearing horse (Plate 330A) is in the pattern that resembles Andrade. His counterpart may be found many times over, always holding very closely to the basic outline of the horse and rider. The border is executed in the manner of the French pen portraitists of the latter part of the eighteenth century. The same type of oval border surrounds the portrait of Andrew Jackson (Plate 330B) – or John C. Calhoun as some would have it. The provenance of this work is not known; the Kennedy Galleries has information that it was found in Indianapolis, Indiana, as one of a group of portraits. The illustration that reads *Mary Newton Her Book* (Plate 330C) has figures that could have been copied directly from Cocker. Such mementoes as the florid testimonial (Plate 330D), given by the village of Yonkers, New York, to the firemen of Morrisania for their help, may be found in the files of historical societies through-

out the country; this one is the property of the New-York Historical Society. *The Duke of Orleans* (Plate 331A) and the *Bird and Fish* (Plate 331B) were done by A. F. DAVENPORT, who taught penmanship in North Adams, Massachusetts. The first is a typical 'steel-pen drawing'; the latter is entirely the result of the flourishing technique. Birds and fish may be found aplenty in the instruction books of the English writing-masters. The verses entitled *Presume not on Tomorrow* (Plate 332A) are from the writing book of Clarissa Jewitt. They were written in 1830 at Middlebury, Vermont; and the book, along with others, is now the property of the Shelburne Museum in that state. *Three Birds* (Plate 332D) is a rather unusual arrangement of pen textures in color. The type of hackneyed pattern used by the instructors in penmanship to show their virtuosity and interest their students is represented by the swan from the collection of the Newberry Library in Chicago (Plate 332C). The deer (Plate 332B) is probably of middle-western origin. The best of these drawings and flourished creations were done about mid-century, which is about the time most of the illustrations were produced. There is a definite sterility toward the century's end.

There is no literature to speak of on the subject of these pen drawings and flourished patterns. There are a number of American penmanship books that tell, in a vague way, how flourishing was done. Even the collecting of such materials is of comparatively recent date. Edith Gregor Halpert believes that much of the interest in this type of popular art had its start among artists who were associated with Hamilton Easter Field in the Ogunquit, Maine, artists' colony. They began to collect Americana of this sort in the early 1920s. Mrs Halpert formally opened an American folk art section in her Downtown Gallery in 1929; and, gradually, such drawings and pen productions became highly salable. The two Davenports, the horse and rider, and the three birds are part of her present collection.

One of the curious, almost un-American, facts that strike the student of penmanship art is that, in its professional sphere, it was altogether a masculine form of endeavor. This is true, on the whole, for all of the history of writing. There were of course exceptions, such as MARIA STRICK, the Dutch writing-mistress of the early-seventeenth century. In the amateur or student sense, however, there were many copybooks and some drawings turned out by the distaff side.

For the study of the influences and basic patterns that affected most of the popular penmanship art in America one can do no better than look into the many instruction books of the seventeenth- and eighteenth-century European masters of the pen. These patterns, several generations away from Europe, underwent a kind of metamorphosis. With the admixture of local American naïveté and a peculiar provincial taste our country produced a folk art that was amusing, charming and often surprising.

No subjects for reference, save those mentioned, are available.

TOOLS OF EARLY
INDUSTRIES

By LORING McMILLEN

INTEREST in the early industries of the United States is the most recent expression of appreciation of material aspects of American history. The first occurred during the last quarter of the nineteenth century when collections began to be formed of the fine furniture, silver, china and glassware of our forebears. Shortly this appreciation spread to all furnishings of the old American home, and collectors began to take an interest in lighting equipment, pewter, paperweights, samplers and needlework, toys, buttons and other subjects. However, for many years the tools and implements of the early American industries, as well as the kindred utensils of the kitchen and hearth, were neglected.

In the light of history the early lack of interest in tools was understandable. Industry is composed of three factors, the worker, the tools and the product. The worker and his product have long been a subject of concern for their vital role in the economic and political life of a people. Tools and the knowledge of their use were jealously guarded by the craftsman and handed down by example or word of mouth from father to son, or through the guild system. Any change which it was thought might eliminate a worker by the substitution of a machine or a shorter method was strongly resisted. Thus, until the advent of the machine age during the nineteenth century, tools and the methods of production remained virtually unchanged since before the days of the Greeks and the Romans. Even to this day the claw-hammer of the Roman carpenter is the claw-hammer of the modern woodworker.

However, the machine age changed this.

The country fairs of the nineteenth century and particularly the great expositions such as the Centennial Exposition in 1876 and the Columbian World's Fair of 1893 emphasized mechanical progress in industry, agriculture and the home. As early as 1861 J. Leander Bishop published a *History of American Manufacturers*, an important reference book describing the progress of American industry up to that date. In the preface the author quotes from another source: '... the world might well afford to lose all record of a hundred ancient battles or sieges, if it could thereby gain the knowledge of one lost art and even the pyramids bequeathed to us by ancient Egypt in her glory would be well exchanged for a few of her humble work-shops and manufactories. ...' Bishop was among the first to appreciate and record the history of American industry. However, neither he nor the authors of the various trade publications, encyclopedias of arts and sciences, and mechanical dictionaries of the nineteenth century, valuable as they are for contemporary descriptions, realized that they were witnessing the passing of many ancient industries together with their tools and their uses.

Alice Morse Earle was probably the first writer and historian to realize that the machine age was driving out the early industries. In 1898, in the preface to *Home Life in Colonial Days*, she wrote that the 'different vocations and occupations had not only implements but a vocabulary of their own and all have become almost obsolete. ...' Mrs Earle was the first writer to study carefully the vanishing evidence of these early American occupations.

However, interest was slowly awakening in early American industries, a natural result of the growth of state and local historical societies. These were organized in great numbers during the last half of the nineteenth century. Some of them, such as the Pocumtuck Valley Memorial Association of Deerfield, Massachusetts, which was organized in 1870, had the foresight to collect not only fine house furnishings but also the common utensils of the kitchen and home, and to a lesser extent the tools and implements of the early industries.

Early collections: the greatest credit for extensive saving of tools and preserving of information regarding their use should go, however, to the private collector, for it was he who quietly went about acquiring both the knowledge and the tools of the fast disappearing crafts. The pioneers among these collectors were the Landis brothers, Henry K. and George D., who began collecting as early as 1880. Their collection is one of the largest and is now owned by the state of Pennsylvania, displayed in a museum opened privately in 1924 and publicly in 1941 at Landis Valley near Lancaster, Pennsylvania. The collection consists of 30,000 reference books and other literature and 250,000 objects relating to the arts and crafts of the Pennsylvania Germans.

Another Pennsylvania collector, Henry Chapman Mercer, archeologist, antiquarian and inventor, was active slightly later than the Landis brothers. Dr Mercer was born at Doylestown, Pennsylvania, on June 24, 1856, and died there March 9, 1930. He began to collect during the 1890s and by 1916 had accumulated one of the largest collections of early American industries. In that year he built a unique and imposing fireproof building at Doylestown to hold his possessions. Before 1916 he had begun to turn his collection over to the Bucks County Historical Society, which now administers the museum and its activities. Dr Mercer is well known for his definitive *Ancient Carpenters' Tools*. No other book on early American industries has so carefully described the use and purpose of each tool of a particular craft.

The twentieth century saw rapid growth in the appreciation of the early American craftsman and his tools. The private collectors still continued to lead the way. Singly they worked to gather the objects of their interest, waiting only for some propitious moment to unite as an articulate group. This moment arrived on August 31, 1933, when 'there gathered at Wiggins Old Tavern, Northampton, Massachusetts, a number of men and women interested in preserving for posterity the tools and implements used by our forefathers in maintaining life, as well as forming the adjuncts of life'. The meeting had been called at the suggestion of William B. Sprague of New York, lawyer and collector. Sixteen people attended the first meeting, including Stephen C. Wolcott, Albert B. Wells, Joseph A. Skinner and Lewis N. Wiggins. The Early American Industries Association was organized at this meeting, 'to encourage the study and better understanding of early American industry, in the home, in the shop, on the farm, and on the sea, and especially to discover, identify, classify, preserve and exhibit obsolete tools, implements, utensils, instruments, vehicles, appliances and mechanical devices used by American craftsmen, farmers, housewives, mariners, professional men and other workers'. The Association publishes *The Chronicle*, a quarterly magazine which after nearly twenty-five years is the chief reference source for subjects relating to early American industries.

Museums and historic sites: several of the collections formed privately by members of the Association provided the working material for the preservation and restoration of historical landmarks which revive an impression of the life once in existence there. These 'live' museums are doing a remarkable service in bringing home to the American people the manner in which their ancestors lived and worked. Stephen C. Wolcott's collection of more than five thousand items went to Colonial Williamsburg, Williamsburg, Virginia, where a faithful portrayal of colonial life and the methods of work of the colonial craftsmen can be seen, including that of the blacksmith, the cabinetmaker, the shoemaker, the printer and book-binder, the silversmith, and others.

The New York State Historical Association

owns and administers the Farmer's Museum at Cooperstown, New York. One of the most extensive and complete collections of farm and other implements, pertaining largely to New York, is displayed here. The collection of William B. Sprague forms the largest part of this collection of more than five thousand objects. The Farmers Museum represents an imaginary community, in this instance a typical mid-nineteenth-century cross-roads village of central New York State. In such reconstructed communities typical and varied buildings of the period are moved from other sites, restored, and furnished in such a way as to give a graphic picture of former activities.

Old Sturbridge Village, Sturbridge, Massachusetts, owes its existence to another founder of the Early American Industries Association, Albert B. Wells, and to his brother J. Cheney Wells. The village was begun in 1936 and after ten years of planning and construction was opened to the public in 1946. As at Cooperstown, old structures, architecturally interesting in themselves yet portraying some early craft or profession, are assembled around a village green according to New England custom.

Mrs J. Watson Webb, long a collector of material belonging to the early American crafts, has assembled a similar museum at Shelburne, Vermont. Her collections are displayed in various old buildings arranged as they may have been in a typical Vermont village of the early-nineteenth century.

Old Museum Village of Smith's Clove, Monroe, New York, is the setting for the collection of Roscoe W. Smith, who for over forty years collected early tools and implements. In 1940 Mr Smith began to assemble a group now numbering sixteen old buildings to display his collections. Among these is a blacksmith's shop, cobbler's shop and country store, and among his collections are found vehicles, fire-fighting apparatus, farm and other early machinery. The collections do not pertain to a certain locality nor do they represent a single period. The museum was opened to the public in 1950.

The largest and most representative collection of early American industry is in the Henry Ford Museum and Greenfield Village, Dearborn, Michigan. The museum and collections are the result of Henry Ford's personal interest. The vast museum was opened and dedicated to Thomas Alva Edison in the fall of 1929. There are a total of twenty-six craft shops in operation; twelve are contained within the exhibition hall together with miscellaneous exhibits of tools and implements, and fourteen shops are within Greenfield Village, an assemblage of over ninety historic buildings. The shops portray among other crafts, those of the pewterer, candlemaker, harness-maker, shoemaker, combmaker, gun and locksmith, carpenter, cabinetmaker, wrought-iron worker, wood-turner and carver.

Among collections displayed along with other historic material are those of the Smithsonian Institution, Washington, D.C., the Goyette Museum at Peterborough, New Hampshire; the Essex Institute and Peabody Museum at Salem, Massachusetts; the New York State Museum, at Albany, New York; the Rochester Institute of Arts and Sciences, Rochester, New York; the Museum of the Buffalo Historical Society, Buffalo, New York; the Newark Museum and the New Jersey Historical Society, Newark, New Jersey; the Ohio State Museum, Columbus, Ohio; the Chicago Historical Society, Chicago, Illinois; the Kansas State Historical Museum, Topeka, Kansas; the San Joaquin Pioneer Museum, Stockton, California.

In the city of New York the only collection is that of the Staten Island Historical Society, Staten Island, opened to the public as a museum in 1935. The Society and the Park Department of the City of New York are now collaborating on a restoration of the old eighteenth- and nineteenth-century village of Richmondtown where the museum is located.

Several collections pertain to a single industry or profession, such as the restoration of the first successful iron-works in America at Saugus, Massachusetts; the Old Salt Museum at Syracuse, New York; and the Mystic Seaport at Mystic, Connecticut. Many collections, in a growing group, are maintained by a modern industry, such as the Corning Glass Center of the Corning Glass Company, Corning, New York.

Historic house museums where the kitchen

or a dependency is furnished with typical utensils or implements, number into the thousands throughout the country. Some examples are Mount Vernon, Virginia; Philipsburg Manor, Tarrytown, New York; more than fifty buildings maintained by The Society for the Preservation of New England Antiquities; the several buildings maintained by the State Education Department of the State of New York; and the buildings operated by the Ohio Historical Society.

It is estimated that there are between two and three thousand collectors, public and private, of the tools and implements of early American industries, in the United States and Canada.

Period of tools collected: the period of the early American industries is generally accepted as beginning with the first settlements and extending to the continually changing and advancing dates when certain tools or machines became obsolete. Thus age is only of academic or historic interest and what is of prime importance is whether the tool has been superseded and is thereby likely to be destroyed and forgotten. Space, personal interest and resources will dictate what can be collected. Many collectors and large institutions are actively saving automobiles, steam locomotives, early farm tractors and sewing machines. The Staten Island Historical Society has stored for future display, among other late accessories, out-of-date radio sets, electric light and gas fixtures and talking machines. The early American industry collector is primarily interested in saving and studying the tool or the machine. The product of these is of chief interest only for demonstration purposes. The tool has to be first an instrument of production and it is of secondary interest whether the tool itself is the product of an industry. The old-time blacksmith made many of the iron tools for the farmer and others in his community. His product, however, became a tool in the hands of the new owner. Collections are not limited to the simple cutting, piercing or forming tool of the carpenter, tinsmith or shoemaker, but include the mechanical application of these simple tools to machines. These machines extend from the ancient woodturner's lathe, the household spinning wheel and mechanical apple-parer to the more complicated farm machinery, such as the reaper, the mower, the threshing machine and the steam tractor. The machine can be hand- or foot-driven, or powered by water, wind or steam.

Display: methods of displaying early American tools vary with the means of the collector. However, the craft shop or industry in actual operation is the ultimate objective. No static display will take the place of a live demonstration of tools and techniques. Where this method is not possible modified settings of the tools to simulate a demonstration is next best, followed by raised panels upon which the smaller tools can be attractively arranged and described. The glass display case is generally not suitable for the exhibition of tools unless they be the small tools or instruments of the watchmaker or physician.

Preservation: preservation of tools from oxidation and decay and the extent of their restoration are serious matters with the institution or private collector. If the tool needs no repair or replacement of parts, a cleansing with soap and water or gentle rubbing with fine steel wool will suffice to remove dirt. Care should always be used to preserve the original finish and a tool should be preserved as it was used. Rust requires more stringent action, namely tapping with a small hammer to loosen scale, followed by the use of a wire brush to remove smaller particles. Further smoothing with file or emery paper is prohibited since original contours and markings are inevitably removed in the process. Missing parts, which prevent the full understanding of the tool, should be replaced and broken parts repaired. These should not be forgeries, but honest, sympathetic replacements or repairs, clearly indicated. Finally, one or two applications of equal parts of boiled linseed oil and turpentine brushed on will not only feed the wooden parts but brighten them. The same application to iron will prevent further rust as well as refresh the appearance. Brass and other metals are best cleaned with one of the patent liquid or paste metal polishes.

Stubborn cases can first be rough-cleaned with fine steel wool and the buffer, followed by the polishes.

Classification: no adequate classification of the tools of early American industries has been attempted and wisely so. For there is no better classification than the historical identification as to trade, and any other classification such as cutting, sawing, clamping, boring or shaping tools tends only to confuse and to lose sight of the craftsman and his techniques.

Samples of historical classification can be found in many of the early records of the provinces, colonies and sub-divisions. An example from the records of the province of Virginia, dated 1620, shows a great variety and lists the tradesmen that were desirable in the new colony: '*Husbandmen, Gardners, Brewers, Bakers, Sawyers, Carpenters, Joyners, Shipwrights, Boatwrights, Ploughwrights, Millwrights, Masons, Turners, Smiths of all sorts, Coopers of all sorts, Weavers, Tanners, Potters, Fowlers, Fish-hookmakers, Netmakers, Shoemakers, Papermakers, Tilemakers, Edge tool makers, Brickmakers, Bricklayers, Dressers of Hemp and Flax, Lime-burners, Leatherdressers, Men skillful in vines, Men for ironworkers, Men skillful in mines.*'

As the early crafts and industries of the blacksmith, the cooper, the miller, the basket maker, and the home crafts of spinning and weaving become a memory, unidentified tools and utensils increase. Collectors and institutions are becoming keenly apprehensive because of this fact and are increasing their efforts to capture, by photographs, interviews and recordings both verbal and graphic, the craftsman at work. Research in a reference library is invaluable in aiding the collector to gain a fuller knowledge of the early industries, and the following list of books, while far from complete, will serve as a guide.

BOOKS FOR
FURTHER READING

APPLETON & CO., D.: *Appleton's Dictionary of Machines, Mechanics, Engine Work, etc.* (1850).

EARLE, ALICE MORSE: *Home Life in Colonial Days* (1898).

HAZEN, EDWARD: *Panorama of Professions and Trades* (1837).

KNIGHT, EDWARD H.: *American Mechanical Dictionary* (1872).

MERCER, HENRY C.: *Ancient Carpenters' Tools* (1929).

RAWSON, MARION NICHOLL: *Handwrought Ancestors* (1936).

TOMLINSON, CHARLES: *Cyclopedia of Useful Arts* (1852).

URE, ANDREW: *Dictionary of Arts, Manufactures and Mines* (1850).

VAN WAGENEN, JARED, JR.: *The Golden Age of Homespun* (1953).

Chronicle of the Early American Industries Association (1933 to present).

PATENT OFFICE MODELS

By JACK E. BROWN

ONE of the richest and most unusual sources of information concerning the early social and economic growth of the United States is to be found in a collection of approximately 155,000 models assembled by the United States Patent Office during the period 1790 to 1890. These models, all of which are miniature or working models of objects submitted for patent rights, depict an era when American inventive genius was coming into its own.

The collection, once maintained as a unit but now widely scattered, was the outgrowth of early patent laws which required that each applicant for a patent submit not only a drawing but also a model of the device under consideration. In many cases the models were indispensable parts of the patent record, for the drawings of early patents were often sketchy and incomplete. The importance which was attached to the maintenance of such a collection is indicated by the remarks of the United States Commissioner of Patents in his annual report for 1890. Here he states that 'the models contained in the model halls are not only of great interest to the public at large ... but they are of almost inestimable advantage to the examiners by enabling them to conduct their investigations expeditiously'.

The models composing the collection are unlimited in their variety and represent countless phases of human ingenuity. Included among the more famous models are Samuel Morse's telegraphs patented during the years 1832 to 1846, Thomas Edison's first phonograph patented in 1877, Graham Bell's original telephone transmitter and receiver dated 1876, a gas-driven automobile invented by George Selden in 1895, and a device for buoying up vessels in shallow waters which

surprisingly enough was patented by Abraham Lincoln in 1849. One of the largest groups of models consists of early sewing machines beginning with the Howe patent of 1846, which for the first time placed the eye of the needle in the point instead of the heel. This machine (Plate 337) led the way for a whole series of similar devices incorporating the improvements of Wilson, Singer, Grover & Baker, and Willcox & Gibbs. Equally well represented were models of thousands of items which played an integral part in the everyday life of the family and the nation and ranging from flycatchers, stoves, beds, dentist chairs and pianos to shoemaking machines, farm machinery and firearms.

As might be expected, this feature of the patent laws requiring the submitting of a model brought about a thriving model-making business. Many inventors were of course able to construct their own models, but the less gifted ones turned for help to model-making firms which sprang up in various communities. The net result was the production of many handsome models exhibiting the perfect workmanship of the hand craftsman. The type and size of the model required was outlined in the patent laws which stated 'the model must clearly exhibit every feature of the mechanism which forms the subject of a claim or invention, must not be more than one foot in length, width or height, and must be substantially made'.

During the middle 1880s much thought was given to the development of an efficient typewriting machine. Two machines were invented within a year of each other (Plates 338A, 340B). The more elaborate (Plate 338A) was the work of C. L. Sholes, invented in 1868 and covered by patents 79,265 and 79,868. In his description of the machine Sholes says 'the types are arranged in a radiating series, and are pivoted to a disk at whose center each type is made to act upon the paper through an opening against a platen'. As in our modern machines, the impression was made on the paper through the use of a moving inked tape. An even more famous invention, and one which has changed little since it was first patented in 1870, is the so-called Stillson wrench (Plate 338B), the work of Daniel C. Stillson. The wrench is an improved version of an earlier model which was patented June 23, 1868.

The first patent issued under United States Patent Laws was granted on July 31, 1790, to a Samuel Hopkins for a new method of making pot and pearl ashes. From this time until the rescinding of the model requirement, the collection of models suffered a series of mishaps which threatened its very existence. On December 14, 1836, the Patent Office in Washington was ravaged by fire. There is considerable divergence of opinion regarding the number of models destroyed, for one authority states that all models collected prior to 1836 were burned, while another source places the loss at approximately 7,000 models. In any case, the loss was of such a serious nature that the United States Congress voted an appropriation for their restoration, and within twelve years an almost complete replacement of both models and records was achieved. A second fire, on September 24, 1877, again resulted in the destruction of models, which one report placed as high as 86,000. Once again Congress, recognizing the historical importance of the models, took immediate steps for their restoration.

By 1890 the size of the collection had reached such proportions that the housing and exhibiting of the models became a major problem to the Patent Office. To alleviate the situation the patent laws were amended and models were no longer required except at the request of the Commissioner of Patents. Patent officials of the period regarded this decision as a grave mistake, a feeling which was voiced by the Commissioner of

Patents in his report for 1890 in which he said, 'I regard it as nothing less than a public calamity that the office was several years ago compelled to suspend the reception of models, excepting in special instances, for want of space in which to store and exhibit them'. He then went on to say, 'I venture to express the hope that the time will come when models will again be required in connection with all applications, and that when that time arrives an effort will also be put forth to obtain specimens of the more important inventions which have been patented during the intervening period'. Unfortunately, his hope was not realized, and the model collection ceased to expand after 1890. This move, drastic as it was, did not solve the problem of where to exhibit the existing models, and in 1908 all of the 155,000 models, except for a few of the more important ones, were crated in some 7,500 boxes and placed in storage. Finally, in 1925, an economy-minded Congress decided that the cost of this arrangement was prohibitive, and ordered the disposal of the collection by public auction.

Prior to the actual sale, a Commission, which included the Commissioner of Patents and the Secretary of the Smithsonian Institution, was appointed to arrange for the disposal of selected groups of models to various governmental agencies and national museums. The Smithsonian Institution made the first selection and retained in the neighborhood of 12,000 models of lasting and historical importance. A small number of models was retained by the United States Patent Office, where they are now on display, and about 2,500 were returned to heirs of the patentees. Approximately 3,000 items were sent to museums and institutions which had expressed an interest in a particular category. On this basis the Henry Ford Museum in Dearborn, Michigan, acquired a collection of models relating to the domestic and agricultural life of the nation. Among the models in the Ford collection is one of Edison's early phonographs (Plate 339A) or speaking machines, which was patented on February 19, 1878, carrying the patent number 200,521. The model itself is about fifteen inches in length. In applying for the patent, Edison anticipated much of the record industry. He noted that the tin foil used on this model to take impressions of sound waves could be removed from the machine and duplicated either by stereotyping or by making a plaster cast, and then pressing fresh tin foils upon it, in this way reproducing the original many times over.

A model of patent number 230,609, patented on August 3, 1880, by Edwin M. Burt of Harvard, Illinois, measuring fifteen inches in length, shows the construction of a farm-yard gate (Plate 999B) which can be opened either by swinging it in the conventional manner or by lifting it up so that it collapses upon itself like a set of parallel rulers.

The exquisite workmanship to be found in many of the models is well illustrated in the working model of a reaper (Plate 340A) which measures about twenty-six inches long and is nine inches high. The patent, number 16131, was granted on November 25, 1856, to W. Whiteley.

With the completion of this preliminary distribution, an arrangement which more or less guaranteed the lasting preservation of at least 18,000 models, there remained approximately 144,000 pieces for public auction. The lot was purchased by Sir Henry Wellcome, of Burroughs Wellcome & Co., for $6,540. This purchase marked the beginning of a series of sales and resales which even in 1957 has not reached its conclusion.

Wellcome planned the erection of a permanent museum for the display of the models, which upon completion would be presented to the American people as a public service. It is unfortunate the plans never materialized and the models remained in storage until the owner's death in 1936. At that time they were again placed on the market as a lot and acquired by a syndicate calling itself American Patent Models Corporation. This organization prepared various exhibits which were rented to schools, museums, stores and fairs. Many were displayed at the New York World's Fair in 1939. The undertaking proved financially unsuccessful and in 1942 the Corporation went into bankruptcy.

Once more the group of models was put up for auction, but this time the main body of the collection was whittled down through the sale of several small groups. One such group of 350 items was purchased by the Rushford Collection in Salem, Massachusetts, where they are now on exhibition and available to commercial organizations seeking material for advertising or public relations programs. This collection includes such categories as bedroom furniture, lighting devices, toys and games, and kitchen utensils.

In spite of these splinter sales the main body of the original collection of 144,000 pieces was kept intact and acquired by Mr O. Rundle Gilbert of New York City. Mr Gilbert arranged several exhibits and sales, all of which proved unsuccessful. A final sale, held in 1950 at Gimbel Brothers in New York City, also failed to catch the imagination of collectors of antiques and Americana. Mr Gilbert ceased his efforts to dispose of the collection and established a museum of 5,000 items at Plymouth, New Hampshire. Here are displayed models of the first Fairbanks scale, the original Gatling gun, an early rotary printing press, and the Mergenthaler type-casting machine. The remaining items are stored in some 1,900 cases at Mr Gilbert's home in Garrison, New York. The specific items included in these cases are still unknown, and their unpacking should reveal many surprises.

BOOKS FOR
FURTHER READING

BREARLY, J. A.: 'Old Patent Office Models' in *Patent Office Society, Journal*, Vol. 8 (February 1926).
BYRN, EDWARD W.: 'The Museum of Patent Office Models' in *Scientific American*, Vol. 95 (August 11, 1906).
COYNE, JOAN: 'Riding a Patent Hobby Horse' in *Scholastic*, Vol. 34 (February 25, 1939).
LARSON, CEDRIC: 'The Patent Office Models, 1836–1890' in *Patent Office Society, Journal*, Vol. 33 (April 1951).
MACGREGOR, DONALD: 'Passing of Uncle Sam's Old Curiosity Shop' in *Mentor*, Vol. 13 (September 1925).
'Models for Some Famous Patents' in *Life*, Vol. 8 (April 15, 1940).
U.S. Department of the Interior: Commissioner of Patents: Report, 1890, Washington, D.C., Government Printing Office (1891).

Sewing machine patented September 10, 1846, by Elias Howe. *Smithsonian Institution.*

PLATE 337

(A) Typewriter invented by C. L. Sholes in 1868. *Smithsonian Institution.*

(B) An earlier model of this Stillson wrench of 1870 was patented June 23, 1868. *Smithsonian Institution.*

PLATE 338

(A) This model of one of Edison's early phonographs was patented February 19, 1878. *Henry Ford Museum, Dearborn, Michigan.*

(B) A farmyard gate patented in 1880 by Edwin M. Burt. *Henry Ford Museum, Dearborn, Michigan.*

PLATE 339

(A) This intricate model represents a reaper patented in 1856 by W. Whiteley. *Henry Ford Museum, Dearborn, Michigan.*

(B) Thomas Hall's typographic machine patented June 18, 1867. *Smithsonian Institution.*

PLATE 340

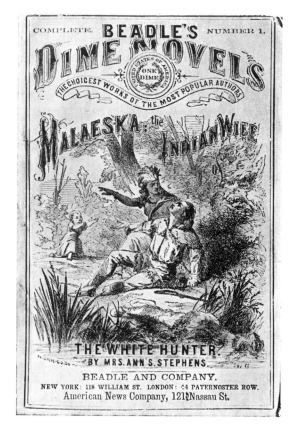

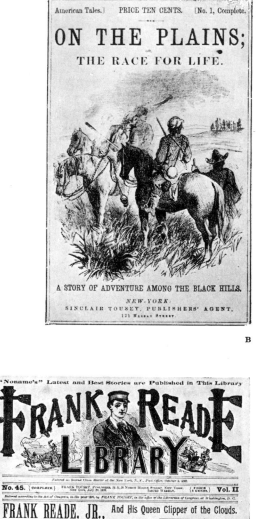

B

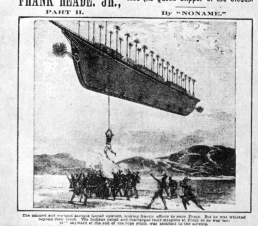

(A) Beadle's first dime novel, *Malaeska: The Indian Wife of the White Hunter*, by Mrs Ann S. Stephens, 1860.

(B) An early western, *On the Plains: or The Race for Life*, Sinclair Tousey.

(C) *Frank Reade, Jr., and His Queen Clipper of the Clouds*, Part 2, July 29, 1893. Frank Reade Library, Frank Tousey, publisher.

All illustrations by courtesy of Charles Bragin, Brooklyn, New York.

PLATE 341

(A) *Pawnee Bill the Prairie Shadower: or The Gold Queen's Secret*, from Beadle's Half Dime Library, 1888.

(B) The Five Cent Wide Awake Library; *Frank Reade and his Steam Man of the Plains* by "Noname", January 24, 1883.

PLATE 342

(A) *Bulto:* 'Humanist' type, *c.* 1810; from cotton-wood root. Ht 34 cm. *Coll. of Cady Wells, Museum of New Mexico.*

(B) *Santo:* Archangel Raphael. Priest painting dated 1780. Note the Rio Grande catfish. Ht 1 m. 25 cm. *Museum of New Mexico, Santa Fe.*

(C) *Bulto:* Cordova style. Ht 62 cm. *Coll. of Cady Wells, Museum of New Mexico.*

PLATE 343

(A) *Santo:* 'St Martin and the Beggar'. School of José Raphael Aragon. Tempera on gesso on pine. Ht 35 cm. *Amerind Foundation.*

(B) Gesso relief *retablo:* San José. Gesso on pine panel. Ht 79 cm. *Coll. of Cady Wells, Museum of New Mexico.*

(C) *Santo* by the Calligraphic Painter. Detail from panel of San Francisco Xavier. *Coll. of Cady Wells, Museum of New Mexico.*

PLATE 344

(A) *Santo:* 'St Vincent Ferrer'. Quill pen painter. Ht 26 cm. *Coll. of Charles D. Carroll.*

(B) *Bulto, above, right:* Anonymous Santero style, classic period. Ht 63 cm. *Coll. of Mr and Mrs Stanley Marcus.*

(C) *Bulto, left:* Arroyo Hondo style. Ht 66 cm. *Coll. of Charles D. Carroll.*

(D) *Bulto, right:* Mora style. 'St Isidore the Farmer.' Ht 39 cm. *Coll. of Cady Wells, Museum of New Mexico.*

PLATE 345

(A) Pine chest on legs, one of three known; generally on stands. Mortise and tenon construction, c. 1800–25. *Photo by Ernest Knee, Historical Society of New Mexico.*

(B) Pine chest for church vestments, dove-tailed construction; carved rosette, lion and pomegranate motifs. Eighteenth century. *Photo by Ernest Knee, Historical Society of New Mexico.*

PLATE 346

(A) Sconce decorated with applied straw. Northern Rio Grande, before 1850. *Historical Society of New Mexico.*

(B) *Trastero* (cupboard); gesso on native pine, painted in tempera, *c.* 1840. *Coll. of Florence McCormick, Museum of New Mexico.*

(c) Trinket box decorated with corn husks. Northern Rio Grande, before 1850. *Historical Society of New Mexico.*

PLATE 347

(A) Tin *nicho* or shrine, tin pierced and stamped with leather tooling dies; glass panels over marbleized painted paper. *Museum of New Mexico.*

(B) Left: candlesconce, tin; five pieces, punched with nail and cold chisel. Right: sconce of fourteen pieces stamped with leather tooling dies. *Museum of New Mexico.*

PLATE 348

Silver mounted saddle, Mexican, late-nineteenth century. Owned by Sheriff Eugene Biscailuz of Los Angeles County, California. *Los Angeles County Sheriff's Department.*

PLATE 349

(B) Leather bullet pouch, handsewn and embroidered with hemp threads in eighteenth-century style. *Museum of New Mexico.*

PLATE 350

(A) *Jerga* or floor cloth, light and dark natural wool; single ply; wool warps and wefts woven in diagonal twill pattern. New Mexico, *c.* 1860. *Museum of New Mexico.*

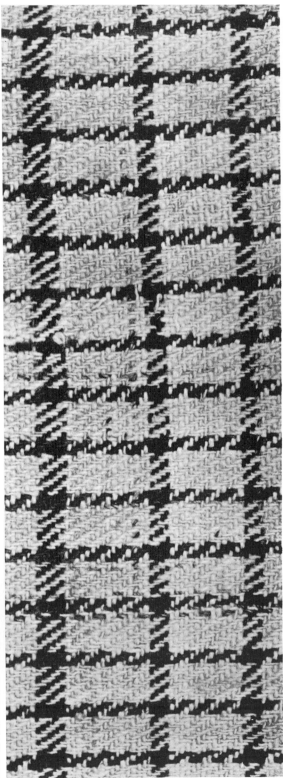

(B) Wool embroidery on wool homespun, worked in *colcha* stitch solidly embroidered; indigo, light and dark natural wool, *c.* 1860. *Museum of New Mexico.*

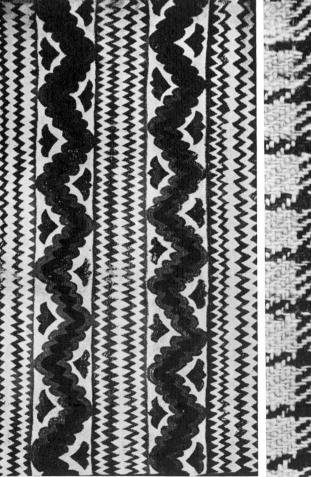

PLATE 351

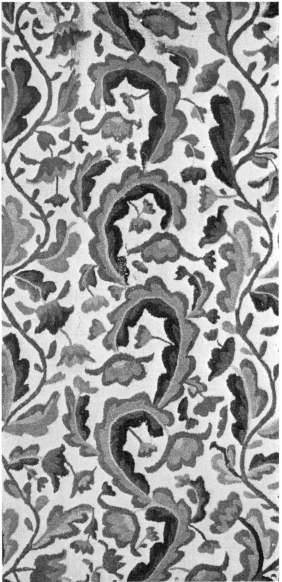

(B) Wool on homespun; *colcha* stitch; solidly worked ground. Colours: red (*bayeta* or raveled red Manchester cloth), indigo, yellow (*chamiso* dye), rose-tan (mountain mahogany), green (mixed indigo and *chamiso*), natural light and dark wool, *c.* 1860. *Museum of New Mexico.*

(A) Wool embroidery in *colcha* stitch on cotton twill; single ply homespun yarns and Saxony three-ply yarns; indigo, cochineal, yellow and green (native dyes); natural wool; and (Saxony) rose, pale pink, French blue, light tan and brown, *c.* 1870. *Museum of New Mexico.*

PLATE 352

DIME NOVELS

By MARY NOEL

THE collector of dime novels is not merely a connoisseur of the outlandish. More seriously, he helps to preserve from decay a source of material of great value to the historian. Morison and Commager, in their *Growth of the American Republic*, agree with many other historians in observing the importance of the reading habits of the common man as a key to the temper of an age. Merle Curti, in a scholarly article for the *Yale Review*, grants to the dime novel a privileged position as the most truly 'proletarian' literature of its period, an accurate gauge of popular taste and opinion, a guide to the history of such popular ideals as patriotism, rugged individualism, and social democracy.

The collector who wishes to specialize could follow the particular enthusiasms of the American public during the entire age of dime novel literature. He would find a flood of bicycle stories during the craze of the 1890s, a flood of railroad stories during the period when the fast expresses were developing, and a flood of motor stories during the early automobile and air age of the twentieth century. Any of these, as well as stories about baseball, football, fire-fighting, and the circus, would make an invaluable supplement to the collections of pamphlet, magazine, newspaper and broadside literature on these special subjects. A search for bicycle stories reveals such interesting titles as: *Bicycle Ben, the Knight of the Wheel; Frank Merriwell's Bicycle Boys, or The Start across the Continent;* and *Bicycle Bob's Hot Scorch, or Shaking up the Street-Steerers: A Story of the Schoharie County Hayseed in New York.* Again, a collector could follow the headlines. In the *Work and Win* 'library', Fred Fearnot rushes to the Klondike to work the 'Dark-Horse' claims; then he is off to Manila, *Plotting to Catch Aguinaldo.* Then

world events necessitate his presence in Russia, where he is *Banished by the Czar;* and then he is back again to deal with *The Masked Fiends of the Mines* at our own Cripple Creek strike.

The collector who wishes to track down a given author must be something of a detective in his own right. Johannsen lists fourteen different pen names used by EDWARD S. ELLIS in writing for Beadle alone. And Ellis's concealed activities were by no means confined to Beadle publications. Nor will the discovery of a pen name attached definitely to a known author be altogether conclusive. EUGENE T. SAWYER and FREDERICK VAN RENSSELAER DEY were only two of the many authors who posed as 'Nick Carter'. GILBERT PATTEN complained bitterly that his pen name of Burt. L. Standish was used for the Frank Merriwell stories of *Tip Top Weekly* long after he had quit writing them.

Even dime novels themselves are not entirely easy to identify, since many of them sold at a nickel, and many novels which sold at a dime are *not* generally classified as dime novels. But the problem of when a dime novel is not a dime novel is not really as difficult as it seems. In general, love stories are disdained by the collector. Dime novels are strictly blood-and-thunder, where the heroines are made to be rescued, not kissed. Pirated English novels, American classics, or translations from the French, all frequently selling at ten cents, are definitely excluded, no matter how lurid their deceptive covers may be.

In general, dime novels are said to begin with BEADLE'S first series, in 1860. As Johannsen points out, Beadle did not start from scratch – he was simply the first to issue a continuous series of sensational adventure stories at a fixed price of a dime. Some of the Beadle inspiration no doubt came from the tremendous success of Robert Bonner's *New York Ledger*, a weekly in newspaper format which emphasized serial stories by Mrs E. D. E. N. Southworth and Sylvanus Cobb, Jr. The railroad boom of the 1850s had first made it profitable to ship large quantities of cheap paper print to local news-agents; and the *New York Ledger*, as well as other story papers, had been a major factor in building up the news-stand business in America. In 1860 Beadle began shipping off his first batch of dime novels to these news-stands, starting with MRS ANN S. STEPHENS's *Malaeska* (Plate 341A), quite in the story-paper tradition. The Civil War undoubtedly gave Beadle his opportunity. The soldier in the field might miss an indispensable installment of his favorite story-paper serial; but the dime novel, complete in one issue, was a sure thing. Beadle shipped them off to the camps done up like bales of hay. By April 1, 1864, five millions of his dime books had been sold, over half of them novels, the rest song collections, handbooks, and biographies. Competitors soon entered the field, and the dime novels continued to flourish, in one form or another, until about 1910. Then, with the rise of the pulp magazines, catering to every taste, the dime novel fell off rapidly until about 1925, when it was practically extinct.

The first Beadle dimes and their imitators were generally of pocket size, about $6\frac{1}{2} \times 4\frac{1}{2}$ inches with black wood engravings or 'cuts', as they were called, on solid-color covers. This, with only slight variations in size, remained a standard type throughout the nineteenth century. Soon experiments were made with cover illustrations in bright colors, laid on over the 'cuts'. Color was a sensation on the news-stands of those days, and it proved too expensive for wide use. Instead, the prevalent form soon became a mere pamphlet, thin and broad, about $11\frac{3}{4} \times 8\frac{1}{2}$ inches, uncut, about thirty-two pages for a dime, and sixteen pages for a half-dime. The slashing lines of their luridly dramatic black-and-white illustrations were quite conspicuous enough for all their lack of color. But with the development of cheap color lithography in the 1890s a fourth major type entered the field and drove out all the others by their gaudy covers, about 11×8 inches in size. These were the famous Nickel libraries, dozens of them, issued by Street & Smith and Frank Tousey.

GLOSSARY OF PUBLISHERS

Beadle & Adams: New York, 1859–98. (Under name of Irwin P. Beadle & Co., 1859–60; Beadle & Co., 1860–72. Sold in 1898 to M. J. Ivers, who continued to issue dime novels, mostly reprints of earlier ones, for a few years. All have black line illustrations on the cover unless otherwise indicated.)

Beadle's Dime Novels (Plate 341A), 1860–74. The first books to be generally classified as dime novels. Pocket size, orange covers. All but the very early issues have black line illustrations on the covers. Series runs heavily to western stories, with some sea and Revolutionary tales. Authors include PRENTISS INGRAHAM, JOSEPH E. BADGER, FREDERICK WHITTAKER, WILLIAM J. HAMILTON, MAYNE REID, EDWARD WILLETT, and EDWARD S. ELLIS.

Beadle's Dime Novels, New Series, 1874–85. Really a continuation of the first series, but with a good many reprints. The 'cuts' on the covers are printed first in black, but have an overprint in several colors.

Beadle's Boy's Library of Sport, Story and Adventure, quarto edition, 1881–4. Difficult to obtain, according to Johannsen. Contains such popular boys' writers as MAYNE REID, T. C. HARBAUGH, FREDERICK WHITTAKER, OLL COOMES, PRENTISS INGRAHAM. Octavo edition, 1884–90.

Beadle's Half Dime Library, 1877–1905. Total of 1,168 issues: 16-page quarto pamphlets. Indian, pioneer (Plate 342A) and sea stories in the beginning, but many detective stories later on. Contains over 120 'Deadwood Dick' stories by EDWARD L. WHEELER. Famous for its alluringly alliterative titles, such as *Dandy Dick Decoyed; or The Terrible Tussle at Satan's Delight* (No. 1,064); and *Brooklyn Bob's Bulge; or Dodger Dot's Diamond*

Snap. A Story of the Willy-Wally Wipe-out (No. 956).

Beadle's New York Dime Library, 1878–1905. Similar to the Half Dime Library, but thicker pamphlets, with stories running 70,000-80,000 words, instead of half that length as in the Half Dime.

Beadle's Pocket Library, 1884–93. Pamphlets, $8\frac{1}{2} \times 5\frac{3}{4}$ inches, without wrappers. Westerns and detective stories. Many reprints.

Beadle's Pocket Novels, 1874–84. Consists entirely of reprints of stories appearing in other Beadle libraries.

Frank Starr's American Novels, 1869–77. Beadle published this series under the imprint of his foreman; almost entirely westerns.

Frederick A. Brady: New York.
Brady's Champion Stories, 1869. Brightly illustrated covers, pocket size.

Camp Fire Company: New York.
Camp Fire Library, 1887-8. Pamphlets with black-and-white illustrations on covers.

T. R. Dawley & Company: Boston.
Camp and Fireside Library, 1864.

Dawley's Ten Cent Novels, 1864–5. Dawley experimented with gaudy colored covers, very unusual in such cheap printing at this date.

Robert M. DeWitt, New York, 1848–77 (succeeded by Clinton DeWitt, 1877–80).

Champion Novels, 1872–8. Bought from Brady, who had issued them as Brady's Champion Stories. Brightly-colored illustrations on the covers. Westerns for the most part.

DeWitt's Ten Cent Romances, 1867–77. About 118 issues, monthly. Gaudy yellow or orange covers with black illustrations. Pocket size.

Elliott, Thomes & Talbot, Boston (1863(?) –85(?)).

Ten Cent Novelettes, 1863–?. 87 issues, pocket-size. First 24 in pink, later blue. Many of them reprints of early story-paper novels, including those that SYLVANUS COBB, JR., wrote for the *Flag of Our Union*.

George Munro, New York, 1863–?.
Munro's Ten Cent Novels, 1863 75. Pocket size, light brown pictorial covers for some, bright colors over black 'cut' for other issues. Various pseudonyms are given on the covers,

but according to George Waldo Browne, ARTHUR L. MESERVE wrote every one of them. Nos. 1–6 published as Irwin P. Beadle's Ten Cent Novels, since Irwin Beadle at that time was in partnership with Munro.

Old Sleuth Library, 1885–1905, 101 issues (quarterly). Pamphlets, $8\frac{1}{2} \times 12$ inches with black-and-white cover illustrations. Perhaps the best-selling of all dime novel series. Written by HARLAN P. HALSEY, one-time member of the Brooklyn Board of Education.

Norman L. Munro: New York, 1868–?.
Old Cap Collier Library, 1883–1900. 822 issues. Both ten cent and five cent editions for first hundred issues. Five cent edition more highly prized because of lurid black-and-white illustrations. Author unknown. Probably the pseudonym of W. I. James, used throughout the series, represented many different authors.

Ornum & Co's Ten Cent Indian Novels, 27 listed in 1870.

Ornum & Co's Ten Cent Popular Novels, 1870–?. Pocket size with illustrated covers in bright colors. Includes pirated Jack Harkaway and highwaymen stories; but also some westerns. Munro published under name of Ornum & Co. for the first few years.

Nickel Library Company: New York.
Little Chief Library, 1885–91. Black-and-white pictorial covers.

Pictorial Printing Company: Chicago.
Nickel Library, 1875–92. Taken over by Nickel Library Company in later years.

Street and Smith: New York, 1859–present time.
(Unless otherwise indicated, all have color lithograph covers.)
Adventure Weekly, 1897. Boxer Rebellion stories.

All-Sports Library, 1905–6. 'Jack Lightfoot' is the hero.

Army & Navy Weekly, 1897. Includes pseudonymous tales by UPTON SINCLAIR.

Bowery Boy, 1905–7. Using imprint of Winner Library Company. Detective stories by JOHN R. CONWAY.

Brave and Bold, 1903–11. Largely story-paper reprints, especially 'Oliver Optic' and 'Horatio Alger Jr.'

Buffalo Bill Stories, 1901–12, 591 issues. Succeeded by *New Buffalo Bill Weekly* for 364 reprints. Authors include EUGENE T. SAWYER and W. BERT FOSTER.

Comrades, 1900–1. Mostly railroad tales with a single hero.

Diamond Dick Jr Weekly, 1896–1912. 762 issues – a tribute to the success of Beadle's earlier 'Deadwood Dick Jr.'

Jesse James Stories, 1901–4. Mainly reprints from Log Cabin Library.

Log Cabin Library, 1889–97. Black-and-white cover. Includes sea tales by 'Ned Buntline', westerns, etc.

Motor Stories, 1909. Motor cycle, airship, submarine, and automobile adventures of 'Motor Matt'.

Nick Carter Library, 1891–7. Black-and-white covers.

Nick Carter Weekly, 1897–1912.

Nick Carter Stories, 1912–15.

New York Five Cent Library, 1892–6. Black-and-white covers. Later issues have the first 'Diamond Dick' tales.

Nugget Library, 1889–93. A nickel library with black-and-white covers.

Red White and Blue Weekly, 1896–7. War stories.

Rough Rider Weekly, 1904–7.

Tip Top Weekly, 1896–1913. These are the famous 'Frank Merriwell' stories written by GILBERT PATTEN at the rate of 20,000 words a week – more than a million a year – for 17 years.

True Blue, 1899. UPTON SINCLAIR, writing under the pseudonym of Ensign Clark Fitch about Naval Academy life.

War Library (Date ?). Civil War stories under the imprint of the Novelist Publishing Company.

Frank Tousey: New York, 1878–1920. (The firm was sold to Wolff and Westbury, who continued for a number of years with the last of the dime novel publications. In these latter years most of the long libraries consisted of reprints of earlier issues. All of the publications listed below have colored covers unless otherwise indicated.)

Blue and Gray Weekly, 1904–5. Civil War stories by George Waldo Browne under pen name of Lt Harry Lee.

Boy's Star Library, 1887–96. Includes stories of the inventor 'Jack Wright' who, like 'Frank Reade Jr', had strange adventures with strange devices, such as an Electric Torpedo. A nickel library with black-and-white covers.

Fame and Fortune Weekly, 1905–28. Later issues were simply reprints of earlier ones. Wall Street speculation, provided one risks everything, now takes on an heroic cast.

Frank Reade Library, 1892–8. A nickel library with black-and-white covers. This, together with the Wide Awake Library, contains the stories of LU SENARENS, written under the pseudonym of Noname, about the hero's marvellous contraptions (Plate 341c) – a 'catamaran of the air' which penetrates the wilds of Australia; an Electric Snow-Cutter; or an Electric Boomerang, etc.

James Boys Weekly, 1901–3. Reprints from the New York Detective Library. This series in general violated the dime novel canons against the exaltation of crime and was therefore not advertised by Tousey in his more respectable publications.

New York Detective Library, 1882–98. Black and-white covers. 'Old King Brady' and 'James Boys' stories.

Pluck and Luck, 1898–1929. Boy heroes who go anywhere for adventure. Lurid color illustrations.

Secret Service Weekly, 1899–1927. Stories of 'Old' and 'Young King Brady' by 'a New York Detective', thought by some to be FRANCIS DOUGHTY, the archeologist.

Wide Awake Library, 1878–98. Includes many 'Frank Reade' (Plate 342B) stories. Black-and-white covers with fantastic illustrations.

Wide Awake Weekly, 1906–9. 168 fire-fighting stories.

Wild West Weekly, 1902–28.

Work and Win, 1896–1924. 'Fred Fearnot' trying to outdo 'Frank Merriwell'.

Yankee Doodle, 1898. 14 timely stories on the Spanish American War.

Young Glory, 1898. Also on the Spanish American War, but at sea.

Young Klondike, 1898. This gold rush happened right in the dime novels' own time.

Arthur Westbrook: Cleveland.

Boys' Best Weekly, 1908. Another 'Merriwell' imitation.

Old Sleuth Weekly, 1908–12. Reprints of Old Sleuth tales in the earlier Munro library.

BOOKS FOR
FURTHER READING

BRAGIN, CHARLES: *Chills and Thrills; Dime Novels, 1860–1928,* a dealer's catalogue illustrating all of the best-known subjects (Brooklyn, New York).

CURTI, MERLE: 'Dime Novels and the American Tradition' in *Yale Review,* XXVI (1937).

CUTLER, JOHN LEVI: *Gilbert Patten and His Frank Merriwell Saga,* University of Maine Studies: Second Series, No. 31, University Press, Orono, Maine (1934).

JOHANNSEN, ALBERT: *The House of Beadle and Adams,* 2 vols, Norman, University of Oklahoma Press (1950).

MONAGHAN, JAY: *The Great Rascal. The Life and Adventures of Ned Buntline,* Little Brown & Co., Boston (1952).

NOEL, MARY: 'Dime Novels' in *American Heritage* (February 1956).

NOEL, MARY: *Villains Galore. The Heyday of the Popular Story Weekly,* The Macmillan Company, New York (1954).

PEARSON, EDMUND LESTER: *Dime Novels,* Little Brown & Company, Boston (1929).

ARTS OF THE SOUTHWEST

By E. BOYD

IT may be remarked, in explanation of the usage of the areal term, New Mexico, that under Spanish rule, this embraced what is now divided into New Mexico, Arizona, Colorado and Texas, where the frontier between Spanish territory and that of French Louisiana was indefinite, while there was no political border between present New Mexico and the Mexican states of Chihuahua and Sonora. Necessity was the mainspring which kept Spanish colonists on the northern Rio Grande busy making their own textiles, cabinetwork, and other objects. When a few Franciscan priests in mid-eighteenth century made religious images for missions in their charge the village craftsmen learned the techniques, and so was launched the New Mexican *santero* school. Innocence of academic art training and the limitations of materials produced a distinctive style, in evidence chiefly between 1800 and 1860. It fell into disfavor until recent decades, when artists and collectors have recalled New Mexican folk art to its proper place among the folk arts of other parts of the world.

With few exceptions, a similar development did not take place in Spanish California, where luxury goods were easily sent from Mexico by ship to a well-to-do Spanish minority of barely 2,000 people, in contrast to the more than 26,000 Spanish mostly in humble circumstances in New Mexico. Due to isolation on the internal frontier, there was no visible change except, perhaps, more poverty, after Mexico declared itself a Republic in 1822. Minor influences were felt when the Santa Fe Trail trade brought better hand tools and novelty goods. More impact upon the old culture was effected after annexation by the United States in 1846. The inauguration of the Diocese of Santa Fe,

bringing non-Spanish religious into the area; the Civil War; and completion of the railroad combined to affect the distinctive character of the Spanish colonial period, so that it may be said to have ended about 1880.

RELIGIOUS FOLK ART

The Spanish word, *santo*, means saint, or the image of a holy person or even thing, such as a cross or monstrance. It is also an adjective, *holy*. The second definition, a holy image, applies to all media; stone, wood, metal, plaster, painting, prints, etc. To Spanish-speaking New Mexicans *un santo* still refers to any religious image, but in recent years the English-speaking New Mexicans have appropriated the term to describe the indigenous folk images. A maker of a *santo* is called a *santero*, who also, in former times, repaired old ones. New Mexican *santos* are of two main classes: pictures painted on wood panels over a gesso ground, called *retablos*—these may be full-sized church altar-pieces or no larger than notepaper, for domestic purposes; and *bultos*, or figures in the round, of wood covered with gesso and painted.

California missions possessed oil paintings on canvas and gilded; also polychromed figures from Mexico and Peru; but relatively few of these academic works made their way to New Mexico. Thus the presence of oil painting, canvas, hardwoods and gilding indicates an importation. Cottonwood roots, pine, gesso made of native gypsum and locally made mineral and vegetable pigments were the materials of the New Mexican *santero*. An exception were two pigments: indigo and cochineal, sent from Mexico for weaving and used also by the *santeros*. *Santos* were often treated with native varnish: a brew of

825

rosin and wax, which served as protection to the water-soluble paint and added a golden film.   Many *santeros* remain anonymous, as few of their works are signed.

Retablos: identified by maker or by style:

Priest paintings: usually in oil on wood or, rarely, canvas, timid compositions after academic Mexican models, often with cartouche giving name of donor and date. Franciscans noted in archives who did such works were Father Andres Garcia, 1747–79, service in New Mexico, and Father Benito Pereyro, 1798–1818, service in New Mexico, although whether the latter actually made images or supervised their making is uncertain (Plate 343B).

Anonymous, eighteenth-century novice paintings: oil or tempera over gesso on native pine panels. Fully covered with dark earth red paint on which opaque light keyed over-painting was added. These are crude and primitive. Dated by tree-rings[1] 1766–89.

José Aragon: tempera on gesso on pine—white gesso used, as in nearly all true *santero* examples, instead of white paint. Precise drawing, conservative iconography, panels often after eighteenth-century Mexican engravings, often lettered with name of image, place where made, prayers, date and signature, or at least one or more of these inscribed facts. Dated works, 1822–35.

The Calligraphic painter: anonymous *santero* with pronounced style of drawing and usage of design elements, prolific output. Dated panel, 1827. Dated by tree-rings; bark-date, 1814 (Plate 344C).

Molleno (given name unknown; surname probably local corruption of the Spanish name, Moreno): prolific output, style changed over lifetime from dark background tempera paintings derived from Mexican prints to santero style; white gesso backgrounds with striking mannerisms in shorthand drawing; use of 'chile pepper' forms (actually roughly sketched acanthus forms), and usage of red color. Dated works, 1828–45. Dated by tree-rings; bark date, 1805.

José Rafael Aragon and workshop: two signed pieces by him are known. Lived at Cordova, a hill village south of Taos, New Mexico. Classic *santero* style and usage of two-dimensional drawing over white gesso backgrounds. Worked 1839, probably to 1850s. At least two followers learned their craft from him, and all three seem to have made *bultos* also (Plate 344A).

A. J.: anonymous *santero*, one of whose panels bears these initials. Naïve style of drawing, brown used for all outlines. Dated panel, 1822.

Dot-and-Dash painter: anonymous *santero*, rather empty compositions and frequent usage of dots and dashes in color to make borders and corner fillers. Not dated.

Quill Pen artist: anonymous, very naïve drawing with fine pen or stylus outlining instead of brushwork. Tree-ring dated board, post-1830 (Plate 345A).

Of miscellaneous, unidentified styles, some were as late as 1880.

Gesso relief retablos: an outgrowth of the sophisticated rococo stucco work of the early-eighteenth century in Latin countries. The latter, however, was modeled over an armature with almost free-standing figures and architectural details, while the New Mexican gesso work (Plate 344B) was built up in low relief over a pine panel to supply a minimum of modeling instead of attempting to carve pitchy wood. A series of these shows some knowledge of iconography and color usage. Tree-ring dated panels; bark date, 1796; six others; mean average 1778–85. A minor series of these by another anonymous *santero* is crude in modeling and detail and not dated.

Bultos: identified by maker or style; due to the fact that figures in the round cannot as a rule be dated by tree-rings, their history

---

[1] Dendrochronology, or the science of dating certain woods by their annual ring sequence, was developed over thirty years ago by Dr A. E. Douglass in his work on meteorology under the auspices of the Carnegie Institution. Starting with wood from living trees which overlap in age, tree-ring plots have been worked out reaching back two thousand years and more. With these plots many archeological sites and specimens have been dated in the south-western United States, where pine and pinyon are native woods and grow only a single ring each year. Trees which grow more than one ring a year cannot be accurately dated.

is less precisely documented. A *bulto* in the Taylor Museum, Colorado Springs, is dated on its pedestal 1820. A few large and conventionally modeled figures are recorded as the work of Father Andres Garcia, also noted in section on *retablos* as stationed in New Mexico, 1747–79. More often made of cottonwood roots than of pine, a *bulto* was carved of several parts pegged together and smoothly covered with gesso. If complicated drapery was wanted it was made by dipping cotton cloth in wet gesso and applying this in sculptural folds to the wooden figure. Painting materials were the same used for *retablos*. Figures made late in the nineteenth century are as a rule crudely finished, except for the head and hands, since the rest was intended to be clothed in fabric garments at all times. Late-eighteenth-century figures attempted to follow Mexican baroque models, but without the elements of hardwoods, *estofado* and oil painting. One type is isolated as of 'humanist' style (Plate 343A) because of its Gothic appearance. The most popular style of *bulto* is the Cordova type (Plate 343C), from the village of its origin, and is thought to have been made by the *santero* José Rafael Aragon and his two or more helpers; hence its estimated dates are those of the working period of José Rafael Aragon, 1839–50, or later. These are tall, rather elegant in form, with calm faces and clear colored painted detail.

An even larger series is in the Mora style, named for the river, valley, town and county of its origin. This region east of the Sangre de Cristo mountains was not successfully settled until after the United States had built Fort Union in 1851 as a protection against Plains Indian raids. Hence the Mora *santero* worked from that time through the Civil War and probably into the 1870s. Highly stylized and non-realistic, these figures have a strange appeal and a homogeneity of treatment which marks them unmistakably. The frequent appearance of pointed black shoes on this type of *bulto* and the hoop skirts and pinafores of the female figures reflect contemporary costume of the 1850s (Plate 345D).

A series of oval-headed *bultos* with peculiar clam-shell shaped ears and vacant expressions were made in *Arroyo Hondo*, Taos County, during the 1870–80 period (Plate 345C). Perhaps the last of the great *santeros* was Juan Ramon Velasquez of Canjilon, New Mexico, who died in 1902 when he was over eighty. An Indian fighter in territorial militia during the 1850s, he lived in so remote a region that his creative imagination was not impaired by the example of plaster images and chromos. His pieces are dramatic, stylized and well carried out, and over his working period he used first tempera pigments and, later, commercial oil paints.

From many hands came the somewhat repetitious and crude figures commissioned for *moradas*, or meeting houses of a penitent order of laymen, which were made on into the twentieth century with commercial materials on both sides of the New Mexico-Colorado border. These represented Christ crucified, during the Passion, and entombed; the sorrowing Virgin; and a somewhat medieval figure of Death.

Unidentified types exist which appear to have been made from the late-eighteenth century until the decline of the art.

With the gradual rise in monetary value of the *santos* during the past thirty-five years a flourishing cottage industry of reproductions and reconstructions of damaged fragments has sprung up to supply tourist demand. While these may be acceptable as decorative pieces, the serious collector should be cautious in acquiring such examples, often sold as authentic old ones by unscrupulous dealers. The new examples are made of sawmill lumber (or sometimes worked over old wood); plaster of Paris; commercial paints; and lack the tactile surfaces of honest craftsmanship. They are often copied from a photograph of some old piece, so that one angle of the copy is correct and the rest is done from imagination, while the color schemes are totally unconvincing.

CABINET WORK

Western yellow pine was the principal material used with cottonwood and juniper in lesser amounts. Tools were few; the small Spanish axe, adz, small bucksaw, chisel, knife and a sawtoothed knife, awl, and sandstone slabs of several degrees of coarseness used to smooth wood as well as for sharpening blades. Boards made before better hand tools were brought over the Santa Fe Trail in the 1830s were shaped with the ax and adz. After better hand tools were available in the southwest the marks of small block planes are visible on woodwork, as well as fancy grooves and rabbets made with a molding planer. No sawmill was in operation until the 1870s in New Mexico, but such innovations reached California earlier in the century and after the conclusion of the War with Mexico in 1846.

Colonial southwestern cabinet work utilized mortise and tenon, dovetailing and dowels for joining. The presence of nails, although square and hand-wrought, indicates later repairs, as no metal was used in construction except for small eyelet hinges and locks. Church and house doors were of the puncheon type.

Design followed tradition of the Renaissance period with simplifications imposed by limitations of materials and tools. Beds, tables and chairs were little used except in the dwellings of governing and clerical officials. Settlers prepared food before the hearth and cooked in the fireplace or in outdoor ovens and pits; wool ticks, sheep pelts and small stools were their seats on packed earth floors, so tables were low, whether round or oblong. The same pelts and wool ticks served at night as beds, with each person wrapping up in a blanket which hung on a pole below the ceiling beams by day.

The principal pieces of furniture were cupboards or *trasteros* (Plate 347B), and chests (Plate 346A), which held food, dishes, valuables and grains. A chair was reserved for the visits of the priest, while large armchairs were used within the church sanctuary during mass. As a result this type of chair is still called a priest chair. Benches with back and arms were church pews, while flat benches made of a long slab on pole legs were for washing and outdoor use.

The style of tables, benches, cupboards and chairs was markedly Spanish in angularity of line, restraint of ornament and sense of proportion. The appearance of Duncan Phyfe lines in chairs, and exposed drawers in cupboards and tables marks the influence of eastern American furniture after 1840.

Bench: made of pine. The straight back usually had hand-shaped splats with a design often different from that of the deep front apron under seat. The size varied from that for two persons to one ten feet long.

Chair: made of pine with either solid plank seat or rawhide seat. Back and apron either with hand-carved spindles or small, repeated design elements on rails.

Chair, priest's: made of pine, large in scale. Solid plank seat, open arms with slightly outward curving rests, back with small carved designs on rails.

Chests: large pine chests made of single slabs for sides; top and bottom were carved in low relief with the rosette, pomegranate and Castillian lions divided by panels (Plate 346B). Those for church usage had inside drawers at one end, and long strap hinges and hasp over a lacy round escutcheon with huge key. This hardware was sent from Mexico.

The domestic chest for clothing was more often set on a wooden stand than built with legs (Plate 346A). Simply proportioned panels and moldings were the more usual ornamentation. The chest for wheat, corn, flour and such staples was often large enough to accommodate two or three people and had built-in legs and severely plain paneled decoration. The wagon boxes, other than those of rawhide described under the heading *Leather Work*, were plain pine with small eyelet hinges and iron lock and served to carry provisions; also served as seats.

Chests, painted: pine chests painted with architectural views and groups of small figures in contemporary dress, all surrounded by floral borders, were made in Chihuahua, Mexico, at the turn of the eighteenth century. These were brought to New Mexico by travelers who went to the annual Chihuahua Fair. They were used as containers for their wedding finery, since it was some such great event which led them to make such a journey. The painted chest was copied in New Mexico during the first part of the nineteenth century, but the professional quality of the Mexican chests was replaced by a naïve folk style in the handling of figures and composition.

Chests, lacquered: Spanish families in California owned many of the red lacquered Chinese chests studded with brass nails. Very few of these found their way into the interior.

Chests, hutch-topped: pine boxes with hutch top and Yankee locks and hinges were made after 1850.

Cupboard, or **trastero:** was unpainted pine, or else pine covered with gesso and painted in tempera like the religious figures. The traditional form was a frame on low legs with a solid pair of doors divided into panels whch opened on shelves (Plate 347B). These had a pediment at front and sides in the form of one or three fluted shells which slipped into grooves in the frame and were not permanently attached. The more imposing *trastero* resembled a chest-on-chest with hand-carved spindles forming a grille on the upper doors, and solid doors on the lower part. In it were drawers shaped like shoe boxes, every other one functional and the alternates blind. These spaces contained similar drawers which could be reached from the back – a survival of the secret drawers of Renaissance desks. With the arrival of emigrants from the eastern states the 'meat safe' or food safe with punched tin panels on front and sides, to admit air and keep out flies, also arrived. Today these are mistaken for old Spanish pieces.

Shelves, hanging: the shelf with brackets and a scrolled apron was in every home, high up on the wall, to hold images of the family saints, candles and flowers. Sometimes gessoed and painted, they were more often of natural pine. Rarely a double shelf was made.

Stools: the low stool to sit on varied from a block of pine with legs hollowed from the block, or slab of cottonwood with pole legs

set into it, to a daintier form with front apron of scrolls and beading.

Tables: the dining table was no more than twelve or fourteen inches high, as a convenience to those seated or reclining on the floor. The oblong form had legs joined on by mortise and tenon, a solid slab top and fluted and scrolled aprons. When joints grew loose they were tightened by rawhide thongs around the apron and corners. Other forms of tables had a square frame with hand-carved spindles and leg turnings and a round top made of a single slab of pine. The Americans living in Santa Fe in connection with trade during the 1830s and 1840s required tables of standard height, and from after that time the design and size of tables had no traditional pattern.

Treen: bowls, dippers, ladles and cheese presses were fashioned from cottonwood or pine, using natural burls and deformities. The truly circular bowl or form shaped by steaming was not attempted. Non-edible gourds raised especially for the purpose were also used to make ladles, jars and water containers, usually covered with rawhide. Hollowed-out logs served in different forms as water and feed troughs, corn bins, wine barrels and even baptismal fonts.

Applied straw decoration: bits of straw applied as ornament was a craft of Moorish countries, and so crossed into Spain with the Moors, thence to Mexico and north along the Rio Grande. Mexican straw work like that of eighteenth-century Europe, developed into elaborate pictorial compositions in full color, but in New Mexico the straw was never dyed. The natural range of golden tones provided an inexpensive substitute for gilding, and the applied patterns were geometric, ornamenting small chests and boxes (Plate 347C), shelves, sconces (Plate 347A) and panels.

The pine box or object was covered with a preparation of pine rosin and soot, which served as background and adhesive. The wheat straw was cut into tiny patches and strips and laid on without pattern or stencil so that it was freehand and irregular in symmetry. The craft was abandoned by 1850 when tin became common in New Mexico.

METAL WORK

For practical purposes the Spanish quest for precious metals was unsuccessful in the southwest. Copper, gypsum and talc were mined for local uses, but the imbalance of commercial credit with Mexico did not allow importation of gold, silver, or even iron to New Mexico. Hence fancy grilles, locks and decorative ironwork traditional in other Spanish countries were absent in New Mexico. Supply caravans carried one lock, key, pair of hinges and a limited number of nails for the building of a new mission church, together with one axe, one adze and one or two spades and crowbars. Colonial smiths reworked iron scraps into eyelet hinges, hasps and plough points; even the tempered steel Solingen sword blade was resharpened and cut down until it served only as a butcher knife. The finer horse trappings brought from Mexico were highly prized, but as they were worn out they were replaced with country-made wooden stirrups and plain iron bits and spurs trimmed with copper jinglers. While the spade bit with attached 'jawbreaker' ring is now called 'Navajo', because it was widely copied by Navajo Indians when they learned to be blacksmiths, it must be recalled that it was Spanish in origin, and many examples of these were used by Spanish colonials.

Jewelry and plate of gold or silver, although said to have been owned by early settlers, were mostly converted into specie when a cash economy supplanted the barter system in 1846. Therefore the hand-hammered silver dish or church plate which is rarely found today, although perhaps two centuries old, is of Mexican or Peruvian origin. Filigree jewelry was introduced into the southwest in the latter part of the nineteenth century by merchants who brought Italian craftsmen to do the work, using western-mined silver and gold. Every type of trinket was made for some years, including solid filigree lifetime railroad passes of gold for the most privileged holders, but the craft was primarily commercial, not indigenous, and recent in time.

Bronze bells: church and mission, cast on Spanish or long-waisted lines in Mexico, many at Zacatecas, were sent to New Mexican and California missions; the Franciscan missions built before 1680 having been destroyed in the Pueblo Rebellion, their bells were broken. Replacements sent from Mexico are often dated from 1710 to 1730, with the name of the patron of the church, and a cross, of bas-relief diamond-shaped forms cast with the bell, around shoulder and waist. Clappers of bronze in nine-pin form. Many bells were not tolled, but struck with a rock by a man in the belfry, causing the side of the bell to be worn smooth. In New Mexico cracked bells were recast after 1790 until 1860, but these are rough, clumsy in shape and often cracked in casting. Bells marked 1856 with a defect in casting are often misread as 1356, which has led to confusion.

In California some mission bells are of Russian make with Russian inscriptions and fanciful figures; traded from the Russian settlements before 1846.

Bronze bell wheels: a wooden wheel on a stand with a series of small bronze bells used at mass. These have survived in California.

Bronze mortars: plain or ornamented; the mortar and pestle was used by the Spanish for crushing ore and in smaller form for kitchen and medicinal herb preparation. These were brought from Mexico or Spain.

Brass and copper: brass kettles with cast brass lugs, together with iron axes and flintlock muskets, came into the southwest with French agents from the Mississippi Valley during the eighteenth century as trade goods to the Indians in exchange for furs. The more common hammered copper kettle with lugs riveted to the rims were standard equipment for fireside use as well as for the traveler. Every horseman rode with a copper on his saddle bow for use as drinking, cooking and bathing, just as later G.I. helmets were used. Originally a monopoly of European gypsies, copper pots were made in Mexico in the same forms: constricted necked pots; *chocolateros*; and plates as well as kettles. They are still made today at the town of Santa Clara de Cobre, Michoacan. Large tubs for boiling over the fire, brandy stills and other copper items were made, mostly in Mexico, but some pieces were hammered out of native ore in New Mexico. Small copper pieces were tobacco flasks, candlesticks, altar cruets and church censers.

Tin: lack of precious metals and even gilding marked Spanish colonial crafts in the southwest with an austerity in marked contrast to the Mexican until tin-plate came over the Santa Fe Trail. While tinned copper plates had been in use especially by the military Spanish, tin containers were a novelty, and tinned mirror frames brought from the eastern states became so popular that they are recorded in New Mexican churches by dozens. The tin cans of oil and lard discarded by Americans were cut up and reworked by Spanish craftsmen to fashion frames and *nichos* (Plate 348A), or little shrines, trinket caskets and candle sconces (Plate 348B) as fast as they were available. The earlier New Mexican tin pieces are all made up of odd-sized scraps and often show factory stamps or trade marks and even United States Army supply marks on the tin. The color and sheen of this old tin resembles pewter, and it is actually heavier in thickness than the modern, white-toned sheet tin. Decoration was sometimes done with the dies and stamps already in use in leather tooling, and with nail points and cold chisels. In the vein of Spanish ornament in general, decorative designs consisted of small motifs as simple as crescents or dots, repeated to fill given spaces. The earlier picture and mirror frames followed the Federal or Regency shapes with corner bosses and pediment or lunette at top.

Other novelties arriving with tin for Spanish-speaking settlers were glass panes, colored wallpapers and prints, engraved, lithographed or in chromolithography. Prior to the period of English-speaking trade, religious prints were sent north from Mexico, either wood engravings or copperplate, but the volume was scant compared to the flood of mission cards distributed after 1851 by French priests.

These were framed with fancy tin and thus the closing of the older *santo*-making school was hastened. Prints of religious subjects by N. Currier were issued with English and Spanish titles for the new territory of New Mexico after 1848; these are still to be found. The oldest tin frames were glazed with thin sheets of native mica, but few of these have survived. Most contain heavy plate glass scraps to cover inlaid bits of wallpaper, often of the William Morris period. In cases where wallpaper was not obtainable the tinsmith painted marbleized inlays (Plate 348A) or combed particolored ribbon stripes. Today collectors prefer these freehand painted inlays in tin pieces to those with wallpaper.

After 1880 railroads brought mass-produced merchandise to rural stores. Tin pieces daubed with house paints appeared, and while this added gaudy color to the tin, it brought about a deterioration in the quality of the stamped ornaments. The delicate proportions of older pieces were no longer in evidence.

LEATHER WORK

Over the southwest hides were commonly available and formed a great part of commercial exports as well as supplying colonial needs. Such things as trunks, ore and water buckets, winnowing sieves and door-pulls were made of rawhide instead of metal, while 'armored' coats and shields, breeches, shirts, grain sacks, saddle bags, shoes, and even panels for painting were made from tanned buck and buffalo skins.

Bridles: finely-braided buckskin or rawhide head stall, throat latch and reins put together with loops, knots and tassels of same. Hand-wrought metal chains attach reins to bit.

Coats, military: long, sleeveless, of seven thicknesses of deerskin quilted in lozenge patterns, bound with tape. Collar turned up to ears. Worn by militia until United States annexed New Mexico and California in 1846.

Coats, cowherders: long, with sleeves, made of one thickness of deerskin.

Hats, military: low-crowned, flat-brimmed, of patent leather.

Hats, men's: of felt or straw, low-crowned, flat-brimmed, trimmed with gold and silver galloon and embroidery. The tall peaked 'sombrero' is an innovation of the past seventy-five years.

Leggings (Californian and Mexican): for riding, worn before boots or chaps were used.

Tanned buck or soft calf skins tied around the knees with flaring bottoms and cuffs at tops. Stamped in elaborate patterns, embroidered with hemp, gold or silver thread, bound with metal galloon. Sometimes perforated showing colored velvet linings.

Leggings (New Mexican): without silver or gold ornamentation, with red Manchester cloth linings showing through perforated patterns, with colored silk embroideries (Plate 350A).

Pouches, cartridge boxes: flat pouches worn on long strap to carry bullets, of buckskin or dressed leather, embroidered in floral motifs with hempen threads. In the nineteenth century these were copied by Navajo without embroidery, but trimmed with silver buttons. Cartridge boxes to tie on belt were made in the same way over a wooden frame, hempen embroidery on the leather (Plate 350 B).

Saddles: the Spanish saddle used by the Conquistadores had a high, narrow pommel and horn and straight cantle. It resembled the Moorish saddle and was covered with a fancy saddle cloth. The tree suited the Spanish rider's way of sitting erect with legs hanging naturally in long stirrups. None of these have survived except for the Indian-made copies, which show the same tree. The Mexican Charro saddle (Plate 349) was developed much later, with a low, raking cantle and pommel and flat, thick horn. Examples of these from Spanish California and Mexico are heavily covered with stamped and tooled designs and incrustations of silver, and are sought by collectors.

Shields: the *adarga*, or shield shaped in double, overlapping oval, was made of two

or three thicknesses of bull hide laced together, painted with the regimental insignia, names of the reigning Spanish king and floral ornaments. The round shield or *rodela* was the same in construction.

Tobacco flasks: small rawhide bottles of two parts sewn around sides with the moccasin stitch, stamped with borders, initials and sometimes dates. The hand-carved wooden stopper tied on with thong. These were used by men and women to carry *punche*, the Spanish tobacco grown in New Mexican mountains. With a corn husk taken from a small flat container, a small cigarette was made.

Trunks, boxes and kayaks: rawhide stretched over a light pole framework with the hair outside. Rawhide thongs laced over exterior in geometric patterns above squares of red, blue and yellow velvet and Manchester cloth. Fine trunks had fancy iron lock, hasp and hinges, buckskin linings.

TEXTILES

Pre-Columbian Indians in the southwest had practised weaving with cotton and other vegetable fibres for over a thousand years. Wool was adopted after Spanish importation of domestic animals, including sheep. These were the Merino breed with long-fibred silky wool, but the yield per clip was limited. In the later nineteenth century American stockmen introduced the Rambouillet sheep to western ranges, where they proved hardy and gave heavier wool clips. Unfortunately, Rambouillet wool is short-fibred, harsh and brittle, and so does not lend itself to fine spinning or weaving.

Pueblo Indians went on weaving after the Spanish conquest, for their own needs and to provide tribute levies, but retained their techniques and designs. In Spanish colonial homes there were, of necessity, a spinning wheel and one or more looms to supply bedding, carpets, clothing and so on. Textiles made on the horizontal harness loom by Indian household servants sometimes show odd combinations of the techniques of two cultures. When the semi-nomadic Navajo learned sheep management and weaving in historic times they adopted the upright loom, but invented their own designs, not having previous tradition, just as they have done with silversmithing and other newly-learned crafts. Also typical of Navajo flexibility, their designs vary with each generation.

Spinning: the Indian spindle was a slender stick of no more than eighteen inches with a whorl two to four inches in diameter which might be made of wood, gourd rind or potsherd. The spinner crouched on one knee with the other leg doubled under the body, pressed the spindle shaft against the right thigh and kept spinning with the right hand while the left fed rovings on to the spindle. As the rovings made a thread it fell on the floor and went on twisting. An alternate method was the use of the same sort of spindle set in a supporting frame. Many Spanish woven textiles of the Rio Grande valley may have been made of yarns spun in this way by Indian servants, but the hardwood spinning wheels which the Spanish brought with them resembled in shape those used in Flanders in the sixteenth century. As these wore out they were replaced by country-made makeshifts much like a sawhorse with wheels at each end, of native pine. Single- or two-ply yarns spun on these were, of course, irregular and thick in comparison with yarns spun on a well-turned wheel.

Weaving: looms brought into the southwest with early settlers have not survived; the older looms now to be seen are country-made horizontal harness looms of pine, with mortise and tenon construction and without metal parts. Spools, pulleys and most tools were made of cottonwood or scrub oak, while shuttles were as a rule fashioned from juniper. Looms were narrow, so weaving was done in long strips from twenty-two to twenty-six inches wide, sewn or woven together. There was little technical variety; plain weaving, diagonal, herringbone and diamond twills. The last seems to have been rare and is called *ojo de perdiz* or partridge eye, by Spanish weavers. The Navajo used herringbones and diamond twill in the past century for many fancy saddle blankets.

The first departures from handspun yarns occurred when three-ply Saxony was brought in through trade about 1860, and soon after this commercial dyes were introduced. About 1880 Germantown yarns arrived in quantity, and Spanish and Indian weavers used them in riotous color schemes, developing new, bold patterns which superseded the older traditional stripes, lozenges and points. By 1900 cotton string warps replaced wool and four-ply factory yarns were used. At the same time that weaving markedly declined, manufactured bedding, clothing and other articles became commonly available so the cottage loom was discarded except in the Chimayo valley north of Santa Fe, where weaving for the tourist trade is still active. Because this is the chief place of survival of non-Indian weaving in the southwest, old Rio Grande blankets have recently been mis-named 'Chimayo', when in fact they were once produced from the Mexican border to the San Luis valley in Colorado, a distance of more than four hundred miles. It has not been determined as yet whether the hand-woven diagonal twilled cotton which was widely used in the southwest in Spanish and Mexican times was actually woven there or imported.

Dyes: from the first period of colonization in 1598 indigo and cochineal were sent from Mexico to the southwest for weavers. Except for these colors yarns were dyed with vegetable colors brewed from bark, lichens, roots and juices. A soft tan-rose, miscalled 'brazil', because it is said to have been made by an infusion of tropical logwood, was actually derived from native mountain mahogany, a slender shrub of the lower mountain levels. Another popular fallacy is the myth that fine-textured scarlet yarns found in mid-nineteenth-century textiles and called *bayeta* were raveled from Spanish soldiers' trousers. In point of fact, Spanish power had declined before the Mexican Republic was proclaimed to an extent that left local militia in the southwest for defensive purposes, and members of these companies more often wore their personal clothing for lack of uniforms. What *bayeta* did come from was Manchester cloth, woollen yardage made in many English factories and exported under this general name to Mexico in the second quarter of the nineteenth century. Finely spun, the true scarlet color of Manchester cloth supplied a wanted red which was woven with other colored hand-spun in many fine blankets. On the other hand, raveled yardage of pink, green and other colors has also been found woven with native hand-spun yarns in textiles of the same period. Today some textiles alleged to contain *bayeta* threads actually do not.

Basic fabric: natural wool yardage in plain weave was woven in lengths and made up as clothing, mattress ticks and served as the support for embroideries. This was called *sabanilla*, or little sheet, from the Spanish *savana*, a sheet.

Blankets: these were made for bedding and also to wear in lieu of cloak or coat. Unlike the Mexican *poncho* or *sarape*, New Mexican blankets seldom had the slit at the centre to put over the wearer's head, but were wrapped around the shoulders. To distinguish them from Indian blankets they are called Rio Grande, and are most easily identified by their being woven in two strips sewn together down the centre and the multiple warps at the selvedges as well as by their designs. Spanish weavers did not apply the overlaid yarn border finish used by Indian weavers, nor does the lazy stitch, so often a part of Navajo weaving, appear on pieces made on the harness loom.

Textiles of the eighteenth century have not survived in the Spanish southwest except in the form of church vestments which were not locally made, but it is of record that weaving had declined to so low a level by 1800 that the current governor of New Mexico arranged to bring master weavers from Mexico to revive the craft. The brothers Bazan arrived about 1806 and soon settled in the Chimayo valley, where their skill and their Mexican *sarape* models influenced the villagers. Mexican *sarapes* often had hempen warps which could not be found in the northern Rio Grande, so the finest weaving and most complicated patterns of Mexico could not be copied. However, simplified versions of the fancy borders, lozenges and zig-zag

designs were made locally during the finest period of Rio Grande weaving, 1860–80.

Jerga: this served the same purpose as drugget or floor cloths in our eastern states for those who did not own oriental rugs. Woven of coarse, often single-ply, homespun in strips of some two feet in width and as long as the room for which they were intended, the *jerga* was sewn together to make wall to wall carpet and laid on packed earth floors. Diagonal and herringbone twill weaves were most common, often appearing at random in the same strip, which may indicate a change of weavers on the work. The possible varieties of checks and plaids that could be woven from light and dark natural yarns were most popular, but more ambitious *jerga* was woven in plaids of red, orange, yellow, green and brown. A scarcer kind was the *ojo de perdiz* or diamond twill in two or more colors. Newly-arrived customs and country store merchandise after 1880 introduced rag rugs and linoleum; the later *jerga* had cotton string warps and rag wefts, but were soon abandoned altogether. While many were worn to shreds, a fair number have survived in good condition (Plate 351A).

Embroidery, wool-on-wool fabric: it is not possible to prove that New Mexican embroideries now termed 'old' are any more than one hundred and ten or so years of age, so the origin of the local style of embroidering is still open to discussion. Some writers have ascribed the patterns to Oriental influences from Manila galleon goods, others to Spanish, Arabic and Mexican-Indian sources. Still others see an imitation of needlework counterpanes brought from New England and New York by women emigrants after 1846. Rustic as they were, the latter clearly stemmed from English embroidery of the Queen Anne period (Plate 351B) which in turn was inspired by East India Company imports, so a certain Oriental influence may be said to have existed from either direction. Except for some work in hempen threads on leather goods, New Mexican needlework was nearly all done in wool, and its chief characteristic is the *colcha* stitch (Plates 352A and B); a long stitch with short holding stitch across it at a 45 degree angle. The interest of texture was achieved by opposed directions of parallel rows of these stitches, which enlivened the work as much as the color contrasts and patterns. The name, *colcha*, is a local term, since in classic Spanish it means a quilt, but in New Mexico a quilt is called *colchone*. In tracing the source of this stitch one naturally looks first to Mexico, where similar designs and colors were worked in wool-on-wool, but the *colcha* stitch itself is not found, nor does it appear in Spanish needlework of the eighteenth and nineteenth centuries.

The embroidered wool bed cover (also called *colcha*), may be presumed to date from the 1840s, when bedsteads became fashionable, since except by a few high officials they were not used in colonial times. Older specimens were worked in all over parti-colored checks or closely-spaced floral motifs; the 1860–70 type had parallel bands of floral elements and wavy scallops. In all designs worked on wool the supporting fabric was entirely covered by solid embroidery. The old *colchas*, hand-spun, woven and dyed in the traditional indigo, cochineal and vegetable colors of the country, were of merino wool and so have a silky texture. In the last thirty years tourist influence has produced a revival of this work, resulting in a new series with saints, Indians, wagons, tepees, etc. worked in commercial yarns, but often on old homespun fabrics reclaimed from mattress ticks. These may be classed as 'folk embroideries', but are not to be confused with the authentic *colchas* of a century or so ago.

Wool embroidery on cotton twill: another local expression is the use of the name *sabanilla* for this class of needlework in New Mexico since it is not done on the plain weave woollen cloth of the same name. Wool-on-cotton work (Plate 352A) was used for altar cloths in rural chapels as well as for domestic decoration. The same *colcha* stitch is employed, but the design elements are less formal and less planned, and the cotton ground is left exposed. Color schemes range from a combination of indigo and natural wool to a full gamut of colors from local and imported sources. Crochet, cross-stitch, calico yard goods, factory lace curtains and, lately, plastics, have completely replaced the old country embroidery which, presumably, was also employed on articles of dress, although nothing has been saved from oblivion. Examples of nineteenth-century embroideries are still found in old family collections.

BOOKS FOR FURTHER READING

BOYD, E.: *Saints and Saintmakers*, Santa Fe, New Mexico (1946).

BOYD, E.: 'Antiques in New Mexico' in *Antiques* (August 1943).

BOYD, E.: 'Decorated Tinware' in *Antiques* (September 1954).

CHRISTENSEN, ERWIN O.: *Index of American Design*, New York (1951).

CHRISTENSEN, ERWIN O.: *Popular Art in the United States*, Penguin, London (1948).

CHRISTENSEN, ERWIN O.: *Early American Woodcarving*, New York (1952).

HORGAN, PAUL: *Great River*, for general background, New York (1955).

WHEELWRIGHT, MARY CABOT: *Some Embroideries from New Mexico*, Bulletin of the Needle and Bobbin Club, New York, V. 16, No. 2 (1932).

WILDER, MITCHELL A. AND BREITENBACH, EDGAR: *Santos – the Religious Folk Art of New Mexico*, Colorado Springs (1943).

INDEX

OF NAMES AND PLACES

References to Plates are shown in italics

Q

R

U

V

W